W9-BMG-912

How to Find Your Family Roots

How to Find Your Family Roots

by Timothy Field Beard with Denise Demong

McGraw-Hill Book Company

New York · St. Louis · San Francisco · Düsseldorf · Mexico · Toronto

*This book is dedicated to the Reference Librarians,
past and present, of the New York Public Library,
a national treasure that should be a national trust*

Book design by Judith Michael.

1 2 3 4 5 6 7 8 9 0 D O D O 7 8 3 2 1 0 9 8 7

Library of Congress Cataloging in Publication Data

Beard, Timothy Field.
How to find your family roots.
1. Genealogy.   I. Demong, Denise, joint author.
II. Title.
CS16.B35   929'.1   77-9411
ISBN 0-07-004210-1

Acknowledgments

There are so many people who have helped to make this book a reality that it would be impossible to mention them all by name. Without Denise Demong this book could not have been contemplated. My wife, Annette Huddleston Beard, Kevin P. Hayes, and the Reverend Timothy Allen have helped us in many ways with the manuscript, and the latter executed the genealogical charts. Lynne Norris typed much of the manuscript. Lyn Martens and Marion Walsh undertook historical research. Kathleen Cameron, William Epstein, Howard Schamest, and Denise Demong are responsible for most of the photography connected with the book. Henry Hoff and Eugenia Ray kindly read the manuscript for errors, as did Rosemary Tucci and Charry D. Boris.

I must go back to the beginning to acknowledge the help that was given to me by so many members of my family who are now deceased. My parents, Stuart-Menteth and Natalie S. T. Beard; my grandmother, Gertrude Field Finley Beard; my brothers, Stuart-M. Beard III, and Henry Sudler Beard; my aunts, Kate Taylor Turner, Alice Smith Hill, Mabel Smith Burdge, Sara Kirk Turner, and Minnie Ricords Sudler; my cousins, Philadelphia S-M. Vines, Emma M. Finley, Sally Sudler Whitehill, Nan Kenney Fooks Campbell, May Kenney, the Honorable C. Sudler Richards, Sallie Bacon, Col. C. E. Vines, Gratia S-M. Walmsley Harral, Herbert and Cora S. Goold, Maud Sudler Rankin, Bessie Ruding, Addie G. Robinson, and the Reverend James Richards all contributed material which aided my progress.

Relatives still living around the world, who gave me a great deal of help, include Sarah E. Cooper, Evelyn Merriam, Mary Dudley Thomas, Lillian Sudler Virden, Alice H. Beard, Capt, Wells L. Field, Field Curry, Rixford Beals, Glorianna Agner, Rear Adm. Brooks J. Harral, Gratia H. Dexter, Sir James Stuart-Menteth, Charles G. Stuart-Menteth, Alexander Stuart-Menteth, Margaret H. Gilman, Ann T. Pistell, Alice T. Anderson, Edith T. O'Connor, Isobel Beard, Patricia Evans, Doris Warrington-Jackson, Jeremy Cole, Mary Lou Phillips, Elizabeth S-M. Laird, Angus I. Macnaughten, Joseph S. Turner, Ludivina S-M. How, Bonnie Beard Sack, Joan V. and Charles

Brookman, and Betty V. and John Dawes, Dorothy L. Harral Bruce, Richard Carville, Alice V. Rowe, and John Field.

Fellow genealogists, writers, researchers, and members and employees of genealogical societies to whom I owe a great debt include Elizabeth Eliot (the Lady Elizabeth Kinnaird), Arthur J. Willis, Hugh Peskett, Liza Lawrence-Dow, William V. Norris, John Eldridge Frost, Louis Gaffen, Malcolm Stern, Rosemary De Saumarez, Winston DeVille, Frank E. Bradley, Henry Hoff, Rosalie Fellows Bailey, the late Gertrude A. Barber, Kenneth Scott, Marie Maffie, Philip W. Marsden, the late Eleanor B. Forbes, Gano Bailey, Olga Carney, Percy H. Goodsell, the late Gerald B. McDonald, J. Orton Buck, Elizabeth B. B. Hamilton, Howard L. Hamilton, Grahame T. Smallwood, Harold Hazelton, Louis Duermeyer, Ann R. Hardy, B-Ann Moorhouse, Robert S. Wilson, Brian G. C. Brooks, Cornelia V. R. Strong, the late Monson M. Burr, Bradley Ridge, Francis and Mary Anne Wells, Elizabeth Burnley-Bentley, Samuel J. Cardozo, Effingham P. Humphrey, Baldwin Maull, David Lowe, Clifford Webster, Bridget Laken, Mrs. Harold I. Meyer, Nellie Holmead Fowler, William R. M. Houston, Mrs. Harry C. Boden IV, Clare McV. Ward, Wilson R. Gathings, John Frazer, William Y. Prior, Betty B. Feenaughty, John Frederick Dorman, Miss Martha P. Miller, Robert S. Greenway, Jean S. Scott, P. William Filby, S. Allyn Peck, the late Carl Greenway, Florence Fisher, the late Ross K. Cooke, Helen L. Hultz, James D. Walker; Freda, Lady Slade; Walter Lee Sheppard, John I. Coddington, Cameron Allen, Virginia P. Livingston, Thomas S. Wilson, Gary Roberts, David Dearborn, Robert Charles Anderson, Arthur and Peggy Hoenig, Grace Knowles, Joyce Lindsay, Ralph Martin, Louise Hall Tharp, Robert L. Crawford, Bruce F. E. Harvey, Donald M. Liddell, Robert Boddington, Henry Darlington, Alexander and Anne Cannon, Nicholas D. Ward, and the staffs of the New York Genealogical and Biographical Society, and the New York Public Library. The special support and interest of my friends, Katherine Viele Platten, Margaret Cobb Westervelt, Josephine Hamilton, Elizabeth Babington Champness, Suzanne Delooz, Monique Devaux, Andrew Westervelt, Sidney Shore, Frances Higgens, Mary Janice Thornton, James and Eugenia Ray, Henry and Esther Trebert, Liza Seifert, Ida Sheppard, Cecil and Libby Good, John Taylor, and Herbert Williams, and my mother-in-law, Alma R. Huddleston, has been invaluable to me.

Contents

[Illustration sections follow pages 368 and 556]

1 Introduction

Do the members of your family treasure a special tradition about your ancestors? Have you always been told that your mother's great-great-grandfather was a pirate, or that your great-grandmother was descended from a noble family? Setting out to discover the truth behind such stories is precisely the impulse that sparks many people's interest in genealogy, the study of their family's history.

Others begin tracing their ancestry because of a more general desire to discover their "roots"—to understand something about "who they are" by learning more about where they came from. For many, the mobility of modern society and the recent passing of this country's two-hundredth birthday have intensified this longing for a sense of the past and knowledge of the people from whom they are descended.

There are, of course, those whose chief goal is to reveal a grand and illustrious family line. The tremendous success of companies that sell coats of arms by mail is an indication of how many people would like to be able to demonstrate to others that theirs was at one time a great family. Because of the social mobility that has marked American society since its inception, it is entirely possible that an average person may find that his family does connect with one or more noble lines, but it makes no sense to be disappointed if one discovers, four or five generations back, that one's immigrant ancestor was a farmer or laborer. Most genealogists soon discover that the pleasure is not in discovering rich or titled ancestors but in learning the details of the lives of the real people—good or evil, great or common—from whom they are descended.

Regardless of the motives that bring them to genealogy, beginners discover a fascinating and compelling hobby that demands the kind of persistence and deductive reasoning ability that are required to solve a detective mystery. Genealogy's special appeal is that the mystery is a very personal one—the story of one's own origins.

I started putting together the puzzle of my own family's past when I was still a child, after I learned that the great-great-

great-great-grandfather for whom I had been named was a captain in the Revolutionary War. The first sources for my research were a variety of old documents and letters stored by my family in a black tin box. Among them I found an abstract from an English parish register recording the baptism of Joseph Anthony Beard, my great-great-grandfather; his will, in which he named several relatives; and a family history his son had prepared for his children, which included not only information about his Beard ancestors but about the ancestors of Mary Grover Beard, Joseph's wife. As the years passed I found additional clues in family Bibles and scrapbooks, government records and published histories. The story that I've pieced together now stretches back over more than forty generations, to the ancestors of the Holy Roman Emperor Charlemagne.

I became so caught up in the study of genealogy that in time I decided to make it my profession. I joined the staff of the New York Public Library's Local History and Genealogy Division in 1962 and have been helping people of all nationalities and races search for their ancestors ever since.

When you trace your family's history you'll discover much more than your ancestors' names and the dates on which they were born and died. You'll find out, sometimes in surprisingly vivid detail, what these people were like and how they lived. A portrait may reveal that you bear a remarkable resemblance to your great-grandmother. Letters found in the bottom of an old trunk may give you a very personal glimpse of another ancestor's experiences and feelings. A diary may reveal not only the year in which ancestors immigrated to this country but the reasons they felt compelled to make such a dramatic move.

You'll develop a new appreciation and understanding of history and geography, even if they haven't really interested you before. The most exciting historians write about the day-to-day experiences of individuals in order to make the period in which they lived come alive. In the same way, as you reconstruct the lives of your forebears, the places where they lived and the events that shaped their lives will become very real to you. In the course of your research you may learn that one early American ancestor settled in upstate New York because he received a grant of land there as payment for his service during the Revolutionary War, that another ancestor died in California during the Gold Rush, that yet another immigrated from Ireland because of the potato famine in his homeland. These remote historical events you've read about will suddenly become vivid as you grasp, in very personal terms, the impact they had on the lives of your ancestors and people like them.

Almost every family passes along some favorite stories about earlier generations; nearly always these tales imply a noble lineage—that the family is descended from an illegitimate child of a prince, or from a passionate countess who ran off with a man far beneath her station. It's best to take such stories with a grain of salt, since they rarely turn out to be true. But every family history yields its share of fascinating and verifiable tales.

For many years, for example, I had been told that an artist had helped my great-grandfather, a Southerner, pass through enemy lines during the siege of New Orleans in the Civil War. When, among some family keepsakes, I found some old playing cards glued into a block and cut into the shape of the official seal on my great-grandfather's British passport, I was at last able to figure out what had happened. The passport was forged, and it was the artist I had heard about who had meticulously carved the seal of the British Consulate and impressed it on the document that guaranteed my ancestor's safe passage. As you proceed in your research you will piece together equally remarkable stories about your own family (Illustration 1).

You can probably count both the famous and the infamous among your ancestors. Perhaps, like one woman I recently helped in the search for a Revolutionary War ancestor, you'll trace your line straight to a signer of the Declaration of Independence. Or you may be able to prove that your family is entitled to a legitimate coat of arms. (If not, you can create one of your own, using symbols with real meaning to you and the other members of your family.)

It's just as likely, of course, that you will uncover some rather seedy stories. My own family line goes back to Jonnetta Stewart, Lady Fleming, the illegitimate daughter of James IV by his illegitimate cousin Agnes Stewart, the illegitimate daughter of the Earl of Buchan. (In time, Lady Jonnetta carried on the family tradition; she went to France and bore the illegitimate child of Henry II, the husband of Catherine de Médicis.)

As a genealogist you'll be joining a tradition that stretches across all cultures and eras. Throughout history the study of ancestry has played an important role in the social and religious order. Even before the invention of writing, family histories were passed on in many cultures through an oral tradition.

One of our oldest written genealogical records appears in the First Book of Chronicles in the Old Testament—the "begats"—in which Adam and Eve are given as the progenitors of all humanity. In the Orient the religiously based custom of ancestor worship persists to the present day. Genealogy was also important, although to a lesser extent, in the European Catholic Church because the devout prayed for the salvation of the souls of deceased parents and other ancestors and relatives. Sometimes they contributed money to the church in exchange for prayers for departed family members, and written records of some of these donations, especially those made by great noble families, often contain detailed genealogical information. In our own country members of the Church of Jesus Christ of the Latter-day Saints—popularly known as the Mormons—trace their ancestors and seal their names in the Tabernacle because their religion holds that the family is a sacred unit throughout eternity. The Mormons have done very valuable genealogical work in recent years, going all over the world to preserve and restore records that might otherwise have been lost forever.

Historically, genealogy was a necessity to cultures ruled by a hereditary monarchy or aristocracy in which whole kingdoms, as well as personal property, were passed on through family lines. Members of royal families frequently squabbled about questions of descent and title, just as families today fight over property; but in the case of royal families, the disputes were often settled on the battlefield.

In some European countries, minor offices, all the way down to the sheriff of a district or the constable of a town, were also hereditary. The patronage that went with these offices made them extremely valuable to the families entitled to them, and they were passed along to heirs, just like property. Before they married into the Scottish royal family themselves, the ancestors of the Stewart family were chief stewards to the king, and it is from that office that they derived their surname.

Not all contemporary genealogical researchers trace their own ancestry. The resources of the Local History and Genealogy

Room of the New York Public Library are constantly utilized by authors and historians. At one time, Mrs. Mackinlay Kantor, wife of the Pulitzer-Prize–winning historical novelist, was an almost daily visitor as she did research for her husband's books. Charles B. Flood, Harnett T. Kane, Thomas B. Costain, Barbara Tuchman, Marchette Chute, David Lowe, Samuel Eliot Morison and Lady Antonia Fraser, among others, have done a great deal of research into the intricacies of royal, noble or American genealogy as background for their books.

People who make a hobby of tracing the genealogies of royal or well-known people often turn up intriguing connections. In 1976, for example, it was revealed that former Presidents Richard Nixon and Gerald Ford are actually ninth cousins, three times removed (Chap. 30). Numerous books on the ancestry of notable people are listed in Chapter 30, "Popular Ancestors."

Most people would like to think that they are related to all the famous people who share their surname, but this is usually not the case, as one surname may derive from various roots—including the professions, residences and even the physical characteristics of people who bore it—and spellings may have changed over the years. A "carter" is one who carries items in carts or wagons, but the surname "Carter" may be a corruption of "carder," as in "woolcarder." Nearly everyone named Carter (pronounced Key-yarder in Virginia) used to claim descent from Robert "King" Carter (1663–1732) of Virginia. Today they are claiming relationship to the President of the United States. Since there were many people with this professional surname in all parts of Great Britain, and numerous immigrants of the surname who settled in the southern colonies, it is unlikely that most of the present-day Carters are related to either "King" Carter or the President, but it makes a good story, and a good story is the beginning of many a family tradition.

Genealogy remains important today in determining the ownership of private property. In some parts of this country, if a person dies without leaving a will, state law requires an extensive search for distant relatives who are entitled to his estate, and there are professional genealogists who devote all their time to searching for missing heirs.

This book will take you step by step through the process of finding your ancestors. Each genealogical case begins like a mystery, and if the proper clues are followed, the case is solved—or nearly so. A genealogy, unlike a mystery story, never comes to a completely satisfactory conclusion; you're always left with the feeling that you can carry your line back just one more generation.

An amazing number of people try to begin their research by going to a library and consulting a famous genealogical reference work, such as *Burke's Peerage*, the standard source on British noble families, or the *Libro d'Oro*, which lists Italian nobility. These people are making two mistakes. First, although nearly every beginning genealogist seems convinced that he is descended from a prince or disinherited peer, it's usually unrealistic to expect to find your ancestors among the peerage of the country from which they immigrated. Second, even if you do find someone with your family name listed in such a reference, you have no way of knowing whether you are actually descended from him.

In researching family history—just as in solving a detective mystery—you first assemble the facts of which you are already sure and then, through careful research, piece together the clues that will lead you from the known to the unknown. In order to establish clearly the connection between yourself and your ancestors, you must begin your research with your immediate family and work backward.

You'll start by talking to all of your relatives—especially the older ones—and making notes of everything they can remember about your family—names, relationships, dates of birth and death, residences and so on.

Then you'll look for documents and heirlooms. Some relatives may have records—a family Bible in which ancestors wrote down births, deaths and marriages; an old photograph album or a box of miscellaneous papers, such as deeds, diaries and letters, which contain important clues. Family jewelry and silver may be engraved with your ancestors' names or initials and the dates of important events in their lives.

In libraries and historical societies you'll study old maps and histories of the areas where your forebears lived, discover what information others have published about branches of your family, and look through indexes of old newspapers for accounts of your ancestors' lives. You'll send away for copies of their birth, death and marriage certificates, visit the cemeteries in which they are buried and dig through musty records in old county courthouses for copies of their wills and deeds. In this way, piecing together facts turned up from a multitude of sources, you'll follow your family line back, generation by generation.

If you're able to establish the identity of one of the ancestors who came to this country from abroad, additional documents, such as ship passenger lists and naturalization papers, may enable you to carry your line back to his homeland. You can continue your research by mail, or you may decide to travel abroad and do your digging in person, searching for any records of your family that have survived overseas, just as you did in this country.

Each chapter describes in detail the techniques you'll use and the resources you'll consult at every stage of your research. The steps are presented in the order in which they are most likely to occur, but it's good to remember that each person's genealogy is unique and that your research on the various branches of your family will progress at different rates. You'll need to be logical and flexible, trying first one avenue and then another, varying the procedure to suit the particular problems you encounter as you trace your family line.

That's where the detective work comes in. The records left behind by each of your ancestors are like so many fingerprints— clues that will help you follow your line back further and further. As you learn some of the details of an ancestor's life, you'll try to figure out what sort of records he may have left. If you know he attended a certain church, you'll go there to look for records of his birth, marriage or death. If you learn how he made his living, you may be able to find him listed in a trade directory. If a black ancestor was a slave, you won't look for a will, since he couldn't own property, but you may be able to locate information about him in plantation documents or in the wills of his owners.

Many years ago genealogy was largely the pastime of upper-class families of European origin. However, with the increase in leisure time and the growth of ethnic consciousness and pride among Americans during this century, popular interest in searching for ancestors has spread to people of all nationalities. Alex Haley's acclaimed book, *Roots,* published in 1976, is an account of how one black American, through years of persistent work, was able to trace his family back through the period of slavery to its origin in Africa.

The bibliographies in this book include the most comprehensive list of references for foreign genealogical research ever published, a panoramic overview of sources that reveal the movements of ethnic groups and individuals from their places of origin to other parts of the world, particularly to the western hemisphere. There are also lists of archives, record offices, libraries and genealogical societies in foreign countries to which you can write when you're ready to carry your line "across the water" to the place from which your ancestors emigrated.

After you've traced your family through several generations you can put together a scrapbook made up of an ancestor chart, written accounts of your forebears' lives and some of the more intriguing pictures and documents you've turned up in the course of your research. It will be a memento valued by your family now and for generations to come. You may want to have your genealogy printed so that you can distribute copies to relatives and to libraries and historical societies where other genealogists and scholars can consult it.

If you're eligible, you may decide to join one of the many lineage societies in this country in which membership is based on descent from an individual who lived in a particular time and place or rendered a particular patriotic service. The most famous of these organizations is the Daughters of the American Revolution, or D.A.R., in which membership is open, by invitation, to women who can prove descent from someone who performed military or other service to the American side during the Revolutionary War. Membership in a hereditary society will bring you in touch with others who share your interest in history and genealogy. Most of these groups hold occasional social functions and are active in various historical preservation projects.

Searching for your ancestors is an ideal project for the whole family to work on together. Your research may be the inspiration for a vacation trip. You may decide to spend some time looking for early records in the town where your first American ancestors settled or even travel overseas to the country where they originally lived.

One of your most rewarding experiences may be corresponding

with or meeting long-lost relatives, in this country or abroad. When I was about sixteen, I placed an ad in *The New England Historical and Genealogical Register,* asking whether any readers had information about one of my family lines. Someone who saw the ad pointed it out to a first cousin of my grandmother, a woman who had attended my mother's wedding some thirty years before but with whom we had since lost contact. She came to visit us, and the entire relationship was reborn. I frequently visited her in the old family home in Delaware and located many other people in the area to whom I was related. I learned a great deal about my ancestry as a result of these contacts, and the friendship between my branch of the family and those I found in Delaware flourished for many years.

On another occasion I noticed that the last name of a man who did research every day at the library was the same as that of my great-great-grandmother. When I looked into it I learned that my great-great-grandmother and his great-great-grandfather were brother and sister; there were even photographs of his ancestors in my family album. It was especially fun for me to find a relative with similar interests who had done a great deal of research into our family history.

How far back will you be able to trace your family? That depends on your persistence and a certain amount of luck in the amount of information that has survived over the years. If you're among the first or second generation of your family to live in the United States, you probably know the name of the foreign town or city from which your family came. The number of past generations you can uncover will depend on the survival of records there.

If your family came to America at the turn of the century and you are not sure just where they lived overseas, you may learn this by locating copies of your ancestors' marriage or death certificates in this country or by finding them in the records of the federal census of 1900, in which immigrants were required to give the year of their arrival in this country and the date and place of their birth. With clues like these you can extend the family tree a generation or more into the old country, to people born 125 or 150 years ago. How much further you can go will depend, once more, on the existence of records in your forebears' homeland.

If you're descended from the vast wave of immigrants who came to this country in the middle of the 1800's, you may find a great deal of information in the federal census records of the last half of that century, particularly the 1880 census, in which individuals were asked to identify their parents' state or country of birth. Without too much effort you should be able to find ancestors born as many as 175 years ago.

If ancestors on several sides were here during the early 1800's, you'll probably find a Revolutionary War soldier lurking in your background, which means that your family in America dates at least from the middle of the eighteenth century, some 225 years ago. If several lines go back to the Revolution, your ancestry probably includes some of the colonists who settled in the North between 1620 and 1700 or in the South between 1607 and 1700. It can be quite difficult to uncover the birthplace and parentage of one of these foreign-born colonial Americans, but if you succeed in doing so, you can "cross the water" and carry your line back even further.

If you are able to trace your family back into the 1500's, you need to run into a titled line in order to keep going, since prior to the sixteenth century, on the whole, the only recorded genealogies were those of royal, noble and gentle families. By the time you get back that far, it's quite possible that you'll find one or two ancestors who have some connection to the gentry and, through the gentry, to the nobility. Once you've established this link, you can go back much further—in a few European royal lines, to ancestors who lived in the third or fourth centuries.

One of the oldest firmly established lineages is that of Charlemagne (A.D. 742–814), the first Holy Roman Emperor. His ancestry can be traced back to Clovis, the Riparian, Frankish king of Cologne of the Merovingian Family, who is known to have been living in A.D. 420. Connecting their family to the descendants of Charlemagne has become the goal of many dedicated genealogists. If you succeed in finding a line that leads back to Charlemagne—as thousands of people have—you will have traced your family over a period of more than 1,500 years (Illustration 2).

Establishing a similar royal connection in the Mideast might take you back as far as the seventh century. In India you might be able to follow a line back a thousand years. The emperors of

Japan and Ethiopia both claim lineages stretching back before the time of Christ. There are some older pedigrees, if one starts investigating the semi-mythological genealogies of the Norse and Saxon kings, and there have even been genealogies published by Americans in the last few years that purport to show descent all the way from Adam and Eve. The later parts of these lineages—from the Middle Ages on—can be verified against records. While the earlier portions may have some basis in truth, it is impossible to establish the extent to which they are valid.

The different nationalities that have immigrated to America throughout its history have steadily merged, turning each family into a miniature "melting pot," and most Americans will discover that their lineage encompasses many heritages. It is not at all unusual for one person to have Jewish ancestors who arrived at the turn of the twentieth century; Irish ancestors who arrived during the middle of the nineteenth century; English, French and German ancestors who fought in the Revolution; and Colonial progenitors descended from Charlemagne.

Once you have established the identity of an immigrant or other prominent or intriguing ancestor, it can be fascinating to reverse the search process, beginning with him and working forward in time, tracing all of his descendants in this country. When I traced the descendants of Samuel Beals of Boston, a Revolutionary War soldier who was my ancestor, I found among them an English playwright, an American judge at the Nuremburg trials, the stepmother of Harriet Beecher Stowe, the first wife of Vincent Astor, some grandchildren of former Vice President Rockefeller, a few members of Congress, bankers, doctors, lawyers and a wide variety of "average" citizens in the United States, Great Britain, Europe and Africa.

A two-volume genealogy by Mary L. Quist (see New York State bibliography) shows how another genealogist uncovered an entire United Nations in a single family in this way. Beginning with a Colonial ancestor—Walter Covey, an obscure Dutchess County, New York, farmer—and working forward with great persistence, she turned up descendants and their spouses who bear Spanish, Chinese, Japanese, German, Jewish, Arab, Scottish, Irish, French, Dutch, Polish, Russian and Hungarian names and who represent an awesome variety of races and religions.

A work with a similar intention but a much different focus is

Le Sang de Louis XIV (see French bibliography), published in Portugal in 1962. It traces the descendants of France's Louis XIV, which today include people in all walks of life, both Christian and Jewish, living throughout Europe and the United States. Interestingly enough, two of Louis' descendants through illegitimate lines are once again at the seat of French power. They are Valéry Giscard d'Estaing, the French President, and his wife.

You can give as much time as you choose to the search for your ancestors. If you become as engrossed as I have you'll stay with it for a lifetime. No matter how far you go, the search hasn't really ended. There's always the irresistible challenge of seeing whether you can carry your line back through just one more generation.

Part One

How to Find Your Ancestors

X

2 Roadmaps for the Search

Once you begin talking to relatives about your family's history, you'll accumulate a surprisingly large volume of information in a very short time. From the very beginning you can organize this material by transferring the facts you uncover to standard genealogical charts as you go along. These partially filled-in charts serve as the roadmaps for your search; they help you keep track of what you've already learned, and blank spaces show at a glance where more work needs to be done.

You're probably eager to start collecting information about your ancestors, but take a little time first to read through this chapter's general guidelines about the charts and filing system you can use to keep your materials in order as they accumulate. Establishing good record-keeping habits from the outset will simplify all the research ahead and can spare you much needless backtracking later on.

A variety of large decorative charts on which you can show your complete ancestry can be purchased from genealogical supply stores (see Chap. 32), and eventually you may want to fill one out and mount it as a gift or wall display. For the time being, however, your charts are tools, and the most easily manageable forms are those on standard 8½-inch by 11-inch paper, which can be kept in a looseleaf notebook and carried with you on research trips. You need two kinds of "working sheets"—biographical worksheets for recording the facts about each family member (see Illustration 3) and pedigree charts for graphically mapping the line of descent from one generation to the next (Illustration 4).

You can purchase these charts, which are available in a variety of formats, from genealogical bookstores (see Chap. 32) or you can make your own, following the examples shown in this book and making as many photocopies as you need. To start out, you need about ten pedigree charts and thirty biographical worksheets.

As shown, the individual biographical worksheets provide space for recording very detailed personal information about each family member—his or her profession and military service, religion, education, residences, memberships and hobbies—as well as basic genealogical data about birth, marriage and children. A genealogy that consists simply of names and dates is neither fun to research nor interesting to read. You want to discover the *people* from whom you're descended—how they looked, what they thought and how they spent their time. By finding answers to as many of the questions on the worksheets as possible you'll be developing full-blown portraits of your ancestors. Referring to the sheets while you do your research will remind you of the questions to pursue.

In addition, the seemingly minor details developed in the biographical worksheets may prove crucial to your basic research. For example, if you're having trouble learning the identity of your grandmother's parents but have found out where she went to school, a search of the school records may turn up the names you're looking for. Knowing that your great-grandfather was a merchant in a particular city may lead you to an early city directory in which you will find additional facts.

A pedigree chart is a simple, graphic representation of your direct line of descent through four or five generations. It contains spaces for the most basic genealogical data—date and place of birth, marriage and death—for each ancestor. Keeping working pedigree charts makes it easy to see at a glance where lines and facts need to be fleshed out by additional research.

A four-generation chart like the one shown has spaces for information about fifteen family members. It is somewhat easier to use than a five-generation chart, because there is more room for writing in names, dates and places. Your first chart, with your own name as the first entry, has room for data about yourself, your parents, grandparents and great-grandparents. When you've filled it, you can use additional copies to extend your line further.

A simple numbering system will enable you to connect one chart to another and cross-reference the pedigree charts to the biographical worksheets. Your own name is the first entry on the first pedigree chart; it goes in blank number 1. As indicated, your father's name and data go in blank 2, your mother's in 3 and so on. Proceeding in this fashion, you'll enter the name of one of your great-grandfathers in space 8. What do you do with his parents?

Take a second chart and enter your great-grandfather's name

in the first blank, but renumber it 8. Continue to fill in this chart just as you did the first, but renumber each blank, In every case, the number of an individual's father will be equal to twice the individual's number; in this example, your great-great-grand-father will be number 16 (Illustration 4a). A woman's number is one more than her husband's; in this case, your great-great-grandmother will be number 17.

Any name appearing in the far-right column of one pedigree chart can be moved into the first position on a new chart as sufficient information becomes available. While the numbering system I've described may seem complicated at the moment, its logic and consistency will become apparent as soon as you actually begin to use it. I've found it simpler and more useful than any of the many numbering systems devised by genealogists.

The number that identifies your ancestor on the pedigree chart is also used to identify him on his individual biographical sheet; it goes in the space in the upper right of each page. Because the same name often turns up in several generations of a family, failure to use these identifying numbers can make your charts very confusing.

Make all entries on both pedigree charts and biographical worksheets as complete and accurate as you can. Use full names (noting nicknames in parentheses) and be careful to check spellings and dates. Identify a married woman by her maiden name, because when you go back one generation further this will become one of the family names you're tracing. If you have tentative information, fill it in with pencil until you're able to confirm it.

As you research earlier generations you may find that some surnames are spelled differently in various records. The spelling of names wasn't standardized until the latter part of the last century, when centralized record keeping was undertaken in some areas and the majority of adult Americans learned to write their names. Still, you may find that one of your nineteenth-century ancestors signed his own name two different ways on the same day. Record any variant spellings in parentheses after the most common spelling. Later on, when you're searching census and other government records, you'll need to check all possible spellings if you have any trouble locating your ancestors.

Information on biographical worksheets should be as detailed as possible. In the space for education, for example, fill in the names and addresses of schools your ancestor went to and the years he attended or graduated, if you can learn them. It's most convenient to list all the children of a marriage on the father's worksheet. On the mother's, in the space provided for children, refer to her husband's worksheet: "see Hamilton, John Caldwell."

The very first biographical worksheet you fill out should be your own. Although you may feel silly writing down facts about yourself that you know only too well, remember that your genealogy will be preserved, read and perhaps continued by future generations.

On the back of each pedigree chart and in the spaces provided on the biographical worksheets, carefully and completely identify the sources from which your information is taken. If you've consulted birth, marriage or death certificates, identify them by number. If your source is a book, record the title, author, publisher, date of publication and the page numbers on which the facts appear. Being painstaking about these details now will make it easy for you to return to these sources later, if necessary. An accurate record of your sources will also be essential if you decide you want to join a hereditary society, for which you will have to show proof of your lineage.

The numbering system you've established for your charts serves as the basis for a convenient filing system you can use to keep track of the research materials you acquire as your genealogy progresses. Although you may need to subdivide your files as the volume of material you have increases, begin by keeping all the notes, correspondence, photographs and documents that pertain to the ancestors on one pedigree chart in a single file. An additional, sundry file for each chart can be used to store undocumented stories, general information about surnames and other miscellaneous material.

If one person's name appears on two pedigree charts, store the documents that pertain to him in the file of the chart on which his name is the first listed. Keep your files in numerical order, according to the number of the first name given on the chart.

One or more additional files can be used to store information about collateral ancestors—early family members from whom you are not directly descended, such as your grandfather's brother. Since these individuals aren't direct ancestors, their names won't appear on your pedigree charts, but it's good to keep files on them, since some of their descendants may have family Bibles and other documents that contain facts about your direct ancestors. You'll also need information about collateral ancestors later, if you want to prepare a complete genealogy, beginning with an early ancestor and working forward, showing all his descendants. You may want to fill out biographical worksheets for those collateral ancestors who lived to adulthood and had families. To avoid confusion resulting from similar names, you can expand your numbering system to include them by the addition of letters. If your great-great-grandfather is number 16, his eldest child is 16a, the next 16b, and so on.

Your final organizational tool is a divided notebook that will serve as a record of your research. In one section keep track of all the letters you send—whether to individuals who may have knowledge of your ancestry or to government and church offices for copies of birth, death and marriage records. Make note of when letters were sent and for what purpose and when they were answered and with what result. An occasional check of this correspondence diary will tell you when it's time to follow up an unanswered letter with a second inquiry. It's also a good idea to file copies of all the letters you write.

In another section of your notebook record the research you've done in person, when and with what result. If you've used books, write down the author and title and the pages consulted. Be sure to make note of people and printed references that don't yield useful information. Knowing what sources have proved unproductive will help you plan future research more effectively and will save you, months later, from going back to sources you've already tried but have forgotten about.

In a third section note which family members have Bibles, scrapbooks, photo albums and other family documents.

Calendars and "Double Dating"

When you've worked back to records dating from before 1753, you may encounter entries such as "13 February 1702/03" or "11 January 1731/32" and other discrepancies in dating that can be explained by a brief review of the history of our modern calendar.

The calendar we use today, known as the Gregorian Calendar, was devised by Pope Gregory XIII in 1582 and was adopted by countries under the influence of the Roman Catholic Church in that year.

England and her colonies, however, continued to use the older, so-called Julian Calendar until 1752, by which time there was an eleven-day discrepancy between the two systems. When Parliament decided to adopt the Gregorian Calendar it directed that eleven days be dropped from the calendar—that September 2, 1752, be followed by September 14—and that New Year's Day, previously considered to be March 25, be changed to January 1.

We can understand the contradictions that resulted from these changes most clearly by considering the birth date of George Washington. Although it was originally recorded as February 11, 1731, we now say that Washington was born on February 22, 1732. When the calendar was changed in 1752, Washington, like many other people, added eleven days to his birth date in order to continue to commemorate the actual anniversary of his birth; this accounts for the change from February 11 to February 22. Moreover, since New Year's Day was commemorated on March 25 when Washington was born, 1732 was still a month away. But by modern reckoning, with January 1 as the start of the new year, he was born in 1732.

To resolve this confusion, the people of the time frequently used "double dates" such as "1731/32" to clarify dates falling in the first three months of years prior to 1752. You may also find dates recorded as 1731 O.S. (old style) or 1732 N.S. (new style). Because many people began to use the Gregorian system long before the government actually adopted it, you may find such double dates noted many years before the official change took place.

When you encounter apparent contradictions in the dates given in early records, you will often find that they can be explained by these calendar changes. Suppose, for example, that a Bible record reveals the astonishing fact that one of your female ancestors bore children on April 5, 1718, and March 20, 1718. Taking into account the eventual change in the beginning of the new year, you'll understand that the second child, according to today's calendar, was actually born in March 1719.

Imagine that a gravestone inscription says that an ancestor

died on August 28, 1812, "aged 80 years, 6 months and 12 days." You calculate, mathematically, that he was born on February 16, 1732, but when you uncover a birth record the date is given as February 5, 1731. That apparent contradiction is eliminated when you recall that February 16, 1732, is the new-style equivalent of February 5, 1731 O.S.

It's also important to remember these calendar changes when you encounter old records in which months are represented by numbers rather than by names, as in "4, 2nd month, 1659." The Quakers, in particular, favored this system of writing dates. Since March was regarded as the first month of the year in 1659, the date represented is April 4, 1659.

In most numerically represented dates, the sequence used is day, month, year, but it's always a good idea to check enough dates in a given record to be sure. If your ancestor's birth date is noted as 3:29:1644, it's clear that the dating sequence used in this particular document must be month, day, year, since there is no twenty-ninth month. But if he was born 4:11:1644, you can't be sure of how to interpret the date unless you can find another in the same record, such as 23:4:1644, which clarifies the sequence. In this case, it is day, month, year, as usual, and your ancestor was born on 4 November 1644.

Prepared now with notebooks, charts and—by far your most valuable tool—an inquiring and selective mind, you're ready to start contacting all the people you know who may have knowledge of your ancestry and to begin your research in earnest.

3 Interviewing Relatives

The American family is more fractured and isolated today than it has been at any time in the country's history. Because of the steady urbanization and increased mobility of our society, it is less and less common for a family to remain in one house—or even one region—over several generations. It is also increasingly rare to find more than two generations living together under the same roof, so children are no longer likely to grow up with grandparents nearby to regale them with stories about "the good old days."

For a genealogist, the time spent re-establishing contact with older relatives by interviewing them about the family's history can be the most fascinating and emotionally gratifying phase of research. If relatives live so far away that you can't visit them, you can learn a great deal by contacting them by phone or mail, but by far the most pleasant and most productive interviews are those you do in person.

Before you visit, give your relative a general idea, perhaps in a brief note, of the kind of information you're going to need. This will give him a few days to start recalling people and events he may not have thought about in years and to look for any old scrapbooks or mementos he has stored away.

You'll want to learn more than names and relationships. Where were your ancestors born? What church did they attend? What were their politics? In what country did they live before coming to America, and when and why did they emigrate? If you take along copies of your flow charts and biographical sheets when you go to see your relatives, they'll remind you of many of the questions you need to ask.

Make careful notes of everything you find out; you might even use a tape recorder. Try to get the person you're interviewing to be as specific as possible about exact names and places. If he refers to one of your ancestors by a nickname, write it down, but try to get the proper name as well. If he has difficulty remembering dates, you may be able to zero in on approximate dates through skillful questioning.

For example, if your relative doesn't know when his grandfather died, you can ask questions like "Was he alive when you were born?" "Can you remember him?" "How old were you when he died?" You may also be able to determine the date of a family event if your relative can place it in historical context. If he says, "I don't know just when Aunt Mary died, but I do remember that it was at the time of the exposition in Buffalo," you may, with a little research, be able to find out when that exposition was. After you've interviewed a few relatives, you'll find yourself becoming quite adroit at working back and forth from one event to another, helping the person whom you're interviewing to remember more, perhaps, than he thinks he does.

Write down any interesting or amusing anecdotes that will add life and vividness to your family's story, including the inevitable one that alleges that your family has some royal blood. It's possible that your ancestors may have moved up or down the social scale, but if all your grandparents were humble people, it's not very likely that you'll find truth in stories about your ancestors' "blue blood." Eventually, though, you may discover just how such a story started.

Carefully label your notes with the name of the person interviewed, and preserve them even after you've transferred the information in them to your charts and biographical sheets. Later, if you need to check certain facts or pursue them further, it will be easy to find out which relative gave you the original information.

After you've accumulated more facts and raised some new questions, go back and talk to your relatives a second and even a third time. Repeat visits are almost always worthwhile, as older people, in particular, tend to recall more and more information the more they talk about their early memories. If your family came from a relatively small town, remember that you may be able to learn a great deal not only from your blood relatives but from any "old-timers" living there who knew your family well.

When you can't visit one of your relatives in person, a well-thought-out inquiry sent by mail can produce a lot of helpful information. The secret is to be very specific about the facts you're looking for. Probably the most effective method for doing research by mail is to make up an informal questionnaire containing some of the details you already know, with blank spaces where your relative can fill in names and dates you need:

Your father, _____ _____
Ross, married Catherine Mary Davis on _____
_____, 18_____, in _____ church, in
_____, Wisconsin. He was born on _____
_____, 18_____, in _____, Massachusetts. He
died on _____ _____, 19_____, in _____,
Wisconsin, and is buried in _____ Cemetery
in _____, Wisconsin.

You can also send your relative a copy of a partially filled-in flow chart and ask him to fill in any blanks he can.

Be careful not to ask too much; if you overwhelm the person to whom you're writing, you may get no answer at all. One or two typewritten pages of questions are all you should send. If your first letter draws a good response, then you can follow up with additional queries.

Send a warm, chatty letter along with your questionnaire. If you and the person to whom you're writing have never met, introduce yourself and tell him how you acquired his name and address. Describe what you're trying to accomplish and give a general summary of what you've already learned, both to stimulate your relative's memory and to give him a chance to correct any errors. Stress that any information at all is valuable, that he should return your questionnaire even if he can fill in only a few blanks and that he should feel free to change any facts you've given which he thinks are incorrect. Be sure to enclose a stamped, self-addressed envelope for the reply. Save all the answers to your letters, making a careful note of who sent them.

As your research progresses, you'll find yourself writing more and more often to people whom you've never met, whose names have been given to you by others. Make it a rule to follow up every lead of this sort with at least a brief note asking whether the person does, in fact, know something about your ancestry.

When I was working on my own genealogy I mentioned to another genealogist at the library that a line I was tracing included a Floyd family on the eastern shore of Virginia. He had been corresponding with a Mrs. Walker Parish of Richland, Georgia, who knew something about a Floyd family in Virginia and suggested that I write to her. Although there was only a remote possibility that this might be the family in which I was interested, I wrote to Mrs. Parish, explaining that I needed information about the family of Berry Floyd of Northampton County, Virginia. This was indeed the family to whom she was related, and she sent me the name of a relative in Maryland who, she thought, might be able to give me further details.

Again I followed up the lead with a letter, and to my amazement my second correspondent, Mrs. Bessie Mears of Baltimore, sent me numerous facts abstracted by her mother from three different family Bibles. Included were the 1749 birth date of my great-great-great-great-grandmother, Kesiah Floyd; the names of her parents, Berry Floyd and Esther Dalby; the date of her marriage; the name and birth date of her husband, Archibald Garrison; and the names and birth dates of all of their children. This was an absolutely incredible discovery, since few public or church vital records have survived from eighteenth-century Virginia. Mrs. Mears was also able to tell me the location of the original records, which her mother had copied many years before.

To follow up such a remote connection and discover detailed information that led me to so many new lines was remarkable. And when you consider how easy and inexpensive it is to write someone a letter, it seems foolish to let even a tenuous lead slip by without making some effort to pursue it.

4 Using Family Records

At one time the great houses of England had "muniments rooms" in which letters, deeds and other documents of ownership were stored. Many genealogists owe their success in tracing back English family lines to the fact that the records of many of these great families have been given to local or county record offices. Even the descendants of humble families have benefited, since in the manorial rolls one may find a record of five or six generations of a tenant family.

This is but one example of the importance of privately kept records. A few generations ago, when families were likely to settle in one place for many years, attics were treasure troves of their memorabilia. Such attics are rarer today, but most modern families have their own equivalent of a muniments room, even if it's just a tin box of family papers like the one my father kept.

Whether you interview relatives in person or by mail, be sure to ask whether they have any family documents or keepsakes that might contain genealogical information. Since public records weren't kept routinely until the mid- to late 1800's, earlier records saved by your family—Bibles, letters, diaries, account books, newspaper clippings and official documents—will be extremely valuable. Such heirlooms as engraved jewelry and silver, portraits and photographs, samplers and quilts may also bear useful clues (Illustration 5).

The custom of writing down births, deaths and marriages on the pages of a family Bible dates back to the sixteenth century in Europe. Such a record is one of the most valuable finds you can make. If it predates the keeping of public records, or if church and local records of the period have been destroyed, it may be your only source for many facts. If public records have survived, the Bible can confirm their accuracy and reveal additional information. Whenever possible, it's good to have at least two sources for your facts.

If a relative who lives far away has a Bible that contains a family record, you can ensure the accuracy of the information you'll receive by asking him to have a photostatic copy made. If he protests that the Bible is too fragile to copy, point out that the copy will still be around after the original has crumbled. Urge him to have one made for his own use, too, so that he can avoid handling the fragile pages. If you can't get a photostatic copy for some reason, ask your relative to transcribe the Bible record and have the transcript notarized. The notary should check the transcript against the original and testify that they are identical.

Look for clues in any old books that have been in your family's possession for some time—for inscriptions on their frontispieces, or clippings or pictures tucked between their pages. A book inscribed "To Jennifer on her tenth birthday, July 5, 1879, from Aunt Martha Stone" will confirm a relationship and provide you with a birth date (Illustration 6). A story that one of my ancestors was related to Scottish nobility was partially confirmed when I found a little book that had belonged to my great-grandmother inscribed, "To my dear little niece, Philly, from her affectionate Aunt Philadelphia, Countess of Mar and Kellie." Just a name and address written in the front of a book by the owner can help you find a town in which your family once lived.

Every little scrap of paper in the "family archives" must be investigated. I have a slim diary, given to me by a cousin, in which my great-great-great-grandmother recorded the date that her family left Ireland to come to this country; the dates that different members of the family moved from Canandaigua, New York, to California and New Orleans; the date of her marriage in Wicklow, Ireland, in 1812; and the birth dates of her children. All of this was extremely helpful, and it's all in a small notebook that someone might easily have thrown out.

You can often unravel a lot of details about your family from information found in old letters. There were several valuable letters in my father's black box, including one my great-grandfather wrote in 1852 to his future father-in-law, asking for his daughter's hand, and another with an account of a trip to attend a cousin's wedding. Letters are especially important in the South, where few vital records survived the devastation of the Civil War.

The still-popular custom of keeping a wedding book signed by the minister, the bridal couple, the members of the wedding party and the guests dates from at least the early part of this century. If you find one, you can be quite sure that some of those who signed are relatives of the bride or groom, although additional research will be necessary to determine the exact relationships. If you ask older family members "Who is this person?" "How is she related?" you may well find that the names in the book stir their imaginations and help them recall a great deal of fresh information.

Portraits and Photographs

Today, having a portrait painted seems a rather elegant idea. Before the advent of photography, however, it wasn't unusual for even humble people to have portraits painted or silhouettes cut out by itinerant artists. Louis Daguerre, a Frenchman, invented the daguerreotype process, the first practical photographic method, in 1839, and by 1841 most of the principal cities of the United States had a "Daguerrean" Parlor or at least a visiting Daguerreotypist. After that time most people had a daguerreotype made at least once in their lives, often for a special occasion, such as a wedding.

Portraits, daguerreotypes and photographs add an important dimension to your finished genealogy by showing what your ancestors looked like. They can also provide important clues for furthering your research. Check the frames and backs of paintings for the names of either the subject or the artist. If you find an old family album, be sure to check the backs of the pictures for the names of the photographers or sitters, dates and places. Look for wedding pictures, which became popular in the 1840's, as they were frequently inscribed (Illustration 7).

For a good genealogical sleuth, the name of a portraitist or photographer can be a very valuable clue. Suppose you find a picture of a bridal couple who you believe are your great-grandparents with the legend "I. Day, Syracuse, N.Y." on the back. If you can find out, by looking in early city directories (Chap. 7), when I. Day did business as a photographer in Syracuse, you'll have narrowed down the period in which your great-grandparents were married and can begin the search for their marriage record.

Images themselves may also contain clues. If you have a picture of an ancestor in uniform, its style may indicate a particular war or historical period, and this in turn may lead you to his service record in the National Archives (Chap. 10).

There are people who collect old portraits, and many books have been published about them; so if your ancestor had his portrait painted or was sketched by a famous silhouette artist, his picture may turn up in a portrait collection or in a book or article. In Chapter 22 is a list of references in which you can find old portraits, silhouettes and photographs from many countries.

John Lockwood's "The Wortham Worthies," one of the articles cited, describes how between the years 1827 and 1877 in the town of Wortham, England, the Reverend Richard Cobbold made watercolor sketches of many of the people of the town in his parish poorbook. All of these pictures—about 100 of them—have been identified and preserved. Now, clearly, only a few genealogists will be able to count these eighteenth-century people of Wortham among their ancestors, but the possibility that you'll find something similar in the course of your own research is what makes genealogy so much fun.

The American Library Association's *Index to Portraits in Printed Works*, often referred to as the "A.L.A. Portrait Index," is an extensive three-volume guide to portraits in works published up to 1906, the year in which the index first appeared. Through it I located a delightful caricature of an ancestor, Sir Charles Stuart-Menteth. Although Sir Charles was made a baronet by Queen Victoria, he wasn't a particularly important person, and the index lists many portraits of quite ordinary people. Nothing as complete has been published since.

Jewelry and Silver

Important dates can often be found engraved on jewelry. My great-grandmother's wedding ring, for example, comes apart, revealing the initials and wedding date of my great-grandparents. A ring that belonged to my great-great-great-great-grandmother, Ludivina Loughnan, is the only source I have for the date of her birth on the island of Madeira on March 12, 1772. I also have a pair of cuff links that my great-grandmother presented to her husband on their twenty-fifth wedding anniversary. The years are worked into the design—1852, the year of their wedding, on one cuff link, and 1877, the year of their anniversary, on the other. On the back of each is their wedding date, May 10, You may find a tiny portrait of one of your ancestors concealed in a locket (Illustration 8).

Mourning jewelry was a popular custom from the seventeenth to the nineteenth centuries. In his will, a person would instruct that rings or other pieces of jewelry bearing his initials and the date he died be made for relatives and friends. Sometimes the hair of the deceased was entwined in the jewelry, or the jewelry was woven entirely of hair, with the name and date of death on the back (Illustration 9).

Christening cups, popular as baby gifts since the seventeenth century, were engraved with the baby's baptismal date, which was in most cases quite close to his date of birth, although if a family lived far from a church or a child were born in the dead of winter, several months might elapse before he was baptized. The date on a christening cup may lead you to church records of the baptism, which often include the actual birth date (Illustration 10).

If you find a silvermark on family silver, books about silver listed in Chapter 22 may help you determine where it was made and, in some cases, the year in which it was made. If you learn that a piece of wedding silver was made in Baden-Baden, and if you know that the ancestors who owned it were German, you may find out that they were from that kingdom themselves.

Quilts, Embroideries and Other Heirlooms

Wedding quilts, in which the squares were made, signed and dated by friends and relatives of the bridal couple, were popular in the nineteenth century. Samplers and memorial embroideries that date from the eighteenth century may also contain important dates and names. Some samplers were specific genealogical records, perhaps stitched in the shape of a family tree (Illustration 11). A dower or hope chest that belonged to one of your ancestors may have her initials and wedding date carved on the front.

If you own a camera, you'll find that it's a useful recording tool when you're searching through family heirlooms. Even with a simple camera it's often possible to get a good rough copy of a portrait, a coat of arms or an old document. If you visit the home of an ancestor, take a picture of that, too; it will be an interesting addition to your completed genealogy.

5

Stones Can Speak

f you've exhausted family sources, at least for the time being, you're ready to turn your attention to the myriad genealogical records maintained outside the family. This and the next several chapters describe many basic sources, such as cemeteries, libraries, government record offices, churches and other institutions, from which you will learn the facts that will enable you to trace your family line back beyond the reach of any of your living relatives' memories.

Keep in mind that there is no set order in which you should utilize these resources. The path you take in following your family lines will depend on the particular problems posed by your individual genealogy. You'll often find yourself using several types of records simultaneously, piecing together information from all of them to reconstruct your family's history.

Don't worry that you'll have too many sources for your genealogy; the more references you have to back up each fact, the more likely you are to produce an accurate family history. Remember that even original documents sometimes contain errors. If you find records that contradict one another—and you will—you'll have to do additional work to determine which is correct.

Cemeteries

Old cemeteries are storehouses of genealogical information, which can be gleaned from the inscriptions on the tombstones and from the records of the cemetery superintendent. Locating the grave of just one of your ancestors can lead you to an enormous amount of new data if it turns out that several other members of the family are buried in the same plot (Illustration 12).

Relatives should be able to tell you where some family plots are located. In other cases you will find the name of the cemetery in which a person is buried listed on his or her death certificate (see Chap. 8). If you have no other leads but know the approximate date and place of an ancestor's death, you can find out from historical societies in the area what cemeteries were operating at that time and begin checking their records for the name of your ancestor. *The Directory of United States Cemeteries*, published in 1974 by Cemetery Research, Inc., may be helpful. Often I've found the cemetery I was looking for just by checking the area yellow pages. If cemeteries that you're interested in are now defunct, it's possible that their records have been preserved by the local historical society.

When you've learned where an ancestor is buried, write to the superintendent of the cemetery and ask for a list of all the interments in his plot. Do this even if you live close enough to visit the cemetery, since the superintendent's files often contain information that is not revealed in the inscriptions on your ancestors' tombstones. Sometimes there aren't even tombstones for everyone buried in a plot. The Brandywine Cemetery in Wilmington, Delaware, contains only a curbstone reading, "J. Elliott," but when I obtained the interment record I learned that both my great-grandmother, Jane Elliott (1827–1908), and her son, Henry Turner (1849–1897), my grandfather, were buried there.

Since cemetery records are often kept chronologically, and to avoid confusion with other families of the same name, give the name and burial date of one ancestor in your letter to the superintendent. You might write, "Please send me a list of all the interments in the plot of John S. Barker, who was buried in late November 1905. He was my grandfather, and I need this information for genealogical purposes." Send a stamped, self-addressed envelope for the reply and enclose a check for five dollars to cover the cost of looking up this information and to convey the seriousness of your inquiry.

Record-keeping policies vary from cemetery to cemetery. Some will be able to tell you only the names of those buried in the family plot and the dates on which they were buried. Others may send very complete information about each ancestor, such as "Frank M. Jacobs was born August 10, 1865, in Adrian, Michigan. He died April 3, 1941, from a fracture in the skull and was buried April 6, 1941. His last address was 112 Academy Street, Buffalo. His wife, Martha Jacobs, survived him."

Some cemeteries will send all the information they have in response to your first inquiry, and several will even return your check, because they consider this to be one of their normal services. Other cemeteries will send a list of names and burial dates, along with a notice that if you require the more complete information recorded on individual "interment cards" you must request it for each ancestor and pay a fee—generally from $1 to $5—for each request.

Visit every family plot within traveling distance to see what you can learn from the inscriptions on your ancestors' tombstones (Illustration 13). When I located my wife's great-great-grandmother's stone in Tuskegee, Alabama, it identified her as Emmeline, wife of Rev. Alfred J. Williams and daughter of Newnam Reynolds. This was marvelous luck, because in 1883, the year she died in Alabama, parents' names weren't recorded on death certificates filed there. Her tombstone was the first source I found that identified her father. After I learned his name I was able to locate the will of Newnam Reynolds, probated in 1863 in the Macon County Courthouse, which confirmed their relationship. Eventually I found the stones for Newnam Reynolds and his wife, Lucy Scarborough, which revealed that they were natives of Caswell County, North Carolina.

Often tombstones may give the military unit in which a veteran served, information that can lead you to pension and other service records kept by the federal government (see Chap. 10). Some inscriptions, such as "Mary Dyer, widow of Thomas, who was lost at sea in 1873," will tell you something about people not buried in the plot. These are the kinds of things you can miss if you rely only on the interment record.

If a cemetery is too far away to visit, write to the superintendent and ask whether he knows of a local person whom you can hire to photograph your ancestors' tombstones for you. If you visit the cemetery yourself, copy the inscription on every stone in the plot, then make a photograph or rubbing (Chap. 5) of each to keep with your records.

Published Epitaphs and Interment Records

Many genealogists find the hours they spend searching among early American gravestones and deciphering the quaint, barely legible inscriptions to be one of the most fascinating parts of their research. For some, this has led to a second avocation— recording and preserving the epitaphs on early cemetery stones in various parts of the country, creating invaluable records for future researchers.

Among the most delightful and painstaking of the people who have done this kind of work was Nona Parkin of Reno, Nevada, who published extensive transcripts of cemetery inscriptions in the American Southwest. Fond of calling herself "Nona, the Nutty Necrologist," she also wrote several lively, amusing and instructive accounts of her experiences exploring old graveyards.

Another researcher, John Eldridge Frost, has compiled several bookshelves full of transcriptions of old tombstones in York County, Maine. He has located abandoned public and private cemeteries hidden deep in the woods, sometimes finding buried graveyards by probing in the ground with a long metal rod. On one occasion he unearthed seventeen pre-Revolutionary War stones, copied them, then carefully buried them again in order to preserve the inscriptions.

Several printed collections of epitaphs and interment records are included in the bibliography of resources in Part II of this book, and their value has been demonstrated in my own research many times. In 1970 I enjoyed wandering through the beautiful grounds of Greyfriars Cemetery in Edinburgh, where, beneath the ramparts of Edinburgh Castle, many of my Murray, Johnston, Menteth and Nisbet ancestors are buried, but I found it nearly impossible to read the inscriptions on the stones. Fortunately, the Scottish Record Society published the interment records in 1902. In 1973 I searched the churchyard of King's Chapel in Boston for the monument of Samuel Beals, my four-times great-grandfather, whom Thomas Bridgman, in his book on the King's Chapel burial ground, had said was interred there. Around 1853 Bridgman had found the stone inscribed, "In Memory of Mr. Samuel Beals who died Novr 15h 1795 aged 39 years," but I searched in vain for the tomb of this man, whose daughter, Lydia Beals, married the Reverend Lyman Beecher and became the stepmother of Harriet Beecher Stowe and Reverend Henry Ward Beecher.

In London in 1975 I took a taxi to St. Mary's Paddington, where, I knew from reading Daniel Lysons' work on London churches, my great-great-great-great-grandfather Thomas Loughman was buried in 1789. As the cab approached the church I had an ominous feeling. A wide new highway to Heathrow Airport passed almost in front of the church door, and there were no tombstones in sight. Many English and European churches, I have discovered, have pulled up their tombstones and either piled them against the church or tossed them in the rubbish.

When I visited New Orleans and looked for the Girod Cemetery, the old Protestant cemetery in which many of my father's relatives were buried, I learned that it had been eliminated during the construction of a new speedway, and all the bodies had been placed in one large marble building. Fortunately, a nostalgic book, *To Glorious Immortality* by Leonard V. Huber, contained a picture of one Beard tomb, and a list of interments can be found on cards in the Pontalba Library on Jackson Square in New Orleans.

Any time you visit an ancestral burying ground, take pictures and copy all the inscriptions, for the next time you visit you may find that your ancestors' monuments have been destroyed by man or nature. Many years ago, when I was a teenager, I was taken to see a Baptist cemetery at Sycamore, Delaware, where Philip Short (1787–1858) and his wife, Sally Hill Short (1794–1855), ancestors of my mother, were buried. I was able to read the quaint Victorian inscriptions then, but thirty years later they are almost illegible. Her stone read, "Dear Husband Hardly Could My Voice Say Adieu to Thee, When Death Had Taken For Its Choice my Form So Loved By Thee," and his "Language of Itself Can Never Tell the Feelings Of My Heart, When We Were Forced To Say Farewell and Knew We Had to Part." These may have been standard inscriptions sold by the makers of tombstones, but my ancestors' choice of them suggests that they were a devoted couple and gives an added dimension to their characters. I'm glad I copied the inscriptions before pollution virtually erased them.

It is also fortunate that I photographed the tombstones in the West Avenue Cemetery plot of my ancestors, the Finleys, in Canandaigua, New York as, the next time I visited, the handsome wrought-iron railing around the plot had been taken down and the stones flattened, apparently for the convenience of the man who mowed the grass.

Tips on Research in Older Cemeteries

Deciphering the legends on early cemetery stones often demands considerable patience. When you visit older cemeteries, take along a stiff scrub brush, a wire brush and a small trowel for use in removing any lichens that obscure the lettering. Use the softer brush whenever possible, working carefully to avoid breaking flaking sandstone.

Passing a damp sponge across the surface of a stone darkens it while leaving the engraved letters dry, causing them to show up more clearly. Rubbing grass vigorously over the stone's surface accomplishes the same effect but is less desirable, since it leaves a long-lasting stain. Tracing the lettering with chalk is another way to make the inscriptions stand out, especially when you want to photograph them. Viewing stones at different hours of the day can also help, since light falling at a particular angle may throw the letters into sharper relief.

Check all sides of tombstones for information. Some may have been used more than once, and others may have a coat of arms or other significant design on the back. If an inscription extends close to the ground, dig away enough dirt at the base to be sure that none of it has been buried. As Nona Parkin noted in her writings, a buried surname completely alters the significance of a stone. In every case, refill any holes you dig and make every effort to leave things as you found them.

If you're working in an old cemetery and have the time, you can perform a great service by copying the inscriptions from all the stones there, not just those of your own ancestors. Work in an orderly fashion, row by row, being careful not to omit any stones. You can keep track of which inscriptions you've transcribed by marking each with a colored crayon. The mark will withstand a sudden rainstorm but won't do any lasting damage.

Work slowly. To be of value, this type of record must be absolutely accurate. When you transcribe, use a slash to indicate the point at which lines of the original are broken, and put question marks in brackets to indicate letters or dates you cannot make out. When you think you know what a word is but are not absolutely sure, fill it in but enclose it in brackets. Using a landmark such as the cemetery entrance gate as the starting point, number rows and stones so that others can find them. Your record will look something like this:

Row 17, no. 1: Frank/ Son of/ George and Rena/ Hamilton/ Born July 29, 1841/ Died Nov. 8, 1856/ Our First-Born Child

If a stone is very old, it may have quaint spellings and be hard to read in places. Then your transcript will look more like this:

Row 3, no. 16: Her lies the corps/ of [?????] Bell who/ lived in [Belloch] and died/ the 10 Apr 1802/ aged 53/ don by Mary his wife

Share your work by depositing copies with local libraries and historical societies.

How to Make Rubbings

Many genealogists like to make rubbings of tombstone inscriptions, since they are at once accurate reproductions of the originals and themselves interesting graphic designs. Some people make rubbings with rice paper and block wax purchased from an art supply store, while others make do with wrapping paper and an unwrapped crayon or soft pencil (Illustration 14).

Clip away any weeds growing in front of the tombstone and gently brush off any lichens or soil that obscure the lettering. Cut a piece of paper slightly larger all around than the surface to be rubbed and attach it with masking tape to the top of the stone's center. Pull the paper taut and tape it at the bottom, then use enough additional tape at the top and sides to be sure that the paper is stretched tightly and immovably across the stone's surface.

Warm the wax in your hands for a few moments so that it will adhere easily, then begin rubbing it onto the paper, using a small, circular motion. Work lightly, letting the wax build up gradually until the rubbing is as dark as you want it. Experiment with different strokes to learn which produce the most attractive results. When you're going over letters, rub up and down along their lengths to avoid catching chunks of wax on the letter edges.

When you're finished, remove the tape from the bottom and side edges first, then from the top of the stone by pulling the tape out toward the stone's edge. Use a pencil to mark the place and date of the rubbing in one corner, then roll it loosely and slip it into a long cardboard tube for protection.

6 Libraries and Historical Societies

By the time you've talked to relatives and dug what you can out of the old family records, you'll probably have gathered enough information to begin searching in the reference books and other printed sources maintained by libraries and historical societies. Early maps and atlases, local histories and genealogies, city directories, files of old newspapers and magazines and specialized genealogical guides and indexes can all be invaluable tools in your pursuit of your family line. In the photographic archives maintained by some libraries and societies you may find pictures of ancestral homes or businesses.

You should pay your first visit to your local library as soon as you've gathered a few clues about your family. Get acquainted with the reference materials that are available there and spend some time planning your research. Study early maps and histories of the area where your family lived and find out where most of the settlers originated; this may be a clue to the residence of earlier ancestors. Make note of any changes in boundaries or place names that may be important when you're trying to track down local records. Even if your ancestors lived at a great distance from the place where you live now, your local library will have some references—directories of historical societies, for example—that will be a help in your research.

If you live in a large city, your public library may have a specialized genealogical collection or department that will be particularly useful. If not, your librarian can direct you to the nearest library that does. There may also be a genealogical or historical society with a good library in your vicinity or in the area where your ancestors lived. To find out, consult the *Directory of Historical Societies and Agencies in the United States and Canada*, published by the American Association for State and Local History.

Genealogical collections in the United States may be as vast as the New York Public Library's Local History and Genealogy Division, with its nearly 100,000 books, or as small as Ellen Morris' specialized Morris Genealogical Library in Allenhurst, New Jersey, with its few thousand volumes. The three largest genealogical collections in the country are those maintained by the Genealogical Society of the Church of Jesus Christ of Latter-day Saints, the New York Public Library Research Libraries and the Library of Congress. Other excellent collections are those of the Daughters of the American Revolution and the National Genealogical Society in Washington, D.C., the Newberry Library in Chicago, the New England Historic Genealogical Society in Boston, the Bancroft Library at the University of California's Berkeley campus, the Western Reserve Historical Society in Cleveland and the Fort Wayne, Indiana, Public Library.

The addresses of state archives, historical societies and libraries are given in Part III, which deals with resources in individual states. Major genealogical collections abroad are identified in Part IV, which covers research in other nations. You'll also find the addresses of the national archives of every country in those chapters. When you're ready to extend your research into an ancestor's homeland, you can write the archives to find out whether there's a local history society in the region from which your ancestor came.

When you start doing research in printed sources, it's extremely important to maintain precise records of the work you do. Make a careful and complete note of every reference you consult so that you can easily find it again. I can't count the number of people who wander into the New York Public Library's enormous Local History and Genealogy Division and ask to see the "big red book" or the "little black book" that they consulted during their last visit.

Doing some preliminary work at your local library will give you a chance to familiarize yourself with the use of the library catalogue and other reference guides before you start doing research in larger institutions, such as the NYPL, which can sometimes overawe or annoy newcomers. Because there are very few volumes on open shelves in most research libraries, you need to go to the catalogue to locate the books you want. Although every library has a catalogue, it's often possible to find what you want without using it in small libraries in which all shelves are open to the public, so many people never learn good library habits. If you're accustomed to pulling books off the shelf for yourself in the libraries with which you're familiar, take some time to learn the proper use of the catalogue. Inevitably, it will broaden the scope of your research, since catalogues contain much cross-referencing and indexing of periodicals that can lead you to new resources.

An enthusiastic librarian with a thorough knowledge of the use of historical reference materials can guide you to many sources that will help you advance your family line. Unfortunately, every genealogist on occasion meets another kind of librarian—an overburdened or impatient sort who not only isn't interested in genealogy but can't figure out why anyone else should be. In any case, it's always worthwhile to seek assistance the first time you visit a new research facility. Describe your project to the person in charge and ask whether he or she can suggest any references that will be of use. You have the best chance of getting a helpful response if your research is well organized and you have some definite questions to which you hope to find answers.

Most libraries do not lend out genealogical materials or make them available through interlibrary loan, but if you can't visit a library, you can write for information. Keep your questions brief, giving specific dates and details, and be sure to enclose a self-addressed, stamped envelope for the reply.

Remember that few libraries have enough staff to do a significant amount of research for you. If your query is too long or complicated, the library may send you a list of local researchers whom you can hire directly to do your library work for you. You can also get a list of professional researchers from the Board of Certification of Genealogists in Washington (1307 New Hampshire Avenue, N.W., Washington, D.C. 20036). Fees vary widely, from $3 an hour in some rural areas to $10 or $15 an hour in major cities.

The Genealogical Society of the Church of Jesus Christ of Latter-day Saints

The Genealogical Society of the Church of Jesus Christ of Latter-day Saints (LDS), popularly known as the Mormons, maintains the largest collection of primary genealogical records in the world at their central offices in Salt Lake City. The Mormons' interest in genealogy is directly related to the tenets of their faith, which hold that families are sacred units linked in heaven "for time and all eternity." Each Mormon has a religious obligation to keep complete and accurate records of his immediate family, trace his direct line back as far as possible and arrange the temple baptism of his ancestors.

In 1894 several Mormons organized a genealogical society to facilitate the carrying out of this obligation; in 1944 it was incorporated as the Genealogical Society of the Church of Jesus Christ of Latter-day Saints. Today the Church spends $10 million a year to maintain its enormous collection of genealogical records.

In the 1930's the Mormons began the immeasurable task of microfilming the records of towns, cities, churches and private organizations in this country and around the world. They have amassed over 850,000 100-foot rolls of microfilmed records, which are protected from disaster in deep vaults carved out of a granite mountainside near the city of Salt Lake. The collection is still growing, at the rate of about 50,000 reels a year.

This worldwide microfilming project is of inestimable value to all genealogists. Already some of the original records from which the Mormons made copies have been destroyed by a variety of man-made and natural causes. Moreover, the availability of many foreign records—and genealogists trained to read them—means that it may be possible to do a great deal of "overseas" research without even leaving the United States.

The Mormons also have extensive transcripts of old Bible records, account books, diaries and so on, most copied from original records that have not been published elsewhere. These are also valuable but must be used with somewhat more caution than the microfilmed records, since their accuracy depends on the care taken by the individual who copied them. You should make an effort to substantiate the information taken from such transcripts by locating the original documents.

The facilities of the Genealogical Society Library, free to Mormons and non-Mormons alike, are used by some 6,500 researchers a week. You can write to the Society (50 East North Temple Street, Salt Lake City, Utah 84150) for a complete list of the services they provide. If you want to avail yourself of this storehouse of genealogical records but are unable to travel to Salt Lake City, you can get answers to brief queries by mail and can have photocopies of information sent to you for about 15 cents a sheet from books and 25 cents a sheet from films. (Current fees are quoted in this book to give you a general idea of the cost involved in engaging a particular service. Since costs change frequently, request up-to-date information on services and prices when you contact any institution.) If you want extensive research done, the library will send you a list of private genealogists who specialize in the area you're working in and who have been accredited by the Society to do research in their facilities. You can also get a list of their 190 branch libraries in this country and abroad, through which most of the microfilmed records stored in Salt Lake City can be borrowed.

Among the Society's special sources are their Archives, an alphabetized card file of data on over seven million family groups from the United States and abroad, and the Index Bureau, an alphabetized file of data on 30 million individuals from all countries and eras. Copy service is available for information from the Archives, and searches of the Index Bureau are made by trained personnel. Searches of the Society's Computer File Index—in which information on over 28 million names is stored by computer, alphabetically and by location—must be done in person or through a private genealogist. For $10 you can have the library conduct a survey to determine if others have submitted information on a given pedigree line and to suggest possible sources that can be used to extend that line.

The New York Public Library
While Salt Lake City boasts the largest collection of genealogical raw material in existence, it isn't the answer to every research problem. Many secondary sources such as biographical dictionaries, local histories and family histories are also essential. One of the world's largest and most usable collections of such printed material is located in the New York Public Library at Fifth Avenue and 42nd Street in Manhattan. The Local History and Genealogy Division (Room 315G) has family histories, periodicals, books and pamphlets on the subject of genealogy from all over the world and local histories of the United States and Great Britain, including a great deal of material in typewritten, mimeographed or scrapbook form. Some of these works were acquired more than a century ago by the Astor and Lenox libraries.

Other divisions of the library house several hundred thousand more books that can be useful in family research. The resources of the General Research and Humanities Division (315), for example, include biographies, group biographies and foreign local histories. In the American History Division (315A) you can find state histories, local histories of the Americas outside the United States and information about American Indians and other ethnic groups in this country. The Art and Architecture Division (313) has books dealing with portraits, pictures of houses in certain regions and information about artists' families and sitters. In the Map Division (Room 117) you can consult atlases that identify nineteenth-century property owners. The Science Division (121) has books about the ships and shipping lines that carried many immigrants to this country, while the resources of the Economics Division (228) include military pension records, documents relating to government land distribution and similar publications filled with details important to genealogists. The Manuscript Division (319) has original letters, diaries and other documents that might shed light on the personalities of your ancestors and those connected with them. Some vital records, such as the Methodist Church Records of New York City, are also deposited there.

The library's special collections can also be helpful for tracing certain lines: the Arents' Collection tells much about the families involved in the early Virginia and Maryland tobacco trade, while the Berg Collection includes letters dealing with literary figures. A card is issued in Room 214 for the use of special collections when such use is deemed warranted.

The catalogues of most of the library's divisions are now in print or in the process of being printed, so that they may be consulted in the majority of the large libraries in the United States. They are excellent bibliographies for research in any large institution, and it is especially important to consult them before writing or visiting the NYPL in order to save your time and the time of the librarians who are there to assist you.

The holdings of the library's Local History and Genealogy Division catalogued through 1971 are listed in the eighteen-volume *Dictionary Catalog of the Local History and Genealogy Division*, which was published in 1974 by G. K. Hall & Co. and is available in many libraries. The references in this catalogue are arranged by author and subject; subjects include town and county histories in the United States and Great Britain, family names, genealogy, heraldry and related topics on an international scale. This listing is supplemented by G. K. Hall's two-volume *United States Local History Catalog,* a modified shelf list of local histories, arranged alphabetically by state and by location within states. Books in the subject fields of Room 315G catalogued since January 1, 1972, appear in the constantly changing and expanding blue and red volumes of the automated *Dictionary Catalog of the Research Libraries* intermingled with the works of the other reference divisions of the New York Public Library Research Libraries. All of these more recent volumes are now given a fixed location number, as well as an NYPL classification mark. With this new system, titles, as well as authors and subjects, are listed alphabetically by the computer. In addition, because this collection is extensive and accessible, I have given the NYPL class mark or call number in bibliographical references throughout this book, where it is identified by the prefix NN.

The fact that NYPL genealogical materials aren't available through interlibrary loan can seem a hardship if you live far from New York, but it means that books don't leave the library unless they have to be sent to the bindery, so you can be virtually certain of finding the resources in which you're interested if you do visit. Again, if that's not possible, you can get some information by mail (NYPL, Local History and Genealogy Division, Fifth Avenue and 42nd Street, 315G, New York, NY 10018). The staff of the genealogy division is small and can handle only brief queries. If you need extensive research done, ask the library to send you a list of professional genealogists whom you can employ to do the work for you.

If you think a book listed in the G. K. Hall catalogue or in this book is relevant to your family history, first inquire whether your library has it or can obtain it from a large library nearby through interlibrary loan. If not, you can write the NYPL and ask if the book is indexed and whether an ancestor is listed: "I notice in your catalogue a genealogy of the Gilman family of Exeter, New Hampshire. Can you please check the index to see if my great-grandmother, Alicia Morton, who married Roger Gilman, is mentioned." If you get an affirmative response, you can write for photocopies of the pages that trace your great-grandmother to her immigrant ancestor.

To get photocopies from the library you must pay a $3 service charge in advance for each title in which you are interested. In return, the library will furnish an estimate of the cost of photocopy service. When copies are ordered there is an additional $3.75 service charge for each volume, and the current cost of quick copies is 30 cents for each two-page spread. Though more expensive than quick-copying, photostating—which employs a camera pointed down at, but not touching, the printed page—is less harmful to books. The NYPL will use only the photostatic process to copy rare, delicate or profusely illustrated books. The cost of photostating by the library currently runs from $3.00 to $6.00 a page, depending on whether a negative, a negative and positive or a direct positive is required. (The less expensive negative is sufficient for fact-finding purposes, but you may want a negative and positive if you plan to incorporate the copy in a finished genealogy or display.)

If you can't go to the library in person but are quite certain that a book will be of special value to you, it makes sense to send your $3.00 and request a photocopy estimate (Photographic Services Division, NYPL, 42nd Street and Fifth Avenue, New York, NY 10018). If you need information from a variety of books, it's more practical to hire a genealogist to go to the library for you. If you need copies of several pages from a rare work or a volume in poor condition, check the catalogues of book dealers who specialize in out-of-print genealogical references (see Chap. 32). If one of them has a book you need, you may find that you can buy it for less than it costs to have the pages photostated.

Having material copied by the NYPL staff can be very expensive, but it must be remembered that the library spends a fortune to maintain its excellent local history and genealogy collection so that these volumes will be available for future generations to consult. Books that are subjected to repeated quick-copying—in which the open volume is turned face down and pressed against the copy machine—are often practically destroyed. Rebinding is costly, and if a volume is in very poor condition rebinding is impossible. Moreover, the time spent in preparing a photocopy estimate is rarely covered by the $3 service charge, and an enormous number of these requests are never followed up by the people who make them.

It should also be remembered that the Research Libraries are not supported by public funds but by the inadequate income of the Astor, Lenox, Tilden Foundation and private donations. The New York Public Library was formed in 1895 by the consolidation of the Astor and Lenox Libraries with the residue of the estate of Samuel Jones Tilden, a former governor of New York. While the city paid for the construction of the landmark library building and has been responsible for its upkeep, the contents of the building are owned by the foundation and the salaries of the librarians are paid by private funds. Only the circulating libraries receive support from city funds.

In addition to the main reference library at 42nd Street and Fifth Avenue, reference sections of the library located elsewhere in Manhattan may also be useful in your research. The NYPL Annex at 43rd Street between Tenth and Eleventh avenues houses such important genealogical resources as newspapers, city directories after 1869, college alumni compilations and some religious and legal material of a genealogical nature. The Music, Theater and Dance collections at Lincoln Center are rich in biographical material on people connected with those fields, and the Schomburg Center for Research in Black Culture (103 West 135th Street) contains important volumes dealing with black history and genealogy as well as microfilms of the federal census records of the United States from 1790 to 1880, which are of great value to ancestor hunters of all races (see Chap. 9 for the use of census information). Library hours have been changed frequently in recent years because of financial problems; if you're planning a visit, be sure to write or call ahead to find out when the library will be open.

Library of Congress
As the official copyright library of the United States, the Library of Congress (Washington, D.C. 20540) has a genealogical collection that rivals that of the NYPL in size and scope. It is also the library *for* Congress, however, and every Congressperson has the right to withdraw materials, which means researchers can't always count on finding the books they need. Furthermore, because service to members of Congress and government agencies is the first priority of the Library of Congress, its staff answers only a limited number of written queries from general researchers and declines requests for research in heraldry or family history.

The Library of Congress is not an easy library in which to do research. Because books seem to be misshelved frequently, you may be told a book is not available when in fact it's just not where it should be. A Washington researcher once told me that some years ago he was upset that so many of his book request slips were returned marked "in use" or "not on shelf." He found out how to get into the library stacks and discovered, to his amazement, that the books he had asked for were right on the shelves. Since then he rarely accepts a negative report from a Library of Congress page or librarian without requesting a double check. Despite these drawbacks, the Library of Congress is the largest library in the United States, and it would be a mistake to ignore its enormous genealogical collection, which includes many resources not available elsewhere.

Genealogical Book Dealers and Publishers

The list in Chapter 32 includes not only book dealers and publishers who specialize in genealogical materials, but selected general out-of-print book dealers from whom it is sometimes possible to obtain genealogical references. Included are many of the publishers cited frequently in bibliographies in this book; since most genealogical publishers are also dealers, you can write directly to the publisher to order a book in which you're interested.

For general purposes, you may find a store located in your area. If not, a variety of genealogical charts are available by mail from Bookcraft, Everton, Goodspeed's, Tuttle and many of the other sources listed.

The catalogues of some of these dealers are themselves such important bibliographic sources that older ones are kept and catalogued by the New York Public Library. They are extremely easy to use, as they usually contain lists of genealogies arranged by surname and lists of local histories arranged by locality. If you're not looking for a specific work, you may, just by checking the listing under the state in which your ancestors lived, turn up a book which is relevant to your research.

The leading out-of-print genealogical sources in this country are Goodspeed's in Boston, the Tuttle Company in Rutland, Vermont, and the Genealogical Publishing Company in Baltimore. Although there are many, many more, few publish genealogical catalogues on the scale that these three do.

The holdings of overseas dealers, also listed, are not confined to subjects in the country in which stores are located; in the catalogue of a Dutch dealer, for example, you may find valuable works on South American history and genealogy.

Conferences, Seminars and Family Associations

The first International Congress of Genealogical and Heraldic Sciences, featuring famous genealogical lecturers from all over the world, met in Barcelona in 1929. This was the first great international genealogical meeting, and another was not held until 1953, twenty-four years later, in Italy. Since then, eleven more Congresses have been held approximately every two years: in Madrid in 1955; Brussels, 1958; Stockholm, 1960; Edinburgh, 1962; The Hague, 1964; Paris, 1966; Bern, 1968; Vienna, 1970; Liège, 1972; Munich, 1974; London, 1976. An extensive range of topics relating to genealogy and heraldry in all countries and all eras are discussed at these conferences, and in many cases the lectures have been transcribed and published and can be found in libraries with genealogical collections.

The establishment of these valuable international meetings has been reflected at national and regional levels in many countries, and in the United States today there are genealogical seminars, courses and meetings available to all. The National Archives sponsors the National Institute on Genealogical Research, a course given in February and July in recent years. Current information can be obtained by writing the Central Reference Division ([NNC], National Archives [GSA], Washington, DC 20408). The New England Historical Genealogical Society, the University of Connecticut, Sanford University in Birmingham, Alabama, the Ohio Genealogical Society, the Maryland Historical Society, the Long Island Historical Society, the Central Texas Genealogical Society and the Black Hawk Genealogical Society of Rock Island, Illinois, are among the many other educational institutions and groups that sponsor genealogical conferences, workshops and meetings on a regular basis.

One of the most important meetings ever held in this country was the Bicentennial Conference on American Genealogy and Family History, held in Cleveland, Ohio, in August 1976 by the Western Reserve Historical Society in collaboration with the American Society of Genealogists, the History Department of Case Western Reserve University and the Ohio Genealogical

Society. The speakers included some of America's best-known genealogists, among them John I. Coddington, Francis J. Dallett, Winston DeVille, John F. Dorman, Margaret Dickson Falley, P. William Filby, Lida F. Harshman, Willard Heiss, George E. McCracken, Milton Rubincam, Walter Lee Sheppard, Malcolm H. Stern, Harriett and Kenn Stryker-Rodda, Lowell Volkel, James Walker, Robert E. Ward, Mary Bondurant Warren and George O. Zabriskie. A meeting of this scope and stature may never take place again, but it's possible that your local, county or state genealogical or historical society may sponsor a lecture by one or two of these genealogists, or others of equal merit, during the year. In 1964 Mrs. Harry J. Morris of Dallas compiled a *Handbook of Seminars in Genealogical Research*, which is a useful guide for any society or group that would like to sponsor a seminar or workshop.

Just as the number of local historical and genealogical society conferences has burgeoned over the past twenty years, there has been a revival of old-fashioned family reunions sponsored by family associations—or "one-name societies," as they are called in England and on the Continent. One of the best lists of these family associations and family publications appears once a year in *The Genealogical Helper*. J. Konrad, in *Directory of Genealogical Periodicals*, includes a list of American and foreign one-name societies, and the number of West German one-name societies is starting to catch up with the American ones. Konrad doesn't list any English family bulletins, but some of these fast-proliferating publications, such as the *Higginbottom Family Bulletin*, published by Frank Higginbottom (17 Glenside Avenue, Canterbury, CT1 1DB, Kent), and the *Harrington Family Miscellany*, published by Duncan Harrington (143 Sturry Road, Canterbury, CT1 1DF, Kent), might be found by contacting these men or the Federation of Family History Societies (care of the Hon. Secretary, Mrs. Elizabeth Simpson, Peapkin's End, 2 Stella Grove, Tollerton, Nottinghamshire NG12 4EY).

Some family associations and periodicals deal with the descendants of a certain person of the surname. For example, the descendants of Edward Howell (1584–1655), an early settler of Southampton, Long Island, comprise the large and active Howell Family Association. By contrast, such folksy American family publications as *Berry Pickin'*, *Fisher Facts*, *Franklin Fireplace*,

Kennedy Clues, Parrott Talk and *Poplin Platter* seek to involve everyone who shares the particular surname. These family bulletins can be valuable clearinghouses for genealogical information and lost connections.

Family reunions may be small affairs with relatives whom you already know or large meetings of many unrelated people who bear the same name. The descendants of Sholem Aleichem, the Yiddish writer, have met every year since his death in 1916 to read his stories, as he requested in his will. The New England families of the nineteenth century who returned annually to the family farm and began to publish family bulletins were following traditions established by the members of many European families who had left the land to follow trades in the towns and cities. A family reunion held by Count and Countess Charles-Albert de Lichtervelde at Chateau de la Follie, Ecaussinnes, Belgium, on May 9, 1976, to celebrate the 100th anniversary of the marriage of ancestors, included only the adult descendants of the marriage, and thus old and young were not able to mingle as they might have done at more old-fashioned family reunions. This trend may be easy on the host and hostess, but it was at meetings such as these in the old days that young children, now elderly adults, first heard the tales of their ancestors that they can now pass down to their own descendants. Today, with apartment living, adult communities that prohibit children and nursing homes that isolate the aged, there is often little chance for old and young to mix. Family reunions on any scale can be important links between generations and should include all ages (Illustration 15).

7 About Printed Sources

Because genealogy is closely tied to many other fields, among them history, geography, biography, law, handwriting and heraldry, the variety of printed references that may prove useful for tracing your genealogy is endless. Among the basic sources that are essential in virtually every genealogical search are maps and atlases, local histories, genealogies, newspapers and periodicals, directories and special genealogical guides.

While these secondary resources are of great value, you must evaluate the accuracy of each printed reference you use and locate original records that substantiate the information drawn from it whenever possible. In any written work there is the possibility of error—either of fact or interpretation—and even the most scrupulous author's accuracy can be undermined by a typographical error. While even original documents are occasionally incorrect, more steps—transcription, writing, rewriting, typesetting—go into the publication of printed information, so there are more opportunities for a small but crucial error—a change in one figure of a date, for example—to occur.

Maps, Atlases and Local Histories

Because we Americans live in a stable political environment, it's possible to forget that parts of the world are in a state of continual unrest. A look at a series of world maps drawn at intervals of many years shows how radically and frequently political boundaries have been redrawn after major upheavals, such as the world wars. Poland, for example, disappeared entirely from the map of Europe for several generations, from the late 1700's until 1918.

In our own country, during the period of colonization, revolution and expansion to the West Coast, the face of the nation changed dramatically in a relatively short period. Today we see more subtle but continuing change, as the boundaries of counties are redrawn or the names of towns and cities changed.

Before you can really pursue the genealogy of your family, you must, in a sense, do the genealogy of the counties and states in which your ancestors lived. Because records such as wills and deeds that are important to your family history are kept in county courthouses, for example, your research could run into a seeming blind alley if you didn't know that the town in which your ancestors resided a hundred years ago was part of a different county then than it is today. Even if several generations of ancestors lived in the same dwelling, it's possible that because of boundary changes your genealogy will require a search of the records in several counties or towns.

Suppose one branch of your family resided in Delaware. You should know that it was at the time of the Revolution that the three lower counties of Pennsylvania acquired a new identity as the state of Delaware. In addition, before earlier boundary settlements between Pennsylvania and Maryland, some of the land that eventually became Sussex County, Delaware, had made up Worcester County and parts of Dorchester County, Maryland. Moreover, in 1742, Worcester County had been formed from Somerset County, Maryland.

In most cases, when one county is formed out of part of another, any prior records are maintained by the office where they were originally filed. If your ancestors' residence in Delaware dates to before the Revolutionary War, records of their lives may be found in the offices of several counties in three states.

A helpful reference work on the "genealogy" of U.S. counties is *The Handy Book for Genealogists* by George B. Everton, Sr. E. Kay Kirkham's *The Counties of the United States and Their Genealogical Value* is also useful, and the *United States Postal Guide* identifies the counties in which towns are presently located.

During the first stage of your library research you should spend some time studying old maps and atlases and local histories, soaking up the background of the region where your ancestors lived. Almost any library that's been in existence for some time should have older atlases that were acquired years ago when they were new. See if you can find maps drawn during the period when your ancestors were actually living in the area (Illustration 16). In addition to looking for boundary and name changes, get acquainted with the area surrounding your ancestors' hometown; if they lived in the region for any length of time, their records may be spread throughout the area. If ancestors lived in a small town where there was no newspaper, for example, there may be news items about them in the newspaper published in the county seat or in a neighboring community.

If your ancestors lived in a large city, city maps of the period will be indispensable when you want to locate them in federal census records, since census schedules (see Chap. 9) are arranged by addresses, with urban addresses arranged by wards. If you know the number of the ward in which ancestors lived, you should be able to locate them in the census with relative ease; without the ward number, you might have to spend days paging through the records of an entire city. A valuable reference is E. Kay Kirkham's *Maps for Census Searching in Larger Cities*.

From the 1860's to the early part of this century, many county atlases that showed the names of individual residents were published, usually on a subscription basis by vanity presses. Some large libraries such as the New York Public Library (Room 117) and the Library of Congress maintain separate map divisions. In other libraries, such maps are kept in a local history collection.

From histories of the town, county or region in which your ancestors lived, you'll learn the origins of early settlers. Accounts of the churches, schools and industries of the area during different historical periods will guide you in your search for records. If your ancestors were among the area's founding families or prominent citizens, local histories may even include accounts of their lives. Guides to such local histories are Clarence Stewart Petersen's *Consolidated Bibliography of County Histories in Fifty States in 1961* and the recent local history publications of the Library of Congress and the NYPL.

When your research has led you to one of your immigrant ancestors, you'll want to return to the library to acquire additional background, this time by consulting histories of the country from which he or she came. If you're tracing a black line that extends into Africa and have reason to believe your ancestors came from the area around Nigeria, for example, you'll study the history of Nigeria, find out the names of tribes that lived there in the past and tribes that live there today and try to narrow your search down to a particular region.

Finding answers to some basic questions about the country

from which your ancestors came will help you plan your subsequent research. When did most immigrants from that country come to the United States? Where did they settle? What events or economic conditions prompted them to leave their homeland? What are the political, social and religious traditions of the country from which they came? Part IV of this book contains general information, addresses of public records offices and lists of reference works pertaining to genealogical research in different countries around the world.

Published Genealogies

It's quite possible that you'll find a genealogy of one of your family's branches, perhaps prepared and printed at personal expense by one of your ancestors, right on the shelves of a library or historical association. The value of such a volume depends, of course, on the accuracy of the research that went into it. Private genealogies are often very helpful, but they are also more likely to contain errors of fact than perhaps any other class of secondary resource. If you find a genealogy pertaining to your family line, you must subject it to careful scrutiny, checking its contents against a variety of original and published sources, before you accept what it says as true.

Much depends on the motivation of the author. Some amateur genealogists who publish books are bent only on proving an elaborate and illustrious line of descent, and their genealogies are often unintentional fabrications. Such authors may be well-meaning people, and their books are often beautifully bound and printed, but the information between the expensive covers is sometimes such drivel that I just feel the books should be burned.

I remember one really delightful old clergyman, now deceased, who published an elegant but totally unreliable book about his family line. In one case he claimed that his ancestor Richard Westmoreland was actually a member of the prestigious Neville family of England but that on arriving in Virginia in the 1600's he had proclaimed, "I will no longer be called by the name of Neville. I am now Richard Westmoreland." While there was no evidence to support this story, he went on from there to claim descent from the earls of Westmoreland and several kings of England.

Because he was descended from a John Washington of Surrey County, Virginia, the clergyman decided that he must also be related to George Washington, although no one has ever been able to prove this connection. Nonetheless, so caught up was this man in his own fantasies that in the last years of his life he would sit so that the light fell across his face at a certain angle and ask, "Who do I remind you of? Don't I look like George?"

By contrast, many genealogies recorded in New England during the 1800's are remarkably accurate in their American generations, probably because the authors were more interested in documenting the histories of their families than in claiming prestigious lineages. During the nineteenth century many New Englanders departed their family farms for the industrialized cities and points South and West. The sprawling genealogies recorded during the period reflect the migrants' longing for roots and heritage.

If you find a printed record of your family line you may experience a feeling of disappointment because someone else has already done the work you set out to do, or elation at finding familiar names in print. Actually, the more information you find in print, the better. Starting from scratch on some family lines is difficult or nearly impossible, and even when you have a published genealogy in hand you'll have to do hours of digging to prove its accuracy. This is one reason you should have all older relatives give you any information that may fill in gaps.

Try to check significant dates and facts against other sources. For example, if the genealogy gives an ancestor's death date, see if you can find a death certificate or probate record (Chapter 8) that backs it up. The authors of early genealogies generally just wrote down their stories without giving any indication of the sources of their information. Modern genealogies are easier to evaluate, since the wills, deeds and other documents from which facts are drawn are usually cited, and sometimes photostats of the originals are bound into the books.

You don't have to confirm every fact in a printed genealogy, but you do want to do enough checking to determine whether the line of descent is correct. Even if the work in question turns out to contain significant errors, chances are it will yield useful clues that will help you to decide the direction in which you should go with your search in the future.

The New York Public Library, the Library of Congress and other libraries with substantial genealogical collections have acquired enormous numbers of private genealogies. People doing research in the NYPL often volunteer, "I'm sure you don't have anything about my family; they weren't famous people," but they're frequently mistaken. Among the noted New England family records, for example, is the Hyde genealogy, published in 1864. An enormous and amazingly accurate document, it tells the story of a typical rural Colonial family and follows them down from the seventeenth to the nineteenth century in both male and female lines.

Check the library catalogue to find out whether it has genealogies of any of the branches of your family. In addition, Marion J. Kaminkow's *Genealogies in the Library of Congress*, in two volumes, is a valuable reference, and *Founders of Early American Families* ... by Meredith B. Colket, Jr., evaluates a large number of genealogies dealing with Colonial families. Libraries with genealogical collections should have these books, but you may want to purchase them so that you can consult them at home.

Genealogical Magazines

There are hundreds and hundreds of genealogical magazines published today, many of them specializing in information about a particular region or field of research. They range from mimeographed family publications of a few pages to sophisticated, scholarly journals of 50 to 100 pages, in which much of the most important genealogical work being done today is first published.

All sorts of topics of a genealogical nature are discussed in these magazines; their contents include genealogies, local histories, biographical sketches, book reviews and general how-to information. Often there are transcripts or abstracts of original records—all the inscriptions in a particular cemetery, for example, or the registers of a certain church. Old genealogies are updated and corrected, and the newest discoveries of significance to genealogists are noted.

You can publish queries in many of these periodicals, asking other readers who have information about your ancestors to write to you. Frequently, the privilege of submitting queries is restricted to subscribers, who may do so free, although some periodicals will allow anyone to place a query for a fee. If your research is concentrated in a particular area, it's a good idea to subscribe to a regional publication, such as *The Maryland and Delaware Genealogist, The Virginia Genealogist* or *The Pennsylvania Genealogical Magazine.* (For information about newspapers that publish genealogical query columns, see Chap. 7.)

The oldest continuously published genealogical magazine in the world is *The New England Historical and Genealogical Register*, which has been published by the New England Historic Genealogical Society since January 1847 and has set high standards in genealogical scholarship. *The New York Genealogical and Biographical Record* dates from 1869. *The American Genealogist*, founded by Donald Lines Jacobus and carried on by Dr. George E. McCracken, and the *National Genealogical Society Quarterly*, published in Washington, D.C., are the major American genealogical periodicals of a general nature. *The Genealogical Helper*, issued by Everton Publishers in Logan, Utah, is another national genealogical periodical that can be of great value.

Quite different and also valuable are numerous small, weekly, query newsletters published in various parts of the country. Among these are *Family Puzzlers*, a compilation of queries and occasional articles with a Southern regional focus, which has been published for years by Mary Bondurant Warren of Danville, Georgia; *The Tri-State Trader*, a hobby, auction and antiques newspaper published since 1968 in Knightstown, Indiana, which includes a section of genealogical booknotes and queries; and *Genealogy News Weekly*, a newsletter of reviews and queries established in Opa-Locka, Florida, in 1976.

Today there is a specialized genealogical periodical dealing with research in virtually every region of the country; many of these are listed in the section pertaining to the individual states (Chap. 33). For names and addresses of additional magazines, consult *The Directory of Historical Societies and Agencies in the United States and Canada* or *Directory of Genealogical Societies in the United States and Canada* by Mary K. Meyer. Another recent pamphlet, J. Konrad's *A Directory of Genealogical Publications*, lists family newsletters and genealogical magazines published in foreign countries as well as in the United States. A "union list" detailing the genealogical magazine holdings of libraries and other institutions around the world should also be available soon, as Roger Scanland, head of the reading room in the LDS Genealogical Library in Salt Lake City, is now preparing one for publication.

Any library with a genealogical collection probably subscribes to several of the more important genealogical magazines. The NYPL Local History and Genealogy Division, the Library of Congress and the LDS Genealogical Library in Salt Lake City each receive several hundred every year. In addition to subscribing to a magazine that deals with the area where your inquiry is based, you should familiarize yourself with the others in your library's collection. Even those with a different regional focus are likely to touch on topics pertinent to your study. For example, *The Virginia Magazine of History and Biography*, which publishes many genealogical articles about Virginia families, often contains important items about families in England, New England or elsewhere who had Virginia connections. If you're tracing ancestors in the West, be sure to consult publications dealing with the original colonies where earlier generations of your family lived before migrating.

The information in a genealogical magazine, like that in any other secondary source, must be checked for accuracy against original records. You should survey what's been published in the magazines early in your study; even if some of the details in accounts of your family are wrong, the information given will probably make it much easier for you to locate the original documents that will reveal the correct information. At the same time, you can begin to evaluate the work of individual genealogists who have published articles related to your research.

If you decide to publish a query in a genealogical periodical, be brief and precise, giving some specific information about the places and dates of your ancestor's birth, death and marriage, or any other identifying places and dates. Your query might read:

Seek information about John Palmerton (Palmeter), born 1834 in Corning, Chemung County, New York. Married Christa Mary Gardner in 1856.

Several indexes to the articles published in genealogical

magazines will help you find those that include references to your ancestors. Some periodicals publish indexes to their own articles at regular intervals, and state libraries and historical societies frequently prepare indexes to regional publications. But it's most efficient to begin by consulting the large composite indexes—those that cover several publications—before moving to the more detailed regional and individual indexes.

The earliest composite index, *Bibliographia Genealogica Americana*, was published in 1868 by Joel Munsell Publishers. With the fourth edition, issued in 1895, it was renamed *Index to American Genealogies*. The fifth and final edition, published in 1900, contains 50,000 entries, including all those in the earlier editions. A *Supplement 1900 to 1908 to the Index to Genealogies Published in 1900*, issued in 1908 by Joel Munsell's Son, listed many articles that were published before 1900 but had been omitted from the earlier volume.

The Munsell enterprise also published *List of Titles of Genealogical Articles in American Periodicals and Kindred Works* in 1899 and *The American Genealogist: Being a Catalogue of Family Histories* in 1900. *Munsell's Genealogical Index*, printed in 1933, was intended to bring *Index to American Genealogies* up to date, but only a small portion of the project was ever completed.

Donald Lines Jacobus' classic *Index to Genealogical Periodicals*, in three volumes, covers a great many magazines published between the turn of the century and 1952 and a few beginning in the 1870's and 1880's. Inez Waldenmaier's *Genealogical Newsletter and Research Aids* and *Annual Index to Genealogical Periodicals and Family Histories* cover the period between 1956 and 1962. The latest composite index is the *Genealogical Periodical Annual Index*, edited between 1962 and 1965 by Ellen Stanley Rogers, taken over in 1966 by George Ely Russell and now published by Laird C. Towle (3602 Maureen Lane, Bowie, MD 20715).

Periodicals issued from 1952 through 1956 and from 1970 through 1973 are not covered by any of these indexes. Many researchers have expressed the hope that, with the aid of computers, a single volume might someday be produced that would consolidate all of the entries in existing indexes and supply new ones for the years that have never been indexed. The

Genealogical Committee of the American Library Association announced plans for such a work, intended to cover the period from 1845 to 1970, several years ago, but so far nothing has come of it.

Some of the indexes mentioned in this section are arranged by surnames only; others, by surnames, place names and article titles. Read the preface or introduction for an explanation of the one you're using.

Three indexes to the names discussed in queries in genealogical magazines have been issued at various times. Two—*The Genealogist's Weekly Query Index* and the *Query Name Index*—have been discontinued, in 1961 and 1975, respectively. *Linkage for Ancestral Research* is still published, although on an irregular basis. Fortunately, most publications that publish queries issue their own indexes. Be sure to look for queries related to your family line; in addition to facts, you can learn the names and addresses of other researchers who are working on the same lines you are.

Newspapers

Newspapers are vital genealogical sources too often ignored by beginners. While any news item pertaining to an ancestor may prove useful, marriage notices and obituaries are the most consistently helpful from a genealogical point of view (Illustration 17). Information found in newspapers tends to be fairly accurate, since it was recorded during your ancestor's lifetime, or—in the case of an obituary—immediately after his death, with the facts usually supplied by a close relative. Some rather flowery obituaries, however, do make exaggerated claims for the deceased.

You may find some newspaper clippings preserved in a scrapbook or other collection of papers kept by members of your family. To locate others, begin by finding out the names of newspapers published in the area where your ancestors lived during the time they were living there. Any good library should have several directories, such as Ayer's *Directory of Newspapers and Periodicals*, R. R. Bowker's *National Directory of Weekly Newspapers* and Clarence Saunders Brigham's *History and Bibliography of American Newspapers 1690–1820*, in which you can find this information. Winifred Gregory's *American Newspa-*

pers, 1821–1936; A Union List of Files Available in the United States and Canada is especially useful because it describes the newspaper holdings of North American libraries. To find out what newspapers have been copied on microfilm, consult Richard W. Hayes's *Guide to Photocopied Historical Materials in the United States and Canada* or the Library of Congress' *Newspapers in Microform United States 1948–1972,* published in 1973, which covers papers in all states from their earliest years until 1972.

The indexing of the marriage and death notices in certain newspapers by genealogists and librarians has made some of the genealogical data buried in newspaper files more accessible to researchers. The American Antiquarian Society of Worcester, Massachusetts, has indexed and abstracted marriages and deaths noted in Boston's *Columbian Centinel* and *Massachusetts Centinel* between 1784 and 1840 and indexed deaths in the *Boston Evening Transcript* from 1875 to 1930. G. K. Hall's *Boston Athenaeum Index of Obituaries in Boston,* in three volumes, covers abstracts of deaths within Boston from 1794 to 1800 and deaths outside Boston between 1704 and 1795. The late Gertrude Barber abstracted and indexed the marriages and deaths that were reported in the *New York Evening Post* from 1801 to 1890 and in the *Brooklyn Eagle* from 1841 to 1880.

These indexes are especially important because the New York and Boston papers reported news not only about local people but about noteworthy people from all over the country and the world. While the Boston indexes are available in most major libraries with genealogical collections, Mrs. Barber's works are not widely distributed. The New York Public Library, the New York Genealogical and Biographical Society, and the New York Historical Society have them in their collections.

Kenneth Scott, a prominent abstractor of newspaper material, has done some extremely valuable work compiling vital records and other genealogical information printed in the *New York Post-Boy* and other eighteenth-century national, New York and Philadelphia papers through the period of the Revolution. His abstracts, published in the *New York Genealogical and Biographical Record* and in some separate volumes, contain facts that are available nowhere else.

The New York Times and the *London Times* are among the few newspapers that have been continually indexed since their inception, although there are some gaps in *The New York Times* index for the early parts of this century. *The New York Times Obituary Index* covers the period from 1851, when the paper was established, to 1968 in a single volume, but it is incomplete, especially for the years before 1930.

Published indexes of marriage and death notices in many other cities are given in this book in the section listing resources for research in individual states (Chap. 33). You should also check with your local library to find out whether any typescript indexes are available. If the newspaper in your ancestor's hometown has never been indexed, you can still locate accounts of a marriage or death if you know the approximate date of the event and have the patience to go through the newspaper files until you find what you're looking for.

State libraries usually have good files of newspapers from all over the state. If you know the exact date and location of the marriage or death of one of your ancestors, some state libraries will locate newspaper accounts and send you photocopies. When you write to libraries requesting this type of service, send along a check for $5 or a blank check marked "this check for not more than $10"—or $15, depending on how much help you're asking. This money helps pay for the librarian's time and the cost of photocopying and demonstrates the seriousness of your inquiry.

At one time not only newspapers but certain periodicals used to run notices of births, marriages, deaths, bankruptcies and military and government promotions. The notices that appeared in two British periodicals—*Gentleman's Magazine* and *Scot's Magazine*—from the 1730's until well into the 1800's have been indexed annually by surname. These are extremely valuable references for English and Scottish genealogies, and there are also many Americans in these listings.

Genealogical Columns in Newspapers

The most famous and ambitious genealogical column in an American newspaper was instituted in 1876 by the *Boston Evening Transcript*. By 1894 the paper had established a separate genealogy department, and the column, "Notes and Queries," continued to appear regularly until the *Transcript* went out of existence in 1941.

Over the years the paper featured contributions by noted

genealogists, aired arguments over disputed genealogical points, printed valuable transcripts of many kinds of records and even printed entire genealogies. In the query section of the column both questions and answers were published.

The queries that appeared in the *Transcript* from 1902 until 1941 are on microcards at the New York Public Library and other libraries with genealogical collections; those from 1904 to 1937 are also in scrapbooks at the NYPL. Names discussed in the *Transcript* columns between 1906 and 1941 can also be found in the revised edition of *The American Genealogical-Biographical Index*. This vast work, begun by the late Freemont Rider in 1942, indexed individuals mentioned in a variety of genealogical and biographical sources, such as the 1790 census, many volumes of Revolutionary War records, local histories, vital records and family genealogies. By the time the first series from A to Z was compiled in 1952, it contained 48 volumes. The revised edition, begun in that year and still in progress, is being expanded to include information from many more genealogies and local histories as well as the material in the *Boston Evening Transcript* columns and will eventually run to close to two hundred volumes.

The *Hartford Times* had a genealogical department in its Saturday issue for many years beginning in 1933. Queries and answers printed between July 1935 and December 1950 are in print and on microfilm in genealogical libraries.

Today, newspapers of all sizes publish genealogical columns, and many of them accept reader queries. You can locate such columns by checking the directories listed at the end of this chapter. Whether or not it publishes a special genealogical column, use the newspaper printed in the town where ancestors lived to find out more about them or even to locate unknown relatives. Take an ad, giving specific identifying information about your ancestors. Some papers may print your query without charge, in the form of a letter to the editor.

City Directories and Telephone Directories
Long before there were telephones—or telephone books—there were city directories, which listed businesses and the names, addresses and occupations of people—usually the heads of households or the working members of a family—in a city. In

general, directories began appearing in small and large cities in America and Europe during the eighteenth century, although London's earliest directory is dated 1677. In New York City, a directory was issued annually from 1786 until 1933, when the city's sheer size made the task of compiling a directory overwhelming. A few years ago *Cole's Directory of the New York City Area* began publication, but these volumes are not like the old city directories, as they merely reverse the information in telephone books, giving the names of people who live at a particular address. While this information can sometimes be useful, these directories contain only the names of people who have telephones and maintain a listing in the telephone book. Old-fashioned city directories are still published in London, as well as in many towns and cities in this country.

The later a directory was published, the more detailed information it is likely to contain about each individual listed. Modern directories sometimes give the occupation, business and residential addresses and spouse's name of every person in a household.

Most large libraries have extensive collections of city directories. All of those listed in Dorothea N. Spear's *Bibliography of American Directories Through 1860* have been microfilmed and are available in major libraries. (In the NYPL they are in the Microform Reading Room—315M—with the classmark *XMG-156.) Many American directories for the period 1861 to 1881 (NN *ZAN-G67) and London directories 1677 to 1900 (NN *ZAN-G68) have also been copied on film. Two additional English research aids are Jane Norton's *A Guide to Directories* and Charles W. F. Goss's *The London Directory, 1677–1855, a Bibliography with Notes*. All three of these volumes cite the libraries in which listed directories can be found.

You can often learn a great deal about an ancestor by tracing him through successive directories. His first appearance in a directory may indicate the year he moved to a particular city, or the year he left his parents' home, married and established his own household. The disappearance of his name from the directory suggests that he has moved or died; in some cases a new listing—"Jones, Mary, widow of Harold"—will make it clear that he has died. You can then begin to look for his death certificate or will.

In response to a query, I once searched New York City directories for records of a Mary Ann Jube, who had worked as a daguerreotypist during the last century. The information I found in successive volumes, abstracted below, shows that I was able to develop a remarkably detailed picture of this woman and several members of her family without consulting any other sources:

1847/48—Jube, Thomas S., trimmer, house 146 Ave 3
1848/49—Jube, John P., hardware, 83 Bowery, house Newark
1850/51—Jube, John P., hardware, 83 Bowery, house Newark
    Jube, Thomas S., coachtrimmer, 83 Bowery
1852/53—Jube, John P., hardware, 83 Bowery, house Newark
    Jube, Mary Ann, artist, 83 Bowery
    Jube, Thomas S., clerk, 83 Bowery
1853/54—Jube, John P., hardware, 83 Bowery, house 83 Mulberry, Newark
    Jube, Mary Ann, daguerreotypes, 83 Bowery, house 83 Bowery (first as photographer)
    Jube, Thomas S., trimmer, 83 Bowery, house 83 Bowery
1859/60—Jube, John P., hardware, 83 Bowery, house Newark
    Jube, Mary A., ambrotypes, 83 Bowery
    (last at this address)
    Jube, Thomas S., hardware, 83 Bowery
1860/61—Jube, John P. & Co., hardware, 83 Bowery, house New Jersey
    Jube, Thomas S., photographer, 220 Bowery
    (no Mary Ann)
1861/62—Jube, John P. & Co. hardware, 83 Bowery, house New Jersey
    Jube, Mary Ann, photographs, 220 Bowery
    Jube, Thomas S., hardware, 83 Bowery, house 220 Bowery

Because you can find an individual's exact street address in them, city directories are of particular value when you want to locate an ancestor in the federal census records, which are arranged geographically rather than by name. After finding his address in the directory, you can consult a period map of the city to find out what ward he lived in. You can then search the census records for just that ward—a relatively small task—rather than for the entire city.

Current telephone directories are also often helpful in genealogical research. The most basic way to use them is to go through those in an area where your ancestors lived, searching for families with the same name, whom you can then contact to find out whether and how they are descended from your ancestors and whether they have any information or records that may further your line. This method is most practical if you're doing research in a rural area, but I've known people who have gone through New York City phone books looking for relatives, and they've sometimes had remarkable results. If the name you're looking for is an unusual one, your chances of success are improved, and a distinctive first name can also be a clue. When I began looking for some of my Sudler relatives in telephone books, I knew that any Arthur E. Sudler I found was almost surely a member of the family, as Ann Emory, who married Joseph Sudler in the mid-1700's, was the daughter of Arthur Emory, and there had been Arthur Emory Sudlers and Emory Sudlers in the family ever since. When I found an Arthur E. Sudler, a New York advertising man, in the phone book, I was quite sure he was a relative. Although I never contacted him, I eventually saw his obituary in the newspaper and learned just how he fitted into the family line.

I also used telephone books frequently when I was tracing all the descendants of Timothy Field, the Revolutionary War captain from whom I am twice descended, and his wife Anna Dudley. When I'd followed a line far enough into this century so that I knew that certain descendants or their children should be living, I'd begin going through telephone books in the appropriate area, looking for people with the name I was tracing at that point. Then I'd write a letter, explaining my project and asking whether the person was the child of a particular individual. Nearly everyone I contacted responded, and most of them confirmed the relationship I'd suspected. I've also used telephone books successfully to locate relatives when doing research overseas.

Genealogical Texts

Among the other printed sources you'll consult during your research are a variety of genealogical texts and guides that will supplement the information contained in this book with additional, specialized material about particular research problems. Because no single reference can cover every source a genealogist will use in the course of tracing a family line over several generations, these additional texts are cited throughout this book whenever appropriate.

Gilbert Doane's *Searching for Your Ancestors*, perhaps the

best-known general guide to genealogical research, was first published in 1933 and has been revised and updated four times— most recently in 1973—in the course of numerous printings. With its heavy emphasis on records maintained in the original thirteen colonies, especially in New England, Doane's book is most valuable as a reference for people with long American lineages.

Val Greenwood's *The Researcher's Guide to American Genealogy* contains extensive, detailed information about the location and availability of all kinds of genealogical records in the United States and Canada. While not a good book for beginners, as it tends to be rather dry and long-winded, it can be a valuable handbook as your research progresses.

After you've done some preliminary investigation, you may also want to read *Sources for Genealogical Research*, a two-volume work compiled by the American Society of Genealogists, with chapters contributed by various Society members. The sections on Europe provide a useful overview of the history, population movements and predominant religious denominations in different areas.

Noel Stevenson's *Search and Research* is particularly useful for its information about the existence and location of state census records, as well as for addresses of state records sources (see also the section on individual states in this book, Chap. 33. George Everton's *Handy Book for Genealogists*, another well-known reference, contains especially good material on counties in the United States, including the names of county seats, the "genealogies" of counties and the scope of records available in each. E. Kay Kirkham's *The Counties of the United States and Their Genealogical Value* is also an aid to research in this area. Kirkham has written several other specialized guides that are extremely valuable; among them are *Research in American Genealogy*, which contains excellent maps of the eastern United States, and *A Survey of American Church Records, Major Denominations Before 1880*.

A recent volume by A. F. Oates, *The Art of Collecting Genealogy and History*, may prove helpful. If you want to get the younger members of your family interested in your search, give them a copy of Suzanne Hilton's *Who Do You Think You Are? Digging for Your Roots*, a genealogical guide for children.

A wide variety of public records and official documents are useful for genealogical purposes. Among the most important local records are certificates of birth, marriage and death, church records, wills and deeds (Illustration 18). Depending on the particular circumstances of your ancestors, other documents, such as school records, tax lists and records of town meetings, may also be helpful.

Birth, Marriage and Death Records

Certificates of birth, marriage and death will substantiate the facts that you have uncovered thus far and provide valuable additional information. Imagine, for example, that a family Bible has revealed that your great-grandfather died on July 28, 1884, in Boston. With that information you can write to the state of Massachusetts for a full copy of his death certificate, which will confirm the place and date of his death and give you his age or birth date and place of birth—if not the specific town, then at least the county or state. The certificate should also contain the name of your ancestor's wife if he was married or widowed, his occupation and, in some states, his military service, if he was a veteran. In most cases the certificate will advance your search another generation, as it should also tell you the name and birthplaces of both your great-grandfather's parents. Interment information may lead you to a cemetery plot where several generations of your ancestors are buried.

For every birth, death and marriage that has occurred in the United States since the early part of the twentieth century an official certificate should be on file in the appropriate Bureau of Vital Statistics (Illustration 18a). These events were originally recorded at the town or county level, and while the federal government doesn't maintain any central registration, the individual states have maintained central vital statistics offices from various dates, ranging from 1841 in Massachusetts to 1919 in Georgia. Divorces have been centrally recorded only in recent years.

For fees ranging from one dollar in Missouri and Ohio to four dollars for a marriage in New York County (Manhattan), you can obtain copies of these records by mail from the appropriate state or local office. The section of this book containing state sources lists the addresses of vital records offices and the dates for which records are available in each state. Three brief federal government pamphlets—"Where to Write for Birth and Death Records," "Where to Write for Marriage Records" and "Where to Write for Divorce Records"—also contain detailed information about how and where to write. These guides can be found in your local library or purchased for a nominal fee from the U.S. Government Printing Office (Washington, DC 20402). In general, if you know the name of the individuals involved and the date and place of the event, you can obtain a copy of the certificate you desire.

If the event in question occurred before state record-keeping began, a record may still be on file in the local town or county courthouse. New York State's vital records date from 1880, for example, but the records in many towns go back as far as 1830; and New York City's death records date from 1798, although they are sketchy in the early period. Even in cases where records are on file with the state, you may be able to obtain them much more quickly from the city or town. You may be able to visit the local office and search the bound volumes of early records yourself. If not, you can make your request by mail; the government pamphlets on obtaining records list the appropriate offices to contact.

In New York State in particular it's always best to write to the clerk of the town where the event in which you're interested took place, since the state office frequently takes as long as six months to answer requests for copies of vital records. New Jersey's records for the period from May 1848 to May 1878, by contrast, are especially well organized. They are maintained in a single alphabetical file by the State Education Department (later records are kept by the Bureau of Vital Statistics), so for this thirty-year period in New Jersey it's quite possible to obtain certificates even if you don't know the exact town or city in which a birth, death or marriage took place.

In every case, be sure to request a "full copy" of the certificate required. Short forms, useful for such purposes as obtaining passports, will not contain the information the genealogist needs about parents and their places of birth. Request particular certificates and be specific about names, dates and addresses. A typical query might read, "Please send me a full copy of the death certificate of Michael Thomas Warren, who died in Johnstown on June 24, 1902. He was my grandfather, and I need this record for genealogical purposes." You may request several certificates at one time, as long as you give specific details about each. Enclose the appropriate fee and a stamped, self-addressed envelope for the reply.

If you don't know the exact date of the birth, death or marriage in which you're interested but can place it approximately in time—say, within a five-year span—some offices will conduct a search of their records for an additional hourly fee. When you write to them you can establish a budget limit that they will not exceed. You might, for example, authorize a four-hour search, which, if the fee is $3 an hour, will cost a maximum of $12. Send a blank check marked "this check for not more than $12" and let the vital-records office fill in the correct amount when the search has been completed. This extra expense can be extremely worthwhile if it turns up facts that you haven't been able to locate elsewhere.

Since they must protect the confidentiality of living people, vital-records offices are sometimes reluctant to issue copies of birth or marriage certificates to individuals other than those named on the documents. Death certificates and older marriage certificates—records of marriages that took place more than fifty years ago—can usually be obtained without difficulty. Since a full copy of a death certificate usually includes all the information found on a birth certificate, begin by obtaining copies of death certificates for your ancestors if you know the dates and places of death. Write for copies of birth records when you don't have the information necessary to locate a death record or when the information given on the death certificate is incomplete. If you're requesting a copy of the birth or marriage record of a living person, have the individual sign the request himself, if possible.

The first record you should obtain is your own birth certificate. It may seem absurd, but the facts you can discover from your own birth certificate are often surprising. Among the information you'll find will be the dates and places of birth of both your parents, facts you may be unsure of if your parents are no longer living.

If your parents are alive, obtain copies of their birth and marriage records. If they are deceased, obtain full copies of their death certificates. Continue working back, obtaining the appropriate records for all your ancestors as soon as you turn up the places and dates necessary to locate them.

Vital records are always maintained at the place where the event actually occurred, so you may need to do some extra sleuthing if an ancestor died or gave birth while traveling away from home. The records of American citizens who were born or died overseas can often be obtained from the government of the country where the event occurred. See the section on overseas research (Chap. 16) for places to write. You may also get some assistance from the American consulate in the foreign country.

During the American Colonial period, marriage bonds had to be obtained in colonies such as New York. The equivalent of a modern marriage license, a bond was purchased and witnessed as assurance of a man's intention to marry a particular woman (Illustration 19). If you're doing research in the South, you'll find that in some places the tradition of marriage bonds kept by county clerks is still retained.

Church Records

Registers of baptisms, marriages and burials and other church records are particularly valuable to genealogists because they are often available for years before government records of vital statistics were maintained, or for years for which government records have been lost or destroyed. The tradition of maintaining meticulous church records dates to medieval Europe (in the city of Madrid, the baptismal records of San Gines survive from 1498), when members of the clergy were an elite group set apart by their ability to read and write. Moreover, in early America, the church was a vital community center in which most people were active, and some records, such as the Dutch Church records in New York City, date back to the formation of the colonies, although many others have been lost over the years.

The amount of detail contained in church records varies. A baptismal record will contain at least the name of the individual and the date of baptism. It may also include the date and place of birth and the names of the child's parents and sponsors.

It is important to remember that while baptism was usually

performed soon after birth, a considerable amount of time might pass if, for example, a child were born at the beginning of a long, cold winter or if the family lived in a rural area served by a traveling minister. Nonetheless, the date of baptism will be helpful in establishing the approximate date of your ancestor's birth. In the same way, a burial date should not be confused with a death date, although it is an important clue in determining the actual date of death.

Marriage records will, in some cases, include the names of parents and witnesses (Illustration 20). The posting of marriage banns—a sign of a couple's intent to marry—was recorded even more consistently by some early churches than were the marriages themselves, but bear in mind that the posting of the banns, in and of itself, does not indicate whether the marriage actually took place.

If your ancestors' church maintained membership lists, they will include notations of confirmations and admissions to the church rolls. You may find a letter of transference or letter of admission that an ancestor brought from his former parish as an introduction to the new church. Such a letter may be your first indication of where your ancestors came from and when they moved.

The clue to your ancestors' religious affiliation may lie in your family's current affiliation or national origin or may be revealed in a family record, will, deed, tombstone inscription or obituary. If the church or synagogue your ancestors attended is still in existence, contact the minister, priest or rabbi, who may be able to locate the records you need or tell you where they can be found. Be very specific in your query, just as when requesting copies of government records. Since some research will be required to turn up the information you need, include a check for $5 to defray the cost.

If your ancestors' church is no longer in existence, a local historical society may know the location of its records. If not, check the denomination to find out whether it maintains archives of the records of now defunct parishes. At the end of this section you'll find the addresses of national societies or libraries of several religious denominations, some of which serve as central repositories of records. Also check your state historical society and state library to see if they have records on file.

Among printed references, E. Kay Kirkham's *A Survey of American Church Records: Major Denominations Before 1880* is especially valuable for locating early records in Eastern states. Another important aid is the collection of church record inventories prepared during the Depression by the Historical Records Survey under the auspices of the Works Progress Administration. Forty states—all except Connecticut, Delaware, Maine, Maryland, Ohio, Pennsylvania, South Carolina and Vermont, as well as Alaska and Hawaii, which were not yet states—participated in this project to compile a list of available vital records.

The WPA inventories and guides, which cover vital records and county archives as well as church records, included information about where and how vital statistics were filed. Unfortunately, many records have been moved since these inventories were compiled in the late 1930's and early 1940's. In the case of church records, the inventories often indicate when particular parishes ceased operation and where the congregations moved.

Copies of the WPA inventories are maintained by major libraries and historical societies, especially in the states concerned. You can check with your state library or another large institution to find out whether there are any such records pertinent to your search.

If you read that a nineteenth-century ancestor was "pious," as printed genealogies often note, and you know the denomination of the church to which he or she belonged, you might look for a religious newspaper that served the denomination. Ray Sawyer abstracted the marriages and deaths published in the *Christian Intelligencer* of the Reformed Dutch Church between 1830 and 1871, and her work is full of details that might not be found in any other source. Ms. Sawyer, incidentally, was the sister of Gertrude Barber, who was well known by genealogists for her work in abstracting similar notices from New York City newspapers.

Scots, French, Dutch and Germans in their own countries often noted the maiden names of mothers in baptismal and marriage records, and many religious groups continued this custom in the churches they established in the New World. Among religious denominations in this country, the Dutch, Episcopal and Catholic churches have some of the best records, although the Roman

Catholic Church sometimes imposes restrictions on access to this material.

The early marriage records of the Dutch Church in the City of New York include information about the place each person was born. The Dutch were very exacting in their record-keeping, and the preserved records of their early church in this country are great social documents.

Illustration 21 is a chart of the extensive genealogy of a New York City black family, originally from Angola, between the 1630's and the 1730's, which I was able to construct through the use of these church records. As the chart shows, the naming system used by the Dutch during this period holds clues to both the national origin and lineage of the individuals involved. A man who bore the surname "van Angola" was from the country of Angola. A patronymic naming system was also employed, so the researcher knows that "Francis Bastiensen" was literally "Francis, son of Sebastien" (Bastien being a nickname for Sebastien). These clues in names are a great help in piecing together a family line, but one has to examine all the baptismal records, marriage records and wills that survive in order to confirm the links between generations.

Early Presbyterian, Methodist and Baptist records in this country are among the hardest to locate, since many of them were maintained privately by ministers who considered them their own property. The problem is particularly severe in parts of the South where nineteenth-century Methodist circuit riders traveled around the countryside ministering to far-flung church members. From time to time a descendant of one of these ministers comes across a book of marriage or other valuable records that have been preserved among the family's possessions. Many such volumes have been published, but there is little doubt that many others have been lost or remain hidden away in attic trunks. Finding records like these is a matter of considerable luck. Sometimes a record book kept privately by a minister duplicates information in official church records but includes notations and additional information that can be helpful to a genealogist.

An article written by J. L. Cartwright, the vicar of Oundle, England, and published in 1976 in *Northamptonshire Past and Present*, one of England's finest county record publications, describes the discovery of a register kept by one John Clifton, a parish clerk or sexton at Oundle during the mid-1700's. Clifton apparently made a hobby of recording the weddings and burials of the parish church, and his accounts compare well with the official parish register in terms of the accuracy of names and dates. But Clifton's personal record is enlivened by the use of nicknames and occasional derisive comments about the people of Oundle. One entry reads, "24 July, 1770: Little Bob Spectacles and Beth Fitzjohn married today," and another notes leeringly, "9 April, 1770: Today Old Ireland, aged 76, is married to Miss Dillingham of 25, an agreeable young lady with a Cambridge fortune. Horns, boys, horns." The adventure of genealogy is that any researcher might discover just this sort of supplemental material, which does so much to bring the people of the past to life.

The particular problems encountered in tracing Jewish ancestry and the techniques and resources that can be used to overcome them are discussed in detail in Chapter 14.

Religious Record Repositories, Historical Societies and Libraries

American Baptist Historical Library
1106 South Goodman Street
Rochester, NY 14620

American Catholic Historical Association
The Catholic University of America
Washington, DC 20017
(*The Catholic Historical Review*)

American Society of Church History
James H. Smylie, Secy.
Union Theological Seminary
3401 Brook Rd.
Richmond, VA 23227

Church of Jesus Christ of Latter-day Saints
(Genealogical Society, Chapter 9)
50 East North Temple Street
Salt Lake City, UT 84105

Drew Theological Seminary (Methodist)
Madison, NJ 07940

Friends Historical Association (Quaker)
Swarthmore College
Swarthmore, PA 19081

North American Baptist Archives
1605 Euclid
Sioux Falls, SD 57105

Presbyterian Historical Society
425 Lombard Street
Philadelphia, PA 19147

Society of the United Lutheran Church in America
Lutheran Theological Seminary
Gettysburg, PA 17325

United States Catholic Historical
Society
St. Joseph's Seminary
Seminary Avenue
Yonkers, NY 10704

For sources of Jewish records, see Chapter 14.

Wills

The tradition of recording wills was brought to this country by
settlers from Europe and England, where some wills survive
from the 1300's. In this country it is quite possible to locate wills
dating from the seventeenth century. Like church records, they
are especially useful for research during the period before vital
records were maintained by government offices. Wills often
describe in complete detail the relationships among family
members, and it is not at all unusual to find one that identifies
four generations of a family covering a span of perhaps one
hundred years.

Wills of immigrant ancestors often yield clues to their origins
overseas. When I was researching my own line, I knew that my
great-great-grandfather Joseph Beard had been born in England, but it wasn't until I found his will in New Orleans, in which
he left a watch to a brother living in Manchester, that I had a
clue to his actual birthplace. The will left by the same man's wife
named a sister and several other relatives living on the Isle of
Guernsey, in the English Channel, and was a great help to me
when I went abroad and began piecing together her line.

If an ancestor died *intestate*—that is, without leaving a will—
you may find other documents relating to the distribution of his
estate if he owned land or personal property. A petition for
administration or an accounting made by a court-appointed
administrator may include a list of heirs. Whether or not there
is a will, there may also be letters of administration, records of
litigation, notices to creditors, inventories and newspaper
advertisements for missing heirs that may yield genealogical
information. If a copy of the distribution of the estate has
survived, you may learn that certain heirs who were living at the
time the will was submitted for probate are listed as "now
deceased," that a daughter who was unmarried has married, or
even that the widow has remarried.

The location of these probate records in this country varies from state to state, but in most cases they are maintained in county courthouses, where copies are kept in bound volumes called libers and can be approached through the use of bound or card indexes arranged by surname. You can use the *U.S. Post Office Department Directory of Post Offices* to find out what county a particular town is in and George Everton's *Handy Book for Genealogists* to determine the date and origin of the county and the date from which records survive. The further back you go, the more important period maps and gazetteers will be in helping you discover the location of these records, as counties may have moved or towns disappeared since the time your ancestors were alive.

As a rule, if you know where your ancestor lived and the approximate date of his death, you can obtain a photostatic copy of his will by mail. Often you will receive a white-on-black negative—the first stage in the photostatic process. While a positive can be obtained for an additional fee, the negative is quite adequate and may even be easier to read than a positive, in the case of old documents.

The cost of copies, again, varies from state to state. In New York, even if you know the exact date of death, an initial fee of $10 is charged to determine whether a will is on file, and an additional fee is levied for the copy. Across the border in New Jersey, the initial fee is only $3. I suggest sending a check marked "for not more than $10" with your request; in most places, you'll get your copy for that amount or less. If there's an additional charge, as there is in New York, you'll be billed, but sending a check at the outset speeds up the whole process.

Because of the fees charged for searching county records, it is worthwhile to visit the courthouse in person if you're searching for numerous wills. Write ahead of time to find out if you will be permitted to search through the records. Looking through the files yourself will also give you an opportunity to examine all the documents pertaining to the probate of your ancestors' estates. The wills on file in libers are copies, and you should ask whether any originals have been preserved so that you can examine the signatures and seals. Since many people in this country were unable to read and write as late as the mid-1800's, your ancestor's signature on an early document is an indication that he was an educated person. If the seals bear heraldic emblems, it suggests that your family may have been entitled to a coat of arms.

If you have written to the courthouse and been informed that your ancestor's will is not on file but later find yourself in the area, go there and try to check the records yourself, as hasty or uninterested clerks are often not very thorough in their searches. If you do visit the courthouse, you may be able to turn up additional documents pertaining to your ancestors' lives. For example, if an ancestor died leaving minor children or an incompetent widow, there may be relevant orphan's court records. In rural areas, records of naturalization are kept in the county courthouse. If you have reason to believe that such documents exist, be sure to look for them while you're at the courthouse. If a visit is not possible, write to the local historical society or to the courthouse and inquire whether a local searcher is available. A professional genealogist will generally prepare "abstracts" of wills and other documents—copying down just the information containing genealogical clues.

The meaning of some terms used in early wills, letters and other records has changed over the years. Today we use the word "spinster" to refer to an unmarried woman, but during the eighteenth century and before, it identified any woman who lived alone, even though she might be a widow. It is not uncommon to find a will made by a woman identified as a "spinster" in which she mentions her late husband and leaves all her property to her children.

The further back you go in your research, the more likely it is that you'll encounter unfamiliar usages of words you think you understand. In particular, the terms used to describe the relationships among family members have evolved to have different or more specific meanings than they did during the seventeenth and eighteenth centuries. The word "cousin," for example, was a general term that might be used to refer to any relative outside the immediate family circle. Most commonly it identified a niece or nephew. The beginning researcher who encounters the word "cousin" in an early will and automatically ascribes the contemporary meaning to it may be making a mistake that will seriously confuse or distort the accuracy of his research. Before tackling early documents, familiarize yourself with the early meanings of the following terms of relationship:

brother—In addition to its strict modern meaning, "brother" might refer to a stepbrother, a brother-in-law, or the husband of a sister, stepsister or sister-in-law. Even more loosely it could signify a "brother in the church" or a good friend. *Sister* was used with the same variations.

daughter—Usually used in the modern sense, "daughter" might also refer to a daughter-in-law or a stepdaughter. *Father, mother* and *son* were subject to the same variations.

daughter-in-law—This term might have the same significance it has today, or it might refer to a stepchild. *Father-in-law, mother-in-law* and *son-in-law* were used similarly; "in-law" simply signified any relationship established by marriage.

german—The word "german"(or *germane*) clarified general terms of relationship. "Brothers german" were children of the same parents, distinct from half brothers or brothers-in-law. "Cousins german" were the children of brothers or sisters—first cousins, as we identify them today.

junior, senior, III, etc.—These labels were used to distinguish living family members with the same name, often uncles and nephews, and did not imply a father-son relationship. In small communities they might even be used to distinguish people of the same name who were not related by blood at all. The eldest person was "senior"; the next, "junior," and so on. These identifications were not permanent. If John Tyler, Sr., died or moved away, John Tyler, Jr., became "Sr." and John Tyler III became "Jr."

nephew—This word was usually employed with its modern meaning. In very early records, however, it sometimes identified a niece or even a male or female grandchild.

It is also a good idea to familiarize yourself with titles and labels that were indicators of an individual's social status. Class consciousness in America grew out of British roots, and these terms were used most strictly during Colonial times. As years passed, they developed new meanings or went out of use altogether.

freeman—A person so designated was, quite literally, a "free man" and was entitled to the rights of a citizen—specifically, the right to vote and the right to conduct business.

gentleman—A descendant of an aristocratic family, a gentleman received his income from the rental of lands; he was a member of the *landed gentry*. Strictly speaking, if the son of a gentle family left home and became a tradesman, he lost his title. If he continued to live on rental income or took up a respected profession such as law or the ministry, he was still considered a gentleman.

goodman—A goodman was a respected member of the community, ranked socially above a freeman but beneath a gentleman. His wife was called a *goodwife*, a term that was frequently shortened to *goody*. It is a common error to mistake "Goody Jones" for a proper name.

indentured servant—During the early years of colonization, impoverished European laborers often contracted to work in America for a fixed period—usually four to seven years—in exchange for passage to the New World. During the period of indenture they had few rights. At its conclusion they became *admitted freemen*.

mister—In Colonial New England, "Mister" was a term of respect applied to gentlemen, office holders and clergy. *Mistress*, and its contracted form, *Mrs.*, were used similarly, in recognition of a woman's social position or age, without regard to whether she was married.

The general glossary in Chapter 20 includes technical and legal terms and phrases that you need to know the meanings of when consulting wills, deeds and similar documents.

Deeds

In Europe, individuals kept their own deeds and as a rule did not record them centrally. But in the United States, for the most part, copies of deeds, like wills, are kept in bound volumes in county courthouses. These volumes are indexed by the names of *grantor* (the person transferring title to property) and *grantee* (the person to whom title is transferred). It is usually possible to obtain copies of deeds in person or by mail, although in certain places, such as New Castle County, Delaware, only lawyers are permitted to search deeds. As the originals were kept by the parties involved, you may also find these records among family papers.

If your ancestors lived in a rural county in the last century, chances are they owned, rather than rented, a farm. If you've been able to locate family members in a particular area during a specific time period, you should look in the "Index of Conveyances" at the courthouse to see if they owned land.

The earliest deed in your family's name in a given region is an indication of when your ancestors moved to an area and may state their former residence. The first deed of my ancestor James Tobin in Ontario County, New York, in 1834, for example, identifies him as " formerly of the city of Dublin in the Kingdom of Ireland." A deed for the sale of land held by your family for a long time may include a statement of how they originally obtained the land and name several previous ancestors. Deeds covering the division of land among heirs after an ancestor's death may include the names and addresses of all his children and the names of the husbands of married daughters.

A deed was crucial in establishing the lineage of my ancestress Nancy Selby. I knew she was the granddaughter of Captain John Selby, but in his will in 1790 Captain Selby had mentioned two granddaughters named Nancy, one the daughter of his son Parker and the other the daughter of his son James. It was in a deed she made in Worcester County, Maryland, in 1823 (Worcester County Deeds Liber AO 1823, p. 494) that Nancy Selby, then the wife of David Pennewill, stated that she was the daughter of James Selby, son of Captain John Selby.

The procedure for obtaining copies of deeds from courthouses is the same as that for obtaining wills. Additional land records, such as mortgages, leases and contracts, should also be searched.

School Records
School records at all levels can be helpful as you hunt for your ancestors. They almost always reveal a student's residence and parentage and often provide a great deal of additional genealogical and personal data.

Public and private school records dating well back into the last century can be found in many parts of the country. In New York City the nineteenth-century records of the Board of Education were recently presented to the Columbia University Teachers College. The accessibility of the records of particular schools depends on how they are stored and whether there is personnel available to help you.

You can begin your search by checking local histories to find out what schools were operating in the area where an ancestor lived at the time he was of school age. For schools that are no longer in existence, ask the local historical society whether any records have been preserved.

The higher the educational level of a school, the more records are likely to be available. If your ancestor attended a college or university, chances are the school has published a "hundred year" book or some other sort of alumni roster. Sometimes they're extremely biographical.

One of the oldest letters kept in my family's black tin box of important papers was written by my great-great-grandmother to her father in 1821, while she was attending the Emma Willard School in Troy, New York. The letter, which described her life at school, led me to inquire whether Emma Willard, one of the first women's secondary schools in this country, had any records from the time of my great-great-grandmother's attendance. I discovered that they had published a biographical book about their alumnae, which included an account of my ancestress. Such books are more commonly issued by colleges, but if an ancestor of yours attended a prominent secondary school such as Emma Willard, you may locate a similar volume.

Records of Clubs and Organizations

Depending on the life an ancestor led, you may find him or her listed in the membership roster of some club or organization. While the possibilities are innumerable, your ancestor's religion, education and profession are all clues to special-interest organizations to which he may have belonged. If he was a lawyer, for example, he may have been a member of a professional association of lawyers. Among the groups whose records are most likely to contain valuable biographical information are social fraternities and fraternal organizations.

The records of fraternities and sororities, quite naturally, give information about the educations of their members. In addition, because these groups generally give membership priority to the children of previous members, their records may include good genealogical data. If you are able to determine that an ancestor was a member of a fraternity, the secretary of the local chapter may be able to help you find his records.

If your ancestor was a member of the Masons, the Elks, the Odd Fellows or any similar fraternal organization, his membership records may turn out to be extremely useful. Sometimes they list only an individual's name and the date and place where he became a member, but often they are full of biographical information—the names and even the birth dates of parents, wife and children; facts about religion, education and profession; and photographs. The local secretary of your ancestor's organization may be able to help you locate his records.

9   Census Records

ounting people is one of the oldest activities of government. Some form of census taking has been employed in civilizations going back as far as Babylonia of 3800 B.C. and ancient China, usually by rulers who want to raise an army or impose taxes.

The word *census* originally referred to a Roman register of adult male citizens and their property, which determined political status, military obligation and taxation. Instituted by Servius Tullius, sixth King of Rome, about 550 B.C., the census was eventually extended under Caesar Augustus to take in the entire Roman Empire. Thus the New Testament tells that Mary and Joseph traveled to Bethlehem to be counted among the descendants of David, in response to a decree that "all the world should be taxed."

Among modern nations the Scandinavian countries recorded some of the earliest censuses. In Finland the records of a 1635 census have been preserved, and the first census of Iceland, taken in 1703, has also survived. Norway's first census was recorded in 1769 and Denmark's in 1787. Among other European nations, Austria took its first census in 1754, but the records no longer exist. Spain's census dates from 1798 and Great Britain's from 1801, although in that country few records prior to 1841 have survived.

Very early population counts were also made in some European possessions in the New World, some in Latin America in the sixteenth century. The first survey of the population of Mexico was made between 1579 and 1582, and the original manuscript of this count is preserved in the University of Texas Library at Austin. Censuses were taken in Barbados in 1680 and 1715, in the Bahamas in 1731, in Venezuela in 1772 and in Cuba in 1774. Some of these colonial censuses were inaccurate or incomplete, however, and the records of many have not survived. The amount of data about individual people in census records varies from country to country.

84

The United States Federal Census

A federal population census has been taken in the United States every ten years since 1790. A federal law passed in 1976 calls for future censuses to be taken every five years, because the American people have become so mobile that modern census statistics go out of date very quickly. The first mid-decade census is scheduled for 1985.

The records of all but two of the American censuses have survived virtually intact to the present day. The 1890 census was almost totally destroyed by fire—only fragments, including a list of widows of Civil War pensioners, remain—and some parts of the 1790 census were destroyed but have been reconstructed from tax lists of the period. Smaller portions of the 1800 and 1810 censuses were destroyed during the War of 1812, and there are no surviving census records for New Jersey before 1830. On the whole, however, America's census records are more complete over a longer period than those of most nations.

Early American censuses were posted publicly, in order to facilitate corrections or additions. Beginning in 1850, however, the information contained in the censuses was declared confidential by the government, in order to ensure the greatest possible accuracy in responses. Although no law has yet been passed concerning the sealing of these records, an informal agreement between the National Archives and the Census Bureau in 1952 called for their release after seventy-two years. Today only the censuses conducted through 1880 are available to the general public (the 1890 schedules having been destroyed). The 1900 census was opened on a limited basis in 1975; its relevant sections can be consulted only by genealogists researching their own family lines or authorized by another family to do research for them. Some information about individuals listed in later censuses may be obtained under special circumstances.

Like many other documents, the records of the American census include some inconsistencies, omissions and errors, the fault of either the census takers or the subjects themselves. However, the comprehensiveness of the information they contain, the generally high level of accuracy and the considerable success of early census takers in reaching the vast majority of the American population combine to make them valuable research tools for the genealogist.

By tracing a single family through several censuses it is possible to piece together an incredible amount of information, not only about family relationships but about how your ancestors lived—their movements, their educations and their professions. Locating as many census records pertinent to a particular family as possible also enables you to detect and eliminate any errors in the original records.

The American census was originally intended for the purpose of apportioning taxes and legislative representation among the states, and for the first census in 1790 federal marshals rode out with a list of six sample questions. Over the years, as the government has made the census a tool for social planning, it has grown into an extensive survey of detailed information about the American people that is invaluable to genealogists. The data collected in a particular census determine its specific usefulness.

The 1790 census identified only heads of households by name, then enumerated the people in each household in five categories: white males over sixteen, white males under sixteen, white females, other free persons and slaves. While succeeding censuses sought additional information, those conducted through 1840 continued to summarize the data for each household, identifying only the head by name. Nonetheless, it is possible, by comparing successive census entries and relating them to any facts you've turned up in other records, to determine the approximate ages and death dates of individuals within the family.

In 1850 a major innovation of great significance to genealogists was made. For the first time every individual in the count was identified by name, age, sex and color. Birthplaces of children, also recorded for the first time in 1850, are clues to earlier residences of migrant families.

In 1860 American Indians were included for the first time in census tallies (Chap. 13). Information on the value of individual property holdings, added in 1870, provides a clue to the existence of wills and deeds in county courthouses.

In 1880 still more additions of particular genealogical significance were made. Census information included the relationship of each person to the head of the family, the marital status of each person and the place of birth of his or her mother and father. (While relationships were not described in earlier schedules, they can often be inferred, but your assumptions should be confirmed through other sources before you accept them as facts.)

Information in the 1900 census included months and years of birth, the lengths of marriages and the number of children of each adult woman. If immigrant ancestors were alive at the time of the 1900 census, you can learn the year of their immigration, a fact which may lead you to ship passenger lists (Chap. 10) and other documents that will help you carry your search abroad. A one-page summary of the information covered in each census from 1790 to 1970 can be obtained from the U.S. Department of Commerce (Bureau of the Census, Pittsburg, KS 66762). *n/a*

You can try to locate census records any time you've pieced together sufficient data on an ancestral family during a census year, but it's most likely that you'll first find your ancestors in the later, 1880 or 1900, schedules and then, with additional clues, trace them back into earlier censuses. Because the 1880 and 1900 censuses collected so much detailed information, locating your ancestors in them can be like opening a genealogical goldmine.

By searching the census records in person at an institution that has microfilm copies, you can investigate a variety of surnames, check for variations in spelling and compare the information in one census to that in another. In order to get the greatest use out of census records, be absolutely scrupulous in researching them. Be sure to copy down every bit of information contained in the records, as some details that don't seem relevant at first may prove useful later, when you've discovered additional facts.

One Family Seen through Censuses

The path I followed in tracing the line of my ancestor John Finley demonstrates how information from early census records, supplemented with a few key facts from a variety of other sources, can be pieced together to create a remarkably detailed family picture. I first discovered John Finley's signature on a petition to have Bethel, Vermont, made a town in 1787. I then found him listed in the 1790 census of Bethel as the head of a household consisting of

1 male over 16
2 males under 16
1 female

[handwritten in right margin: Fruitland, Maryland (301) 457-4608 History Dept (301) 457-1167]

I surmised that the people listed were Finley's wife and children, as I knew that he had had two sons. In 1800 his household was once again in the Bethel census, this time with

    2 males under 16
    1 male over 45
    1 female between 26 and 45

At first glance this entry seems to represent the same family group as the 1790 census. But from cemetery inscriptions in the Old Yard at Bethel I had learned that John Finley died September 17, 1823, aged 69, and that his wife Sarah died July 15, 1796, aged 37. Reinterpreted in this light, the 1800 census suggests that John either took a second wife or engaged a housekeeper after Sarah's death. (The census enumerated all individuals living in a household, whether or not they were family members.)

While the name of a second wife doesn't appear in any vital records, an additional clue is the burial of a child, Frances Findlay (the name is spelled various ways in different records), the daughter of John and Mehitabel, on November 18, 1798, in the Episcopal Cemetery near where Finley lived.

By 1810, the census records reveal, John Finley had moved from Bethel to Stockbridge, Vermont, which is in the same county. By then the household included

    2 males between 16 and 26
    1 male over 45
    1 female 10 to 16
    1 female over 45

While it's possible that John and his second wife had had another daughter by 1810, the fact that the additional female in the household is over ten makes it more likely that she was a hired girl or a relative. By 1820 John Finley was still in the census of Windsor County but had moved back to Bethel. The household included

    1 male 26 to 45
    1 male 45 and up
    1 female 45 and up

The implication is that one of John's sons had established his own household by 1820, and, in fact, there is also a listing in the census for John Finley, Jr., who, cemetery records reveal, married a woman named Deborah. In 1820 their household consisted of

1 male under 10
1 male 16 to 26
1 male 26 to 45
1 female under 10
1 female 26 to 45

From this I gather that John and Deborah had a son and daughter both under the age of ten and a hired man between the ages of sixteen and twenty-six. From previous censuses we know that John Finley, Jr., is the male between twenty-six and forty-five and can guess that the female in the same age bracket must be his wife.

By 1830 John Finley, Sr., had, of course, disappeared from the census listing, as we know he died seven years earlier. The younger John Finley remained, no longer identified by the suffix "Jr." His household included

1 male 15 to 20
1 male 40 to 50
1 female 10 to 15
1 female 30 to 40
1 female 60 to 70

The younger male is no doubt John's son Marshall Finley, my great-great-grandfather, and the younger female his daughter. The older woman may well be Mehitabel, the widow of the elder John Finley.

The same census reveals that William Finley, John's brother, had married since 1820 and established his own household, which included

1 male 5 to 10
1 male 15 to 20
1 male 40 to 50
1 female 5 to 10
1 female 30 to 40
1 female 60 to 70

Probably William had two young children and a hired man between the ages of fifteen and twenty. The elderly woman in his household might, again, be his father's widow, as she might have taken up residence with either son. The other elderly woman is probably a mother-in-law of one of the Finleys.

By 1840, I knew, John Finley and his family had moved to upstate New York. In 1850 I found John Finley, a farmer aged sixty-four and a native of Vermont, listed in the federal census of Bristol, Ontario County, New York, with his wife Deborah, a native of Massachusetts, aged sixty-four. Their ages are slightly wrong, as he was actually sixty-three and she sixty-five—perhaps a matter of chivalry on John's part.

Such age discrepancies are not unusual in census records, and it appears that Deborah Finley may have shaved several more years off her age when questioned for the earlier, 1820 census. As English genealogist and writer Pauline Litton once noted when discussing the question of "exact age" in census records, women most often started young and aged rapidly, once their husbands had discovered their true age, whereas men were more likely to give their correct age during the early years and start subtracting later in life, when jobs became harder to come by and it paid to appear young.

I found the Finleys again in the 1855 New York State census (Chap. 9), an extremely valuable record because it required a great deal more information than federal censuses of the same period. In it I found John Finley, sixty-seven, a native of Vermont who had lived in Bristol for seventeen years. This told me that he had left Bethel for Bristol in about 1838, and in time I located the 1837 deed for the purchase of his Bristol home. Deborah Finley gave her correct age as sixty-nine in the 1855 census and identified her birthplace as Massachusetts. Living with them was Jane Finney, their servant, a twenty-eight-year-old native of Bristol.

From cemetery records I learned that Deborah Finley died December 15, 1856, at the age of seventy-one. She was buried in West Avenue Cemetery in Canandaigua, New York, where her gravestone can still be seen in the family plot. John Finley died in Canandaigua March 31, 1861, at the age of seventy-three and was buried next to her.

Their son, Marshall Finley, continued to live in Canandaigua, in Ontario County. The 1860 federal census revealed that he was forty-seven years old and a native of Vermont and was married to Ann E. Finley, forty-four, who was born in England. They lived with their four children.

The path I followed in tracing the line of Marshall's wife Ann exemplifies the usefulness of later, more detailed census records. In preliminary research I had learned that she was born in Cumnor, England, the daughter of James and Ann Bailey, and that her family lived near the church. Indeed, an English correspondent in Cumnor found a copy of the 1831 census in the parish records that showed the family living in a house near Cumnor Church. The abstract she sent me listed the following family members (ironically, the name of Ann, the daughter from whom I am descended, is missing):

James Bailey, shoemaker	52
Ann, wife	41
James, son	20
Jane, daughter	14
George, son	11
Charles, son	9
Alfred, son	7
Robert, son	5
Emma, daughter	1

For the most part, the earliest surviving English census that mentions people by name is that taken in 1841, but scattered copies of others can occasionally be found. In this case, the vicar of Cumnor, who may well have been the census taker, had preserved a copy of the 1831 record. I was especially lucky in this regard, for, as I learned from other sources, the family emigrated to America the following year.

From family sources I knew that the Baileys had settled for some time in upstate New York—where Ann met and married Marshall Finley—and then moved on to Michigan. A daguerreotype of the parents, James and Ann, suggested that they might still have been alive in 1850, since daguerreotypes didn't become popular in this country until the 1840's. While I might have searched for the family in the 1840 federal census of New York State, I was more interested in the 1850 and later schedules, which would identify each family member by name.

Thus the next census in which I located the Baileys was the

federal count in Sandstone, Jackson County, Michigan, in 1850. In four dwellings in a row, members of the family were named and identified by age, sex and place of birth. Information about property holdings was also given. James and Ann's children Jane, George and Charles now had families of their own:

1850 Federal Census, Sandstone, Jackson Co., Michigan, 29 Aug. 1850
p. 581

1022	Harrington, Theron	31m	N.Y.	$600 real
"	, Jane	31f	Eng.	
"	, Sarah	9f	N.Y.	sch.
"	, Bradley	5m	Mich.	sch.
"	, Alfred	2m	Mich.	
1023	Bailey, George A.	30m	Eng.	$700 real
"	, Mary	28f	N.Y.	
"	, Ann	3f	Mich.	
"	, James	1m	Mich.	
1024	Bailey, Charles	28m	Eng.	$1000 real
"	, Elizabeth	21f	Eng.	
"	, John	2m	Mich.	
"	, Horace	1/12m	Mich.	
	Welch, George	9m	Mich.	
1025	Bailey, James	70m	Eng.	$800 real
"	, Ann	60f	Eng.	
"	, Robert	22m	Eng.	
"	, Emma	20f	Eng.	
"	, William	15m	N.Y.	sch.
"	, Edwin	13m	N.Y.	sch.

From other records I confirmed that Jane Harrington had been born Jane Bailey. The minor discrepancy in her age (based on the 1831 English census, she should have been thirty-two or thirty-three by 1850) may represent an error made by one of the census takers, or perhaps Jane lied rather than admit that she was older than her husband. Had I not already known that the family had settled for a period in New York, the fact that New York is given as the birthplace of several of the children would have been an important clue.

Family records show that both James and Ann Bailey died before 1860. But various of their children continued to dwell in Jackson County, as the information from successive censuses, shown below in the form in which it was abstracted for me by Nellie Holmead Fowler, a professional researcher in Silver Spring, Maryland, reveals.

In the 1860 census George's family was not listed, but in 1870 their names reappeared:

1870—2nd ward, City of Jackson, Jackson Co., Mich.—Dwelling 228; Family 218 p. 27. Taken by D.G. Palmer Aug. 2, 1870.

BAILEY,   George—51m shoe merchant $3500 real; $4000 pers.; b. Eng.; parents foreign born.
"   Mary J. 49f   keeping house; b. N.Y.
"   James M. 21m   travelling agent; b. Mich.; father foreign born
"   Anna E. 23f   teaching sch.; b. Mich.

By 1880, the census revealed, George's wife had died and he was living alone.

1880—4th ward—Main St., Jackson City, Jackson Co., Mich.—Dwelling 135; Family 414
BAILEY, George A.   61m wid.; clerk in store; b. Eng.; parents foreign born

Between 1850 and 1860 Charles and Elizabeth had added three children to their family:

1860—Sandstone Township, Jackson Co., Mich. p. 146 or 147 (marked over), taken by T.G. Shippey Aug. 30, 1860—Dwelling & Family 1140
NOTE—2 doors from Robert Bailey.

BAILEY, Charles 39m farmer; $3000 real; $800 pers.; b. Eng.
"   Elizabeth   32f; b. Eng.
"   John   12m sch. b. Mich.
"   Horace   10m sch. b. Mich.
"   Fanny   7f sch. b. Mich.
"   Anna   2f b. Mich.
"   Herbert   7/12m b. Mich.

Charles and Elizabeth's family were not listed in the 1870 census schedule, but they reappeared, having produced five more sons, in 1880:

1880—Sandstone Township, Jackson Co., Mich. taken June 12, 1880 p. 17—Dwelling 170; Family 179.

BAILEY, Charles	58m farmer b. Eng.; parents foreign born
" Elizabeth	51f wife keep. house; b. Eng.; parents for. b.
" Horace G.	30m son; single; farmer; b. Mich., par. b. Eng.
" Herbert	20m son; single; farm laborer; b. Mich.; par. b. Eng.
" Frank A.	18m son; single; farm lab.; b. Mich.; par. b. Eng. sch.
" Eugene W.	15m son; sch.; b. Mich.; par. b. Eng.
" Irving	12m son; sch.; b. Mich.; par. b. Eng.
" Joseph	10m son; sch.; b. Mich.; par. b. Eng.
" Walter	7m son; sch.; b. Mich.; par. b. Eng.

Charles and his family may have been omitted from the 1870 count accidentally, or they may have moved away from Jackson County for a while. If a family you're tracing disappears from one census, always check one or two others before concluding that they have in fact left the area or died.

Robert, who was living with his parents in 1850, married and started a family during the next ten years:

1860—Sandstone Township, Jackson Co., Mich.; p. 146 or 147; taken Aug. 30, 1860 by T.G. Shippey—NOTE: 2 doors from Chas. Bailey.

BAILEY, Robert	32m farmer; $1200 real; $400 pers; b. Eng.
" Maryette	25f b. N.Y.
" Alice	4f b. Mich.
" Arthur	2m b. Mich.
GODFREY, Frances	17f dom.; sch.; b. N.Y.

Ten years later Robert's family was growing, he had changed professions and his fortunes were on the rise:

1870—2nd ward, City of Jackson, Jackson Co., Mich., p. 63—Dwelling 496; Family 480—NOTE: Alfred Bailey next house.

BAILEY, Robert   42m photographer; $5000 real; $2000 pers.; b. Eng.; parents foreign born.

"   Marietta   37f keep. house; b. N.Y.
"   Arthur   11m at home; sch.; b. Mich.
"   Edwin   7m at home; sch.; b. Mich.
"   Ella   5f at home; sch.; b. Mich.
"   Willard   2m at home; b. Mich.
"   Alice ·   14f at home; sch.; b. Mich.

The year 1880 found Robert with a new wife:

1880—Blackstone St., Jackson City, Jackson Co., Mich., p. 21—E.D. #117—Dwelling 239; Family 335.

       BAILEY, Robt.   54m mar.; photographer; b. Eng.; par. for. born.
**   "   Emily J.   41f wife; photographer; b. Mich.; father b. Vt.; mother b. Conn.
      "   Edwin D.   17m son; single; painter?; b. Mich.; father b. Eng.; mother b. Pa.*
      "   Ela J.   15f daug.; single; sch.; b. Mich.; father b. Eng.; mother b. Pa.*
      "   Willard G.   11m son; single; sch.; b. Mich.; father b. Eng.; mother b. Pa.*

      *   mother b. Pa. evidently error as two previous censuses show N.Y.

**   NOTE: the residents of the next dwelling must be related to Emily J. Bailey—she may have been a widow—MOON.

MOON Allen B.   20m <u>step-son</u>; mar.; photographer; b. Minn.; father b. Pa.; mother b. Mich.
      "   Sarah A.   18f <u>dau-in-law</u>; mar.; b. Canada; father b. Eng.; mother b. Canada
      "   Robert E.   1m <u>grandson</u>; b. Iowa; father b. Minn.; mother b. Canada

The underlining and notes marked with asterisks were contributed by the woman who abstracted the census returns for me and are typical of the kind of guidance and additional information you can expect from a competent researcher.

I have surmised that William and Edwin Bailey, listed in the household of James Bailey in 1850, may have been grandsons rather than sons, as a list of the children of James and Ann Bailey in a family Bible mentions neither of them. I know that their oldest son, James H., who appears with his parents in the 1831 English census but in none of the Michigan schedules, married and had children. Since he ran a circus, it seems quite possible that he might have left his children to be raised by his parents.

Clearly, the information found in censuses—even in the detailed censuses after 1850—is of greatest value when it can be supplemented by facts from other sources. When I found the following biography of Charles Bailey in a nineteenth-century history of Sandstone Township, it answered many questions left by the census information.

> *Charles Bailey was born in the borough of Abingdon, England, July 27, 1821. His parents came to America in 1832, and located in Seneca County, N.Y. In the spring of 1843 Mr. Bailey came West and bought land in secs. 23 and 24 in this tp. He married Elizabeth Welch, of England; their family is as follows—Chas. J., merchant in Boston; Horace G., Fannie E., Annie M., Herbert A., Frank A., Eugene, Irvin R., Jos. W. and Ernest Walter. In 1852 Mr. Bailey went to California, returning in 1854; since that time has been farming; owns 200 acres of land in secs. 23 and 24 where he now resides. He devotes very little attention to politics, but votes with the Republican party. P.O., Parma.*

Access to Census Records

The 1790 original and reconstructed census has been published and completely indexed and is widely distributed in libraries.

Copies of other censuses are maintained on microfilm or in bound volumes in the National Archives in Washington, D.C., where on any given day you can find dozens of amateur and professional genealogists poring over the old records. Copies are also available in regional Federal Records Centers (Chap.10), and it is possible to borrow microfilmed records from them through your local library, a recent development that has greatly enhanced the accessibility of census records to researchers all over the country. Complete copies of federal census records are also maintained by the Genealogical Society of the Church of Jesus Christ of the Latter-day Saints in Salt Lake City, which makes them available through its branch libraries, and in the Schomburg Center for Research in Black Culture, a division of the New York Public Library.

There are complete or partial collections in other libraries and historical societies around the country; large libraries, for example, often have copies of the records of their own state. The Microform Reading Room (315M) of the New York Public Library at 42nd Street, for instance, has the census records of New York State from 1790 to 1880, all the surviving census records of neighboring New Jersey from 1830 to 1880 and those for Connecticut from 1790 to 1810 and 1850 to 1880. Soundex indexes (Chap. 9) for the 1880 census in these states are also maintained, and there are scattered additional census records on film and in print and a variety of census indexes. The catalogue for these materials is maintained by the Local History and Genealogy Division (315G).

A major problem for researchers has traditionally been that census records are arranged geographically, by address, rather than by family name. The 1790 census, as noted, has been completely indexed by surname, and the 1880 and 1900 censuses have been partially indexed by Soundex indexing (Chap. 9), but in order to search for ancestors in the records of censuses conducted between 1800 and 1870 you need to know at least the county in which they lived during the census year. If your ancestors lived in a large city, you'll also need to know the ward in which they lived. Thus maps and directories are extremely important for searching census records, especially in larger cities and towns. E. Kay Kirkham's *Census Searching in Major Cities*, which contains maps of the major cities in America in census years, is a valuable tool.

Fortunately, a great number of alphabetical census indexes have been issued in the last few years by private publishers, and we can look forward to a time when all census records will be indexed and the entire task of census searching greatly simplified. One of the major firms in the field is Accelerated Indexing Systems, which has been producing indexes, broken down into volumes by state and year, at an incredible rate. These books may be purchased for use at home or found in a library in your area. You can get up-to-date information on the indexes and other research aids that are available by writing to the company (3346 South Orchard Drive, Bountiful, UT 84010).

As when using any secondary source, the researcher using a printed census index must be aware of possible errors or omissions. Because the original documents are often difficult to read, the people preparing indexes can easily confuse vowels or initial letters, substituting an *H* for a *K*, for example.

The spelling variations I encountered when searching in census indexes for the unusual old Dutch name of Keteltas (or Ketteltas) illustrate the kind of errors that can be made by indexers who are not acquainted with the family names of a region and have difficulty reading the poor or faint writing of the original transcripts on film. In *New York in 1800*, an index published by Gendex Corporation, two spellings—Ketteltas (Gerrit and Philip) and Kettletas (Sarah, Stephen, William and William N.)—appear on the same page, but as William Nicoll Ketteltas was the son of Gerrit Ketteltas, they probably spelled their names the same way. Accelerated Indexing System's *New York 1810 Census Index* contains several more variations in spelling—Ketteltas (William, p. 177), Kettletas (Benjamin, p. 178), Kettletos (Philip D., p. 178), Kettlilas (Stephen, p. 178), Kittletash (William N., p. 181) and Kittletask (John, p. 181)—although my research reveals that all of these people were members of the same family. The three entries in the AIS *New York City 1850 Census Index* are still further afield from the original—Ketellas (Eugene), Ketletas (William A.) and Kettlihu (Edward W.)—though all appear on the same page. In the actual 1850 census film, the name appears only as Keteltas and Ketteltas, and Edward's middle initial is N. (for Nicoll, an important family name), not W.

Despite such errors, the census indexes are invaluable, and I have frequently used them with great success. Considering the enormous scope of the indexing task and the poor quality of many of the original census records, the errors are understandable, but they mean that special care is required when using indexes. If you're sure a family lived in a particular location during a census year but can't find them in an index, the name may have been misspelled or omitted, so you should use your imagination and check a variety of phonetic spellings. If you still can't find it, an investigation of the original records is in order.

The Soundex Index
The government's development of "Soundex" indexing for the 1880 and 1900 census schedules represented a major improve-

ment in the accessibility of census information. It is a partial index; only those households in which there was a child ten years of age or younger are included, because the index, which was prepared during the 1930's, was primarily intended to enable people without birth records to use census data as proof of age for Social Security purposes.

Under the Soundex system, names are coded by sound, then alphabetized by state. The code for the family surname consists of the first letter of the name, followed by three numbers representing consonant sounds, as follows:

1-b, p, f, v
2-c, s, k, g, j, q, x, z
3-d, t
4-l
5-m, n
6-r

There is no code for the letters a, e, i, o, u, y, w or h. Employing the Soundex system, the name Stern would be represented by the code S365. Making a search within a state for this code would produce a variety of similar names and variant spellings: Styron, Sternn, Sternman, Southern and so on. This feature makes the Soundex index especially useful for the genealogist whose ancestors varied or simplified the spelling of their name over the years.

If two letters with the same code appear in sequence, they are represented by a single number, as in the name Packard, coded P263, or Schumacher, coded S526. If there are not enough consonants in a name to warrant three code numbers, the remaining spaces are filled with zeros, as for the name Shea, coded S000.

Census Records by Mail

The National Archives and Records Service conducted limited searches of census records in response to mail inquiries until late 1976, when the practice was discontinued because of the prohibitive cost involved. It is still possible to obtain photocopies of particular pages of census schedules by mail, but only if you can supply the state, county and exact page of the records on which a family is enumerated. If you have uncovered this information through the use of published indexes or other sources, you can write (Correspondence Branch-Census [NNCC], National Archives [GSA], Washington, DC 20408) for a photocopy. You will be billed a nominal fee after your order is filled.

You can also purchase a microfilm copy of the records of a county (current price, $12) from the Publication Sales Branch ([NEPS], National Archives [GSA]). This can be useful if you have access to a microfilm reading machine, perhaps at a local library.

While 1900 and later census schedules have not been released for general public use, information about individuals (not complete families) contained in them can be obtained by writing the U.S. Department of Commerce (Bureau of the Census, Pittsburg, KS 66762). A special form, BC-600, "Application for Search of Census Records," must be filed and signed by the individual if he is still living, or signed by a member of the immediate family or a direct descendant and accompanied by a death certificate or other proof of death if he is deceased.

The information furnished is the individual's name; his relationship to the head of the household, whose name may also be shown; age; place of birth and citizenship data. The current cost of this service, $8.50, covers a search of two censuses suggested by the person making the request. For an additional $2 charge, genealogists can obtain a "full schedule," which may also reveal the birthplaces of the individual's parents, his or her race, sex and marital status and educational and occupational information, depending on the questions asked by enumerators during the census year in question.

Mortality Schedules

Beginning in 1850, census enumerators completed separate schedules listing all the people who died during the year prior to June 1 of the census year (i.e., June 1, 1849, through May 31, 1850). These records, called the mortality schedules, were completed during every census year through 1900 and on a limited basis in 1885. After 1900 most states had established central registration of deaths, so the mortality schedules were done away with. Records for each state were turned over to state libraries, and those not claimed were deposited in the library of the Daughters of the American Revolution. In time, however, the National Archives and Records Service reassessed the value of these documents and now maintains copies of them on microfilm, but the mortality schedules of 1890 and 1900 are no longer in existence. Some of the mortality schedules have been published and are listed in the bibliographies for individual states.

The information recorded for each person listed in the mortality schedules includes his name, age, sex, color, birthplace, occupation, marital status and month and cause of death. During certain years information on parents' birthplaces was also noted.

The mortality schedules can often provide vital records that appear in no other place. For example, on page 42 of the published 1850 mortality schedules for Arkansas, which were copied by Bobbie J. McLane and Capitola H. Glazner (see Arkansas bibliography), it is noted that Lewis Tackett, aged eighty and a native of Virginia, died in Pope County, Arkansas, in February 1850—more than sixty years before the state began keeping vital records.

In Augusta Fothergill's *Virginia Taxpayers 1782–1787*, which supplements the reconstructed 1790 census of Virginia published by the Bureau of Census in 1908, there is a Lewis Tackett listed in Augusta County, Virginia, as a white male taxpayer over sixteen years of age. Since the man who died in Arkansas in early 1850 would have been born in about 1769, he would have been about sixteen in 1785 and might well have been a taxpayer during that period. Christian Tackett, listed in the same county, was almost certainly his father or a near relative, as Tackett was not a very common surname. Further research would be needed to substantiate these assumptions, but they illustrate how information culled from the mortality schedules can lead you back in your genealogical search.

Unfortunately, some published mortality schedules leave much to be desired. The Idaho schedules for 1870 were published along with the territorial census by the Idaho Genealogical Society in 1973 (see Idaho bibliography), but all the Chinese have been omitted from the published record, their entries summarized in phrases such as "114-71 through 117-73, all Chinese." This entire census should be republished with the full names of the Chinese residents.

Additional Censuses

Censuses conducted by the various states in years other than those in which federal population counts were carried out may provide additional genealogical information. Some of them may take the place of the missing 1890 federal census records. In New York State, for example, a census was taken in 1892. There's an exception here, too, however; the census for New York County, including Manhattan, has not survived. But there was a police census in New York City in 1890 that is maintained by the Municipal Archives (23 Park Row, New York, NY 10007).

In order to find out about the availability of such records in the state in which you're doing research, consult Noel Stevenson's *Search and Research* or send an inquiry to the state archives.

Earlier, during the Colonial period, a total of thirty-eight regional censuses were recorded between 1600 and 1789. Most of the surviving records have been published.

Part IV of this book gives the addresses of offices to which you can write for census data in other countries. In order to facilitate your search for records, the precise years when censuses were conducted in foreign countries are also noted in cases where that information is available. These dates are not exclusive, and censuses may have been recorded in other years as well. Census years are noted even in cases when records are thought not to have survived, because, as my experience with the 1831 English census in Cumnor illustrates, fragments of early census records believed to be lost may sometimes be discovered in local offices.

Published Census Guides
A variety of printed sources describe in greater detail the availability of particular census schedules. The *Guide to Genealogical Records in the National Archives*, which can be purchased for less than a dollar from the U.S. Government Printing Office in Washington, discusses not only census records but other federal documents, such as land and pension records, of use to ancestor hunters. A publication of the National Archives and Records Service, *Federal Population and Mortality Census Schedules, 1790–1890, in the National Archives and in the States*, describes the records that have survived and the libraries and institutions that have copies.

Index to Census Schedules in Printed Form, by Mary Marie Brewer, is a guide to federal and local census records, tax lists and so on that have been published or indexed by genealogical societies and other groups and individuals. *The Census Compendium*, issued by Gendex Corporation of Salt Lake City, is a directory to the locations of censuses and census indexes. Both have been updated by periodic supplements.

Another useful volume is *A Century of Population Growth from the First Census of the United States to the Twelfth,* an analysis of information in censuses conducted between 1790 and 1900, originally published in 1909 by the Bureau of Census. Included are maps that show the changes in county boundaries since 1790, which will help you locate your ancestors correctly in order to find them in the census. The book also contains a lengthy table of the names recorded in the 1790 schedules, noting their geographical distribution and the various spellings used at that time.

Directory of Census Information Sources, a pamphlet by J. Konrad, covers printed copies of census schedules by state, county and year; the areas for which rental or search service is available; and vendors of census information. *Census Records,* a catalogue of the Genealogical Publishing Company in Baltimore, is itself valuable as a bibliography.

Since our nation's inception, millions and millions of individuals have had dealings of some sort with the federal government, and virtually all of these transactions have involved written records of some sort. As vast and valuable as the federal census schedules are, they comprise only a tiny part of the extensive storehouse of records of genealogical value that have been preserved by the government.

The federal records that are most often of genealogical value include applications by veterans or their heirs for pensions or bounty land warrants and lists of immigrants and other passengers arriving by ship at major ports during the nineteenth century. Additional service records, applications for passports and records of land transactions between individuals and the federal government may also be helpful in specific cases. The majority of those documents that have been preserved are maintained at the National Archives in Washington, D.C. Because the Archives' records are so vast, nearly every genealogist tracing an American line will find a visit to Washington worthwhile. Even without going in person, a lot of information can be secured by mail or through one of the many regional Federal Records Centers and their branch archives (see end of this Chapter).

This chapter discusses the history, availability and usefulness of federal records most frequently of value in tracing ancestry. For information on other records and precise lists of which documents are available, consult *Guide to Genealogical Records in the National Archives.*

Pension Records

The system of rewarding military service with pensions dates back to the early days of the Revolution. In 1776 the Continental Congress passed a pension act providing that all officers who served for the duration of the war would earn half pay for seven years after its conclusion. In time a succession of additional Revolutionary pension laws were passed, each extending pensions to a larger number of veterans and their heirs.

In 1790, under advice by Congress, the states began providing for invalid veterans, and in 1808 the federal government assumed responsibility for these pensions. In 1818 pensions were granted to all veterans who had served nine months or more in the Revolution and could demonstrate need; in 1832 the required period of service was reduced to six months.

With the passage of the Widow's Act in 1836, pensions were made available to widows of Revolutionary soldiers who were married before the end of the war. Later laws granted pensions to widows who had married later, so that by 1868, although there were no Revolutionary veterans living, there were 888 widows receiving pensions, and as late as 1893 there were still thirteen widows receiving pensions.

The pension records of the Revolution are most often cited for their genealogical worth, probably because they are often part of the proof submitted by people seeking to join the Daughters of the American Revolution or other patriotic societies in which the requirement for membership is descent from a soldier or patriot of the Revolutionary period.

However, the National Archives houses a total of seven series of valuable pension records. In addition to those for Revolutionary invalids and Revolutionary veterans, there are records for soldiers who fought in the "Old Wars," the War of 1812, the Mexican War, the Indian Wars and on the Union side in the Civil War.

Information in Pension Records

The Revolutionary veteran seeking a pension had to submit proof of his military service and his need. After 1820, when a veteran was required to submit a schedule of his estate, deeds were often presented to show that he had disposed of his property. As the earlier section on deeds suggests, pension files that contain such land records are often especially rich in genealogical data.

Many pension applications include statements about the veteran's birth and parentage, marriage and movements. Affidavits prepared by fellow soldiers or friends to support the veteran's claim may provide still more information along these lines. (Those who prepared these affidavits also recorded a good deal of information about themselves, but as there is no index to these papers, finding an affidavit written by your ancestor for another veteran is largely a matter of luck.)

Because a widow claiming a pension was required to prove her relationship to the deceased veteran and list the children they had together, her application is often of greater value than her husband's (Illustration 22). Marriage certificates and transcripts of family Bible records are often included. From the widow's pension application you should also learn the date and place of the veteran's death.

Locating Pension Records

In order to make positive identification of an ancestor in the pension records, you need to know the year of his birth or death and where he lived at the time of enlistment and during the period when he claimed a pension.

Most pension records are arranged or indexed alphabetically by the veteran's surname. If your ancestor served in the Revolution, you can determine whether he filed a pension application by consulting the National Genealogical Society's *An Index of Revolutionary War Pension Applications*, which has recently been revised and is available in most libraries with genealogical collections. Indexes for pension records of other wars are on microfilm in the National Archives, as are the records themselves.

To obtain information by mail, request form 6751—"Order for Copies of Veteran's Records"—from the National Archives and Records Service (Correspondence Branch, National Archives [GSA], Washington, DC 20408). After locating your ancestor's file, they will photocopy a selection of those documents that are most often useful to genealogists and bill you for the cost. If questions remain unanswered, you can inquire about the cost of copying any remaining documents.

When I obtained copies of the documents in my grandfather's pension application file I learned for the first time that my mother was a Civil War pensioner. Her father's file included my mother's and uncles' birth certificates, my grandparents' marriage record and a great amount of additional information that I had found nowhere else. It was from this source that I first learned that my grandmother, who had left her three children to be raised by her mother, had remarried after my grandfather's death.

Sometimes letters and other personal effects of soldiers who died may be among the papers in their pension files. When one woman I know sent for copies of the documents in the pension application file of an uncle who had served in the Civil War, she found among them a letter that he had written to his parents from Andersonville, the military prison where he had died. The letter, which had never been sent, wound up in his file in the National Archives.

After the Civil War, federal pensions were granted only to those who fought on the Union side. Some Confederate veterans did apply, however, so you may find a Southern ancestor's application on file. Some of the states in the South granted their own pensions to Confederate veterans; check with the appropriate state archives for information. Other military records of the Confederacy have been deposited in the National Archives, and I obtained the service record of my great-grandfather, Major Cornelius C. Beard of Louisiana, by sending for it (Illustration 23).

If you fail to turn up a pension record for an ancestor, it doesn't mean that you are mistaken about his service record. He may not have sought a pension or may not have qualified under the laws of the time. Perhaps he applied for bounty land but not for a pension as reward for his military service.

Bounty Land Records

Grants of free land to veterans or their heirs, as well as pensions, were used by the early American government as inducements to enlist or rewards for past service, first during the Revolution and later for the War of 1812, the Indian Wars and the Mexican War. In 1862 the Homestead Act's liberal soldier provisions made land warrants unnecessary during the Civil War, so they were abandoned.

Bounty land application files are maintained at the National Archives in two series: Revolutionary War and post-Revolutionary War. They include the warrant application, the veteran's discharge certificate and a record of how the application was resolved. Like pension records, these files contain a variety of information that may include the veteran's name, rank, unit, period of service, age or birth date, residence and sometimes a personal description. If the application was filed by a widow or heir, it should also include the applicant's name and relationship to the deceased veteran and the place and date of the veteran's death.

Copies of bounty land application records, like copies of pension records, can be obtained by mail from the National Archives and Records Service by filing form GSA 6751.

Additional Service-Related Records

A variety of other service-related records may also be helpful in your search for your ancestors. The payrolls of the Continental Army, among the oldest documents in the National Archives, are frequently used as a proof of pedigree for admission to the D.A.R. and other patriotic societies. A helpful pamphlet, "Military Service Records in the National Archives of the United States," can be obtained free from the National Archives and Records Service.

You may be able to obtain service records for soldiers who did not receive pensions by writing the Defense Department in Washington or the office of the adjutant general of the state from which the soldier served.

While World War I records are generally not yet available, the state adjutant general may again be able to provide some assistance. In addition, the files of Selective Service cards maintained at the time of both world wars—which should cover every draft-age male of the period—are now considered public records, and information from them can be obtained at no charge by writing the Atlanta Federal Records Center (1557 St. Joseph Avenue, East Point, GA 30344). They will send you the necessary form, which must be filled out with your ancestor's name, approximate date of birth, date and place of draft registration and any identifying data you can provide. The information you may learn when a copy of your ancestor's registration is returned to you includes his exact date of birth and birthplace, his residence, marital status, age and next of kin at the time he registered for the draft.

Passenger Arrival Lists

Beginning in 1820, ships' captains were required by the federal government to record identifying information about each passenger on ships arriving in America from overseas. These passenger lists are useful for identifying the immigrant founders of American families and often provide vital links for the researcher attempting to carry his line "across the water."

Some of the lists in the National Archives date back to 1798, but the majority date from 1820, when federal law made them mandatory, or later. Those over fifty years old have been copied on microfilm and can be consulted by genealogists. Transcripts of arrivals between October 1, 1819, and September 30, 1820, and between September 1821 and December 1823 can also be found in two printed volumes, issued by the Genealogical Publishing Company and the Magna Carta Book Company, respectively.

The surviving passenger lists, which contain many gaps, are for arrivals at Atlantic and Gulf of Mexico ports. San Francisco's arrival lists were destroyed by fires in 1851 and 1940, and those of other Pacific ports, if they exist, have never been transferred to the National Archives. Fortunately, Louis J. Rasmussen's *San Francisco Ship Passenger Lists*, four volumes of lists reconstructed from newspaper announcements, covers passenger arrivals from the beginning of 1850 through January 1853—a period of intense migration into California as a consequence of the discovery of gold there in 1848 (see bibliography of California resources).

The passenger arrival lists exist in two major groups: Customs Passenger Lists and Immigration Passenger Lists. The Customs Passenger Lists, so called because they were first filed with the collectors of customs, include each passenger's name, age, sex and occupation; the name of the vessel on which he sailed; the port of embarkation and the port and date of entry.

The Immigration Passenger Lists (which recorded information about visitors to this country and Americans returning from abroad, as well as actual immigrants) are especially valuable. In addition to the information listed above, they include the passenger's place of birth and last place of residence. After 1893 they include the name and address of an American relative of the immigrant, if he had any, and after 1907 the name and address of his nearest relative in his homeland.

Unfortunately, the passenger lists are arranged chronologically, and indexes are scarce. In order to find an ancestor in the unindexed Customs Passenger Lists you need to know his name, the port through which he entered this country and either the name of the vessel and its approximate date of arrival or the name of the port from which it sailed and the exact date of arrival. To locate an ancestor in the Immigration Passenger Lists you need to know his name and age, the port of entry, the name of the vessel and the date of its arrival.

In those lists that have been indexed you may be able to locate your ancestor if you know only the port of entry and the year of arrival. Indexes, which are on microfilm in the National Archives and some libraries, primarily cover the years 1820 to 1846, while most of the lists of arrivals from 1846 until after the turn of the twentieth century remain unindexed. It was through the index to the lists for the Port of New York, 103 reels of microfilm available in the New York Public Library, that I discovered the arrival in 1833 of my great-great-grandparents, Joseph and Mary Beard, with their sons Joseph R. and "Corny"—or Cornelius—my great-grandfather, on the ship *Hannibal.* Detailed information about indexes can be found in *Guide to Genealogical Records in the National Archives,* and the more recent *National Archives Microfilm Publications.*

If you have only part of the information necessary to locate your ancestor in the passenger arrival lists, you may be able to find what you need, or at least narrow your search, by consulting the records of vessel entrances that were maintained at ports and are now housed at the National Archives. These give the names of ships, their dates of arrival in various ports and the countries from which they sailed.

If necessary, you can make a general search of all the passenger arrival lists for a particular port, but the sheer size of this undertaking makes it a course of last resort. If you know the name of the port from which your ancestor sailed, however, you have already reduced the task significantly.

If family papers don't provide enough information to enable you to find your ancestor in the passenger arrival lists, naturalization papers, which sometimes give the name of the ship on which an immigrant traveled and the date and port of his arrival in this country, may prove helpful. Naturalization papers are found in the courts where naturalization took place, and if you don't know where your ancestor was naturalized, you may find out by consulting voter lists of the county in which he resided. The information in naturalization papers issued since the turn of the century is often quite detailed, while earlier records are more cursory.

When you have enough data to find an ancestor in the passenger arrival lists you can obtain a copy of his entry by mail by filing form GSA 7111 with the National Archives and Records Service.

Passport Applications

In the early years of America, passports were carried by individuals traveling from state to state or into Indian territory. Records of such early passports may be useful to you if your ancestors settled in the area that eventually became Alabama, Mississippi and Louisiana. Some of these documents have been published; the passports issued by the governors of Georgia between 1785 and 1820, for example, were transcribed by the late Mary Givens Bryan and printed in two special publications of the National Genealogical Society, as indicated in the bibliography of Georgia resources.

Modern passport applications filed between 1791 and 1905 are now maintained in the Diplomatic Records Branch of the National Archives. Although passports were not required by law during that period, except during the Civil War, many were secured for the protection they afforded. Immigrants traveling home often obtained passports in order to avoid the military draft in their home country.

Passport applications dated between 1810 and 1905 are kept in bound volumes at the National Archives, and indexes are available for the years 1834 to 1905. While the earliest applications were simple letters of request, expired passports, birth certificates, certificates of citizenship or similar documents may be on file with them.

After the Civil War, passport applications were more detailed. Information usually includes the applicant's name, signature, residence, age, personal description and the names or number of family members traveling with him. If he was a naturalized American, the date and place of his naturalization is given. Early passport applications for naturalized citizens also include birth dates, the name of the vessel and date and port of arrival, and length of uninterrupted residence in the United States.

If you have reason to believe an ancestor traveled and applied for a passport before 1905, you can obtain information from his application from the Diplomatic Records Branch of the National

Archives by submitting his name and residence and the place and approximate date of his application. If the records you need are located, a nominal fee will be charged for copies.

Passport applications filed since 1906 are maintained by the Passport Office (Department of State, Washington, DC 20524). To request information from these records, you must supply your ancestor's full name, the date and place of his or her birth and at least an approximate indication of the time and place of application. In some cases an approximate birth date may suffice. You can facilitate the location of your ancestor's application by also supplying the passport number, if you've learned it; information on whether he or she was included in another's passport; and any possible variations in the spelling of your ancestor's surname. If the individual whose passport application you are seeking is still alive, he must sign your request. If he is deceased, you should submit evidence of your relationship.

The current fee for requesting a post-1905 passport application is $2 for the search and the first photocopied page plus sixty cents for each additional page. The Passport Office will bill you after the search is completed.

The amount of data contained in these applications varies. In addition to the information supplied in pre-1905 records, more recent passport applications may identify the applicant's spouse and may include the names, birth dates and birthplaces of children if they were included in the passport. A picture of your ancestor will be included if the application was filed in 1915 or later.

Information from passport applications is sometimes very helpful to genealogists but will be available only if your ancestor was a citizen and sought a passport. Before World War I, passports were required only for travel to certain countries. For additional details, consult *The United States Passport, Past, Present, Future*, a recent publication available from the U.S. Government Printing Office (Washington, DC 20402) for $5.10.

Federal Records Centers
The National Archives and Records Service operates a nation-wide system of depositories that includes not only the National Archives Building in Washington, D.C., but fifteen Federal

Records Centers. Two of these—the Washington National Records Center in Suitland, Maryland, and the National Personnel Records Center in St. Louis—are national in scope. Eleven of the others include branch archives established in 1969.

With the establishment of these regional archives and the development of a system under which you can borrow microfilmed records through your local library, a wealth of information has been made available to genealogists all over the country— information that previously could be obtained only by paying a sometimes costly visit to the nation's capital. The collections in the branch archives consist of holdings that are chiefly of regional interest, along with microfilm copies of the most significant records in the National Archives, such as the federal census schedules.

You can study these microfilms in the research room of your regional archives branch or borrow them through any library or other research institution that has a microfilm reading machine. This means you can now search the census and other valuable federal documents in a library close to your home, at no charge. Only the 1900 census cannot be borrowed; it must be seen in person at the archives branch.

Some of the regional centers have published catalogues of their microfilm holdings, and *Prologue: The Journal of the National Archives* (currently $8 for four issues a year from the Cashier, National Archives, Washington, DC 20408) periodically lists the microfilm publications deposited in the regional archives branches.

To find out what's available in your area, request a list of microfilm holdings from the Chief, Archives Branch, Federal Archives and Records Center, at the appropriate address listed below. If your local librarian isn't already familiar with them, you can also request a sample standard Interlibrary Loan Order form.

Archives Branch	Address and Phone	Area Served
Boston	380 Trapelo Road Waltham, MA 02154 617-223-2657	Connecticut, Maine, Massachusetts, New Hampshire, Rhode Island, Vermont

New York	Building 22—MOT Bayonne Bayonne, NJ 07002 201-858-7164	New Jersey, New York, Puerto Rico, the Virgin Islands
Philadelphia	5000 Wissahickon Avenue Philadelphia, PA 19144 215-951-5591	Delaware, Pennsylvania; for microfilm loans, also serves District of Columbia, Maryland, Virginia, West Virginia
Atlanta	1557 St. Joseph Avenue East Point, GA 30344 404-763-7474	Alabama, Georgia, Florida, Kentucky, Mississippi, North Carolina, South Carolina, Tennessee
Chicago	7358 South Pulaski Road Chicago, IL 60629 312-353-8541	Illinois, Indiana, Michigan, Minnesota, Ohio, Wisconsin
Kansas City	2306 East Bannister Road Kansas City, MO 64131 816-926-7271	Iowa, Kansas, Missouri, Nebraska
Fort Worth	4900 Hamphill Street (building address) PO Box 6216 (mailing address) Fort Worth, TX 76115 817-334-5515	Arkansas, Louisiana, New Mexico, Oklahoma, Texas
Denver	Building 48, Denver Federal Center Denver CO 80255 303-234-5271	Colorado, Montana, North Dakota, South Dakota, Utah, Wyoming
San Francisco	1000 Commodore Drive San Bruno, CA 94066 415-876-9001	California except southern California, Hawaii, Nevada except Clark County, the Pacific Ocean area
Los Angeles	24000 Avila Road Laguna Niguel, CA 92677 714-831-4242	Southern California counties of Imperial, Inyo, Kern, Los Angeles, Orange, Riverside, San Bernardino, San Diego, San Luis Obispo, Santa Barbara, Ventura; and Clark County, Nevada
Seattle	6125 Sand Point Way NE Seattle, WA 98115 206-442-4502	Alaska, Idaho, Oregon, Washington

11 Regional Differences within the United States

$\mathfrak{T}$he particular sources you will use to uncover your family's history will depend on the religion and nationality of the people whom you are tracing and the area in which they lived in this country and abroad. When I began to move into the professional sphere of genealogy in New York I discovered that many ancestor hunters shied away from doing research in the southern United States because the obstacles they encountered there were quite different from those with which they had become familiar in the North. An understanding of the different approaches and resources that are appropriate when doing genealogical research in the North and South must begin with a consideration of the patterns of English Colonial settlement and the subsequent histories of these two regions of the country.

The North

In the harsh climate of New England, settlers clustered together in towns, with their farms and common grazing lands arranged around the outskirts. A structured town government developed early, with a town clerk keeping track of the births, marriages and deaths of the inhabitants. The evangelical church of the community, the Congregational Church, was a powerful force, and the minister, too, kept records—of baptisms, marriages and burials. A town burial ground was set aside, and native granite tombstones were erected.

Because such a variety of records were maintained in early New England, many have survived to the present day, and it is often easy for a genealogist doing research in this area to accomplish a great deal. If a fire destroyed a church in a New England town, the town hall might still survive. Or at least the crisp, clean air kept the inscriptions on the tombstones legible, leaving solid and accurate sources for researchers.

The middle of the nineteenth century saw the movement of many of the younger members of New England farming families into the industrialized cities. The consequent sense of uprootedness inspired many individuals to begin compiling vast family histories that have become standard works in the field of genealogy.

The South

In the South, once the major Indian problems had been overcome, there was no reason for people to band together in the moderate climate, and while certain cities were established, the majority of people settled on farms. In the late seventeenth century, as black slaves were imported from Africa in ever-increasing numbers, small farms gave way to plantations of several hundred or more acres. Each was like a private community, in which the services of everyday life were provided by the owner's family and slaves.

In each county a courthouse was set up to house the deeds, probate records and, sometimes, marriage bonds of the area. There was usually an established Church of England near the courthouse and a store that provided any necessities the plantations were unable to produce for themselves. A few professional people, such as lawyers and doctors, built houses nearby, forming the nucleus of a typical county seat. While the people who lived in these towns might be buried near the church, those in the countryside were usually buried on their own plantations, often in unmarked graves or in graves identified only by wooden tomb markers.

As the eighteenth century waned, Methodist, Baptist and various evangelical faiths took the place of the established church, which often fell into decay. Circuit-riding ministers officiated at baptisms, marriages and burials on outlying plantations, and the records of these events often remained in the possession of the ministers and their descendants or were lost.

The records of the early South were scarcer and less well maintained than those of the North. In addition, the bulk of the devastation of the Civil War of the 1860's was visited on the South, and many of those records that did exist were destroyed.

While family Bibles were popular in the South, many of them were lost or destroyed in fires. County records are important because towns and cities did not keep records, but many county records were burned, or counties were divided and the early records left in the county seat of a distant county. Southern church records may be helpful to genealogists, but many of the Protestant wooden churches were destroyed during the war or as a consequence of natural disasters, and no trace remains of many of the private family cemeteries. Because so few local records have survived, federal census schedules are of special importance to researchers in Southern states.

Nonetheless, while the North took the lead in genealogy during the nineteenth and early twentieth centuries, the South began to close the gap in the middle part of this century, when the various Southern states, realizing that their heritage was endangered, began to build up their state archives. The Mormons undertook the extensive task of microfilming many of the precariously housed Southern county records, and with these microfilms as a basis, Southern archives have become in many ways better organized than those in the North. New York State, for example, probably has one of the poorest archives in the country, while Virginia has one of the best. New York, at one time, didn't allow the Mormons to microfilm state records, although this decision was subsequently reversed, and this work of preservation is now going on. New York's county courthouses maintained a great deal of independence in record-keeping, and many of the documents in them are not yet on microfilm in the state archives. New York City, in particular, retained a great deal of autonomy in keeping many of its own records. In addition, a fire in Albany in 1911 destroyed many New York State records.

By contrast, many of the archives in Southern states have gathered together not only existing state and county records but federal census schedules, church and cemetery records, some pension records and private papers such as family Bibles, letters and diaries. In this effort, they have been aided by the Daughters of the American Revolution, the United Daughters of the Confederacy and many other patriotic organizations.

Southern Place Names as Genealogical Clues

In many parts of the United States, towns and cities bear the names of early settlers. In the South, more interestingly, settlers often named their parcels of land after the places in England or Europe with which they had been associated. You must be cautious about making assumptions on this basis, however, for if an ancestor owned a parcel of land called Bohemia, he may have bought it from someone else who came from Bohemia and gave the name to the property.

My ancestor John White was fairly prominent in Somerset

County, on the eastern shore of the Chesapeake Bay in Maryland, in the late 1600's. He had arrived there around 1660, but his origins were unknown; in fact, some of the printed volumes in the Maryland state archives bemoaned the fact that White's roots were lost to history, as he was not only a notable man but was the brother-in-law of Colonel William Stevens, a very wealthy man in the same county, who was originally from Buckinghamshire County, England.

I was interested to learn that White had named one parcel of land that he owned Caldicot; another, Newport-Pagnell; and another, Buckinghamshire. In going through various general sources on the surname White—and it is a very common name—I found one White family that lived at a house called Caldicot, in the parish of Newport-Pagnell, in the county of Buckinghamshire, England. And sure enough, the family had a son by the name of John who was the age of the man I was searching for.

In addition, the pedigree chart of this particular White family included many sets of twins, all the way back into the 1500's. I knew there were many twins among the descendants of the John White for whom I was searching, right down to my great-great-grandmother, who was a twin, and my first cousin, who gave birth to twins.

The White pedigree chart also revealed that John had a sister Elizabeth, about whom no further information was given. John White had married a woman named Sarah Keyser in Somerset County in the 1670's, and it had long been assumed, because William Stevens and John White referred to one another as "brother" in various records, that Stevens' wife Elizabeth was the sister of Sarah Keyser. When I found the genealogically detailed will of one of Sarah Keyser's unmarried brothers, however, there was no mention in it of any sister Elizabeth. I now believe that Elizabeth, the wife of William Stevens, was actually John White's sister and that they all emigrated from Buckinghamshire together. Stevens may have married Elizabeth in England. In America, the family first settled in Virginia and then moved up into Maryland.

It's interesting to note that so many "official" sources said that the origins of John White were unknown. It is not unusual for the individual genealogist, because of his or her greater personal interest, to accomplish much more than the professional historian.

Nineteenth-Century American Genealogy

In any culture, people generally begin to investigate their past during periods of stability and prosperity. In the United States, local history and genealogy first flourished during the period of peace that followed the War of 1812.

In New England, people began to write town histories, and families that had been scattered by urbanization began to reunite at periodic family reunions, from which grew family histories. As a group, the authors of the large, nineteenth-century New England genealogies generally didn't try to prove that they had a great ancestry. While they might include some background on the family name in England and list Crusaders or other notable people who bore the same surname, this information was presented as general background, and for the most part direct descent wasn't claimed unless it could be proven. Instead, the New England genealogies focused on the immigrant ancestor and his descendants, and many of these works can be verified by other historical documents that have been published since they were written. For example, the vital records of many Massachusetts towns from the earliest point up to 1850 have been published by the New England Historic Genealogical Society and the Essex Institute, and it's remarkable how well the dates in them correspond with those noted in the early New England genealogies. The people who wrote these histories apparently did careful research, checking family records and talking to older people who still had a good memory of earlier generations.

By contrast, nineteenth-century Southern genealogies tended to be quite fanciful and often had little basis in fact. If the family name was Montague, for example, the author would try to establish a link with the very greatest English families of the same name. There was a general tradition that all Southern families were of gentle origin, although in truth they were no more gentle than the people of New England.

In fact, on the whole, the English who first settled both Massachusetts and Virginia were people of the middle or lower middle class who were seeking economic advancement. Generally, they had been able to save enough money to pay their passage to the colonies. There were, of course, those who came as indentured servants because they could not afford the passage money, and most of these settled in the South. But many indentured servants were also members of good families who had simply fallen on hard times as a consequence of the English Civil War of 1642.

Many other early settlers were hard-working people whose opportunities in England were limited by the law of primogeniture, under which a father's estate went to his oldest son. This system of inheritance prevailed from the very top of the social order to the bottom. Noblemen and gentlemen might be able to set aside a little property to give to a younger son, or arrange for him to go into the military or clergy so that he would be provided for, but merchants and farmers could do very little for their younger sons, except, perhaps, give them a small amount of money. Often it was this money that paid their way to America.

Early documents reveal that numerous early American settlers could write their names, so it's obvious that many of them had at least some education. In America, with little money and a great deal of ambition, industrious immigrants were able to find land and position and become very prosperous.

At one time I was asked to do some research into the lineage of a family by the name of Frisby. James Frisby was a fairly elegant man in seventeenth-century Maryland, an officer of the county in which he lived. His descendant was sure the family must have had an illustrious origin in England, as various Colonial American Frisbys were high sheriffs and members of the Maryland Assembly.

In fact, when I followed the line back to London, I learned that James was the son of William Frisby, who had gained some wealth and position as a dyer of cloth. He belonged to a guild and was a warden of the Church of St. Peter in Paul's Wharf, London. In the early parish registers, which have been published by the Harleian Society, there are the names of family members who were buried in the churchyard, but when William Frisby died he was buried in the church, an indication of his social and financial ascendancy.

William's son James, who probably received some education, married Mary Maddox, the daughter of John Maddox, whom records identify as a "chirurgeon" (a Middle English term for a surgeon) and a citizen of London—that is, an established member of the middle class. He belonged to the same church as William Frisby, and he, too, was a prosperous man. According to his will, probated in the Prerogative Court of Canterbury in

1658 (p. 629) and now preserved in the Public Record Office in London, he left Mary some money when he died.

When it came time for James and Mary to decide what they were going to do in life, they undoubtedly saw that there was little chance for advancement for them in London. So they emigrated, settling first in Virginia and then in Maryland, where they became members of the gentry, which they never could have done in England with the amount of money they had. The Frisbys are typical of many of the people who held office in Colonial America.

The Movement West

The nineteenth century saw the expansion of young America as people of both North and South began moving west in search of new land and opportunity. By 1820 the Industrial Revolution was beginning in the North, and many people left their farms to go to the cities, then changed their minds and headed west. New Englanders first migrated into Vermont and New Hampshire and across upper New York State, then into the Middle West.

At the same time, Eli Whitney's cotton gin made cotton "king" in the South. Farms along the East Coast were deserted as the soil was ruined by the continuous planting of tobacco and cotton, and plantations, farms and small county seats that resembled the ones the pioneers left behind began sprouting up in Kentucky, Missouri, Tennessee, the western Carolinas, Georgia, Alabama, Mississippi, Louisiana, Arkansas and Texas.

The differences in the type and survival of records in the North and South are reflected farther west, as the migrating settlers carried their religious and political customs with them. Many upstate New York towns have vital and church records dating from the 1830's. In Michigan, which was settled by Northerners, good records date from the 1860's. But in Missouri, settled by Southerners, early records are scarce. In some parts of the Middle West the influences of North and South converge.

As the nineteenth century progressed, expansion to the Pacific proclaimed the "manifest destiny" of the United States. Texas, which had won its own independence from Mexico, was annexed in 1845. By the treaty of Guadalupe Hidalgo after the Mexican War, the United States acquired California and the present

American Southwest. By the Gadsden Purchase from Great Britain in 1853, the United States gained its Pacific Northwest.

With the discovery of gold in California in 1848, many people from both North and South headed for the far west, some traveling across the country by wagon train and others "sailing around the Horn"—going by sea around the southern tip of South America. Both were long and dangerous journeys. Travel by wagon train was slow and arduous and there were conflicts with Indians. Many pioneers didn't survive the trip to the West Coast, and others stopped and settled at some point along the way.

The Mormons, seeking religious freedom, moved into Utah. The devastation wrought by the Civil War provided further impetus for many Southerners to move west. The development of transcontinental railroads in the late 1860's and early 1870's spurred the nation's continuing expansion. As these railroads opened up travel in both directions across the country, they also carried some of the first Chinese settlers from the West Coast to New York City's Chinatown. Some had immigrated by ship to the West Coast, and others were born there of immigrant parents.

Extensive settlement of the southwestern states of Arizona and Nevada came in the 1870's and 1880's, after the Indians in those areas had been overcome. In the last part of the nineteenth century there was rapid growth of the American economy, based on steel, oil, railroads and machines, and waves of immigrants poured in.

Tracing Pioneer Families

The less migration a family participated in, the easier it is to trace them, whether they originated in the North or South. Following the paths of some of America's pioneer families as they moved from one area to another constitutes a true detective mystery.

Census records are helpful in tracing some of the early settlers of the Midwest. If deeds can be located in county courthouses, they are also very important, as they may reveal the former residences of early families. If Midwestern settlers lived into the 1860's or 1870's, when vital statistics were first recorded, you may find death certificates that will tell you their birthplaces and parentage. There are also some valuable marriage records in various parts of the Midwest dating from as early as the 1870's.

As the great mass of migration to the West Coast began around 1850, it is fortunate for genealogists that in that year federal census schedules, for the first time, listed each person by name and identified his or her place of birth, making it possible to trace some pioneer families to their origins in the East. Currently, a variety of individuals and organizations are indexing the 1850 to 1880 census records of such western states as California, Nevada, Arizona, the Dakotas and Montana, indicating which of the enumerated people were born in Connecticut, which in Virginia, and so on. These works, cited in the bibliography of resources for individual states, are extremely helpful to ancestor hunters.

The names of some of the early California settlers who traveled around the tip of South America by ship can be found in the reconstructed passenger lists of San Francisco, many of which have been published (Chap. 10).

Family records are especially helpful in the search for the roots of migrant families. At one time I traced a family named Lightfoot, who had originally moved from Virginia into Kentucky, then to Tennessee and Alabama, across Mississippi and into Texas, scattering descendants and marrying into various families all along the way. To trace their movements through county after county in different states was extremely difficult. If I hadn't had access to a manuscript genealogy written by an elderly woman who remembered hearing her older relatives talk about the numerous states and counties in which the family had lived, I couldn't have accomplished anything. This woman's manuscript wasn't specific about dates and places, but it included the names of counties and the approximate periods during which the family had lived in them. With this information as a guide, I succeeded in uncovering the marriage bonds, death records, deeds and wills that enabled me to reconstruct the family's history.

Local printed sources such as town and county histories are of great value in research at the regional level. The books and articles cited in Part III of this book ("Genealogical Sources in Every State") include statewide sources and sources for research in the largest cities and counties of each state. It is also possible to find a great many excellent sources—particularly local histories and transcripts, abstracts or indexes of censuses, vital, church, cemetery and probate records—for smaller towns and counties. You can locate these references by checking library and book dealers' catalogues, through correspondence with historical and genealogical societies (many of which publish this type of material), in periodical indexes and in the specialized bibliographies and guides cited throughout this book.

12   Black American Ancestry

The last fifteen years have seen a tremendous upsurge in interest on the part of black Americans in tracing their family histories. This phenomenon is reflected not only in the work of numerous individual black genealogists but in the institution of classroom projects in black genealogy in schools and colleges, the formation of black genealogy societies (the first being the Orangeburg Historical and Genealogical Society in Orangeburg, South Carolina), a proliferation of workshops in black genealogy sponsored by academic and historical groups and the publication of several books dealing with black genealogy and black history. Much of the interest of blacks in searching for their origins can be attributed to the emergence of black pride, while at the same time the materials for this research have become more accessible as racial inequality and prejudice in this country have steadily, if slowly, diminished.

To date, the climax of this growing interest in black genealogy is the 1976 publication of Alex Haley's *Roots: The Saga of An American Family*, which was a best-selling book even before it was turned into an eight-day, twelve-hour television serial that on several evenings in January 1977 drew the largest American television audiences in history.

Twelve years of research and writing went into Haley's account of seven generations of his family, beginning with the story of his four-times-great-grandfather, Kunta Kinte, who was captured in Africa and brought to America as a slave in 1767. The book concludes with a description of how, as a child in Tennessee, Haley had listened to his grandmother and great-aunts talking each evening, recounting in pieces the long family narrative that had been passed down for generations. The "furthest-back person" they ever spoke of was "the African," who had been brought on a slave ship to "Naplis" in this country. Although the African had been named "Toby" by his master, they said, he was a proud man who always insisted on calling himself by his African name, "Kin-tay."

Haley's relatives told how Kintay had taught his American-born daughter, Kizzy, some of the words of his native tongue, calling a guitar a "ko" and referring to the river that ran near the place in Virginia where they lived as slaves as "Kamby Bolongo." He told her stories of his people and homeland and related that he had been out in the forest, chopping wood to make a drum, when he was kidnapped into slavery.

Haley's relatives also recalled the stories of each generation descended from Kintay, using the names of individuals and telling what each did and where each lived and how each had carefully passed on the story of the African who was their ancestor.

Haley became a professional writer when he grew up. While on assignment in London, he visited the British Museum and saw the Rosetta Stone. This tablet, discovered near Rosetta, Egypt, in 1799, is inscribed with the same message in Greek, Egyptian hieroglyphics and Demotic. Its discovery enabled scholars to "crack" the previously undecipherable hieroglyphics in which some of earliest written history had been recorded. As Haley stood in the museum, it occurred to him that, like a personal Rosetta Stone, the African words he had learned as a child were the key to his family's lost origins in Africa.

Doing research in tax offices, archives and libraries, Haley carefully documented the stories he had heard about the American generations of his ancestors. He also consulted an African linguist and learned that the words passed down by his family were of the Mandinka tongue, spoken by the Mandingo people. "Bolongo" meant river, he was told, and "Kamby Bolongo" probably meant the Gambia River.

In time, Haley traveled to the Gambia, where he arranged a meeting with a *griot*—one of the men who are "walking archives of oral history" in black Africa, trained from childhood to narrate the histories of their people. The *griot*, who was very knowledgeable about the "Kinte" clan, recounted the lineage of these people generation by generation from ancient times, telling how they had left a place called Old Mali and migrated into Mauritania and how one Kariaba Kunta Kinte had moved into the Gambia and settled in the village of Juffure. Some two hours into his monologue, the *griot* related that one of Kariaba Kunta Kinte's grandsons, also named Kunta, had gone away from his village to chop wood and was never seen again.

While Haley had been able to find records which verified the stories his relatives told about the American generations of his ancestors, there are no records against which one can check the *griot's* account. The linguistic clues which led Haley to the Gambia leave little doubt that he actually located the tribe of his ancestors, however, and Haley offers considerable evidence from British and American records that he identified the ship on which his ancestor "Toby" was imported to America from the Gambia in 1767. Oral history, in the form of stories told by relatives, is the starting point for almost all genealogical research. It is also the form in which some of the early genealogies—those of the Welsh, Irish and Scandinavians—were passed down. In countries like the Gambia, where there are no written records to fall back on, oral history may be the only source of genealogical material.

Haley's stunning accomplishment in piecing together his genealogy and his subsequent fictionalized recreation of his ancestors' lives brought the common heritage of innumerable blacks descended from African slaves to life in terms of one particular family. *Roots* has inspired many more blacks to begin their search for origins, and indeed Haley's persistence and ultimate success are an inspiration to genealogists of any race and any nationality.

In 1977, accompanied by his two brothers, Haley, by then the recipient of a special Pulitzer Prize for *Roots*, paid a joyous and triumphant visit "home" to the Gambian village of Juffure, which his work had made world-famous.

Tracing Black Ancestors Through the Period of Slavery
Working back as far as about 1870, the genealogist tracing a black American lineage will utilize all of the resources described in preceding chapters. As Haley's family story illustrates so well, not only are there *griots*, or oral historians, in black Africa, but this cultural tradition has persisted, and there are many *griots* in American black communities today. While oral histories are immensely valuable in tracing any family's genealogy, they are especially important to black researchers because black Americans were denied the right to learn to read and write for so many years.

Before 1870, if ancestors were slaves, the search is complicated but not impossible, and a variety of different records must be relied on. To trace families through the period of slavery it is essential to learn the name of the slaveowner; in fact, tracing black genealogy generally requires tracing the genealogy of white slaveowners as well. There will be no wills or deeds left by slave ancestors. Because slaves were regarded as property, the property records of slaveowners must be consulted (Illustration 24). Their wills sometimes include estate inventories listing the names of slaves, their ages and the names of their children (Illustration 26). As owners often passed slaves from generation to generation, a study of a single white family's wills may in some cases produce abundant data about a black family's lineage. In my work in the wills and inventories of eighteenth-century Worcester County, Maryland, I have been able to trace some black families into the seventeenth century.

The identity of a slaveowner may be found through oral accounts of elderly relatives, in family records, in the National Archives' files on the Bureau of Refugees, Freedmen and Abandoned Lands or the Freedmen's Saving and Trust Company. It may be revealed in a newspaper account of a slave who became famous in his own right for a particular skill, or in a reward poster seeking the return of a runaway that has been preserved by a local historical society. Often the clue lies in the black family's name, as slaves often bore the surnames of their owners. If a search of nineteenth-century census records of the state or county where your ancestors lived turns up white families with the same name, you may subsequently be able to establish that one of them owned your ancestors during the period of slavery.

Once you have this essential piece of information you can begin the search for wills and other records in the slaveowner's name that may include information about his slaves. If a slave was subject to taxation or was sold or freed, there may be local county court documents that identify him by name, age and sex. Often slaveowners themselves kept careful records of their slaves, especially their house servants, and reading through such papers may provide valuable clues. Plantation records can be very helpful, and family Bibles of slaveowning families should also be located if possible, as the families frequently listed in them their most valuable assets—their slaves. Some slaves were buried in their owner's family plots, and tombstone inscriptions, if still legible, may provide further information.

Inventories of slaves may be located in Southern county

courthouses where records have survived, in state libraries, among records that remain on old farms or in the possession of the descendants of slaveowners, or in black history collections such as those listed at the conclusion of this chapter.

Many accounts of slaveowning families' collections of letters, estate inventories and other documents that include information about enslaved families have been published or preserved in historical societies. Among the manuscripts of Robert "King" Carter (Chap. 30) preserved by the Virginia Historical Society (Virginia resources, Chap. 33) is an elaborate inventory of his estate that lists his slaves. Material dealing with "King" Carter and other Virginia slaveowners can also be found in the Robert A. Brock Collection of the Henry E. Huntington Library in San Marino, California.

Many slaves remained as servants to their former owners after the Emancipation, and their vital records may be found in white family sources even after the end of the period of slavery. A page in the family Bible of my great-great-grandfather, Dr. John Ralston Sudler, of Bridgeville, Delaware, bears the notations "Lilie Oney colored child daughter of Lude Oney Born September 28th 1868" and "Elizabeth Cannon colored child daughter of Elmira Cannon was born 10th September 1876."

Black people, like white people, must be realistic in tracing their ancestry, and considering the history of slavery and race relations in America, the black genealogist may encounter some particularly unpleasant reality. Some of the words commonly used to describe ancestors in early records—Negro, colored, mulatto, octaroon, quadroon, nigger, neger—bear derogatory connotations today, but the grim side of black history will be no surprise to any researcher. In fact, because many of these words were used in a strict descriptive sense, they can actually be helpful in following the family line. The general terms used to describe people with dark skin included "Negro," "black" and "colored." According to the *Oxford New English Dictionary*, the term "Negro" was first used in the seventeenth century to describe the black people of Guinea (where the Niger River flows) and later became loosely applied to all black people. Niger and Nigeria are two countries in Africa today that bear forms of this place name. The term "mulatto" was applied specifically to someone who was half black and half white. A quadroon was one-forth black—the offspring of a mulatto and a white—and an octaroon had one-eighth black blood, so if ancestors are described by any of these three terms you know that there are both blacks and whites among your forebears.

One of the sensitive points about which black genealogists must be realistic is that they may find white slaveowners or overseers among their ancestors. Many members of slave-owning families fathered black children, and in some instances acknowledgment of paternity can be found in written records. This information is part of the truth of the past. During the early growth of interest in black genealogy most researchers were primarily interested in tracing their black African heritage, but this attitude has begun to broaden into an acceptance of and curiosity about intermingled white and American Indian ancestry as well.

Because federal censuses identify only free blacks by name during the period of slavery, they are not particularly useful to families of slave ancestry. Some state census records list blacks, but only by first names. Censuses of slaves, taken in slave states in 1850 and 1860, may be of some value. The schedules show the owner's name and the number of slaves owned. Slaves are identified by age, sex and description, not by name, but by comparing the census descriptions with the owner's will, estate inventory or church records it may be possible to establish an accurate identification of a slave ancestor.

Records of relief societies that worked for the freedom of blacks, such as the American Colonization Society in Philadelphia, may be found in church archives, historical societies and university manuscripts. Records of the Underground Railroad are virtually nonexistent, as it was essential to preserve the anonymity of runaway slaves, but it may be interesting and helpful to study the routes used, as revealed in Robert C. Smedley's *History of the Underground Railroad*.

There are many published personal narratives of slaves written or dictated to historians or abolitionist societies in the last century that give genealogical details and clues for further research. The memoir of Isaac Jefferson, one of Thomas Jefferson's slaves, for example, confirms many of the details revealed in other sources about the family of Sally Hemmings, the slave who was a blood relative of Thomas Jefferson's wife and with whom Thomas Jefferson had several children (Illustration 25). It is not impossible that you'll find a published memoir by one of your slave ancestors. If not, you may find one attributed to a slave from the same area or plantation that may mention your ancestors in particular or simply provide background and a vivid sense of the life of your forebears. There are collective as well as individual memoirs, such as Charles Nicholas' *Many Thousands Gone*.

Free Blacks

It's important to keep in mind that your ancestors may have been among those blacks in this country who were free long before the Civil War. The relationship between slaveowners and their house servants was a particularly complex one, as there was always close contact and, in some cases, blood relationship, and many slaveowners—among them Thomas Jefferson, who died in Virginia in 1826—freed house slaves in their wills.

If your black ancestors were free before the Civil War, their pre-1870 records should be among those of the general population, although some states, such as Kentucky, took special censuses of free blacks. If, as you trace free black ancestors, you suddenly "lose" them in general records, you may subsequently learn that prior to that date they were enslaved, and you will then proceed in your research as you would if your ancestors weren't freed until the conclusion of the Civil War, by determining the identity of the slaveowner and searching his family papers and property records.

Some early blacks, of course, arrived on these shores as free people. There has been a nucleus of free blacks in the United States throughout its history, and there was a free black community in New York City as early as the 1640's. By the time of the Revolution there were a great many free black people both in this country and in the Caribbean, and there were a great many more free black people in this country prior to the Civil War than most people imagine.

You can trace the ancestry of these people, who generally lived in the more northern states, through the use of church, land, probate, military and census records. Two important printed sources are Carter Woodson's *Free Negro Heads of Families in the United States Census of 1830* and Deborah Newman's *List of Free Black Heads of Families in the First Census of the United States*.

Jean Sampson Scott, a schoolteacher from Mount Vernon, New

York, and the wife of Lieutenant Colonel Osborne Scott, a retired Army chaplain, began the search for her black heritage several years ago. I remember when she first came into the library to search in printed sources for material that would document the family papers and oral traditions of her forebears, who lived in Butler County, Ohio. Recently when she visited the library I learned that she had succeeded in finding pension records of Sampson ancestors who served in the War of 1812 and indications of their origins in Maryland in the late 1700's, as well as New England ancestors in the eighteenth and nineteenth centuries.

The chart in the illustrations section which shows the lineage of a group of free black Angolans living in New York City between the 1630's and 1730's, suggests the amount of genealogical data about some early black Americans that can be uncovered in printed sources. I found most of the information for this family tree in the published records of the Dutch Church of New York City and was able to verify it with facts from I. N. Phelps Stokes's *Iconography of Manhattan Island.*

How Far Back Can You Go?

In this hemisphere in the sixteenth century there were Spanish and Portuguese slaves in South and Central America and the Caribbean Islands, and it is possible that there were some in the Spanish colony of Florida. However, 1619 is usually given as the date of the first arrival of black people in what is now the United States.

I have not been able to find the names of any of these early black people, and since it is quite difficult to construct a pedigree for early white settlers, it would seem that one would not be able to form any black pedigrees in America until the second quarter of the seventeenth century.

The ultimate goal of many black genealogists is to succeed, like Haley, in tracing their ancestry to its African birthplace. His success required a remarkable combination of luck and determination, however, and it would be unreasonable to suppose that all black lineages might be extended that far. The first step is to trace the family history as far as possible on this side of the ocean, and discovering the identity of an ancestor imported from Africa as a slave is itself a major genealogical accomplishment. On the other hand, if Haley's family so faithfully and accurately memorized and handed on the family history that began with a progenitor brought from Africa on a slave ship in the eighteenth century, it seems quite possible that there may be other black families in America that have done the same.

If the immigrant ancestor is identified, establishing the link to his homeland will still be extremely difficult. There are only six slave-ship manifests in the National Archives, and they are not particularly helpful, as slaves were considered "cargo" and listed by number. Establishing the overseas origins of free blacks should be considerably easier. For many black families of either free or slave origin the names of the earliest ancestors living in America often suggest links to particular parts of Africa, as the chart of early black Angolans in New York illustrates.

Published Sources and Societies

People continually express amazement that there are records for blacks to use in tracing their family histories, but as the bibliography for research in black ancestry indicates, there has been a proliferation of published materials since the turn of the century (Illustration 27). Among them are numerous biographies and biographical compendiums. For example, the second volume of G. B. Caldwell's *History of the American Negro and His Institutions*, published in 1920, includes an account of the grandfather of Martin Luther King, Jr., the Reverend Adam D. Williams, who was born in Georgia in 1863. The first volume of *Who's Who Among Black Americans*, published in 1976, contains some 10,000 entries, and a second volume is in progress.

Benjamin Wheeler's genealogy of the Varick family of New York, published in 1906, is an excellent example of an early illustrated black family history.

Of particular interest is *Black Genesis*, a genealogical guide written by James Rose and edited by Dr. Alice Eicholz of Queens College in New York. Kamuyu-Wa-Kange'the's *What Is Your African Name?* and Newbell Puckett's *Black Names in America: Origins and Usage* are two sources that may help black Americans discover the link to their origins in Africa through their ancestors' names.

Westward Soul, compiled and edited by Paul Stewart and Fray Marcos Purdue, may be useful for descendants of early black pioneers in the American West. Utilizing history books, business directories and taped interviews with early settlers, the editors discovered the stories of blacks, most of whom migrated after the

Civil War, who lived as cowboys, miners, ranchers, hotel owners, lawmen and outlaws in the old West. Additional volumes are planned. Stewart, who heads the Black American West Foundation, Inc. (P.O. Box 6589, Denver, CO 80205), has collected books, private papers, heirlooms, photographs, newspaper articles, handbills and documents that deal with early blacks in the American West. While the collection is not yet catalogued, he anticipates making some of its resources available to researchers once this organizational work is completed. A related institution is the Black American West Museum, located at the Colorado State University Family Action Center (3607 32nd Avenue, Denver, CO 80205).

The recently formed Afro-American Historical and Genealogical Society in Washington, headed by James D. Walker, genealogist with the National Archives, is yet another reflection of rising interest in black family history. The *AAHGS Journal* (c/o James D. Walker, 1700 Sheppard Avenue N.W., Washington, DC) began publication in 1977. Jean Sampson Scott, whose work I've mentioned, is a founding member. One of her goals it to extract the names of all blacks listed in the 1870 federal census of Virginia, preparing a thorough analysis of that state's first post-slavery census. Other black history organizations are listed below.

Afro-American Cultural and Historical Society Museum
8716 Harkness Road
Cleveland OH 44106

Black Military History Museum, Inc.
2602 Agnes St.
Kansas City, MO
(Mail: Box 6027, Kansas City, MO 64110)

East Bay Negro Historical Society, Inc.
3651 Grove Street
Oakland, CA 94609

Museum of Afro-American History
8 Smith Ct.
Boston, MA 02114

Negro History Society of Nebraska, Inc.
2444 Evans Street
Omaha, NE 68131

San Francisco African American Historical and Cultural Society, Inc.
680 McAllister Street
San Francisco, CA 94102

Schomburg Center for Research in Black Culture
103 West 135th Street
New York, NY 10030

13 American Indian Ancestry

In the past several years not only blacks but other American ethnic and racial groups have discovered a sense of pride in their origins. This has led to an intense desire to re-examine and sometimes rewrite history—because minority groups were so often misrepresented or ignored in conventional sources—and to begin the search for individual family roots.

People of known Native American descent are becoming interested in tracing their lineages, and an additional number of genealogists who are not aware they have Indian ancestors when they begin their research eventually find themselves tracing Indian lines in one or another of their family's branches.

The late American humorist Will Rogers (1879–1935), of Oologah, Oklahoma, one of the most popular men of his day, was proud of his Indian blood, as is another well-known Oklahoman, Senator Fred Harris, who has been a contender for the Democratic candidacy for President of the United States.

During the past fifteen years large payments made to various Indian tribes by the federal government have been an additional impetus to research in American Indian ancestry. As these "judgment awards"—the consequence of lawsuits filed by the Indians—have been announced, numerous descendants of Indians who merged with the general population long ago have sought to establish their tribal connections in order to share in the financial settlements. Similarly, many young people have attempted to establish tribal membership in order to qualify for educational assistance available to those of Indian blood. In both cases, appeals for additions to tribal membership rolls are filed with the Secretary of the Interior and reviewed for approval by the Tribal Enrollment Section of the Bureau of Indian Affairs in Washington, D.C.

Just how far an Indian lineage can be traced depends on the tribe involved and the area in which it was located. You may find quite early records for some Indians who lived in the eastern United States (Illustration 28), for some of those who had contact with Spanish missionaries in the Southwest and for those who were converted to Christianity by the French in Michigan and

Canada. The Indians of the Northwest, however, continued to have mostly hostile contact with non-Indians until well into the latter part of the nineteenth century. The famed Sitting Bull, chief of the Sioux, defeated Custer at the Little Bighorn in 1876 and was himself killed by Indian police on December 15, 1890, less than a century ago. The infamous massacre at Wounded Knee, South Dakota, in which some 200 Sioux men, women and children held captive by the U.S. 7th Cavalry were shot down, occurred two weeks later. While the name of Sitting Bull's father is known, it is doubtful that his ancestry can be followed back any further.

Though some earlier Indian records survive, reliable documents of use to ancestor hunters generally date from about 1880. Nonetheless, because of the distinct genealogical nature of some of these papers, it may be possible, through their use, to extend an Indian line back into the eighteenth century. For example, in 1901, the federal government paid a judgment to the Six Nations of New York. In order to establish their right to part of this award, tribal Indians living at that time had to establish their ancestry back to 1838, using forms that required them to provide the names of their parents and grandparents. Some of the older Indians who filed these papers were themselves born before 1838, and the information they gave about their family extends their line back into the late 1700's. Similar records exist for some other tribes (Chap. 26).

The records that exist for research in American Indian ancestry reflect the unique status of Indians throughout this country's history. In the early years of the United States attempts to assimilate Indians into the white culture soon gave way to federal laws that first removed them from eastern states to lands in the West and then isolated them on specific parcels of land called reservations. Thus tribal Indians have existed within, but distinctly separate from, the rest of society. Tribal Indians (as well as natives of unincorporated territories and children of foreign ambassadors) were excluded from the provisions of the 14th Amendment to the Constitution, which was passed in 1868 to guarantee national (rather than state) citizenship and extend it to all persons born or naturalized in the United States and subject to its jurisdiction.

Moreover, tribal Indians were not included in any early federal censuses. When plans for the first census were made in 1787, they specifically excluded "Indians not taxed"—that is,

Indians in tribes—and in truth counting them would have proved difficult, as frontier skirmishes between Indians and white settlers were still very common. There was no reference to Indians in any census until 1860—those few who were counted before that were probably numbered among "free colored"—and it was not until 1890, one hundred years after the first census was taken, that an attempt was made to include all Indians in the decennial population count.

As late as the 1960's some 80 percent of American Navajos—the largest and most independent American Indian tribe and the one with the highest proportion of full-blooded members—did not speak English. While tribal Indians have remained separate from mainstream America, however, the government has by no means ignored them, and a variety of federal Indian records can be of use to anyone attempting to trace a Native American lineage. There were, of course, numerous Indians who were assimilated into the non-Indian population, and their records must be sought in the basic public and private sources employed by all genealogists. This chapter concerns itself with some of the special records of Indians who maintained their tribal status.

If you are tracing an American Indian line, begin by learning as much as possible from older relatives, accumulating facts and stories that you can document and build on with information found in printed sources and public records. Names present a particular problem, as a Native American might bear several different Indian names during his lifetime and might use yet another, English name when dealing with census takers and other non-Indians. You should make a special attempt, when talking to family members, to learn both the Indian and English names of your ancestors. These names, the name of the Indian tribe and specific or approximate years of births, deaths and other major events in your ancestors' lives are needed to gain access to information in government records.

Repositories of Indian Records

There are three major repositories for the government records that pertain to research in American Indian genealogy: the National Archives, the Federal Archives branch in the region where the tribe is located and the agency office in charge of Indian records in the particular area of the tribe in question.

The records at the National Archives, arranged by tribe and

dated chiefly 1830 to 1940, include various Indian censuses, muster rolls of Indians removed from the eastern United States during the first half of the nineteenth century, records of claims filed by the eastern Cherokees against the federal government and estate files for Indians who made wills with the approval of the Commissioner of Indian Affairs after 1910.

As the consequence of a lawsuit instituted by a Washington tribe against the National Archives and the Secretary of the Interior in 1976, Indian records in the National Archives have been temporarily sealed and cannot be used by the general public. The resolution of the case might take years, but fortunately access to records is still given to individuals doing research into their own family history.

A search of National Archives Indian records other than the Cherokee Claim files can be made for you if you provide your ancestor's name (preferably both Indian and English), the name of his tribe and the approximate date of his tribal association. For a search of the Cherokee Claim files you need the name of the claimant or the number of the claim and the claimant's birth date or his age at the time the claim was filed. Additional information about your ancestor's residence at the time his claim was made and the names of his wife, parents or children are also helpful. You can search the National Archives records for Indians yourself if you know the name of your ancestors' tribe and some approximate dates pertaining to your ancestors' lives.

Information about Indian records is included in the free pamphlet *Genealogical Records in the National Archives*, and in the more extensive *Guide to Genealogical Records in the National Archives*. Edward E. Hill's two-volume *Preliminary Inventory of Records of the Bureau of Indian Affairs at the National Archives*, published in 1965 and available from the Archives Publication Sales Branch, lists and describes records and identifies the agencies responsible for their creation.

Among the regional records maintained by each Regional Archives Branch (Chap. 25) are the records of field offices of federal agencies located in the region served by that branch, including records of the Bureau of Indian Affairs from the mid-nineteenth century until 1952. These may include birth, death or marriage registers, censuses of tribes and school records.

In the office of the agency in charge of records for your ancestors' tribe you may find documents not on file in the

National Archives or its regional branches. A list of the names and locations of these agencies can be obtained from the Bureau of Indian Affairs (1951 Constitution Avenue N.W., Washington, DC 20245).

Use of Indian Records

The first public records to be consulted once family sources have been exhausted are the rolls of annual Indian censuses authorized by law in 1884, begun in 1885 and continued on most reservations until 1940. The existence, completeness and accuracy of these records vary from reservation to reservation and from year to year. On the Navajo reservation in Arizona, for example, a census was recorded in 1885, but another wasn't taken until 1915. The information recorded for each individual in the Indian censuses includes his or her Indian or English name (sometimes both), sex, age, relationship to the head of family and sometimes to another Indian named on the roll. Earlier rolls often show the names of people who were born or died during the year and give the dates of birth or death; after 1924, this information was recorded on separate, interfiled rolls.

You may also find information about Indian ancestors in the schedules of the regular federal censuses beginning in 1860, when the category of "Indians taxed"—that is, living among the white population—was first included in the census categories. The information on those Indians counted in this and succeeding censuses, however, is scanty and often inaccurate, and many Indians gave the enumerators their "census names" while keeping their Indian names secret. In 1890 the government undertook the enumeration of all Indians, including those on reservations and roaming over unsettled tracts of country, numbering among them not only full-blooded American Indians but "persons of mixed white and Indian blood ... if they are enrolled on an Indian tribal or agency roll or if they are regarded as Indians in their community." In 1890 most Indians lived on reservations, and special agents who knew the land were hired to count them. The barriers of social and geographical isolation, language, illiteracy and distrust of whites meant that accurate Indian enumerations were impossible for many decades. Nonetheless, if schedules contain information about your particular ancestors, they can be extremely valuable.

Among the Indian records in the National Archives are four

volumes—covering only certain tribes in the Dakota and Washington Territories and California—of a "Special Census of Indians Not Taxed" that was conducted in 1880. There are also a few very early Indian censuses taken in the East prior to the period of removal, including the 1832 Census of the Creek Nation and the 1835 Census of the Cherokee Nation. A special Indian issue of the *Georgia Genealogical Society Quarterly* published in 1967 contains census records and other genealogical details of Georgia Indians, and additional Indian censuses in printed form are included in the bibliography.

Beginning in 1830 the federal government undertook a policy, carried out over the next twenty-five years, of "removing" Indians from eastern areas and concentrating them on lands west of the Mississippi. The removal muster rolls of Indians who were moved in this way sometimes enumerate the number of persons in each family by age and sex and identify the original residence of each head of family in the East. They are maintained in the National Archives and are chronologically arranged and indexed.

The largest and most consistently kept set of records of the reservation period, 1850 through 1887, are the annuity rolls. The federal government, in some of its treaties with tribes, guaranteed a certain amount of money or goods to be paid annually to the heads of Indian families. When these payments were made the Indians had to have their names noted by a government agent and sign, usually with their marks, to indicate that they had been paid. Often the age and sex of each family member are contained in these rolls. During the same period the Bureau of Indian Affairs undertook a number of school censuses that listed Indian children, their ages, where they were born and sometimes the names of their parents.

Beginning in 1887, under the terms of the General Allotment Act, the federal government allotted each Indian a parcel of land to be turned over to him when he proved himself able to manage his own affairs. The allotment registers from this period are among the most accurate and detailed Indian records in existence and often contain a great deal of genealogical information. By law an Indian who wanted to sell his allotment, even to his tribe, had to have the permission of all other Indians who had any interest in it. At the death of an allotted Indian all his heirs and their specific relationship to him had to be identified. While terms of relationship are used very loosely in some Indian records—the same word might identify a brother, sister or cousin, for example—relationships are strictly defined in the allotment registers, as they were the basis for determining the amount of an allotment that passed from the deceased to each of his heirs. While allotment registers date from about 1905—the allotment period continued until about 1930—some of the family information in them goes back to the early part of the nineteenth century. It includes the allotted individual's Indian and English names, age and birth date and the names, ages and relationships of many family members.

Another record kept by the Bureau of Indian Affairs that is rich in genealogical data is the *Sanitary Record of Sick, Injured, Births, Deaths, etc.*, dating from the late 1800's, in which information about all Indians who were treated by the Bureau's health service was recorded. If the individual died, the date of death is noted. In the case of births, the date and the names of the parents are given. You may be able to locate other scattered vital records, kept by non-Indians or by the tribal government, depending on the tribe and period you are researching.

Among the earliest claims filed against the federal government by Indians are the Cherokee claims authorized by a law passed in 1902 (Illustration 29). The Cherokee Claims Commission Records—some 48,000 files of individuals who registered claims against the government—are in the National Archives, as is the two-volume index to them. Each Indian had to defend his claim by proving descent from an Indian who appeared on an earlier roll of the tribe, and the files reveal not only the name, date and place of birth and residence of the claimant but genealogical information about numerous family members. Many more recent Court of Claims records relating to tribes throughout the country are in the National Records Center in Suitland, Maryland, and still others are in the hands of the lawyers who represented the Indians.

An Indian who wanted to make a will after 1910 could do so, with the approval of the Commissioner of Indian Affairs. Information on family relationships can be found in the estate files containing wills, reports of heirship and related papers, which are kept in the National Archives.

Church Records

During the earlier years of contact between Indian and white man, many churches sent missionaries to convert Indians to Christianity, and you should try to locate the records of any churches that might have been active in this work in your ancestors' tribe. In the Catholic Church some of these documents date back to the mid-1500's, though more complete records begin about 1730. Unfortunately, when an Indian was baptized, he was usually given a Christian name, and only in certain cases was his Indian name noted.

Native American Lineages in Published Sources

As interest in American Indian ancestry is just beginning to blossom, not a great deal has yet been published in the way of genealogical guides. However, there is a tremendous amount of general information about Indians in print. In the catalogue of the New York Public Library there are literally thousands of entries under the heading "Indians, North American tribes." Ricardo J. Martinez of Falls Church, Virginia, himself an Indian of Aztec and Apache descent, has been at work for many years on a bibliographical index of all books on North America Indians, and by early 1977 he had indexed some 400,000 works. This long-range project, expected to comprise about one hundred volumes, may be of future value to genealogists working on Native American lineages.

The bibliography of references for Native Americans in Part Two of this book includes a selection of general works, books about individual tribes, research bibliographies, published records and a few printed genealogies. Using just these sources, I have been able to construct descents from several noted Indians of various eras in different parts of the country—among them Pocahontas, famous in romantic legend for saving the life of the English colonist Captain John Smith by staying the hand of her father, Chief Powhatan.

It was not John Smith but Captain John Rolfe, an English tobacco planter, who married the Indian princess Pocahontas Mataoka, alias Rebecca, in Jamestown, Virginia, on about March 5, 1614. Following their marriage, perhaps the most celebrated of the Colonial period, the couple carried on in great style, and in 1616 Pocahontas was presented at the court of King James I, where she was received with the honors accorded a foreign princess. Unfortunately, the damp English climate proved too much for Pocahontas; she died on the eve of the couple's scheduled return to Virginia at Gravesend, Kent, on the English coast, where she was buried under the altar of St. George's Church. She was not the first of her race to succumb to the English climate; a Virginia Indian, Raleigh, brought to that country by Sir Richard Grenville, had been buried in the church at Bideford, Devonshire, in 1589.

The line of Pocahontas, who bore one son, was a slender thread for nearly ninety years, as can be seen from Illustration 30, which shows three generations of only children. In the fifth generation, with the birth of the six children of Pocahontas' great-grandson, John Bolling, the family began to flourish. These six produced some forty-two children, assuring the continuation of Pocahontas' line of descent. Today there are thousands of her descendants, who are eligible to be members of the Order of First Families of Virginia, living in this country and around the world. Daisie D.W.S. Howe's *Some Midwest Descendants of Rebecca Mataoka Pocahontas* . . . is a 101-page work dealing with just the descendants of one branch of her bloodline.

Not all Indians of the Powhatan Federation fared as well as Pocahontas. Thomas Rolfe, her son, was prohibited by the Colonial government in Virginia from visiting his aunt Cleopatre and his great-uncle, Opechancanough, who was executed by white settlers on October 4, 1645, in retaliation for his marauding attacks. Such tribes of the Federation as the Pamunkey, Mattaponi, Chickahominy, Nansamond, Rappahanock, Potomac and Accomack Indians still exist in Virginia, but their survival has not been easy, and their names are familiar to us mainly as place names given to towns, rivers and counties in that state.

One of the Virginia Pamunkey who survived and carried the traditions of his race into the twentieth century was George M. Cook, living in 1928. Photographs of his children Ottigny, Capitola, Pocahontas, Tecumseh and George M. Cook, Jr., wearing Native American dress, appeared in an article on the Powhatans by Frank G. Speck published in *Indian Notes and Monographs* in that year. Surnames common to the Mattaponi in Virginia in the 1920's were Allmond, Collins, Custello, Langston, Major, Ried and Tuppins, and it is possible that some of the descendants of these families who drifted to the cities and have little knowledge of their Indian heritage may rediscover it when searching such documents as the federal census records.

Major General Sir William Johnson of Johnson Hall (1715–1774), one of the most important men in Colonial America, can also be connected to an Indian line. Johnson, 1st Baronet and the nephew of British admiral Sir Peter Warren, led the British forces to victory over the French at Lake George, New York, in 1755. He was the founder of a line still listed in *Burke's Peerage*, but there is no mention there of his illegitimate liaison with Molly Brant, sister of Joseph Brant, also known as Tayendanega (1742–November 24, 1807), a great Mohawk chief whose portrait appeared on a United States postage stamp in 1976. Johnson provided for Molly Brant and their eight children in his will. One of their daughters married Dr. Robert Kerr of Niagara, and they had three sons, Colonel William Johnson Kerr, Walter Kerr and Robert Kerr. Colonel William J. Kerr married his cousin Elizabeth Brant (living 1865), one of the seven children of Chief Joseph Brant and his third wife. When Joseph Brant's wife died at the age of seventy-eight on November 24, 1837, she named Tekarihogea, William and Elizabeth Kerr's eldest son, as the heir of the line of Chief Joseph. All of this information is contained in William L. Stone's two-volume *Life of Joseph Brant*, published in 1865. Using the county records and census schedules of Erie County, New York, one might be able to trace the descendants of these people to the present day.

It is possible that some Americans of Indian descent could trace their lines to one of the children of the Shawnee warrior Puckeshinewa, who was born in Florida in the 1720's and died at the Battle of Point Pleasant, in what is now West Virginia, in 1774. He took as his wife Methoataske, a Muskogee Creek from the Tuckabatche Town in Alabama. Their twin sons Tecumseh and Tenskwatawa, also know as the Prophet, born about March 1768, became noted Indian chiefs. Tecumseh was made a brigadier general by the British, fought against the American forces in the War of 1812 and was mortally wounded at the Battle of the Thames on the Thames River near Chatham, Ontario, in 1813. By his wife Manete he had a son, Pugeshawhenwa, born about 1796. The Prophet led the Indians at the Battle of

Tippecanoe on November 7, 1811, where he was defeated by General William Henry Harrison, who later became President of the United States. The Prophet, whose likeness was painted by the noted Indian portraitist George Catlin, died in Wyandotte, Kansas, about 1834. He and Tecumseh also had sisters who may have left descendants.

Pontiac (c. 1718–1769), chief of the Ottawa Indians, made a name for himself as the leader of the so-called Pontiac's Rebellion against the British and was the leading force in the siege of Detroit in 1763 and 1764. In 1766 Pontiac signed a treaty with Sir William Johnson and was pardoned. He had a son, Shegenasa, living in 1769, and one of his later wives, Kantuckee-gan, was living from 1807 until after 1815 in an Ottawa village at the mouth of the Maumee River with their son, Otussa, according to Howard H. Peckham's *Pontiac and the Indian Uprising*. A Chief Tus-saw, who was reportedly preparing a biography of Pontiac in 1825, may have been this son or a grandson of Pontiac, and many others, some of whom have borne the surname Pontiac, have claimed descent from him.

Native American Historical Societies, Libraries and Museums

American Indian Historical Society
1451 Masonic Avenue
San Francisco, CA 94117
(*The Indian Historian*)

Cherokee Historical and Preservation Society, Inc.
413 E. Rutledge Avenue
Gaffney, SC 29340

Choctaw Nation Historical Society
204 College Avenue, Poteau
Tuskahoma, OK 74953

Colorado River Indian Tribes Museum—Library
4 Corners and Mojave Road
Parker, AZ 85344
(Mail: Rt. 1, Box 23-B)

Five Civilized Tribes Museum
Agency Hill—Honor Heights Drive
Muskogee, OK 74401
(*Five Civilized Tribes Museum Newsletter*)

Indian House Memorial, Inc.
Main Street
Deerfield, MA 01342

Institute of American Indian Arts Museum
Cerrillos Road
Santa Fe, NM 87501

Koshare Indian Museum, Inc.
18th and Santa Fe
La Junta, CO 81050

Mohican History Society
203 East Main Street
Loudonville, OH 44842

Museum of the Cherokee Indian,
   Inc.
Box 398, Highway 441N
Cherokee, NC 28719

Museum of Navaho Ceremonial
   Art, Inc.
Box 5153, 702 Camino Lajo
Santa Fe, NM 87501

Owasco Stockades Indian Village
Emerson Park
203 Genesee Street
Auburn, NY 13021

Plains Indians and Pioneer Historical Foundation
Box 292
2009 Williams Avenue
Woodward, OK 73801

Seminole Nation Historical Society
Box 1079
520 S. Wewoka
Wewoka, OK 74884

We generally think of Jewish immigration to America as taking place in the late nineteenth century, during the period of the Russian pogroms, and in fact at least two million Jewish people of East European stock came to the United States during the huge, forty-year wave of immigration just prior to and during World War I. A second wave of Jewish immigration followed the rise of Naziism and the opening of the concentration camps in Europe.

But there are Jewish families that go back many generations in this country. Some are descended from seventeenth- and eighteenth-century immigrants—Spanish and Portuguese Jews of Dutch or French nationality, German and English Jews—and others from early and middle nineteenth-century immigrants from Western Europe, predominantly Germany, masses of whom poured into the United States following the failure of republican revolutions in 1848.

I first became interested in Jewish genealogy when I learned that my first cousins had Jewish ancestors who lived in Pennsylvania prior to the Revolution and later moved into Virginia. My aunt, whose grandmother was Jewish, told me that her great-grandfather, Solomon Jacobs, had been mayor of Richmond in the early 1800's. According to family tradition, the Richmond synagogue had shared a parking area with the Episcopalian church, and all of Solomon Jacobs' daughters had married Episcopalians. One of them, Isabel DeLeon Jacobs, my aunt's grandmother, married James Marshall Taylor, a nephew of Chief Justice John Marshall.

I found confirmation of my aunt's story in *The Universal Jewish Encyclopedia*. Solomon Jacobs (1775–1827) was the city recorder of Richmond, served as acting mayor in 1818 and was the president of the Richmond congregation, Kaal Kaadosh Beth Shalome (Holy House of Peace). His likeness, painted by Thomas Sully, the famous British-born American painter of portraits and historical scenes, appears in that book and in Hannah London's *Portraits of Jews*.

In an article by Malcolm Stern in the *American Jewish*

Historical Society Quarterly, I learned that Barnard (Barent) Jacobs, Solomon's father, lived in Lancaster County and was the "mohel," or ritual circumcisor, of Pennsylvania prior to the Revolutionary War. The recently established Museum of American Jewish History in Philadelphia has discovered some of the marvelous records he kept.

Jewish Settlement in America

The Bible, one of the oldest genealogical documents in existence, contains a great deal of information on the family lines of ancient Jews in the "begats" of Genesis and in the books of Kings and Chronicles, and it's probable that these accounts are quite accurate. But the narrative ends at the time of Christ, when the Jews were dispersed from the area of Palestine. From there they fled to many parts of the world: some to Spain, others to Turkey and up into Russia and Europe and some to England. They were expelled from England in the thirteenth century and from Spain and Portugal in the late fifteenth century. Because political and social persecution have made the Jews a nomadic people throughout modern history, the genealogist in search of Jewish ancestors faces large, though not insurmountable, problems.

Historically, those Jews who settled in the Iberian Peninsula, and their descendants, came to be known as Sephardic Jews, and those who settled in Germany, and their descendants, came to be known as Ashkenazic Jews. Most American Jews are descended from these two groups, which differed in language, religious rites, social customs and style of names. North America's first Jewish settlers were Sephardic, and the vast majority of early American congregations followed Sephardic rites. By 1750, however, Ashkenazim outnumbered Sephardim, and today the distinctions are blurred, as most Jews of Sephardic descent have been assimilated through intermarriage with Ashkenazic Jews and Christians. Solomon Jacobs was Ashkenazic, while his wife, Hetty Nones, was the daughter of a Sephardic Jew, Benjamin Nones (1757–1826), a native of Bordeaux who fought in the Revolutionary War.

The very first Jewish community in this hemisphere was in the Dutch colony of Recife in Brazil. During the Colonial period many "New Christians"—Sephardic Jews who in 1492 had been forced to convert, at least outwardly, to Catholicism—followed the Spanish and Portuguese to Latin America. Initially thwarted in their search for religious freedom, they at last settled in the Dutch provinces of Brazil. From about 1630 there was a thriving congregation at Recife and shortly thereafter another on the adjacent island of Mauricia. When the Dutch were expelled by the Portuguese around 1654 many of them, including most of the Jews, returned to Amsterdam, and others fled into Dutch-British possessions in the Carribbean. A French ship, the *St. Charles*—or, according to some records, the *St. Catherine*—carried, among others, more than twenty Jewish exiles from Recife to New Amsterdam, where they landed on September 6 or 7, 1654. They had been preceded by one month by Jacob Barsimon, who had arrived from Holland on August 22 and was the first Jew to become a permanent resident of New Amsterdam. After some protest, the refugees were allowed to remain in the city, and they founded the Congregation Shearith Israel, the oldest Jewish community in the United States. Many of these refugees bore typically Sephardic names that suggest Iberian or Arabic origins. Among their number were Asser Levy, Jacob Cohen Henriques, Solomon Pietersen, David Israel, Moses Lucena, Salvador D'Andrada, David de Ferera and Moses Ambrosius. Asser Levy was admitted to the burgher right—that is, became a freeman—on April 26, 1657, paving the way for the careers of Jewish businessmen who came after him during the next three centuries.

The congregation founded by the early Jewish refugees in New Amsterdam still functions today as the Spanish-Portuguese Congregation Shearith Israel. The early group is known to have purchased a cemetery in 1656, but records of it have disappeared. Those of the next three cemeteries maintained by the Manhattan Jewish community have been preserved, however, in Rabbi David deSola Pool's *Portraits Etched in Stone, 1682–1831*, which lists all burials and includes biographical sketches.

Moses Raphael Levy, evidently no relation to Asser, was one of the most opulent merchants in New York when he died in 1728, according to Pool's book (Illustration 31). His tombstone, which survives in the Old Jewish Cemetery in New York City, is inscribed in both Hebrew and Portuguese, and portraits of Levy and several members of his family are in the possession of the Jewish Historical Society. His descendants today (Illustration

32) live on several continents and can be traced through a variety of published sources, including Malcolm Stern's *Americans of Jewish Descent* and *Burke's Peerage*. They include the children of the late Arthur Hays Sulzberger, publisher of the *New York Times;* Pamela Harriman, wife of Averell Harriman, the former governor of New York; the Earl of Rosebery; young Winston Churchill; and the Dowager Duchess of Norfolk, as well as thousands of other Jews and Christians.

There were other early Jewish communities in Newport, Rhode Island; Richmond, Virginia; and Charleston, South Carolina. In time, many Jews moved from the original East Coast centers of Jewish life into the opening Midwest and South. Those who were assimilated into the non-Jewish society can be traced through such general genealogical sources as public documents, family mementos and tombstone inscriptions.

Problems and Resources

Any researcher tracing Jewish ancestors will employ traditional sources and rely heavily on public records and should consult the sections of this book that deal with research in his ancestors' country of origin. In addition he will face certain obstacles and utilize resources that are peculiar only to Jewish genealogy.

One basic problem is a dearth of written family records. As a persecuted people Jews were generally preoccupied with making a living and preserving basic security in their lives, and few had the opportunity to record family history. Certain descendants of outstanding rabbis did record their ancestry. The oldest such family that can be traced to the present is the de Sola family, whose earliest known ancestor lived in ninth-century Navarre, in northern Spain. Other European Jewish lines can be traced back several centuries. A Viennese family, the Schiffs, can be followed back to the 1300's, and among the ancestors of Anthony Armstrong-Jones are German Jewish forebears of the fifteenth century.

Jewish naming customs present additional obstacles. Through the Middle Ages most European Jews were identified by a simple Hebrew patronymic, such as David ben Abraham, meaning David, son of Abraham. In some areas Jews acquired one name by which they were known in the business community and retained their Hebrew name for synagogue records of birth, circumcision, marriage and death. Names were changed as migrant Jews moved from country to country or were converted, willingly or otherwise, to Christianity. Some English Jews anglicized their names to such an extent that it is impossible to determine their origin, and the practice of name changing among American Jews persists to the present day.

The extensive patronymics used by early Sephardic Jews in America included the first names of both father and grandfather and can therefore provide valuable genealogical information. But the fact that most European Jews didn't take last names until the first decade of the nineteenth century, when they were legally required to do so, places practical limitations on how far back certain lines can be traced. Arthur Kurzweil, co-editor of *Toledot: The Journal of Jewish Genealogy*, relied on traditional genealogical resources—family interviews, death certificates and naturalization papers, city directories and town histories— to trace his family five generations to his great-great-great-grandparents who lived in Poland in the early 1800's and whose gravestones survive there. As noted in a 1977 article by Dorothy Gallagher in *The New York Times Magazine* (see Jewish bibliography, Chap. 28), it is not likely that he will find any earlier records, as the Kurzweil name probably didn't exist before that time.

The genealogical value of synagogue and cemetery records is similar to that of church and cemetery records of people of other faiths, but if they are written in Hebrew and you are not fluent in that language, you may have to engage a translator in order to use them. In some Jewish cemeteries, tombstone inscriptions are written in English, while in others, such as Mt. Hebron Cemetery in Queens, New York, they are mostly in Hebrew. If you identify a family plot in such a cemetery, you can photograph all the stones and have the inscriptions translated later. Dates in both synagogue and cemetery records will frequently be noted according to the Jewish calendar, and the date in terms of our Gregorian calendar will have to be calculated accordingly. While synagogue sources may include records of circumcision and bar mitzvah—the ceremony commemorating a boy's passage into manhood— there is often little mention in them of women. (The bas mitzvah, a similar ceremony for adolescent girls, is a modern development.) For women, marriage and cemetery records may be the only ecclesiastical sources in existence.

Special Problems for Eastern Europeans

You face special genealogical problems if you are descended from East European Jews who came to America in the late nineteenth and early twentieth centuries. While you can probably identify your immigrant ancestors easily and may even know them personally, you may encounter major obstacles in searching for their European roots.

Most turn-of-the-century Jewish immigrants were refugees from a vast territorial band stretching along the western boundary of Imperial Russia. Like their Christian compatriots, they were fleeing the cruel social and economic conditions of Eastern Europe, but they were also fleeing repressive government persecution and widespread anti-Semitism. Because many crossed illegally into Western Europe en route to the United States, few carried with them identifying documents or incriminating papers.

Once in America, many of these immigrants changed or simplified their names and cast off their former identity as they struggled to build a new life. Many told their children little about their European forebears or the places from which they came. Patronymics of ancestors, family lines and the names of towns and counties where ancestors lived have in many cases been passed on incorrectly or forgotten altogether. Repositories of Jewish records from Europe in the United States have excellent sources for historical research, but there is a scarcity of the kind of primary records so essential to genealogists in their collections, as well as in the private papers of immigrant families.

The very existence of pre-World War I records for Jews of Eastern Europe is in doubt. Russia of the period (which included areas that became Poland, Lithuania, Latvia and eastern Czechoslovakia) had no bureaus of vital statistics; civil registration didn't begin until after the Russian Revolution in 1918. While it's possible that Eastern European governments might have at least a few records of Jews who lived in the area before that time, the Soviet Union has so far rebuffed all efforts to locate such documents or even determine whether they exist. Ecclesiastical records were kept on the premises of synagogues or in the homes of rabbis or other community leaders, and it is unlikely that many of these documents could have survived the period of political turmoil, disease epidemics, famine and population upheaval that preceded World War I or the rise of fascism, persecution of Jews and destructive battles of World War II that came later. There are, however, Jewish cemeteries still in existence in the area.

After the extermination of European Jewry in the Holocaust of World War II, Jerusalem's Central Archives of the History of the Jewish People began to concentrate on recovering the archival remains of destroyed communities. By 1974 they had accumulated 1,400 archives or parts of archives of communities, organizations and individuals covering a period of 500 years; and some three million documents of Jewish interest, covering the twelfth to the twentieth centuries, had been filmed. All of these materials are available for research, but those in greatest abundance are from Germany, Austria, France and Italy rather than from Eastern Europe. Most of those records from Eastern Europe pertain to the period between the world wars or after World War II, rather than to the pre-World War I era.

The Central Jewish Archives (Hebrew University [Givat Ram Campus], Sprinzak Building, P.O.B. 1149, Jerusalem, Israel) does hold some hope for people tracing lines in Imperial Russia, nonetheless. Because the staff can give only limited time to requests for information by mail, the Archives' resources are most useful if you are able to travel to Israel to search in person. As little material has been translated into English, a knowledge of Hebrew and Yiddish is essential, and an acquaintance with the language of the country in which your ancestors lived is also helpful. You need to know the place where your family came from and some dates relating to your ancestors' lives, as there were frequent changes in the map of Europe during the period in question, and the Archives are arranged in national sections according to the geography of Europe between the world wars.

Published Sources

The bibliography of Jewish research sources which appears later in this book includes numerous general works as well as references for research in Jewish ancestry in the individual states of this country and in various nations around the world.

Dan Rottenberg's new *Finding Our Fathers: A Guidebook to Jewish Genealogy* should be consulted by anyone pursuing a Jewish family line. Rottenberg, who began the search for his own ancestors by copying information from tombstone inscriptions at his grandmother's funeral and spent a great deal of time doing research in the NYPL's Local History and Genealogy Division, eventually succeeded in tracing one branch of his family to the Middle Ages. Another new reference in the field is *Toledot: The Journal of Jewish Genealogy*, established in 1977.

The *American Jewish Historical Society Quarterly*, formerly known as the AJHS *Publications*, has printed genealogies and family histories, biographies, vital records and other items of interest to genealogists since it was founded in 1892.

Malcolm H. Stern's "Americans of Jewish Descent: Sources of Information for Tracing Their Genealogy," was originally published as an article in the *National Genealogical Society Quarterly* and later issued as NGS Special Publication No. 20. It provides a background in the history of Jewish migrations, the origins and cultural distinctions between Ashkenazim and Sephardim and their bearing on the genealogical search, Jewish naming customs and early Jewish settlements and congregations in the United States. Stern, a rabbi and the official genealogist of the American Jewish Archives in Cincinnati, Ohio, is also author of *Americans of Jewish Descent, A Compendium of Genealogy*, which contains family trees of many Jewish families established in the United States before 1840. Originally published in 1960, it is being reissued in a greatly expanded second edition.

Descendants of immigrants who arrived on these shores during the late nineteenth or early twentieth century will learn much from "The Ancestors of George M. Gross," printed in two issues of *Virginia Tidewater Genealogy* in 1975 and 1976. The author, then fifteen, described how he used public records and family interviews to follow his ancestors—turn-of-the-century Jewish immigrants—back to Europe.

Record Repositories

A number of Jewish institutions in this country have records of American and European Jews that can be of value to genealogists. In addition, several large libraries, including the Jewish Division (Room 84) of the New York Public Library, have large collections of Judaica.

The American Jewish Archives (AJA), on the campus of Hebrew Union College in Cincinnati (3101 Clifton Avenue,

Cincinnati, OH 45220), has collected a great many congregational and organizational records, family documents and periodicals pertaining to American Jewry, primarily before 1900. Other repositories of Jewish historical records are listed below.

American Jewish Historical Society
2 Thornton Road
Waltham, MA 02154
(*AJH Quarterly*)

B'nai B'rith Museum
1640 Rhode Island Avenue, N.W.
Washington, DC 20036

Greater Boston Jewish Historical
Society
2 Thornton Road
Waltham, MA 02154

Hebrew Immigrant Aid Society
200 Park Avenue South
New York, NY 10003
(Network of international offices;
New York office has microfilm
records of every immigrant met
by HIAS workers since 1911.)

Indiana Jewish Historical Society
215 East Berry Street, Room 303
Fort Wayne, IN 46802

Jewish Division/Room 84
New York Public Library
42nd Street and Fifth Avenue
New York, NY 10018

Jewish Historical Society of
Greater Washington
1330 Massachusetts Avenue, N.W.
Washington, DC 20005

Jewish Historical Society of Maryland, Inc.
5800 Park Heights Avenue
Baltimore, MD 21215

Jewish Historical Society of
Michigan
163 Madison Avenue
Detroit, MI 48226
(*Michigan Jewish History*)

Jewish Historical Society of New
York, Inc.
8 West 70th Street
New York, NY 10023

Jewish Theological Seminary
Library
3080 Broadway
New York, NY 10027

Leo Baeck Institute
129 East 73rd Street
New York, NY 10021
(Emphasis is on German Jewry,
but records cover other Ger-
man-language areas as well.)

Rhode Island Jewish Historical
Association
209 Angell Street
Providence, RI 02906
(*RIJH Notes*)

Society for the History of Czechoslovak Jews
25 Mayhew Avenue
Larchmont, NY 10538

Southern California Jewish Histor-
ical Society
590 North Vermont Avenue
Los Angeles, CA 90004
(*Western States Jewish Historical
Quarterly*)

Western Jewish History Center of Judah L. Magnes Memorial Museum
2911 Russell Street
Berkeley, CA 94705

World Federation of Hungarian Jews
136 East 39th Street
New York, NY 10016

Yeshiva University Library
Yeshiva University
500 West 185th Street
New York, NY 10033

The Yivo Institute for Jewish Research
1048 Fifth Avenue
New York, NY 10028
(Best American source for material on East European Jewry.)

15 Adoptees in Search of Their Natural Parents

My first experience and awareness of the cruel aspect of bureaucracy came some fifteen years ago when a woman in her seventies, who had been adopted as an infant, came to the New York Public Library hoping to learn at least the names of her natural parents. The Board of Health had refused to allow her to see her original birth record; the courts would not let her see her adoption papers; her church had been of no help; and at every New York City office she had visited in her search she had been treated with disdain and contempt. The woman felt beaten and battered by the time she arrived in the Local History and Genealogy Division, and as I could suggest no more places where she might go, there was nothing left for her to do but sit down at a table, bow her head and cry. It was unnerving, and it seemed so unnecessary. If there was a law that prohibited this woman from seeing her original birth certificate, I felt, then someone should just break the law and give it to her. What harm could it do, when, in all probability, her parents were long dead?

Today there is a place where adopted people like that woman can go and receive not only sympathy but constructive help. It is the result of the work of Florence Fisher, another adopted woman, who began coming into the Local History and Genealogy Division in 1970 to pursue the search for her natural parents. Day after day this pretty, diminutive redhead would rush down from her uptown office and spend her lunch hour going through old directories and other records that might help. Florence had already been searching for nearly twenty years, and although adoption records are sealed by law, she had managed, through a combination of persistence, luck and persuasion, to obtain copies of her original birth certificate and order of adoption and thus had learned the names of her natural parents and her maternal grandparents. Her goal was to locate her parents and meet them.

Unlike the elderly woman I had encountered years before, Florence Fisher was not about to give up and cry. The emotional power behind her search was overwhelming, and her determination convinced me that she would find her parents, even though her clues were over forty years old. Often I would help her, recommending sources, going through directories with her and employing the kind of deduction I'd used during so many years of genealogical research to suggest that "this person might be the one." In a 1933 Brooklyn directory we located the names of her grandparents and mother living in one household. After that, Florence was able to obtain copies of her mother's birth certificate and her grandparents' death certificates, and in June 1970 she at last located and met her mother, whose home was not far from the address where she had lived in 1933. The following year, with a clue provided by her mother, Florence found her father, a Hollywood stuntman, in a matter of days.

She recounted her quest in *The Search for Anna Fisher*, published in 1973, a true-life detective story written in so compelling and appealing a manner that many readers find themselves literally unable to put it down before they have finished it. In the book Florence described how, as a child raised as "Florence Ladden," she had discovered a paper that bore the names of the people she considered her parents, the name "Anna Fisher" and the word "adopted." Although her mother repeatedly denied that she had been adopted, Florence was haunted by the memory of the paper she had seen, and at the age of twenty-two, after her mother's death, she confirmed the fact of her adoption and began to search in earnest for her original identity. In her book she poignantly described the problems she faced as she searched for her parents, whose names she didn't know and was prohibited by law from learning.

In 1971 Florence, determined to make the road smoother for others like her, founded the Adoptees' Liberation Movement Association, known as ALMA, which has as one of its main goals the opening of records to any adopted person over eighteen years old who wants, for any reason, to see them. With its motto "The truth of his origin is the birthright of every man," the organization is actively challenging the laws of sealed adoption records as far as adult adoptees are concerned, hoping ultimately to win a Supreme Court declaration of the unconstitutionality of these laws and an injunction against their continued enforcement. In addition ALMA, which has regional branches throughout this country and in some places overseas, conducts "search workshops" for its members and maintains an international registry of adopted children who are seeking their parents and natural parents who are seeking the children they once gave up for adoption. The ALMA newsletter, "Searchlight," is often filled with remarkable accounts of "Registry Match-ups."

At the conclusion of *The Search for Anna Fisher*, Florence related that, while her father had received her with unreserved joy, her mother, after several loving encounters, had severed her connection with Florence because she was unable to face the pain and embarrassment of telling her family of Florence's existence. Although she had told her husband of her brief teenage marriage, she had been unable to bring herself to tell him that she had given up her child for adoption and had said, instead, that her baby had been born dead. I am glad to be able to provide a happier postscript. After Florence's book was published, the same persistence that had carried her through twenty years of searching prevailed once more. When I addressed an ALMA meeting in New York in 1975 I met both Florence's mother and stepfather, who were enthusiastic ALMA volunteers. I know that many people are inclined to discount the importance of heredity, but even though Florence had never set eyes on her mother until she was very much an adult, the two women resembled each other remarkably in voice, mannerisms and taste in clothes and makeup. It was fascinating to see mother and daughter together, knowing the background of the events that had brought them together at last.

The inheritance of physical characteristics is often intriguing and frequently provides a clue in genealogical research. Historians have written of such distinctive family features as the "Hapsburg lip" or the "Talbot fingers," and many of us are told while we're growing up that we resemble our ancestors: "You've got your grandfather's big hands," perhaps, or "You've got a Roscoe chin." My mother grew up feeling that she wasn't pretty, because Cousin Lizzie, an austere, elderly relative who visited often, used to remark in one breath that the Sudlers (my grandmother's family) were among the handsomest men and the homeliest women in Delaware and in the next that my mother looked just like the Sudlers. Looking at early daguerreotypes in old family albums I discovered that Cousin Lizzie was right—my mother did resemble many of the Sudler women and was the very image of her grandfather's sister, Sally. But these women were unusual-looking rather than homely; their features had an

Oriental quality that can be traced to their ancestor Augustine Herman, who was born in 1621 in Prague, where Eastern and Western blood had mingled throughout the Middle Ages. I am certain that there were strong Tartar genes in their distant past.

If the outward manifestation of physical inheritance is intriguing, the inward manifestation—the inheritance of disease or deformity—is a matter of serious consequence. Queen Victoria of Great Britain unwittingly became a sort of "Typhoid Mary" of the European royal houses, transmitting hemophilia, through her daughters and her daughters' daughters, to the heirs to the thrones of Spain and Russia, among others. The existence of such hereditary disorders is one of the important reasons why I believe that every adult should have access to his original birth certificate and information about his biological family. Those of us who take this freedom for granted can have difficulty empathizing with the frustrations, fears, heartbreaks and disappointments of adopted people who are denied it by law. The case of a young women who was desperately trying to locate her natural parents when I met her a few years ago comes to mind. Her three small children were all suffering from a rare blood disease that could not be traced to her husband's family, and their doctor said it was imperative to learn the medical history of her family. The New York City Board of Health and the adoption agency involved were not sympathetic, however, and as ALMA was not yet in existence, there was no place for her to turn.

As a consequence of my contact with adopted people in search of their parents I have become convinced that every adult adoptee should have access to information about his family origin, even when there is no question of hereditary disease. Again, those of us who were raised by our natural parents may find it somewhat difficult to appreciate the longing of many adoptees to see and talk with their natural parents, or at least to learn some scrap of information about their background. Throughout her search Florence Fisher was chided by innumerable people from whom she sought assistance. "What's the matter with you?" they would ask. "Weren't your adoptive parents good to you? Don't you owe your loyalty to them?" It wasn't until she placed a newspaper ad seeking other adoptees who wanted to find their natural parents—the first step in the founding of ALMA—that Florence learned that many, many other adopted persons were driven by an intense desire to know their family origins, regardless of the amount of love they felt for the family that had raised and cared for them. The feeling that motivates these people is very much akin to the longing for heritage that prompts many genealogists to search for lost origins, but for adoptees the urge to find something of themselves in their parents or grandparents and establish a continuity with the past can be especially urgent.

In this country, adoption proceedings are governed by state laws, the details of which vary. In almost every case provision is made for maintaining confidentiality through the issuance of a modified birth certificate after the adoption decree has been granted and through provision for sealed records and files. The name and status of the child as it exists after adoption is recorded in the public birth record, but accurate and complete records are maintained that might enable the adoptee to establish his true identity in later life should the need arise. Most laws permit these original records to be opened by court order for "good cause," but traditionally, access to them has almost always been denied. The adoptee searching for information about his family continually encounters people—doctors, lawyers, hospital and agency personnel, public officials—who know or have access to the information that he is seeking but who refuse, usually with good intentions, to disclose it.

Without question, rewriting the law to allow adult adoptees access to the names of their natural parents would present some problems. At one time adoption papers were part of the public record, and it was through experience with intrusions into adoptive families and other abuses that the practice of sealing records began. For parents who gave a baby up for adoption years ago a sudden phone call or visit from their child might prove traumatic or embarrassing, and some adoptive parents feel threatened by the idea that the children they are raising as their own might someday seek their natural parents. Any legal changes might have to take into account the fact that parents who have already given up children for adoption did so with assurances that their privacy would not be violated.

At the same time, we live in a period when social conditions and attitudes are changing rapidly and radically. The widespread practice of birth control and abortion and a reduction in prejudice against women bearing children out of wedlock have sharply reduced the number of adoptable babies, and many childless couples have adopted older children or children of other races. While adoptive parents at one time went to great lengths to prevent their children from learning of their adoption, social workers and child-care authorities now counsel that children should be told of their adoption as soon as they are able to grasp the concept.

As adoption is no longer shrouded in secrecy, the adoptive history of some well-known Americans has come to light. Gerald Ford was the first American President who was adopted. Born Leslie Lynch King, Jr., he was raised by his natural mother and her second husband, Gerald Rudolf Ford, who adopted him and gave him his name. The facts about his birth and adoption were kept secret from Ford until he was sixteen, and his younger half brothers didn't learn the truth until later, when they stumbled on the formal adoption papers while rummaging through the attic. Ford met his real father twice—once while he was in high school in Grand Rapids and once as a law student at Yale, but didn't choose to follow up his father's pleas for further contact. Leslie Lynch King, Sr., died in Tucson, Arizona, in 1941.

In two articles in the *Ladies' Home Journal* in 1974 and 1975, another prominent American, television personality Steve Allen, recounted his successful ten-year search for his half brother, whom his mother, vaudevillean Belle Montrose, had given up for adoption many years before she met and married Steve's father, Billy Allen.

When I read Jerry Hulse's *Jody*, the story of a husband who tracked down the family medical history of his desperately ill wife, who had been adopted, I was gratified to learn that an enlightened attitude had prevailed and the public agencies in Fort Wayne, Indiana, had cooperated because of the medical crisis. The publication of Florence Fisher's book and later books of a similar nature, such as Rod McKuen's *Finding My Father*, have generated new awareness and understanding of the psychological yearning for completion experienced by some children who are not raised by their biological parents, and today there are adoptive parents who are willing to help their children find their natural parents. With the formation of ALMA, a great advance has been made and there are now many supportive and knowledgeable people waiting to help adoptees break the barriers of bureaucracy and find their families.

Troubling questions remain for the future. What of the rights and heritage of "test-tube babies"—the children of artificial insemination donation (A.I.D.), who are conceived with donated semen and raised as the "natural" offspring of their mothers and their mothers' husbands? Their number in this country is currently estimated around the half-million mark, and each year another ten to twenty thousand American babies are conceived by this means. What of children who have been adopted through the "black market" created by the shortage of available white babies? What of the children of mixed national and racial heritage fathered and left behind by American servicemen in other countries?

My own conviction is that adopted adults should have access to the medical history of their natural family, as well as to their actual genealogy, for any reason that motivates them. Natural parents can have eighteen years to resolve the personal problems that made them give up their babies, but I feel very strongly that they should accept the fact that some day they may have to face up to the responsibility of having fathered or given birth to a child.

How to Search

Any adopted person who wants to find his natural parents should begin by contacting ALMA (P.O. Box 154, Washington Bridge Station, New York, NY 10033) to learn the location of the nearest regional chapter—in order to participate in workshops and rap sessions—and to obtain a copy of their "Handbook for the Search." A moderate annual membership fee, currently $20, is charged. If by some chance one of your parents has been trying to find you, his or her name may already be on file in the ALMA Registry; although the possibility seems remote, numerous ALMA members have been reunited with their families in just this way.

Your search really involves two steps. It is the first—learning the identity of your natural parents—that is obstructed by the fact of sealed adoption records. If you break through this barrier and learn your parents' names, the second stage—tracing them to their location in the present—involves investigating the same public sources—death and marriage records, probate papers, voting registrations, census and immigration records—that genealogists use in their work.

You should write for a copy of your birth certificate at the outset. If luck is with you, you might, through a bureaucratic oversight, receive a copy of the original, which bears the names of your natural parents, as one woman I know did. Even if you receive a copy of the altered certificate, the date and place of your birth will be correct, and you may learn the name of the hospital in which you were born. The number on the altered certificate will bear some relation to—and may even be the same as—the number on the original, which may be an important clue in finding the family surname.

Occasionally an adoption is first discovered when a birth certificate is obtained, because an altered certificate may be dated significantly after the date of birth. A regular birth certificate is usually issued within a week of birth. If there's a gap of months, some irregularity—perhaps adoption—is indicated.

You should also try to find the court order for your adoption. If you can't obtain a copy, you might get someone to tell you the number, which you can use in future attempts.

Your sealed records may be kept in several places—in the hospital where you were born, in the Surrogate's Court of the county in which your adoption took place and in the records of the agency that arranged your adoption, the lawyer who handled it and the doctor who delivered you. As there is no law that affirms the right of adopted people to know their family origins, you may find yourself in the position of having to wheedle and cajole people to help. Every source must be pursued, and everyone who might know something about your birth must be questioned, in the hope that somewhere a break may be made.

In one case I know of, a doctor told a woman of about twenty that he had arranged her adoption and that her natural mother, like her adoptive mother, was still his patient. No matter how this woman pleaded, however, he refused to tell her mother's name. In such a case it may be possible to persuade the doctor to tell your natural mother that you want to meet her and find out if she's willing.

Anyone who takes up this search must realize that a parent, if found, may react with hostility, refuse any contact or deny outright that he or she ever gave up a child for adoption. Any overture to a natural parent must be made with great care and discretion. In a great many cases the parent first denies the relationship, then capitulates and consents to a meeting. One girl I spoke with traced her mother, an unmarried woman who was past forty when she gave birth, to her home in Massachusetts. She telephoned the woman and told her that she was sure she was her mother. While the woman denied it, she did suggest that they meet some day for lunch. After a pause she asked the girl, "Is there something wrong with your lip?" This clinched the identification for the girl, as she knew she had been born with a harelip. Having given herself away, the woman acknowledged that she was the girl's mother, and they were reunited.

Adoption and Family History

An individual tracing his family tree sometimes runs into a case of adoption in an earlier generation; in order to reconstruct an accurate genealogy, he must determine the identity of the adopted ancestor's biological parents. This is often relatively easy, as in earlier years orphans were frequently taken in by people who knew their families or were related to them, and adoptions were not bound up in great secrecy.

Many early adoptions were extremely casual. In the 1850 census of Wilmington, Delaware, my grandfather, Henry C. Elliott, born a year earlier, was enumerated with his mother, Jane Elliott, in the household of a Captain Brooke Turner and his wife, Elizabeth Turner. In the 1860 schedule the same individuals were listed but were indentified as Captain Brooke Turner; his wife, Elizabeth Turner; his son, Henry C. Turner; and Jane Elliott.

In her will Elizabeth Turner left her estate to my grandfather, whom she identified as " Henry C., the son of Jane Elliott, commonly known as Henry C. Turner." When Jane Elliott, who outlived her son, died in 1908, she left her estate to her three grandchildren—Joseph, Natalie and Henry Turner—the children of her son, Henry C. Turner. I've never located any documents of adoption, and I doubt that there ever were any. As Jane Elliott never married, it's probable that Henry was given the name Turner for social reasons.

One man for whom I did some genealogical research had an

ancestress who died in upper New York State in 1881. According to the history of the town where she died, she had been adopted. In order to pursue his lineage, the man wanted to learn her original identity; it was particularly important because he hoped to join the St. Nicholas Society, in which membership is based on descent from a pre-1785 resident of New York State, and there were indications that this woman might have been born in New York (see Chap. 18, "Hereditary Societies and Popular Ancestors").

We obtained her death certificate from New York State, which began keeping records in 1880. As she was ninety years old when she died, it seemed unlikely that the individual who supplied the facts for her death certificate would have had any knowledge of the woman's family origins in the late 1700's. Nonetheless, to our joy and amazement, the certificate bore her original name—Griswold—and the fact that she had been born in Connecticut.

The name Griswold had appeared in no other record that we had turned up. But the Griswolds were an early Connecticut family, and we immediately found the names of this woman's parents—they had died when she was a child—in a published genealogy. Her mother's maiden name was given as Landon, and a genealogy of the Landon family revealed in turn that the woman's natural mother and adoptive mother were sisters. It also showed early New York State residents among the woman's ancestors, so her twentieth-century descendant was able to join the St. Nicholas Society, as he had hoped.

Among the references on adoption listed in the final section of this book are an alphabetical index of *Divorces and Names Changed in Maryland by Act of the Legislature 1634–1854*, *An Index to Changes of Name . . . 1760–1901* for London, and a *List of Persons whose Names have been Changed 1780–1892*, issued by the Massachusetts Secretary of the Commonwealth. The names of the people listed in such indexes may have been changed for any number of reasons, including adoption. With the index as a starting point, original records, containing more complete information, might be located.

16

Crossing the Water

Tracing a family back several generations in this country is challenging, but the greatest genealogical detective story of all is the search for the lineage of an immigrant ancestor. If you're able to trace your American line back far enough, you will, unless you're a full-blooded American Indian, discover the identity of one or more forebears who emigrated to this country. If you can learn an ancestor's approximate date of migration and connect him to a town or parish overseas, there's a good chance you'll be able to "cross the water" and begin tracing your ancestry in his homeland.

If you're lucky enough to have the time and resources, you can travel overseas to search for records in churches, public offices and libraries, just as you've done in this country. If any people living in the town bear your family name, you may be able to establish their relationship to you. Often they can provide information and family documents. Before returning home you can enlist someone to carry on your research.

If you can't make a trip abroad, you can continue your work by mail and in published sources here and accomplish a great deal, probably with some assistance from a professional researcher living in your ancestor's native country. Even if you do plan to go abroad, it's a good idea to work by mail ahead of time, gathering as much information and establishing as many contacts as possible before you go.

Sources Abroad

The process of tracing your family in another land is the same as it is here, but the sources vary somewhat from country to country. If you've traced English ancestors to a certain parish, you can write to the rector for records of baptisms, marriages and burials. In France you'll want to identify the town in which ancestors lived, so that you can write to the *hôtel de ville*, or town hall, for information. In German and Austrian towns you'll write to the *standesamt*.

The more recent your ancestor's immigration, the more likely it is that you will be able to find traces of your family in his

167

birthplace. The more stable the country—and the fewer natural or man-made disasters that have occurred—the more likely it is that records will have survived. England is unique among foreign countries in that it is an ancient land and has not been invaded since the Norman Conquest in 1066. It has been attacked, and some records were destroyed as a consequence. During the bombing of Exeter in the Second World War, for example, all the wills of the southwest part of the country, which had been deposited at Devon, were lost. On the whole, however, there are numerous types of genealogically valuable records dating almost back to the Conquest. In some European countries repeated invasions have destroyed a great many records, and in areas such as Latin America, where governments have been subject to frequent revolution and the climate is destructive, research is often difficult.

A tradition of education is a positive influence on record-keeping and family history. In England and Wales there has been central registration of births, marriages and deaths since 1837 and in Ireland and Scotland since 1855. Germany, India and Norway all have well-preserved archives and abundant geneal-ogical material, but before Germany became a united country in 1848 it consisted of numerous little duchies and principalities and unless you know the exact area from which your ancestors came, tracing them can be difficult Some European countries have ancient and well-preserved records because certain nationalities, among them Dutch and Belgian, were traditionally interested in family history. There are excellent genealogical documents in some British and European colonies and dependencies because settlers were concerned about preserving proof of their family history and evidence of their origins.

At one time prospects for genealogical research in the Soviet Union and Iron Curtain countries were quite dim, but the ac-cessibility of records is much greater today than it was twenty years ago. People I know have done successful research in Czechoslovakia, Rumania and Poland, and one genealogist of my acquaintance recently went to visit long-lost relatives in Russia.

If your ancestors came from a small, poorly developed country, you may not be able to find any records at all, or you may find, as Alex Haley did in his Gambian research, that the dearth of written records is overcome by a rich oral history. In some places valuable genealogical information survives but has never been assembled in a central location, and you may have to do truly original research—something one always hopes to do—using records that haven't been turned over for a century.

Some countries are "virgin territory" for genealogists and record-keepers. In the Sudan, for instance, the government conducted a pilot census in 1953, asking each individual his name and the names of his parents and grandparents, his age and where he lived. Some people didn't have surnames; residences were uncertain, as a young wife often shared the cooking pot of her parents until she bore a child, and relationships were frequently unclear. The Sudan took a complete census a few years later, but its value is questionable. In places with high illiteracy rates, people are often reluctant to cooperate with record-keepers because they fear they may take advantage of them. In some countries no census has ever been taken, and in others whole classes of people have been ignored because of prejudice.

Establishing the Link to a Foreign Home

Once you've learned the name of an immigrant ancestor, find out as much as you can about him in family accounts, original records and published sources. The name of his home overseas may be revealed in one of the documents used to trace him in this country, such as his death certificate, a town, county or family history or a record of naturalization or immigration. In some cases, however, there may be no record that identifies the place where he lived before coming to America, and you will have to consult additional sources.

Generally, family tradition, public records or the nature of the family name will reveal your ancestor's country of origin, and your task will be to identify the exact parish, town or county from which he came, in order to continue your research there. With the information you've gathered, you can go to the library and make a survey of the surname in the country. If your ancestor was French, for example, you will begin by looking through the French bibliography in this book for works dealing with his surname and see whether any of them mention the part of France in which the name originated. Find out in the library whether there are other bibliographies or source books for

French research. If you don't locate books dealing with your family's surname in particular, general works of French surnames may be helpful. Gaston Saffroy's *Bibliographie Généalogique Héraldique et Nobiliare de la France*, for example, contains a great deal of information on surnames, although it deals primarily with gentle and noble families, and many French emigrants to America were humble people. Check the library catalogue under "France—Genealogy" for additional sources, and remember that more and more works on family history in other lands are being published all the time—currently, the average Frenchman is becoming very interested in the subject— so even if you're stymied now, a later visit to the library may prove fruitful. Study histories of the country from which your ancestor came and, being realistic about his station in life, try to imagine him within the context of that history.

While you're pursuing your library research, write to the national archives in your ancestor's homeland (addresses are given in Part Four) and ask whether they have any knowledge of the regional origin of your family name and whether any indexes of surnames exist. England has *Boyd's Marriage Index* (Illustration 33) and other recent marriage indexes based on entries in parish registers, and as interest in genealogy builds, there may be similar references in other countries in the future. These indexes are most likely to lead to the area from which a family came if the surname is somewhat unusual; in the case of very common names, they are of little value. When you write to the archives, ask whether the government has published a guide to genealogical research—many have—and if so, how you can obtain a copy.

In instances where it is difficult to determine even the national origin of your ancestor, Elsdon Smith's *The New Dictionary of American Family Names* and other general works on the history of surnames may offer clues. Each genealogical case is unique, and every lead should be pursued in hopes that one will reveal the name of your ancestor's home overseas. Once a woman approached me in the library for assistance with her research into the surname Givodan. She had no idea of the nationality of the ancestor who bore it, but I felt certain, from the sound, that it must be a French name. The woman had traced her ancestry in this country to West Virginia, so I looked in an index of deeds in that state and found several variants of the surname, including Gevaudan, listed there. I learned the origin of the name in Virginia when I located an article by Cameron Allen in *The Virginia Magazine of History and Biography* about Antoine Gevaudan of Manakin Town, one of the French Huguenot settlers of the early eighteenth century. In subsequent research I discovered Louis Bran's *Le Livre d'Or de Quelques 6000 Familles de Velay, Auvergne, Gevaudan . . .*, published in Lyon in 1910, which revealed that Gevaudan was a French place name. It is almost certain that the family took its name from the place, and further research in the area might turn up people of the surname still living there.

The case of my search for my ancestor John White, in which I connected the names of his Maryland properties to the home of his family in England, is another example of how place names may provide the link between an American immigrant and his overseas origin.

Corresponding with Foreign Sources

Part Four of this book contains the addresses of archives, public record offices, libraries and historical and genealogical societies in countries around the world as well as basic information about the existence of vital and census records. (These addresses change continually, but in most cases, letters will be forwarded to new offices.) To simplify your search for records, the exact years when censuses were conducted in foreign countries are also noted in many cases, but these years should not be considered exclusive; censuses may have been taken in other years as well.

Your queries to foreign offices should be concise and clear and should contain precise identifying information about your ancestors. You can write in English, but you should type your letter, as the office you're contacting may have to have your questions translated before they answer.

Foreign archives and record offices will not undertake extensive research for you but can provide the names of professional genealogists whom you can hire to do so. Just as in this country, there are fees for copies of vital records, which you can pay with international money orders purchased from the post office or with international bank drafts from your bank.

Inflation has affected genealogy, just as it has affected all other areas of life, and the cost of copies of records, though generally moderate, has quadrupled in some countries in the past several years. It now costs six Australian dollars (a little over six dollars in American currency) to obtain a copy of a certificate in that country, and a search of post-1871 census records in England costs about six pounds (roughly ten dollars), even if you know your ancestor's exact address. This is an important reason to do very thorough preliminary research; if you can narrow down dates, places and names, you can minimize your expenses. At one time, when I was researching a line of the Tilt family in England, I located all the marriages and deaths of the surname Tilt between 1837 and 1850 and ordered copies of each record from the Registrar General's Office. There must have been forty or fifty documents in the stack I received, and while this approach was practical at the time, it would cost a small fortune today.

In your initial query to an overseas library, try to establish the existence of local histories, books about families in your ancestor's region and other published references that may enable you to extend your family line. In England, for example, you might ask whether the library has a history of your ancestor's parish, abstracts of records from the parish or books dealing with the surname. Some libraries may send you photocopies of information from these sources, and most, if extensive research is required, will supply the names of genealogists in the area who can do the work for you.

Genealogical and historical societies in your ancestor's country of origin may be particularly helpful because of their interest in family research. The information they can provide about your family or the region from which they came depends on the resources they have accumulated; some, like the Royal Netherlands Society for Genealogy and Heraldry in The Hague, have detailed indexes to genealogical publications and a large collection of family archives and manuscripts. You may need to hire a researcher to utilize these sources or you may, like some genealogists I've known, be able to work out a trade, having someone in the foreign society do research on your lineage there, while you pursue the lines of family members of theirs who migrated to America. The Royal Netherlands Society and the

Society of Genealogists in London, among others, commonly arrange contacts between genealogists who are interested in the same families.

American Sources for Foreign Lineages

While you're engaged in correspondence with offices, libraries and societies abroad, you can continue to pursue your foreign ancestry using published sources in libraries and other research institutions in this country. This book's bibliographies for other nations list genealogical guides, family histories, works on families in particular localities and bibliographies of vital records. Many of these are written in the language of the country, and it is important that you overcome the mental block that many beginning genealogists have about the language barrier and at least look at these books before deciding you can't learn anything from them. When using many foreign sources, especially those of a specific genealogical nature, it is often a relatively easy matter to figure out the words or abbreviations that represent birth, death and marriage, and names and dates written in another language are often not very different from their English equivalents. If a work in a foreign language deals at great length with your family, you may decide that it is worthwhile to have someone translate it for you.

The microfilmed records from various countries that are maintained by the Genealogical Society of the Church of the Latter-day Saints in Salt Lake City are another valuable tool for pursuing foreign lineages in this country. You may also get some assistance from ethnic societies in the United States. Some may have records and others, although not genealogically oriented, may be able to give you background in national customs and the kinds of records that are available in your ancestor's homeland, or help you find someone who can assist you in translating books and records written in the language of the country. Foreign embassies and consulates in this country are also potential sources of assistance.

Various countries offer unique resources related to their particular religious, political and social structure. When doing research in England, for example, you may make use of the records of the Visitations made by the Heralds of the College of Arms, who periodically rode out into the countryside to examine pedigrees and verify the rights of certain families to bear arms. Many of the Visitations, which span the period from about 1532 to 1686, have been published, and others are available in manuscript in the British Museum and the College of Arms in London. These records are accurate as a rule for the generations closest to the person who provided the information—for his parents and grandparents, children and grandchildren—but may be somewhat more fanciful in their references to ancestors from the time of William the Conqueror. Some of the more recently published Visitations, such as the Harleian Society's Visitation of Wiltshire in 1623, have been annotated with entries from public records that verify the information in them.

I used the Visitations to establish the English origin of Richard Wright, who died in Northumberland County, Virginia, in 1663. In his will, Wright mentioned a cousin, Matthew Merriton, of London. Another document, a court deposition filed on August 20, 1655, gave Wright's age as twenty-two, so I knew that he was born in or about 1633.

In the Visitation of London in 1664, I found Matthew Merriton listed as the son of John Merriton of Moulton, Yorkshire, who died around 1650, and the grandson of George Merriton, Dean of York, who died December 23, 1624. The Visitation of Yorkshire taken by Dugdale on August 26, 1655, gave the pedigree of the Meryton family of Castle Leventon, Yorkshire. It revealed the same information found in the Visitation of London of the previous year, plus the fact that among his other children George Meryton had a daughter, Anne, the wife of "Franc" Wright of Boulton upon Swaile, Yorkshire. The family of Francis Wright by his wife Anne Meryton was also noted in the 1665 Visitation of Yorkshire. They had been married in 1626, and their fourth son, Richard, was born about 1633.

Piecing Together a British Lineage

The course I followed in tracing the British line of my great-great-grandfather, Joseph Anthony Beard, illustrates how facts uncovered in family papers, church and government records, books and correspondence can all be pieced together to trace a family across the water and back into history.

I was very lucky, when I began researching my ancestry, that my father had such an abundance of family records preserved in the black tin box I've already described. More accurately, I might never have begun that search were it not for the existence of that box, for in it were the seeds of my fascination with genealogy. Even when I was a child it was a great joy to me when my father could be prevailed upon, perhaps as a special treat on a rainy day, to bring out the box and go through the hodgepodge of records inside.

There before me was a profusion of papers that documented events in the lives of five generations of my ancestors. Many people are told stories of earlier generations when they're growing up, but all those pieces of paper, palpable objects that I could handle and read for myself, made my ancestors real to me in a way that mere stories couldn't. Probably few children have the opportunity to perceive so vividly the reality of history and their own link to past generations.

My birth certificate was in that box, along with those of my father and brothers , and there was a marriage booklet from my parents' wedding in 1921, in which the guests had signed their names. From there the records went back further and further. Among the mass of letters, clippings and photographs were an invitation to the wedding of my grandparents in 1888 and a newspaper clipping noting the marriage of my great-grandparents in 1852, as well as the letter the groom wrote to the bride's father to ask for her hand. There were the wills of my great-great-grandparents, Joseph Anthony Beard, who died in New Orleans in 1857, and his wife Mary Grover Beard, who died in Blackpool, Lancashire, on a return visit to England in 1859, and there was an abstract from a family Bible that recorded his birth in Portsea, Hampshire, England, the son of John and Ann Beard, in 1804.

This store of records that had been passed down from one generation to the next in my family was the written equivalent of the oral history passed down by Alex Haley's ancestors, and it is by uncovering just such caches of family papers that a great many people begin the investigation into their family trees. Unfortunately, when an elderly person dies, such envelopes and boxes of irreplaceable family documents are often disposed of by well-meaning relatives or friends who are bent on getting everything in order. I constantly hear stories of family Bibles, family albums and other heirlooms that were thrown out in the rubbish. That's why I feel very strongly that if you're young, you should keep in touch with older relatives and, if you are older, should see to it that younger relatives will inherit the family documents they will someday treasure, even though they may not seem interested now.

In the early part of this century my grandfather's sister, who died in 1912, wrote an account of the family for my father, his sister and his cousins, although they were still children and had little interest in the past. There was also, in the black tin box, the rather brief account written in 1876 by her father, Cornelius C. Beard, who was my great-grandfather and the son of Joseph Anthony Beard.

From this combination of family records I was able to piece together a very sketchy account of the Beards' arrival in the New World: My great-great-grandfather, Joseph Anthony Beard, of Portsmouth, England, married Mary Grover of the Isle of Guernsey in 1824, and they had two children, Joseph Robert and Cornelius Collins Beard. Joseph Anthony Beard came to the United States to join a gold rush in Georgia, and the family settled there until they moved to New Orleans in 1836.

As I began to pursue other sources, my search branched out in several directions. I first sought to document the family story in public records in this country (Illustration 34). I had no idea what port Joseph Anthony Beard and his family came through when they arrived in this country, but I knew that most immigrants sailed to major ports, and I decided to check the index of passenger lists for the Port of New York, 1820 to 1846, because it covered the period of their immigration. Lo and behold, there I found the arrival of Joseph A. Beard, twenty-eight, Mary Beard, thirty-four, Joseph Beard, eight, and "Corny" Beard, four, on June 3, 1833, aboard the *Hannibal* from England. Then, in Augusta, Richmond County, Georgia, I found deeds and property records that showed that the family had owned property there in the 1830's.

I also found several records that confused me for some time about Joseph Anthony Beard's early life in America. When I located his naturalization paper it was dated 1836, but I knew that he should have been required to live here five years before he was naturalized. He became a major in the United States Army around the same time, which also seemed odd. My original family story had indicated that he had come to this country to join a Georgia gold rush, and historical sources revealed that there had been such a gold rush—a false one—around Augusta in the mid-1820's. Then I found Joseph Anthony Beard listed as the executor of a Georgia will in 1825. Still, I had the information from the ship passenger lists that indicated he had emigrated with his family in 1833.

After some time I understood that my ancestor had come to this country for the gold rush in the 1820's (probably the will he executed was that of another prospector), had acquired property in Georgia during that time and then returned to England, where he stayed, presumably, until he returned to this country with his family in 1833. On his first trip to America he must have sailed to a Southern port, because his arrival in the 1820's was not recorded in the index of passenger lists for the Port of New York.

Now it was time to try to "cross the water" and pursue my ancestors' lineages in their homelands—to find records of Joseph Anthony Beard in Portsmouth and of Mary Grover on the Isle of Guernsey. I wrote to the Greffe, or Archives, in St. Peterport on the Isle of Guernsey and was sent a chart from the parish church that showed that Mary Grover, born June 21, 1798, the daughter of John and Marie (Mollet) Grover, had married Joseph Anthony Beard, son of John Beard of Portsea, on July 20, 1824, and had given birth to a son, Joseph Robert, on April 15, 1825.

A few years later I was able to visit the Greffe in person. I found an advertisement in an 1824 edition of a newspaper, *The Guernsey Star,* in which John Beard, Jr., of the old and established shoemaking firm of John Beard & Son, announced that he was opening a store in the Pollet—that is, on the main street—and would welcome the patronage of the gentry. In the same paper a Mrs. Grover advertised lodgings. It seems quite probable to me that John Beard and his brother, Joseph, took rooms with Mrs. Grover, and that is how Joseph Beard met Mary Grover. In a history of Guernsey I found a plate showing the hotel that John Grover, Mary's father, had erected on the New Ground in St. Peterport.

My search for Joseph Anthony Beard's English origin was a good deal more complicated and demonstrates how it may sometimes be necessary to follow a circuitous route—pursuing the lines of your direct ancestors' relatives—in order to extend the line of your direct ancestors themselves.

The abstract in my father's black tin box that noted that

Joseph Anthony Beard was born in Portsea, Portsmouth, in 1804 had been attested by a Reverend John R. Beard to be a true copy of a Bible record. I found this name again in Joseph Anthony Beard's will, in which he mentioned his brothers, the Reverend John Relly Beard of Manchester and James R. Beard of Blackpool, England. In Cornelius Beard's written account of the family, I learned that his uncle, the Reverend John Relly Beard, was a Unitarian minister and that James Rait Beard had settled in Natal, Africa, in 1860.

I turned to library sources and found the Reverend John Relly Beard (1800–1876) listed in the *Dictionary of National Biography*, but his parents weren't identified. Another volume, *The Records of a Family*, written by the Reverend Herbert McLachlan and published by the University of Manchester, contained a good deal of information about the Reverend John Relly Beard, his son, the Reverend Charles Beard, and his grandson, Sir Lewis Beard. A family chart showed that John Beard (1775–1831) of Portsea, Hampshire, married Ann Paine, and they had six children—John Relly, Joseph Anthony, James Rait, George Richard, Augusta and Ann Beard. Ann Beard had married a Cornelius Collins, and the chart showed George Beard to be the father of Cornelius C. Beard of New Orleans, but I knew from my family records that this was an error and he was the son of Joseph Anthony Beard.

I engaged Arthur Willis, an expert in Hampshire research, to examine the parish registers of Portsea for me, and there he found the records of the marriage of John Beard to Ann Pibram (not Paine) in 1798 and the baptisms of their children, including Joseph Anthony.

While *The Records of a Family* concentrated on the lives of the Reverend John Relly Beard and his descendants who were active in the field of education, it contained two genealogical clues from an old letter that were to prove extremely important in my search for my ancestors. John Beard of Portsea came from an old Devonshire yeoman family, it was noted, and he had a brother, Richard Bowden Beard, living in Newton Abbot, Devon, in the early 1800's.

I lived in Devonshire for several months in 1958 and had the opportunity to do a great deal of research there in person. I joined the Devon and Cornwall Record Society, whose extensive library of parish register copies and other manuscript volumes were then housed in the old Exeter Public Library (today they're in a special room in the new library) and began to abstract all the information I could find concerning the surnames Beard and Bowden in Devonshire, expecially around Newton Abbot. The marriage bond of Anthony Beard of East Stonehouse with Ann Cleverton, widow, of Plystock, in 1755 was the only record that seemed particularly interesting at the time, since my ancestor Joseph Beard's middle name was Anthony. But I copied and abstracted a great many records and eliminated many leads during the hours I spent poring over these manuscripts.

Also in 1958 I began a series of letters to relatives in England. The first was to Lady Beard, the widow of Sir Lewis Beard, who died in 1919, whose address I found in *Debrett's Peerage*. She answered my letter graciously and in a firm hand but said that she had little knowledge of family origins in Devonshire. At the conclusion of her four-page letter she told me that she was ninety-eight years old and had been born in Edisto Island, Georgia, before the outbreak of the Civil War. Her daughter later wrote to let me know that her mother had died at the age of 102. These two women put me in touch with a number of other descendants of John Beard, until as last I contacted Isobel Beard of Gerrards Cross, Buckinghamshire, who had a family Bible that stated that John Beard was born in Devonport in 1774 and died at Portsea, Portsmouth, on March 7, 1831, and that his wife, Ann Pibram, was born in 1777 and died in Manchester on January 7, 1864.

Their parents were not identified, and this presented a major obstacle, as the county records of Devon, including any wills that existed before 1858, were destroyed during the bombing of Exeter in the Second World War, and some of the parish registers in the vicinity of Plymouth and Devonport were also destroyed or damaged almost beyond repair. I knew, however, that for many of these parishes the bishop's transcripts—annual copies of parish registers—had survived and were now deposited in the Devon Record Office in Exeter.

I wrote there and asked whether there was a record of the baptism of John Beard, suggesting that he might have been the son of Anthony Beard, because custom indicated that Joseph Anthony Beard, named for his mother's father, Joseph Pibram, might also have been named for his father's father. The Record Office sent me records of the baptisms of some children of Anthony and Elizabeth Beard of East Stonehouse, including a son, "Richard Bander Beard," who was baptized March 12, 1773. A. M. Wherry, a researcher whom I employed to search further into the surviving parish registers and bishop's transcripts, examined this entry and found that it actually read "Richard Bawden Beard." To this day I haven't found a record of the baptism of John Beard, but as original letters published in *The Records of a Family* identified him as the brother of Richard Bowden Beard, I know that he too must have been the son of Anthony Beard and his wife Elizabeth.

When Mr. Wherry found the marriage of Anthony Beard and Elizabeth, or Betty, Skinner in the parish register of Plympton, St. Mary, I knew that he'd located the right couple, because several of the children whose baptismal certificates I had received from Devon bore the middle name Skinner. This was definitely the same Anthony Beard whose marriage bond with Ann Cleverton I had discovered years before, but if that marriage ever took place, I have never found any record of it. My belief that Ann Cleverton must have been the mother of Anthony Beard's children, who were born after the date of the marriage bond, obstructed my research for many years. A marriage bond mustn't be confused with a marriage, and even if you do find a marriage record, you can't assume that the two people named on it had all their children with each other. In earlier centuries many more people died at a young age, and it is not unlikely that some of your ancestors might have married and had children with more than one spouse.

When Mr. Wherry moved away, Hugh Peskett, then of Exeter, took up the search and found parish records, chancery depositions, leases and other documents that started to make the Beard pedigree fall into place. When Liza Lawrence, a genealogist from Richmond, Virginia, traveled to England, I put her in touch with Mr. Peskett, and she showed great persistence in helping him, charming vicars into showing her parish registers that were still in the hands of the clergy. On one occasion she was even taken into a bank vault where parish records were preserved, and there, in the parish register of Shaugh Prior, she found the marriage of Robert Beard to Mary Bowden, who brought that name into the family in 1698.

With the help of these researchers I eventually carried the line back to John Beard of Ugborough, who was born before 1538. In all, some fourteen generations of the Beards can be traced from him, even though many records have been destroyed and the family moved around, first just within the Devon area, then in various counties of England and finally around the world. Much of what I've learned about the earliest generations of my Beard ancestors is set forth in the following chapter, as an example of how a traditional genealogy is presented.

In constructing this lineage I spent perhaps $2,500 for the services of professional genealogists and for copies of English records. Spread out over the twenty years I worked on it, this averages out to a little over $100 a year, certainly no more than people spend on many other pastimes, and the search has afforded me a great deal of pleasure throughout that time.

Parish registers, Bishops' Transcripts, leases, apprentice records, Bible records, newspaper accounts, wills, deeds, city directories and family letters and tradition worked together to form this pedigree, and there is much additional material to be found. The Devonshire Lay Subsidy for 1332, published by the Devon and Cornwall Record Society in 1969, shows that John atta Beare and Nicholas Baudewyn were living in the parish of Brenta (South Brent), and it is possible that some further research in manorial and public records will show the link to these men as my Beard and Bowden ancestors. (For more on English documents, see Chap. 42.) Somehow, when you think you have gone as far as you can go, there are always more branches to be found on your family tree. This is part of the intrigue of genealogy.

17 Presenting Your Genealogy

Each individual's genealogy unfolds into stories of his particular set of ancestors that reflect in a very personal way the history of the times and places in which they lived. Most genealogists, after they've pieced together an account of several generations, want to put their work into a form in which they can easily share it with other people.

You can present the results of your research in a pedigree chart, a scrapbook that combines pictures, signatures and documents with the story of your forebears, or a published genealogy that can be distributed to historical and genealogical libraries, as well as to other members of your family.

Charts and Scrapbooks

If you've accumulated daguerreotypes, photographs and signatures of several ancestors, you can incorporate them into an ancestral chart to make an attractive wall hanging. Decorative charts, large enough to show your direct ancestry as far as you've been able to trace it, can be purchased for a few dollars from genealogical suppliers. After you've filled in the chart, mount reproductions of pictures of ancestors or copies of their signatures next to their names or around the border, and frame it (Illustration 35).

A scrapbook is another popular and appealing way to present your family's history and, like a wall chart, is a favorite gift for relatives. You can mount page-sized pedigree charts in the front and fill the rest with written narratives and anecdotes about your family, pictures of ancestors and family homes, newspaper clippings, wedding invitations, letters, maps and similar documents (Illustration 36). Select items that give life and flow to your story. For some early forebears you may not have an extensive choice of pictures or records, but in the case of ancestors for whom you have accumulated many documents, pick those that are the most interesting and represent milestones in their lives.

Don't use original pictures or records in charts or scrapbooks. Have them photographed or photocopied and carefully preserve the originals.

Any documents or photographs on paper will deteriorate as time passes, but you can prolong their lives by seeing that they're properly stored and cared for. Keeping them in acid-free acetate envelopes is one way to forestall their deterioration. It is also possible to have documents laminated, although I would hesitate to do so, because the process is often irreversible. Store papers in a cool, dry place. You should avoid hot attics or damp basements, but humidity is more destructive than dry heat, if you have to choose between evils.

If you have valuable historical documents and pictures, it's a good idea to deposit either the originals or copies in an interested library or historical society. In this way, you can share what you have with historians and other genealogists, and if the originals finally crumble or are inadvertently destroyed, at least the copies will survive. You'll probably find, incidentally, that your oldest documents are the most resilient, because older papers, often of 100 percent rag content, are generally more durable than newer papers made with synthetic fibers and chemical additives.

Publishing Your Genealogy

If you have completed a lot of research and traced your family through several generations, consider putting the results into book form, incorporating charts and illustrations. The simplest and least expensive way to do this is to prepare your genealogy in typewritten form, have several photocopies made and enclose them in manuscript binders. Maps, charts and photocopies of documents or signatures can be included, and some copying machines make fairly good reproductions of photographs and daguerreotypes. Pictures of ancestors, pages from family Bibles, letters and certificates will give personality to the dry facts and add authenticity to your story.

If you're willing to spend more money, you can have your book printed and bound. The development of offset printing has made this a less expensive option than it once was, and offset pages can be printed directly from a typewritten manuscript. If you choose to spend still more, you can have the book set in type. Including photographic plates and choosing a handsome binding will, of course, add to your costs.

A local printer can produce your genealogy, but if you're contemplating a full-length book, you may appreciate the guidance offered by one of the many genealogical publishers who specialize in this type of work (see list, Chap. 32). Among the best known are Charles E. Tuttle in Rutland, Vermont; Polyanthos in New Orleans, Louisiana; Genealogical Publishing Company in Baltimore, Maryland; and Edwards Brothers in Ann Arbor, Michigan. Perhaps interested relatives will share the cost— roughly $2,000 to $3,000 for a few hundred copies of an attractively bound 200-page book. Regardless of who does the printing, the time taken in preparation by the printers—rather than running a number of copies through the press—is the chief expense, so careful organization on your part is essential.

It is a fairly common practice for genealogists to sell printed genealogies by mailing notices to relatives and other descendants of families named in the manuscript and to libraries and genealogical and historical societies, but I don't think you should look on this particular publishing venture as a money-making one. You cannot hope to be compensated for the time and money you've spent in research, but presumably your main motivation has been the fun and satisfaction derived from searching for your ancestry. If you do decide to sell your book, I would suggest you base the price on the cost of printing alone.

My own feeling is that if you can, you should make a gift of copies to any libraries that are interested and certainly to those where you found materials and assistance that enabled you to trace your lineage. In many cases you can claim an income-tax deduction for such donations, and people who see your book in a library may decide to purchase a copy. Sending copies to genealogical periodicals for review can also lead to sales to others interested in the families you've traced.

Giving copies of your genealogy to libraries provides a means to share your work with others and may result in your receiving feedback and additional information from researchers working on related lines. It also protects your material against destruction in case of a fire or similar disaster in your home. Not long ago I spoke with a man who had lost the results of thirty years of genealogical research in a house fire. While I didn't feel it was appropriate at that point to ask why he had never given copies of his family history to relatives or institutions, you can learn from his tragic experience. Even if the day when you might publish a "complete" genealogy is a long way off, you should periodically distribute copies of what you've learned so far to family members and libraries.

Writing Your Genealogy

Whether you intend to include your written genealogy in a family scrapbook or in a published work, you'll want to arrange it in a form that will be easily understood by the reader. While your research and working charts have of necessity progressed from present to past, a finished genealogy in written form begins with a person or couple and traces their descendants to the present day. You may choose to begin yours with the earliest ancestor whose identity you have been able to establish, or with an ancestor who emigrated to this country. If you want to present your complete ancestry, you'll write up each line separately, beginning with the progenitor and coming forward.

A numbering system, completely different than that used in tracing your line back on working charts, is used to give clarity to your written genealogy. Each person in the family line is identified by an individual number, assigned consecutively, and by a generation number. Thus in the example that follows, my earliest established Beard ancestor, John Beard of Ugborough, is assigned the individual number 1 and is identified as John^1 Beard, to signify that he is of the first generation. His children are numbered in birth order—the eldest is number 2—and each of their given names is followed by a raised numeral 2, indicating that they are of the second generation. As my example shows, this double identification system makes the genealogy easy to follow, even if the same name, as so often happens, turns up several times along the line.

Each time a new surname is introduced, alternate spellings that have been found in various records are indicated in parentheses after the primary spelling.

The genealogy begins with a biographical paragraph about John^1 Beard containing information about his probable parentage; his birth, marriage and death; his occupation and accomplishments; and the sources in which these facts were discovered. Any known facts of his wife's birth, death and parentage are also described. Their children are listed in birth order, and any information about their births, marriages and deaths that has been learned is given.

In this genealogy I have chosen to describe in detail only my direct ancestors. The sign + in front of the name of Andrew² Beard, the eighth child of John¹, indicates that he will be described more fully in a following paragraph.

The Beard Family
of Devonshire, Hampshire and New Orleans

1. John¹ Beard (Beere, Beare), of Ugborough, Devonshire, was probably the son of Edward and Margaret Beard of Ugborough, who had Mary Beard baptized in 1538, Robert Beard in 1540, Margerie in 1546, and William Beard in 1548. Edward Beard was buried in Ugborough on 9 Jan. 1558, and his wife Margaret on 17 Nov. 1557. John¹ Beard married Emline Bynmoore (Binmore) in Ugborough, on Jan. 18, 1573. Presumably he was a yeoman, tilling the soil of this parish on the edge of Dartmoor, as Beards are still doing in the 1970's. John¹ Beard was buried at Ugborough on 12 Feb. 1602, and his widow Emline was buried there on 6 Feb. 1613. They had nine children baptized at Ugborough.

    2. John² Beard, baptized 5 July 1579.
    3. Johan² Beard, baptized 17 Sept. 1581.
    4. Thomas² Beard, baptized 8 Nov. 1583.
    5. William² Beard, baptized 2 Sept. 1585.
    6. Agnes² Beard, baptized 25 Oct. 1587.
    7. Ralph² Beard, baptized 23 July 1589.
    8. Margery² Beard, baptized 16 Feb. 1590.
 + 9. Andrew² Beard, baptized 18 May 1593, of whom further.
    10. Richard² Beard, baptized 9 June 1595, probably buried at Buckfastleigh.

9. Andrew² Beard, the son of John¹ and Emline (Bynmoore) Beard, was baptized at Ugborough, Devon, 18 May 1593, and he was undoubtedly the man of the same name buried at South Brent, Devon, 6 May 1688, which was an unusually long life span for this period. Andrew Beard was only eleven when his father died, and he was the fifth son of the family. The family farm at Ugborough, probably held by lease from the lord of the manor, traditionally would have gone to the eldest son, John² Beard. Therefore, Andrew² Beard went to the neighboring parish of Buckfastleigh, where there were

Beards and Binmores who were probably relatives. Andrew Beard signed his name to the Protestation against Popery in Feb.–March 1641/42 at Buckfastleigh. For these early generations, supposition is all there is to go on to interpret the facts from the parish registers and bishop's transcripts. Andrew Beard was first married on 7 May 1618 at Buckfastleigh to Petronella Bovy, who was buried there on 10 May 1626. He married secondly Richoard ———— at South Brent in 1627, where the parish registers have not survived and the bishop's transcripts which start in 1597 are incomplete and mutilated at this entry. She was buried at Buckfastleigh, 3 Sept. 1656. Andrew Beard and his first wife, Petronella Bovy, were the parents of four children, all baptized at Buckfastleigh.

11. Christian[3] Beard, baptized 13 Sept. 1618.
12. Edmund[3] Beard, baptized 14 May 1620.
+ 13. Andrew[3] Beard, baptized 13 Oct. 1622, of whom further.
14. John[3] Beard, baptized 15 June 1625.

13. Andrew[3] Beard, the son of Andrew[2] Beard and Petronella Bovy, was baptized at Buckfastleigh, 13 Oct. 1622, and he was buried at South Brent, Devon, 14 Feb. 1697. His name appears on the Protestation List for Feb–Mar. 1641/42 as a male over 18 at South Brent. He is the first of his family to come alive in documents of the period other than parish registers (Illustration 37). In 1689 he made a deposition in connection with a chancery proceeding, now in the Exeter Record Office, stating that he was aged 68 or thereabouts. It was probably this Andrew Beard who was in possession of Flexie Meadow, part of Binnamore (the maiden name of his grandmother), on 7 Dec. 1669. His son Bartholomew was in possession of lands at Binnamore in South Brent in 1696, and in 1701, according to leases in the Ilbert Estate Papers in the Devon Record Office, the lands were called Binnemore Barton (meaning farm). The name of his wife is unknown, but she may have been from a parish at some distance from Dartmoor in the Tavistock area, as the chancery proceeding concerned lands in which Andrew Beard may have had some interest in that section of Devon. From leases in the Petre and Ilbert Estate Papers in the Devon Record Office, it can

be determined that Andrew Beard had at least four children.

    15.   Bartholomew[4] Beard, of full age in 1676, and termed "lately deceased" in 1730, married Margaret Beard at South Brent, 25 Jan. 1695, and had no issue.

    16.   Andrew[4] Beard, of full age by 1689, married Sarah Pomeroy of Chagford, at South Brent, 7 Dec. 1695, and had no issue.

+17.   Robert[4] Beard of Shaugh Prior, of whom further.

    18.   Susanna[4] Beard, who married Richard Cole, weaver, at Ugborough on 15 Nov. 1698.

17.   Robert[4] Beard, the son of Andrew[3] Beard, was mentioned in a lease of his brother Andrew[4] Beard on 9 May 1685, dealing with lands in South Brent Manor. In a lease of his brother, Bartholomew[4] Beard, dated 25 March 1701, he is noted as living in the parish of Shea (Shaugh) and having a son, Bartholomew. He was buried at South Brent on 9 June 1721. Robert[4] Beard married Mary Bowden at Shaugh Prior on 9 Nov. 1698. She was buried at South Brent 18 Dec. 1708. They had two children, baptized at Shaugh Prior, Devon.

+19.   Bartholomew[5] Beard, baptized 21 Nov. 1699, of whom further.

    20.   Joan[5] Beard, born 18 Oct. 1702, and baptized 27 Oct. 1702, married Edmund Not of South Brent, both living 9 July 1739, when they sold "Moore Park" in Ugborough.

19.   Bartholomew[5] Beard, the son of Robert[4] and Mary (Bowden) Beard, was baptized at Shaugh Prior, 21 Nov. 1699. He was living in Plymstock, Devon, in the 1730's and was alive 9 July 1739, when he sold "Moore Park" in Ugborough, inherited from his uncle Bartholomew. Bartholomew[5] Beard was mentioned in the lease of his uncle Bartholomew[4] Beard in 1701, and he was termed of the parish of Shaw (Shaugh), yeoman, on 25 March 1722, in a lease dealing with Binnemore Barton in South Brent. It was Bartholomew[5] Beard who started the movement of the Beards of this branch away from the land. As Bartholomew Beard of Ugborough, he married Agnes Bury of Alvington, Devon, at Brixton, 20 June 1726. They settled at Plymstock, next to

Plymouth, where he may have been involved in activities dealing with this port, and he certainly apprenticed his son, Anthony Beard, to a ropemaker. Agnes (Bury) Beard was buried at Plymstock, 4 Sept. 1755, but no information has been found concerning her husband's death or burial. They had at least three children.

+21.   Anthony[6] Beard, baptized at Plymstock, 29 Aug. 1726, as "Anthony son of Bartholomew Bayrd," of whom further.

22.   Mary[6] Beard, baptized at Plymstock, 23 Jan. 1731/32.

23.   Robin[6] (Robert) Beard, baptized at Plymstock, 8 Feb. 1734/35

21.   Anthony[6] Beard, baptized at Plymstock, Devon, 29 Aug. 1726, son of Bartholomew[5] and Agnes (Bury) Beard, was apprenticed as a ropemaker, at which time he was noted as the son of Bartholomew Beard. He is first found in records as an adult when he had a license as Anthony Beard of East Stonehouse, ropemaker, to marry Ann Cleverton, widow, of Plymstock, in 1755. The marriage evidently did not materialize, as the record cannot be found in any parish, and Anthony Beard, ropemaker, of East Stonehouse, had a license to marry Betty Skinner of Plympton St. Mary in 1762. He was bound in £200 to Thomas Skinner not to have any impediment to the proposed marriage. This was a large sum for that period, and it is possible that the Skinners knew that he had jilted Ann Cleverton. This time the marriage took place, in the parish church at Plympton St. Mary on 28 Nov. 1762. The baptisms of six of their children appear in the registers of East Stonehouse, and the burial of their son Thomas occurred in the same parish in 1769, while the burials of three others were in Plymstock. Betty or Elizabeth (as she is called at the baptisms of her children) Skinner Beard may have been the Elizabeth Skinner, daughter of John Skinner, who was baptized at Plymstock on 6 Dec. 1730. It is uncertain who her relative, Thomas Skinner, the bondsman at her marriage, was. He may have been her father, uncle, grandfather, brother or cousin. No death record of Betty (Skinner) Beard has been found, and it is possible that she married again after the death of her

husband, Anthony[6] Beard, who was buried at Plymstock, 23 Jan. 1780.

24. Thomas[7] Beard, baptized 2 June 1765, buried at East Stonehouse, 21 July 1769.

25. Anthony[7] Beard, Jr., baptized 15 Oct. 1766, buried at Plymstock, 21 Sept. 1780.

26. James Skinner[7] Beard, baptized 2 Sept. 1768.

27. William Skinner[7] Beard, baptized 21 Apr. 1770, buried at Plymstock, 20 Apr. 1776.

28. Betty Skinner[7] Beard, baptized 27 Dec. 1771, buried at Plymstock, 15 Mar. 1772.

29. Richard Bowden[7] Beard, baptized 7 Mar. 1773, living at Newton Abbot, Devon, about 1810, when John[7] Beard visited him.

+ 30. John[7] Beard, stated in the family Bible to have been born in Devonport in 1774, and in the printed family genealogy, *The Records of Family*, in 1775, of whom further.

30. John[7] Beard, the son of Anthony[6] and Betty (Skinner) Beard, was born in Davenport in 1774 or 1775 and died in Portsea, Portsmouth, 7 Mar. 1831. The early events of his life and the reason for his removal to Portsea are unknown. He obviously received a good education, as he wrote excellent letters and served as a lay preacher in the Unitarian Chapel at Portsmouth. In an advertisement in the *Guernsey Star* in 1824, when his son was opening a branch of the family shoe business in Guernsey, it was stated that John Beard & Son was an old, established firm of shoe manufacturers in Portsmouth. It would seem that the business was successful enough to support and educate his family fairly well, but according to family tradition, he fell on hard times toward the end of his life, possibly because of a long period of ill health. John[7] Beard married Ann Pibram at Portsea 24 July 1797. She was born in 1777, according to the family Bible, and she was probably the daughter of Joseph Pibram, widower, who married Ann Bone at Portsea on 25 Jan. 1781. They were evidently from another parish, as his former marriage and the baptism of Ann Pibram do not appear in the Portsea records. Ann Beard survived her husband for many years

and died at Manchester, Lancashire, 7 Jan. 1864. A search of the 1851 and 1861 census records so far has been unable to locate her. Either of these censuses would give the parish of her birth. In spite of the fact that the Beards were Non-conformists (from the established church), their children were baptized in the Church of England, as Non-conformists were not allowed to vote until 1828.

31. John Relly[8] Beard, D.D., born at Portsea, 4 Aug. 1800, Unitarian minister, died at Ashton-on-Mersey, Lancashire, 22 Nov. 1876. He married Mary Barnes, daughter of Charles Barnes, at Portsea, 28 June 1826, and had issue. He authored *Cassell's Latin-English Dictionary*, etc. (See *Dictionary of National Biography*.)

+ 32. Joseph Anthony[8] Beard, born 16 Nov. 1804 and baptized at St. Mary's Church, Portsea, 14 Aug. 1806, died at his home, 120 Canal Street, New Orleans, La., 20 Aug. 1857, of whom further.

33. Ann[8] Beard, whose baptism has not been discovered, but she was evidently the eldest daughter. She married Cornelius Collins, for whom her nephew, Cornelius Collins Beard of New Orleans, was named.

34. Elizabeth[8] Beard, born 30 June 1807, baptized 28 June 1810.

35. Amelia[8] Beard, born 27 Sept. 1809, baptized 28 Jan. 1810.

36. Augusta[8] Beard, baptized 12 Jan. 1812.

37. George Richard[8] Beard, born 25 Sept. 1815, baptized 25 Dec. 1815, died at Jefferson, Texas, 23 Oct. 1892. Not long before he died, George R. Beard was baptized in the Episcopal Church, not realizing that his Non-conformist parents had had him baptized when he was an infant so that he could claim full rights as a British subject. He has many descendants living in Louisiana, Tennessee, Texas and Oklahoma.

38. James Rait[8] Beard, baptized 1 Feb. 1818, emigrated to Natal, South Africa, suddenly in 1860, after his unmarried daughter became pregnant. His date of death (which probably took place in Pietermaritzburg, Natal) has not been discovered. He has many

descendants, mostly legitimate (as his daughter's illegitimate son left no issue), in South Africa and Rhodesia.

39.   Sarah Ann[8] Beard, baptized 3 Nov. 1820.

A finished genealogy would continue in the same manner, tracing all fourteen generations descended from John Beard of Ugborough to the present day. Even in this succinct form, the paragraphs of biographical information about my direct ancestors give some dimension to their characters and show the movement and changing lifestyles of succeeding generations. The term "yeoman," used to describe John[1] Beard, creates a picture of my earliest ancestor tilling the soil and tending his farm. In later generations we learn that his descendants eventually moved off the land, assumed professions and broke with the established church.

The same basic form can be used to present a detailed genealogy of all the descendants of the progenitor of the family line. In that case the mark + would appear in front of the name of each individual who lived to maturity, and a biographical paragraph and list of children would be included for each. A genealogy of this scope is generally divided into chapters for the second, third and succeeding generations, to make it easy to read and understand.

At the beginning of each biographical paragraph I restated the birth and parentage of my ancestor in order to establish an exact identification. In many genealogies, including most of the published nineteenth-century New England genealogies, an alternate style is used to identify the successive generations from the progenitor: Robert[4] (Andrew[3] Andrew[2] John[1]). This technique, which places each individual clearly in the line of family descent, is an excellent device to use if you're publishing your genealogy.

My genealogy is written in the American style, which I find preferable to certain European variations. In both England and Europe it is customary to list all the sons of a couple first, in the order in which they were born, and then list all the daughters. The children in the list are identified only by their given names; the surname is not repeated. While this may make for smoother reading, it can be extremely confusing when one is tracing a female line. If, for example, I had listed the children of Susanna[4] Beard and Robert Cole and identified them only by their first names, a reader might easily mistake them for Beards, because this is the Beard genealogy.

Dates can be expressed in the English form—2 May 1788—or in the American—May 2, 1788. Over the years I have come to prefer the former, because there is no chance that the numbers of days and years will be run together and confused.

A book on my complete ancestry would trace several lines, each beginning with the earliest known ancestor and continuing to the present. Thus, I might publish a genealogy of *The Beard, Finley, Stuart-Menteth and Related Families,* beginning with the line of the Beards, then the next known surname of my ancestors. In the best of such works a chart before each line shows how it connects to the author's family.

If I chose to publish my genealogy, I would include a bibliography of the references used in my research, citing the author, title and date of publication of all printed sources. I would also prepare an index, to make the book more useful for other genealogists and scholars.

If, in the future, I succeeded in tracing the Beard line further, positively identifying Edward and Margaret Beard as the parents of John[1] Beard, perhaps, or even connecting him to the John atta Beare listed in the Devonshire Lay Subsidy for 1332, it would be a relatively simple task to rewrite my genealogy, adding the earlier generations and revising my numbering system accordingly. You can never really be sure that you have reached the conclusion of your genealogical search, but if you continually put off writing your genealogy for that reason, you will probably never do it, and the charts and raw records you leave behind after your death will not be easily understood by your heirs, unless they, too, are genealogists. It is best to write your genealogy after you've traced several generations, and then revise it periodically as you discover earlier ancestors.

18 Hereditary Societies and Popular Ancestors

There is a vast number of hereditary societies in this country in which membership is based on proven descent from an individual who can be connected with a particular event, location or period. These differ from genealogical societies, which exist to further the pursuit of family history in general and are open to all. The best-known hereditary and patriotic society, the Daughters of the American Revolution, is one of many that commemorate descent from an ancestor who provided patriotic and military service to the American side during the Revolutionary War. There are others in which membership is based on descent from a forebear of a certain ethnic origin, such as the St. Andrew's Society, for descendants of ancestors born in Scotland; or from an individual who performed a particular professional service, such as the Hereditary Order of Descendants of Colonial Physicians and Chirurgiens; or from an ancestor who served in another American war, such as the General Society of the War of 1812 and the United States Daughters of 1812. There are also regional organizations, including the Daughters of the Republic of Texas, the Daughters of Utah Pioneers and the Sons of Utah Pioneers. Other societies, such as the Order of the Crown of Charlemagne in the United States of America, are open to descendants of European royal families, and there is even an organization for Descendants of the Illegitimate Sons and Daughters of the Kings of Great Britain.

For some genealogists membership in a hereditary society presents a challenge and a goal, and they search for the link that will qualify them to join. Some people just want to prove their ancestry or commemorate their descent from a particular individual.

Joining a society is also a means of registering and preserving your genealogy. You can learn just how valuable this is by making use of the lineage papers of others whose admission to a society was based on descent from one of your ancestors. In most cases societies will provide you with copies of these papers if the member who filed them is deceased or has dropped out of the organization, or if an active member has given permission for his or her papers to be made available to others. Some hereditary societies maintain excellent genealogical libraries for use by both members and nonmembers or issue publications that contain valuable genealogical and biographical information.

Most of the organizations that commemorate a particular historical period are active in preserving buildings, churches, records and cemeteries and erecting plaques on the sites of major events of the era. The cost of these activities is covered by annual dues, which vary from group to group but is generally quite moderate, and by bequests from deceased members. Joining a hereditary society will enable you to participate in meetings and historical outings that will bring you in touch with other people who share your interest in genealogy.

The membership requirements of one organization, even for the period of the Revolution, may be quite different from those of another. To join the Daughters of the American Revolution, founded in 1890, or the Sons of the American Revolution, formed in 1889, you must prove descent from an individual who provided patriotic aid to the American side during the Revolution, of which military service is but one acceptable form. You might also base your application on descent from a civil officer of one of the colonies or states, an ancestor who rendered material aid to the American cause, a Signer of the Declaration of Independence, or a female patriot such as Mary Ludwig Hays, who aided her husband, a Pennsylvania artillery private, at the Battle of Monmouth in 1778, carried water for the soldiers there and is known to history as Molly Pitcher. On the other hand, to join the Sons of the Revolution, formed in 1876, or the Daughters of the Revolution, formed in 1895, you must be descended from a man who performed military or civil service at the state or federal level.

Mrs. Benjamin Harrison, the wife of the President of the United States, was the First President General of the D.A.R., and the wives of seven presidents—including Mrs. James Earl (Jimmy) Carter, the former Rosalynn Smith—have been members. Other First Ladies who belonged to the D.A.R. are Mrs. Ulysses S. Grant, Mrs. Theodore Roosevelt, Mrs. Warren G. Harding, Mrs. Franklin D. Roosevelt and Mrs. Dwight D. Eisenhower.

The ultimate in Revolutionary War societies is the oldest—the Society of the Cincinnati, formed in 1783. To become a member you must prove descent from an officer in the Continental Army or a state militia officer who was killed in battle. (Each state had regiments in the Continental line, which formed the regular forces of the Revolutionary War, as well as militia regiments, which served for various periods of time at home and at times with the regular forces in other states.) If the officer in question died without issue or has no descendants today, a collateral descendant from a brother or sister may represent him.

George Washington himself was the first president of the Society of the Cincinnati, and his successor today still wears the handsome jeweled badge of office sent to him from France by the Marquis de Lafayette. (Because so many French fought in the Revolution, there is a branch of the Society of the Cincinnati in France, which has a substantial membership.) A descendant must join the Society in the state from which his progenitor served, and only one member at a time can represent a Revolutionary figure. It was for this reason that the Sons of the Revolution was formed in 1876, the Centennial Year, by the younger sons and brothers of Cincinnati members, together with descendants of militia officers and soldiers. The distaff equivalent is the Daughters of the Cincinnati, for which the requirements of the ancestor are the same, but any number of women can represent an eligible officer.

To join the Descendants of Loyalists and Patriots you must prove descent from two ancestors—one who was a patriot and the other a Loyalist relative of the patriot. The lineages filed by members reflect the great number of families who were divided by the War of Independence, a phenomenon so common in civil wars and revolutions.

For the young, there is the Children of the American Revolution, in which membership is open to both males and females between the ages of one day and eighteen years of age.

The existence of these societies is, in a sense, the closest American parallel to the landed gentry of Europe, in that members have proven lines of descent from a certain period. But it is a great deal more democratic, and many people who qualify to join have very mixed lineages. Membership doesn't depend on wealth, status or family name, as long as descent can be proven generation by generation, and in most societies this can be done through either male or female lines. I know one man whose father was a Russian-born Jew who was eligible for membership in several Revolutionary and Colonial societies through the ancestry of his mother, the daughter of a Congregational clergyman from Canandaigua, New York. Many black soldiers and their widows received pensions for Revolutionary service, and it is hoped that with the recent interest in black genealogy their descendants will be encouraged to prove their family lines for membership in these organizations.

There are certain organizations for which descent must be shown through male lines only. Membership in the Holland Society, for example, is open to men with male descent from someone who settled in New Amsterdam before 1672. To join the Order of Founders and Patriots you must prove a male line— through either your father or mother—to an ancestor who resided in the Colonies before 1657 and another ancestor in the same line who served in the Revolution.

Joining A Hereditary Society

The names, addresses and membership requirements of some of the most active hereditary, patriotic and ethnic societies in this country are listed in Chapter 29. Many more can be found in *The Hereditary Register* or in Summit Publications' *List of 60 Hereditary Organizations for Which Membership Is Based Upon Ancestral Background*. The procedures for joining vary, but generally you must be sponsored by at least two people who are already members. Some societies welcome the opportunity to introduce prospective members to sponsors and others do not. One must be invited to join the Colonial Dames and, according to the etiquette of the Society, should never request permission to do so. Many national societies require that membership be secured through state societies or chapters.

You should be well along in your genealogical research before you consider trying to join a hereditary society; too many would-be members start with hearsay, rather than with the cold facts needed to prove descent from an appropriate ancestor. When you've found the name of a society in which you are interested and for which you think you qualify, write directly to them for details about their rules for eligibility, procedures for joining and standards for evidence of ancestry.

In the early years of their existence, hereditary societies

accepted a great many undocumented claims of ancestry, and their early lineage papers are quite sketchy as far as proof goes. Today, however, applicants must submit ample evidence of descent with their lineage papers. You will usually be required to fill out a pedigree worksheet that has spaces for information about the birth, marriage and death of each individual in your line, starting with yourself and working back to the ancestor upon whose identity you are basing your application (Illustration 38). In order to establish proof of your line, you must back up every name, place and date with references listed on the application and keyed by number to each generation. Published sources should be identified by author, title, volume and page, and your application should be accompanied by photocopies or certified transcripts of unpublished sources such as vital and church records, pages from family Bibles, tombstone inscriptions and letters.

Always cite the most authoritative reference for each fact set down in your lineage. Primary records—vital statistics, church records, wills and similar documents—are considered better evidence than information from published sources. Genealogies are excellent research guides and can be used to support your lineage, but if you've used some of the older works that didn't list references, you should submit original records that back up the information taken from them. Family tradition is not accepted as proof of ancestry.

You must prove beyond doubt the line of descent from one generation to the next, but in cases where it is impossible to ascertain the exact date of a birth, marriage or death, it is generally permissible to note the approximate date. If you can, you should delineate an exact time period. For example, rather than say that an ancestress married her second husband "circa 1874," you could note that the marriage took place between July 7, 1873 (the date of her first husband's death), and March 30, 1875 (the date of the first known record in which she is identified as the wife of her second husband).

In addition to charting and documenting your lineage, you must establish proof of the military service (Illustration 39), profession or other qualification of the ancestor upon whom you are basing your application, according to the requirements of the society in which you are seeking membership. For Revolutionary

War societies, evidence of military service may be found in original documents kept by your family, in payrolls of the Continental Army or pension or other military records (Chap. 25) maintained at the National Archives, or in sources preserved by the society itself. The *DAR Patriot Index*—which covered more than 105,000 names when it was issued in 1966 and has been expanded in three supplements since then—lists the name, dates and pension number, if any, of each Revolutionary patriot on whose service membership applications have been approved. If you find your ancestor listed in it, you can get a photocopy of the application of another descendant (unless that file is closed) by submitting a nominal fee to the Treasurer General of the National Society (1776 D Street, N.W., Washington, DC 20006), but if it is one of the earlier, poorly substantiated applications, you will have to gather additional records that back up the information found in it. Many state and local chapters have published books about the Revolutionary War ancestors of members, and the *Daughters of the American Revolution Magazine*, published under various titles since 1892, includes biographical and genealogical information about Revolutionary patriots in virtually every issue. Various indexes have been published that will enable you to find this genealogical material. The D.A.R.'s extensive genealogical library in Washington is open to the general public, and the staff will send you a list of professional researchers if you cannot go there in person.

The application forms for hereditary societies are sometimes intimidating to novices, but they are not difficult to fill out once you have gathered proof of your descent and your ancestor's qualification. An initiation fee will cover the time spent in checking your references and verifying your lineage. You should keep copies of your application and proofs, as the society will probably file the records you submit if your lineage is accepted.

A D.A.R. pamphlet, "Is That Lineage Right?", discusses in detail the types of evidence that may be submitted as proof of ancestry, the form in which they should be submitted and guidelines for their evaluation. Prepared as a training manual for those who examine lineage papers, it is equally useful for a genealogist preparing an application for membership in any hereditary society and can be purchased for less than a dollar from the National Society in Washington.

Popular and Gateway Ancestors

Revolutionary War soldiers are but one group of individuals from whom numerous genealogists hope to find and prove descent. Signers of the Declaration of Independence, passengers on the *Mayflower* and lords of Colonial manors are some of the other groups of "popular ancestors," and hereditary organizations exist for the descendents of each (see list, Chap. 29).

Not all of the people who comprised these groups were prominent figures. Most of the *Mayflower* passengers (Illustration 40) were not well known, and many of their descendants continued in a fairly humble way of life. They formed the backbone of early New England society, then set out for Vermont, New Hampshire and Connecticut, moved into upper New York State and gradually worked their way south and west. Today, the network of descendants of *Mayflower* passengers is spread all over the country, and they bear names that represent all races, colors and creeds, because of the great intermingling in the melting pot of America that has taken place since the landing at Plymouth Rock in 1620.

Bing Crosby (Harry Lillis Crosby) has proven his twelve generations of descent from William Brewster and is a member of the Society of Mayflower Descendants, with the National Number of 48,193.

There are also individual historical figures who have become known as popular ancestors. Because of their prominence in early American life, their descendants may qualify for membership in a variety of hereditary organizations.

Isaac Allerton (c. 1586–1658/59) is a popular ancestor who spread his seed from one end of the Colonial coast to the other. A *Mayflower* passenger who was Assistant Governor of the Plymouth Colony, he settled for a time in New Amsterdam and died in New Haven. He also owned land in Virginia, and his son, Isaac Allerton, Jr. (by his second wife, Fear Brewster), left descendants there. Allerton's descendants are eligible for membership in the Society of Mayflower Descendants, the St. Nicholas Society (founded by Washington Irving in 1835 and open to men descended from pre-1785 residents of New York State) and the Society of Colonial Wars.

Augustine Herman, a Bohemian, was born in Prague about 1621 and immigrated to New Amsterdam about 1643 (Illustration 41). His descendants are eligible for the St. Nicholas Society, the

Society of Colonial Wars and the Order of Colonial Lords of Manors in America, because in exchange for drawing the first map of Maryland and Virginia, Lord Baltimore granted him some 30,000 acres in what is now Maryland and Delaware, which included Bohemia Manor in Cecil County, Maryland, where he died in 1686.

Descendants of Theopolus Eaton (1591–1658), first Governor of the New Haven Colony, qualify for membership in the Society of Descendants of Colonial Governors as well as in the Society of Colonial Wars, because of his status as Governor. The descendants of his second wife, Anne Lloyd, who had some royal ancestors, are eligible to be members of the Order of the Crown of Charlemagne.

Anne Lloyd herself is a popular ancestress. A very powerful woman in her time, she was first married to Thomas Yale, who left her a widow, and was the wife of Theopolus Eaton when she arrived in this country in 1637. She was an Anabaptist and refused to go to church—apparently a strong and independent woman, for her father, George Lloyd, had been Bishop of Chester. After Eaton's death, Anne Lloyd took her daughter, Hannah Eaton, and her grandson, Elihu Yale, to London, where she died in 1659. Her grandson, who never returned to this country, amassed a great fortune in England and left money in his will for the founding of Yale College in New England. Anne's daughter Hannah married an Englishman, William Jones, and returned with him to New Haven, and he eventually became Lieutenant Governor of Connecticut.

There are several other American women who are honored as ancestresses. One is Anne Marbury Hutchinson (1591–1643), a courageous and determined woman who founded a settlement in Rhode Island after she was banished from the Massachusetts Bay Colony in 1637 because of her religious beliefs and was later killed by Indians on Long Island. She was a descendant of King Edward I. Pocahontas is another popular ancestress.

Priscilla Mullen wasn't famous in her time, but she was one of the few women who survived the first winter at Plymouth and was made famous by Longfellow in "The Courtship of Miles Standish." Whether there was any truth to Longfellow's tale cannot be determined, but Priscilla did marry John Alden and became the ancestress of thousands of Americans.

While the "popular ancestor" is essentially an American

phenomenon, genealogists in other countries sometimes aspire to prove descent from a royal figure or a national hero. The Irish would like to be descended from Brian Boru or Neil of the Nine Hostages; the Scotch, from Robert the Bruce, John Knox or Annie Laurie; and Russians from Yaraslav. In Spain, one may hope to trace a line to El Cid; in England, to Alfred the Great, William the Conqueror or a Magna Carta signer; in France, to St. Louis or Joan of Arc; and in Germany, to Woden, Charlemagne or Martin Luther.

Certain individuals can be identified not only as popular ancestors but as "gateway ancestors"—like Anne Hutchinson, people through whom one can establish a connection to a royal line in a foreign country. Until the sixteenth century genealogy was concerned almost exclusively with the nobility and royalty. By the time you've traced your family back to the 1500's you need to locate an ancestor with a noble lineage in order to keep going.

The descendants of Clovis, the King of Cologne, an ancestor of Charlemagne, can be traced quite accurately through royal lines. If you want to establish your descent from Charlemagne, your goal is actually a "gateway ancestor" who lived much later. Once you've documented your connection to him, your connection to Charlemagne, and through Charlemagne to Clovis, is automatically established.

In democratic countries such as Great Britain and the United States, where social classes mixed quite freely, there are many gateway ancestors to royal lines among rather humble people. This is much less common in European countries, where the middle class and the nobility rarely mixed. In England, the daughter of a king might marry a nobleman, and their daughters in turn might marry into the gentry, gradually bringing the royal blood down into lower classes more and more removed from the king.

The Neville family, for example, married into the English royal family and then had many children who spread out and married into various classes in succeeding generations. Through the Nevilles you might establish a link to an ancestor who signed the Magna Carta—a document as important to the English as the Declaration of Independence is to Americans—or to a Knight of the Garter.

Long lists of legitimate descendants of Edward I and Edward

III who lived in Shropshire in the seventeenth and eighteenth centuries—many of them minor gentlepeople or townspeople—were published in Volume 5 of the *Shropshire Archaeological Society Publications* in 1881–1882.

Very often, establishing your link to a single gateway ancestor will connect you to a variety of royal or otherwise noteworthy ancestors (Illustration 42). If you can prove descent from William the Conqueror—a popular ancestor in his own right—and his wife, Matilda Flanders, then you're also descended, through her, from both Alfred the Great and Charlemagne.

Numerous American historical figures are gateway ancestors to European royal families. The line of Peter Bulkeley (d. 1658/ 59), a Massachusetts clergyman, goes back to Charlemagne through Edward I. Maria Horsmanden (d. 1699), the wife of Colonel William Byrd of Westover, Charles County, Virginia, was descended from Charlemagne through Edward III.

Other people of royal descent who came to the New World were not so well known or well regarded. Jasper, Richard and Ellen More, who came here on the *Mayflower*, were illegitimate children of Katherine More, a descendant of Edward I, by her lover Jacob Blakeway. They were shipped off to New England by their relatives so that their presence wouldn't remind them of this disgrace, according to documents turned up within the last decade and published in the *New England Historic Genealogical Register* in 1970 (v. 124, pp. 85–87). There are numerous descendants of Richard More around the country.

The bibliography in Chapter 30 identifies numerous popular American ancestors and gateway families and lists published sources of information about their lineages. Like every other step in the genealogical search, tracing your way to these people begins in the present and leads into the past. You will probably become a member of a Colonial or Revolutionary hereditary society before you're ready to join the Order of the Crown of Charlemagne. At every stage you'll be gathering the vital records, deeds, wills and other documents that will serve as proof of your ancestry.

Titles

Titles often perplex Americans, who have seldom come into contact with the system, and the terms "royalty" and "nobility" are often confused. There is only one royal family in most countries, and the royal leader may be designated the emperor, king, prince, duke, count, mikado, emir, shah or sultan. Those who bear a myriad of lesser titles constitute the nobility. In France, *comte* (count) can be a royal title, as in *Comte de Paris*, while in England the equivalent title of earl is seldom royal and, when it is, is a minor title held by a royal duke or prince.

It is often difficult to sort out European titles, as the royal regimes of Austria, France, Germany, Italy and Russia have long since disappeared, and many people have taken advantage of this fact to claim titles that their ancestors never possessed. Books dealing with the national nobility or peerage of countries that had such a system, such as the Gotha series on the various degrees of German nobility, are cited in the bibliographies for research in individual nations.

The Titled Nobility of Europe, written in 1914 by the Marquis de Ruvigny and Raineval (a suspect title), is the best general work on European titles and provides a good overview of the titles of Europe on the eve of World War I, which brought about the downfall of the old regimes.

In the case of England, there is little room for fraudulent claims to titles, as the system has maintained a certain rigidity. *Burke's Peerage* and *Debrett's Peerage*, current volumes, help us to understand the network of titles from top to bottom, and *The Complete Peerage*, first edited by George E. Cockayne, sets the record straight about all titles granted from the earliest period until 1945.

Today, of course, the head of English royalty is Elizabeth II, the Queen of England. Just below her in the line of succession is her son and heir, Charles, Duke of Cornwall and Prince of Wales; followed by her other children, the Royal Princes Andrew and Edward and Princess Anne; and her immediate family—her sister, Princess Margaret, and her children. Elizabeth's cousins, the Royal Dukes of Gloucester and Kent, follow as possible successors to the throne. Her husband, Prince Philip, the Duke of Edinburgh, is a royal duke but is not in the line of royal succession. Two other members of the royal family are Wallis (Warfield), the American-born Duchess of Windsor and widow of the former King Edward VIII, the Duke of Windsor; and the Queen Mother, Queen Elizabeth, widow of George VI, also not in line for the throne. *Burke's Guide to the Royal Family* further clarifies the line of succession.

England's hereditary noble titles, in descending order, are duke, marquess, earl, viscount, baron and baronet. A knighthood cannot be passed to descendants, and today there are many nonhereditary life peers created. The gentry of England—the hereditary untitled landed families—are covered in *Burke's Landed Gentry*, and some of them are knights.

19 Heraldry: The Possible Fruit of a Family Tree

merica today is in the midst of a heraldry craze, with people displaying coats of arms on walls, blazers, bank checks, ashtrays and jewelry, purchased in most cases from unethical heraldic firms. While most of this enthusiasm is innocent enough, it constitutes an unfortunate abuse of heraldry, the use of hereditary family symbols.

Heraldry is properly the end product of the genealogical search. Coats of arms were, and still are, granted by a heraldic body in a kingdom to individuals for the use of that person and his descendants; they were not granted to families or surnames. Not everyone is descended from an armigerous, or arms-bearing, ancestor. Morever, two brothers might have two different coats of arms if each received a grant, so there are often many different coats of arms borne by people of the same surname, and the descendants of a third brother might not be entitled to a coat of arms at all. You can only learn whether you are legitimately entitled to a coat of arms by carefully tracing your lineage, for arms, like property, are passed down from generation to generation within a family, according to strict rules of inheritance.

Heraldry in History

While the use of some sort of family insignia dates to ancient times, coats of arms as we know them originated in England and the Continent in the twelfth century, when fighting men wore metal suits of armor with closed helmets that made knights in full battle dress indistinguishable from one another. To prevent friend from attacking friend, each knight identified himself by painting a colorful pattern on his battle shield. In time these heraldic devices might also be displayed on a man's horse, on a pennant on his lance, or on an embroidered cloth surcoat worn over his armor—hence the term "coat of arms."

As this practice grew more popular it became increasingly likely that two knights might use the same insignia, so records began to be kept concerning the right of a specific individual to a particular heraldic design. Noblemen and knights already employed household officers called heralds and pursuivants, among whose duties was that of introducing their master on public occasions by reciting his family history and military feats. To them fell the additional task of devising and recording coats of arms.

In time the royal heralds of various kingdoms were formed into colleges, beginning with the French heralds in 1407. In England, King Richard III incorporated the Royal Heralds and Pursuivants into the College of Arms in 1484, and similar institutions were subsequently set up in other countries. The chief of the Scottish heralds is the Lord Lyon, whose office was in existence some three hundred years before it was established by Parliament as the sole authority to grant arms in that kingdom in 1672. When mail-clad warriors became a thing of the past, inherited heraldic devices were retained as identifying marks on carriages, jewelry, silver, houses, bookplates and tombstones (Illustration 43).

While the essential elements of heraldry were the same throughout Western Europe, the system governing the inheritance of arms varied from kingdom to kingdom. Under English law, arms were passed down through the male line from a father to his eldest son, while younger sons would be entitled to "differenced" versions of the arms. It was permissible to "quarter" a woman's arms with those of her husband—that is, combine them in a single design—provided she had no brothers and was heiress of the arms.

Between 1528 and 1704 the College of Arms in England conducted a series of "Visitations" to determine what arms were borne and who was entitled to them. The heralds recorded rolls of arms and preserved thousands of pedigrees, many of which exist today in various repositories in Britain and in printed form and which constitute a valuable storehouse of genealogical records. French heralds also conducted Visitations from the fourteenth through the seventeenth centuries, with the most thorough being recorded between 1666 and 1674.

In countries such as England, where a monarchy persists, the use of coats of arms is still carefully regulated. The Heralds of the College of Arms in London still function as officers of the Royal Household, and there are also royal heralds in Sweden and Denmark. In Scotland, anyone who uses arms without the proper sanction is subject to a fine or even to imprisonment. Some form of heraldry also persists in many democratic countries. Ireland and South Africa have state heralds; Australia has published a Roll of Australian Arms; and Canada has a growing heraldic society.

Heraldry has its own language to describe its strictly defined forms and symbols. A diagonal stripe across a shield, for example, is a *bend;* a horizontal stripe, a *fess;* and a vertical stripe, a *pale.* The "tinctures" of heraldry are also described in special terms, such as *or* for gold, *argent* for silver, *gules* for red and *azure* for blue. Heraldic terms are mostly of French origin, as this was the court language of Western Europe in the Middle Ages, and there are heraldic glossaries and dictionaries that explain them.

To "blazon" is to describe arms briefly but precisely in heraldic language, while to "emblazon" is to translate this description into an accurate rendering of the arms. Within the limits of the blazon, the heraldic artist is free to add his own stylistic touches.

The basis of a man's arms is a shield, but the arms of an unmarried woman, unless she is a queen ruling in her own right, are emblazoned on a lozenge or diamond shape, as women did not carry arms into battle.

Heraldry in the United States

In the United States there is no authority to grant arms and no deterrent to usurping the arms of others, except for the regard of people who know something about heraldry. Abuses by heraldic artists are not new and not surprising, as the country has been a democracy for over two hundred years, and the College of Arms lost control of the situation in 1775.

In the Colonial period, with few exceptions, coats of arms were used only by those who had a right to them. After the Revolution, when the sounds of war and the hatred of monarchy began to fade, increasing prosperity brought time for reflection and nostalgia among those who had found a comfortable situation in the new social and political structure. In Maryland, Virginia and the Carolinas, plantation owners imitated the ways of English and European gentry and many families assumed the arms of families with the same name in Europe, without regard for their right to do so.

As the nineteenth century progressed, an interest in genealogy and heraldry became apparent with the publication of large volumes of the histories of New England families. The scholarship of these genealogies was generally excellent back to the immigrant ancestor, and, as noted previously, the subsequent publication of volumes of church and vital records, tombstone inscriptions, census records and other source materials has substantiated their contents to a surprising degree. However, the portions of the books dealing with European ancestry usually leave much to be desired. Many of the authors felt that even if they couldn't establish a link between their family in this country and forebears abroad, it was appropriate to give an account of the most noble family of the same surname and use their coat of arms as the frontispiece of the book. They didn't suggest any actual relationship to the armigerous family, and little did they realize that a hundred years later many of the descendants of families mentioned in the genealogy—perhaps without even reading the text—would be claiming the coat of arms as their own and displaying it on the walls of their homes. This was the beginning of the misappropriation of heraldic devices in the United States on a large scale. Modern genealogical research has revealed that certain of these New England families were armigerous but that the coat of arms to which they were entitled were not those illustrated in their Victorian family histories.

The nineteenth century also saw the birth of genealogical groups—the New England Historic Genealogical Society, formed in 1845, being the oldest. In their publications these societies, at first hesitantly and then sometimes militantly, began to dispel the inaccuracies and misconceptions set forth in undocumented genealogies. In increasingly scholarly articles they began to investigate the actual origins of American immigrants, and it is in the periodical literature of genealogy (Chap. 29) that some of the best work in the field has been done. It is sometimes in these articles that one may discover the identity of an ancestor who actually bore a coat of arms.

Nonetheless, vanity-press publications of such firms as the American Historical Company, active from the early part of the 1920's to the 1960's, continued to work against the proper application of heraldry. The main series issued by this firm—*The Colonial and Revolutionary Families of Pennsylvania, The*

Colonial and Revolutionary Lineages of America and *The National Americana Publication*—are filled with coats of arms, the majority of which are correct in their visual representation but incorrect and inappropriate as far as the right of the particular family to bear arms. In their innocent shenanigans with regard to heraldry, the American Historical Company and others like them were the forerunners of the more unscrupulous heraldic peddlers who began doing business in the 1960's and 1970's.

In the late 1950's the Sanson Institute of Boston began advertising coats of arms in newspapers and magazines, listing family names of various ethnic origins for which they could supply heraldic achievements. While the American Historical Company had attempted to supply a genealogy and coat of arms for a large sum of money, this firm, for a few dollars, would supply a rough picture of the coat of arms, a report on your surname and no genealogy. For larger amounts of money you were invited to purchase the coat of arms in the form of a blazer patch, a framed painting or a wall plaque.

It remained for Halbert's of Bath, Ohio, to computerize American telephone listings in order to make personalized direct-mail solicitations for coats of arms. The one I received began "Dear Mr. Beard, Did you know that the family name of Beard was recorded with a coat of arms in ancient heraldic archives hundreds of years ago?" and concluded by offering to send me an artist's rendering of the arms, along with information about my family name, all in an attractive one-page report "suitable for framing" for just two dollars. (Having done my genealogical research, I knew, of course, that my Beard ancestors were of yeoman stock and had no right to a coat of arms.)

Admittedly, Sanson's, Halbert's and the dozens of other firms like them are not breaking any laws, but what they are doing is in direct contradiction of heraldic traditions and principles. Working with a library of heraldic reference books, they do produce copies of authentic heraldic achievements, usually the earliest recorded arms for a given surname, but they make no attempt to ascertain whether a customer is in any way connected to the family that originally bore the arms.

The chances are infinitesimal that a coat of arms arbitrarily selected from a book on heraldry would have any connection to your ancestors, and even it it did, it is unlikely that you would be a heraldic heir—that is, descended through a male line. In any case, mail-order heraldry firms protect themselves with a disclaimer, in both their offerings and their reports, to the effect that "no genealogical representation is intended or implied."

(Another group of mail-order firms, among them the American Heraldry Foundation of Clearwater, Minnesota, offers customers a selection of motifs representing hobbies, professions, personal characteristics—and, yes, even zodiac symbols—from which they may select four to be combined into a "personal" coat of arms. While it is quite acceptable to create your own arms in this country, the designs offered by these companies are extremely expensive and completely contrary to correct principles of heraldic design.)

I will never forget a woman who stormed into the library a few years ago, covered with jewelry engraved with a coat of arms. She had gone overboard with a ring, earrings, pin and bracelet, all in heavy gold, and she was in a terrible emotional state, as she had just returned from a visit to Italy, where she had learned that the actual coat of arms borne by her family—ironically, they did have one—was completely different from that on her jewelry, which had been engraved by an American heraldic firm. She had little recourse, however, as she should have consulted her Italian relatives or a heraldic researcher in that country before she went to the expense of having her jewelry engraved.

Perhaps the most unfortunate consequence of the explosion in mail-order heraldry is that the information dispensed by these firms has begun to creep into printed genealogies. James D. Rorabaugh, in his book *John R. Rohrbach (Rohrabaugh) 1728–1821: Descendants and Marriage Connections*, included a report from the Sanson Institute with an unprepossessing illustration of a coat of arms, and C. A. Weslager, in his *Notes About the Families of William Lowe and Eliza Perry Lowe of Pittsburgh, Pennsylvania*, presents a coat of arms and report from Halbert's that has little scholarly or artistic merit. Like the nineteenth-century New England genealogists, these authors haven't claimed the coats of arms as their own, but their books are now in libraries, where they will undoubtedly be read by researchers who will accept the implied connection as fact.

I have learned, with a mixture of amazement and dismay, that the business of ready-made heraldry has even spread to kingdoms where there are still heraldic bodies. When I was in Bath, England, a few years ago, I passed a shop right on the square where they were selling coats of arms for various surnames on plaques.

It may be discouraging for a serious genealogist who has not discovered an armigerous ancestor to see a coat of arms displayed on the wall of a neighbor who has done no research at all, but one has to be a bit philosophical about it. It is almost impossible to convey the truth to such people; they purchased the arms because they want to believe that they are entitled to them. But it is they who are losing out, for they have missed the satisfaction of actually tracing their ancestors and relating them to the events that molded our culture. At its best, genealogy is not a path to status but an honest search for true forebears, wherever they ranked on the social ladder.

Any American interested in genealogy and heraldry must be realistic about his ancestors, realizing that most emigrants to this country were laborers, farmers and merchants who were not entitled to coats of arms, although there were a few professional men and a smattering of gentlemen among early Americans, mostly younger sons with no prospects in the Old World. In searching for immigrant ancestors who might lead to descents from Magna Carta signers, barons, kings or other arms-bearing figures, I have often had to disappoint their descendants, for many members of the Colonial gentry were from relatively obscure European families.

Heraldry should not even be a consideration during the early stages of your research, although it might be interesting to note that some people with your surname bore coats of arms. If they lived in a certain part of your ancestor's country or origin, it might be a clue for your research, and you should pursue the history of that locality. But you can't assume you have a right to a coat of arms until you have proven a line of descent from an armigerous ancestor.

If you find that an early immigrant ancestor in your direct male line had a coat of arms, you may want to seek confirmation of those arms from the heraldic body that granted them, if it still exists. Should you turn up a coat of arms that belonged to an ancestor of another surname, it would be entirely appropriate to illustrate this heraldic device in a history of your family, and in your home it would certainly be better to display a coat of arms that has something to do with your family than one that belonged to someone who had the same name but to whom you are not related.

If you find that your ancestors were not armigerous and you still wish to have a coat of arms, it is possible to obtain a grant of arms from an official heraldic institution in a country where a monarchy or structured nobility still exists, provided you can prove descent from a direct male ancestor of your surname who was once a subject of that kingdom. In England, you would apply to the College of Arms (Secretary of the Earl Marshall, College of Arms, Queen Victoria Street, London, EC4V 4BT). It might be best first to consult an English genealogist or an organization such as Achievements, Ltd. (Northgate, Canterbury, Kent, England CT1 1BA) or Debrett Ancestry Research (67 Parchment Street, Winchester, England S023 8AT). Both specialize in heraldic and genealogical research and artwork and have acted as a liaisons with the College of Arms. Having your own representative in England could save you a great deal of time and money. Before you take such a step, however, you must realize that the basic cost of the grant of arms may run between $750 and $1,000 or more. A less expensive solution would be to design your own arms, according to the directions in Jack A. Reynolds' *Heraldry and You.*

Interest in heraldry has led to repeated attempts to set up a college of arms in this country, although it's really not possible to do so in a democracy. The American College of Arms, established in Baltimore in 1966, was one of the more serious of these groups, but it eventually collapsed because it lacked any authority to proclaim itself as a heraldic body. Today there is an American College of Heraldry in New Orleans.

Books on Heraldry

Heraldic bodies that exist today, such as the College of Arms in London, maintain archives of heraldry, but some of the records of the coats of arms granted by former kingdoms, as well as by surviving ones, can be found in libraries. Numerous volumes dealing with heraldry are noted in the national bibliographies in this book, and the heraldic bibliography in Chapter 31 brings together in one place for your convenience general works and sources for different countries.

J. B. Rietstap's *Armorial General*, two volumes of text first published in 1863, is still one of the great standard works on European heraldry. The companion volumes by V. and H. Holland, *General Illustrated Armorial*, illuminate Rietstap's text. These books have been reprinted many times, and if a library could afford to have only one general work on the subject of heraldry, they comprise the best choice.

The much more elaborate compilation of central European heraldry that is placed under the authorship of the seventeenth-century heraldic scholar Johann Siebmacher and known familiarly as "Siebmacher's Wappenbuch" is in the process of being reprinted, but only a large, well-endowed library could afford this extensive set of volumes. The index by Hanns Jäger-Sunstenau, which is a guide as well as an index to surnames included in Siebmacher, is a book that smaller libraries might have in their collections.

For British coats of arms, the basic work is still Burke's *General Armory* of 1884, which has been reprinted many times and has been updated with a supplement by Cecil R. Humphrey-Smith. (An excellent project would be for someone to revise, correct and update the entire work to bring it into focus with this century.)

Papworth's Ordinary of British Armorials and Renesse's *Dictionnaire des Figures Héraldique* are of special interest, because they will help to identify coats of arms when the name of the family is unknown. Antique dealers, art historians, bibliophiles and genealogists should all be aware of these books, which can be useful in establishing the identity of the owner of a piece of jewelry or china, the sitter for a painting or the benefactor of an artist, the private library from which a certain volume came or the ancestor to whom a piece of silver or a seal belonged. Renesse's work, which is in French, reverses the coats of arms illustrated in Rietstap by noting the marks of identification on the arms, and Papworth's does the same for Burke's *General Armory*.

Eugene Zieber's *Heraldry in America*, first issued in 1895 and followed by a second edition in 1909, is still an excellent handbook. It was reprinted by Haskell House in New York in 1969 in 427 pages, exactly the same number as in the 1895 edition, but the new version is half the size of the original and has no color plates. The 1895 edition contained one of the best plates in heraldic work, which showed examples of the tinctures of heraldry and illustrated how they are depicted in black and white renderings by various linear patterns. Reproduced in black and white opposite page 254 in the 1969 edition, this plate is completely meaningless.

The New England Historic Genealogical Society's Committee on Heraldry has investigated claims and published rolls of authentic coats of arms borne by Americans that contain a simple illustration of each heraldic device and a brief biographical description of the person who originally bore it. There are also periodicals that deal extensively with heraldry, among them *The Coat of Arms*, a quarterly published by the Heraldry Society in London.

ab nepos: a great-great-grandson

ab neptis: a great-great-granddaughter

abstract: a summary of the relevant information in a document

A.D.: anno domini—in the year of our lord

Adels: *German.* nobility

administration: the process of settling an estate

administration cum testamento annexo (C.T.A.): administration with will annexed—an administration granted by the proper court when the decedent has left a valid will but failed to name an executor, named an incapable executor or named an executor who refused to act. The estate is settled by a court-appointed administrator.

administration de bonis nom: administration of goods not already disposed of, as when one is appointed to succeed an administrator or executor who has died before completing the settlement of an estate

administrator: a person appointed by a court to settle the estate of a deceased person who has died without leaving a valid will or without appointing a capable executor

alias: otherwise, at another time, formerly; also, in sixteenth-century Europe, used to link the names of a man and wife if she had a good dowry and was the last of her line, thus perpetuating her family name, as Davies *alias* Clarke. In later centuries a hyphen might serve the same purpose.

ancestor: a person from whom one is descended

ancestress: feminine form of ancestor

anno regni: designating a specific year of a monarch's reign, calculated from the date of accession

apprentice: one bound by legal agreement to work for another for a specific period of time, in exchange for instruction in a trade, art or business

A.R.: anno regni

armiger: a person entitled to heraldic arms

armigerous: entitled to heraldic arms

Ashkenazim: Central or Eastern European Jews, generally Yiddish-speaking

assignee: a person to whom some right, privilege or property is transferred by a court

assignor: a person who signs over the title or interest in something to another individual or party

avia: grandmother or ancestress

avus: grandfather or ancestor

band: *German.* volume

banns of marriage: a spoken or published announcement in a church of an intended marriage

barber: in earlier centuries, one who performed the functions of contemporary barbers, as well as some of the functions of physicians, such as bleeding people

bar mitzvah: the ceremony conferring and celebrating the passing into manhood of a thirteen-year-old Jewish male, signifying the assumption of certain moral and religious responsibilities

baron: a feudal tenant holding rights and title directly from a monarch or other feudal superior; a lord or nobleman; a member of the lowest rank of nobility in Great Britain, certain European countries and Japan

baronet: British hereditary title of honor, ranking next beneath baron

B.L.W.: bounty land warrant

bounty land: land given by the government to induce men to enter military service

bounty land warrant: a gift of bounty land due a person or his heirs, entitled by military service

brasier, brazier: a brass worker

bris: the Jewish ceremony of circumcision

canon, canon law: a rule or statute of a church

Cavalier: a supporter of King Charles I of England in his struggles against Parliament; a royalist during the Revolution; a gentleman or knight, from the French *chevalier*

charter chest: in Europe, a receptacle for family papers, deeds and other documents

chattel: an article of movable personal property; in early times, a synonym for slave

chevalier: *French.* nobleman or knight

chirurgeon: surgeon

Churtos: pork-eating Jews

circumcision: a Jewish ceremony in which a male infant is circumcised

citizen: a resident of a town or city, entitled to vote; a person owing loyalty to and entitled by birth or naturalization to the protection of a certain state

clerk: a lay minister of the Anglican Church; a person who keeps the records of a court or legislative body

codicil: a supplement to a will

connubium: marriage

consanguinity: relation by blood; descendance from a common ancestor

consort: a spouse, especially of a monarch

cooper: a barrel maker

cordwainer: a shoemaker

court of common pleas: in some states, a court having general jurisdiction; in early Great Britain, a court that hears civil cases between commoners

C.P.: Common Pleas, Court of

creole: a person of European descent born in the West Indies or Spanish America; a person descended from the original French settlers of the Southern United States, especially Louisiana; a person descended from the Spanish and Portuguese settlers of the Gulf states; a person of Negro descent born in the western hemisphere, distinguished from a Negro brought from Africa, also a "creole Negro"; a person of mixed European and Negro ancestry who speaks a creole dialect

crypt: a room or vault beneath a church

deed: an instrument conveying title to real estate

denization: the act of making a foreigner a citizen

denizen: an adopted or naturalized citizen; a person admitted to residence in a foreign country

descendant: a person who is descended from another

devise: to grant real property by will; the gift of real property by will

diocese: the district or churches under the jurisdiction of a bishop

dowager: a widow having a dower from her deceased husband

dower: the lands and tenements to which a widow has claim after the death of her husband, usually one third in value of all real estate he held during the marriage

draper: a dealer in cloth or clothing

d.s.p.: died *sine prole*—without issue

d.s.p.m.: died without male issue

earl: a British peer ranked above a viscount and below a marquis

elder: senior

entailment: limitation of an inheritance to a specified, unalterable succession of heirs

et ux, et uxor: and wife

executor: the person designated in a will to carry out its provisions

executrix: feminine form of executor

extract: a word-for-word copy of information in a document

fee: an inherited or heritable estate in land; also, in feudal law, an estate held on condition of some service or homage to the lord, a "fief"

fee simple: an absolute inheritance, without limitation to any particular class of heirs

fee tail: an estate of land limited in inheritance to a specified, unalterable succession of heirs

feet of fine: the bottom portion of an indenture or deed, retained by the appropriate record office

fief: a feudal estate held on condition of service to the proprietor

fine: a tax or compensation, such as a fine paid on the renewal of a tenure

f.n.; free Negro

frater: brother

freehold: land held in fee simple, or for life

freeholder: a landowner, entitled to vote and hold office

freeman: a person entitled to the rights of a citizen, specifically the rights to vote and conduct business

Freiherr: *German.* baron

fuller: a person who fulls (increases the weight and bulk of fabric by shrinking and beating or pressing it)

Fürst: *German.* prince

Fürstin: *German.* princess

generous: of noble lineage

genus: ancestry

geschichte: *German.* history

girdler: a person who makes girdles

glebe: land belonging to a parish church or assigned to a minister as part of his salary

goods and chattels: a comprehensive term for all personal property

graf: *German.* earl or count

grant: a gift or conveyance of real property; to transfer real property by deed

grantee: a person to whom a grant is made
grantor: one who makes a grant

heft: *German.* part, as part of a volume
holographic will: a will entirely in the handwriting of the testator
husbandman: a farmer

indenture: an agreement in which two or more parties are bound by reciprocal obligations—it is signed by both; a contract in which a person, as an apprentice, is bound over for service
inquisition post mortem: petition for probate exam
interred: buried
intestate: having made no legal will; a person who has died without leaving a valid will
inv.: inventory
inventory: a list of all goods and valuables in the estate of a deceased person, filed in probate court by an executor or administrator
I.p.m.: *Latin. Inquisitione post mortem*
issue: offspring, progeny

jahr: *German.* year
jahrgang: *German.* annual volume
joiner: carpenter or cabinetmaker

knight: a medieval tenant giving military service to a feudal landholder; a medieval gentleman-soldier; the holder of a nonhereditary honor conferred by a monarch in recognition of personal merit or service to the country
laborer: a person who works for wages rather than for profits
landgrave: a title of rank in early South Carolina, the holder of 48,000 acres of land; in medieval Germany, a court with jurisdiction over a certain territory; the title of certain German princes
land warrant: a negotiable government certificate entitling the holder to receive a designated quantity of public land
leasehold: property held by lease
limner: a painter

maltster: a brewer
manumission: freeing of a slave
maritus: husband
marquis: a nobleman ranking below a duke and above an earl or count
Marrano: Christianized Jew or Moor of medieval Spain converted to avoid persecution
mater: mother
mercer: a dealer in textiles, especially silks
merchant: a person who sells goods for profit
messuage: a dwelling house with adjacent lands and buildings
mestizo: a person of mixed European and Indian ancestry
miles: *German.* knight
moiety: a half
mortality schedules: a special federal census taken in the United States between 1850 and 1900, recording all persons who died during the year prior to the census count
mulatto: a person having one white and one Negro parent
muniments: written and other evidence that supports title to property
muniments room: a room in European manor houses in which muniments and other documents were stored

naturalize: to grant full citizenship to one of foreign birth

necrology: a register of deaths, especially in a church

nepos: grandson

neptis: granddaughter

noble: possessing hereditary rank

notary: a person officially authorized to draw up or attest to contracts, wills, deeds or similar documents, to protest bills of exchange and so on

nuncupative will: an oral will declared by the testator in the presence of witnesses and later reduced to writing by someone other than the testator

nuptial: marriage

obit: died

octaroon: a person having one-eighth Negro ancestry

ordinary: in some states (Georgia and formerly South Carolina and Texas), a probate judge

parson: a clergyman

pater: father

P.C.C.: the Prerogative Court of Canterbury—the court in which all the wills of southern England were probated from the fourteenth century unitl 1858

P.C.Y.: the Prerogative Court of York—the court in which all the wills of northern England were probated from the fourteenth century until 1858

personality: personal property, goods and chattels

per stirpes: a method of dividing an estate so that children act as a group, rather than individually, taking only the share to which their deceased ancestor would have been entitled had he been living

poll: a register of individuals for the purpose of taxation

posthumous: born after the father's death

primogeniture: the right of inheritance by the eldest son, to the exclusion of daughters and younger sons

progeny: children or descendants

prothonotary: a chief notary or clerk; in some states, a registrar or chief clerk of a court

quadroon: a person having one-quarter Negro ancestry

quit claim deed: a deed conveying the interest of the grantor at the time it is delivered

quit rent: a rent of land so called anciently because the tenants thereby went free and quit of other service to the lord

real property, realty: relating to lands, as distinguished from personalty

rector: a clergyman charged with managerial as well as spiritual duties

regnal years: see anno regni

revista: *Spanish.* magazine

saddler: a person who makes, repairs or sells saddles

salter: a person who makes or sells salt; a person who treats meat, fish or other foods with salt

sawyer: one who saws wood

Sc: Schomburg Center for Research in Black Culture

schedule: a formal list of items in tabular form, as a census schedule

scrivener: a clerk or notary; before general literacy, a professional copyist who wrote wills and similar documents

seisen, seizin: legal possession of land; the act of taking such possession; property thus held

Sephardim: Spanish or Portuguese Jews and their descendants

sep., sepulchered, sepultured: buried

sepulture: burial

sine prole: without issue

skinner: a person who dresses or sells animal skins; in the western United States, a mule driver

sorar: sister

spouse: husband or wife

spurrier: one who makes spurs

S.S.: *Latin—supra scriptum—*as written above; that is to say; also, a form of greeting used to open documents

surety: a guarantee or security; a person who makes himself liable for another's debts or obligations, should that person default

surgeon: in earlier times, one who performed the functions of a modern barber, as well as certain medical functions such as bleeding people

surrogate: in some states (New York and New Jersey), a judicial officer presiding over probate matters

tafel: *German.* plate or illustration

tallow chandler: a wax or candle merchant

tanner: a person who tans hides

témoin: *French.* a witness

tenements: anything held by occupancy; houses and other buildings

tertius: a third person; third generation

testament: a will—a formal instrument disposing of property, intended to take effect at the death of the testator

testate: leaving a valid will at death; a person who leaves a valid will

testator: a person who dies leaving a valid will

testatrix: feminine form of testator

tome: *French.* volume

transported: deported or banished, often from England to her colonies

tutor: In Scotland and France (and therefore Louisiana) a guardian; found in documents

union list: a bibliography containing information about the libraries and institutions where listed references can be found

ux, uxor: wife

vicar: a clergyman

victualer: a grocer

vidua: widow

vintner: a wine merchant

virgin, virgo: in bonds or licenses of England, an unmarried woman

viscount: a peer ranking below an earl and above a baron

visitations: periodic travels by the Heralds of the British College of Arms into counties to inspect pedigrees and verify individual claims to coats of arms (Chap. 18)

viz't: namely, to wit, that is to say

wappen: *German.* shield

warranty deed: a deed conveying and continuing the usual convenants of seisen and against incumbrances on the title

wheeler: a wheel maker

writ: writing issuing from a court or officer of law

yeoman: an independent farmer; especially a member of a former class of small free-holding farmers in England

The following abbreviations and symbols are frequently encountered in printed pedigrees, charts and old records.

abt.	about
ae.	age, aged
aft.	after
als.	alias
ante	before
b.	born
bap.	baptized
bd.	buried
bef.	before
bet.	between
biog.	biography
bpl	birthplace
bpt.	baptized
bro.	brother
B.T.	Bishop's Transcripts
bur.	buried
c., ca.	circa, about
cem.	cemetery
cens.	census
cent.	century
cer., cert.	certificate
chn.	child(ren)
chr.	christened
cir.	circa, about
co.	county
coh.	co-heir, co-heiress
con.	country
csn.	cousin
d.; dd	died
d & coh	daughter and co-heir
dau.; dau^r	daughter
dec.; dec^d	deceased
desc.	descendant
div.	divorced
do	ditto, the same
d/o	daughter of
dpl	deathplace
d.s.p.	(decessit sine prole) died without issue

d.s.p.m.	(decessit sine prole mascula) died without male issue
dum; d. unm.	died unmarried
d.v.p.	died during father's lifetime
F.	father
fam.	family
fb	family Bible
F-in-l	father-in-law
filia	daughter
filius	son
fl.	(floruit) he/she flourished
g.	great
gent.	gentleman, gentlewoman
gf.	grandfather
gff.	great-grandfather
gm.	grandmother
ggm.	great-grandmother
gp.	grandparents
h.	husband; also heir, heiress
ibid.	the same
inf.	infancy
info.	information
int.	interred; interested
Jr.	Junior
kt.	knight
li.; liv.	lived, living
M.	mother
m.; md.	married
m/1	married first
m/2	married second
mat.	maternal
m.i.	monumental inscription
M-in-l	mother-in-law
mvd.	moved
nr.	near
ob., obit.	died
o.s.p.; ob.s.p.	died without issue
p.; pp.	page(s)
pat.	paternal
par., psh	parish
prob.	probably

QV.	which see
rec.	record
relecta	widow
relectus	widower
res.	resided
ret.	retired
s.	son
s & h	son and heir
sen.	senior
sis.	sister
s/o	son of
sol.	soldier
s.p.	(sine prole) without issue
s.p.l.	(sine prole legitima) without legitimate issue
s.p.m.	(sine prole mascula) without male issue
s.p.s.	(sine prole superstite) without survivor
Sr.	Senior
unc.	uncle
ux; uxor	wife
w.	wife
wid.	widow
w/o	wife of
vide	see
v.m.	(vita matris) during mother's life
v.p.	(vita patris) during father's life
w.d.	will dated
w.p.	will proved
yeo	yeoman
*	born
(*)	born illegitimate
X; ;	baptized or christened
o	betrothed
∞ ; =	married
o/o	divorced
o-o	common law marriage
↑	issue
+	lineage continued (In American genealogies)
++; (+)	no further issue
+; /	died (In European genealogies)
▢	burial
▽	cremation

The abbreviations listed below are used in bibliographical entries for frequently cited terms, sources and place names. Abbreviations for states are those used by the United States Postal Service.

Because, as noted in the section on libraries, the New York Public Library has one of the most extensive and accessible genealogical collections in the world, I have included the NYPL call number or classification mark in bibliographical entries whenever possible; it is identified by the prefix NN.

If you can't find volumes noted in this book in your local library or in some larger library in your state through interlibrary loan, you may be able to obtain photocopies of pertinent pages of items that interest you by mail from the NYPL, depending on the copyright laws and the condition of the books involved. Details and fees are discussed in Chapter 6.

AAS—American Antiquarian Society

AASP—*American Antiquarian Society Proceedings*

AH—*Anelecta Hibernica*

AIS—Accelerated Indexing System

AJHSQ—*American Jewish Historical Society Quarterly*

ALA—American Library Association

alpha—alphabetical

AME—American Methodist Episcopal

APS—American Philosophical Society

assoc.—association

Beds.—Bedfordshire (England)

Berks.—Berkshire (England)

bib.—bibliography

Bucks.— Buckinghamshire (England)

Cambs.—Cambridgeshire (England)

CDA—Colonial Dames of America

CDS—Coutant de Saisseville, Guy. *Les Maisons Impériales et Royales D'Europe.* Paris, Editions du Palais Royal, 1966. 587 p.

c.—circa, about

c of a—coat of arms

col.—column

CP—*Complete Peerage*, by G. E. Cokayne

CWAAST—*Cumberland and Westmoreland Antiquarian and Archaelogical Society Transactions*

DAB—*Dictionary of American Biography*

DAC—Daughters of the American Colonists

DAR—National Society, Daughters of the American Revolution

DARM—Daughters of the American Revolution Magazine

DC—David and Charles

DCHS—Dutchess County Historical Society (New York)

DNB—*Dictionary of National Biography*

DSGRM—Detroit Society for Genealogical Research Magazine

ed.—edited, edition

FCAGR—*French Canadian Acadian Genealogical Review*

f, ff—following (pages)

gen.—genealogy, genealogical

GGSQ—*Georgia Genealogical Society Quarterly*

GH—*Genealogical Helper*

GHF—*Genealogisches Handbuch der Fürstlichen Häuser*

Gloucs.—Gloucestershire (England)

GM—*Genealogists' Magazine*

GPC—Genealogical Publishing Company

Hants.—Hampshire (England)

Herefs.—Herefordshire (England)

Herts.—Hertfordshire (England)

hist.—history, historical

HMSO—Her Majesty's Stationery Office

Hunts.—Co. Huntingdon (England)

IF—*Irish Families*, by Edward MacLysaght

inst.—institute

JNH—*Journal of Negro History*

JHSE—Jewish Historical Society of England

JPS—Jewish Publication Society

Lancs.—Lancashire (England)

LC—Library of Congress

LDS—Church of Jesus Christ of Latter-day Saints (Mormons)

Leics.—Leicestershire (England)

Lincs.—Lincolnshire (England)

LHQ—Louisiana Historical Quarterly

LSU—Louisiana State University

MGH—*Miscellanea Genealogica et Heraldica*

MHM—*Maryland Historical Magazine*

MI—*Monumental Inscription*

MIF—*More Irish Families*, by Edward MacLysaght

MQ—*Mayflower Quarterly*

NARS—National Archives and Record Service

NCGSJ—North Carolina Genealogical Society Journal

n.d.—no date

NEHGR— *New England Historical and Genealogical Register*

NGSQ—*National Genealogical Society Quarterly*

NGSSP—*National Genealogical Society Special Publication*

NHCHS Journal—New Haven Colony Historical Society Journal

NIPR—*National Index to Parish Registers* (sponsored by the Society of Genealogists, London)

NN—New York Public Library classification mark

Northants.—Northamptonshire (England)

Notts.—Nottinghamshire (England)

n.p.—no place

NPP—*Northamptonshire Past and Present*

n.s.—new series

NSCDA—National Societies of Colonial Dames

NYGBR—*New York Genealogical and Biographical Register*

NYHS—New York Historical Society

NYPL—New York Public Library

NYT—*New York Times*

OGS—Ontario Genealogical society

p.—page, pages
P—press
pbk—paperback
PGM—*Pennsylvania Genealogical Magazine*
ports.—portraits
Pub.—Publisher, publication
p.v.—pamphlet volume

quart.—quarterly

rep.—reprint, reprinted
RKP—Routledge and Kegan Paul

SAR—Society of the Sons of the American Revolution
SG—Scottish Genealogist
SGSB—Saskatchewan Genealogical Society Bulletin
SIF—*Supplement to Irish Families*, by Edward MacLysaght
soc.—society
SR—Society of the Sons of the Revolution

Staffs.—Staffordshire (England)
sup.—supplement

TAG—*The American Genealogist*
t of c—table of contents
trans—transactions

U.—University
U.S.W.P.A.—United States Works Progress Administration
UDC—United Daughters of the Confederacy

v.—volume
VG—*Virginia Genealogist*
VM—*Virginia Magazine of History and Biography*

Wars.—Warwickshire (England)
Westm.—Westmorelandshire (England)
Wilts.—Wiltshire (England)
WMCQ—*William and Mary College Quarterly*
Worcs.—Worcestershire (England)

Part Two

Books to Help You Search

22   Family Records

General

Carpenter, Ralph E.
The Arts and Crafts of Newport, 1640–1820.
Newport, Preservation Soc. of Newport, 1954. 216 p.
NN MAWC (Newport)

Crosby, Everett V.
Books and Baskets, Signs and Silver of Old-Time Nantucket.
Nantucket, 1940. 72 p.
NN IQH (Nantucket)

Ormsbee, Thomas H.
Know Your Heirlooms.
New York, McBraide, 1957. 128 p.
NN MAVC

DIARIES

Mathews, William.
American Diaries.
Boston, J.S. Canner, 1959. 383 p., index.
NN *RB-AGZ

Matthews, William.
American Diaries in Manuscript 1580–1954; A Descriptive Bibliography.
Athens, GA, U. of GA, 1974. 176 p., index.
NN *RS-AGZ 75-6856

PORTRAITS, PHOTOGRAPHS, BRASSES, SEPULCHRAL MONUMENTS

General

Adair, Virginia.
Eighteenth Century Pastel Portraits.

London, 1971. 203 p.
NN MET+ 73-1333

Adams, C. Kingsley.
Portraiture Problems and Genealogy.
(IN: *GM, London, 1964. v. 14, p. 382–388*)
NN ARCA

A.L.A. Portrait Index.
New York, Burt Franklin, 1967 (orig. 1906). 3 v. alpha.
NN *R- Room 313

Gernsheim, Helmut and Allison.
The History of Photography.
New York, McGraw-Hill, 1969.
NN *R-MFC 75-641

Hickman, Peggy.
Silhouettes, A Living Form of Art.
Newton
David & Charles, 1975. 96 p.
NN 3-MBT 77–399

Johnson, Peter.
What Are You Doing with That Photograph.
(IN: *New Zealand Genealogist, Auckland, 1975. v. 6, p. 246–*)
NN APW

Leach, Terence R.
Recording Family Portraits.
(IN: *The Amateur Historian, London, 1964. v. 6, p. 74–78*)
NN CA

Welling, William B.
Photography in America: The Formative Years, 1839–1900.

231

New York, Crowell, 1977. c. 517 p., 400 illus. (Includes the first daguerreotype by Marshall Finley taken in 1842)

United States

Appleton, Marion B.
Index of Pacific Northwest Portraits.
Seattle, WA, 1972. 210 p.
NN IX 73-843

Bolton, Charles F.
The Founders Portraits of Persons Born Abroad Who Came to the Colonies Before the Year 1701.
Baltimore, MD, GPC, 1976 (orig. 1919–1926). 3 v. in 2.
NN JFD 76-563

Bolton, Theodore.
Early American Portrait Painters in Miniature.
New York, F.F. Sherman, 1921.
NN MCW

Butler, Joseph T.
Family Collections at Van Cortlandt Manor.
Tarrytown, NY, Sleepy Hollow Restorations, c. 1967. 127 p.
(Portraits, furniture, silver, papers, etc., all tied together; excellent illustrations, family tree p. 20)
NN IRM (Croton-on-Hudson)

Carrick, Alice Van Leer.
Shades of Your Ancestors: American Profiles and Profilists.
Boston, MA, Little, Brown, 1928. 205 p.
(Covers the major American silhouettists)
NN MBC

Detroit Institute of Arts.
Portraits of Eight Generations of the Pitts Family.
Detroit, MI, 1969. 59 p.
NN APV (Pitts) 75-393

Dictionary of American Portraits, 4045 Pictures from Earliest Times to the Beginning of the Twentieth Century.
New York, Dover Press, 1967. 756 p., index.
NN *R American History

Essex Institute. Salem MA.
Catalogue of Portraits at Essex Institute ... Covering Three Centuries.
Salem, MA, 1936. 306 p.
NN MCW

Gibbs, George.
The Gibbs Family of Rhode Island and Some Related Families (Channing, Wolcott, Hosmer)
New York, the author, 1933. 193 p., index.
(Many family portraits, handsome layout)
NN APV (Gibbs)

Hoover, Gladys W.
The Elegant Royalls of Colonial New England.
New York, Vantage Press, 1974. 115 p., t of c, no index.
(Superb color plates of portraits of the family of Isaac Royall, father-in-law of Sir William Pepperell, by Feke and Copley, etc.)
NN APV (Royall) 76-926

Lee, Cuthbert.
Early American Portrait Painters.
New Haven, CT, Yale U. Press, 1929. 350 p.
NN MCW

Lee, Cuthbert.
Portrait Register.
Ashville, NC, Biltmore Press, 1968.
  v. 1 (725 p.)
NN MBT

Little, Nina Fletcher.
Paintings by New England Prov-
  incial Artists, 1775–1800.
(IN: *Antiques, New York, 1976. v.
  CX, p. 994–1005*)
NN MAA +

Luckey, Lura C.
Family Portraits in the Museum of
  Fine Arts, Boston.
(IN: *Antiques, New York, 1976. v.
  CX, p. 1006–1110*)
(Berkeley, Royall, Winslow, Cop-
  ley, Greenwood, Hope, Atwood
  and Hollingsworth family
  groups)
NN MAA +

National Society of Colonial
  Dames, Alabama.
Alabama Portraits Prior to 1870.
Mobile, AL, c. 1969. 417 p.
NN JFF 74-49

National Society of Colonial Dames
  of America, Delaware.
Portraits in Delaware, 1700–1850:
  A Checklist.
Wilmington, DE, 1951. 176 p.
NN MCW

NSCDA, North Carolina.
The North Carolina Portrait In-
  dex, 1700–1860.
Chapel Hill, NC, U. of NC Press,
  1963. 272 p.
NN F-10 8438

NSCDA, Tennessee.
Portraits in Tennessee Painted
  Before 1866; Preliminary
  Checklist.

Nashville, TN, 1964. 147 p.
NN D-19 5683

NYHS.
Catalogue of American Portraits
  in the New York Historical
  Society.
New York, 1974. 2 v.
NN MAVY (New York) 75-263

Oliver, Andrew.
Connecticut Portraits at the Conn.
  Hist. Soc.
(IN: *Antiques, New York, 1973. v.
  CIV, p. 418–435*)
NN MAA +

Prown, Jules D.
John Singleton Copley.
Cambridge, MA, Harvard U. Press,
  1966. 2 v.
(Genealogical charts of sitters)
NN MCX

U.S.W.P.A. N.J.
American Portrait Inventory:
  1440 Early American Portrait
  Artists (1663–1860) ...
Newark, NJ, Hist. Record Survey,
  1940. 305 p.
NN MCW

Vernay, Arthur S.
The Collection of American Silhou-
  ette Portraits Cut by August
  Edouart.
New York, Van Benthuysen, 1913.
  183 p.
NN MBC

Weekley, Carolyn T.
Artists Working in the South
  1750–1820.
(IN: *Antiques, New York, 1976. v.
  CX, p. 1046–1055*)
NN MAA +

Australia, New Zealand and Pacific

Nan Kivell, Rex de Charembac.
Portraits of the Famous and Infamous: Australia, New Zealand and the Pacific, 1492–1970.
London, R. Nan Kivell and S. Spence, 1974. 332 p.
(Catalogue of portraits of the R. Nan Kivell Collection of Australiana now in the National Library, Canberra)

Belgium

Bois de Ryckholt, Philippe du.
Nos Beaux Portraits de Famille-Les Geelhand.
(IN: *Le Parchemin, Brussels, 1973. v. 20, p. 321–323*)
(A series in this publication)
NN APA

Mauquoy-Hendrikx, Marie.
Portraits Graves Belges.
Brussels, Office de Publicité, 1960. 62 p.
(Plates pp. 33–62)
NN K-10 2392 no. 3

Europe

Aubert, Joachim.
Handbuch der Grastatten Beruhmter Deutscher, Osterreicher und Schweizer.
Munich, 1973. 201, 8 p.
NN JFC 75-1408

France

Du Pasquier, Jacqueline.
Pierre-Edouard Dagoty 1775-1871 et la Miniature Bordelaise au XIXe Siècle.
Chartres, 1974. 223 p.
NN MCO D 127.D9

Horsin-Deon, Léon.
Essai sur les Portraitistes Français de la Renaissance Contenant un Inventoire Raisonne de tous les Portraits du XVIe Siècle des Musées de Versailles et du Louvre.
Paris, P. Larousse, 1888. 212 p.
NN 3-MCN

Great Britain

Burgess, Frederick B.
English Churchyard Memorials.
London, Lutterworth Press, 1963. 325 p.
NN MRIF

Bushy, Richard J.
A Companion Guide to Brasses and Brass Rubbings.
London, Pelham Books, 1973. 264 p.
NN ARC 74-481

Callam, G. Marion Norwood.
The Norwoods.
Bushey Heath, Herts, A.E. Callum, 1963–65. 2 v.
(Brasses)
NN ARZ (Norwood)

Franklyn, Julian.
Brasses . . .
London, Arco Pub., 1964. 156 p.
NN MRIL

Gough, Richard.
Sepulchral Monuments in Great Britain . . .
London, T. Payne, 1786–96. 2 v. in 3.
NN 3-MRIF + + +

Haines, Herbert.
A Manual of Monumental Brasses . . . a List of Those Remaining in

the British Isles with Two
Hundred Illustrations.
Oxford, Parker, 1861. 2 v.
NN 3-MRIL

Jackson, Emily.
Catalogue of 5,200 Named and
Dated English Silhouette Por-
traits by August Edouart,
1789–1861.
London, Walbrook, 1911. 56 p.
NN*ZM-41 film

Lockwood, John
The Wortham Worthies.
(IN: *East Anglian Magazine, Ipswich, 1976. v. 35, p. 234–237*)
(This article has nine of the 100
sketches by the Rev. Richard
Cobbold, 1797–1888, of the ordinary people of Wortham, Suffolk,
with which he illustrated a
parish poorbook.)
NN CO (East Anglia)

National Portrait Gallery, London.
Catalogue 1856–1947...
London, 1949. 320 p.
... Sup. 1948–1953.
London, 1953. 30 p.
NN MAVY (London)

National Portrait Gallery, London.
Catalogue of Seventeenth Century
Portraits, 1625–1714. comp. by
David Piper.
Cambridge, U. Press, 1963. 409 p.
NN MAVY (London)

National Portrait Gallery, London.
Tudor and Jacobean Portraits.
comp. by Roy Strong.
London, HMSO, 1969. 2 v.
NN MAVY (London)

Ormond, Richard.
Early Victorian Portraits (Catalogue).

London, 1973. 2 v.
NN MAVY (London) 75-420

Strong, Roy C.
The English Icon; Elizabeth and
Jacobean Portraiture.
London, Paul Mellon Foundation
for British Art, 1969. 388 p.
(Studies in British Art)
NN MCT +

Germany

Boehn, Max von.
Miniaturen and Silhouetten ...
Munich, F. Bruckmann, 1919. 207
p.
NN 3-MBO

Rudenhausen, Germany. Schloss.
Die Portrats im Schloss Rudenhau-
sen (Katalog von).
Wurburg, Freunde Main-Frank-
ischer, 1966. 164 p.
NN ELS

Wilckens, Hans J. von.
Portraitbilder im den Leichen-
preigten des 17–18, Jahrun-
derts.
Hildesheim, 1967. 91 p.
NN JFE 73-2830

India

Archer, William C.
Paintings of the Sikhs. London,
HMSO, 1960.
London, HMSO, 1960. 284 p.
(Victoria and Albert Museum
Monograph no. 34)
NN MAF

Ireland

National Portrait Gallery, Dublin.
Irish Portraits, 1660–1860. comp.

by Ann Crookshank and the Knight of Glin.
London, Paul Mellon Foundation, 1969. 106 p.
NN MCT 74-1472

Potterton, Homan.
Irish Church Monuments, 1570–1880.
Belfast, 1975. 98 p.
NN 3-MGI 76-1308

Netherlands

Feith, P.R.
Dreihonderd Jaar Geschilderde Familie Portretten Uitgegeven door Familie-Vereniging Feith.
n.p., 1973. 169 p.
(A family genealogy in portraits)
NN AVDI (Feith) 75-106

Russia

Chubinashvili, Nikolai G.
Khandisi.
Tbilsi, 1972. 122, 5 p. 95 plates.
(Georgian sepulchral monuments)
NN*QDZ + 74-5969

Sideau, F.G.
La Cour de l'Impératrice Catharine II ... Cent Quatre-Vingt Neuf Silhouettes.
St. Petersberg, 1899. 2 v.
NN *QDZ

Spain

Spain. Junta de Iconografia Nacional.
Iconografía Española.
Madrid, 1966–
NN MAA 73-2833

Switzerland

Perrchon, Henri.
Portraits et Silhouettes du Passe Vaudois.
Lausanne, 1969. 239 p.
NN JFB 71-93

Turkey

Inan, Jale.
Antalya Bolgesi Roma Devri Portreleri.
Ankara, 1965. 94p.
(Portraits of the Province of Antalya, Turkey)
NN 3MGH + 73-1036

Istanbul Topkapi Sarayi Muzes.
Portraits of the Sultans.
Istanbul, 1967. 13 p.
NN MAVZ + (Istanbul) 75-2336

JEWELRY, SILVER, CLOCKS

Belshaw, C.S.
Changes in Heirloom Jewelry in the Central Solomons.
(IN: *Oceana, Sydney, March 1950. p. 169–184*)
NN QPH

Bohan, Peter, and Philip Hammerslough.
Early Connecticut Silver, 1700–1840.
Middletown, CT, Wesleyan U. Press, 1970. 288 p.
NN-MNO

Boston Museum of Fine Arts.
American Silver 1655–1825.
Boston, 1972. 2 v.
NN MNO 73-728

Buhler, Kathryn C.
American Silver: Garvan and
Other Collections in the Yale
University Art Gallery.
New Haven, CT, 1970. 2 v.
NN MNO 72-400

Carlisle, Lilian B.
Vermont Clock and Watchmakers,
Silversmiths and Jewelers.
Burlington, VT, 1970. 313 p.
NN MOF 71-241

Cutten, George Barton.
Silversmiths of North Carolina
1696–1850.
Raleigh, NC, Division of Archives
and History, 1973. 140 p.
NN 3-MNO 74-2224

Cutten, George Barton.
Silversmiths of Virginia, Together
with Watchmakers and Jewelers, 1694–1850.
Richmond, VA, Dietz Press, 1952.
259 p.
NN MNO

Cutten, George Barton.
The Silversmiths, Watchmakers
and Jewelers of the State of New
York Outside New York City.
Hamilton, NY, 1939. 47 p.
NN MNO

Davis, Edward M.
Virginia Families and Their Silver.
(IN: *American Collector, New
York, April 1941. p. 10–11, 20*)
NN MAA +

Flower, Margaret C. C.
Victorian Jewelry.
New York, Duell,Sloan and Pearce,
1951. 271 p.
NN MNR

Harrington, Frank L.
Massachusetts Silver in the Frank
L. and Louise C. Harrington
Collection.
Worcester, MS, 1965. 121 p.
NN MNO

Harrington, Jessie.
Silversmiths of Delaware 1700–
1850.
Wilmington, NSCDA Del., 1939. 132
p.
NN MNO

Hiatt, Noble W.
The Silversmiths of Kentucky To-
gether with Watchmakers and
Jewelers, 1785–1850.
Louisville, KY, Standard, 1954. 135
p.

Hirshorn, A. S.
Mourning Fans.
(IN: *Antiques, New York., 1973. v.
103, p. 801–804*)
NN MAA +

Martin, Mary.
Glooms and "Hair-looms."
(IN: *House and Garden, Green-
wich, 1928. v. 54, p. 67–71, 134,
138*)
NN MSA +

Morgan John Hill.
Memento Mori: Mourning Rings,
Memorial Miniatures and Hair
Devices
(IN: *Antiques, Concord, 1936. v. 17,
p. 226–230*)
NN MAA +

NSCDA, Pennsylvania
... Three Centuries of Historic
Silver
Philadelphia, the Society, 1938. 191
p.
NN MNO

Museum of the City of New York.
Silver by New York Makers Late
   17th Century to 1900. comp. by
   V. Isabelle Miller.
New York., 1937. 71 p.
NN MNO

Pleasants, Jacob Hall.
Maryland Silversmiths 1715–1830.
Baltimore, Lord Baltimore Press,
   1930. 324 p.
NN MNO +

Postnikova-Loseva, M. M.
Russkoe Chernevoe Iskusstvo.
Moscow, 1972. 143 p.
(Russian silver)
NN *QDZ+ 73-3142

Smith, Helen Burr.
Early American Silversmiths.
New York., 1941–45. 2 v.
NN MNO

Steingraber, Erich.
Antique Jewelry: Its History in
   Europe from 1800 to 1900.
London, Thames and Hudson,
   1957. 191 p.
(Translated from German)
NN MNR

Summersgill, Revah, and Jean P.
   Allen.
Mourning Miniatures.
(IN: *Hobbies, Chicago, July 1939. v.
   44 p. 42*)
NN MAA

Wenham, Edward.
Domestic Silver of Great Britain
   and Ireland.
New York, Oxford U. Press, 1931.
   186 p.
NN 3-MNO

Wilkinson, Wynard R. T.
Indian Colonial Silver.
London, 1973. 171 p.
NN MNO + 74-1714.

Williams, Carl M.
Silversmiths of New Jersey
   1700–1825 with Some Notice of
   Clockmakers.
Philadelphia, G. S. Mac Manus,
   1949. 164 p.
NN MNO

QUILTS, EMBROIDERIES

Bacon, Lenice I.
American Patchwork Quilts.
New York., Morrow, 1973. 190 p.
NN MOT 74-76

Colonial Coverlet Guide of Amer-
   ica.
Heirlooms from Old Looms.
Chicago, R. R. Donnelley, 1940. 246
   p.
NN 3-MON

Finley, Ruth E.
Old Patchwork Quilts and the
   Women Who Made Them.
Boston, C. T. Branford, 1929 (re-
   print 1970). 202 p.
NN MOT

Holstein, Jonathan.
The Pieced Quilt, an American
   Design Tradition.
Greenwich, CT, N.Y. Graphic Soc.,
   1973. 187, 5 p.
NN MOT 74-630

Mainardi, Patricia and others.
Quilt articles.
(IN: *Ms., New York, 1973. v. II, no.
   6, p. 58–63, 86*)
(With a brief bibliography of addi-

tional references by Linda H. Adams)
NN

Orlofsky, Patsy and Myron.
Quilts in America.
New York., McGraw-Hill, 1974. 368 p.
NN MOT 75-68

Ring, Betty.
Collecting American Samplers Today.
(IN: *Antiques, New York., June 1972. v. CI, no. 6, p. 999, 1012–1018*)
NN MAA +

PROFESSIONS

Arlott, John.
Island Camera, The Isles of Scilly in the Photography of the Gibson Family ...
Newton Abbot, DC, 1972. 110 p., gen. table, ports.
NN ARZ (Gibson) 76-2788

Atherton, Ralph S.
Beyond the Workhouse: An Edwardian Mystery.
(IN: *GM, London, 1973–1974. v. 17, p. 261–265, 604–610*)
(Records of various types for people who were often unemployed)
NN ARCA

Austin, John Osborne.
American Authors' Ancestry.
Providence, E. L. Freeman, 1915. 107 p., index.
(With blank charts to add your favorite authors)
NN APK

Burchall, Michael J.
Huggetts on Sunday—A Clerical Family.
(IN: *Sussex Family Historian, Brighton, Sussex, 1976. v. 2, no. 6, p. 186–191*)

Catlow, Richard.
The Pendle Witches.
Nelson, Hendon Pub. Co., 1976. 44 p., gen. table, no index.

Chapuis, Alfred.
... Le Grand Frédéric et Ses Horlogers; une Emigration d'Horlogers suisses au XVIIIe Siècle ...
Lausanne, Journal Suisse d' Horlogerie, 1938. 95 p.
(Swiss clockmakers in Germany)
NN OMY+

Coldham, James D.
A Northamptonshire Cricket Song.
(IN: *NPP, Delapre Abbey, 1976. v. 5, p. 363–365*)
(With notes on some players, including eight Kingston brothers who played cricket 1874–1909)
NN CO (Northamptonshire)

Duncan, Louis C.
Medical Men in the American Revolution 1775–1783.
New York., Augustus M. Kelley, 1970 (orig. 1931). no index or t of c; list of illus.
(Includes an alphabetical list of "medical men" in the back)
NN IG

Ericson, Carolyn R.
Fires and Firemen of Nacogdoches, Texas, A History of the Fire Department with a Roster of the Men ... 1840 to 1974.
Nacogdoches, C. R. Ericson, c. 1976. 241 p., index.

NN ITRM (Nacogdoches, TX)
76-2367

Fales, Martha Gandy.
Joseph Richardson and Family,
    Philadelphia Silversmiths.
Middletown, CT, Wesleyan U.
    Press, 1974. 340 p.
NN MNO 75-1113

Farrie, Geoffrey.
The Sugar Refining Families of
    Great Britain.
London, Tate and Tate, 1951. 35
    pp.
(Includes the Tate, Martineau,
    MacFie, Farrie and other
    families.)
NN ARF

ffolliott, Rosemary.
The Swift Rise and Slow Decline of
    Frederick Buck.
(IN: *Irish Ancestor, Dundalk, 1975.*
    v. 7, p. 15–24) Irish artist
NN ARCA 72-1448

Fothergill, Gerald.
A List of Emigrant Ministers to
    America, 1690–1811. Baltimore,
    GPC, 1965. (orig. 1904) 65 p.,
    alpha.
NN APK

Gaythorpe, Harper.
Two "Old Masters": The Crankes
    of Urswick.
(IN: *CWAAST, 1906. n.s. v. 6, p.*
    128–142)
NN CO (Cumberland)

Gibson, Jeremy S.W.
Trouble Over Sheep Penns. (IN:
    Cake and Cockhorse. Banbury,
    Eng. 1977. v. 7, p. 35–48) (Excel-
    lent depositions from sheep
farmers, etc., in a chancery
    case.)
NN CO (Banbury)

Godfrey, Lieut. Commander M.
British Military Records as
    Sources of Biography and
    Genealogy.
(IN: *GM, London, 1969. v. 16, p. 1–5*)
NN ARCA

Jensen, Michael C.
The Financiers: The World of the
    Great Wall Street Investment
    Banking Houses.
New York., Weybright and Talley,
    1976.
NN

Langdon, John E.
Canadian Silversmiths and Their
    Marks 1667–1867.
Lunnenburg, VT, Stinehour Press,
    1960. 190 p.
NN MNO

Love, William DeLoss 2nd
Hamilton College and Her Family
    Lines.
San Francisco, the author, 1963.
    498 p., alpha index in front.
(Genealogical charts show interre-
    lationships among families who
    have attended Hamilton Col-
    lege)
NN APK

Neely, Donald Owen.
One Hundred Summers: The His-
    tory of Wellington Cricket.
Aukland, The Wellington Cricket
    Assoc., 1975. 229 p.
NN

Oak-Rhind, HH.
Clay Tobacco Pipe Makers of
    Suffolk.

(IN: *The Suffolk Review, Bulletin of the Suffolk Local History Council, Ipswich, Winter 1975–76. v. 4, no. 4, p. 195–211*)
(Biographical details from apprentice records, parish records, 1851 and 1861 censuses, directories, etc.)
NN CO (Suffolk)

Smith, D.T.
Mousehole Forge.
(IN: *The Hunter Archaeological Society Transactions. Sheffield, 1975. v. 10, p. 182–198*)
(Several generations of people involved with Mousehole Forge, in the manor of Owlerton, Sheffield, England)
NN CO (Hallamshire)

Stapleton, Guy.
A Family in Transition: The Weaving Bushys of Moreton, Gloucestershire.
(IN: *GM, London, 1972. v. 17, p. 67–74*)
NN ARCA

Unwin, Philip.
The Printing Unwins: A Short History of the Unwin Brothers, The Gresham Press, 1826–1976.
London, Allen Unwin, 1976. 159. p., gen. tables, index.
NN JFE 76-3554

Washington County Museum of Fine Arts
The Peale Heritage 1763–1963.
Hagerstown, MD, 1963. 1,116 p., no index. (American artists.)
NN 3-MCX P35. W3

Cemeteries and Cemetery Inscriptions

Bosio, Antonio (1811–1880)
Iscrizioni Torinesi ...
Turin, c. 1971. 325 p.
(Turin, Italy, epitaphs)
NN JFF 72-110

Bridgman, Thomas.
Memorials of the Dead in Boston ... King's Chapel Burial Ground.
Boston, B.B. Musey, 1853. 339 p.
(Samuel Beals, p. 152)
NN APR (Boston)

Caillot, Antoine.
Voyage Religieux et Sentimental aux Quatre Cimetières de Paris ...
Paris, 1809. 368 p.
(Paris, France, epitaphs)
NN DOH

Carr, David H.
Where to Find Cemetery Records in the London, Ontario Area.
(IN: *Families Toronto, 1973. v.12, p. 3–24*)
(It is noted that the records of some 40 cemeteries are deposited in the London Room of the London Public Library, London, Ontario)
NN APW 73-2794

Cemetery Research Inc.
Directory of United States Cemeteries.
San Jose, CA 95150; Cemetery Research, P.O. Box 6616; 1974. v. 1 (343 p.).
NN APK 75-1060

Chamberlayne, Tankerville J.
Lacrimae Nicossienses ...
Paris, Quantin, 1894. 172 p.
(Nicosia, Cyprus, epitaphs
NN BVX+

Clarke, Richard Samuel Jessup.
Gravestone Inscriptions.
Belfast, Ulster Scot Historical Foundation, 1966–1976. 16 v. in progress. (All volumes so far deal with County Down)
NN ARF

Clarke, R.S.J.
The Value of Tombstone Inscriptions with Special Reference to County Down.
(IN: *Irish Ancestor, Dundalk, 1969. v. 1, p. 17–22*)
(More than a hundred references to emigrants who died in the U.S., Australia, etc.)
NN ARCA 72-1448

Codman, Ogden.
Graveyard Inscriptions and Records of Tomb Burials in the Central Burying Ground, Boston Common ...
Salem, Essex Inst., 1917. 167 p.
NN APR (Boston)

Darnell, Anita W.
Cemetery Records of Fort Campbell, Kentucky.
Clarksville, TN, 1970. 46, 30 p.
NN APR (Fort Campbell, KY) 76-801

Edinburgh, Scotland.
Greyfriars Burying-Ground, Edin-
burgh, 1658–1700, ed. by Henry
Paton.
Edinburgh, Scottish Rec. Soc., 1902.
722 p., alpha.
NN ARX (Edinburgh)

Firminger, Walter K.
The Dutch Cemetery at Chin-
surah.
(IN: *Bengal Past and Present,
Calcutta, 1918. v. 16 p. 195–207*)
NN*OHM

Fisher, Payne.
Catalogue of the Tombs in the
Churches of the City of London.
1885 (orig. 1668) 94 p.
NN ARX (London)

Fitzpatrick, William John.
History of the Dublin Catholic
Cemeteries.
Dublin, 1900. 235 p.
NN CT (Dublin) 73-2184

Forbes, Harriette M.
Gravestones of Early New Eng-
land and the Men Who Made
Them.
New York, De Capo, 1967. 141 p.
NN MRIF

Grose, Erich.
Katalog der Fruhchristlichen In-
schriften in Trier.
Berlin, Mann, 1958. 129 p. (Trierer
Grabunger und Forschunger
bd. 3)
(Trier, Germany, epitaphs)
NN G-10 1037

Holmes, Mrs. Basil.
The London Burial Grounds.
New York, Macmillan, 1896. 339 p.
NN CO (London)

Irvin, Mrs. John M.
Tombstone Inscriptions of Ceme-
teries in Green County, Wis-
consin.
Monroe, WI, 1971. 1 v., v.2.
NN APR (Green Co. WI) 75-681

Jervey, Clare.
Inscriptions on the Tablets and
Gravestones in St Michael's
Church and Churchyard,
Charleston, S.C.
Columbia, SC, The State Co., 1906.
333 p., index.
NN APR

Kippax, John R.
Churchyard Literature, A Choice
Collection of American Epi-
taphs ...
Detroit, Singing Tree Press, 1969
(orig. 1877). 213 p.
NN APM 72-1635

Klein, Samuel.
Judisch-Palatinisches Corpus In-
scriptionum.
Hildesheim, 1971. 106 p.
(Jewish epitaphs in the Palatinate)
NN *PWN 72-1014

Kull, Andrew.
New England Cemeteries.
Brattleboro, VT, S. Greene Press,
1975. 253 p.
NN IQ 75-2794

Laurain, Ernest.
... Epigraphie de Notre-Dame de
Noyon ...
Noyon, Soc. Arch. de Noyon, 1941.
276 p.
(Noyen, France, epitaphs)
NN F-10 2871

Le Neve, John, 1679–1741.
Monumenta Anglicana, Being In-

scriptions on the Monuments of
Several Eminent Persons ...
Since 1600 ...
London, 1717–1719. 5 v.
NN ARF

Light, Alfred W.
Bunhill Fields ... Old London
Cemetery.
London, C.J. Fanncombe, 1915–
1933. 2 v.
(Dissenters' burial ground with
bios.)
NN AGH

Lysons, Daniel.
The Environs of London: Being an
Historical Account of the
Towns, Villages and Hamlets
within Twelve Miles of that
Capital.
London, 1792–96. 4 v., index each v.
(Many of the interments noted are
in cemeteries now destroyed.
The tomb of my ancestor,
Thomas Loughnan [d. 1789], in
St. Mary's, Paddington, is one of
these.)
NN Co+ (London)

Norman, James.
Ancestral Voices, Decoding An-
cient Languages.
New York, Four Winds Press, 1975.
242 p.
NN JFE 76-1081

Oliver, Vere Langford.
The Monumental Inscriptions in
Churches and Churchyards of
the Island of Barbados, British
West Indies.
London, Hughes and Clarke, 1915.
223 p.
(100 Jewish inscriptions included)
NN APW

Parkin, Nona.
Nona, the Nutty Necrologist.
(IN: *Genealogist's Post, Miami,
FL, 1964. v. 1, no. 9, p.1; no. 10, p.
7–18; no. 11, p. 1–12, 30*)
(Lively adventures in Nevada
cemeteries)
NN APGA

Pinchart-Staes, Henry de.
Epitaphes en Brabant.
Brussels, 1957–1967. 14 v. in 1 v.
(Brabant, Belgium, epitaphs)
NN M-11 589

Pool, David de Sola.
Portraits Etched in Stone; Early
Jewish Settlers 1682–1831.
New York., Columbia U. Press,
1952. 543 p.
NN *PXY (New York City)

Potter, Gail M.
The Stories Behind the Stones.
South Brunswick, NJ, 1969. 244 p.
NN JFF 70-70

Sequin, Jean.
Corpus des Inscriptions Tumu-
laires (Ante 1789) de Mortainais
...
Avranches, c. 1932. 95 p.
(Mortain, France)
NN BTE p. v. 487

Speakman, Mary N. and Walter F.
Cemeteries of Clay County, Texas.
Wichita Falls, the authors, 1973.
322 p.
NN APR (Clay Co., TX) 74-1097

Wallis, Charles L.
Stories on Stone, A Book of Ameri-
can Epitaphs.
New York., Oxford U. Press, 1954.
272 p., index.
NN APM

Weever, John.
Ancient Funeral Monuments of Great Britain and Ireland.
London, 1767. 608 p., index.
NN ARS

Wilson, Charles R.
List of Inscriptions on Tombs and Monuments in Bengal ...
Calcutta, 1896. 248 p.
(*Indian Monumental Inscriptions V. 1.*)
NN OHN++

CHURCH RECORDS

American Catholic Historical Society.
Researches.
Pittsburgh, Philadelphia, 1884–1912. 29 v., index v. 1–29, 1916.
NN IAA

The American Catholic Who's Who.
Washington, DC, National Cath. News Service.

Cartwright, J.L.
Oundle in the Eighteenth Century Through the Eyes of John Clifton.
(IN: *NPP, Kettering, 1976. v. 5, no. 4, p. 339 ff.*).
NN Co. (Northants.)

Curry, Cora C.
Records of the Roman Catholic Church in the U.S. as a Source of Authentic Genealogical and Historical Material.
Washington, DC, 1935. 41 p.
(*NGSSP No. 5*)
NN APGA

The Encyclopedia of American Quaker Genealogy.

Ann Arbor, Edwards Bros., etc., 1936–1975. v. 1–7, v. 7 in 6 parts (v. 1–6 ed. by Wm. W. Hinshaw; v. 7 ed. by Willard Heiss, pub. by IN Hist. Soc; v. 1—NC; v. 2—Phila. and vic.; v. 3—NYC and Long Is.; v. 4–5—OH; v. 6—VA; v. 7—IN)
NN APK

Kinsella, Thomas H.
A Centenary of Catholicity in Kansas. 1822–1922.
Kansas City, 1921. 251 p.
NN IWB (Miami Co.) 73–1802

Kirkham, E. Kay.
A Survey of American Church Records: Major Denominations Before 1880. 3rd ed. revised and enlarged.
Logan, UT, Everton, 1971. 264 p. (Arranged by state)
NN APK 73-1887

Mode, Peter G.
Source Book and Bibliographical Guide for American Church History.
Boston, J.S. Canner & Co., 1964. (orig. 1921) 735 p.
NN AD-10 1231

O'Rourke, Timothy J.
Maryland Catholics on the Frontier: The Missouri and Texas Settlements.
Parson, KS, Belfrey Press, 1973. 952 p., index.
NN APK 75-1849

Parisot, Rev. P. F. and Rev. Christopher J. Smith.
History of the Catholic Church in the Diocese of San Antonio, Texas, 1685–1897.

San Antonio, Carrico and Bowen, 1897. 214, 4 p.
NN ITRM (San Antonio)

Parker, Jimmy B., and Wayne T. Morris.
A Definitive Study of Major U.S. Genealogical Records: Ecclesiastical and Secular.
Salt Lake City, The Gen. Soc. of LDS, 1969.

Sawyer, Ray C.
Deaths Published in Christian Intelligencer of the Reformed Dutch Church 1830–71.
New York., typescript, 1932–34. 10 v. surname index each v. Marriages . . . 1830–71. 1931–32 7 v.
(Excellent work by the sister of Gertrude A. Barber).
NN APK

U.S. and Canada Church Records, ed. by Constance H. Jacquet.
Nashville, TN, Abingdon Press, 1974.

Warner, Mikel D. W. and Harriet Duncan Munnick.
Catholic Church Records of the Pacific Northwest: Vancouver, v. 1 and 2 and Stellamarris Mission.
St. Paul, OR, French Prairie Press, 1972. various paging, 2 v. in 1, index.
NN APR (Northwest Pacific) 73–2225

UNIVERSITY AND COLLEGE REGISTERS

Dallett, Francis James.
University Archives as a Genealogical Resource.

(IN: *NGSQ Washington, 1977. v.65, no.1, p. 57–74*)
(Includes bibliography of alumni biographies in the United States and Great Britain.)
NN APGA

Brown University

Brown University.
Historical Catalogue of Brown University.
1950 Edition.
Providence, Brown, 1950. 1,212 p.
NN *RR-STG

Harvard

Harvard Alumni Directory, 1970.
Cambridge, Harvard U. Alumni Assoc., 1970. 1,910 p.
NN *RR-STG

Harvard University Quinquennial Catalogue of the Officers and Graduates, 1636–1930.
Cambridge, Harvard, 1930. 1,463 p.
NN *RR-STG

Sibley, John L., etc.
Biographical Sketches of Graduates of Harvard University in Cambridge, Mass.
Cambridge, Harvard, 1873–1975. 17 v. (Covering 1642–1771 in progress).
NN *RR-AGZ

West Point

U.S. Military Academy, West Point.
Register of Graduates and Former Cadets 1802–1974 of the U.S. Military Academy.
West Point, Assoc. of Graduates, 1974. 816 p.
NN *RR-AGZ 74-50

Yale

Catalogue of the Officers and Graduates of Yale University in New Haven, Conn., 1701–1924.
New Haven, Yale, 1924. 822 p., index.
NN *RR-STG

Dexter, Franklin.
Biographical Sketches of the Graduates of Yale College with Annals of the College History ... 1701–1815.
New York, H. Holt, 1885–1912. 6 v.
NN JFF 22-1042

Yale University Alumni Directory. 1956.
(52nd series, no. 7)
New Haven, Yale, 1956. 1,751 p.
NN *RR-STG

American Library Directory. 30th ed. 1976/77.
New York., R. R. Bowker, 1976. (A biennial pub.)
NN Pub. Cat.

American Association of State and Local History.
Directory of Historical Societies and Agencies in the United States and Canada. Tenth Edition. 1976/77.
Nashville, AASLA, 1975 (Bienniel pub). 434 p. index
(Next edition late 1978)
NN IXZ

Besterman, Theodore.
A World of Bibliographies. 4th ed.
Lausanne, Societas Bibliographicas, 1965–66. 5 v.
NN*RR-RG

A Bibliography of the Cox Library.
Tucson, AR, Americana Unlimited, 1976.
(Amer. Unlimited, P.O. Box 50447, 1701 N. 11th Ave., Tucson, AR 85703)

Cleveland Public Library.
European Origins: A Selective Guide to Genealogical Aids in the Cleveland Public Library.
Cleveland OH, 1976.
(Cleveland Pub. Lib, 325 Superior Ave., Cleveland, OH 44114)

Cunningham, Ronald, and Evan Evans.
A Handy Guide to the Genealogical Library.

Salt Lake City, UT; Logan, UT; Everton, 1969. 45 p.
NN APB 75-1959

Directory of State and Provisional Archives 1975.
Chicago, Soc. of American Archivists, 1975. 71 p.
(The Library, Soc. of American Archivists, P.O. Box 8198, U. of IL, Chicago, IL 60680)

Encyclopedia of Library and Information Science.
New York., M. Dekker, 1968– 17 v. by 1976
(v. 9, p. 200–211, genealogy section by Gilbert H. Doane).
NN *RR-*HB

Guide to American Libraries. 9th ed.
Coral Springs, FL, B. Klein Pub., 1975. 496 p.

Guide to the Research Collection of the New York Public Library, comp. by Sam P. Williams, under the direction of Wm. V. Jackson and James W. Henderson.
Chicago, IL, ALA, 1975. 336 p.
LHG p. 266–269
NN Desk Room 315G

Hobbs, John L.
Local History and the Library.
London, Andre Deutsch, 1962. 338 p.
NN CAB

International Guide to Library Archives and Information Sci-

ence Association, ed. by Josephine R. Fang and Alice H. Song.
New York., R. R. Bowker, 1976. 35 p.
NN *R-*HA 76-5898

Lombard Suburban Genealogical Society.
Genealogical Holdings of the Dupage Library System.
Lombard, IL, 1975.
(Lombard Sub. Gen. Soc., 23 W. Maple St., Lombard, IL 60148)

Morand, Julia P. M.
Catalogue or Bibliography of the Library of the Huguenot Society of America. 2nd ed.
Baltimore, MD, GPC, 1971. (orig. 1920) 351 p., alpha.
NN AP 74-495

Newberry Library. Chicago.
Genealogical Index of the Newberry Library.
Boston, MA, G. K. Hall, 1960. 4 v.
NN AP+ and AP+ 76-228

New York Public Library. The Research Libraries.
Dictionary Catalog of the Local History and Genealogy Division.
Boston, G. K. Hall, 1974. 18 v., alpha by author and subject (Family names, places, etc.).
NN AP+ 74-762

New York Public Library. The Research Libraries.
Local History and Genealogy Division.
United States Local History Catalog.
Boston, MA, G. K. Hall, 1974. 2 v.
NN AP+ 74-763

Radenwald, Bette Miller.
The Library Handbook, Simplified Methods and Terms for the Genealogist.
Riverside, CA 92507, the author, RE: Genealogy, 639 Sandalwood Ct., 1974. 94 p., index.
NN APG 75-1408

San Francisco Public Library Dept. of Rare Books and Special Collections.
Genealogy Recent Additions.
San Francisco, CA, 1964–1971. v. 1–7, 7 v. in 1.
(NN lacks Apr. 1966–Feb. 1967)
NN AP 76-1557

U.S. Library of Congress.
Genealogies in the Library of Congress, comp. by Marion Joan Hume Kaminkow.
Baltimore, MD, Magna Carta, 1972. 2 v. v. 1 (A–J), v. 2 (K–Z).
NN *R-AP+ 72-1038

U.S. Library of Congress.
United States Local Histories in the Library of Congress, A Bibliography, comp. by Marion Joan Hume Kaminkow.
Baltimore, MD, Magna Carta, 1974–1976. 4 v.
(v. 1 Atlantic states, Maine to NY; v. 2 Atlantic states, NJ to Florida; v. 3 Middle West, Alaska, Hawaii; v. 4 the West; v. 5 Supplement and Index)
NN *R-IXZ 75-1346

MICROFILM

Auerbach on Microfilm Readers/ Printers.
Princeton, NJ, Auerbach Pub., 1972. 133 p.
NN JFF 72-1032

Baker, G. G.
A Guide to Microfilm Readers and
Reader-Printers.
Guildford, Surrey, England; G. G.
Baker Assoc. (54 Quarry St.);
1976. 192 p., index.

Ballou, Hubbard W.
Guide   to   Microreproduction
Equipment.
Silver Spring, MD, 1971. 793 p.
NN JFD 74-2240

Library Microfilms Annual. 1977.
Palo Alto, CA, 1977. 117 p. plus
section on equipment and sup-
plies
(Library   Microfilms,   737   Loma
Verde, Palo Alto, CA 94303)

National Microfilm Association.
Guide   to   Microreproduction
Equipment.
Annapolis, MD, 1968. 493 p.
NN JSK 76-20

National Microfilm Association.
Introduction to Micrographics.
Silver Spring, MD, 1973. 26 p.
NN JFF 74-490

Powell, Ted F.
Genealogists Gain Exciting Ad-
vantages Through the Use of
Microfilm.
(IN: *Genealogy Digest. Salt Lake
City, UT, 1975. v. 6, p. 41–43, 45*)
(Powell was manager of microfilm
operations of the Gen. Soc. of LDS
at the time he wrote this
article.)

U.S. National Archives and Rec-
ords Service.
Office of Records Management.
Microfilm Retrieval Equipment.
Washington, 1975. 88 p.
NN JSF 75-1256

COMPUTERS
Gagan, David.
The Genealogist, the Historian,
the Computer.
(IN: *Families, Toronto, 1973. v. 12,
p. 103–108*)
NN APW 73-2794

Montgomery, Austin H., Jr.
Speeding Indexing of Genealogical
Data by Computer.
(IN: *NGSQ, Washington, Mar. 1976.
v. 64, p. 35–44*)
NN APGA

MAPS AND ATLASES
Atlas of Early American History:
The Revolutionary Era 1760–
1790. Lester J. Cappon, ed. in
chief.
Princeton, NJ, Princeton U. Press,
1976. 157 p.
NN Map Div. 76-524

Atlas Historyczny Polaski ...
Warsaw, 1930–1973. 3 v.
NN *QR + 73-5850

Banks, Arthur.
A World Atlas of Military History.
London, 1973. v. 1, 1 v.
NN Map Div. 74-346

Bartholomew's Survey Gazetteer
of the British Isles.
Edinburgh, J. Bartholomew and
son, 1927. 7th ed., 768 p., 47
maps.
(The older editions of this work
are excellent for locating small
parishes, hamlets and manor
houses that are sometimes ignored by more recent gazetteers.)
NN Desk Room 315 G

Chew, Allen F.
An Atlas of Russian History,

Eleven Centuries of Changing Borders. revised ed.
New Haven, CT, Yale, 1970 (orig. 1967). 127 p., index.
NN Map Div. 72-77

Columbia Lippincott Gazetteer of the World (with 1961'supp.).
New York, Columbia U. Press, 1962. 2148, 22 p., alpha.
NN Map. Div.

Everton, George B.
Genealogical Atlas of the United States of America.
Logan, UT, Everton, 1966. 118 p., plus 2 folding maps.
NN APB

Gilbert, Martin.
American History Atlas.
New York, Macmillan, 1968. 112 p.
NN Map Div.

Grosser Historischer Weltatlas.
Munich, Bayerischer Schibuch Verlag, 1954–1970. 3 v. (Tiel 1.: Vorgeschichte und Altertum [1954]; Tiel 2.: Mittelalter [1970]; Tiel 3.: Neuzeit [1957]; Maps in color overlays, index)
NN Map Div.

Hammond, Inc.
Man and History.
Maplewood, NJ, 1971. 192 p.
NN Map Div. 72-157

Hayt, Franz.
Atlas d'Histoire Universelle (et d'Histoire de Belgique).
Namur, 1967. 144 p.
NN Map Div. 72-479

Kirkham, E. Kay.
A Handy Guide to Record Searching in the Larger Cities of the United States.

Logan, UT; Everton, 1974. 137 p., t of c, no index.

Lord, Clifford L., and Eliza H. Lord.
Historical Atlas of the United States. Revised.
New York, Johnson Reprint, 1969 (orig. 1944). 238 p., index.

McEvedy, Colin, and Sarah McEvedy.
The Atlas of World History.
London, 1970–1972. 3 v.
(v. 1: Beginning to Alexander the Great; v. 2: The Classical World; v. 3: Dark Ages)
NN Map Div. 71-41

Muir's Historical Atlas, Ancient and Mediaeval and Modern.
London, George Phili, 1962. 96, 24 p.
NN Map Div.

Newby, Eric.
The Rand McNally World Atlas of Exploration.
New York, 1975. 288 p., index.
NN Map Div. 76-788

Pergamon General Historical Atlas.
Oxford, Pergamon Press, 1970. 85 p.
NN Map Div. 73-340

Shepherd, William R.
Shepherd's Historical Atlas. 9th ed. revised.
New York, Barnes & Noble, 1973. 216, 115 p., index.
NN Map Div. 75-422

Webster's New Geographical Dictionary.
Springfield, MA, G & C. Merriam, 1972. 1,370 p., alpha.
NN Map Div. 73-317

Wesley, Edgar B.
Our United States, Its History in Maps.
Chicago, Denoyer-Geppert, 1956. 96 p.
NN Map Div.

Wilson, Andrew.
The "Observer" Atlas of World Affairs.
London, The Observer, 1971. 111 p.
NN Map Div. 73-62

PERIODICALS

The American Genealogist.
New Haven, CT & Des Moines, IA, 1922–. Edited by Donald Lines Jacobus from 1922–1965 and from 1966 to date by Dr. George E. McCracken, 1232 39th Street, Des Moines, IA 50311. (Volumes 1–8 were issued under the title *New Haven Genealogical Magazine*.)
(Excellent scholarship has prevailed for fifty-five years in this periodical.)
NN APGA

A Brief Guide to American Genealogical Societies and Periodicals.
Lansing Mid-Michigan Gen. Soc., 1975.
NN APR (Michigan) 74-227-No. 6

Cappon, Lester J.
American Genealogical Periodicals, A Bibliography with a Chronological Finding-List.
NY, NYPL, 1964. 32 p.
NN APG

Directory of Genealogical Periodicals, edited by J. Konrad.
Munroe Falls, OH 44262; Summit Publications, P.O. Box 222, 1975. 61 p.
(Covers USA and some family or "one name" newsletters in the USA and Europe.)

Directory of Genealogical Societies in the U.S.A. and Canada, edited by Mary Keysor Meyer.
Pasadena, MD 21122; the editor, Rt. 10, Box 138-A; 1976. 73 p.

Directory of Historical Societies and Agencies in the United States and Canada.
Tenth Edition 1975–1976, edited by Donna McDonald.
Nashville, TN 37303; American Association for State and Local History, 1400 Eight Avenue South; 1975. 434 p.
(4,405 entries) Index
(Lists names and addresses of historical societies by state and province. The next edition is due in late 1978.)
NN IXZ

Federation of Genealogical Societies Newsletter.
Midlothian, IL, 1976– v. 1–
(A clearinghouse for genealogical information)
(John P. Megaris, ed., 9161 W. Forest Drive, Hickory Hills, Il 60457; Federation of Genealogical Societies, P.O. Box 743, Midlothian, IL 60445)

Genealogical Periodical Annual Index.
Bladensburg, MD. Bowie, MD, 1962–
Edited first by Ellen S. Rogers, then George E. Russell and now by Laird C. Towle, 3602

Maureen Lane, Bowie, MD 20715.
NN *R-APG

Genealogy Library Quarterly
Harbor City, CA 90710, Augustan Soc., 1617 W. 261st Street, 1976– v. 1–.

Jacobus, Donald Lines.
Index to Genealogical Periodicals.
New Haven, the author, 1932– 1953. 3 v. (v. 1 & 2 reprinted by GPC in 1963 and 1969)
NN *R-APG

Journal of Genealogy.
Omaha, NE, 1976– v. 1–.
(Robert D. Anderson, ed., Box 31097, Omaha, NE 68131)
(Articles in first issue dealing with Fort Wayne, IN, Public Library and Newberry Library, Chicago)

Munsell, Joel.
Index to American Genealogies.
5th ed. 1900.
(With supplement 1900 to 1908)
Baltimore, GPC, 1967. 352, 107 p.
NN *R-APG

National Genealogical Society Quarterly.
Washington, DC, 1912–.
This society, which was established in 1903, has its headquarters at 1921 Sunderland Place, N.W., Washington, DC 20036. It also issues a series of interesting special publications. Articles from the quarterly are noted in this book. The editorship of this periodical rotates among the members; George Ely Russell is the current editor.

(Topical Index to NGSQ Volumes 1–5, 1912–1962, edited by Carleton E. Fisher, Washington, DC, 1964. 155 p.) (*NGSP No. 29*)
NN APGA

The New England Historical and Genealogical Register. Boston, 1847–.
The New England Historic Genealogical Society with its library and headquarters at 101 Newbury Street, Boston, MA 02116, issues this venerable periodical which is the oldest continuous genealogical quarterly in the world. The quality of its content on the whole has been of the highest caliber, as the result of the work of the late Henry F. G. Waters, the late G. Andrews Moriarty, and many others.
——Index of (Persons, Places, Subjects): Volumes 1–50 (1847–1896). Baltimore, MD, GPC, 1972 (orig. 1907–1911) 5 v. in 4 v.
——Index (Abridged) NEHGR Volumes 51–112 (1879–1958), compiled by Margaret W. Parsons, Marlborough, MA, 1959, 406 p.
NN APGA

(See the bibliographies in Sections III and IV for additional periodicals.)

NEWSPAPERS
Ayer Directory of Publications ... Newspapers ... Magazines ...
Philadelphia 19106, Ayer Press, 210 W. Washington Sq., 1869– (1976 ed., 1,278 p.).
NN Pub. Cat.

Barnes, Timothy M.
Loyalist Newspapers of the American Revolution 1763–1783; A Bibliography.
(IN: *AASP, Worcester, MA, 1973. v. 83; p. 217–283*)
NN IAA

Brigham, Clarence Saunders.
History and Bibliography of American Newspapers, 1690–1820.
Worcester, MA, Amer. Antiquarian Soc., 1947 (orig. 1913–1928). 2 v. (1,508 p.)
NN NARE

Crane, R. S., etc.
Census of British Newspapers and Periodicals, 1620–1800.
Chapel Hill, NC, U. of NC, 1927. 205 p. (Studies in Philology v. 24)
NN*R-*D

Gregory, Winifred.
American Newspapers, 1821–1936; A Union List of Files Available in the United States and Canada.
New York, Kraus Reprint, 1967 (orig. 1937). 791 p.
NN Pub. Cat., Desk Room 315G, etc.

Hale, Richard W., Jr.
Guide to Photocopied Historical Materials in the United States and Canada.
Ithaca, NY, Cornell U. Press, 1961. 241 p.; index.
NN Desk Room 315A

Hartford Times Gen. Dept.
Queries and Answers from the Saturday Issues. July 1935–Dec. 1950.

NN *ZAN-G13 (film) and APR+ (Conn.)

Haskell, Daniel C.
Checklist of Newspapers and Periodicals in the New York Public Library.
New York, NYPL, 1915. 579 p.
NN *RS-*A 75-7819

Library of Congress.
Newspapers in Microform Foreign Countries 1948–1972.
Washington, DC, Library of Congress, 1973. 264 p.
NN Pub. Cat.

Library of Congress.
Newspapers in Microform United States 1948–1972.
Washington, DC, Library of Congress, 1973. 1,056 p.
NN Pub. Cat. 74-117

New York Weekly Newspapers Representatives.
New York, 1959–
NN M-11 619 and TWA+

Scott, Kenneth.
Genealogical Abstracts from the American Weekly, 1719–1746.
Baltimore, MD, GPC, 1974. 180 p., index.
NN APK 74-677

Tri-State Trader, Weekly Hobby, Antique, Auction and Collectors' Newspaper.
P.O. Box 90, Knightstown, IN 46148.
(Published since 1968; includes genealogy section with booknotes and queries, and each issue includes a surname index to queries.)

DIRECTORIES
Goss, Charles W. F.
The London Directory, 1677–1855, A Bibliography with Notes.
London, D. Archer, 1932. 146 p.
NN CO (London)

Norton, Jane.
A Guide to the National and Provincial Directories of England and Wales Excluding London Published Before 1856.
London, Royal Hist. Soc., 1950. 241 p.
NN C

Spear, Dorothea.
Bibliography of American Directories through 1860.
Worcester, MA, AAS, 1961. 389 p.
NN AZE

BIOGRAPHIES
Biographical Directory of Congress 1774–1971.
Washington, U.S. Gov. Print. Office, 1971. 1,972 p.
NN *R-Economics (18)
(1961 ed. 1,863 p. in *R-AGZ and JFF 75-1464)

Biographical Dictionaries Master Index. 1975/76
Detroit, Gale, 1975 3 v. (A-2)
NN*AA-75-6969

Celebrity Register, ed. by Earl Blackwell.
New York, Simon and Schuster, 1973. 562 p.
NN Pub. Cat.

Chicorel Index to Biographies.
Chicorel Index Series.
New York, Chicorel Library Pub.

Co. (275 Central Park West), 1974, v. 15, 15A (A-Z)
NN *RS-A 74-617

Dictionary of American Biography.
New York, Charles Scribner's Sons, 1928–1974. 13 v.
(The original 20 volumes plus 4 supplements covering the period from the early history of this country to 1950. Further supplements are in progress.)
NN *R-AGZ

Encyclopedia of American Biography, ed. by John A. Garraty.
New York, Harper & Row, 1974. 1,241 p., alpha.
NN *R-AGZ 75-4258

Havlice, Patricia P.
Index to Literary Biography.
Metuchen, Scarecrow, 1975. 2 v., alpha.
NN *RS-A 75-6697

International Celebrity Register. U.S. Section. Cleveland Amory, ed.
New York, 1959–
NN M-10 3984

The National Cyclopedia of American Biography.
Clifton, NY, James T. White, 1891–1975. 56 v.
(Cumulative index v. 1–54) (Also included current v. A–L; numbered series deals on the whole with deceased Americans and the lettered series with living people.)
NN *R-APK

Notable American Women, 1607–1950.

Cambridge, MA, Belknap Press of
Harvard, 1971. 3 v., alpha.
NN *R-SNE

Sobel, Robert.
Biographical Directory of the
United States Executive
Branch 1774–1971.
Westport, CT, Greenwood, 1971.
491 p., alpha plus indexes.
NN *R-AGZ 75-29

Who's Who in America.
Chicago, A. N. Marquis, 1976/77.
39th ed. 2 v., alpha. (v. 1 1899/
1900)
NN *RR-AGZ

Who's Who of American Women
1975/76. 9th ed.
Chicago, Marquis, 1975. 988 p. alpha
NN *RR-AGZ

Who's Who in the East. 1974/75.
14th ed.
Chicago, Marquis, 1974. 929 p.
NN *RR-AGZ

Who's Who in the Midwest. 1976/
77. 15th ed.
Chicago, Marquis, 1976. 823 p.
NN *RR-AGZ

Who's Who in New England.
Chicago, Marquis, 1909–1949. 4 v.
NN AGZ

Who's Who in the South and Southwest. 1976/77 15th ed.
Chicago, Marquis, 1976. 904 p., alpha.
NN *RR-AGZ

Who's Who in the West. 1976/77.
15th ed.

Chicago, Marquis, 1976. 823 p., alpha.
NN *RR-AGZ

Who Was Who in America.
Chicago, Marquis, 1943–1976. 7 v.
v. H (Historical) 1607–1896; v. 1
1897–1942; v. 2 1943–1950; v. 3
1951–1960; v. 4 1961–1968; v. 5
1969–1973; v. 6 1974–1976; cumulative index in v. 6.
NN *R-AGZ

GENEALOGICAL GUIDES
The American Genealogical-Bio-
graphical Index, ed. by the late
Freemont Rider and others.
Revised ed.
Middletown, CT, 1952–1977 plus v.
1– (Alpha unpaged). 1st ed.
1942–1952 48 v. A–Z.
NN *R-APK

American Society of Genealogists.
Genealogical Research: Methods
and Sources.
Washington, DC, the Society,
1960–1971. 2 v., t of c each v.,
no index.
NN APB 72-1848

Bennett, Archibald F.
Finding Your Forefathers in
America.
Salt Lake City, UT, Bookcraft,
1957. 444 p., index.
NN APG

Besterman, Theodore.
Family History, A Bibliography
of Bibliographies.
Totowa, NJ, Rowman & Little-
field, 1971 (orig. 1939). 149 p.
NN AP 72-1406

Bremer, Ronald A.
Selected American Historical

Sources, An Annotated Bibliography.
Salt Lake City, UT 84101, Gencor, 322 Crandall Bldg., 10 W. 1st South, 1974. 28 p., t of c, no index.
NN APB 75-2176

Cox, E. E.
Ancestry Climbing in the Midwest: Illinois, Indiana, Iowa, Kansas, Missouri, Nebraska.
Ellensburg, VA, E. E. Cox, c. 1967.

Doane, Gilbert H.
Searching for Your Ancestors. 4th ed.
Minneapolis, MN, U of MN Press, 1973. 212 p., index.
NN APG 75-1025

Encyclopedia of Local History and Genealogy.
Bountiful, UT, AIS, 1976. 200 p. Series 1, v. 1.

Everton, George B.
Handybook for Genealogists. 6th ed.
Logan, UT, Everton, 1971. 297 p.
NN APB 72-624

Filby, P. William.
American and British Genealogy and Heraldry.
Chicago, American Library Assoc., 1975. 2nd edition 467 p. index.
NN APG 76-2108

Genealogy Beginners Manual.
Chicago, Newberry Library, 1973. 20 p.

Genealogical Books in Print, ed. by Nettie Schreiner-Yantis.
Springfield, VA 22150, the editor, 6818 Lois Drive, 1975. 311 p., index.
(2nd ed.—Springfield, the editor, 1976. 410 p., 5,000 titles, no repetition from 1st ed.)
NN APG 75-1842

Gobble, J.R.
Who's Where in Your Genealogical Records, A Filing and "Finding" System.
Idaho Fall, ID 83401, the author, P.O. Box 2442. 29 p.
NN APB 75-2535

Greenwood, Val D.
The Researcher's Guide to American Genealogy.
Baltimore, MD, GPC, 1973. 535 p.
NN APG 74-801

Groene, Bertram H.
Tracing Your Civil War Ancestors.
Winston-Salem, NC, John F. Blaire, 1973. 124 p., index.
NN APG 74-676

Haley, Curtis E.
The Ancestor Hunting Kit.
Coral Gables, FL, the author, 1969. 32 leaves.
NN APB 72-1952

Hembold, F. Wilbur.
Tracing Your Ancestry, A Step-by-Step Guide to Researching Your Family Tree.
Birmingham, AL, Oxmoor House, 1976. 2 v.

Hilton, Suzanne.
Who Do You Think You Are? Digging for Your Roots.
Philadelphia, PA, The Westminster Press, 1976. 189 p.
NN APB 76-1617

Jaussi, Laureen R., and Gloria D. Chaston.
Fundamentals of Genealogical Research.
Salt Lake City, UT, Deseret, 1972. 400 p., t of c, no index.
NN APB 72-2297

Jones, Vincent L., Alene H. Eakle and Mildred H. Christensen.
Family History for Fun and Profit.
Salt Lake City, UT, Publishers Press, 1972. 326 p., index.
NN APB 74-1523

Kirkham, E. Kay.
The Counties of the United States and Their Genealogical Value. 3rd ed.
Salt Lake City, UT, Deseret, 1964. (2nd ed. 1961, 77 p.)
NN IXZ

Kirkham, E. Kay.
The Land Records of America and Their Genealogical Value.
Washington, DC, 1963. 60 p.
NN APB p. v. 144

Kirkham, E. Kay.
Professional Techniques and Tactics in American Genealogical Research.
Logan, UT, Everton, 1973

Kirkham, E. Kay.
Research in American Genealogy, A Practical Approach to Genealogical Research.
Salt Lake City, UT, Deseret, 1956. 447 p.
NN APB

Morris, Mrs. Harry J.
Handbook of Seminars in Genealogical Research.

Dallas, TX, Local History and Genealogy Society, 1964. 100 p., p. v. 159.
NN APB

Oates, Addison Ford.
The Art of Collecting Genealogy and History.
n.p., the author, 1971. 170 p
NN APV (Oates) 72–1981

Pine, Leslie G.
Genealogist's Encyclopedia.
Newton Abbot, DC, 1969. 360 p., index.
NN APB

Rottenberg, Dan.
Finding Our Fathers: A Guidebook to Jewish Genealogy.
New York, Random House. 1977. 401 p.
NN APB 77-1002

Sheppard, Walter Lee, Jr.
A Bicentennial Look at Genealogy Methods, Performance, Education and Thinking.
(IN: *NGSQ, Washington, 1977. v. 65, no.1, p. 3–15*)
NN APGA

Stevenson, Noel C.
Search and Research: The Researcher's Handbook. New Edition.
Salt Lake City, UT, Deseret, 1964. 364 p.
NN APG

Tarte, Robert J.
Your Genealogical Heritage: New England States.
Ashland, MA, Frank Genealogical Forms, 1977. 40 p.

Wakefield, Roberta P., ed.
General Aids to Genealogical Research.

Washington, DC, 1957. 50 p.
(*NGSSP, no. 14*)
NN APGA

Wakefield, Roberta P., ed.
Special Aids to Genealogical Research in Northeastern and Central States.
Washington, DC, 1957. 70 p.
(*NGSSP, no. 16*)
NN APGA

Wakefield, Roberta P., ed.
Special Aids to Genealogical Research on Southern Families.
Washington, DC, 1957. 106, 16, 2 p.
(*NGSSP, no. 15*)
NN APGA

Wellauer, Maralyn A.
A Guide to Foreign Genealogical Research. Revised and enlarged.
Milwaukee, WI, the author, 1976. 227 p.
NN AP 76-2614

Westin, Jeanne Eddy.
Finding Your Roots: How Every American Can Trace His Ancestors at Home and Abroad.
Los Angeles, CA, J. P. Tarcher, Inc., 1977. 243 p.

Willoughby, Miranda Goodrie.
The Search for a Family History; How a Search Was Conducted for Ancestors in the Early Northwest.
Riverside, RI, Farwill Pub. Co., 33 Arnold St., 02915 81 p.
NN APB (Goodrie) 73-1705

Wright, Norman.
Building an American Pedigree, A Study in Genealogy.
Provo, UT, BYU, 1974. 639 p.
NN APK 75-495

Zabriskie, George Olin.
Climbing Our Family Tree Systematically.
Salt Lake City, UT, Parliament Press, 1969. 222 p., index.
NN APB

PUBLISHING GENEALOGY AND HISTORY

Barnett, Mitzi.
How to Publish Genealogical and Historical Records.
Fort Worth, TX, American Ref. Pub., 1971. 12 p.
NN APG 72-209

Cumming, John.
A Guide for the Writing of Local History.
Lansing, MI, American Rev. Bicen. Comm., 1974. 53 p.
NN IVMB 76-1770

Walder, Alisa H.
Sharing My Family Research.
(IN: *Relatively Speaking, Edmonton, Alberta, 1976. v. 2, no. 2, p. 11–14*)

GENERAL AMERICAN REFERENCES

American Archivist.
Menasha, WI, 1938– index v. 1–20 (1938–1957), 1 v.
NN *HA

American Legal Records Series.
Washington, DC, 1933–1964. 9 v.
NN XP

American Historical Views: A New Edition, Revised and Enlarged, of American Historical Print Catalog of the Phelps, Stokes Collection.
New York, 1977.

The American Revolution, 1763–1793, A Bicentennial Collection, ed. by Richard B. Morris. Columbia, SC, U. of SC Press, 1971. 361 p.
NN IG 71-593

Brown, Mary J., and Kendall H. Williams.
Compendium of American Historical Sources.
Salt Lake City, UT, Gencor, 1973.

Deák, Gloria-Gilda.
American Views, Prospects and Vistas: An Introduction by James T. Flexner
New York, Viking Press, 1976. 134 p.
NN MOZ+ 76-1855

Dornbusch, Charles Emil.
Histories, Personal Narratives, U.S. Army; A Checklist.
Cornwallville, NY, Hope Farm Press, 1967. 400 p.
(Covers World Wars I and II and the Korean War; revision of 1956 edition)
NN I

Dornbusch, Charles Emil.
Regimental Publications and Personal Narratives.
New York, NYPL, 1961–1972. 3 v., index each v.
v. 1 Northern States; v. 2 Southern States; v. 3 General
NN IK

Encyclopedia of United States Counties.
Bountiful, UT, AIS, 1976. 292 p.

Guide to Archives and Manuscripts in the United States, ed. by Philip M. Hamer.

New Haven, CT, Yale, 1961. 775 p., index.
NN I

Lawrence, Ruth.
Colonial Families of America.
New York, National Americana, 1920–1965. 30 v.
NN APK+

Leventhal, Herbert, and James E. Mooney.
A Bibliography of Loyalist Source Material in the United States.
(IN: *AASP, Worcester, MA, 1975. v. 85, p. 73–308, 405–460*)
NN IAA

McMullin, Phillip W.
Grass Roots of America, A Comprehensive Index to the American State Papers—Land Grants and Claims (1789–1837) with Other Aids to Research.
Salt Lake City, UT, Gendex, 1972. 489 p.
NN *R-IAG 72-2143

The National Register of Historic Places.
Washington, U.S. Department of Interior, National Park Service, 1976. 961 p. Index.
NN IXZ 73-2678

Peterson, Clarence Stewart.
Known Military Dead During the American Revolutionary War 1775–1783.
Baltimore, MD, GPC, 1967 (orig. 1959). 188 p., alpha.
NN APK

Powell, William H.
List of Officers of the Army of the United States from 1779–1900.

Detroit, MI, Gale, 1967 (orig. 1900).
863 p., index.
NN *RR-AGZ 72-922

Smith, Elsdon.
The New Dictionary of American
Family Names.
New York, Harper & Row, 1973.
570 p., alpha.
NN APD 76-737

U.S. Congress.
American State Papers. Class 8, v.
1–8; Class 9, v. 1.
Washington, DC, 1832–1861, 9 v.
(Indexed by McMullin's *Grass
Roots*)
NN *R-IAG+

GENERAL WORLD REFERENCES

The Annual Register of World
Events ...
London, Longman,1758–
NN *RR-*AL and BAA

Burke's Royal Families of the
World.
London, Burke's Peerage, 1977. v.
1: Europe and Latin America.

(Presumably to be followed by volumes dealing with other continents)

Freeman-Grenville, G.S.P.
Chronology of World History: A
Calendar of Principal Events
from 3000 B.C. to A.D. 1973.
London, Rex Collins, 1975. 753 p.,
index.
NN *R-BAH 76-3303

Hymanson, Albert M.
A Dictionary of Universal Biography of All Ages and All People. 2nd ed. entirely rewritten.
London, RKP, 1951. 679 p.
(Indexes *DAB, DNB, Jewish Encyclopedia, Encyclopedia Bri-
tannica,* etc.)
NN *R-AA 73-1101

Miles, Joyce C.
House Names Around the World.
Detroit, MI, Gale, 1972 (orig. DC,
1972). 135 p., brief t of c, no
index.
NN APD 75-1892

New Cambridge Modern History.
Cambridge, U. Press, 1957–1970.
14 v.
(Covers 1493–1945)

CENSUS

Alterman, Hyman.
Counting People, the Census in History.
New York, Harcourt, Brace, 1969. 368 p., index.
NN SDK

Brewer, Mary Marie.
Index to Census Schedules in Printed Form.
Huntsville, AR, Century Enterprises. 69, 63 p. . . . 1970–71 Supplement, 76 p.
(M. M. Brewer, 4400 Howe Lane, Milwaukie, OR 97222)
NN APG

The Census Compendium.
Salt Lake City, UT, Gendex Corp., 1972.

Federal Population Censuses, 1790–1890. A Catalog of Microfilm Copies of the Schedules.
Washington, DC, NARS Administration, 1975. 90 p. plus order forms.

Dubester, Henry J.
State Censuses; An Annotated Bibliography of Censuses of Population Taken After the Year 1790 by States and Territories of the United States.
New York, Burt Franklin, 1967 (orig. 1948). 73 p.

Franklin, W. Neil.
Federal Population and Mortality Census Schedules, 1790–1890, in the National Archives and in the States.
Washington, DC, 1971. vii, 89 p. (NARS Spec. List No. 24)
NN JLF 74-191

Kirkham, E. Kay.
A Handy Guide to Record-Searching in the Larger Cities of the United States.
Logan, UT, Everton Publishers, Inc., 1974. 137 p.

Kirkham, E. Kay.
A Survey of American Census Schedules . . . 1790 to 1950.
Salt Lake City, UT, Deseret Book Co., 1959, 102 p.
NN IXZ p.v. 622

Konrad, J.
Directory of Census Information Sources.
Munroe Falls, OH, Summit Publications. 23 p.
(P.O. Box 222, Munroe Falls, OH 44252)

Richardson, Lorraine J.
History of My Family and the 1880 Census of Ozark Co., Missouri.
Beebee, AR, the author, 1969. 147 p.
NN APV (Richardson) 75–1895

Surnames in the United States Census of 1790.
Baltimore, GPC, 1969. 441 p., index.
(Rep. from annual report of the American Hist. Assoc. for the year 1931. Includes ethnic breakdown.)
NN APD 70-9

Taeuber, Irene.
General Censuses and Vital Statistics in the Americas
Detroit, MI, Baline Ethridge Books, 1974 (orig. 1943). 151 p.
NN APF 75-1295

U.S. Census Office.
First Census, 1790, Heads of Families.
U.S. Gov. Printing Office, 1907–1908.
(Covers RI, NH, VT, MA, ME, CT, NY, PA, MD, VA [Reconstructed], NC, SC)
NN *R-APR (U.S.)

U.S. Bureau of the Census.
A Century of Population Growth from the First Census of the United States to the Twelfth, 1790–1900.
Washington, DC, U.S. Gov. Print. Office, 1909, 303 p.
NN Desk Room 315G

Warren, Mary B.
Census Enumerations: How Were They Taken? Do Local Copies Exist?
(IN: *Family Puzzlers, Danielsville, GA, 1976. no. 475, p. 1–17*)
NN APA+

Wells, Robert V.
The Population of the British Colonies in America before 1776; a Survey of Census Data.
Princeton, NJ, Princeton U. Press, 1975. 342 p., index.
NN JLE 76-1159

NATIONAL ARCHIVES
Colket, Meredith B., and Frank E. Bridges.

Guide to Genealogical Records in the National Archives.
Washington, DC, National Archives, 1964. 145 p., t of c, no index.
NN APB 74-11

Genealogical Records in the National Archives.
17 p.
(*National Archives Leaflet no. 5*)

Genealogical Sources Outside the National Archives.
8 p.
(*National Archives Leaflet no. 6*)

Military Service Records in the National Archives of the United States.
15 p.
(*National Archives General Leaflet no. 7*)

Regional Branches of the National Archives.
(*National Archives General Information Leaflet no. 22*)

Walker, James Dent.
Records in the National Archives. Washington, D.C.
(IN: *DSGRM, Detroit, MI, 1976–1977 v. 40 p. 55–58, 101–105.*)
(This article updates some of the information in Colket's guide.)
NN APGA

PENSION
Index of Revolutionary War Pension Applications.
Washington, DC, 1976. 658 p., alpha.
(Bicentennial Edition, revised and enlarged)
(*NGSSP No. 40*)
NN APGA

United States Pension Bureau.
Rejected or Suspended Applications for Revolutionary War Pensions.
Baltimore, MD, GPC, 1969 (orig. 1852). 402 p.
NN APK

U.S. Pension Office (Int. Dept.)
List of Pensioners on the Roll Jan. 1, 1883. Washington, 1883. 5 v. (v. 1—ME, NH, VT, MA, RI, CT, NJ, DC; v. 2—NY, PA; v. 3—OH, IL, IO; v. 4—Dakota Ter., New Mexico Ter., Mont. Ter., Wash. Ter., Idaho Ter., Utah Ter., Ariz Ter., Alaska Ter., Wyom. Ter.; v. 5—DE, WV, VA, MD, NC, SC, GA, FL, AL, MS, LA, TX, AR, TN, KY, MO)
NN *R-APK

U.S. State Dept.
A Census of Pensioners for Revolutionary or Military Services 1840: General Index.
Baltimore, MD, GPC, 1965. 382 p.
NN *R-APK

U.S. State Dept.
A Census of Pensioners for the Revolution or Military Service with Their Names, Ages and Places of Residence Taken in 1840.
Baltimore, MD, GPC, 1967 (orig. 1841). 195 p.
NN *R-APK

U.S. War Dept.
Letter from the Secretary of War Transmitting a Report of the Names, Rank and Line of Every Person Placed on the Pension List in Pursuant of the Act of the 18th March 1818 ...

Baltimore, MD, GPC, 1955 (orig. 1920). 672–.
NN *R-APK

U.S. War Dept.
Message from the President of the United States ... a List of All Pensioners ...
Washington, DC, Southern Book, 1959 (orig. 1818). 358 p.
NN APK

U.S. War Dept.
Report from the Secretary of War ... in Relation to the Pension Establishment of the United States.
Washington, DC, D. Green, 1835. 3 v.
NN APK

IMMIGRATION

Bolton, Ethel S.
Immigrants to New England 1700–1775.
Baltimore, MD, GPC, 1966 (orig. 1931). 235 p., index (Exact origins in a few cases)
NN APR (New England)

Coleman, Terry.
Passage to America, A History of Emigrants from Great Britain and Ireland to America in the Mid-Nineteenth Century.
London, Hutchinson, 1972. 317, 25 p.
NN JLE 73-1335

Ghirelli, Michael.
Emigrants from England to America 1682–1692.
Baltimore, MD, Magna Carta, 1968. 106 p., index.
NN APK

Kaminkow, Jack, and Marion Kaminkow.

A List of Emigrants from England to America, 1718–1759.
Baltimore, MD, Magna Carta, 1964. 288 p., alpha index of places.
NN APK

Kaminkow, Jack, and Marion Kaminkow.
Original List of Emigrants in Bondage from London to the American Colonies, 1719–1744.
Baltimore, MD, Magna Carta, 1967. 211 p., alpha.
NN APK

Lancour, Harold.
A Bibliography of Ship Passenger Lists, 1538–1825; Being a Guide to Published Lists of Early Immigrants to North America. 3rd ed., rev. and enlarged by Richard J. Wolfe. With a list of passenger arrival records in the National Archives by Frank E. Bridgers. New York, New York Public Library, 1963, 137 p.
NN APG and APG 77-219

Miller, Olga K.
Migration, Emigration, Immigration.
Logan, UT, Everton, 1977. 278 p.
NN APG 77-219

Morton Allan Directory of European Passenger Steamship Arrivals.
New York., N.Y. Information Bureau, 1931.
(About vessels arriving N.Y. 1890–1930; Baltimore, Boston and Philadelphia 1904–1926)
NN Desk Room 315G

Neagles, James C. and Lila L. Neagles,

Locating Your Immigrant Ancestor, A Guide to Naturalization Records.
Logan, UT, Everton, 1975. 153 p.

Port Arrivals and Immigrants to the City of Boston 1715 and 1716 and 1762–1769, comp. by William H. Whitmore with a Reconstructed Index.
Baltimore, MD, GPC, 1973 (orig. 1900). 111 p.
NN APR (Boston) 73-2973

U.S. National Archives.
Index to Passenger Lists of Vessels Arriving at New York 1820–1846.
Washington, DC, 1958. 103 reels of microfilm arranged alphabetically.
NN *ZI-80

U.S. State Dept.
Passenger Lists of Vessels Arriving at New York 1820–1897.
Washington, DC, 1967.
(NN has reels covering Jan. 7, 1820–1860 and is gradually adding more reels.)
NN *ZI-131

U.S. State Dept.
Passenger Arrivals 1819–1820; a Transcript of the List of Passengers Who Arrived in the United States from the 1st of October 1819 to the 20th Sept. 1820.
Baltimore, MD, GPC, 1967. 342 p.
NN APK

U.S. State Dept.
Passenger Arrivals . . .
Baltimore, MD, Magna Carta, 1969. 427 p.
NN APK

26 Emerging Groups

AMERICAN ETHNIC GROUPS

Bailey, Rosalie Fellows.
Dutch Systems in Family Naming:
New York–New Jersey.
Washington, 1954. 21p.
(*NGSSP no. 12*)
NN APGA

The Ethnic Contribution to the
American Revolution, ed. by
Frederick F. Harling and Martin Kaufman.
Westfield, MA, History Dept.,
Westfield State College, 1976.

Johnson, Harry A.
Ethnic American Minorities, a
Guide to Media and Materials.
New York., R. R. Bowker, 1976.
304 p., index.

Miller, Wayne Charles
A Handbook of American Minorities.
New York, NYU Press, 1976. 225
p., t of c, no index.
NN *R-IE 77-97

Miller, Wayne Charles with Faye
Nell Vowell, etc.
A Comprehensive Bibliography
for the Study of American Minorities.
New York, NYU Press, 1976. 2 v.
NN IE 77-198

Sutherland, Ann.
Gypsies, the Hidden Americans.
London, Tavistock Pub., 1975. 330
p., index.
NN IEE (Gypsies) 75-939

NATIVE AMERICANS

Alterman, Hyman.
Counting People, the Census in
History.
New York, Harcourt, Brace, 1969.
(American Indians p. 291–304)
NN SDK

Apache Indians I by Albert H.
Schroeder.
New York, Garland, 1974. 1 v.
NN HBC 75-2804

Archives of the Episcopal Diocese
of Nevada in the Nevada Historical Society.
(IN: *Nevada Historical Society
Quarterly, Reno, 1975. v. 18, p.
288*)
(Included are Pyramid Lake Reservation vital records from the
Nixon, NV, Mission to the
Northern Paiute Tribe.)
NN IAA

Bell, George M., Sr.
Genealogy of Old and New Cherokee Indian Families.
Bartlesville, OK, G.M. Bell, 1972.
567 p., t of c, no index.
NN APK 73-179

Bennett, Archibald.
Finding Your Forefathers in
America.
Salt Lake City, UT, Bookcraft,
1957. p. 410–126.
(Pocahontas and her descendants)
NN APB

Biographical and Historical Index
of American Indians and Persons Involved in Indian Affairs.

266

U.S. Department of the Interior (Washington, DC).
Boston, MA, G.K. Hall, 1966. 8 v., alpha by subject.

Biographies and Legends of New England Indians.
Wakefield, MA, Bonnell Pub., 1968. 1 v.
NN HBM 73-2185

Brent, Chester Horton.
The Descendants of Col. Giles Brent, Capt. George Brent and Robert Brent, Gent, Immigrants to Maryland and Virginia.
Rutland, VT, Tuttle, 1946. p. 50*ff.*
NN APV (Brent)

Brown, John P.
Old Frontiers: the Story of the Cherokee Indians from Earliest Times to the Date of their Removal to the West, 1838.
Kingsport, TN, Southern Press, 1938. 570 p.
NN HBC

Burns, Annie Walker.
Ward Families History. Records of the Eastern Cherokee Indian Tribe Copies at the National Archives in Washington, DC (Room 5-W).
Washington, DC, A.W. Burns, 1958. 86 p., index.
(Petitions for claims for land due to Indian blood by various people named Ward—many other names included)
NN APV (Ward)

Carselowey, James M.
Pryor Cemetery.
Adair, OK, the author, 1962. 55 p.
NN APR (Pryor, OK)

Coe, Charles H.
Red Patriots.
Gainesville, FL, U. of FL Press, 1974 (orig. 1898). 290, 5 p.
(Seminole Indians)
NN HBC 74-1716

Debo, Angie.
A History of the Indians of the United States.
Norman, OK, U. of OK Press, 1970. 386 p., index.
(Many illus. and ports., including Joseph Brant by George Romney)
NN HBC 76-246

Dennis, Henry C.
The American Indian, 1492–1970.
Dobbs Ferry, NY, Oceana, 1971. 137 p.
NN HBC 72-2678

Dewdney, Selwyn H.
The Sacred Scrolls of the Southern Ojibway.
Toronto, U. of Toronto Press, 1975. 199 p., index.
NN HBC 75-937

Fehrenbach, T.R.
Comanches, the Destruction of a People.
New York, Alfred A. Knopf, 1974. 553, xiv p., index.
NN HBC 74-7406

Flexner, James T.
Mohawk Baronet: Sir William Johnson of New York.
New York, Harper, 1959. 400 p.
NN D-12 1142

Gabarino, Merwyn S.
Big Cypress, a Changing Seminole Community.

New York, Holt, Rinehart, 1972.
132 p., t of c, no index.
NN HBC 72-2889

Gibson, Arrell M.
The Chickasaws.
Norman, OK, U. of OK Press, 1971.
312 p., index.
(109th volume of the Civilization
of American Indian series, full
list p. 308–312)
NN HBC 71-585

Grassman, Thomas.
The Mohawk Indians and their
Valley ... to the end of 1693.
Schenectady, NY, E. Hugo, 1969.
722 p.
NN HBC 70-176

Green, Norma Kidd.
Iron Eye's Family: The Children
of Joseph La Flesche.
Lincoln, NB, Johnson Publ. Co.,
1969. 225 p.
(Joseph La Flesche, 1822–1889, an
Omaha Indian)
NN HBM (La Flesche)

Gridley, Marion E.
Indians of Today.
n.p., 1971, 494 p.
NN HBC 72-782

Hall, Ted Bryon.
Oklahoma Indian Territory.
Fort Worth, TX, Amer. Ref. Pub.,
752 p., index.
NN APR (Oklahoma) 72-2202

Hill, Edward E.
Preliminary Inventory of Records
of the Bureau of Indian Affairs
at the National Archives.
Washington, DC, 1965. 2 v.
(Available from National Archives
Publication Sales Branch)
NN HBB

Hodge, Frederick W.
... Handbook on Indians of Can-
ada.
Ottawa, C.H. Parmerlee, 1913. 632
p.
(Also Bulletin no. 31, Bureau of
American Ethnology)
NN HBC

Hodge, William H.
A Bibliography of Contemporary
North American Indians Se-
lected and Annotated with
Study Guides. 2nd enlarged
printing.
New York, Interland Pub., 1975.
296 p., index by author and
subject.
NN HBC 76-718

Howe, Daisie D.W.S.
Some Midwest Descendants of Re-
becca Mataoka Pocahontas;
The Line of Susan Elizabeth
Branch Howe, Lafayette
County, Missouri, Who Married
Robert Mitchell Howe.
Kansas City, MO, c. 1961. 101
leaves.
NN APV+ (Howe)

Hyde, George E.
The Pawnee Indians.
Norman, OK, U. of OK Press, 1974.
372 p., index.
NN HBC 74-1362

Kelly, Lawrence C.
Indian Records in the Oklahoma
Historical Society Archives.
(IN: Chronicles of Oklahoma,
Oklahoma City, 1976. v. 54, p.
227–244)
NN IAA

Klein, Bernard, and Daniel Ico-
lari.

Reference Encyclopedia of the American Indian.
New York, B. Klein, 1967. 536 p., alpha.
NN *R-American History

Mails, Thomas E.
The People Called Apache.
Englewood Cliffs, NJ, Prentice-Hall, 1974. 447 p.
NN HBC+ 75-2080

Massey, George Valentine II.
Ancestry of Richard Dorsey Morgan.
n.p., 1953. p. 84–97, etc.
NN APV (Morgan)

Minnesota Historical Society.
Chippewa and Dakota Indians: A Subject Catalog of Books ...
St. Paul, MN, 1969. 131 p.
NN HB 72-1710

Momaday, N. Scott.
The Names.
New York, Harper & Row, 1976.
NN JFD 77-1185

Morgan, Lewis Henry.
Houses and House Life of the American Aborigines.
Chicago, IL, U. of Chicago Press, 1965. 319 p.
NN HBC

New York State Adjutant General's Office.
Index of Awards on Claims of the Soldiers of the War of 1812 ...
Albany, NY, 1860 (rep., GPC, 1969).
(Section on Indian Tribes Mustered into the Service of the United States: Seneca Nation, p. 563–572; Oneida Nation, p. 573; Tuscarora Nation, p. 573.)
NN ITH 72-2317

Olsen, Evelyn Guard.
Indian Blood.
Parsons, WV, McClain, 1967. 253 p., t of c, no index.
NN ISC

Oregon Indians by Robert J. Suphan and Herbert C. Taylor, Jr.
New York., Garland, 1974. 2 v.
NN HBC 75-2083

Parker, Arthur C.
Notes on the Ancestry of Cornplanter.
Canandaigua, NY., 1927. 22 p.
(IN: *NY State Arch. Assoc. Lewis H. Morgan Chapt. Researches and Trans. v. 5, no. 2*)
NN HBA

Parker, Jimmy B.
American Indian Genealogical Research.
(IN: *NGSQ, Washington, DC, 1975. v. 63, p. 15–21*)
NN APGA

Peckham, Howard H.
Pontiac and the Indian Uprising.
Princeton, NJ, Princeton U. Press, 1947. 346 p., index.
NN HBM (Pontiac)

Phillips, George Harwood.
Chiefs and Challengers: Indian Resistance and Cooperation in Southern California.
Berkeley, CA, U. of CA Press, 1975. 222 p., index.

Puckett, James M., Jr.
Indian Issue of Georgia Genealogical Society Quarterly.
(IN: *GGSQ, Atlanta, GA, 1967. v. 3, series 3, p. 414–482, t of c, p. 519*)
(Genealogy of the Ross family, Cherokee Census Records of the 1830's, etc.)
NN APGA

Pueblo Indians I, by Florence H. Ellis, etc.
New York., Garland, 1974. 1 v.
NN HBC 75-2478

Reference Encyclopedia of the American Indian.
Rye, NY, 1974. 1 v, v. 2.
NN HBC 75-68

Reynolds, Charles R.
American Indian Portraits.
Brattleboro, VT, 1971. 123 p.
NN HBC+ 72-1576

Robertson, Wyndham.
Pocahontas Alias Matoaka and Her Descendants through Her Marriage at Jamestown, Virginia, in April 1614.
Baltimore, MD, GPC, 1956 (orig. 1887). 84 p.
(See also *GM, London, 1976. v. 18, p. 227* NN ARCA)
NN APV (Pocahontas)

Ruttenber, Edward M.
History of the Indian Tribes of Hudson's River.
Port Washington, NY, 1971. 415 p.
NN HBC 75-1494

Sac, Fox and Iowa Indians I, by Zachary Gussow.
New York, Garland, 1974. 1 v.
NN HBC 75-2806

Seaver, James E.
Life of Mary Jemison, Deh-Ne-Wä-Mis. 5th edition
Buffalo, NY, 1877 (orig. 1824). 303 p.
NN *KF-1877

Silfer, David.
The Eastern Cherokees: A Census of the Cherokee Nation in North Carolina, Tennessee, Alabama and Georgia in 1851.
New Orleans, LA, Polyanthos, 1977. 150 p., index.

Smith, Dwight L., ed.
Indians of the United States and Canada: A Bibliography.
Santa Barbara, CA, ABC Clio, 1974. 453 p., index.
(Clio Bib. Series, v. 3)

Speck, Frank G.
Chapters on the Ethnology of the Powhattan Tribes of Virginia.
(IN: *Indian Notes and Monographs, New York, 1928, v. 1, p. 227-455*)
NN HBA

Stone, William Leete (1792–1844)
Life of Joseph Brant—Thayendanega . . .
Albany, NY, J. Munsell, 1865. 2 v., index v. 2.
NN HBM (Brant)

Thompson, Ray.
Walking Hoax Purchase of 1737.
Fort Washington, PA, Bicentennial Press, 1973. 112 p., t of c, no index.
(Delaware Indians)
NN HBC 74-186

Tucker, Glenn.
Tecumseh, Vision of Glory.
Indianapolis, IN, Bobbs-Merrill, 1956. 399 p., index.
NN HBM (Tecumseh)

U.S. National Archives and Records Service.
The American Indian; A Selected Catalog of National Archives Microfilm.

Washington, DC, 1972. 50 p.
NN HB 73-2748

Ute Indians I, II, by Julian H.
Seward, etc.
New York, Garland, 1974. 2 v.
NN HBC 75-1990

Vestal, Stanley.
Sitting Bull, Champion of the
Sioux.
Boston, MA, Houghton Mifflin,
1932. 350 p., index.
NN HBM (Sitting Bull)

Weaver, William O.
Hail to the Chief, True Tales of
Old Wapello.
Wapello, IA, Louisa Pub. Co., 1974.
132 p., index.
NN IVO (Wapello) 76-1383

Wheeler-Voegelin, Ermine and
Helen H. Tanmer.
Indians of Northern Ohio and
Southeastern Michigan.
New York., Garland, 1974. 374 p.

Wilson, Edmund.
Apologies to the Iroquois with a
Study of the Mohawks in High
Steel by Joseph Mitchell.
New York, Farrar, Straus, 1960.
310 p.
NN HBC

Wilson, Edmund.
Red, Black, Blond and Olive: Stud-
ies in Four Civilizations, Zuni,
Haiti, Soviet Russia, Israel.
New York, Oxford, 1956. 500 p.
NN HBC

Woodward, Grace Steele.
Pocahontas.
Norman, OK, U. of OK Press, 1969.
227 p., index, excellent illus.
NN HBM (Pocahontas)

Wright, Harry A.
Indian Deeds of Hampden County
(Massachusetts).
Springfield, MA, the author, 1905.
194 p., index.
NN IQH (Hampden)

REFERENCES FOR ADOPTEES

Allen, Steve.
How I Found My Missing Brother.
(IN: *Ladies' Home Journal, NY,
July 1975. p. 69, 30, 32.* Also
LHJ, December 1974.)

Bander, Edward J.
Change of Name and Law of
Names.
Dobbs Ferry, NY, Oceana, 1973.
116 p.
NN JLC 73-1390

Brown, Christine.
Goodbye Patrick.
London, Arlington Books, 1973.
186 p.
NN JLD 74-1934

Cabanes, Auguste.
Le Mal Héréditaire.
Paris, A. Michael, 1945–50. 2 v.
(Series 1: the descendants of
Charles V of Austria; Series 2:
the Bourbons of Spain)
NN BXD

Fisher, Florence.
The Search for Anna Fisher.
New York, A. Fields Books, 1973.
270 p.
(Fawcett Crest Book P2083 paper
edition 1974)
NN JLD 74-1628

Hulse, Jerry.
Jody.
New York, McGraw-Hill, 1976.

Johnston, Tracey.
Torment over the Viet Non-Orphans.
(IN: *The New York Times Magazine, New York, May 9, 1976. p. 14–15, 76– 78, 83–87*)

Knight, Alva.
Find Happiness in Your Name.
New York, Vanguard Press, 1973. 239 p.

Leeson, Francis.
The Talbot Fingers.
(IN: *GM*, London, 1969. v. 16, p. 8–10)
NN ARCA

Litton, Pauline.
Fact, Fiction and a Foundling.
(IN: *The North Cheshire Family Historian*, Stockport, Cheshire, Feb. 1976. v. 3, no. 1, p. 7–9)
NN ARX (Cheshire) 76-1670

Massachusetts Secretary of the Commonwealth.
List of Persons Whose Names Have Been Changed 1780–1892.
Boston, MA, Wright & Potter, 1893. 522 p., index.
NN APR (Massachusetts)

McKuen, Rod.
Finding My Father, One Man's Search for Identity.
New York, Cheval Books, 1976. 253 p.

Meyer, Mary Keysor.
Divorces and Names Changed in Maryland by Act of the Legislature 1634–1854.
Baltimore, MD, M.K. Meyer, 1970. 143 p., alpha.
NN APR (Maryland)

Millhouse, Leslie W.

Adopted Children and Family Trees.
(IN: *Cheshire Family Historian. Chester, Eng., Apr. 1974. no. 2, p. 13ff.*)
NN ARX (Cheshire) 76-1670

Muller, Herman J.
Studies in Genetics; Selected Papers of H. J. Muller.
Bloomington, IN, IN U. Press, 1962. 618 p.
NN AE-10 370

Phillimore, W.P.W., and Edward A. Fry.
An Index to Changes of Name ... 1760–1901.
London, Phillimore & Fry, 1905. 357 p., alpha.
NN ARF

Ridge, C. Harold.
How Many Ancestors Have We?
(IN: *The Amateur Historian*, London, 1952. v. 1, p. 18–23) (Examples of the Hapsburg lip illustrated)
NN CA

Schwartz, Harold, M.D.
Abraham Lincoln and the Marfan Syndrome.
(IN: *The Journal of the American Medical Association. Chicago, 1964. v. 187, p. 473–479.*)

Triseliotis, John B.
In Search of Origins—The Experiences of Adopted People.
London, RKP, 1973. 177 p., index.
NN JLD 74-1838

Woods, Frederick Adams.
The Influence of Monarchs; Steps in a New Science of History.
New York, Macmillan, 1913. 422 p.
NN SED

Woods, Frederick Adams.
Mental and Moral Heredity in Royalty, A Statistical Study in History and Psychology.

New York, Henry Holt, 1906. 312 p., t of c, no index, many gen. charts and ports.
NN QOP

GUIDES

Black Americans
(IN: *Miller, Wayne C. A Comprehensive Bibliography for the Study of American Minorities.*
New York, New York University Press, 1976. v. 1 p. 3–262.)
NN IE 77-198

The Bicentennial Genealogy and Oral Historical Institute.
New York, Black Librarians' Caucus, Inc., 1976.
(Pamphlet prepared for seminar in the Harlem State Office Building, Sat., Oct. 2, 1976)

Gamarekian, Barbara.
Blacks Searching for the Long-Lost Past.
(IN: *The New York Times, New York, Feb. 21, 1977. p. 28*)
NN NY *Times* microfilm Room 315M

Haley, Alex.
My Furthest-Back-Person—"The African."
(IN: *The New York Times Magazine, Sunday, July 16, 1972. p. 12–16*)
NN NY *Times* film Room 315M

Haley, Alex.
Roots, The Saga of an American Family.
Garden City, NY, Doubleday, 1976. 587 p., no index, no t of c.
NN APV (Haley) 77-56

Johnson, Thomas A.
"Roots" has Widespread and Inspiring Influence. Babies Being Named after Characters in Best-Seller. "Roots" also Inspiring Interest in Africa and Genealogy.
(IN: *NYT, New York, March 9, 1977. p. 46, col. 1–4*)

Journal of Negro History.
Washington, DC, 1916–
NN IEC

Kamuyu-Wa-Kange'the
What Is your African Name.
Jamaica, NY, 1972. 23 p.
NN APD 72-3024

Kaplan, Sidney.
The Black Presence in the Era of the American Revolution, 1770–1800.
Washington Nat. Port. Gallery, Smithsonian, 1973. 241 p., no index.
NN IG 75-362

Marsh, Louise D.
Slave Genealogy.
(IN: *Ebony, Chicago, 1976. p. 22ff.*)
NN *DA+

Murrell, Peggy J.
Black Genealogy.
(IN: *The Wall Street Journal, New York, March 9, 1972. p.1, etc.*)
NN Room 227 (microfilm)

Newman, Debra L.
List of Free Black Heads of Families in the First Census of the United States.
Washington, DC, 1973. 73 p.
NN Sc. 929.3-N

(Also *National Archives Special List, Washington, 1973, No. 34.* *44 p.* NN APK 77-936)

Porter, Dorothy B.
Family Records, a Major Source for Documenting the Black Experience in New England.
(IN: *Old-Time New England. Boston, 1973. v. 63, p. 69–72*)
NN IAA

Puckett, Newbell W. Niles.
Black Names in America: Origins and Usage.
Boston, MA, G. D. Hall, 1975. 561 p.
(Several alphabetical lists in Chapt. 5. Dictionary of African Origins, p. 347–469, may give some clues to the country from which your family came.)
NN APD 76-2024 & Sc 929.4-P

Roderick, Thomas H.
Negro Genealogy.
(IN: *The American Genealogist, Des Moines, IA, 1971. v. 47, p. 88–91.*)
NN APGA

Rose, James, and Alice Eicholz.
Black Genesis. . .
Detroit, MI, Gale, 1977. c. 350 p.

Scarupa, Harriet Jackson.
Black Genealogy.
(IN: *Essence, New York, July 1976. v. 7, p. 56–57, 84–87*)
NN JFM 72-137 & Sc. Ser.-M.E865

Sloan, Irving J.
Blacks in America: 1492–1976; A Chronology and Fact Book, 4th ed. revised.
Dobbs Ferry, NY, Oceana, 1977. 169 p., index.
NN IEC 77-615

Thompson, Era B.
The Baughan Family, a Tale of Two Continents.
(IN: *Ebony, Chicago, 1975. v. 30, p. 53–64*)
NN *DA+

U.S. National Archives and Records Service.
Black Studies: Select Catalog of National Archives and Records Service Microfilm Publications.
Washington, DC, 1971. 71 p.
NN IEC 74-2364

U.S.W.P.A. Illinois.
Directory of Negro Baptist Churches in U.S.
Chicago, 1942. 2 v.
NN ZVLW

Whiteman, Maxwell.
Problems, Sources, Methodology. Black Genealogy.
(IN: *Research Quarterly, Chicago, 1972. v. 11, p. 311–319*)
NN L-10 6126

Woodson, Carter Goodwin, 1875–1950
Free Negro Heads of Families in the United States Census of 1830.
Assoc. for the Study of Negro Life and History, 1925. 296 p., index.
NN IEC

GENERAL SOURCES

Adler, Bill.
The Black Soldier from the American Revolution to Vietnam.
New York, 1971. 248 p.
NN IEC 72-293 & Sc 355.1-A

Afro-American Encyclopedia.
North Miami, FL, Educational

Book Pub., 1974. 10 v., alpha, index in v. 10.
NN IEC 74-2374

Alford, Sterling G.
Famous First Blacks.
New York, 1974. 105 p.
NN Sc 920.073-A

Atlanta University.
General Catalogue of Atlanta University, Atlanta, Georgia ... 1867–1929.
Atlanta, GA, 1929. 162 p.
NN STG

Bell, Barbara L.
Black Biographical Sources: An Annotated Bibliography.
New Haven, CT, 1970. 20 p.
(*Yale U. Library Bibliography Series 1*)
NN *RB-*GAA

Birmingham, Stephen.
Certain People. . . (301 p.)
Boston, MA, Little, Brown, 1977.
(Black aristocracy with portraits)

The Black American in United States History.
Boston, MA, Allyn & Bacon, 1973. 280 p.
NN Sc. 073-T

Black American Reference Book.
New York, Phelps Stokes Foundation, 1976.
(Mabel Smythe, ed., 1976 ed.)

Bracey, John H.
Free Blacks in America.
Belmont, CA, 1971. 160 p.
NN IEC 72-607

Caldwell, A.B.
History of the American Negro and His Institutions.

Atlanta, GA, A.B. Caldwell, 1917–1923. 7 v., index in each.
v. 1 (1917. Georgia, c. 220 bios.)
v. 2 (1920. Georgia, c. 160 bios.)
v. 3 (1919. South Carolina, c. 275 bios.)
v. 4 (1921. North Carolina, c. 250 bios.)
v. 5 (1921. Virginia, c. 230 bios.)
v. 6 (1922. Washington, DC, c. 125 bios.)
v. 7 (1923. West Virginia, c. 125 bios.)
NN IEC

Calendar of the Manuscripts of the Schomburg Collection.
New York, Andronicus, c. 1974 (orig. 1942). 548 p., index.
NN Pub. Cat. 74-315

Christopher, Maurine.
Black Americans in Congress. Revised and enlarged.
New York, Thomas Y. Crowell, 1976 (orig. 1971). 329 p., index.
NN IEC 77-171

Conyers, James.
Black Elected Officials.
New York, Russell Sage Foundation, 1976. 190 p., index.
NN IEC 76-1395

Dannett, Sylvia G.L.
Profiles of Negro Womanhood.
New York, M. W. Lads, 1964. v. 1 (1619–1900), 352 p., index. (Negro Heritage Library)
NN IEC

Davis, John P.
The American Negro Reference Book.
Englewood Cliffs, NJ, Prentice Hall, 1966. 969 p., index.
NN IEC

Directory of Afro-American Resources.
New York, R.R. Bowker, 1970. 485 p.
NN Pub. Cat. 72-342

Dobler, Lavinia.
Pioneers and Patriots: The Lives of Six Negroes of the Revolutionary Era.
Garden City, NY, Doubleday, 1965. 118 p.
NN IEC

A Documentary History of Slavery in North America, ed. by Willie Lee Rose.
New York, Oxford, 1976. 537 p.
NN IIR 76-557

Dunn, Lynn P.
Black Americans, A Study Guide and Source Book.
San Francisco, CA 1970. 112 p.
NN Sc 917.307-D

Ebony.
The Negro Handbook.
Chicago, IL, Johnson Pub., 1966. 535 p.
NN *R-IEC

Ebony Patriots (in the NYC area, 1776-1779).
New York, Institute of Afro-American Affairs, NYU, 3rd floor, 70 Washington Square, New York, NY 10012, 1976. 18 p.

Fletcher, Marvin.
The Black Soldier and Officer in the U.S. Army, 1891-1917.
Columbia, SC, 1971. 205 p.
NN Sc 355. 1-F

Foner, Jack D.
Blacks and the Military in American History.

New York, Praeger, 1974. 278 p., index.
NN IEC 74-2147

Fowler, Arlen L.
The Black Infantry in the West 1869-1891.
Westport, CT, Greenwood, 1971. 167 p.
NN IEC 72-676

Gutman, Herbert G.
The Black Family in Slavery & Freedom, 1750-1925.
New York, Pantheon, 1976. 664 p., index.
NN Sc 301.421-G

Hamilton, Green P.
Beacon Lights of the Race.
Memphis, TN, E.H. Clarke, 1911. 546 p.
NN AGZ

Hartshorn, William N.
An Era of Progress and Promise 1865-1910, the Religious, Moral and Educational Development of the American Negro Since His Emancipation.
Boston, MA, Priscilla, 1910. 576 p.
NN IEC

Horne, Lena, and Richard Schickel.
Lena
New York, Doubleday, 1965. 224 p., no index.
NN *MEC (Horne, L.)

Jefferson, Isaac.
Memoirs of a Monticello Slave, as dictated to Charles Campbell in the 1840's by one of Thomas Jefferson's Slaves.
Charlottesville, VA, U. of VA Press, c. 1951. 86 p.
NN E-10 4239

Johnson, Jesse.
The Black Soldier (Documented 1619–1815); Missing Pages in United States History.
Hampton, VA, 1969. 174 p.
NN IEC 72-1623

Journal of Black Studies.
Beverly Hills, CA, Sage Pub., 1970–
v. 1–.
NN JFK 72-53

LaBrie, Henry G.
The Black Newspaper in America, A Guide.
Iowa City, IA, U. of IA, c. 1970. 64 p.
NN JFF 72-272

McPherson, James M., etc.
Blacks in America, Bibliographic Essays.
New York, Doubleday, 1971. 430 p., index.
NN IEC 72-2123

The National Cyclopedia of the Colored Race, Clement Richardson ed.-in-chief.
Montgomery, AL, National Pub. Co., 1919. 619 p., plus index, alpha by state.
NN AGZ +

New York Public Library. Schomburg Collection of Negro Literature.
Dictionary Catalog of the Schomburg Collection.
Boston, MA, G.K. Hall, 1962. 9 v. 1st sup., 1967, 2 v.; 2nd sup., 1972, 4 v.
(Now the Schomburg Center for Research in Black Culture, 103 W. 135th St., New York, NY 10030.)
NN Pub. Cat. 1962

Nichols, Charles H.
Many Thousands Gone. The Ex-Slaves' Accounts of Their Bondage and Freedom.
Leiden, Netherlands E.J. Brill, 1963. 229 p.
NN E-12 3347

Penn, I.G., & J.W.E. Bower.
The United Negro, His Problems and His Progress.
Atlanta, GA, D.E. Luther, 1902. 600 p., long t of c called index. (Many ports., illus. of churches, etc.)
NN IEC

Penn, Irvine G.
The Afro-American Press and its Editors ... with contribution by Frederick Douglass.
New York, Arno, 1969 (orig. 1891). 565 p.
NN IEC & NARF

Reuter, Edward B.
The Mulatto in the United States.
New York, Haskell House, 1969 (orig. 1918). 417 p., index.
(Leading Men of the Negro Race, p. 183–215)
NN IEC 72-872

Rogers, Joel A.
World's Great Men of Color ...
New York, J.A. Rogers, 1946–49.
v. 1–2.
NN AA

Schomburg Center for Research in Black Culture.
Journal.
New York, 1976– v. 1–.

Simmons, William J.
Men of Mark; Eminent, Progressive and Rising.
Cleveland, OH, G.M. Rewell and

Co., 1887. 1,141 p. (Reprinted
by Arno)
NN AGZ & IEC

Smedley, Robert C.
History of the Underground Rail-
road.
New York, Arno, 1969. 407 p.
NN IEC

Sprading, Mary Mace.
In Black and White: Afro-Ameri-
cans in Print ... 1619–1969.
Kalamazoo, MI, K. Library Sys-
tem, 1971. 127 p., alpha.
NN IEC 72-20008

Stewart, Paul, and Fray Marcos
Purdue.
Westward Soul!
Denver, CO, Com. College of Den-
ver, 1976. 59 p., illus.
(Black American West Founda-
tion, P.O. Box 6589, Denver, CO
80206)

Toppin, Edgar A.
A Biographical History of Blacks
in America Since 1528.
New York, McKay, 1971. 499 p.
NN IEC 71-745 & Sc. 973-T

Wesley, Charles H.
The Negro's Struggle for Freedom
in Its Birthplace.
(IN: *JNH, Washington, DC, 1945.
v. 30, p. 62–81*)
NN IEC

Who's Who Among Black Americans. Wm. C. Matney, ed.
Northbrook, IL, Educational Communications, 1976– v. 1 (772 p.),
10,000 bios., v. 2 in progress.
Sc 920.073W

Who's Who in Colored America.
New York, WWCA Corp., 1927–
1950. 7 v. plus sup. to v. 7. Each
v. alpha, ports.
NN IEC

Who's Who in the Colored Race.
Chicago, IL, Frank L. Mather,
1915. v. 1– (269 p.) alpha.
NN IEC

Woodson, Carter Goodwin, 1875–
1950.
A Century of Negro Migration.
New York, AMS Press, 1970 (orig.
1918). 221 p.
NN IEC

Woodson, Carter Goodwin.
Free Negro Owners of Slaves in
the United States in 1830, To-
gether with Absentee Owner-
ship of Slaves in the United
States.
New York, Negro Universities
Press, 1968 (orig. 1924). 78 p.
NN IEC 72-1699

UNITED STATES

Alabama

Moorman, J. H., and E. L. Barrett.
Leaders of the Colored Race in
Alabama.
Mobile, AL, News Pub., 1928. 98 p.
NN IEC

Reynolds, Alfred W.
The Alabama Negro Colony in
Mexico, 1894–1896.
(IN: *Alabama Review, Tuscaloosa,
1952. v. 5 p. 243–268*)
NN IAA

California

Abajian, James deT.
Blacks and Their Contribution to
the American West, a Bibliog-
raphy ... (San Francisco Public
Library).
Boston, MA, G. K. Hall, 1974.
NN IEC 75-1577

Beasley, Delilah L.
The Negro Trail Blazers of Cali-
fornia.
Los Angeles, CA, *Times Mirror*,
1919. 323 p.
NN IEC

Holte, Clarence L.
The Black Settlers of Northern
California.
(IN: *The Westerners, New York,
1968. v. 15, p. 78–79, 87–88*)
NN IW

Thurman, Sue Bailey.
Pioneers of Negro Origin in Cali-
fornia.
San Francisco, CA, Acme, 1952. 70
p.
NN IEC

Colorado

Harvey, James R.
Negroes in Colorado
(IN: *Colorado Magazine, Denver,
1949. v. 26, p. 165–176*)
NN IAA

Connecticut

Schmoke, Kurt.
The Dixwell Avenue Congrega-
tional Church, 1829–1896.
(IN: *NHCHS Journal, New Haven,
1971. v. 20 p. 1–21*)
NN IQM

Warner, Robert A.
New Haven Negroes, a Social His-
tory.
New Haven, CT, Yale U. Press,
1940. 309 p.
NN IEC

White, David O.
Connecticut's Black Soldiers,
1775–1783. 71 p.
NN Sc. 973.23-W

Delaware

Liveway, Harold C.
Delaware Negroes, 1855–1915.
(IN: *Delaware History, Wilming-
ton, 1966. v. 13, p. 87–123*)
NN IAA

District of Columbia

Brown, Letitia Wood.
Free Negroes in the District of
Columbia.
New York, 1972. 226 p.
NN Sc 975.302-B

Caldwell (see General Sources), v.
6

Shannon, Alexander H.
The Negro in Washington ...
New York, W. Neale, 1930. 332 p.
NN IEC

Twentieth Century Union League
Directory ... A Historical, Bio-
graphical and Statistical Study
of Colored Washington.
Washington, DC, 1901. 174 p.
NN IEC

Florida

Porter, Kenneth W.
Florida Slaves and Free Negroes

in the Seminole Indian Wars, 1835–1842.
(IN: *JNH, Washington, DC, 1943. v. 28, p. 390–421*)
NN IEC

Georgia

Caldwell (see General Sources), v. 1–2.
(V. 1 [1917], p. 210–214: Bio. of Rev. Adam D. Williams [born Penfield, Greene Co., GA, 2 Jan. 1863], pastor of Ebenezer Baptist Church, Atlanta. Son of Willis and Creecy Williams, husband of Jennie C. Parks, daughter of William and Fannie Parks of Atlanta. Their daughter, Alberta Christine Williams, married Rev. Martin Luther King and was the mother of Rev. Martin Luther King, Jr. Ports.)

Gordon, Asa H.
The Georgia Negro, a History.
Spartanburg, SC, The Reprint Co., 1972 (orig. 1937).
426 p., index.

Harvey, Diana.
The Terri, Augusta's Black Enclave.
(IN: *Richmond County History, Augusta, 1973. v. 5, p. 60–75.*)
NN ITK (Richmond Co.) 75–496

Illinois

The Negro in Illinois
(IN: *Illinois History, Springfield, IL, 1960. v. 14 p. 51–71.*)
NN IAA

Spear, Allan H.
Black Chicago: The Making of A Negro Ghetto, 1890–1920.
Chicago, U. of Chicago, 1967. 254 p.
NN IEC

Indiana

Thornbrough, Emma Lou.
The Negro in Indiana, A Study of a Minority (period prior to 1906).
Indianapolis, 1957. 412 p.
(Indiana. History Bureau. Indiana Historical Collections. v. 37)
NN IEC

Iowa

Bergman, Leola.
The Negro in Iowa.
(IN: *Iowa Journal of History, Iowa City, 1948. v. 46, p. 3–90*)
NN IAA

Kentucky

Bellardo, Lewis J., Jr.
Frankfurt, Kentucky, Census of Free Blacks.
(IN: *NGSQ, Washington, DC, 1975. v. 63, p. 272–275*)
NN APGA

Louisiana

Blassingame, John W.
Black New Orleans, 1860–1880.
Chicago, IL, 1973. 301 p.
NN Sc. 976.3-B

Everett, Donald E.
Emigres and Militiamen: Free

Persons of Color in New Orleans, 1803–1815.
(IN: *JNH, Washington, DC, 1953. v. 38 p. 377–402*)
NN IEC

Fleming, Margaret M. Jackson.
Contributions of the Negro in Lake Charles, A Pictorial Review.
Lake Charles, L.C. Letter Shop, 1967. 138 p.
NN ITQ (Lake Charles)

McConnell, Roland C.
Negro Troops of Antebellum Louisiana: A History of the Battalion of Freemen of Color.
Baton Rouge, LA, LSU Press, 1968. 143 p., index.

Roherer, John H.
The Eighth Generation: Cultures and Personalities of New Orleans Negroes.
New York, Harper, 1960. 346 p.
NN IEC

The Sepia Socialite.
... The Negro in Louisiana: Seventy-eight Years of Progress.
New Orleans, Sepia Socialite, 1942. 168 p.
NN IEC+

Winston, James E.
The Free Negro in New Orleans.
(IN: *LHQ, New Orleans, 1938. v. 21, p. 1075–1085*)
NN IAA

Maryland

Brackett, Jeffrey P.
The Negro in Maryland.
Freeport, NY, Books for Libraries, 1969. 268 p.
NN IIR 71-669

Bragg, George Freeman.
Men of Maryland. Revised edition.
Baltimore, Church Advocate Press, 1925. 160 p.
NN IEC

Genealogical Marylandia.
Genealogical Studies of Black Families.
(IN: *MHM, Baltimore, 1976. v. 71, p. 103–104*) (See also v. 66, 1971, p. 79–81)
NN IAA

Kimmel, Ross M.
Free Blacks in Seventeenth Century Maryland.
(IN: *MHM, Baltimore, 1976. v. 71, p. 19–25*)
NN IAA

Secretary in Maryland-Tax Lists.
(IN: *Maryland Genealogical Society Bulletin, Baltimore, 1977. v. 18, p. 9–12*)
(Many Negroes are mentioned by name in this 1740 tax list of Anne Arundel County.)
NN APR (Maryland)

Massachusetts

Batchelder, Samuel F.
Notes on Col. Henry Vassall (1721–1769) ... and His Slaves Tony and Darby.
Cambridge, MA, Cambridge Hist. Soc., 1917.
NN APV (Vassall)

Boston Registry Department.
Records ... Boston, 1883–1903. v. 9 (Births, Marriages, Deaths, 1630–1699) p. 272 (Negroes); v. 24 (Births, 1700–1800) p. 378–379 (Negroes); v. 28 (Marriages, 1700–1751) p. 464–466

(Negroes); v. 30 (Marriages 1752–1809) p. 690–702 (Negroes).
NN IQH (Boston)

Brookline Vital Records.
Salem, Essex Inst., 1929.
(Births, p. 81–82; marriages, p. 175; deaths, p. 242–244)
NN APR (Brookline)

Christ Church, Boston, Records, 1725–1774.
(IN: *NEHGR, Boston, 1948. v. 102, p. 32–37*)
NN *R-APGA

Greene, Lorenzo J.
The Negro in Colonial New England, 1620–1776.
Port Washington, NY, Kennikat, 1966 (orig. 1942). 404 p.
NN IEC

Michigan

Banner, Melvin E.
The Black Pioneer in Michigan
Midland, MI, 1973. 1 v.
NN Sc 977.4-B

Minnesota

Spangler, Earl.
The Negro in Minnesota. Introduction by Carl T. Rowan.
Minneapolis, T. S. Denison, 1961. 211 p.
NN IEC

Mississippi

Adams, Rev. Revels A.
Cyclopedia of African Methodism in Mississippi.
Natchez, 1902. 215 p.
NN ZTR

William Johnson's Natchez.
The Ante-Bellum Diary of a Free Negro, ed. by William Ransom Hogan and Edwin A Davis.
Baton Rouge, LA, LSU Press, 1951. 812 p., index.
NN ITOM (Natchez)

Mosley, Mrs. Charles C.
The Negro in Mississippi.
Jackson, Herderman Bros., 1950. 151 p.
NN IEC

Wallace, Jesse T.
A History of the Negroes of Mississippi from 1865 to 1890.
Clinton, MS, 1927. 188 p.
NN IEC

New York

Abyssinian Baptist Church, N.Y.
The Articles of Faith, Church Discipline . . .
New York, 1833. 17 p.
(Members are listed alphabetically by their first name, with last name and the date they joined the church also given, p. 11–14.)
NN IRIB

Baptismal Records of the 1st Dutch Reformed Church, Albany, 1809–1823.
(IN: *Dutch Settlers of Albany Yearbook, Albany, 1961–62. v. 36, p. 21–28*)
NN IRM (Albany)

Census of Slaves 1755, New York.
(No records for Albany, New York or Suffolk counties.)
NN APRF (New York)

Korbin, David.
Black Minority in Early New
York.
Albany, NYS Amer. Bicen. Comm.,
1971. 45 p.
NN Sc 326.974-K

Mabee, Carleton
Early Black Public Schools
(IN: *Long Island Forum, Islip,
1973. v. 36, p. 214–216*)
NN IRM (Long Island)

Ottley, Roi, and Wm. J. Weath-
erby.
The Negro in New York, an Infor-
mal Social History.
New York, NYPL, 1967. 328 p.
NN IRGC 72-2162

Reynolds, Helen W.
The Negro in Dutchess County in
the Eighteenth Century.
(IN: *DCHS Yearbook, Poughkeep-
sie, 1941. v. 26, p. 89–99*)
NN IRM (Dutchess Co.)

Tomkins, Calvin.
Profiles: The Black People of
Bridgehampton.
(IN: *The New Yorker, New York,
Sept. 10, 1973. v. 49, p. 47–101*)
NN *ZAN-3174

Wheeler, Benjamin F.
The Varick Family.
Mobile, AL, 1906. 58 p., no index.
ports.
(Des. of Rev. James Varick of the
AME Church)
NN APV (Varick)

Who's Who in Harlem, 1949–50.
1st ed.
New York, B.S.B. Trottman, 1950.
index.
NN IEC

Wortis, Helen.
Black Inhabitants of Shelter Is-
land.
(IN: *Long Island Forum, Islip,
NY, Aug. 1973. v. 36, p. 146–153*)
NN IRM (Long Island)

Yoshpe, Harry B.
Record of Slave Manumissions in
New York, During the Colonial
and Early National Periods.
(IN: *JNH. Washington, D.C., 1941,
v. 26, p. 78–107.*)
NN IEC

Yoshpe, Harry B.
Record of Slave Manumissions in
Albany, 1800–1828.
(IN: *JNH. Washington, D.C., 1941,
v. 26, p. 499–522.*)
NN IEC

North Carolina

Caldwell (See General Sources) v. 4

Farrison, William E.
The Negro Population of Guilford
County, North Carolina Before
the Civil War.
(IN: *North Carolina Historical Re-
view. Raleigh, 1944. v. 21 p. 319–
329*)
NN IAA

Logan, Frenise A.
The Movement of Negroes from
North Carolina, 1876–1894.
(IN: *North Carolina Historical Re-
view. Raleigh, 1956. v. 33 p. 45–65.*)
NN IAA

Logan, Frenise A.
The Negro in North Carolina,
1876–1894.
Chapel Hill, NC, U. of NC Press,
1964. 244 p.
NN IEC

Padgett, James A.
From Slavery to Prominence in North Carolina.
(IN: *JNH Washington, 1937. v. 22 p. 433–487*)
NN IEC

Slave and Former Slave Marriages.
(IN: *Randolph County Historical Society Genealogical Journal. Asheboro, NC 27203; Randolph Co. Public Library, 201 Worth St.; 1977. v. 1 p. 36*) covers 1840–1866.
NN current

Ohio

Davis, Russell H.
Black Americans in Cleveland ... 1796–1969.
Washington, DC, Assoc. Pub., 1972. 525 p., index.
NN IEC 75-485

Hill, Leonard W.
John Randolph's Freed Slaves Settle in Western Ohio.
(IN: *Cincinnati Hist. Soc. Bulletin, Cincinnati, OH, 1965. v. 23, p. 179–187*)
NN IVB (Cincinnati)

Kusmer, Kenneth L.
A Ghetto Takes Shape: Black Cleveland, 1870–1930.
Urbana, IL, U. of IL, 1976. 305 p. index.
(Blacks in the New World)
NN IEC 76-2312

Pennsylvania

Johnson, Richard.
Slaves and Indentured Blacks in Berks Co. Before 1800.

(IN: *Hist. Review of Berks Co., Reading, 1971–72. v. 37, p. 8–14*)
NN ISD (Berks Co.)

Oblinger, Carl D.
Ellipses, the Black Masses and Local Elan: A Review of the Sources for a History of the Ante-Bellum Negro in Southeastern Pennsylvania.
(IN: *Lancaster Co. Hist. Soc. Journal, Lancaster, 1970. v. 74, p. 124–131*)
NN ISD (Lancaster Co.)

White, Charles F.
Who's Who in Philadelphia.
Philadelphia, AME Book Concern, 1912. 206 p.
NN IEC

Willson, Joseph.
Sketches of the Higher Classes of Colored Society in Philadelphia.
Philadelphia, 1969. 116 p.
NN IEC 74-1889

Wolf, Edwin, 2nd.
Negro History: 1553–1903. An Exhibition ... from the Shelves of the Library Company of Philadelphia and the Hist. Soc. of Pennsylvania ...
Philadelphia, 1969. 83 p.
NN *KAB (Library Co. . . .)

South Carolina

Caldwell (see General Sources), v. 3.

Fitchett, E. Horace.
The Free Negro in Charleston, S.C.
Chicago, U. of Chicago thesis, 1950. 376 leaves.
NN *ZH-43 film

Newby, Idus A.
Black South Carolinians: History of the Blacks in South Carolina from 1895–1968.
Columbia, U. of SC Press, 1973. 388 p.
NN Sc 975.7-N

Tennessee

Taylor, Alrutheus A.
The Negro in Tennessee, 1865–1880.
Spartanburg, SC, The Reprint Co., 1974 (orig. 1941). 306 p., index.
NN IEC (1941 ed.)

Texas

Barr, Alwyn.
Black Texans: History of Negroes in Texas, 1528–1971.
Austin, Jenkins Pub. Co., 1973. 259 p., index.
(Negro Heritage Series no. 12)
NN Sc 976.4-B

Brewer, John M.
Negro Legislators of Texas and Their Descendants.
Austin, 1970. 154 p.
NN Sc. 976.4-B

Rice, Lawrence D.
The Negro in Texas, 1874–1900.
Baton Rouge, LA, Louisiana State University Press, 1971. 309 p.
NN IEC 71-586

Sapper, Neil Gary.
A Survey of the History of the Black People of Texas, 1930–1954.
Nashville, TN, 1954. 549 leaves.
NN Sc Micro R-779

Utah

Davis, Lenwood G.
Blacks in the State of Utah.
Monticello, IL, 1974. 12 p.
NN Sc 016.9792-D

Virgin Islands

Valle, Lionel.
The Negro Family of St. Thomas.
Ithaca, NY, 1964. 244 leaves.
NN Sc. Micro R-455

Virginia

Caldwell (see General Sources), v. 5.

Chamberlayne, Churchill Gibson.
Births from the Bristol Parish Register of Henrico, Prince George and Dinwiddie Counties.
Baltimore, MD, GPC, 1974 (orig. 1898). Negroes p. 2 (1725), 4 (1761), 6 (1720–22), 11 (1732), etc. More or less alpha index.
NN APR (Virginia) 75-1127

Coleman, Mary H. B.
Virginia Silhouettes.
Richmond, VA, Dietz, 1934. 59, 64 p.
(Letters concerning Negro slavery in Virginia)
NN SEKK

Culmer, Frederick A.
Fleming Terrell of Virginia and Missouri and the Curious Case of his Slaves.
(IN: VM, *Richmond, 1950. v. 58, p. 193–208*)
NN *R-APR (Virginia)

Douglas, Rev. William.
The Douglas Register.

Richmond, VA, J. W. Fergusson, 1928. Negro marriages, births 1721–1779 p. 347–348, 378
NN APR (Virginia)

Morgan, Edmund S.
American Slavery, American Freedom. The Ordeal of Colonial Virginia.
New York, W. W. Norton, 1975. 454 p., index.
NN IIR-76-271

The Parish Register of Christ-Church Middlesex County, Virginia from 1653 to 1812.
Richmond, NSCDA, 1897. Negroes p. 11 (bapt. 1663–1672), 31–32 (bur. 1686), 45 (bapt. 1690–94), 48–50 (bapt. 1701–1706), 58–60 (1698–1714), 62 (bapt. 1694–1703), 73–75 (bapt. 1698–1710), 143 (1735), 161 (1769–1776).
(170 p. out of 313 deal with black people)
NN APR (Middlesex Co., VA)

U.S.W.P.A.
Inventory of the Church Archives of Virginia ... Negro Baptist Churches in Richmond.
Richmond, Hist. Records Survey, 1940. 59 f.
NN ZVL

U.S.W.P.A.
The Negro in Virginia.
New York., Hastings, 1940. 30–.
(Sponsored by Hampton Institute)
NN IEC

Washington State

Washington State. State Library.
The Negro in the State of Washington, 1788–1967.

Olympia, 1968. 14 p.
NN *XMB-712

West Virginia

Caldwell (see General Sources), v. 7.

Morton, Oren F.
History of Monroe Co., West Virginia.
Dayton, VA, Ruebush-Elkins, 1916. p. 188–190. (List of free blacks 1806, etc.)
NN ITB (Monroe Co.)

CANADA

Armstrong, F. H.
The Toronto Directories and the Negro Community in the Late 1840's.
(IN: *Ontario Historical Society Papers and Records, Toronto, 1969. v. 61, p. 111–119*)
NN HWA

Canadian Black Studies Bibliographies.
London, Ontario, 1971. 96 leaves, various foliations.
NN HWH 75-2419

Clairmont, Donald H.
Africville: The Life and Death of a Canadian Black Community.
Toronto, 1974. 272 p.
NN JLD 76-104

Clairmont, Donald H.
Nova Scotian Blacks.
Halifax, 1970. 151 p.
NN Sc 917.16-C

Grant, John N.
Chesapeake Blacks Who Immigrated to New Brunswick, 1915.

(IN: *NSGQ*, Washington, DC, 1972.
v. 60, p. 194–198)
NN APGA

Henry, Frances.
Forgotten Canadians.
Don Mills, Ontario, c. 1973. 215 p.
NN HXK 75-1344

Howay, Frederic W.
The Negro Immigration into Vancouver Island in 1956.
(IN: *British Colonial History Quarterly*, Victoria, 1939. v. 3,
p. 101–13)
NN HYE

Tanser, Harry A.
The Settlement of Negroes in Kent
Co., Ontario ...
Chatham, Shepherd, 1939. 187 p.
NN YEM

Tullock, Headley,
Black Canadians.
Toronto, 1975. 186 p.
NN HWH 76-827

Walker, James W. St. G.
The Black Loyalist: The Search
for a Promised Land in Nova
Scotia and Sierra Leone, 1783–
1870.
London, Longman, 1976. 438 p.,
index.
(Dalhousie African Studies Series)

Winks, Robin W.
The Canadian Negro: An Historical Assessment.
(IN: *JNH*, Washington, DC,
1968–69. v. 53, p. 283–300, v. 54,
p. 1–18)
NN IEC

28 Jewish Ancestry in the United States and Around the World

GENEALOGIES AND GUIDES

Aaron and Leah Herschlikowitz Family Association ... History Book and Family Tree.
New York, I. M. Hirsch, c. 1938. 47 p.
NN *PWO (Herschlikowitz)

Alexander, Henry Aaron.
Notes on the Alexander Family of South Carolina and Georgia and Connections.
Alanta?, the author, 1954. 143 p., no index.
NN *PWO

Birmingham, Stephen.
The Grandees: America's Sephardic Elite.
New York, Harper & Row, 1971. 368 p.
NN *PXY 71-302

Birmingham, Stephen.
Our Crowd: The Great Jewish Families of New York.
New York, Harper & Row, 1967. 404 p.
NN *PXY

Cohen, Caroline Meyers.
Records of the Meyers, Hays and Mordecai Families, from 1707 to 1913.
Baltimore, MD, the author, typescript, c. 1913. 57 leaves, index.
NN *PWO

Corti, Egon C., Count.
The Rise of the House of Rothschild.

New York, Cosmopolitan Book, 1928. 3 v.
NN *PWO

Costa, Isaac da.
Noble Families Among the Sephardic Jews ...
London, Oxford U. Press, 1936. 219 p.
NN *PWO+

D'Aranda Pedigree.
(IN: *MGH, London, 1874. v. 1*)
NN ARCA

Draznin, Yaffa.
It Began with Zade Usher: The History and Records of the Families Bernstein-Loyev/Lewis-Mazur.
Los Angeles, CA, Jamy Pub., 1972. 255 p., index.
NN APV (Bernstein) 75-110 and *PWO (Mazur) 73-220

Draznin, Yaffa.
Jewish Genealogical Research and Central Archives.
(IN: *NGSQ, Washington, DC, 1975. v. 63, p. 204–208*)
NN APGA

Epstein, Louis M.
The Jewish Marriage Contract.
New York, Arno, 1973 (orig. 1927) 316 p., index.
NN *PIV 74-604

Evans, Eli N.
The Provincials, a Personal History of the Jews in the South.

289

New York, Atheneum, 1973. 369 p., index.
NN *PXY 74-923

Friedman, Lee M.
Rowland Gideon, an Early Boston Jew and his Family.
New York, 1939. 11 p. (*AJHS pub. no. 35, p. 27–37*)
NN *PBM p.v. 366

Foraboschi, Daniele.
Onomasticon Alternum Papyrologicum.
Milan, Varese, 1967–1971. 2 v.
(Semitic names)
NN *OBKQ+ 73-768

Gallagher, Dorothy.
Tracing Their Roots.
(IN: *The New York Times Magazine, Feb. 20, 1977. p. 48–55, 58*)
(This article discusses the ancestral search of Arthur Kurzweil, co-editor of *Toledot: The Journal of Jewish Genealogy.*)
NN *N.Y. Times* microfilm Room 315M

Genealogical Research: Methods and Sources.
Washington, DC, American Society of Genealogists, 1971. v. 2, p. 291–311.
(Chapter on Jewish migrations)
NN APB 72-1848

Gilbert, Martin.
Jewish History Atlas.
New York, Macmillan, 1969. 112 p. plus index and bib.
NN Map Div. 76-166

Goldberg, M. Hirsh.
The Jewish Connection.
New York, Stein & Day, 1976.

Gross, George M.
The Ancestors of George M. Gross.
(IN: *Virginia Tidewater Genealogy, Hampton, VA, 1975–1976. v. 6, p. 101–104; v. 7, p. 23–33*)
(A 15-year-old boy traces both sides of his family back to Europe)

Howe, Irving.
World of Our Fathers.
New York, Harcourt, Brace, 1976. 714 p.
NN *PXY 76-4205

Hubmann, Franz.
The Jewish Family Album: Yesterday's World in Old Photographs.
London, RKP, 1975. 318 p.
NN *PYA+ 76-3790

Jackson, Stanley.
The Sassoons.
New York, E. P. Dutton, 1968. 304 p., index.
(Jews from Baghdad who settled in England)
NN ARZ (Sassoon)

Kolatch, Alfred J.
The Names Dictionary, Modern English and Hebrew Names.
New York, Jonathan David, 1967. 418 p.
NN APD

Lauterbach, Leo.
Chronicle of the Lauterbach Family ... 1800–1960. New ed.
Jerusalem, Lauterbach Family Fund, 1961. 184 p., index.
NN *PWO

Lemann, Bernard
The Lemann Family of Louisiana.

Donaldsonville, LA, Lemann and
Bro., 1965. 181, 30 p., index.
NN APV (Lemann)

Liebeschutz, Rachel.
The Wind of Change, Letters of
Two Generations from the
Biedermeier Period.
(IN: *Leo Baeck Institute Yearbook,
New York, 1967. v. 12, p. 227–256*)
(August Belmont family chart, p.
239)
NN *PXA

Majer-Leonhard, Hans.
Nachkommen des Salomon Bene-
dikt Goldschmidt in Frankfurt
+ 1812.
Frankfurt, n.d. 132 p., index.
(Available at Leo Baeck Institute)

Manners, Andre.
Poor Cousins.
New York, Coward McCann, 1972.
318 p., index.
(The other side of the tracks from
Our Crowd)
NN *PXY 72-1160

Moise, Harold.
The Moise Family of South Caro-
lina.
Columbus, SC, R. L. Bryan Co.,
1961. 304 p.
NN APV (Moise)

Morpurgo, Edgardo.
... La Famiglio Morpurgo di
Gradisca Sull'Isonzo 1585–1885.
Padua, 1909. 110 p.
NN *PWO+

Morton, Frederic.
The Rothschilds, a Family Por-
trait.
New York, Atheneum, 1962. 305 p.

(Excellent family chart)
NN D-13 7980

New Standard Jewish Encyclope-
dia, edited by Cecil Roth and
Geoffrey Wigoder.
New revised edition.
London, W.H. Allen, 1975 (pre-
vious ed. 1970). 2,028p.

New York Public Library.
Dictionary Catalog of the Jewish
Division.
Boston, MA, G. K. Hall, 1960. 14 v.
... Supplement 1976. 8 v.

Newmark, Leo.
California Family Newmark: An
Intimate History and a Com-
mentary by Wm. M. Kramer
and Norton B. Stern.
NN APV (Newmark)

Noren, Catherine Hanf.
The Camera of My Family.
New York, Knopf, 1976. 240 p.
(100-year album of a German Jewish family)

Postal, Bernard, and Samuel H.
Abramson.
Landmarks of a People: A Guide
to Jewish Sites in Europe.
New York, Hill & Wang, 1962. 270
p. (pbk. 1971)
NN *PXK

Rosenstein, Neil.
The Unbroken Chain.
New York, Shengold Pub., 1977.
716 p.
(The descendants of Rabbi Meir
Katzenellenbogen [living in
1482], including Helena Ruben-
stein, Karl Marx, Felix Men-
delssohn and Martin Buber)

Roth, Cecil.
The House of Nasi: Dona Gracia.
Philadelphia, JPS, 1948. 208 p.
(About Gracia Mendesia, 1510–1569)
NN *PBX (J.P.S.)

Roth, Cecil.
The House of Nasi, Dukes of
    Naxos.
Philadelphia, PA, JPS, 1948. 250 p.
(Joseph Nasi, Duke of Naxos, d.
    1579)
NN *PBX (J.P.S.)

Rothschild, Nathaniel M. V.
Rothschild Family Tree, 1450–1973.
London, Curwen Press, 1973. 26 p.
    gen. charts, index.

Rottenberg, Dan.
Finding Our Fathers. A Guide-
    book to Jewish Genealogy.
New York, Random House, 1977.
    401 p. alpha sections, no index.
NN APB 77-1002

Saltzstein, Joan Weil.
Liebman Adler: His Life Through
    His Letters.
Napco Grafic Arts, 1975. 130 p.

Samuel, Edgar.
Jewish Ancestors and Where to
    Find Them.
(IN: *GM, London, 1953. v. 11, p.
    412–424*)
NN ARCA

Shankman, Sam.
The Peres Family.
Kingsport, TN, Southern Pub.,
    1938. 241 p., no index.
NN *PWO

The Sheftalls of Georgia.
(IN: *Georgia Historical Quarterly,
    Savannah, 1943. v. 27, p. 339–349*)
NN IAA

Shenker, Israel.
Now, Jewish Roots.
(IN: *NYT Magazine, March 20,
    1977. p. 42–45*).

Stern, Malcolm H.
Americans of Jewish Descent;
    Sources of Information for Trac-
    ing Their Ancestry.
(IN: *NGSQ, Washington, DC, 1958.
    v. 46, p. 63–72*)
(Also available as *NGSSP no. 20*)
    NN APGA

Stern, Malcolm H.
American Jewish Genealogy.
(IN: *NGSQ, Washington, DC, 1977.
    v. 65, no. 1, p. 45–56*)
NN APGA

Stern, William.
On the Fascination of Jewish Sur-
    names.
(IN: *Leo Baeck Institute Yearbook,
    New York, 1974. v. 19, p. 219–235*)
NN *PXA

Stryker-Rodda, Harriet.
Price-Goldsmith-Lowenstein and
    Related Families, 1700–1967.
New York, 1967. 49 p. gen. tables.
NN APV (Price)

Vroonen, E.
Encyclopédie des Noms des Per-
    sonnes Etude par Groupes Lin-
    guistiques.
Paris, Editions Universitaire,
    1973.
(Azkenazim p. 30–40, Neerlandais
    p. 66–68, English Jews p. 84–86,
    Spanish Jews p. 168–170, Italian
    Jews p. 229–233, etc.)
NN APD 76-439

Wagner, Anthony R.
The Ancestry of Mr. Anthony Arm-
    strong-Jones.

(IN: *GM, London, 1959. v. 13, p. 97–103, 129–133*)
(Families; Messel, Stern, etc.)
NN ARCA

Weill, Ernest B.
Weil-De Veil. A Genealogy. 1360–1956.
Scarsdale, NY, the author, 1957. 44 p., plus chart.
NN APV (Weill)

Zumoff, Abraham.
Our Family, A History of Five Generations in Pictures and Script, 1831–1956.
New York, Academy Photo Offset, 1956. 127 p., index. Heavily illustrated.
(Excellent example of illustrated family trees)
NN APV+(Zumsky)

UNITED STATES
AJHS News
Waltham, MA, 1968–

American Jewish Historical Society (AJHS) Quarterly (formerly Publications).
New York, 1892–
Now at 2 Thornton Road, Waltham, MA 02154.
NN *PXX

Biographical Encyclopedia of American Jews.
Jacobs & Glassman, 1935. 606 p.
NN *PWR 73-2899

Fishman, Priscilla.
The Jews of the United States.
New York, Quadrangle, 1973. 302 p.
(NYT Library of Jewish Knowledge)
NN *PXY 74-5174

Friedman, Lee E.
Jewish Pioneers and Patriots.
New York, Macmillan, 1943. 430 p., index.
NN *PXY

Jewish Historical Association of Chicago.
Bibliography of Publications about Jews in America in Five Chicago Libraries.
Chicago, the Association, 1955. 144 p.
NN *PXY

Joseph, Samuel.
Jewish Immigration to the United States from 1881 to 1910.
New York, Arno Press, 1969 (orig. 1914). 211 p.
NN *PYN

London, Hannah R.
Miniatures of Early American Jews.
Springfield, MA, Pond-Ekberg, 1953. 154 p. (p. 79–149 ports.)
NN *PWW

London, Hannah R.
Portraits of Jews.
New York, W. E. Rudge, 1927. 197 p., index.
NN *PXY

London, Hannah R.
Shades of My Forefathers.
Springfield, MA, Pond-Ekberg, 1941. 199 p. (Silhouettes)
NN *PXY

Marcus, Jacob R.
The Colonial American Jew, 1492–1776.
Detroit, MI, Wayne State U., 1970. 3 v.
NN *PXY

Marcus, Jacob R.
Memoirs of American Jews, 1775–1865.
Philadelphia, PA, JPS, 1955–56. 3 v., index in v. 3.
NN *PXY

The National Jewish Blue Book; an Elite Directory.
Philadelphia, Blue Book, 1927. 1 v. (582 p.).
NN *PWR

Postal, Bernard, and Lionel Koppman.
A Jewish Tourist's Guide to the U.S.
New York, Hill & Wang, 1954. 705 p. (pbk. 1971)
NN *PXY

Rezneck, Samuel.
Unrecognized Patriots: The Jews in the American Revolution.
Westport, CT, Greenwood Press, 1975. 299 p.
NN *PXY 75-7483

Rosenbloom, Joseph R.
A Biographical Dictionary of Early American Jews.
Lexington, KY, U. of Kentucky Press, 1960. 175 p.
NN APK

The Saint Charles Review . . .
Camden, NJ, 1935– 1 v. (all published)
(Devoted to the history and genealogy of the ancestors, founders and descendants of Jewish families in America prior to 1789)
NN *PWO and APA 72-1134

Sloan, Irving S.
Jews in America, A Chronology and Fact Book.
Dobbs Ferry, NY, Oceana, 1971. 151 p.
NN *PXY 73-985

Stern, Malcolm.
Americans of Jewish Descent, A Compendium of Genealogy.
Cincinnati, OH, Hebrew Union College, 1960. 307 p., index. (2nd ed. 1977, c. 600 p.)
NN APK+

Toledot: The Journal of Jewish Genealogy.
Flushing, NY, 1977–. v. 1–.
(P.O. Box 1126, Flushing, NY 11367)
(Arthur Kurzweil and Steven W. Siegel, eds.; Malcolm Stern, contributing ed.)

Alabama

Elovitz, Mark H.
A Century of Jewish Life in Dixie: The Birmingham Experience.
Tuscaloosa, U of AL, 1974. 258 p., index.
NN *PXY 75-6891

Alaska

Glanz, Rudolf.
The Jews in American Alaska 1867–1880.
New York, 1953. 46 p.
NN *PBM p.v. 587

California

Cogan, Sara G.
The Jews of San Francisco and Greater Bay Area 1848–1919, an Annotated Bibliography.
Berkeley, 1973. 127 p., index.

Cogan, Sara G.
Pioneer Jews of California,
Mother Lode, 1849–1880, an An-
notated Bibliography.
Berkeley, 1968. 49 p., index.
(Western Jewish American Series.
Publications. v. 1–2)
NN *PXY 72-1481

Glanz, Rudolf.
The Jews in California from the
Discovery of Gold until 1880.
New York, Walden Press, 1960.
188 p., no index.
NN *PXY

Stern, Norton.
California Jewish History: A De-
scriptive Bibliography . . .
Glendale, A. H. Clark, 1967. 175 p.,
index.
NN *PXY

Stern, Norton B.
The Franklin Brothers of San
Diego.
(IN: *Journal of San Diego History,
San Diego, 1975. v. 12, p. 32–42*)
NN IXH (San Diego)

Vorspan, Max, and Lloyd P. Gart-
ner.
History of the Jews of Los Angeles.
San Marino, Huntingdon Library,
1970. 362 p., index.
NN *PXY

Colorado

Breck, Allen duPont.
The Centennial History of the
Jews of Colorado, 1859–1959
Denver, U of Denver, The Hirsch-
feld Press, 1960. 360 p., index.
NN *PXY

Uchill, Ida Libert.
Pioneers, Peddlers and Tsadikim.
Denver, A. Swallow, 1957. 327 p.
NN *PXY

Connecticut

Silverman, Morris.
Hartford Jews, 1659–1970.
Hartford, Conn. Hist. Soc., 1970.
449 p., no index. (Alpha bio sec-
tions, p. 121–314)
NN*PXY 72-407

Sulman, Esther.
A Goodly Heritage, the Story of
the Jewish Community in New
London, 1957. 81 p.
NN *PXY

Delaware

Geffen, M. David.
Delaware Jewry: The Formative
Years, 1872–1889.
(IN: *Delaware History. Wilming-
ton, 1975. v. 16, p. 269–297*)
NN IAA

Saretsky, Samuel.
History of the Jew in Delaware.
Wilmington, A. R. Saylor, 1922. 20
leaves
NN *PBM p.v. 29 no. 3.

District of Columbia

Marany, Hillel.
Jews in Greater Washington, a
Panoramic History of Washing-
ton Jewry for the Years 1795–
1860.
Washington, 1961. 143 p.
NN *PMX p.v. 847

Georgia

Herzberg, Fannie.
Pioneer Members and History of Temple Beth El (West Point, GA) 1859–1959.
West Point, GA, 1959. 47 p. (*Chattahoochee Valley Hist. Soc. Bul. no. 4*)
NN ITI

Illinois

Bregstone, Philip Pollack.
Chicago and its Jews: A Cultural History.
Chicago, the author, 1933. 423 p., index.
NN *PXY

Gutstein, Morris Aaron.
A Priceless Heritage: the Epic Growth of Nineteenth Century Chicago Jewry.
New York, Bloch, 1953. 488 p., index.
NN *PXY

Indiana

Dunn, Jacob P.
Greater Indianapolis.
Chicago, Lewis, 1910. v. 1 p. 628–630 (Jewish Community)
NN IVD

Iowa

Glazer, Simon.
Jews of Iowa.
Des Moines, Koch, 1904. 359 p., no index.
NN *PXY

Shuman, Bernard.
A History of the Sioux City Jewish Community, 1869–1969.

Sioux City, Jewish Federation, 1969. 209 p.
NN *PXY

Wolfe, Jack.
A Century of Iowa Jewry, 1833–1940.
Des Moines, Iowa Print., 1941. 280 p., no index.
NN *PXY

Kentucky

Bernheim, Isaac W.
History of the Settlement of Jews in Paducah and Lower Ohio Valley.
Paducah, 1912. 78 p.
NN *PXY

Louisiana

Korn, Bertram Wallace.
The Early Jews of New Orleans.
Waltham, MA, AJHS, 1969. 382 p., index.
(American Jewish Communal Histories no. 5)
NN *PXY

U.S.W.P.A.
Inventory of Church and Synagogue Archives of Louisiana. Jewish Congregations . . .
Baton Rouge, LSU, 1941. 183 p.
NN *PXY

Maine

Band, Benjamin.
Portland Jewry: Its Growth and Development.
Portland, Jewish Hist. Soc., 1955. 117 p., no index.
NN *PXY

Maryland

Blum, Isador.
Jews of Baltimore.
Baltimore, Hist. Review Pub. Co.,
  1910. 470 p., no index (t of c, p.
  ix *ff.*).
NN *PXY

Fein, Isaac.
The Making of an American Jew-
  ish Community: the History of
  the Baltimore Jewry, 1773–1920.
Philadelphia, PA, JPS, 1971. 348 p.
NN *PBX (J.P.S.)

Rosenwaike, Ira.
The Jews of Baltimore to 1810.
(IN: *AJHQ, Waltham, MA, 1975. v.
  64, p. 291–320*)
NN *PXX

Massachusetts

Ehrenfried, Albert.
A Chronicle of Boston Jewry from
  Colonial Settlement to 1900.
Boston, Irving Berstein, 1963. 771
  p., no index (t of c).
NN *PXY

Horwitt, Pink, and Bertha Skole.
Jews in Berkshire County.
Williamstown, MA, DOR Co., 1972.
  74 p., index.
(Moses and Louis England from
  Baiersdorf, Bavaria, opened
  their first store in Pittsfield,
  Mass., in 1857, the forerunner
  of England Brothers, the larg-
  est department store in the
  county)
NN *PXY 74-148

Michigan

Congregation Beth El Detroit.
The Beth El Story with a History

of the Jews in Michigan before
  1850 by Irving Katz.
Detroit, Wayne U. Press, 1955. 238
  p., index.
NN *PXY

Mayer, Albert J.
Flint Jewish Population Study,
  1967.
Flint, MI, 1969. 94 p.
NN *PXY 74-716

Minnesota

Plant, W. Gunther.
The Jews in Minnesota, the First
  Seventy-five Years.
New York, AJHS, 1959. 347 p., in-
  dex.
(American Jewish Communal His-
  tories no. 3)
NN *PXY

Mississippi

U.S.W.P.A.
Inventory of the Church and Syn-
  agogue Archives of Mississippi.
Jackson, State Conference of B'nai
  B'rith, 1940. 41 leaves.
NN *PXY

Missouri

Bush, Isador.
The Jews of St. Louis.
(IN: *Missouri Hist. Rev., Colum-
  bia, MO. 1951. p. 60–70*)
NN IAA

Makovsky, Donald L.
The Philipsons, the First Jewish
  Settlers in St. Louis, 1807–1858.
St. Louis, Judaism Sesquicent.
  Comm., 1958. 28 p.
NN *PBM p. v. 1024

Sach, Howard.
Development of the Jewish Community of Kansas City 1864–1908.
(IN: *Missouri Hist. Rev., Columbia, MO. 1961. v. 60, p. 350–360*)
NN IAA

New Jersey

Brandes, Joseph.
Immigrants to Freedom; Jewish Communities in Rural New Jersey since 1882.
Philadelphia, PA, U. of PA Press, 1971. 424 p.
NN *PXY

History of Pioneers.
Toms River, NJ, Congregation B'nai Israel, 1976. 70, 4 leaves.
(Jews in Toms River)
NN *PXY 76-3259

New York

Adler, Selig, and Thomas E. Connolly.
From Ararat to Suburbia: The History of the Jewish Community of Buffalo.
Philadelphia, 1960. 498 p.
(Jacob R. Schiff Library of Jewish Contributions to American Democracy no. 13)
NN *PXY

Gritstein, Hyman.
The Rise of the Jewish Community of New York 1654–1860.
Philadelphia, PA, JPS, 1945. 645 p.
NN *PBX (J.P.S.)

Kohn, S. Joshua.
The Jewish Community of Utica, New York 1847–1948.
New York, AJHS, 1959. 221 p., index.
(American Jewish Communal Histories no. 2)
NN *PXY

Pool, David de Sola, and Tamar de S. Pool.
An Old Faith in a New World. A Portrait of Shearith Israel 1654–1954.
New York, Columbia U. Press, 1954. 595 p., index.
NN *PXY

Pool, David de Sola.
Portraits Etched in Stone, Early Jewish Settlers, 1682–1831.
(Tombstone and portrait of Moses Levy p. 197–201)
New York, Columbia U. Press, 1952. 543 p.
NN *PXY

Postal, Bernard, and Lionel Koppman.
Jewish Landmarks in New York, An Informal History and Guide.
New York, Hill & Wang, 1965. 277 p.
(Index of synagogues, p. 275–277)
(pbk)
NN IRGV

Rosenburg, Stuart E.
The Jewish Community of Rochester 1843–1925.
New York, Columbia U. Press, 1954. Index.
(American Jewish Communal Histories no. 1)
NN *PXY

Ohio

Cleveland Jewish Society Book.
Cleveland, Jewish Independent
Pub. Co., 1915-.
NN *PXY

Michael, Ann D.
The Origins of the Jewish Community of Cincinnati, 1817–1860.
(IN: *Cincinnati Hist. Soc. Bulletin. Cincinnati, 1972. v. 30 p.
155–182.*)
NN IVB (Cincinnati)

Oregon

Nodel, Julius J., and Alfred Ap-
sler.
The Ties Between: A Century of
Judaism on America's Last
Frontier: The Human Story of
Congregation Beth Israel,
Portland Oregon, the Oldest
Jewish Congregation in the Pa-
cific Northwest.
Portland, 1959. 194 p.
NN *PXY

Pennsylvania

Burnett, Robert.
The Jewish Community of Colon-
ial Reading.
(IN: *Hist. Review of Berks Co.,
Reading, 1972. v. 37, p. 58–59,
79–80*)
NN ISD (Berks Co.)

Klein, Esther M.
Guide to Jewish Philadelphia: His-
tory, Landmarks ... 1703–1965.
Philadelphia, Phil. Jewish Times
Inst., 1965. 191 p.
NN *PXY

Morais, Henry S.
The Jews of Philadelphia ...
Philadelphia, Levytype, 5654–
1904. 576 p.
NN *PXY

Stern, Malcolm.
Two Jewish Functionaries in Colonial Pennsylvania.
(IN: *AJHQ, Waltham, MA, 1967. v.
57, p. 24–51*)
(Barnard Jacobs, d. after 1790, ritual circumciser [Mohel]; Mordecai Moses Mordecai [1727–
1809], lay reader [Hazzan])
NN *PXX

Trachtenberg, Joshua.
Consider the Years: The Story of
the Jewish Community at Eas-
ton, 1752–1942.
Easton, 1944. 327 p.
NN *PXY

Wold, Edwin.
The History of the Jews of Phila-
delphia from Colonial Times to
the Age of Jackson.
Philadelphia, JPS, 1957. 543 p.
NN *PXY

Rhode Island

Gutstein, Morris A.
The Story of the Jews of Newport,
Two and a Half Centuries of
Judaism 1658–1908.
New York, Bloch, 1936.
NN *PXY

Gutstein, Morris A.
To Bigotry No Sanction: A Jewish
Shrine in America 1658–1958.
New York, Bloch Pub. Co., 1958.
191 p.
NN *PXY

Gutstein, Morris A.
The Touro Family in Newport.
Newport, RI Hist. Soc., 1935. 39 p.
NN *PBM p. v. 253

South Carolina

Elzas, Barnett A.
The Jews of South Carolina from
    Earliest Times to the Present
    Day.
Philadelphia, PA, J. B. Lippincott,
    1905. 352 p., index.
NN *PXY

Rezinkoff, Charles.
The Jews of Charleston . . .
Philadelphia, JPS, 1950 (5711). 343
    p.
NN ITH (Charleston)

Tennessee

Frank, Fedora S.
Beginnings on Market Street,
    Nashville and Her Jewry 1861–
    1901.
Nashville, the author, 1976. 227
    p., index, gen. charts p. 128–147.
NN *PXY 76-7172

Shankman, Sam.
Baron Hirsch Congregation: From
    Ur to Memphis.
Memphis, the Congregation, 1957.
    153 p., no index.
NN *PXY

Texas

Cohen, Anne Nathan.
The Centenary History, Congre-
    gation Beth Israel of Houston,
    1854–1954.
Houston, c. 1955. 95 p.
NN *PXY

Institute of Texan Cultures.
The Jewish Texans.
San Antonio, U. of Texas, 1974. 32
    p.
(The Texians and Texas)

Utah

Brooks, Juanita.
History of the Jews of Utah and
    Idaho.
Salt Lake City, Western Epics,
    1973. 252 p.
NN *PXY 75-2860

Walthers, Leon L.
The Pioneer Jews of Utah.
New York, AJHS, 1952. 199 p., in-
    dex.
(Studies in American Jewish His-
    tory no. 2)
NN *PXY

Vermont

The Story of the Jewish Commu-
    nity of Burlington, Vermont.
Burlington, Myron Samuelson,
    1976. 87 p., t of c, no index.
NN *PXY 76-7586

Virgin Islands

Paiewonsky, Isidor.
Jewish Historical Development in
    the Virgin Islands.
St. Thomas, the author, 1959. 24
    p., no pagination, no index.

Virginia

Ezekiel, Herbert, and Gaston
    Lichtenstein.
The History of the Jews of Rich-
    mond from 1769 to 1917.
Richmond, H. T. Ezekiel, 1917. 374
    p., index.
NN *PXY

Ginsburg, Louis.
History of the Jews of Petersburg
1789–1950.
Petersburg, 1954. 118 p., no index.
NN *PXY

West Virginia

Shinedling, Abraham I.
West Virginia Jewry 1850–1958.
Philadelphia, PA, Maurice Jacobs,
1963. 3 v., index in v. 3.
NN *PXY

Wisconsin

Guide to the Wisconsin Jewish Ar-
chives at the State Historical
Society of Wisconsin.
Madison, 1974. 28 p.
NN *XM 710

Levitats, Isaac.
The Story of the Milwaukee Jewish
Community.
Milwaukee, 1954. 38 leaves.
NN *PBM p. v. 683

BY COUNTRY

Africa (North)

Attal, Robert.
Les Juifs d'Afrique du Nord.
Jerusalem, Institute Ben-Zvi,
1973. 248, 12 p.
NN *PXL 76-1305

Millás Vallicrosa, José M.
Lapidas Sepulcrales Antropomo-
morfas en los Cementerios Is-
raelitas de Xauen y Tetuan
(IN: *Sefarad, Madrid, 1946. a no 6,
fasc. 1, p. 63–72*)
NN *PBL

Nesry, Carlos de.
Le Juif de Tangier et le Maroc.
Tangier, Editions Internationales,
1956. 148 p.
NN *PXL

Wolkowicz, Steven D.
... Mission to Morocco, a Report
on Moroccan Jewry.
New York, World Jewish Con-
gress, 1947. 41 p.
NN *PBM+ p. v. 526

Africa (South)

Hertman, Louis.
A History of the Jews in South
Africa from Earliest Times to
1895.
Johannesburg, S.A. Jewish Board
of Deputies, 1935. 288 p., index.
NN *PXZ

Saron, Gustav, and Louis Hotz.
The Jews in South Africa, A His-
tory.
Capetown, Oxford U. Press, 1955.
422 p., index.
NN *PXZ

Africa (West)

Williams, Joseph J.
Hebrewism of West Africa.
New York, Dial Press, 1930. 443
p., index.
NN *PXZ

Australia

Joseph, Anthony.
On Tracing Australian Jewish Ge-
nealogy.
(IN: *GM, London, 1964. v. 14, p.
425–435.*)
NN ARCA

Levi, John S.
Australian Genesis.
Adelaide, 1974. 360 p.
NN *PXZ 75-7247

Medding, Peter Y., ed.
Jews in Australian Society.
South Melbourne, Vic., Clayton, Victoria, Macmillan, 1973. 299 p., index.
NN *PXZ 74-5842

Austria

Gedelte Juedishe Familien.
Salzburg, 1891. 112 p., index.
(Available at Leo Baeck Institute)

Kann, Robert.
German Speaking Jewry during the Austro-Hungarian Constitutional Era 1867–1918.
(IN: *Jewish Social Studies, New York, 1948. p. 239–256*)
*NN *PBC*

Peller, Sigismund.
Ueber die Böhmischen und Österreichischen Juden zur zeit Maria Theresias.
(IN: *Monatsschrift für Geschichte und Wissenschaft des Judentums.*
Frankfurt, 1926. Jahr. 70, p. 284–288)
NN *PBC

Bulgaria

Chary, Frederick B.
The Bulgarian Jews and the Final Solution 1940–1944.
Pittsburgh, PA, c. 1970. 246 p.
NN *PXM

Canada

Chiel, Arthur A.
Jewish Experience in Early Manitoba.
Winnipeg, Manitoba Jewish Pub., 1955. 125 p., no index.
NN *PXY

Cohen, Zvi, ed.
Canadian Jewry, Prominent Jews of Canada.
Toronto, Canadian Jewish Hist. Pub. Co., 1933. 304 p., index.
NN *PXY

Leonoff, Cyril Ede.
Wapella Farm Settlement.
Winnipeg, joint pub., Hist. & Scient. Soc. of Manitoba and Jewish Hist. Soc. of Western Canada, 1970. 36 p.
(First successful Jewish farm settlement in Canada)

Rome, David.
Canadian Jewish Archives ...
Montreal, 1974–1975. 2 v.

Caribbean

Emmanuel, Isaac Samuel.
History of the Jews of the Netherlands Antilles.
Cincinnati, OH, 1970. 2 v. (1,165 p.)
NN *PXX 74-4716

Emmanuel, Isaac S.
Precious Stones of the Jews of Curaçao, Curaçaon Jewry 1656–1957.
New York, Bloch Pub. Co., 1957. 584 p., index .
NN APY

Judah, George F.
The Jew's Tribute in Jamaica.

(IN: *AJHS Publications, Baltimore, MD, 1909. p. 149–177*)
NN *PXX

Margolinsky, Julius.
299 Epitaphs from the Jewish Cemetery in St. Thomas, W.I. 1837–1916.
Copenhagen, 1957. 34 leaves.
NN *PXZ+

Shilstone, Emmanuel.
Monumental Inscriptions in the Burial Ground of the Jewish Synagogue at Bridgetown, Barbados.
New York, AJHS, 1956. 205 p.
NN *PXZ

China

Leslie, Donald D.
The Survival of the Chinese Jews: The Jewish Community of Kaifeng.
Leiden, Brill, 1972. 270 p.
NN *OAA 73-2597 v. 10

Czechoslovakia

Kisch, Guido.
In Search of Freedom, a History of American Jews from Czechoslovakia with a foreword by Jan Masaryk.
London, E. Goldstone, 1949. 373 p.
NN *PXY

Muneles, Otto.
Starý Židovský Hřbitov v Praze.
Praha, 1955. 480, 39 p.
(Židovské Památky v Čechach a na Moravě [sv] 3)
(Jewish epitaphs in Czechoslovakia)
NN *PXT

Egypt

Herrmann, Siegfried.
Israel in Eqypt.
Naperville, IL, c. 1973. 98 p.
NN L-10 1922 2nd series, 27

France

Annuaire de la Noblesse de France.
Paris, 1897. v. 53, p. 383–403.
(Titled French banking families of Jewish origin: Erlanger, Cahen D'Anvers, Gunzburg, Hirsch, Koenigswarter, Rothschild, etc.)
NN ASA

Blumenkranz, Bernhard.
Bibliographie Des Juifs En France.
Toulouse, Edouard Privat, 1974. 349 p. (Bibliography of French Jews)
NN PXP 74-1699

Gygès
Les Israélites dans la Société Française.
Paris, Librarie Française, 1956. 238 p.
NN *PXP

Kobler, Franz.
Napoleon and the Jews.
New York, Schocken Books, 1976. (c. 1975) 220 p.
NN *PZV 76-4522

Levy, Paul.
Les Noms des Israelites en France, Histoire et Dictionnaire.
Paris, Presses Universitaires de France. 1960. 210 p.
NN APD

Germany

Czellitzur, Arthur.
... Mein Stammbaum eine Geneal-
ogische Anleitung für Deutsche
Juden.
Berlin, Philo, 1934. 32 p. (Guide to
family trees of German Jewish
families)
NN *PBM

Friederich, Heinz F.
Juden und Judenregister in Hes-
sen.
(IN: *Hessesche Familienkunde,
Frankfurt, 1956. Bd. 3, Heft 11/
12, col. 621–624.*)
NN ATF (Hesse)

Gesellschaft für Jüdische Familienforschung ... Verzeichnis
der Mitglieder und Mitarbeiter.
Berlin, 1935–
NN *PWO

Jacobson, Jacob.
Judische Trauungen in Berlin
1859–1913. Walter de Gruyter,
ed.
Berlin, 1968.
(Verffentlihungen de Historische
Kommission zu Berlin. Band 28
Quellenwerke Band 4)
NN *PWO (Jacobson)

Judische Familien Forschung:
Mitteilungen de Gesellschraft
für Judische Familien For-
schung.
Berlin, 1924–1938. 14 v. in 2.
NN *PWO

Kahn, Ludwig.
Judische Familienkunde.
(IN: *Genealogie Deutsche Zeit-
schrift für Familienkunde,
Neustadt (Aisch), 1966. Jahrg.
Bd. 8, Heft 4, p. 157–164*)
NN ATA

Leo Baeck Institute, New York
LBI News.
New York, 1959–
NN *PXA

Leo Baeck Institute, New York
Yearbook.
New York, 1956–. v. 1–.
NN *PXA

Lowenthal, Marvin.
The Jews in Germany, A Story of
Sixteen Centuries.
Philadelphia, JPS, 1936. 444p.
NN *PXS

Reinemann John Ott.
Carried Away ... Recollections
and Reflections.
Philadelphia, Mrs. J. O. Reine-
mann, 1976. 216 p., index.
NN

Semigothaische Genealogisches
Taschenbuch Ari(st)okratish-
Jüdischer Heiraten ...
Munich, 1912–1914. 3 v.
(Available at Leo Baeck Institute)
NN *ZAN-*P148

Wenzl, Stefi.
Judische Burger and Kommunale
Selbstverwaltung in Preus-
sischen Stadten 1808–1848.
Berlin, W. de Gruyter, 1967. 265 p.
(Berliner Historische Kommission
Veroffentlichungen band 21)
NN *PXS

Gibralter

Serfaty, Abraham B.M.
The Jews of Gibralter Under Brit-
ish Rule.
Gibralter, Beanland, Malin Co.,
1933. 36 p.
NN *PBM p.v.269

Great Britain

Adler, Rev. Michael.
British Jewry Book of Honour.
London, Caxton, 1922. 636, 364 p.
 ports.
(WWI soldiers)
NN *PXQ

Bermant, Chaim.
The Cousinhood, the Anglo-Jewish
 Gentry.
London, Eyre & Spottiswoode,
 1971. 466 p., index.
NN *PXQ 72-1241

Bermant, Chaim.
Troubled Eden: An Anatomy of
 British Jewry.
London, Vallentine, 1969. 274 p.
NN *PXQ

Dobson, R. B.
The Jews of Medieval York and
 the Massacre of March 1190.
York, St. Anthony Press, 1974. 50
 p.
(Borthwich Institute Papers no.
 45)
NN CO (York)

Emden, Paul H.
Jews of Britain.
London, Sampson Low Marston,
 1944. 577 p., index.
NN *PXQ

Godber, Joyce.
Sheba's Marriage Portion.
(IN: *Bedford Magazine, 1975. v.
 15, p. 69–72*)
NN CO (Bedfordshire)

Jewish Historical Society of England.
Anglo-Jewish Notabilities, Their
 Arms and Testamentary Dis-
 positions.

London, JHSE, 1949. 233 p.
NN *PXQ

Jewish Historical Society of Eng-
 land.
Transactions.
London, 1893–
(33 Seymour Place, London, S.W.1)
NN *PXQ

Jewish Year Book.
London, 1896–
NN *PXQ

The Jews' Who's Who.
London, 1920. 255 p.
(Jews in Soviet Russia p. 239, Jews
 in Hungary p. 250, etc.)
NN *PXQ

Joseph, Anthony P.
Jewry of South West England and
 Some of Its Australian Connec-
 tions.
(IN: *JHSE Transactions, London,
 1974. v. 24, p. 24–27*)
NN *PXQ

Lehmann, Ruth P.
Anglo-Jewish Bibliography 1937–
 1970.
London, JHS, 1973. 364 p.
NN *PXQ 73-2422

Levine, Harry.
The Jews of Coventry.
Coventry, 1970. 100 p., no index.
NN *PXQ 77-22

Levy, E. Lawrence.
Birmingham Jewry 1870–1929.
Birmingham, 1929.
NN *PXQ 76-7430

Lipman, V. D.
The Jews of Medieval Norwich.

London, JHSE, 1967. 355, 45 p.,
index.
NN *PXQ

Roper, Donald.
Ipswich Jews Last Rest.
(IN: *East Anglian Mag., Ipswich,
1975. p. 265*)
NN CO (East Anglia)

Roth, Cecil.
A History of the Jews of England.
3rd ed.
Oxford, Clarendon Press, 1964. 311
p.
NN *PXQ

Roth, Cecil.
Medieval Jews at Oxford.
Oxford, 1951. 194 p.
(Oxford Hist. Soc. n.s. no. 9)
NN CA

Samuel, Edgar.
The Jews.
(IN: *Steel, D.J., Sources for Roman
Catholic and Jewish Genealogy
and History, Chichester, Philli-
more, 1974. NIPR v. 3, p. 959–
991*)
NN ARS 72-1119

Spanish and Portuguese Jews'
Congregation. London. Bevis
Marks Records.
Oxford, Oxford U. Press,
1940–1949. 2 v.
NN *PXQ

Thirteen London Jews and Conversion: Problems of Apostasy
in the 1280's.
(IN: *Institute of Historical Research Bulletin, London, 1972.
v. 45, p. 214–229*)
NN BAA

Willims, Bill.
The Making of Manchester Jewry
1740–1875.

Manchester, Manchester U. Press,
1976. 454 p., index.
NN *PXQ 76-7390

Greece

Argenti, Philip.
Religious Minorities of Chios: The
Jews and Roman Catholics.
Cambridge, Cambridge U. Press.
1970. 581 p., index
NN *PXR

Hungary

Manuscript Census of the Jews of
Dej, Hungary.
Dej, 1944. 140 leaves.
NN PXT+ 75-9463

McCagg, William O.
Jewish Nobles and Geniuses in
Modern Hungary.
Boulder, CO, East European
Quarterly, 1972. 254 p., index.
NN *PXT 74-623

Israel

Avi-Yonah, Michael.
The Jews of Palestine: A Political
History from the Bar Kokhba
War to the Arab Conquest.
Oxford, Blackwell, 1976. 286 p.
(c. A.D. 135-640)

Registration of Births, Deaths
and Marriages in European
Jewish Communities in Palestine and Israel.
(IN: *Archivum, Paris, 1961. v. 9,
p. 101–119*)
NN BAA

Who's Who in the State of Israel.
Tel Aviv, 1949. 336 p.
NN *PWR

Italy

Gli Israeliti Italiana: Nella Guerra 1915–1918.
Turin, I. Servi, 1921. 314 p., 2 parts, alpha, no index.
NN *PWR

Roth, Cecil.
History of the Jews in Italy.
Philadelphia, JPS, 1946. 575 p.
NN *PXN

Latin America

Wiznitzer, Arnold.
Cryto Jews in Mexico . . .
(IN: *AJHSQ, NY, 1962. v. 51 p. 168–214, 222–268.*)
(covers sixteenth and seventeenth centuries)
NN *PXX

Wiznitzer, Arnold.
The Records of the Earliest Jewish Community in the New World. [Brazil]
New York, AJHS, 1954. 108 p.
NN *PXX

Latvia

The Jews in Latvia.
Tel Aviv, Assoc. of Latvian Estonian Jews in Israel, 1971. 384 p.
NN *PXW 76-5880

Near East

Gilbert, Martin,
The Jews of Arab Lands: Their History in Maps.
London, the author, 1976. 34 p.
NN Map Div. 76-166

Netherlands

Jewish Ancestry Charts.
[IN: *Gens Nostra, Amsterdam, 1966, v. 21 p. 130–131* (Isaac Da Costa, 1798–1860), *v. 21 p. 154–155* (Emanuel Querido, 1866–1943), *v. 21 p. 324–325* (Prof. Dr. Tobias M. C. Asser, 1838–1913]
NN AVD

Villiers, C. G. S.
Jewish Genealogy in Holland
(IN: Familia, Capetown, 1966. Year 3, p. 27–28)
NN AVH (Africa, South)

Winkel, H.
Genealogisch Onderzoek naar Joodse Voorouder.
(IN: *Gens Nostra, Amsterdam, 1971. v. 26, p. 401–415.*)
NN AVD

Poland

Korwin, Ludwik.
Szlachta Mojzeszowa.
Krakow, 1938–39. 2 v.
NN *PWO

Weinryb, Bernard D.
The Jews of Poland . . . 1100 to 1800. Philadelphia, JPS, 5733/ 1973. 424 p. index
NN *PXV 74-1648

Portugal

Schwarz, Samuel.
As Lapides Hebraicas do Musem Arquelogico do Carmo en Lisboa.
(IN: *Arquelogia e Historia, Lisbon, 1922. v. 1, p. 126–168*)
NN MTA

Russia

Baron, Salo W.
The Russian Jews under Tsars and Soviets.
New York, Macmillan, 1976. 468 p., index.
NN *PXW 76-5868

Dubnow, Simon M.
History of the Jews in Russia and Poland.
New York, KTAV Pub. House, 1975 (orig. 1916). 3 v.
(Includes events of Russian and Soviet Jewry 1912–1974 by Leon Shapiro)
NN *PXW (4916 ed.)

Israel, Gerard.
The Jews in Russia, trans. by Sanford L. Chernoff.
New York, St. Martin's Press, 1975. 329 p.
NN *PXW 75-5286

Koestler, Arthur.
The Thirteenth Tribe: The Khazar Empire and Its Heritage.
London, Hutchinson, 1976. 255 p., index.
NN JFD 76-8132

Koestler, Arthur.
Ukrainians and Jews.
NY, Ukrainian Congress of America, 1966. 199 p.
NN *PXW 72-1265

Spain

Moore, Kenneth.
Those of the Street: The Catholic Jews of Mallorca.
Notre Dame, IN, U. of N.D. Press, 1976.

Ortega, Manuel L.
... Los Hebreos en Marruecos ...
Madrid, Ediciones Nuestra Raza, 1934. 369 p.
(Expulsion from Spain 1492)
NN *PXL

Roth, Cecil A.
A History of the Marranos.
Philadelphia, PA, 1932. 422 p.
NN *PXI

Singerman, Robert.
The Jews in Spain and Portugal, a Bibliography.
New York, London, Garland, 1975. 364 p., index.
(Garland Reference Library of Social Sciences Series v. 11)
NN *PXO 76-4414

Torroba Bernaldo de Quirós, Felipe.
The Spanish Jews. 5th ed.
Madrid, Rivadeneyra, 1961. 161 p.
NN *PXO 74-2813

Sweden

Ivarsson, Martin.
Svensk-Judiska ...
Jönköping, 1956. 284 p., gen. table.
NN *PXR

Turkey

Goodblatt, Maurice.
Jewish Life in Turkey in the XVIth Century.
New York, Jewish Theo. Sem. of Amer., 1952. 240 p.
NN *PWZ (Medina)

Lewis, Bernard.
Notes and Documents from Turkish Archives. A Contribution to the History of the Jews in the Ottoman Empire.
Jerusalem, 1952. 52 p.

(Oriental Notes and Studies no. 3)
NN *OAA

Mayer, N.
The Jews of Turkey.
London?, 1913. 46 p.
NN *PXL 76-1678

Venezuela

Emmanuel, Isaac S.
The Jews of Coro, Venezuela.
Cincinnati, Amer. Jewish Archives, 1973. 63 p.
NN *PXX 75-8898

GENERAL SOURCES

Davies, Wallace Evans.
Patriotism on Parade. The Story of Veterans' and Hereditary Organizations in America. 1783–1900.
Cambridge, MA, Harvard U., 1955. 385 p.
NN APGA

The Hereditary Register.
Washington, DC, Hereditary Pub., Inc., 1972–
(Hereditary ·Register Publications, 444 West Camelback Road, Suite 305, Phoenix, AZ 85013)
NN APGA 73-514

Hood, Jennings, and Charles T. Young.
American Orders and Societies and Their Decorations.
Philadelphia, Bailey, Banks and Biddle, 1917. 107 p., index.
NN APGA

MAJOR SOCIETIES AND THEIR PUBLICATIONS

The Ancient and Honorable Artillery Company of Massachusetts (founded 1637)—male membership; members in the company or descendants from a member prior to 1738. Address: Executive Secretary, The Armory, Faneuil Hall, Boston, MA 02109.

Roberts, Oliver Ayer.
History of the Military Company of Massachusetts, now called the Ancient and Honorable Artillery Company of Massachusetts, 1637–1888.
Boston, MA, A. Mudge & Son, 1895–1898. 3 v., index.
NN IQH (Boston)

Baronial Order of Magna Charta (1898)—male membership based on descent from one of the twenty-five Magna Charta Sureties 1215. Address: c/o Mr. Grahame T. Smallwood, Jr., The Union League, Philadelphia, PA 19102.

Adams, Arthur, and Frederick L. Weis.
Magna Charta Sureties 1215. The Barons Names in the Magna Charta 1215 and Some of Their Descendants Who Settled in America 1607–1650, revised by Walter Lee Sheppard.
Baltimore, MD, GPC, 1968 (orig. 1955). 138 p., index.
NN APK

National Society of Children of the American Revolution (1895)—male and female membership; same ancestral requirements as the Daughters of the American Revolution. Address: Executive Secretary, 1776 D Street, N.W., Washington, DC 20006.

The Society of the Cincinnati (1783)—male membership based on descent from an officer of the Continental line with three years of service, or any officer killed in battle (regular or militia). Address: Anderson House, 2118 Massachusetts Avenue, N.W., Washington, DC 20008. Only one member may represent an eligible ancestor at a time.

Heitman, Francis B.
Historical Register of Officers of the Continental Army During the War of the Revolution Apr. 1775 to Dec. 1783. New revised and enlarged edition of 1914, with addenda by Robert H. Kelby, 1932.
Baltimore, MD, GPC, 1967 (orig. 1914). 698 p., alpha.
NN *R-APK

Metcalf, Bryce.
Original Members and Other Officers Eligible to the Society of the Cincinnati,
Strasburg, VA, Shenandoah Pub. for the Connecticut Society, 1938. 390 p., index.
NN APGA (Cincinnati)

Thomas, William Sturgis.
Members of the Society of the Cincinnati, Original Hereditary and Honorary.
New York, Tobias A. Wright, 1929. 188 p., alpha, index.
NN APGA (Cincinnati)

The Daughters of the Cincinnati (1894) Female membership based on the same requirements as the Society of the Cincinnati; however, more than one member at a time may represent an eligible ancestor. Address: 122 East 58th Street, New York, NY 10022.
(A volume dealing with the ancestors of the members of the so-

ciety with many portraits of Revolutionary War officers will be published by Columbia University Press in 1977)

Society of the Descendants of Colonial Clergy (1933)—male and female membership. Address: c/o Mrs. Frederick W. Johnson, Secretary General, 255 Madison Street, Dedham, MA 02026.

Society of the Descendants of Colonial Clergy.
Pedigrees of Descendants of the Colonial Clergy, ed. by Robert Glenn Thurtle . . .
Lancaster, MA, the Society, 1976. 688 p., no index.
(Alphabetical list of ancestors at end listing pedigrees of descendants and their page numbers in book.)
NN APK 76-2082

Order of the Crown of Charlemagne in the United States of America (1939)—male and female membership based on descent from the Emperor Charlemagne. Address: c/o Mrs. Henry Haskins Farrell, Jr., Corresponding Secretary General, 511 Cathedral Drive, Alexandria, VA 22314.

Von Redlich, Marcellus D. A.
Pedigrees of Some of the Emperor Charlemagne's Descendants. Order of the Crown of Charlemagne in the USA, 1941–1977.
3 v. (V. 1 [1941] by Marcellus D. A. von Redlich, foreword by Arthur Adams [p. xvii-xxix]; v. 2 [1974] by Aileen Lewers Langston and J. Orton Buck, fore-

word by Timothy Field Beard [p. xvii-c], index [p. 389–408]; v. 3 [1978] by J. Orton Buck and Timothy Field Beard.)
NN APK (Redlich)

Colonial Dames of America (1890)—female membership based, generally, on descent from an officer of the militia or a high civil official, such as a Colonial governor; accepts service prior to April 18, 1775. Address: Executive Secretary, 421 East 61st Street, New York, NY 10021.

Colonial Dames of America.
The Colonial Dames of America 1890–1904.
New York, Irving Press, 1904. 4 p.
NN APGA

Colonial Dames of America. Chapter 1, Baltimore.
Ancestral Records and Portraits: A Compilation from the Archives of Chapter 1.
New York, Grafton Press. 2 v.
NN APK

National Society of Colonial Dames of America (1891)—female membership based on descent from an ancestor in America prior to 1750 who rendered service or held civil office prior to July 5, 1776; includes all signers of the Declaration of Independence. Address: Dumbarton House, 2715 Q Street, N.W., Washington, DC 20007.

Lamar, Mrs. Clarinda H. P.
A History of the National Society of Colonial Dames of America from 1891 to 1933.

Atlanta, GA, Walter E. Brown, c. 1934. 272 p.
NN APGA (Colonial Dames)

National Society of Colonial Dames of America. Virginia.
History and Register of Ancestors and Members of the Society . . . 1892–1930.
Richmond, VA, the Society, 1930. 544 p.
NN APGA

National Society of Colonial Dames in the State of New York. Register . . .
New York, 1926–1931. 2 v. v. 1: 1926, 534 p.; v. 2: 1941, 204 p.
(Covers ancestors and members, 1893–1941)
NN APGA

Hereditary Order of the Descendants of Colonial Governors (1896)—male and female membership based on descent from a governor prior to July 4, 1776. No national headquarters.

Hereditary Order of the Descendants of Colonial Governors.
Colonial Governors and Acting Governors Serving the Divers Colonies Prior to July 4th, 1776. 2nd revised list.
Verona, NJ, 1963. 21 columns.
NN APGA (Colonial Governors)

Hereditary Order of the Descendants of Colonial Physicians and Chururgiens (1975)—male and female membership based on descent from a physician or midwife in the Colonies before July 4, 1776. Address: c/o Edward Hungerford, Pinecroft Road, Berwyn, PA 19312.

Order of Colonial Lords of Manors in America (1911)—male and female membership based on descent from a Lord of a Manor with right of Court Leet in Colonial Maryland and New York. Address: T. F. Beard, Registrar, 38 Barrow Street, New York, NY 10014.

Order of Colonial Lords of Manors in America.
Publications.
New York, 1914–1976 (in progress)
NN APGA

General Society of Colonial Wars (1893)—male membership. No national headquarters. Write: c/o Lawson E. Whitesides, Secretary General, 840 Woodbine Ave., Glendale, OH 45256; or Society of Colonial Wars in the State of New York, 122 East 58th Street, New York, NY 10022.

Society of Colonial Wars.
Index of Ancestors.
New York, Baltimore, MD, 1922–1976. 3 v. (1922, 1941, 1976)
NN APGA

Society of Colonial Wars in the State of Connecticut.
Hartford, the Society, 1941. 1,394 p., index.
NN APGA

National Society Daughters of the American Revolution (1890)—female membership based on descent from one who served the cause of Independence in a military or civil capacity or by rendering material aid. Address: 1776 D Street N.W., Washington, DC 20006.

Daughters of the American Revolution Magazine.
Washington, DC 1892–
(DAR Genealogical Guide. Master Index of Genealogy in the DAR Magazine. v. 1–84, 1892–1950. Washington, 1951. 137 p. ... sup. v. 85–89, 1950–1955. Washington, 1956. 26 p., 2 leaves)
NN APGA

DAR Patriot Index.
Washington, DC, NSDAR, 1967. 771 p. alpha, index.
... First Sup. (1969) 85 p.; ... Second Sup. (1973) 95 p.; ... Third Sup. (1976) 116 p.
NN APGA

Dorman, J. Frederick, and Martha Porter Miller.
Index to the Genealogical Department of the DAR Magazine.
Washington, 1958–1968. 11 v. covering v. 91–101, 1957–1967 bound with DARM.
NN APGA

Esker, Katie-Prince.
The Genealogical Department: Source Records from the DAR Magazine 1947–50.
Baltimore, GPC, 1975. 693 p. index
NN APK 77-827

National Society Daughters of Colonial Wars (1932)—Female membership. Address: 1307 New Hampshire Avenue, N.W., Washington, DC 20009.

Daughters of Colonial Wars.
Membership List and Index of Ancestors.
Somerville, MA, Somerville Print. Co., 1941. 542 p.
NN APGA

Daughters of the Republic of Texas (1891)—female membership. Address: The Alamo, San Antonio, TX 78205.

Daughters of the Republic of Texas.
Founders and Patriots of the Republic of Texas.
2nd edition. Dallas, the society, 1963. 684 p. index.
NN APR (Texas)

National Society Daughters of the Revolution, 1776 (1891)—female membership based on the same requirements as the Sons of the Revolution. Address: 132 Nassau Street, New York, N.Y. 10038.

Daughters of the Revolution.
Magazine of the Daughters of the Revolution. New York, 1893–1896, 4 v.
NN APGA

The Patriot.
New York, 1914–1917, 1938–.
NN APGA (DR)

National Society of the Daughters of Utah Pioneers (1901)—female membership. Address: 300 North Main Street, Salt Lake City, UT 84103

Order of Founders and Patriots of America (1896)—male membership based on descent from a direct male ancestor of mother or father resident in the Colonies before 1657 and an ancestor of the same line who served in the American Revolution. Address: % Asa E. Phillips, Jr., 53 State Street, Boston, MA 02109.

Colket, Meredith B.
Founders of Early American Families: Emigrants from Europe 1607–1657 ...
Cleveland, General Court of the Order, 1975. 366 p., alpha.
NN APK 76-310

Order of Founders and Patriots of America.
Register 1926.
New York., the Order, 1926. 578 p.
... first sup. to the Register of 1926, 1926–1940.
New York, 1940. unpaged.
NN APGA

The Holland Society of New York (1885)—male membership based on descent in the direct male line from a resident of New York prior to 1675. Address: 122 East 58th Street, New York, NY 10022.

Holland Society of New York.
Der Halve Maen.
New York, 1922–
NN APGA

Holland Society of New York.
Year Book.
New York, 1886–1937.
(Index to the Publications ... New York, 1959. 46 p.)
NN APGA

National Huguenot Society—male and female membership; descendants of French Protestants who adhere to the principles of the Huguenot faith. Address: 1307 New Hampshire Avenue N.W., Washington, DC 20036.

Descendants of the Illegitimate Sons and Daughters of the Kings of Britain (c. 1950)—male and female membership. Address: Mr. Brainerd T. Peck, Secretary-Treasurer, Lakeside, CT 06758.

Descendants of the Illegitimate Sons and Daughters of the Kings of Britain.
Lineages of Members. Havertown, PA, 1950–.
NN APGA (Descendants Illegitimate) 71-6

General Society of Mayflower Descendants (1897)—male and female membership based on descent from a *Mayflower* passenger. Address: The Mayflower Society House, 4 Winslow Street, Plymouth, MA 02360.

The Mayflower Descendants.
Boston, MA Soc., 1899–1937. v. 1–34, index 2 v.: v. 1 A–G, v. 2 H–Z
NN APGA

Mayflower Families Through Five Generations. Plymouth, MA 02360; Mayflower Families, P.O. Box 297 NE; 1976. v. 1 (All male descendants of Francis Eaton, Samuel Fuller & William White in the 1st five generations.)
(See *MQ Warwick, RI, 1977. v. 43 p. 25* and other issues for additions and corrections)
NN APR (Massachusetts) 76-1937

Mayflower Index. Revised Edition.
Boston, General Society, 1960. 3 v.
NN *R-APK

The Mayflower Quarterly.
NY, Warwick, RI, 1935–

(c/o Mrs. Robert M. Sherman, ed., 128 Massasoit Drive, Warwick, RI 02888)
NN APGA

Shaw, Hubert Kinney.
Families of the Pilgrims. Boston, Massachusetts, Soc. of Mayflower Descendants, 1956. 178 p. index.
NN APK

The Saint Andrew's Society (Charleston, 1729; Philadelphia, 1747; Savannah, 1750; New York, 1756; Alexandria, 1780; St. John's, N.B., 1798; Albany, N.Y., 1803; Montreal, 1835; Quebec, 1835; Ottawa, 1846; Washington, DC, 1855)—male membership descended from an ancestor born in Scotland. Address: The Saint Andrew's Society of the State of New York, 281 Park Avenue South, New York, NY.

Kimmear, Peter.
Historical Sketch of the Saint Andrews Society of the City of Albany, 1803–1903 . . .
Albany, Weed-Parsons, 1903. 126 p.
NN SHOD

MacBean, William M.
Biographical Register of the Saint Andrews Society of the State of New York.
New York, the Society, 1922–1925. 2 v.
NN SHOD

Saint Andrews Society of the City of Charleston.
History of the Saint Andrews Society of Charleston, South Carolina, 1729–1929.

Charleston, SC, the Society, 1929.
154 p.
NN SKA

Saint Andrews Society of the State
of New York.
200th Anniversary 1756–1956.
New York, the Society, 1956. 453
p., index.
Members 1906–1956—p. 372–392—
alpha, not included in index.
NN IEG

Saint Andrews Society of Philadelphia.
An Historical Sketch of the Catalogue of the Saint Andrews Society of Philadelphia with Biographical Sketches of Deceased
Members 1749–1913.
Philadelphia, PA, the Society,
1907–1913. 2 v.
NN SHOD

St. Nicholas Society of the City of
New York (1835)—male mem-
bership based on descent from
a resident of New York City or
State before 1785. Address: 122
East 58th Street, New York, NY
10022.

St. Nicholas Society of the City of
New York.
Genealogical Record: Advance
Sheets.
New York, the Society, 1902. 113 p.
NN APGA

St. Nicholas Society of the City of
New York.
Genealogical Record . . .
New York, the Society, 1905–1968.
8 v.
NN APGA

National Society of the Sons of the
American Revolution (1889)—

male membership based on descent from a soldier or patriot
of the American Revolution.
Address: 2412 Massachusetts
Avenue, Washington, DC 20008.

Sons of the American Revolution
Magazine. Washington, 1906–.
NN APGA

General Society of the Sons of the
Revolution (1876)—male mem-
bership based on descent from
a soldier, sailor, etc., in the
American Revolution, or from
certain civil officials, such as
members of the Continental
Congress. Address: Fraunces
Tavern, 54 Pearl Street, New
York, NY 10004.

Sons of the Revolution. California
Society.
Register . . .
Los Angeles, CA, 1899–1907. 7 v.
NN APGA

Sons of the Revolution in the State
of New York.
Year Book 1925.
New York, the Society, 1925. 671
p., alpha.
NN APGA

Sons of the Revolution. Pennsyl-
vania Society.
Decennial Register . . . 1888–1898.
Philadelphia, PA, J. B. Lippincott,
1898. 457 p.
NN APGA

Sons of the Revolution. Virginia.
Genealogy of Members Sons of the
Revolution in the State of Vir-
ginia.
Richmond, VA, Mitchell & Hotch-
kiss, 1939. 590 p., index.
NN APGA

National Society of the Sons of Utah Pioneers—male membership. Address: 2009 Connor Street (2150 East), Salt Lake City, UT 84109.

National Society United States Daughters of 1812 (1892)—female membership based on descent from soldiers in the War of 1812. Address: 1461 Rhode Island Avenue N.W., Washington, DC 20005.

National Society United States Daughters of 1812.
1812 Ancestor Index 1892–1970.
Washington, DC, the Society, 1970. 576 p., alpha.
NN APK 73-191

General Society of the War of 1812 (1814)—male membership based on lineal descent from soldiers, sailors, etc., in the War of 1812; in the absence of lineal descendants, collateral descent from a sister or brother. Address: c/o Mr. John W. W. Loose, Secretary General, 3311 Columbia Pike, Lancaster, PA 17603

Society of the War of 1812.
Register of the General Society, ed. by Col. Frederick I. Ordway and John G. R. Rountree.
Washington, DC, the Society, 1972. 688 p., index.
NN APGA (War of 1812) 73-1931

Society of the Descendants of Washington's Army at Valley Forge 1777–1778 (1976)—Male and female membership from Revolutionary soldiers who served at Valley Forge. Address: % Donald G. Cronan, P.O. Box 608, Manhasset, NY 11030

GENERAL SOURCES

American Historical Company.
Colonial and Revolutionary Lineages of America. NY, American Hist. Co., 1939–1968. 25 v.
NN APK

Amory, Cleveland.
The Last Resorts. NY, Harper, 1952. 527 p. index.
NN IDS

Amory, Cleveland.
The Proper Bostonians. NY, E.P. Dutton, 1947. 381 p. index.
NN IQH (Boston)

Amory, Cleveland.
Who Killed Society. NY, Harper, 1960. 599 p. index.
NN D-12 9636

Burke's Presidential Families of the United States of America, edited by Hugh Montgomery-Massingberd. London; Burke's Peerage, Ltd.; 1975. 673 p. surname index.
NN APK 75-891

Burt, Nathaniel.
First Families: The Making of an American Aristocracy.
Boston, MA, Little, Brown, 1970. 503 p.

Call, Michael L.
Royal Ancestors of Some LDS Families. Orem, UT 84057; the author, 1312 N. 725 W.; 1975.

Colket, Meredith B.
Founders of Early American Families: Emigrants from Europe 1607–1657 . . .
Cleveland, Order of Founders and Patriots, 1975. 366 p., alpha.
NN APK 76-310

Crowther, G. Rodney
Surname Index to Sixty-five Volumes of Colonial and Revolutionary Pedigrees. Washington, 1964. 143 p., alpha. (*NGSSP no. 27*) (Indexes to the volumes by Ruth Lawrence and the American Historical Company.)
NN APGA

Howe, Helen.
The Gentle Americans, 1864–1960; Biography of a Breed. NY, Harper & Row, 1965. 458 p.
NN IQH (Boston)

Lawrence, Ruth.
Colonial Families of America.
New York, National Americana, 1928–1965. 30 v., index each v.
NN APK +

Savage, James.
A Genealogical Dictionary of the First Settlers of New England Showing Three Generations of Those Who Came Before May 1692 . . . With Genealogical Notes and Errata (1873) and a Cross Index (1884).
Baltimore, GPC, 1965 (orig. 1860–62) 4 v., alpha.
NN *R-APR (New England)

Smith, Elsdon C.
New Dictionary of American Family Names.
New York, Harper & Row, 1973. 570 p., alpha.
NN APD 76-737

Thorndike, Joseph J., Jr.
The Very Rich, A History of Wealth. NY, American Heritage, 1976. 344 p., index.
NN JLF 76-551

Tucker, R. Whitney.
The Descendants of the Presidents. Charlotte, NC, Delmar Printing Co., 1975. 222 p., index (covers only the direct descendants of the presidents but it has some information not in the volume by Burke's Peerage, and it is easier to read.)
NN APK 76-905

Ward, Robert Leigh.
English Ancestry of Seven Mayflower Ancestors: Tilley, Sampson and Cooper.
(IN: *TAG, Des Moines, IA, 1976. v. 52, p. 198–208*)
NN APGA

The Wall Street Journal.
The New Millionaires and How They Made Their Fortunes.
New York, B. Geis, 1961. 187 p.
NN E-11 5902

Wecter, Dixon (1906–1950)
The Saga of American Society: A Recount of Social Aspiration 1607–1937. New York, Scribner's, 1937. 504 p.
NN IDS

Weis, Frederick Lewis.
Ancestral Roots of Sixty Colonists Who Came to New England Between 1623 and 1650, The Lineage of Alfred the Great, Charlemagne, Malcolm of Scotland, Robert the Strong and Some of Their Descendants. 5th ed. with Additions and Corrections by Walter Lee Sheppard, Jr.
Baltimore, GPC, 1976. 186 p., index.
NN APR (New England)

SOME POPULAR AMERICAN NAMES AND GATEWAY FAMILIES

ADAMS—A Presidential family

Adams Addenda.
St. Louis, MO, 1971– v. 1–
NN APV (Adams) 74-757

Adams, Andrew N.
A Genealogical History of Henry Adams of Braintree, Mass. and His Descendants, also John Adams of Cambridge, Mass.1632–1897.
Rutland, VT, Tuttle, 1898. 2 v. (1,298 p.)
(Needs much revision)
NN APV (Adams)

Adams, Enid E.
Ancestry and Descendants of Jeremiah Adams, 1794–1883 (7th in Descent from Henry Adams of Braintree).
Victor, OH, Ancestor Hunters, 1974. 716 p., index.
(Clears up the early generations)
NN APV (Adams) 75-2308

President John Adams and His Alden Ancestry.

(IN: *MQ, Warwick, RI, 1976. v. 42, p. 87–90*)
NN APV (Adams) 76-2133

ALDEN—*Mayflower* passenger

Alden, Augustus E.
Pilgrim Alden: the Story of the Life of the first John Alden in America ... and some account of the later Aldens ...
Boston, MA, J. H. Earle, 1902. 232 p.
NN APV (Alden)

Alden, Ebenezer.
Memorial of the Descendants of the Hon. John Alden.
Randolph, MA, S. P. Brown, 1867. 164 p.
NN APV (Alden)

Alden Kindred of New York City and Vicinity.
New York, 1929–1945. nos. 1–46.
NN APV (Alden)

ALEXANDER—Scottish exiles, a Revolutionary War general and Jewish Colonial settlers

Alexander, Charles C., and Virginia W. Alexander.
Alexander Kin.
Columbia, TN, 1965. 173 p., index.
(Six signers of the Mecklenburg Declaration, p. 4)
NN APV (Alexander)

Alexander, De Alva Stanwood.
The Alexanders of Maine.
Buffalo, NY, 1898. 129 p., index.
NN APV (Alexander)

Alexander, Henry Aaron.
Notes on the Alexander Family of South Carolina and Georgia and Connections.

The author, 1954. 143 p., no index.
NN *PWO

Boggs, Marion B.
The Alexander Letters 1787–1900.
Savannah, GA, G. J. Baldwin, 1910. 387 p., no index.
NN APV (Alexander)

Lanphier, Beatrice Howell.
The Alexander and Howell Families.
Dixon, IL, 1964. 240 p., cursory index.
NN APV (Alexander)

Rogers, Charles.
Memorials of the Earl of Stirling and the House of Alexander.
Edinburgh, W. Paterson, 1877. 2 v.
NN ARZ (Alexander)

ALLERTON—Isaac the Pilgrim was a man for all seasons in Massachusetts, New York and Virginia

Allerton, Walter S.
History of the Allerton Family in the United States 1585 to 1885. 2nd ed.
Chicago, IL. 1900. 144 p., index.
NN APV (Allerton)

Greenwood, Isaac.
Allertons of New England and Virginia.
(IN: *NEHGR, Boston, MA, 1890. v. 44, p. 290–296*)
NN *R-APGA

Johanna Swinnerton: Third Wife of Isaac Allerton, Sr.
(IN: *NEHGR, Boston, MA, 1970. v. 124, p. 133*)
NN *R-APGA

ALSTON(ALLSTON)—Colonial Carolinian planters and soldiers of English origin

Groves, Joseph A. and Silas Emmett Lucas.
Alstons and Allstons of North and South Carolina ... With Supplementary Materials on the LaBruce, Pawley and Ward Families of Waccamaw. Easley, SC, Rev. Silas E. Lucas, 1976. (some material orig. 1901, 1957) 534 p., index to p. 1-367.

ANTHON—A New York name

Fish, Stuyvesant.
Anthon Genealogy.
New York, 1930. 214 p.
NN APV (Anthon)

APPLETON—Merchants, industrialists and politicians

Davis, Walter Goodwin.
The Ancestry of Mary Isaac c. 1549–1613, wife of Thomas Appleton ...
Portland, ME, 1955. 401 p.
(One of the great classic genealogies)
NN ARZ (Isaac)

Jewett, Isaac Appleton.
Memorial of Samuel Appleton of Ipswich, Mass. ...
Boston, MA, 1950. 183 p.
NN APV (Appleton)

Tharp, Louise Hall.
The Appletons of Beacon Hill.
Boston, MA, Little, Brown, 1973. 368 p., index.
NN APV (Appleton) 74-284

ARCHER—Virginia planters, descendants of Pocahontas

Randolph, Wassell.
George Archer I of the Umberslade Archers of Henrico County, Virginia, and His Descendants.
Memphis, TN, 1965. 63 p., plus index.
NN APV (Archer)

ASTOR—Fur and real estate in New York and England

Kavaler, Lucy.
The Astors: A Family Chronicle of Pomp and Power.
New York, Dodd Mead, 1966. 354 p., index.
NN APV (Astor)

O'Connor, Harvey.
The Astors.
New York, Alfred A. Knopf, 1941. 488, xvi p., index.
NN APV (Astor)

Thomas, Lately.
A Pride of Lions, the Astor Orphans: The Chanler Chronicle.
New York, William Morrow, 1971. 304 p., index.
NN APV (Astor) 72-1959

ATWATER—Connecticut pioneers

Atwater, Francis.
Atwater History and Genealogy.
Meriden, CT, Journal Pub. Co., 1901–1956. 4 v.
NN APV (Atwater)

BANCROFT—Yankees who went West

Bancroft, Margaret.
Bancroft Family History.
Denver, CO. 2 v., plus 1 v. index.
NN APV (Bancroft) 75-1908

BARCLAY—Early settlers in New York and New Jersey

Moffat, R. Burnham.
The Barclays of New York ...
New York, R. G. Cooke, 1904. 474
  p., index.
NN APV (Barclay)

BATCHELDER—Ancestor of at least two Presidents, Nixon and Ford

Batchelder, Batcheller, Genealogy
  of the Descendants of Rev. Stephen Batchelder of England.
Chicago, IL, W. B. Conkey, 1898.
  623 p., index.
NN APV (Batchelder)

Hurst, Lise.
President Ford and Richard
  Nixon Are Blood Relatives.
(IN: *National Enquirer, Lantana,
  FL, Nov. 6, 1976, p. 61*)
(They are ninth cousins three
  times removed through Rev.
  Stephen Batchelder, as found by
  David Dearborn of Boston)

BEAUREGARD—A Louisiana general popular in the Civil War

Basso, Hamilton.
Beauregard, the Great Creole.

New York, Charles Scribner's Sons,
  1933. 333 p.
NN AN (Beauregard)

Seebold, Herman de B.
Old Louisiana Plantation Homes
  ...
New Orleans, LA, Pelican Press,
  1941. v. 2, p. 145–147.
NN APR (Louisiana)

BEEKMAN—Dutch settlers in New York

Gibson, James Renwick.
Some Records of the Beekman
  Family.
(IN: *NYGBR, New York, 1888. v.
  19, p. 41–52*)
NN APGA

White, Philip L.
The Beekmans of New York in
  Politics and Commerce 1647–1877.
New York, NYHS, 1956. 705 p.,
  index.
NN APV (Beekman)

BEVERLEY—Popular Virginians

McGill, John.
The Beverly Family of Virginia,
  Descendants of Maj. Robert
  Beverley, 1641–1877, and Allied
  Families.
Columbia, SC, R. L. Bryan, 1956.
  1,117 p., index.
(Male and female lines of descent)
NN APV (Beverley)

BLISS—Pioneers and patrons of the arts

Bliss, John Homer.
... Genealogy of the Bliss Family

in America from about the Year 1550 to 1880.
Boston, the author, c. 1881. 810 p., index.
NN APV (Bliss)

Moffett, Lauren R.
Record of the Descendants of Aaron Sage Bliss 1797–1853 with Lineal Antecedents to the Immigrant Ancestor Thomas Bliss (1580 or 1585–1640).
Cleveland Heights, OH, 1960. 41 leaves.
NN APV (Bliss)

BOLLES—Rugged New Englanders descended from Charlemagne

Williams, George E.
A Genealogy of the Descendants of Joseph Bolles of Welles, Maine. West Hartford, CT 06107; the author, 16 Royal Oak Drive; 1970. 846 p. (European ancestry with line to Charlemagne p. 1-13)
NN APV (Bolles) 72-1879

BOLLING—Ancestors of a first lady—Edith Bolling Wilson

Bolling, Robert.
A Memoir of a Portion of the Bolling Family in England and America.
Richmond, VA, W. H. Wade, 1868. 68 p.
NN APV (Bolling)

BOONE—The Kentucky frontiersman

Boone Sierra Echoes.
Boone Family Assoc. of Cal., 1968–.
NN APV (Boone) 73-2814

Spraker, Ella H.
The Boone Family, a Genealogical History of George and Mary Boone Who Came to America in 1717 ... also a Biographical sketch of Daniel Boone. ...
Rutland, VT, Tuttle, 1922. 691 p.
NN APV (Boone)

BRADFORD—The Plymouth Colony Governor

Governor William Bradford Compact.
New York, 1945–, ed. by Ruth Hall.
NN APV (Bradford)

Hall, Ruth Gardiner.
Descendants of Governor William Bradford (Through Seven Generations).
Ann Arbor, MI, 1951. 1 v.
NN APV (Bradford)

Kennedy, Sophia F.
Bradford: from the Mayflower and Plymouth Colony to Missouri, with Related Families.
Kansas City, MO, S. F. Kennedy, 1975. 134 p.
APV (Bradford) 76-1105

BREWSTER—A popular and prolific Pilgrim ancestor whose descendants include a movie star.

Jones, Emma C. Brewster.
The Brewster Genealogy 1566–

1907 ... Descendants of William
Brewster.
New York, Grafton Press, 1908. 2
v., index each v. (Bing Crosby's
line from Brewster appears in
the *Mayflower Index*)
NN APV (Brewster)

BROWN—Rhode Island Baptists who endowed a university

Hedges, James B.
The Browns of Providence Plan-
tations.
Providence, RI, Brown U. Press,
1968. 2 v., index each v.
NN APV (Brown)

Ogden, Galen B.
The Jeremiah Brown Family Gen-
ealogy 1802–1974.
Elgin, IL, 1974. 133 p.
NN APV (Brown) 75-721

BULKELEY—Pioneer clergymen in Massachusetts

Bell, Patricia.
Odell, Two Notable Rectors, Edward Bulkeley and His Son Peter.
(IN: *Bedfordshire Magazine, Bedford, MA, 1975. v. 15, p. 119–124*)
NN CO (Bedfordshire)

Jacobus, Donald Lines.
Bulkeley Genealogy, Rev. Peter
Bulkeley.
New Haven, CT, 1933. 2 v. (1,066 p.)
NN APV (Bulkeley)

CABOT—Boston Brahmins

Briggs, L. Vernon.
History and Genealogy of the Ca-

bot Family 1475–1927.
Boston, MA, C. E. Goodspeed,
1927. 2 v.
NN APV (Cabot)

CALVERT—The Lords Baltimore of Maryland and Their American descendants

Hastings, Mrs. Russell.
Calvert and Darnell Gleanings
from England.
(IN: *MHM, Baltimore, MD,
1926–1927. v. 21, p. 303–324; v.
22, p. 1–22, 115–138, 211–245,
307–349*)
NN IAA

O'Gorman, Ella Foy.
Descendants of Virginia Calvert.
Los Angeles, CA, 1947. 766 p., in-
dex.
NN APV (Calvert)

Nicklin, J. B. C.
Calvert Family.
(IN: *MHM, Baltimore, MD, 1921,
1924–1925. v. 16, p. 50–59,
189–204, 313–318, 389–394; v. 24,
p. 126–132; v. 25, p. 30–49*)
NN IAA

CARDOZO—Sephardic South Carolina merchants and a Justice of the Supreme Court

Hellman, George S.
Benjamin N. Cardozo, American
Judge (1870/1938).
New York, Whittlesey House,
1940. 339 p.
NN E-13 7253

Cardozo Family.
(IN: *Stern, Malcom H., Americans*

*of Jewish Descent. Cincinnati,
OH, 1960, p 23*)
APK+

CARROLL—Maryland Signer of the Declaration of Independence

"Anywhere So Long As There Be
Freedom" Charles Carroll of
Carrollton, His Family and His
Maryland. Baltimore, Balti-
more Museum of Art, 1975.
NN APV (Carroll) 76-739

Grove, William Jarboe.
History of Carrollton Manor,
Frederick County, Maryland.
Frederick, MD, Marken & Biel-
feld, 1928. 496 p., no index.
NN ISH (Frederick Co.)

CARTER—King Carter of Virginia, New England Puritans and a President of the United States

Carter, Howard W.
A Genealogy of the Descendants
of Thomas Carter of Reading
and Weston, Mass. ... Also
Some Account of his Brothers
Eleazer, Daniel, Ebenezer and
Ezra, the Sons of Thomas
Carter and Grandsons of the
Rev. Thomas Carter, First Min-
ister at Woburn Mass., 1642.
Norfolk, CT, 1909. 341 p., index.
NN APV (Carter)

Carter, Robert Randolph of Shir-
ley.
The Carter Tree.
Santa Barbara, CA, Channel Litho
Co., 1951. 243 p., index.
NN APV (Carter)

Harvey, Mr. and Mrs. W. D.
Sumter County, Georgia, Cemetery
Records.
Americus, GA 31709; Mazie Mun-
son Harvey, 214 W. College St.,
1972, p 29. James Earl Carter
(father of the President),
Nina Pratt, wife of William Car-
ter (grandmother of JEC, Jr.).
NN APR (Sumter Co., GA) 72-2914

Miller, Joseph L.
The Descendants of Thomas
Carter of Barford, Lancaster
Co., Virginia, 1652–1912.
Thomas, WV, J. L. Miller, 1912.
388 p., no index.
NN APV (Carter)

Thomas, Kenneth H., Jr.
Georgia Family Lines. Carter-
Gordy. (IN: *Georgia Life. Atlanta, 1976. v. 3 no. 3 p. 40–41,
46*) (The paternal and maternal
lines of President Carter.)
NN APTF (Carter, James Earl)

Wallace, George S.
The Carter of Blenheim.
Richmond, VA, Garrett & Massie,
1955. 139 p., index.
NN APV (Carter)

Warner, Charles W. H.
Thomas Carter of Corotoman,
Lancaster County, Virginia ...
Williamsburg, VA, *Gazette*, 1958.
58 p., t of c, no index.
(Thomas Carter in VA, 1637, Skip-
with and Dales)
NN APV (Carter)

Wulfeck, Dorothy.
Carter of Virginia ...
Naugatuck, CT, 1962. 59 p.
NN APV (Carter)

CHASE—A Secretary of the Treasury, a Signer and Nantucket whalers

Chase, John C., and G. W. Chamberlain.
Seven Generations of the Descendants of Aquila and Thomas Chase.
Derby, NH, 1928. 624 p., index.
(Salmon P. Chase p. 376–378)
NN APV (Chase)

Hultz, Helen Lorraine.
Charles Gardiner Chase, His Ancestors and Descendants.
Cottonport, LA, Polyanthos, 1973. 393 p., index.
(Printed in the handwriting of the author)
NN APV (Chase 74-937)

Sons of the American Revolution. Maryland.
Maryland Signers of the Declaration of Independence. Baltimore, the society, 1912. p. 1–6
(Samuel Chase, 1741–1811)
NN APGA

NN IRAT
CLARK(E)—A Rhode Island gentleman, a Kentucky explorer, loyalists and patriots

Bryant, George Clarke, and D. L. Jacobus.
Deacon George Clark(e) of Milford, Conn., and Some of His Descendants.
Ansonia, CT, 1949. 258 p., index.
NN APV (Clark)

Gould, Robert F.
Thompson Clark's Ancestors.
Bethesda, MD, 1975. 672 p., index.

(New Milford, CT, families)
NN APV (Clark) 76-1780

Johnson, Carol Clark.
A Genealogical History of Clark and Worth Families and Other Puritan Settlers ...
Cygnet, OH, 1970. 551, 25 p., index.
NN APV (Clark) 72-75

Justice, Alfred R.
Ancestry of Jeremy Clarke of Rhode Island and Dungan Genealogy.
Philadelphia, PA, Franklin Print. Co., 1923. 538 p., index.
NN APV (Clarke)

Thruston, R. C. Ballard.
Some Recent Finds Regarding the Ancestry of Gen. George Rogers Clark.
(IN: *Filson Club Hist. Quart., Louisville, KY, 1935. v. 9, p. 1–34*)
NN IAA and reprint in APT p.v. 74

Watson, Estelle Clark.
Loyalists Clarks, Badgleys and Allied Families ...
Rutland, VT, Tuttle, 1954. 327 p., index.
NN APV (Clark)

CLARKE—The family of Hyde Hall, Cooperstown, NY

Linaker, R. H.
A Short Account of the Life of George Clarke, Lieutenant Governor of New York 1736–1745.
(IN: *Chester and North Wales Architectural, Archaeological &*

*Historic Soc. Chester, 1920. n.s.v.
23, p. 55–63*)
NN CO (Chester)

COOPER—Our first novelist and some Southerners of the name

Cooper, James Fenimore.
The Legends and Traditions of a Northern County.
New York, G. P. Putnam's, 1921. 263 p.
NN IRM (Otsego)

Cooper, Murphy Rowe.
The Cooper Family History and Genealogy, 1681–1931.
Richmond, VA, Garrett and Massie, 1931. 116 p.
NN APV (Cooper)

Cooper, Wyatt.
Families, A Memoir and Celebration.
New York, Harper & Row, 1975. 199 p., no index.
(Photos of the author, his wife, Gloria Vanderbilt, their children, etc., between p. 110 and 111)
NN APV (Cooper) 76-293

Grossman, James.
James Fenimore Cooper.
New York, W. Sloane, 1949. 286 p.
NN *R-NCB

Ward, Clare McVickar.
Descendants of Katherine Lemoine (Guy) Fenimore Cooper through the Spottiswoode Lineage.
n.p., 1969. gen. table. (the compiler and illuminator is a foremost heraldic artist)
NN APV+++ (Cooper)

DAVIS—New England Yankees and the President of the Confederate States

Davis, Harry Alexander.
The Davis Family (Davies and Davids) in Wales and America.
Washington, DC, H. A. Davis, 1927. 445 p., index.
(Jefferson Davis p. 96–97)
NN APV (Davis)

Davis, Walter Goodwin.
The Ancestry of Nicholas Davis 1753–1832 of Limington, Maine.
Portland, ME, The Anthoensen Press, 1956. 239 p., index.
NN APV (Davis)

Davis, William Church.
The Ancestry and Posterity of Joseph Davis 1773–1865 of Norway, New York, and His Wife Elizabeth Hallock Davis.
Walton, NY, 1927. 161 p., index.
NN APV (Davis)

DELAFIELD—A Norman family who settled in New York

Delafield, Brig. Gen. John Ross.
Delafield Family History.
New York., J. R. Delafield, 1945. 2 v., index v. 2.
NN APV (Delafield)

DESLOGE—Missouri merchants and pioneers

Huger, Lucie Furstenberg.
The Desloge Family in America.
St. Louis, MO, Nordmann, 1959. 64 p.
NN APT p.v. 156

DIODATI—An Italian Family in Colonial New Haven

Dorian, Donald Clayton.
The English Diodatis.
New Brunswick, NJ, Rutgers U. Press, 1950. 365 p., index.
(William Diodati of New Haven p. 318–327)
NN ARZ (Diodati)

Salisbury, Edward E.
Mr. William Diodati of New Haven from 1717 to 1751 and His Italian Ancestry.
New Haven, CT, 1876. 39 p.
NN APV (Diodati)

DOMINQUEZ—Early California ranchers

Gillingham, Robert C.
The Rancho San Pedro; The Story of a Famous Rancho in Los Angeles County and Its Owners, the Dominquez Family.
Los Angeles, CA, Cole-Holmquist Press, 1961. 473 p., index.
NN APV (Dominquez)

DORSEY—A noted family in Maryland

Dorsey, Maxwell Jay.
The Dorsey Family: Descendants of Edward Darcy-Dorsey of Virginia and Maryland for Five Generations.
n.p., c. 1947. 270 p.
NN APV (Dorsey)

DOWD—Mamie Doud Eisenhower's ancestors

Brandon, Dorothy B.
Mamie Doud Eisenhower, a Portrait of a First Lady.
New York, Scribner's, 1954. 307 p.
NN AN (Eisenhower, M.)

Dowd, Willis Wentworth.
The Descendants of Henry Doude Who Came from England in 1639.
Hartford, CT, Case, Lockwood & Brainard, 1885. 355 p., index.
NN APV (Doude)

DRAKE—Yankee farmers and mariners

Gay, Frank B., and Harrie Beekman Drake.
The Descendants of John Drake of Windsor, Conn.
Rutland, VT, Tuttle, 1933. 358 p., index, use care.
NN APV (Drake)

Thompson, Alice Smith.
The Drake Family of New Hampshire ... with an Introduction by Sir Anthony Wagner.
Concord, NH, Hist. Soc., 1962. 342 p., index.
(Excellent documentation and style)
NN APV (Drake)

DUDLEY—The family of Governor Thomas of Mass. and others

Dudley, Dean.
The History of the Dudley Family ...
Montrose, MA, 1894. 1201, 52 p.
NN APV (Dudley)

DUPONT—The French family of the Delaware chemical empire

DuPont, Pierre Samuel.
Genealogy of the DuPont Family 1739–1949.

Wilmington, DE, 1949. 2 v., index
each v.
NN APV (DuPont)

American Historical Co.
DuPont and Allied Families
New York, 1965. 497 p., index.
NN AZ+

EISENHOWER—The German ancestors of the popular general and President

Cook, Ross K.
The Eisenhower Family in America.
(IN: *NYGBR, New York, 1945. v. 76, p. 51–68, 139*)
NN APGA

Richardson, Fannie Belle (Taylor)
Eisenhower Lineage and Reference, a Series of Bulletins on Eisenhower, Eisenhauer, Isenhour ...
Greenwood, IN, 1958. 5 v.
(Various paging)
NN APV (Eisenhower)

Friederichs, Heinz F.
The Eisenhower Genealogy; A Post Script.
(IN: *PGM, Philadelphia, DA, 1961. v. 22, p. 144–146*)
NN APR (Penn)

ENO—This family invented the salts

Eno, Henry Lane.
The Eno Family, New York Branch.
Princeton, NJ, Princeton U. Press, 1920. 35 p.
NN APV (Eno) 73-2319

FIELD—Marshall Field, Cyrus W. Field, Stephen J. Field and many others

Field, Emilia A. R.
Record of the Life of David Dudley Field, his Ancestors and Descendants.
Denver, CO, 1931. 181 p., no index.
NN APV (Field)

Field, Wells L., and Elizabeth D. Field.
Our Children's Ancestors.
West Hartford, CT, W. L. Field, 1966–1971. 2 v.
NN APV (Field)

Pierce, Frederick Clifton.
Field Genealogy.
Chicago, W. B. Conkey, 1901. 2 v.
(Thomas Jefferson v. 2, p. 1,059–1,079; Marshall Field v. 2, p. 690–706; the Field Brothers v. 2, p. 608–658)
NN APV (Field)

FISH—Preserved Fish and New York social leaders

Fish, Job.
Job Fish Pioneer Teacher 1828–1923.
Batavia, NY, 1964. 2 v.
NN APV (Fish)

Fish, Lester W.
The Fish Family in England and America.
Rutland, VT, Tuttle, 1948. 530 p., index.
NN APV (Fish)

Fish, Stuyvesant.
Ancestors of Hamilton Fish and Julia Ursin Niemcewicz Kean, His Wife.

New York, 1929. 177 p.
NN APV (Fish)

Hale, Nathan, and Lillian Boynton Hale.
The Ancestors and Descendants of Simeon Fish, Minuteman of Mason, N.H., and Pioneer of Lincoln County, Maine.
Gardiner, ME, The Simeon, Asa and Amos Fish Cemetery Assoc., 1969. 88 p., index.
NN APV (Fish) 76-1263

FORD—Many patriots and pioneers, but not Henry; the first adopted President (born King)

Anderson, Robert C., William A. Reitwiesner and Gary B. Roberts.
The Matrilinear Line of President Ford.
(IN: *TAG, Des Moines, IA, 1977. v. 53, p. 56–57*)
NN APGA

Ford Family Genealogy.
Great Neck, NY, Hannibal C. Ford, 1950. 9 v., index.
NN APV (Ford)

Ford, Frederick W.
Ford History and Genealogy ... One Line of ... William Ford Who Landed at Plymouth, Mass., Nov. 20, 1621.
Oak Ridge, TN, 1960. 253 p., long t of c, no index.
NN APV (Ford)

FROST—The Maine ancestors of a great poet

Frost, John Eldridge.
The Nicholas Frost Family (with Sup. 1 & 2).

Milford, NH, The Cabinet Press, 1943. 142 p.
(Sup. 1, 1944; Sup. 2, 1946)
NN APV (Frost)

GARDINER—The family of Lion Gardiner, whose island manor is intact

Gardiner, John Lion.
Gardiners of Gardiner's Island.
East Hampton, NY, Star Press, 1927. 326, xix p., index.
NN APV (Gardiner)

GILMAN—New Hampshire aristocrats

Noyes, Mrs. Charles P. (Emily H. Gilman)
A Family History in Letters and Documents 1667–1837 ...
St. Paul, MN, the author, 1919. 692 p., index.
NN APV (Gilman)

GOULD—New York Financiers

Hoyt, Edwin Palmer.
The Goulds: A Social History.
New York, Weybright & Talley, 1969. 346 p.
NN E-13 8526

DE GRAFFENRIED—A Swiss baronial Family in the Colonial south

de Graffenried, Thomas.
The de Graffenried Family Scrap Book 1191–1956 ...
Charlottesville, VA, U. of VA Press, 1958. 271 p., index.
NN APV (Graffenried)

de Graffenried, Thomas.
History of the de Graffenried
Family from 1191 A.D. to 1925.
Binghamton, NY, the author,
1925. 282 p., index.
NN APV (Graffenried)

GREEN(E)—The family of Revolutionary War Gen. Nathaniel Greene

Greene, George S., and Louise B.
Clarke.
The Greenes of Rhode Island with
Historical Record of English
Ancestry 1534–1902.
New York, 1903. 892 p., index.
(The English ancestry is incor-
rect)
NN APV (Greene)

Devereux, Margaret Green
The Land and The People: an
American Heritage.
New York, Vantage Press, 1974.
394 p., index.
NN APV (Green) 75-1321

GREGG—Scottish southern planters with illustrious connections

Gregg, E. Stuart.
A Crane's Foot—or Pedigree of
Branches of the Gregg, Stuart,
Robertson, Dobbs and Allied
Families.
Columbia, SC, R. L. Bryan, 1975.
index.
(Lewis of Warner Hall p. 237–244;
Warner p. 245–249; Reade with
lines to royal houses p. 251–279;
Martiau p. 282–286; Taylor fam-
ily of Pres. Zachary p. 218–226;

Michaux p. 357–364; Watkins p.
372–377; etc.)
NN APV (Gregg) 76-1842

HAMILTON—The ancestry of the Dukes of Hamilton and Alexander of New York

Hamilton, George.
A History of the House of Hamil-
ton.
Edinburgh, J. Skinner, 1933. 1,168
p., 2 indices (name and place).
(Alexander of N.Y. p. 1,069)
NN ARZ (Hamilton)

Hamilton Letter.
(IN: *SG, Edinburgh, 1970. v. 17, p.
56–59*)
NN ARCA

Reynolds, Cuyler.
History of Southern New York and
Hudson River Valley.
New York, Lewis Publishing Co.,
1914. v. 3, p. 1,376–1,392. port.
NN APR (New York State)

Parish, Verel Hamilton.
Hamilton, Mullins, Fleming and
Related Families of Kentucky,
West Virginia, North Carolina,
and Tennessee.
Stamping Ground, KY, 1975. 80 p.
NN APV (Hamilton) 76-313

HAWTHORNE—They gave us a great American writer

Loggins, Vernon.
The Hawthornes, the Story of
Seven Generations of an Ameri-
can Family.
New York, Greenwood Press, 1968
(orig. 1951). 365 p., index.
NN APV (Hawthorne)

HOUSTON—Scottish baronets in Georgia

Johnston, Edith Duncan.
The Houstons of Georgia.
Athens, U. of GA Press, 1950. 430 p.
NN APU (Houston)

Moore, Clarence E.
The Houston Family.
(IN: *Fort Worth Gen. Soc. Bul, Forth Worth, TX, 1961. v. 4, p. 3–7*)
NN APR (Fort Worth)

Shuffler, Ralph H.
The Houstons at Independence.
Waco, TX, Texian Press, 1966. 101 p.
NN E-12 7179

Whyte, Donald.
The Houstons of Houston.
(IN: *SG, Edinburgh, 1968–69. v. 15, p. 86–92; v. 16, p. 53–60*)
NN ARCA

HOWELL—Seventeenth-century Long Island pioneers and the wife of Jefferson Davis

Finch, Jessie Howell.
The Ancestral Lines of Chester Everts Howell 1867–1949, of Elmira, New York.
Elmira, NY, Howell Assoc., 1965. 130, 43 p., index.
NN APV (Howell)

Ross, Emma Howell.
Descendants of Edward Howell Bapt. 1584, d. 1655 ... of Buckinghamshire ... and Southampton, L.I., New York.
Holliston, MA 01746; Mrs. Elbert Ross, 31 Norland St., 1968. 357 p., index.

(Revision in progress)
NN APV (Howell)

Leach, Joseph Granville.
Genealogical and Biographical Memorial of the Reading, Howell, Yerkes, Watts, Latham and Elkins Families.
Philadelphia, PA, Lippincott, 1898. 285 p.
(Gov. Richard Howell of NJ and his granddaughter, Varina Davis)
NN APV (Reading)

Ross, Ishbel.
First Lady of the South; Mrs. Jefferson Davis.
New York, Harper, 1958. 475 p.
(Varina Howell Davis, 1826–1906)
NN D-11 2283

HOWLAND—Pilgrim father and Hetty Green

Emory, William M.
The Howland Heirs, Being the Story of a Family and a Fortune and of a Trust Established for Mrs. Hetty H. R. Green.
New Bedford, MA, E. Anthony, 1919. 484 p., index.
NN APV (Howland)

Howland, Franklyn.
A Brief Genealogical and Biographical History of Arthur, Henry and John Howland and Their Descendants.
New Bedford, MA, 1885. 2 v., index.
NN APV (Howland)

The Howland Quarterly.
Boston, the Pilgrim John Howland Soc., 1936–. (40 v. by 1976)

% Mrs. W. R. Greenwood, 73 Pound Hill Rd., N. Smithfield, Woonsocket, RI 02895.
NN APV (Howland)

HUME—Scottish exiles in Virginia

Hume, Edgar Erskine.
A Colonial Scottish Jacobite Family.
Richmond, VA, Old Dominion Press, 1931. 103 p., plus chart.
(Letters and documents that prove the Scottish link)
NN APV (Hume)

McCurdy, Mrs. James, and Mabel R. Smith.
Tiger by the Tail.
(IN: *NGSQ, Washington, DC, 1969–1970. v. 57, p. 193–198, 262–268; v. 58, p. 258–268*)
NN APGA

HYDE—Most claim kin to Anne Hyde, wife of James II

Walworth, Reuben.
Hyde Genealogy, the Descendants in the Female as Well as Male Lines of William Hyde of Norwich.
Albany, NY, J. Munsell, 1864. 2 v., index v. 2.
(This book set the style for the big Victorian genealogy)
NN APV (Hyde) and AZ

ISELIN—Swiss bankers and sportsmen

Weiss, Frey.
Heinrich Iselin of Rosenfeld and His Descendants. 2nd ed., Basle, O'Donnell Iselin, 1963. 273 p.,
index, gen. chart in rear cover.
NN APV (Iselin)

JONES—Welsh settlers at Jones Beach and points north and south

Cunningham, Caroline.
Jones Records.
Raleigh, NC, 1964–1965. 2 v.
NN APV (Jones)

Jones, Carroll Brewster.
Jones and Related Families.
Milford, NH, Cabinet Press for the author of Marcellus, MI, 1951. 436 p., index.
(Francis Jones from Ireland to PA)
NN APV (Jones)

Jones, John H.
The Jones Family of Long Island, Descendants of Major Thomas Jones 1665–1726 . . .
New York, Tobias A. Wright, 1907. 435 p., index.
NN APV (Jones)

Jones, Mabel Merryfield.
Some other Joneses Descendants of Increase Jones 1752–1825 of Minerva, New York.
(Descendant of Cornelius Jones of Rhode Island)
Middletown, CT, Dorothy J. Manny, 1967. 263 p., index.
NN APV (Jones)

JOHNSON—A Texas President and a PA descendant of Peter Paul Rubens

Johnson, Rebekah Baines.
A Family Album.

New York, McGraw-Hill, 1965. 146 p.
NN APV (Johnson)

Johnson, Robert W.
The Ancestry of Rosalie Morris Johnson ...
Philadelphia, 1905–08. 2 v., index each v.
(Rubens family, v. 1, p. 205–211; v. 2, p. 26; Lords Baltimore, v. 1, p. 9–48)
NN APV (Johnson)

JOHNSTON(E)—Scots and Scotch-Irish at home and abroad

Johnston, Henry Poellnitz.
The Gentle Johnstons and Their Kin.
Birmingham, AL, Featon Press, 1966. 550 p. index.
NN APV (Johnston)

Johnstone, C. L.
History of the Johnstones 1191–1909.
Edinburgh, Johnston, 1909. 396 p., index plus 8 charts.
NN APV (Johnstone)

Thomas, Elizabeth Wood.
Genealogy of Lyndon Baines Johnson, Descendant of a Revolutionary Soldier.
(IN: *Ala. Gen. Reg, Tuscaloosa, AL, 1964. v. 6, p. 3–15, 53–57*)
NN APR (Alabama)

KENNEDY—Boston Irish who gave us a President and two Senators

Brennan, Rev. J. F.
The Evolution of Everyman (An-

cestral Lineage of John F. Kennedy).
Dundalk, Ireland, Dundalgan Press, 1968. 259 p., index.
NN APV (Kennedy)

Buck, Pearl S.
The Kennedy Women.
New York, Cowles Book, 1970. 218 p.
NN APV (Kennedy)

The Kennedys.
New York, Time Inc., 1968. 95 p.
NN APV+ (Kennedy)

KEY—The "Star-Spangled Banner" author

Lane, Julian C
Key and Allied Families.
Macon, GA, J. W. Burke, 1931. 495 p., index.
(Francis Scott Key p. 10–32, 58–64, etc.)
NN APV (Key)

KING—Seventeenth-century immigrants and a twentieth-century black hero

Bennett, Lerone.
What Manner of Man: A Biography of Martin Luther King, Jr.
Chicago, IL, Johnson Pub., 1964. 227 p.
NN E-12 2949

King, Coretta Scott.
My Life with Martin Luther King, Jr.
New York, Holt, 1969. 372 p.
NN E-13 8500

Morrison, George A.
King Families of New England.

New York, typescript, 1911–12. 4.
v. plus 1 v. index.
NN APV (King)

Rey, Luise K.
The Singing Kings ...
Salt Lake City, UT, Deseret, 1969.
1 v.
NN *MEC (King)

LANIER—A popular American poet

Ingersoll, Louise Lanier.
Lanier.
n.p., the author, 1965. 695 p., index.
(Sidney Lanier, 1842–1881, p. 338.)
NN APV (Lanier)

LEE—Signer of the Declaration and Civil War general

Hogg, O.F.G.
The Lees of Virginia.
(IN: *GM, London, 1961. v. 13, p. 332–344, 372–384*)
NN ARCA

Lee, Edmund Jennings.
Lee of Virginia 1642–1892.
Baltimore, MD, GPC, 1974 (orig. 1895). 586 p., index.
NN APV (Lee) 75-263

LEVY—Naval heroes, the Dowager Duchess of Norfolk and seventeenth-century Jewish pioneers

Fish, Sidney M.
Aaron Levy (1742–1815), Founder of Aaronsburg.
New York, AJHS, 1951. 181 p.
(Studies in AJH no. 1)
NN *PXY

Fitzpatrick, Donovan, and Saul Saphire.
Navy Maverick: Uriah Phillips Levy (1792–1862).
Garden City, NY, Doubleday, 1963. 273 p.
NN D-15 5064

Levy, Nathan.
The "Green Book"; Records of the Levy, Goodwin and Many Other Families.
Montclair, NJ, 1931. 41 leaves.
NN APT p.v. 139

Levy Family.
(IN: *Stern, Malcolm H., Americans of Jewish Descent. Cincinnati, OH, 1960, p. 109–121*)
NN APK+

LEWIS—Washington's kin and western pioneers

Anderson, Sarah T. S.
Lewises, Meriwethers and Their Kin.
Richmond, VA, Dietz Press, 1938. 652 p.
NN APV (Lewis)

Lewis, Morgan Milton.
Genealogical and Biographical Record of the Lewis and Grissell Families from the Years 1751 and 1763 to the Year 1903.
Battle Creek, MI, M. M. Lewis, 1903. index.
NN APV (Lewis)

Sorley, Merrow E.
Lewis of Warner Hall, History of a Family.
Columbia, MO, E. W. Stephens, 1937. 887 p.
NN APV (Lewis)

LINCOLN—Massachusetts Puritans and a Kentucky-born President

Kaye, Ruth Lincoln.
Thomas Lincoln of Taunton and Joseph Kellogg of Hadley and 144 Related Families.
Washington, DC, Professional Printing, 1973. 410 p., index.
(Abe Lincoln chart p. 20; George Washington chart p. 21; John Adams chart p. 22; U. S. Grant and Grover Cleveland charts p. 23–24)
NN APV (Lincoln) 74-702

The Lincoln Kinsman.
Fort Wayne, IN, 1938–1942. no. 1–54.
NN APV (Lincoln)

Lincoln, Waldo.
History of the Lincoln Family: An Account of the Descendants of Samuel Lincoln of Hingham, Mass., 1637–1920.
Worcester, MA, Commonwealth Press, 1923. 718 p., index.
(Abe Lincoln p. 469–471)
NN APV (Lincoln)

LIVINGSTON—Scottish Lords of the Manor in New York

Livingston, Edwin Brockholst.
The Livingstons of Callendar.
Edinburgh, U. Press, 1920. 511 p., index.
(The New York family chart p. 487)
NN ARZ (Livingston)

Livingston, Edwin Brockholst.
The Livingstons of Livingston Manor.
New York, Knickerbocker Press,

1910. 590 p., sup. Jan. & Feb. 1910, 150 p.
NN APV (Livingston)

Kinkead, Rev. George B.
Gilbert Livingston and Some of His Descendants.
(IN: *NYGER, New York, 1953–1957. v. 84, p. 4–15, continuing in issues through 88 p. 39–48*)
NN *R-APGA

Van Rensselaer, Florence.
The Livingston Family in America and Its Scottish Origins Arranged by William Laimbeer.
New York, 1949. 413 p., index. (Needs much revision.)
NN APV (Livingston)

LONGSTRETH—Philadelphia Quakers

Taylor, Agnes Longstreth.
The Longstreth Family Records; Revised and Enlarged.
Philadelphia, PA, Ferris & Leach, 1909. 804 p., sup. 1914.
NN APV (Longstreth)

LOWELL—They knew the Cabots in Boston

Greenslet, Ferris.
The Lowells and Their Seven Worlds.
Boston, MA, Houghton Mifflin, 1946. 442 p., index.
NN APV (Lowell)

Lowell, Delmar R.
The Historic Genealogy of the Lowells in America from 1639 to 1899.

Rutland, VT, Tuttle, 1899. 826 p.,
index.
NN APV (Lowell)

MCDONALD—The Lords of the Isles and Flora Macdonald

Macdonald of Clanranald.
(IN: *Burke's Landed Gentry, 18th
ed., London, 1972. v. 3, p. 566–572*)
NN ARF 73-1915

Williams, Mrs. Flora McDonald.
The Glengary McDonalds of Virginia.
Louisville, KY, George G. Fetter,
1911. 340 p., t of c, no index,
ports.
NN APV (McDonald)

MACLEOD—The late Dame Flora was the 28th chief from 1934–1976

Grant, I. F.
The MacLeods, History of a Clan,
1200–1956.
London, Faber & Faber, 1959. 653
p., index.
NN ARZ (MacLeod)

MacKenzie, Alexander.
History of the MacLeods with Genealogies of the Principal Families of the Name.
Inverness, Scotland, A. & W. MacKenzie, 1889. 463 p., index.
NN ARZ (MacLeod)

MacLeod of MacLeod.
(IN: *Burke's Landed Gentry, 18th
ed., London, 1965. v. 1, p. 484–486*)
NN ARF 73-1915

MACNEIL—One of the clans with an American chief, Ian Roderick, 46th in line

MacNeill of Barra.
(IN: *Burke's Landed Gentry, 18th
ed., London, 1972. v. 3, p. 592–593*)
NN ARF 73-1915

MASON—Distinguished Virginia leaders and Maine pioneers

Copeland, Ramelia C., and Richard K. MacMaster.
The Five George Masons, Patriots
and Planters of Virginia and
Maryland.
Charlottesville, VA, U. of VA
Press, 1975. 341 p., index.
NN APV (Mason) 76-1037

Mason, Edith W.
Descendants of Capt. Hugh Mason
. . .
New Haven, CT, Tuttle Morehouse, 1937. 867 p., index.
NN APV (Mason)

MASSEY (MASSIE)—Canadian Americans with a Governor General, an actor who played Lincoln and Virginia pioneers

Massie, Evelyn Hepworth.
A Massie Family History.
Kennewick, WA, 1972. 272 p., index.
NN APV (Massie) 73-162

Nicholson, Marian L. M.
The Massey Family 1591–1961.
Saskatoon, Sask., 1961. 24 p., gen.
tables.
NN APWL+ (Massey)

Owen, Phyllis E.
Vincent Ancestors of the Masseys.
(IN: *Families, Toronto, 1973. v. 12,
   p. 3–9*)
NN APW 73-2794

MELYN—A patroon who had to flee from his manor

Cornelis Melyn, Patroon of Staten
   Island and Some of His Descendants.
(IN: *NYGBR, New York, 1937. v.
   68, p. 3–17, 132–145, 217–231,
   357–365*)
NN *R-APGA

MORGAN—Financiers, patrons of the arts and philanthropists, J.P., Sr., and Jr.

Hoyt, Edwin P.
The House of Morgan. NY, Dodd,
   Mead, 1966. 428 p.
NN E-12 8685

Massey, George Valentine.
Ancestry of Richard Dorsey Mor-
   gan.
(Dover, Del.) the author, 1953. 160
   p. index
(Indian blood through Kittama-
   qund of the Piscataways p.
   93–97, Brent Family p. 83–90.
   Carroll Family p. 101–106)
NN APU (Morgan)

Morgan, [James] Appleton.
History of the Family of Morgan
   from the Year of 1089 to Pres-
   ent Times.
NY, the author, 1897–1902. 297 p.,
   index.
(J. P. Morgan p. 77–80)
NN APU (Morgan)

MORRIS—A Signer of the Declaration and Lords of the Manor of Morrisania

Carhart, Lucy A. M.
Genealogy of the Morris Family,
   Descendants of Thomas Morris
   of Connecticut.
New York, A. S. Barnes, 1911. 478
   p.
NN APV (Morris)

Lefferts, Elizabeth M. W.
Descendants of Lewis Morris of
   Morrisania b. 1671 d. 1746.
New York, T. A. Wright, 1907. 106
   leaves.
NN APV+++(Morris)

Moon, Robert C.
The Morris Family of Philadel-
   phia, Descendants of Anthony
   Morris (1654–1721).
Philadelphia, PA, 1890–1959. 6 v.
(v. 6, 1959 by Morris Family Pub.
   Co.)
NN APV (Morris)

National American Society
Morris, Hennen, Shepard, Vander-
   bilt and Allied Families.
New York, 1934. 66 p., index.
NN APV+ (Morris)

Wilkinson, Kathryn Y.
Some Descendants of Richard Mor-
   ris and Sarah Pole of Morrisania
   . . .
Milwaukee, WI, 1966. 292 p.
NN APV (Morris)

MURRAY—Jennie Jerome's grandmother and an electrical tycoon

Birmingham, Stephen.
Real Lace, America's Irish Rich.

New York, Harper & Row, 1973.
322 p.
(Thomas E. Murray p. 35)
NN IEH 74-474

Corry, John.
The Golden Clan. Boston, Hough-
ton Mifflin, 1977. 203 p., index,
(The story of the family of
Thomas E. Murray which in-
cludes Vanderbilt and Detroit
Ford connections.)

Johnston, George H.
The Heraldry of the Murrays.
Edinburgh, Johnston, 1910. 111 p.
NN ARZ (Murray)

Murray, William B.
The Descendants of Johnathan
Murray of East Guilford.
Peoria, IL, Valley Pub., 1956. 376
p., index.
(Jerome family p. 54–56)
NN APV (Murray)

OGDEN—New Jersey and New
York pioneers, some of whom
went west

Wheeler, William Ogden.
The Ogden Family in America,
Elizabethtown Branch. NY,
1907. 531 p. index plus 1 v. of 37
charts.
NN APV (Ogden)

PALMER—Seventeenth-century
residents of New York, Massachusetts, Connecticut and the
sister of Mrs. U. S. Grant

Palmer, Horace W.
Palmers in America.
Typescript, 195–. 48 v.
NN APV (Palmer)

Palmer, Horace W., and Nellie M.
Palmer.
Palmer Family in America Lt.
William Palmer of Yarmouth,
Mass.
Neshanic, NJ, 1966. 1 v.
(v. 2 of Palmer gen. above)
NN APV (Palmer)

Ross, Ishbel.
Silhouette in Diamonds, the Life
of Mrs. Potter Palmer.
New York, Harper, 1960. 276 p.
(Bertha Honore Palmer 1849–1918)
NN D-13 2936

PANKEY—Descendants of a
prolific Huguenot

Pankey, George Edward.
John Pankey of Manakin Town,
Virginia and His Descendants.
Rushton, LA, the author,
1969–1972. 2 v.
NN APV (Pankey) 72-2299

PARDEE—Connecticut
Yankees who formed the
backbone of many communities

Jacobus, Donald Lines.
The Pardee Genealogy.
New Haven, CT, N. H. Colony
Hist. Soc., 1927. 693 p., index.
NN APV (Pardee)

PEABODY—Educators,
clergymen, diplomats

Hoyt, Edwin P.
The Peabody Influence: How a
Great New England Family
Helped Build America. NY,
Dodd, Mead, 1968. 302 p.
NN E-13 4937

Peabody, Selim Hobart.
Peabody (Paybody, Pabody, Pabodie) Genealogy, ed. by Charles H. Pope. Boston, MA, C. H. Pope, 1909, 596 p., index.
NN APV (Peabody)

PATTERSON—A Baltimore Bonaparte and the founder of Chambersburg, PA.

Bell, Edmund Ayres, and Mary Hall Colwell.
James Patterson of Conestoga Manor and His Descendants.
Lancaster, PA, Wickersham Print., 1925. 314 p., index.
(Betsey Patterson p. 290–291, Benjamin Chambers p. 259–287)
NN APV (Patterson)

Patterson, and Pattison Family Association.
The Patterson and Pattison Family, Record Book.
Minneapolis, Norman Patterson, 1963–67. 4 v.
NN APV (Patterson)

RANDOLPH—Planter ancestors of T. Jefferson, J. Marshall and J. Randolph of Roanoke

Randolph, Robert Isham.
The Randolphs of Virginia, a Compilation of the Descendants of William Randolph of Turkey Island and his Wife, Mary Isham of Bermuda Hundred.
Chicago, IL, 1936. 404 p., index.
(Just the bare bones of the family given)
NN APV (Randolph)

Daniels, Jonathan.
The Randolphs of Virginia.
Garden City, NY, Doubleday, 1972. 362 p.
NN APV (Randolph) 73-2610

ROBINSON (ROBESON, ROBERTSON)—The pastor of the Pilgrims, variants of the surname of Scottish descent and a black baseball hero

Anderson, William Kyle.
Donald Robertson and Rachel Rogers of King and Queen Co., Virginia . . .
Detroit, MI, 1900. 263 p., index.
NN APV (Robertson)

Osborne, Kate Hamilton.
An Historical and Genealogical Account of Andrew Robeson of Scotland, East Jersey and Pennsylvania and His Descendants from 1653 to 1918.
Philadelphia, PA, J. B. Lippincott, 1916. 760 p., index.
NN APV (Robeson)

Robinson Genealogical Society Publications.
Salem, MA, etc., 1926–c.195–.
(v. 1 deals with Rev. John Robinson, pastor of the Pilgrims)
NN APV (Robinson)

Robinson, John Roosevelt.
I Never Had It Made. NY, G. P. Putnam's, 1972. 287 p. (Jackie Robinson)
NN JFD 73-7751

ROCKEFELLER—A German family who has given us oil and Governors of Arkansas, New York and West Virginia plus a VP

Rockefeller Family Association Transactions.
New York, Knickerbocker Press, etc., 1910–195–. 4 v., index each v.
NN APV (Rockefeller)

Collier, Peter, and David Horowitz.
The Rockefellers.
New York, Holt, 1976. 746 p., index, chart on endpapers.
NN *R-AN (Rockefeller) 76-3725

ROOSEVELT—Dutch merchants, a Catholic bishop and two Presidents

The Ancestry of Theodore Roosevelt, A Genealogical Record from 1649 with Notes on the Families of Bailee, Bulloch, Douglas, Elliott, Irvine, Stewart, Van Schaack.
New York, Wm. M. Clemons, 1914. 20 p., index.
NN APV (Roosevelt)

Churchill, Alan.
The Roosevelts, American Aristocrats.
New York, Harper & Row, 1965. 341 p., index.
NN APV (Roosevelt)

Johnson, Alvin Page.
Franklin D. Roosevelt's Colonial Ancestors.
Boston, Lothrop. Lee, Shepard, 1933. 222 p., index.
NN APV (Roosevelt)

Schriftgiesser, Karl.
The Amazing Roosevelt Family.
New York, Wilfred Funk, 1942. 367 p., index.
NN APV (Roosevelt)

Whittelsey, Charles B.
The Roosevelt Genealogy 1649–1902.
Hartford, CT, J. B. Burr, 1902. 121 p., index.
(Watch out for errors)
NN APV (Roosevelt)

SALTONSTALL—Massachusetts gentry and a famous senator

Saltonstall, Leverett
Ancestry and Descendants of Sir Richard Saltonstall, First Associate of the Massachusetts Bay Colony and Patentee of Connecticut.
Riverside Press, 1897. xii, 265 p.
NN APV (Saltonstall)

SELIGMAN—Bankers, authors, patrons of the arts

Hellman, George S.
The Family Register of the Descendants of David Seligman.
Baltimore, MD, 1913. 93 leaves.
NN APV+ (Seligman) and *KP+ (Cleland)

Hellman, George S.
The Story of the Seligmans.
New York, 1945. 329 leaves.
NN APV (Seligman)

Mott, Harper Stryker.
Isaac N. Seligman.
(IN: *NYGBR, New York, 1918. v. 94, p. 321–326*)
NN *R-APGA

Wagner, Anthony R.
Ancestry of Mr. Anthony Armstrong-Jones.
(IN: *GM, London, 1959–1960. v. 13, p. 97–103, 129–133*)
(Isaac Seligman wed Lina Messel in 1869, great-grandaunt of A. A-Jones)
NN ARCA

SHARPLESS—Solid Pennsylvania Quakers

Anderson, Bart.
The Sharples-Sharpless Family.
Westchester, PA, the author, 1966.
2 v., index v. 2.
NN APV+ (Sharpless)

SHIPPEN—Pretty Peggy Shippen fled with Benedict Arnold

Klein, Randolph Shipley.
Portrait of an Early American Family, the Shippens of Pennsylvania across Five Generations.
Philadelphia, PA, U. of PA Press, 1975.
NN APV (Shippen) 76-790

SMITH—There are few places or professions where this name is not found

Allen, Maud Bliss.
Absalom Walmsley Smith; His Ancestry and Descendants; Nine Generations of the Smith Family.
Salt Lake City, UT, the author, 1962. 391 p.
NN APV (Smith) 76-1113

Smith, Frederick.
The Family of Richard Smith of Smithtown, L.I., Ten Generations.
NN APV (Smith)

Smith Number.
(IN: *TAG, New Haven, CT, 1949. v. 25, p. 65–144*)
NN APGA

STEWART (STUART)— Presbyterian ministers in Kentucky and a Scottish baronet in New York

Kinsey, Frank Stewart.
Stewarts, Dressers, Tafts, Cones.
Los Angeles, CA, Amer. Offset, 1956. 388 p., index (front).
(Wm. H. Taft p. 32)
NN APV (Stewart)

Johnston, G. Harvey.
The Heraldry of the Stewart.
Edinburgh, Johnston, 1906. 92 p., index.
(Sir James Stuart-Menteth of Canandaigua, NY p. 65, chart 6)
NN ARZ (Stewart)

White, Francenia Stewart.
Genealogy of Hugh Stewart and Descendants.
Columbus, OH, F. J. Heer, 1912. 181, 12 p., 3 indexes.
NN APV (Stewart)

Sanders, Rev. Robert Stuart.
The Rev. Robert Stuart D.D., 1772–1856, a Pioneer in Kentucky . . .
Louisville, KY, Dunne Press, 1962. 167 p., t of c, no index.
NN APV (Stuart)

STRONG—Massachusetts pioneers who spread far across the land

Swight, Benjamin W.
The History of the Descendants
of Elder John Strong of Northampton, Mass.
Baltimore, MD, Gateway, 1975
(orig. 1871). 2 v.
(Too bad that no additions were
made to the reprint.)
NN APV (Strong) 75-1201

STUDEBAKER—Colonial Germans who built wagons, then automobiles

The Studebaker Family in America, 1736–1976.
Tipp City, OH, The Studebaker National Assoc., 1976. 910 p., index.
(Wagons, etc. p. 75–116)
NN APV (Studebaker) 76-2451

TROWBRIDGE—Colonial warriors, patriots, their descendants are legion

Trowbridge, Francis Bacon.
The Trowbridge Genealogy, His-
tory of the Family in America.
New Haven, CT, the author, 1908.
840 p., index.
NN APV (Trowbridge)

UPSHUR—Early Virginia immigrants and a Secretary of State

Upshur, John Andrews.
Upshur Family in America.
Richmond, VA, Dietz Press, 1955.
221 p., index.
NN APV (Upshur)

VALLEJO—Spanish aristocrats in California

Emparan, Madie Brown.
The Vallejos of California.
San Francisco, CA, U. of San Fran-
cisco, 1968. 464 p., index.
NN APV (Vallejo)

VANDERBILT—They forged a transportation empire on sea and land and gave England a duchess

Andrews, Wayne.
The Vanderbilt Legend, the Story
of the Vanderbilt Family 1794–
1940.
New York, Harcourt, Brace, 1941.
454 p., index.
NN APV (Vanderbilt)

Hoyt, Edwin Palmer.
The Vanderbilts and Their For-
tunes.
Garden City, NY, Doubleday,
1962. 434 p.
NN E-11 7620

Hix, Charlotte Megill.
Sophia Johnson, Wife of Commo-
dore Cornelius Vanderbilt.
(IN: *NYGBR, New York, 1976. v.
107, p. 201–212*)
NN *R-APGA

VAN RENSSELAER—Dutch patroons up the Hudson

Hoffman, William J.
The Older Generation of the Van
Rensselaer Family.
(IN: *TAG, New Haven, CT, 1952.
v. 28, p. 178–188*)
NN APGA

Van Rensselaer, Florence.
Van Rensselaer in Holland and America.
New York., 1956. 103 p., index.
NN APV (Van Rensselaer)

Van Rensselaer, Kiliaen.
Rensselaerwyck Patroonship and Manor, the Pedigree of the Van Rensselaer Family.
Baltimore, MD, 1929. (Order of OCLMA Pub. no. 21). 93 p., no index.
NN APGA

WARFIELD—They nearly gave us a queen, but supplied us with a duchess instead

Ballenger, Evelyn.
Warfield Records.
Annapolis, MD, Thomas Ord Warfield, 1970. 861 p., index.
(Bessie Wallis Warfield, Duchess of Windsor, pp. 558, 647)
NN APV (Warfield) 73-2749

Warfield, Joshua Dorsey.
The Warfields of Maryland.
Baltimore, MD, Daily Record Co., 1898. 102 p., no index.
NN APV (Warfield)

Martin, Ralph G.
The Woman He Loved, The Story of the Duke and Duchess of Windsor.
New York, Simon and Schuster, 1973. (1974). 608 p., index.

WASHINGTON—The father of our country who had many ancestors and collateral descendants and the founder of Tuskegee Institute

Goff, John.
An Aspect of the Washington Pedigree.
(IN: *Northamptonshire and Bedfordshire Life, St. Ives, 1976. v. 5, p. 24–27*)
NN

Headley, W. Percy.
The Early Washington of Washington Co. Durham.
(IN: *CWAAST*, Kendal, England, 1964. n.s. v. 64, p. 110–122)
NN CO (Cumberland)

Hoppin, Charles W.
Washington Ancestry.
Greenfield, OH, 1932. 3 v.
NN APV (Washington)

Longden, Henry Isham.
The History of the Washington Family.
(IN: *GM, London, 1925. v. 1, p. 47–54, 109–116; v. 2, p. 12–18*)
NN ARCA

Nicholson, T.
The Washington Ancestry.
(IN: *Antiquary of Sunderland and Its Vicinity, Sunderland, England 1960. v. 22, p. 1–10*)
NN CO (Sunderland)

Wagner, Anthony R.
Queen Elizabeth's American Ancestry and Cousinship to George Washington.
(IN: *GM, London, 1939. v. 8, p. 368–376*)
NN ARCA

Washington, Booker Taliaferro (1856–1915).
Up from Slavery.
New York, Doubleday, 1901. 330 p., index.
(Married three times, left three children, Portia, Baker Taliaferro and Ernest Davidson Washington)
NN AN (Washington, B.)

Washington, George.
The Washington Surname in Northamptonshire and One Branch of the Virginia Washingtons.
(IN: *NPP, Delapre Abbey, 1976. v. 5, p. 335–338*)

Washington Family.
(IN: *Herts Countryside, Hitchin, Herts., England, 1976. v. 30, p. 18–21*)
NN COB (Herts)

WATTS—Colonial New Yorkers with Southern connections

Stryker-Rodda, Harriet.
Watts Ancestry of Ridley Watts with Additional Information on the Families of Izard and Deas. New Orleans, Polyanthos, 1976. 116 p.

WHITNEY—The inventor of the cotton gin, financiers, and diplomats of early New England origin.

Hoyt, Edwin P.
The Whitneys, an Informal Portrait, 1635–1975.
New York, Weybright and Talley, 1976. 280 p., index.
NN APV (Whitney) 77-92

WILLIAMS—The founders of Rhode Island and Williams College, and an eighteenth-century artist, a Signer and a senator from New Jersey

Anthony, Bertha Williams.
Roger Williams of Providence, Rhode Island. Cranston, RI,

the author, 1949–1966. 2 v., index each v.
NN APV (Williams)

Williams, E. Ray.
Williams Families of Henry County, Tennessee. Paris, TN, the author, 1971. 159 p., index.
NN APV (Williams) 73-1125

The Williams' Family Bulletin Genealogical Research Quarterly. Miami, FL, Richard T. & Mildred C. Williams, 1966–1973. 8 v.
NN APV (Williams) 75-289

Williams, Harrison.
The Life, Ancestors and Descendants of Robert Williams of Roxbury ... Massachusetts ... 1607–1693. Washington, DC, W.F. Roberts, 1934. 216 p., index. (Ephraim Williams, founder of Williams College, p. 108ff; Harrison Williams III, p. 203; William Williams, the Signer, p. 128ff.)
NN APV (Williams)

Williams, John F.
The Ancestor. The World of William Williams. Philadelphia, Dorrance and Co., 197. 184 p., no index (William Williams, artist and writer).
NN APV (Williams) 74-113

WINSLOW—A Pilgrim and Puritans in Massachusetts

Holton, David Parson.
Winslow Memorial, Family Records of Winslows and Their Descendants in America with the English Ancestry ... of Kenelm Winslow.

New York, 1877. 2 v.
NN APV (Winslow)

Raymond, William O.
Winslow Papers A.D. 1776–1826.
Boston, MA, 1972. 732 p.
NN HXN 74-1457

WINTHROP—Early Massachusetts Bay Governors

Mayo, Lawrence Shaw.
The Winthrop Family in America.
Boston, MA, Mass. Historical Soc.,
    1948. 507 p., index.
NN APV (Winthrop)

WOOD—Numerous immigrants of this name settled in most colonies

Wood, John Sumner.
The Wood Family Index . . .
Germantown, MD, 1966. 578 p.,
    alpha by given name.
NN APV (Wood)

GENERAL SOURCES

Boutell, Charles.
Boutell's Heraldry, revised by J. P. Brooke-Little.
London, Frederick Warne, 1973. 355 p. index
NN AWB and AWB 76-397

Briggs, Geoffrey.
National Heraldry of the World.
London, J. M. Dent, 1973. 147 p.
NN AWB 76-1359

Brooke-Little, John P.
An Heraldic Alphabet, New revised edition
London, Macdonald & Jane's, 1975. 226 p.
NN AWP 76-474

Chivalry.
Harbor City, CA, 1976. v. 1–

Dennys, Rodney.
The Heraldic Imagination.
London, Barrie & Jenkins, 1975. 224 p., index.
NN AWB 76-2402

Fairbairn, James.
Fairbairn's Book of Crests of the Families of Great Britain and Ireland. 4th edition revised and enlarged. Baltimore, MD, GPC, 1968. (orig. 1905) 2 v. in 1 v. (50,000 names with mottoes and 314 plates of crests)
NN AWS

Fox-Davies, Arthur C.
A Complete Guide to Heraldry, revised and annotated by J. P. Brooke-Little.

London, Thomas Nelson, 1969. 513 p.
NN AWB

Franklyn, Julian, and John Tanner.
An Encyclopedic Dictionary of Heraldry.
Oxford, Pergamon Press, 1970. 367 p., index.
NN AWD

Grant, Francis J.
The Manual of Heraldry.
Detroit, MI, Gale, 1975 (orig. 1929). 142 p.
NN AWB 76-1182

Heraldic Art.
(IN: *Family History, Canterbury, 1967. v. 5, n.s. no. 2, p. 36–44, 53–56)*
NN ARCA+

Heraldry.
Harbor City, CA, 1976. v. 1–

Papworth, John W.
Papworth's Ordinary of British Armorials ... introduction by G. D. Squibb and A. R. Wagner.
London, Tabard, 1961 (orig. 1874). 1,125 p.
(Watch out for errors; based on Burke's General Armory, 3rd ed. of 1847)
NN Desk Room 315G

Parker, James.
A Glossary of Terms Used in Heraldry.
Rutland, VT, Tuttle, 1971 (orig. 1894). 659 p.
AWB 71-20

Pine, Leslie.
International Heraldry.
Newton Abbot, Devon, David &
Charles, 1970. 244 p.
NN AW

Puttock, Arthur G.
A Dictionary of Heraldry and Re-
lated Subjects.
London, Gifford, 1970. 256 p.
NN AWD 72-1435

Renesse, Théodore de, Comte.
Dictionnaire des Figures Héraldiques.
Brussels, Société Belge de Libraire, 1894–1903. 7 v., index v.
7.
NN AWD

Rietstap, Johannes B. (1828–1891)
Armorial General; Precede d'un
Dictionaire des Termes du Bla-
son.
Baltimore, MD, GPC, 1972 (orig.
1861, GPC 1950) 2 v., alpha.
NN AWD

General Illustrated Armorial, by
Victor and Henri Rolland.
Lyon, France, 1950 (orig.
1903–1926) 6 v. (GPC 1967). 6 v.
in 3 v.; plates for the Rietstap
work.
NN AWD +

Supplement to the Armorial General, by Victor and Henri Rolland. Baltimore, MD, GPC,
1969–1971 (orig. 1904–1954). 9 v.
in 3 v.
NN AWD

Royalty and Monarchy.
Harbor City, CA. v. 1–

Summers, Peter.
How to Read a Coat-of-Arms.

London, W.C. 1, The National
Council for Social Service, 26
Bedford Sq., 1967.
24 p.

Volbroth, Carl A. von
Heraldry of the World.
London, Blandford Press, 1973.
251 p.
NN AWB 75-132

Woodward, John, and George Bur-
nett.
Woodward's a Treatise on Her-
aldry British and Foreign, with
English and French Glossaries.
Rutland, VT, C. E. Tueele, 1969
(orig. 1891 in 2 volumes). 858 p.
NN AWB 71-44

BY AREA AND COUNTRY

Europe

Dielitz, J.
Die Wahl-und Denkspruche.
Frankfurt, Wilhelm Rommel,
1887. 476 p., index.
(Mottoes for Continental families)
NN AWG +

Central Europe

Jäger-Sunstenau, Hanns.
General-Index zu den Sieb-
macher'schen Wappenbuchern
1605–1961.
Graz, Austria, Akamdemische
Druck, 1964. 586 p.
NN Desk Room 315G

Siebmacher, Johann (d. 1611)
Grosses und Allgemeines Wappen-
buch ... mit Heraldischen.
Nürnberg, 1854–1961. 101 v.
(For reprints: Neustadt/Aisch,
Degner, 1970–)
NN AWR and AWR 75-135

Australia

The Escutcheon, Official Journal
of the Heraldry Society of Australia.
1966–, v. 1–.
NN AWA 75-1424

Low, Clarence.
A Roll of Australian Arms Corporate and Personal Borne by
Lawful Authority, illustrated
by Allan K. Chatto, foreword
by Sir Anthony Wagner.
Sydney, Rigby Ltd., 1971. 184 p.,
index.
NN AWN 72-2799

Austria-Hungary

Gritzner, Maxmillian.
Wappenalbumnder   Graflichen
Familien   Deutschlands   und
Oesterreich-Ungarns.
Leipzig, 1895. 4 v.
NN AWR

Hermann, Hermann.
Genealogie und Heraldik Burger-
licher Osterreich-Ungarns.
Vienna, 1899. 2 v.
NN ATK

Belgium

Annuaire de la Noblesse Belge.
Brussels, 1847–1950. 81 v.
NN AVE

Annuaire des Nobles et Patri-
ciennes de Belgique.
Brussels, 1900–1945. 6 v.
NN AVE

Annuaire des Familles Patri-
ciennes de Belgique.
Brussels, 1940–1968. 7 v.
NN AVE

Canada

Heraldry in Canada.
Ottawa, 1966–, v. 1–.
NN AWA 74-123

Massicotte, Edouard Z.
Armorial du Canada Français.
Montréal, 1915. 152 p.
NN AWN

Roll of Arms of Members of Heraldry Societies.
(IN: *Heraldry in Canada, Sept.,
1976. v. 10, no. 3, whole issue,
99 p.*)
NN AWA 74-123

Todd, Herbert G.
Armory and Lineages of Canada
. . .
Yonkers, NY, 1918. 122 p.
NN APW

Denmark

Achen, Sven Tito.
Danske Adelsvabener en Heral-
disk Nogle.
Copenhagen, 1973. 624 p.
NN AWT 74-1571

Achen, Sven Tito.
Identifikation af Anonyme Vaben-
skjolde. Copenhagen, Dansk
Historisk   Faellesforenings
Handboger, 1972. 96 p. (A guide
to identifying anonymous coats
of arms.)
NN AWB 74-98

Denmark Adels Aabog.
Copenhagen, 1884–1976. 87 v.
NN AVC

Finland

Finlands Ridderskaps och Adels
Kalender.
Helsinki, 1911–1974. 21 v.
NN AVH (Finland)

France

Annuaire de la Noblesse de France.
Paris, 1843–1961. 90 v.
NN ASA

Jougla de Morenas, Henri.
Grand Armorial de France ...
Paris, Éditions Héraldiques, 1934–1952. 6 v. and supplement.
NN AWP +

Germany

Deutsches Geschlechterbuch.
Charlottenburg, 1889–1975. 172 v.
NN ATC

Gothaischer Genealogischer ... (Gesamtverzeichnis der im Gothaischen Hofkalender und in der Genealogischen Taschenbuchern ...)
Gotha, 1934. 143 p.
NN APC

Kenfenheuer, Johann J.
Alphabetisches Namenregister Bürgerlischer Deutscher Wappenvorkommen.
Hoffnungsthal-Köln, 1937. 264 p.
NN AWR

Leonhard, Walter.
Das Grose Buch der Wappenkunst.
Munich, Georg D. W. Callwey, 1976. 368 p., illus.
NN AWB 76-1741

Stammfolgen-Verzeichnisse.
Limburg/Lahn, C. A. Starke, 1963. 240 p.
NN ATC

Great Britain

Brooke-Little, John P.
An Heraldic Alphabet, new revised ed.
London, Macdonald and Jane's, 1975. 226 p.
NN AWD 76-474

Burke, Sir Bernard.
General Armory of England, Scotland, Ireland and Wales ...
London, Burke's Peerage. 1961 (orig. 1884). 1,185 p.
AWN and AWN 74-1288

Burke's Landed Gentry of Great Britain ...
London, 1833–1972. 18 editions.
ARF and ARF 73-1915 for 18th ed.

Burke's Peerage ...
London, 1826–1970. 105 editions.
NN ARM

Coat of Arms. . . . London, 1950–, v. 1–.
London, The Heraldry Society.
(28 Museum St., London WC1A 1LH)
NN AWA

Debrett's Peerage ...
London, 1802–1976+. (1973/74 edition is the last with the Knightage. Due to mergers with other publishers the foundation date is now given as 1769.)
NN ARM

Fox-Davies, Arthur C.
Armorial Families, A Directory of Gentlemen of Coat-Armour.
Newton Abbot, DC, 1970 (orig. 1929). 2 v., alpha, many black and white and some color illus.

Grantees of Arms Named in Docquets and Patents to the End

of the Seventeenth Century ...
ed. by W. Harry Rylands.
London, 1915. 290 p., alpha.
(Harleian Society Publications v.
66)
NN ARCA

Grantees of Arms, 1687–1898.
London, 1916–17. 411 p.
(Harleian Society Publications v.
67–68)
NN ARCA

Howard, David Sanctuary.
Chinese Armorial Porcelain, with
a foreword by Sir Anthony Wagner.
London, Faber & Faber, 1974. 1,-
034 p., index.

Humphrey-Smith, Cecil R.
General Armory Two.
Baltimore, MD, GPC, 1974. 230 p.,
alpha, index.
NN AWN 74-200

Pinches, John H. and R. V.
The Royal Heraldry of England.
London, Heraldry Today, 1974.
334 p., index.
(Illus. of the arms and seals of
members of the British Royal
Family from 1054 to date.)
NN AWN 75-2008

Roll of Arms, Henry III.
London, 1961–62. 281 p.
(Harleian Society Publications v.
113/114)
NN ARCA

Wagner, Sir Anthony R.
A Catalogue of English Medieval
Roll of Arms.
London, 1950. 176 p.
(Harleian Society Publications v.
100)
NN ARCA

Wagner, Sir Anthony R.
Heralds of England, a History of
the Office of the College of
Arms.
London, HMSO, 1967. 609 p., xlii
plates.
NN AWN+

Wagner, Sir Anthony R.
Records and Collections of the
College of Arms.
London, Burke's Peerage, 1952. 84
p.
NN APB p.v. 68.

Hungary

Nemesi Évkönyv.
Budapest, 1923–43. 21 v.
NN ATNA

Turul; A Magyar Heraldkai és Ge-
nealogiai Társaság Közlönye.
Budapest, 1883–1942. 56 v.
NN ATNA

Ireland

Burke's Irish Family Records.
London, Burke's Peerage, 1976.
1,237 p. (This may also be considered the 5th edition of
*Burke's Landed Gentry of Ire-
land.*)
NN ARF 77-357

Burke's Landed Gentry of Ire-
land.
London, 1899–1958. 4 v.
NN ARF

Lodge, John.
Peerage of Ireland, revised by
Mervyn Archdall.
Dublin, 1789–1799. 7 v.
NN ARM

MacLysaght, Edward.
Irish Families, Their Names,
Arms and Origins.
New York, Crown, 1972 (orig.
1957). 365 p., 27 plates.
NN ARF 72-2357

Italy

Crollalanza, Giovanni B. di (d.
1819)
Dizionario Storico-Blasonico.
Bologna, Forni, 1965 (orig.
1886–1890). 3 v.
NN ASX

Dallari, Umberto.
Motti Araldici Editi di Famiglie
Italiane.
Bologna, Forni, 1965 (orig. 1918).
221 p., index.
NN AWG

Libro D'Oro Della Nobilità Ital-
iana.
Rome, 1910–1969. 16 v.
NN ASTA

Mannucci, Silvio, Conte
Nobiliario E Blasonario Del
Regno D'Italia.
Rome, Collegio Araldico, 1929. 5 v.
NN AWT

Padiglione, Carlo.
I Motti delle Famiglie Italiane.
Bologna, Forni, 1972. 140 p.
NN AWG 73-2677

Spreti, Vittorio, Marchese
Enciclopedia Storico Nobiliare It-
aliana.
Bologna, 1969 (orig. 1928–1935). 8
v.
NN ASX

Japan

Japan Gazette, Peerage of Japan.
Yokohama, 1912. 951 p.
NN AVH (Japan)

Parish, H. Carroll.
The Mon, Japanese Equivalent of
the European Coat-of-Arms.
(IN: *The Augustan, Harbor City,
CA, 1971. v. 14, p. 122–137*)
NN APA

Niwa, Motoji.
Kamon Daizukan.
Tokyo, Akita Shoten, 1971. 678 p.
NN*R-Oriental 75-982

Luxembourg

Loutsch, Jean-Claude.
Armorial du Pays de Luxem-
bourg.
Luxembourg, 1974. 869 p.
NN AWT 75-2223

Mexico

Academia Mexicana de Genealo-
gía y Heraldica. Memorias.
Mexico City, 1945–1968. 14 v.
NN APY

Netherlands

De Nederlandsche Leeuw.
's-Gravenhage, 1883–1976+. 93 v.
+.
NN AVD

Laars, T. Van Der.
Nederlandsche Heraldief.
Hilversum, 1924. 2 v.
NN AWT

Nederland's Patriciat.
's-Gravenhage, 1910–1975. 61 v.
NN AVD

Leenaerts, Remy J.
Genealogisch-Heraldisch Repertorium voor de Zuidelijke Nederlanden Handzame, 1969–1972.
1 v. in 4.
NN AVE 74-2124

Nederlands Adelsboek.
's-Gravenhage, 1903–1975. 62 v.
NN AVD

Vorsterman van Oyen, Anthonie
A.
Stam-en Wapenboek van Aanzien-
lijke Nederlandsche.
Te Groningen, 1885–90. 3 v.
NN AVD+

Wapenheraut, De ...
's Gravenhage, 1902–1920. v. 6–24.
NN AVD

Norway

Norsk Sletshistorisk Tidsskrift.
Oslo, 1927–.
NN AVB

Poland

Gumowski, Majan.
Handbuch der Polnischen Heral-
dick.
Graz, Akamdemische Druck Aus-
tria, 1969. 84 p., 60 plates.
NN AWB

Konarski, Szymon (Simon)
Armorial de la Noblesse Polon-
naise Titrée.
Paris, 1958. 478 p.
NN AWT

Portugal

Armorial do Ultramar Portugues.
Lisbon, 1966. 2 v.
NN AWT+ 75-603

Velho, Antonio Jose Vaz.
Tesouro Heraldic de Portugal.
Lisbon, 1958–1963. 4 v.
NN AWT+ 73-1128

Russia

Noblesse de Russie.
Paris, 1957–1966. 26 v.
NN ATW

Scotland

Douglas, Sir Robert.
The Peerage of Scotland ... , sec-
ond edition revised.
Edinburgh, 1813. 2 v.
NN ARO+

Innes, Sir Thomas.
Scots Heraldry, second edition re-
vised.
Edinburgh, Oliver & Boyd, 1952.
xxiv, 258 p.
NN AWN

Ordinary of Arms Volume II ...
Edinburgh, Lyon Office, 1976. 540
p.
(Public register of all arms and
bearings in Scotland 1902–1973)
(Court of the Lord Lyon, HM New
Register House, Edinburgh
EH1 3YT, Scotland, UK)

Paul, Sir James B.
An Ordinary of Arms Contained
in the Public Register of all the
Arms and Bearings in Scotland,
second edition.

Baltimore, MD, GPC, 1969 (orig. 1903). 428 p. (Arms up to 1902)
NN AWN

The Scots Peerage, edited by Sir James B. Paul.
Edinburgh, 1904–1914. 9 v.
NN ARO

Scandinavia

Lexicon Over Adelige Familier Denmark, Norge og Hertugdommene.
Copenhagen, 1814. 2 v.
NN AVC

Spain

Atienza, Julio de.
Nobiliario Español.
Madrid, 1954. 1,081 p.
NN AWT

Garcia Carraffa, Alberto y Auturo.
Diccionario Heraldico y Genealogico de Apellidos Espanoles y Americanos.
Madrid, 1919–1956. 88 v.
NN APY

Piferrer, Francisco, 1813–1863.
Nobiliario de los Reinos y Señorios de España. 2nd ed.
Madrid, La Redaccion, 1857–1860. 6 v.
NN ASM

Sweden

Sveriges Ridderskapoch Adels Kalender.
Stockholm, 1854–1975. 93 v.
NN AVB

Switzerland

Schweizer Archive fur Heraldik. Archives Héraldiques Suisses.
Zurich, 1887–1976. 90 v.
NN AWT

Schweizerrasches Geschlectterbuch. Almanach Généalogique Suisse.
Basel, 1905–1955.
NN AVG

United States

American College of Heraldry.
Journal.
New Orleans, 1973–1975. v. 1, no. 1–15.
NN AWA 76-850

The American Heraldic Challenger-Informer.
Crockett, TX, 1976–. v. 1–.
(F. B. Keopnick, ed., Rt. 1, Box 124 A, Crockett, TX 75835)

Crozier, William A.
Virginia Heraldica, Being a Registry of Virginia Gentry Entitled to Coat Armor ... ed. by William A. Crozier.
Baltimore, MD, GPC, 1965 (orig. 1908). 116 p., index.
NN Desk Room 315G 75-110

New England Historic Genealogical Society. Heraldic Committee.
Roll of Arms.
(Originally published in the NEHGR, 1928, 1932, 1936, 1940, 1946, 1954, 1958, 1971)
Boston, 1928–1971. 8 parts.
NN AWS

Heraldry.
Harbor City, CA, 1976–. v. 1–.

(The Hartwell Co., 1617 W. 261st St., Harbor City, CA 90710)

Holden, Edward S.
A Primer of Heraldry for Americans.
Detroit, MI, Gale, 1973 (orig. 1898). 105 p.
(Still interesting)
NN AWB 74-1609

Johnson, David P.
The American College of Heraldry, A Handbook of Distinctively American Coats of Arms.
New Orleans, LA, American College of Heraldry, 1972. 52 p.
NN AWS 72-3047

Newman, Harry Wright.
Heraldic Marylandiana.
Washington, DC, H. W. Newman, 1968. 188 p.
NN AWS

Pratt, David H.
The Family Crest Sham.
(IN: *Genealogy Journal, Salt Lake City, UT, 1976. v. 5, p. 96–99*)

Reynolds, Jack Adolphe.
Heraldry and You: Modern Heraldic Usage in America.
Edinburgh, Scotland, and New York, Nelson, 1961. 176 p.

(With information on how to make your own coat of arms)
NN AWB

Stephenson, Jean.
Heraldry for the American Genealogist. Washington, 1959. 44 p.
(*NGSSP no. 25*)
NN APGA

Zieber, Eugene.
Heraldry in America. 2nd ed.
New York, Haskell House, 1969 (orig. 1895, 1909). 427 p., index.
(One half the size of the earlier editions, no color plates. Plate op. p. 254 of 1895 ed. especially good for tinctures or heraldic colors)
NN AWS 71-120 and AWS for 1895 ed.

Wales

Dwnn, Lewys.
Heraldic Visitations of Wales.
Llandovery, 1846. 2 v.
NN Desk Room 315 G

Royal and Princely Heraldry in Wales.
London, Tabard Pub., 1969. 24 p.
NN AWN 75-1742

32

Book Dealers and Publishers in the United States and Foreign Countries

UNITED STATES

Accelerated Indexing Systems, Inc.
3346 South Orchard Drive
Bountiful, UT 84010

American History Publications
4800 West Market St., R.D. 6
York, PA 17404

American Reference Publisher, Inc.
Ridglea Bank Bldg., Suite 246–250
3327 Winthrop St.
Fort Worth, TX 76116

Ancestor Publishers
P.O. Box 19465
Denver, CO 80219

American Society of Genealogists
(see Genealogical Methods)

Arco Publishing Co.
219 Park Ave. South
New York, NY 10003

Area Keys
P.O. Box 19465
Denver, CO 80219

Argosy Book Stores, Inc.
116 East 59th St.
New York, NY 10022

Arms & Ancestors Institute, Division of Genealogical Printing and Supply Co., Inc.
321 South Beverly Drive
Beverly Hills, CA 90212

Arno Press
New York Times Company
330 Madison Ave.
New York, NY 10017

Augustan Society
1510 Cravens St.
Torrance, CA 90501.
(Also the Hartwell Co.)

Beehive Press
321 Barnard St.
Savannah, GA 31401

Bookcraft
1186 South Main St.
Salt Lake City, UT 84101

Booklover's Answer
Box 157
Webster, NY 14580

The Bookmark
P.O. Box 74
Knightstown, IN 46148

Borderland Books
P.O. Box 3021
Bartlesville, OK 74003

British Book Centre
153 E. 78th St.
New York, NY 10021

Burke's Peerage Ltd. /U.S.A. Representative
(See: Arco Pub. Co.)

Byron Sistler & Associates
1626 Wash. St.
Evantson, IL 60202

Cambridge University Press
32 E. 57th St.
New York, NY 10022

Century Enterprises Genealogical
Services
P.O. Box 312
Huntsville, AR 72740

Charles E. Tuttle Co., Inc.
Rutland, VT 05701
(Catalogue #380, *Genealogy and
Local History*, 1976. $2.00)

Chedwato Service
R.F.D. 3, Box 120A
Middleboro, MA 02346

Cherokee Book Shop, Inc.
P.O. Box 3427
6607 Hollywood Blvd.
Hollywood, CA 90028

Dauber & Pine Bookshop, Inc.
66 Fifth Ave.
New York, NY 10011

Deseret Book
44 E. South Temple
P.O. Box 659
Salt Lake City, UT 84110

Elizabeth F. Dunlap
Books and Maps
6063 Westminster Place
St. Louis, MO 63112

J. W. Edwards
2500 South State St.
Ann Arbor, MI 48104

Edwards Brothers
Ann Arbor, MI 48106

Everton Publishers, Inc.
P.O. Box 368
Logan, UT 84321
(*The Genealogical Helper*, etc.)

Gale Research Co.
Book Tower
Detroit, MI 48226

Gateway Press
(See: Genealogical Publishing Co.,
Inc.)

Genealogical Books in Print/Netti
Schreiner-Yantis
6818 Lois Drive
Springfield, VA 22150

Genealogical Methods and Sources
Mrs. Donna R. Hotaling
Agent for the American Society of
Genealogists
2255 Cedar Lane
Vienna, VA 22180

Genealogists Book Shelf/Karen
Stineheifer
330 E. 85th St.
P.O. Box 468
New York, NY 10028

Gendex Corporation
P.O. Box 299
Provo, UT 84601

Goodspeed's Book Shop, Inc.
18 Beacon St.
Boston, MA 02108
(Catalogue #582, *Family and Local History* $1.50)

Greenwood Press
51 Riverside Ave.
Westport, CT 06880

Gencor
Ronald A. Bremer, President
15 North West Temple
Salt Lake City, UT 84103

Harbor Hill Books
P.O. Box 407
Harrison, NY 10528

The Hartwell Company
1617 West 261st St.
Harbor City, CA 90710

Robert G. Hayman
Antiquarian Books
R.F.D.#1
Carey, OH 43316

Her Majesty's Stationery Office
(See: United States Outlet)

Heritage House
Rt. 1, Box 211
Thompson, IL 61285

G. F. Hollingsworth
P.O. Box 1725
Manhattan Beach, CA 90266

Holmes Book Co.
274 Fourteenth St.
Oakland, CA 94612

Hope Farm Press
Strong Road
Cornwallville, NY 12418

Thomas P. Hughes
4140 Chanwil Ave.
Memphis, TN 38117

Illiana Genealogical Publishing
Company
(See: Heritage House)

Jenkins Co.
Rare Books & Documents
Box 2085
Austin, TX 78767

Johns Hopkins University Press
Baltimore, MD 21218

Kelly, Arthur C.M. (see Palatine
Transcripts)

H. P. Kraus
16 W. 46th St.
New York, NY 10017

Laurence Lingle, Bookseller
5012 Stoneleigh Ave.
Dallas, TX 75235

Rev. Silas Emmett Lucas
(see Southern Historical Press)

George S. MacManus Co.
1317 Irving St.
Philadelphia, PA 19107

Magna Carta Book Co.
5502 Magnolia Ave.
Baltimore, MD 21215

Mickler's Floridiana
Chuluota, FL 32766

Microfilm Review
P.O. Box 1297
Weston, CT 06880

Miran Publishers
(See: American Reference Publishers., Inc.)

Edward Morrill and Son, Inc.
25 Kingston
Boston, MA 02111

National Archives Microfilm Pub-
lications
National Archives and Records
Service
General Service Administration
Washington, DC 20408

Harold Nestler
13 Pennington Ave.
Wildwick, NJ 07463

The New York Public Library
Astor, Lenox and Tilden Founda-
tions
Fifth Avenue and 42nd St.
New York, NY 10018

Oceana Publications, Inc.
75 Main St.
Dobbs Ferry, NY 10522

Ohio University Press
Administrative Annex
Athens, OH 45701

David L. O'Neal/Antiquarian Bookseller
New Ipswich, NH 03071

Gary Owen Press
P.O. Box 543
New Brunswick, NJ 08903

Owens and Tanco
1307 South Davis Dr.
Arlington, TX 76013

Owl Pen/Barbara Probst
Washington County
Greenwich, NY 12834

Oxford University Press
16–00 Pollitt Dr.
Fair Lawn, NJ 07410

Palatine Transcripts
Arthur C. M. Kelly
Box 79A, R.D. 1
Rhinebeck, NY 12572

The Pequot Press
Chester, CT 06412

Polyanthos, Inc.
Drawer 51359
New Orleans, LA 70151

Princetown University Press
Box AAA
Princeton, NJ 08540

Readex Books
101 Fifth Avenue
New York, NY 10003.

Readex Microprint Publications
5 Union Square
New York, NY 10003

Reprint Company/Thomas E. Smith,
pub.
P.O. Box 5401
114–118 Hillcrest Offices
Spartanburg, SC 29301

Research Publications, Inc.
12 Lunar Dr.
P.O. Box 3909
New Haven, CT 06525

Roger Butterfield, Inc.
Antiquarian Bookseller
White House, Rt. 205
Harwick, NY 13348

Saddleback Book Shop
P.O. Box 10393
Santa Ana, CA 92711

Scarecrow Press
52 Liberty St.
Box 656
Metuchen, NJ 08840

Nettie Schreiner-Yantis
6818 Lois Drive
Springfield, VA 22150

Southern Historical Press, Pub-
lishers
P.O. Box 738
Easley, SC 29640
(Formerly Georgia Genealogical
Reprints)

Strand Book Store, Inc.
828 Broadway
New York, NY 10003

F. J. Sypher
Gracie Station, Box 570
New York, NY 10038

Taylor, R. J., Jr., Foundation
P.O. Box 38176, Capitol Hill Station
Atlanta, GA 30334

Tuttle Co., Inc.
(See: Charles E. Tuttle Co., Inc.)

Unigraphic, Inc.
1401 N. Fares Ave.
Evansville, IN 47711

United States Outlet
Her Majesty's Stationery Office
Pendragon House, Inc.
2595 East Bayshore Rd.
Palo Alto, CA 94303

University Microfilms
300 North Zeeb Rd.
Ann Arbor, MI 48106

University of Minnesota Press
Minneapolis, MN 55455

University Press of Virginia
Box 3608, University Station
Charlottesville, VA 22903

University of Washington Press
Seattle, WA 98105

Virginia Book Company
Berryville, VA 22611

Volkel, Lowell M.
(See: Heritage House)

Wantagh Book Co.
P.O. Box A73
Wantagh, NY 11793

Joseph W. Watson
406 Piedmont Ave.
Rocky Mount, NC 27801

Western Hemisphere, Inc.

1613 Central St.
Stoughton, MA 02072

Fred White, Jr./Bookseller
Box 3698
Bryan, TX 77801

ARGENTINA
Libreria de Antano Buenos Aires
Sanchez de Bustamente 1876
Buenos Aires, Argentina

AUSTRALIA
Messrs. Berkelouw
19 Boundary St.
Rushcutters Bay
Sydney 2011

BELGIUM
Familia et Patria/p.v.b.a.
Kortemarkstr. 26–8120
Handzame

Librairie Gaston
Rue Marie Henriette, 44–46
B. 4800
Verviers

BRAZIL
Livraria Losmos Editora
Matriz, 135–137 Rua do Rosario
Rio de Janeiro

CANADA
Editions Bergeron
9247 24e Avenue
Montréal, Québec H12 4A2

Canadiana House
P.O.Box 306
Toronto, Ontario M4Y 2L7

Centre Canadien des Recherches
   Généalogiques
P.O. Box 845, Upper Town
Québec City 4

Librarie D'Anton
355 Rue Emory
(Coin St. Denis entre de Maisonneuve et Ontario)
Montréal, Québec H2X 1J2

Mansfield Book Mart Ltd.
2065 Mansfield St.
Montréal, Québec H3A 1Y7

Mika Publishing
P.O. Box 536
200 Stanley Street
Belleville, Ontario K8N 5B2

Omnicraft Enterprises
P.O. Box 261
North Vancouver, B.C.

Real Deslauriers Libraire
G251 Rue d'Iberville
Montréal H2G 2C5, Québec

La Société Héraldique du Canada
900 Pinecrest Road
Ottawa, Ontario

Specialty Book Concern
3 Dundas St. East
Waterdown, Ontario

William P. Wolfe
222 Rue de l'Hopital
Montréal, Québec H2Y 1V8

(See Canadian bibliography—Parish Registers—for additional
   publishers.)

DENMARK
Arnold Busck International
Andrew Frederick Host ud Son/
   Booksellers
49 Kobmagergade
DK-1150 Copenhagen K, Denmark

FRANCE
Bartholoni, Fernand
Guide du Blason
Editions Stock
14 Rue de l'Ancienne—Comédie
75006 Paris

Diffusion Frankelve/& Editions
   du Palais Royal
8 Rue Clapeyron
F 75008 Paris

Jeanne Lafitte
106 Bd. Longchamp
13001 Marseilles
(Publisher of reprints and dealer)

Gaston Saffroy
Librairie Ancienne
4 Rue Clément
Paris 6 (Zone Bleue)

R. Clavreuil
Librairie Historique
37 Rue Saint-André-Des-Arts
37 75006 Paris

GERMANY
Antiquariat Stenderhoff
Alter Fischmarkt 21
Postfach 7620
4400 Münster

Auvermann & Reiss K G
Wissenschaftliches Antiquariat
D-6246 Glashütten Im Taunus

Zum Talblick 2
Frankfurt, Germany
(Catalogue #30, Spain, Portugal,
    Latin America, 1976)

Verlag Degener & Co.
Imhard Gerhard Gessner
P.O. Box 1340
D 8530 Neustadt/Aisch
West Germany

Rudolf Patzer, Antiquariat
Buch—Export und-Import
D-6731 Weidenthal (Germany),
    Mainzer Berg 23

C.A. Starke Verlag
625 Limburg/Lahn
West Germany

GREAT BRITAIN

England

A. J. Coombes Bookseller
25 Tynedale Rd.
Strood Green
Betchworth Surrey RH3 750

Alfred Koffler/Books
60 Holland Park
London W11 3SJ
or 28 Museum St.
London WC1

Anglebooks Ltd.
12 Boxwell Road
Berkhamsted, Hertfordshire

Antiquarian Booksellers
Waplington Hall
Allenthorpe
Yorks YO4 4RS

A. R. Heath
15 Badminton Rd.

Dowend Bristol
(Catalogue #33, 1976, catalogue of
    interesting books and pam-
    phlets, 17–19th centuries, in-
    cluding a selection of auto-
    graphs, letters and historic
    documents)

Barstable Books
28 Ravensbourne Dr.
Chelmsford

BCM/Pinhorns
London WC1V 6XX United King-
    dom
(Pinhorn Handbooks)

Beeleigh Abbey Books
Beeleigh Abbey
Maldon, Essex
(A branch of W. and G. Foyle,
    Ltd., 119–125 Charing Cross
    Rd., London WC2H OFB)

Bernard Quaritch, Ltd.
5–8 Lower John Street
Golden Square
London W1R 4AU

Brian W. Keogh
P.O. Box 12
Princes Risborough
Buckinghamshire

British Book Sellers
George's
89 Park Street
Bristol BS1 5PW

Bow Windows Bookshop
128 High Street
Lewes, Sussex

C. K. Broadhurst & Co., Ltd.
5 & 7 Market St.
Southport, PR8 1HD

Burke's Peerage Ltd.
56 Walton St.
London SW3 1RB

Castle Bookshop
A. B. Doncaster
37 North Hill
Colchester, Essex

Chancery Lane Bookshop see E.
C. Nolan

Charles W. Traylen
Castle House
49–50 Quarry Street
Guildford, Surrey

Coombes, A. J. see A. J. Coombes

Ian H. R. Cowley
233 Mansfield Road
Nottingham NG1 3FT

Craven Books
23 Newmarket St.
Skipton-in-Craven
North Yorkshire

David & Charles
South Devon House
Newton Abbot
Devon TQ12 2DW

Dawsons of Pall Mall
16 and 17 Pall Mall
London SW1Y 5NB

Dawsons of Pall Mall
Folkestone Office
Cannon House
Folkestone, Kent CT19 5EE

Debrett's Peerage
67 Parchment St.
Winchester SO23 8AT

Deighton, Bell and Co./Frank
Hammond
13 Trinity Street
Cambridge CB2 1TD

Dillon's University Bookshop
1 Malet St.
London WC1
(British Local History)

E. C. Nolan
The Chancery Lane Bookshop
6 Chichester Rents
Chancery Lane
London WC2A 1EC

Eileen Ryley
The Basement Bookshop
104 Risbygale St.
Bury St. Edmunds

E. M. Lawson & Co.
Kingsholm
East Hagbourne
Berkshire

E. P. Publishing Ltd.
Bradford Road
East Arsley
Wakefield, West Yorks WF3 2JN

E. T. Webster/Antiquarian & Export Bookseller
Stonham Parva
Stowmarket
Suffolk

Export Book Co.
63 Havelock Terrace
Garstang Road
Preston, Lancaster

Fisher & Sperr
46, Highgate High Street
London N6 5JB
(Catalogue #71)

Francis Edwards, Ltd.
83 Marylebone High St.
London WIM 4AL
(British Topography and Local
    History)

Frank Hammond
(see Deighton, Bell and Co.)

F. Weatherhead and Son Ltd.
New & Second Hand Booksellers
58 Kingsbury
Aylesbury, Buckhamshire

George W. Walford
186 Upper St.
London N1 1RH

Henry Stevens, Son, and Stiles
Upper Church Lane
Farnham, Surrey

Heraldry Today
10 Beauchamp Place
London, SW3 and
Parliament Piece, Back Lane
Ramsbury, Nr. Marlborough,
    Wilts

Hofmann & Freeman/Antiquarian
    Booksellers
Shoreham, Kent, or
Cambridge, MA, U.S.A.

Holland Bros.
The Barn House
New Street
Ledbury, Herefordshire HR8 2DX

H. Pordes
529B Finchley Road
London NW3 7BH

Hudsons Bookshop
New Street
Birmingham

Ian H. R. Cowley
233 Mansfield Road
Nottingham
(Catalogue #40, Heraldry, Geneal-
    ogy, Topography)

H. T. Jantzen
East Grinstead
Sussex, RH19 3NE

Ken Spelman, Bookseller
70 Micklegate
Yorkshire

Kohler & Coombes/Local History
    Publishers
141 High Street
Dorking, Surrey RH4 1AQ
and
The Gatehouse
Coldharbour Lane
Dorking
Surrey, RH4 3BH

Liles Weedon
near Aylesbury, Bickhamshire
(50-room country mansion fitted
    with books on 1,001 subjects)

McDowell and Stern/Booksellers
Fine and Antiquarian
37 Fossgate
York

Maggs Bros. Ltd.
50 Berkeley Square
London W1X GEL

Minster Gates Books of York
41 Fossgate
York

Monarchist League
The Secretary-General
Brigadier-General J. E. Craik
201 Fulham Palace Road
London, W.6

N. T. Leslie/Rare Books
15 and 17 Hepworth's Arcade
Silver Street
Hull

Peter Eaton/Antiquarian Bookshop
80 Holland Park Ave.
London W11 3RE

Peter Murray Hill
Rare Books
72 Sloane Ave.
Chelsea S.W. 3, London

Phillimore & Co., Ltd.
Shipwyke Hall
Chichester, Sussex PO2O 6BQ

Piccadilly Rare Books
31 Savile St.
London W1X 1DB

P. J. Radford
Sheffield Park
Nr. Uckfield
Sussex

Research Pub.
52 Lincoln's Inn Fields
London WC2A 3NW

R. G. Hill
Westbury
Wilts

Richard Hatchwell Antiquarian
Books
The Old Rectory
Little Somerford
Chippenham, Wiltshire

Ridings Pub. Co.
33 Beverly Rd.
Driffield, Humberside

Robert Hale
63 Old Brompton Rd.
London, SW7 35U

Robin Waterfield
P.O. Box 57
Oxford

Serif Books
Harrow House
Chipping Campden
Gloucestershire

Stanley Crowe
5 Bloomsbury St.
London WC1B 3QE
(Catalogue #80, Ireland and the
Irish; Catalogue #84, Great
Britain and Ireland and all his
other Catalogues are scholarly
classics.)

Sterling Books
11 Cecil Bond
Weston-Super-Mare
Avon BS23 2NG

Stratford Trevers
Picton House, Broadway
Worcestershire

Sussex Record Soc.
44 Lewes
Sussex

Thomas Thorp
170 High St.
Guilford GU1 3HP
Surrey
also: 47 Holborn Viaduct
London EC1

University of York
Borthwick Institute of Historical
Research
St. Anthony's Hall
York Y01 2PW

W. Heffer & Sons Ltd.
20 Trinity Street
Cambridge, CB2 3NG

White Rabbit Bookshop
47 North Bar
Beverley

William Dawson and Sons, Ltd.
10/14 Macklin St.
London WC2B 5NG

Channel Islands

Button's Limited, Book Sellers to
   the Bailiwick
21 Smith St.
St. Peterport, C.I.

Guernsey Press Shops
8 Smith St.
St. Peterport
Channel Islands, British Isles

Northern Ireland

Cathedral Book Store
18 Gresham St.
Belfast, N.I.

Emerald Isle Books
539 Antrim Road
Belfast BT15 3BU, N.I.

HMSO (Her Majesty's Stationery
   Office)
Chichester Street
Belfast, N.I.

University Bookshop, Inc.
50 University Road
Belfast, N.I.

Scotland

Alex. M. Frizzell
Castlelaw, West Linton
Peeblesshire, Scotland

James Thin
53–59 South Bridge St.
Edinburgh

John Smith & Son (Glasgow) Limited
57 St. Vincent St.
Glasgow G2 5TB

MacInnes Bookseller
9 Chapel St.
Aberdeen

Oliver and Boyd
Tweedale Court
Edinburgh 1

IRELAND

Brian W. Keogh
P.O. Box 12
Princes Risborough
Buckinghamshire
(Irish Books)

C. P. Hyland
The Old Rectory, Wallstown
Castle Roche
County Cork, Ireland

Desmond Kenny
High St.
Galway

Figgis Rare Books Ltd.
15 South Frederick St.
Dublin 2

Hodges Figgis and Co.
5 and 6 Dawson St.
Dublin 2

Stanley Crowe
5 Bloomsbury St.
London WC1B 3QE
(Catalogue #80, Ireland and the
   Irish; Catalogue #84, Great
   Britain and Ireland)

ITALY
Arnaldo Forni Editore
Via Gramsci 164
40010 Sala Bolognese

MALTA
Sapienzas Bookshop
26 Republic St.
Valletta, Malta

MEXICO
Buletin Bibliografico Mexicano
Libreria de Porrua
Anos y Cia Sr.
Argentina y Justo
Sierra, Mexico 1D.F.

NETHERLANDS
Antiquariaat "De Tille" B.V.
Eewal 56, 58, P.O. Box 233
Leeuwarden (Netherlands)

E. J. Brill of Leiden
Oude Riijn 33a-35
Leiden, Netherlands

Martinus Nijohff
P W S & Bookseller (est. 1853)
P.O. Box 269
Lange Voorhout 9-11
The Hague, Netherlands

NEW ZEALAND
Smith's Bookshop Ltd.
34 Mercer St.
Wellington 1, New Zealand

POLAND
Bibliothèque Polonaise
6 Quai d'Orléans
75004 Paris, France

PORTUGAL
Livraria D. Pedro V
Rua 1D. Pedro V, 16
Lisbon 2

RUSSIA
Iskander Ltd.
12 McGregor Road
London W11, England

SWEDEN
Thulins Antikvariatab
Old and Rare Books
570-60 Österbymos
Sverige (Sweden)

URUGUAY
Norberto E. Piccioni
P.O. Box 941
Montevideo, Uruguay

WALES
The University of Wales Press
6 Gwennyth St.
Cathays
Cardiff CF2 4YD, Wales

YUGOSLAVIA
Bibliothèque Slave
14 bis, rue d'Assas
75006 Paris, France

CONSULATE
of Her Britannic Majesty
NEW ORLEANS

Whereas Doctor Cornelius Beard, together with two witnesses, has presented himself before me, James Coppel, Her Britannic Majesty's Act'g Consul for the port of New Orleans, filed his affidavit, and by oath of said witnesses and by other evidences and documents proven that he was born in the town of Portsmouth, Hampshire, England, on the 23d day of November 1828.

Be it hereby known to all authorities, friendly to England, that said Cornelius Beard is by me duly recognized as a loyal subject of Her Britannic Majesty and entitled to whatever rights, privileges and immunities appertaining to such.

Given under my hand and the seal of Great Britain, at New Orleans, this 24th day of September 1862.

James Coppel

Act'g Consul for Her Britannic Majesty, for the port of New Orleans.

1. According to family tradition, the holder of this passport, Dr. Cornelius C. Beard, had passed through enemy lines from New Orleans to his home in Biloxi during the Civil War with the aid of an artist friend. When a deck of playing cards carved into the shape of the seal on the passport was found among family papers, it became clear that the artist had forged the passport. While searching through documents and heirlooms kept by relatives you may uncover many intriguing stories about your ancestors (see page 3).

2. The line of Clovis, King of the Franks (who lived about A.D. 466), through Charlemagne (crowned emperor of the Romans in A.D. 800) to Matilda of Flanders, wife of William the Conqueror. This is one of the earliest established family lines, and proving descent from Clovis through Charlemagne is a goal for many genealogists (see page 10).

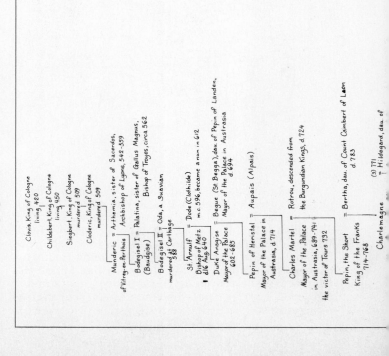

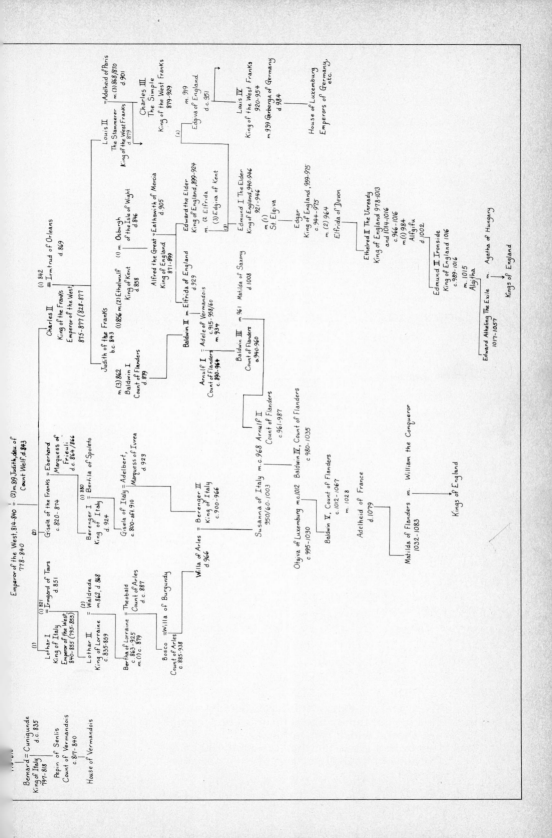

BIOGRAPHICAL WORK SHEET

NAME: _____ NO.: _____

BIRTH date: _____ place: _____

   birth cert. no.: _____

BAPTIZED (ETC.) date: _____ place: _____

   church, synagogue: _____

FATHER: _____ MOTHER: _____

MARRIED to: _____

   date: _____ place: _____

   church, synagogue: _____

   marriage cert. no.: _____

   spouse's b'date: _____ place: _____

   father: _____ mother: _____

MARRIED (if a 2nd time) to: _____

   date: _____ place: _____

   church, synagogue: _____

   marriage cert. no.: _____

   spouse's b'date: _____ place: _____

   father: _____ mother: _____

DIED date: _____ place: _____

   death cert. no.: _____ cemetery: _____

RELIGIOUS AFFILIATION (S): _____

_____

MILITARY SERVICE: _____

_____

_____

_____

_____

SOURCES (cont. on back)

3. Personal and genealogical information about each individual in your family line is recorded on biographical work sheets, which you can make or buy. The sheets serve as a guide for your research and enable you to develop a detailed portrait of each ancestor (see page 15).

BIOGRAPHICAL WORK SHEET 2

NAME: _____ NO. : _____

RESIDENCES: town   country   state   dates

_____

_____

_____

_____

EDUCATION: _____

_____

OCCUPATION (S): _____

_____

MEMBERSHIPS: _____

_____

INTERESTS: _____

CHILDREN: name   b'date and place   married to

_____

_____

_____

_____

_____

_____

_____

_____

_____

_____

_____

SOURCES (cont. on back)

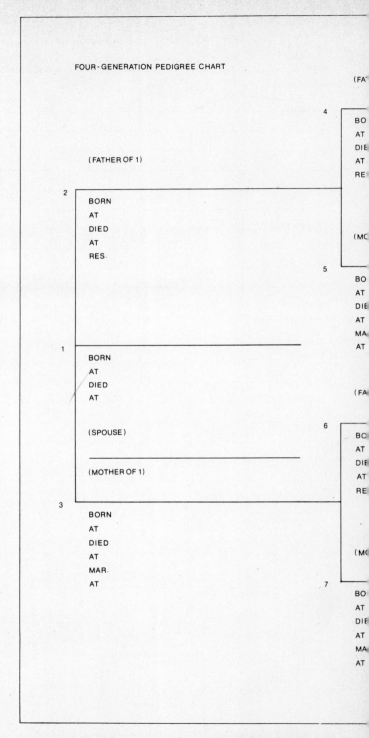

FOUR-GENERATION PEDIGREE CHART

(FATHER OF 1)

2 BORN
AT
DIED
AT
RES.

1 BORN
AT
DIED
AT

(SPOUSE)

(MOTHER OF 1)

3 BORN
AT
DIED
AT
MAR.
AT

4 BO
AT
DIE
AT
RE

(MO

5 BO
AT
DIE
AT
MA
AT

(FA

6 BO
AT
DIE
AT
RE

(MO

7 BO
AT
DIE
AT
MA
AT

(FA

4. A pedigree chart is used to express graphically the direct line of descent from one generation of your family to the next (see page 15).

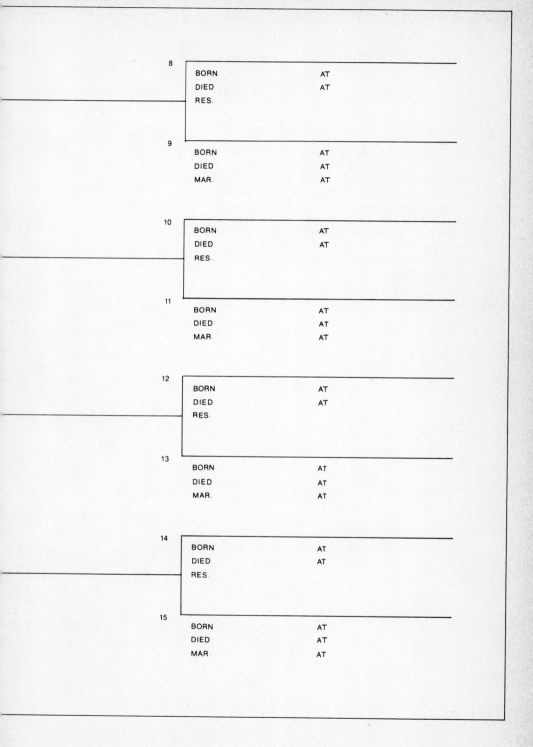

8

BORN	AT
DIED	AT
RES.	

9

BORN	AT
DIED	AT
MAR.	AT

10

BORN	AT
DIED	AT
RES.	

11

BORN	AT
DIED	AT
MAR.	AT

12

BORN	AT
DIED	AT
RES.	

13

BORN	AT
DIED	AT
MAR.	AT

14

BORN	AT
DIED	AT
RES.	

15

BORN	AT
DIED	AT
MAR.	AT

4a. Renumbering successive pedigree charts according to a simple system enables you to link one chart to the next as you follow your family line back over many generations. You should leave spaces for missing names, place names and dates that you may discover later. While you can record limited data about your ancestors' professions and educations here, detailed information will go on individual work sheets. Working charts can be typed or neatly hand-lettered (see page 17).

FOUR-GENERATION PEDIGREE CHART

(FATHER OF 1)

16 Marshall Finley

BORN July 6, 1813
AT Bethel, Vt.
DIED   1893
AT Canandaigua, N.Y
RES.
    Musician, Photog
    Schoolteacher
    ed. Randolph Aca
    Randolph, Vt.

8 Horace Marshall Fi

BORN   1838
AT Bristol, N.Y.
DIED July 15, 1901
AT Canandaigua, N.Y
    Photographer

(SPOUSE)

    Louise Howell

(MOTHER OF 1)

17 Ann Eliza Bailey

BORN March 8, 1816
AT Cumnor, Berks, E
DIED Apr. 13, 1897
AT Canandaigua, N.
MAR.   18
AT Canandaigua, N.

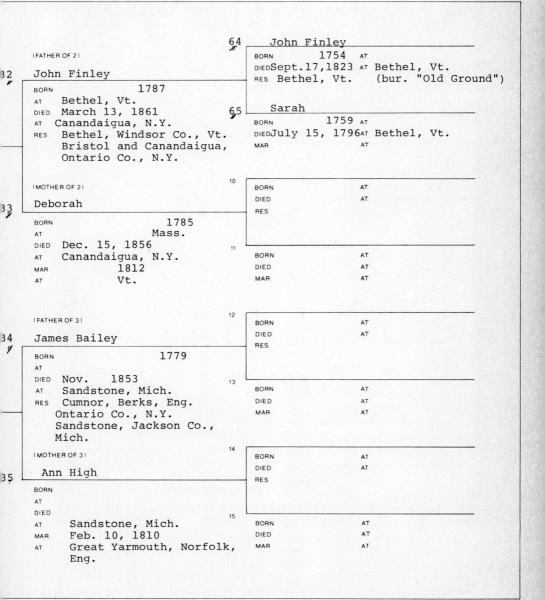

64 John Finley
BORN 1754 AT
DIED Sept.17,1823 AT Bethel, Vt.
RES Bethel, Vt.   (bur. "Old Ground")

32 (FATHER OF 2)
John Finley
BORN 1787
AT Bethel, Vt.
DIED March 13, 1861
AT Canandaigua, N.Y.
RES Bethel, Windsor Co., Vt.
Bristol and Canandaigua,
Ontario Co., N.Y.

65 Sarah
BORN 1759 AT
DIED July 15, 1796 AT Bethel, Vt.
MAR AT

33 (MOTHER OF 2)
Deborah
BORN 1785
AT Mass.
DIED Dec. 15, 1856
AT Canandaigua, N.Y.
MAR 1812
AT Vt.

10
BORN AT
DIED AT
RES

11
BORN AT
DIED AT
MAR AT

34 (FATHER OF 3)
James Bailey
BORN 1779
AT
DIED Nov. 1853
AT Sandstone, Mich.
RES Cumnor, Berks, Eng.
Ontario Co., N.Y.
Sandstone, Jackson Co.,
Mich.

12
BORN AT
DIED AT
RES

13
BORN AT
DIED AT
MAR AT

35 (MOTHER OF 3)
Ann High
BORN
AT
DIED
AT Sandstone, Mich.
MAR Feb. 10, 1810
AT Great Yarmouth, Norfolk,
Eng.

14
BORN AT
DIED AT
RES

15
BORN AT
DIED AT
MAR AT

6. Inscriptions on the frontispieces of books given a
gifts may reveal family relationships and birth o
wedding dates (see page 27)

RECORD

OF

MOSES BLOWERS!

MOSES BLOWERS, now a resident of Pompey, Onondaga County, N. Y.; was born in the Town of White Creek, Washington County, N. Y., Dec. 15th, 1774.

He came to Pompey at the age of 17 years, in company with SAMUEL SHERMAN and WILLAM BENSON; was married by O. BURR, Esq., in 1797, to Miss BATHSHEBA LEWIS, a daughter of BENJ. LEWIS, and lived with her until her death, March 28th, 1822.

Then he was married by the Rev. JOHN PECK, July 3d, 1823, to Miss LUCY LEWIS, a daughter of MATHEW LEWIS, and lived with her until her death, July 8th, 1832.

Then he was married by the Rev. D. BLAKESLEE, Oct. 22, 1844, to Mrs. DOROTHY STEWART, a daughter of ABRAM WILLIAMSON, and lived with her until her death, June 26th, 1850.

Then he was married by the Rev. J. P. SMITH, July, 1854, to Mrs. ANNA HORTON, a daughter of CHUNCEY MASON, and lived with her until her death, Aug. 4th, 1858.

The first wife died at the age of 42, the second at the age of 34, the third at the age of 52, and the last wife at the age of 66 years.

MOSES BLOWERS had eight children while living with his first wife, and three by the second.— Names and births as follows :

ABEL L. BLOWERS born Aug. 6th, 1798.

HIRAM BLOWERS born October 8th, 1801.

AMANDA BLOWERS born November 20th, 1803.

ALVIN BLOWERS born June 16th, 1806.

ALANSON BLOWERS born February 19th, 1810.

MARIA S. BLOWERS born August 11th, 1812.

MOSES BLOWERS, Jun. born January 18th, 1816.

NEWMAN BLOWERS born October 12th, 1820.

CHANCEY M. BLOWERS born December 18th, 1824.

IRENE S. BLOWERS born January 19th, 1827.

NORMAN BLOWERS born May 25th, 1832.

All of the eleven children lived to be men and women, and are now living but AMANDA, ALANSON and IRENE S. The three daughters married MOSES VAIL, SETH BENSON and ANSEL BALDWIN.

MOSES BLOWERS is in the 86th year of his age ; is now the oldest settler in the town, and is living upon the same farm he located upon 68 years ago when all was wilderness, and but 3 or 4 familes in the town.

Dalia Pompey April 1st 1860

5. This unusual family record, apparently printed at the request of Moses Blowers when he was in his old age, was passed down by his descendants for several generations. You may find genealogical records in family Bibles and other family papers (see page 26). (Courtesy Sylvia Shoebridge)

From

The Countess of Mar

To her affectionate Brother

Capt. T. L. Stuart Menteath

Feby. 23. 1833.

7. Silhouettes of Sir Charles Stuart-Menteth (1769–1847) and his wife, Ludivina (Loughnan) (1772–1852), cut in Paris by August Edouard, were given to their son, James, on March 19, 1835, according to a note on the frame. Old portraits, daguerreotypes, photographs and silhouettes show what your ancestors looked like, and often dates, places and other genealogical clues are written on the back (see page 28).

8. (Top) Likenesses of ancestors are often found in lockets, and important dates in their lives may be found engraved on various kinds of jewelry. The ring at right is inscribed with the initials of Ludivina (Loughnan), Lady Stuart-Menteth, and her date of birth, March 12, 1772 (see page 29).

9. This bracelet, ear bob and brooch are each woven of hair. From the seventeenth to the nineteenth centuries it was common for a person to instruct in his will that rings or other pieces of jewelry be made of his hair as mementos for relatives and friends. Often the deceased person's initials and date of death are engraved on such jewelry (see page 30).

11. Sally Nearing of Pompey, New York, stitched the names and birth dates of her parents, her brothers and sisters and herself in this sampler, made about 1830. Handmade quilts and memorial embroideries may also contain genealogical information about your ancestors (see page 30). (Courtesy Sylvia Shoebridge)

10. A christening cup presented in 1855 by Mrs. Mary (Grover) Beard to Alice M. Stuart-Menteth, her daughter-in-law's much younger sister. Such silver cups often reveal birth dates and names of relatives (see page 30).

Sally Nearing is my name
America is my nation
Pompey is my dwelling place
And Christ is my salvation

Alson Nearing was born Oct 28 1781
Eliza Nearing was born March 2 1791

George Nearing was born June 18 1810
Polly Nearing was born August 10 1812
Asahel Nearing was born Sept 18 1814
And died July 15 1816
Sally Nearing was born May 18 1817
Elzady Nearing was born May 6 1819
Harriet Nearing was born August 31 1821
Lucius Nearing was born Dec 10 1824

IN MEMORIAM
1863 Henry Pettit Corbin & foster Son
fell in Battle June 14.

HOMAGE
to a loving
WIFE
MOTHER
Sister Friend.
By her
HUSBAND & CHILDREN.

THY HOME.

MRS. LUCIA PETTIT.

12. A genealogy in stone: Four sides of a single tombstone reveal the maiden and married names, birth, marriage and death dates and parentage of Lucia (Peck) Pettit, as well as the name and death date of a foster son. Adjacent stones in the family plot contain similar details about two sons and a daughter (see page 31).

13. According to local tradition, in Fabius, New York, where this tombstone is located, the parents of young Freddie R. H. Mihlback had shoes and socks carved on his monument because he became ill and died after a group of older boys made him walk barefoot in the snow. This is an example of the kind of family or town legend that might be verified through research (see page 33).

14. This inscription from the gravestone of Shakespeare was reproduced in a wax rubbing. Rubbings are easily made, provide exact records of the information carved on your ancestors' tombstones and are themselves interesting and decorative designs (see page 37).

Penney Reunion – Sept. 1st 191

15. A typical turn-of-the-century family reunion. It is at such gatherings that older relatives often pass on the stories of their ancestors to younger generations (see page 50).

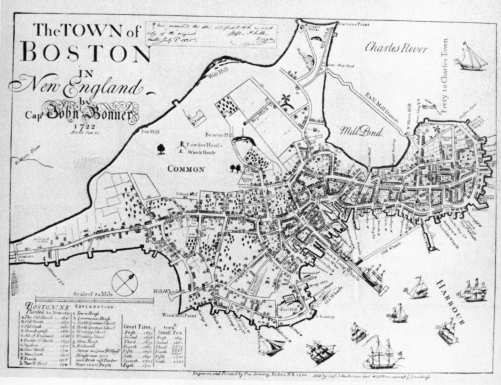

16. Colonial Boston nearly one hundred years after its establishment. Studying maps and atlases of the area where your ancestors lived, drawn during the period they lived there, can help you locate records in newspapers and government offices (see page 52).

THE LATE SIR CHARLES GRANVILLE STUART MENTEATH OF CLOSEBURN, BART. *1818*

We are sorry indeed to have to record the demise of this much respected and esteemed gentleman. He died at 27, Abercromby Place, his residence in Edinburgh, on Friday, the 3d curt. He had almost reached the patriarchal age of fourscore years: In the touching language of Scripture, so beautifully appropriate in reference to one, all whose labours tended to the blessed maturities of harvest, he has thus " come to his grave in a full age, like as a shock of corn cometh in his season."

The funeral of the venerable Baronet took place on Friday last. He was buried in the family burying-ground, in the old church-yard of Dalgarno, a secluded spot on the banks of the Nith. The solemn rites were paid to him by a large host of mourners with unaffected sorrow: " Dust to dust !"

The funeral sermon was preached in Closeburn Church, on Sabbath last, by the Rev. Andrew Bennet, Minister of the Parish. An affecting tribute it was to the dead, and an impressive lesson to the living.

By the surviving partner of his honoured life, Lady Menteath, who comes of those old Dumfries-shire families, the Fergussons of Craigdarroch, and the Johnstones of Westerhall, Sir Charles has left a family of seven sons and two daughters: These are, Philadelphia, Countess of Mar, and Miss Menteath, who resides with the Dowager Lady Menteath, Edinburgh; James, now Sir James Menteath, Baronet of Closeburn; Thomas, late Captain of the 16th Lancers; Chas. G. S. Menteath, Barrister, Lincoln's Inn Fields; William, Major, H.E.I.C.S.; the Rev. Francis Hastings, Rector of Thornpark, Yorkshire; Alexander, Writer to the Signet, Edinburgh; and the Rev. Granville Wheeler, Rector of Ranceby, Lincolnshire.

The deceased Baronet was long eminent as an agriculturist. Long were his sagacity and invention the very foremost feelers on the advancing front of Scottish improvement, gradually encroaching upon rudeness, waste, and national poverty. And thankful were the body of our people to follow on, with ever widening resources, to the instinctive delicate wisdom that was leading the way. In mechanics, also, and in all the practical, economical applications of Art and Science, the late Sir Charles was a master. Nature had given him that high quality of genius,

" The shaping mind."

17. An 1847 newspaper obituary of Sir Charles Stuart-Menteth is full of genealogical details. Newspaper marriage notices are also important genealogical sources. You may find clippings among family papers, or search for them in newspaper files and indexes (see page 60).

Si monumentum quæris, circumspice : Look at the beautiful valley of Closeburn, remembering what it formerly was.

On a lovely day, in the summer of 1846, as we were passing along Princes Street, Edinburgh, by the side of its western gardens, we were struck with the profile of the head of some one reading, close within the window of the New Club-room, on the opposite side of the street. The face seemed purged from all the grossness of earth, thin, and keen, and spiritual-looking, yet placid withal ; the whole head being beautiful with the sanctifying beauty of old age : In the words of Cicero, with all his Asiatic softness, and sweetness, and fulness, here was obviously, *" quiete, et pure, et eleganter actæ ætatis, placida ac lenis senectus."* The large pane framed that perfect head, and nothing more of the man was seen—what a fine old picture ! We were affected to see that it was our southern neighbour, the worthy old Baronet of Closeburn. This was the last time we saw that venerable head.

" A nation of shopkeepers " we are indeed ; else, instead of giving our successful ploughmen at ploughing matches prizes of money, we would give them medals struck with the heads of such eminent agriculturists as Sir John Sinclair and Sir Charles Menteath, at once to honour the dead, and provoke the living to equal deeds. " De Serres, in 1559," says the elder D'Israeli, " composed a work on the cultivation of mulberry trees, in reference to the art of raising silk-worms. He taught his fellow-citizens to convert a leaf into silk, and silk to become the representative of gold. Our author encountered the hostility of the prejudices of his times, even from Sully, in giving his country one of her staple commodities ; but I lately received a medal recently struck in honour of De Serres, by the Agricultural Society of the Department of the Seine. We are too slow in commemorating the genius of our own country, and our men of genius are still defrauded of the debt we are daily incurring of their posthumous fame. Let monuments be raised, and let medals be struck ! They are sparks of glory which you scatter through the next age ! " Monuments are not so easily raised ; but they are by no means the sole mode of perpetuating glory, or of rousing emulation. It may even be questioned whether, in this respect, they are more influential than medals. They are more imposing, certainly ; but then they are fixed, and cannot, like medals, be

A— $\frac{199}{97}$

Uimh.
No.

ÉIRE

IRELAND

Deimhniú báis arna eisiúint de bhun na hAchtanna um Chlárú Breitheanna agus Básanna 1863 go 1952.

DEATH CERTIFICATE issued in pursuance of Births and Deaths Registration Acts 1863 to 1952.

FOIRM B.

FORM B.

Básanna a Cláraíodh i gCeantar
Deaths Registered in the District of .... *Dunkilly* .... i gCeantar an Chláraitheora Maoirseachta do .... *Donegal* .... i gContae .... *Donegal* ....
in the Superintendent Registrar's District of .... in the County of ....

Uimh. No. (1)	Dáta agus Ionad Báis Date and Place of Death (2)	Ainm agus Sloinne Name and Surname (3)	Gnéas Sex (4)	Staid Condition (5)	Aois an Lá Breithe is Déanaí Age an last Birthday (6)	Céim, Gairm nó Sli Bheatha Rank, Profession or Occupation (7)	Cúis Bháis Dheimhnithe agus Fad Tinnis Certified Cause of Death and Duration of Illness (8)	Síniú, Cáilíocht agus Ionad Cónaithe an Fhaisnéiseora Signature, Qualification and Residence of Informant (9)	An Dáta a Cláraíodh When Registered (10)	Síniú an Chláraitheora Signature of Registrar (11)
294.	*23rd September 1920 Crolly*	*Biddy L Sullivan*	*Woman*	*Widow*	*93 years*	*Farmers certified*	*Senile Decay*	*George Gallagher Grandson Present at death Crolly*	*Twenty fourth September 1920 Crolly*	*W. O'Donnell Registrar*

Is fíor cóip í seo de thaifid atá i gClár-leabhair na mBás in Oifig an Ard-Chláraitheora i mBaile Átha Cliath.
Certified to be a true Copy taken from the Certified Copies of Entries of Deaths in Oifig an Ard-Chláraitheora, Dublin.

Tugtha faoi Shéala Oifige an Ard-Chláraitheora

an .... *fifth* .... lá seo de

Given under the Seal of Oifig an Ard-Chláraitheora

this .... day of .... *March* .... 19 *44*.

Ath-Scríofa
Copied.

Scrúdaithe
Examined.

Scrúdaithe
Examined. *No .*

IS CION TROM É AN DOICIMÉAD SEO A ATHRÚ, NÓ É A CHUR FEIDHME TAR ÉIS A ATHRAITHE

TO ALTER THIS DOCUMENT OR TO UTTER IT SO ALTERED IS A SERIOUS OFFENCE

18. An Irish death record. By writing to record offices in the country from which your ancestors emigrated, you can often obtain copies of birth, death and marriage records that will help you follow your family line back for several generations in that country (see page 68).

18a. (Below) An American death certificate. You can obtain copies of your ancestors' death records by mail from local or state vital record offices. They usually contain a great deal of important genealogical information, including the deceased person's birth date, birthplace and parentage (see page 68).

---

1. FULL NAME Virginia Stewart	DISTRICT NO. 3801 REGISTRAR'S NO. 3602

2. PLACE OF DEATH: (A) CITY AND COUNTY OF SAN FRANCISCO
  IF OUTSIDE CITY OR TOWN LIMITS, WRITE RURAL
  (C) NAME OF HOSPITAL OR INSTITUTION 545 Post St.
  IF NOT IN HOSPITAL OR INSTITUTION, GIVE STREET NUMBER OR LOCATION
  (D) LENGTH OF STAY: (SPECIFY WHETHER YEARS, MONTHS OR DAYS)
  IN HOSPITAL OR INSTITUTION:
  IN THIS COMMUNITY 70 Yrs   IN CALIFORNIA 70 Yrs
  (E) IF FOREIGN BORN, HOW LONG IN THE U.S.A. Life   YEARS

3. USUAL RESIDENCE OF DECEASED:
  (A) STATE California
  (B) COUNTY San Francisco
  (C) CITY OR TOWN San Francisco
  IF OUTSIDE CITY OR TOWN LIMITS, WRITE RURAL
  (7) STREET NO. 545 Post St.

20. DATE OF DEATH: MONTH May DAY 14 YEAR 1947 HOUR 6 MINUTE 50 A.M.

3. (E) IF VETERAN, NAME OF WAR No
3. (F) SOCIAL SECURITY NO. None

4. SEX Female   5. COLOR OR RACE White   6. (A) SINGLE, MARRIED, WIDOWED OR DIVORCED Single

6. (B) NAME OF HUSBAND OR WIFE
6. (C) AGE OF HUSBAND OR WIFE IF ALIVE YEARS

21. MEDICAL CERTIFICATE
  I HEREBY CERTIFY, THAT I ATTENDED THE DECEASED
  FROM May 1 1936
  TO July 19 1947
  THAT I LAST SAW H__ ALIVE
  ON May 14 1947
  AND THAT DEATH OCCURRED ON THE DATE STATED ABOVE, AND HOUR STATED ABOVE.
  IMMEDIATE CAUSE OF DEATH Myocarditis
  DUE TO __
  DUE TO __
  OTHER CONDITIONS __ (INCLUDE PREGNANCY WITHIN THREE MONTHS OF DEATH)
  MAJOR FINDINGS OF OPERATIONS __ DATE OF OPERATION __
  OF AUTOPSY __

22. CORONER'S CERTIFICATE
  I HEREBY CERTIFY, THAT I HELD A__
  AUTOPSY, INQUEST OR INVESTIGATION
  ON THE REMAINS OF THE DECEASED AND FIN__ FROM SUCH ACTION THAT DECEASED CAME T__
  __ DEATH ON THE DATE AND HOU__
  DURATION
  PHYSICIAN
  UNDERLINE THE CAUSE TO WHICH DEATH SHOULD BE CHARGED STATISTICALLY

7. BIRTHDATE OF DECEASED October 3rd, 1862
  MONTH   DAY   YEAR

8. AGE 84 YRS 7 MOS 11 DAYS   IF LESS THAN ONE DAY OLD HRS MIN
9. BIRTHPLACE New Orleans, Louisiana
10. USUAL OCCUPATION School Teacher
11. INDUSTRY OR BUSINESS Retired
12. NAME Thomas Stewart (FATHER)
13. BIRTHPLACE Scotland
14. MAIDEN NAME Frances Tobin (MOTHER)
15. BIRTHPLACE Ireland
16. (A) INFORMANT Agnes M. Waite
    (B) ADDRESS 545 Post St.
17. (A) Cremation (B) DATE May 15th. 1947
    (C) PLACE Cypress Lawn Mem. Park
18. (A) EMBALMER'S SIGNATURE __ LICENSE NO. 3005
    (B) FUNERAL DIRECTOR Halsted & Co.
    ADDRESS 1123 Sutter St.
    BY John J. Toomey
19. (A) MAY 15 1947 (B) __
    DATE FILED

23. IF DEATH WAS DUE TO EXTERNAL CAUSES, FILL IN THE FOLLOWING:
  (A) ACCIDENT, SUICIDE, OR HOMICIDE (B) DATE OF INJURY
  (C) WHERE DID INJURY OCCUR?
  CITY OR TOWN COUNTY STATE
  (D) DID INJURY OCCUR IN OR ABOUT HOME, ON FARM, IN INDUSTRIAL PLACE, OR IN PUBLIC PLACE? WHILE AT WORK?
  SPECIFY TYPE OF PLACE
  (E) MEANS OF INJURY Alex Thibodeau MD

24. CORONER'S OR PHYSICIAN'S SIGNATURE Alex Thibodeau
  (SPECIFY WHICH)
  ADDRESS 1200 Taylor St DATE Mar 14

STATE OF CALIFORNIA
DEPARTMENT OF PUBLIC HEALTH

CERTIFICATE OF DEATH

U.S. DEPT. OF COMMERCE
BUREAU OF THE CENSUS

THIS IS TO CERTIFY THAT, IF BEARING THE SEAL OF THE SAN FRANCISCO DEPARTMENT OF PUBLIC HEALTH, THIS IS A TRUE COPY OF THE DOCUMENT FILED IN THIS OFFICE.

NO. 21277

DATED: JUNE 14, 1968

SAN FRANCISCO, CALIFORNIA

ELLIS D. SOX, M.D.
DIRECTOR OF PUBLIC HEALTH AND
LOCAL REGISTRAR

20. An unusual marriage certificate, dated 188
contains portraits of the bride and groom. Resear
among descendants of the couple revealed that th
minister, also pictured, was the uncle and guardia
of the bride (see page 7

COMMONWEALTH OF KENTUCKY,
NELSON COUNTY, } To-wit:

To any authorized Minister of the Gospel.

These are to license and permit you to solemnize the Rites of Matrimony between *James M Doom & Sarah C. Nourse*

according to the forms and ceremonies of the Church to which you belong; the said

J. M. Doom having executed bond with security in my

Office as required by law: *and Cha. Nourse father*
of said Sarah C. having Consented
in person father, license to issue

Given under my hand as Clerk of the County Court for the county aforesaid, this
6 day of *June* 18 *43*

Nath. Wickliffe

I certify, that on the *6* day of *Jun* 18 *43* the above named persons were married by me, as authorized by this License.

H. S. Dickson

19. A nineteenth-century Kentucky marriage bond
for the marriage of James M. Doom to Sarah C.
Nourse. Because the bride was a minor, the bond
was authorized by her father, Charles Nourse, providing an additional and important piece of genealogical information. Marriage bonds are still issued
in some Southern states (see page 71).

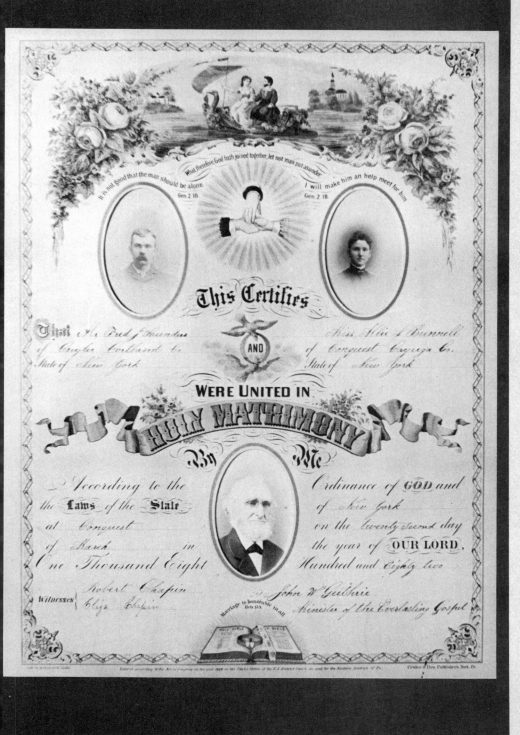

22. Pension record of Matilda (Lowe) Tovera, a widow
of Bartly Tovera, a Union soldier. If you learn of the
military service of an ancestor, you may be able to
obtain his pension record, or that of his widow, by
mail from the National Archives in Washington, D.C.
In it you will often find a great deal of information
about a soldier's birth, parentage, marriage, children,
and death (see page 106).

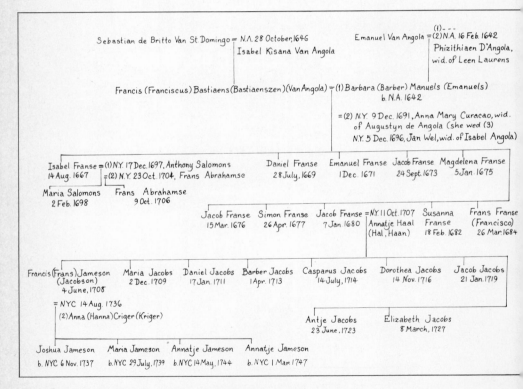

21. Some descendants of black Angolans living in
New Amsterdam in the early seventeenth century.
The information for their lineage was found in the
published records of the city's old Dutch church. Surnames borne by individuals on this chart contain
clues to both their parentage and their national origin (see page 74).

WIDOW'S DECLARATION FOR PENSION OR INCREASE OF PENSION.

This must be Executed before a Court of Record or some Officer thereof having Custody of the Seal.

State of _Illinois_, County of _Randolph_, ss.

On this _first_ day of _March_ A. D., one thousand, eight hundred and eighty _Three_ personally appeared before me _Clerk_ of the _County Court_ a Court of Record within and for the County and State aforesaid _Matilda Tovera, widow Bartly Tovera, deceased_ aged _72_ years, who, being duly sworn according to law, makes the following declaration in order to obtain the Pension provided by Acts of Congress granting pension to widows: That she is the widow of _Bartly Tovera, died_ who _enlisted_ under the name of _Bartly Tovera_ at _Sparta, Ill_, on the _10_ day of _Sept_, A. D. 18_61_ in _Company "K" 5th Ill Cav_ (Company and Regiment of service, if in the army; or vessel and rank if in the navy.) in the war of _Rebellion_ who _died, from the effects of disease contracted in the Service, and for which he was Pensioned, by Cert No. 163.061 from which disease, Chronic Diarrhea, he died as will be shown by testimony_, on the _2nd_ day of _February_ A. D. 18_83_ at _Chester, Illinois_ ["In the service aforesaid," or otherwise.]

that she was married under the name of _Matilda Lowe_ to said _Bartly Tovera_ on the _3rd_ day of _January_ A. D. 18_33_ by _Saml Dickey a J.P._ at _Knox Co, Tenn_, — there being no legal barrier to such marriage; that neither she nor her husband had been previously married _previous to their marriage with each other,_

that she has to the present date remained his widow;

There are not any Children under 16 years of age

of soldier by	, born	18	
of soldier by	, born	18	
of soldier by	, born	18	
of soldier by	, born	18	
of soldier by	, born	18	
of soldier by	, born	18	

[For such children as are not under her care claimant should account.]

that she has not in any manner been engaged in, or aided or abetted, the rebellion in the United States; that _no_ prior application has been filed

[If prior application has been filed, either by soldier, or widow on state, giving number assigned to it.]

that she hereby appoints, with full power of substitution and revocation _R. A. Thompson_ of _Chester Ill_ her attorney to prosecute the above claim; that her residence is _Chester_ _Randolph Co, Ill_ and her Post Office address is _Chester Randolph County Illinois_

James L. Douglas

Lewis Dudenbostel

Matilda X Tovera
her mark
(Signature of Claimant)

<table>
<tr><td>

(Confederate.)

B | 1 (Nelligan's) | **La.**

C. Beard, M.D.

Surgeon, 1 Regiment Louisiana Infantry.

Appears on

Field and Staff Muster Roll

of the organization named above,

for *Date Apr 28,* 186*1*.

Enlisted :
When *Received in the Service of the Confederate States Apr 28,* 186*1*.
Where *New Orleans*
By whom *Capt Galt*
Period *one year*

Last paid :
By whom ....
To what time ...., 186 .

Present or absent *Present*

Remarks : ....

Book mark : ....

A Mercosby Copyist.

(643)

</td><td>

(Confederate.)

B | 1 (Nelligan's) | **La.**

C C Beard

Surg & Maj, 1 Regiment Louisiana Infantry.

Appears on

Field and Staff Muster Roll

of the organization named above,

for *April 28 to June 30,* 186*1*.

Enlisted :
When *April 28,* 186*1*.
Where *New Orleans*
By whom *Capt Galt*
Period *1 year*

Last paid :
By whom ....
To what time ...., 186 .

Present or absent *Absent*

Remarks : *On duty as Medical Director at Division Head Quarters*

Book mark : ....

A Mercosby Copyist.

(643)

</td></tr>
</table>

23. This original commission of Dr. Cornelius C. Beard in the Confederacy was preserved among family papers. A copy of his service record was obtained from the National Archives (see page 107).

Beard

Surgeon, 1 Regiment Louisiana Infantry.

Appears on a

Record*

of the Field and Staff of the organization named
above,

for *Apl. 28 1861 to Mar. 22*, 186 *5*,

(under the head of, "Roster of Commissioned
Officers.")

Appointment:
Rank *Surgeon*
Date of *Apl. 28*, 186 *1*.
Authority of *Gov Moore*

Commission Expired:
When _____, 186 .
Where *Norfolk Va*
Cause *Commuted Div Surgeon*

Remarks: _____

Book mark: _____

(645)   *Copyist.*

(Confederate.)

B	1	La.
	(Nelligan's.)	

Beard

Surgeon, 1 Regiment Louisiana Infantry.

Appears on a

"Record"*

of the Field and Staff of the organization named
above,

from *Apl. 28 1861 to Mar. 22*, 186 *5*,

Enlisted:
When _____, 186
Where _____
Period _____

Born—(State) *La.*
Occupation *Surgeon*
Residence—(Nearest P. O.) _____
Age when enlisted _____
Married or single *M.*
Remarks: *Never with Regt.*

*From copy (made in the R. & P. Office, War Department,
May, 1903.) of an original record borrowed from the Louisiana
Historical Association at New Orleans, La.—R. & P. 722177.

(654)   [OVER.]   *Copyist.*

---

24. (Following page) A bill of sale for Joshua, a slave
purchased in 1859 by Dr. Cornelius C. Beard, to cure
him of his cataracts, and subsequently free him.
The lines of black families descended from slaves can
often be traced through papers kept by slave-owning
families (see page 128).

State of Louisiana.

KNOW ALL MEN BY THESE PRESENTS.

That I Mc Guilvery Geo W Jones Bell of this City

for, and in consideration of the sum of Four hundred Dollars at nine month's credit bearing Eight per cent interest paid by Dr C Beard of this City

do by these Presents, BARGAIN, SELL, CONVEY, TRANSFER AND DELIVER unto the said Dr C Beard a certain negro boy named Joshua aged about twelve years having a double Catar on both eyes otherwise fully guaranteed

To Have and to Hold, the said Slave Joshua unto the said Dr C Beard his heirs, executors, administrators and assigns, forever: and I the said Mc G G W J Bell do bind myself my heirs, executors, administrators and assigns, to protect and defend said property against all claim or claims whatever.

Dated at New Orleans, this Twenty sixth day of March in the year of our Lord, one thousand eight hundred and fifty- nine

WITNESS:

R. W. Long

J. H. Mague

M. G G W J Bell

Lavinia M. Bell

Part Three

Tracing Your Family's History in America

33 Genealogical Sources in Every State

ALABAMA

State Archives

Alabama Archives and History Department
War Memorial Building
Montgomery, AL 36104
(*Alabama Historical Quarterly*, 1930–) NN IAA

Vital Records

Division of Vital Statistics
Department of Public Health
Montgomery, AL 36130
Births and deaths: 1908–
Marriage: Probate Judge, County Courthouse. Dates vary from county to county, some as early as 1800

Libraries

Birmingham Public Library
2020 7th Avenue North
Birmingham, AL 35203

Huntsville, Alabama, State Branch Library
106 Sanders Drive S.W.
Huntsville, AL 35802

Samford University Library
Birmingham, AL 35209

Societies and Periodicals

Alabama Genealogical Society, Inc.
P.O. Box 35
Epes, AL 35460
(*AGS Inc. Magazine*, 1967–)
NN APR (Alabama)

Birmingham Genealogical Society, Inc.
P.O. Box 2432
Birmingham, AL 35201
(*Pioneer Trails*)

Dothan District, the Latter-day Saints Church
c/o E. H. Hayes
13 Bird Circle
Ozark, AL 36360
(*Dothan District Genealogical Exchange*)

The Genealogical Gazette
Genealogical Micro/Publishing Co.
Jacksonville, AL 36265

Genealogical Society of East Alabama
c/o Mrs. John R. Fuller, 1109 3rd Avenue, Opelika, AL 36801
(*Tap Roots*, 1963–)
NN APR (Alabama)

Mobile Genealogical Society
P.O. Box 6224
Mobile, AL 36606
(*Deep South Genealogical Quarterly*, 1963–1971. v. 1–9)
NN APGA

Northeast Alabama Genealogical Society
P.O. Box 674
Gadsden, AL 35902
(*Settlers of Northeast Alabama*, 1962–)
NN APR (Alabama) 72-1216

Pea River Historical and Genealogical Society

c/o Miss Mabel E. Willoughby
107 George Wallace Drive
Enterprise, AL 36330
(*PRH&GS Quarterly; Pea River Trails*, 1976–)

Southern Society of Genealogists
Stewart University
Centre, AL 35960
(c/o Mrs. Frank R. Stewart for early issues of *Alabama Genealogical Society, Inc. Magazine*)

Tennessee Valley Genealogical Society
P.O. Box 1512
Huntsville, AL 35807
(*Valley Leaves*, 1965–)
NN APR (Alabama) 75-619

Books and Articles

Alabama Census Returns 1820 and Abstract of Federal Census of Alabama 1830.
Tuscaloosa, 1960 (orig. 1944).
NN APR (Alabama)

Alabama 1830 Census Index.
Bountiful, UT, AIS, 1976.

Alabama 1840 Census Index.
Bountiful, UT, AIS, 1977.

Alabama 1850 Census Index.
Bountiful, UT, AIS, 1976. 242 p.

Alabama Records, compiled by Pauline Jones Gandrud and Kathleen P. Jones, Tuscaloosa, 1932–. 250 plus v. (Complete set in the State of Alabama Department of Archives and History; NN has incomplete set)
NN APR (Alabama) 74-212

Andrews, Johnnie, Jr., and William D. Higgins.
The Mobile Registers, 1770–1813.
Prichard, AL, Bienville Hist. Soc., 1974.

DAR of Alabama.
Index to Alabama Wills, 1808–1870.
Ann Arbor, MI, Edwards Bros., 1955. 180 p. incomplete index, alpha.
NN APR (Alabama)

1850 Census of Benton Co. (now Calhoun Co.), Alabama.
(IN: *Settlers of Northeast Alabama*, Gadsden, AL, Northeast Alabama Gen. Soc., 1969. 1st instal. v. 7, no. 3, p. 18–24; 1975, 27th instal., v. 15, no. 1, p. 19–24) (full census abstract, well annotated).
NN APR (Alabama) 72-1216

England, Flora D.
Alabama Source Book.
Selma, 1964. 1 v.
NN APR (Alabama)

England, Flora D.
Notes on Central Alabama Families.
Marion, AL, 1956. 101 leaves.
NN APR (Alabama)

Gandrud, Pauline Jones.
Alabama Index to the 1830 U.S. Census.
Hot Springs, AR, Bobbie J. McLane, 1973. 397 p., alpha.
NN APR (Alabama) 73-1541

Index to Compiled Service Records, Alabama Units—Creek War, 1836–1837.
Shreveport, LA, Benjamin Achee

and Margery Wright, 1971. 2 v., alpha.
NN (Alabama) 76-1517

Johnson, Dorothy Scott.
Madison Co., Alabama, Orphans Court Minutes, 1810–1817.
Huntsville, Johnson Hist. Pub., 1972.

Kilduff, Eleanor M., comp.
1850 Census, City of Mobile, Alabama.
Mobile, Mobile Gen. Soc., 1966. 161 p., index (unpaged).
NN APR (Mobile) 75-607

Mallon, John and Mrs.
Bay and Bayou Burials of South Mobile Co., Ala., vol. 1.
Mobile, Mrs. Lester E. Taylor, 1974. 2 v.
NN APR (Mobile Co.) 74-2362

Mitchell, Lois Dumas, and Dorothy Ivison Moffett, comp.
Mobile Co., Alabama, Burial Records.
Mobile, Mobile Gen. Soc., 1963–71. 2 v. (Covers 1820–1870)
NN APR (Mobile Co.)

Nelson, Soren and Mrs., comp.
A History of Church Street Graveyard, Mobile, Alabama.
Mobile, Historic Mobile Preservation Soc., 1963. 111 p.
NN APR (Mobile)

Peck, Lou E., Mrs.
Connecticut Born Residents of Alabama from the 1850 Census.
(IN: *Connecticut Ancestry*, Stamford, CT, Stamford Gen. Soc., 1973. v. 16, p. 18–22, 58–63, 129–134)
NN APR (Connecticut) 76-234

Spence, Ruth S.
Bibliography of Birmingham, Alabama, 1872–1972.
Birmingham, Oxmoor Press, 1973. 136 p.
NN ITNM (Birmingham) 74-1285

U.S.W.P.A.
Church Archives.
Birmingham, 1942. 238 p., index.
NN APR (Alabama)

U.S.W.P.A.
Vital Statistics.
Birmingham, 1942. 73 p., alpha by county.
NN APR (Alabama)

Ward, Wyley Donald.
Early History of Covington County, Alabama, 1821–1871.
Huntsville, the author, 1976. 382 p., index.
NN ITVM (Covington Co.) 77-204

Webb, Mary Frances.
Alabama—Its Development and Records.
(IN: *NGSQ. Washington, DC, 1969. v. 57, p. 3–12*)
NN APGA

ALASKA

State Archives

Alaska Historical Library and Museum
Juneau, AK 99801

Vital Records

Bureau of Vital Statistics
Department of Health and Welfare

Pouch "H"
Juneau, AK 99801
Births, deaths and marriages
1913–

Libraries

Alaska Division of State Libraries
Pouch "G," State Capitol
Juneau, AK 99801

Societies and Periodicals

Alaska Historical Commission
Higher Education Consortium Library
3211 Providence Avenue
Anchorage, AK 99504

Alaska Historical Society
635 Alder Street
Juneau, AK 99801

Bristol Bay Historical Society
Naknek, AK 99633

Church of Jesus Christ of Latter-
day Saints
Anchorage, Alaska, State Genealogical Library
2501 Maplewood Street
Anchorage, AK 99501

Cook Inlet Historical Society
121 West 7th Avenue
Anchorage, AK 99501

Fairbanks Genealogical Society
1552 Noble Street
Fairbanks, AK 99701

Genealogical Society of Southeastern Alaska
518 Deermount
Ketchikan, AK 99901

Kenai Historical Society, Inc.
Kenai, AK 99611

Kodiak Historical Society
101 Marine Way
Kodiak, AK 99615

Resurrection Bay Historical Soci-
ety
City Building
Seward, AK 99664

Tongass Historical Society, Inc.
629 Dock Street
Ketchikan, AK 99901

Valdez Historical Society
Egan Drive
Valdez, AK 99686

Books and Articles

Alaska—Who's Here—What's Do-
ing—Who's Doing it.
Anchorage, Jeffrey, 1955. 212 p.
NN AGZ

Bank, Ted, II.
Birthplace of the Winds.
New York, T. Y. Crowell, 1956.
274 p., no index.
NN IXQ (Aleutian)

Chaffin, Yule.
Alaska's Southwest Koniag to
King Crab.
Chaffin, 1968. 252 p., index.
IXQ (Kodiak)

Chance, Norman A.
The Eskimo of North Alaska.
New York, Holt, 1966. 107 p.
NN HBC

Chase, Wm. Henry.
Pioneers of Alaska, the Trail
Blazers of Bygone Days.
Kansas City, MO, Burton, 1951.
203 p.
NN IXP

De Armond, Robert N.
Subject Index to *The Alaskan*,
1885–1907, a Sitka Newspaper.
Juneau, Alaska Div. of State Li-
brary, 1974. 107 p. (Alaska State
Lib., Monograph no. 3)
NN IXQ (Sitka) 76-580

Orth, Donald J.
Dictionary of Alaska Place
Names.
Washington, DC, U.S. Gov. Print.
Office, 1967. 1,084 p., plus maps,
alpha.
NN *RR-KAT 75-6324

Ray, Dorothy.
The Eskimos of the Bering Strait,
1650–1898.
Seattle, WA, U. of WA Press, 1975.
305, 16 p., index.

Tewkesbury's Who's Who in
Alaska.
Juneau, 1947–.
NN L-10 9600

Tourville, Elsie.
Alaska: A Bibliography, 1570–
1970, with Subject Index.
Boston, MA, G. K. Hall, 1974. 738
p., alpha, index.
NN IXP

Wells, James K.
Ipani Eskimos: A Cycle of Life in
Nature.
Anchorage, Methodist U. Press,
1974, 112 p.

ARIZONA

State Archives

Arizona State Library
Department of Library, Archives
and Public Records
1700 W.Washington
Phoenix, AZ 85007

Vital Records

Division of Vital Records
State Department of Health
P.O. Box 3887
Phoenix, AZ 85030
Births and deaths: 1909–
Births and deaths prior: abstracts
from counties
Marriages: Clerk of Superior Court
of County. Dates vary from
county to county, begin 1863 or
later.

Libraries

University of Arizona
Arizona State Museum Library
Tucson, AZ 85721

Colorado River Indian Tribes Mu-
seum-Library
4 Corners and Mojave Road
Parker, AZ 85344

Tucson Public Library
200 South 6th Avenue
Tucson, AZ 85701

Societies and Periodicals

Apache County Historical Society
Box 454
St. Johns, AZ 85936

Arizona Historical Foundation
Hayden Memorial Library
Arizona State University
Tempe, AZ 85281

Arizona Pioneer's Historical Society
949 East Second Street
Tucson, AZ 85719
(*Journal of Arizona History*, 1960–)
NN IAA

Arizona State Genealogical Society
Box 6027
Tucson, AZ 85733

Casa Grande Valley Historical Society
404 N. Marshall Street
Casa Grande, AZ 95222

Church of Jesus Christ of Latter-day Saints
Tucson Arizona Branch Genealogical Library
500 South Langley
Tucson, AZ 85710

Cochise Co. Historical and Archeological Society
Box 818
Douglas, AZ 85607
(*The Cochise Quarterly*, 1968–)

Eastern Arizona Museum and Historical Society, Inc. of Graham County
North Main Street
Puma, AZ 85543

Mohave Pioneers Historical Society, Inc.
400 W. Beale
Kingman, AZ 86041

Navajo Co. Historical Society
Drawer 1060, Winslow Civic Center

Airport Road
Winslow, AZ 86047

Northern Arizona Pioneer's Historical Society, Inc.
Fort Valley Road
Flagstaff, AZ 86001

Pioneer Arizona
Interstate 17
Pioneer Road Exit
Phoenix, AZ 85061
(*Wagon Train Report*)

Sharlot Hall Historical Society
W. Gurley Street
Prescott, AZ 86301

Southern Arizona Genealogical Society
P.O. Box 6027
Tucson, AZ 85716
(*Copper State Bulletin*, 1965–; formerly *SAGS Quarterly*)
NN APGA

Yuma County Historical Society, Inc.
2405 Madison Avenue
Yuma, AZ 85364

Books and Articles

Barnes, William C.
Arizona Place Names, Revised and enlarged by Byrd H. Granger
Tucson, U. of AZ Press, 1960 (orig. 1935). 519 p., index and alpha arrangement.
NN IXBB

Schreier, Jim and Mary.
An Index to the 1864 Census of the Arizona Territory.

Phoenix, AZ, 1975. 83 p.
NN APR (Arizona) 75-2692

Senate Document 13, 89th Congress, 1st Session. Washington, DC, 1965.
(Contains 1864 Census of the Territory of Arizona; 8th and 9th, 1860 and 1870, U.S. Censuses of New Mexico and Arizona)
NN APR (Arizona)

Territory of Arizona; Index to the 1880 Federal Census.
Phoenix, Southern Arizona. Gen. Soc., 1870. 4 reels of film.
NN *ZI-204

Tinker, George H.
Northern Arizona and Flagstaff in 1887, the People and Resources.
Glendale, CA, A. H. Clark, 1969. 62 p., index.
NN IXB (Flagstaff, Glendale, CA)

U.S.W.P.A.
Directory of Churches and Religious Organizations in Arizona
. . .
Phoenix, 1940. 113 p.
NN ZAY

U.S.W.P.A.
Guide to Public Vital Statistics Records in Arizona.
Phoenix, 1941. 62 p.
NN APT p.v. 214

U.S.W.P.A.
Inventory of County Archives of Arizona.
Phoenix, 1938.
NN IXBB

U.S.W.P.A. Historical Records Survey.

1864 Census of the Territory of Arizona.
1938. 210 p.
NN APR (Arizona)

Yavapai Cowbelles.
Echoes of the Past: Tales of Old Yavapai.
Prescott, Yavapai Cowbelles, 1955–64. 2 v.
NN IXB (Yavapai)

ARKANSAS

State Archives

Arkansas State History Commission
Old State House Road
Little Rock, AR 72201

Vital Records

Bureau of Vital Statistics
State Department of Health
4815 West Markham Street
Little Rock, AR 72201

Births and deaths: February 1914–
Marriages: 1917–
Some births and deaths: Little Rock and Fort Smith 1881–

Libraries

Little Rock Public Library
700 Louisiana Street
Little Rock, AR 72201

Societies and Periodicals

Arkansas Ancestry
Mrs. Gerald B. McLane
112 Leach Street
Hot Springs, AR 71901

Arkansas Genealogical Society
4200 "A" Street
Little Rock, AR 72205
(*Arkansas Family Historian*,
1962–)
NN APR (Arkansas) 76-87

Arkansas Genealogical Research
Aid
c/o Mrs. William H. Counts
3812 Glenmore Road
North Little Rock, AR 72116
(1966–1971, 2 v. in one, ceased publication, a quarterly)
NN APR (Arkansas) 76-87

Arkansas Historical Association
History Department
University of Arkansas
Fayetteville, AR 72701
(*Arkansas Historical Quarterly*,
1942–)
NN IAA

Arkansas Historical Society
422 South 6th Street
Van Buren, AR 72956

Arkansas Records Association
314 Vine St.
Newport, AR 72112
(*Arkansas Records Survey*, 1972–)
(*Arkansas Gazette Marriages*,
1822–1824 appear in v. 1, no. 1–3,
p. 3–6)

Carroll County Historical Society
Berryville, AR 72616
(*Carroll County Historical Quar-
terly*)

Craighead County Historical Society
Box 1011
615 Warner
Jonesboro, AR 72401

(*Craighead County Historical
Quarterly*, 1963–)
NN ITVM (Craighead Co.)

Crawford County Historical Soci-
ety
417 Webster Street
Van Buren, AR 72956
(Mail: 1012 Cedar Street, Van
Buren, AR 72956)
(*The Heritage*, 1958–)
NN ITVM (Crawford Co)

Faulkner County Historical Society
Conway, AR 72032

Garland County Historical Society
914 Summer Street
Hot Springs, AR 71901
(*The Record*)

Grand Prairie Historical Society
1009 East 9th Street
Stuttgart, AR 72160

Independence County Historical
Society
Box 1412
115 North 4th Street
Batesville, AR 72501
(*Independence County Chronicle*)

Izard County Historical Society
Dolph, AR 72528
(*Izard County Historian*)

Mississippi County Historical and
Genealogical Society
505 Southwest Parkway
Blytheville, AR 72315

North Arkansas Genealogical Society
Mountain Home, AR 72653

North Central Arkansas Genealogical Society and Northeast

Arkansas Genealogical Society
314 Vine Street
Newport, AR 72112

Northwest Arkansas Genealogical
Society
1004 North 9th Street
Rogers, AR 72756
(*The Backtracker*, 1972–)

Phillips County Historical Society
623 Pecan Street
Helena, AR 72342
(*Phillips County Historical Quarterly*, 1963–)
NN ITVM (Phillips Co.)

Pulaski County Historical Society
653 Palm
Little Rock, AR 72201
(*Pulaski County Historical Society Review*, 1953–)
NN ITVM (Pulaski Co.)

Southern Arkansas Genealogical
Society
976 Lyons Lane S.W.
Camden, AR 71701

Texarkana USA Genealogical Society
901 State Line Avenue
Texarkana, AR 75501
(*Texarkana USA Quarterly*)

White County Genealogical Society
P.O. Box 327
Searcy, AR 72143

Books and Articles

Arkansas 1840 Census Index.
Bountiful, UT, AIS, 1976. 119 p.

Arkansas 1850 Census Index.
Bountiful, UT, AIS, 1976. 98 p.

Christensen, Katherine.
Arkansas Military Bounty Grants
(War of 1812).
Hot Springs, Arkansas Ancestors,
1971. 255 p.
NN APR (Arkansas) 72-1627

DAR, Arkansas.
A Roster of the Arkansas Daughters of the American Revolution, 1893–1968.
Mrs. Winslow Clement Spousta,
ed., 1971. 321 p., index.
NN APGA

U.S.W.P.A.
Vital Records of Arkansas;
Church Records.
Little Rock, 1942. 2 v., (620 p.)
NN APR (Arkansas)

CALIFORNIA

State Archives

California State Archives
Room 200, 1020 "O" Street
Sacramento, CA 95814

Vital Records

Bureau of Vital Statistics Registration
State Department of Health
410 N Street
Sacramento, CA 95814
Births and deaths: July 1905–
Births and deaths prior: County
Recorder
Marriages: also from state office;
at county level, begin 1850 or
later.

Libraries

California State Library
Sacramento, CA 95814

California State Library (Sutro
    Branch)
Temescal Terrace and Golden
    Gate Avenue
San Francisco, CA 94118

Church of Jesus Christ of Latter-
    day Saints
Los Angeles, California, Branch
    Genealogical Library
10741 Santa Monica Blvd.
Los Angeles, CA 90025

Church of Jesus Christ of Latter-
    day Saints
Los Angeles, California, East
    Branch Genealogical Library
106 South Hillview Avenue
Los Angeles, CA 90022

Church of Jesus Christ of Latter-
    day Saints
Sacramento, California, Branch
    Genealogical Library
2745 Eastern Avenue
Sacramento, CA 95821

Genealogical Research Center
Department of Special Collections
San Francisco Public Library
Civic Center
San Francisco, CA 94102

Long Beach Public Library
Ocean at Pacific Avenue
Long Beach, CA 90802

Los Angeles Public Library
630 West Fifth Street
Los Angeles, CA 90017

Oakland Public Library
14th and Oak Streets
Oakland, CA 94612

San Diego Public Library
820 "E" Street
San Diego, CA 92101

Societies and Periodicals

Amador County Historical Society
Box 157
Sutters Creek, CA 95685

Association for Northern Califor-
    nia
Records and Research
Box 3024
Chico, CA 95926

Calaveras County Historical Soci-
    ety
16 Main Street
San Andreas, CA 95249
(Mail: Box 542, Angels Camp, CA
    95222)
(*Las Calaveras*)

California Central Coast Genea-
    logical Society
P.O. Box 832
Morro Bay, CA 93442
(*Bulletin*)

California Genealogical Society
2099 Pacific Avenue
San Francisco, CA 94109
(*Newsletter*)

California Historical Society
2090 Jackson Street
San Francisco, CA 94109
(Mail: 1120 Old Mill Road, San
    Marion, CA 91108)
(*California Historical Quarterly*,
    1922-)
NN IAA

California Pioneers of Santa Clara
    County
Box 8208

San Jose, CA 95155
(*The Trailblazer*)

Contra Costa County Genealogical
Society
P.O. Box 910
Concord, CA 94522
(*The Diablo Descendants*)

Escondido Genealogical Society
P.O. Box 2190
Escondido, CA 92025
(*Newsletter*)

Fresno Genealogical Society
P.O. Box 2042
Fresno, CA 93718
(*Ash Tree Echo*, 1966–)
NN APR (Fresno)

Genealogical Society of Riverside
P.O. Box 2664
Riverside, CA 92506
(*Lifeliner*, v. 1, 1965–)
NN APR (Riverside, California)
73–246

Genealogical Society of Santa Cruz
County
P.O. Box 72
Santa Cruz, CA 95060
(*Newsletter*)

Genealogical Society of Siskiyou
County
P.O. Box 225
Yreka, CA 96097
(*Bulletin of Genealogical Society of
Siskiyou Co.*)

Historical Society of Long Beach
6400 Bixby Hill Road
Long Beach, CA 90815
(*Long Beach Journal; Los Fierros*)

Historical Society of Southern California
200 East Avenue 43

Los Angeles, CA 90031
(*Southern California Quarterly*)

Humboldt County Genealogical So-
ciety
P.O. Box 868
Arcata, CA 95527

Kern County Genealogical Society
P.O. Box 2214
Bakersfield, CA 93303
(*Kern-Gen*, 1964–)
NN APR (Kern Co.) 72–3106

Lake County Historical Society
Box 1011
Lakeport, CA 95453
(*Pomo Bulletin*)

Lake Tahoe Historical Society
Box 404
South Lake Tahoe, CA 95705

Madera County Historical Society
Box 478
210 W. Yosemite Avenue
Madera, CA 93637
(*Madera County Historian*)

Mariposa County Historical Soci-
ety
Box 606
5119 Jessie Street
Mariposa, CA 95338
(*Sentinel*)

Mojave Desert Genealogical Soci-
ety
P.O. Box 1320
Barstow, CA 92311
(*Mojave Nugget*, 1971–)

Moraga Historical Society
St. Mary's College
Moraga, CA 94575
(Mail: Box 103, Moraga, CA 94556)
(*Los Ranchos*)

Napa County Historical Society
Box 832
928 Coombs Street
Napa, CA 94558
(*Gleanings*)

Napa Valley Genealogical and Biographical Society
P.O. Box 385
Napa, CA 94558

Native Sons of the Golden West
414 Mason Street
San Francisco, CA 94102
(*Native Son*)

Nevada County Historical Society
Box 1300
214 Main Street
Nevada City, CA 95959
(*Nevada County Historical Society Bulletin*)

Orange County Genealogical Society
P.O. Box 1587
Orange, CA 92668
(*Orange County Genealogical Society Quarterly*, 1964–)
NN APR (Orange Co.)

Pacific Coast Branch—American Historical Association
History Department
University of Southern California
Los Angeles, CA 90007

Palo Alto Historical Association
Box 193
Palo Alto, CA 94302
(*Tall Tree*)

Paradise Genealogical Society
P.O. Box 335
Paradise, CA 95969

(*Genealogical Goldmine*, 1968–)
(This is a goldmine of abstracts of original records.)
NN APR (Butte Co.) 76-364

Placer County Historical Society
Box 643
Auburn, CA 95603

Plumas County Historical Society
Box 695
Quincy, CA 96103
(*Plumas Memories*, 1959–)
NN IXH (Plumas Co.)

Pomona Valley Genealogical Society
% Georgia E. Morgan, President
714 South Hillward Avenue
West Covina, CA 91791
(*The Bulletin of the Pomona Valley Genealogical Society*, 1965–)
NN IXH (Pomona Valley, California)

Redwood Genealogical Society
P.O. Box 645
Fortuna, CA 95540
(*Redwood Researchers*, 1968–)
NN APR (Humbolt Co.)

Sacramento County Historical Society
Box 1175
Sacramento, CA 95806
(*Golden Notes; Golden Nuggets*)

San Benito County Historical Society
Hollister, CA 95023

San Bernardino Valley Genealogical Society
P.O. Box 2505
San Bernardino, CA 92406
(*The Valley Quarterly*, 1962–)

San Diego Genealogical Society
The Studio 30, Spanish Village, Balboa Park
San Diego, CA 92101
(*Leaves and Saplings*, 1973–)

San Diego Historical Society
Box 81825
2727 Presidio Drive
San Diego, CA 92103
(*Journal of San Diego History*, 1955–)
NN IXH (San Diego)

San Fernando Valley Historical Society
10940 Sepulveda Blvd.
Mission City, CA 91345

San Gabriel Valley Genealogical Society
Pasadena Public Library
285 East Walnut Street
Pasadena, CA 91101

San Joaquin County Historical Society
Box 21, 11793 N. Micke Grove Road
Lodi, CA 95240
(*San Joaquin Historian*, 1965–)
NN IXH (San Joaquin) 73-2516

San Leandro Historical Society
Casa Peralta
384 W. Estudillo Avenue
San Leandro, CA 94577
(*San Leandro Recollections*)

San Luis Obispo County Historical Society
696 Monterey Street
San Luis Obispo, CA 93401
(*La Vista*)

San Mateo County Historical Association

1700 W. Hillsdale Blvd.
San Mateo, CA 94402
(*La Peninsula*)

Santa Barbara County Genealogical Society
P.O. Box 1174
Goleta, CA 93017
(*Ancestors West*, 1974–)

Santa Clara County Genealogical Society
2635 Homestead Road
Santa Clara, CA 95051
(*Santa Clara County Historical and Genealogical Society Quarterly*, 1964–)
NN APR (Santa Clara Co.)

Santa Cruz Historical Society
Box 1581
Santa Cruz, CA 95061
(*News and Notes*)

Santa Maria Valley Genealogical Society
P.O. Box 1215
Santa Maria, CA 93454

Shasta Historical Society
Box 277
Redding, CA 96001
(*The Covered Wagon*)

Sierra Madre Historical Society
405 Manzanita
Sierra Madre, CA 91024

Society of California Archivists
University Archives
The Bancroft Library
Berkeley, CA 94720
(*Society of California Archivists Newsletter*, 1971–)

Society of California Pioneers

456 McAllister Street
San Francisco, CA 94102

Society of Mayflower Descendants
in the State of California
681 Market Street, Room 670
San Francisco, CA 94105

Sonoma County Genealogical Society
P.O. Box 2273
Santa Rosa, CA 95405

Sons of the Revolution
672 S. Lafayette Park Place
Los Angeles, CA 90057

Sutter-Yuba Genealogical Society
P.O. Box 1274
Yuba City, CA 95991
(*Digger's Digest*)

Southern California Genealogical
Society, Inc.
P.O. Box 7665
Bixby Knolls Station
Long Beach, CA 90807
(*The Searcher*, 1963–)
NN APR (California)

Tuolumne County Historical Society
Box 695
158 W. Bradford Avenue
Sonora, CA 95370
(*Chispa*, 1962–)

Ukiah Tree Tracers
1620 South Dora Street
Ukiah, CA 95482
(*Ukiah Tree Tracers Flash News*)

Books and Articles

Avina, Rose Hollengaugh.
Spanish and Mexican Land Grants
in California.

San Francisco, R. and E. Research
Assoc., 1973. 109 p., index (orig.
1932, U. of CA thesis).
NN APR (California) 75-1821

Bowman, Alan P.
Index to the 1850 Census of the
State of California.
Baltimore, MD, GPC, 1972. 605 p.,
alpha under county.
NN APR (California) 73-1475

California 1850 Census Index.
Bountiful, UT, AIS, 1977

California Register.
Beverly Hills, Social Blue Book of
Cal., Inc., 1966 v. 5, 983 p.
NN *R-IZ

Eason, Edwin M.
Vintage Fresno, Pictorial Recollections of a Western City.
Fresno, Huntington Press, 1965.
150 p., index.
NN IXH (Fresno)

Fresno County Blue Book ...
Fresno, 1941. 555 p., index.
NN IXH (Fresno)

Handbook for Local Registrars of
Births and Deaths.
State of California Dept. of Health.
California Office of the State Registrar of Vital Statistics, 1973. 113
p.
APB 74-362

Haskins, Charles Warren.
Index to the Argonauts of California, by Libera Martina Spinazze
New Orleans, LA, Polyanthos,
1975. 514 p., alpha.

Kinnard, Lawrence.
History of the Greater San Francisco Bay Region.

New York, Lewis Hist. Co., 1966.
3 v., index.
NN IXH (San Francisco Bay)

Lingenfelter, Keith.
Northern California Bounty Land
Grantees Under Acts of 1847–
1955.
(IN: *NGSQ, Washington, DC, Dec.
1976. v. 64, p. 294–311*)
NN APGA

Lingenfelter, Keith, and Robert
Fulton.
Northern California Marriages,
1850–1860.
(IN: *NGSQ, Washington, DC, 1966.
v. 54, p. 125–48, 170–192, 260–291*)
(Includes Sacramento, El Dorado,
Placer, Nevada, Yuba, Sutter,
Butte, Plumas, Tehama, Shasta,
Siskiyou, Solano, Yolo, Colusa,
Sonoma, Mendocino and Trinity
counties)
NN APGA

Mucatine, Doris.
San Francisco, the Biography of a
City from the Early Days to
the Earthquake.
New York, G. P. Putnam's, 1975.
450 p., index.
NN IXH (San Francisco) 76-684

Northrup, Marie E.
Spanish-Mexican Families of Early
California: 1769–1850.
New Orleans, LA, Polyanthos,
1976. v. 1, 396 p., index.
NN APR (California) 77-323

Pompey, Sherman Lee.
Genealogical Records of California.
Fresno, CA, S. L. Pompey, 1968. 31
p. plus misc. Cal. records, unpaged sect.
NN APR (California) 74-511

Pourade, Richard F.
The History of San Diego.
San Diego, Union Tribune Pub.
Co., 1960–65. 5 v., index.
NN IXH (San Diego)

Rasmussen, Louis J., comp. and
ed.
Railway Passenger Lists of Overland Trains to San Francisco
and the West.
San Francisco, 1966–68. 2 v.
NN APR (San Francisco)

Rasmussen, Louis J., comp. and
ed.
San Francisco Historic Record and
Genealogy Bulletin.
San Francisco, 1963–65. 3 v.
NN APR (San Francisco)

Rasmussen, Louis J.
San Francisco Ship Passenger
Lists.
San Francisco, 1965–70. 4 v. (Cov-
ers arrivals from 1850– Jan.
1853)
NN APR (San Francisco)

Saddleback Ancestors, Rancho
Families of Orange County.
Orange, Co., CA, Orange Co. Gen.
Soc., 1969. 187 p.
(Sepulveda, Peralta, Yorba, Avila,
Carrillo, Dominquez, etc.)
NN APR (Orange Co.) 72-2867

San Joaquin Gen. Soc.
1850 Census of San Joaquin
County, California.
Stockton, CA, 1959. 70 p., index.
NN APR (San Joaquin)

San Joaquin Gen. Soc.
Marriage Records of San Joaquin
Co., California, August 1850–
December 1884.

Stockton, CA, 1969–73. 2 v.
NN APR (San Joaquin)

San Joaquin Gen. Soc.
Old Cemeteries of San Joaquin Co.,
California.
Stockton, CA, 1960–64. 3 v.
NN APR (San Joaquin)

Smith, A. McCall, ed.
A Modern History of Tulare
County (Hist. and Bio.).
Visalia, CA. Limited Editions of
Visalia, Inc., 1974. 203 p., 2 in-
dexes.
NN IXH (Tulare Co.) 75-1319

Who's Who in Los Angeles.
Los Angeles, c. 1925–c. 1930, 1950–
1953.
NN IXH (Los Angeles)

COLORADO

State Archives

Colorado Division of State Archives and Public Records
1530 Sherman Street
Denver, CO 80203

Vital Records

Records and Statistics Section, Col-
orado Department of Health
4210 East 11th Avenue
Denver, CO 80220
Births: 1910–
Births prior: some counties
Deaths: 1910–
Marriages: statewide index of rec-
ords for all years except 1940–
1967
Write county clerk for certified
copies.

Libraries

Church of Jesus Christ of Latter-
day Saints
Denver, Colorado, Branch Genealogical Library
Denver Stake Center
740 Hudson Street
Denver, CO 80201

Denver Public Library
1357 Broadway
Denver, CO 80203

Historical Society Library
14th and Sherman
Denver, CO 80203

Societies and Periodicals

Adams County Historical Society
9755 Henderson Road
Brighton, CO 80601

Area Keys Genealogical Magazine,
1976–
Box 19465
Denver, CO 80219

Arvada Historical Society
6047 Flower Street
Arvada, CO 80003
(Mail: Box 419, Arvada, CO 80001)
(*The Arvada Historian*)

Boulder Genealogical Society
P.O. Box 3246
Boulder, CO 80302
(*The Boulder Genealogical Society,*
c.1969–)
NN APR (Boulder)

Clear Creek Canyon Historic Society of Chaffee County
27500 County Road 390
Vicksburg, CO 81228
(Mail: Box 2181, Granite, CO
81228)

Colorado Division of State Archives and Public Records
1530 Sherman Street
Denver, CO 80302
(*Checklist of Colorado Publications*)

Colorado Genealogical Society
P.O. Box 9654
Denver, CO 80209

Colorado State Historical Society
912 Harrison Avenue
Leadville, Co 80461

Colorado Military Historians
3966 South Mariposa Street
Englewood, CO 80110

Columbine Genealogical and Historical Society
P.O. Box 2060
Littleton, CO 80121

Delta County Historical Society
Box 125
Delta County Courthouse
5th and Palmer
Delta, CO 81416

East Yuma County Historical Society
140 West 4th Street
Wray, CO 80758

Fremont—Custer Historical Society, Inc.
423 Hazel Avenue
Canon City, CO 81212
(*Historical Flashbacks*)

Gilpin County Historical Society
Box 244
Central City, CO 80427

Gunnison County Pioneer and Historical Society

East Adams Street and Hwy. 50
Gunnison, CO 81230

Historical Museum and Institute of Western Colorado
4th and Ute Streets
Grand Junction, CO 81501

Historic Denver, Inc.
1059 9th Street
Denver, CO 80204

Jefferson County Historical Society, Inc.
Box 703
Evergreen, CO 80439

Lake County Civic Center Association, Inc.
Box 962
100–102 East 9th Street
Leadville, CO 80461
(*Mountain Diggings*)

Larimer County Genealogical Society
℅ Mrs. John C. Simpson, President
2211 West Mulberry Street, #5
Fort Collins, CO 80521

Logan County Historical Society
Box 272
Sterling, CO 80751

Park County Historical Society, Inc.
Box 43
Bailey, CO 80421

Pioneer Historical Society of Bent County
414 Grand
Las Animas, CO 81054

Prowers County Historical Society
Box 362, N. Santa Fe Trail
Lamar, CO 81052

Rio Blanco County Historical Society, Inc.
565 Park Street
Meeker, CO 81641

San Juan Historical Society
Box 154
Courthouse Square
Silverton, CO 81433

San Luis Valley Historical Society, Inc.
Box 982
Alamosa, CO 81101
(*The San Luis Valley Historian*)

State Historical Society of Colorado
200 14th Avenue
Denver, CO 80203
(*The Colorado Magazine*, 1923–)
NN IAA

The Colorado Genealogist, 1939–
7244 South Platte Canyon Drive
Littleton, CO 80123
NN APR(Colorado)

Weld County Genealogical Society
P.O. Box 278
Greeley, CO 80631

Books and Articles

Brown, Robert L.
Ghost Towns of the Colorado Rockies.
Caldwell, ID, Caxton Printers, 1968. 401 p., index.
NN IWQB

Brown, Robert L.
Jeep Trails to Colorado Ghost Towns.
Caldwell, ID, Caxton Printers, 1963. 239 p., no index, alpha.
NN IWQB

Early Colorado Marriages.
(IN: *Colorado Genealogist*. Denver,
1941–1976; v. 2, no. 5 and 6, p. 73 ff; v. 37, no. 2, p. 86–95)
(Covers 19 May 1862–28 Apr. 1917)
NN APR (Colorado)

Frandsen, Maude L.
The Counties of Colorado: Sixty-three on the Flying "C."
Boulder, Johnson Pub. Co., 1960. 104 p.
NN IWQB

Frech, Mary L.
Chronology and Documentary Handbook of the State of Colorado.
Dobbs Ferry, NY, Oceana Pub., 1973. (*Chronologies and Documentary Handbooks of the States*, v. 6)

Griswold, Don, and Jean Griswold.
Colorado's Century of Cities, 1858–1958.
Denver, Smith Brooks, 1958. 307 p., no index.
NN IWQB

Jones, Wm. C., and Kenton Forrest.
Denver: A Pictorial History from Camp to Queen City of the Plains.
Boulder, Pruett Pub. Co., 1973. 336 p., t of c, no index.
NN IWQ (Denver) 74–975

Pease, Janet K.
Jefferson County Colorado Marriage Records.
Moline, IL, the author, 1972. 2 v.
v. 1, 1868–81; v. 2, 1881–95.
NN APR (Jefferson Co.)

Pease, Janet K.
Jefferson Co., Colorado, Marriage
    Records, 1868–1881.
Moline, IL, J. K. Pease, 1972. 45
    leaves.
NN APR (Jefferson Co.) 73-410

Perkin, Robert L.
The First Hundred Years: An In-
    formal History of Denver and
    the Rocky Mountain News.
Garden City, NY, Doubleday,
    1959. 624 p., index.
NN IWQ (Denver)

Perry, Eberhart.
Guide to Colorado Ghost Towns.
Denver, Sage Books, 1959. 479 p.,
    index.
NN IWQB

Pompey, Sherman L.
Confederate Soldiers Buried in
    Colorado.
Independence, CA, Hist. & Gen.
    Pub. Co., 1965.

U.S. Census Office.
Seventh Census—1850; Index to
    1850 Colorado Census.
Greeley, Weld Co. Gen. Soc., 1976.

CONNECTICUT

State Archives

Connecticut State Library
231 Capitol Street
Hartford, CT 06115

Vital Records

Public Health Statistics Section
State Department of Health

79 Elm Street
Hartford, CT 06115
(Births, marriages, deaths since
    July 1, 1897. Earlier records
    with the town and city clerks
    and in the Barbour Collection
    at the State Library.)

Libraries

Godfrey Memorial Library
134 Newfield Street
Middletown, CT 06457
(Publishes *The American Geneal-
    ogical Index*, now being revised)

Hartford,   Connecticut   State
    Branch
Genealogical Library
30 Woodside Avenue
Manchester, CT 06040

Societies and Periodicals

Connecticut Historical Society
1 Elizabeth Street
Hartford, CT 06105
(*Connecticut Historical Soc. Collec-
    tions*)
NN IQL

Connecticut Society of Genealo-
    gists, Inc.
16 Royal Oak Drive
West Hartford, CT 06107

The Connecticut Nutmegger
Connecticut Society of Genealo-
    gists
P. O. Box 435
Glastonbury, CT 06033
NN APR (Connecticut) 74-726

Darien Historical Society
Leroy Avenue
Darien, CT 06820

Fairfield Historical Society
636 Old Post Road
Fairfield, CT 06430

Litchfield Historical Society
Litchfield, CT 06759

New Canaan Historical Society
13 Oenoke
New Canaan, CT 06380

New Haven Colony Historical Society
114 Whitney Avenue
New Haven, CT 06510
(*NHCHS Papers*, 1865–1918)
NN IQM (New Haven)

New London County Historical Society
Shaw Mansion
11 Blinman Street
New London, CT 06320
(*Quarterly Bulletin*, 1976–; *New London County Historical Society Journal*, 1953–)
NN IQH (New London)

Stamford Genealogical Society
Box 249
Stamford, CT 06904
(*Connecticut Ancestry*, 1971–)
NN APR (Connecticut) 76–234
(Formerly *Stamford Genealogical Society Bulletin*, 1959–70, NN APR [Stamford])

Trumbull Historical Society
Trumbull Town Hall
Trumbull, CT 06611

Wilton Historical Society
150 Danbury Road
Wilton, CT 06897

Books and Articles

Bailey, Frederic W.
Early Connecticut Marriages, as Found in Ancient Church Records Prior to 1800. Baltimore, MD, GPC, 1968. 7 books in 1, 7 indexes (orig. 1869–1906).
NN APR (Connecticut)

Barbour, Lucius Barnes.
Families of Early Hartford, Connecticut, edited and indexed by the Connecticut Society of Genealogists. Baltimore, GPC, 1977. 736 p.

Barlow, Claude.
Sources for Genealogical Searching in Connecticut.
Worcester, MA, C. W. Barlow, 1972.

Bixby, William.
Connecticut: A New Guide.
New York, Charles Scribner's Sons, 1974. 386 p., index.
NN IQL 74-1423

Connecticut 1800 Census Index.
Bountiful, UT, AIS, 1976

Connecticut 1810 Census Index.
Bountiful, UT, AIS, 1976

Connecticut 1820 Census Index.
Bountiful, UT, AIS, 1977. 124 p.

Connecticut 1830 Census Index.
Bountiful, UT, AIS, 1977

Connecticut 1840 Census Index.
Bountiful, UT, AIS, 1977

Connecticut 1850 Census Index.
Bountiful, UT, AIS, 1977

Connecticut State Library
Checklist of Probate Records in the Connecticut State Library.

Hartford, CT State Lib. RG4; Probate Courts Descriptive Report no. 1, May 6, 1972, rev. June 7, 1976. 19 p.

Connecticut State Library
List of Church Records in the Connecticut State Library, rev. ed.
Hartford, June 15, 1976. 35 p.

Connecticut State Library
Revised Preliminary Checklist of Court Records in Connecticut State Library, 1636–1944.
Judicial Dept. Descriptive Report no. 1, 2nd rev. ed. RG3.
Hartford, Sept. 9, 1975. 33 p.

Conway, Rosanne L., and Kenneth Scott, comp. and ed.
Abstracts from Colonial Connecticut Newspapers.
New Haven, 1755–75.
New Orleans, LA, Polyanthos, 1977. 600 p., index.

Culter, Charles C.
Connecticut's Revolutionary Press.
Chester, CT, Pequot Press, 1975. 61 p. (Connecticut Bicentennial Series, v. XIV)

French and Indian War Rolls, 1755–1762.
Hartford, 1903–05. 2 v.
(Connecticut Hist. Soc. Collections, v. 9–10)
NN IQL

General Index of the Land Records of the Town of Hartford from the Year 1639 to the Year 1839.
Hartford, Wiley, Waterman and Eaton, 1973. 613, 4 p.
NN APR (Hartford)

Grant, Marion H.
The Fenwick Story.
Connecticut Hist. Soc., 1974. 224 plus p., cursory index.
(A beautiful book)
NN IQM

Hughes, Arthur H, and Morse S. Allen.
Connecticut Place Names.
Hartford, Connecticut Hist. Soc., 1976. 907 p., index.
NN IQMB 77-828

Jacobus, Donald Lines.
...Families of Ancient New Haven.
Baltimore, MD, GPC, 1974 (orig. 1923–32). 8 v. in 3 v. with cross-index. (This work forms the first 8 volumes of *The American Genealogist*, often called *TAG*, which is now being published by Dr. George E. McCracken, 1232 39th St., Des Moines, IA 50311.)
NN APGA (*American Genealogist*)

Jacobus, Donald Lines.
...Families of Old Fairfield.
Baltimore, MD, GPC, 1976 (orig. 1930–32). 2 v. in 3 v. (another famous work by the "dean" of American genealogists)
NN APR (Fairfield Co.) 76-1538

Jacobus, Donald Lines.
List of Officials of the Connecticut and New Haven Colonies.
New Haven, Roland Mather Hooker, 1935. 65 p., alpha.
*R-APR (Connecticut)

Love, William DeLoss.
The Colonial History of Hartford.
Chester, CT, Centinel Hill Press, 1974 (orig. 1935). 369 p., index.
NN IQM (Hartford) 75-2304

Lyme, Connecticut, Bicentennial Commission.
Lyme Vital Records, 1665–1850, a Literal Transcription.
Hadlyme, CT 06439; the Commission, Box 56, 1977.

Mainwaring, Charles.
Digest of the Early Connecticut Probate Records, Hartford District, 1635–1750.
Hartford, 1904–1906. 3 v., index in each v.
NN APR (Connecticut)

New London, Connecticut
Probate Records, 1713–24.
(IN: *DAR Magazine*, Washington, DC, NSDAR, 1953. p. 925–933, 1,017–1,026)
NN APGA

Society of Colonial Wars in the State of Connecticut.
Register of Pedigrees and Services of Ancestors.
Hartford, CT, The Case, Lockwood, Brainard Co., 1941. 1,394 p., index.
NN APGA

Frech, Mary L.
Chronological and Documentary Handbook of the State of Connecticut.
Dobbs Ferry, NY, Oceana, 1973. 139 p.
NN IRL 74-128

Tyler, John W.
Connecticut Loyalists: An Analysis of Loyalist Land Confiscations in Greenwich, Stamford, and Norwalk.
New Orleans, LA, Polyanthos, 1977. 125 p., index.

U.S.W.P.A., Connecticut.
Guide to Vital Statistics in Church Records of Connecticut.
New Haven, 1942. 190 p.
NN APR (Connecticut)

DELAWARE

State Archives

The Public Archives Commission
Hall of Records
Dover, DE 19901

Vital Records

Bureau of Vital Statistics
Division of Public Health
Department of Health and Social Services
Jesse S. Cooper Memorial Bldg.
Dover, DE 19901
Births, deaths and marriages: 1861–1863, 1881–

Libraries

Division of Historical and Cultural Affairs
Department of State
Hall of Records
Dover, DE 19901

Morris Library
University of Delaware
Newark, DE 19711
(*Delaware Genealogy*, 1974. 4 p.)

Societies and Periodicals

Division of Historical and Cultural Affairs
Department of State
Hall of Records
Dover, DE 19901

Duck Creek Historical Society
Box 413
Duck Creek Village
Smyrna, DE 19977
(*Footprints of the Past*)

Historic Red Clay Valley, Inc.
Box 1374
Wilmington, DE 19899

Historical Society of Delaware
505 Market Street
Wilmington, DE 19801
(*Delaware History*, 1946–)
NN IAA

Lewes Historical Society
199 West 3rd Street
Lewes, DE 19958

Milford Historical Society
Box 352
501 N.W. Front Street
Milford, DE 19963
(*Kent*)

Books and Articles

Biographical and Genealogical History of the State of Delaware.
Chambersburg, PA, J. M. Runk and Co., 1899. 2 v., index v. 2.
(This work is familiarly called "Runk.")
NN APR (Delaware)

Calendar of Delaware Wills, New Castle Co., 1682–1800.
New York, Frederick H. Hitchcock, 1911. 218 p., index.
NN APR (New Castle)

Calendar of Sussex Co., Delaware, Probate Records.

Edited by Leon de Valinger.
Dover, 1964. 310, 87 p.
NN APR (Sussex Co.)

Delaware 1810 Census Index.
Bountiful, UT, AIS, 1976.

Delaware 1820 Census Index.
Bountiful, UT, AIS, 1977. 27 p.

Delaware 1830 Census Index.
Bountiful, UT, AIS, 1977.

Delaware 1840 Census Index.
Bountiful, UT, AIS, 1977.

Delaware 1850 Census Index.
Bountiful, UT, AIS, 1977.

Delaware Archives.
Wilmington, Delaware Archives Commission, 1911–1916. 5 v., v. 1–3. Revolution, v. 5–6 post-Revolution to War of 1812, index v. 3, 5.
NN APR (Delaware)

Ehinger, Aline N.
Bridge Across the Years: A History of the Presbyterian Church of Dover.
Dover, 1975. 419 p., index.
NN ISF (Dover) 77-754

Fields, Dale.
Genealogical Source Material in the Historical Society of Delaware.
(IN: *PGM, Philadelphia, PA, 1973. v. 28, p. 86–93*)
NN APR (Pennsylvania)

Fields, Dale.
Records in the Historical Society of Delaware, Wilmington, Delaware.
(IN: *Maryland Gen. Soc. Bulletin,*

Baltimore, MD, 1971. v. 12, p. 15–20)
NN APR (Maryland)

Frech, Mary L., ed.
Chronological and Documentary Handbook of the State of Delaware.
Dobbs Ferry, NY, Oceana Pub., 1973.
(Also known as Chronologies and Documentary Handbooks of the States, vol. 8.)

Gehring, Charles T., ed.
New York Historical Manuscripts: Dutch Volumes xx–xxi—Delaware Papers (English period, 1664–1682).
Baltimore, MD, GPC, 1977. 395 p., index.

History and Biography; Encyclopedia of Delaware.
Wilmington, Aldine Pub., 1882. 572 p.
NN ISE+

Hoffecker, Carol E.
Wilmington, Delaware, Portrait of an Industrial City, 1830–1910.
Charlottesville, VA, U. of VA Press, for Eleutherian Mills-Hagley Foundation, 1974. 187 p., index.
NN ISF (Wilmington) 74-2339

Jackson, Ronald V.
Delaware in 1800.
Salt Lake City, UT, AIS, 1972. 171 p., alpha.
NN APR (Del.) 73-976

Keen, Gregory B.
The Descendants of Jöran Kyn of New Sweden, Delaware.

Swedish Col. Soc., 1913. 318 p., index and list of members.
NN APV (Kyn)

Maddux, Gerald M. and Doris O.
1800 Census, Delaware.
Montgomery, AL, 1964. 200 p.
NN APR (Delaware)

Montgomery, Elizabeth.
Wilmington.
Cottonport, LA, Polyanthos, 1971 (orig. 1851). 367 p., plus index.

New Castle County, Delaware, Naturalization Records, 1826–1858.
(IN: *Maryland and Delaware Genealogist*, St. Michael's, MD, 1977. v. 18, p. 38–39 ff.)
NN APR (Maryland)

Scharf, John Thomas, 1843–1898.
History of Delaware, 1609–1888.
Port Washington, NY, Kennikat Press, 1972 (orig. 1888). 2 v., 1,358 p.
(Poor index in this work, but a new index has been recently compiled by the Delaware Historical Society.)
NN ISE 73-1637

Tunnell, James M., Jr.
A Genealogy of the Tunnell Family of Delaware.
Georgetown, DE, 1954. 100 leaves, t of c, no index.(p. 79–80, James Mitler Tunnell, U.S. Senator for Delaware, 1940–46; p. 87, Ebe Walter Tunnell, Governor of Delaware, 1897–1901)
NN APV (Tunnell)

Valinger, Leon de, ed.
A Reconstructed 1790 Census of Delaware.
Washington, DC, 1962. 83 p.

(*NSGQ Special Pub. # 10*)
NN APGA

Virdin, Donald.
Virdins of Delaware and Related
    Families.
Arlington, VA, privately printed,
    1976. 142 leaves.

DISTRICT OF COLUMBIA

Archives

National Archives and Records
    Service
National Archives
Constitution Avenue
Washington, DC 20408
(*Prologue: The Journal of the Na-
    tional Archives*)

Vital Records

District of Columbia Department
    of Public Health
Vital Records Division
300 Indiana Avenue N.W., Room
    1022
Washington, DC 20001
Births: 1871–
Deaths: 1855– but none during the
    Civil War.
Marriages: Clerk, District of Co-
    lumbia Court of General Ses-
    sions, Washington, DC 20001

Libraries

Congressional Library
Washington, DC 20540

Library of Congress
Washington, DC 20540

The Public Library
499 Pennsylvania Avenue N.W.
Washington, DC 20001

Societies and Periodicals

American Historical Association
400 "A" Street S.E.
Washington, DC 20003
(*American Historical Review*)

Columbia Historical Society
1307 New Hampshire Avenue N.W.
Washington, DC 20036

Genealogy Department
Library of Congress Annex
Washington, DC 20540

National Genealogy Society
1921 Sunderland Place N.W.
Washington, DC 20036
(*National Genealogy Society Quar-
    terly*, 1912–)
NN APGA

National Society of Colonial Dames
    of the XVII Century
1300 New Hampshire Avenue N.W.
Washington, DC 20036
(*Seventeenth Century Review*)

National Society of the Daughters
    of the American Revolution
1776 "D" Street N.W.
Washington, DC 20006
(*Daughters of the American Revo-
    lution Magazine*, 1892–)
NN APGA

National Society of the Sons of the
    American Revolution
2412 Massachusetts Avenue N.W.
Washington, DC 20008
(*Sons of the American Revolution
    Magazine*, 1906–)
NN APGA

Books and Articles

Babbel, June A.
Lest We Forget. A Guide to Genealogical Research in the Nation's Capitol. 4th ed.
Annandale, VA, 1976. 135 p.

Bicentennial Register of the Society of Mayflower Descendants in the District of Columbia, 1976.
Washington, DC, the Society, 1976. 918 p., index (includes 1970 Register, 1973 Supplement, 1976 Bicentennial Supplement).
NN APR (District of Columbia) 77-510

McGhee, Lucy Kate.
Revolutionary, War of 1812 and Indian Wars' Pensioners' List of Washington, DC, and Alexandria, Virginia.
Washington, DC, c. 1955. 50, 21 leaves.
NN APR (Washington, DC)

Walker, Homer A.
Historical Court Records of Washington, District of Columbia ... Death Records.
Washington, DC, 1955. 2 v. (covers 1801–1878).
NN APR (Washington, DC)

Walker, Homer A.
Historical Court Records of Washington, District of Columbia ... Marriages.
Washington, DC, c. 195-. 14 v. in 5 (covers 1811–1858).
NN APR (Washington, DC)

Washington, DC 1800 Census Index.
Bountiful, UT, AIS, 1976.

Washington, DC 1820 Census Index.
Bountiful, UT, AIS, 1976, 86 p.

Washington, DC 1830 Census Index.
Bountiful, UT, AIS, 1977.

Washington, DC 1840 Census Index.
Bountiful, UT, AIS, 1977.

Washington, DC 1850 Census Index.
Bountiful, UT, AIX, 1977.

FLORIDA

State Archives

Florida Division of Archives, History and Records Management
401 East Gains Street
Tallahassee, FL 32304

Vital Records

Department of Health and Rehabilitative Services
Division of Health
Bureau of Vital Statistics
P.O. Box 210
Jacksonville, FL 32201
Births, some: April 1865–
Deaths, some: August 1877–
Births and deaths, most: January 1917–
Marriages: June 6, 1927– or write County Judge's Office for earlier records

Libraries

Florida State Library
Supreme Court Bldg.
Tallahassee, FL 32301

Jacksonville Public Library
122 North Ocean Street
Jacksonville, FL 32202

Hillsborough County Historical
Commission
Museum, Historical and Geneal-
ogical Library
County Courthouse
Tampa, FL 33602

Polk County's Genealogical and
Historical Library
P.O. Box 511
Bartow, FL 38830

St. Augustine Historical Society
Library
1883 Webb Memorial Bldg.
22 St. Francis Street
St. Augustine, FL 32084

St. Petersburg Public Library
3745 Ninth Avenue North
St. Petersburg, FL 33713

Tampa Public Library
900 North Ashley Street
Tampa, FL 33602

Societies and Periodicals

Brevard Genealogical Society
P.O. Box 1123
Cocoa, FL 32922

Florida Historical Society
P.O. Box 3645
University Station
Gainesville, FL 32601
(*Florida Historical Quarterly*,
1908–)
NN IAA

Florida Genealogical Society
P.O. Box 18624

Tampa, FL 33609
(*Florida Genealogical Society Jour-
nal*, 1965–, v. 1–)
NN APR (Florida) 76-880

Genealogical Society of Gainesville
% Helen Garner Reed
2132 N.W. 7th Pl.
Gainesville, FL 32603

Genealogical Society of South Bre-
vard County
P.O. Box 786
Melbourne, FL 32901

Jacksonville Genealogical Society
P.O. Box 7076
Jacksonville, FL 32210
(*Jacksonville Genealogical Maga-
zine*, 1973–)

Magnolia Monthly, 1963– Box 8
Crawfordville, FL 32377
(A magazine of news, features and
history about Wakulla County
and North Florida)
NN ITM (Wakulla Co., Florida)

Palm Beach County Genealogical
Society
P.O. Box 1746
West Palm Beach, FL 33402
(*Ancestry*, 1966–)
NN APGA 72-995

St. Augustine Historical Society
1883 Webb Memorial Bldg.
22 St. Francis Street
St. Augustine, FL 32084
(*El Escribano* 1955–)
NN ITM (St. Augustine)

Southern Genealogist's Exchange
Society
P.O. Box 2801
Jacksonville, FL 32202

(*Southern Genealogist's Exchange Quarterly*, 1957–1958.)
NN APR (Southern states)

South Florida Pioneers (1974–)
Richard M. Livingston, ed.
P.O. Box 166
Fort Ogden, FL 33842

Books and Articles

Avant, David A., Jr.
Florida Pioneers and Their Alabama, Georgia, Carolina, Maryland, and Virginia Ancestors.
Tallahassee, FL, D. A. Avant, Jr.
500 p., index.
(includes names of slaves and other blacks)
NN APR (Florida) 75-1619

Brownell, Daphne.
Cemetery Records of West Volusia County, Florida.
Melbourne, FL, S. Brevard Hist. Soc., c. 1974. 3 v.
NN APR (Volusia Co., Florida) 75-1382

Covington, James W.
The Story of Southwestern Florida.
New York, Lewis Historical Pub. Co., 1957. 2 v., index.
NN ITL

Davis, T. Frederick.
History of Jacksonville and Vicinity, 1513–1924.
Gainesville, U. of FL Press, 1964. 513 p., subject index only.
NN ITM (Jacksonville)

Dovell, J. F.
Florida, Historic, Dramatic, Contemporary.

New York, Lewis Historical Pub. Co., 1952. 4 v., index.
NN ITL

Florida 1830 Census Index.
Bountiful, UT, AIS, 1976.

Florida 1840 Census Index.
Bountiful, UT, AIS, 1976.

Florida 1850 Census Index.
Bountiful, UT, AIS, 1976.

Florida State Library.
Genealogy and Local History: A Bibliography. 5th ed.
Tallahassee, Florida State Library, 1975.

Frech, Mary L., ed.
Chronological and Documentary Handbook of the State of Florida.
Dobbs Ferry, NY, Oceana Pub., 1973.

Frisbie, Louise.
Peace River Pioneers.
Miami, E. A. Seaman Pub. Co., 1974. 136 p., index.
(See p. 135–136 for other Florida books published by E. A. Seaman.)
NN ITM (Charlotte Co.) 75-2367

Fritot, Jessie Robinson
Pension Records of Soldiers of the Revolution Who Removed to Florida.
Jacksonville, DAR, 1946. 86 p.
NN APR (Florida)

Gismer, Karl H.
History of St. Petersburg, Historical & Biographical.
St. Petersburg, Tourist News, 1924. 299 p.
NN ITM (St. Petersburg) 73-783

Harris, Michael H.
Florida History.
Metuchen, NJ, Scarecrow Press,
  1972. 257 p.
NN ITL 73-1392

Hawes, Frank M.
New Englanders in the Florida
  Census of 1850.
(IN: *NEHGR*, Boston, MA, 1922.
  v. 76, p. 44–54)
NN *R-APGA

Index to the Archives of Spanish
  West Florida, 1782–1810.
New Orleans, LA, Polyanthos,
  1975. 365 p.

Isern, J.
Pioneros Cubanos en U.S.A., 1575–
  1898.
Miami, c. 1971. 128 p.
NN ICM (Cuba) 74-214

King, Virginia.
Interesting Facts About Leading
  People and Families of Duval
  County, Florida.
Jacksonville, V. King, 1972.

McKay, D. B.
Pioneer Florida.
Tampa, Southern Pub. Co., 1959. 3
  v., index.
NN ITL

Marks, Henry S.
Who Was Who in Florida.
Huntsville, Al, 1973. 276 p.
NN JFF

Martin, Richard.
The City Makers.
Jacksonville, Convention Press,
  1972. 334 p., index.
NN ITM (Jacksonville) 73-439

Morris, Allen.
Florida Place Names.
Coral Gables, U. of Miami Press,
  1974. 160 p.
NN ITL 75-1008

Nance, Ellwood Cecil.
The East Coast of Florida.
Delray Beach, Fl, Southern Pub.
  Co., 1962. 3 v., index.
NN ITL

Pieru, Charles W.
Pioneer Life in Southeast Florida.
Coral Gables, U. of Miami Press,
  1970. 264 p., index.
NN ITM (Palm Beach Co.)

Pompey, Sherman L.
The 1850 Census Record of Dade
  Co., Florida.
Independence, CA, Hist. and Gen.
  Pub., 1965. 5 leaves.

Rosselli, Bruno.
The Italians in Colonial Times: A
  Repertory of Italian Families
  Who Settled in Florida under
  the Spanish, 1513–1762, 1784–
  1821, and British, 1762–1784.
Jacksonville, Drew Press, 1940. 56
  p.
NN IAG p.v. 678

Servtes, James A.
Pensacola and Western Florida.
Pensacola, 1970. unpaged
NN ITM (Pensacola) 73-1906

Shaw, Aurora.
1830 Florida U.S. Census Index.
Jacksonville, 1969. 37 p.
NN APR (Florida)

Shaw, Aurora.
1840 Florida U.S. Census.
Jacksonville, 1968. 44 p.
NN APR (Florida)

Tebeau, Charlton W., and Ruby L. Carson
Florida from Indian Trail to Space Age.
Delray Beach, Southern Pub Co., 1965. 3 v., index.
NN ITL

U.S.W.P.A., Florida.
Guide to Vital Statistics Records in Florida.
Jacksonville, Florida Hist. Records Survey, 1941. 70 f.
NN APR (Florida)

U.S.W.P.A., Florida.
The Seminole Indians in Florida.
Tallahassee, 1941. 87 p.
NN HBC p.v. 303

U.S.W.P.A., Florida.
Land Grants in Florida.
Tallahassee, State Library Board, 1940–41. 5 v.
NN TE

Wey, John
Palm Beach.
Boston, MA, Little, Brown 1966. 303 p. no index.
(Families who were very different from the pioneers)
NN ITM (Palm Beach)

GEORGIA

State Archives

Georgia Department of Archives and History
330 Capitol Avenue
Atlanta, GA 30334

Vital Records

Vital Records Service
State Department of Public Health
47 Trinity Avenue S.W.
Atlanta, GA 30334
Births and deaths: January 1, 1919–
Marriages: June 9, 1952–
Earlier marriages from county clerks or Clerk of the Ordinary Court, county courthouses.

Libraries

Atlanta Public Library
126 Carnegie Way N.W.
Atlanta, GA 30303

Georgia Historical Society Library
501 Whittaker Street
Savannah, GA 31401
(*Georgia Historical Quarterly*, 1917–)
NN IAA

Georgia State Library
301 State Judicial Bldg.
Capitol Hill Station
Atlanta, GA 30334

Georgia State University Archives
104 Decatur Street S.E.
Atlanta, GA 30303

Societies and Periodicals

Family Puzzlers (weekly), 1967–
Mary Bondurant Warren, ed.
Heritage Papers
Danielsville, GA 30633
NN APA+

Georgia Communications/South, Inc.
P.O. Box 7750
Atlanta, GA 30309

Georgia Genealogical Society, Inc.
P.O. Box 38066
Atlanta, GA 30334

(Georgia Genealogical Society Quarterly, 1964–)
NN APR (Georgia)

Georgia Genealogical Magazine, 1961
Rev. Silas Emmett Lucas, ed.
(Founded by Folks Huxford)
P.O. Box 229
Easley, SC 29640
NN APR (Georgia)

Master Index of Georgia Genealogical Magazine
(1961–1972), v. 1–46, 888 p.
(Georgia Genealogical Magazine, Fall 1974, p. 246–248, shows t of c for issues up to 1974 [v. 1–54].)

Northwest Georgia Historical and Genealogical Society
P.O. Box 2484
Rome, GA 30161
(Northwest Georgia Historical and Genealogical Society Quarterly, 1969–)
NN APR (Georgia) 76-703

Richmond County Historical Society
%Augusta College Library
2500 Walton Way
Augusta, GA 30904
(Richmond County Historical Society, 1969–)
NN ITK 75-496

They Were Here, 1965–
Frances Wynd, ed.
2009 Gail Avenue
Albany, GA 31705
NN APR (Georgia)

Books and Articles

Beckemayer, Frances Howell.
Abstracts of Georgia Colonial Conveyance Book C-1, 1750–1761.

Atlanta, R. J. Taylor, Jr., Foundation, 1975. 429 p., index.
(Handsome book, good example)
NN APR (Georgia) 76-1614

Brooke, Ted O.
Georgia Wills 1733–1860: "In the Name of God, Amen," an index . . .
Atlanta, Pilgrim Press, 1976. 224 p., alpha.
NN APR (Georgia) 77-394

Bryan, Mary Givens.
Genealogical Research in Georgia.
(IN: *NSGQ*, Washington, DC, 1952. v. 40, p. 37–49)
NN APGA

Bryan, Mary Givens.
Passports Issued by Governors of Georgia (1785–1820).
Washington, DC, 1962–1964. 2 v., index in v. 2. v. 1, 1785–1809; v. 2, 1810–1820.
(NGS Spec. Pub. no. 21, 28)
NN APGA

DAR, Georgia.
Catalog of the Georgia DAR Collection of Genealogical and Historical Records in the Georgia Department of Archives and History, ed. by Mary Givens Bryan.
Atlanta, 1956. 232 p.
NN APR (Georgia)

Frech, Mary L., ed.
Chronology and Documentary Handbook of the State of Georgia.
(Chronologies and Documentary Handbooks of the States, v. 10)
Dobbs Ferry, NY, Oceana Pub., 1973. 119 p.
NN ITI 75-110

Georgia Department of Archives.
Some Early Tax Digests of Georgia, comp. by Ruth Blair.
Vidalia, GA, Georgia Gen. Reprints, 1971 (orig. 1926).
316, 174 p., index.
NN APR (Georgia)

Georgia 1820 Land Lottery and 1821 Land Lottery.
Easely, SC, Georgia Gen. Reprints, 1972. 2 v.

Georgia 1820 Census Index.
Bountiful, UT, AIS, 1976.

Georgia 1830 Census Index.
Bountiful, UT, AIS, 1976.

Georgia 1840 Census Index.
Bountiful, UT, AIS, 1977.

Georgia 1850 Census Index.
Bountiful, UT, AIS, 1976. 298 p.

The Georgia Genealogist.
Danielsville, GA, Heritage Papers, 1969–.
NN APR (Georgia) 76-1578

Georgia Historical Society.
Index to the United States Census of Georgia for 1820. 2nd ed., rev. ed.
Savannah, 1969 (orig. 1966). 167 p., alpha.
NN APR (Georgia)

Gnann, Pearl Rahn, comp. ed.
Georgia Salzburger and Allied Families. 2nd ed. with additions.
Easley, SC, Southern Historical Press, Sept. 1976. 873 p., index.

Hathaway, Beverly West.
Primer for Georgia Genealogical Research.

West Jordan, UT, Allstates Research Co., 1973. 27 p., no index.
NN APR (Georgia) 74-2198

History of the Baptist Denomination in Georgia.
Easley, SC, Southern Historical Press, n.d.
(Reprint of 1881 edition.) 274, 613 p., alpha bio., bio. index.

Huxford, Folks.
Pioneers of Wiregrass Georgia.
Homersville, the author, 1948–77. 7 v.
NN APR (Georgia)

Krakow, Kenneth K.
Georgia Place Names.
Macon, GA, Winship Press, 1975. 272 p.
NN ITKB 76-580

Lucas, Silas Emmett.
Index of Headright and Bounty Grants of Georgia, 1765–1909.
Vidalia, GA, Georgia Gen. Reprints, 1970. 741 p., alpha.
NN APR (Georgia)

Lucas, Silas Emmett.
The 1832 Gold Lottery of Georgia.
Easley, SC, Southern Historical Press, 1976. 596 p., alpha.

Lucas, Silas Emmett.
The Second or 1807 Land Lottery of Georgia.
Vidalia, GA, Georgia Gen. Reprints, 1968. 215 p.
NN APR (Georgia)

Maddox, Joseph T., and Mary Carter.
37,000 Early Georgia Marriages.
Irwinton, GA, 1975.

National Society of Colonial Dames, Georgia.
Abstracts of Colonial Wills of the State of Georgia 1733–1777, ed. by Mary Givens Bryan, et al.
Atlanta, 1962. 152 p., index.
NN APR (Georgia)

Nichols, Frederick D.
The Architecture of Georgia.
Savannah, The Beehive Press, 1976. 436 p., index.
NN MQWO + 77-751

Overby, Mrs. James C.
Marriages Published in the Christian Index, 1828–1855.
Shady Dale, GA, 1971. 130 p.
NN APR (Georgia) 72-1871

Rainer, Vessie Thrasher.
Henry County, Georgia: The Mother of Counties.
McDonough, GA, 1971. 374 p., no index, long t of c.
NN ITK (Henry Co.) 76-792

Register, Alvaretta K.
Index to the 1830 Census of Georgia.
Baltimore, MD, GPC, 1974. 520 p., alpha.
NN APR (Georgia) 74-1834

Reprint of Official Register of Land Lottery of Georgia, 1827, comp. by Martha Lou Houston.
Easley, SC, Southern Historical Press, 1976 (orig. 1928). 315 p., alpha by county, index.

Savannah Morning News.
Annals of Savannah, 1850–1891.
Savannah, 1961–1976.
NN ITK (Savannah)

Shaw, Aurora C.

U.S. Census (of Counties) of Georgia.
Jacksonville, 1961. 3 pamphlets.
NN APR (Georgia)

Sheffield, Eileen, and Barbara Woods, comp.
1840 Index to Georgia Census. rev. ed.
Baytown, TX, 1971. 315 p.
NN APR (Georgia) 72-1963

Smith, James F.
The 1832 Cherokee Land Lottery

Vidalia, GA, Georgia Gen. Reprints, 1968 (orig. 1838). 413, 73 p.
NN APR (Georgia)

Substitutes for Georgia's Lost 1790 Census.
Albany, GA, Delwyn, 1975. 178 p.
NN APR (Georgia) 77-265

Townsend, Brigid S.
Indexes to Seven State Census Reports for Counties in Georgia 1838–1845.
Atlanta, R. J. Taylor, Jr., Foundation, 1976. 152 p.
NN APR (Georgia) 76-890 no. 1

U.S. Census Office.
7th Census—1850 Georgia Mortality Census.
Jacksonville, FL, 1971. 26, 43 p.
NN APR (Georgia) 75-312

Warren, Mary Bondurant.
Georgia Genealogical Bibliography.
Danielsville, GA, Heritage Papers, 1969.

Warren, Mary Bondurant.
Marriages and Deaths, 1763–1830,

Abstracted from Extant Georgia Newspapers.
Danielsville, GA, Heritage Papers, 1968–71. 2 v. (v. 1, 1763–1820; v. 2, 1820–1830)
NN APR (Georgia) 73-1308

Wood, Ralph V., and Virginia S. Wood.
1805 Georgia Land Lottery.
Cambridge, MA, 1964. 393 p.
NN APR (Georgia)

HAWAII

State Archives

Hawaii State Archives
Iolani Palace Grounds
Honolulu, HI 96813

Vital Records

Research and Statistics Office
State Department of Health
P.O. Box 3378
Honolulu, HI 96801
Births, deaths and marriages since 1853.

Libraries

DAR Memorial Library
1914 Makiki Heights Drive
Honolulu, HI 96822

Laie Hawaii State Branch
Genealogical Library
Church College of Hawaii
Laie, HI 96762

Library of Hawaii
King and Punchbowl Streets
Honolulu, HI 96813

Societies and Periodicals

Daughters of Hawaii
2913 Pali Highway
Honolulu, HI 96817

Hawaii County Library
Box 471
Lihue, HI 96766

Hawaiian Historical Society
560 Kawaiahao Street
Honolulu, HI 96813
(*The Hawaiian Journal of History*, 1967–; *Genealogical Notes*, 1915–1922, v. 1–3)

Hawaiian Mission Children's Society
553 South King Street
Honolulu, HI 96813

Maui County Free Library
Box B
Wailuku, HI 96793

Books and Articles

Bailey, Paul D.
Those Kings and Queens of Old Hawaii.
Los Angeles, CA, Westernlore Books, 1976. 381 p., index, ports.
NN IXS 76-1979

Bradley, Harold W.
The American Frontier in Hawaii: The Pioneers, 1789–1843.
Stanford, CA, Stanford U. Press, 1942. 488 p.
NN *RR-BIC

Brennan, Joseph.
The Parker Ranch of Hawaii: The Saga of a Ranch and a Dynasty.
New York, John Day, 1974. 220 p., index.
NN IXS 75-449

Gallagher, Charles F.
Hawaii and Its Gods.
New York, Weatherhill, 1975. 150
p., t of c, no index.
NN IXS 76-339

Hawaiian Gazette Co., Ltd.
Hawaii Nei ... Biographical
Sketches . . . Including the His-
tory of Honolulu for a Hundred
Years.
Honolulu, 1899. 123 p.
NN BIB+

Joesting, Edward.
Hawaii: An Uncommon History.
New York, W. W. Norton, 1972.
353 p., index.
NN IXS 73-1288

Kort, Blanch L.
A Biographical Record of Ameri-
cans of Japanese Ancestry
(State of Hawaii).
Honolulu, Stowe, 1963. 106 p.
NN F-109975

Kuykendall, Ralph S.
The Hawaiian Kingdom.
Honolulu, U. of Hawaii Press,
1947-67. 3 v., index each v.
NN IXS

Mellen, Kathleen D.
The Lonely Warrior: The Life and
Times of Kamehameha the
Great of Hawaii.
New York, Hastings House, 1949.
179 p.
NN BIC

Men and Women of Hawaii.
Honolulu, P. E. Hilleary, 1954–.
NN *R-AGS and AGS

Pole, James T.
Hawaii's First King.

Indianapolis, IN, Bobbs-Merrill,
1959. 191 p.
NN D-12 1997

Porteus, Stanley D.
Calabashes and Kings.
Rutland, VT, Tuttle, 1974. 129 p.
NN IXS 72-1957

Pukui, Mary W.
Place Names of Hawaii.
Honolulu, U. of Hawaii Press,
1974. 289 p., alpha.
NN IXS 75-2293

Rubincam, Milton.
The Hawaiian Royal Family.
(IN: *NSGQ*, Washington, DC, Spe-
cial Pub. #43, 1976, 15 p.; *NSGQ*,
Washington, DC, 1962, v. 50, p.
79–81; *TAG*, New Haven, CT,
1956, v. 32, p. 65–71)
NN APGA

Slidell, John W.
Men of Hawaii.
Honolulu, Star Bulletin, 1917–1921.
2 v., 291, 464 p.
NN AGS

Smith, Carl Thurman.
They Went West
(IN: *PGM*, Philadelphia, PA, 1972.
v. 27, p. 248–255)
NN APR (Pennsylvania)

The Story of Hawaii and Its Build-
ers.
Honolulu, Star Bulletin, 1925. 915
p. NN AGS

Waldron, Elsie.
Honolulu 100 Years Ago.
Honolulu, the author, 1967. 106 p.,
t of c, no index.
NN IXT (Honolulu)

Who's Who in Hawaii.
Honolulu, 1947–.
NN AGS

IDAHO

State Archives

Idaho State Historical Society
610 North Julia Davis Drive
Boise, ID 83706

Vital Records

Bureau of Vital Statistics
State Department of Health
State House
Boise, ID 83720
Births and deaths: 1911–
Births and deaths: 1907–11,
County Recorder
Marriages: 1947–
Early marriages: County Recorder

Societies and Periodicals

Bannock County Historical Society
Box 253
Pocatello, ID 83201

Bonner County Historical Society
Second Avenue
Sandpoint, ID 93964

Church of Jesus Christ of Latter-day Saints
Boise Idaho Branch Genealogical Library
325 State Street
Boise, ID 83702

Historical Society of Boundary County, Idaho

% Mrs. Gale Plato
Route 1, Box 91
Bonners Ferry, ID 83805

Idaho Genealogical Society
325 State Street
Boise, ID 83702
(*Idaho Genealogical Society Quarterly*, 1958–)
NN APR (Idaho)

Idaho State Historical Society
610 North Julia Davis Drive
Boise, ID 83706
(*Idaho Yesterdays*, 1957–)
NN IXL

Intermountain Historical and Genealogical Society
% Frank L. Fry, Jr.
Box 788
McCall, ID 93638

Lemhi County Historical Society
Box 1114
Salmon, ID 83467

Minidoka County Historical Society
625 "E" Street
Rupert, ID 83350

Owyhee County Historical Society
Murphy, ID 83650
(*Owyhee Outpost*)

Twin Falls County Historical Society, Inc.
Route 2
Filer, ID 83326

Upper Snake River Valley Historical Society
24 College Avenue
Rexburg, ID 83440
(*Upper Snake River Valley Historical Society Quarterly*)

Books and Articles

Idaho Genealogical Society.
The First Census of Idaho, 1870, Plus Mortality Schedules Indexed.
Boise, ID, Idaho Gen. Soc., 1973. 218 p.
NN APR (Idaho) 74-1350

Idaho Poet's and Writer's Guild.
The Idaho Story.
Iona, Ipas Pub., 1967–68. 2 v., index each v.
NN IXMB

An Illustrated History of North Idaho.
n.p., Western Hist. Pub. Co., 1903. 1,238 p.
NN IXL +

Pompey, Sherman Lee.
The 1870 Census Records of the Lincoln Valley, Oneida Territory, Idaho Territory.
Bakersfield, CA, Hist. and Gen. Pub. Co., c. 1966.

Williams, Thomas H.
Miracle of the Desert: A History of Thomas Ward and Surrounding Counties.
Blackfoot, ID, 1957. 617 p., index to family histories.
NN IXM (Bingham)

ILLINOIS

State Archives

Illinois State Archives
Archives Bldg.
Springfield, IL 62706

Vital Records

Office of Vital Records
State Department of Public Health
535 West Jefferson Street
Springfield, IL 62761
Births and deaths: 1916–
Marriages: 1962–
Births, deaths and marriages prior: county clerk

Libraries

Clark County Genealogical Society and Library
P.O. Box 153
Marshall, IL 62441

Church of Jesus Christ of Latter-day Saints
Champaign, Illinois, State Branch Genealogical Library
Illinois State Center
604 West Windsor Road
Champaign, IL 61820

Illinois State Historical Library
Old State Capitol
Springfield, IL 62706
(*Illinois State Historical Society Collections*, 1903–)
NN IAA

Newberry Library
60 West Walton Street
Chicago, IL 60610

Societies and Periodicals

Blackhawk Genealogical Society
P.O. Box 912
Rock Island, IL 61201
(*Blackhawk Genealogical Society Quarterly*, 1974–)

Bloomington–Normal Genealogical Society

P.O. Box 432
Normal, IL 61761
(*Gleanings from the Heart of the Cornbelt*, 1967–)
NN APR (Bloomington)

Chicago Genealogical Society
P.O. Box 1160
Chicago, IL 60690
(*Chicago Genealogist*, 1967–)
NN APR Chicago 73-254

Chicago Historical Society
North Avenue and Clark Street
Chicago, IL 60657

Coles County Historical Society
Box 255
Charleston, IL 61920
(*Coles Historical Series*)

Commission on Archives and History
1121 North Park Street
Bloomington, IL 61701
(*The Historical Messenger*)

Cumberland and Coles County of Illinois Genealogical Society
Route 1, Box 141
Toledo, IL 62468
(*Quarterly*, 1971–)

Cumberland County History and Genealogical Society of Illnois
Greenup, IL 62428
(*The Happy Hunter*, 1966–)
NN APR (Cumberland Co.)

Decatur Genealogical Society
P.O. Box 2068
Decatur, IL 62526
(*Central Illinois Genealogical Quarterly*, 1965–)
NN APR (Macon Co.)

DeWitt County Genealogical Society

Box 329
Clinton, IL 61727

Evanston Historical Society
225 Greenwood Avenue
Evanston, IL 60201
(*Fountain Square Recalls*)

Federation of Genealogical Societies
333 North Michigan Avenue
Suite 1500
Chicago, IL 60601

Frankfort Area Historical Society of Will County
27 Ash Street
Frankfort, IL 60423
(Mail: % Marie Tewes, Route 1, Frankfort, IL 60423)
(*Frankfort Lore*)

Fulton County Historical and Genealogical Society
% Mrs. Charles V. Petrovich
1040 North Main Street
Canton, IL 61520

Genealogical Society of DeKalb County, Illinois
P.O. Box 295
Sycamore, IL 60178
(*Cornsilks*)

Genealogical Society of Southern Illinois
% John A. Logan College
Carterville, IL 62918
(*Newsletter*, 1972–)

Great River Genealogical Society
% Quincy Public Library
Quincy, IL 62301
(*Yellowjacket*)

Illiana Genealogical and Historical Society

P.O. Box 207
Danville, IL 61832
(*Illiana Genealogist*, 1965–)
NN APR (Illinois)

Illinois Mennonite Historical and
Genealogical Society
918 South University
Normal, IL 61761
(*Mennonite Heritage*, 1974–)

Illinois State Genealogical Society
P.O. Box 2225
Springfield, IL 62705
(*Illinois State Genealogical Society
Quarterly*, 1969–)
NN APR (Illinois) 73-2861

Illinois State Historical Society
Old State Capitol
Springfield, IL 62706
(*Journal of the Illinois State His-
torical Society*)

Iroquois County Genealogical So-
ciety
Old Courthouse Museum
103 West Cherry Street
Watseka, IL 60970
(*The Iroquois Stalker*)

Jacksonville   Area   Genealogical
and Historical Society
P.O. Box 21
Jacksonville, IL 62651
(*Genealogical Journal*)

Kankakee Valley Genealogical Society
304 South Indiana Avenue
Kankakee, IL 60901
(*Theakiki*)

Knox County Genealogical Society
(Illinois)
P.O. Box 13
Galesburg, IL 61401

(*Knox County Genealogical Society
Quarterly*, 1973–)

Lexington Genealogical and Historical Society
304 North Elm Street
Lexington, IL 61753
(*Ancestors, Yours and Mine*, 1975–)

Marissa Historical and Genealogi-
cal Society
P.O. Box 27
Marissa, IL 62257
(*Branching Out from St. Clair
County, Illinois*)

Moultrie County Historical and
Genealogical Society
P.O. Box MM
Sullivan, IL 61951
(*Moultrie County Heritage*, 1973–)

Northern Illinois Historical Soci-
ety
Box 50
Grayslake, IL 60030 (*Northern
Historical Record*)

Peoria Genealogical Society
P.O. Box 1489
Peoria, IL 61602
(*Prairie Roots*, 1974–)

Poplar Creek Genealogical Society
of Streamwood
209 Egan Drive
Streamwood, IL 60103
(*Poplar Creek Genealogical Newsletter*)

Rockford Historical Society
211 North Main Street
Rockford, IL 61101
(Mail: 1614 Huffman Blvd, Rock-
ford, IL 61103)
(*Nuggets of History*)

Sangamon County Genealogical Society
P.O. Box 1829
Springfield, IL 62705
(*The Circuit Rider/Sangamon County Genealogical Society Quarterly*, 1968–)

Schuyler-Brown Historical Society
Congress and Madison Streets
Rushville, IL 62681
(*Schuylerite*)

Southern Illinois Genealogical Society
901 Roberta Drive
Murphysboro, IL 62966

South Suburban Genealogical Society
P.O. Box 96
South Holland, IL 60473
(*Where the Trails Cross*, 1970–)

Thornton Township Historical Society/Genealogical Section
154 East 154th Street
Harvey, IL 60426
(*Thornton Township Historical Society Newsletter*)

United Methodist Church Central Illinois Conference Commission on Archives and History
1121 North Park Street
Bloomington, IL 61701

Waukegan Historical Society
1917 North Sheridan Road
Waukegan, IL 60085
(*Historically Speaking*)

Zion Historical Society
1300 Shiloh Blvd.
Zion, IL 60099
(*What's in Zion*)

Books and Articles

Brichford, Maynard J., et al.
Manuscripts Guide to Collections at the University of Illinois at Urbana-Champaign, Ill.
Urbana, U. of IL Press, 1976. 384 p., index.

Chicago Census Report and Statistical Review.
Chicago, Rich Edwards, 1871. 1,-264 p.
(Name of head of household, address, occupation, ward number, number of males and of females, total number in house, place of birth, county or state)
NN IVF (Chicago)

Chicago City Directories.
1839/1850–1917/1923/1928/1929.
Chicago, U. Of Chicago, n.d. 74 reels.
NN *ZAN-G80

Decatur Genealogical Society
Agenda for County, State and National Research.
Decatur, IL, 1967. 34 p.
NN APB 75-2095

Downs, Robert B.
Guide to Illinois Library Resources.
Chicago, 1974. 564 p.
NN *R-*HND 75-4875

1850 Federal Census of Illinois: Champaign, Stark, Wabash and Winnebago Counties.
Chicago, Chicago Gen. Soc., c. 1975–, 4 v.

1850 Federal Census of Illinois: Saline, Henry, Hancock, Johnson, and Gallatin Counties (counties so far completed)

Richland, WA, Tri-City Gen. Soc.,
c. 1975–, 5 v.

Gill, James V., and Maryan R.
Gill, comp.
Index to the 1830 Federal Census
... Illinois.
Danville, Heritage House,
1968–1970. 2 v.
NN APR (Illinois) 72-89

A Guide to Record Holdings of
the Illinois State Archives.
Springfield, IL, Sec. of State, c. 1976.

Illinois 1820 Census Index.
Bountiful, UT, AIS, 1977. 155 p.

Illinois 1830 Census Index.
Bountiful, UT, AIS, 1976.

Illinois 1840 Census Index.
Bountiful, UT AIS, 1977

Illinois 1850 Census Index.
Bountiful, UT, AIS, 1977

... Illinois Marriage Records.
Litchfield, IL, W. R. Sanders, 1969–,
c. 1970. 7 v. in 2.

Illinois Periodical Index.
(IN: *Illinois State Gen. Soc. Quarterly*, Springfield, 1969. v. 1 p. 9–42)
NN APR (Illinois) 73-2861

Lee, George R.
The Beaubiens of Chicago.
Canton, MO, 1973. 84 p.
NN APV (Beaubien) 74-1386

Lowe, David.
The Chicagoans.
New York, Lippincott, 1978.

Lowe, David.
Lost Chicago.
Boston, MA, Houghton Mifflin,
1975. 241 p., index.
NN IVF (Chicago) 76-1420

The Mereness Calendar: Federal
Documents on the Upper Mississippi Valley, 1780–1890.
Boston, MA, G. K. Hall, 1971. 13 v.

Taylor, Lola B.
Gleanings from Old Newspapers,
Clay and Richland Counties, Illinois.
Olney, IL, Taylor Print Shop, 1975.
2 v., 375 p.
NN APR (Richland Co.) 72-1887

Vital Records from Chicago Newspapers.
Chicago, Chicago Gen. Soc.,
1971–76. 5 v. (Covers 1833–46).
NN APR (Chicago) 73-21

Volkel, Lowell M.
1850 Indiana Mortality Schedules.
Danielsville, IL, 1971. 3 v.
NN APR (Indiana) 74-1000

Volkel, Lowell M.
Genealogy in Illinois.
(IN: *NGSQ*, Washington, DC, 1975.
v. 62 p. 163–71)
NN APGA

Volkel, Lowell M. and James V
Gill.
1820 Federal Census of Illinois.
Danville, Illiana Pub. Co., 1966. 1
v., unpaged. NN APR (Illinois)

U.S.W.P.A. Illinois.
Macon County Marriage Records
(1829–1880)

Decatur Co. Hist. Soc., 1967–69.
(orig. 1940). 4 v.
NN APR (Macon Co., Illinois

Wolf, Joseph C.
A Reference Guide for Genealogical Research in Illinois.
Detroit, MI, Detroit Soc. for Gen. Research, 1963. 140 p.
NN APR (Macon Co., Illinois)

Wormer, Maxine E.
Illinois 1840 Census Index.
Thomson, IL, Heritage House, 1973–75. 3 v.
(Adams-Marshall Co.)
NN APR (Illinois) 75-2092

INDIANA

State Archives

Genealogy Division
Indiana State Library
140 North Senate Avenue
Indianapolis, IN 46204

Vital Records

Division of Vital Records
State Board of Health
1330 West Michigan Street
Indianapolis, IN 46206
Births: October 1907–
Deaths: 1900–
Births and deaths prior: Health Officer of county or city
Marriages: 1958–: For earlier records write Clerk of Circuit Court or Clerk of Superior Court.

Libraries

American Legion National Headquarters Library

700 North Pennsylvania Street
Indianapolis, IN 46204

Byron R. Lewis Historical Library
Vincennes University
1002 North 1st Street
Vincennes, IN 47591

Church of Jesus Christ of Latter-day Saints
Indianapolis, Indiana, Branch Genealogical Library
State Center
900 East Stop 11 Road
Indianapolis, IN 46206

Indiana Historical Society Library
William Henry Smith Memorial Library
140 North Senate Avenue
Indianapolis, IN 46204
Genealogical Section
(*Hoosier Genealogist*, 1961–)
NN APR (Indiana)

Public Library of Fort Wayne and Allen County
900 Webster
Fort Wayne, IN 46802

Societies and Periodicals

Allen County–Fort Wayne Historical Society
1424 West Jefferson Street
Fort Wayne, IN 46804
(*Old Fort News; Old Fort Bulletin*)

Archives of DePauw University and Indiana Methodism
Roy O. West Library
DePauw University
Greencastle, IN 46135

Conner Prairie Pioneer Settlement
30 Conner Lane

Noblesville, IN 46060
(*Conner Prairie Peddler*)

Daviess County Genealogical Society
% Eleanor Purdue, Secretary
703 Front Street
Washington, IN 47501
(*The Forks*)

Delaware County Genealogical Society
Rodney Qualkinbush, President
2314 Rosewood Avenue
Muncie, IN 47305

East Chicago Historical Society
2401 East Columbus Drive
East Chicago, IN 46312

Elkhart County Genealogical Society
660 Strong Avenue
Elkhart, IN 46514
(*Michiana Searcher*, 1969–)

Francis Vigo Chapter of the Daughters of the American Revolution
3 West Scott Street
Vincennes, IN 47591
(Mail: 427 North Second Street, Vincennes IN 47591)

Fulton County Historical Society
Race Street
Rochester, IN 46975
(Mail: Route 2, Rochester, IN 46975)
(*Fulton County Historical Society Quarterly*)

Henry County Historical Society
614 South 14th Street
New Castle, IN 47362
(*Henry County Historicalog*)

Illiana Genealogical and Historical Society
P.O. Box 207
Danville, IL 61832
(*Illiana Genealogist*, 1965–)
NN APR (Illinois)

Indiana Historical Society
140 North Senate Avenue
Indianapolis, IN 46204
(*Indiana Magazine of History*, 1905–)
NN IAA

Indiana Historical Society
Indiana University
Bloomington, IN 47405

Jasper County Historical Society
624 West Clark Street
Rensselaer, IN 47978
(*Historical Society Bulletin of Jasper County*)

Kosciusko County Genealogical Society
% Mrs. Cloice E. Metzger, President
Route 2, Box 463
Warsaw, IN 46580
(*Kosciusko County Genealogical Newsletter*)

Miami County Genealogical Society
% Ray Bakehorn
Rural Route 3
Kokomo, IN 46901
(*The Genealogist*)

Northeastern Indiana Historical Society
Route 1
LaGrange, IN 46761

Northern Indiana Historical Society

112 South Lafayette Blvd.
South Bend, IN 46601
(*Old Courthouse News*)

North Central Genealogical Society
% Mrs. Floyd Bixler
609 Maple Street
Monticello, IN 47960

Northwest Indiana Genealogical Society
Purdue-North Central
Westville, IN 46391

Pulaski County Genealogical Society
% Mrs. Orval Burgess
Rural Route 1
Winamac, IN 46996

Society of Indiana Pioneers
140 North Senate Avenue
Indianapolis, IN 46204

Sullivan County Historical Society, Inc.
P.O. Box 326-G
Sullivan, IN 47882
(*Sullivan County Historical Society Newsletter*)

The Wesleyan Church Archives and Historical Library
50th Street and State Road 37
Marion, IN 46952
(Mail: Box 2000, Marion, IN 46952)
(*The Wesleyan Advocate*)

Tippecanoe County Historical Association
Lafayette, IN 47901
(*Weatenotes*)

University of Notre Dame Archives
Box 513

University of Notre Dame
South Bend, IN 46556

Vigo County Historical Society
1411 South 6th Street
Terre Haute, IN 47802
(*Leaves of Thyme*, 1950–)
NN ISD (Vigo Co.)

Books and Articles

Family Fare.
Fort Wayne, 1961–. (A quarterly list of additions to the Reynolds Hist. Collection of the Fort Wayne Pub. Lib.)
NN APGA 73-388

Heiss, Willard, comp.
1820 Federal Census for Indiana.
Indianapolis, Indiana Hist. Soc., 1966. 461 columns.
NN APR (Indiana)

Heiss, Willard.
Guide to Research in Quaker Records in the Midwest.
Indianapolis, Indiana Quaker Rec., 1962. 30 p.
NN APB p.v. 169

Heiss, Willard.
Who's Your Hoosier Ancestor?
(Reprint of columns in Indianapolis *Times*, Sunday edition)
Indianapolis, 1963–65. 3 v., index each v.
NN APR (Indiana)

Hoosier Ancestor Index
(1963–73), comp. by Eloise R. Means.

Indianapolis, 1969–74. 4 v.
NN APR (Indiana) 72–171

Indiana 1820 Census Index.
Bountiful, UT, AIS, 1976.

Indiana 1830 Census Index
Bountiful, UT, AIS, 1976.

Indiana 1840 Census Index.
Bountiful, UT, AIS, 1977.

Indiana 1850 Census Index.
Bountiful, UT, AIS, 1977.

Indiana 1850 Census Index.
Indianapolis, Indiana State Lib.
Gen. Div., 1975.

McCay, Leonard G.
Indiana Ancestors Index.
Indianapolis, 1975. v. 1.
NN APR (Indiana) 76–099

United States Census Office. 6th
Census of Indiana.
Index to 1840 Federal Population
Census of Indiana.
Indianapolis, Indiana Hist. Soc.,
1975. 374 p., index.
NN APR (Indiana) 76-2143

Volkel, Lowell M.
1850 Indiana Mortality Schedule.
Thomson, IL, V. M. Volkel, 1971.
(v. 1, Adams through Harrison
counties; v. 2, Hendricks
through Posey counties; v. 3,
Pulaski through Whitley counties; index each volume)
NN APR (Indiana) 74–1000

Wendell, Carolynne L.
Aids for Genealogical Searching in
Indiana. rev. ed

Detroit, MI, Detroit Soc. for Gen.
Research, 1970 (orig. 1962). 154
p.
NN APR (Indiana)

IOWA

State Archives

Iowa State Department of History
and Archives
East 12th Street and Grand Ave-
nue.
Historical Bldg.
Des Moines, IA 50319

Vital Records

Division of Records and Statistics
State Department of Health
Des Moines, IA 50319
Births and deaths: July 1880–
Marriages: also from state office.
Early marriage records, kept by
clerks of district courts, begin
1837 or after.

Libraries

Church of Jesus Christ of Latter-
day Saints
Des Moines State Branch Genealogical Library
3301 Ashworth Road
West Des Moines, IA 50265

Iowa Historical and Genealogical
Library
Iowa Department of History and
Archives
East 12th Street and Grand Ave-
nue
Des Moines, IA 50319
(*Annals of Iowa*, 1863–)
NN IAA

State Historical Society of Iowa Library
University of Iowa
Box 871
Iowa City, IA 52240

Societies and Periodicals

Adair County Anquestors Genealogical Society
Mrs. Ethel Handley
Route 2, Box 113
Greenfield, IA 50849

Boone County Historical Society
811 Keeler Street
Boone, IA 50036
(Mail: 1521 Carroll Street, Boone, IA 50036)
(*Trail-Tales*)

Central Iowa Genealogical Society
P.O. Box 493
Albion, IA 50005

Des Moines County Genealogical Society
P.O. Box 493
Burlington, IA 52601
(*Des Moines County Genealogical Quarterly*)

Dubuque County Historical Society
Box 305
Dubuque, IA 52001

Iowa County Historical Society
Box 237
Williamsburg, IA 52361
(*Vignette*)

Iowa Genealogical Society
P.O. Box 3815
6000 Douglas
Des Moines, IA 50322

(Has many local chapters in counties and towns)
(*Hawkeye Heritage*, 1966–)
NN APR (Iowa) 74-860

Key City Genealogical Society
% Dubuque Public Library
1862 Central Avenue
Dubuque, IA 52001

Lee County Genealogical Society of Iowa
P.O. Box 303
Keokuk, IA 52632

Linn County Heritage Society, Inc.
P.O. Box 175
Cedar Rapids, IA 52402

Midwest Old Settlers and Threshers Association, Inc.
Route 4
Mount Pleasant, IA 52641

Muscatine Area Heritage Association, Inc.
705 West 4th Street
Muscatine, IA 52761
(*Muscatine Area Heritage Review*)

North Central Iowa Genealogical Society
% Mrs. Merle Behne
Route 3, 35th Street N.E.
Mason City, IA 50401
(*Genie Bug*)

Southwest Iowa Genealogical Society
P.O. Box 93
New Market, IA 51646

State Historical Society of Iowa
402 Iowa Avenue
Iowa City, IA 52240
(*The Palimpsest*, 1920–)
NN IAA

Sunday Gazette
Box 175
Cedar Rapids, IA 52406
("Dear Genie" column; must have
Iowa connections)

Wright County Genealogical
Searchers
1002 First Avenue S.E.
Clarion, IA 50525

Books and Articles

Gingerich, Mary A.
Cemetery Directory of Amish and
Mennonites in Iowa, Johnson,
and Washington Counties of
Iowa.
Kalowa, IA, 1972. 279 p., index.
NN APR (Iowa Co.)

Iowa 1850 Census Index.
Bountiful, UT, AIS, 1976. 115 p.

Iowa Territorial 1836 Census Index.
Bountiful, UT, AIS, 1976.

McCracken, George E.
Genealogical Resources in the
Iowa Archives.
(IN: *NSGQ*, Washington, DC, 1953.
v. 41, p. 67–69)
NN APGA

Obert, Rowene T., Helen M. Blum-
hagen, and Wilma Adkins.
The 1840 Iowa Census; Census of
the 18 Original Counties and
Several Precincts Which Comprised the Area Then Known
as Iowa.
Salt Lake City, UT, H. M. Blum-
hagen, 1968. 342 p., index.
NN APR (Iowa)

Swisher, Emelyn.
Some Sources of Genealogical Ma-
terial in Iowa.
(IN: *The Kansas City Genealogist*,
Kansas City, MO, 1963. v. 3, p.
3–6)
NN APR (Kansas City)

Who's Who in Des Moines.
Des Moines, 1929–. 1 v., 280 p.,
alpha, ports.
NN IVO (Des Moines)

KANSAS

State Archives

Kansas State Historical Society
Memorial Bldg.
120 West 10th Street
Topeka, KS 66612
(*Kansas Historical Quarterly*,
1931–)
NN IAA

Vital Records

Division of Registration and
Health Statistics
6700 S. Topeka Avenue
Topeka, KS 66620
Births and deaths: July 1911–
Births and deaths prior: county
clerk
Marriages: May 1913–
Marriages prior: dates vary, 1860
and later.
Write Probate Judge of county.

Libraries

Bethel Historical Library
Bethel College
North Newton, KS 67114

Church of Jesus Christ of Latter-
day Saints
Wichita, Kansas, State Branch Genealogical Library
7011 East 13th Street
Wichita, KS 67206

Mennonite Library and Archives
Bethel College
North Newton, KS 67117

Public Library
Sixth and Minnesota Streets
Kansas City, KS 66101

Wichita City Library
220 South Main Street
Wichita, KS 67202

Societies and Periodicals

Ameri-Kan Genealogical Society
2200 Hope Street
Topeka, KS 66604

East Central Kansas Genealogical
Society
P.O. Box 78
Iola, KS 66749

Finney County Genealogical Society
Garden City Public Library
210 North 7th
Garden City, KS 67846

Fort Hayes, Kansas, Genealogical
Society
% Marc Campbell, Librarian
Kansas College Library
Fort Hayes, KS 67601

Heritage Genealogical Society
W. A. Rankin Memorial Library
Neodesha, KS 66757

(*Heritage Genealogical Society
Quarterly*, 1971–)
NN APR (Wilson Co., Kansas) 74-
538

Johnson County Genealogical Soci-
ety
P.O. Box 8057
Shawnee Mission, KS 66208
(*The Johnson County Genealogist*)

Kansas Council of Genealogical Societies
10821 West 91st Street
Overland Park, KS 66214
(*Newsletter*)

Kansas East Commission on Archives and History
606 8th Street
United Methodist Historical Library
Baldwin City, KS 66006

Kansas Genealogical Society
P.O. Box 103
Dodge City, KS 67801
(*Tree Searcher*, 1959–)
NN APR (Kansas)

Midwest Genealogical Society, Inc.
2911 Rivera
Wichita, KS 67211
(*Midwest Genealogical Register*,
1966–)
NN APR (Kansas)

Montgomery County Genealogical
Society
Box 444
Coffeyville, KS 67337
(*The Descender*, 1968–)
NN APR (Montgomery Co.) 73-
1050

Old Fort Genealogical Society of
Southeast Kansas

2108 South Horton Street
Fort Scott, KS 66701

Riley County Genealogical Society
908 Kearney Street
Manhattan, KS 66502
(*Kansas Kin*, 1963–)
NN APR (Riley Co.)

Shawnee County Historical Society
Box 178
Topeka, KS 66601
(*Bulletin*)

Sherman County Historical and
  Genealogical Society
P.O. Box 684
Goodland, KS 67735
(*Sherman County Historical and
  Genealogical Society Newsletter*)

Southeast Kansas Genealogical Society of Crawford County
% Pittsburg Public Library
109 West Jackson Street
Pittsburg, KS 66762

Thomas County Genealogical Society
% Thomas County Historical Society
375 West 4th Street
Colby, KS 67701

Topeka Genealogical Society
P.O. Box 4048
Topeka, KS 66604
(*Topeka   Genealogical   Society
  Quarterly*, 1971–)
NN APR (Topeka) 74-116
(*Textbook*, 1970, 93 leaves)
NN APR (Kansas) 73-2842

Wilson County Historical Society
Courthouse
Fredonia, KS 66736
(*Our Yesteryears*)

Books and Articles

Anderson, Lorene.
A Bibliography of Town and
  County Histories of Kansas.
(IN: *Kansas Historical Quarterly*,
  Topeka, 1955. v. 21, p. 513–551)
NN IAA

Curtis, Mary Barneet.
Kansas, the Formative Years.
(IN: *Magazine of Bibliographies*,
  ed. by Lalla Campbell Critz.
  Fort Worth, TX, Dec. 1972. v. 1,
  no. 2)

Heiss, Willard.
The Census of the Territory of
  Kansas, February, 1855, with
  Index and Map of the Kansas
  Election Districts in 1854.
Knightstown, IN, Eastern Indi-
  ana Pub. Co.; 1968. 38 p.
NN APR (Kansas)

Kansas Pioneers.
Topeka, Topeka Gen. Soc., 1976. v.
  1, index.
NN APR (Kansas) 77-387

Kansas Territorial 1855 Census
  Index.
Bountiful, UT, AIS, 1976

Miller, Nyle H.
Why the West Went Wild: A Contemporary Look at Some of the
  Antics of Some Highly Publi-
  cized Kansas Cowtown Personalities.
Topeka, Kansas State Hist. Soc.,
  1963. 685 p.
NN IWA

Pantle, Alberta.
Death Notices from Kansas Territorial Newspapers, 1854–1861.

(IN: *Kansas Historical Quarterly*, Topeka, 1950. v. 18, p. 302–323)
NN IAA

Pantle, Alberta.
Marriage Notices from Kansas Territorial Newspapers, 1854–1861.
(IN: *Kansas Historical Quarterly*, Topeka, 1955. v. 21, p. 445–486)
NN IAA

Pioneers of the Bluestem Prairie: Kansas Counties—Clay, Geary, Marshall, Pottawatomie, Riley, Waubaunsee, and Washington.
Manhattan, Riley Co. Hist. Soc., 1976. 608 p.
NN APR (Riley Co.)

Robertson, Clara H.
Kansas Territorial Settlers of 1860 Who Were Born in Tennessee, Virginia, North Carolina and South Carolina.
Baltimore, MD, GPC, 1976. 187 p., alpha.
NN APR (Kansas) 77-209

Shackleton, Bernice C.
Handbook on the Frontier Days of Southeast Kansas.
Kansas Centennial, 1861–1961. Pittsburg, KS, 1961. 141 p.
NN IWBB

Shawnee County Cemeteries. Volume I: Small Cemeteries in the City of Topeka.
Topeka, KS, Topeka Gen. Soc., 1973. 57 p.

Swan, Robert A., Jr.
The Ethnic Heritage of Topeka, Kansas, Immigrant Beginnings.

Topeka, 1974. 178 p. t of c, no index.
NN IWB (Topeka) 75-1193

U.S.W.P.A., Kansas.
Guide to Public Vital Statistics.
Topeka, 1942. 262 F.
NN APR (Kansas)

Wichita Century: A Pictorial History of Wichita, Kansas, 1870–1970.
Wichita, McCormick, Armstrong, 1970. 272 p., no index.
NN IWB (Wichita) 71-623

KENTUCKY

State Archives

Kentucky Historical Society Library
200-202 Broadway
Frankfort, KY 40601

Vital Records

Office of Vital Statistics
State Department of Health
275 East Main Street
Frankfort, KY 40601
Births and deaths: January 1911–
Births and deaths prior for Louisville and Lexington: Write State Department of Health. Births and deaths prior for Covington: City Health Department.
Marriages: July 1958–
Earlier marriages: clerk of county court

Libraries

Filson Club Library
118 West Breckinridge Street
Louisville, KY 40203

John Fox Memorial Library
DAR Shrine
Duncan Tavern Street
Paris, KY 40361

Louisville Free Public Library
Fourth and York Streets
Louisville, KY 40203

Owensboro-Daviess County Public
   Library
Kentucky Room
Local History and Genealogy
450 Griffith Avenue
Owensboro, KY 42301

Societies and Periodicals

Ancestral Trails Historical Society
P.O. Box 573
Vine Grove, KY 40175

Central Kentucky Genealogical So-
   ciety
P.O. Box 153
Frankfort, KY 40601
(*Bluegrass Roots*)

(*East Kentuckian*, 1965–) NN APR
   (Kentucky) 72-964
P.O. Box 107
Stanville, KY 41659

(*Falling Leaves*, 1971–) NN APR
   (Kentucky) 75-233
1640 Newport Boulevard, S-41
Costa Mesa, CA 92627

Filson Club
118 West Breckinridge Street
Louisville, KY 40203
(*Filson Club History Quarterly*,
   1926–)
NN IAA +

Fulton Genealogical Society

Fulton, KY 42041
(*The Society*, 1974–)

Hart County Historical Society
Hart County Library
Box 86, Third Street
Munfordville, KY 42765
(*Hart County Historical Quart-
   erly*)

(*Kentucky Genealogist*, 1959–) NN
   APR (Kentucky), index each v.
Martha Porter Miller, ed.
Box 4894
Washington, DC 20008

Kentucky Historical Society
P.O. Box H
Frankfort, KY 40601
(*Kentucky Ancestors*, 1965–) NN
   APR Kentucky; (*The Register*,
   1903–)
NN IAA

Madison County Historical Society
120 West Main Street
Richmond, KY 40475
(*Kentucky Pioneer*)

Northern Kentucky Historical Society, Inc.
37 East 4th Street
Newport, KY 41071
(*Northern Kentucky Bulletin*)

Research Historians
Route 23 and 460 North
Paintsville, KY 41240
(*The Eastern Kentucky Historian*)

South Central Kentucky Genea-
   logical Society
% Mrs. David Reneau
Route 1, Box 285
Glasglow, KY 42141

Southern Historical Association

% University of Kentucky
Lexington, KY 40506

Taylor County Historical Society
Box 14
Campbellsville, KY 42718
(*The Central Kentucky Researcher*)

West Central Kentucky Family
Research Association
P.O. Box 1465
Owensboro, KY 42301
(*Kentucky Family Records*, 1971–)
NN APR (Kentucky) 72-3023

Books and Articles

Bolin, Daniel Lynn.
Ohio Valley History, Westpoint to
Lewisport: A Bibliography of
Breckinridge, Hancock, Meade,
Hardin, Grayson, Ohio and
Davies Counties in Kentucky
and Their Indiana Neighbors
of Perry, Crawford and Harrison.
New Orleans, LA, Polyanthos,
1976. 141 p., index.

Clift, G. Glenn.
The "Corn Stalk" Militia of Kentucky, 1792–1811.
Frankfort, KY, 1957. 265 p.
NN APR (Kentucky)

Clift, G. Glenn.
Kentucky Marriages, 1797–1865.
Baltimore, MD, GPC, 1966. 1 v.,
index.
(Reprint from *Kentucky Hist.
Mag.*)
NN APR (Kentucky)

Clift, G. Glenn.
"Second Census" of Kentucky,
1800.

Frankfort, 1954. 333 p.
NN APR (Kentucky)

Conley, Joan W.
History of Nicholas County, Kentucky.
Carlisle, KY, Nicholas Co. Hist.
Soc., 1976. 549 p., index.
NN ITZ (Nicholas Co.) 77-264

Dorman, John Frederick.
Some Sources for Kentucky Research.
Washington, DC, 1957. (*NGSSP*, no.
15, p. 43–48)
NN APGA

Hathaway, Beverly.
Inventory of County Records of
Kentucky.
West Jordan, UT, Allstates, 1974.
164 p.
NN APR (Kentucky) 75-1476

Heineman, Charles B.
"First Census" of Kentucky, 1790.
Washington, DC, G. M. Brumbaugh, 1940.
NN APR (Kentucky)

Hinds, Charles F.
Kentucky Records: How to Use
Them and Where They Are Located.
(IN: *NGSQ*, Washington, DC, 1971.
v. 59, p. 3–7)
NN APGA

Kentucky 1810 Census Index.
Bountiful, UT, AIS, 1976.

Kentucky 1820 Census Index.
Bountiful, UT, AIS, 1976.

Kentucky 1830 Census Index.
Bountiful, UT, AIS, 1976.

Kentucky 1840 Census Index.
Bountiful, UT, AIS, 1977.

Kentucky 1850 Census Index.
Bountiful, UT, AIS, 1976. 469 p.

Kentucky Family Records, ed. by
Mrs. Edgar L. Coy.
Owensboro, West Central Ken-
tucky Families Research As-
soc., 1971–72. v. 1–3.
NN APR (Kentucky) 72-3023

Kentucky Genealogy and Biography, ed. by Thomas Wester-
field.
Owensboro, Gen. Ref. Co., 1970–72.
4 v.
NN APR (Kentucky) 72-929

Kentucky Issue.
Antiques, New York, April 1974.
v. CV, no. 4
NN MAA+

Kentucky State Historical Society
Portraiture in the Kentucky His-
torical Society, with Notes on
the Subjects and Artists, by G.
Glenn Clift.
Frankfort, 1951. 14 p., 149f.
NN MAVY (Frankfort)

Kentucky Wills.
Bountiful, UT, AIS, 1976. alpha.

Kozee, William C.
Pioneer Families of Eastern and
Southeastern Kentucky.
Baltimore, MD, GPC, 1973 (orig.
1957). 272 p., alpha.

The Louisville Directory for the
Year 1832.
Louisville, 1970. 198 p.
NN AZE (Louisville) 73-2129

Smith, Dora Wilson.
Kentucky 1830 Census Index.
Thomson, IL, Heritage House,
1973–74. 6 v.

Swinford, Frances K., and Rebecca
S. Lee.
The Great Elm Tree: Heritage of
the Episcopal Diocese of Lex-
ington.
Lexington, Faith House Press,
1969. 456 p., index.
NN ITZB 72-1609

U.S. Census, 3rd Census, 1810.
An Index to the 1810 Federal Cen-
sus of Kentucky, comp. by Low-
ell M. Volkel.
Springfield, IL, 1971–72. 4 v.
NN APR (Kentucky) 72-973

U.S. Census, 4th Census, 1820.
An Index to the 1820 Federal Cen-
sus of Kentucky, comp. by Low-
ell M. Volkel.
Thomson, IL, 1974–75. 2 v.
NN APR (Kentucky) 75-1102

LOUISIANA

State Archives

Louisiana State Library
State Capitol Ground
Baton Rouge, LA 70804

Vital Records

Division of Public Health Statistics
State Department of Health
P.O. Box 60630
New Orleans, LA 70160
Births and deaths: July 1914–
Marriages: 1946–
Marriages prior: Early nineteenth
century and later. Marriage
records are in clerk's office of
local parishes (counties).
For city of New Orleans: births,

1790–; deaths, 1803–; marriages: Bureau of Vital Statistics, City Health Dept., 1W03 City Hall, Civic Center, New Orleans, LA 70112.

Libraries

Church of Jesus Christ of Latter-day Saints
Baton Rouge, Louisiana, Branch Genealogical Library
Louisiana State University Library
Baton Rouge, LA 70803

Hill Memorial Library
Louisiana State University
Baton Rouge, LA 70803

Howard Tilton Library
The Map and Genealogy Room
Tulane University
New Orleans, LA 70118

Societies and Periodicals

Ark-La-Tex Genealogical Association
P.O. Box 4462
Shreveport, LA 71104
(*The Genie*, 1967–)
NN APR (Louisiana) 73-2815

Attakapas Historical Association
Box 107
105 South New Market Street
St. Martinville, LA 70582
(*Attakapas Gazette*)

Baton Rouge Genealogical Society
% Shelton B. McAnelly, President
1340 Monterrey Blvd.
Baton Rouge, LA 70815

DeSoto Historical Society
Box 523

Mansfield, LA 71052
(*DeSoto Plume*)

Genealogical Research Society of New Orleans
P.O. Box 51791
New Orleans, LA 70150
(*New Orleans Genesis*, 1962–)
NN APR (New Orleans)

Louisiana Genealogical and Historical Society
P.O. Box 3454
Baton Rouge, LA 70821
(*Louisiana Genealogical Register*, 1953–)
NN APR (Louisiana)

Louisiana Historical Association
1515 Choctaw
Baton Rouge, LA 70804
(*Louisiana History*)
NN IAA

Louisiana Historical Society
509 Cotton Exchange Bldg.
231 Carondelet Street
New Orleans, LA 70130
(*Louisiana Historical Society Quarterly*, 1917–)
NN IAA

Northeast Louisiana Genealogical Society
P.O. Box 2743
Monroe, LA 71201

North Louisiana Historical Association
Louisiana Tech.
Ruston, LA 71270
(*North Louisiana Historical Association Journal*)

Southeast Louisiana Historical Association
200 Rumsie Drive
Hammond, LA 70401

Southern Historical Association
Tulane University
New Orleans, LA 70118
(*Journal of Southern History*,
1935–)
NN IAA

Southwest Louisiana Genealogical
Society
% Mrs. Yvonne Yongue Guidroz
1927 East Prien Lake Road
Lake Charles, LA 70601

Books and Articles

Ardoin, Robert Bruce L., comp.
Louisiana Census Records.
Baltimore, MD, GPC, 1970–72. 2 v.
(v. 1, 1810 and 1820 Census of
Avoyelles and St. Landry Par-
ishes; v. 2, 1810 and 1820 Cen-
sus of Iberville, Natchitoches,
Pointe Coupee and Rapides
parishes)
NN APR (Louisiana) 73-282

Buller, Talmadge L.
Louisiana Successions.
Fort Worth, TX, 1968–. v. 1–.
NN APR (Louisiana) 75-247

Childs, Marlete, ed.
North Louisiana Census Reports,
Vol. I: 1830 and 1840.
Schedules of Catahoula, Concordia,
Ouachita, Caldwell, Carrol,
Madison and Union Parishes.
New Orleans, LA, Polyanthos,
1975. 115 p., index.

Confirmaciones.
New Orleans, New Orleans Genealogical Research Soc., 1967.
187 p. (First Book of Confirmations of the Parish of St. Louis)
NN APR (New Orleans) 76-1427

Conrad, Glenn R.
St. Charles, Abstracts of the Civil
Records of St. Charles Parish,
1700–1803. Lafayette, LA, U. of
Southwestern LA, USL History
Series, 1974. 554 p., index.
NN APR (St. Charles Parish) 76-
101

Deville, Winston.
Acadian Church Records, 1679–1757.
Mobile, AL, 1964–. v. 1–.
NN APW

DeVille, Winston.
Avoyelles Parish.
Baton Rouge, 1961. xiii, 50 p.
(Louisiana Archives and Records
Commission, *Calendar of Loui-
siana Colonial Documents*, v. 1)
NN ITP

DeVille, Winston.
Gulf Coast Colonials: A Compen-
dium of French Families in
Early 18th Century Louisiana.
Baltimore, MD, GPC, 1968. 69 p.
(Refers to early settlers of Louisi-
ana and Mississippi)
NN APR (Louisiana)

DeVille, Winston.
Louisiana Recruits, 1752–1758.
Cottonport, LA, Polyanthos, 1973.
99 p.
NN APR (Louisiana) 73-2983

DeVille, Winston.
The New Orleans French, 1720–
1733.
Baltimore, MD, GPC, 1973. 113 p.,
index.
NN APR (New Orleans) 74-983

DeVille, Winston.
St. Landry Parish.
Baton Rouge, 1964. xiii, 33 p.

(Louisiana Archives and Records Commission, *Calendar of Louisiana Colonial Documents*, v. 2)
NN ITP

DeVille, Winston.
Louisiana Troops, 1720–1770.
Fort Worth, TX, Amer. Ref. Pub., 1965. 136 p.
NN ITP

Forsyth, Alice D.
German "Pest Ships," 1720–1721.
New Orleans, 1969, 53 p.
NN APR (Louisiana) 75-115

Herbert, Donald T.
Southwest Louisiana Records.
Eunice, LA, 1974–76. 4 v.
NN APR (Louisiana) 75-364

Jennings, Virginia Lobdell.
The Plains and the People: A History of Upper East Baton Rouge Parish.
New Orleans, Pelican Pub. Co., 1962. 396 p., cursory index and partial alpha. arrangement.
NN ITQ (East Baton Rouge Parish)

Leeper, Clare D'Artois.
Louisiana Place Names: A Collection of the Columns from the Baton Rouge *Sunday Advocate*, 1960–1970.
Baton Rouge, Legacy Pub. Co., 1976. 264 p.
NN ITQB + 77-616

Louisiana 1810 Census Index.
Bountiful, UT, AIS, 1976.

Louisiana 1820 Census Index.
Bountiful, UT, AIS, 1976.

Louisiana 1830 Census Index.
Bountiful, UT, AIS, 1976.

Louisiana 1840 Census Index.
Bountiful, UT, AIS, 1977.

Louisiana 1850 Census Index.
Bountiful, UT, AIS, 1977.

Maudell, Charles R., Jr.
Census Tables for the French Colony of Louisiana, 1699–1732.
Baltimore, MD, GPC, 1972. 171 p.
NN APR (Louisiana) 73-525

Maudell, Charles R., Jr.
Federal Land Grants in the Territory of Orleans. The Delta Parishes. Adapted from American State Papers, Public Lands, Volume II.
(Arranged by counties as they existed in 1812)
New Orleans, Polyanthos, 1975. v, 406 p., indexes.

Maudell, Charles R, Jr.
Marriage Contracts, Wills and Testaments of the Spanish Colonial Period in New Orleans, 1770–1804.
New Orleans, C. R. Maudell, 1969. 1 v., various paging.
NN APR (New Orleans)

Maudell, Charles R., Jr.
Marriages and Family Relationships of New Orleans, 1830–1840.
New Orleans, C. R. Maudell, 1969. 180, 9 p., index.
NN APR (New Orleans) 72-2740

Meyers, Rose.
A History of Baton Rouge 1699–1812.
Baton Rouge, LSU Press, 1976. 149 p., index.
NN ITQ (Baton Rouge) 76-2729

Orleans Parish, LA, Courts, General Index of All Successions

Opened in the Civil District Court, Parish of Orleans, Louisiana.
New Orleans, 1895–1902 (Aug. 1, 1885–Jan. 1, 1902).
2 v. in 1, alpha.
NN APR (Orleans)

Quinones, Estevan de.
Love, Honor and Betrayal: The Notorials Acts of Estevan de Quinones, trans. by Elizabeth B. Gianelloni.
Baton Rouge, 1964–66. 2 v. (Louisiana Ancestry Series)
NN APR (Louisiana)

Robichaux, Alfred J.
Louisiana Census and Militia Lists, 1770–1789.
Harvey, LA, 1973–74. 2 v.
NN APR (Louisiana) 74-659

Siegel, Martin.
New Orleans.
Dobbs Ferry, NY, Oceana, 1975. 140 p.
NN ITQ (New Orleans) 76-645

Troups, Neil J.
Mississippi Valley Pioneers.
Lafayette, LA, 1970. 135 p.
NN APR (Louisiana) 71-27

Voorhies, Jacqueline K.
Some Late Eighteenth Century Louisianians. Census Records, 1758–1796.
Lafayette, LA, USL, 1973. 613 p., index.
NN APR (Louisiana) 74-1075

Young, Perry.
The Mistick Krewe: The Chronicles of Comus and His Kin.
New Orleans, Louisiana Heritage Press, 1969. 268 p., no index.

(Full details and chronologies of Mardi Gras, with many names of kings, queens and supporters; too bad no index)
NN ITQ (New Orleans) 75-2719

MAINE

State Archives

Maine State Library
Archives Bldg.
State House
Augusta, ME 04330

Vital Records

Office of Vital Records
State Department of Health and Welfare
State House
Augusta, ME 04333
Births and deaths: 1892–
Births and deaths prior: town clerk
Marriages: also from state office or town clerk.
Some local records date from early nineteenth century.

Libraries

Church of Jesus Christ of Latter-day Saints
Augusta, Maine, State Branch Genealogical Library
Augusta Ward Chapel
Hasson Street
Farmington, ME

Societies and Periodicals

Bar Harbor Historical Society
24 Mt. Desert Street
Bar Harbor, ME 04609

Camden Historical Society
80 Mechanic Street
Camden, ME 04843

Gray Historical Society
Gray, ME 04039
(*Gray Matter*)

Hancock County Historical Society
Box 691
Ellsworth, ME 04605

Lincoln County Cultural and Historical Association
Box 61
Federal Street
Wiscasset, ME 04578

(*Maine Genealogical Enquirer*, 1968–1975)
NN APR (Maine)
Box 253
165 Main Street
Oakland, ME 04963

Maine Genealogical Society
P.O. Box 221
Farmington, ME 04936

Maine Historical Society
485 Congress Street
Portland, ME 04111
(*Maine Historical Society Newsletter*, c. 1962–)

Maine League of Historical Societies and Museums
10 Brann Avenue
Lewiston, ME 04240
(*Maine History News*)

Maine Old Cemeteries Association
% Mr. Nathan Hale
River Road
Newcastle, ME 04553

National Society of Colonial Dames of America in Maine

The Tate House
1270 West Brook Street
Portland, ME 04102
(Mail: % Mrs. M.S. Peabody, 4 Walker Street, Portland, ME 04102)

Books and Articles

Bibliography of the State of Maine.
Boston, MA, G. K. Hall, 1962. 803 p., 1 v.

Fisher, Carleton E.
Research in Maine.
(IN: *NGSQ*, Washington, DC, 1967. v. 55, p. 83–88)
NN APGA

Flagg, Charles A.
An Alphabetical Index of Revolutionary War Pensioners Living in Maine.
Baltimore, MD, GPC, 1967 (orig. 1920). 91 p., alpha.
NN APR (Maine)

Frost, John Eldridge.
Guide to Maine Vital Records in Transcript.
New York, the author, 1963. 107 p.
(Available at Maine Hist. Soc.)

Frost, John Eldridge.
Maine . . .
(IN: *NEHGR*, Boston, Oct., 1977. v. 131
(The information in this article is not a repetition of the author's excellent 1977 guide but a complement to it.)
NN APGA

Frost, John Eldridge.
Maine Genealogy: A Bibliographical Guide.
Portland, Maine Hist. Soc., 1977. 46 p., index.

(A superb survey of Maine material that includes general references and those for other New England states)

Genealogy of French Canada, Acadia and Franco-America at the Maine State Library.
Augusta, Maine State Library, c. 1976. 7 p.

Kershaw, Gordon E.
Gentlemen of Large Property and Judicious Men: The Kennebeck Proprietors, 1749 –1775.
Somersworth, NH, New Hampshire Pub. Co. for Maine Hist. Soc., 1975. 343 p.
NN IQA 77-771

King, Marquis Fayett.
Changes of Names by Special Acts of the Legislature of Maine, 1820–1895.
Portland?, M. F. King, 1901. 66f. p.
NN APR (Maine)

Maine (Colony)
Province and Court Records of Maine.
Portland, Maine Hist. Soc., 1928–75. 6 v. (covers 1636–1727)
NN IQA

Maine 1800 Census Index.
Provo, UT, AIS, 1974. 425 p., alpha.
NN APR (Maine) 76-1272

Maine 1810 Census Index.
Bountiful, UT, AIS, 1976.

Maine 1820 Census Index.
Bountiful, UT, AIS, 1976.

Maine 1830 Census Index.
Bountiful, UT, AIS, 1977.

Maine 1840 Census Index.
Bountiful, UT, AIS, 1977.

Maine 1850 Census Index.
Bountiful, UT, AIS, 1977.

Morris, Gerald E.
Atlas of Maine.
Portland, Maine Hist. Soc., 1976.

Maine Library Association. Bicentennial Committee.
Bibliography of Maine, 1960–1975.
Orono, ME, Maine Library Assoc., 1976. 109 p.

Microfilm List, Maine Town and Census Records (rev.).
Augusta, Maine State Archives, 1976. 31 p.

Noyes, Sybil, Charles Thorton Libby and Walter Goodwin Davis.
The Genealogical Dictionary of Maine and New Hampshire.
Baltimore, MD, GPC, 1972 (orig. 1928–1939, 5 pts.). 1 v.
NN APR (Maine) 73-1427

Pope, Charles Henry.
The Pioneers of Maine and New Hampshire 1623 to 1660 ... with a foreword by James Phinney Baster.
Baltimore, MD, GPC, 1965. 252 p., index.
NN APR (Maine)

Ring, Elizabeth.
Maine Bibliographies: A Bibliographical Guide.
Portland, Maine Hist. Soc., 1973. 34 p.
NN *XM-7787

Sargent, William M.
Maine Wills, 1640–1760.
Portland, Brown Thurston and Co., 1887. 953 p., index.
NN APR (Maine)

Stackpole, Everett.
Old Kittery Families.
n.p., 1970 (orig. 1903). 822 p., index.
NN APR (Kittery)

MARYLAND

State Archives

Hall of Records
College Ave. and St. John's St.
Annapolis, 21404
(*Publications*, 1943–)
NN ISG

Vital Records

Division of Vital Records
State Department of Health
State Office Building
201 West Preston Street
P.O. Box 13146
Baltimore, MD 21203
Births and deaths: 1898–
Births and deaths, city of Baltimore: January 1875–
Marriages: June 1951–
Marriages prior: Write clerk of Circuit Court.
Marriages, city of Baltimore: Clerk of Court of Common Pleas of Baltimore.

Libraries

Church of Jesus Christ of Latter-day Saints
Washington, DC, Genealogical Library
500 Randolph Road
Silver Spring, MD 20904

Enoch Pratt Free Library
400 Cathedral Street
Baltimore, MD 21201

Maryland State Library
Court of Appeals Bldg.
361 Rowe Blvd.
Annapolis, MD 21401

Societies and Periodicals

Anne Arundel Genealogical Society
P.O. Box 221
Pasadena, MD 21122
(*Anne Arundel Speaks*)

Baltimore Conference United Methodist Historical Society
Baltimore, MD 21218

Baltimore County Historical Society
Genealogy Committee
9811 Van Buren Lane
Cockeysville, MD 21030
(*History Trails*)

Caroline County Historical Society
Maple Avenue
Preston, MD 21655
(*Gazette*)

Garrett County Historical Society
The Courthouse
Oakland, MD 21550

Historical Society of Charles County, Inc.
Box 336
Port Tobacco, MD 20677
(*The Record*)

Historical Society of Hartford County, Inc.
324 Kenmore Avenue
Bel Air, MD 21014
(*Hartford Heritage*)

Maryland Delaware Genealogy, 1959–, NN APR (Maryland)
Box 352
St. Michaels, MD 21663

Maryland Genealogical Society
201 West Monument Street

Baltimore, MD 21201
(*Maryland Genealogical Society Bulletin*, 1960–)
NN APR (Maryland)

Maryland Historical Society
201 West Monument Street
Baltimore, MD 21201
(*Maryland Historical Magazine*, 1906–)
NN IAA

Maryland Historical Trust
2525 Riva Road
Annapolis, MD 21401
(*SWAP*)

Mid-Atlantic Regional Archives Conference
% Mary Boccaccio
Maryland Room, McKeldin Library
University of Maryland
College Park, MD 20742
(*Maryland Archivist*)

Montgomery County Historical Society
103 West Montgomery Avenue
Rockville, MD 20850
(*The Montgomery County Story*)

Prince George's County Genealogical Society
Box 819
Bowie, MD 20715
(*Prince George's County Genealogical Society Bulletin*)

St. Mary's County Historical Society
Box 212
Leonardtown, MD 20650
(*Chronicles of St. Mary's*, 1953–)
NN ISH (St. Mary's)

Society for the History of the Germans in Maryland

231 St. Paul Place
Baltimore, MD 21202

Unitarian and Universalist Genealogical Society
10605 Lakespring Way
Cockeysville, MD 21030

Books and Articles

Annapolis.
(IN: *Antiques*, New York, 1977. v. cxi, p. 145ff.)
MAA +

Barnes, Robert.
Maryland Marriages, 1634–77.
Baltimore, GPC, 1975. 233 p., index.
NN APR (Maryland) 76-619

Barnes, Robert.
Maryland Pioneers to the Frontiers.
(IN: *The Maryland and Delaware Genealogist*, St. Michael's, MD, 1977. v. 18, 6–7 and following issues.) Alpha clues from land records, etc., to pioneers to Kentucky, Ohio, etc., who were from Maryland.
NN APR (Maryland)

Barnes, Robert.
Marriages from the Maryland Gazette, 1727–1839.
Baltimore, GPC, 1973. 234 p., index.
NN APR (Maryland) 74-1382

Beard, Timothy Field, and Nellie Holmead Fowler.
Abstracts of the Wills of Worcester County, Maryland, 1742–1790, with Annotations Concerning Some of the Families of the County. (In preparation)

Brown, Helen M.
Marriage Licenses of Prince George's County, Maryland, Index 1777–1886.
College Park, MD, 1971. 249 p.
NN APR (Prince George's Co., Maryland) 73-218

Carothers, Bettie.
Maryland Source Records.
Lutherville, MD, privately printed, 1975. 72 p.

Carr, Lois Green, and David William Jordan.
Maryland's Revolution of Government, 1689–1692.
Ithaca, NY, Cornell U. Press, 1974. 321 p., index.
NN ISG

Clark, Raymond B., Jr.
Maryland Revolutionary Records: How to Find Them and Interpret Them, with an introduction by P. William Filby.
St. Michael's, MD 21663, the author, 1976.

Clark, Raymond B., and Sarah Seth Clark.
Baltimore County, Maryland, Tax Lists, 1699–1706.
Washington, DC, 1964. 78 p., index.
NN APR (Baltimore) 73-2725

Clark, Raymond B., and Sarah Seth Clark.
Genealogical Research in Maryland. A monograph.
Washington, DC, 1963. 14 p.

Cotton, Jane B.
Maryland Calendar of Wills (1635–1743).

Baltimore, GPC (orig. 1901–28). 8 v., index each v.
NN APR (Maryland)

Cox, Richard J.
Some Maryland Recruits of 1776.
(IN: *NGSQ*, Washington, DC, Dec. 1976. v. 64, no. 4, p. 261–270)
NN APGA

DAR, Maryland Daughters' Directory of Maryland State Society: Daughters of the American Revolution and Their Revolutionary Ancestors, 1892–1965.
Bel Air, MD, Services Unlimited, for Maryland State Soc., DAR, 1966. 785 p., no index, alpha in 2 sec. (sec. 1, members; sec. 2, ancestors; from many states, not just Maryland)
NN APGA

Hienton, Louise Joyner.
Prince George's County, Maryland, Piscataway or St. John's Parish Index to Register, 1689–1878.
Baltimore, GPC, 1961.

Hienton, Louise Joyner.
Prince George's Heritage: Sidelights on the Early History of Prince George's County, Maryland, from 1696 to 1800.
Baltimore, Maryland Hist. Soc., 1972. 223 p.
NN ISH (P. G. Co.) 73-2039

Hume, Joan.
Index of Maryland Wills: Allegany Co., 1784–1960, Vol. I; Harford Co., 1774–1960, Garrett Co., 1872–1960, Vol. II; Howard Co., 1840–1950, Kent Co., 1642–1960, Vol. III; and St. Mary's Co., 1662–1960, Somerset Co., 1664–1955, Vol IV.

Baltimore, Magna Carta Book, 1970.
NN APR (Maryland)

Jacobsen, Phebe R.
Quaker Records in Maryland.
Annapolis, 1966. 154 p., index.
(Hall of Records Commission, pub. #14)
NN ISG

Ljungstedt, Mrs. Milnor (1858–1942), ed.
The County Court Note-Book Volumes 1–10, and Ancestral Proofs and Probabilities, Numbers 1–4, introduction by Mary K. Meyer.
Baltimore, GPC, 1972 (orig. 1921–1936).
NN APGA 72-1944

McCay, Betty L.
Sources for Genealogical Searching in Maryland.
Indianapolis, IN, 1972.

Magruder, James.
Magruder's Maryland Colonial Abstracts, Wills Accounts and Inventories, 1772–1777.
Baltimore, GPC, 1968 (orig. 1934–39). 5 v. in 1.
APR (Maryland)

Magruder, James.
Index of Maryland Colonial Wills, 1634–1777 in the Hall of Records, Annapolis, Maryland, and Additions (by Louise E. Magruder).
Baltimore, GPC, 1967 (orig. 1933). 3 v. in 1.
NN APR (Maryland)

Marks, Lillian Bayly.
Reister's Desire. The Origin of

Reisterstown, Maryland, Founded 1758. With a Genealogical History of the Reister Family and Sketches of Allied Families.
Baltimore, Maryland Hist. Soc., 1975. xv 236 p.
NN APV (Reister) 76-1774

Maryland Colonial Wills, Abstracts.
Annapolis, Annie Walker Burns, 1937–38. 15 v.
(Maryland Archives Wills, Libers 24–38)
NN *ZI-217

Maryland 1800 Census Index.
Bountiful, UT, AIS, 1976.

Maryland 1810 Census Index.
Bountiful, UT, AIS, 1976.

Maryland 1820 Census Index.
Bountiful, UT, AIS, 1976.

Maryland 1830 Census Index.
Bountiful, UT, AIS, 1976. 119 p.

Maryland 1840 Census Index.
Bountiful, UT, AIS, 1977.

Maryland 1850 Census Index.
Bountiful, UT, AIS, 1977.

Maryland Tax List, Baltimore County, 1783, from the Maryland Historical Society.
Philadelphia, Historic Pub., 1970. 165 p. (facsimile).
NN APR (Baltimore Co.) 72-1830

Meyer, Mary Keysor.
Genealogical Research in Maryland: A Guide. 2nd rev. ed.
Baltimore, Maryland Hist. Soc., 1976. 109 p.

Montgomery County, Maryland, 1800 Census.
Baltimore, Maryland Gen. Soc., 1972.

Muster Rolls of Maryland Troops in the American Revolution, 1775–1783.
Baltimore, GPC, 1972 (orig. 1900). 736 p., index.
ISG + 75-261

Newman, Harry Wright.
Anne Arundel Gentry (rev.).
Annapolis, H.W. Newman, 1970–71 (orig. 1934). 2 v.
NN APR (Anne Arundel)

Newman, Harry Wright.
Heraldic Marylandianna.
Washington, DC, H. W. Newman, 1968. 188 p., index.
NN AWS

Newman, Harry Wright.
The Flowering of the Maryland Palatinate.
Washington, DC, H. W. Newman, 1961. 359 p., index.
(Possible passengers on ship *Ark and Dove*, arriving in Maryland 1634)
NN ISG

Passano, Eleanor Phillips.
An Index of the Source Records of Maryland, Genealogical, Biographical, Historical.
Baltimore, GPC, 1967 (orig. 1940). 478 p., alpha.
NN APR (Maryland)

Pedley, Avril I. M.
The Manuscript Collections of the Maryland Historical Society.
Baltimore, Maryland Hist. Soc., 1968. 390 p., index.
NN ISG

Pogue, Robert E. T.
Old Maryland Landmarks.
Baltimore, R.E.T. Pogue, 1972. 353 p., index.
NN ISG 73-683

Radoff, Morris L.
The County Courthouses and Records of Maryland.
Annapolis, 1960–63.
(Hall of Records Commission, pub. #12–13)
(v. 1, the courthouses; v. 2, the records)
NN ISG

Schuyler, Montgomery, comp.
Material for the Study of the Maryland Manors.
New York, John B. Watkins Co., 1944. 62 p.
(The Order of Colonial Lords of Manors in America, pub. no. 30)
NN APGA

Semmes, Raphael.
Captains and Mariners of Early Maryland.
Baltimore, Johns Hopkins Press, 1937. 856 p., index.
NN ISG

Skordas, Gust.
The Early Settlers of Maryland: An Index of Names of Immigrants, Compiled from Land Patents, 1633–1680.
Baltimore, GPC, 1968. 525 p.
NN APR (Maryland)

Skordas, Gust, and Elizabeth Hartsook.
Land Office and Prerogative Court Records of Colonial Maryland.
Baltimore, GPC, 1968 (orig. 1946). 124 p.

(Hall of Records Commission, Annapolis, pub. #4)
NN ISG

Smith, Mrs. Dorothy H.
Orphans and Infants of Prince George's County, Maryland, 1696–1758.
Annapolis, D. H. Smith, 1976. 116, viii p.

Society of Colonial Wars in the State of Maryland., ed. by Francis Barnum Culver.
Baltimore, The Williams & Wilkins Co., for the Society, 1940. 398 p., alpha.

Van Horn, R. Lee.
Out of the Past: Prince Georgians and Their Land.
Riverdale, MD, Prince George's County Hist. Soc., 1976.

Vokel, Charlotte A., Lowell M., and Timothy W. Wilson.
Index to the 1800 Federal Census of Maryland.
Danville, IL, 1967–68. 4 v. in 1, unpaged.
NN APR (Maryland)

Wyand, Jefrey A., and Florence L. Wyand.
Colonial Maryland Naturalizations.
Baltimore, GPC, 1975. 104 p., indexes.
NN APR (Maryland) 76-894

MASSACHUSETTS

State Archives

Massachusetts State Library
Beacon Hill
Boston, MA 02133

Vital Records

Registrar of Vital Statistics
Rm. 103, McCormack Bldg.
1 Ashburton Place
Boston, MA 02108
Births, deaths and marriages: 1841–
Births, deaths, and marriages prior: city or town clerk
Births, deaths and marriages: Boston, 1848– and
Births, deaths, and marriages: Boston, 1639–, write: City Registrar, Registry Division, Health Department, Room 705, City Hall Annex, Boston, MA 02133

Libraries

American Antiquarian Society Library
185 Salisbury Street
Worcester, MA 01609

Boston Public Library
P.O. Box 286
Boston, MA 02177

Church of Jesus Christ of Latter-day Saints
Boston, Massachusetts, State Branch Genealogical Library
Brown Street and South Avenue
Weston, MA 02193

Societies and Periodicals

American Antiquarian Society
185 Salisbury Street
Worchester, MA 01520
(*AAS Proceedings*, 1812–)
NN IAA

Berkshire County Historical Society, Inc.

113 E. Housatonic Street
Pittsfield, MA 01201
(*Berkshire History*)

Bostonian Society
Old State House
206 Washington Street
Boston, MA 02109
(*Proceedings of the Bostonian Society*, 1882–)
NN IAA

Braintree Historical Society, Inc.
786 Washington Street
Braintree, MA 02184

Car-Del Scribe, 1965–
Chedwato Service
R.F.D. 3, Box 120A
Middleboro, MA 02346

Commission on Archives and History
Southern New England Conference
United Methodist Church
745 Commonwealth Avenue
Boston, MA 02215

Congregational Christian Historical Society
14 Beacon Street
Boston, MA 02108
(*Newssheet*)

Danvers Historical Society
Danvers, MA 01923

Dedham Historical Society
612 High Street
Dedham, MA 02026

Essex Institute
132A Essex Street
Salem, MA 01970
(*Essex Institute Historical Collections*, 1859–)
NN IQH (Essex)

Historical Society of the Stockbridge Library
Main Street
Stockbridge, MA 01262

Historic Deerfield, Inc.
Box 321
Deerfield, MA 01342

Huguenot Memorial Society of Oxford
Fort Hill Road
Oxford, MA 01540
(Mail: 2 Maple Road, Oxford, MA 01540)

Ipswich Historical Society
53 South Main Street
Ipswich, MA 01938

Lexington Historical Society
Box 514
Lexington, MA 02173

Longyear Historical Society
120 Seaver Street
Brookline, MA 02146
(*Quarterly News*)

Massachusetts Historical Commission
40 Beacon Street
Boston, MA 02133

Massachusetts Historical Society
1154 Boylston Street
Boston, MA 02215
(*Massachusetts Historical Society Proceedings*, 1791–)
NN IAA

Massachusetts Society of Genealogists
P.O. Box 215
Ashland, MA 01721

Mayflower Descendants General Society

P.O. Box 297NE
Plymouth, MA 02360
(For *Mayflower Quarterly*, see
Rhode Island)

Medford Historical Society
10 Governors Avenue
Medford, MA 02155

Middleborough Historical Association
Box 272, Jackson Street
Middleborough, MA 02346
(*Middleborough Antiquarian*)

Nantucket Historical Association
Box 1016
Old Town Bldg.
2 Union Street
Nantucket, MA 02554
(*Historical Nantucket*)

New England Document Conservation Center
800 Massachusetts Avenue
North Andover, MA 01845

New England Historic Genealogical Society
101 Newbury Street
Boston, MA 02116
(*New England Historical and Genealogical Register*, 1847–)
Index of persons, places, subjects.
   v. 1–50 (1847–1896); abridged index, v. 51–112 (1897–1968)
NN *R-APGA

Old Colony Historical Society
66 Church Green
Taunton, MA 02780

Old Dartmouth Historical Society
18 Johnny Cake Hill
New Bedford, MA 02740
(*The Bulletin from Johnny Cake Hill*)

Pilgrim John Howland Society, Inc.
Jabez Howland House
33 Sandwich Street
Plymouth, MA 02895
(*The Howland Quarterly*)

Plymouth Antiquarian Society, Inc.
27 North Street
Plymouth, MA 02360

Rowe Historical Society, Inc.
Zoar Road
Rowe, MA 01367
(*The Bulletin*)

Sandwich Historical Society
129 Main Street
Sandwich, MA 02563
(*The Acorn*)

South End Historical Society
52A Union Pike
Boston, MA 02118

Weston Historical Society
Box 343
Weston, MA 02193
(*Weston Historical Society Bulletin*)

Books and Articles

American Antiquarian Society.
The Boston Evening Transcript
   Index of Obituary Notices.
Worcester, MA, 1937. 2 v.
   (1875–1899); 1940, 3 v. (1900–1930).
NN APK

American Antiquarian Society.
Index of Deaths in the *Massachusetts Centinel* and The *Columbian Centinel*, 1784–1840.
Worcester, MA, 1952. 12 v., alpha.
(Marriages pub. in 1961, 4 v. in
   the same classification)
NN APR (Massachusetts)

Anderson, Robert C.
Directions of a Town.
Harvard, MA, Harvard Common Press, 1976. 180 p.

Banks, Charles E.
The Winthrop Fleet.
Baltimore, MD, GPC, 1968 (orig. 1930). 119 p.
NN APK

Boston Athenaeum Index of Obituaries in Boston Newspapers.
Boston, G.K. Hall, 1968. 3 v.
(v.1, Boston deaths, 1704–1800; v. 2 and 3, deaths outside Boston, 1704–1795)
NN APR (Boston)

Boston Registry Department.
Records Relating to the Early History of Boston.
Boston, 1876–1909. v. 1–39.
v. 9 [1883] births, 1630–1699; v. 24 [1894] births, 1700–1800; v. 28 [1898] marriages, 1700–1750; v. 30 [1902] marriages, 1752–1809; v. 21 [1890] Dorchester Vital Records, to 1825; v. 36, Dorchester V.R., 1829–1849)
NN IQH (Boston)

Bowen, Richard LeBaron.
Massachusetts Records: A Handbook for Genealogists, Historians, Lawyers and Other Researchers.
Rehoboth, MA, R. LeB. Bowen, 1957. 66 p., index.
NN APR (Massachusetts)

Bunting, W. H.
Portrait of a Port: Boston, 1852–1914.
Cambridge, Belknap Press of Harvard, 1971. 519 p., index, many illus. of ships and harbor views.
NN IQH (Boston) 72–2834

Cincinnati, Society of the, Massachusetts.
Memorials of the Massachusetts Society, Bradford Adams Whittemore, comp.
Boston, The Society, 1964. 852 p. index
NN APGA

Falmouth, Massachusetts, Vital Records to 1850, comp. by Oliver Brown.
Warwick RI, Soc. of Mayflower Descendants in Rhode Island, 1976. 272 p., alpha.
NN APR (Falmouth) 77–228

Flagg, Charles.
An Index of Pioneers from Massachusetts to the West.
Salem, MA, Salem Press, 1915. 86 p.
NN APR (Massachusetts)

Gladden, Sanford C.
An Index to the Vital Records of Boston, 1630–1699.
Boulder, Co, S.C. Gladden, 1969. 188 p.
(Fully indexed old volume of vital records for this period, pub. in v. 9 of the Boston Registry Dept.)
NN APR (Boston)

Jones, Howard Mumford, and Bessie Z. Jones, ed.
The Many Voices of Boston: An Historical Anthology, 1630–1975.
Boston, Little, Brown, 1975. 488 p., no index, t of c p. v–x.
NN IQH (Boston)

Massachusetts: A Bibliography of Its History, ed. by John D. Haskell, Jr.
Boston, G. K. Hall, 1976. 583 p., index

(Bibliographies of New England
   History v. 1)
NN IQHB 77-794

Massachusetts Courts, Probate
   Court, Worcester County.
Index to the Probate Records of
   the County of Worcester, Mass.
   . . .
Worcester, 1898–1907. 6 v., alpha,
   each v. alpha.
(Series A, July 17, 1731–July 1,
   1881, 2 v.; Series B, July 1,
   1881–Jan. 1, 1907, 4 v.)
NN APR (Worcester)

Massachusetts 1800 Census Index.
Bountiful, UT, AIS, 1976.

Massachusetts 1810 Census Index.
Bountiful, UT, AIS, 1976. 192 p.

Massachusetts 1820 Census Index.
Bountiful, UT, AIS, 1976. 222 p.

Massachusetts 1830 Census Index.
Bountiful, UT, AIS, 1977.

Massachusetts 1840 Census Index.
Bountiful, UT, AIS, 1977.

Massachusetts 1850 Census Index.
Bountiful, UT, AIS, 1977.

Massachusetts (Colony) Courts.
   Probate Court
The Probate Records of Hamp-
   shire County 1660–1820 . . .
Springfield, MA, 1969. 12 reels.
NN *ZI-130

Massachusetts   Commonwealth
   Secretary. Massachusetts Sol-
   diers and Sailors of the Revolu-
   tion.
Boston, 1896–1908. 17 v., A-Z.
NN *R-APR (Massachusetts)

Monroe, J. B.
A List of Alien Passengers from
   January 1, 1847, to January 1,
   1851, for the Use of the Over-
   seer of the Poor. (Boston).
Baltimore, MD, GPC, 1971 (orig.
   1851).

Plymouth Colony.
Plymouth Colony Records (1620–
   1697/98).
Boston, William White, 1855–61.
   12 v. (v. 12, Indian Deeds)
NN IQ + (New Plymouth)

Pope, Charles H.
The Pioneers of Massachusetts.
Baltimore, MD, GPC, 1975 (orig.
   1900). 550 p., alpha, cross-index.
NN APR (Massachusetts)

Records of the Court of Assistants
   Colony of Massachusetts Bay.
Boston, 1901–28. 3 v. (reprint 1968)
NN IQG 73-2589

The Records of the First Church
   in Boston, 1630–1868, Richard
   D. Pierce, ed.
Boston, Colonial Soc. of Mass.,
   1941. 3 v., index in last v.
(Colonial Society of Massachusetts
   Collections, v. 39–41)
NN IAA

Records of Massachusetts (1628–
   1686).
Boston, William White, 1853–54. 5
   v. (reprint NY, AMS, 1968)
NN IQG 76-136

U.S.W.P.A. Massachusetts.
Guide to Public Vital Records.
Boston, Hist. Rec. Survey, 1942.
342 p.
(Births, marriages, deaths, 3 sections arranged by county in each section, then by town under the counties)
NN APR (Massachusetts)

Voye, Nancy S., ed.
Massachusetts Officers in the French and Indian Wars, 1748–1763.
Boston, NEHGS, etc., 1976. 6,611 entries, alpha, no pagination.

Yarmouth, Massachusetts, Vital Records to 1850, comp. by Robert M. and Ruth W. Sherman.
Warwick, RI, Soc. of Mayflower Descendants, 1975. 2 v.
NN APR (Yarmouth) 76–1587

MICHIGAN

State Archives

Michigan State Library
735 East Michigan Avenue
Lansing, MI 48933

Vital Records

Vital Records Section
Michigan Department of Public Health
3500 North Logan Street
Lansing, MI 48914
Births and deaths: 1867–
Marriages: April 1867–
Births, deaths, and marriages, prior: Check with county clerk's office.
Detroit: City Health Department
Births: 1893–
Deaths: 1897–

Libraries

Church of Jesus Christ of Latter-day Saints
Midland, Michigan, State Branch Genealogical Library
Mid-Michigan State Center
1700 West Sugnut Road
Midland, MI 48540

Saginaw Public Library
505 James Street
Saginaw, MI 48607
(Genealogies in the Eddy Historical Collection, Saginaw, Michigan, Public Libraries, rev. 1975 [orig. 1971], 131 p.)

Societies and Periodicals

Battle Creek Historical Society
196 Capital Avenue N.E.
Battle Creek, MI 49017
(*Up-to-date*)

Bay County Genealogical Society
P.O. Box 27
Essesville, MI 48732
(*Chips and Ships*, 1969–)

Bishop Baraga Association
239 Baraga Avenue
Marquette, MI 49855
(*Bishop Baraga Bulletin*)

Detroit Conference Commission on Archives and History of the United Methodist Church
Flint, MI 49221

Detroit Historical Commission
Detroit Historical Museum
5401 Woodward Avenue
Detroit, MI 48202

Detroit Society for Genealogical Research
℅ Burton Historical Collection

Detroit Public Library
5201 Woodward Avenue
Detroit, MI 48202
(*Detroit Society for Genealogical Research Magazine*, 1937–)
NN APGA

Elkhart County Genealogical Society
Route 5, Box 148
Elkhart, IN 46514
(*Michiana Searcher*, 1969–)
NN APR (Elkhart County) 73-2697

Flat River Historical Society
302 South Lafayette Street
Greenville, MI 48834

Flint Michigan Genealogical Society
2085 Kingswood Drive
Flint, MI 48507
(*Flint Genealogical Society Quarterly*, 1959–)
NN APR (Flint)

Genealogical Association of Southwestern Michigan
P.O. Box 573
St. Joseph, MI 49085
(*The Pastfinder*, 1972–)
NN APR (Michigan) 76-835

Grand Rapids Historical Society
Public Museum
54 Jefferson S.E.
Grand Rapids, MI 49502
(*The Friendly Visitor Newsletter of the Grand Rapids Historical Society*)

Historical Society of Michigan
2117 Washtenaw Ave.
Ann Arbor, MI 48104
(*Chronicle*)

Iron County Historical and Museum Society

Route 424, Museum Street
Caspian, MI 49915
(*Past-Present Prints*)

Kalamazoo Valley Genealogical Society
Kalamazoo Public Library
315 South Rose Street
Kalamazoo, MI 49006
(*Kalamazoo Valley Family Newsletter*, 1971–)
NN APR (Kalamazoo) 75-585

Lake Odessa Area Historical Society
Page Bldg, 4th Avenue
Lake Odessa, MI 48849
(*Bonanza Bugle*)

Macomb County Historical Society
Box 243
Mount Clemens, MI 48043
(*News Bulletin*)

Marquette County Historical Society
213 North Front Street
Marquette, MI 49855
(*Harlow's Wooden Man*)

Mason County Historical Society, Inc.
305 East Filer Street
Ludington, MI 49431
(*Mason Memories*)

Michigan Department of Education
State Library Serivces
735 East Michigan Avenue
Lansing, MI 48913
(*Family Trails*, 1967–
NN APR [Michigan] 73-2580; *Family Tree Talk*)

Michigan Genealogical Council
Mrs. Mary Jane Trout, Secretary
Michigan State Library
735 East Michigan Avenue
Lansing, MI 48913

Michigan Heritage (1959–1973)
730 Parker Avenue
Kalamazoo, MI 49001
NN APR (Michigan)

Michigan Historical Collections
Bentley Historical Library
1150 Beal Avenue
Ann Arbor, MI 48105
(*Michigan Gazette*)

Michigan Historical Commission
208 North Capitol
Lansing, MI 48918

Michigan History Division
208 North Capitol Avenue
Lansing, MI 48918
(*Michigan History*, 1917–)
NN IAA

Midland County Historical Society
1801 West St. Andrews Drive
Midland, MI 48640
(*Midland Log*)

Mid-Michigan Genealogical Society
528 Charles Street
East Lansing, MI 48823

Muskegon County Genealogical Society
3301 Highland
Muskegon Heights, MI 49444

Northwest Oakland County Historical Society
423 North Saginaw Street
Holly, MI 48442
(*Lantern Light News*)

Oakland County Pioneer and Historical Society
405 Oakland Avenue
Pontiac, MI 48016
(*Oakland Gazette*)

Riverside Heritage Association
Box 184
Port Huron, MI 48060
(*Riverside Heritage Association Newsletter*)

Saginaw Genealogical Society
% Saginaw Public Library
505 James Street
Saginaw, MI 48607
(*Timbertown Log*, 1972–)

Washtenaw Historical Society
2708 Brockman Blvd.
Ann Arbor, MI 48104

Western Michigan Genealogical Society
% Grand Rapids Public Library
111 Library Street
Library Plaza N.E.
Grand Rapids, MI 49502
(*Michigana, 1955–*
NN APR (Michigan)

Books and Articles

Conot, Robert.
American Odyssey.
New York, William Morrow, 1974.
735 p., index.
NN IVH (Detroit 74-1980)

Hagman, Arthur, ed.
Oakland County Book of History
Sesqui-Centennial Pub., 1820–1970.
Oakland, Oakland Co. Board of

Supervisors, 1970. 623 p., no index.
NN IVH (Oakland) 75-2377

Index to the 1840 Federal Population Census of Michigan, ed. by Estelle A. McGlynn.
Detroit, Detroit Soc. for Gen. Research, 1977. 176 p.

Index to the 1850 Federal Population Census of Michigan.
Lansing, DAR Michigan, 1976. 463 p., alpha.

Kellogg, Lucy.
A Guide to Ancestral Trails.
(IN: *U.S. Census Office, 5th Census, 1830 Federal Population Schedule*. Detroit, DSGR, 1961. p. 139–150.)
NN APR (Michigan)

Lydens, Z. Z.
The Story of Grand Rapids.
Grand Rapids, Kregel Publications, 1966. 682 p., index.
NN IVH (Grand Rapids)

Michigan 1830 Census Index.
Bountiful, UT, AIS, 1977.

Michigan 1840 Census Index.
Bountiful, UT, AIS, 1977.

Michigan 1850 Census Index.
Bountiful, UT, AIS, 1977.

Miller, Alice Turner.
Soldiers of the War of 1812 Who Died in Michigan.
Ithaca, MI, 1962. 335 p., alpha.
NN APR (Michigan)

Schadenbrand, Peter S.
Death Records of St. Mary's German Catholic Church of Detroit, Michigan, 1835–1847.
(IN: *DSGR Magazine*, Detroit, 1976. v. 40, p. 76–80)
NN APGA

Vital Statistics Holdings by Government Agencies in Michigan.
Detroit, Michigan Hist. Rec. Survey, 1941–42. 4 v.
(Birth, marriage, death and divorce records)
NN APR (Michigan)

Wiedeman, Ruby, and Larry Bohannan.
Fourth Census of the United States, 1820, Michigan Population.
Huntsville, AR, Century Enterprises, 1968. 35 p.
NN APB p.v. 170

MINNESOTA

State Archives

Minnesota Historical Society
690 Cedar Street
St. Paul, MN 55101
(*Minnesota History News*, 1959–)
NN IVMB

Vital Records

Minnesota Department of Health
Section of Vital Statistics
717 Delaware Street S.E.
Minneapolis, MN 55440
Births and deaths: January 1908–
Births and deaths prior: clerk of district court of county
For Minneapolis or St. Paul: City Health Dept.
Marriages: Statewide index since January, 1958. Section of Vital

Statistics, State Dept. of Health, 717 Delaware St. S.E., Minneapolis, MN 55440.
Earlier marriages: clerk of district court

Libraries

Church of Jesus Christ of Latter-day Saints
Minneapolis, Minnesota, State Branch Genealogical Library
2801 Douglas Drive N.
Minneapolis, MN 55422

Minneapolis Public Library
300 Nicollet Avenue
Minneapolis, MN 55401

Public Library
90 West 4th Street
St. Paul, MN 55102

University of Minnesota Library
Minneapolis, MN 55455

Societies and Periodicals

Anoka County Genealogical Society
1900 Third Avenue
Anoka, MN 55303

Catholic Historical Society of St. Paul
2260 Summit Avenue
St. Paul, MN 55105

Commission on Archives and History for the United Methodist Church
122 West Franklin Avenue
Minneapolis, MN 55404

Dakota County Historical Society
125 Third Avenue North

South St. Paul, MN 55075
(*Over the Years*)

Fillmore County Historical Society
County Courthouse
Preston, MN 55965

Goodhue County Historical Society
1166 Oak Street
Red Wing, MN 55066
(*Goodhue County Historical News*)

Hennepin County Historical Society
2303 3rd Avenue South
Minneapolis, MN 55404
(*Hennepin County History*)

Minneapolis Genealogical Society
P.O. Box 16006
St. Paul, MN 55105
(*The Minnesota Genealogist*, 1970–)

Minnesota Heritage Enterprises, Inc.
100 Government Road
Taylor Falls, MN 55084
(*The Dalles Visitor*)

Mower County Genealogical Society
P.O. Box 145
Austin, MN 55912

North Hennepin Pioneer Society, Inc.
Box 406
Osseo, MN 55369

Olmstead County Historical Society
3103 S.W. Salem Road
Rochester, MN 55901

Ramsey County and St. Paul Historical Society
75 West 5th Street

St. Paul, MN 55102
(*Ramsey County History*)

Range Genealogical Society
Box 726
Buhl, MN 55713
(*Northland Newsletter*, 1969–)
NN APR (Minnesota) 73-574

St. Louis County Historical Society
2228 East Superior Street
Duluth, MN 55812

Southern Minnesota Historical
Center
Memorial Library
Mankato State College
Mankato, MN 56001

Southwest Minnesota Historical
Center
Southwest Minnesota State College
Marshall, MN 56258

Twin Ports Genealogical Society
% Ray E. Ecker
2121 East Second Street
Duluth, MN 55812

Western Hennepin County Pi-
oneers Association
Highway 12
Long Lake, MN 55356

Books and Articles

Bjornsenn, Val.
History of Minnesota.
West Palm Beach, FL, Lewis Hist.
Pub. Co., 1969. 4 v., index.
NN IVL

Harpole, Patricia C., and Mary D.
Nagle
Minnesota Territorial Census
1850.

St. Paul, 1972. 115 p.
NN APR (Minnesota) 73-161

Jones, Thelma.
Once Upon a Lake: A History of
Lake Minnetonka and Its Peo-
ple.
Minneapolis, Ross and Haines,
1957. 285 p., no index.
NN IVM (Minnetonka)

Kane, Lucile M.
The Waterfall That Built a City:
The Falls of St. Anthony in Min-
neapolis.
St. Paul, Minnesota Hist. Soc., 1966.
224 p., index.
NN IVM (Minneapolis)

Minnesota Historical Society.
Reference Guide to Minnesota His-
tory, by Michael Brook.
St. Paul, 1974. 132 p. index.
NN IVL 74-2047

Minnesota Historical Society.
Guide to the Personal Papers in
the Manuscript Collections.
St. Paul, 1935, 1955. 2 v.
NN IVL

MISSISSIPPI

State Archives

Mississippi Department of Ar-
chives and History
Box 571
100 South State Street
Jackson, MS 39201
(*Journal of Mississippi History*,
1939–)
NN IAA

Vital Records

Division of Public Health Statistics
State Board of Health
P.O. Box 1700

Jackson, MS 39205
Births and deaths: 1912–
Births and deaths, prior: check
with circuit clerk of county
Marriages: January 1926–
Marriages, prior: write circuit
clerk of county

Societies and Periodicals

Aberdeen Genealogical Society
Mrs. William Nickles, President
Aberdeen, MS 39730

Choctaw-Pioneer Historical Soci-
ety of French Camp on the
Natchez Trace
% Patty Ann Hall
Carthage
French Camp, MS 39051

Homochitto Valley Historical Soci-
ety
Box 337
Crosby, MS 39633
(*The Lumberjack*)

Mississippi Baptist Historical
Commission
Box 51
Mississippi College Library
Clinton, MS 39056

Mississippi Coast Historical and
Genealogical Society
P.O. Box 513
Biloxi, MS 39530
(*Mississippi Coast Historical and
Genealogical Quarterly*, 1968–)

*Mississippi Genealogy and Local
History*, 1969–)
NN APR (Mississippi) 73-2552
P.O. Box 9114
Shreveport, LA 71109

Mississippi Genealogical Society
Richard S. Lackey, President
438 East 1st Street
Forest, MS 39704
(*Mississippi Genealogical Ex-
change*, 1955–)
NN APR (Mississippi)

Mississippi Methodist Conference
Historical Commission
Millsaps College
Jackson, MS 39210

Skipwith Historical and Genealogical Society
% Mary Buie Museum
510 University Avenue
Oxford, MS 38655

Sons of the Confederacy
James B. Butler
P.O. Box 1055
Jackson, MS 39205

Books and Articles

Crocker, Mary Wallace.
Historic Architecture in Missis-
sippi.
Jackson, U. and College Press of
Mississippi, 1973. 194 p., index.
NN MQWO + 74-2068

DAR of Mississippi.
Mississippi Daughters and Their
Ancestry.
Starkville, MS, Starkville Pub. Co.,
1965. 2 v.
(v. 1, daughters, alpha.; v. 2, ancestry, alpha.)
NN APGA (DAR—Mississippi) 76-
666

Flanders, Robert B.
Nauvoo, Kingdom of the Mississippi.

Urbana, IL, U. of IL, 1965. 364 p.,
index.
NN IVF (Nauvoo)

Fly, Jean.
Marriage and Death Notices in
Natchez Newspapers, 1805–1840.
(IN: *Journal of Mississippi History*, Jackson, 1946, v. 8, p. 163–
226)
NN IAA

Gillis, Irene G.
Mississippi 1850 Mortality Schedules.
Shreveport, LA, Gillis Pub., 1973.
59, 17 p., alpha.
NN APR (Mississippi) 75-209

Gillis, Norman E., and Irene S.
Gillis.
Mississippi 1820 Census.
Baton Rouge, LA, 1963. 147 p.
NN APR (Mississippi)

Gillis, Norman E, and Irene S. Gillis.
Mississippi 1830 Census.
Baton Rouge, LA, 1965. 236 p.
NN APR (Mississippi)

Gillis, Norman E., and Irene S.
Gillis.
Mississippi Surname Index to the
1850 Census.
Shreveport, LA, 1972. 521 p.
NN APR (Mississippi) 73-1803

King, Junie E. S.
Mississippi Court Records, 1799–
1835.
Beverly Hills, CA, 1936. 181 p.,
index.
NN APR (Mississippi)

McBee, May Wilson.
Mississippi Court Records from
the May W. McBee Papers.

Greenwood, MS, 1958. 94 p., index.
NN APR (Mississippi)

Mississippi Courts, High Court of
Errors and Appeals.
Mississippi Court Records from
the Files of the High Court of
Errors and Appeals, 1799–1859,
comp. by Mary L. Hendrix,
1950. 373 p., index.
NN APR (Mississippi)

Mississippi 1820 Census Index.
Bountiful, UT, AIS, 1976.

Mississippi 1830 Census Index.
Bountiful, UT, AIS, 1976.

Mississippi 1850 Census Index.
Bountiful, UT, AIS, 1977.

Mississippi Provincial Archives,
1701–1743, French Dominated
. . ., ed. and trans. by Dunbar
Rowland and H.G. Sanders.
New York, AMS Press, 1973 (orig.
1927–1932). 3 v.
NN ITO

Natchez District, Province of Louisiana.
The Natchez Court Records,
1767–1805. Abstracts of Early
Records, comp by May Wilson
McBee.
Greenwood, c. 1953. 635 p., index.
NN APR (Natchez)

The Story of Jackson.
Jackson, J. F. Hyer Pub. Co., 1953.
2 v., index.
NN ITOM (Jackson)

U.S. Census Office 6th Census,
1840.
Index to the U.S. Census of 1840,
comp. by Given Platt, et al.

Santa Ana, CA, G.A.M. Pub., 1970–71. 2 v., surname index each v.
(Southern and Northern Districts)
NN APR (Mississippi) 76-309

MISSOURI

State Archives

Records and Archives
Office of Secretary of State
Capitol Bldg.
Jefferson, MO 65101

Vital Records

Bureau of Vital Records
Division of Health
State Department of Public Health and Welfare
Jefferson City, MO 65101
Births and deaths: January 1910–
Births and deaths prior: write county clerk's office
Marriages: indexes since July 1948
Earlier marriages: recorder of deeds of county

Libraries

Church of Jesus Christ of Latter-day Saints
Kansas City, Missouri, Branch Genealogical Library
8144 Holmes
Kansas City, MO 64131

Harry S. Truman Library and Museum
Independence, MO 64050
(*Whistlestop*)

Heritage Library
Johnson County Historical Society
135 East Pine Street
Warrensburg, MO 64093

Kansas City Public Library
311 East 12th Street
Kansas City, MO 64106

Missouri State Library
308 East High Street
Jefferson City, MO 65101

St. Louis Public Library
1301 Olive Street
St. Louis, MO 63103

Societies and Periodicals

Archives of the City of St. Louis
1200 Market Street
St. Louis, MO 63103

Cape Girardeau County, Missouri, Genealogical Society
204 South Union Avenue
Jackson, MO 63755

Chariton County Historical Society, Inc.
Salisbury, MO 65281
(*Chariton County Historical Society Newsletter*)

Concordia Historical Institute
801 DeMun Avenue
Clayton, MO 63105
(*Concordia Historical Institute Quarterly*)

Dent County Historical Society
Salem, MO 65560
(*Historical Review*)

Florissant Valley Historical Society
No. 1 Traille de Noyer

Florissant, MO 63031
(Mail: Box 298, Florissant, MO 63032)
(*Florissant Valley Historical Society Quarterly*)

Genealogical Society of Central Missouri
c/o Mrs. Sandra Hayton
55 East Park Lane
Columbia, MO 65201

Heart of America Genealogical Society
1828 Walnut Street, Room 501
Kansas City, MO 64108
(*Kansas City Genealogist*, 1960–)
NN APR (Kansas City, Missouri)

Heritage Seekers
819 South Home Street
Palmyra, MO 63461

Jackson County Historical Society
217 North Main Street
Independence, MO 64050
(*Jackson County Historical Society Journal*, 1958–)
NN IVQ (Jackson Co.) 75-616

Johnson County Historical Society
Main and Gay
Warrensburg, MO 64093
(Mail: 410 Grover, Warrensburg, MO 64093)
(*Johnson County Historical Society Bulletin*)

Kingdom of Callaway Historical Society
7th and Westminster Avenue
Fulton, MO 65251
(Mail: c/o W.C. Murphy, 501 East 10th Street, Fulton, MO 65251)
(*Bulletin*)

Lawrence County Historical Society

210 North Main Street, Box 406
Mount Vernon, MO 65712
(*Lawrence County Historical Society Bulletin*)

Missouri Baptist Historical Society
William Jewell College Library
Liberty, MO 64068

Missouri Historical Society
Jefferson Memorial Bldg.
Forest Park
St. Louis, MO 63112
(*Missouri Historical Review*, 1906–)
NN IAA

Missouri Pioneers
7231 Sycamore
Kansas City, MO 64133

Moniteau County, Missouri, Historical Society
California, MO 65081

Native Sons of Kansas City, Missouri
4200 West 54th Street
Shawnee Mission
Kansas City, MO 66205
(Mail: Box 1111, Mission, KS 66222)

Niangua Chapter, Daughters of the American Revolution
c/o Ilene Sims Yarnell
Versailles, MO 65084

Perry County Lutheran Historical Society
Altenburg, MO 63732

Peter Willcocks Society
4141 Terrace, Box 1832
Kansas City, MO 64141
(*Journal of the Peter Willcocks Society*)

Ray County Historical Society
Box 2, Westend of Royle
Richmond, MO 64085
(*Ray County Mirror*)

Raytown Historical Society
6335 Blue Ridge Blvd.
Raytown, MO 64133
(*Trail News*)

The Researcher (1966–)
c/o Elizabeth Prather Ellsberry
Box 206
Chillicothe, MO 64601
NN APR (Missouri) 73-2820

Ridge Runners
William A. Yates
Sparta, MO 65753

St. Charles County Genealogical
   Society
P.O. Box 715
St. Charles, MO 63301
(surname index)

St. Louis Genealogical Society
1617 South Brentwood Blvd, Suite
   268
St. Louis, MO 63144
(*St. Louis Genealogical Society
   Quarterly*, c.1967–)
NN APR (St. Louis) 73-607

St. Mary's Pioneer Historical Society
611 North Liberty
Independence, MO 64050

State Historical Society of Missouri
Hitt and Lowry Streets
Columbia, MO 65201
(*Missouri Historical Review, 1906–*)
NN IAA

West Central Missouri Genealogical Society and Library, Inc.

312 Johnson Avenue
Warrensburg, MO 64093
(*Prairie Gleaner*, 1969–)

Western Historical Manuscripts
   Collection
23 Ellis Library
University of Missouri
Columbia, MO 65201

Westport Historical Society, Inc.
Box 10064, Suite D
23 Westport Square
Kansas City, MO 64111
(*Westport Historical Society Quart-
   erly*)

Books and Articles

Carter, Genevieve L.
Early Missouri Marriages to and
   including 1840.
Sedalia, MO, Mrs. J. R. Carter,
   197–. 3 v.
NN APR (Missouri)

Chadwell, Patricia.
Missouri Land Claims, with a New
   Index.
New Orleans, Polyanthos, 1976
   (orig. 1835) 421 p. plus maps
   and index.

Coppage, A. Maxim.
Missouri Cousins.
Antioch, CA, Raines Pub. Co.,
   1969. 145 p.
NN APR (Missouri)

Coppage, A. Maxim, and Dorothy
   F. Wulfeck.
Virginia Settlers in Missouri.
Naugatuck, CT, D. F. Wulfeck, c.
   1964. 151 p.
NN APR (Virginia)

DAR in Missouri.
Cemetery Records of Missouri.
Chillicothe, E. P. Ellsberry, 1965.
3 v.
NN APR (Missouri)

Ellsberry, Elizabeth P.
Bible Records of Missouri.
Chillicothe, E. P. Ellsberry, 1963–
c. 1966. 8 v.
NN APR (Missouri)

Ellsberry, Elizabeth P.
Early Wills of North Central
Counties of Missouri.
Chillicothe, 1960. 7, 75 leaves.
NN APR (Missouri)

Haynes, Shirley.
Index to Missouri Obituaries.
Gillian, Saline Sentiments, c. 1974.
4 v.
NN APR (Missouri) 75-420

The History of Jackson County,
Missouri.
Cape Giradeau, Ramfre Press,
1966 (orig. 1881) 1,006 p., index
added.
NN IVQ (Jackson Co.)

Hodges, Nadine.
Missouri Pioneers: County and
Genealogical Records.
Kansas City, Mrs. Howard W.
Woodruff, 1967–76, 30 v.
NN APR (Missouri)

Houts, Alice K., and Hazel East-
man.
Revolutionary Soldiers Buried in
Missouri.
Kansas City, 1966. 286 p.
NN APR (Missouri)

Gambrill, Georgia.
Genealogical Material and Local

Histories in the St. Louis Public
Library.
St. Louis, St. Louis Public Lib., rev.
1965–66. 356 p.
1st Supplement, 1971 (orig. pub.
1941, rev. in 1953)
NN AP

Green, George F.
A Condensed History of the Kan-
sas City Area, Its Mayors and
Some VIPs.
Kansas City, Lowell Press, 1968.
342 p., no index.
NN IVQ (Kansas City)

McManus, Thelma S., and Grace
E. Burlison.
Come Over into Macedonia: The
Charles Thompson Line from
Dinwiddie County, Virginia, to
Ripley County, Missouri, 1760–
1974.
Doniphan, Vitronic Division,
Penn. Corp., 1974.
Various paging, 65, 17, 49, 74 plus
p., index.
NN APR (Macedonia, Missouri)
75-1369

Missouri 1830 Census Index.
Bountiful, UT, AIS, 1976.

Missouri 1840 Census Index.
Bountiful, UT, AIS, 1976.

Missouri 1850 Census Index.
Bountiful, UT, AIS, 1977.

Petty, Gerald M.
Composite Index of the 1830, 1840,
1850, 1860, 1870, and 1880
United States Census of Ran-
dolph County, Missouri.
Columbus, OH, G. M. Petty, 1970.
138 p., index, alpha.
NN APR+ (Randolph Co.)

St. Louis Genealogical Society.
Index of St. Louis Marriages.
1973. 2 v. (Covers 1804–1876)
NN APR (St. Louis)

St. Louis Genealogical Society.
Index of the 1850 Census of St.
Louis and St. Louis Co., MO,
1969. 1 v., unpaged, arranged
alpha.
NN APR (St. Louis) 73-2348

St. Louis Genealogical Society.
Tracing Family Trees in Eleven
States: Missouri, Illinois, Ken-
tucky, Virginia, Georgia, Ohio,
North Carolina, South Carolina,
Tennessee, Indiana, Pennsyl-
vania.
Brentwood, MO, 1920. 290 p.,
maps.
NN APB 72-1707

Thruston, Ethylene Ballard.
Echoes of the Past: A Nostalgic
Look at Early Raytown and
Jackson County.
Kansas City, Missouri, The Low-
erll Press, 1973. 483 p., t of c,
no index. (Interesting local his-
tory, filled with pictures and
good layout; too bad no index)
NN IVQ (Raytown) 75-1330

Vexler, Robert I.
St. Louis: A Chronological and Doc-
umentary History, 1762–1970.
Dobbs Ferry, NY, Oceana, 1974.
153 p.
NN IVQ (St. Louis) 71-3

Williams, Jacqueline H., and
Betty H. Williams.
Resources for Genealogical Re-
search in Missouri.
Warrensburg, 1969. 60 p.
NN APR (Missouri)

MONTANA

State Archives

Montana Historical Society
225 North Robert Street
Helena, MT 59601
(*Montana: The Magazine of West-
ern History*, 1951–)
NN IAA

Vital Records

Bureau of Records and Statistics
State Department of Health and
Environmental Sciences
Helena, MT 59601
Births and deaths: 1907–
Births and deaths prior: county
clerk's office
Marriages: July 1943–
Earlier marriages: clerk of dis-
trict court

Libraries

Church of Jesus Christ of Latter-
day Saints
Helena, Montana, State Branch
Genealogical Library
Helena State Center
1610 East 6th Avenue
Helena, MT 59601

Societies and Periodicals

Central Montana Historical Association
Box 592
408 N.E. Main
Lewistown, MT 59457

Eastern Montana Historical and
Archeological Society
Box 549
Miles City, MT 59301

Great Falls Genealogical Society
4705 Carol Drive
Great Falls, MT 59405
(*Treasure State Lines*)

Historical Society of Montana
Helena, MT 59601

Pioneer Historical Circle
Box 393
Circle, MT 59215

Western Heritage Center
29th Street and Montana Avenue
Billings, MT 59101

Books and Articles

Abbot, Newton C.
Montana in the Making. 13th ed.
   rev.
Billings, MT, Gazette Print. Co.,
   1964. 485 p.
NN IWL

Burlingame, Merrill G, and K.
   Rosstoole.
A History of Montana.
New York, Lewis, 1957. 3 v.
NN IWL

Campbell, William C.
From the Quarries of Last Chance
   Gulch: A Newspaper History of
   Helena   and   Its   Masonic
   Lodges.
Helena, Montana Record Pub. Co.,
   1951–64. 2 v., t of c, no index.
NN IWM (Helena)

Davis, Jean W.
Shallow Diggin's: Tales from Mon-
   tana's Ghost Towns.
Caldwell, ID, Caxton Printers,
   1962. 375, 2 p.
NN IWL

Miller, Don C.
Ghost Towns of Montana.
Boulder, CO, Pruett Pub. Co.,
   1974. 178 p., t of c, no index,
   towns   alpha   (Cemeteries   in
   many of them).
NN IWMB 75-2183

Speiser, James and Mildred.
Changing West.
Miles City, MT, H. & T. Quality,
   1975. 186 p.
NN IWM (Ekalaka) 75-2224

U.S.W.P.A.
Guide to Public Vital Statistics in
   Montana.
Bozeman, 1941. 85 p.
NN APR p.v. 211

U.S.W.P.A.
Inventory of Vital Statistics Rec-
   ords of Churches and Religious
   Organizations in Montana.
Bozeman, 1942. 117f. p.
NN APR (Montana)

Woole, Muriel V.S.
Montana Pay Dirt: A Guide to the
   Mining Camps of the Treasure
   State.
Denver, CO, Sage Books, c. 1963.
   436 p.
NN IWMB

NEBRASKA

State Archives

Nebraska State Historical Society
1500 "R" Street
Lincoln, NE 68508
(*Nebraska History*, 1918–)
NN IAA

Vital Records

Bureau of Vital Statistics
State Department of Health
Lincoln Building
1003 "O" Street
Lincoln, NE 68508
Births and deaths: 1904–
Births and deaths prior: write
state for information
Marriages: January 1909–, Bureau of Vital Statistics, State
Dept. of Health, State Capitol,
Lincoln NE 68509
Marriages prior: county court

Libraries

Church of Jesus Christ of Latter-
day Saints
Omaha, Nebraska, State Branch
Genealogical Library
11027 Martha Street
Omaha, NE 68144

Nebraska Conference United
Methodist Historical Library
Lucas Bldg.
Nebraska Wesleyan University
50th and St. Paul
Lincoln, NE 68504

Nebraska Daughters of the American Revolution Library
202 West 4th Street
Alliance, NE 69301

Nebraska State Historical Society
Library
1500 "R" Street
Lincoln, NE 68508

Omaha Public Library
19th and Harney
Omaha, NE 68102

Public Library
136 South 14th Street
Lincoln, NE 68508

University of Nebraska Library
Lincoln, NE 68503

Societies and Periodicals

Adams County Historical Society
Box 102
Hastings, NE 68901
(*Historical News*)

Brownville Historical Society, Inc.
Box 186—Second and Main
Brownville, NE 68321
(*Brownville Bulletin*)

Centennial Historical Committee
148 West 4th
Ainsworth, NE 69210

Chappell-Chapter Historical Soci-
ety
Box 321—190 Vincent Avenue
Chappell, NE 69129
(*Historical Review*)

Eastern Nebraska Genealogical
Society
% Gene Bang
4011 North Somers Street
Fremont, NE 68025
(*Eastern Nebraska Genealogical
Society Quarterly*)

Eastern Nebraska Genealogical
Society
% Mrs. R. L. Baum
6812 Minne Lusa Blvd.
Omaha, NE 68112

Nebraska Genealogical Society
% Nebraska State Historical Society

1500 "R" Street
Lincoln, NE 68508
(*Records*, v. 1–22, 1923–44)
NN APGA

North Central Nebraska Historical Society, Inc.
Stuart, NE 68780

North Platte Genealogical Society
% North Platte Public Library
4th Street and Vine
North Platte, NE 69101
(*Newsletter*, 1965–)
NN APR (North Platte) 76-702

North Platte Valley Historical Association, Inc.
Box 495, 11th and J Street
Oregon Trail Park
Gering, NE 69341

Books and Articles

Brevet's Nebraska.
Historical Markers and Sites.
Sioux Falls, 1974. 220 p.
NN IWC 75-1659

DAR, Nebraska.
Nebraska DAR History.
Lincoln, 1929, 558 p., index.
NN APGA

Fitzpatrick, Linda L.
Nebraska Place-Names.
Lincoln, U. of NE Press, 1960. 227 p.
NN IWDB

Gilman, Musetta.
Pump on the Prairie.
Detroit, MI, Harlo, 1975. 223 p.
NN IWD (Platte River Valley) 76-442

Green, Norma Kidd.
Iron Eye's Family: The Children of Joseph LaFleshe.
Lincoln, Johnson Pub. Co., 1969. 225 p. (J. LaFleshe, 1822–1889, Omaha Indian)
NN HBM (LaFleshe)

Guide to the Archives and Manuscripts of the Nebraska State Historical Society, comp. by William F. Schmidt and Harold E. Kemble, Jr.
Lincoln, 1966. 93 p.
(*Nebraska State Historical Society Bulletin, no. 2*)
NN IAA 74-22 no. 2

Heil, Lelia R.
Genealogical Abstracts from the *Tecumseh Chieftain*, Johnson County, Nebraska, Official Newspaper, 1873–1900. n.p., L.R. Hill, 1970. 310 p., index, alpha.
NN APR (Johnson Co.) 71-118

Kucera, Vladimir.
Czechs and Nebraska.
Ord, NE, Quiz Graphics, c. 1967. 424 p.
NN IEE (Czechs)

National Society of U.S. Daughters of 1812, Nebraska.
Heroes of 1812.
Omaha, 1930. 228 p.
NN APGA

Nebraska Census, 1954, Second District.
(IN: *Genealogist's Post*, Miami, FL 1967–68. v. 4, no. 11, p. 31–35; v. 4, no. 12, p. 27–29; v. 5, no. 2, p. 29–33)
NN APGA

Shippey, Melda Haynes.
Nebraska Pioneer, William Butler, Ancestors and Descendants.
Cottonport, LA, Polyanthos, 1973.
166 p., index.
NN APV (Butler) 74-2321

U.S.W.P.A., Nebraska.
Guide to Vital Statistics.
Lincoln, 1941. 94f. p.
NN APR (Nebraska)

NEVADA

State Archives

State, County, Municipal Archives
Capitol Bldg. Annex
Carson City, NV 89701

Vital Records

Department of Human Resources
Division of Health
Section of Vital Statistics
Capitol Complex
Carson City, NV 89710
Births and deaths; July 1, 1911–
Births and deaths prior: county
recorder
Marriages: county recorder. Dates
vary—as early as 1860, as late
as 1919—by county.

Libraries

Church of Jesus Christ of Latter-
day Saints
Las Vegas, Nevada, Branch Genealogical Library
509 South 9th Street
Las Vegas, NV 89010

Nevada State Historical Society Li-
brary
P.O. Box 1192
Reno, NV 89501

Societies and Periodicals

Carson Valley Historical Society
Box 545
Minden, NV 89423

Nevada State Historical Society
1650 North Virginia Street
Reno, NV 89503
(*Nevada State Historical Society
Quarterly*, 1957–)
NN IAA

Pueblo Grande de Nevada
Box 127, Highway 12
Puerton, NV 89040

Southern Nevada Historical Society
2900 Capistrano Avenue
Las Vegas, NV 89121
(*Back Trails*)

White Pine County Historical Soci-
ety
White Pine County Library
Box 789
Ely, NV 89301

Books and Articles

Ashbaugh, Don.
Nevada's Turbulent Yesterdays:
A Study in Ghost Towns.
Los Angeles, CA, Western Lore
Press, 1963. 346 p., index.
NN IXFB

Daughters of American Colonists.

Nevada Collections of Genealogies.
Reno, 1956. 6 v. in 1 (church, cemetery, Bible records).
NN APR (Nevada)

Early Nevada Churches, etc.
(IN: *Genealogists Post*, Miami, FL., 1964. v. 1, no. 11, p. 13–26)
NN APGA

Hafner, Arabell Lee.
One Hundred Years on the Muddy.
Springville, UT, Art City Pub. Co., 1967. 384 p., long t of c, no index, many illus.
NN APR (Clarke Co.) 72-2074

Kelly, J. Wells.
First Directory of Nevada Territory, 1862.
Los Gatos, CA, Talisman Press, 1962. 264, 24, 265, 266 p.
NN AZE (Nevada)

Parkin, Nona.
List of Registered Voters in Various Nevada Precincts [sic] Years 1882 and Other Lists of Nevada Citizens.
Reno, c. 1964. 1 v. 7 parts in 1 v.
NN APR (Nevada)

Parkin, Nona.
Nevada Cemeteries Inscriptions from the Tombstones of Sixteen Cemeteries.
Reno, c. 1964. 1 v. 17 parts.
NN APR (Nevada)

Paher, Stanley W.
Las Vegas, As It Began—As It Grew.
Las Vegas, Nevada Pub., 1971. 181 p., index.
NN IXF (Las Vegas) 72-1237

Paher, Stanley W.
Nevada Ghost Towns and Mining Camps.
Berkeley, CA, Howell North, 1970. 492 p., index.
NN IXE 72-111

Ratay, Myra Sauer.
Pioneers of the Ponderosa ...
Sparks, NV, Western Printing, 1973. 470 p., index.
NN IXF (Washoe Co.) 73-1783

Sullivan, John J.
State of Nevada Dept. of Health and Welfare, Division of Health, Section of Vital Statistics, Carson City, Nevada.
(IN: *Genealogist's Post*, Miami, FL., 1964. v.1, no. 10, p. 19–21)
NN APGA

Wright, William (Dan DeQuille).
The Big Bonanza: Comstock Lode of Nevada.
New York, Knopf, 1947. 436, viii p., index.
NN IXE

Yerrington *Times*.
Draft and Enlistment Lists, Lyon County, 1917–1918, Together with Notices of Marriages, Divorces, Births and Deaths from the Yerrington *Times*, comp. by Nona Parkin.
Reno, c. 1964. 1 v., 3 parts.
NN APR (Yerrington)

NEW HAMPSHIRE

State Archives

New Hampshire State Library
20 Park Street
Concord, NH 03303

Vital Records

Department of Health and Welfare
Division of Public Health
Bureau of Vital Statistics
61 South Spring Street
Concord, NH 03301
Births, deaths and marriages: 1640–. Also may write city or town clerk for vital records

Libraries

Baker Memorial Library
Dartmouth College
Hanover, NH 03755

Dartmouth College Archives
Baker Library
Hanover, NH 03755

Societies and Periodicals

American-Canadian Genealogical Society of New Hampshire
% Jean Tellerin
145 Oakdale Avenue
Manchester, NH 03103

Association of Historical Societies of New Hampshire, Inc.
Durham, NH 03824

Conway Historical Society
Lord House
Main Street
Conway, NH 03818

Exeter Historical Society
27 Front Street
Exeter, NH 03833

Historical Society of Cheshire County
104 West Street

Keene, NH 03431
(Mail: 117 Washington Street, Keene, NH 03431)

Manchester Historical Association
129 Amherst Street
Manchester, NH 03104

New Hampshire Genealogical Society
% North Hampton Public Library
North Hampton, NH 03862

New Hampshire Historical Society Library
30 Park Street
Concord, NH 03301
(*Historical New Hampshire*, 1944–)
NN IAA
(NHS ... Family Names in New Hampshire Town Histories. Concord, 1946. 78 p.)
NN APR (New Hampshire)

New Hampshire Society of Genealogists
P.O. Box 795
Laconia, NH 03246

New Hampshire State Historical Commission
71 South Fruit Street
Concord, NH 03301

Northam Colonists
% Donald Bryant
Washington Street
Dover, NH 03820

Portsmouth Historical Society
State and Middle Streets
Portsmouth, NH 03801

Rochester Historical Society
Box 2114
Rochester, NH 03867

Sandwich Historical Society
Maple Street
Center Sandwich, NH 03227
(*Excursion*)

Books and Articles

Cole, Luane.
Patterns and Pieces 1761–1976.
Canaan, Lyme Historians, 1976.
381 p., index.
NN IQD (Lyme) 77-623

Dearborn, David C.
New Hampshire Genealogy: A
Perspective.
(IN: *NEHGR*, Boston, MA, Oct.
1976. v. 130, p. 224–55)
NN *R-APGA

Gill, Maryan R.
An Index to the 1800 Federal Census of Grafton and Hillsborough Counties in the State of
New Hampshire.
Danville, IL, Maryan R. Gill, 1972.
88 p., alpha for each co.
NN APR (Grafton Co.) 74-1439

Goss, Mrs. Charles C.
Colonial Gravestone Inscriptions
in the State of New Hampshire.
Baltimore, MD, GPC, 1974 (orig.
1942). 160 p., no index, cemeteries alpha by town.
NN APR (New Hampshire) 75-2078

Hammond, Otis G.
Notices from the New Hampshire
Gazette, 1765–1800.
Lambertville, NJ, Thomas B. Wilson's Hunterdon House, 1970.

Hanrahan, E.J.
Hammond's Checklist of New
Hampshire History, new ed.

Somersworth, NJ Pub. Co., 1971
(orig. 1925). 129 p., index.
NN IQDB 72-2159

Holbrook, Jay Mack.
New Hampshire 1776 Census.
Oxford, MS 01540, Holbrook Institute, 57 Locust St., 1977. 9,000
names.

New Hampshire (Colony) Probate
Court.
Probate Records of the Province
of New Hampshire, 1635–1771.
Concord, Hist. Soc., 1907–41. 9 v.
(New Hampshire State Papers
Series, v. 31–39)
NN IQC

New Hampshire 1800 Census Index.
Bountiful, UT, AIS, 1976.

New Hampshire 1810 Census Index.
Bountiful, UT, AIS, 1976.

New Hampshire 1820 Census Index.
Bountiful, UT, AIS, 1976. 66 p.

New Hampshire 1830 Census Index.
Bountiful, UT, AIS, 1977.

New Hampshire 1840 Census Index.
Bountiful, UT, AIS, 1977.

New Hampshire 1850 Census Index.
Bountiful, UT, AIS, 1977.

Threlfall, John Brooks.
Heads of Families at the Second
Census ... 1800, New Hampshire.

Madison, WI, 1973. 222 p., index.
NN APR (New Hampshire) 74-
1593

Towle, Laird C.
New Hampshire Genealogical Re-
search Guide.
Bowie, MD, Prince George's Co.
Gen. Soc., 1973. 43 p.
NN APR (New Hampshire) 75-
2256

Two Hundred Years Plus
1771–1776: Bradford, New
Hampshire, in Retrospect.
Canaan, Phoenix Pub. for the
Town of Bradford, 1976. 286 p.,
index. (A good example of a New
Hampshire local history com-
piled with Bicentennial spirit)
NN IQD + (Bradford) 77-829

Woodbury, George.
John Goffe's Legacy.
New York, W.W. Norton, 1955. 272
p., no index.
NN IQD (Bedford)

NEW JERSEY

State Archives

New Jersey Bureau of Archives
and History
185 West State Street
Trenton, NJ 08618

Vital Records

State Department of Health
Bureau of Vital Statistics
Box 1540
Trenton, NJ 08625
Births and deaths: June 1878–
Marriages: state office or county
clerk. Local records begin as
early as 1795.

Births, marriages and deaths for
May 1848–May 1878: write Archives and History Bureau,
State Library Division, State Department of Education, Trenton, NJ 08625

Libraries

Church of Jesus Christ of Latter-
day Saints
Caldwell, New Jersey, Branch
Genealogical Library
Short Hills Ward
140 White Oak Ridge Road
Summit, NJ 07901

Gardiner A. Sage Library
21 Seminary Place
New Brunswick, NJ 08901
(The repository for many of the
Dutch Reformed Church rec-
ords)

Rutgers University Library
New Brunswick, NJ 08903
(The New Jersey Genealogical So-
ciety records are housed here)

Societies and Periodicals

Batsto Citizens Committee
Batsto R.D. 1
Hammonton
Batsto, NJ 08215
(*Batsto Citizens Gazette*)

Bergen County Historical Society
Box 61
River Edge, NJ 07661
(*Bergen County History*)

Bergen-Passaic Military History
Society
98 Van Winkle Avenue
Passaic, NJ 07055

Burlington County Historical Society
457 High Street
Burlington, NJ 08016

Camden County Historical Society
Park Blvd. and Euclid Avenue
Camden, NJ 08103
(*The Bulletin*)

Cape May Historical Society
Courthouse
Cape May, NJ 08204

Cemetery Hounds
Committee of the Genealogical Society of New Jersey
% Dorothy A. Stratford
123 West Franklin Street
Bound Brook, NJ 08805

Clark Historical Society
Clark Public Library
303 Westfield Avenue
Clark, NJ 07066
(*The Avalanche*)

Cumberland County Historical Society
Box 16, Ye Greate Street
Greenwich, NJ 08323

English Neighborhood Historical Society
130 Grand Avenue
Leonia, NJ 07605

Genealogical Society of New Jersey
P.O. Box 1291
New Brunswick, NJ 08903
(*Genealogical Magazine of New Jersey*, 1925–)
(*Index to the Genealogical Magazine of New Jersey*, compiled by Kenn Stryker-Rodda, New Orleans, Polyanthos, 1973–. 3 v. to date (covers v. 1–40, 1925–65)
NN APR (New Jersey)

Gloucester County Historical Society
58 North Broad Street
Courthouse Annex, Room 202
Woodbury, NJ 08096
(*Gloucester County Historical Society Bulletin*)

Historical Society of Hudson County
Public Library
472 Jersey Avenue
Jersey City, NJ 07392

Historical Society of Princeton
158 Nassau Street
Princeton, NJ 08540

Historical Society of the Southern New Jersey Annual Conference of the United Methodist Church
Library of the Pennington School
Pennington, NJ 08534

League of Historical Societies of New Jersey
Box 531
Elizabeth, NJ 07201

Mercer County Cultural and Heritage Commission
640 South Broad Street
Mercer County Administration Bldg.
Trenton, NJ 08607
(*The Mercer Oak*)

Monmouth County Historical Association
70 Court Street
Freehold, NJ 07728
(*Monmouth Historian*)

Montclair Historical Society
Box 322, Orange Road
Montclair, NJ 07042

New Jersey Genesis, Carl M. Williams. ed., 1955–. NN APR (New Jersey)
151 East 81st Street
New York, NY 10028
(*Index to the New Jersey Genesis, 1955–1971*. Albuquerque, NM, NM Gen. Soc., 1973.)

New Jersey Historical Commission
State Library
185 West State Street
Trenton, NJ 08625

New Jersey Historical Society
230 Broadway
Newark, NJ 07104
(*New Jersey History*, 1845–)
NN IAA

North Jersey Highlands Historical Society
Box 1
Newfoundland, NJ 07435
(*Highlander*)

Paramus Historical and Preservation Society, Inc.
650 East Glen Avenue
Ridgewood, NJ 07450

Pascack Genealogical Society
% Mrs. Edna Falter
5 Ackerman Avenue
Woodcliff Lake, NJ 07675
(*The Archivist*)

Pascack Historical Society
Box 285, 19 Ridge Avenue
Park Ridge, NJ 07656
(*Relics*)

Passaic County Historical Society
Box 1729
Lambert Castle
Garret Mountain Reservation
Paterson, NJ 07509

(*Remembrances of Passaic County*)

Revolutionary Memorial Society of New Jersey, Inc.
Washington Place
Somerville, NJ 08876

Salem County, New Jersey, Historical Society
81–83 Market Street
Salem, NJ 08079

Trenton Historical Society
Box 213
Trenton, NJ 08620

Van Voorhees Association
151 George Street
New Brunswick, NJ 08901

Vineland Historical and Antiquarian Society
108 South 7th Street
Vineland, NJ 08360

Books and Articles

Beck, Henry C.
The Jersey Midlands.
New Brunswick, Rutgers U. Press, 1962 (orig. 1939) 460 p., index.
NN ISBB

Bergen Records: Records of the Reformed Protestant Dutch Church of Bergen in New Jersey, 1666 to 1788.
Baltimore, MD, GPC, 1976 (orig. 1913–1915) 3 v. in 1, index.
NN APR (Bergen)

DAR, New Jersey.
State History of the New Jersey DAR.
Sea Isle City, 1929. 369 p.
NN APGA

Gerlach, Larry R.
Prologue to Independence: New Jersey in the Coming of the American Revolution.
New Brunswick, Rutgers U. Press, 1976. 535 p., index.
(p. 361–79, appendix 1, members of the Council, 1760–70, A–Z; members of the Provincial Congress, 1775–76)
NN ISA 76-1955

Gibson, G. & F., comp.
Gloucester County, New Jersey 1850 Census.
Woodbury, Gloucester Co. Hist. Soc., 1971.

Groff, Sibyl McC.
New Jersey's Historic Houses.
South Brunswick, A.S. Barnes, 1971. 247 p., index.
NN ISBB 71-563

McMahon, William.
South Jersey Towns, History and Legend.
New Brunswick, Rutgers U. Press, 1973. 382 p., index.
(A modern gazetteer)
NN ISBB 75-620

Mack, Helen Leek.
The Leek Family of Southern Jersey.
Woodbury, Gloucester Co. Hist. Soc., c. 1974. 193 p., index.
NN APV (Leek) 76-161

Military Men of New Jersey, 1775–1815.
Bountiful, UT, AIS, 1976. alpha.

Minotty, Paul.
Records of the Moravian Church at Oldman's Creek.
Woodbury, Gloucester Co. Hist. Soc., 1968. 134 p., index.

NN APR (Gloucester Co.) 76-15 and 76-430

New Jersey Bureau of Archives and History and Genealogical Research.
Trenton, 1971. 36 p.
NN APR (New Jersey) 74-739

New Jersey 1830 Census Index.
Bountiful, UT, AIS, 1976.

New Jersey 1840 Census Index.
Bountiful, UT, AIS, 1977.

New Jersey 1850 Census Index.
Bountiful, UT, AIS, 1976. 386 p.

New Jersey Historical Society Archives, First Series, Calendar of Wills, 1670–1817.
Trenton, 1901–49. v. 1–13.
(v. 23, 30, 32, 33, 34, 35, 36, 37, 38, 39, 40, 41, 42)
NN APR (New Jersey)

New Jersey Index of Wills, with an introduction by Kenn Stryker-Rodda.
Baltimore, MD, GPC, 1969 (reprint; orig. 1912–13)
(Covers period prior to 1901)
NN APR (New Jersey)

Norton, James S.
New Jersey in 1793.
Salt Lake City, UT, 1973. 515 p., alpha.
NN APR (New Jersey) 75-2301

Richards, Kenneth W., Rebecca B. Colesar, David C. Munn, comp.
Genealogical Research: A Guide to Source Materials in the Archives and History Bureau of the New Jersey State Library.
Trenton, Gen. Soc. of NJ for the

Archives and History Bureau, Feb. 1971. 36 p.
NN APR (New Jersey) 74-739

Smith, Herbert F.
A Guide to the Manuscript Collection of the Rutgers University Library.
New Brunswick, Rutgers U. Lib., 1964. 179 p.
NN E-11 9482

Stryker-Rodda, Kenn.
New Jersey: Digging for Your Ancestors in the Garden State.
Detroit, MI, DSGR, 1970. 38 p.
NN APB p.v. 175

Stryker-Rodda, Kenn.
Revolutionary Census of New Jersey: An Index, Based on Ratables of the Inhabitants of New Jersey During the Period of the American Revolution.
Cottonport, LA, Polyanthos, 1972. xi, 248, 13 p., alpha.
NN APR (New Jersey) 73-1850

Stryker-Rodda, Harriet.
Some Early Records of Morris County, New Jersey, 1740–1799.
New Orleans, LA, Polyanthos, 1975. 243 p., index.

Tanco, Barbrae Owens and Marguerite D. Owens.
The 1850 Census ... New Jersey
Arlington, Fort Worth, TX, Owens & Tanco, 1973–74. 2 v.
(v. 1, Atlantic, Bergen, Burlington Co; v. 2, Gloucester, Hunterdon, Hudson Co.), index each v.
NN APR (Atlantic Co.) 75-1365 and APR (Gloucester Co.) 75-1364

Thayer, Theodore.
Colonial and Revolutionary Morris County, New Jersey.

Morristown, Morris County Heritage Comm., 1975. 325 p., index
ISB (Morris Co.) 76-2183

Van Benthuysen, Robert F.
Monmouth County, New Jersey: A Bibliography of Published Works, 1676–1973.
Sea Bright, Ploughshare Press, 1974. 170 p., index.
NN ISB (Monmouth) 75-1503

Van Benthuysen, Robert F.
Monmouth County During the Revolution: A Bibliography of Published Works.
West Long Branch, Monmouth College Lib., 1971. 23 p.
NN ISM (Monmouth Co.) 76-910

New Mexico

State Archives

Historical Services Division
State Records Center and Archives
404 Montezuma Street
Santa Fe, NM 87501

Vital Records

Vital Records
New Mexico Health and Social Services Department
PERA Building, Room 118
Santa Fe, NM 87501
Births and deaths: 1880–
Births and deaths prior: check with county clerk
Marriages: county clerk. Dona Ana County marriage records begin 1816; most counties, mid to late nineteenth century.

Libraries

Church of Jesus Christ of Latter-day Saints

Albuquerque, New Mexico,
Branch Genealogical Library
5709 Haines Avenue N.E.
Albuquerque, NM 87110

History Library Museum of New
Mexico
Palace of the Governors
Santa Fe, NM 87501

New Mexico State Library Commission
301 Don Gasper
Santa Fe, NM 87501

Public Library
423 East Central Avenue
Albuquerque, NM 87101

University of New Mexico Library
Albuquerque, NM 87131
(*New Mexico Historical Review*,
1926–)
NN IAA

Societies and Periodicals

Dona Ana County Historical Society
3963 University Park Station
Las Cruces, NM 88003

Genealogy Club of the Albuquerque Public Library
% Albuquerque Public Library
501 Copper Way
Albuquerque, NM 87102

Historical Society of New Mexico
1201 Madeira S.E., Apt. 193
Albuquerque, NM 87108

Historical Society of Southwest New
Mexico
Box 962
Silver City, NM 88061

Lea County Genealogical Society
P.O. Box 1044
Lovington, NM 88260

Llano Estacado Heritage, Inc.
Box 2446
925 West Copper Avenue
Hobbs, NM 88240
(*Southwest Heritage*)

Luna County Historical Society
300 South Nickel
Deming, NM 88030

New Mexico Genealogical Society
P.O. Box 8734
Albuquerque, NM 87108
(*New Mexico Genealogist*, 1962–)
NN APR (New Mexico)

Rio Grande Historical Collections
Box 3475
University Library
New Mexico State University
Las Cruces, NM 88003
(*Rio Grande History*)

Roswell Genealogical Society
P.O. Box 994
Roswell, NM 88201

Sierra County Historical Society
Box 1029, 325 Main Street
Truth or Consequences, NM 87901

Socorro County Historical Society,
Inc.
Box 923
Socorro, NM 87801
(*Publications in History*)

Southeastern New Mexico Historical Society
505 South Mesquite
Carlsbad, NM 88220

Taos County Historical Society,
Inc.

Box 398
Taos, NM 87571
(*Historical News*)

Tucumcari Historical Research
Institute
416 South Adams
Tucumcari, NM 88401

Western Echoes Genealogical Society
2411 South 8th Street
Deming, NM 88030

Books and Articles

Adams, Eleanor, and Fray Angelico Chavez.
The Missions of New Mexico, 1776.
Albuquerque, NM, New Mexico Press, 1956. 387 p., index.
(Handsome book)
NN IWR

Chavez Angelico, Fray (Brother), comp.
Archives, 1678–1900.
Washington, DC, Academy of Franciscan History, 1957. 283 p.
NN IWR

Chavez Angelico, Fray (Brother), comp.
Addenda to New Mexico Families.
(IN: *El Palacio*, Santa Fe, 1955. v. 62, no. 11, p. 324–39+)
NN HBC

Chavez Angelico, Fray (Brother).
New Names in New Mexico, 1820–1850.
(IN: *El Palacio*, Santa Fe, 1957. v. 64, no. 9–10, p. 291–318)
NN HBC

Chavez Angelico, Fray (Brother).
Origins of New Mexico Families in the Spanish Colonial Period in

Two Parts: The Seventeenth (1658–1693) and the Eighteenth (1693–1821) Centuries.
Santa Fe, Hist. Soc. of New Mexico, 1954. 339 p., no index, alpha.
NN APR (New Mexico)

Curtis, Janet A., and Virginia L. Olmstead.
The Location of Early Spanish Records of New Mexico.
(IN: *Stirpes*, Fort Worth, TX, March 1975. v. 15, p. 4–5)
NN APR (Texas)

Koogler, C. V., and Virginia Koogler Whitney.
Aztec: A Story of Old Aztec from the Anasazi to Statehood.
Fort Worth, TX, Amer. Ref. Pub. Co., 1972. 242 p., index.
NN IWS (Aztec) 74-1848

La Farge, Oliver.
Santa Fe: The Autobiography of a Southwestern Town.
Norman, OK, U. of OK Press, 1959. 436 p., index.
NN IWS (Santa Fe)

New Mexico.
Spanish Archives of New Mexico, 1621–1821.
Santa Fe, 1967. 22 reels.
NN *ZH-287

New Mexico 1850 Census Index.
Bountiful, UT, AIS, 1977.

New Mexico Province.
Calendar of the Mexican Archives of New Mexico, 1821–1846.
Santa Fe, 1970. 43 reels.
NN *ZH-329 and *ZH-329+

New Mexico Territory.
Territorial Archives of New Mexico.

Santa Fe, 1971–74. 189 reels.
NN *ZH-333 and *ZH-333+

Olmstead, Virginia L.
New Mexico Spanish and Mexican
    Colonial Censuses 1790–1823–
    1845.
Albuquerque, New Mexico Gen.
    Soc., 1975. 303 p.

Simmons, Marc.
Spanish Government in New Mex-
    ico.
Albuquerque, U. of NM Press,
    1968. 238 p., index.
NN IWR

Stanley, F. (pseudonym).
Ciudad Santa Fe.
Denver, CO, 1958–65. 3 v.
NN IWS (Santa Fe)

Stanley, F.
The Duke City: The Story of Albu-
    querque, New Mexico, 1706–1956.
Pep, TX, 1963. 267 p., index.
NN IWS (Albuquerque)

Twitchell, Ralph E.
Spanish Archives of New Mexico.
Cedar Rapids, IA, Torch Press,
    1914. 2 v., 525, 683 p., index each
    v. (Valuable sources, facsimile
    of documents with signatures,
    etc.)
NN IWR

U.S.W.P.A.
Directory of Churches and Reli-
    gious Organizations in New
    Mexico.
Albuquerque, 1940. 385 p.
NN ZAY

U.S.W.P.A.
Inventory of the County Archives
    of New Mexico.

Albuquerque, 1942. 135 p.
NN APR (New Mexico)

Voght, Evon Z., and and Ethel M.
    Albert.
People of Rimrock: A Study of Val-
    ues in Five Cultures.
Cambridge, MA, Harvard U. Press,
    1966. 342 p., index.
NN IWS

NEW YORK STATE (for New York City, see page 476)

State Archives

New York Office of State History
The State Education Department
Empire State Plaza
Albany, NY 12234

Vital Records (except New York City)

Bureau of Vital Records
State Department of Health
Empire State Plaza
Albany, NY 12237
Births and deaths: 1880–
Births and deaths prior: City Reg-
    istrar of Vital Statistics
Births and deaths prior to 1914 for
    Albany, Buffalo and Yonkers:
    write City Registrar of Vital Sta-
    tistics
Marriages: January   1880–
    December 1907; May 1915–;
    January 1908–April 1915, write
    county clerk
Marriages: January   1880–
    December 1907 for Albany,
    Buffalo and Yonkers, write
    city clerk

Libraries

Buffalo and Erie County Public
Library
Lafayette Square
Buffalo, NY 14203

Church of Jesus Christ of Latter-
day Saints
Rochester, New York, State
Branch Genealogical Library
Rochester 2nd Ward
1250 English Road
Rochester, NY 14616

New York Public Library
Fifth Avenue and 42nd Street
New York, NY 10018

New York State Library
Empire State Plaza
Albany, NY 12234

Rosewell P. Flower Genealogical
Library
229 Washington Street
Watertown, NY 13601

Western New York Collection of
the Walter C. Hinkle Memorial
Library
State University of New York Ag-
ricultural and Technical College
Alfred, NY 14802

Societies and Periodicals

Adirondack Historical Association
Blue Lake, NY 12812

Adjutant General
Bureau of War Records
112 State Street
Albany, NY 11207

Albany County Historical Association

9 Ten Broeck Place
Albany, NY 11210

American Baptist Historical Society
1106 South Goodman Street
Rochester, NY 14620
(*Foundations: A Quarterly Journal of History and Theology*)

Association of Suffolk County Historical Societies
% J. Emma
15 Saywood Lane
Stony Brook, NY 11790

Broome County Historical Society,
Inc.
30 Front Street
Binghamton, NY 13905

Buffalo and Erie County Histori-
cal Society
25 Nottingham Court
Buffalo, NY 14216
(*Niagara Frontier*, 1953–)
NN IRM (Niagara)

Catskill Valley Historical Society
Oak Hill, NY 12460

Central New York Genealogical So-
ciety
Box 104, Colvin Station
Syracuse, NY 13205
(*Tree Talks*, 1961–)
NN APR (New York State)

Chemung County Historical Society, Inc.
304 William Street
Elmira, NY 14901
(*Chemung County Historical Journal*, 1955–)
NN IRM (Chemung)

Cohocton Historical Society
Route 1

Cohocton, NY 14826
(*Cohocton Journal*)

Columbia County Historical Society
Broad Street
Kinderhook, NY 12106

DeWitt Historical Society
121 East Court Street
Ithaca, NY 14850

Dutchess County Historical Society
P.O. Box 88
Poughkeepsie, NY 12602

Dutch Settlers Society of Albany
6 DeLucia Terrace
Albany, NY 12211
(*Yearbooks*, 1924/25–)
NN IRM (Albany)

Eastchester Historical Society
60 Crescent Place
Eastchester, NY 10709
(Mail: % Tuckahoe, NY 10707)

Erie County Historical Federation
11 Danforth Street
Cheektowaga, NY 14227

Franklin County Historical and Museum Society
51 Milwaukee Street
Malone, NY 12953
(*Franklin Historical Review*, 1964–)
NN IRM (Franklin Co.) 74-477

Genealogical Research Group
118 Sunshine Drive
North Tonawanda, NY 14120

Genealogical Roundtable
% Mrs. Harry F. Zobel
130 Dale Road
Rochester, NY 14621

Genealogical Section of the Suffolk County Historical Society
300 West Main Street
Riverhead, NY 11901
(*The Register*, 1975–)

Greene County Historical Society
R.D. Rt. 9W
Coxsackie, NY 12051

Historical Society of Middletown and Walkill Precinct, Inc.
25 East Avenue
Middletown, NY 10940

Historical Society of Rockland County
Box 587, 20 Zukor Road
New City, NY 10960
(*South of the Mountains*, 1957–)
NN IRM (Rockland Co.)

Historical Society of the Town of Chester, Inc.
Town Hall
Chestertown, NY 12817
(*Chester History Today*)

Historical Society of the Town of Minerva
Minerva, NY 12851
(*Quarterly of the Historical Society of the Town of Minerva*)

Historical Society of the Town of North Hempstead
200 Plandome Road, Manhasset
North Hempstead, NY 11030

Huguenot Historical Society
Box 339, Huguenot Street
New Paltz, NY 12561
(*Huguenot Historical Society Yearbook*)

Huguenot–Thomas Paine National Historical Association

983 North Avenue
New Rochelle, NY 10804

Huntington Historical Society
Box 506
2 High Street and 434 Park Avenue
Huntington, NY 11743
(HHS *Quarterly*, 1961–)
NN IRM (Huntington)

Jefferson County Historical Society
228 Washington Street
Watertown, NY 13601
(*Jefferson County Historical Society Bulletin*, 1960–)
NN IRM (Jefferson)

Landmark Society of Western New York
130 Spring Street
Rochester, NY 14608

Lewis County Historical Society
Box 286, Dayan Street
Lowville, NY 13367
(*Lewis County Historical Society*, c. 1966–)
NN IRM (Lewis Co.) 74-150

Long Island Historical Society
128 Pierpont Street corner of Clinton Street
Brooklyn, NY 11201
(*The Journal of Long Island History*, 1961–)
NN IRM (Long Island)

Nassau County Historical Society
Box 207
Garden City, NY 11530
(*Nassau County Historical Journal*, 1937–)
NN IRM (Nassau)

New York Genealogical and Biographical Society
122–126 East 58th Street

New York, NY 10022
(*New York Genealogical and Biographical Record*, 1870–)
NYGBR
Subject Indexes v. 1–76. 3 v.
Surname Indexes v. 1–40. 4 v.
(Indexes mainly the work of Gertrude A. Barber)
NN *R-APGA

New York State Historical Association
Fenimore House, Lake Road
Cooperstown, NY 13326
(*New York History Quarterly*, 1919–)
NN IAA

Northeastern New York Genealogical Society
% Mrs. Mark H. Fish, President
Chestertown, NY 12817

Old Saratoga Historical Association of Schuylerville
Schuylerville, NY 12871

Onondaga Historical Association
311 Montgomery Street
Syracuse, NY 13202

Ontario County Historical Society
55 North Main Street
Canandaigua, NY 14424

Orange County Genealogical Society
Old Courthouse Bldg.
Goshen, NY 10924

Oswego County Historical Society
Richardson–Bates House
135 East 3rd Street
Oswego, NY 13126

Oyster Bay Historical Society
Box 142, 20 Summit Street
Oyster Bay, NY 11771

Putnam County Historical Society
63 Chestnut Street
Cold Spring, NY 10516

Rensselaer County Historical Society
59 Second Street
Troy, NY 12180

Rochester Historical Society
485 East Avenue
Rochester, NY 14607
(*Genesee Country Scrapbook*, c. 1950–)
NN IRM (Rochester)

Rome Historical Society
133 West Court Street
Rome, NY 13440
(*Annals and Recollections*)

St. Lawrence County Historical Association
Box 8, 3 East Main Street
Canton, NY 13617
(*The Quarterly*, 1956–)
NN IRM (St. Lawrence Co.) 74-361

St. Lawrence County History Center
Box 43, Court House
Canton, NY 13617
(*Historic Comment*)

Saratoga County Historical Society
Box 426
Fairground Road and Charlton Street
Ballston Spa, NY 12020

Schenectady County Historical Society
32 Washington Avenue
Schenectady, NY 12305

Schoharie County Historical Society

Old Stone Fort Museum
North Main
Schoharie, NY 12157
(*Schoharie County Historical Review*, 1937–)
NN IRM (Schoharie Co.)

Schuyler County Historical Society, Inc.
Box 116, 108 North Catherine Street
Montour Falls, NY 14865
(*Schuyler County Historical Society Journal*, 1965–)
NN IRM (Schuyler Co.) 73-2693

Sons of the Revolution in the State of New York
54 Pearl Street
New York, NY 10004

Southhold Historical Society
Southhold, Long Island, NY 11971

Steuben County Historical Society
R.D. 4
Cameron Street
Bath, NY 14810

Suffolk County Historical Society
300 West Main Street
Riverhead, NY 11901
(Register, 1975–)

Tappantown Historical Society
Box 71
Tappan, NY 10983
(*Drummer Boy*)

Three Village Historical Society
Box 965
Stony Brook, NY 11790
(*Three Village Historian*)

Twin Tiers Genealogical Society
230 Devonshire Drive
Elmira, NY 14903

Ulster County Genealogical Society
Box 41
Stone Ridge, NY 12484
("Family Tree" column in *Saugerties News Post*)

Upper Susquehanna Historical Society and Museum
203 River Street
11 Ford Avenue
Oneonta, NY 13820

Wayne County Historical Society
21 Butternut Street
Lyons, NY 14489

Westchester County Historical Society
43 Read Avenue
Tuckahoe, NY 10707; (*Westchester Historian*, 1925–)
NN IRM (Westchester)

Western New York Genealogical Society, Inc.
209 Nassau Avenue
Kenmore, NY 14217
(*Western New York Genealogical Society Journal*, 1974–)

Yesteryears Magazine, 1957– NN IRN
Box 52
Aurora, NY 13026

Books and Articles

Aber, Ted, and Stella King.
The History of Hamilton County.
Lake Pleasant, Great Wilderness Books, 1965. 1,209 p., index. (Excellent use made of the New York State Census Records for this superb county history.)
NN IRM (Hamilton Co.)

An Account of Her Majesty's Revenue in the Province of New York, 1701–09: The Customs Records of Early Colonial New York, ed. and intro. by Julius M. Bloch, Leo Hershkowitz, Kenneth Scott and Constance D. Sherman of City University of New York.
Ridgewood, NJ, The Gregg Press, 1967. 288, lxx p.
(Ports. of Caleb Heathcote, op. p. xiv; Adolph Phillipse, op. p. xxviii)
NN APRN+

Austin, John D.
Genealogical Research in Upstate New York
(IN: *TAG*, New Haven, CT, 1960. v. 36, p. 163–68)
NN APGA

Balloting Book and Other Documents Relating to Military Bounty Lands in the State of New York.
Albany, 1825.
NN *KF+

Barck, Dorothy C.
Some References for Genealogical Searching in New York State.
Detroit, MI, Detroit Soc. for Gen. Research, 1959. 22 p.
NN APB p.v. 129

Bergen, Tunis.
Register in Alphabetical Order of the Early Dutch Settlers of Kings County, Long Island, New York, new introduction by Mrs. Harriet Mott Stryker-Rodda.
Cottonport, LA, Polyanthos, 1973 (orig. 1881). 452 p.
NN APR (Kings Co.) 74-2224

Carman, Harry J., and Arthur W. Thompson.
A Guide to the Principal Sources for American Civilization, 1800–1900, in the City of New York.
New York, Columbia U. Press, 1962. 630 p.
NN *RH-I

Church of Jesus Christ of Latter-day Saints.
Eastern States Mission, New York State Cemetery Records, 1943–1968. 23 v.
NN *ZI-205

Comstock, Frederick H.
An Index to Wills, Deeds and Other Instruments ... State of New York.
New York, Miller and Miller, 1896. 247 p., alpha.
NN APR (New York State)

DAR, New York State.
Master Index, New York State DAR Genealogical Records.
New York, DAR in New York State, 1972. 371 p., alpha.
(Indexes 600 v. of Bible, cemetery, church and town records—most of these volumes are in the New York Public Library, and all are in the DAR Library in Washington & NY State Library, Albany)
NN APR (New York State)

Descendants of Peter and Mary (Blue) Van Vleet of Seneca County, New York.
(IN: *Detroit Society for Genealogical Research Magazine. Spring 1974. v. 37, no 3, p. 109*)
APGA

Dutch Settlers Society of Albany, Year Book, 1924–25.

Albany, v.1–.
NN IRM (Albany)

Early Architecture in Ulster County.
Kingston, Junior League, 1974. 222 p., index.
(Excellent illus.)
NN IRM (Ulster) 75–2258

Eastchester Historical Society.
Records of the Town of Eastchester, Westchester County, New York, and St. Paul's Church (Mount Vernon).
Eastchester, 1964–. Many volumes.
(Covers 1664–1909)
NN IRM (Eastchester)

Ellis, David M., et al.
History of New York State. 2nd ed.
Ithaca, New York State Hist. Assoc., Cornell U. Press, 1967 (orig. 1957). 732 p.
NN IR

Evers, Alf.
The Catskill, from Wilderness to Woodstock.
Garden City, Doubleday, 1972. 821 p., index.
NN IRM (Catskill) 73–395

Fernow, Berthold.
Calendar of Wills ... in the Offices of the Clerk of the Court of Appeals of the County Clerk of Albany and of the Office of the Secretary of State.
New York, Colonial Dames, 1896. 657 p.
NN APR (Albany)

Fernow, Berthold.
New York in the Revolution.
New Orleans, Polyanthos, 1972

(orig. 1887). 638 p., index and alpha list.
NN *R-APR (New York State) 73-2851

Finch, Jesse Howell.
Vital Records from the *Ovid Bee*, Published at Ovid Village, Seneca County, New York, 1822–1869.
n.p., J.H. Finch Committee, 1971. 174 p., 3 indexes.
NN APR (Seneca Co.)

French, J. H.
Gazetteer of the State of New York.
Syracuse, R. P. Smith, 1860. 752 p., index.
NN IRN

Gredel, Stephen.
Pioneers of Buffalo: Its Growth and Development.
Buffalo, Commission on Human Relations, 1966. 48 p., no index, biblio. p. 46. (Sections on different nationalities; map, p. 41 showing location of turn-of-the-20th-century ethnic groups; Negroes, p. 34–36)
NN IRM (Buffalo) 72-2251

Grimes, Marilla.
Some Newspaper References to Irish Immigrants in Oneida County, New York.
(IN: *Irish Ancestor*, Dundalk, Ireland, 1974. v. 6, p. 97–98)
NN ARCA 72-1448

Kelly, Arthur C.M.
Settlers and Residents.
Rhinebeck, NY, 12572, the author, 1973–. (v. 1, Germantown, Columbia Co., 1710–1889; v. 2, parts 1 and 2, Clermont, Columbia Co, 1756–1899)

(Mr. Kelly has published many volumes of transcripts of church records of this area of New York State.)
NN APR (New York) 74-580

Kenney, Alice P.
Albany: Crossroads of Liberty.
Albany, Albany American Revolution Bicentennial Committee, 1976. 82 p.
(Available from Institute of History and Art, Albany)

McMullin, Philip.
New York in 1800: An Index to the Federal Census Schedules of the State of New York.
Provo, UT, Gendex (now Gendata), 1971. 272 p., alpha.
NN *R-PAR (New York State) 72-1208p

Meyers, Carol M.
Early New York State Census Records, 1663–1772. 2nd ed.
Gardena, CA, Ram, c. 1965. 176, 66 p.
NN APR (New York State)

Nestler, Harold.
A Bibliography of New York State Communities, Counties, Towns, Villages.
Port Washington, NY, I. J. Friedman, 1968. 1 v., unpaged.
(Empire State Hist. Pub. Series, 51)
NN IRN

New York 1800 Census Index.
Bountiful, UT, AIS, 1976.

New York 1810 Census Index.
Bountiful, UT, AIS, 1976. 364 p.

New York 1820 Census Index.
Bountiful, UT, AIS, 1976. 537 p.

New York 1830 Census Index.
Bountiful, UT, AIS, 1977.

New York 1840 Census Index.
Bountiful, UT, AIS, 1977.

New York 1850 Census Index.
Bountiful, UT, AIS, 1977.

New York Marriages Previous to
1784.
Baltimore, MD, GPC, 1968 (orig.
1860). 618 p., index, alpha.
NN *R-APR (New York)

New York State Comptrollers Office.
New York in the Revolution as
Colony and State, by James A.
Roberts.
Albany, 1898. 534 p., index.
... sup. Albany, 1901. 336 p., index.
NN *R-APR (New York State)

O'Callaghan, Edmund B.
Calendar of Dutch Historical Manuscripts in the Office of the Secretary of State, Albany, New
York, 1630–1664.
Ridgewood, NJ, Gregg Press, 1968
(orig. 1865). 423 p., index.
NN *R-IR 72-763

O'Callaghan, Edmund B.
New York State Calendar of British Historical Manuscripts,
1664–1676.
Ridgewood, NJ, Gregg Press, 1968.
892 p., index.
NN *R-IR 72-771

Pearson, Jonathan.
Early Records of the City and
County of Albany and Colony of
Rensselaerwyck ... translated
from the original Dutch.
Albany, 1869–1919. 4 v.

(v. 1, 1656–75; v. 2, Deeds 3 and 4,
1678–1704; v. 3, Notarial Papers
1 and 2, 1660–93; v. 4, Mortgages
1658–1660, Wills 1 and 2, 1681–
1765)
NN IRM (Albany)

Pearson, Jonathan.
Genealogies of the First Settlers of
the Ancient County of Albany,
from 1630 to 1800. 1st ed.
Baltimore, MD, GPC, 1976 (orig.
1872). 182 p., index.
NN APR (Albany)

Prindle, Paul W.
New York Church Records.
(IN: *TAG*, New Haven, CT, 1958.
v. 34, p. 162–63)
NN APGA

Quist, Mary Lancaster.
Ancestors and Descendants of
Walter Covey, Dutchess
County, New York, 1750–1834.
Santa Ana, CA, the author, 1971 2
v. (1660 p.) index
NN APV (Covey) 73-1489

Rattray, Jeanette Edwards.
Perils of the Port of New York,
Maritime Disasters from Sandy
Hook to Execution Rocks.
New York, Dodd, Mead, 1973. 301
p., index.
(Chronological lists of vessels in
distress, p. 241–78)
NN IRM 75-2013

Reynolds, Helen W.
Notices of Marriages and Deaths
... Published in Newspapers
Printed at Poughkeepsie, New
York, 1778–1825.
Poughkeepsie, Dutchess Co. Hist.
Soc., 1930. v. 4, 140 p.
NN IRM (Dutchess Co.)

Scott, Kenneth.
New York State Census of Albany
County Towns in 1790.
Baltimore, MD, GPC, 1975. 68 p.
NN APR (Albany Co.) 76-588

Scott, Kenneth.
Suffolk County, Long Island, New
York, 1778 Census.
(IN: *NGSQ*, Washington, DC, 1975.
v. 63, p. 276–83)
NN APGA

Scott, Kenneth.
Ulster County, New York, Court
Records, 1693–1775.
(IN: *NGSQ*, Washington, DC,
1972–73. v. 60, p. 276–85; v. 61,
p. 60–68, 137–40, etc.)
NN APGA

Sealock, Richard B., and Pauline
A. Seely.
Long Island Bibliography.
Baltimore, MD, 1940. 338 p. (p.
88–92, directories index; p.
67–87, biography; p. 126–52, history and description; p. 257–77,
societies; p. 93–111, documents)
NN IRM (Long Island)

Southern Tier Library System.
A Local Guide to the New York
Histories, Held by the Libraries
of the Southern Tier Library Sys-
tem, comp. by Jacqualine G.
Roony. 2nd rev. ed.
Corning, 1968. 101 p.
NN IRN (75-839)

Stryker-Rodda, Kenn, and Herbert
F. Seversmith.
Long Island Genealogical Source
Material: A Bibliography.
Washington, DC, 1962. (*NSGQ Spe-
cial Pub. #24*)
NN APGA

U.S.W.P.A.
New York State Guide to Public
Vital Statistics Records.
Albany, Hist. Records Survey, 1942.
alpha by county and town. 3 v.
(v. 1, births; v. 2, marriages; v.
3, deaths)
NN APR (New York State)

Vital Statistics of Churches (exclu-
sive of New York City).
Albany, 1942. 2 v. (v. 1, Albany–
Montgomery; v. 2, Nassau–Yates)
NN APR (New York State)

Willis, Edmund P.
George Washington's New York:
A Socio-Economic Profile of the
City in 1789.
New Orleans, Polyanthos, 1976. c.
500 p.
(Has complete tax list of 1789)

Yoshpe, Harry B.
Record of Slave Manumissions in
Albany 1800–1828.
(IN: *JNH*, Washington, DC, 1941.
v. 26, p. 499–522)
NN IEC

Yoshpe, Harry B.
Record of Slave Manumissions in
New York During Colonial and
Early National Periods.
(IN: *JNH*, Washington, DC, 1941.
v. 26, p. 78–107)
NN IEC

NEW YORK CITY—Borough of Bronx

Vital Records

Births 1898– and deaths 1898–:
Bronx Bureau of Vital Records
1826 Arthur Avenue
Bronx, NY 10457

(1865–1897 in Municipal Archives)
Marriages: 1914–
Office of City Clerk
1780 Grand Concourse
Bronx, NY 10457
(Records for 1908–1913 for Bronx
are on file in Manhattan office)

Libraries

Bronx Public Library
The Fordham Branch
2556 Bainbridge
Bronx, NY 10458

Fordham University Library
Fordham University (Rose Hill
Campus)
Fordham Road
Bronx, NY 10458

Societies and Periodicals

Bronx County Historical Society
3266 Bainbridge Avenue
Bronx, NY 10467
(*Bronx County Historical Society
Journal*, 1964–)
NN IRM (Bronx Co.)

NEW YORK CITY—Borough of Brooklyn

Vital Records

Births 1898– and deaths 1898–:
Brooklyn Bureau of Vital Records
295 Flatbush Avenue Ext.
Brooklyn NY 11201
(1866–1897 in Municipal Archives)
Marriages: 1866–
Office of City Clerk
208 Joralemon Street
Brooklyn, NY 11201

Libraries

Brooklyn Public Library
Grand Army Plaza
Brooklyn, NY 11238

City University of New York Library
Midwood Campus
Bedford Avenue and Avenue H
Brooklyn, NY 11210

St. Francis College
Historic Library
180 Remsen Street
Brooklyn, NY 11201

Societies and Periodicals

Gravesend Historical Society
1937 West 6th Street, Gravesend
Brooklyn, NY 11223

James A. Kelly Institute for Local
History Studies
180 Remsen Street
Brooklyn, NY 11201

Kingsborough Historical Society
2001 Oriental Blvd.
Brooklyn, NY 11235

Long Island Historical Society
128 Pierrepont Street
Brooklyn, NY 11201

NEW YORK CITY—Borough of Manhattan

Vital Records

Births 1898– and deaths 1898–:
Department of Health of New
York City
Bureau of Vital Statistics
125 Worth Street
New York, NY 10013

(Births 1866–1897, Deaths 1798–
1897 in Municipal Archives)
Marriages: 1866–
Marriage License Bureau
Room 265, Municipal Building
New York, NY 10007
(1847–1865 in Municipal Archives)
Note: New York City was incorporated on January 1, 1898. Prior
to this date New York City consisted of Manhattan Island
(New York County) and a portion of the Bronx.

Libraries

Church of Jesus Christ of Latter-
day Saints
New York, New York, State Branch
Genealogical Library
2 Lincoln Square
New York, NY 10023

City College
Convent Avenue and West 138th
Street
New York, NY 10031

City University of New York Libraries
City University of New York: Bernard M. Baruch College
155 East 24th Street
New York, NY 10010

Columbia University Libraries
Columbia University
116th Street and Broadway
New York, NY 10027

Fordham University Library
Fordham University at Lincoln
Center
Columbus Avenue and West 60th
Street
New York, NY 10023

Hunter College
695 Park Avenue
New York, NY 10021

Jewish Division—Room 84
New York Public Library
42nd Street and Fifth Avenue
New York, NY 10018

Local History and Genealogical
Division, Room 315G
New York Public Library
Fifth Avenue and 42nd Street
New York, NY 10018

New York University Library
Washington Square
New York, NY 10012

Religious Society of Friends Li-
brary
Haviland Records Room
15 Rutherford Place
New York, NY 10003
(New York Quaker Archives)

Schomburg Center for Research in
Black Culture
103 West 135th Street
New York, NY 10030
(Collection contains all U.S. Census
records on microfilm 1790–1818)

Yeshiva University Library
Yeshiva University
500 West 185th Street
New York, NY 10033

Societies and Periodicals

Municipal Archives and Record
Center
23 Park Row
New York, NY 10038
(New York City birth and death
records prior to 1898 and marriages 1847–1865)

Museum of the City of New York
Fifth Avenue at 103rd Street
New York, NY 10029

New York Genealogical and Biographical Society
122 East 58th Street
New York, NY 10022
(*New York Genealogical and Biographical (NYGBR) Record,*
1871–)
NN *R-APGA

New York Historical Society
170 Central Park West
New York, NY 10024
(*New York Historical Society
Quarterly,* 1917–, NN IAA or
IRGA; *Collections,* 1809–, NN
IAA)

Sons of the Revolution in the State
of New York
Fraunces Tavern Museum
54 Pearl Street
New York, NY 10004

NEW YORK CITY—Borough of Queens

Vital Records

Births 1898– and deaths 1898–:
Queens Bureau of Vital Records
90-37 Parsons Blvd.
Jamaica, NY 11432
Marriages 1898–:
Office of City Clerk
120-55 Queens Boulevard
Borough Hall Station
Jamaica, NY 11424

Libraries

Queens Public Library
8911 Merrick Blvd.
Jamaica, NY 11432

Historical Documents Collections
Queens College (CUNY)
% Paul Klapper Memorial Library
Room 101
Flushing, NY 11367

Societies and Periodicals

Flushing Historical Society
% F. M. Pokorney
153-10 60th Avenue
Flushing, NY 11355

Queens Historical Society
143-35 37th Avenue
Flushing, NY 11354

NEW YORK CITY—Borough of Staten Island

Vital Records

Births 1898– and deaths 1898–:
Richmond Bureau of Vital Records
51 Stuyvesant Place
Staten Island, NY 10301
Marriages 1898–:
Borough Hall
St. George
Staten Island, NY 10301

Libraries

Staten Island Public Library
St. George Library Center
10 Hyatt Street, St. George
Staten Island, NY 10301

Societies and Periodicals

Staten Island Historical Society
302 Center Street
Staten Island, NY 10306
(*Staten Island Historian*)
NN IRM (Staten Island)

Books and Articles

Bailey, Rosalie Fellows.
Guide to Genealogical and Biographical Sources for New York City (Manhattan), 1783–1898.
Rosalie F. Bailey, 1954. 96 p., subject index.
NN APRN

Barber, Gertrude A.
Abstracts from Brooklyn *Eagle*.
New York, 1963–66. index each v.
(Covers 1841–80: deaths, 27 v.; marriages, 14 v.)
NN APRN

Barber, Gertrude A.
Abstracts from New York *Evening Post*.
New York, 1934–51. index each v.
(Covers 1801–90: deaths, 54 v.; marriages, 23 v.)
NN APRN

Barber, Gertrude A., comp.
Index to the Letters of Administrations Filed in New York County, 1743–1875.
New York, Gertrude Barber, 1950–51. 6 v.
NN APRN

Barber, Gertrude A., comp.
Index of Wills Probated in Kings County, New York, Jan. 1, 1850–Dec. 31, 1890.
New York, Gertrude A. Barber, 1949. 2 v., alpha.
NN APR (Kings Co.)

Bloch, Julius M., and Leo Hershkowitz.
New York City Assessment Roll, February 1730.
(IN: *NYGBR*, New York, 1964. v. 95, p. 27–33, 166–74, 196–202)
NN *R-APGA

Breton, Arthur J.
A Guide to the Manuscript Collections of the New York Historical Society.
Greenwood, 1972. 2 v.
NN IR 75–2337

Carman, Harry James and Evarts B. Greene.
A Guide to the Principal Sources for Early American History (1600–1800) in the City of New York. rev. ed. New York, Columbia U. Press 1962 (orig. 1929) 630 p.
NN *RH-I and Desk Room 315A

Cole Directories.
New York, Cole, 1971–.
NN Westchester JXN 76-2, latest in IZ
Bronx AN-10 203
Manhattan AN-10 200
Suffolk AN-10 201
Nassau AN-10 202
Queens AN-10 202
Brooklyn AN-10 199
Staten Island IXN-76-3

Earliest Trinity Church Marriages (1746–1778).
(IN: *NYGBR*, New York, 1888. v. 19, p. 147–49)
*R-APGA

1850 Census, Rochester, Monroe County, New York.
(IN: *DAR Cemetery, Church, and Town Records*. Albany, 1934–36. v. 87, 1st–5th wards v. 88, 6th–9th wards)
NN APR (New York State)

Evjen, John O.
Scandinavian Immigrants in New York, 1630–1674.
Minneapolis, MN, K. C. Holter, 1916. 438 p.

(Jonas and Peter Bronck, p. 167–83)
NN APRN

Furer, Howard B.
New York: A Chronological and Documentary History, 1524–1770.
Dobbs Ferry, NY, Oceana, 1974. 153 p.
NN IRGC 75-922

Grim, Charles F.
An Essay Towards an Improved Register of Deeds. City and County of New York to December 31, 1799, Inclusive.
New York, Could, Banks & Co., 1832. 371 p. (4 sections, each alpha.; New York Co. Grantor and Grantees, 1st 2 sections; Sec. of State Grantors and Grantees, last 2 sections)
NN IRGC

Guernsey, Rocellus S.
New York City and Vicinity During the War of 1812–15: A Military, Civic and Financial Local History of the Period.
New York, C. L. Woodward, 1889. 2 v., index in each v.
NN IRGC

The Heritage of New York, preface by Whitney North Seymour.
New York, Fordham U. Press, 1970. 402 p. (Buildings with plaques showing photos of each plaque and building)
NN IRH 76-1137

Holland Society.
Index to the Publications of the Holland Society of New York.
New York, Holland Soc., 1959. 46 p.
NN APGA

Index of Passenger Lists of Vessels Arriving at the Port of New York, 1820–1846.
Washington, DC, U.S. National Archives, microfilm, 103 reels, after 1846, no index.
(National Archives has latter indexes, 1897–1902)
NN *ZI-80

McGenn, Rev. James H.
The Earliest Baptismal Register of St. Peter's Church, New York City.
(In: *U.S. Catholic Hist. Soc., Historical Records and Studies*, Philadelphia, 1899–1904. v. 1, p. 97–107, 387–99; v. 2, p. 148–62, 454–63; v. 3, p. 217–25, 506–15)
NN IAA

Moriarty, John H.
Directory Information Material (Printed) for New York City Residents, 1626–1786: A Bibliographic Study.
New York, NYPL, 1942. 60 p.
NN IRGC p.v. 58

New York (City) Department of Health.
Borough of Manhattan, Register of Deaths, Aug. 1, 1798–1865.
Salt Lake City, UT, 196–. 25 reels
NN *ZI-201

New York City Directories. 1786–1933/34.
New York, 1954. 77 reels.
NN *ZAN-G61

New York City 1850 Census Index.
Bountiful, UT, AIS, 1976. 382 p.
APRN 76-596

NYGBS Collections.
New York, 1890–1969. 10 v. (v.1, 1890, marriages in the Dutch

Church, New York, 1639–1800; v.2, pts. 1–2, 1901–1902, baptisms in the Dutch Church, New York, 1639–1730, 1731–1800)
(*Genealogical Data from New York Administration Bonds*, 1753–1799, abstracted by Kenneth Scott, New York, 1969, v. 10, 194 p., alpha by name, index)
NN APR (New York)

New York Times Obituaries Index 1858–1968.
New York, *New York Times*, 1970. 1,136 p. alpha (not at all complete).
NN APK

Olsson, Nils William.
Swedish Passenger Arrivals in New York, 1820–1850.
Chicago, Swedish Pioneer Hist. Soc., 1967. 392 p.
NN APK

Sawyer, Ray C.
Gravestone Inscriptions of Trinity Cemetery, New York City, 155th Street and Broadway.
New York, R.C. Sawyer, 1931. 2 v., index each v.
NN APRN

Sawyer, Mrs. Ray C., and Gertrude A. Barber.
Abstracts of Wills of New York County.
New York, Sawyer & Barber, 1934–51. 20 v. (Covers 1801–56)
NN APRN

Sawyer, Mrs. Ray C., comp.
Index of New York County Wills, 1662–1850
New York, Mrs. Ray C. Sawyer, 1931 and 1950–51. 3 v. (Covers 1851–1875)
NN APRN

Sawyer, Ray C.
Marriages Performed by the Various Mayors and Aldermen of of the City of New York, as Well as Justices of the Peace, etc. 1830–1854.
New York, Ray C. Sawyer, 1935. 63 p. plus index.
NN APRN

Scott, Kenneth.
Genealogical Data from New York Administration Bonds, 1753–1799.
New York, 1969. 194 p. (*NYGBS Collections*, v.10)
NN APR (New York)

Scott, Kenneth.
Genealogical Data from Administration Papers from the New York State Court of Appeals in Albany.
New York Nat'l Soc. of Colonial Dames in New York State, 1972. 506 p., index. (Numerous other works of abstracts from newspapers in pub. doc.)

Scott, Kenneth.
Genealogical Data from the New York *Gazette and Weekly Mercury* and Genealogical Data from the New York *Mercury*.
(IN: *NYGBR*, 1966–Oct. 1976+. v. 97–107+)
(Covers 1760's and 1780's)
NN *R-APGA

Scott, Kenneth.
Genealogical Data from the New York Post-Boy, 1743–1773.
Washington, DC, 1970. 188 p., index. (*NSGQ Special Pub. #35*)
NN APRN

Scott, Kenneth.
New York Marriage Bonds, 1753–1783.

New York, St. Nicholas Soc., City of New York, 1972. 570 p., alpha, index.

Scott, Kenneth.
Records of the Chancery Court Province and State of New York, Guardianships, 1691–1815.
New York, Holland Soc., 1971. 297 p., index.

Scott, Kenneth.
Rivington's New York Newspaper: Excerpts from a Loyalist Press, 1773–1783.
New York, NYHS, 1973. 470 p., index.
NN APRN 75-2343

Scott, Kenneth, and James A. Owre.
Genealogical Data from Inventories of New York Estates, 1666–1825.
New York, NYGBS, 1970. 220 p.

Scott, Kenneth, and Kristin L. Gibbons, ed.
The New York Magazine, Marriages and Deaths: 1790–1797.
New Orleans, LA, Polyanthos, 1975. 306 p.

Smith, Thomas E. V.
The City of New York in the Year of Washington's Inauguration . . ., introduction (short) by Joseph Veach Noble.
Riverside, CT, Chatham Press, 1972 (1st ed. 1889). 244 p.
NN IRGV 75-352

Stokes, Isaac N. P.
The Iconography of Manhattan Island, 1498–1909.
New York, R.H. Dodd, 1915–28. 6 v. (index, v. 6).
NN IRGC

U.S. Census Office.
10th Census, 1880, New York City Guide to the Use of . . .
New York, New York Public Library, 1963. Various pagination.
NN Desk, Room 315G

U.S. National Archives.
Index to Passenger Lists of Vessels Arriving at New York, 1820–1846.
Washington, DC, n.d. 103 reels of film arranged alpha. by the name of passengers
NN *ZI-80

U.S. State Department.
Passenger Lists, Arriving at New York, 1820–1897.
NN has 1820–1860+ (National Archives has records 1820 to present day)
NN *ZI-13

U.S.W.P.A.
New York City Guide.
New York, Octagon Press, 1970 (orig. 1939). 708 p., index.
NN *R-Art 72-769 and IRGU

U.S.W.P.A.
New York City Guide to Statistics. Churches: Manhattan, Bronx, Brooklyn, Queens, Richmond.
New York, 1942. 5 parts.
NN APRN

U.S.W.P.A.
New York City Inventory of Church Records, Eastern Orthodox Churches and Armenian.
New York City, Hist. Rec. Survey, 1940. 178 p., index.
NN IRI

U.S.W.P.A.
New York City, Inventory of Church Records, Methodist.

New York, 1940. 216 p., index.
NN IRI

U.S.W.P.A.
New York City Inventory of
Church Records, Presbyterian.
New York, 1940. 160 p., index.
NN IRI

U.S.W.P.A.
New York City, Inventory of
Church Records, Protestant
Episcopal Church.
New York, 1940. (v. 1, Diocese of
Long Island, Kings and Queens
Counties, 67 p., index; v. 2, New
York Co., Bronx, Richmond, 153
p., index)
NN IRI

U.S.W.P.A.
New York City, Inventory of
Church Records, Reformed
Church in America.
New York, 1939. 95 p., index. (Man-
hattan, 1639–)
NN IRI

U.S.W.P.A.
New York City, Inventory of
Church Records, Religious Soci-
ety of Friends.
New York, 1940. 224 p., index.
NN IRI

U.S.W.P.A.
New York City, Inventory of
Church Records, Roman Cath-
olic.
New York, 1941. 181 p. (Arch-
diocese of New York)
NN IRI

U.S.W.P.A.
New York City, Inventory of
Church Records, Lutheran.
New York, 1940. 152 p., index.
NN IRI

NORTH CAROLINA

State Archives

Division of Archives and History
North Carolina Department of
Cultural Resources
109 East Jones Street
Raleigh, NC 27611
(*North Carolina Historical Review*,
1924–)
NN IAA

North Carolina Department of Ar-
chives and History
Salisbury and Edenton Streets
P.O. Box 1881
Raleigh, NC 27602

Vital Records

Vital Records Section
State Board of Health
P.O. Box 2091
Raleigh, NC 27602
Births and deaths: October 1913–
and some delayed records prior
Marriages: January 1962.
Marriages prior: Register of Deeds
in county

Libraries

Church of Jesus Christ of Latter-
day Saints
Raleigh, North Carolina, Branch
Genealogical Library
5100 Six Forks Road
Raleigh, NC 27609

Public Library of Charlotte and
Mecklenburg Counties
310 North Tyron Street
Charlotte, NC 28202

North Carolina State Library
109 East Jones Street
Raleigh, NC 27611

Societies and Periodicals

Carolinas Genealogical Society
306 South Thompson Street
Monroe, NC 28110
(*Carolinas Genealogical Society Bulletin*, 1964–)

Chapel Hill Historical Society
Box 503
Franklin Street Station
Chapel Hill, NC 27514

Commission on Archives and History of the United Methodist Church
Box 488, 39 North Lake Shore Drive
Lake Junaluska, NC 28745
(*Methodist History*)

Cumberland County Historical Society
% Mrs. William D. Sherman
312 Devane Street
Fayetteville, NC 28305

Eastern North Carolina Genealogical Society
P.O. Box 395
New Bern, NC 28560

Genealogical Society of the Original Wilkes County
% May R. Hayes, Editor
Route 4, Box 663
North Wilkesboro, NC 28659

Halifax County Historical Association
301 West Burnette Avenue
Enfield, NC 27823

Historical Foundation of the Presbyterian and Reformed Churches
Box 847

Montreat, NC 28757
(*Historical Foundation News*)

Historical Society of North Carolina
Department of History
Elon College
Elon, NC 27244

Johnston County Genealogical Society
% Public Library of Johnston County and Smithfield
305 Market Street
Smithfield, NC 27577
(*Johnston County Genealogical Society Newsletter*)

Lower Cape Fear Historical Society, Inc.
Box 813, 126 South Third
Wilmington, NC 28401
(*Lower Cape Fear Historical Society Bulletin*)

Murfreesboro Historical Association, Inc.
Box 3, Robers Village Center
Main Street
Murfreesboro, NC 27855
(*Renaissance in Carolina*)

North Carolina Baptist Historical Collection
Wake Forest University
Winston-Salem, NC 27109
(Mail: Box 7777, Reynolds Station, Winston-Salem, NC 27109)

North Carolina Genealogical Society
P.O. Box 1492
Raleigh, NC 27602
(NCGS *Journal*, 1975–)

North Carolina Literary and Historical Association, Inc.
109 East Jones Street
Raleigh, NC 27611

North Carolina Genealogy, 1955–
75, 21 v. in 9.
NN APR (North Carolina)
P.O. Box 1770
Raleigh, NC 27602

Northwest North Carolina Histor-
ical Association, Inc.
Box 165, Main Street
East Bend, NC 27018

Northwest North Carolina Histor-
ical Association, Inc.
Government Center
Winston-Salem, NC 27101

University of North Carolina
Drawer 870
Chapel Hill, NC 27514

Western North Carolina Historical
Association
346 Montford Avenue
Asheville, NC 28801

Wilkes Genealogical Society, Inc.
P.O. Box 1629
North Wilkesboro, NC 28659
(*Wilkes Genealogical Bulletin*)

Books and Articles

Broughton, Carrie L.
Marriage and Death Notices from
Raleigh Register and *North
Carolina State Gazette*, ... 1799–
1897.
Raleigh, State Library, 1944–52. 6
v., alpha by year.
(Volumes for 1799–1845 reprinted
by GPC, 1962–68)
NN APR (North Carolina)

Draughon, Wallace R., and William Perry Johnson, comp. and
ed.

North Carolina Genealogical Reference: A Research Guide for
All Genealogists Both Amateur
and Professional, new ed.
1966. 571 p.
NN APR (North Carolina)

Durden, Robert F.
The Dukes of Durham, 1865–1929.
Durham, Duke U. Press, 1975. 295
p., index.
NN APV (Duke) 76-1438

Fries, Adelaide.
Records of the Moravians in North
Carolina.
Raleigh, 1922–64. 9 v. (Covers 1752–
1847)
NN ITE

Guide to Research Materials in the
North Carolina State Archives,
Section B: County Records. 3rd
ed.
Raleigh, Dept. of Cultural Re-
sources, Archives and Records
Section, c. 1976. 262 p.
(Best new guide for genealogy for
any state archives)

Johnson, William Perry.
Index to North Carolina Wills,
1663–1900.
Raleigh, 1963 to date. 3 v.+.
NN APR (North Carolina)

Livingston, Virginia Pope.
Some Migrations from Virginia to
North Carolina.
(IN: *NCGSJ*, Raleigh, 1976–77. v. 2,
p. 122–28, 192–97; v. 3, p. 32–38.
108–113, ff.)

McBride, B. Ransom.
Divorces and Separations Granted
by Act of North Carolina Assembly from 1790–1808.

(IN: *NCGSJ*, Raleigh, 1977. v. 3, p. 43–47)

McBride, B. Ransom.
Legal Name Changes by Act of North Carolina Assembly from 1805 through 1808.
(IN: *NCGSJ*, Raleigh, 1976. v. 2, p. 162–67)

McCubbins, James Franklin.
McCubbins Collection.
Salisbury, Salisbury Pub. Lib., n.d. 78 reels of microfilm.
NN *ZI-147

North Carolina 1820 Census.
Tullahoma, TN, Dorothy W. Potter, 1970–72. 56 v.
NN APR (North Carolina) 75-2960

North Carolina 1800 Census Index.
Bountiful, UT, AIS, 1976.

North Carolina 1810 Census Index.
Bountiful, UT, AIS, 1976.

North Carolina 1820 Census Index.
Bountiful, UT, AIS, 1976.

North Carolina 1830 Census Index.
Bountiful, UT, AIS, 1976. 210 p.

North Carolina 1850 Census Index.
Bountiful, UT, AIS, 1976. 342 p.

Petty, Gerald M.
Index of the 1840 Federal Census of North Carolina.
Ann Arbor, MI, Edwards Brothers, for G.M. Petty, 1974.
273 p., alpha.
NN APR (North Carolina) 75-518

Powell, William S.
The North Carolina Gazetteer.

Chapel Hill, U. of NC, 1968. 561 p., index, alpha.
NN ITFB

Register, Alvaretta K., comp.
State Census of North Carolina, 1784–1787.
2nd ed.
Norfolk, VA, the author, 1973 (orig. 1971). 240 p.
NN APR (North Carolina) 75-2558

Roster of Soldiers from North Carolina in the American Revolution.
Baltimore, MD, GPC, 1972 (orig. 1932). 709 p., index.
APR (North Carolina)

Smith, Evelyn F.
Charn Cuimhne: To Our Scots of North Carolina.
Jacksonville, FL, E. F. Smith, 1969. 309 p., index.
NN APR (North Carolina)

Spence, Wilma C.
Tombstones and Epitaphs of Northeastern North Carolina ...
Baltimore, MD, Gateway Press, 1973. 323 p., index.
NN APR (North Carolina) 74-1928

Tompkins, Robert M.
Marriage and Death Notices from the *Western Carolinian* (Salisbury, North Carolina), 1820–1842.
Raleigh, The Author, 1975. 255 p., alpha, index.
NN APR (North Carolina) 76-776

U.S. Census Office. 4th Census North Carolina.
1820 Federal Census of North Carolina.

Tullahoma, TN 37385, Dorothy W.
   Potter, 1970–. v. 1 (Anson Co.);
   v. 53 (Warren) in NN
NN APR (North Carolina) 73-2960

NORTH DAKOTA

State Archives

State Library Commission
Liberty Memorial Bldg.
Bismarck, ND 58505

Vital Records

Division of Vital Statistics
State Department of Health
Bismarck, ND 58505
Births and deaths: July 1893–, but
   1894–1920 incomplete
Births and marriages prior: clerk
   of district court
Marriages: July 1925–, or county
   judge of county
Marriages prior: county judge of
   county

Societies and Periodicals

Barnes County Historical Society
Box 767
Valley City, ND 58072

Bismarck–Mandan Historical and
   Genealogical Society
Box 485
Bismarck, ND 58505
(*Bismarck—Mandan Historical
   and Genealogical Society News-
   letter*, 1972–)
NN Current

Burke County and White Earth
   Valley Historical Society
Box 286
Powers Lake, ND 58773

Cass County Historical Society
% Ken McIntyre, Harwood
West Fargo, ND 58042

Divide County Historical Society
Crosby, ND 58730

Fargo Genealogical Club
1105 South University
Fargo, ND 58102

Fort Seward Historical Society, Inc.
Box 1002
321 Third Avenue S.E.
Jamestown, ND 58401

Foster County Historical Society
37 North Central
Carrington, ND 58421

Grand Forks County Hist. Soc.
323 1/2 DeMers Avenue
Grand Forks, ND 58201

Griggs County Historical Society
Copperstown, ND 58425

Hettinger County Hist. Soc.
% Mrs. Delores Tollefson
Regent, ND 58650

McKenzie County Museum and
   Historical Society, Inc.
Watford City, ND 58854

McLean County Historical Society
Washburn, ND 58577

North Dakota Historical Society,
   Inc.
% Mrs. Dave Robinson, Secretary
Coleharbor, ND 58531
(*Trails and Smoke Signals* 1967–)
NN IWHB 76-1352

North Dakota Historical Society of
   Germans from Russia
Box 371
Bismarck, ND 58505
(*Heritage Review*, c. 1973–)

Oliver County Historical Society
Center, ND 58530

Pembina County Pioneer Daughters
% Clifton Jenson
Cavalier, ND 58220

Red River Valley Historical Society
Minard Hall
North Dakota State University
Fargo, ND 58102
(*Red River Historian; Red River Valley History News*)

Richland County Historical Society
Second Street and 7th Avenue
Wahpeton, ND 58075

State Historical Society of North Dakota
Liberty Memorial Bldg.
Bismarck, ND 58501
(*North Dakota History: Journal of the Northern Plains*, 1926–)
NN IAA

Steele County Historical Society
Main Street
Hope, ND 58046

University of North Dakota Library
Grand Forks, ND 58201

Walsh County Historical Society
Carnegie Bookmobile Library
Griggs and 7th
Grafton, ND 58237

Walsh County Historical Society
Minot, ND 58261
(*Walsh Historical News*)

Wells County Historical Society, Inc.
Box 96
Fessenden, ND 58438

Books and Articles

Aberle, George P.
Pioneers and Their Sons: One Hundred Sixty-five Family Histories.
Dickinson, c. 1969. 2 v., index.
NN APR (North Dakota)

Dakota Territory.
NN APR (South Dakota) 74-758

Handler, Mabel J.
Towner County Long Beach, CA, the author, 1958–62. 6 v.
NN APR (Towner Co. ND)

Williams, Mary A. B.
Origins of North Dakota Place Names.
Washburn, Bismarck *Tribune*, 1966. 354, 2 p., no index, alpha.
NN IWHB

U.S.W.P.A. North Dakota.
Guide to Public Vital Statistics Records.
Bismarck, 1941. 76 p.
NN APT p. v. 211

OHIO

State Archives

Ohio State Library
65 South Front Street
Columbus, OH 43215

Vital Records

Division of Vital Statistics
State Department of Health
G-20 State Departments Bldg.
65 S. Front Street
Columbus, OH 43215
Births and deaths: December 20, 1908–

Births and deaths prior: Probate
Court of county
Marriages: September 1949—
Marriages prior: probate judge of
county

Libraries

Akron Public Library
55 South Main Street
Akron, OH 44309

Church of Jesus Christ of Latter-
day Saints
Cincinnati, Ohio, State Branch Genealogical Library
5505 Bosworth Place
Cincinnati, OH 45212

Cincinnati Public Library
800 Vine Street
Cincinnati, OH 45202

Cleveland Public Library
325 Superior Avenue
Cleveland, OH 44114

Ohio Historical Society Library
1982 Velma Avenue
Columbus, OH 43211

Peninsula Library and Historical
Society
6105 Riverview Road
Peninsula, OH 44264

Public Library of Cincinnati and
Hamilton County
Eighth and Vine Streets
Cincinnati, OH 45202

Toledo Public Library
Local Historical and Genealogical
Department
325 Michigan Street
Toledo, OH 43624

University of Cincinnati Library
Cincinnati, OH 45221

Societies and Periodicals

Allen County Historical Society
620 West Market Street
Lima, OH 45801
(*Allen County Reporter*)

Ashtabula County Genealogical So-
ciety
P.O. Box 885
Ashtabula, OH 44004
(*The Ancestor Hunt*)

Association of Historical Societies
of Ohio
10829 Valley View Road
Northfield, OH 44067

Bellevue Area Historical Society
Box 304
Bellevue, OH 44811
(*Four County Crossroads*)

Canal Fulton Heritage Society
Box 607, 623 Cherry Street
East Canal Fulton, OH 44614

Centerville Historical Society
89 West Franklin Street
Centerville, OH 45459
(*Curator*)

Cincinnati Historical Society
Eden Park
Cincinnati, OH 45202
(*Cincinnati Historical Society Bul-
letin*)
NN IVB (Cincinnati)

Clark County Historical Society
300 West Main Street
Springfield, OH 45504
(*Clark County Historical Society
Newsletter*)

Franklin County Historical Society
280 East Broad Street
Columbus, OH 43215
(*Sights and Sounds of Cosi*)

Geauga County Historical Society
Box 153, 14653 East Park
Burton, OH 44021
(*The Quarterly*)

Genealogical Workshop
331 Fifth Avenue
Elyria, OH 44035

Greater Cleveland Genealogical Society
P.O. Box 963
Cleveland, OH 44140

Great Lakes Historical Society
480 Main Street
Vermilion, OH 44089
(*Inland Seas*)

Hardin County Archeological and Historical Society
121 North Detroit Street
Kenton, OH 43326
(*Hardin County Museum Bulletin*)

Hudson Historical Society and Library
22 Aurora Street
Hudson, OH 44236
(*Flashback*)

Johnstown Genealogical Society
P.O. Box 345
Johnstown, OH 43031

Kinologists of the Firelands Historical Society
4 Case Avenue
Norwalk, OH 44857

Lake County Genealogical Society
% Mrs. Earl Williams, Secretary
7468 McKinley Street
Mentor, OH 44060

Maumee Valley Historical Society
1031 River Road
Maumee, OH 43537
(*Northwest Ohio Quarterly*)

Meigs County Pioneer and Historical Society
Butternut Avenue
Pomeroy, OH 45769

Miami Valley Genealogical Society
P.O. Box 1364
Dayton, OH 45401

Montgomery County Historical Society
The Old Court House
7 North Main Street
Dayton, OH 45402
(*Ionic Columns*)

National Documentation Institute
Marietta College
Marietta, OH 45750

New England Society of Cleveland and the Western Reserve
633 Huron Road
Cleveland, OH 44115

Northwestern Ohio Genealogical Society
Mrs. David J. Read, Secretary
5711 Vail Avenue
Toledo, OH 43623

Northwest Ohio Great Lakes Research Center
214-A Graduate Building
Bowling Green State University
Bowling Green, OH 43403

Ohio Academy of History
Heidelberg College
Tiffin, OH 44883

Ohio Association of Historical Societies
Box 483
Canton, OH 44701

Ohio Genealogical Society
P.O. Box 2625

West Mansfield, OH 44906
(*The Report*, 1961–)
NN APR (Ohio) 75-254 and *ZAN-G71 (1961–69 film)

Ohio Historical and Philosophical Society
Ohio State Museum
Columbus, OH 43215

Ohio Historical Society
I-71 and 17th Avenue
Columbus, OH 43211
(*Ohio History*)

Ohio Records and Pioneer Families
Esther W. Powell, ed.
36 North Highland Avenue
Akron, OH 44303
(*Ohio Records and Pioneer Families*, 1960–)
NN APR (Ohio)

Ohio Society of the Daughters of the American Revolution
Waldschmidt House
Camp Dennison, OH 45111

Pictorial and Historical Society of Ohio
4491–93 Pearl Road
Cleveland, OH 44109

Pike County Chapter Ohio Genealogical Society
P.O. Box 224
Waverly, OH 45690
(*Newsletter*)

Pioneer and Historical Society
Box 2201
304 Woodlawn Avenue
Zanesville, OH 43701

Ross County Genealogical Society
P.O. Box 395

Chillicothe, OH 45601
(*Newsletter*)

Sandusky County Historical Society
% Rutherford B. Hayes Library
1337 Hayes Avenue
Fremont, OH 43420
(*Kin Hunters Guide*)

Shaker Historical Society
16740 South Park Blvd.
Shaker Heights, OH 44120
(*The Journal*)

South Central Ohio Genealogical Society
P.O. Box 33
Chillicothe, OH 45601

Studebaker Family National Association
6555 South Street, Rt. 202
Tipp City, OH 45371
(*The Studebaker Family*)

Tri-County Lineage Research Group
% Mrs. Fred Fish, President
Route 3
Fostoria, OH 44830

Tuscarawas County Genealogical Society
P.O. Box 141
New Philadelphia, OH 44663
(*Newsletter*)

United Methodist Historical Society of Ohio
Ohio Wesleyan University
Beeghly Library
Delaware, OH 40315

University of Akron Archival Services
Bierce Library

The University of Akron
Akron, OH 44325

Washington County Historical So-
ciety, Inc.
401 Aurora Street
Marietta, OH 45750
(*The Tallow Light*, 1966–)
NN APR (Washington Co.) 73-2800

West Augusta Historical and Genealogical Society
1510 Prairie Drive
Belpre, OH 45714

Western Reserve Historical So-
ciety
10825 East Blvd.
Cleveland, OH 44106
(*Western Reserve Historical Society
News*)

Wood County Historical Society
301 Sand Ridge Road
Bowling Green, OH 43402
(*Black Swamp Chanticleer*)

Books and Articles

Bolin, Daniel Lynn.
Ohio Valley History: West Point to
Lewisport.
New Orleans, LA, Polyanthos,
1976. 141 p., plus index.

Budd, Anne Lockwood Dallas.
Richland County, Ohio, Abstracts
of Wills, 1813–1873.
Mansfield, Ohio, Gen. Soc., 1974. v.
1 (241 p.), 2 indexes (people and
place).
NN APR (Richland Co.) 76-2215

DAR, Ohio Society.
Soldiers of the American Revolu-
tion Who Lived in the State of
Ohio.

Mineral Ridge, Trumbul Co.
Chapt., OGS, c. 1976 (orig. 1929,
1939, 1958). 3 v.
NN APR (Ohio)

Douthit, Ruth L.
Ohio Resources for Genealogists
and Some References for Ge-
nealogical Searching in Ohio.
Detroit, MI, Detroit Soc. for Gen.
Research, 1971 (orig. 1960). 51 p.
NN APB p. v. 144

Grismer, Karl H.
Akron and Summit Counties.
Akron, Summit Co. Hist. Soc., 1952.
834 p., index.
(Contains large indexed biograph-
ical section)
NN IVB (Akron)

Guide to the Manuscripts and Ar-
chives of the Western Reserve
Historical Society.
Cleveland, 1972. 425 p.
(Western Reserve Hist. Soc., Cleve-
land Pub., no. 124)
NN IAA

Guide to Manuscripts Collections
and Institutional Records in
Ohio.
Columbus, 1974. 315 p.
NN JFE 75-1586

Hartinger, Rosalie L.
Researching in Ohio.
(IN: *Maryland Genealogical So-
ciety Bulletin*, Baltimore, MD,
1971. v. 12, p. 104–107)
NN APR (Maryland)

Ohio Adjutant General.
Roster of Ohio Soldiers in the War
of 1812.
Columbus, Adj. Gen. of Ohio, 1916.
157 p., no index.
NN APR (Ohio)

Ohio Area Key: A Guide to the Genealogical Records of the State of Ohio.
Logan, UT, Everton, 1977. 254 p.

Ohio Early Census Index.
Bountiful, UT, AIS, 1976.
(Includes Federal 1810, 1800 and state 1803 for Washington County)

Ohio 1820 Census Index.
Bountiful, UT, AIS, 1977. 222 p.

Ohio 1830 Census Index.
Bountiful, UT, AIS, 1977

Ohio 1840 Census Index.
Bountiful, UT, AIS, 1977.

Ohio 1850 Census Index.
Bountiful, UT, AIS, 1977.

Ohio Family Historians.
Index to the 1850 Federal Population Census of Ohio.
Mineral Ridge, Lida Flint Harshman, 1972. 1,098 p., 526,819 entries.
NN APR (Ohio) 73-2728

Ohio Library Foundation.
Index to the 1820 Federal Census of Ohio.
Columbus, 1964. 831 p.
NN APR (Ohio)

Ohio Tax List, 1800–1810.
Bountiful, UT, AIS, 1976. alpha.

Petty, Gerald M.
Ohio 1810 Tax Duplicate.
Columbus, G. M. Petty, 1977. 231 p.

Powell, Esther Weygandt.
Early Ohio Tax Records.

Akron, E. W. Powell, 1971. 459 p., index.
NN APR (Ohio) 73-1401

Powell, Esther Weygandt.
Stark County, Ohio, Early Church Records and Cemeteries.
Akron, E. W. Powell, 1973. 269 p. index
NN APR (Stark Co.) 74-962

Short, Anita, and Ruth Bowers.
Index to Ohio Wills and Intestate Estates.
(In preparation; will cover 1788–1850 for the 87 counties existing in 1850)

Smith, Clifford Neal.
Virginia Land Grants in Kentucky and Ohio.
(IN: *NGSQ*, Washington, DC, 1973. v. 61, p. 16–27)
NN APGA

Smith, Clifford Neal, comp.
Federal Land Series: Archival Material on the Land Patents Issued by the United States Government, with Subject, Tract, and Name Indexes.
Chicago, IL, ALA, 1972–73. 2 v.
NN APG 76-579

U.S. Census, 5th Census.
1830 Federal Population Census of Ohio Index, comp. by Ohio Family Historians.
Columbus, Ohio Library Foundation, 1963. 2 v.
NN APR (Ohio)

Western Reserve Historical Society, Cleveland.
A Guide to the Manuscripts and Archives of the Western Reserve Historical Society.

Cleveland, 1972. 425 p. (*WRHS Pub. no. 124*)
NN IAA

Wilkens, Cleo G., and J. Howard Wilkens, comp.
Index to 1840 Federal Population Census of Ohio, 1969–71. 3 v.
NN APR (Ohio).

Who's Who, A Society Register. Cincinnati, Olive M. Avery and C.A.R. Devereux, 1892.
111 p., alpha.
NN IVB (Cincinnati)

OKLAHOMA

State Archives

Oklahoma State Library
109 Capitol
Oklahoma City, OK 73105

Vital Records

Vital Records Section
State Department of Health
Northeast 10th Street and Stone-wall
P.O. Box 53551
Oklahoma City, OK 73105
Births and deaths: October 1908–
Marriages: clerk of court in county where license issued; records begin late 19th or early 20th century.

Libraries

Capitol Hill Branch Library
834 S.W. 26th Street
Oklahoma City, OK 73109

Church of Jesus Christ of Latter-day Saints

Tulsa, Oklahoma, Branch Genealogical Library
12110 East 7th Street
Tulsa, OK 74138

Oklahoma City Library
131 N.W. Third Street
Oklahoma City, OK 73102

Public Library
220 South Cheyenne
Tulsa, OK 74103

State Daughters of the American Revolution Library
History Bldg.
Oklahoma City, OK 73102

Tulsa Central Library
400 Civic Center
Tulsa, OK 74103

Societies and Periodicals

Canadian County Historical Society
Wade and Grand
El Reno, OK 73036
(Mail: 400 South 10th Street, Yukon, OK 73099)
(*Canadian County Historical Society Bulletin*)

Coal County Historical and Genealogical Society
Route 5, Box 16
Coalgate, OK 74538

Genealogical Institute of Oklahoma
3813 Cashion Place
Oklahoma City, OK 73112

Indian Territory Genealogical Society
321 West Shawnee Street
Tahlequah, OK 74464

Oklahoma Baptist Historical Society
1141 North Robinson
Shawnee, OK 74801
(Mail: Oklahoma Baptist University, Shawnee, OK 74801)
(*Oklahoma Baptist Chronicle*)

Oklahoma Genealogical Society
P.O. Box 314
Oklahoma City, OK 73101
(*Oklahoma Genealogical Society Quarterly*, 1955–)
NN APR (Oklahoma)

Oklahoma Heritage Association
201 N.W. 14th Street
Oklahoma City, OK 73101
(*Oklahoma Heritage*)

Oklahoma Historical Society
History Bldg, Capitol Sub-Station
2100 North Lincoln Blvd. at N.E. 19th Street
Oklahoma City, OK 73105
(*Chronicles of Oklahoma Historical Society*, 1921–)
NN IAA

Oklahoma State Historical Society
2100 North Lincoln
Oklahoma City, OK 73105

Pioneer Genealogical Society
P.O. Box 2028
Ponca City, OK 74601

Pontotoc County Historical and Genealogical Society
Box 1646, 221 West 16th Street
Ada, OK 74820
(*Pontotoc County Quarterly*, c. 1969–)
NN APR (Pontotoc Co.) 75-760

Southwestern Oklahoma Historical Society

916 1/2 "B" Avenue
Lawton, OK 73501
(*Prairie Lore*)

Tulsa Genealogical Society
P.O. Box 585
Tulsa, OK 74101
(*Tulsa Annals*, 1966–)
NN APR (Tulsa)

Tulsa Genealogical Society
1507 East 21st Street
Tulsa, OK 74114

Western Trails Historical and Genealogical Society
P.O. Box 574
Altus, OK 73521

Books and Publishers

Butler, William J.
Tulsa 75: A History of Tulsa.
Tulsa, Metro Tulsa Chamber of Commerce, c. 1974. 228 p.
NN ITTM+ (Tulsa)

DAR of Oklahoma.
A Roster of Oklahoma Society, DAR, 1909–1959, and Register of Ancestors.
Oklahoma DAR, 1959. 199 p., index.

Hall, Ted Bryon.
Oklahoma Indian Territory.
Fort Worth, TX, American Reference Pub., 1971. 752 p., index.
NN APR (Oklahoma) 72-2202

Kerr, William F. and I. Gainer.
The Story of Oklahoma City, Oklahoma.
Chicago, IL, S. J. Clarke Pub. Co., 1922. 2 v., index v. 2.
NN ITTM (Oklahoma City)

Smith's First Directory of Oklahoma Territory for the Year Commencing August, 1890.
Guthrie, OK, J. W. Smith, 1890. 331 p.
NN *KSB

Society of Mayflower Descendants, Oklahoma.
Lineages of Society of Mayflower Descendants in State of Oklahoma, comp. by Lewis E. Neff.
Tulsa, 1959, 174 p.
NN APR (Oklahoma)

U.S.W.P.A.
Guide to Public Vital Statistics Records in Oklahoma.
Oklahoma, 1941. 85 p.f.
NN APR (Oklahoma)

Woods, Frances.
First Census of Oklahoma, Reprint of Indian Lands West of Arkansas (Oklahoma), Population Schedule of the United States Census of 1860.
Austin, TX, Arrow Printing Co., 1964.

OREGON

State Archives

Oregon State Archives
1005 Broadway N.E.
Salem, OR 97301

Vital Records

Vital Statistics Section
Oregon State Health Division
P.O. Box 231
Portland, OR 97207
Births and deaths: July 1903–
Births and deaths, city of Portland: some 1880–

Marriages: January 1907–
Marriages prior: county clerk's office

Libraries

Church of Jesus Christ of Latter-day Saints
Portland, Oregon, East Branch Genealogical Library
Portland 8 and 14 Wards
2215 N.E. 106th Street
Portland, OR 97220

Oregon Historical Society Library
1230 S.W. Park Avenue
Portland, OR 97205

Portland Library Association
801 S.W. Tenth Avenue
Portland, OR 97205

Societies and Periodicals

Columbia County Historical Society
45 South 21st Street
St. Helens, OR 97051

Coos Genealogical Forum
P.O. Box 476
Coos Bay, OR 97420
(*Coos Genealogical Forum Bulletin*, 1964–)
NN APR (Coos Bay) 77-150

Crook County Historical Society
Bowman Museum
246 North Main Street
Prineville, OR 97754

Deschutes Pioneers Association
2 Greenwood Avenue
Bend, OR 97701

Douglas County Historical Society

Route 2, Box 759
Roseburg, OR 97470

Genealogical Forum of Portland
1410 S.W. Morrison, Room 812
Portland, OR 97205
(*Bulletin*)

Harney County Historical Society
Box 646
North Broadway
Burns, OR 97720

Josephine County Genealogical So-
  ciety
% Wainwright, 1013 S.W. "L"
  Street
Grants Pass, OR 97526
(*Josephine County Researcher*)

Lane County Historical Society
740 W. 13th Avenue
Eugene, OR 97402

Lincoln County Historical Society
  579 S.W. 9th Street
Newport, OR 97365

Linn Genealogical Society
925 West 19th Street
Albany, OR 97321

Marion County Historical Society
Box 847
Salem, OR 97308

Mid-Valley Genealogical Society
3960 N.W. Elizabeth Place
Corvallis, OR 97330
(*Newsletter*)

Mount Hood Genealogical Forum
P.O. Box 703
Oregon City, OR 97045
(*The Trackers*)

Old Church Society, Inc.

1422 S.W. 11th Avenue
Portland, OR 97201

Oregon Genealogical Society
P.O. Box 1214
Eugene, OR 97401
(*Oregon Genealogical Bulletin*,
  1959–)
NN APR (Oregon) +

Oregon Heritage Council
P.O. Box 3424, Salem, OR 97302

Oregon Historical Society
1230 S.W. Park Avenue
Portland, OR 97205
(*Oregon Historical Quarterly*,
  1906–)
NN IAA

Polk County Historical Society
Box 200
Dallas, OR 97338
(*Historically Speaking*)

Portland Genealogical Society
2215 N.E. 106th Street
Portland, OR 97205

Rogue Valley Genealogical Society
P.O. Box 628
Ashland, OR 97520
(*Rogue Digger*)

Southern Oregon Historical So-
  ciety, Inc.
Box 480, 206 Fifth Street
Jacksonville, OR 97530

Washington County Hist. Soc.
641 East Main Street
Hillsboro, OR 97123

Willamette Valley Geneal. Soc.
P.O. Box 2083
Salem, OR 97302
(*Beaver Briefs*)

Yamhill County Historical Society
Box 484, 6th and Market
Lafayette, OR 97127

Books and Articles

DAR, Oregon.
Oregon State Roster of Ancestors.
Tillamook, 1964. 402 p.
NN APR (Oregon)

End of the Trail Researchers.
Lebanon, 1970–. v. 1–.
(145 24th St. S.E., Salem, OR 97301)
NN APR (Oregon)

Genealogical Forum, Portland, Oregon.
Genealogical Material in Oregon
Donation Land Claims, Abstracted from Applications.
Portland, GFPO, 1957–62. 4 v.
NN APR (Oregon)

Genealogical Research in Oregon.
(IN: *NGSQ*, Washington, DC, 1959.
v. 47, p. 115–148)
NN APGA

Index to Clackamas County, Oregon, Marriage Records.
Oregon City, Mt. Hood Gen. Forum
of Clackamas Co., 1973. v. 2.
NN APR (Clackamas Co.) 72-2570

Lepschat, May Ringle, and Gyneth
S. Balfour.
Washington County, Oregon, Records: Vol. 1, Marriage Records,
1842–1880.
Portland, Genealogical Forum,
1972. v. 1, 91 p., index.
NN APR (Washington Co.) 74-203

Lynch, Vera M.
Free Land, Free Men: A Story of
Clackamas County.

Oregon City, V. M. Lynch, 1973.
680 p., index.
NN IXK (Clackamas Co.) 74-918

Oregon 1850 Census Index.
Bountiful, UT, AIS, 1977.

U.S. Census, 7th Census.
Pioneer Families of the Oregon
Territory, 1850. 2nd ed. Bulletin
#3, Pub. #17.
Oregon State Archives, 1961.
NN IXI+ (Oregon State Archives)

U.S. National Archives.
Index to Oregon Donation Land
Claims, Filed in the National
Archives.
Portland, 1953. 166 p., alpha.
NN APR (Oregon)

PENNSYLVANIA

State Archives

Pennsylvania Historical and Museum Commission
William Penn Memorial Museum
and Archives Bldg., Rm. 1026
3rd and North Streets
Harrisburg, PA 17120

Vital Records

Division of Vital Statistics
State Department of Health
Central Bldg.
101 South Mercer Street, P.O. Box
1528
Newcastle, PA 16103
Births and deaths: January 1906–
Births and deaths prior: Register
of Wills, Orphan's Court, county
seat

Marriages: January 1941–
Marriages prior: Marriage License Clerk County Court House
Births and deaths, Pittsburgh, 1870–1905, and births and deaths, Allegheny City (part of Pittsburgh), 1882–1905, write: Office of Biostatistics, Pittsburgh Health Dept., City-County Bldg., Pittsburgh, PA 15219
Births and deaths, city of Philadelphia, 1860–1915, Vital Statistics, Philadelphia Dept. of Public Health, City Hall Annex, Philadelphia, PA 19107

LIBRARIES

Altoona Public Library
"The Pennsylvania Room"
1600 Fifth Avenue
Altoona, PA 16602

Carnegie Library
4400 Forbes Avenue
Pittsburgh, PA 15213

Centre County Library and Historical Museum
203 North Allegheny Street
Bellefonte, PA 16823

Church of Jesus Christ of Latter-day Saints
Philadelphia, Pennsylvania, State Branch Genealogical Library
Pennsylvania State Center
721 Paxon Hollow Road
Broomall, PA 19008

Franklin Institute Library
Benjamin Franklin Parkway and 20th Street
Philadelphia, PA 19103

Free Library of Philadelphia
Logan Square
Philadelphia, PA 19141

Friends Historical Library
Swarthmore, PA 19081

Lutheran Historical Society Library
Gettysburg, PA 17325

Lutheran Theological Seminary Library
Mt. Airy
Philadelphia, PA 19119

Pennsylvania State Library
Walnut and Commonwealth Avenue
Education Bldg.
Harrisburg, PA 17126

University of Pennsylvania Library
Central Bldg.
34th Street below Woodland
Philadelphia, PA 19104

Washington County Historical Society Library
LeMoyne House
49 East Maiden Street
Washington, PA 15301

York County Historical Society Library
250 East Market Street
York, PA 17403

Societies and Periodicals

Adams County Historical Society
Old Dorm
Lutheran Theological Seminary Campus
Gettysburg, PA 17325

Allegheny-Kiskiminetas   Valley
  Historical Society
224 East 7th Avenue
Tarentum, PA 15084
(*Historia*)

American Catholic Historical Soci-
  ety of Philadelphia
Box 84
Philadelphia, PA 19105

Balch Institute
123 South Broad Street
Philadelphia, PA 19109

Blair County Historical Society
P.O. Box 1083
Altoona, PA 16603
(*The Mansion*)

Bucks County Historical Society
Mercer Museum
Pine and Ashland Streets
Doylestown, PA 18901
(*Bucks County Historical Society
  Journal*, 1909–)
NN ISD (Bucks Co.)

Cambria County Historical Society,
  Museum and Library
201 West Sample Street
Ebensburg, PA 15931
(Mail: 604 N. West Street, Ebens-
  burg, PA 15931)

Central Pennsylvania Genealogical Society and Library
629 Holmes Street
State College, PA 16801

Chester County Historical Society
225 North High Street
West Chester, PA 19015

Chestnut Hill Historical Society
8505 Germantown Avenue
Philadelphia, PA 19118

Clarion County Historical Society
Courthouse
Clarion, PA 16214

Clearfield County Historical Society
104 East Pine Street
Clearfield, PA 16830

Clinton County Historical Society
East Water Street
Lock Haven, PA 17745

Colonial   Philadelphia   Historical
  Society
292 St. James Place
Philadelphia, PA 19106
(*The Calendar*)

Columbia County Historical Soci-
  ety
Box 105,
Bakeless Humanities Center
Bloomsburg State College
Bloomsburg, PA 17815
(*The Columbian*)

Community Historians of Lancas-
  ter County
College and James Streets
Lancaster, PA 17603

Cornerstone Genealogical Society
P.O. Box 547
Waynesburg, PA 15370
(*Cornerstone Clues*)

Cumberland County Historical Society and Hamilton Library Association
21 North Pitt Street
Carlisle, PA 17013

Delaware County Historical Society
Wolfgram Memorial Library

15th and Walnut Streets
Chester, PA 19013
(Mail: Box 1036, Widener College,
Chester, PA 19013)
(*The Bulletin*)

Elk County Historical Society
The Country Courthouse
Ridgway, PA 15853
(*Elk Horn*)

Ely Family Association
11 West Chestnut Hill Avenue
Chestnut Hill, PA 19118
(*The Ely Reunion*)

Erie Society for Genealogical Research
The Y.M.C.A.
130 West 8th Street
Erie, PA 16507
(*Keystone Kuzzins*, 1972–)

Erie Society for Genealogical Research
P.O. Box 991
Erie, PA 16502
(*Journal of Erie Studies*)

Evangelical and Reformed Historical Society
555 West James Street
Lancaster, PA 17603

Friends Historical Association
Haverford College Library
Haverford, PA 19041
(*Quaker History*)

Genealogical Society of Southwestern Pennsylvania
Citizen's Library
55 South College Street
Washington, PA 15301
(*The Keyhole*, 1973–)

Genealogist's Post (1964–1971, v. 1–8, NN APGA)

R. T. and M. C. Williams, Editors
Danboro, PA 18916

Harmonist Historic and Memorial Association
Main and Mercer Streets
Harmony, PA 16037
(*Der Harmonist*)

Historical and Genealogical Society of Somerset County, Inc.
Box 533, R.D. 2
Somerset, PA 15501
(*Laurel Messenger*)

Historical Society of Berks County
940 Centre Avenue
Reading, PA 19601
(*Historical Review of Berks County*)
NN ISD (Berks Co.)

Historical Society of Cocalico Valley
249 West Main Street
Ephrata, PA 17522

Historical Society of Eastern Pennsylvania Conference
United Methodist Church
326 New Street
Philadelphia, PA 19106

Historical Society of the Evangelical and Reformed Church
Archives and Libraries
College Avenue and James Street
Lancaster, PA 17604

Historical Society of Montgomery County
1654 DeKalb Street
Norristown, PA 19401
(*Bulletin of the Historical Society of Montgomery County*, 1936–)
NN ISD (Montgomery Co.)

Historical Society of Pennsylvania
1300 Locust Street
Philadelphia, PA 19107
(*Pennsylvania Magazine of History and Biography*, 1877–)
NN IAA

Historical Society of Perry County
Headquarters and Museum
129 North Second Street
Newport, PA 17074

Historical Society of Schuylkill County
14 North Third Street
Pottsville, PA 17901

Historical Society of Western Pennsylvania
4338 Bigelow Blvd.
Pittsburgh, PA 15213
(*Western Pennsylvania Historical Magazine*, 1918–)
NN IAA

Historical Society of York County
250 East Market Street
York, PA 17403
(*York Gazette and Public Advertiser*)

Historic Bethlehem, Inc.
Main and Church Streets
Bethlehem, PA 18018

Historic Schaefferstown, Inc.
Box 1776
Schaefferstown, PA 17088

Huntingdon County Historical Society
P.O. Box 305
106 4th Street
Huntingdon, PA 16652

Jefferson County Historical Society
% Mr. Arthus Altman

54 Jenks Street
Brookville, PA 15825

Juniata County Historical Society
% Mr. David Shellenberger
Star Route
Mifflintown, PA 17059

Lackawanna County Historical Society
232 Monroe Avenue
Scranton, PA 18510

Lancaster County Historical Society
230 N. President Avenue
Lancaster, PA 17603
(*Journal of the Lancaster County Historical Society*, 1896–)
NN ISD (Lancaster Co.)

Lancaster Mennonite Conference Historical Society
2215 Mill Stream Road
Lancaster, PA 17602
(*Mennonite Research Journal*)

Lehigh County Historical Society
414 Walnut Street
Allentown, PA 18102
(*LCHS Proceedings*)
NN ISD (Lehigh Co.)

Lutheran Historical Society of Eastern Pennsylvania
7301 Germantown Avenue
Philadelphia, PA 19119
(Mail: % Mrs. Arthur S. Deibert, 2452 Main Street Schnecksville, PA 18078)
(*The Periodical*)

Lycoming County Historical Society
858 West 4th Street
Williamsport, PA 17701

(*Journal of the Lycoming County Historical Society*, 1955–)
NN ISD (Lycoming Co.)

Mayflower Descendants in the Commonwealth of Pennsylvania
1300 Locust Street
Philadelphia, PA 19107

Mercer County Historical Society
119 South Pitt Street
Mercer, PA 16137
(*Mercer County History*)

Methodist Historical Center
326 New Street
Philadelphia, PA 19106

Mifflin County Historical Society, Inc.
17 North Main Street
Lewistown, PA 17044
(Mail: 53 North Pine Street, Lewistown, PA 17044)

Monongahela Historical Society
904 Lincoln Street
Monongahela, PA 15063

Monroe County Historical Society
9th and Main Streets
Stroudsburg, PA 18360

Moravian Historical Society
210 East Center Street
Nazareth, PA 18064
(*Moravian Historical Society Transactions*)

Muncy Historical Society and Museum of History
44 North Main Street
Muncy, PA 17756
(*The Now and Then*)

Newcomen Society in North America

412 East North Ship Road, Exton
Downingtown, PA 19341
(*Newcomen Publications in North America*)

Northampton County Historical and Genealogical Society
101 South 4th Street
Easton, PA 18042

Northumberland County Historical Society Library
228 Arch Street
Sunbury, PA 17801
(Mail: 1019 Susquehanna Avenue, Sunbury, PA 17801)
(*Proceedings of the Northumberland County Historical Society*)

Old York Road Historical Society
% Abington Library Society
York Road
Jenkintown, PA 19046
(*Old York Road Historical Society Bulletin*)

Pennsylvania Dutch Folk Culture Society, Inc.
Lenhartsville, PA 19534

Pennsylvania Genealogical Society
1300 Locust Street
Philadelphia, PA 19107
(*Pennsylvania Genealogical Magazine*, 1895–)
NN APR Pennsylvania

Pennsylvania German Society
Fackenthal Library
Franklin & Marshall College
Lancaster, PA 17602

Pennsylvania German Society
Route 1, Box 469
Breinigsville, PA 18031
(*Der Reggeboge*)

Pennsylvania German Society

Times Herald Bldg.
Norristown, PA 18401

Pennsylvania Historical Association
806 New Liberal Arts Bldg.
University Park, PA 16802

Pennsylvania Traveler-Post, 1964–
P.O. Box 307
Danboro, PA 18916
NN APR (Pennsylvania)

Philadelphia Historical Commission
1313 City Hall Annex
Juniper and Filbert Streets
Philadelphia, PA 19107

Pittsburgh Historical and Landmarks Foundation
906 Benedum Trees Bldg.
Pittsburgh, PA 15222

Potter County Historical Society
308 North Main Street
Coudersport, PA 16915
(*Potter County Historical Society Bulletin*)

Presbyterian Historical Society
425 Lombard Street
Philadelphia, PA 19147
(*Journal of Presbyterian History*)

Quakertown Historical Society
44 South Main Street
Quakertown, PA 18951
(*Town Crier*)

Scottish Historic and Research Society of the Delaware Valley
2137 MacLarie Lane
Broomall, PA 19008

Snyder County Historical Society
Dr. George Dunkelberger Library
Seibert Hall

Susquehanna University
Selinsgrove, PA 17870

South Central Pennsylvania Genealogical Society
P.O. Box 1824
York, PA 17405
(*Our Name's the Game*)

Susquehanna County Historical Society and Free Library Association
Monument Square
Montrose, PA 18801

Tulpehocken Settlement Historical Society
Box 53
Womelsdorf, PA 19567
(*Tulpehocken Settlement Historical Society Newsletter*)

Union County Historical Society
Mrs. Jeanne Sampsell, Secretary
Laurelton, PA 17835

Valley Forge Historical Society
Valley Forge, PA 19481
(*The Picket Post*)

Warren County Historical Society
Box 427, 210 Fourth Avenue
Warren, PA 16365
(*Stepping Stones*)

Western Pennsylvania Conference of the United Methodist Church Commission on Archives and History
817 Caldwell Avenue
Portage, PA 15946

Western Pennsylvania Genealogical Society
4338 Bigelow Blvd.
Pittsburgh, PA 15213
(*The Quarterly; Jots from the Point*, 1974–)

Westmoreland County Historical
Society
Museum of Art Bldg.
221 North Main Street
Greensburg, PA 15601

Women's Historical Society of
Pennsylvania
4338 Bigelow Blvd.
Pittsburgh, PA 15213

Wyoming Historic and Genealogical Society
49 South Franklin Street
Wilkes-Barre, PA 18701
(*Proceedings of the Wyoming Historic and Genealogical Society*)

Your Family Tree, 1948– NN APR
(Pennsylvania)
414 Montgomery
P.O. Box 208
Hollidaysburg, PA 16648

Books and Articles

Anderson, Bart, Dorothy B. Lapp
and Marwood Darlington.
Index of Chester County, Pennsylvania, Wills and Intestate Records 1713–1850.
Danboro, R. T. and M. C. Williams,
1970. 224 p.
NN APR (Chester Co.) 72-503

Barnes, Anthony C., and Andrew
Allen, Jr.
Notes on the Last Will and Testa-
ment of Mrs. John Penn (Anne
Allen).
(IN: *Lehigh Co. Hist. Soc. Proceed-
ings*, Allentown, 1972. v. 29, p.
10–45, ports., houses, etc.)
NN ISD (Lehigh Co.)

Brace, Edwin T., and Alta Peck-
enpaugh Brace.

Descendants of Johann Adam and
Anne Maria Beckenbach (Peck-
inpaugh, Pickenbaugh, etc.).
Baltimore, MD, GPC, 1975. 438 p.,
index.
NN APV (Peckinpaugh) 75–1457

Brackbill, Martin H.
Family Data in Some Pennsylvania
Land Patents,1760–1761.
(IN: *NGSQ*, Washington, DC, Dec.
1976. v. 64, no. 4, p. 275–83)
NN APGA

Burt, Nathaniel.
The Perennial Philadelphians:
The Anatomy of an American
Aristocracy.
Boston, MA, Little, Brown, 1963.
625 p., index.
NN ISD (Philadelphia)

Carousso, Dorothee Hughes.
How to Search for Your Revolutionary Patriot in Pennsylvania.
Philadelphia, Gen. Soc. Pennsylvania, 1975. 12 p.

Chester County, Pennsylvania,
Court Records.
Danboro, R. & M. Williams, 1975.
v. 5–6.
(Orphans Court Records, 1747–61,
transcribed by Dorothy B.
Lapp)
NN ISD (Chester Co.)

Cox, Jean White, and Della Reagan Fischer.
1850 Census of Fayette County,
Pennsylvania, mimeographed.
Connellsville, J. W. Cox, et al.,
1972. (Full alpha by borough
and/or township, surname, etc.)
NN APR (Fayette Co.) 73-1861

Curtis, Martha B.
Public Records in County Court
　Houses.
(IN: *Pennsylvania History*, Eas-
　ton, PA, 1958. v. 25, p. 269–305)
NN IAA

Davis, Allen F., and Mark H.
　Haller.
1850 Census, Fayette County,
　Pennsylvania.
Connellsville, PA, Jean White Cox
　and Della Reagan Fischer, 1972.
　4 v., alpha by township, cross-
　index in v. 4 to stray names.
NN APR (Fayette Co.) 73-1861

The Peoples of Philadelphia: A
　History of Ethnic Groups and
　Lower-Class Life, 1790–1940.
Philadelphia, Temple U. Press,
　1973. 301 p., index.
NN ISD (Philadelphia) 75-2262

Erie Society for Genealogical Re-
　search.
A Surname Index to the 1876 Erie
　County Historical Atlas.
Erie, c. 1973. 118 leaves.
NN APR (Erie Co.) 74-1474

Fischer, Charles A.
Wills and Administrations of Nor-
　thumberland County, Pennsyl-
　vania, Including Wills and
　Administrations of Union, Mif-
　flin, and Indiana Counties. All
　Formerly Part of Northumber-
　land County.
Baltimore, MD, GPC, 1974 (orig.
　1950). 77 p., index.
NN APR (Northumberland Co.) 75-
　983

Fischer, Della R.
8736 Marriages 1866–1899 from

Westmoreland County, Penn-
　sylvania, Old Newspapers.
McKeesport, Della R. Fischer,
　1970, 2 v.
NN APR (Westmoreland Co.) 73-
　1610

Flake, G. Raymond, under aus-
　pices of Bucks County Histori-
　cal Society.
An Index of Persons and Subjects
　for Collection of Papers Read
　Before the Bucks County His-
　torical Society, Doylestown,
　Pennsylvania.
Danboro, Rich T. and Mildred C.
　Williams, 1972.
263 p., v. 1–8 (1908–40).
NN ISD (Bucks Co.)

Fulton, Eleanore Jane, and Bar-
　bara Kendig Mylin.
An Index to the Will Books and
　Intestate Records of Lancaster
　County, Pennsylvania, 1729–
　1850.
Baltimore, MD, GPC, 1973 (orig.
　1936). ix, 136 p., illus.
NN APR (Lancaster Co.) 75-2023

Hoenstine, Floyd G.
Guide to Genealogical and Histor-
　ical Research in Pennsylvania.
　3rd ed.
Hollidaysburg, PA 16648, F.G.
　Hoenstine, 1972. 474 p., index.
NN APR (Pennsylvania) 74-759

Hogg, O.F.G.
William Penn and His Descend-
　ants.
(IN: *GM*, London, 1959–60. v. 13,
　p. 115–19, 133–42)
NN ARCA

Koger, Marvin V.

Index to the Names of 30,000 Im-
migrants.
Pennington Gap, VA, 1935. 232 p.
(See Rupp)
NN APR (Pennsylvania)

Long, George F., and Margaret W.
Long.
John Long of Lancaster County,
Pennsylvania.
New Orleans, Polyanthos, 1974, c.
1975 219 p., index.
NN APV (Long) 75-2460

McCay's, Betty.
Sources for Genealogical Searching
in Pennsylvania.
Indianapolis, IN, 1968. 1 sheet of
microfiche
NN *XMG-169

MacReynolds, George.
Place Names in Bucks County,
Pennsylvania. 2nd ed.
Doylestown, Bucks Co. Hist. Soc.,
1955. 454 p., alpha arranged in
a historical narrative.
NN ISD (Bucks Co.)

Marriages and Death Notices from
the Philadelphia *Saturday Evening Post.*
(IN: *PGM*, Philadelphia, 1971–73.
v. 27, p. 241–43; v. 28, p. 32–34)
NN APR (Pennsylvania)

Mayhill, R. Thomas.
Lancaster County, Pennsylvania,
Deed Abstracts and Revolution-
ary War Oaths of Allegiance.
Knightstown, IN, 1973. 283 p.
NN APR (Lancaster Co.) 74-935

Myers, Albert Cook.
Quaker Arrivals at Philadelphia,
1682–1750: Being a List of Certificates of Removal Received

by Philadelphia Monthly Meet-
ing of Friends. 2nd ed.
Baltimore, MD, GPC, 1957. 131 p.
NN APR (Philadelphia)

Pennsylvania (Colony) Land Of-
fice.
Early Pennsylvania Land Records
... with a new introduction by
George E. McCracken.
Baltimore, MD, GPC, 1976 (orig.
1893). 787 p.
NN APR (Pennsylvania) 77-182

Pennsylvania (Colony) Courts, Su-
preme Court.
Persons Naturalized in the Prov-
ince of Pennsylvania, 1740–
1773. Indexed edition
Baltimore, MD GPC, 1967. 139 p.
(Extracted and reprinted from
Pennsylvania Archives, series
2, v. 2)
NN APR (Pennsylvania)

Pennsylvania 1800 Census Index.
Bountiful, UT, AIS, 1976.

Pennsylvania 1810 Census Index.
Bountiful, UT, AIS, 1976. 314 p.

Pennsylvania 1820 Census Index.
Bountiful, UT, AIS, 1976. 406 p.

Pennsylvania 1830 Census Index.
Bountiful, UT, AIS, 1976. 531 p.

Pennsylvania 1840 Census Index.
Bountiful, UT, AIS, 1977.

Pennsylvania 1850 Census Index.
Bountiful, UT, AIS, 1976. 2 v.
NN APR (Pennsylvania) 76-1593

Pennsylvania Folklife.
Lancaster, 1949–.
(Formerly *Pennsylvania Dutch-*

man, 1949–1957. Many articles of a genealogical nature have appeared in this publication, including passenger lists.)
NN IEK+ and *ZAN-H9

Pennsylvania State Library.
Genealogical Research in the State Library.
Harrisburg, 1973. 10 p.
(State and Local Historical Collection, General Library Bureau, State Library of Pennsylvania, Dept. of Education)
NN Desk Room 315G

Philadelphia Marriages and Obituaries, 1857–1860, Philadelphia *Saturday Bulletin*, ed., comp. by Maryly B. Penrose.
Franklin Park, NJ, Liberty Bell Assoc., 1974. 294 p., index (Heads of family, index, 1850 federal census, city of Philadelphia).

Ohio Family Historians.
Index to 1810 Census of Pennsylvania.
Columbus, OH, 1966. 297 p.
NN APR (Pennsylvania)

Roach, Hannah Benner.
The Pennsylvania Militia in 1777.
Philadelphia, Gen. Soc. Pennsylvania. 69 p., index.

Rubincam, Milton.
Genealogical Research Materials Relating to Pennsylvania.
(IN: *TAG*, New Haven, CT, 1958. v. 34, p. 195–98)
NN APGA

Rubincam, Milton.
Researching European Origins of Pennsylvania German Families.

(IN: *PGM*, Philadelphia, 1968. v. 25, p. 227–45)
NN APR (Pennsylvania)

Rupp, Israel D.
A Collection of Upwards of Thirty Thousand Names of German, Swiss, Dutch and French, and Other Immigrants in Pennsylvania, for 1725–1776. 2nd ed. rev. and enlarged. (See Koger)
Baltimore, MD, GPC, 1965 (orig. 1876). 583 p.
NN APR (Pennsylvania)

Scott, Kenneth.
Abstracts from Franklin's *Pennsylvania Gazette*, 1728–1748.
Baltimore, MD, GPC, 1975. 720 p., index.
NN APR (Pennsylvania) 75-1912

Scott, Kenneth.
Abstracts (Mostly deaths) from the *Pennsylvania Gazette*, 1775–1783.
Baltimore, MD, GPC, 1976. 58 p., index.

Scott, Kenneth.
Genealogical Data from the *Pennsylvania Chronicle*, 1767–1774. (NGS, Special Pub. #37)
Washington, DC, 1972.
NN APGA

Scott, Kenneth.
Pennsylvania Birth and Baptismal Certificates.
(IN: *Pennsylvania Gen. Mag.*, 1974. v. 38, p. 128–31) (48 certificates in New York Hist. Soc.)
NN APR (Pennsylvania)

Scott, Kenneth.
Runaways: Excerpts from the

Pennsylvania Gazette, 1775–1783.
(IN: *NGSQ*, Washington, DC, Dec. 1976. v. 64, no. 4, p. 243–60)
NN APGA

Sheppard, Walter Lee, Jr., and George E. McCracken, eds.
The Welcome Society Publications, 1970. 2 v.
(v. 1, Passenger and Ships Prior to 1684; v. 2, Welcome Claimants Proved, Disproved, and Doubtful with an Account of Some of Their Descendants)
NN APR (Pennsylvania) 72-241

Stemmons, John D.
Pennsylvania in 1800.
Salt Lake City, UT, Gendata, 1972. 687 p.
NN APR (Pennsylvania) 73-1188

Stover, Robert.
Abstracts from the *Republican Compiler*, Adams County, Pennsylvania.
Baltimore, MD GPC, 1976. v. 2, index.
NN APR (Adams Co.) 76-2563

Tepper, Michael.
Emigrants to Pennsylvania 1641–1819: A Consolidation of Ship Passengers Lists from the *Pennsylvania Magazine of History and Biography* ...
Baltimore, MD, GPC, 1977 (orig. 1877–1934). 292 p., new indexes.

Who's Who in Philadelphia.
Philadelphia, 1925–26. v. 1–3 index
NN APR (Philadelphia)

Williams, Richard T., and Mildred C. Williams.
Index of Wills and Administration

Records, Philadelphia, Pennsylvania.
Danboro, 1971–72. 4 v. (v. 1, 1682–1782; v. 2, 1783–1810; v. 3, 1811–31; v. 4, 1832–50)
NN APR (Philadelphia) 72-2018

Williams, Richard T., and Mildred C. Williams.
Index of Bucks County, Pennsylvania, Wills and Administrations, 1684–1850.
Danboro, 1971. 192 p.
NN APR (Bucks Co.)

Williams, Richard T., and Mildred C. Williams.
Index of Wills and Administration Records of Delaware County, Pennsylvania, 1789–1850.
Danboro, 1975. 96 p.
NN APR (Delaware Co.) 74-2398

Williams, Richard T., and Mildred C. Williams.
Index of Wills and Administration Records of Northampton County, Pennsylvania ... 1752–1850, and Lehigh County, Pennsylvania ... 1812–1850.
Danboro, 1971. 169 p.
NN APR (Northampton) 72-2528

Williams, Richard T., and Mildred C. Williams.
Oaths of Allegiance in Bucks County, Pennsylvania, 1776–1786.
Danboro, 1973.

Williams, Richard T., and Mildred C. Williams.
1779 Transcript Tax of Bucks County, Pennsylvania.
Danboro, 1973.

Wion, John H.

Deaths in Central Pennsylvania: An Index to the Obituaries Appearing in the *Democratic Watchman*, Bellefonte, Pennsylvania.
New York, John H. Wion, 1969. (Covers 1889–1920) 2 v. in 1.
NN APR (Pennsylvania)

Wolff, Raymond A.
The Wolf, Wolfe, Wolff Families of Pennsylvania.
Baltimore, MD, Delford and Co., 1971. 2 v., index in v. 2.
NN APV (Wolfe)

Wright, Norman E.
Genealogist's Notebook, Part 1— Pennsylvania Genealogical Sources.
(IN: *Ancestors West*, Santa Barbara, CA, 1976. v. 2, no. 7, p. 75–81)

RHODE ISLAND

State Archives

314 State House
Providence, RI 02900

Vital Records

Division of Vital Statistics
State Department of Health
Health Bldg., Room 101
Davis Street
Providence, RI 02908
Births, marriages and deaths: 1853–
Births, marriages and deaths prior: town clerk

Libraries

John Hay Library
Brown University
Providence, RI 02912

Providence Public Library
229 Washington Street
Providence, RI 02903

Rhode Island State Library
82 Smith St. State House
Providence, RI 02903

Societies and Periodicals

Blackstone Valley Historical Society
% Howard B. Whitney
27 Nickerson Street
Pawtucket, RI 02860

Block Island Historical Society
Old Town Road
Block Island, RI 02807

Bristol Historical and Preservation Society
48 Court Street
Bristol, RI 02809
(Mail: 21 Constitution Street, Bristol, RI 02809)

Burrillville Historical and Preservation Society
Box 94
Pascoag, RI 02859

Coventry Historical Society
Read School House
Route 117
Coventry, RI 02816
(Mail: % Margaret Tripp, Flat River Road, Coventry, RI 02816)

Cranston Historical Society
1351 Cranston Street

Governor Sprague Mansion
Cranston, RI 02920

Diocese of Providence Archives
Cathedral Square
Providence, RI 02903

Hopkinton Historical Association,
    Inc.
Hopkinton City
Hopkinton, RI 02833
(Mail: Box 13, Wood River Jct.,
    Hopkinton, RI 02894)

Jamestown Historical Society
Narragansett Avenue
Jamestown, RI 02835

League of Rhode Island Historical
    Societies
Box 6
Lincoln, RI 02865

Little Compton Historical Society
West Road
Little Compton, RI 02837

Massasoit Historical Association
37 Sowamset Avenue
Warren, RI 02885

Mayflower Quarterly (1935–) NN
    APGA
Ruth W. Sherman, Editor
128 Massasoit Drive
Warwick, RI 02888

Newport Historical Society
82 Touro Street
Newport, RI 02840
(*Newport History*, c. 1957–)
NN IRK (Newport)

North Smithfield Heritage Associ-
    ation
Box 413, Slatersville
North Smithfield, RI 02876

Pettaquamscutt Historical Society
1348 Kingston Road
Kingston, RI 02881
(*Pettaquamscutt Reporter*)

Rhode Island Historical Society
52 Power Street
Providence, RI 02906
(*Rhode Island History*, 1942–)
NN IAA

Rhode Island Society of the Sons of
    the American Revolution
132 Adams Point Road, Barring-
    ton
Providence, RI 02806

Richmond Historical Society
Richmond Town Hall
Richmond, RI 02898

Society of Friends of Touro Syn-
    agogue
85 Touro Street
Newport, RI 02840

Tiverton Historical Society
Chace-Cory House
Main Road
Tiverton, RI 02878

Warwick Historical Society
22 Roger Williams Avenue
Warwick, RI 02888

Westerly Historical Society
Westerly, RI 02891

Western Rhode Island Civic His-
    torical Society
Paine House
1 Station Street, Coventry
Providence, RI 02816
(Mail: % Mrs. William L. Mullins,
    365 Plainfield Street, Provi-
    dence, RI 02909)
(*Hinterlander*)

Books and Articles

Alphabetical Index of the Births, Marriages and Deaths Recorded in Providence, Rhode Island. Providence: City Registrar, 1879–1940.
Providence (Covers 1636–1935) 25 v., alpha.
(If only every city and town would have published its records in this manner!)
NN APR (Providence)

Austin, John O.
Genealogical Dictionary of Rhode Island: Comparing Three Generations of Settlers Who Came Before 1690.
Baltimore, MD, GPC, 1969. Reprint with additions and corrections by G. Andrews Moriarty. 496 p.
NN APR+ (Rhode Island)

Beaman, Alden G.
Rhode Island Vital Records
New Series
East Princeton, MA, the author, 1975–1977. 3 v.
NN APR (Washington Co.) 77-227 and 77-879

Cowell, Benjamin.
1781–1860, Spirit of '76 in Rhode Island.
Baltimore, MD, GPC, 1973 (orig. 1850). 560 p., index.
NN APR (Rhode Island) 74-1405

Jackson, Ronald V.
Rhode Island 1800 Census.
Salt Lake City, UT, AIS, 1972. 222 p., alpha.
NN APR (Rhode Island) 75-233

James, Sydney V.
Colonial Rhode Island: A History.

Charles Scribner's Sons, New York, 1975. 423 p., index.
NN IQI 76-2021

Klyberg, Albert T., ed.
Rhode Island Land Evidences, Volume I, 1648–1696.
Baltimore, MD, GPC, 1970 (orig. 1921). 246 p., index (i–xxv p.).

MacGunnigle, Bruce C.
Rhode Island Freeman, 1747–1755: A Census of Registered Voters.
Baltimore, MD, GPC, 1977. 49 p.

Rhode Island 1810 Census Index.
Bountiful, UT, AIS, 1976.

Rhode Island 1820 Census Index.
Bountiful, UT, AIS, 1976.

Rhode Island 1830 Census Index.
Bountiful, UT, AIS, 1977.

Rhode Island 1840 Census Index.
Bountiful, UT, AIS, 1977.

Rhode Island 1850 Census Index.
Bountiful, UT, AIS, 1976. 125 p.

Sherman, Ruth Ann Wilder.
Lineages of the Society of Mayflower Descendants in the State of Rhode Island and Providence Plantations.
Warwick, Society of Mayflower Descendants, 1966. 397 p., sup. 1968, 407–452 p.
NN APR (Rhode Island)

Waterman, Katherine U., trans.
The Rhode Island Census of 1782.
(IN *NEHGR*, Boston, MA, 1973–75.
v. 127, p. 3–17, 138–50, 216–29, 302–12; v. 128, p. 49–63, 124–35, 215–24, 293–304; v. 129, p. 53–67, 270–77, 379–87)
NN *R-APGA

SOUTH CAROLINA

State Archives

South Carolina Department of Archives and History
1430 Senate Street
Columbia, SC 29211
(*New South Carolina State Gazette*, 1968–)

Vital Records

Division of Vital Records
Bureau of Health Measurement
South Carolina Dept. of Health and Analysis Environmental Control
2600 Bull Street
Columbia, SC 29201
Births and deaths: January 1915–
City of Charleston: births, 1877–; deaths, 1821–
Charleston County Health Dept.
Ledger entries for:
  Florence County Health Dept.: Births and deaths, 1895–1914.
  Newberry County Health Dept.: Births and deaths, late 1800's.
Births and deaths prior: only from county health dept. listed.
Marriages: July 1, 1950–
Marriages prior: County Probate Judge, July 1911–

Libraries

Richland County Public Library
1400 Sumter Street
Columbia, SC 29201

South Carolina State Library
1500 Senate Street
Columbia, SC 29201

South Caroliniana Library
University of South Carolina
Columbia, SC 29208

Societies and Periodicals

Aiken County Historical Society
Route 2, Box 322
Aiken, SC 29801

Anderson County Historical Society
1100 Stratford Drive
Anderson, SC 29621

Beaufort County Historical Society
Box 55
Beaufort, SC 29902

Carolina Genealogist (1969–)
NN APR (South Carolina) 76-870
Danielsville, GA 30633

Carolina Low Country Historical Society
% John G. Smith
Sea Pines Company
Hilton Head Island, SC 29928

Charles Towne Landing 1670
1500 Old Towne Road
Charleston, SC 29407

Citadel Archives-Museum
Citadel Station
The Citadel
Charleston, SC 29409

Colonel William Bratton Chapter
Sons of the American Revolution
% H. M. McCallum
Box 206
Fort Mill, SC 29715

Dalcho Historical Society of the Protestant Episcopal Church in South Carolina
1020 King Street
Charleston, SC 29403

Fort Prince George Chapter
Daughters of the American Revolution
Hampton Avenue
Pickens, SC 29671

Horry County Historical Society
1008 Fifth Avenue
Conway, SC 29526
(*The Independent Republic Quarterly*)

Huguenot Society of South Carolina
94 Church Street
Charleston, SC 29401
(*Transactions*, 1889–)
NN IAA

Kith and Kin Genealogical Society
9 Tomassee
Greenville, SC 29605

Lancaster County Historical Commission
101 Connelly Bldg.
Lancaster, SC 29720

Laurens County Historical Society
Box 150, 1 Clay Street
Clinton, SC 29325

Newberry County Historical Society
Box 364
Newberry, SC 29108
(*Bulletin*)

Ocones County Historical and Recreational Society, Inc.
P.O. Box 1615, College Station
Orangeburg, SC 29115

South Carolina Annual Conference of the United Methodist Church, Commission on Archives and History
Box 550
Cheraw, SC 29520

South Carolina Baptist Historical Society
Furman University Library
Greenville, SC 29613

South Carolina Genealogical Society
P.O. Box 11353
Columbia, SC 29211
(*Carolina Herald*, 1972–)

South Carolina Historical Society
100 Meeting Street, Fireproof Bldg.
Charleston, SC 29401
(*South Carolina Historical Magazine*, 1900–) *R- NN APR (South Carolina)

South Carolina Magazine of Ancestral Research (1973–)
Brent Holcomb, Editor
Box 21766
Columbia, SC 29221

Spartanburg County Historical Association
501 Otis Blvd.
Spartanburg, SC 29302
(Mail: Route 4, Box 245, Spartanburg, SC 29302)
(*Grovers Post*)

University South Caroliniana Society
South Caroliniana Library
University of South Carolina
Columbia, SC 29208

York County Historical Society
Box 707
Rock Hill, SC 29730

Books and Articles

Black, James M.
The Counties and Districts of South Carolina.

(IN: *Genealogical Journal*, Salt Lake City, UT, 1976. v. 5, no. 3, p. 100–13)

Charleston, South Carolina, City Council.
Census of the City of Charleston, South Carolina, for the Year 1861.
Charleston, Evans and Cogswell, 1861. 271 p.
NN *KF 1861

Cyclopedia of Eminent and Representative Men of the Carolinas of the Nineteenth Century.
Spartanburg, Reprint Co., 1972 (orig. 1892). 1 v.
NN ITG 74-1458

DAR, Fort Sullivan Chapter, Charleston, South Carolina.
American Revolution Roster of Fort Sullivan (later Fort Moultrie), 1776–1780, Charleston Harbor . . .
Charleston, Fort Sullivan Chapter, DAR, 1976.
NN

De Saussure, William Henry.
South Carolina Courts: Court of Chancery Reports of Cases, Arguments and Debates. The Court of Chancery of the State of South Carolina, 1784–1816.
Columbia, 1817–19. 4 v.
NN XN

Easterby, James H.
A Guide to the Study and Reading of South Carolina History . . .
Columbia, 1949–50. 2 v. (new ed. with sup. by Noel Polk)
Spartanburg, South Carolina Reprint Co., c. 1975.
NN ITG

Esker, Katie-Prince Ward.
South Carolina Memorials. . . 1731–1776.
New Orleans, LA, Polyanthos, 1973–1977. 2 v.
NN ITG 73-2189

Frazier, Evelyn McD.
Hunting Your Ancestors in South Carolina.
Jacksonville, FL, 1974. 42 p.
NN *XMG-383

Hazelwood, Jean Park, Fred L. Hazelwood, Jr., and T. L. Smith.
Index, 1830 Census, South Carolina.
Fort Worth, TX, Gen. Re Put, 1973. 433 p.
NN APR (South Carolina) 74-2181

Hendrix, Ge Lee Corley, and Morn McKoy Lindsay.
The Jury Lists of South Carolina, 1778–1779.
Greenville, Mrs. Ge Lee Corley, 1975. 131 p., index, partial substitute for a statewide tax list.
NN APR (South Carolina) 75-1261

Hoff, Henry B.
The Gignilliat Ancestry.
(IN: *Huguenot Society of South Carolina Transactions*, Charleston, 1974. no. 79, p. 78–85)
NN IAA

Holcomb, Brent.
Some South Carolina County Records, Volume 1.
Easley, Southern Historical Press, 1976. 146 p., index, maps.

Holcomb, Brent.
Upper South Carolina Marriage and Death Notices, 1843–1865.
Easley, Southern Historical Press, 1977.

Meriwether, James B.
South Carolina, Journals and Journalists.
Spartanburg, The Reprint Co., 1975. 348 p.
(Lists South Carolina periodicals and newspapers in South Carolina libraries)
JFD 76-2254

Moore, Caroline T.
Abstracts of Wills of the State of South Carolina . . .
(Columbia, R. L. Bryan, 1960–74. 4 v., index each v.)
(Covers 1670–1800)
NN APR (South Carolina)

Moore, John Hammond, comp., ed.
Research Materials in South Carolina: A Guide.
Columbia, U. of South Carolina Press, 1967. 346 p., index.
NN ITG

Quattlebaum, Paul.
The Land Called Chicora. The Carolinas Under Spanish Rule, with French Intrusions, 1520–1670.
Spartanburg, The Reprint Co., 1973 (orig. 1956). 153 p., index.
NN ITG

Register of St. Phillips Parish Charles Town, 1720–1758, ed. by A. S. Salley, Jr.
Columbia, U. of South Carolina Press, 1971 (orig. 1904). 355 p., index.
NN APR (Charleston) 72–2255

Register of St. Phillips Parish Charles Town, or Charlestown, South Carolina, 1754–1810, ed. by D. E. Huger Smith and A. S. Salley, Jr.
Columbia, U. of South Carolina

Press, 1971 (orig. 1927). 505 p., index.
NN APR (Charleston) 72-2322

Reynolds, Emily R., et al.
Biographical Directory of the Senate of the State of South Carolina, 1776–1964.
Washington, DC, J. Stephenson, 1971. 137 p.
NN APR (South Carolina) 72-393

South Carolina 1810 Census Index.
Bountiful, UT, AIS, 1976.

South Carolina 1820 Census Index.
Bountiful, UT, AIS, 1976.

South Carolina 1830 Census Index.
Bountiful, UT, AIS, 1976.

South Carolina 1840 Census Index.
Bountiful, UT, AIS, 1977.

South Carolina Land Grants, 1784–1800.
Bountiful, UT, AIS, 1976. alpha.

South Carolina Revolutionary Soldiers, Sailors and Patriots, and Descendants, comp. by Joseph T. Madox and Mary Carter.
Albany, GA, Georgia Pioneers Pub. 1976. v. 1, no index, alpha.
NN APR (South Carolina) 76-2474

Stephenson, Jean.
Scotch-Irish Migration to South Carolina 1722: Rev. Martin and Five Shiploads of Settlers.
Washington, DC, J. Stephenson, 1971. 137 p.
NN APR (South Carolina) 72-393

U.S. Census Office, 2nd Census.
1800 Census of South Carolina.
Provo, UT, AIS, 1973.

•

U.S. Census Office, 4th Census.
1820 Federal Census for the State
of South Carolina.
Tustin, CA, G.A.M. Publications,
1972.

U.S. Census Office, 5th Census.
1830 South Carolina Census Index,
comp. by Jean Park Hazelwood,
et al.
Fort Worth, TX, Gen. Re Put, c.
1973. 433 p., alpha.
NN APR (South Carolina) 74-2181

U.S. Census Office, 7th Census.
1850 Census Index of South Carolina.
Bountiful, UT, AIS, 1976. 174 p.

Wakefiled, Roberta P.
Genealogical Source Materials in
South Carolina.
Washington, DC, 1957.
(*NGSSP*, no. 15)
NN APGA

Warrants for Lands in South Carolina, 1672–1711.
Columbia, U. of South Carolina
Press, for South Carolina Dept.
of Archives and History, 1973
(orig. 1910–15). 724 p., index.
NN ITG 73-2411

Watson, Alan D.
The Quit Rent System in Royal
South Carolina.
(IN: *William and Mary Quarterly*,
Williamsburg, VA, April 1976.
3rd series, v. 32, no. 2, p. 183–211)
NN *R-APR (Virginia)

SOUTH DAKOTA

State Archives
Department of History, Historical
Resource Center, Soldiers' and
Sailors' Memorial Bldg.
East Capitol Avenue

Pierre, SD 57501
(Has published a genealogical bibliography)

Vital Records

Division of Public Health Statistics
State Department of Health
Pierre, SD 57501
Births and deaths: July 1905– and
holds some prior to that date
Marriages: July 1905–
Marriages prior: clerk of court of
county

Societies and Periodicals

Aberdeen Area Genealogical Society
% Alexander Mitchell Library
519 Kline Street
Aberdeen, SD 57401

Bennett County Historical Society
Martin, SD 57551

Brookings County Historical Society
Volga, SD 57071

Brown County Museum and His-
tory Society, Inc.
Box 395, 21 South Main Street
Aberdeen, SD 57401

Butte County Historical Society
% Mrs. Dewey Holdren,
Vale, SD 57788

Charles Mix County Historical So-
ciety
Public Library
Box 297
Wagner, SD 57380

Clay County Historical Society, Inc.
Box 170
Vermillion, SD 57069

Custer County Historical Society
Box 27
Custer City, SD 57730

Dakota Territory (1969–) NN APR
(South Dakota) 74-758
Bernice L. Rogers, Editor
Phoenix, AZ 85026

Fall River County Historical Soci-
ety
Everett Gillis
Route 1
Hot Springs, SD 57747

Faulk County Historical Society
Faulkton, SD 57438

Grant County Historical Society
101 Park Avenue East
Milbank, SD 57252

Gregory County Historical Society
Burke, SD 57523

Hughes County Historical Society
300 South Highland
Pierre, SD 57501

Hyde County Historical and Genealogical Society
Highmore, SD 57345

Jackson-Washabaugh County His-
torical Society
Box 15
Kadoka, SD 57543

James Valley Historical Society
Box 397
Huron, SD 57350
(*James Valley Historical Society
Quarterly*)

Lake County Historical Society
% Dakota State College
Madison, SD 57042

Lyman County Historical Society
Presho, SD 57568

Minnehaha County Historical Society
Sioux Falls, SD 57105

Mitchell Area Genealogical Society
1004 West Birch Street
Mitchell, SD 57301

Moody County Historical Society
Box 283, East Park Road
Flandreau, SD 57028

Old Stanley County Historical Society
410 West Main
Fort Pierre, SD 57532

Potter County Historical Associa-
tion
Box 164
Gettysburg, SD 57442

Rapid City Society for Genealogical
Research
P.O. Box 1495
Rapid City, SD 57701
(*Black Hills Nuggets*, 1968–)
NN APR (South Dakota) 77-59

Roberts County Historical Society
122 First Avenue West
Sisseton, SD 57262

Sioux Valley Genealogical Society
P.O. Box 655
Sioux Falls, SD 57101

Society of Black Hills Pioneers
2115 Main Street
Deadwood, SD 57732

South Dakota Historical Society
Soldiers' and Sailors' Memorial
Bldg.

East Capitol Avenue
Pierre, SD 57501
(*South Dakota History*, 1902–)
NN IAA and IAA-73–548

Yankton County Historical Society
Box 412
West Side Park
Yankton, SD 57078

Books and Articles

Casey, Robert J.
The Black Hills and Their Incredible Characters.
Indianapolis, IN, Bobbs-Merrill, 1949. 383 p., index.
NN IWF (Black Hills)

Collins, Charles.
Collins History and Directory of the Black Hills, Central City, Dakota Territory.
Central City, DT., C. Collins, 1878. 91 p.
NN IWE+

Early Churches and Towns in South Dakota.
(IN: *Genealogist's Post*, Brookings, SD, 1964. v. 1, p. 13–20)
NN APGA

Fox's Who's Who Among South Dakotans.
Pierre, Statewide Service Co., 1924. 238 p., alpha.
NN AGZ

Frederickson, Roger.
God Loves Dandelions.
Waco, TX, Wood Books, 1975. 168 p.
NN IWF (Sioux Falls) 76-338

Hall, Bert L.
Round-Up Years: Old Muddy to

Black Hills. 2nd ed. Pierre, 1956. 608 p. plus index.
NN IWE

Inhabitants of Dakota, 1 Jan. 1861.
(IN: *Wi-iyohi*, Pierre, 1961. v. 14, no. 10)
NN IWFB 72-2414

Who's Who for South Dakota, 1956.
Pierre, South Dakota Trade Mark Reg., 1955. 281 p.
NN M-10 418

TENNESSEE

State Archives

State Library and Archives
411 7th Avenue North
Nashville, TN 37219
(*Index to County Records on Microfilm*, 1967–)
NN APR (Tennessee) 75-2072

Vital Records

Division of Vital Statistics
State Department of Public Health
Cordell Hull Building
Nashville, TN 37219
Births: January 1914–, and
Nashville, June 1881–
Knoxville, July 1881–
Chattanooga, January 1882–
Deaths: January 1914–, and
Nashville, July 1874–
Chattanooga, March 6, 1872–
Knoxville, July 1887–
Births and deaths enumeration records by school district: July 1908 through June 1912
Births: Memphis, April 1874–
December 1887, November 1898–
January 1914
Deaths: Memphis, May 1848–
January 1914
Write: Memphis-Shelby County

Health Dept., Division of Vital
Statistics, Memphis, TN 38103
Births and deaths prior: check with
county clerk's office
Marriages: July 1945–
Marriages prior: dates vary, early
19th century, and later, county
clerk's office

Libraries

Cossitt-Goodwyn Library
33 South Front Street
Memphis, TN 38103

Memphis Public Library and Information Center
1850 Peabody
Memphis, TN 38104

Memphis State University Library
Mississippi Valley Collection
Memphis, TN 38104

Public Library of Knoxville and
Knox County
McClung Historical Collection
217 Market Street
Knoxville, TN 37902

Public Library of Nashville and
Davidson County
222 Eighth Avenue North
Nashville, TN 37203

Tennessee State Library and Archives
Nashville, TN 37219

Societies and Periodicals

Bedford County Historical Society
Shelbyville, TN 37160

Chattanooga Area Historical Society Association
Box 1663

Chattanooga, TN 37401
(*Chattanews*)

Coffee County Historical Society
Box 524
304 South Irwin Street
Manchester, TN 37355
(*Coffee County Historical Society
Quarterly*)

Dickson County Historical Society
133 West Lake Circle
Dickson, TN 37055

East Tennessee Historical Society
Lawson McGhee Library
217 Market Street
Knoxville, TN 37902
(*Echoes*, 1955–)
NN APR (Tennessee)

Fentress County Historical Society
Box 457
Jamestown, TN 38556

Greene County Historical Society
Greeneville Light and Power Bldg.
Greeneville, TN 37743

Henry County Historical Society
Box 356
Paris, TN 38242

Heritage Foundation of Franklin
and Williamson Counties
Box 723
Franklin, TN 37064

Historical Associates of Wilson
County
112 South Hatton Avenue
Lebanon, TN 37087

Historical Commission of the
Southern Baptist Convention
127 9th Avenue North
Nashville, TN 37234
(*Baptist History and Heritage*)

Historic Nashville, Inc.
Box 40342
2700 12th Avenue South
Nashville, TN 37204
(*Historic Nashville Quarterly*)

Humphreys County Historical Society
Waverly, TN 37185

Lawrence County Historical Society
Box 431
Lawrenceburg, TN 38464
(*Annals of Lawrence County*)

Lincoln County Historical Society, Inc.
Wyatt Bldg.
202 East Washington
Fayetteville, TN 37334

McClung Historical Collection
Lawson McGhee Library
Knoxville Public Library System
217 Market Street
Knoxville, TN 37902

McMinn County Historical Society
Box 416
Athens, TN 37303

Maury County Historical Society
Columbia, TN 38401
(Mail: Box 127, Culleoka, Columbia, TN 38451)
(*Historic Maury*, 1965–)
NN ITX (Maury) 73-2860

Mid-West Tennessee Genealogical Society
P.O. Box 3175
Murray Station
Jackson, TN 38301
(*Family Findings*, 1969–)
NN APR (Tennessee) 73-2710

Mississippi Valley Collection
Memphis State University

John W. Brister Library
Memphis, TN 38111
(*Mississippi Valley Collection Bulletin*)

Montgomery County Genealogical Society
Route 1, Box 70
Adams, TN 37010

Montgomery County Historical Society
512 Madison Street
Clarksville, TN 37040
(*Montgomery County Genealogical Journal*, 1971–)

Morgan County Historical Society
Wartburg, TN 37887

National Society of Colonial Dames in Tennessee
Travellers Rest Historic House
Farrell Parkway
Nashville, TN 37220

Overton County Historical Society
207 East University Street
Livingston, TN 38570

Polk County Historical Society
Benton, TN 37307

River Counties, The
610 Terrace Drive
Columbia, TN 38401

Roane County Historical Society
Box 165
Rockwood, TN 37854

Robertson County Historical Society
Gorham McBane Library
White Street
Springfield, TN 37172

Rutherford County Historical Society

Box 1139
Murfreesboro, TN 37130

Tennessee Genealogical Society
P.O. Box 12124
Memphis, TN 38112
(*Ansearchin News*, 1954–)
NN APR (Memphis)

Tennessee Historical Society
403 7th Avenue North
Nashville, TN 37210
(*Tennessee Historical Quarterly*,
1942–)
NN IAA

Tipton County Historical Society
535 South Tipton
Tipton, TN 38019

Upper Cumberland Genealogical
Society
% Juanita Heard
P.O. Box 145
Algood, TN 38501

Watauga Association of Genealo-
gists
Sherrod Library, Room 301
East Tennessee State University
Johnson City, TN 37601
(*WAG Bulletin*, 1972–)

Wayne County Historical Society
Box 451
Waynesboro, TN 38485

West Tennessee Historical Society
157 South Fenwick Road
Memphis, TN 38111

Books and Articles

Bell, Annie Walker Burns, trans.
Major Index to Wills and Inventories of Tennessee at the DAR
Library, Washington, DC.
Washington, DC, A.W.B. Bell, 196–.
6 v. (incomplete), alpha (Covering Bedford through Meigs
counties).
NN APR (Tennessee)

Cartwright, Betty G. C., and L. J.
Gardiner.
North Carolina Land Grants in
Tennessee, 1778–1791.
Memphis, The Authors, 1958. 199
p. (reprinted 1973)
NN ITW

Cobb, Cully Alton.
The Cobbs of Tennessee.
Atlanta, GA, Ruralist Press, 1968.
114 p., index.
NN APR+ (Cobb)

D'Armand, Roscoe C., and Virginia
C. D'Armand.
Knox County, Tennessee, Mar-
riage Records, 1792–1900.
Knoxville, Family Record Soc. of
Knoxville, 1970. 1,144 p.
NN APR (Knox Co.)

DAR of Tennessee.
Membership Roster and Soldiers.
1961–1970. 2 v.
NN APR (Tennessee)

Hathaway, Beverly West.
Genealogy Research Sources in
Tennessee.
West Jordan, UT, Allstates Re-
search Co., 1972. 107 p.
NN APR (Tennessee) 73-1307

Johnson, Lillian B.
Historical Cane Ridge and Its
Families.
Nashville, Blue and Gray Press,
1973. 452 p., index.
NN APR (Davidson Co.) 74-2359

Kelley, Sarah Foster.
Children of Nashville ... Lineage from James Robertson.
Nashville, Blue and Gray Press, 1973. 337 p., index.
NN APV (Robertson) 74-475

McCown, Mary Hardin.
Soldiers of the War of 1812, Buried in Tennessee.
Johnson City, Tennessee Society, United Daughters of 1812, 1959, 156 leaves, alpha.
NN APR (Tennessee)

Memphis, Shelby County, Tennessee, Index to 1865 Census.
(IN: *Ansearchin' News.* Memphis, 1976. v. 23, no. 1, p. 30–39 [A-H]; no. 2, p. 13–22 [H-N]; no. 3, p. 135–44 [O-Z])
NN APR (Memphis)

Nashville in the 1890's.
Nashville, Vanderbilt U. Press, 1970. 342 p., index.
NN ITX (Nashville) 72-1749

Presley, Mrs. Leister.
Biographical Index to the History of Tennessee.
Searcy, AR, 1970–71. 3 v. in 1.
NN APR (Tennessee)

Sistler, Byron.
1830 Census East Tennessee.
1830 Census Middle Tennessee.
1830 Census West Tennessee.
Evanston, IL, 1969–72. 3 v.
NN APR (Tennessee) 74-1652

Sistler, Byron and Barbara, trans.
1850 Census of Tennessee.
Evanston, IL, Byron Sistler & Assoc., 1974–77. 8 v., cross-index.
NN APR (Tennessee) 75-208

Smith, Sam B., and Luke H. Banker.
Tennessee History: A Bibliography.
Knoxville, U. of TN Press, 1974. 498 p., index (county history, p. 320–452).
NN ITW 75-2243

Tennessee 1820 Census Index.
Bountiful, UT, AIS, 1976.

Tennessee 1830 Census Index.
Bountiful, UT, AIS, 1977.

Tennessee 1840 Census Index.
Bountiful, UT, AIS, 1976. 260 p.

Tennessee 1850 Census Index.
Bountiful, UT, AIS, 1977.

TEXAS

State Archives

Texas State Library
1201 Brazos Street
Austin, TX 78701
(Mail: Box 12927, Capitol Station, Austin, TX 78711)
(*Texas Libraries*)

Vital Records

Bureau of Vital Statistics
State Department of Health
410 East 5th Street
Austin, TX 78701
Births and deaths: 1903–
Births and deaths prior: some counties have records before 1903; check with county clerk
Marriages: county clerk. Dates vary widely from county to county—as early as 1824, as late as 1918.

Libraries

Church of Jesus Christ of Latter-
day Saints
Houston, Texas, East State Branch
Genealogical Library
Houston State Center
3000 Broadway
Houston, TX 77034

Clayton Library
5300 Caroline
Houston, TX 77004

Dallas Public Library
Texas History and Genealogy Department
1954 Commerce Street
Dallas, TX 75201

Ector County Public Library
Genealogical and Historical Room
622 North Lee Street
Odessa, TX 79761

El Paso Genealogical Library
3651 Douglas
El Paso, TX 79903

El Paso Public Library
Document-Genealogy Department
501 North Oregon Street
El Paso, TX 79901

Fort Worth Public Library
Ninth and Throckmorton Streets
Fort Worth, TX 76102

Genealogical Research Library
4524 Edmondson Avenue
Dallas, TX 75205

Houston Public Library
Houston, TX 77004

Lyndon Baines Johnson Library
2313 Red River
Austin, TX 78705

McLennan County Library
1717 Austin Avenue
Waco, TX 76701
(*Family Tree*)

Mirabeau B. Lamar Library
University of Texas
Austin, TX 78712

San Antonio Public Library
203 South St. Mary's Street
San Antonio, TX 78205

Scarborough Library of Genealogy,
History and Biography of the
South and Southwest
% McMurry College Library
McMurry Station
Abilene, TX 79605

Southeast Texas Genealogical, Historical and Sociological Library
2870 Driftwood Lane
Beaumont, TX 77703

Southwestern Genealogical Library
5301 Hanawalt Avenue
El Paso, TX 79903

Societies and Periodicals

Amarillo Genealogical Society
Amarillo Public Library
10th and Polk Streets
P.O. Box 2581
Amarillo, TX 79101

Austin Genealogical Society
P.O. Box 774
Austin, TX 78767
(*Austin Genealogical Society Quar-
terly*, 1960–)
NN APR (Austin) 74-326

Castro County Genealogical Society

P.O. Box 911
Dimmitt, TX 79027
(*Castro County News*)

Central Texas Genealogical Society
% Waco-McLennan County Library
1717 Austin Avenue
Waco, TX 76701
(*CTGS Bulletin, Heart of Texas Records*, 1958–) NN APR (Texas) v. 1–14 and APR (Texas) 76-155 for v. 15–

Chaparral Genealogical Society
P.O. Box 606
Tomball, TX 77375
(*Roadrunner*, 1974–)

Church Historical Society
606 Rathervue Place
Austin, TX 78705
(*The History Magazine of the Protestant Episcopal Church*)

Confederate Research Center
Hill Junior College
Hillsboro, TX 76645

Daughters of the Republic of Texas
112 East 11th
Austin, TX 78711

East Texas Historical Association
Box 6223, SFA Station
Nacogdoches, TX 75961
(*East Texas Historical Journal*, 1963–)
NN IAA

El Paso County Historical Society
Box 28, El Paso Chamber of Commerce
Civic Center Plaza
El Paso, TX 79901
(*The Password*, 1956–)
NN ITRM (El Paso)

Fort Worth Genealogical Society
P.O. Box 864
Fort Worth, TX 76101
(*Footprints*, 1958–) NN APR (Fort Worth)

Galveston Historical Foundation
Box 302
212 Kempner Avenue
Galveston, TX 77550
(*The Saccarappa*)

Genealogical Society of the Big Spring
% Howard County Library
Big Spring, TX 79720
(*Signal Peak*)

Hale County Historical Society
8th and Quincy
Plainview, TX 79072
(*Hale County History*)

Harris County Genealogical Society
P.O. Box 3329
Pasadena, TX 77501
(*Living Tree News*)

Houston Genealogical Forum
7130 Evans Street
Houston, TX 77017
(*Genealogical Record*, 1958–) NN APR (Houston)

Hutchinson County Genealogical Society
Hutchinson County Library
625 Weatherly Street
Borger, TX 79007
(*Cenotaph*, 1965–72)

Labor of Love Genealogical Society
Box 606
Tomball, TX 77375
(*Texas Legacy*)

Lamesa Area Genealogical Society
Box 1090
Lamesa, TX 79331
(*Lamesa Area Genealogical Society
Bulletin; Threads of Life*)

Local History and Genealogy Society
1954 Commerce Street
Dallas, TX 75201
(*Local History and Genealogy Society—The Quarterly*, 1955–) NN
APR (Texas)

Mesquite Historical and Genealogical Society
P.O. Box 165
Mesquite, TX 75149
(*Mesquite Historical and Genealogical Society*, 1965–)
NN APR (Mesquite)

Methodist Historical Society
Fondren Library
Southern Methodist University
Dallas, TX 75222

Northeast Texas Genealogical Society
P.O. Box 458
Mineola, TX 75773
(*Northeast Texas Genealogical Society Quarterly*, 1970–)

Pampa Genealogical and Historical Society
430 North Sumner Street
Pampa, TX 79065

Panhandle–Plains Historical Society
2400 4th Avenue
Canyon, TX 79016
(*Panhandle–Plains Historical Review*)

Parker County Genealogical Society

% Parker County Library
318 South Main Street
Weatherford, TX 76086
(*Trails West*, 1975–)

Permian Basin Genealogical Society
% Ector County Library
622 North Lee Street
Odessa, TX 79761
(*The Treeshaker*, 1963–) NN APR
(Texas)

Pioneer Heritage Preservation Society
616 Arkansas Street
South Houston, TX 77587

San Angelo Genealogical and Historical Society, Inc.
P.O. Box 3453
San Angelo, TX 76901
(*Stalkin' Kin*)

San Antonio Genealogical and Historical Society
P.O. Box 6383
San Antonio, TX 78209
(*Our Heritage*, 1959–)
NN ITRN (San Antonio)

San Jacinto Descendants, Inc.
5705 Shoalwood
Austin, TX 78756

Smith County Historical Society
and Survey Committee
624 North Broadway
Tyler, TX 75701
(Mail: Route 6, Box 310-C, Tyler,
TX 75701)
(*Chronicles of Smith County, Texas*)

Sons of the Republic of Texas
2426 Watts Road
Houston, TX 77025
(The Texian, 1955–)
NN APGA

Southeast Texas Genealogical and
Historical Society
2870 Driftwood Lane
Beaumont, TX 77703
(*Yellowed Pages*, 1971–)

South Plains Genealogical Society
% Lubbock Public Library
4215 University Avenue
Lubbock, TX 79408

South Texas Genealogical and His-
torical Society P.O. Box 40
Gonzales, TX 78629
(*South Texas Genealogical and His-
torical Society Quarterly*, 1966–)
NN APR (Texas)

Southwest Collection
102 Social Science Bldg.
Texas Tech. University
Lubbock, TX 79409

Southwestern Texas Genealogical
Society
5301 Hanawalt Drive
El Paso, TX 79903

Southwest Genealogical Society
% San Antonio College Library
1300 San Pedro Avenue
San Antonio, TX 78212

Southwest Texas Genealogical Association
208 Avenue "K"
Del Rio, TX 78840

Texas Catholic Historical Society,
Inc.
Catholic Archives of Texas
Chancery Bldg.
N. Congress and West 16th
Austin, TX 78711

Texas Family Heritage, Inc.
P.O. Box 17007
Fort Worth, TX 76102

Texas State Genealogical Society
"Hacienda Tejas"
2515 Sweetbrier Drive
Dallas, TX 75228
(*Stirpes*, 1961–) NN APR (Texas)

Texas State Genealogical Society
2528 University Drive South
Fort Worth, TX 76109

Texas State Historical Association
Sid Richardson Hall 2/306
University Station
Austin, TX 78712
(*Southwestern Historical Quar-
terly*, 1897–)
NN IAA

Tip O' Texas Genealogical Society
% Harlingen Public Library
502 East Taylor Street
Harlingen, TX 78550
(*Genealogical Tips*, 1963–) NN APR
(Texas)

West Texas Genealogical Society
2825 South 11th Street
Abilene, TX 79605
(*West Texas Genealogical Society
Bulletin*, 1959–)
NN APR+ (Texas)

Books and Articles

Abstract of Land Titles, Tarrant
County, Texas.
Fort Worth, Fort Worth Gen. Soc.,
1969. 88, 15+p., index, maps.
NN APR (Tarrant Co.) 75-383

Bexar County, Texas, 1860 Surname Census.
(IN: *Our Heritage*, San Antonio,
1971–73. v.12, p. 40–45, 76–83; v.
13, p. 2–13, 48–59, 96–108, 147–58;
v.14, p. 50–60, 92–101, 140–49)
NN ITRN

Bolton, Herbert E.
Texas in the Middle Eighteenth Century.
Millwood, NY, Kraus Reprint Co., 1974 (orig. 1915) 501 p.
NN STG (California. University. Publications: History v. 3.)

Bowden, J. J.
Spanish and Mexican Land Grants in the Chihuahuan Acquisition.
El Paso, Texas Western Press, 1971. 231 p.
NN ITR 73-1226

Bryant, Stella Vinson.
Pioneers of Yesteryear, Pleasant Mound "Public"
Cemetery and Memorial Park, 1848–1973.
Dallas, Pleasant Mound "Public" Gen. Assoc., 1974. 277 p.,index.
NN APR (Dallas) 75-275

Catefoot, C.J.
What Is the State Archives?
(IN: *Stirpes*, v.14, Dec. 1974, p. 100–106; v.15, March 1975, p. 61–71) (Regular features by state archivist, etc.)
NN APR (Texas)

Clark, Anne.
Historic Homes of San Augustine.
Austin, San Augustine Hist. Co., 1972. 72 p.
ITRM (San Augustine) 74-1500

Conway, James.
The Texans.
New York, 1976. 262 p.
NN JLD 76-1716

Corbin, John Boyd.
Catalog of Genealogical Materials in Texas Libraries.
Austin, State Library and Historical Commission, 1965–66. 2 v.

NN M-10 8859 no. 2, part 1 also in NN AP 75-470

Daughters of the Republic of Texas.
Founders and Patriots of the Republic of Texas: Lineages of the Members, comp. by Mrs. H. J. Morris.
Austin, 1963. 684 p., index.
NN APR (Texas)

The Roster of Texas Daughters' Revolutionary Ancestors.
Houston, 1976. 4 v. (A–C, D–H, I–Q, R–Z); alpha.
NN APGA (DAR) 77-368

Ericson, Carolyn R.
Kissin Kuzzins (Query column).
Fort Worth, Mar. 18, 1970. 6 v. in 1.
NN APR (Nacogdoches) 72-2627

Everett, Donald E.
San Antonio: The Flavor of Its Past, 1845–1898.
San Antonio, Trinity U. Press, 1975. 162 p., index.
NN ITRM (San Antonio) 76-1102

Foster, Pearl (O'Donnell).
Trek to Texas, 1770–1870.
Fort Worth, Branch-Smith, 1966. 200 p.
NN APR (Texas)

Geue, Chester W., and E. H. Geue.
A New Land Beckoned: German Immigrants to Texas, 1844–1847 ... Fort Worth, 1966. 174 p.
NN APR (Texas)

Gracy, Alice Duggan, Jane Sumner and Emma G. S. Gentry.
Early Texas Birth Records, 1838–187
Austin, Mrs. H. R. Gentry, 1970–71. 2 v., alpha.

(73 county courthouses were visited by the authors; map of Texas in front, showing counties from which records were taken)
NN APR (Texas) 73-2141

Grammer, Norma Rutledge.
Marriage Records of Early Texas, 1824–1846.
Fort Worth, Fort Worth Gen. Soc., 1972.

Grimm, Agnes G.
Llanos, Mestanas: Mustang Plains.
Waco, Texian Press, 1968. 189 p., index.
NN ITR

Hauser, Frankies, and Edith K. Zuber.
Society of Mayflower Descendants in the State of Texas.
San Antonio, Naylor Co., 1967–71. 2 v.
NN APR (Texas)

Houston: A History and Guide.
Houston, Anson Jones Press, 1972. 363 p., index.
NN ITRM (Houston)

McComb, David G.
Houston: The Bayou City.
Austin, U. of TX Press, 1969. 315 p., index.
NN ITRM (Houston)

Miller, Thomas Lloyd.
Bounty and Donation Land Grants of Texas, 1835–1888.
Austin, 1967. 894 p., index.
NN APR (Texas)

Mullins, Marion D.
The First Census of Texas, 1829–1836 ... Citizenship Lists 1821–45.

Washington, DC, 1959. 63 p., no index.
(*NGSSP.* no. 22)
NN APGA

Mullins, Marion Day.
Republic of Texas: Poll Lists for 1846.
Baltimore, MD, GPC, 1974. 189 p., index.
NN APR (Texas) 74-1407

Nacogdoches Archives, 1835 Entrance Certificates and Citizenship Applications.
(IN: *Stirpes*, Fort Worth, June 1975. v. 15, p. 43–50, 82–112, 151–57)
NN APR (Texas)

Purl, Benjamin F., and Alma N. W. Barnes.
Republic of Texas, Second Class, Headrights, March 2, 1836–Oct. 1, 1837.
Houston, Mrs. J. N. Barnes, 1974. 261 p., alpha.
NN APR (Texas) 76-1464

Quensell, Carl W. A.
From Tyranny to Texas: A German Pioneer in Harris County.
San Antonio, Naylor Co., 1975. 100 p., t of c, no index.
NN ITRM (Harris Co.) 76-366

Race, Lila Bunch.
Pioneer Fort Worth, Texas ... Families of South Tarrant County, Texas.
Dallas, Taylor Pub. Co., 1976. 279 p., t of c, no index.
NN APR+ (Fort Worth) 76-2375

Records of East Texas.
Lufkin, TX, 1966–.
NN APR (Texas)

Rogers, John William.

The Lusty Texans of Dallas, new
ed.
New York, E. P. Dutton, 1960. 415
p., index. NN ITRM (Dallas)

St. Mark's (Episcopal) Baptisms,
San Antonio, Texas, 1858–1876.
(IN: *Our Heritage*, San Antonio,
1973–74. v. 1, p. 136–37, 167–71;
v.15, p. 71–75, 134–35.)
NN ITRN

Sanders, Leonard.
How Fort Worth Became the Tex-
asmost City.
Fort Worth, Amon Carter Mu-
seum, 1973. 214 p., index.
NN ITRM (Fort Worth) 74-858

Scott, Florence Johnson.
Royal Land Grants North of the
Rio Grande, 1777–1821.
Rio Grande City, 1969. 116 p.
NN ITRM (Rio Grande City) 72-
1277

Smith, Bennett.
Marriage by Bond in Colonial
Texas.
Fort Worth, c. 1972. 102 p., index.
(Contains illustrations of early
bonds and lists of marriage
bonds with names of both groom
and bride and place of mar-
riage)
NN JLF 75-1082

Special Census, Texas 1856, Enu-
meration of Free White Popu-
lation.
(IN: Central Texas Genealogical
Society Bulletin, *Heart of Texas
Records*, Waco, 1926. v. 10, no.
2, p. 43–53)
NN APR (Texas)

Texas Cousins.
Dallas, 1967–71. NN APR (Texas)
75-960

Texas 1850 Census Index.
Bountiful, UT, AIS, 1976.

Texas General Land Office.
An Abstract of Titles of Records
in the Office of the General
Land Office. Austin, Pemberton
Papers, 1964. 182 p.
NN APR + (Texas)

Texas Issue.
(*Antiques*, New York, Sept. 1975. v.
CVIII, no. 3)
NN MAA+

White, Gifford.
The 1840 Census of the Republic
of Texas.
Austin, 1966. 236 p.
NN APR (Texas)

Winfrey, Gorman.
Gone to Texas: Sources for Genea-
logical Research in the Lone
Star State.
(IN: *Stirpes*, Fort Worth, 1969. v.
9, p. 87–95)
NN APR (Texas)

UTAH

State Archives

Utah State Historical Society
603 East South Temple
Salt Lake City, UT 84102
(*Utah Historical Quarterly*)

Vital Records

Division of Vital Statistics
Utah State Department of Health
554 South Third East
Salt Lake City, UT 84113
Births and deaths: 1905–

532 • *Tracing Your Family's History in America*

Births and deaths, Salt Lake City
or Ogden, 1890–1904, write City
Board of Health
Births and deaths elsewhere in
state, 1898–1904, write county
clerk
Births and deaths prior: late nineteenth century, check with
county clerks's office
Marriages: county clerk of county;
records begin late nineteenth or
early twentieth century.

Libraries

Brigham Young University Library
Provo, UT 84601

Church of Jesus Christ of Latter-
day Saints
Ogden, Utah, Branch Genealogical
Library
339 21st Street
Ogden, UT 84401

Dixie Genealogical Library
St. George, UT 84770

Genealogical Society of the Church
of Jesus Christ of Latter-day
Saints
50 East North Temple Street
Salt Lake City, UT 84105

Temple Area Genealogical Library
Manti, UT 84642

University of Utah Library
Salt Lake City, UT 84112

Societies and Periodicals

Daggett County Historical Society
109 South Blvd.
Dutch John, UT 84023

History Department of the Church
of Jesus Christ of Latter-day
Saints
47 East North Temple Street
Salt Lake City, UT 84150

Iron County Historical Society
Southern Utah State College
Cedar City, UT 84720

National Society of the Daughters
of Utah Pioneers
300 North Main Street
Salt Lake City, UT 84103
(*Our Pioneer Heritage*)

Utah Genealogical Association
P.O. Box 1144
Salt Lake City, UT 84110
(*Genealogical Journal*, 1972–) In-
dex 1–5

Utah Heritage Foundation
603 East South Temple
Salt Lake City, UT 84102

Western History Association
Box 8005
Salt Lake City, UT 84108

Books and Articles

Bennett, Archibald F.
Genealogical Sources in Salt Lake
City.
(IN: *TAG*, Des Moines, IA, 1966. v.
42, p. 89–94)
NN APGA

Carter, Kate B., comp.
Heart Throbs of the West . . .
Salt Lake City, 1939–51. 12 v.
NN IXC

Carter, Kate B., comp.
Treasures of Pioneer History.

Salt Lake City, 1952–55. 4 v.
NN IXC

Foy, Leslie.
The City Bountiful. Bountiful, Horizon Pub., 1975.
350 p., index.
NN IXD (Bountiful) 77–637

Jaussi, Laureen R., and Gloria D. Chaston.
Genealogical Records of Utah.
Salt Lake City, Desert Book Co., 1974. 312 p., subject index, detailed t of c.
NN APR (Utah) 75–1427

McFarland, Drucilla H., and Ruth M. White.
Mormon John Martin, Utah Pioneer Family History.
Bountiful, UT, Carr Print. Co., 1969. 356 p., no index.
NN APV (Martin) 74–319

The Palatine Immigrant: Quarterly Publication of the Palatines in America. Charles M. Hall, ed.
Salt Lake City, 1976–. v. 1–.
(The Palatines in America, 157 N. State St., Salt Lake City, UT 84103)

Papanikolas, Helen Z.
The Peoples of Utah.
Salt Lake City, Utah Hist. Soc., 1976.

Stout, Wayne.
The History of Utah.
West Palm Beach, FLA, Lewis Hist. Co., 1967–71. 3 v., index.
NN *R-IXC

Utah 1850 Census Index.
Bountiful, UT, AIS, 1977.

Veterans Buried in Utah.
Salt Lake City, Utah State Archives, 1965–. 7 v.
(Beaver to Morgan)
NN APR (Utah)

VERMONT

State Archives

Vermont Historical Society
State Street
Montpelier, VT 05602
(*Vermont History: The Proceedings of the Vermont Historical Society*, 1870–)
NN IAA

Vital Records

Secretary of State
Vital Records Department
State House
Montpelier, VT 05602
Births and deaths: approx. 1760–
Marriages: 1857–
For information on vital statistics laws: Public Health Statistics Division, Dept. of Health, Burlington, VT 05401

Libraries

General Library
Bennington Museum
Bennington, VT 05201

Vermont Department of Libraries
Law and Document Unit
Montpelier, VT 05602

Societies and Periodicals

Bellows Falls Historical Society, Inc.

Adams' Old Stone Grist Mill Museum
Mill Street
Bellows Falls, VT 05101

Bethel Historical Society
Cushing Avenue
Bethel, VT 05043

Bradford Historical Society
Box 92
Bradford, VT 05033

Braintree Historical Society, Inc.
Braintree Hill
Braintree, VT 05060
(Mail: 6 Weston Street, Randolph, VT 05060)

Chittenden County Historical Society
Bailey Library
University of Vermont
Burlington, VT 05401
(*Bulletin*)

Danville Historical Society
Town Hall
Danville, VT 05828

Dorset Historical Society
Dorset, VT 05251

Fairfax Historical Society
Box 105, Route 104
Fairfax, VT 05454

Genealogical Society of Vermont
% Miss V. Gassette
21 Heath Street
South Burlington, VT 05401
(*Branches and Twigs*, 1972–)

Grafton Historical Society, Inc.
Main Street
Grafton, VT 05146

Green Mountain Perkins Academy and Historical Society, Inc.
South Woodstock, VT 05071

Historical Society of Marlboro
Main Street
Marlboro, VT 05344

Historical Society of Windham County, Inc.
R.D. 1
Newfane, VT 05345

Island Pond Historical Society, Inc.
Island Pond, VT 05846

Londonderry Historical Society, Inc.
Londonderry, VT 05148

Manchester Historical Society
Manchester, VT 05255

Middletown Springs Historical Society, Inc.
Middletown Springs, VT 05757

Missisquoi Valley Historical Society
North Troy, VT 05859

Newbury Historical Society
Newbury, VT 05085

Norwich Historical Society
Norwich, VT 05055

Orleans County Historical Society, Inc.
The Old Stone House
Brownington, VT 05860

Peacham Historical Association
Peacham, VT 05862

Pittsford Historical Society
Pittsford, VT 05763

Poultney Historical Society
Poultney, VT 05764

Putney Historical Society
Town Hall, Main Street
Putney, VT 05346

Randolph Historical Society, Inc.
Main Street
Randolph, VT 05060
(Mail: Box 15, Randolph, VT 05061)

Reading Historical Society
Reading, VT 05062

Rowland E. Robinson Memorial
Association
Route 7, Rokeby
Ferrisburg, VT 05456
(*Rokeby Messenger*)

Royalton Historical Society
Royalton, VT 05063

Rutland Historical Society, Inc.
101 Center Street
Rutland, VT 05701
(*Quarterly of the Rutland Historical Society*)

St. Albans Historical Society, Inc.
109 Congress Street
St. Albans, VT 05478

Saxtons River Historical Society,
Inc.
Box 205
Saxtons River, VT 05154

Shaftsbury Historical Society, Inc.
U.S. Route 7
Shaftsbury, VT 05262
(Mail: Box 101, Route 1, Shafts-
bury, VT 05262)

Shoreham Historical Society
Shoreham, VT 05770

Springfield Art and Historical Society
9 Elm Hill
Springfield, VT 05161

Strafford Historical Society
Strafford, VT 05072

Thetford Historical Society
Thetford, VT 05074

Vermont Old Cemetery Association
308 South Prospect Street
Burlington, VT 05401

Vershire Historical Society, Inc.
Vershire, VT 05079

Waterbury Historical Society
% Alice Post, Secretary
Waterbury Center, VT 05677

Weathersfield Historical Society
Weathersfield Center
Perkinsville, VT 05151

Westminster Historical Society,
Inc.
Main Street
Westminster, VT 05158

Weston Historical Society
Weston, VT 05161

Books and Articles

Anderson, Robert Charles.
Ancestry of President Calvin Cool-
idge.
(IN: *TAG*, Des Moines, 1977. v 53,
p. 65–74)
NN APGA

Anderson, Robert Charles.
Vermont ...
(IN: *NEHGR*, Boston, 1978. v. 132)
    (A Genealogical Guide)
NN APGA

Cushing, Irene, and Irene Stafford.
Bethel: The Early Years.
Bethel, The Spaulding Press for the
    Bethel Hist. Soc., 1974. 84 p., no
    index.
NN IQF (Bethel) 75–2119

Hill, Ellen C.
Revolutionary War Soldiers of East
    Montpelier.
East Montpelier, East Montpelier
    Bicentennial Committee, 1976.
    110 p.

Nichols, Joan H., comp.
Some Vermont Ancestors: The Bi-
    centennial Project of the Ge-
    nealogical Society of Vermont,
    1776–1976.
Brattleboro, VT, Mrs. A. G. Nich-
    ols, c. 1976. 83 p.

State of Vermont.
State Papers of Vermont.
Montpelier, 1918–69. 17 v. (peti-
    tions, v. 5, 8, 9–11)
NN IQE

Vermont 1810 Census Index.
Bountiful, UT, AIS, 1976.

Vermont 1820 Census Index.
Bountiful, UT, AIS, 1977. 94 p.

Vermont 1830 Census Index.
Bountiful, UT, AIS, 1977.

Vermont 1840 Census Index.
Bountiful, UT, AIS, 1977.

Vermont 1850 Census Index.
Bountiful, UT, AIS, 1977.

VIRGINIA

State Archives

Virginia State Library
1101 Capitol
Richmond, VA 23219

Vital Records

Bureau of Vital Records and
    Health Statistics
State Department of Health
James Madison Bldg., Box 1000
Richmond, VA 23208
Births and deaths: January
    1853–December 1896; June 4,
    1912–
Births and deaths: December
    1896–June 4, 1912, write city or
    town health department
Marriages: January 1853–
    Marriages prior: check with
    clerk of circuit court of county

Libraries

Church of Jesus Christ of Latter-
    day Saints
Richmond, Virginia, State Branch
Genealogical Library
5600 Monument Avenue
Richmond, VA 23226

College of William and Mary Li-
    brary
Williamsburg, VA 23185

Kirn Norfolk Public Library
301 East City Hall Avenue
Norfolk, VA 23510

Public Library
345 West Freemason Street
Norfolk, VA 23510

Societies and Periodicals

Albemarle County Historical Society, Inc.
220 Court Square
Charlottesville, VA 22901
(*Magazine of Albemarle County History*)
NN ITD (Albemarle Co.)

Alexandria Historical Society
307 South St. Asaph Street
Alexandria, VA 22314

Arlington Historical Society
1805 South Arlington Ridge Road
Arlington, VA 22202
(*Arlington History Magazine*)

Augusta County Historical Society
Box 686
Staunton, VA 24401
(*Augusta Historical Bulletin*)
NN ITD (Augusta Co.)

Bath County Historical Society, Inc.
Box 212
Warm Springs, VA 24484

Clark County Historical Association
Berryville, VA 22611

Eastern Shore of Virginia Historical Society, Inc.
Kerr Place
Onancock, VA 23417

Franklin County Historical Society
221 Claiborne Avenue
Rocky Mount, VA 24151

Goochland County Historical Society
River Road, Route 6
Goochland, VA 23063

(*Goochland County Historical Society Magazine*)

Hanover County Historical Society
% Edward C. Taylor
Hanover, VA 23069

Henry County Historical Society
Bassett, VA 24055

Historical Society of Washington County, Inc.
Box 484
Abingdon, VA 24210

Historic Richmond Foundation
2407 East Grace Street
Richmond, VA 23223

Institute of Early American History and Culture
Box 220
Williamsburg, VA 23185
(*William and Mary Quarterly*, 1892–) NN*R-APR (Virginia)

Kenmore Association, Inc.
1201 Washington Avenue
Fredericksburg, VA 22401
(*Kenmore News Notes*)

King and Queen County Historical Society
King and Queen, VA 23085

Loudoun County Historical Society
Box 344
Leesburg, VA 22075
(*Loudoun Historical Society Bulletin*, 1958–)
NN ITD Loudoun

Louisa County Historical Magazine (1969–)
NN ITD Louisa (76–1349)
Louisa, VA 23093

Mathews County Historical Society, Inc.
% Benjamin M. Thompson
Mathews, VA 23109

Norfolk Historical Society
Box 708
Professional Arts Building
Norfolk, VA 23510

Northern Neck of Virginia Historical Society
Montross, VA 22520
(*Northern Neck of Virginia History Magazine*, 1951–)

Nottoway County Historical Association
Route 1, Box 23
Blackstone, VA 23824

Orange County Historical Society
Box 591
Orange, VA 22960

Portsmouth Historical Association
221 North Street
Portsmouth, VA 23704

Princess Anne County Historical Society
1124 Bay Colony Drive
Virginia Beach, VA 23451

Prince William County Historical Society
9213 North West Street
Manassas, VA 22110

Roanoke Valley Historical Society
Box 1904
Roanoke, VA 24008
(*Journal*)

Rockingham County Historical Society
Harrisonburg, VA 22801

Smyth County Historical and Museum Society, Inc.
Stadium Road
Marion, VA 24354
(Mail: 230 North Church Street, Marion, VA 24354)

Spotsylvania Historical Association, Inc.
Box 64
Spotsylvania, VA 22553

Tidewater Genealogical Society of Virginia
Drawer K, Riverdale Post Office
Hampton, VA 23666
(*Virginia Tidewater Genealogy*, 1970–)

United Methodist Historical Society of Northern Virginia
5001 Echols Avenue
Alexandria, VA 22311

Virginia Baptist Historical Society
Box 95
University of Richmond
Richmond, VA 23173

Virginia Genealogist [*VG*] (1957–)
NN APR (Virginia), index each v.
Box 4883
Washington, DC 20008

Virginia Genealogy Society
P.O. Box 1397
Richmond, VA 23211
(*Virginia Genealogy Society Quarterly*, 1961–)
NN APR (Virginia)

Virginia Historical Society
428 North Blvd.
Richmond, VA 23220
(Mail: Box 7311, Richmond, VA 23221)

(*Virginia Magazine of History and Biography* [VM], 1894–)
NN *R-APR (Virginia)

Virginia History Federation
12th and Capitol Streets
Richmond, VA 23219
(*Virginia Phoenix*)

Virginia Place Name Society
Manuscripts Department
University of Virginia
Charlottesville, VA 22903
(*Occasional Papers*)

Winchester–Frederick County Historical Society
610 Tennyson Avenue
Winchester, VA 22601

Wythe County Historical Society
Wytheville, VA 24382
(*Wythe County Historical Review*)

Books and Articles

Barbour, Philip.
Pocahontas and Her World.
Boston, Houghton Mifflin, 1970. 320 p., index.
NN ITD (Jamestown) 71-12

Boddie, John Bennett.
Virginia Historical Genealogies.
Baltimore, GPC, 1975 (orig. 1954). index.
NN APR (Virginia)

Brown, Stuart E., Jr.
Virginia Genealogies: A Trial List of Printed Books and Pamphlets.
Berryville, Virginia Book Co., 1967. 310 p., index.
NN APR (Virginia)

Chamberlayne, Churchill Gibson.
Births from the Bristol Parish Register of Henrico, Prince George and Dinwiddie Counties, 1720–1798 . . . with a new index.
Baltimore, Baltimore Gen. Pub., 1974 (orig. 1898). 133 p.
NN APR (Virginia) 75-1127

County Court Note-Book, ed. by Milnor Ljungstedt.
Baltimore, GPC, 1972 (orig. 1921–36). 10 v. in 1 with index.
(Important for Eastern Shore of Virginia and Maryland)
NN APGA 72-1944

Crickard, Madeline W.
Index to the 1810 Virginia Census.
Parsons, WV, McClain, 1971. 293 p., index, alpha by counties but without references to the pages in original census.
NN APR (Virginia) 72-1466

Crozier, William Armstrong.
Virginia Colonial Militia, 1651–1776.
Baltimore, GPC, 1965 (orig. 1905). 144 p., index.
(*Virginia County Records*, v. 2)
NN APR (Virginia)

Currer-Briggs, Noel.
Colonial Settlers and English Adventurers.
Baltimore, MD, GPC, 1971. 393 p., index.
NN APR (Virginia) 73-584

Currer-Briggs, Noel.
English Wills of Colonial Families.
Cottonport, LA, Polyanthos, 1972. 209, 23, xlv p., index.
NN APR (Virginia) 73-688

Currer-Briggs, Noel.

Similarity of Surnames in York County, Virginia, and County Norfolk, England.
(IN: *VM*, Richmond, 1970. v. 78, p. 442–46; p. 445, Mary Scot incorrect information.)
*R-APR (Virginia)

Currer-Briggs, Noel.
Virginia Settlers and English Adventurers.
Baltimore, MD, GPC, 1970. 3 v. in 1, index.
NN APR (Virginia)

Dabney, Virginius.
Richmond: the Story of a City.
Garden City, NY, Doubleday, 1976. 412 p., index.
NN ITD (Richmond) 77-51

Des Cognets, Louis.
English Duplicates of Lost English Records.
Princeton, NJ L. Des Cognets, 1958. 380 p.
NN APR (Virginia)

Dorman, John Frederick.
Virginia Revolutionary Pension Applications.
Washington, DC, Cason-Chappell, 1958–75. 21 v.
NN APR (Virginia)

Dorman, John Frederick, see West Virginia for his Virginia state guides.

Elliott, Katherine B.
Emigration to Other States from Southside Virginia.
South Hill, VA, 1966. 2 v.
NN APR (Virginia)

Fairfax County, Virginia, 1800 Tax List.

(IN: *VG*, Washington, DC, 1975. v. 19, p. 261–64)
APR (Virginia)

Felldin, Jeanne R.
Index to the 1820 Census of Virginia.
Baltimore, MD, GPC, 1976. 487 p., alpha.
NN APR (Virginia) 76-2180

Foley, Louise Pledge Heath.
Early Virginia Families Along the James River.
Richmond, L.P.H. Foley, 1974. 138 p.
NN APR (Virginia) 75-947

Forman, Henry Chandler.
The Virginia Eastern Shore and Its British Origins.
Easton, MD, Eastern Shore Pub. Assoc., 1975. 402 p.

Fothergill, Augusta B., and John Mark Naugle.
Virginia Tax Payers, 1782–87, Other Than Those Published by the United States Census Bureau.
Baltimore, MD, GPC, 1966 (orig. 1940). 142 p., alpha.
NN APR (Virginia)

Gamble, Robert S.
Sully: The Biography of a House.
Chantilly, Sully Foundation, 1973. 228 p., index.
(Lee Family)
NN ITD (Sully) 76-530

Genealogical Research in the Virginia State Library.
Richmond, Richmond, Virginia, State Library, 1973.

Hamlin, Charles Hughes.

They Went Thataway.
Baltimore, MD, GPC, 1974 (orig. 1964–66). 3 v. in 1.
NN APR (Virginia) and APR (Virginia) 75-1624

Hamlin, Charles Hughes.
Virginia Ancestors and Adventurers.
Richmond, 1967–73. 3 v.
NN APR (Virginia) 73-1129

Hayden, Horace Edwin.
Virginia Genealogies: A Genealogy of the Glassell Family of Scotland and Virginia.
Baltimore, MD, GPC, 1966 (orig. 1891). 759 p., alpha by families, index.
APR (Virginia)

Jester, Annie L., and Martha W. Hidden.
Adventurers of Purse and Person, Virginia, 1607–1625. 2nd ed.
Princeton, NJ, Order of the First Families of Virginia, 1607–1624, 1964. 462 p., index.
NN APR (Virginia)

Lackey, Richard S.
Notes on the Massengil Family of Virginia and North Carolina.
(IN: *Stirpes*, Dallas, TX, June 1976. v. 16, p. 51–60, 99–105, 155–62)
APR (Texas)

Lawrence, Liza.
The Vistas at Eagle's Nest: The Fitzhugh-Grymes Family Home, King County, Virginia.
King George, 1969. 12 p.
NN APV (Fitzhugh) 72-1297

McCay, Betty L.
Sources for Genealogical Searching in Virginia and West Virginia.

Indianapolis, IN, 1971
NN APR (Virginia) 72-177

McDonald, Cecil D.
Virginia Marriages, 1700–1799.
Seattle, WA, 1972–1976. 16 v.
NN APR (Virginia) 74-635

McMillion, Lynn C., and Jane K. Wall, comp.
Fairfax County, Virginia, 1820 Federal Population Census and Census of Manufactures.
n.p., 1976. 54 p., index.

Meredith, Joseph N.
Genealogical Resources for 18th Century Research Found in the Library of Congress. (IN: *Virginia Tidewater Genealogy*, Hampton, Dec. 1975, v. 6, no. 4, p. 121–26)
(Strange for a librarian, no dates of publication, certainly no places of publication, surnames only for authors, no classmarks given; one would expect L. C. classmarks at least)

Nottingham, Stratton.
Wills and Administrations of Accomack County, Virginia, 1663–1800, with New Introduction by Timothy Field Beard.
Cottonport, Polyanthos, 1973 (orig. 1931). 484 p., 2 v. in 1.
NN APR (Accomack) 73-2939

Nugent, Nell Marion.
Cavaliers and Pioneers, Abstracts of Virginia Land Patents and Grants, 1623–1666.
Baltimore, MD, GPC, 1969 (orig. 1934). v. 1, 766 p.
(All that was orig. pub.), index.
NN APR (Virginia) and APR (Virginia) 71-88

Schreiner-Yantis, Netti.
A Supplement to the 1810 Census
of Virginia.
Tax Lists of the Counties for
Which the Census Is Missing.
Springfield, N. S.-Yantis, 1971. Ar-
ranged by counties, index, var-
ious pagination.
NN APR (Virginia) 73-1242

Selby, John E.
A Chronology of Virginia and the
War of Independence, 1763–1783.
Charlottesville, U. Press of Vir-
ginia for Virginia Independent
Bicentennial Commission, 1973.
48 p.
NN ITC 74-1674

Semple, Robert Baylor.
History of the Baptists in Virginia.
Cottonport, LA, Polyanthos, 1972
(orig. 1810). 536 p., index.

Some Marriages in the Burned
Record Counties of Virginia.
Richmond, Virginia Gen. Soc., 1972.
139 p.
(VGS Special Pub. #4)
NN APR (Virginia) 73-2241

Stanard, W. G.
Some Emigrants to Virginia. 2nd
ed.
Baltimore, MD, GPC, 1964 (orig.
1915). 94 p., alpha.
NN APR (Virginia)

Stewart, Robert A.
Index to Printed Virginia Geneal-
ogies . . .
Baltimore, MD, GPC, 1965 (orig.
1930). 265 p., alpha.
NN APR (Virginia)

Swem, Earl G.

Virginia Historical Index.
Gloucester, MA, Peter Smith, 1965
(orig. 1934). 2 v. in 4.
NN APR (Virginia)

Tanner, Douglas W.
Place Name Research in Virginia:
A Handbook.
Charlottesville, 1976. 52 p.

Torrence, Clayton.
Virginia Wills and Administra-
tions, 1632–1800.
Baltimore, MD, GPC, 1965 (orig.
1930). 483 p., alpha.
NN APR (Virginia)

Turman, Nora Miller.
The Eastern Shore of Virginia,
1603–1964.
Onancock, *Eastern Shore News*,
1964. 306 p., index.
NN ITD (Accomac Peninsula)

Virginia Book Company.
VBAPPA: Virginia Books and
Pamphlets Presently Available,
comp. by Stuart E. Brown, Jr.
Berryville, Virginia Book Co.,
1972. 430, 69 p.
NN ITC 74-142

Virginia Calendar of Virginia State
Papers, 1652–1869.
New York, Kraus, 1968 (orig.
1875–1893). 11 v.
NN ITC 72-790

Virginia 1810 Census Index.
Bountiful, UT, AIS, 1976.

Virginia 1820 Census Index.
Bountiful, UT, AIS, 1976.

Virginia 1830 Census Index.
Bountiful, UT, AIS, 1976. 309 p.

Virginia 1840 Census Index.
Bountiful, UT, AIS, 1977.

Virginia 1850 Census Index.
Bountiful, UT, AIS, 1976. 628 p.,
alpha.

Virginia Local History: A Bibliography.
Richmond: Richmond, Virginia,
State Library, 1971.

Virginia Tithables from Burned
Record Counties, comp. by Robert F. Woodson and Isobel B.
Woodson.
Richmond, 1970. 122 p. (Covers
1763–75)
NN APR (Virginia) 73-2638

Withington, Lothrop.
Virginia Gleanings in England.
(IN: *VM*, Richmond, 1914–17. v. 22
(1914), p. 396–400, etc.)
*R-APR (Virginia)

Waldemaier, Inez R.
Virginia Marriage Records Before
1853.
Washington, DC, 1956. 49 p.
NN APR (Virginia)

William and Mary Quarterly Index, 3rd series. v. 16–30, 1959–73.
Williamsburg, Inst. of Early
Amer. Hist. and Cult., 1974. 156
p.
NN *R-APR (Virginia)

Wulfeck, Dorothy F.
Marriages of Some Virginia Residents, 1607–1800.
Naugatuck, CT, the author,
1961–1967. 7 v. (series 1 v. 1–7)
NN APR (Virginia)

WASHINGTON

State Archives

Washington State Library
State Library Bldg.
Olympia, WA 98501

Vital Records

Bureau of Vital Statistics
Department of Health and Society
Services
P.O. Box 709
Olympia, WA 98504
Births and deaths: July 1907–
Seattle, Spokane, Tacoma: records
also obtainable from City Health
Dept.
Marriages: January 1968–
Earlier births, marriages and
deaths: county auditor

Libraries

Church of Jesus Christ of Latter-day Saints
Seattle, Washington, North State
Branch Genealogical Library
State Center
5701 8th N.E.
Seattle, WA 98105

Genealogical Library
1101 Second S.E.
Quincy, WA 98848

Public Library
4th Avenue and Madison
Seattle, WA 98104
(Since 1955 the general genealogical collection of the State Library has been in this library.)

Regional Public Library
7th and Franklin Street
Olympia, WA 98501

Seattle Public Library
4th Avenue and Madison
Seattle, WA 98104

University of Washington Library
Seattle, WA 98105

Washington State Historical Society
    Library
State Historical Bldg.
315 North Stadium Way
Tacoma, WA 98403

Societies and Periodicals

Benton County Museum and His-
    torical Society, Inc.
Box 591
Prosser, WA 99350

Chelan County Historical Society
112 Cottage Avenue
Cashmere, WA 98815

Clallam County Historical Society
Box 1024
Pioneer Memorial Museum
Port Angeles, WA 98362

Clark County, Washington, Gen-
    ealogical Society
% Mrs. John Finley, Editor
8205 N.E. 9th Street
Vancouver, WA 98664

Cowlitz County Historical Society
4th and Church Streets
Kelso, WA 98626
(*Cowlitz County Historical Quar-
    terly*)

Eastern Washington Genealogical
    Society
P.O. Box 1826
Spokane, WA 99210
(Genealogical collection in refer-

ence room of Spokane Public
    Lib., 906 W. Main, Spokane, WA)
(*Eastern Washington Genealogical
    Society Bulletin*, 1963–)
NN APR (WA) 75–517 & APR (WA)
    75–715

Ferry County Historical Society
Box 114
Republic, WA 99166

Ft. Vancouver Historical Society
1511 Main Street
Vancouver, WA 98660
(*Clark County History*)

Franklin County Historical Society
Box 1033, 716 Henry Street
Pasco, WA 99301
(*Franklin Flyer*)

Genealogical Society of North Cen-
    tral Washington
P.O. Box 613
Wenatchee, WA 98801

Grant County Historical Society
Box 1141
Ephrata, WA 98823

Island County Historical Society
Coupeville, WA 98239

Jefferson County Historical Society
City Hall
Port Townsend, WA 98368

King County Historical Associa-
    tion
Box 162
6046 Lake Sammamish Parkway
    N.E.
Redmond, WA 98052

Kittitas County Historical Society
Box 265
4th and Nanum Streets
Ellenburg, WA 98926

Klickitat County Historical Society
Goldendale, WA 98620

Lake Chelan Historical Society
Box 697
202 East Woodin Avenue
Chelan, WA 98816
(*Lake Chelan History Notes*)

Lewis County Historical Society
1070 Washington
Chehalis, WA 98531

Lincoln County Historical Society
Box 585, 7th and Park Streets
Davenport, WA 99122

Lower Columbia Genealogical Society
P.O. Box 472
Longview, WA 98632

Mason County Historical Society
Star Route 2, Box 310
Belfair, WA 98528

Okanogan County Historical Society
Box 1129
Okanogan, WA 98840
(*Okanogan County Heritage*)

Olympia Genealogical Society
% Olympia Public Library
7th and Franklin
Olympia, WA 98502
(*The Quarterly*)

Olympia Genealogical Society
Route 5, Box 747-F
Bremerton, WA 98310
(*Backtracking*)

Pacific County Historical Society
and Museum Foundation
Highway 101, South Bend
Raymond, WA 98577

(Mail: Box 384, Raymond, WA
98577)
(*The Sou'wester*)

Skagit County Historical Society
Box 32, 4th Street
LaConner, WA 98273

Skamania County Historical Museum
Box 396, Vancouver Avenue
Stevenson, WA 98648
(*Skamania County Heritage*)

Snohomish County Museum and
Historical Association
Legion Park
Everett, WA 98201

State Capitol Historical Association
211 West 21st Avenue
Olympia, WA 98501

Stevens County Historical Association
137 North Wynne Street
Colville, WA 99114
(Mail: 958 South Rae, Colville, WA
99114)

Tacoma Genealogical Society
P.O. Box 11232
Tacoma, WA 98411
(*Researcher*, 1969–)

Tri-City Genealogical Society
Box 191, Route 1
Richland, WA 99352
(*Tri-City Genealogical Society Bulletin*, 1961–)
NN APR (Kennewick) 75-380

Walla Walla Valley Genealogical Society
P.O. Box 115
Walla Walla, WA 99362
(*Blue Mountain Heritage*)

Walla Walla Valley Pioneer and
Historical Society
Box 1616
Walla Walla, WA 99362

Washington State Historical Society
315 North Stadium Way
Tacoma, WA 98403
(*Pacific Northwest Quarterly*)

Whatcom County, Washington,
Genealogical Society
924 South 16th Avenue
Yakima, WA 98902
(*Bulletin of the Whatcom County Society*)

Yakima Valley Genealogical Society
P.O. Box 2967
Yakima, WA 98902
(*YVGS Bulletin*, 1969–)
NN APR (Yakima Valley)

Books and Articles

Catholic Church Records of the
Pacific Northwest: Vancouver I
and II . . .
St. Paul, OR, French Prairie Press,
1972. 1 v, various paging (Baptisms 1838–60)
NN APR (Pacific Northwest) 73–
2226

Garner, Grace, and Lorena Wildman.
1880 Census, Spokane County,
Washington Territory.
Spokane, Eastern Washington Gen.
Soc., 1973. 95 p.

Newell, Gordon.
Rogues, Buffoons, and Statesmen.

Seattle, Hangman Press (Superior
Pub. Co.), 1975. 506 p., index.
NN IXO (Olympia) 76-1634

Sheldon, Mary, and Lorena Wildman.
Early Wills of Spokane, Washington, July 7, 1891 to Jan. 1, 1900.
Spokane, Eastern Washington Gen.
Soc., 1973. 63 p., index.

U.S.W.P.A.
Guide to Church Vital Statistics
Records in Washington.
Seattle, 1942. 93 p.
NN APR (Washington) p. v. 219

U.S.W.P.A.
Guide to Public Vital Statistics
Records in Washington.
Seattle, 1941. 131 p. *f.*
NN APR (Washington)

WEST VIRGINIA

State Archives

West Virginia Department of Archives and History
400 East Wing
State Capitol
Charleston, WV 25305
(*West Virginia History*, 1939–)
NN IAA

Vital Records

Division of Vital Statistics
State Department of Health
State Office Bldg., No. 3
Charleston, WV 25305
Births and deaths: January 1917–
Marriages: 1921–
Earlier births, marriages and
deaths: clerk of county court

Societies and Periodicals

Barbour County Historical Society
Volga, WV 26238

Boone County, West Virginia, Genealogical Society
% Janet E. Hager
P.O. Box 146
Hewett, WV 25108
(Query column in *Coal County News*)

Brooke County Historical Society
Brooke County Court House
Wellsburg, WV 26070

Fayette County Historical Society
Ansted, WV 25812

Grant County Historical Society
Box 665
Petersburg, WV 26847

Greenbrier Historical Society
100 Austin Street
Lewisburg, WV 24901
(Mail: % Mrs. K. D. Swope, Archivist, 205 Lee Street, Lewisburg, WV 24901)
(*Greenbrier Historical Society Journal*)

Hancock County Historical Society
New Cumberland, WV 26047

Harrison County Historical Society
Box 2074, 123 West Main Street
Clarkburg, WV 26301

Jefferson County Genealogical Society
% Mrs. Dorothy Feigley
Route 1, Box 83
Kearneysville, WV 25430

Lewis County Historical Society
Weston, WV 26452

Mason County Genealogical Society
% Mrs. Violette Machir
2100 Mason Blvd.
Point Pleasant, WV 25550

Methodist Historical Society
West Virginia Wesleyan College Library
Buckhannon, WV 26201

Mineral County Historical Society, Inc.
35 East Queen Street
Keyser, WV 26726

Mingo County Historical Society
Box 365
Kermit, WV 25674

Monroe County Historical Society
Union, WV 24983

Pendleton County Historical Society
Main Street
Franklin, WV 26807

Pocahontas County Historical Society
Box 51, Route 219
Marlinton, WV 24954

Preston County Historical Society
215 Jackson Street
Kingwood, WV 26537

Raleigh County Historical Society
117 Hill Park Drive
Beckley, WV 25801
(*Proceedings*)

Randolph County Historical Society
Box 1164
Elkins, WV 26241
(*Magazine of History and Biography*)

Ritchie County Historical Society
Genealogical Committee
200 South Church Street
Harrisville, WV 26362
(*Ritchie County Historical Society
Newsletter*)

Summers County Historical Society
107 ½ Miller Avenue
Hinton, WV 25951

Taylor County Historical Society
R.F.D. 5
Grafton, WV 26354

Upshur County Historical Society
118 Barbour Street
Buckhannon, WV 26201

West Augusta Historical and Genealogical Society
118 11th Street
Parkersburg, WV 26101
(*WAHGS Newsletter*, 1955–)
NN APR (West Virginia) 73-1087

West Virginia Collection
University of West Virginia
Morgantown, WV 26506

West Virginia Echoer, 1967–
Mary F. Warrell, Editor
398 National Road
Wheeling, WV 26003

West Virginia Historical Society
State Department of Archives and
History
400 East Wing, State Capitol
Charleston, WV 25305

Books and Articles

Dorman, John Frederick.
A Guide to the Counties of Virginia.

(IN: *VG*, Washington, DC, 1959. v.
3, p. 38–42 (Accomack) ff.)
(This series of articles lists West
Virginia counties as well as
those of Virginia.)
NN ITA 75-1372

Kelly, Richard A., ed.
Outstanding West Virginians of
1969–1970. 1st ed.
Charleston, 1969. 415 p., index.
NN APR (West Virginia) 75–1372

Munn, Robert F.
Index to West Virginia.
Charleston, Education Foundation, 1960. 154 p. (indexes several
West Virginia periodicals.)
NN ITA

Sims, Edgar B.
Sims' Index to Land Grants in West
Virginia.
Charleston, State Auditor's Office,
1952. 866 p.
Supplement, 1956, 16 p.
NN APR+ (West Virginia)

West Virginia University Library.
West Virginia Collection Guide to
Manuscripts and Archives ...
Morgantown, 1974. 317 p.
NN ITA 75-1743

WISCONSIN

State Archives

State Historical Society of Wisconsin
University of Wisconsin
816 State Street
Madison, WI 53701
(*Wisconsin Then and Now; Wisconsin Magazine of History*, 1917–)
NN IAA

Vital Records

Bureau of Health Statistics
Wisconsin Division of Health
P.O. Box 309
Madison, WI 53701
Births and deaths: some 1814–, but
early records are incomplete
Marriages: April 1835–

Libraries

Church of Jesus Christ of Latter-
day Saints
Milwaukee, Wisconsin, State
Branch
Genealogical Library, State Center
9600 West Grange Avenue
Hales Corner, WI 53130

Milwaukee Library
University of Wisconsin
P.O. Box 604
Milwaukee, WI 53211

Milwaukee Public Library
814 West Wisconsin Avenue
Milwaukee, WI 53233

Societies and Periodicals

Adams County Historical Society
Box 261, 101 South Main Street
Adams, WI 53910

Barron County Historical Society
425 South 5th Street
Barron, WI 54812

Brown County Historical Society
3319 Delahaut Street
Green Bay, WI 54301

Burnett County Historical Society
Box 124
Webster, WI 54893

Calumet County Historical Society
State 57 and Irish Road
Chilton, WI 53014

Chippewa County Historical Society
Rutledge Bldg.
404 Bridge Street
Chippewa Falls, WI 54729

Clark County Historical Society,
Inc.
Route 2, Box 117
Loyal, WI 54446

Columbia County Historical Society
917 West Pleasant
Portage, WI 53901

Cranford County Historical Society
Prairie Du Chien, WI 53821

Dane County Historical Society
Room 114, City-County Bldg.
Madison, WI 53709

Door County Historical Society
18 North 4th Avenue
Sturgeon Bay, WI 54235
(*The Peninsula*)

Douglas County Historical Society
906 East 2nd Street
Superior, WI 54880

Dunn County Historical Society
Box 437
Menomonee, WI 54751

Fond Du Lac County Historical
Society
Box 131, 336 E. Pioneer Road
Fond Du Lac, WI 54935

Green County Historical Society
1617 9th Street
Monroe, WI 53566

Iron County Historical Society
Town Hall, Box 88, Gile
Upson, WI 54525

Jackson County Historical Society
South First Street
Black River Falls, WI 54615
(Mail % Mrs. J. Dougherty, Route
4, Evergreen Drive, Black River
Falls, WI 54615

Juneau County Historical Society
Mauston, WI 53948

Kenosha County Genealogical Society
Mrs. Carl Stein, Jr.
% 4902 52nd Street
Kenosha, WI 53140

Kewaunee County Historical Soci-
ety
Old County Jail Museum
Kewaunee, WI 54216
(Mail: 409 Steele Street, Algoma, WI
54201)

Lacrosse County Historical Soci-
ety, Inc.
Box 404
Lacrosse, WI 54601

Langlade County Historical Soci-
ety, Inc.
% Antigo Public Library
Antigo, WI 54409

Manitowoc County Historical Society
1115 North 18th Street
Manitowoc, WI 54220

Marathon County Historical Society
403 McIndoe Street
Wausau, WI 54401

Marinette County Historical Society

Box 262
Marinette, WI 54143

Marquette County Historical Society
Montello, WI 53949

Milwaukee County Genealogical
Society, Inc.
916 East Lyon Street
Milwaukee, WI 53202

Milwaukee County Historical Soci-
ety
910 North 3rd Street
Milwaukee, WI 53203
(*The Historical Messenger*, 1944–)
NN IVK (Milwaukee)

Monroe County Historical Society
Box 422, 418 East Main Street
Sparta, WI 54656
(*Portals of Time*)

Monroe, Juneau, Jackson Counties
Genealogical Workshop
% Carolyn Habelman
Route 3, Box 177-A
Black River Falls, WI 54615
(*Monroe, Juneau, Jackson Coun-
ties, Wisconsin, Genealogical
Workshop Query*)

New Berlin Historical Society
19765 West National Avenue
New Berlin, WI 53151
(Mail: 3730 South Racine Avenue,
New Berlin, WI 53151)
(*New Berlin Almanack*)

Oconto County Historical Society
917 Park Avenue
Oconto, WI 54153

Outagamie County Historical Society
325 West Michigan Street
Appleton, WI 54911

Ozaukee County Historical Society
533 North Meguon Street
Cedarburg, WI 53012
(*Pioneer Village Review*)

Pierce County Historical Association
936 West Maple Street
River Falls, WI 54022
(*Pierce County Heritage*)

Polk County Historical Society
% Willis Erickson
Extension Polk County Center Bldg.
Balsam Lake, WI 54810

Portage County Historical Society
301 Post Road, Plower
Stevens Point, WI 54467
(*The Pinery*)

Price County Historical Society
Fifield, WI 54524

Racine County Historical Society, Inc.
501 South Main Street
Racine, WI 53403

Rock County Historical Society
Box 896, 440 North Jackson Street
Janesville, WI 53545
(*Rock County Chronicle*)

Rusk County Historical Society, Inc.
Route 2, Box 89
Ladysmith, WI 54858

St. Croix County Historical Society
1004 3rd Street
Hudson, WI 54016

Shawano County Historical Society, Inc.
North Franklin Street
Shawano, WI 54166

(Mail: 1003 South Main Street, Shawano, WI 54166

Sheboygan County Historical Society
Box 754, 3110 Erie Avenue
Sheboygan, WI 53081

Southwestern Wisconsin State Old Cemetery Society
% Mrs. Robert Habelman
Route 3, Box 177A
Black River Falls, WI 54615

South Wood County Historical Corporation
Third Street
Wisconsin Rapids, WI 54469

Taylor County Historical Society
Box 6
Rib Lake, WI 54470

Walworth County Historical Society
9 East Rockwell Street
Elkhorn, WI 53121

Washburn County Historical Society
Box G, Auditorium, Fifth Avenue
Shell Lake, WI 54871

Washington County Historical Society
340 Fifth Avenue
West Bend, WI 53095
(Mail: 932A Hickory Street, West Bend, WI 53095)

Waukesha County Historical Society
101 West Main Street
Waukesha, WI 53186
(*Landmark*)

Waushara County Historical Society

Box 129
Wautoma, WI 54982

Western Kenosha County Histori-
cal Society
Box 31
Wilmot, WI 53192

Wisconsin Council for Local History
816 State Street
Madison, WI 53607

Wisconsin State Genealogical Soci-
ety, Inc.
P.O. Box 90068
Milwaukee, WI 53202
(Local chapters throughout the
state)
(*Wisconsin State Genealogical So-
ciety Newsletter*, 1954–)
NN APR (Wisconsin)

Wisconsin State Old Cemetery So-
ciety
% F. Winston Luck, President
4319 North 70th Street
Milwaukee, WI 53216
(*Quarterly Newsletter*)

Books and Articles

Belden, Elvera.
Suggested Sources for Genealogi-
cal Searching in Racine
County, Wisconsin.
(IN: *Wisconsin State Gen. Soc.
Newsletter*, Milwaukee, 1972. v.
19 p. 39–40)
APR (Wisconsin)

Buell, Robert.
Public Records of Wisconsin.
(IN: *TAG*, New Haven, CT, 1960.
v. 36, p. 79–83)
NN APGA

Conzen, Kathleen Niels.
Immigrant Milwaukee, 1836–1860.
Cambridge, MA, Harvard U. Press,
1976. 300 p.
(Harvard Studies in Urban His-
tory)
NN IEK 76-2598

Gleason, Margaret.
Printed Resources for Genealogi-
cal Searching in Wisconsin: A
Selective Bibliography.
Detroit, MI, Detroit Soc. for Gen.
Research, 1964.

Gnacinski, Janneyne L.
Waukesha County Births, 1846–
1879.
West Allis, 1971.

Harper, Josephine L.
Searching for Ancestors in the
Draper Manuscripts ...
(IN: *Indiana Historical Bulletin*,
Indianapolis, IN, 1960. v. 37, p.
107–20)
NN IAA

Still, Bayard.
Milwaukee: The History of a City.
Madison, State Hist. Soc. of Wiscon-
sin, 1948. 638 p., index.
NN IVK (Milwaukee)

Wicklein, Edward C.
The Scots of Vernon and Adjacent
Townships, Waukesha County,
Wisconsin.
Big Bend, 1974. 92 p.
NN APR (Waukesha Co.) 75-2563

Wisconsin 1840 Census Index.
Bountiful, UT, AIS, 1977.

Wisconsin 1850 Census Index.
Bountiful, UT, AIS, 1977.

Wisconsin State Historical Society. Guide to the Manuscripts of the Wisconsin State Historical Society, edited by Alice E. Smith, Supplement 1, 1957; Supplement 2, 1966.
NN IVI

WYOMING

State Archives

Wyoming State Archives and History Department
State Office Building
Cheyenne, WY 82001
(*Annals of Wyoming*) NN IAA

Vital Records

Vital Records Services
Division of Health and Medical Services
State Office Building West
Cheyenne, WY 82002
Births and deaths: July 1909–
Marriages: May 1941–
    Marriages prior: late 19th century, write county clerk

Libraries

Church of Jesus Christ of Latter-day Saints
Cheyenne, Wyoming, State Branch Genealogical Library
Wyoming County Library
2800 Central Avenue
Cheyenne, WY 82001

Laramie County Public Library
Cheyenne, WY 82001

Wyoming State Library
Supreme Court Building
Cheyenne, WY 82001

Societies and Periodicals

Albany County Chapter
Wyoming State Historical Society
1317 Garfield
Laramie, WY 82070

Big Horn County Historical Society
% Jonathan Davis, President
Emblem, WY 82422

Big Horn County Historical Society
Emblem Route
Greybull, WY 82426

Bits and Pieces
Box 746
Newcastle, WY 82701
(Covers North and South Dakota, Wyoming and Montana)

Cheyenne Genealogical Society
% Laramie County Library
Central Avenue
Cheyenne, WY 82001

Heridan County Chapter of Wyoming Historical Society
Box 186
Sheridan, WY 82801

Hot Springs County Historical Society
% Mrs. Bob Milek
836 Mondey
Thermopolis, WY 82443

Johnson County Historical Society
Box 231
Jim Gatchell Memorial Museum
Fort Street
Buffalo, WY 82834

Lincoln County Historical Society
Box 58
Labarge, WY 83123

Niobrara County Historical Society
Box 1396
342 South Main Street
Lusk, WY 82225

Park County Historical Society
Box 1356
Cody, WY 82414

Sublette County Historical Society,
Inc.
Box 666
Pinedale, WY 82941

Sweetwater County Historical
Society
Box 25
50 West Flaming Gorge
Green River, WY 82935

Teton County Historical Society
Box 613
Jackson, WY 83001

Uinta County Historical Society
Box 106
Evanston, WY 82930

Western Historical and Archives
Department
University of Wyoming
Laramie, WY 82070

Weston County Historical Society
Box 698
Newcastle, WY 82701

Books and Articles

Burns, Robert H., Andrew S. Gilles-
pie and Willing G. Richardson.
Wyoming's Pioneer Ranches.
Laramie, Top-of-the-World Press,
1955. 752 p.
NN IWN

Cheyenne Genealogical Society.
Genealogical Records Compiled
from Tombstones and Informa-
tion Found in the Old Register
of Burials of the Cheyenne City
Cemetery, 1875–1910.
Cheyenne, c. 1950. 2 parts, alpha.
NN APR (Cheyenne)

Collection of Genealogical Mate-
rial.
Cheyenne, Daughters of the
American Colonists, Wyoming,
195–. 1 v., 3 parts.
(1st part, parish registers of St.
Matthew's Episcopal Cathedral,
Laramie, 1890–1911; 2nd part,
cemetery records of Newcastle,
Weston County, Wyoming; 3rd
part, family and Bible records)
NN APR (Wyoming)

Erwin, Marie.
Wyoming, Historical Blue Book
. . .1868–1943.
Denver, CO, 1944. 1,471 p., index,
ports.
NN IWN

Flynn, Shirley E.
Our Heritage: 100 Years at St.
Mark's, Cheyenne, Wyoming,
1868–1968.
Cheyenne, St. Mark's Episcopal
Church, c. 1968. 143 p., no index.
NN IWO (Cheyenne)

Homsher, Lola M.
Guide to Wyoming Newspapers,
1867–1967.
Cheyenne, Wyoming State Li-
brary, 1971. 130 p.
NN JFF 72-64

Mokler, Alfred J.
History of Natrona County, Wyoming, 1888–1922 . . .

New York, Argonaut Press, 1966.
477 p.
NN IWO (Natrona Co.)

Pence, Mary Lou, and Lola M.
Homsler.
The Ghost Towns of Wyoming.
New York, Hastings House, c.
1956. 242 p.
NN IWOB

Pioneer Biographies from Original
Manuscripts.
Sheridan, Wyoming Society of Co-
lonial Dames, 1959 to date.
[*Brides of the Open Range, 1875–87.*
(1962). 41 p.]
NN HAE p. v. 805

Triggs, J. H.
History and Directory of Laramie
City, Wyoming Territory . . .
Laramie, Powder River Pub., 1955
(orig. 1875). 91 p.
NN IWO (Laramie)

U.S.W.P.A.
Guide to Vital Statistics Records in
Wyoming.
Cheyenne, 1942.
NN APR (Wyoming)

U.S.W.P.A.
Inventory of the County Archives
of Wyoming.
Cheyenne, 1938–.
NN IWOB

Wall, J. Tom.
Crossing Old Trails to New in
North Central Wyoming.
Philadelphia, Dorrance and Co.,
1973. 242 p., no index.
NN IWO (Johnson Co.) 75-1920

Wasden, David J.
From Beaver to Oil.
Cody, David Wasden, 1973. 350 p.,
index.
NN IWO (Big Horn Basin) 74-180

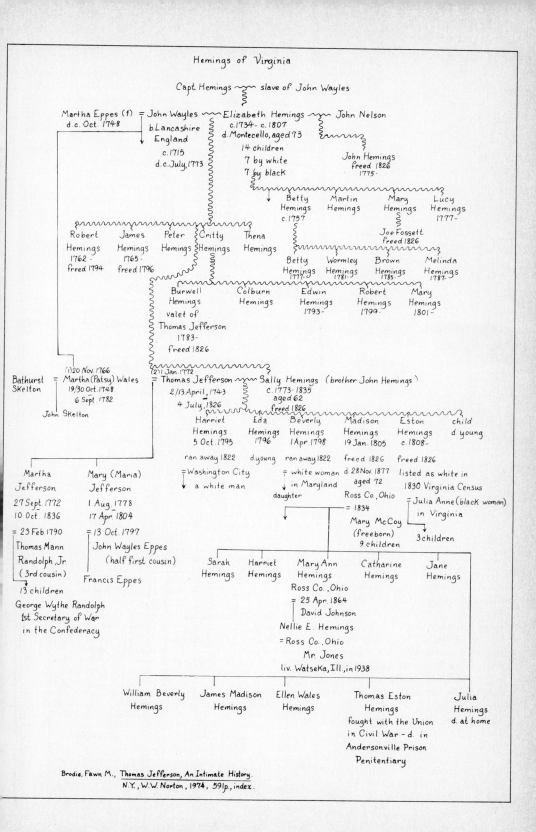

Brodie, Fawn M., _Thomas Jefferson, An Intimate History._ N.Y., W.W. Norton, 1974, 591p., index.

25. (Preceding page) The black descendants of President Thomas Jefferson. Captain Hemings' daughter, Elizabeth, bore six children by John Wayles, the father of Thomas Jefferson's wife. Sally Hemings, thus a half sister of Jefferson's wife, bore Jefferson six children, four of whom survived infancy. (Wavy lines are used on genealogical charts to indicate illegitimacies.) Many members of slave-owning families fathered children with slave women (see page 130).

26. An inventory of the estate of John Purnell of Worcester County, Maryland, dated May 28, 1743, shows the names, ages and professions of his slaves. His will, deposited in the Hall of Records at Annapolis (Maryland Wills Liber 23, Folio 177), tells more about the relationships of some of these slaves to one another and to whom they were bequeathed. The wills of slave-owning families are extremely important sources for black genealogy (see page 128) (courtesy Maryland Hall of Records).

COMMISSIONERS.

1 Rev. Thomas Sanders, Pearson, Miss.
2 Prof. J. A. Mason, Baxter, Ark.
3 Mr. E. J. Young, Charlotte, N. C.
4 Mr. W. P. Burrell, Richmond, Va.
5 Rev. H. H. Waring, Alexandria, Va.
6 Rev. J. E. Bryant, Navasota, Texas.
7 Rev. Henry Taylor, New Orleans, La.
8 Rev. W. A. C. Hughes, Richmond, Va.
9 Prof. J. E. Knox, Brinkley, Ark.
10 Rev. W. E. Partee, D.D., Richmond, Va.

11 Rev. S. H. Brown, Staunton, Va.
12 Prof. O. A. Fuller, A. B., Marshall, Texas.
13 Prof. A. B. Whitby, A. B., Langston, O. T.
14 Rev. S. B. Holmes, B. D., King William, Va.
15 Rev. G. J. Hamilton, Sumter, S. C.
16 Rev. W. H. Jones, Gurden, Ark.
17 Rev. W. S. Snead, Pocahontas, Va.
18 Prof. A. W. Pegues, Ph.D., Raleigh, N. C.
19 Rev. Freeman Parker, Paris, Texas.
20 Mrs. M. M. Bunn, Richmond, Va.

27. Some black leaders in the Southern states in the early 1900's. Many such pictures can be found in old printed references, such as this one from Penn's *The Untitled Negro* (1902), plate between its pages 510 and 511 (see pages 133 and 278).

28. The marks of Wappinger Indians of New York on a seventeenth-century deed are as distinctive as any signatures (see page 135).

SIR:

I hereby make application for such share as may be due me of the fund appropriate: by the Act of Congress approved June 30, 1906, in accordance with the decrees of the Court of Claims of May 18, 1905, and May 28, 1906, in favor of the Eastern Cherokees.   The evidence of identity is herewith subjoined.

------

1. State full name—

   English name: *William Green Edwards*

   Indian name: ....

2. Residence: *Folsom, Ga.*

3. Town and post office: *Folsom,*

4. County: *Bartow*

5. State: *Georgia*

6. Date and place of birth: *Sept. 16, 1848. Tellico Plains, Tenn.*

7. By what right do you claim to share? If you claim through more than one relative living in 1851, set forth each claim separately:

   Through my mother, Agnes Edwards, nee Carnes. The daughter of Hubbard Carnes and Mrs. — Carnes, nee Callahan.

8. Are you married? *Yes.*

9. Name and age of wife or husband: *Katherine Edwards, nee Dowdy. Seventy-four (74) years.*

10. Give names of your father and mother, and your mother's name before marriage.

    Father—English name: *Thomas Edwards.*

    Indian name: ....

    Mother—English name: *Agnes Edwards.*

    Indian name: ....

    Maiden name: *Agnes Carnes.*

11. Where were they born?

    Father: *Virginia.*

    Mother: *South Carolina.*

12. Where did they reside in 1851, if living at that time?

    Father: *Lumpkin County, Ga.*

    Mother: *"   "   "   "*

13. Date of death of your father and mother—

    Father: *1862*   Mother: *1855*

6—524

9. A Cherokee claim obtained from the Commis-
ioner of Indian Affairs in Washington, D.C. Be-
ause each Indian had to defend his or her claim
y proving descent from an Indian who ap-
eared on an earlier roll of the tribe, these files
ften contain an abundance of genealogical de-
ail (see page 141).

30. (Below) The descendants
of Pocahontas and her only
son, Thomas Rolfe, today
include thousands of people
living in the United States
and around the world (see
page 143).

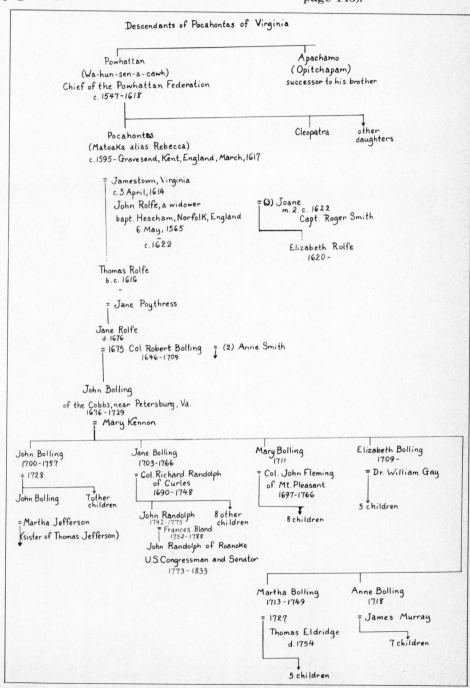

Descendants of Pocahontas of Virginia

Powhattan
(Wa-hun-sen-a-cawh)
Chief of the Powhattan Federation
c. 1547-1618

Apachamo
(Opitchapam)
successor to his brother

Pocahontas
(Matoaka alias Rebecca)
c.1595- Gravesend, Kent, England, March, 1617

Cleopatra

other
daughters

= Jamestown, Virginia
c. 5 April, 1614
John Rolfe, a widower
bapt. Heacham, Norfolk, England
6 May, 1565
c. 1622

= (3) Joane
m. 2. c. 1622
Capt. Roger Smith

Elizabeth Rolfe
1620 -

Thomas Rolfe
b. c. 1616
-

= Jane Poythress

Jane Rolfe
d. 1676
= 1675 Col. Robert Bolling = (2) Anne Smith
1646-1709

John Bolling
of the Cobbs, near Petersburg, Va.
1676 - 1729
= Mary Kennon

John Bolling
1700-1757
= 1728

John Bolling   7 other
children

= Martha Jefferson
(sister of Thomas Jefferson)

Jane Bolling
1703-1766
= Col. Richard Randolph
of Curles
1690-1748

John Randolph   8 other
1742-1775   children
= Frances Bland
1752-1788
John Randolph of Roanoke
U.S. Congressman and Senator
1773 - 1833

Mary Bolling
1711
= Col. John Fleming
of Mt. Pleasant
1697-1766

8 children

Elizabeth Bolling
1709 -
= Dr. William Gay

5 children

Martha Bolling
1713 - 1749

= 1727
Thomas Eldridge
d. 1754

Anne Bolling
1718
= James Murray

7 children

5 children

31–32. Moses Levy, an eighteenth-century New Yor[k]
merchant, has many prominent descendants livin[g]
in the United States and Great Britain. Many suc[h]
Jewish lineages can be traced through printe[d]
sources (see page 149[)]

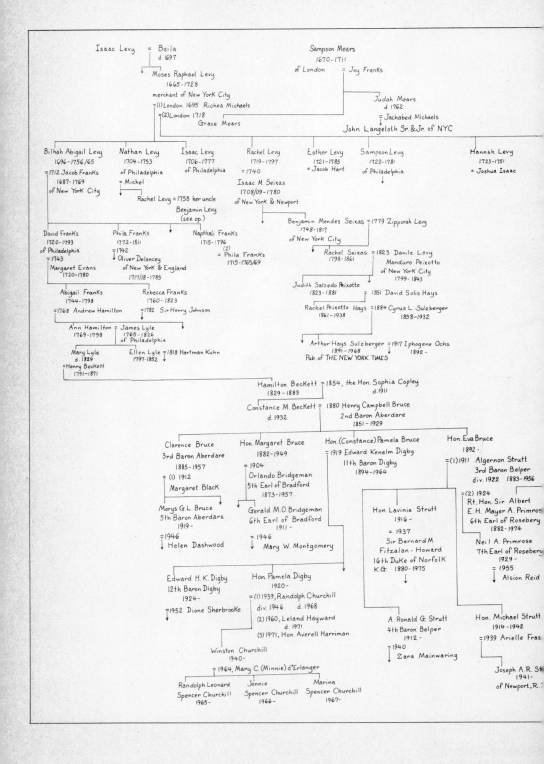

Isaac Levy = Beila
d. 1697

Sampson Mears
1670-1711
of London = Joy Franks

Moses Raphael Levy
1665-1728
merchant of New York City
=(1) London 1695 Richea Michaels
=(2) London 1718
Grace Mears

Judah Mears
d. 1762
= Jachabed Michaels
John Langeloth Sr. & Jr. of NYC

Bilhah Abigail Levy
1696-1756/65
=1712 Jacob Franks
1687-1769
of New York City

Nathan Levy
1704-1753
of Philadelphia
= Michel

Rachel Levy =1758 her uncle
Benjamin Levy
(see op.)

Isaac Levy
1706-1777
of Philadelphia

Rachel Levy
1719-1797
=1740

Isaac M. Seixas
1708/09-1780
of New York & Newport

Esther Levy
1721-1785
= Jacob Hart

Sampson Levy
1722-1781
of Philadelphia

Hannah Levy
1723-1751
= Joshua Isaac

David Franks
1720-1793
of Philadelphia
=1743
Margaret Evans
1720-1780

Phila Franks
1722-1811
=1742
Oliver Delancey
of New York & England
1717/18-1785

Napthali Franks
1715-1796
(2)
= Phila Franks
1715-1765/69

Benjamin Mendes Seixas =1779 Zipporah Levy
1748-1817
of New York City

Rachel Seixas =1823 Danile Levy
1798-1861   Manduro Peixotto
                  of New York City
                  1799-1843

Judith Salzedo Peixotto
1823-1881   =1851 David Solis Hays

Rachel Peixotto Hays =1884 Cyrus L. Sulzberger
1861-1938   1858-1932

Abigail Franks
1744-1798
=1768 Andrew Hamilton

Rebecca Franks
1760-1823
=1782 Sir Henry Johnson

Ann Hamilton = James Lyle
1769-1798   1765-1826
               of Philadelphia

Arthur Hays Sulzberger =1917 Iphogene Ochs
1891-1968   1892-
Pub. of THE NEW YORK TIMES

Mary Lyle
d. 1829
=Henry Beckett
1791-1871

Ellen Lyle =1818 Hartman Kuhn
1797-1852

Hamilton Beckett = 1854, the Hon. Sophia Copley
1829-1883   d. 1911

Constance M. Beckett = 1880 Henry Campbell Bruce
d. 1932   2nd Baron Aberdare
                           1851-1929

Clarence Bruce
3rd Baron Aberdare
1885-1957
= (1) 1912
Margaret Black

Hon. Margaret Bruce
1882-1949
= 1904
Orlando Bridgeman
5th Earl of Bradford
1873-1957

Hon. (Constance) Pamela Bruce
= 1919 Edward Kenelm Digby
11th Baron Digby
1894-1964

Hon. Eva Bruce
1892-
=(1)1911 Algernon Strutt
3rd Baron Belper
div. 1922 1883-1956

Morys G.L. Bruce
5th Baron Aberdare
1919-
=1946
Helen Dashwood

Gerald M.O. Bridgeman
6th Earl of Bradford
1911-
= 1946
Mary W. Montgomery

Hon. Lavinia Strutt
1916-
= 1937
Sir Bernard M.
Fitzalan-Howard
16th Duke of Norfolk
K.G. 1880-1975

=(2) 1924
Rt. Hon. Sir Albert
E.H. Mayer A. Primrose
6th Earl of Rosebery
1882-1974

Neil A. Primrose
7th Earl of Rosebery
1929-
= 1955
Alsion Reid

Edward H.K. Digby
12th Baron Digby
1924-
=1952 Dione Sherbrooke

Hon. Pamela Digby
1920-
=(1)1939, Randolph Churchill
div. 1946   d. 1968
(2)1960, Leland Hayward
d. 1971
(3)1971, Hon. Averell Harriman

A. Ronald G. Strutt
4th Baron Belper
1912-
=1940
Zara Mainwaring

Hon. Michael Strutt
1914-1942
=1939 Arielle Fraz

Winston Churchill
1940-
= 1964, Mary C. (Minnie) d'Erlanger

Joseph A.R. St
1941-
of Newport, R.

Randolph Leonard
Spencer Churchill
1965-

Jennie
Spencer Churchill
1966-

Marina
Spencer Churchill
1967-

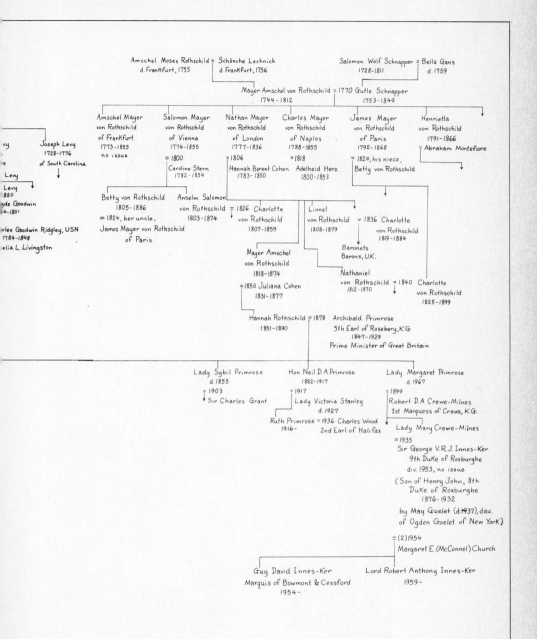

Amschel Moses Rothschild = Schönche Lechnich
d. Frankfurt, 1755   d. Frankfurt, 1756

Salomon Wolf Schnapper = Bella Gans
1728-1811   d. 1759

Mayer Amschel von Rothschild = 1770 Gutle Schnapper
1744 - 1812   1753 - 1849

Joseph Levy
1728-1776
of South Carolina

vy

Levy

Levy
820

de Goodwin
4-1801

rles Goodwin Ridgley, USN
1784-1848

elia L. Livingston

Amschel Mayer
von Rothschild
of Frankfurt
1773-1855
no issue

Salomon Mayer
von Rothschild
of Vienna
1774-1855
= 1800
Caroline Stern
1782-1854

Nathan Mayer
von Rothschild
of London
1777-1836
= 1806
Hannah Barent Cohen
1783-1850

Charles Mayer
von Rothschild
of Naples
1788-1855
= 1818
Adelheid Herz
1800-1853

James Mayer
von Rothschild
of Paris
1792-1868
= 1824, his niece,
Betty von Rothschild

Henrietta
von Rothschild
1791-1866
= Abraham Montefiore

Betty von Rothschild
1805-1886
= 1824, her uncle,
James Mayer von Rothschild
of Paris

Anselm Salomon
von Rothschild
1803-1874

Charlotte
von Rothschild
1807-1859
= 1826

Lionel
von Rothschild
1808-1879
= 1836 Charlotte
von Rothschild
1819-1884

Mayer Amschel
von Rothschild
1818-1874
= 1850 Juliana Cohen
1831-1877

Baronets
Barons, U.K.

Nathaniel
von Rothschild
1812-1870
= 1840

Charlotte
von Rothschild
1825-1899

Hannah Rothschild = 1878 Archibald Primrose
1851-1890   5th Earl of Rosebery, K.G.
                         1847-1929
                         Prime Minister of Great Britain

Lady Sybil Primrose
d. 1855
= 1903
Sir Charles Grant

Hon. Neil D. A. Primrose
1882-1917
= 1917
Lady Victoria Stanley
d. 1927
Ruth Primrose = 1936 Charles Wood
1916-   2nd Earl of Halifax

Lady Margaret Primrose
d. 1967
= 1899
Robert D. A. Crewe-Milnes
1st Marquess of Crews, K.G.

Lady Mary Crewe-Milnes
= 1935
Sir George V. R. J. Innes-Ker
9th Duke of Roxburghe
div. 1953, no issue
(Son of Henry John, 8th
Duke of Roxburghe
1876-1932
by May Goelet (d. 1937), dau.
of Ogden Goelet of New York)

= (2) 1954
Margaret E. (McConnel) Church

Guy David Innes-Ker
Marquis of Bowmont & Cessford
1954-

Lord Robert Anthony Innes-Ker
1959-

7   BAS

Year	Name	Couple	Place
1638	BASTERD	Phil & Honer Brimmin	Exeter S Kerrians
1632	BASTON	Pet & Elnr Sweetland	Brixham
1641		Chas & Dunes Tucker	Exminster
1650		Jn als Ralf & Marie Pain	Feniton
1629	BASTOW	Hen & Jane Lane	Dartmouth
1650	BATH	Walt & Johane French	Exeter S Sidwell
1636	BATHE	Jos & Mgy Loves	Exeter S Laur
1630	BATSTON	Tho & Mary Grabham	Up Ottery
1645		Fran & Joan Clap	Withycombe Raleigh
1649	BATTE	Chas & Mgt Southecot	Bideford
1643	BATTIN	Edw & Tomsin German	Withycombe Raleigh
1631	BATTISHILL	And & Mary Row	Spreyton
1627	BAWDEN	Phil & Mary Michel	Modbury
1627		Rob & Reb Bewford	Bideford
1635		Jn & Agn Wakham	Modbury
1637		Philip & Yackett Smale	Bideford
1639		Jn & Johan Goodchild	do
1639		Jn & Annice Sweet	Dartmouth
1636	BAXONS	Wm & Elz Mitchel	Up Ottery
1640	BEADON	Walt & Alce Hamling	Otterton
1626	BEAL	Jn & Pascoe Eastabrook	Alphington
1633		Phil & Alce Fish	Exeter S Sidwell
1648		Philip & Mary Aushton	Bideford
1626	BEALLET	Rob & Elz Hanks	Stoke Damarell
1635	BEAN	Jn & Xtian Pears	Marwood
1626	BEAR	Laur & Mary Wils	Dartmouth
1626		Tho & Mary Temlet	Tedburn
1629		And & Gillian Davy	Dartmouth
1630		Abr & Alce Vicary	Exeter S Sidwell
1630		Geo & Elz Shepard	Modbury
1633		Hen & Mgy Pulliblank	do
1634		Hum & Peternel Gasworthy	Bideford
1634		Ric & Mary Smale	Drewsteignton
1636		Clement & Xtian Rich	Ashwater
1641		Wm & Johan Dicker	Drews/teignton
1644		Jn & Mgt Fook	Braunton
1645		Pet & Elnr Laurenc	Ugborough
1647		Abr & Elz Kit	Marwood
1648		Jn & Mgt Glowin	Ashwater
1649		Nic & Alce Sunter	Staverton
1626	BEARDE	Tho & Joan Bowthers	do
1628		Mark & Jane Williams	Ashburton
1636		And & Anis Horn	Modbury
1650		Jas & Johane Kingwill	Exeter S Sidwell
1649	BEARDON	Geo & Reb Cornish	Dartmouth
1640	BEARMAN	Edw & Petronell Morrice	Bishops Nympton
1646		Pet & Johan Camins	do
1636	BEATON	Rob & Agn Steel	Molton S
1643		Ric & Tomsin Pickherd	Braunton
1644		Phil & An Fellpott	Dartmouth
1646		Ric & Sus Been	Marwood
1626	BEERE	Gilb & Agn Spicer	Wembury
1628		Rog & Agn Pascole	Bideford
1631		Hugo & Agnet Finch	Ugborough

UNITED STATES OF AMERICA

To all to whom these Presents shall come, Greeting

Nº 4630

DESCRIPTION

49 Years

Stature 5 Feet 7 Inches Engh

forehead rather full

Eyes light hazel

Nose small

Mouth medium

Chin ordinary

Hair grey mixed

Complexion ruddy

Face full

Signature of the Bearer

GRATIS

I the Undersigned, Secretary of State of the **United States of America**, hereby request all whom it may concern, to permit safely and freely to pass Joseph A. Beard

a Citizen of the United States, and in case of need to give him all lawful Aid and Protection

Given under my hand and the impression of the Seal of the **DEPARTMENT OF STATE**, at the City of Washington the 12th Day of July, A.D. 1852 in the Year of the Independence of these United States.

Dan Webster

35. An illuminated sixteenth-century pedigree of the
Hesketh (Heskaith) family of Hesketh and Rufford,
County Lancaster, England. You can prepare your
own version of an illuminated pedigree by attaching
photographs and daguerreotypes of your ancestors to
a completed pedigree chart (see page 182).

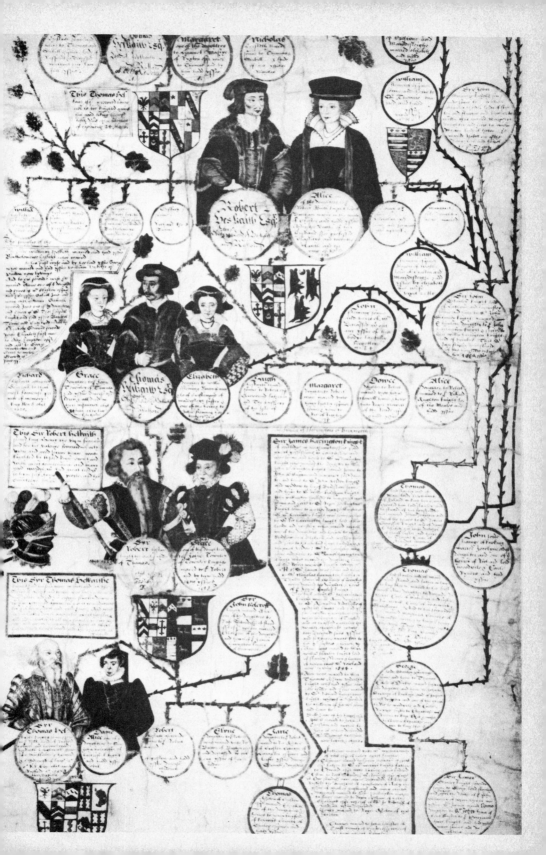

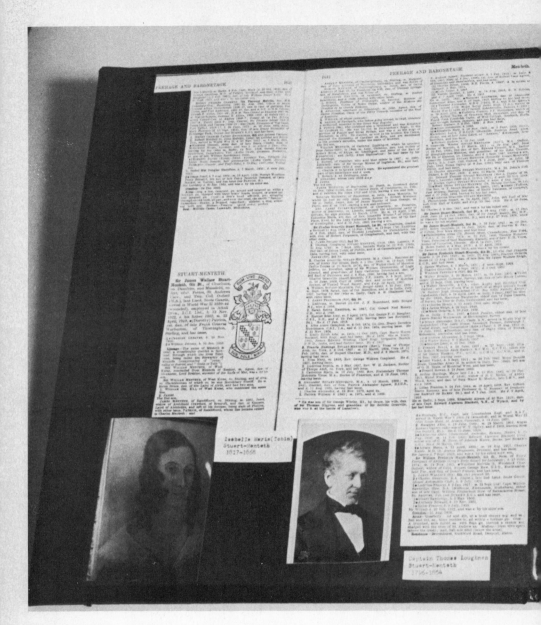

36. You can present your genealogical research in a scrapbook, including family pictures, pages from books, newspaper clippings and other mementos and pedigree charts (see page 182).

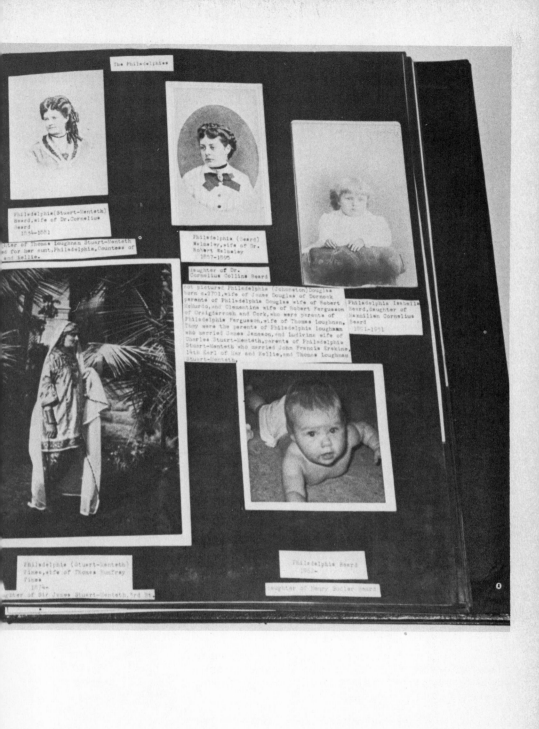

The Philadelphias

Philadelphia(Stuart-Menteth)
Beard,wife of Dr.Cornelius
Beard
1854-1881

...hter of Thomas Loughnan Stuart-Menteth
...ed for her aunt,Philadelphia,Countess of
...and Kellie.

Philadelphia (Beard)
Walmsley,wife of Dr.
Robert Walmsley
1857-1895

daughter of Dr.
Cornelius Collins Beard

...ot pictured Philadelphia (Johnston)Douglas
born c.1701,wife of James Douglas of Dornock
parents of Philadelphia Douglas,wife of Robert
McMurdo,and Clementina wife of Robert Fergusson
of Craigdarroch and Cork,who were parents of
Philadelphia Fergusson,wife of Thomas Loughnan.
They were the parents of Philadelphia Loughnan
who married James Jameson,and Ludivina wife of
Charles Stuart-Menteth,parents of Philadelphia
Stuart-Menteth who married John Francis Erskine,
14th Earl of Mar and Kellie,and Thomas Loughnan
Stuart-Menteth.

Philadelphia Isabelle
Beard,daughter of
Maximilian Cornelius
Beard
1951-1951

Philadelphia (Stuart-Menteth)
Vinse,wife of Thomas Humfray
Vinse
1874-
...ghter of Sir James Stuart-Menteth,3rd Bt.

Philadelphia Beard
1961-
...aughter of Henry Butler Beard

This Indenture

Andrew [mark] +

37. A seventeenth-century English lease dealing
with land in South Brent, Devonshire, bears the
mark of Andrew Beard, whose name was then signed
by another person. Because many early records
survive in England, it is often possible to follow the
lines of yeoman families back into the fifteenth
century (see page 187).

in the Twentyth yeare of the raigne of o[u]r Soueraigne Lord Kinge Charles
...rris of South Brent in the County of Devon yeoman Geard his wife
...thone zeto And Andrew Board of South Brent aforesaid Husbandman
fo[r] ... Robert ferris theire Sonn ffor and in Considera[ti]on of the Summe
...yaids before thensealing & deliu[er]y of these p[rese]nts the receipt
...um doe hereby acknowledge them selues fully sattisfied & paid
...ill & Discharge the said Andrew Board his heires Ex[ecu]tors Adm[inistrato]rs
graunted & sett And by these p[rese]nts doe Demise Lease graunt
...and called Flox hay meadow lying in Bynny moore w[i]thin the said
...theire aboutes To haue and to hold the said meadow and all
...it Pathes waters water courses ... &ffitts Comodytiiis And
...the said Andrew Board his Ex[ecu]tors Adm[inistrato]rs & Assignes ffrom the third
...und of one & Twenty yeares from thence next ensuing full
...the said Thomas ferris his heires or Assignes the yearly Rent of one
... demaunded And the said Andrew Board doth for himselfe his
...graunt & agree w[i]th the said Thomas ferris his heires Ex[ecu]tors
...that ... Ju[s]tm[en]ts dureing the said Terme w[hi]ch shalbe due And
...the said meadow and not to plough the said meadow nor sow any
Thomas ferris Geard his wife & Robert theire Sonn doe for them
...and agree to and w[i]th the said Andrew Board his Ex[ecu]tors Adm[inistrato]rs
...the said meadow by itt selfe or w[i]th any other Lands of the said Thomas
... & theire Ju[s]tments due to the Parson of South Brent as aforesaid,
...that ffences & Gates when and as often as need shall Require
...& Robert theire Sonn and theire heires shall & will att any tyme
...done acknowledged or executed & suffered such further assurance
...ny to bee made & done vppon the Request of the said Andrew
...is not any fformer Graunt made of the p[re]misses to any
...doe the Estate hereby graunted to the said Andrew Board or any
...e hand & Seales haue putt ... downe the day & yeare first

Board

State of New York   County of New York

City, Village or Town of New York

Address   38 Barrow Street

I,   Timothy Field Beard

am the applicant for membership in The Order of Three Crusades (1096-1192).

1. I, the applicant,   Timothy Field Beard

was born at Great Barrington, Massachusetts   on Dec. 19, 1930

Married at New York, New York   ; married on Sept. 12, 1963

to Annette Knowles Huddleston at Montgomery, Ala. on Sept. 20, 1933

died at _____ on _____

Proof: Birth & Marriage Certificates attached

2. The said   Timothy Field Beard   was the child of

Stuart-Menteth Beard II born at Canandaigua, N.Y.   on Nov. 28, 1893

died at Sheffield, Mass.   on Sept. 8, 1955; married on June 30, 1921

to Natalie Sudler Turner   born at Wilmington, Del. on Dec. 20, 1888

died at Great Barrington, Mass. on Jan. 7, 1957 ; married at Asbury Park, N.J.

Proof: Birth, Marriage & Death Certificates attached

3. The said Stuart-Menteth Beard II   was the child of
                                    Beard
Maximilien Cornelius   born at Biloxi, Miss.   on Nov. 27, 1864

died at New Haven, Conn.   on Feb. 19, 1924; married on Sept. 25, 1888

to Gertrude Field Finley   born at Canandaigua, N.Y on June 18, 1869

died at Sheffield, Mass.   on April, 20, 1941; married at Canandaigua, N.Y.

Proof: Aldrich, L.C. History of Ontario County (1893) Family Sketches

p.24; Marriage & Death Certificates, Beard Bible Records, Will of
C.C. Beard attached.

4. The said   Maximilien Cornelius Beard   was the child of

Cornelius Collins Beard born at Portsmouth, Eng.   on Nov. 26, 1828

died at Brookline, Mass.   on May 15, 1906 ; married on May 10, 1852
                    Menteth
to Philadelphia Stuart-   born at Canandaigua, N.Y. on May 17, 1834

died at New Orleans, Louisiana on March 29, 1881; married at Canandaigua, N.Y.

Proof: Ruvigny & Raineval. The Plantgenet Roll of the Blood Royal.

Clarence Volume. London, 1905. p.77; Beard Bible Records & Will &
Death Cert. of C.C. Beard attached.

5. The said Philadelphia Stuart-Menteth   was the child of
                                        Dumfries, Scot.
Capt. Thomas Loughnan S-M born at Closeburn Hall,   on Aug. 31, 1796

died at Canandaigua, N.Y.   on Feb. 22, 1854 ; married on Sept. 7, 1832
                                    Ireland
to Isabella Maria Tobin   born at Delgany, Wicklow Nov. 8, 1817

died at Canandaigua, N.Y.   on Jan. 26, 1868 ; married at Canandaigua, N.Y.

Proof: Ruvigny & Raineval, IBID.; Beard & Stuart-Menteth Bible Records

& letter of Rev. Mr. Rooke attached

38. Membership in a hereditary society is based on proven descent from an individual who can be connected with a particular event, location or period. In order to join you must submit a lineage paper that shows your line back to the ancestor upon whose identity you are basing your application. Proof of your information about each generation must be carefully and completely identified (see page 198).

39. The Colonial commission of David Field in the Connecticut Militia was reproduced in a genealogy of the Field family. This evidence of military service makes his descendants eligible for membership in a variety of Colonial patriotic societies (see page 198).

JONATHAN LAW, Esq;
Governour and Commander in Chief of His
Majesty's Colony of Connecticut in New=England.

To David Field , , , Gent. Greeting.

YOU being by the General Affembly of this Colony Accepted to be Enfign of the 6 Company in Finsbuad in the Town of Colony Repofing fpecial Truft and Confidence in your Loyalty, Courage and good Conduct, I do, by Virtue of the Letters Patents from the Crown of England to this Corporation, Me thereunto Enabling, Appoint and Impower you to take the faid Trainband into your Care and Charge, as their Enfign Carefully and Diligently to Difcharge that Truft ; Exercifing four Inferiour Officers and Souldiers in the Ufe of their Arms, according to the Difcipline of War : Keeping them in good Order and Government, and Commanding them to Obey you as their Enfign for His Majefty's Service. And you are to Obferve all fuch Orders and Directions as from time to time you fhall Receive either from Me, or from other your Superiour Officer, purfuant to the Truft hereby Repofed in you. Given under my Hand and the Seal of this Colony, in Hartford the fird Day of June In the 20 X Year of the Reign of Our Sovereign Lord GEORGE the Second KING of Great Britain, &c. Annoque Domini, 1747.

By his Honour's Command,
Secr.

J. Law

COMMISSION GIVEN DAVID FIELD ON JUNE 1, 1747

41. Augustine Herman (Herrman, Heermans, etc.), born in Prague in 1621, settled in New Amsterdam in 1643. He moved to Maryland in the 1660's, became the first Lord of Bohemia Manor, Cecil County, Maryland, and died in 1686. He is a "popular ancestor" whose descendants are eligible for membership in the St. Nicholas Society (for descendants of early residents of New York), the Society of Colonial Wars and the Order of Colonial Lords of Manors in America (see page 200) (Courtesy Maryland Historical Society).

40. New England's first permanent European settlers. If you can prove your connection to one of them, you are eligible for membership in the Society of Mayflower Descendants (see page 200).

The names of those which came over first, in ȳ year 1620 and were (by the blesing of god) the first begiñers, and (in a sort) the foundation, of all the plantations, and colonies, in New-England (and their families)

mr John Carver
Kathrine his wife
Desire minter; &
2 man-servants
John Howland
Roger Wilder
William Latham, a boy
& a maid servant, & a
child ȳ was put to him
called Jasper More

mr William Brewster
Mary his wife, with
2 sons, whose names
were Loue, & Wrasling
and a boy was put to
him caled Richard More; and another of his brothers
the rest of his children
were left behind & came
over afterwards

mr Edward Winslow
Elizabeth his wife, &
2 men servants, caled
Georg Sowle, and
Elias Story, also a litle
girle was put to him caled
Ellen, the sister of Richard More.

William Bradford, and
Dorothy his wife, hauing
but one child, a sone left
behind, who came afterward.

mr Isaack Allerton, and
Mary his wife; with 3 children
Bartholmew
Remember, &
Mary, and a servant boy,
John Hooke.

mr Samuel fuller, and
a servant caled
William Butten His wife
was behind & a child, which
came afterwards

John Crakston and his sone
John Crakston

Caplin myles Standish
and Rose his wife 2

mr Christopher Martin,
and his wife, and 2 servants
Salamon prower, and
John Langemore 4

mr William mullines, and his
wife; and 2 children
Joseph, & priscila; and a servant
Robart Carter 5

mr William White, and
Susana his wife; and one sone
caled Resolued; and one borne
a ship-bord caled perigrene; &
2 servants, named
William Holbeck, & Edward Thomson 6

mr Steuen Hopkins, &
Elizabeth his wife; and 2
children, caled giles, and
Constanta a doughter, both
by a former wife; And 2 more
by this wife, caled Damaris, &
Oceanus; the last was borne at
sea and 2 servants, caled
Edward Doty, and Edward Litster 8

mr Richard Warren, but his
wife and children were left
behind and came afterwards 1

John Billinton, and Elen his wife
and 2 sones John, & francis 4

Edward Tillie, and Ann his wife
and 2 children that were their
cosens; Henery samson, and Humility Coper 4

John Tillie, and his wife, and
Elizabeth their doughter 3

The List of Pilgrims who Came over on the "Mayflower."

From Bradford's Journal.

Catherine Duer
(Mrs. Clarence Mackay)

42. A modern "gateway" ancestress, Catherine Alexander (Duer) Mackay Blake (1879–1930), first married Clarence H. Mackay and then Dr. Joseph A. Blake. Her daughter, the talented author Ellen Mackay, is the wife of composer Irving Berlin (born Irving Baline in Russia in 1888). Mrs. Blake was descended from the Revolutionary War general William Alexander, claimant of the Earldom of Stirling, and from the Livingstons of Livingston Manor in New York. When you establish your relationship to a gateway ancestor or ancestress you generally connect your family to a variety of well-known figures (see page 203).

43. A topaz and gold watch fob, engraved with the Stuart-Menteth coat of arms, belonged to the Reverend James Stuart-Menteth (1718–1802). If your ancestors bore a coat of arms, you may find it emblazoned on jewelry, silver, book plates, china or tombstones (see page 207).

45. Borgund Stave Church near Laerdal in Norway's fjord country was built in 1138 and is one of the finest and best preserved of these buildings, many of which contain very old records (see page 890) (Courtesy Norwegian National Tourist Office).

44. The oath of allegiance of Bartholomew Beard, then living in the parish of St. Thomas the Apostle, Devon, in the tenth year of the reign of George I (about 1724). These documents, now usually deposited in the county record offices of England, note the parish of residence of each adult male swearing to support the Protestant succession. By searching the parish registers, further details about a family can often be found (see page 950).

Devon. ss.

THese are to certify, that at the General Quarter-Sessions of the Peace held *by Adjournment at ye Sheriffs Ward in St Thomas the Apostle* in and for the said County the *Twelfth* Day of *December* in the *Tenth* ———— Year of the Reign of His Majesty King GEORGE, *Bartholomew Beard now* ——; inhabiting in *St Thomas ye Apostle* within the said County, took and subscribed the Oaths appointed to be taken and subscribed, by the Statute made in the First Year of His said Majesty's Reign, intituled, *An Act for the further Security of His Majesty's Person and Government, and the Succession of the Crown in the Heirs of the late Princess* SOPHIA, *being* Protestants, *and for extinguishing the Hopes of the Pretended* Prince of WALES, *and his open and secret Abettors;* which said Oaths are required to be taken and subscribed by an Act made in the Ninth Year of His said Majesty's Reign, intituled, *An Act to oblige all Persons (being* Papists*) in that Part of* Great-Britain *called* Scotland, *and all Persons in* Great-Britain *refusing or neglecting to take the Oaths appointed for the Security of His Majesty's Person and Government, by several Acts herein-mentioned, to register their Names and Real Estates.*

House of Grimaldi

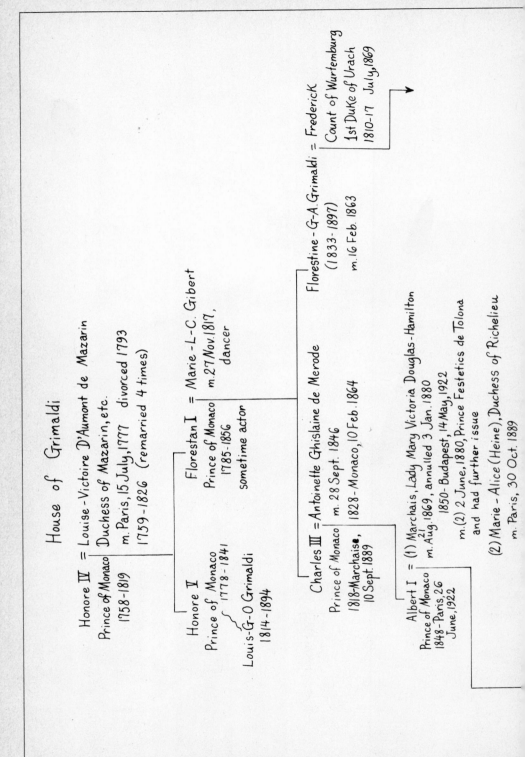

Honore IV = Louise-Victoire D'Aumont de Mazarin
Prince of Monaco   Duchess of Mazarin, etc.
1758-1819   m. Paris, 15 July, 1777   divorced 1793
               1759-1826 (remarried 4 times)

Florestan I = Marie-L-C. Gibert
Prince of Monaco   m. 27 Nov. 1817,
1785-1856   dancer
sometime actor

Honore V
Prince of Monaco
1778-1841
Louis-G-O Grimaldi
1814-1894

Florestine-G-A.Grimaldi = Frederick
(1833-1897)   Count of Wurtemburg
m. 16 Feb. 1863   1st Duke of Urach
                           1810-17 July, 1869

Charles III = Antoinette Ghislaine de Merode
Prince of Monaco   m. 28 Sept. 1846
1818-Marchais,   1828-Monaco, 10 Feb. 1864
10 Sept. 1889

Albert I = (1) Marchais, Lady Mary Victoria Douglas-Hamilton
Prince of Monaco   m. Aug. 1869, annulled 3 Jan. 1880
1848-Paris, 26   1850- Budapest, 14 May, 1922
June, 1922   m.(2) 2 June, 1880, Prince Festetics de Tolona
                   and had further issue

(2) Marie-Alice (Heine), Duchess of Richelieu
m. Paris, 30 Oct. 1889

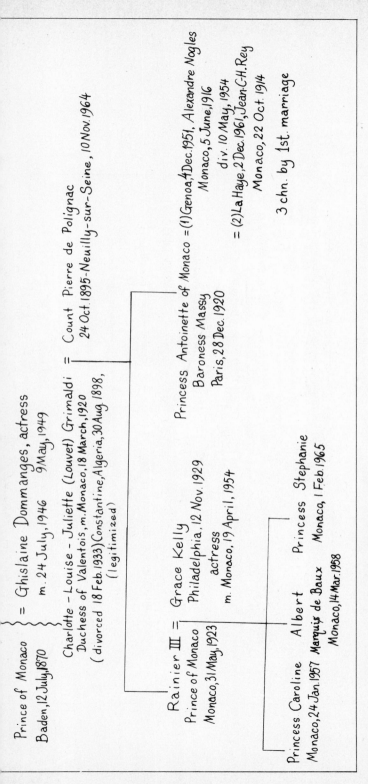

Prince of Monaco = Ghislaine Dommanges, actress
Baden, 12 July, 1870   m. 24 July, 1946   9 May, 1949

Charlotte – Louise – Juliette (Louvet) Grimaldi = Count Pierre de Polignac
Duchess of Valentois, m. Monaco, 18 March, 1920   24 Oct. 1895 – Neuilly-sur-Seine, 10 Nov. 1964
(divorced 18 Feb. 1933) Constantine, Algeria, 30 Aug. 1898,
(legitimized)

Princess Antoinette of Monaco = (1) Genoa, 4 Dec. 1951, Alexandre Nogles
Baroness Massy   Monaco, 5 June, 1916
Paris, 28 Dec. 1920   div. 10 May, 1954
= (2) La Haye, 2 Dec. 1961, Jean-C-H. Rey
Monaco, 22 Oct. 1914

3 chn. by 1st marriage

Rainier III = Grace Kelly
Prince of Monaco   Philadelphia, 12 Nov. 1929
Monaco, 31 May, 1923   actress
m. Monaco, 19 April, 1954

Princess Caroline   Albert   Princess Stephanie
Monaco, 24 Jan. 1957   Marquis de Baux   Monaco, 1 Feb. 1965
Monaco, 14 Mar. 1958

46. The line of the Princes of Monaco from Honore IV to Rainier III includes several theatrical personalities. Princess Grace, the wife of the present ruler, is the former movie actress Grace Kelly, a popular figure in America and around the world (see page 880).

Queen Elizabeth's American Ancestors

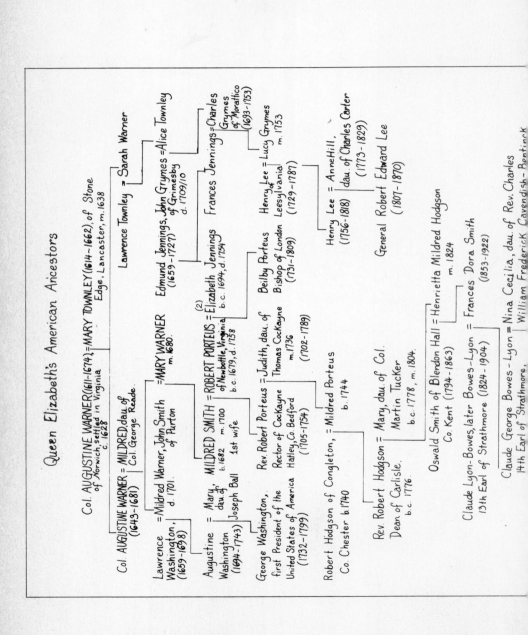

Col. AUGUSTINE WARNER (1611–1674) = MARY TOWNLEY (1614–1662), of Stone
of Norwich, settled in Virginia   Edge, Lancaster, m. 1638
c. 1628

Lawrence Townley = Sarah Warner

Col. AUGUSTINE WARNER = MILDRED, dau. of
(1643–1681) | Col. George Reade.

Edmund Jennings, John Grymes = Alice Townley
(1659–1727) of Grimesby
d. 1709/10

Lawrence = Mildred Warner, John Smith   = MARY WARNER
Washington, d. 1701.   of Purton   m. 1680.
(1659–1698)

Frances Jennings = Charles
Grymes
of Morattico
(1693–1753)

Augustine = Mary, MILDRED SMITH = ROBERT PORTEUS = Elizabeth Jennings
Washington dau. of b. 1682 m. 1700 of Newbottle, Virginia b. c. 1694, d. 1754
(1694–1743) Joseph Ball 1st wife   b. c. 1679, d. 1758   (2)

Beilby Porteus
Bishop of London
(1731–1809)

Henry Lee = Lucy Grymes
Leesylvania m. 1753
(1729–1787)

George Washington, Rev. Robert Porteus = Judith, dau. of
first President of the Rector of CocKayne Thomas CocKayne
United States of America Hatley, Co. Bedford m. 1736
(1732–1799)   (1705–1754)   (1702–1789)

Henry Lee = AnneHill,
(1756–1818) | dau. of Charles Carter
(1773–1829)

Robert Hodgson of Congleton, = Mildred Porteus
Co. Chester b. 1740   b. 1744

General Robert Edward Lee
(1807–1870)

Rev. Robert Hodgson = Mary, dau. of Col.
Dean of Carlisle. Martin Tucker
b. c. 1776.   b. c. 1778, m. 1804.

Oswald Smith of Blendon Hall = Henrietta Mildred Hodgson
Co. Kent (1794–1863)   m. 1824

Claude Lyon-Bowes-Lyon = Frances Dora Smith
13th Earl of Strathmore (1824–1904) (1853–1922)

Claude George Bowes-Lyon = Nina Cecilia, dau. of Rev. Charles
14th Earl of Strathmore,   William Frederick Cavendish-Bentinck

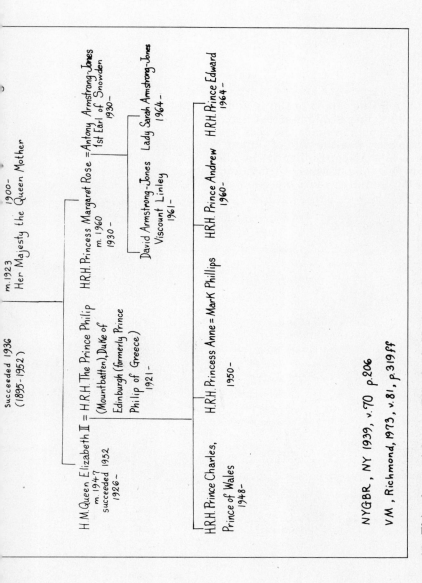

m. 1923
Her Majesty the Queen Mother
1900–

succeeded 1936
(1895–1952)

H.M. Queen Elizabeth II = H.R.H. The Prince Philip
m. 1947   (Mountbatten), Duke of
succeeded 1952   Edinburgh (formerly Prince
1926–   Philip of Greece)
                                        1921–

H.R.H. Princess Margaret Rose = Antony Armstrong-Jones
                          m. 1960   1st Earl of Snowden
                          1930–   1930–

David Armstrong-Jones   Lady Sarah Armstrong-Jones
Viscount Linley   1964–
1961–

H.R.H. Prince Charles,
Prince of Wales
1948–

H.R.H. Princess Anne = Mark Phillips
1950–

H.R.H. Prince Andrew
1960–

H.R.H. Prince Edward
1964–

NYGBR, NY 1939, v.70 p. 206

VM, Richmond, 1973, v.81, p. 319 ff

47. This chart of Queen Elizabeth II shows her relationship to both Robert E. Lee and George
Washington. When you trace your family's history
you may discover a variety of notable, if highly unlikely, connections (see page 946).

48. The line of the Soong family of China and the United States. Ching-ling Soong married Sun Yat-sen, and May-ling Soong, perhaps the best-known member of the family, was the wife of Chiang Kai-shek. H.H. Kung, husband of Ei-ling Soong, allegedly stood seventy-fifth in line of descent from Confucius, who lived some five hundred years B.C. (see page 697).

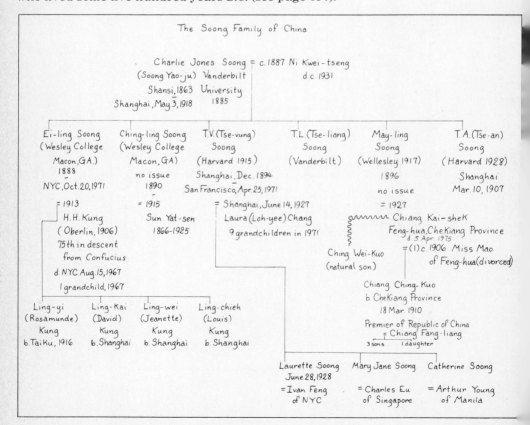

The Soong Family of China

Charlie Jones Soong = c.1887 Ni Kwei-tseng
(Soong Yao-ju) Vanderbilt   d.c.1931
Shansi, 1863 University
Shanghai, May 3, 1918   1885

Ei-ling Soong
(Wesley College
Macon,GA.)
1888
NYC,Oct.20,1971
= 1913
H.H. Kung
(Oberlin, 1906)
75th in descent
from Confucius
d.NYC Aug.15,1967
1 grandchild,1967

Ching-ling Soong
(Wesley College
Macon,GA)
no issue
1890
= 1915
Sun Yat-sen
1866-1925

T.V.(Tse-vung)
Soong
(Harvard 1915)
Shanghai, Dec.1894
San Francisco,Apr.25,1971
= Shanghai, June 14,1927
Laura (Loh-yee) Chang
9 grandchildren in 1971

T.L.(Tse-liang)
Soong
(Vanderbilt)

May-ling
Soong
(Wellesley 1917)
1896
no issue
= 1927
Chiang Kai-shek
Feng-hua,CheKiang Province
d.5 Apr 1975
=(1)c.1906 Miss Mao
of Feng-hua(divorced)

T.A.(Tse-an)
Soong
(Harvard 1928)
Shanghai
Mar.10, 1907

Ching Wei-Kuo
(natural son)

Chiang Ching-Kuo
b.CheKiang Province
18 Mar. 1910
Premier of Republic of China
= Chiang Fang-liang
3 sons   1 daughter

Ling-yi
(Rosamunde)
Kung
b.TaiKu, 1916

Ling-Kai
(David)
Kung
b.Shanghai

Ling-wei
(Jeanette)
Kung
b.Shanghai

Ling-chieh
(Louis)
Kung
b.Shanghai

Laurette Soong
June 28,1928
=Ivan Feng
of NYC

Mary Jane Soong
= Charles Eu
of Singapore

Catherine Soong
= Arthur Young
of Manila

Part Four

Tracing Your Family's History Abroad

Afars and Issas (Djibouti)

France first gained a foothold in this area, formerly known as French Somaliland, in 1862 and organized it as a colony in 1896. It was made a territory within the French Union in 1946 and a member of the French Community in 1958. The Afars, with French support, gained political dominance in 1967 and full independence in 1977. The inhabitants are Somali (Issas and others) and Afars.

Archives

Archives Nationales, Section Outre-Mer
27 rue Oudinot
75007 Paris, France

Books and Articles

Franchetti, Raimondo.
... Nella Dancalia ...
Milan, A. Mondadori, 1935. 424 p.
NN BLM

Jousseaume, F.
Impressions de Voyage en Aphar-ras ...
Paris, J. B. Baillière et fils, 1914. 2 v.
NN BLM

Lewis, Joan Myrddin.
Peoples of the Horn of Africa, Somali, Afar and Saho.
London, International African Institute, 1955. 200 p.
(*Ethnographic Survey of Africa North-Eastern Africa*, pt. 1)
NN L-10 1395 pt.1

Lucas, Maurice.
Renseignements Ethnographiques et Linguistiques sur les Danakils de Tadjourah.
(IN: *Société des Africanistes Journal*, Paris, 1935. v. 5, p. 181–202)
NN QOA

ALGERIA (ALGIERS)

In prehistoric times, present Algeria was made up of people from whom today's Berbers are descended. The Phoenicians settled the area around 1200 B.C. After 146 B.C. much of what is now Algeria became part of the Roman province of Numidia when the Romans established hegemony over the entire North Africa coast. In the seventh century Algeria and all of North

Africa were conquered by the Moslems, and Islam took root. In the eleventh century Algeria was invaded by Saharan nomads, and the coastal Berbers were forced into piracy and an eventual alliance with the Moors in their conquest of Spain. In 1518 Algeria fell to the Turks, who established a bey (governor) and ruled until the arrival in 1830 of the French, who seized Algiers, deposed the bey and established French rule. During the Second World War Algeria served as Allied headquarters, as well as the seat of Charles de Gaulle's provisional French government. In 1954 the Algerians erupted in rebellion against French rule; the rebels' leaders stationed themselves in Cairo and formed a "Provisional Government of Algeria." Algerian independence was finally achieved in 1962.

Censuses were conducted in 1881, 1901, 1906, 1926, 1931, 1936, 1948 and 1954.

The most common surnames in Algiers are Ait, Ali, Brahimi, Hadj and Ould.

Archives

Dépôt Central des Archives Nationales rue Serpagy
Algiers, Algeria

Public and Church Records

Birth and marriage certificates can be obtained from the mayor's office (*La Mairie*) of the place of birth or marriage.

Libraries

Bibliothèque Nationale
avenue Frantz Fanon
Algiers, Algeria

Bibliothèque Municipale
Hôtel de Ville
Constantine, Algeria

Bibliothèque de L'Université
2 rue Didouche Mourad,
Algiers, Algeria

Historical & Genealogical Societies

Société Historique Algérienne
% the Faculty of Arts
University of Algiers
2 rue Didouche Mourad
Algiers, Algeria
(*Révue Africaine*, 1856-)
NN BKA

Books and Articles

Amrouche, Fadhma Aïth Mansour.
Histoire de ma Vie.
Paris, F. Maspero, 1968. 223 p.
NN D-18 7674

Bengana, Bouaziz.
... Le Cheih el Arab: Étude Historique sur la Famille Bengana.
Algiers, J. Carbonel, 1930. 158 p., gen. table.
NN *OFS

Faucon, Narcisse.
Le Livre d'Or de L'Algérie.
Paris, Augustin Challamel, 1890.
v. 1 (617 p.), index.
NN AGC

Grammount, Henri D. de
Histoire d'Alger sous la Domina-
tion Turque, 1515–1830.
Paris, E. Leroux, 1887. 420 p.
NN *OFO

Merad, Ali.
Contribution à l'Histoire de la Dynastie Mu'Minide, 1163–1223.
(IN: Algiers (City). Université, Institut d'Études Orientales, *Annales*. Algiers, 1962. v. 20, pp.
401–79)
NN *OAA

Mouilleseaux, Louis.
Histoire de l'Algérie.
Paris, Product de Paris, 1962. 452
p.
NN D-13 5332

Scherb, Jean Daniel.
Le Soleil ne Chauffe que les Vi-
vants.
Paris, R. Laffont, 1964. 236 p.
(Algerians in France)
NN C-13 3093

Verges, Jacques.
Gli Scomparsi di Algeria, Libro
Verde.
Florence, La Nuova Italia, 1961.
121 p.
NN C-12 1321

ANGOLA (LUANDA)

A southwest African nation, Angola borders South-West Africa,
Zambia and Zaire. The Portuguese settled the region in 1491
and founded the capital city of Luanda in 1575. Angola served
as a slaving center, sending some three million slaves to the
New World by the mid-nineteenth century. By the twentieth,
there were 340,000 white settlers in the country, while the rest
of the population was made up of four major Bantu tribes. In
1961 a rebellion broke out against Portuguese rule. Angola won
independence in 1974. When fighting broke out again in 1975,
after an effort at joint rule by three tribally based political
groups failed, over 3,000 people were killed in Luanda and most
white settlers left the country.

The old Dutch Church records of New Amsterdam reveal that
a number of black Angolans were among the city's inhabitants
as early as the 1640's. The marriage in May 1641 of Lucie
d'Angola, widow of Laurens d'Angola, and Anthony Van Angola,
widower of Cataline d'Angola, is the ninth marriage—and the
first marriage between blacks—noted in these records. The marriage of Jan Fort Orangien, widower of Magdelena Van Angola,

to Marie Grande, widow of Jan Premier, took place on November 24 of the same year. The marriages of Emmanuel Van Angola, "neger," to Phizithiaen D'Angool (Angola), widow of Van Leen Laurens, in 1642, and of Isabel Kisana van Angola to Sebastiaen de Britto van Santo Domingo in 1646 are especially interesting, as these couples were the parents of Barbara Manuels (Emmanuel's daughter) and Francis Bastiaens (Sebastiaen's son), whose genealogical chart appears in illus. 21. It would be interesting to investigate whether the name Kisana, given to Isabel van Angola, holds a clue to her tribal origin.

Archives

Arquivo Histórico Ultramarino (Historical Archives—Overseas Provinces)
Calçada da Boa-Hora 30
Junqueira, Lisbon, Portugal

Libraries

Biblioteca Nazional de Angola
Caixa Postal 1267C
Luanda, Angola

Biblioteca Municipal
Caixa Postal 1227
Luanda, Angola

Books and Articles

Anais de Angola 1630–1635.
Lisbon, 1945. 260 p.
NN Sc P967.3-A

Dias, Antonio A.
Pombeiros de Angola.
Lisbon, 193–. 62 p.
NN *Zan-342 no.35

Gonzaga, Noberto.
Historia de Angola 1482–1963.
Luanda, c. 1969. 380 p.
NN JFD 72-3239

Laszlo, Andreas E.
Doctors, Drums, and Dances.
Garden City, NY, Hanover House, 1955. 284 p.
NN BMP

Miller, Joseph C.
Kings and Kinsmen: Early Mbundu States in Angola.
Oxford, Clarendon Press, 1976. 312 p., index, gen. tables.
(Oxford Studies in African Affairs)
NN JFD 76–9168

BOTSWANA (GABORONE)
(formerly Bechuanaland)

Known as Bechuanaland before gaining its independence in 1966, Botswana is located in southern Africa and bordered by South-West Africa (Namibia), Zambia, Rhodesia and the Republic of South Africa. The area was inhabited by Bushmen in early times, but the direct forebears of today's population are thought to have come from central or eastern Africa in Bantu migrations. In the nineteenth century there were frequent incursions into Botswana by the Boers and by a neighboring tribe called the Matabeles that were finally halted by Khama III, chieftain of the powerful Bamangwato tribe. (Today's President, Sir Seretse Khama, is the grandson of Khama III.) The area was under British protection until 1966. In 1965 a constitution was drawn up, general elections held and the capital city established at Gaborone. In 1966 Bechuanaland became an independent member of the British Commonwealth and adopted the name Botswana.

Archives

Botswana National Archives
Khama Crescent (P.O. Box 239)
Gaborone, Botswana

Libraries

Library
The University of Botswana, Lesotho and Swaziland
P.O. Roma, via Maseru
Lesotho, Southern Africa

Books and Articles

Balima, Mildred Grimes.
Botswana, Lesotho and Swaziland: A Guide to Official Publications, 1868–1968.
Washington, DC, 1971. 84 p.
NN JFF 74-28

Benson, Mary.
Tshekedi Khama.
London, Faber & Faber, 1960. 318 p.
NN D-13 5779

Hole, Hugh M.
The Passing of the Black Kings.
London, P. Allan, 1932. 322 p.
NN BNM

Molema, S.M.
Montshiwa, 1815–1896, Barolong Chief and Patriot.
Cape Town, C. Struik, 1966. 233 p., ports.
NN D-17 6899

Mockford, Julian.
Khama: King of the Bamangwato.
London, J. Cape, 1931. 322 p., charts.
NN BNN

Sillery, A.
Sechele: the Story of an African Chief.
London, G. Ronald, 1954. 224 p.
NN BNN

Sillery, A.
Founding of a Protectorate: History of Bechuanaland 1885–1895.
London, 1965. 267 p.
NN D-16 4762

Stevens, Richard P.
Historical Dictionary of the Republic of Botswana.
Metuchen, NJ, Scarecrow, 1975. 189 p.
NN *R-BNN & Sc 968.1-S

BURUNDI (BUJUMBURA)

The pygmy Twa, the earliest inhabitants of Burundi (east-central Africa), were supplanted by the Bahutu, a Bantu people, and finally the tall Watusi arrived in the fifteenth or sixteenth century and established a lasting supremacy. In 1890 Burundi and neighboring Rwanda were incorporated into German East Africa. In 1916, when Belgium defeated the Germans in Africa, Rwanda and Burundi became a Belgium-mandated territory known as Ruanda-Urundi. In 1962 the kingdom of Burundi attained full independence under the reign of King Mwambutsa IV, but tribal conflict marred the years that followed until, with the abolition of the Watusi monarchy in 1966, the main source of conflict was removed. A republic was established, and former Watusi Premier Michel Micombero became its first President.

Public and Church Records

Officer of Vital Statistics (Officier de L'État Civil)

Libraries

Bibliothèque de l'Université Officielle
B.P. 1320
Bujumbura, Burundi

Bibliothèque Publique
B.P. 960
Bujumbura, Burundi

U.S. Information Service Library
Bujumbura, Burundi

Books and Articles

Gerkens, Georges.
Les Batutsi et les Bahutui: Contribution à l'Anthropologie du Ruanda et de l'Urandi.
Brussels, 1949. 112 p.
(*Institut Royal des Sciences Naturelles de Belgique Bruxelles Memoires. Série 2, Fasc. 31*)
NN PQA +

Maquet, Jacques.
The Premise of Inequality in Ruanda: a Study of Political Relations in a Central African Kingdom.
London, Institute of African Studies, Oxford U. Press, 1961. 199 p.
(Watusi tribe)
NN D-13 2546

Weinstein, Warren.
Historical Dictionary of Burundi.
Metuchen, NJ, Scarecrow Press, 1976. 365 p.
NN JFD 77-966

CAMEROON (YAOUNDÉ)

The west-central African country of Cameroon was given its name in the fifteenth century by Portuguese explorers. Its original inhabitants were the pygmies; today the majority of the people are of Bantu stock. By 1885 Cameroon had become a German colony, but during World War I the British and French occupied the territory and divided it between them under League of Nations mandates. In 1959 the United Nations voted the end of French trusteeship, and a year later French Cameroon became an independent republic. In 1961 the southern part of the British Cameroons voted for reunification with the Cameroon Republic, while the northern part voted for union with Nigeria. A federation of east and west Cameroon was established.

Archives

Archives Nationales
B.P. 1053
Yaoundé, Cameroon

Archives Provinciales de Buea
Buea, Cameroon

Public and Church Records

Certificates are issued by the Office of the Mayor (*La Mairie*) at the place of birth or marriage.

Libraries

Bibliothèque Nationale du Cameroun
B.P. 1053
Yaoundé, Cameroon

Bibliothèque du Centre IFAN de Cameroun
B.P. 339
Yaoundé, Cameroon

Library, Université Fédérale du Cameroun
B.P. 337
Yaoundé, Cameroon

Books and Articles

Delancey, Mark W., and Virginia H. Delancey.
A Bibliography of Cameroon.
New York, Africana Pub. Co., 1975. 673 p., index.
NN *RS-BMH 75-4651

Egerton, F. Clement C.
... African Majesty: A Record of Refuge at the Court of the King of Bangante in the French Cameroons.
New York, Scribner's, 1939. 348 p.
NN QPF

Eyongetah, Tambi.
A History of the Cameroon.
London, 1974. 192 p.
NN JFD 75-4302

Le Vine, Victor T.
Historical Dictionary of Cameroon.
Metuchen, NJ, Scarecrow Press, 1974. 198 p., alpha, biblio., no index.
NN Sc 967.11-L

Personnalités Publiques de l'Afrique Centrale.
Paris, Ediafric, 1972
NN JFM 73-127

CAPE VERDE ISLANDS (PRAIA ON SÃO TIAGO)

The fifteen Cape Verde Islands were uninhabited when the Portuguese discovered them in 1460, but Portuguese colonists arrived to settle in 1462, and African slaves were brought in shortly thereafter. Independence from Portugal was achieved in 1975. Although all the members of the new national assembly belonged to the Party for the Independence of Guinea-Bissau and the Cape Verde Islands, unification with Guinea-Bissau was not achieved.

Archives

Arquivo Histórico Ultramarino (Historical Archives: Overseas Provinces)
Calçada da Boa-Hora 30
Junqueira, Lisbon, Portugal

Books and Articles

Barcellos, Christiano José de Senna.

Subsidios para a historia de Cabo Verde e Guiné; memoria a presentada á Academia real das sciencias de Lisboa.
Lisboa, Academia real das sciencias, 1899–1913.
7 v. in 3. illus, maps
NN G-10 643

CENTRAL AFRICAN EMPIRE/REPUBLIC (BANGUI)

Although many peoples have migrated through the area of today's Central African Republic, its present inhabitants are primarily of Bantu stock. French expeditions penetrated the area in the nineteenth century and named it Ubangi-Shari after its two main rivers. In the twentieth century the territory was linked with that of Chad and became one of the components of French Equatorial Africa. In 1946 the people of Ubangi-Shari were given French citizenship and began sending members to the French parliament, and in 1958 Ubangi-Shari voted to become an autonomous republic within the French Union. Barthélémy Boganda, the first elected President, was killed in a plane crash in 1959 and was succeeded by his cousin, David Dacko. The republic became fully independent in 1965, and President Dacko was ousted in 1966 by Colonel Jean-Bedel Bokassa, chief of the armed forces. Bokassa threw the Communist Chinese mission out of the country and established rule by a Revolutionary Council. In 1976 Colonel Bokassa declared the country an empire and proclaimed himself Emperor Bokassa I.

A census was undertaken in 1959 and during the years 1961–63.

Books and Articles

Kalck, Pierre.
Central African Republic.
New York, 1971. 206 p.
NN JFD 72-5848

Kalck, Pierre.
Histoire de la République Centrafricaine.
Paris, 1974. 341 p.
NN JFD 75-4894

La République Centrafricaine.
Paris, 1966. 96 p.
(*La Cité. Révue de la Cité Universitaire de Paris*, no. 31)
NN *DM+

Vansina, Jan.
Kingdoms of the Savanna.
Madison, WI, U. of WI, 1966. 364 p.
NN D-16 7136

CHAD (FORT LAMY)

The mixed ancestry of present-day Chad reflects centuries of migrations and invasions by Bantu southerners, Sudanese Moslems and Nilotic peoples. Until the last part of the nineteenth century, Chad was dominated by a succession of conquerors and warrior slave traders. The last of these was Sudanese ex-slave Rahan Amoney, a chieftain and slave merchant who conquered the Bornu kingdom. After the beleaguered traditional rulers sought French help against the Sudanese, French troops poured into Chad from Algeria from 1897 to 1900, finally defeating the Sudanese armies. French rule was officially established in 1910 when Chad—along with Gabon, Brazzaville (the present Congo) and Ubangi-Shari—were combined into French Equatorial Africa. In 1940 Chad was the first French territory to join the British fight against the Germans in North Africa. In 1960 France granted Chad full independence, and the Republic of Chad was proclaimed. The major post-independence problem was the antagonism between the Arab population in the north and the Bantus in the south. In 1969 a Moslem uprising was quelled when President Tombalbaye called in French troops.

Archives

Dépôt National d'Archives
Institut National des Sciences Humaines (INSH)
B.P. 503
N'Djamena, Chad

Books and Articles

Malval, Jean Paul
Essai de Chronologie Tchadienne
1707–1940.

Paris, 1974. 156 p.
NN JFF 75-490

Tchad: une Neo-Colonie.
Paris, 1972. 177 p.
NN JFD 73-4251

Vernhes, Monique.
Guerre Coloniale au Tchad.
Lausanne, 1972. 96 p.
NN JFD 74-4226

COMORO ISLANDS (MORONI ON GRANDE COMORE)

These islands were ruled by Moslem Sultans until 1841, when they came under French rule. From 1912 to 1947 they were administered as part of Madagascar. In 1961 they became an autonomous French Overseas Territory. In 1974 all but the non-Moslem island of Mayotte voted for independence in a referendum, and France allowed each island to choose for itself whether to become independent. The Comoro Chamber of Deputies declared the country's independence in 1975 and prevented a Mayotte separatist move.

A census was taken in 1966.

Books and Articles

DeHorsey, Algernon.
On the Comoro Islands.
(IN: *Royal Geo. Soc. of London*, Journal. London, 1864. v. 34, p. 258–63.)
NN KAA

Ferrand, Gabriel.
Les Musulmans à Madagascar et aux Iles Comores. Paris, E. Leroux, 1891–1902. 3 v.
(École des Lettres d'Alger Pub.: *Bull. de Correspondence Africaine. tome 9*)
NN *OBC

Guilloteaux, Erique.
... La Réunion et L'Ile Maurcie, Nossi-Be et les Comores ...
Paris, Perrin et Cie, 1920. 426 p.
NN BLT

Madagascar, Comores, Réunion, Ile Maurice.
Paris, Hachette, 1955. 429 p. (Les Guides Bleu)
NN B-10 18

Tara, Vasile.
Madagascar, Mascareignes et Comores.
Paris, 1969. 383 p.
NN E-13 7508

CONGO (BRAZZAVILLE)

Formerly the French Congo, the Republic of the Congo is in West Africa. The Portuguese explored the area in the 1480's. In 1880 Count Pierre Savorgnan de Brazza (for whom the capital city is named) established French control of the area north of the Congo River. At the Congress of Berlin in 1885 French claims were recognized, and the territory was officially named the Middle Congo. In 1910 it was made a part of French Equatorial Africa. In 1958 the territory became an autonomous member of the French community as the Republic of the Congo. Full independence was achieved in 1960.

One of the first natives of the Congo to live in this country was Anthony de Chongo, who married Francisco (Francesca) de Angola in the Dutch Church in New Amsterdam on November 27, 1644, according to the surviving records, in which surnames provide clues to many early church members' national origins. Emanual Congo was a resident of the city as early as May 6, 1644, when he witnessed the baptism of Phillipe Swartine's daughter, Ann. When his twins, Adam and Eva, were baptized on March 31, 1647, Simon Congo was a witness.

Public and Church Records

Certificates can be obtained from the local Mayor's office (*La Mairie*).

Libraries

Bibliothèque du Centre d'Enseignement Supérieur
B.P. 2025
Brazzaville, Republic of the Congo

Bibliothèque Publique de Brazzaville
B.P. 2025
Brazzaville, Republic of the Congo

Books and articles

Belgian Congo and United States of America Directory.
New York, Moretus Press, 1943–.
NN N-10 183

Belgium Institute Royal Colonial.
Biographie Coloniale Belge.
Bruxelles, G. van Capenhout, 1948–58. 5 v.
NN F-10 9314

Le Congo Belge et ses Coloniaux: Livre d'Or.
Leopoldville, Ed. Stanley, 1953. 552 p.
(Text in French and Flemish)
NN F-10 2250

Encyclopédie de Congo Belge.
Bruxelles, Bieleveld, c. 1950–53. 3 v., no index.
NN *RR BMS

Tangh, B.
Histoire Générale des Migrations des Peuples de l'Ubangi.
(IN: *Congo*, Bruxelles, 1938. année 19, tome 2, p. 361–91)
NN *BMS

DAHOMEY (PORTO NOVO)

The roots of present-day Dahomey stem from the warlike king-dom of Abomey, which lasted from the sixteenth century until 1900. Even the women of the Abomey were soldiers and partici-pated in raids against the Yorubas in the east and the Ashantis in the west. Prisoners taken by the Abomey were sold to Euro-pean slavers. In 1851 the French signed a treaty with King Gezo of Cotonou and established a trading post in the area. When a rebellion broke out within Abomey in 1892, it was put down by the French, who subsequently made the country a part of French West Africa. The territory of Dahomey became fully independent in 1960, with Hubert Maga as its first Presi-dent. In 1963, however, Colonel Chritophe Soglo staged a coup and dissolved the National Assembly. Although national elec-tions were held in 1964, dissension prompted Soglo to intervene once again. In 1968 a military junta overthrew the Soglo govern-ment and almost immediately returned the reins of power to a civilian administration.

Archives

Archives Nationales
Route de l'Inspection
B.P. 6
Porto Novo, Dahomey

Public and Church Records

Birth and marriage certificates are issued by the Mayor's Office (La Mairie) or prefecture at the place where the event took place.

Libraries

Bibliothèque Nationale
Porto Novo, Dahomey

Books and Articles

Akinjogbin, I. A.
Dahomey and Its Neighbors 1708–1818.
Cambridge, Cambridge U. Press, 1967. 234 p.
NN D-18 1828

Bartet, P.
Les Rois du Bas Dahomey.
(IN: Soc. de Geog. De Rochefort, *Bulletin*. Rochefort, 1908. v. 30, p. 179–216)
NN KAA

Dalzel, Archibald.
History of Dahomey, an Inland Kingdom of Africa.
London, Cass, 1967 (orig. 1793). 230 p.
NN F-11 4921

Decalo, Samuel.
Historical Dictionary of Dahomey (People's Republic of Benin)
Metuchen, NJ, Scarecrow Press, 1976. 201 p.
NN JFD 76-5640

Dictionnaire Bio-Bibliographique du Dahomey.
Porto Novo, 1969–.
NN JFK 74-525

Herskovits, Melville J.
Dahomey: An Ancient African Kingdom.
New York, J. J. Augustin, 1938. 2 v.
NN QPE

Le Faivre, Henri.
Les Derniers Rois du Dahomey.
(IN: *Revue d'Histoire des Colonies*, Paris, 1937. année 25, p. 25–76)
NN DS

Le Herisse, A.
L'Ancien Royaume du Dahomey: Moeurs, Religion, Histoire.

Paris, E. Larose, 1911. 384 p.
NN BML

Norris, Robert (d. 1791)
Memoirs of the Reign of Bossa Ahadee, King of Dahomey, an Inland Country of Guiney.
London, Cass, 1968 (orig. 1789). 184 p.
NN D-19 2232

Sarmento, August.
Portugal no Dahome.
Lisboa, Tavares Cardoso, 1891. 134 p.
NN BML

Scholefield, Alan.
The Dark Kingdoms.
London 1975. 194 p.
NN JFD 75-7725

EGYPT (CAIRO)

Egyptian history, under native Egyption rule, is commonly divided into thirty dynasties, beginning with the Menes Dynasty (dated 3400 B.C.) and ending with the conquest of Egypt by Alexander the Great in 332 B.C. At that time Alexandria was founded and became a center of Hellenism. After Alexander's death Egypt fell to General Ptolemy, who founded a dynasty that included the exotic Queen Cleopatra and endured for two centuries, until the Romans took charge of the country after 58 B.C. In A.D. 616 Egypt was conquered by the Persians. They were quickly supplanted by the Arabs in 639, and Islam took the place of Christianity. In 939 Fatimate claimants to the Caliphate invaded Egypt, founded the capital city of Cairo and made Egypt a center of Islamic learning and culture. The Crusades undermined and probably caused the downfall of the Fatimates, who were replaced by the Ayyubite Dynasty founded by the great Saladin. In 1250 the Mamelukes—former slaves— seized the reins of government and maintained a hold on the country until 1517, when the Ottoman Turks arrived. Ottoman rule, as administered by Turkish beys (governors), was frequently disorderly. In 1798 Napoleon conquered Egypt, but he was driven out by the British and the Turks in 1801–05. The Ottoman Emperor appointed a common soldier, Mohammed Ali (1769–1849), as Egyptian Pasha (governor). The office of Pasha was made hereditary, and Egypt became increasingly independent of Ottoman rule. This extravagant dynasty survived until King Ahmed Fouad II (1951–), the infant son of King Farouk (1920–65), was deposed in 1952. In 1869 the Suez Canal was completed, and Ismail Pasha sold increasing numbers of shares in the canal to Britain, leading to almost complete consolidation of British control of the country during the years 1883–1907, with Lord Cromer becoming de facto ruler. Lord Kitchener, who was to become Consul General in Egypt from 1911–14, conquered the Sudan for Britain during this period. In 1914 Turkey joined the Central Powers, and Egypt became a British Protectorate. After World War I Egyptian nationalists, led by Zaghlul Pasha, demanded freedom. A treaty of independence finally went into effect in 1923, and Egypt was proclaimed a constitutional monarchy under Faud I. The monarchy was deposed in 1952 by a military coup led by General Mohammed Naguib, who became the first President of the new Egyptian Republic in 1953. He was replaced by Colonel Gamal Abdul Nasser soon after. In 1958 Egypt and Syria joined to form the United Arab Republic, but Syria withdrew from the federation in 1961.

Censuses were taken every ten years between 1897 and 1947. The most recent Egyptian census was taken in 1976.

The most common surnames in Alexandria are Åbd-al-, Hamīd, Ahmad, Ibrāhīm, Mahmud and Muhammad; in Cairo, Åbd-al-, Hamīd, Ahmad, Hasan, Mahmūd and Muhammad.

Archives

National Archives
Citadel
Cairo, Egypt

Public and Church Records

Birth certificates can be obtained from the appropriate Public Health Office of the Ministry of Municipal and Rural Affairs having jurisdiction over the locality in which the birth occurred. Marriage certificates for foreigners of the same religious denomination (all Christians are considered to be of the same denomination) and same nationality can be obtained from the ecclesiastical authority who performed the marriage. Egyptians and couples with different religious denominations should apply to the Office of the Shahr el Akari (14 Sharia Mahdy, Ezbekieh, Cairo, Egypt).

Libraries

Alexandria Municipal Library
18 Sharia Menasce Moharrem Beey
Alexandria, Egypt

Alexandria University Library
6 Sharia Kenissa El-Inguilizia
Stanley Bay, Ramleh
Alexandria, Egypt

American University in Cairo Library
113 Sharia Kasr El-Aini
Cairo, Egypt

Cairo University Library
Sharia Hadiket El-Ormane
Cairo, Egypt

Egyptian Library
Abdin Palace
Cairo, Egypt

Egyptian (National) Library (Dar-ul-Kutub)
Midan Ahmed
Cairo, Egypt

Library of the Greek Orthodox Patriarchate of Alexandria
166 rue Port Said
Alexandria, Egypt

Books and Articles

Bakri, Muhammad T. al-
A Genealogy of the Family of Al-Bakri ...

Cairo, 1905. 416 p.
NN *OFS

Bergue, Jacques.
Egypt, Imperialism and Revolution.
London, Faber & Faber, 1972. 736 p., index.
NN *R-BLB 73-377

David, Ann Rosalie.
The Egyptian Kingdoms.
London, Elsevier-Phaidon, 1976. 137 p., index.

L'Egypt Nouvelle.
... Livre d'Or—Golden Book.
Cairo, 1938. 127 leaves, illus.
NN BLB+

Holt, Peter M.
Studies in the History of the Near East.
London, 1973. (Egyptian history, 1517–1882)
NN JFD 74-4000

Lane-Poole, Stanley.
The Art of the Saracens in Egypt.
Beirut, 1971. 264 p. (Kings and rulers of Egypt)
NN MAF 72-1539

Lauer, Jean Philippe.
Saqqara: The Royal Cemetery of Memphis: Excavations and Discoveries Since 1850.
London, Thames and Hudson, 1976. 248 p., index.
NN *OBL 76-1722

Legrain, Georges.
Recherches sur la Famille dont fit Partie Montouemhat.
(IN: *Recueil de Traveaux Relatifs à la Philologie et à Archaéologie Égyptiennes et Assyriennes.*

Paris, 1911–14. v. 33, p. 180–92; v. 34, p. 97–104, 168–75; v. 35, p. 207–16; v. 36, p. 57–68, 145–52)
NN *OBKG

Louca, Anouar.
Voyageurs et Écrivains Égyptiens en France au XIXe Siècle.
Paris, 1970. 363 p.
NN JFE 73-1802

Rivlin, Helen A. B.
The Dār al-Wathā'iq in Ābdīn Palace at Cairo as a Source for the Study of the Modernization of Egypt in the Nineteenth Century.
Leiden, 1970. 134 p.
NN *OFP 72-442

Tanner, Henry.
New Millionaires Flourishing in Egypt's Liberalized Economy.
(IN: *New York Times*, NY, 10 Feb. 1976. p. 3, col. 1–6.)

Tugay, Emine Foat.
Three Centuries; Family Chronicles of Turkey and Egypt, with a foreword by the Dowager Marchioness of Reading.
Westport, CT, Greenwood Press, 1974 (orig. London, Oxford U. Press, 1963). 324 p., index, gen. tables.
(The royal family of Egypt by a cousin of King Farouk)
NN AVHH (Mohamed Ali)

Turner, Adrian.
The Ptolemies of Egypt: A Genealogical History.
(IN: *Coat of Arms*, London, 1950. v. 1, no. 2, p. 49–54)
NN AWA

Who's Who in Egypt and the Near East.
Cairo, J. E. Blattner, 1946–58.
NN L-10 3788

Who's Who in the U.A.R. and Near East.
Cairo, J. E. Blattner, 1959–.
(UAR, Sudan, Iran, Libya, Cyprus, Iraq, Saudi Arabia, India, Pakistan, Ceylon, Indonesia, Ethiopia and Aden)
NN *R-Room 219 and L-10 3783

EQUATORIAL GUINEA (SANTA ISABEL)
(formerly Spanish Guinea)

The island territory of Equatorial Guinea was first named Fernando Po, after the Portuguese explorer who discovered it in the fifteenth century. In 1778 the island was ceded to Spain, along with trading rights on the mainland. In the nineteenth century the island port of Santa Isabel was leased to the British, who used it as a naval base, although it also became a haven for freed slaves. In 1958 the island and mainland colony became a province of Spain called Spanish Guinea. Its inhabitants, made up of Fernandinos (descendants of freed African slaves), native Bubis and Spaniards—along with the Fangs, who were the main tribal group on the mainland—began to send members to the Spanish Cortes (parliament). In 1963 the province was renamed Equatorial Guinea, and limited self-government was initiated. Equatorial Guinea became fully independent in 1968.

A census was taken in 1950.

Archives

Dirección General De Archivos, Bibliotecas y Museos Biblioteca Pública
Santa Isabel, Equatorial Guinea

Books and Articles

Cervera Pery, José.
La Marina Española en Guinea Ecuatorial.

Santa Isabel, 1968. 168 p.
NN JFD 73-4765

Pélissier, Réné.
Los Territorios Españoles de Africa.
Madrid, 1964. 94 p.
NN E-12 6774

Unzueta y Yuste, Abelardo.
... Guinea Continental Española.
Madrid, 1944. 394 p.
NN BMP

ETHIOPIA (ADDIS ABABA)

Ethopia traditionally dates its origins from 1000 B.C., when the Queen of Sheba had her first son by King Solomon. Between that time and the first century A.D., Ethopia became pagan. In the fourth century the Aksumite king converted to Coptic Christianity, and Ethiopia remained Coptic even though it became surrounded by hostile Moslem neighbors from the seventh century on with the rise of Islam. In 1270 the Solomonic line was restored, bringing a measure of stability to the country. Foreign embassies were first permitted in the sixteenth century, but with the restoration of Coptic Christianity in the seventeenth, all foreigners were expelled. During the next two centuries civil war and anarchy prevailed, resulting in the destruction of all Ethiopian monuments. In 1855 the chieftain Kasa conquered Tigre and Shoa and extended his rule over most of the country. Later in the nineteenth century a Shoa ruler, Menelik II, united the country with the assistance of the Italians. In 1895 Italy invaded but finally withdrew after sustaining severe losses. In 1916 Menelik's daughter Judith became empress, with her cousin,

Ras Tafari Makonnen, as her regent and heir. At her death in 1930 he became Emperor Haile Selassie (1892–1975). The Italian threat was renewed in the 1930's and this time was successful. The Italians overran Ethiopia and Haile Selassie fled. After Italy's defeat in the East African campaign during World War II, Selassie returned with Ethiopian and British armies to the capital city of Addis Ababa. In 1952 the former Italian colony of Eritrea was federated with Ethiopia. In 1955 the constitution was revised to provide for a popularly elected Chamber of Deputies and the first elections were held. In 1973 HIM Haile Selassie (K.G.) was deposed by a military coup, and in 1975 the monarchy was abolished entirely.

Public and Church Records

Vital record certificates for residents of the capital are obtained from the Municipality of Addis Ababa, Box 356, Menelik II Square, Addis Ababa, Ethiopia. In other cities they are issued by the chief municipal authority. Persons born in outlying villages may in some cases obtain the required data from the Senior Divisional Officer in the district concerned.

Libraries

National Library
P.O. Box 717
Addis Ababa, Ethiopia

University Library
P.O. Box 399
Addis Ababa, Ethiopia

Books and Articles

Abir, Mordechai.
Ethiopia: the Era of the Princes.
London and Harlow; Longman's Green; 1968. 208 p.
NN JFD-72-1528

Bibliography of Ethiopia.
Addis Ababa, 1968. 46 p.
NN JFC 71–1169

Gilkes, Patrick.
The Dying Lion: Feudalism and Modernization in Ethiopia. Devies, Wilts, England, Davison Pub. Ltd., 1975 (orig. London, Friedman, 1975). 307 p., index, gen. tables.

Haile Selassie: HIM Emperor obit. (IN: *The Monarchist*, London, 1975–76. no. 46–47, p. 56–58)

Heeren, Arnold H. L.
Historical Researches into the Politics, Intercourse and Trade of the Carthaginians, Ethiopians and Egyptians.
London, 1850. 520 p.
NN Sc 939-H

Lord, Edith.
Queen of Sheba's Heirs.
Washington, DC, 1970. 320 p.
NN JFE 72-791

Marcus, Harold G.
The Modern History of Ethiopia and the Horn of Africa.

Stanford, CA, Stanford U. Press, 1972. 641 p.
NN JFF 74-924

Mathew, David.
Ethiopia: A Study of a Policy, 1540–1935.

Westport, CT, Greenwood Press, 1974 (orig. 1947). 254 p., index.
NN *R-BLK 76-2762

Pankhurst, Richard K. P.
The Ethiopian Royal Chronicles (Extract).
Addis Ababa, Oxford U. Press, 1967. 210 p.
NN C-13 8784

Pankhurst, Sylvia.
Ethiopia: A Cultural History.
Woodford Green, Essex, Lalibela House, 1971 (orig. 1955).
747 p., index.
NN *R-BLK

Stokvis, A. M. H. J.
Manuel d'Histoire, de Généalogie de Tous les États du Globe ...
Amsterdam, B. M. Israel, 1966 (orig. 1888–93), v. 1, p. 439–46 (Abessinie)
NN APC

Zanutto, Silvio.
Bibliografia Etiopica.
Rome, 1932–36. 2 v.
NN *R-BLK 75-2574

GABON (LIBREVILLE)

Gabon's coastal area was first explored by the Portuguese in the fifteenth century, but the country's interior—a dense jungle—was not penetrated by Europeans until the nineteenth century, when the French made treaties with the coastal chieftains and began exploration inland. In 1890 Gabon became a part of the French Congo and in 1910 was declared a separate colony and incorporated into French Equatorial Africa. In 1913 Albert Schweitzer, an Alsatian doctor, set up a medical mission at Lambarene, his work there eventually leading to a Nobel Peace Prize. After a period of autonomy within the French Community, the republic of Gabon became fully independent in 1960. Leon M'Ba, premier of the provisional government, was elected President. Vice President Albert-Bernard Bongo assumed the presidency at M'Ba's death, which occurred early in his second term, in 1967. Bongo established a one-party system in 1968.

Archives

Archives Nationales
B.P. 1188 ou 2188
Libreville, Gabon

Books and Articles

Deschamps, Hubert J.
Quinze Ans de Gabon, les Débuts
   de l'Establishment Français,
   1839–1853.
Paris, 1965. 345 p.
NN E-13 8110

Meyo-Bebang, Frédéric.
Aperçu Historique du Gabon.
Libreville, c. 1973. 141 leaves, illus.
   t of c at end, no index.
NN JFF 76-489

Patterson, David K.
The Northern Gabon Coast to
   1875.
Oxford, 1975. 167 p.
NN Sc 967.21-P

Reynard, Robert.
Recherches sur la Presence des
   Portugais au Gabon XVe-XIXe
   Siècles.
(IN: French Equatorial Africa, In-
   stitut d'Études Centrafricains,
   Brazzaville, *Bulletin*.
Brazzaville, 1959. no 9, p. 15–66)
NN BMK

Walter, André.
Notes d'Histoire du Gabon.
Montpellier, Charité, 1960. 158 p.
NN F-10 5865

GAMBIA (BANJUL)

Gambia, Africa's smallest nation, is almost surrounded by neighboring Senegal. Claimed by Portugal in the fifteenth century,
when its explorers first discovered the territory, Gambia was
purchased by Britain in 1588 and became that country's first
African colony. French and British disputes over the borders of
Senegal and Gambia were resolved in 1888, and Gambia became
a Crown Colony. Gambia was granted independence in 1965 and
proclaimed itself a republic in 1970.

Archives

Public Records Office
The Quadrangle
Banjul, Gambia

Public and Church Records

Civil registration began in 1845 for
   births, 1835 for marriages and
   1834 for deaths. Local Anglican
   mission records date from 1832
for marriages, 1834 for baptisms
and 1855 for burials. Local mission records conclude in 1887.

Books and Articles

Gailey, Harry A.
Historical Dictionary of Gambia.
Metuchen, NJ, Scarecrow Press,
   1975. 171 p., alpha, biblio., no
   index.
NN *R-BMH 76-5123

Gailey, Harry A.
A history of Gambia.
London, RKP, 1964. 244 p., index.
NN *R-BMH

Gray, John Milner.
A History of Gambia.
Cambridge, Cambridge U. Press,
1940. 508 p., index.
NN *RR-BMB

GHANA (ACCRA)
(formerly the Gold Coast)

In pre-colonial times, what is now Ghana was controlled by various neighboring Negro kingdoms. In the fifteenth century the Portuguese arrived and began a brisk trade in gold, which caused the area to be known as the Gold Coast. Slave trading, which soon replaced gold trading, was banned by the British in the nineteenth century. In 1874 Britain established the colony of the Gold Coast. In 1922 a section of neighboring Togoland, a former German colony, was mandated to Britain by the League of Nations and governed as part of the Gold Coast. In 1942 a movement for independence arose in the area, led by Joseph B. Dangaugh and Kwame Nkrumah, who were imprisoned by the British in 1948. When Nkrumah was released in 1949, he formed the Convention People's Party and initiated a campaign of civil disobedience. In 1951 a new constitution promised greater autonomy for Ghanians, and in the subsequent general election Nkrumah became the Prime Minister. In 1957 the state of Ghana, composed of the Gold Coast and British Togoland, became the first black African colony to achieve independence, and in 1960 Ghana was proclaimed a republic within the Commonwealth.

Censuses were taken in 1960 and 1970.

Archives

Central Government Archives
P.O. Box 3056
Accra, Ghana

Public and Church Records

Vital records date back to 1855.

Registrar-General's Office
P.O. Box 118
Accra, Ghana

Libraries

Accra Central Library
Thorpe Road
P.O. Box 663
Accra, Ghana

Ashanti Regional Library
Bantama Road
P.O. Box 824
Kumasi, Ghana

University of Ghana Library
(Balme Library)

P.O. Box 24
Legon, Ghana

Historical and Genealogical Societies

Historical Society of Ghana
University of Ghana
P.O. Box 25
Legon, Nr. Accra, Ghana

Books and Articles

Advance Pub. Co., Ltd.
Accra-Tema in Pictures.
Accra, 1969. 168 p. (Biographies)
NN Sc 916.67-A

Amedekey, E. Y.
The Culture of Ghana.
Accra, 1970. 215 p.
NN *RS-BMK 72-1838

Apraku, L. D.
A Prince of the Akans.
Accra, Waterville Pub., 1964. 58 p.
NN C-14 2879

Bourret, F. M.
The Gold Coast: A Survey of the
   Gold Coast and British Togo-
   land, 1919–1946.
Stanford, Stanford U. Press, 1949.
   231 p.
NN BKM

Cardinall, Allan W.
A Bibliography of the Gold Coast.
Westport, CT, Greenwood Press,
   1970. 384 p.
NN JFD 72-8433

Claridge, William W.
A History of the Gold Coast and

Ashanti, from Earliest Times to
   the Commencement of the
   Twentieth Century. 2nd ed.
New York, Barnes & Noble, 1964.
   2 v., gen. tables.
NN D-15 8388

Dumett, Raymond E.
Survey of Research Materials in
   the National Archives of
   Ghana.
Basel, Schwäbisch Gmünd, 1974. 48
   p.
NN JFK 74-131 heft 11

Ephson, Issac S.
Gallery of Gold Coast Celebrities,
   1632–1958.
Accra, Ilen Pub., 1969 (c. 1970–71).
   1 v.
NN L-11 4116

Freestone, Basil.
Osei Tutu: The Leopard Owns the
   Land.
London, Dobson, 1968. 183 p.
(Ashanti kings and rulers)
NN D-18 8077

Historical Society of Ghana.
Transactions
Legon, c. 1955–.
NN K-10 3727

Johnson, Albert F.
A Bibliography of Ghana 1930–1961
Evanston, IL, Northwestern U.
   Press, 1969. 210 p.
NN D-15 6208

Meyowitz, Eva L-R.
The Early History of the Akan
   States of Ghana.
London, Red Candle Press, 1974.
   228 p., index.
NN JFD 76-2136

Oppong, Christine.
Marriage Among a Matrilineal Elite.
London, 1974. 186 p.
NN Sc 301.42.0

Ward, W. E. F.
A History of Ghana. 4th ed., revised.
London, Allen & Unwin, 1967. 454 p., index.
NN *R-BMK

GUINEA (CONAKRY)
(formerly French Guinea)

At different times from the tenth through the fifteenth centuries Guinea was a part of the empires of Ghana, Mali and Songhai. The Portuguese, who established trade contact in the fifteenth century, were followed by the Dutch, English and French. In 1849 the French set up a protectorate, but attempts to penetrate the interior of the country were resisted by Malinke and Fulani chieftains. In 1898 the French defeated the popular chieftain Samory Touré. In 1958 Guinea, then a territory of French West Africa, was the only country to refuse membership in the French community. It became an independent republic, with Sékou Touré (who claimed to be a descendant of Samory Touré) its President.

Archives

Direction de La Bibliothèque et des Archives Nationales
B.P. 561
Conakry, Guinea

Libraries

Bibliothèque Nationale
Conakry, Guinea

Books and Articles

Bitteli, Urs.
Die Endeckung des Schwarzen Afrikaners versuch einer Geistesgeschichte der Europäisch-Afrikanischen.
Zürich, Atlantis, 1970. 247 p.
(Guinea coast, 17 and 18th centuries)
NN E-14 2155

Études Guinées.
Conakry, 1947–55. no. 1–13.
NN *ZAN 728 film

Houis, Maurice.
La Guinée Française.
Paris, Ed. Maritimes et Coloniales, 1953. 94 p.
(Pays Africains no. 3)
NN D-12 736

Rouget, Fernand.
La Guinée.
Crete, Corbeil, E., 1906. 459 p.
NN E-10 5096

Unzuetay Yuste, Albelvardo de.
... Islas del Golfo do Guinea (Elobeyes, Corsico, Annobon, Principe y Santo Tomé).
Madrid, 1945. 386 p.
NN BMT

GUINEA-BISSAU (BISSAU)
(formerly Portuguese Guinea)

Guinea-Bissau (Portuguese Guinea) was a Portuguese colony until it won independence in 1974. The Portuguese reached the area in 1446, participated in the slave trade in the seventeenth and eighteenth centuries and colonized the area in the nineteenth century. In the 1960's the African Party for Independence of Guinea-Bissau and the Cape Verde Islands created their own government with an elected national assembly, and guerrilla warfare was conducted against Portuguese troops. The founder of the liberation movement, Dr. Amilcar Cabral, was murdered in 1973, and his brother Luiz became the first President. The Cape Verde Islands did not, as was expected, merge with Guinea-Bissau but achieved their own independence.

Archives

Arquivo Histórico Ultramarino (Historical Archives—Overseas Provinces)
Calçada da Boa-Hora 30
Junqueira, Lisbon, Portugal

Historical and Genealogical Societies

Centro de Estudos da Guine Portuguesa (Includes a library)
Caiza Postal 37
Bissau, Guinea-Bissau

Books and Articles

Aguiar, Armando de.
Guine Minha Terra.
Lisbon, 1964. 174 p.
NN D-16 7262

Barcellos, Christiano José de Senna.
Subsidos para a Historia de Cabo Verde e Guine ...
Lisbon, 1899–1913. 7 v.
NN G-10 643

Carvalho Viegas, Luis Antonio de.
Guine Portuguesa.
Lisbon, 1936–40. 3 v.
NN L-10 9309

Eannes de Azurara, Gomes.
The Chronicle of the Discovery and Conquest of Guinea.
London, Hakluyt Soc., 1896–99. 2 v.
NN KBD Hakluyt no. 95/100

Lyall, Archibald.
Black and White Make Brown: An Account of a Journey to the Cape Verde Islands.
London, W. Heinemann, 1938. 303 p.
NN BYV

Russell, Peter F.
Fontes Documentais Castelhanas para Historia de Expansao Portuguesa na Guinea nos Ultimos anos de D. Afonso V.
(IN: *Portugal, Centro de Estudos Historicals, do Tompo e da Historia.* Lisbon, 1971. v. 4, p. 5–33)
NN L-11 1207 v. 4

IVORY COAST (ABIDJAN)

The Agni, Baoule and Senufo are the chief tribes in the region. In the sixteenth century the Portuguese established coastal trading settlements. By 1842 there was a French military protectorate along the coast, and in 1893 a protectorate over the entire country was proclaimed. Strong resistance by local tribes delayed occupation of the interior, but the Ivory Coast was incorporated into French West Africa, which included Senegal, Guinea, Mali, Upper Volta, Mauritania, Dahomey and Niger. In 1958 the country achieved autonomy within the French community. In 1960 it declared itself independent, and Felix Houphouët-Boigny was elected President.

A census was undertaken in 1956–57.

Archives

Archives Nationales
1 avenue du Gouverneur Général
Van Vollenhoven (B.P. 1770)
Abidjan, Ivory Coast

Public and Church Records

Civil registration for births, deaths, marriages and divorces began in 1893; records are housed in the Mayor's Office, City Hall, of each city. For Catholic Church records, write:

Archevêché de Côte d'Ivoire
B.P. 1287
Abidjan, Ivory Coast

For Protestant records:

Église Methodiste de C.I.
B.P. 121
Abidjan, Ivory Coast

For Islamic records:

Mosquee de Treichville
Treichville, Ivory Coast

Libraries

Bibliotheque de L'Université
d'Abidjan B.P. 1880
Abidjan, Ivory Coast

Bibliothèque du Service d'Information
B.P. 1879
Abidjan, Ivory Coast

Bibliothèque Centrale de Côte d'Ivoire
B.P. 6243
Abidjan-Treichville, Ivory Coast

Centre National de Documentation
B.P. 398
Abidjan, Ivory Coast

Books and Articles

Abidjan, Ivory Coast. Université. Annales. Series F: Ethnosociologie. Abidjan, 1969–.
NN JFL 72-161

Abidjan, Ivory Coast. Université. Annales. Series I: Histoire.

Abidjan, 1972–.
NN JFL 76-316

Davis, Hassoldt.
Sorcerer's Village.
London, Harrap, 1956. 272 p , illus.
NN D-10 248

Janvier, Geneviève.
Bibliographie de la Côte-d'Ivoire.

Abidjan, 1973. 1 v.
NN JFL 75-572

Mouëzy, Henri.
Assinie et le Royaume de Krin-
jabo; Histoire et Coutumes. 2nd
éd.
Paris, Larose, 1953. 286 p.
NN BMG

KENYA (NAIROBI)
(formerly Abyssinia)

In ancient times the coast of Kenya was well known to Phoenicians, Egyptians and Greeks. The Arabs set up colonies on the
coast in the eighth century A.D. The Portuguese began to share
in the already prosperous spice and slave trade in the fifteenth
century. The British became dominant in the nineteenth century
and established a protectorate over the area in 1895. South
African and British settlers began to come in large numbers.
In 1944 the Africans won appointment of the first black member
to the Legislative Council. Jomo Kenyatta, a Mau Mau leader,
was released from prison in 1961 and headed the Kenya African
National Union (KANU) in the Legislative Council. In 1964
Kenya became a republic within the British Commonwealth,
with Kenyatta its first President. In 1968 thousands of Asians
left the country because of the government's policy of "Kenyan-
ization" of business and commerce.

The first census, 1911, and those of 1921, 1926, 1931 did not
include Africans. The first complete census was taken in 1948;
another, in 1969.

Archives

Kenya National Archives
Jogoo House
P.O. Box 30520
Nairobi, Kenya

Public and Church Records

General Address for birth and
marriage certificates:

Registrar General's Office
P.O. Box 30031
Nairobi, Kenya

Divorce registration:

Registrar General of the High
Court

Civil registration of births and
deaths of Europeans and Americans and deaths of any person

in a municipality became compulsory in 1904. Registration of births and deaths of Asians became compulsory on June 9, 1928, and registration for Africans became compulsory, district by district, at various dates between March 12, 1963, and September 1971.

Marriages of Europeans and Americans and Africans contracted under the Marriage Act, since November 1902, have been registered. There is no official registration of Asian or Hindu marriages or African marriages under customary law. Registration of Mohammedan marriages is administered by the Minister of Mohammedan Marriages (P.O. Box 45687, Nairobi).

Burial in a public cemetery—unusual except for immigrants—is recorded in the Office of the District Commissioner. Baptism and burial records are kept by individual churches. For more information:

The Church Missionary Society Office
P.O. Box 40360
First Ngung Avenue
Nairobi, Kenya

Libraries

British Council Library
Kenya Cultural Centre
Government Road
Nairobi, Kenya

Desai Memorial Library
P.O. Box 791
Nairobi, Kenya

United States Information Service Library
P.O. Box 30143
Nairobi, Kenya

University College Library
P.O. Box 30197
Nairobi, Kenya

Historical and Genealogical Societies

Kenya History Society
P.O. Box 14474
Westlands, Nairobi, Kenya

Books and Articles

Abuor, C. Ojwando.
White Highlands No More.
Nairobi, Pan African Researchers, 1971. 440 p.
NN JFD 75-526

Kaggwa, Sir Apolo.
The Kings of Buganda.
Nairobi, East African Pub. House, 1971. 256 p.
NN Sc 967.61-K

King, Kenneth J.
Kenya Historical Biographies.
Nairobi, 1971. 192 p.
NN JFK 72-106

Muriuki, Godfrey.
A History of the Kikuyu, 1500–1900.
Nairobi, Oxford University Press, 1974. 190 p.
NN Sc 572.9676-M

Remole, Robert A.
White Settlers or the Foundations of European Agricultural Settlement in Kenya.
Cambridge, MA, 1959. 421 leaves.
NN Sc Micro R-1758

Salim, A. I.
The Swahili-Speaking Peoples of
  Kenya's Coast, 1895–1965.
Nairobi, 1973. 272 p.
NN Sc 967.62-S

Tignor, Robert L.
The Colonial Transformation of
  Kenya, the Kamba, Kikuyu and
  Masai from 1900 to 1939.
Princeton, NJ, Princeton U. Press,
  1976. 372 p., index.
NN JLE 76-3451

LESOTHO (MASERU)
(formerly Basutoland)

The Basotho people, target of Zulu and Matabele raids in the
early nineteenth century, were united as Basutoland by Moshesh (Moshoeshoe) I. The king sought the protection of the British
Cape Colony when the Boers from the Orange Free State made
incursions into Basutoland. Annexation by the Colony came in
1868, but Basutoland became a separate British protectorate
again in 1884. In 1910 the British administration in Basutoland
set up a Basutoland council consisting of Basotho chiefs. When
Basutoland became independent in 1966 it took the name Lesotho. In 1970 Prime Minister Leabua Sonathon seized control and
suspended the constitution.

Censuses for Basutoland were taken in 1911, 1946 and 1956;
for Lesotho, in 1966.

Archives

Government Archives
Education Department
P.O. Box 47
Maseru, Lesotho

Libraries

British Council Library
P.O. Box 429
Maseru, Lesotho

Library, the University of Bot-
  swana, Lesotho and Swaziland
P.O. Roma, via Maseru
Lesotho, South Africa

Books and Articles

Becker, Peter.
Hill of Destiny: The Life and
  Times of Moshesh, Founder of
  the Basotho.
Harlow, England, Longmans,
  1969. 294 p.
NN D-20 1321

Brading, Barbara.
Basutoland: Portrait of a Protec-
  torate.
London, 1961. 255 p.
NN D-15 2558

Casalis, Eugene.
The Basutos, or Twenty-three
  Years in South Africa.

London, J. Nisbet, 1861. 355 p.
NN QPE

Halper, Jack.
South Africa's Hostages: Basutoland, Bechuanaland, and Swaziland.
Baltimore, MD, Penguin, 1965. 495
p.
NN C-13 1552

Smith, Ernest W.
The Mabilles of Basutoland.

London, Hodder and Stoughton,
1939. 382 p.
NN AN (Mabille, A.)

Stevens, Richard P.
Lesotho, Botswana and Swaziland.
London, Pall Mall Press, 1967. 294
p., index.
NN *R-BNN

Tylden, G.
The Rise of the Basuto.
Cape Town, Juta, 1950. 270 p.
NN BNG

LIBERIA (MONROVIA)

Liberia is a western African nation whose indigenous Kru, Gola,
Mandingo and Vai are thought to be descended from the peoples
of ancient black empires farther north. In 1816 the American
Colonization Society was founded to send freed slaves to western
Africa; in 1822 the first colony was established on Providence
Island, the site of Monrovia, Liberia's capital city. Monrovia was
named after United States President James Monroe in 1824, while
the name Liberia was adopted for the whole territory. The first
settlers endured a great deal of hardship, including attacks by
native tribes. In 1847 the governor of the Liberian Commonwealth, Joseph Jenkins Roberts, a freeman of part-black ancestry,
declared Liberia an independent republic and became its first
President. The years from 1850 to 1920 were difficult; territory
was lost to British and French colonies and the Liberian economy
declined. In 1943 True Whig party candidate William V. S. Tubman
won the presidency and began a policy of integration of the
"Americo-Liberian" (descendants of the first settlers) and the
tribal people. In 1967 Tubman was elected to a sixth successive
term—the longest tenure for any elected head of government
in Africa.

The first census was taken in 1930 and another in 1956.

Public and Church Records

Civil registration for births, deaths and marriages began in 1932; for divorces, in 1925.

Ministry of Public Health and Social Welfare
Monrovia, Liberia

For wills and deeds, write:

Clerk of the Probate Court
Temple of Justice
Monrovia, Liberia

For information on religious records, consult:

Ministry of Information, Cultural and Tourism
Monrovia, Liberia

Libraries

Government Public Library
Ashmun Street.
Monrovia, Liberia

Liberian Information Service Library
Monrovia, Liberia

United States Information Service Library
Broad Street.
Monrovia, Liberia

University of Liberia Library
University of Liberia
Monrovia, Liberia

Books and Articles

American Colonization Society Records, 1792–1964.
Washington, DC, 1971. microfilm 165 feet, 190,000 items.
NN Metro-NNC

Blyden, Edward W., 1832–1912.
Sierra Leone and Liberia: Their Origin, Work and Destiny.
London, 1884. 56 p.
NN Sc Micro R-863 Pt.O

Directory with Who's Who in Liberia. 1st ed. 1970–71.
Monrovia, 1970.
NN JFL 75-500

Foote, Andrew Hull, 1806–1863.
Africa and the American Flag.
New York, D. Appleton, 1854. 390 p.
NN D-19 5874 also 1969 reprint in JFD 70-47

Fraenkel, Merron.
Tribe and Class in Monrovia.
London, International African Institute by Oxford Press, 1964.
NN D-15 5665

Gurley, Ralph R.
Life of Jehudi Ashmun, Late Colonial Agent in Liberia . . . 2nd ed.
New York, Robinson & Franklin, 1839. 396 p.
NN AN (Ashmun, J.)

Holsoe, Svend E.
A Bibliography on Liberia.
Newark, DE, U. of Delaware, 1971–. 1 v.
NN JFM 76-102

Huberich, Charles H.
The Political and Legislative History of Liberia . . .
New York Central Book Co., 1947. 2 v.
NN E-11 743

Innes, William.
Liberia: or the Early History and Signal Preservation of the

American Colony of Free Negroes.
Edinburgh, Waugh & Innes, 1831. 152 p.
NN BMI

Latrobe, John H. B.
Maryland in Liberia. A History of the Colony Planted by the Maryland State Colonization Society ... at Cape Palmas ... Africa 1833–1853.
Baltimore, MD, J. Murphy, 1885. 138 p.
NN BMI

Liberia College, Monrovia, Liberia.
Catalogue of Liberia College (1862), Monrovia, Liberia, West Africa, for 1916 and Historical Register.

Brookline, MA, Riverdale Press, 1919. 46 p.
NN SSR

Marinelli, Lawrence A.
The New Liberia: A Historical and Political Survey.
New York, F. A. Praeger, 1964. 244 p.
NN *R-BMI and D-15 8099

Mower, J. H.
The Republic of Liberia.
(IN: *JHN*, Washington, DC, 1947. v. 32, p. 265–306)
NN IEC

Shick, Tom W.
Emigrants to Liberia 1820 to 1843.
Newark, NJ, 1971. 111 leaves.
NN Sc 929.3-S

LIBYA (TRIPOLI, BENGAZI)

In ancient times Libya was ruled successively by Carthage, Rome and the Vandals. In the seventh century A.D. the Arabs conquered the country. Libya became a part of the Ottoman Empire in 1551, but the local pashas (governors) retained considerable authority. In 1830 Turkish control tightened. After the Turko-Italian War (1911–12) Italy occupied Libya, and until 1933 the Italians were involved in wars of pacification against a Muslim religious brotherhood, the Sanusi. During World War II the Allies took Libya, and two separate military administrations were set up by the French and the British. In 1951 Libya won independence. Idris I, a leader of the Sanusi, became the first king of Libya. In 1969 he was overthrown by a military junta led by Colonel Muammar el-Qaddafi, and the Arab Republic of Libya was proclaimed.

Censuses were taken in 1936 and 1954.

Archives

Department of Antiquities, Archives Section
Tripoli, Libya

Public and Church Records

Civil records can be obtained from the Vital Statistics offices of municipalities or from the Mudirah (Directorate) of an outlying area through the Mutasarrif (District Governor).

Muslim records can be obtained from the Shar'iyah Court (Muslim Canon Law Courts) of municipalities or the Chief of the Qabilah (Tribe) in villages.

For Catholic Church records, write:

Parocco (Priest)
Bengazi Cathedral
Bengazi, Libya

For Jewish records:

Head of the Jewish Community
Umar Mukhtar Street
Bengazi, Libya

Libraries

Government Library

14 Shar'a al-Jazair
Tripoli, Libya

Islamic University Sayid Muhammad Ali Sanusi Library
Beida, Libya

University of Libya Library
Bengazi, Libya

Books and Articles

Dearden, Seton.
A Nest of Corsairs: The Fighting Karamanlis of Tripoli.
London, J. Murray, 1976. 331 p., index.
NN SFD 76-8134

Murabet, Mohammed.
A Bibliography of Libya.
Valetta, Malta, 1959. 868 p.
NN JFD 73-7306

Villard, Henry S.
Libya, the New Arab Kingdom of North Africa.
Ithaca, NY, Cornell U. Press, 1956. 169 p.
NN BKR

Wright, John.
Libya.
New York Praeger, 1969. 304 p.
NN *R-BKR

MALAGASY REPUBLIC/MADAGASCAR (TANANARIVE)

Black Africans and Indonesians reached the island 2,000 years ago, and Indonesian immigration continued until the nineteenth century. In the ninth century Muslim traders visited the island. In 1500 it was discovered by the Portuguese, and in 1600 Portuguese Roman Catholic missionaries tried but failed to convert the Malagasy. Beginning in 1642, the French maintained footholds on the island, and small Malagasy kingdoms were formed. In the eighteenth century the Merina people of the interior united in a kingdom; under Radama I (1810–28) they accepted British aid and missionaries. The French established a protectorate over Madagascar in 1885 and gained full control of the island in 1904. In 1947–48 rebellion broke out against the French; in 1958 the Malagasy Republic was declared autonomous; and in 1960 it gained full independence.

Archives

Service des Archives Nationales
23 rue Aube-Tsaralalana
B.P. 3384
Tananarive, Madagascar

Public and Church Records

Birth certificates can be obtained from the chief of the district (*chef du district*) of the person's birth; marriage certificates, from the chief of the district at the place of marriage—or the place of birth, if the person was born in the Malagasy Republic.

Libraries

Bibliothèque Municipale
Antsirabé, Madagascar

Bibliothèque Nationale
Place de l'Independence
Tananarive, Madagascar

Bibliothèque Universitaire
P.B. 908
Tananarive, Madagascar

U.S. Information Center Library
Tananarive, Madagascar

Books and Articles

Fontieille, Jean R.
Bibliographie Nationale de Madagascar, 1956–63
Tananarive, 1971. 511 p.
NN JFE 74-666

Macau, Jacques.
La Suède et Madagascar, au Début du XVIIIe Siècle.
Aix-en-Province, 1973. 204 leaves.
NN JFM 74-196 no. 7

Poirer, M.
Généalogie des Rois Maroseranana de l'Onilahy. (IN: *Académie, Algasche, Tananarive, Bulletin.* Tananarive, 1953. n.s., tome 31, p. 29–35)
NN BLX

Thompson, Virginia M.
The Malagasay Republic: Madagascar Today.
Stanford, Stanford U. Press, 1965. 504 p.
NN E-12 5693

MALAWI (ZOMBA)

Pygmylike hunter-gatherers lived in the area until Bantus migrated from the west and north in the fifteenth century and formed a Malawi kingdom that remained into the eighteenth century, when it expanded into Rhodesia and Mozambique territories. Internal rivalries then caused the kingdom to decline, and there were incursions by the Yao, who sold Malawis as slaves to Arab and Swahili merchants. In 1859 David Livingstone explored the region and promoted the establishment of Scottish missions and business groups to develop legitimate commerce as a deterrent to the Arab slave trade. Britain prevented encroachment of the Portuguese and Germans in 1891 and in 1907 set up a protectorate named Nyasaland. In 1953 Nyasaland was joined to the new Central African Federation, and in 1959 Dr. Hastings Kamuzu Banda set up the Malawi Congress Party. Britain granted an African majority in the Legislative Council (1960–61), and in 1963 Nyasaland seceded from the Central African Federation. In 1964–75 Nyasaland became independent as Malawi, and in 1966 Malawi became a republic within the British Commonwealth. In 1971 Dr. Banda was made President for life.

A census was taken in 1966.

Archives

National Archives of Malawi
P.O. Box 62
Zomba, Malawi

Public and Church Records

Birth certificates for non-Africans are issued by the Registrar General (P.O. Box 100, Blantyre, Malawi). For Africans born in Malawi an affidavit of birth by a relative can be made available.

Libraries

British Council Library
P.O. Box 456
Blantyre, Malawi

U.S. Information Service Library
St. Andre's St.
Blantyre, Malawi

Library, University of Malawi
P.O. Box 200
Limbe, Malawi

Books and Articles

Bandawe, Lewis Mataka.
Memoirs of a Malawian.
Blantyre, Malawi, 1971. 143 p.
NN Sc B-Bandawe

Boeder, Robert B.
Malawians Abroad.
East Lansing, MI, 1974. 299 leaves.
NN Sc Micro R-1785

Brown, Edward F.
A Bibliography of Malawi.
Syracuse, NY, 1965. 161 p.
NN JFD 75-490

Pachai, Bridglal.
Malawi: The History of a Nation.
London, 1973. 324 p.
NN Sc 968.97-P

Pike, John G.
Malawi.
New York, Praeger, 1968. 248 p.,
  index.
NN *R-BNM

Wills, Alfred John.
An Introduction to the History of
  Central Africa.
London, 1973. 458 p.
NN *R-BMW 74-495

MALI (BAMAKO)

The medieval empire of Mali was at its peak in the fourteenth century as a leading world supplier of gold. A national hero is Mansa Musa, Emperor (1307–1332), who reputedly distributed some 50,000 ounces of gold to the poor as he journeyed to Mecca on a pilgrimage. He conquered Timbuktu and made it a center of trade, learning and culture. In 1590 Gao was shattered by the Moroccan army. During the eighteenth century anarchy prevailed. There was a resurgence of Islam during the 1800's. Emperors resisted French invasion, but in 1898, as French Sudan, the country became part of the Federation of French West Africa. In 1958 it became an automonous Sudanese Republic in the French community. Renamed the Republic of Mali, it obtained full independence in 1960.

Archives

Archives Nationales
Institut des Sciences Humaines
Kouloube, P.B. 159
Bamako, Mali

Libraries

Bibliothèque Nationale
Institut des Sciences Humaines
(Address above)

Bibliothèque Municipale
Bamako, Mali

Centre de Documentation Arabe
Timbuktu, Mali

Centre Française de Documenta-
  tion
Ave. Modibo Keita
Bamako, Mali

Books and Articles

Levtzion, Nehemia.
Ancient Ghana and Mali.
London, 1973. 283 p.
NN JFC 73-3790

Norris, Harry Thirlwall.
The Tuaregs: Their Islamic Legacy and Its Diffusion in the Sahel.
Warminister, England, Aris and Phillips, 1975. 234 p., gen. tables, index.
NN *OGI 76-1908

Tauxier, Louis.
Le Noir du Soudan.
Nendeln Liechtenstein, Kraus Reprint, 1973. 796 p.
NN Sc F 572.966-T

MAURITANIA (NOUAKCHOTT)

During the first millennium A.D., the Berbers pushed the black African inhabitants, especially the Soninke, southward toward the Senegal River. The Hodh region in the southeast was the center of the ancient empire of Ghana (700–1200). Until the thirteenth century southeast Mauritania was a major region on the trans-Siberian caravan route between Morocco and the upper Niger River. During the fourteenth and fifteenth centuries southeast Mauritania was part of the empire of Mali. In 1440 the Portuguese established fishing bases on Arguin Island, near the northwest coast. Beginning in the seventeenth century, Dutch, British and French traders who were interested in gum arabic founded settlements near the Senegal River. France gained control of southern Mauritania by the mid-nineteenth century and declared it a protectorate in 1903. Until 1920 Mauritania was administered as part of Senegal. In 1957 Nouakchott became its administrative center, and in 1958 Mauritania became an autonomous republic within the French community. In 1960 Mauritania gained full independence.

Archives

Archives Nationales
B.P. 77
Nouakchott, Mauritania

Public and Church Records

Birth certificates can be obtained from the Mayor (*Mairie*) of the commune in which the applicant was born. If the birth was not within a commune, the document may be obtained from the *cadi* (Islamic judge) of the place where he was born; or, if there is no *cadi*, from the Commandant du Cercle of the *cercle* (administrative district) where he was born. Marriage certificates can be obtained from the *cadi* of the place where the marriage took place. Marriages of non-nationals (non-Muslim ceremony) are registered with the Commandant du Cercle of the administrative district where they were married.

Libraries

Arab Library
Boutilimit, Mauritania

Arab Library
Chinguetti, Mauritania

Bibliothèque Publique Centrale
B.P. 77
Nouakchott, Mauritania

National Administrative and Historical Library
B.P. 77
Nouakchott, Mauritania

Books and Articles

Desire-Vuillemin, Genevieve M.
Contribution à l'Histoire de la Mauritanie de 1900 à 1934. Dakar, 1962. 412 p.
NN Sc F966.1-D

Gillier, L.
... La Pénétration en Mauritanie: Découverte-Explorations-Conquête ... Paris, P. Geuthner, 1926. 359 p.
NN BM

Maele, Bernard van
Bibliographie Mauritanie. Nouakchott, 1971.
NN Sc F016.966-M

MAURITIUS (PORT LOUIS)

From 1598 to 1710 the island was occupied by the Dutch, who named it after Prince Maurice of Nassau. In 1722 French settlers called it Ile de France, and it became an important way station on the route to India. The French introduced the culture of sugar cane and imported large numbers of African slaves to work the plantations. In 1810 the British captured the island and restored the Dutch name. Slavery was abolished in the British Empire in 1833, making it necessary to bring indentured laborers from India. In 1947 the franchise was extended to Indians. In 1968 independence was declared under an Indian prime minister, and Mauritius joined the Commonwealth of Nations.

The first complete census was taken in 1735; thereafter, in 1776, 1786, 1846, 1851; and after this, every ten years until the 1940's, when the census was taken in 1944. Since 1952 censuses have been taken every ten years.

Archives

Mauritius Archives Department/
Service des Archives de Maurice
52 rue Sir William Newton
Port Louis, Mauritius

Public and Church Records

Civil registration began in 1723 for
births, 1724 for deaths, 1721 for
marriages, and in 1793 for divorces.

For Civil Status registers prior to
1811, write:

Chief Archivist, Archives Depart-
ment
Sunray Hotel
Coromandel, Mauritius

For Civil Status registers 1811 to
date, write:

Registrar General
Sir William Newton Street
Port Louis, Mauritius

Write the Chief Archivist for census information.

For religious information, refer to
the Diocese of Port Louis and
the Diocese of Mauritius.

Libraries

Mauritius Institute Public Li-
brary
P.O. Box 54
Port Louis, Mauritius

Municipal Library
P.O. Box 422
Port Louis, Mauritius

Carnegie Library
Queen Elizabeth II Avenue
Curepipe, Mauritius

Library, University of Mauritius
Moka, Mauritius

Historical and Genealogical Societies

Société de l'Histoire de l'Ile Mau-
rice
Mauritius Institute
Port Louis, Mauritius

Books and Articles

Bechet, Otave.
Inventaire des Registres
Paroissiaux de Ile de France (Ile
Maurice) Compagnie des Indies,
1722–1767.
Port Louis, 1952. 420 p.

Dictionnaire de Biographie Mau-
ricienne
Port Louis, 1947. no. 20
NN JFK 73-334

Hollingworth, Derek.
They Came to Mauritius. Portraits
of the Eighteenth and Nine-
teenth Centuries.
London, Oxford, 1965. 175 p.
NN C-13 3903

Lagess, Marcelle.
L'Ile de France Avant la Bourdon-
nais (1721–1735).
Port Louis, 1972. 111 p.
NN JFE 74-1356

Mauritius. Archives Department.
Bibliography of Mauritius

(1502–1954) ... by A. Touissant and H. Adolphe.
Port Louis, Mauritius, Esclapon, 1956. 884 p.
NN D-11 346

Mauritius.
Blue Book for the Colony of Mauritius.

Port Louis, 1898–.
NN *SF

Toussaint, Auguste.
Histoire de l'Ile Maurice.
Paris, Presses Universitaires de France, 1971. 128 p.
NN JFC 73-2403

MOROCCO (RABAT)

In 685, Arabs brought Islam to the land and created conflict with the native Berbers. In 788 the territory became an independent state under the royal line of Idris I but returned to separate tribal states by 900. In 1062 the Almorabids established a kingdom stretching from Spain to Senegal. From 1259–1550 a Merinid dynasty was limited to Morocco. Meanwhile, Moors (Moroccans) were driven out of Spain. The Portuguese conquered Morocco in 1415 but were defeated in 1578. The Alawite dynasty—the present ruling dynasty—was established in 1660. The Franco-Spanish agreement of 1912 divided Morocco into four administrative zones, of which French Morocco comprised nine-tenths of the territory. A Spanish protectorate included Spanish Morocco, and a southern protectorate of Morocco was administered as part of the Spanish Sahara. Tangier was made an international zone. Germany was ceded territory in French Equatorial Africa in exchange for its claims in Morocco. A nationalist movement and demand for reforms began in 1934. Sidi Muhammad was restored to power in 1955; and in 1956 France gave up its rights in Morocco, the Spanish surrendered their protectorate and Tangier was given to Morocco by an international agreement. In 1958 Spain ceded its southern protectorate, and in 1961 Sidi Muhammad's son, Hassan II, ascended the throne.

Censuses were taken in 1931, 1936, 1947, 1951–52 and 1960.

Archives

Bibliothèque Générale et Archives du Maroc
Avenue Moulay Ali Cherif
Rabat, Morocco

Bibliothèque Générale et Archives de Tétouan
3 avenue Mohammed V
B.P. 41
Tétouan, Morocco

Public and Church Records

Birth certificates can be obtained from the Municipal Services (Bureau de l'État Civil) by European residents or former residents, born after 1912. If Moroccan Muslims and Moroccan Jews are in possession of a *Livret de Famille* they may obtain birth certificates from the civil authorities having jurisdiction over their place of birth. If they are not in possession of a *Livret de Famille* they must obtain one before requesting a birth certificate.

Libraries

Bibliothèque Municipale
Avenue Général d'Amade
Casablanca, Morocco

Al Qarawiyin University Library
Fez, Morocco

Biblioteca Publica Española
Consulado General de España
26 Avenida de España
Tangier, Morocco

Books and Articles

Barber, Forest
An Introduction to Genealogical Research in Morocco.
(IN: *The Augustan*, Torrance, CA, 1977. v. 18, p. 113–14)
NN APA

Barber, Forest
The Sultans and Kings of Morocco.
(IN: *The Augustan*, Torrance, CA, 1976. 18, p. 10–13)
NN APA

Brace, Richard M.
Morocco, Algeria, Tunisia.
Englewood Cliffs, NJ, Prentice-Hall, 1964. 184 p.
NN D-15 9168

Gouvion Saint-Cyr, Marthe.
... Kitab Aayane Al-Marhrib 'l'-Alca.
Paris, Paul Geuthner, 1939. 914 p., gen. tables.
NN BKG

Griguen, Jules.
Précis d'Histoire des Dynasties Marocaines ...
Casablanca, Vigie Marocaine, etc., 1929. 113 p.
NN *OFO

Histoire du Maroc, par Jean Brignon, et al.
Paris, Hatier, etc., 1967. 416 p.
NN E-13 5948

Howe, Marvine.
Fez, Former Morocco Capital, Salvages Some of Its Ancient Glory.
(IN: *The New York Times*. New York, February 23, 1977. p. 2)

Les Sources Inédites de l'Histoire du Maroc.
Paris, E. Leroux, 1905–1961. 28 v.
NN BKG

Levi-Provençal, E.
... Les Historiens des Chorfa.
Paris, E. Larose, 1922. 420 p., gen. tables.
NN *OFO

Maher, Vanessa.
Women and Property in Morocco.
London, 1974. 238 p.
NNSc 301.412-M

Martin, Alfred G.P.
Quarte Siècle d'Histoire Marocaine au Sahara de 1504 à 1902, au Maroc de 1894 à 1912 ...
Paris, F. Alcan, 1923. 591 p.
NN BKG

Maxwell, Gavin.
Lords of Atlas: The Rise and Fall of the House of Glaoua, 1893–1956.

London, Longmans, 1966. 318 p.
NN JFD 73-10263

Ricard, Prosper.
Les Dynasties Marocaines en Dix Tableaux ...

Casablanca, Service Topo. du Maroc., 1919. 33 p.
NN BKB p.v., 22 no. 11

Salmon, G.
Les Chorfa Filala et Ojilala de Fes
. . .
(IN: *Archives Marocaines*, Paris, 1905. v. 3, p. 97–118)
(NN BKG)

Tangier, Morocco (Diocese).
Registos Paroquais da Se de Tanger (Casamentos de 1582 a 1678, Tenconciliacoes de 1611 a 1672).
Lisbon, Academia das Sciencias de Lisboa, 1922. v. 1 (548 p.), index.
NN ASO+ (Tangier)

MOZAMBIQUE (MAPUTO/LOURENÇO MARQUES)
(formerly Portuguese West Africa)

In the first millennium A.D., Bantu-speaking black Africans migrated into the region. In 1000, Arab and Swahili traders operated along the coast. Vasco da Gama visited the coast in 1498, and in 1505 the Portuguese established a settlement at Sofala. In the seventeenth century the Portuguese founded feudal estates that resembled kingdoms; slave-raiding began in 1650. The territory was ruled as part of Goa in India from the end of the seventeenth century until 1752. Between 1820 and 1830 Nguni-speaking people from South Africa invaded the country. One group, the Shangana, remained in control into the late 1800's. In 1891 a treaty defined the boundaries between English and Portuguese holdings in southeast Africa. In 1910 the territory became a colony of Portugal, rather than a province, and in 1951 Mozambique declared itself a "self-governing" state. In 1974 the Frelimo (Mozambique Liberation Force) and a Portuguese military coup overthrew the Portuguese government. Independence was declared in 1975 under Joaquim Chissano as premier, and there was a massive exodus of Europeans from Mozambique.

Archives

Arquivo Histórico de Moçambique
(Mozambique Historical Archives)
Direcção Provincial dos Serviços de
Educação
Lourenço Marques, Mozambique

Public and Church Records

Conservatoria do Registo Civil in
the city of birth or marriage.

Libraries

Biblioteca Arquivo Histórico de
Moçambique
C.P. 493
Lourenço Marques, Mozambique

Biblioteca Municipal
Lourenço Marques, Mozambique

Biblioteca Nacional de Moçambique (National Library of Mozambique)
Lourenço Marques, Mozambique

Books and Articles

Ferraz, Maria de Lourdes Esteves
dos Santos de Freitas.
Documentaçao Histórica Mocambicana.
Lisbon, 1973. 1 v.
NN JFL 74-280

Soares-Zilhão, João.
O Brazao de Moçambique e o Armorial das Colonias Portuguesas.
(IN: *Moçambique Documentario Trimestral*, Lourenço Marques, 1935. no. 3, p. 5–16)
NN BLW

NAMIBIA:

See South-West Africa

NIGER (NIAMEY)

Niger, bordering on the southern Sahara, was a battleground for myriad nations and tribes, including the Berbers, Arabs, Fulanis and Tuaregs, and the Ghana, Mali, Songhai and Bornu empires. In 1901 the French arrived and began the construction of forts; in the following years they put down Tuareg resistance and set up the colony of Niger. In 1946 the people of Niger were granted French citizenship, and in 1958 Niger became a republic within the French community. Army Chief of Staff Lieutenant Colonal Scyni Kountche, supported by military officers, declared himself head of state in 1974. Niger became fully independent in 1960.

The first census was taken in 1968.

Archives

Presidence de la République
Niamey, Niger, West Africa

Service des Archives
B.P. 550
Niamey, Niger, West Africa

Public and Church Records

Civil registration began in 1900.

Presidence de la République
Niamey, Niger, West Africa

Libraries

Centre de Documentation (Library)
Niamey, Niger, West Africa

Books and Articles

Hinkmann, Ulrich.
Niger.
Munich, R. Oldenburg, 1968. 178 p.
NN D-18 7883

NIGERIA (LAGOS)

Nigeria was the home of several rich ancient and medieval cultures, notably the Nok (700–200 B.C.), and one that emerged from Ife, a sacred Yoruba city, in the twelfth century. Islam was established in northern Nigeria in the fourteenth century. From the fifteenth through seventeenth centuries, the British and Portuguese were involved in slave trading along the coast. The British annexed the capital city of Lagos in 1861 and established control over all of Nigeria by 1914. Nigeria became a federal republic within the Commonwealth in 1963. A military government was established in 1966. The secession of the Eastern Region as the independent republic of Biafra in 1967 ended in Biafran defeat in 1970 after thirty months of civil war.

Censuses were taken in 1921 and 1963.

Archives

National Archives of Nigeria
University of Ibadan, Chapel Road
Private Mail Bag 4
University Post Office
Ibadan, Nigeria

National Archives, Enugu Branch
Colliery Road
Private Mail Bag 1050
Enugu, Nigeria

National Archives, Kaduna Branch
Uakubu Gowon Street
Kaduna, Nigeria

Public and Church Records

The registers for births and deaths go back to 1876 and for marriages to 1886. The Principal Registrar for marriages is the

Police Magistrate, Lagos. The Principal Registrar for births, deaths and burials is the Assistant Director of Medical Services (Health). These officials keep original records, while copies are forwarded to the Chief Secretary to the Government.

Libraries

Regional Central Library
Ogui Road
Enugu, Nigeria

National Library of Nigeria
4 Wesley St.
P.M.B. 12626
Lagos, Nigeria

Northern Regional Library
P.M.B. 2061
Kaduna, Nigeria

University of Lagos Library
University of Lagos
Yaba, Lagos, Nigeria

University of Nigeria Library
Nsukka, Nigeria

Western Regional Library
P.M.B. 5082
Ibadan, Nigeria

Historical and Genealogical Societies

Historical Society of Nigeria
Arts Building, Ahmadu Bello University
Zaria, Nigeria
(*Journal; Tarikh; Bulletin of News*)

Books and Articles

Alagoa, Ebiegberi Joe
A History of the Niger Delta.
Ibadan, 1972. 231 p.
NN JFD 74-2663

Basden, George T.
Among the Ibos of Nigeria.
New York, Barnes & Noble, 1966.
   321 p.
NN D-16 9626

Bradbury, R.E.
Benin Studies, ed. by Peter Morton-Williams.
London, Oxford U. Press for the International African Institute, 1973. 293 p., gen. tables, index.
NN JFD 74-5964

Burns, Alan Cuthbert.
History of Nigeria.
London, 1972. 366 p.
NN R-BMM 73-851

Ferguson, John.
Some Nigerian Church Founders.
Ibadan, 1971. 84 p.
NN JFC 74-1057

Hogden, Sidney John.
An Introduction to the History of the Islamic States of Northern Nigeria.
Ibadan, 1967. 351 p.
NN SC 966.9-H

Ibadan, Nigeria U. Library.
Africana Catalogue of the Ibadan University Library (Ibadan, Nigeria).
Boston, G.K. Hall, 1973. 2 v.
NN JFG 74-79

Isichei, Elizabeth Allo.
A History of the Igbo People.

London, St. Martin's Press, 1976.
303 p., index.
NN JFD 76-6884

Last, Murray.
The Sokoto Caliphate.
London, Longmans, 1967. 280 p.,
index, gen. tables in pocket of
back cover.
NN *RR-BMM

Ombu, Jigekuma A.
Niger Delta 1627–1967.
Ibadan, Nigeria, 1970. 138 p.
NN Sc 016.9669-O

Synge, Richard.
Nigeria: The Land and its People.
London, MacDonald Educational,
1975. 63 p.
(MacDonald Countries no. 11)

RHODESIA/ZIMBABWE (SALISBURY)

The first Bantus arrived in Rhodesia sometime between the
fifth and tenth centuries A.D. The Portuguese explored the
region in the 1500's. In 1889 Cecil Rhodes (after whom Rhodesia
is named) formed the British South Africa Company, which,
along with British troops, had subdued the Mashona and Matabele peoples by 1897; British colonists came into the region. In
1923 Southern Rhodesia became a self-governing colony. In 1953
Britain created the Federation of Rhodesia and Nyasaland that
connected Northern Rhodesia (now Zambia), Southern Rhodesia
and Nyasaland (now Malawi); Southern Rhodesian settlers controlled the Federation. In 1964 the Federation was dissolved
and the two northern territories were given independence; Southern Rhodesia, however, was denied independence unless representative government was promised. In 1965 Prime Minister Ian
Smith declared Rhodesia's independence from Britain, and in
1970 a republic was proclaimed.

A census was conducted in 1956.

Archives

National Archives of Rhodesia
Gun Hill, Borrowdale Road
Private Bag 7729
Causeway, Salisbury, Rhodesia

Public and Church Records

Vital records are kept by Deputy
Registrars of births and deaths,
who retain their own registers,
file and keep all forms of information on births and deaths.
Some records of deaths and marriages date from 1891, but official registration did not begin
until 1904.

Libraries

National Free Library of Rhodesia
P.O. Box 1773
Bulawayo, Rhodesia

Public Library
P.O. Box 586
Bulawayo, Rhodesia

Queen Victoria Memorial Library
P.O. Box 1087
Salisbury, Rhodesia

University College of Rhodesia Library
Private Bag 167H
Salisbury, Rhodesia

Books and Articles

Chiwale, Jacques C.
Royal Praises and Names of Lunda Kazembe of Northern Rhodesia.
Lusaka, 1962. 67 p.
NN Sc 572.978-C

Gray, Richard.
The Two Nations ... in the Rhodesias and Nyasaland.

London, Oxford U. Press, 1960. 373 p.
NN D-12 8966

Hanna, Alexander John.
The Story of the Rhodesias and Nyasaland.
London, Faber & Faber, 1960. 288 p.
NN D-12 7605

National Archives of Rhodesia.
Guide to the Public Archives of Rhodesia.
Salisbury, 1969. 1 v.
NN Sc 016.3546-N

Tabler, Edward.
Pioneers of Rhodesia.
Cape Town, C. Struik, 1966. 185 p.
NN E-12 6982

Tanser, George Henry.
Founders of Rhodesia.
Cape Town, Oxford U. Press, 1950. 80 p.
NN AGH

RWANDA (KIGALI)

The region was originally inhabited by the pygmy Twa people and later by the Bantu Hutus. In the fifteenth century the Tutsi, or Watutsi, a cattle-keeping people, imposed a feudal overlordship on the Hutus. European explorers came in the nineteenth century, and the region was taken over by Germany in 1885. After World War I it was ceded to Belgium. The Hutus, meanwhile, sought emancipation from Tutsi domination. In 1959 they overthrew the Tutsi monarchy, and in 1960 the Hutu Emancipation Movement (Parmehutu) established a provisional government that was recognized by Belgium in 1961. Full independence came the following year.

Libraries

Library, Université Nationale du
Rwanda
B.P. 117
Butare, Rwanda

Books and Articles

Gerkens, George.
Les Batutsi et les Bahutu ... du
Ruanda et de l'Urundi.
Bruxelles, 1949. 112 p.
(IN: Institut Royal des Sciences
Naturelles de Belgique, Brux-
elles. *Memoires. Série. 2 fac., 31*)
NN *PQA

Gorju, Julien L.
... Face au Royaume Hamite du
Ruanda; le Royaume Frère de
l'Urundi.
(Bibliothèque-Congo, n.s., no. 3,
Bruxelles, 1938. 117 p.)
NN QPE

Lacroix, Benoit.
Le Rwanda: Mille Heures au Pays
de Mille Collines.
Montreal, Editions du Levrier,
1966. 96 p.
NN D-17 4558

Le Marchand, René.
Rwanda and Burundi.

New York, Praeger, 1970. 562 p.
(Praeger Library of African Af-
fairs)
NN *R-BMS

Louis, William Roger
Ruanda-Urundi 1884–1919.
Oxford, Clarendon Press, 1963. 290
p.
NN D-14 9481

Sasserath, Jules.
Le Ruanda-Urundi ... un Étrange
Royaume Féodal au Coeur de
l'Afrique.
Bruxelles, Editions Germinal,
1948, 77, 1 p.
NN Sc F916.757-S

Shabahoza, Beata.
L'Oeuvre Missionaire au Rwanda
et au Burundi et la Participa-
tion de Fribourg.
Fribourg, 1969. 95 leaves.
NN JFF 72-786

Vansina, Jan.
L'Évolution du Royaume Rwanda
des Origines à 1900.
Bruxelles, 1962. 100 p.
(Académie Royale di Sciences
d'Outre-Mer, Brussels Sciences
Morales et Politiques Class des
Memoires. n.s., t. 26, fasc. 2)
NN L-10 4558 n.s. t. 26 fasc. 2

SÉNÉGAL (DAKAR)

The Tukolor dynasty, which settled in the Senegal River valley
in the ninth century, dominated the region from the tenth to
the fourteenth century, during which time they were converted
to Islam. In the fourteenth century the Mali empire expanded
westward and conquered them. In 1444 Portuguese traders
entered the Senegal River and established trading stations in
the area of present-day Dakar. In the seventeenth century

Portuguese power was displaced by the Dutch and the French; the first French settlement was made at Saint-Louis about 1650. In 1763 Great Britain captured all French posts in Senegal and joined them with its holdings along the Gambia River (the area in which Alex Haley's ancestor, Kunta Kinte, was captured into slavery in 1767), forming Senegambia—Britain's first African colony. Between 1775 and 1783, France regained its holdings. In 1895 Senegal was made a French colony and was part of French West Africa, which was headquartered from 1902 at Dakar. Senegal became an autonomous republic within the French community in 1958.

Censuses were taken in 1904 and 1958.

Archives

Archives du Sénégal
Immeuble administratif,
Avenue Roume
Dakar, Sénégal

Public and Church Records

Birth and marriage certificates are issued by the local Mayor's office (*La Mairie*).

Libraries

Bibliothèque de l'Institut Fondamental d'Afrique Noire
B.P. 206
Dakar, Sénégal

Bibliothèque de l'Alliance Française
10 rue Colbert
B.P. 1777
Dakar, Sénégal

Bibliothèque de l'Université
B.P. 2006
Dakar, Sénégal

Books and Articles

Cultru, Prosper.
Histoire du Sénégal du XVe Siècle à 1970.
Paris, E. Larose, 1910. 375 p.
NN DS

Klein, Martin A.
Islam and Imperialism in Senegal: Sine-Saloum, 1847–1914.
Stanford, CA, Hoover Institute, 1968. 285 p.
NN E-13 1843

Marty, Paul.
L'Islam en Mauretanie et au Sénégal.
Paris, E. Leroux, 1916. 483 p.
(*Rev. du Monde Musulman, v. 31*)
NN *OAA

Robinson, David.
Chiefs and Clerics: Abdul Bokar Kan and Futa Tora, 1853–1891.
Oxford, Clarendon Press, 1975. 239 p., index, gen. tables.

SIERRA LEONE (FREETOWN)

The Temne Tribe lived along the northern coast when the Portuguese landed on the peninsula in 1460 and named it Sierra Leone. In 1500 European traders came and the slave trade began. In the eighteenth century tribes from present-day Guinea converted numerous Temne to Islam. In 1772 slavery was abolished in England, and in 1787 four hundred freed slaves established the Province of Freedom near present-day Freetown, but the colony was destroyed by the Temne in 1790. In 1792 1,100 freed slaves from Nova Scotia landed on Sierra Leone Peninsula and named it Freetown, and in 1800 five hundred free blacks from Jamaica arrived via Nova Scotia. In 1864 50,000 liberated slaves were settled at Freetown. In 1827 Fourah Bay College, now part of the University of Sierra Leone, was founded to educate black Africans. An advisory legislative council was established in 1863 and in 1924 black Africans sat on it. Sierra Leone's interior was made a British protectorate in 1896. In 1961 Sierra Leone became independent, and in 1971 the Parliament declared Sierra Leone a republic.

Censuses were taken in 1911, 1921, 1931 and 1963.

Archives

Public Archives Office
John F. Kennedy Building, 4th
  Floor
Fourah Bay College
Freetown, Sierra Leone

Some records exist from before the beginning of civil registration; baptism records in all churches cover the years 1795–1907 and in certain churches—mostly Methodist—go up to 1924.

Public and Church Records

Civil registration for births and deaths began in 1854, while marriage registers date back to 1796. Birth certificates can be obtained from the Registrar's Office, Ministry of Health, Oxford Street, Freetown; marriage certificates, from the Registrar General's Office, Judicial Department, Westmoreland Street, Freetown.

Libraries

Fourah Bay College Library
University of Sierra Leone
Freetown, Sierra Leone

J.J. Thomas Library
Water St.
Freetown, Sierra Leone

Sierra Leone Library Board
P.O. Box 326
Freetown, Sierra Leone

Books and Articles

Butt-Thompson, Frederick W.
The First Generation of Sierra Leo-
neans.
Freetown, Sierra Leone, 1952. 65 p.
NN BMH

Butt-Thompson, Frederick W.
Sierra Leone in History and Tra-
dition.
London, Witherby, 1926. 275 p.
NN *R-BMH

Fyfe, Christopher.
A History of Sierra Leone.
London, Oxford U. Press, 1962. 773
p., index.
(West Africa Series)
NN D-15 2951

Keup, Peter A.
A History of Sierra Leone 1400–1787.
Cambridge, Cambridge U. Press,
1961. 211 p.
NN D-13 1375

Peterson, John.

Providence of Freedom: A History
of Sierra Leone 1787–1970.
London, Faber and Faber, 1969.
354 p.
NN *R-BMH & JFD 71-414

Salvador, George A.
Paul Cuffe: The Black Yankee,
1759–1817.
New Bedford, MA. 76 p.
NN Sc 966.4-S

Sierra Leone Year Book. 1971–1973.
(Has an alpha Who's Who section)
NN JLK 73-242

West, Richard.
Back to Africa: a History of Sierra
Leone and Liberia.
London, J. Cape, 1970. 357 p.
NN D-20 4217

Williams, Geoffrey J.
A Bibliography of Sierra Leone,
1925–1967.
New York, 1971. 209 p.
NN *RS-BMH 71-179

SOMALIA (MOGADISHU)

Ancient Egyptian writings called this region the Land of Punt (God's Land). Its original inhabitants were Somalis, a blend of Asian and African peoples. From the seventh to the tenth centuries, immigrant Muslim Arabs and Persians established trading ports along the Gulf of Aden and Indian Ocean coasts. In the fifteenth and sixteenth centuries Somali warriors joined the armies of the Muslim sultanates in their battles with Christian Ethiopia. Between 1884 and 1886 the British made agreements with local tribal chiefs and in 1887 established a protectorate. France had acquired a foothold during the 1860's, and in 1888 England and France defined the boundary between their possessions. In 1889 Italy established a protectorate in the central zone and later in the south (territory ceded by the sultan of Zanzibar) and in the north. In 1925 Jubaland, east of the Juba River, was detached from Kenya to become the westernmost part of the Italian colony. In 1936 Italian Somaliland combined with Somali-speaking districts of Ethiopia to form a province of Italian East Africa. In 1956 it became independent and the legislature of the two new states created the United Republic of Somalia, but there was discontent because the Ogaden region, with its large Somali population, had been returned to Ethiopia by the British in 1954. In 1969 the country changed its name to Somali Democratic Republic.

Public and Church Records

Registers, preserved with the Registrar-General, date only from August 1941, the previous records having been lost during the Italian occupation. Application for information should be made to the Chief Secretary of the Government.

Ex-British Somaliland: Birth certificates are issuable by appropriate District Commissioners. Marriage certificates are issued by the Registrar of Marriages.

Ex-Italian Somaliland: Birth and marriage certificates are issued by the municipal authorities.

Libraries

Biblioteca del Istituto Universitario della Somalia Mogadishu, Somalia

Hargeisa Local Government Council Library (Public Library) Hargeisa, Somalia

Musée de La Garesa (Somalia's largest public library) Mogadishu, Somalia

Books and Articles

Ali, Ismail Mohamed. Beautiful Somalia. Paris, c. 1971. 86 p. NN Sc 916.773-A

Burton, Sir Richard F. First Footsteps in East Africa. London, RKP, 1966. 320 p.

Castagno, Margaret. Historical Dictionary of Somalia. Metuchen, NJ, Scarecrow Press, 1975. 213 p. NN JFD 76-2498

Cerulli, Enrico. Somalia ... Rome, 1957. 1 v. NN L-10 1723

Cesari, Casare. ... La Somalia Italiana ... Rome, Palombi, 1935. 207 p. NN BLO

Ferrand, Gabriel. Les Comalis ... Paris, E. Leroux, 1903. 284. NN BLP

Hess, Robert L. Italian Colonialism in Somalia.

Chicago, IL, U. of Chicago Press,
  1966. 234 p.
NN D-17 55

Le Pointe, Henri.
La Colonisation Française au Pays
  des Somalis.
Paris, Jouve, c. 1914. 98 p.
NN BLP

Lewis, Joan M.
The Modern History of Somaliland.
London, Weidenfeld & Nicolson,
  1965. 234 p.
(Asia-Africa Series of Modern His-
  tory 1)
NN D-16 802

McNeill, Malcolm.
In Pursuit of "Mad" Mullah ...
London, C.A. Pearson, 1902. 313 p.
NN BLP

Onor, Romolo.
... La Somalia Italiana.
Turin, Fratelli Bocca, 1925. 365 p.
NN TAH

Pankhurst, E. Sylvia.
Ex-Italian Somaliland.
London, Watts & Co., 1951. 460 p.,
  t of c, no index.
NN *RR-BLO

Rayne, Henry.
Sun, Sand and Somals.
London, H. F. and G. Witherby,
  1921. 223 p.
NN BLP

Wightwick Haywood, Cecil W.I.
To the Mysterious Lorain Swamp
  ... Unknown Jubaland.
London, Seely, Service, 1927. 275 p.
NN BLR

SOUTH AFRICA (CAPE TOWN, PRETORIA)

In 1488, when Portuguese explorers arrived and named the Cape of Good Hope, the southern and central parts of this region were inhabited by Khoikhoi (Hottentots) and San (Bushmen), while Bantu-speaking blacks were entering from east-central Africa and settling in the north and east. In 1652 the Dutch established Cape Colony, giving land to Europeans for farms and bringing black Africans from western and eastern Africa and Malayans as slaves. In 1689 two hundred Huguenot settlers arrived, established a wine industry and intermarried. A smallpox epidemic killed much of the European population in 1713. During the eighteenth century interbreeding between Khoikhoi, slaves and Europeans produced the "Coloured" population. The Congress of Vienna of 1814 assigned the Cape territory to Great Britain, and in 1820 five thousand British settlers were given farms near the Great Fish River. Slavery was abolished in the British Empire in 1833, and between 1835 and 1843 many Boers (Dutch settlers) left the Cape for land beyond the Orange River. In 1838 they defeated the Zulus and established farms in Natal, to the east. Britain annexed Natal in 1843. During the 1850's the Boer republics of Orange Free State and Transvaal were established. In 1860 the first indentured laborers arrived in Natal from India to work on the sugar plantations. Diamonds and gold were discovered in the late 1800's. Between 1870 and the turn of the century there was rapid economic development, and the number of whites in the area increased from 300,000 to about one million. In 1871 Britain annexed the diamond-mining region, despite protests of the Orange Free State. The Boer War, begun in 1899 when Orange Free State and Transvaal declared war on Britain, ended with British victory in 1902. Britain established the Union of South Africa in 1910. In 1961 South Africa left the British Commonwealth of Nations and became a republic.

The first census was taken in 1965.

Archives

Central Archives Depot/Sentrale Argiefbewaarplek
Union Buildings
Private Bag X236
Pretoria, Republic of South Africa 0001

Transvaal Archives Depot/Transvaalse Argiefbewaarplek
Union Buildings
Private Bag X236
Pretoria, Republic of South Africa 001

Cape Archives Depot/Kaapse Argiefbewaarplek
Queen Victoria Street
Private Bag X9025
Cape Town, Republic of South Africa 8000

Orange Free State Archives Depot/ Oranje Vrystaate Argiefbewaarplek

37 Elizabeth Street
Private Bag X20504
Bloemfontein, Republic of South Africa 9300

Natal Archives Depot/Natalse Argiefbewaarplek
231 Pietermaritz Street
Private Bag X9012
Pietermaritzburg, Republic of South Africa 3200

Archives Depot of the Territory
Private Bag 13250
Windhoek, Republic of South Africa 9100

Intermediate Archives Depot
Private Bag X236
Pretoria, Republic of South Africa 0001

Public and Church Records

The registrar for the country has duplicate copies of marriage records and the originals of birth and death registrations. Compulsory registration of births and deaths, according to area, date from: Cape Province: 1894 (voluntary in 1880). Transvaal: 1900. Orange Free State: 1902. Natal: 1867.

Marriage records date from:
Cape Province: 1804.
Transvaal: 1871—Europeans.
1897—Non-Europeans.
Orange Free State: 1859.
Natal: 1846.

For vital record information, write:
Registrar of Births, Marriages and Deaths
Department of the Interior
Private Bag X114
Pretoria, Republic of South Africa 0001

For census information:
Department of Statistics
Private Bag X44
Pretoria, Republic of South Africa 0001

Church records predate civil registration. During the seventeenth and eighteenth centuries the Nederduitsch Gereformeerde Kerk (Dutch Reformed Church) was the only officially recognized denomination, and practically all whites in the Cape belonged to it. Baptismal, marriage and death registers kept by the Dutch Reformed Church Archives date from about 1665. Copies are kept by the Transvaal Archives Depot. In 1778 freedom of religious worship was granted to the Lutherans. The original baptismal and marriage registers (1780–1864) of the Evangelical Lutheran Church are kept in the vault of the church building in Cape Town. Microfilms are kept by the Human Sciences Research Council's section for Genealogy.

Argief Van Die Gereformeerde Kerk in Suid-Afrika (Dutch Reformed Church)
N.G. Kerksentrum
P.O. Box 3171
Grey's Pass, Cape Town, Republic of South Africa

Argief Van Die Gereformeerde Kerk in Suid-Afrika (Dutch Reformed Church)
Corner of Van der Hoff Road and Borcherd Street
Posbus 20004
Potchefstroom, Republic of South Africa

Catholic History Bureau
Oblate Novitiate
44 Parkhill Road, Glebe
Germiston, Republic of South Africa

St. George's Cathedral Monument Room
St. George's Cathedral, Wale Street
Cape Town, Republic of South Africa
(Register of births, deaths and marriages from c. 1834)

Dutch Reformed Church Archives
Queen Victoria Street
Cape Town, Republic of South Africa 8001

For wills and deeds, write to the Master of the Supreme Court of the specific province.

Libraries

Free State Provincial Library Service (Vrystaatse Provinsiale Biblioteekdiens) P.B. X0606
Bloemfontein, Republic of South Africa

University of the Orange Free State Library
Bloemfontein, Republic of South Africa

Cape Town City Libraries
30 Chiappini Street
Cape Town, Republic of South Africa

Library of the Royal Society of South Africa
% University of Cape Town
Rondebosch, Cape Town, Republic of South Africa

South African Library (National Library)
Queen Victoria Street
Cape Town, Republic of South Africa

University of Cape Town Library
Private Bag, Rondebosch
Cape Town, Republic of South Africa

Johannesburg Public Library
Johannesburg, Republic of South Africa

State Library
P.O. Box 397
Pretoria, Republic of South Africa

Transvaal Provincial Library
Private Bag 288
Pretoria, Republic of South Africa

Historical and Genealogical Societies

Hon. Secretary
Genealogical Society of South Africa
15 Queens Road
Tamboerskloof, Cape Town, Republic of South Africa 8001
(*Familia*, 1964–)
NN AVH (South Africa)

Section for Genealogy
Institute for Historical Research
Human Sciences Research Council
Private Bag X41
Pretoria, Republic of South Africa 0001

The Curator
Huguenot Memorial Museum
P.O. Box 37
Franschhoek, Republic of South Africa 7690

The Director
Kaffrarian Museum
3 Lower Albert Road
King William's Town, Republic of South Africa 5600
(For German settlers)

Books and Articles

Arma (Quarterly Bulletin of the Heraldry Society of Southern Africa.)
Cape Town, 1958–1976+ 19 v.+.
(% Maj. L. H. C. Russell, ed., P.O. Box 4839, Cape Town)
NN AWA

Braby's Orange Free State Directory (Including Basutoland and Trades Directory of Kimberley and Aluwal North).
Durban, A. C. Braby, 1921, 1924, 1927. issues no. 15, 18, 21.
NN BAZ (Orange)

Breutz, Paul L.
The Tribes of the Districts of Taung and Herbert.
Pretoria, 1968. 277 p.
NN Sc 572.968-B

Dictionary of South African Biography, W. J. de Kock, ed.
Pretoria, 1972–.
NN *R-AGH 76-6627

Familia (Quarterly Journal of the Genealogical Society of South Africa).
Capetown, 1964–1976+. 13 v+.
(%Dr. C. Pama, ed., P.O. Box 4839, Cape Town)
NN AVH (Africa, South)

Holt, Basil F.
Where the Rainbows Call.
Cape Town, 1972. 176 p.
(Kaffraria)
NN JFD 74-2462

Junod, Henri A.
The Life of a South African Tribe.
New Hyde Park, NY, University Books, 1962 (orig. 1926). 2 v.
(Thonga tribe)
NN *RR-QPF

Kannemeyer, A. J.
... Hugenote-Familieboeck
Kaapstad, Unie-Volkspers, 1940. 282 p.
(Huguenots in South Africa)
NN AVH (Africa, South)

Macmillan, William M.
The Cape Colour Question: an Historical Survey.
Cape Town, A. A., Blakema, 1968 (orig. 1927). 304 p.
(South African Bio. and Hist. Studies no. 6)
NN F-11 5600

Malherbe, Daniel F. du T.
Stamregister van die Suid-Afrikaanse Volk.
Stellenbosch, Tegniek, 1966. 1,208 p.
NN AVH (Africa, South)

Mitford-Barberton, Ivan Graham.
Some Frontier Families: Biographical Sketches of 100 Eastern Province Families Before 1840.
Cape Town, Pretoria, Human & Rousseau, 1968. (i.e., 1969) 303 p.
NN AVH (Cape of Good Hope)

Moletsane, Morena Abraham Aaron, 1878–
An Account of the Autobiographical Memoir, ed. by R. S. Webb.
Paarl, Cape Province, Fisher & Sons for R. S. Webb, 1967. 35 p., t of c at end, many orig. illus. tipped in., short index.
(Written by the grandson of a noted African chieftain)
NN AVHH (Moletsane)

Nienaber, Gabriel S.
Afrikaanse Familienname: 'n Geselsie vir Belangstellende leke oor die Betekenis van ouer Afrikaanse vanne.
Kaapstad, A. A. Balkema, 1955.
NN APD

Ollemans, Pierre Hugo.
Hottentot Hunt.

Bloemfontein, Friend, 1960. 64 p.
NN E-12 1977

Pama, Cornelis.
Die Wapens van die ou Afrikaanse
Families.
Kaapstad, A. A. Balkema, 1959.
194 p., index.
NN AWT

Pama, Cornelis.
Heraldry of South African Fami-
lies.
Cape Town, A. A. Balkema, 1972.
365 p., index.
NN AWT 73-13

Prinsloo, S. M.
Descendants of Frederick Jacobus.
(IN: *Familia*, Cape Town, 1975. v.
12, no. 4, p. 86–98)
(The family of a Malay slave from
Tranquebar on the east coast
of India, south of Pondichery)
NN AVH (Africa, South)

Robert, Brian.
The Zulu Kings.
London, 1974. 388 p.
NN JFD 76-7100

Robertson, George S., Sr.
The Kafirs of Hindu-Kush.
New York, 1970. 658 p.
NN JFD 72-2146

Schapera, Isaac.
The Khosian People of South Af-
rica: Bushman and Hottentots.
London, Routledge and Kegan
Paul, 1965 (orig. 1930). 450 p.
NN D-20 1608

Shooter, Joseph.
The Kafirs of Natal and the Zulu
Country.
New York, 1969. 403 p.
NN JFD 70-54

Smithers, A. J.
The Kaffir Wars, 1779–1977.
London, 1973. 288 p.
NN JFD 75-5333

South African Archival Records.
Natal.
Cape Town, c. 1958–. no. 1-8.
NN M-11 898

Theal, George McCall.
The Republic of Natal: The Origin
of the Present Pondo Tribe.
Cape Town, U. of Cape Town Li-
brary, 1961 (orig. 1886). 69 p.
NN B-10 1932

Villiers, Christoffel C. de.
Geslagregisters van die Kaapse
Families ... (Genealogies of Old
South African Families com-
pletely revised, ed., augmented
and rewritten by C. Pama).
Kaapstad, A. A. Balkema, 1966. 3
v. (1,212 p.)
NN APW

Who's Who in Southern Africa.
Johannesburg, Argus, 1907–1975+.
59 v.
(Includes Malawi, Central and
East Africa, Republic of South
Africa, South-West Africa, Rho-
desia, Zambia and Mauritius)
NN *RR-AGH & AGH

SOUTH-WEST AFRICA or NAMIBIA (WINDHOEK)

The region, administered by the Republic of South Africa, is inhabited by Ovambo, Okavango, Herero; various Nama (Khoikhoi) groups; Bergdama; Bushmen, or San; and whites of South African, German and British descent. Portuguese and Dutch expeditions explored the coastal regions during the fifteenth century. Dutch and British captains briefly claimed parts of the coast in the eighteenth century, and English missionaries arrived. Germany proclaimed a protectorate over the area. Between 1903 and 1908 many thousands of Herero and other black Africans died when a revolt by Namas and Hereros was put down by the Germans. In 1908 diamonds were discovered and a large influx of Europeans began. The country was occupied by South African forces in 1915, and in 1920 South Africa was given a mandate to administer it under the League of Nations. In 1945 South Africa refused to surrender its mandate and place South-West Africa under the United Nations trusteeship system. A United Nations resolution terminated the mandate in 1966 and in 1968 resolved that the country be known as Namibia. In 1971 the International Court of Justice upheld the United Nations action, but the South African government maintains that the UN has no authority over the area and is tying it more closely to itself by organizing it into magisterial districts with representation in the South African government.

The first census was taken in 1898, and others have been conducted approximately every ten years.

Archives

National Archives
Luderitz Street
Private Bag 13250
Windhoek 9100, South-West Africa

Central Archives Depot
Private Bag 236
Pretoria, South Africa

Archives Depot of the Territory
Private Bag 13250
Windhoek 9100, South-West Africa

Public and Church Records

Civil registration began in 1893 for deaths, births and marriages.
Department of the Interior
Private Bag X114
Pretoria, South Africa

For census information since 1915, write:
Department of Census and Statistics
Steyn's Building
Schoeman Street
Pretoria, South Africa

For census information, 1898–1915, and wills, 1893–1915, write the Archives Depot of the Territory. For wills since 1915, write the Master of the Supreme Court, Windhoek.

For religious records concerning the German community, write:
Evangelical Lutheran Church
P.O. Box 5069
Windhoek, South-West Africa
(Records from c. 1880's)

For the Anglican community:
Dutch Reformed Church in S.W.A.
P.O. Box 389
Windhoek, South-West Africa
(Records from c. 1956)

Cape Archives Depot
Private Bag 9025
Cape Town 8000, South Africa
(For earlier records)

Books and Articles

Beiderbecke, Heinrich.
Life among the Hereros in Africa.
New York, E. Kaufmann, 1922.
64 p.
NN ZKVX

François, Hugo von.
Nama und Damara: Deutsch-Sud-West Africa.
Magdeburg, E. Baensch, Jr., 1895.
334 p., ports.; tables.
NN BNL

Hanekom, T.N.
Die Gemeente Namakwaland: in Eeufees-Gedenkboek 1850–1950.
Woodstock, W. G. Kerpers, 1950.
195 p.
NN D-16 5032

Maywald, Fritz.
... Sudwest und seine Helden.
Berlin, 1934. 248 p.
(Deutschlands Kolonialhelden bd. 4)
NN BNL

Paschasius, W.
Die Befreiung Okahandjas Wahrend des Herero-Aufstandes.
Windhoek, 1951. 77 p.
NN D-10 3352

Schapera, Isaac.
Notes on some Herero Genealogies.
Cape Town, 1945. 39 p.
(Cape Town U. African Studies, School of Communication, School of African Studies. n.s., no. 14)
NN QPF+

SPANISH SAHARA (EL AAIÚN)

In 1434 Portuguese explorers came to the northern coast of Africa. Spain claimed a protectorate over the area in 1884. During the 1950's the Spanish began to develop more contact with the interior. They were ousted by a rebel movement in 1957 but regained control a year later with French help. In the same year Spain formed the province of Spanish Sahara and gave it representation in the Spanish Cortes. The area was relinquished to Morocco and Mauritania in February 1976.

Books and Articles

Almagro Basch, Martin.
Prehistoria del Norte de Africa y del Sahara Español.
Barcelona, 1946. 302 p.
NN BKE

Lodwick, John.
The Forbidden Coast: the Story of a Journey to Rio de Oro, a Spanish Possession in North West Africa.
London, Cassell, 1956. 266 p.
NN D-10 2696

SUDAN (KHARTOUM)

The Nubians, who occupied the northern part of Sudan in ancient times, were converted to Coptic Christianity in the sixth century A.D., but Islam took root during the wave of Arab conquests in the fifteenth century. The Egyptians united north and south Sudan in the nineteenth century. Led by Mohammed Ahmed ibn Abdullah—a Muslim mystic known as the Mahdi—the Sudanese rebelled against Egyptian rule in 1881 and by 1885 had control over most of Sudan. In 1898–99 a force of Egyptians and British defeated the Mahdi's followers, and the Sudan came under joint Anglo-Egyptian rule. Elections were held in Sudan for the first time in 1948. In 1956 the country was declared an independent republic.

A census was taken in 1955–56.

Archives

Dar-Al-Wath'ig   Al-Mar-Kaziya (Central Records Office)
P.O. Box 1914
Khartoum, Sudan

Libraries

Library of the University of Khartoum
P.O. Box 321
Khartoum, Sudan

Omdurman Public Library
Omurman, Sudan

Public and Church Records

Birth and marriage certificates can be obtained from the Department of Statistics, Ministry of Social Affairs.

Books and Articles

Alterman, Hyman.
Counting People: The Census in History.

New York, Harcourt, Brace, 1969.
p. 91–117.
(An account of the first census of
Sudan, 1953–56)
NN SDK

Badri, Babakr.
The Memoirs of Babikr Bedri.
London, Oxford U.P., 1969. 250 p.
NN *OFS 71-30

Bennett, Sir Ernest N.
The Downfall of the Dervishes ...
New York, Negro U. Press, 1969
(orig. 1899). 255 p.
NN JFD 70-34

Holt, Peter M.
The Mahdist State in the Sudan
1881–1898.
Oxford, Oxford U. Press, 1970. 295
p.
NN JFD 72-2366

O'Fahey, Rex Sean and J. L. Spalding.

Kingdoms of the Sudan.
London, Methuen, 1974. 235 p., in-
dex.
(Studies in African History v. 9)
NN *R-BLH 75 5039

Seligman, Charles G.
The Kabâbîsh, a Sudan African
Tribe.
(IN: Harvard African Studies,
Cambridge, MA, 1918. v. 2, p.
105–85)
NN *OAC+

Shibeika, Mekki.
History of the Nile Valley Peoples.
Beirut, 1965. 790 p.
NN SC AR962-S

Shibeika, Mekki.
Sudan Across the Generations.
Cairo, 1966. 450 p.
NN SC AR962 4S

SWAZILAND (MBABANE)

The Swazis settled in what is now Swaziland in 1820, after being
driven out of their first home by the Zulus; but the Zulus
continued their harassment, and the Swazis appealed to the
British for protection. The British and Transvaal governments
guaranteed Swaziland independence, and in 1890 a provisional
representative government was established. Following the Boer
War in 1902, the Transvaal's rights in Swaziland passed to the
British commissioner. In 1921 Sobhuza II became Swazi head of
state. In 1949 Britain decided against transferring Swaziland,
Lesotho and Botswana to South African control because of South
Africa's policy of apartheid. Swaziland became a self-governing
nation in 1967 and became fully independent with Sobhuza as
king in 1968.

Censuses were taken in 1911, 1921, 1946 and 1966.

Archives

Director of Archives
P.O. Box 57
Mbabane, Swaziland
Southern Africa

Public and Church Records

Civil registration began in 1907.

Registrar of Births, Marriages and Deaths
P.O. Box 19
Mbabane, Swaziland

Libraries

There are Public Libraries at Mbabane, Bremmersdorp, Goedgegun and Hlatikulu.

Books and Articles

Filmer, Harry J.
Usutu—A Story about the Early Days of Swaziland.
Johannesburg, Central News, 1960. 144 p.
NN D-13 4819

Grotpeter, John J.
Historical Dictionary of Swaziland.
Metuchen, NJ, Scarecrow Press, 1975. 251 p. alpha, biblio., no index.
(African Hist. Dict. no. 3)
NN *R-BNN 76-3217

Matsebula, J. S. M.
A History of Swaziland.
Cape Town, 1972. 131 p.
NN Sc 968.3-M

TANZANIA (DAR ES SALAAM)
(formerly Tanganyika and Zanzibar)

Tanzania represents the union of the two islands of Zanzibar with the mainland country of Tanganyika. Little is known about the area before the Arabs colonized it in the eighth century. The islands and the coast came under Portuguese rule in the sixteenth century, but the Sultans of Muscat reestablished Arab rule during the seventeenth. Trade in ivory and slaves flourished. In 1861 the British separated Zanzibar from the control of Muscat and it became an independent sultanate. In 1885 Germany established a protectorate over the mainland region, which became known as German East Africa. In 1920, after the German defeat in World War I, German East Africa was mandated to Britain. The name was changed to Tanganyika, and German colonists were ordered to leave. In 1961 Tanganyika gained independence within the Commonwealth with Julius K. Nyerere as premier. The following year he became President of the independent Republic of Tanganyika. Zanzibar obtained independence within the Commonwealth in 1963 and became a republic, with Sheik Abeid Karume as President, in 1964. Tanganyika and Zanzibar formed the United Republic of Tanzania in 1964, with Nyerere as President and Karume as Vice President.

A census was taken in 1967.

Archives

National Archives of Tanzania
Ministry of National Culture and
   Youth
P.O. Box 2006
Dar es Salaam, Tanzania

Zanzibar Government Archives
   (History and Administration)
P.O. Box 116
Zanzibar, Tanzania

Public and Church Records

Records dating back to April 1, 1921—and some back to August 28, 1917—are kept by the Registrar-General, Dar es Salaam. Some earlier records may be available for Zanzibar, where registration of births began in 1909, for deaths in 1906 and for marriages in 1907. British Consulate records for the area predate civil registration; births and deaths were noted beginning in 1868 for Zanzibar.

Libraries

British Council Library
P.O. Box 9100
Dar es Salaam, Tanzania

Ladha Maghji Indian Public Library
P.O. Box 70
Mwanza, Tanzania

Tanga Library (formerly, King George VI Memorial Library)
Box 391
Tanga, Tanzania

U.S. Information Service Library
Independence Avenue
P.O.B. 9170
Dar es Salaam, Tanzania

The University College Library
P.O. Box 9184
Dar es Salaam, Tanzania

Books and Articles

Don Nanjira, Daniel D.C.
The Status of Aliens in East Africa: Asians and Europeans in Tanzania, Uganda and Kenya.
New York, Praeger, 1976. 230 p., index.
(Praeger Studies in International Politics and Government)
NN JLE 76-1776

Gray, John M.
History of Zanzibar, from the Middle Ages to 1856.
Westport, CT, Greewood, 1975 (orig. 1962). 314 p.
NN Sc 967.81-G

Hatch, John C.
Tanzania in Profile.
New York, 1972. 214 p.
NN JFD 73-396

Ingrams, William Harold.
Chronology and Genealogies of Zanzibar Rulers.

Zanzibar, The Gov. Printer, 1926.
  10 p., gen. table.
NN AVH+ (Zanzibar)

Lema, Anza A.
Horombo: The Chief Who United
  His People.
London, Longman, 1976. 48 p.
(Makers of African History)

A History of Tanzania.
Nairobi, 1969. 276 p.
NN Sc 967.8-H

Van Pelt, P.
Bantu Customs in Mainland Tan-
  zania.
Tabora, Tanzania, c. 1971. 199 p.
NN JFC 75-57

TOGO (LOMÉ)
(formerly Togoland)

The coast of Togo was raided for slaves by European traders in
the seventeenth and eighteenth centuries. In 1884 the coastal
area was made a protectorate by the Germans, who later linked
Togo and Ghana as the protectorate of Togoland. With the
outbreak of World War I, the British occupied west Togoland
and the French occupied the east. In 1922 France and Britain
received mandates for their respective territories from the
League of Nations. The United Nations changed the mandates
to trusteeships in 1946. In 1956 British Togoland voted to join
the Gold Coast. France ended its trusteeship in 1958, and in
1960 French Togoland became the Republic of Togo.

  Censuses were taken in 1921 (Togoland) and in 1958 and 1961.

Archives

Archives de la Bibliothèque Na-
  tionale
Avenue de la Victoire
B.P. 1002
Lomé, Togo

Public and Church Records

Certificates for residents of the
  capital can be obtained from the
  État Civil de Lomé; for residents of other cities and towns,
  from the Mayor's Office (*La
  Mairie*).

Books and Articles

Buchner, Max.
Aurora Colonialis Bruchstucke
  eines Tagebuchs . . .
Munich, Piloty & Loehle, 1914. 341
  p.
NN BMN

Cornevin, Robert.
Le Togo, Nation-Pilote.
Paris, Nouvelles Editions Latines,
  1963. 159 p.
NN C-12 5423

Gold Coast and Togoland Histori-
cal Society Transactions.
Achimota, 1952–. v. 1–.
NN L-10 779

Hurston, Zora Neale.
Cudjo's Own Story of the Last African Slavery.

(IN: *JNH*, Lancaster, PA, 1927. v.
12, p. 648–63)
NN IEC

Mariox, Jean E.P.
... Le Togo. Pays d'Influence,
Française.
Paris, Larose, 1938. 136 p.
NN BMN

TRANSKEI (UMTATA)

Transkei is a black African homeland, or Bantustan. In the
1830's there was fighting between European settlers and black
Africans over possession of cattle and grazing lands. The territory was annexed by the British in 1848 and joined to Cape
Province in 1865. During the nineteenth century Transkeian
territories were given limited representative government. In
1963 the Transkei was separated from Cape Province to become
one of nine projected internally self-governing black African
areas within South Africa. The Assembly includes a majority of
hereditary chiefs.

Books and Articles

Elliott, Aubrey.
The Magic World of the Xhosa.
London, Collins, 1970. 144 p.
NN F-11 7545

McLean, John F.
A Compendium of Kafir Laws and
Customs, Including Genealogi-
cal Tables of Kafir Chiefs and
Various Tribal Census Returns.

Grahamstown, Cape Province, J.
Slater, 1906. 171 p., 3 tables.
NN QPF

Soga, John Henderson.
The Ama-Xhosa: Life and Cus-
toms.
Lovedale, Cape Province, Love-
dale Press, 1931. 431 p.
NN QPF

TUNISIA (TUNIS)

The capital city of Tunis is near the ancient site of Carthage,
founded in the sixth century B.C. and rebuilt by Julius Caesar
after it was destroyed by Rome in 146 B.C. In the seventh

century the Arabs conquered Tunisia. The Turks incorporated it into the Ottoman Empire in 1574, but the country was under only nominal Turkish control. The French established a protectorate in 1881. In 1934 an independence party was founded by Habib Bourguiba, and in 1956 Tunisian independence was achieved. In 1957 the Turkish bey, Sidi Lamine (the office had become hereditary in 1705), was deposed and a republic was proclaimed; Bourguiba became President.

Censuses were taken in 1926 (Tunis only), 1931, 1936 and 1956.

Archives

Archives Générales
Premier ministère, place du Gouvernement
Tunis, Tunisia

Public and Church Records

Civil registration began in 1911. Certificates are issued by the Controleur Civil in the district where a birth or marriage occurred, or by the Bureau de l'État Civil in a municipality. A central office for vital records is located at:
Municipalité de Tunis
Avenue de Carthage
Tunis, Tunisia

Certificates for Jewish marriages are issued by the rabbi who performed the ceremony. Muslim marriage certificates are issued by the *cadi* of the district where the marriage took place.

Libraries

Bibliothèque Nationale de Tunisie
20 Souk-el-Attarine
Tunis, Tunisia

Central Library
Tunis, Tunisia

Tunis Public Library
Tunis, Tunisia

Books and Articles

Brown, Leon C.
The Tunisia of Ahmad Bey, 1837–1855.
Princeton, NJ, Princeton U. Press, 1974. 409 p.
NN JFE 75-3250

Dessort, C.H. Roger.
. . . Histoire de la Ville de Tunis.
Algiers, E. P. Fister, 1926. 208 p.
NN BKO+

Goitein, S.D.
La Tunisie de XIe Siècle à la Lumière des Documents de la Geniza du Claire.
(IN: *Études d'Orientalisme Dédiés à la Mémoire de Levi-Provençal*, Paris, 1962. v. 2, p. 559–79)
NN *OGC

Guiraud, Amedoe.
Histoire de la Tunisie.
Tunis, 1945. 2 v.
NN BKO

Temimi, Abdeljelil.
Recherches et Documents d'Histoire Maghrebine.
Tunis, 1971. 333 p.
NN *OFO 75-2118

UGANDA (KAMPALA)

Britain set up a protectorate over the state of Buganda in 1894 and eventually extended the protectorate to encompass all of Uganda. In 1953 Kakaka (King) Mutesa II was exiled to London by the British for his refusal to quell local rioting in Buganda. He was allowed to return in 1955 with the understanding that he would rule as a constitutional monarch and ensure the participation of Buganda in Uganda's central government. In 1962 Buganda was given a great deal of autonomy in the federal constitution that marked Uganda's formal independence. Mutesa was elected President by Parliament the following year. In 1966 Prime Minister Milton Obote ousted Mutesa and took full control of the government. In 1967 a republican constitution was adopted that provided for a presidential government headed by Obote. General Idi Amin seized control of the government and was named President in 1971. The following year he ordered all Asians (numbering some 25,000 Indians and Pakistanis who held British passports) to leave the country.

Censuses were taken in 1921, 1931,1941, 1959 and 1969.

Archives

Entebbe Archives
P.O. Box 5
Entebbe, Uganda

Public and Church Records

Civil registration of births, deaths, marriages and adoptions began January 1, 1905, but there are entries in Marriage Register Books back to April 1, 1904, and a register of births kept by the British Vice-Consulate at Entebee also predates civil registration. Birth and death certificates can be obtained from the Registrar of Births and Deaths, Kampala. Marriage certificates should be requested from the district commissioner of the district in which the marriage took place.

Libraries

Makerere University College Library
P.O. Box 16002
Kampala, Uganda

Makerere University College, Albert Cook Library
P.O. Box 2072
Kampala, Uganda

Uganda Library Service
Headquarters: Salisbury Road
P.O. Box 4262
Kampala, Uganda

Books and Articles

Kaggwa, Apolo, Sir.
Ekitabo kya Basekabaka be Buganda, na be Bunyoro, na be Kokis, ne be Toro, na be Nkole.

Kampala, 1971. 332 p.
(Kings and rulers of Uganda)
NN JFC 75-488

Karugire, Samwiri Rubaraza.
A History of the Kingdom of Nkore
    in Western Uganda to 1896.
Oxford, 1971. 291 p.
NN Sc 572.967-K & JFD 73-571

Lamphear, John.
The Traditional History of the Jien
    of Uganda.
Oxford, Clarendon Press, 1976. 281
p., gen. table, index.
(Oxford Studies in African Affairs)

Makerere History Papers.
Kampala, no. 1–.
NN JFK 73-281 (NN has no. 3,
1969–)

Mullins, J. D.
The Wonderful Story of Uganda.
London, 1904. 224 p.
NN Sc 266.3-M

Stacey, John.
Summons to Ruwensori.
London, Secken & Warburg, 1965.
    224 p.
(The Bakonjo Tribe)
NN D-16 910

Weinraub, Bernard.
Uganda Exiles: "In Britain, I Miss
    ..."
(IN: *NYT.* New York, Mar. 14 1976.
    p. 24)

UPPER VOLTA (OUAGADOUGOU)

Between the eleventh and thirteenth centuries the Mossi people came into the region and set up three independent kingdoms, the most powerful of which was the Ouagadougou. The Mossi warred with the nearby empires of Mali and Songhai from the fourteenth through the nineteenth centuries and Mossi power was broken. In 1896 the French established a protectorate. In 1904 the present area of Upper Volta became part of a French colony that also included Niger and Upper Sénégal. Upper Volta became a separate French colony in 1919. In 1932 Upper Volta was divided among the colonies of Sudan, Niger and the Ivory Coast, but in 1947 the old boundaries were restored. In 1958 a self-governing state, called the Voltaic Republic, was established. In 1959 the name was changed to Upper Volta, and the next year it became an independent republic.

Books and Articles

Balima, Salfo A.
Genese de la Haute-Volta.
Ouagadougou, c. 1970. 253 p.
NN JFD 73-9631

Izard, Françoise.
Bibliographie Générale de la
    Haute-Volta, 1956–1965.
Paris, 1967. 300 p.
NN Sc F 016.9662-I

ZAÏRE (KINSHASA)
(formerly Belgian Congo, Republic of Congo)

The Portuguese explored this region in the fifteenth century, at which time the Kingdom of the Congo included present-day Congo and Angola. The area was explored by Henry Stanley in service to King Leopold II of Belgium, from 1879 to 1884, and in 1885 Leopold II established the Congo Free State. In 1908 it was renamed the Belgian Congo. In 1960 the country was granted independence, for which it was poorly prepared. Within a week Premier Patrice Lumumba announced that the Belgians were no longer welcome; the Congolese army mutinied and Belgian troops were called in. Moise Tshombe, Premier of the rich region of Katanga, announced secession, while Joseph Kasavubu, the head of state, and Lumumba, the national premier, each declared the other's dismissal. The chaos was resolved when Colonel Joseph Mobuto, the commander of the army, seized control. In 1961 Mobuto returned the government to Kasavubu. Katanga's secession ended in 1963. In 1964 Tshombe, who had fled the country, was recalled in hopes that he could unite the Congo. Soon after he became premier, a peasant rebellion erupted, and the insurgents took half the country, but Tshombe, aided by mercenaries and Belgian paratroopers, put down the revolt. In 1965 Tshombe was dismissed. Mobuto again deposed the Kasavubu government and went on to provide a relatively stable, centralized government. In 1971 the Democratic Republic of the Congo became the Republic of Zaïre, and the Congo River was renamed the Zaïre River. In 1972 citizens with Christian names were ordered to assume African names.

Archives

Archives Nationales
42/A avenue de la Justice (B.P. 3428)
Kinshasa-Gombé, Zaïre

Books and Articles

Bouveignes, Olivier de.
... Les Anciens Rois de Congo.
Namur, 1948. 160 p.

(Revue Générale des Missions d'Afrique, Grands Lacs)
NN QPF

Challaye, Felicien.
Le Congo Français ...
Paris, F. Alcan, 1909. 311 p.
NN BMR

Cornevin, Robert.
La Zaïre Ex-Congo-Kinshasa.
Paris, 1972. 128 p.
NN JFC 73-3168

Lewis, Thomas.
The Ancient Kingdom of Kongo
. . .
(IN: *Geography Journal*, London,
1902. v. 19, p. 541–58)
NN KAA

Masoin, Fritz.
Histoire de l'État Independant du
Congo.
Namur, Picard-Balon, 1912–13. 2 v.
NN BMS

Olsen, Hal C.
African Heroes of the Congo Re-
bellion.
Kijabe, Kenya, 1973. 94 p.
NN Sc 276.751-0

Stanley, Henry Morton.
The Congo and the Founding of
Its Free State.
Detroit, MI, 1970 (orig. 1885). 2 v.
NN JFD and 72–1384

Thompson, Virginia, and Richard
Adloff.
Historical Dictionary of the Peo-
ple's Republic of the Congo
(Congo-Brazzaville).
Metuchen, NJ, Scarecrow Press,
1974. 139 p. alpha, biblio., no
index.
(African Historical Dictionary no.
2)
NN *R-BMR 076-1517

Witherall, Julian W.
French-Speaking Central Africa.
Washington, DC, 1973. 314 p.
NN JLF 74-197

Zaïre: Revue Congolaise.
Brussels, 1947–60. v. 1–14.
(NN is missing some issues)
NN BMS (Zaïre)

ZAMBIA (LUSAKA)
(formerly Northern Rhodesia)

Zambia is the former British protectorate of Northern Rhodesia.
David Livingstone explored the area in 1851 and 1873, and the
British South Africa Company administered the area until 1924,
when a British protectorate was established. Many Europeans
came into the area between 1930 and 1944, after large deposits
of copper were discovered. In 1964 Northern Rhodesia became
the independent republic of Zambia, and Kenneth Kaunda,
leader of the ruling United National Independence Party, was
elected President by Parliament.
    A census was taken in 1963.

Archives

National Archives of Zambia
P.O. Box R.W. 95
Lusaka, Zambia

Libraries

Ndola Public Library
P.O. Box 388
Independence Way, Ndola, Zambia

National Archives Library
P.O. Box 10, Ridgeway Lusaka, Zambia

Library
The University of Zambia
P.O. Box 2379
Lusaka, Zambia

Books and Articles

Graham, Ivor M.
Guide to the Public Archives of Zambia.
Lusaka, 1970. 1 v.
NN JFL 73-248

Storry, J.G.
Heraldry in Africa.
(IN: *The Coat of Arms*, London, 1974. n.s., v. 1, no. 91, p. 83–85; no. 92, p. 108–111)
(Arms of the Emperor Monomatapa of the Zambesi Region granted by Portugal c. 1569)
NN AWA

Who's Who in Zambia.
Lusaka, Zambia, 1967–68.
107 p., alpha.
JFK 75-233

ZIMBABWE:

See Rhodesia

AFRICA

General Sources

The African Historian (Journal of the Historical Soc. of the U. of Ife)
Ibadan, Nigeria. 1965–.
NN K-10 7525

Ajayi, J.F.A. de, and Michael Crowder.
History of West Africa.
New York, Columbia U. Press, 1973–76. 2 v.
NN Sc 966-A and Sc E 77-29

Becker, Peter.
Trails and Tribes in Southern Africa.
London, Hart-Davis MacGibbon, 1975. 211 p.
NN Sc 572.968-B and JLM 75-593

Chuk-orji, Ogonna.
Names from Africa.
Chicago, 1972. 89 p.
NN APD 73-1710

Cole, Mary.
Dirtroads.
Dublin, Gill & Macmillan, 1975. 246 p.
(Central Africa)

Davies, Helen
Libraries in West Africa, 1960–73.
A Bibliography. 2nd ed.
Aberystwyth, College of Librarianship, 1974. 53 p., index.

Dickie, John.
Who's Who in Africa.
London, 1973. 602 p.
NN Sc 920.06-D

Dictionary of African Biography.
London, 1970–.
NN *R-AGC 72–202

Duignan, Peter.
Handbook of American Resources for African Studies.
Stanford, CA, Hoover Institution, 1967. 218 p.
NN F-11 4307

Duignan, Peter.
The United States and the African
   Slave Trade, 1619–1862.
Stanford, CA, Hoover Institution,
   1963. 72 p.
NN D-16 2000

Dunigan, Peter, et al.
Guide to Research and Reference
   Works on Sub-Saharan Africa.
Stanford, CA, Hoover Institution,
   c. 1971. 1,102 p.
NN JFF 73-650

Encyclopedia of Africa.
New York, Franklin Watts, 1976.

Freeman-Granville G.S.P.
Chronology of African History.
London, Oxford U. Press, 1973. 312
   p.
NN *R-BKC 74-1720

Freeman-Granville, G.S.P.
The East African Coast: Select
   Documents from the First to
   the Earlier Nineteenth Cen-
   tury. 2nd ed.
London, Collings, 1975 (1st ed.
   1962) 314 p., index.
NN Sc D 77-85

Freeman-Granville, G.S.P.
A Modern Atlas of African History
London, Collings, 1976. 63 p., in-
   dex.

Hakim, Dawaud.
Arabic Names and Other African
   Names with Their Meanings.
Philadelphia, PA, 1970. 28 p.
NN Sc 929.4-H

Herdeck, Donald F.
African Authors, a Companion to
   Black African Writing, 1300–
   1973.

Washington, DC, Black Orpheus
   Press, 1973. 605 p.
NN *R-NAB 74-1975

History of East Africa.
Oxford, Clarendon Press, 1963–76.
   v. 1–3
NN *RR-BLN 76-353

History of West Africa, ed. by J.F.
   Ade Ajayi and Michael Crow-
   der. 2nd ed.
London, Longman, 1976.
2 v. in 1 (644 p.).
NN (1973 ed.) Sc 966-A

International African Institute
   (London).
Cumulative Bibliography of Afri-
   can Studies.
Boston, MA, G.K. Hall, 1973. 5 v.
   author cat. 2 v.; classified cat.
   3 v.
NN *RG-BK 75-1262

July, Robert W.
A History of the African People.
   2nd ed.
New York, Scribner's, 1974. 731 p.,
   index.
NN *R-BKC 74-4201

Kamuyu-Wa-Kange' The.
What Is Your African Name?
Jamaica, New York, Pan African
   Students Organization, 1972. 23
   p.
NN APD 72-3024

Lewis, Roy.
The Times Map of the Tribes, Peoples and Nations of Modern Africa.
London, John Bartholomew, 1972.
   map 92 x 74.
NN Map Div. 75-1288

Madubuike, Ihechukwu.
A Handbook of African Names.
n.p., n.d., 1976

Noms de l'Afrique Noire.
(IN: *Vroonen, E., Encyclopedie des Noms des Personnes*. Paris, Editions Universitaires, 1973. p. 691–728)
NN APD 76-439

Retel-Laurentin, Anne.
Les Noms de Naissance Indicateur de la Situation Familiale et Sociale en Afrique Noir.
Paris, 1972. 160 p.
NN JFL 74-236

Rosenthal, Eric.
Encyclopedia of Southern Africa. 6th ed.
London, Frederick Warne, 1973. 662 p.
NN *R-BN 74-3671

Seligman, Charles G.
Races of Africa. 4th ed.
London, Oxford, 1966. 170 p.
NN C-13 3934

Thompson, Virginia, and Richard Adolf.
French West Africa.
London, Allen & Unwin, 1958. 626 p., index.
(Newspapers, p. 551-53)
NN *R-BM

U.S. Library of Congress. African Section.
Africa South of the Sahara: Index to Periodical Literature, 1900–1970. The Library of Congress.
Boston, MA, G.K. Hall, 1971. 4 v. 1st sup. 1973, 1 v.
NN *RG-KAH 72-149

West African Chiefs, Ed. by Michael Crowder.
New York, 1970. 453 p.
NN JLD 72-581

Wills, A.J.
An Introduction to the History of Central Africa. 3rd ed.
London, Oxford U. Press, 1973. 458 p., index.
NN *R-BMW 74-495

BELIZE (BELMOPAN)
(Formerly British Honduras)

Carved out of Central America by English buccaneers in the early seventeenth century, Belize was a British oasis in a Spanish Empire. Most of the people in the country are black, but there are some descendants of the ancient Maya, a few Caribs and many Spanish Americans among the population. While the official language is English, Spanish is widely used. Belize was known as British Honduras until June 1, 1973. The capital is at Belmopan, as the former capital at Belize was badly damaged by a hurricane in 1961.

Books and Articles

Alderman, Ralph H., and Clarence Minkel.
A Bibliography of British Honduras 1900–1970.
East Lansing, MI, 1970. 93 p.
NN HMO 72-1842

Caiger, Stephen L.
British Honduras, Past and Present.
London, Allen & Unwin, 1951. 240 p., index, maps.
NN HMO

Calderon Quijano, José Antonio.
... Belice 1663(?)–1821. Seville, 1944. 503 p., index.
(Abstracts of original documents, maps, signatures)
NN HMO

Carr, David, and John Thorpe.
From Cam to the Cays ... British Honduras 1959–60.
London, Putnam, 1961. 190 p., index.
NN HMO

Gregg, A.R.
British Honduras.
London, HMSO, 1968. 158 p., index, map, illus.
NN HMO

CANAL ZONE

A French company headed by Ferdinand de Lesseps began work on a canal across the isthmus of Panama in 1881, but by 1889 financial problems and disease among the workers brought about the firm's bankruptcy. In 1903, Panama revolted against

Columbia—of which it was a part—when the Columbian senate refused to ratify the Hay-Herrán treaty that would have given the United States the right to build the canal. The United States intervened on the Panamanian side, and Panama declared its independence. The United States was granted exclusive control of the Canal Zone and was assigned the authority to intervene in case of a threat to Panama's independence. In 1939 the treaty was changed, and the United States was denied the right to intervene in Panamanian affairs. A governor appointed by the United States administers the Canal Zone, which extends five miles on either side of the canal. United States sovereignty has been a cause of periodic rioting since 1959, and the ultimate transfer of jurisdiction over the canal from the United States to Panama may take place in the next decade.

Public and Church Records

Birth and death records since May 1940 are maintained by the Vital Statistics Clerk
Health Bureau
Balboa Heights, Canal Zone

For marriage records, write: Balboa Division (Pacific Area)
Clerk, U.S. District Court, Box 2006
Balboa Heights, Canal Zone

Libraries

Canal Zone Library and Museum
Balboa Heights, Canal Zone

Books and Articles

Gause, Frank A., and Charles C. Carr.
The Story of Panama, the New Route to India.
New York, Arno Press, 1970 (orig. 1912). 290 p., index.
NN HDL 72-997

Hoard, Lyon J.
Early Graves of Mount Hope Cemetery, Panama Canal Zone.
(IN: *TAG*, Des Moines, IA, 1976. v. 52, p. 11–13)
NN APGA

Howarth, David.
The Golden Isthmus.
London, Collins, 1966. 285 p., index.
(Excellent book for background of the area; includes the Scottish colony of 1698–1700— 1,200 Scots led by William Patterson, a Scottish economist and a founder of the Bank of England)
NN HDL

McCullough, David.
The Path Between the Seas: The Creation of the Panama Canal, 1870–1914.
New York, Simon and Schuster, 1977. 698 p. index

COSTA RICA (SAN JOSÉ)

The Spanish conquest of this land began with the establishment of the city of Cartago in 1563, although Columbus had visited the site of Puerto Limon earlier, during his fourth and last voyage to the New World. The area was administered by the captaincy general of Guatemala, and the cities of San José, Heredia and Alajuela were settled in the eighteenth century. In 1821 Costa Rica gained its independence from Spain with the other colonies in the area, and it was annexed to the Mexican Empire. From 1823 to 1838 it was part of the Central American Federation and in 1839 became a separate nation, despite attempts at invasion by Nicaragua. In the area around Cartago, few Indians survived, and the hacienda system of other Spanish colonies, which was based on Indian labor, was not feasible. Most of the Spanish settlers became small farmers. In the northeast, a mestizo population developed in the cattle country. Jamaican blacks settled in Costa Rica after the Second World War to work on the banana plantations.

The parish registers of Cartago date from 1564, and from these registers and others in the country census information was developed for 1824, 1836 and 1844. Early censuses of the country were taken in 1864, 1892 and 1927, and more recent counts were recorded in 1963 and 1973.

Archives

Archivo Nacional de Costa Rica
Calle 7, Av. 4 (Apartado Postal 10217)
San José, Costa Rica

Public and Church Records

Certificates for births after January 1, 1888, can be obtained from the Civil Registry of San José (Registro Central del Estado Civil), and baptismal certificates of people born before then may be kept by the Roman Catholic Church. Marriage certificates can also be obtained from the Civil Registry.

Dirección General de Estadística y Censos
(Statistics and Census Office)
Avda. 2-4, C. 6
San José, Costa Rica

Libraries

Biblioteca de la Universidad de Costa Rica
Ciudad Universitaria, Apdo. 3862
San José, Costa Rica

Biblioteca Nacional
Calle 5, Avenidas 1/3
San José, Costa Rica

Books and Articles

Academia Costarricense de Ciencias Genealogicas Revista.
San José, 1953–1962. 9 v.
(Genealogical periodical)
NN *XLG-7 microfiche

Castro y Tosi, Norberto de.
De Vera Nobilitate Costarricense.
San José, pub. del Supremo Tribunal y Colegio de Armas de Costa Rica, 1960. nos. 1–4 1 v., no index.
NN APY

Keith Alvarado, Henry M.
Historia de la Familia Alvardo Barroeta: Genealogía de Manuel Alvarado y Alvarado ...
San José, 1972. 104 p.
NN APY 74-695

Sanabria Martinez, Victor.
Genealogías de Cartago Hasta 1850.
San José, Costa Rica, the author, 1957. 6 v., indexed.
NN APY

GUATEMALA (GUATEMALA CITY)

In 1524 Pedro de Alvarado defeated the Maya-Quiche Indians, whose civilization was a thousand years old, and became captain-general of this area. The colonial capital was first at Ciudad Vieja and then at Antigua, both ruined sites today. Guatemala City was founded in 1776, was destroyed by an earthquake in 1917–18 and was rebuilt on the same site. (In 1976 another earthquake leveled many communities and parts of the capital city.) Guatemala gained its independence from Spain in 1821 along with the other Central American countries, was briefly annexed to the Mexican Empire and became the focal point of the Central American Federation until the republic was established in 1839. About half of the population is of pure Indian descent, while the remainder is of mixed Spanish and Indian origin.

In the early 1970's the most common surnames in Guatemala City were Garcia, González, López, Morales and Rodríguez.

A census was taken in the colonial period in 1778. In 1880 the first national census was taken, and subsequent population counts were made in 1893, 1921, 1940, 1950 and 1964.

Archives

Archivo General De Centro America
4a Av. entre 7a. y 8a calles, Zona 1
Guatemala City, Guatemala

Public and Church Records

Birth and marriage certificates can be obtained from the Registro Civil nearest the place where the event occurred.

Libraries

Biblioteca Nacional de Guatemala
5a Avda. 7-26, Zona 1
Guatemala City, Guatemala

Biblioteca Central de la Universidad de San Carlos
Ciudad Universitaria, Zona 12
Guatemala City, Guatemala

Historical and Genealogical Societies

Institute de Antropología e Historia (Includes colonial history)
Edificio 5 de "La Aurora"
Guatemala City, Guatemala
(*Antropología e Historia de Guatemala*)

Sociedad de Geografía e Historia de Guatemala
3a Avenida No. 8-35
Guatemala City 1, Guatemala

Books and Articles

Aparicio y Aparico, Edgar John.
Conquistadores de Guatemala y Fundodores de Familias Guatemaltecas. 2nd ed.
Mexico, 1961. 81 p.
NN D-13 8809

Cózar, Arnoldo.
Arcon Patrico.
Guatemala, Ministerio de Educación, 1965. 2 v.
NN HMD

Herrera, Marta J.
Semblanzas Figuras de Guatemala.
Guatemala, 1966. 372 p.
NN D-17 6051

Moore, Richard.
Historical Dictionary of Guatemala. rev. ed.
Metuchen, NJ, Scarecrow Press, 1973. 285 p., alpha subject index.
NN HMD 75-1987

HONDURAS (TEGUCIGALPA)

Hernando Cortes explored this area in 1524 and commanded Pedro de Alvarado to establish some settlements on the coast. The Mayan civilization in such cities as Copan had declined greatly by the time the Spanish arrived. Honduras gained independence from Spain in 1821 and became part of Iturbe's Mexican Empire. In 1825 it became a member of the Central American Federation, of which Francisco Morazan of Honduras was President. It became a separate country in 1838, but through the years there has been much interference in the government from foreign elements. About 90 percent of the population is mestizo, and over half the people are illiterate.

Censuses were attempted in 1881, 1887, 1895, 1901 and 1905, but the results were unsatisfactory. More accurate censuses were taken in 1910, 1916, 1926, 1935, 1940, 1950, 1956 and 1960.

Archives

Archivo Nacional Hondureño
4a Av. entre 6a y 7a Calles
Tegucigalpa, Honduras

Public and Church Records

Birth and marriage certificates can be obtained by applying to the civil registry officials in the municipality where the event took place.

Libraries

Biblioteca Nacional de Honduras
6a Ave. "Salvador Mendieta"
Tegucigalpa, Honduras

Biblioteca de la Universidad Nacional
Plaza de la Merced
Tegucigalpa, Honduras

Historical and Genealogical Societies

Asociación de Bibliotecarios y Archivisitas de Honduras
5a Avda. 517 Comayagua, D.C.
Tegucigalpa, Honduras
(*Honduras Bibliotecológica y Archivística*)

Book and Articles

Davidson, William V.
Historical Geography of the Bay Islands, Honduras.
Birmingham, AL, Southern U. Press, 1974. 199 p., index.
(Important for its biblio., p. 151–190).
NN HML 75-1499

Gonzolez y Contreras, Gilberto.
Hombres Entre Lava y Piños.
Mexico, B. Costa Amic, 1946. 315 p.
NN HMH

Pan American Publicity Corp.
Propaganda pro Honduras.
Havana, Molina, 1932. 424 p.
NN HML

Revista del Archivo y Biblioteca Nacionales de Honduras.
Tegucigalpa, 1905–55. v. 1, no. 7–.
v. 33 (incomplete)
NN *ZAN-H50 film and HML+

Saavedra, David.
... Bananas, Gold and Silver.
Tegucigalpa, Talleros, 1935. 436 p.
NN TAH+

Valladares, Paulino.
Hondureños Ilustres.
Tegucigalpa, 1972. 240 p.
NN JFD 74-1168

NICARAGUA (MANAGUA)

In 1524 Francisco Fernandez de Cordoba founded the cities of León and Granada in this area. León was the ancient capital, and the city of Managua, the modern capital, was not founded until 1855. In 1821, after gaining its independence from Spain, Nicaragua was briefly part of the Mexican Empire. It was a member of the Central American Federation from 1825 to 1838, when it became an independent republic.

As a Guatemalan Province, Nicaragua was included in the Spanish population count of that country in 1778. A trial census was taken in 1800, and various censuses were taken in 1813, 1834, 1845–46, 1867, 1890 and 1906. National censuses were recorded in 1920, 1940 and 1950.

Archives

Archivo General De La Nación
Apartado Postal No. 1141
Managua, Nicaragua

Dirección General de Cedulación
Iglesia el Carmen 20 vrs. arriba
Managua, Nicaragua

Public and Church Records

Civil registration for births, deaths and marriages began in 1879; for divorces, in 1893. Certificates can be obtained from the Civil Registrar (Registrar del Estado Civil).

Libraries

Biblioteca Nacional
Calle del Triunfo No. 302, Apdo. 101
Managua, Nicaragua

Biblioteca Central del Universidad Nacional de Nicaragua
León, Nicaragua

Biblioteca Centroamericana
Managua, Nicaragua

Historical and Genealogical Societies

Academia de Geografía e Historia de Nicaragua
Managua, Nicaragua
(*Revista*)

Books and Articles

Aguilar, Arturo.
Hombres de la Independencia de Nicaragua y Costa Rica.
León, Tip La Patria, 1940. 248 p.
NN AGX

Castrillo Gamaz, Manuel.
Proceres Nicaraguenses y Articulos Históricos.
Managua, Tall. Nacionales, 1961. 322 p.
NN E-12 2519

Meyer, Harvey Kessler.
Historical Dictionary of Nicaragua.
Metuchen, NJ, Scarecrow Press, 1972. 503 p., alpha, no index.
NN HMR 76-1959

PANAMA (PANAMA CITY)

The Isthmus of Panama where this republic is located connects Central and South America. The area was visited by Columbus in 1502, having been sighted by his ships the previous year.

Vasco Nuñez de Balboa crossed the isthmus in 1513 and discovered the Pacific Ocean on September 13. The city of Panama was founded in 1519 under the governorship of Pedro Arias de Avila. Francis Drake attacked the area in the late sixteenth century, and the pirate Henry Morgan destroyed the old city of Panama in the late 1660's. The province of Panama became part of the viceroyalty of Peru after this and in 1740 became part of New Granada. In 1821 Panama was freed from Spain and became part of Colombia. Its independence as a country did not come until November 3, 1903, with the help of United States naval forces. On November 18 of that year, Panama granted the United States the use and control of the Canal Zone.

Panama was included in the Colombian census of 1870, but it was not until 1911 that the first national census was taken. Other censuses followed in 1920, 1930 and 1940.

Archives

Archivo Nacional
Av. Peru 31-31 (Apartado 6618)
Panama 5, República de Panama

Public and Church Records

Civil registration began in 1914, and records are maintained at:
Dirección General del Registro Civil
Apartado 5281
Panama 5, República de Panama

For census information:
Dirección General de Estadística y Censo
Contraloria General de la República
Panama 4, República de Panama

For religious records:
Arquidiocesis de Panama
Apartado 6386
Panama 5, República de Panama

Libraries

Biblioteca Nacional
Apartado 3435
Panama, República Panama

Biblioteca de la Dirección de Estadística y Censo
Apartado 5213
Panama 5, República de Panama

Biblioteca de la Universidad de Panama
Apartado 3277
Panama, República de Panama

Books and Articles

Arosemena, Augustin J.
Siluetas Biográficas de Illustres Coclesanos ... 1855–1955.
Panama, 1961. 264 p.
NN D-13 6508

Diez Castillo, Luisa.
Los Cimarroones y la Esclavitud en Panama.

Panama, 1968. 86 p.
NN HDL 71-311

Hedrick, Basil Calvin.
Historical Dictionary of Panama.
Metuchen, NJ, Scarecrow Press,
1970. 105 p.
NN HDL 72-648

Mejia Robledo, Alfonso.
Quien es Quien en Panama.

Medellin, Columbia, Dedout, 1949.
320 p.
NN D-14 803

Panameños Illustres.
Panama, 1950–.
NN HDL

Strasserde Saavedra, Mia.
El Libro d'Oro: The Golden Book.
Panama, 1926. 352 p.
NN HDL

EL SALVADOR (SAN SALVADOR)

Pedro de Alvarado placed El Salvador under the captaincy-general of Guatemala when he conquered the area in 1526. With the other Central American states, it became free from the Spanish yoke in 1821 and was briefly part of the Mexican Empire before joining the Central American Federation. El Salvador protested the continued interference of Guatemala in its affairs, and the capital of the Federation was moved to El Salvador in 1831. In 1839 El Salvador became a republic. Although it is the smallest republic in Latin America, it is densely populated, with 85 percent of the people being of mixed white and Indian descent, 10 percent pure Indian and 5 percent white.

El Salvador appeared as a part of Guatemala in a poll taken in 1776 and as the province of San Salvador in a census of Guatemala in 1807. After it became a republic, censuses were taken in 1878, 1882, 1892, 1901, 1930, 1950 and 1961.

Archives

Archivo General De La Nación
Palacio Nacional, Planta baja costado poniente
San Salvador, El Salvador

Public and Church Records

Civil registration was established in 1881. Birth and marriage certificates can be obtained from the municipality (*alcaldias*) in which they took place. Baptismal certificates are issued by parochial authorities.

Dirección General de Estadísticas y Censos
(Statistics and Census Office)
Calle Arce No. 953
San Salvador, El Salvador

Libraries

Biblioteca Nacional
8a Avenida Norte y Calle Delgado
San Salvador, El Salvador

Biblioteca Universitaria de la
   Universidad de El Salvador
7a Avenida Sur 15
San Salvador, El Salvador

Books and Articles

Album Patriotico.
San Salvador, Imprenta Nacional,
   1915. 266 p.
NN HMH

Anaqueles: Revista de la Biblioteca Nacional.

San Salvador, 1951–. Época 5, no. 1–.
NN *HZD (Salvador)

Dominquez Sosa, Julio A.
Ensayo Histórico Sobre las Tribus
   non Ualcas y Caudillo Anastasio Aquino.
San Salvador, 1964. 202 p.
NN JFE 71-800

Garcia, Miguel Angel.
Diccionario Histórico Enciclopédico
   de la República de El Salvador.
San Salvador, La Lux, 1927–1951.
   13 v.
NN HMH

Osborne, Lilly.
Four Keys to El Salvador.
New York, Funk and Wagnalls,
   1956. 221 p.
NN HMH

BERMUDA (HAMILTON)

A British dependency, Bermuda consists of 360 coral islands, twenty of which are inhabited. The islands were discovered in 1515 by a Spaniard, Juan de Bermúdez. In 1690 a group of colonists under Sir George Somers was wrecked there; the islands were called Somers Islands for a long time and were governed by a chartered company until they were acquired by Britain in 1684. An assembly began in 1620. In 1968, elections, based on the first universal suffrage, were held, and Sir Edward Richards, a black, became Prime Minister in 1971. Censuses were recorded in Bermuda in 1891, 1911, 1921, 1931 and 1960.

Archives

Bermuda Archives
Par-la Ville
Hamilton, Bermuda

Public and Church Records

The Registrar General, Hamilton, has complete registers back to 1866. Some church records of baptisms, weddings and burials date to the seventeenth century.

Libraries

Bermuda Library
Hamilton, Bermuda

Historical and Genealogical Societies

Bermuda Historical Monuments Trust (in charge of Colonial Archives)
Hamilton, Bermuda

Bermuda Historical Society
Par-la Ville
Hamilton, Bermuda

Royal Commonwealth Society, Bermuda Branch
% Bank of Bermuda
Hamilton, Bermuda

St. George's Historical Society
St. George, Bermuda

Books and Articles

Bermuda Historical Quarterly.
Hamilton, 1944–. v. 1–.
(33 v. by 1976)
NN HRX

Eeman, Harold.
The English Branch of the Tucker Family.
(IN: *Bermuda Historical Quarterly*, Hamilton, 1958. v. 15, p. 155–57)
NN HRX

Genealogical Notes from Bermuda.
(IN: *Tyler's Quarterly Magazine*, Richmond, VA, 1942–47. v. 23, p. 176–91, 259–78, 282–97; v. 24, p. 50–59, 220–30; v. 25, p. 44–52, 136–46, 206–17, 278–89; v. 26, p. 33–46, 107–18, 189–200, 295–305; v. 27, p. 27–56, 144–55, 231–41, 319–22; v. 29, p. 136–39)
NN *R-APR (Virginia)

Kennedy, Jean de C.
Biography of a Colonial Town: Hamilton, Bermuda, 1790–1897.
Hamilton, c. 1963. 400 p., index.
NN HRX

Lefroy, Sir. J. H.
Memorials of Bermuda, 1515–1687.
London, 1877–79. 2 v.
NN HRX

Tucker, Beverly R.
Tales of the Tuckers, Decendants in the Male Line of St. George Tucker of Bermuda and Virginia.
Richmond, VA, Dietz, 1942. 170 p., no index.
NN APV (Tucker)

Tucker, Terry.
Bermuda Today and Yesterday, 1503–1973.
London, R. Hale, 1975. 208 p., index.

Wilkinson, Henry Campbell.
Bermuda in the Old Empire: a History of the Island from the Dissolution of the Somers Company Until the End of the American Revolutionary War, 1684–1784.
London, Oxford, 1950. 457 p.
NN HRX

CANADA (OTTAWA)

While the Vikings are believed to have touched on Canada around A.D. 1000, the first recorded landing was that of John Cabot, in service to Henry VII of England, who landed near Newfoundland in 1497 and claimed the area for the English Crown. In 1534 Jacques Cartier claimed the Gaspé Peninsula for France, and the history of Canada for the next two centuries was dominated by territorial rivalry between England and France. The first settlement, made by Sieur de Monts and Samuel Champlain of France in 1604, was removed to Port Royal, and in 1608 Champlain founded Québec. The French went on to expand their claims in Canada, but their settlements were spread out and thinly populated. Late in the seventeenth century Champlain's policy of support for the Huron Indians against the Iroquois almost spelled the extinction of the French when the Iroquois demolished the Huron. The French royal government took over the administration of Québec in 1663.

The French and Indian Wars broke out in 1689, reflecting the concurrent rivalries between the French and English in Europe. In 1759 General James Wolfe defeated Montcalm, which brought about the fall of Québec. The following year saw the fall of Montréal, and the Treaty of Paris in 1763 ended New France and established British rule. Some concessions were made to the French in the Québec Act of 1774. In 1791 a constitutional act divided Lower Canada (now Québec) and Upper Canada (now southern Ontario) and established limited self-government. Rebellions in the two Canadas in 1837–38 caused the British to consider reuniting them for the purpose of making the French Canadians a minority and anglicizing them.

In 1867 the British North America Act created the Dominion of Canada, a confederation consisting of Nova Scotia, New Brunswick and Lower and Upper Canada. The western territories joined the confederation on a later date. In 1931 the Statute of Westminister established the equality of the Canadian Parliament with that of England.

The most common surnames in Montréal in the early 1970's were Bélanger, Côté, Gagnon, Gauthier, Roy and Tremblay; in Toronto, Brown(e), Macdonald (McDonald), Smith, Thompson (Thomson) and Wilson.

The dates of a first census vary from province to province, with the earliest recorded census of Québec taken in 1671.

Eric Jonasson's *Canadian Genealogical Handbook* and Reginald Olivier's *Your Ancient Canadian Family Ties* are useful guides.

Archives

Archives Publiques du Canada / Public Archives of Canada, 395 rue Wellington, Ottawa, Ontario K1A ON3

Public and Church Records

The registration of births, marriages and deaths is generally covered by a Vital Statistics Act of the individual province. Some records, including those of Québec, date back to the seventeenth century, but in most provinces they date from the middle or late 1800's. Indian records are maintained separately, with the registration of Indians organized similarly in each province. The Indian Agents, Dominion Civil Servants, act as District Registrars of births, marriages and deaths and forward their original registrations to the Director of Vital Statistics.

Libraries

National Library of Canada
395 Wellington Street
Ottawa, Ontario K1A ON4

Historical and Genealogical Societies

Canadian Historical Association
National Capital Commission, P.O. Box 81
Ottawa, Ontario K1A ON3
(*Annual Report; Historical Booklets; Canadian Archivist*)

Centre Canadien de Recherches Généalogiques
Case Postale 845, Haute-Ville
Québec, Québec G1R 457

Centre d'Echanges Généalogiques
56 First Avenue
Ottawa, Ontario

Genealogist, Dominion Council
United Empire Loyalists' Association
21 Prince Arthur Avenue, Toronto

North American Genealogical Society
507 30 Avenue, S.W.
Calgary, Alberta

Société Canadienne de Généalogie (Québec)
Case Postale 2234
Québec, Québec G1K 7N8

Société Canadienne de Généalogie (Hull-Ottawa)
119 rue Charlotte, Ottawa, Ontario

Société Généalogique Canadienne-Française
Case Postale 335

Place d'Armes, Montréal, Québec H2Y 3H1

Société Généalogique des Cantons de l'Est
1041 rue Kingston, Sherbrooke, Québec

Sons of Scotland
19 Richmond St. West
Toronto, Ontario

Société Généalogique Trifluvienne
839 rue Richard
Trois-Rivières, Québec

Sources in the United States

Yale University Library
New Haven, CT 06500
(Largest collection of Canadian material in this country)

Alberta

Archives
Provincial Museum and Archives of Alberta
12845-102th Avenue
Edmonton, Alberta T5N OM6

Public and Church Records
Registers date to 1885.
Deputy Registrar-General
Bureau of Vital Statistics
Alberta—Jasper Building
9815 Jasper Avenue
Edmonton, Alberta T5J 0A6

Libraries
Church of Jesus Christ of Latter-day Saints
Cardston, Alberta, Branch Genealogical Library
348 Third Street, West
Cardston, Alberta

University of Alberta Library
Edmonton, Alberta T6G 2E1

Historical and Genealogical Societies

Alberta Historical Society
% H.A. Dempsey
95 Hollywood Avenue
Calgary, Alberta

Alberta Genealogical Society
Box 3151
Edmonton, Alberta T5J 2G7 (Calgary Branch, P.O. Box 45 Calgary, Alberta T2P 2G9)
(*Relatively Speaking*, 1973–)
NN Current and APW

Historical Society of Alberta
11146 91st Avenue
Edmonton, Alberta

British Columbia

Archives

Provincial Archives of British Columbia
Parliament Buildings
Victoria, British Columbia V8V 1X4

Archives of the Ecclesiastical Province of British Columbia
6050 Chancellor Boulevard
Vancouver, British Columbia V6T 1X3

Public and Church Records

Civil registration began in British Columbia in 1872, but some earlier events can be registered if proof is available. All original records are sent from the province's seventy-three registration districts to the Director of Vital Statistics.

Church registrations date to 1836, and some records remain with the churches.

Director, Division of Vital Statistics
Parliament Buildings
Victoria, British Columbia V8V 1X4

Libraries

Provincial Library
Victoria, British Columbia V8V 1X4

University of British Columbia Library
Vancouver, British Columbia V6T 1W5

Vancouver Public Library
Vancouver, British Columbia V6Z 1X5

Historical and Genealogical Societies

British Columbia Historical Association
Provincial Archives
Victoria, British Columbia

British Columbia Genealogical Society
The Library, Langara College
100 West 49th Avenue
Vancouver, British Columbia V5Y 2Z6
(*The British Columbia Genealogist*, 1971–)
NN Current and APW

Manitoba

Archives

Provincial Archives of Manitoba
Room 247 Legislative Building
Winnipeg, Manitoba R3C 0V8

Public and Church Records

Records of births, marriages and deaths deposited with the Division of Vital Statistics date to 1882. Records of church registrations are not complete but go back sixty more years.

Division of Vital Statistics
Department of Public Health and Social Development
327, Legislative Building
Winnipeg, Manitoba R3C 0V8

Libraries

University of Manitoba Library
Winnipeg, Manitoba R3T 2N2

Historical and Genealogical Societies

Manitoba Genealogical Society
% Eric Jonasson
Box 205 St. James P.O.
Winnipeg, Manitoba R3J 3R4

New Brunswick

Archives

Public Archives of New Brunswick
Box 39, Centennial Building
Fredericton, New Brunswick E3B 5H1

Public and Church Records

Compulsory registration dates from 1920 with incomplete records from 1888. Original documents are with the Registrar-General of Vital Statistics, but some earlier registrations are kept by the Sub-Deputy Registrar of the County Boards of Health.

The Registrar General of Vital Statistics
Department of Health
Fredericton, New Brunswick

Libraries

Harriet Irving Library
University of New Brunswick
Fredericton, New Brunswick E3B 5H5

Historical and Genealogical Societies

New Brunswick Historical Society
Historical Museum
St. John, New Brunswick
37

Newfoundland

Archives

Provincial Archives of Newfoundland
Colonial Building
Military Road
St. John's, Newfoundland

Public and Church Records

The Registrar-General has registers since 1892, and earlier records are in the hands of the registering officers.

Registrar-General
Department of Health and Welfare
St. John's, Newfoundland

Libraries

Newfoundland Provincial Reference Library
Arts and Cultural Centre
Allandale Road
St. John's, Newfoundland AIB 3A3

Memorial University of Newfoundland Library
St. John's, Newfoundland AIC 507

Nova Scotia

Archives
Public Archives of Nova Scotia
Coburg Road
Halifax, Nova Scotia B3H 1Z9
Civil Registers are complete from
1909, but some records date
from 1864.

Public and Church Records
Deputy Registrar-General
Provincial Building
Halifax, Nova Scotia B3J 2M9

Libraries
Acadia University Library
Archives Section
Wolfville, Nova Scotia BOP 1XO

Dalhousie University Library
Halifax, Nova Scotia B3H 4H8

Legislative Library and Nova Sco-
tia Historical Society Library
Province House
Halifax, Nova Scotia B3H 3J5

Historical and Genealogical Societies
Nova Scotia Historical Society
Genealogical Committee
Box 865
Halifax, Nova Scotia BOS 1PO

Ontario

Archives
Department of Public Records and
Archives of Ontario
77 Grenville Street, Queen's Park
Toronto, Ontario M7A 1C7

Archives of the Anglican Diocese
of Ontario
90 Johnson Street
Kingston, Ontario K7L 1X7

Mennonite Archives of Ontario
Conrad Grebel College
Waterloo, Ontario N2L 3G6

Public and Church Records
Civil registers date from July 1,
1869, but some church and private records go back to 1812.
The Vital Statistics Act of 1937
contains an unusual provision
that permits cemetery companies, churches, historical societies and other groups or individuals possessing genealogically
useful vital records of Ontario
residents to deposit them with
the Registrar-General.

Registrar-General of Ontario
Macdonald Block, Queen's Park
Toronto, Ontario M7A 1Y5

Libraries
Church of Jesus Christ of Latter-
day Saints
Toronto, Ontario, Branch Genealogical Library
95 Melbert Street
Etobicoke, Ontario

University of Western Ontario Re-
gional History Collection
Lawson Memorial Library
London, Ontario N6A 3K7

University of Toronto Archives
University Library (Department
of Rare Books)
Toronto, Ontario M5S 1A1

Historical and Genealogical Societies

Ontario Genealogical Society
Box 66, Station Q
Toronto 290, Ontario M4T 2L7
(*Families*)
NN APW 73-2794

Ontario Historical Society
40 Eglinton Avenue E.
Toronto, Ontario
(OHS *Papers and Records; Ontario History*)
NN HWA

Prince Edward Island

Archives

Public Archives of Prince Edward Island
P.O. Box 1000
Charlottetown, Prince Edward Island C1A 7M4

Public and Church Records

Records date back to 1906.

Director of Vital Statistics
Department of Health
Box 3000
Charlottetown, Prince Edward Island C1A 7P1

Libraries

Confederation Centre Library (Incorporates Charlottetown Public Library and Legislative Library)
Charlottetown, Prince Edward Island C1A 7M4

Prince Edward Island Provincial Library
University Ave.
Charlottetown, Prince Edward Island RR7 C1A 7N9

Historical and Genealogical Societies

Abegweit Research Group
Box 20
Winsloe, Prince Edward Island

Quebec

Archives

Archives Nationales du Québec
Parc des Champs de Bataille
Québec, Québec G1A 1A3
(*Rapport de l'Archiviste de la Province de Québec, Inventaires des Archives de la Province de Québec*)

Archives Nationale du Québec, Dépot de Montréal
85 rue Sainte-Thérèse
Montréal, Québec H2Y 1E4

Archives de La Ville de Montréal
Hôtel de Ville
275 Nôtre-Dame Est
Montréal, Québec H2Y 1C6

Archives de L'Archevêché de Montréal
2000 ouest rue Sherbrooke
Montréal, Québec H3H 1G4

Archives de L'Archevêché de Québec
2140 chemin Saint-Louis
Sillery, Québec G1T 1P8

Montréal Diocesan Archives
1444 Union Street
Montréal, Québec H3A 2B8

Public and Church Records

Duplicate registers are prepared by each Roman Catholic and Protestant church. One is sent to the Prothonotary of the Superior Court of the district in which the church is located, and the other is kept by the minister or priest. In the case of Roman Catholic missions, the duplicate is sent to the palace of the bishop of the diocese. The registers go back to 1617, when the French colony was established. Birth certificates can be obtained from the Demographer, Department of Health, Québec City, Québec, and marriage certificates from the church or synagogue or the Prothonotary of the District Superior Court.

Libraries

Bibliothèque National du Québec
Departement des Manuscrits
4499 Esplanade, Montréal
(P.O. address: 1700 rue Saint-Denis
Montréal, Québec H2X 3K6)

Libraries of the University of Montréal
Box 6128
Montréal, Québec H3T 1J4

Historical and Genealogical Societies

Société Historique de Montréal
Bibliothèque Nationale du Québec
Departement des Manuscrits
4499 Esplanade, Montréal
(P.O. address: C.P. 60, Station N
Montréal, Québec H2X 3M2)

Saskatchewan

Archives

Saskatchewan Archives Board (Regina Office)
University of Saskatchewan, Regina Campus
Regina, Saskatchewan S4S 0A2

Saskatchewan Archives Board (Saskatoon Office)
University of Saskatchewan, Saskatoon Campus
Saskatoon, Saskatchewan S7N 0W0

Public and Church Records

Registers date from about 1878, but are not complete until 1920.

Division of Vital Statistics
Department of Public Health
Regina, Saskatchewan S4S 0A6

Libraries

Saskatchewan Provincial Library
1352 Winnipeg St.
Regina, Saskatchewan S4R 1J9

Saskatoon Public Library
311 23rd Street E.
Saskatoon, Saskatchewan S7K 0J6

Historical and Genealogical Societies

Saskatchewan Genealogical Society
P.O. Box 1894
Regina, Saskatchewan S4P 3E1
(SGS *Bulletin*, 1970–)
NN APW

Saskatchewan Historical Society
403–4 McCallum Hill Building
Regina, Saskatchewan

Saskatoon Genealogical Society
%Robert M. Black
323 Hilliard Street E.
Saskatoon, Saskatchewan S7O 0E5

Yukon Territory

Public and Church Records

Records date from 1898. There is an index book of statistics for the Forty Mile District of the Yukon Territory from 1894, but the records were destroyed by fire.

Registrar of Vital Statistics
Administration Buildings
Dawson, Yukon Territory

Registrar of Vital Statistics
Territorial Treasurer's Office
Whitehorse, Yukon Territory

Northwest Territories

Public and Church Records
Registers date from 1870.

Registrar-General of Vital Statistics for the Northwest Territories
Department of Northern Affairs and National Resources
Ottawa, Ontario

Books and Articles

Genealogical Sources
Acadian Genealogy Exchange.
Covington, KY 41015, 1972–.
NN APR (Louisiana)

Auger, Roland J.
English and French Archival Research.
(IN: *Families*, Toronto, 1972. v. 11, p. 110–115)
NN APW 73–2794

Auger, Roland J.
Wills, Acts of Donation and Inventories.
(IN: *French Canadian and Acadian Genealogical Review*, Haute-Ville, 1975. v. 5, p. 3–23)
NN APW 72–1700

Baker, Eunice R.
Searching for Your Ancestors in Canada.
Ottawa, Heritage House, 1976. 80 p.
(Heritage House, Box 8544, Ottawa, Ontario K1G 0A0)

The British Columbia Genealogist.
Vancouver, 1971–.
(The Library, Langara College, 110 W. 49th Ave., Vancouver, B.C. V5Y 2Z6)

The Canadian Genealogical Handbook.
Winnipeg, Manitoba, Wheatfield Press, 1976.

Canadian Newspapers (With Dates) Available Through the Canadian Library Association, 63 Sparks Street, Ottawa, Ontario.
(IN: *Lost in Canada?* Sparta, WI, 1976. v. 4, no. 2, p. 188–90)
NN

Census of Canada 1860–61 Enumerated Areas.
(IN: *Lost in Canada?* Sparta, WI, 1976. v. 2 no. 1, p. 27–30)
NN

Dornbusch, Charles E.
Lineages of the Canadian Army 1855–1961: Armour, Cavalry, Infantry. 2nd ed.
Cornwallville, NY, Hope Farm Press, 1961. 1 v., unpaged.
NN D-14 3753

Families.
Toronto, OGS, 1961–. (Formerly OGS *Bulletin*)
NN APW 73–2794

Fellows, Jo-Ann, and Kathryn Calder.
A Bibliography of Loyalist Source Material in Canada.
(IN: *AAS*, Worcester, MA, 1972. v. 82, p. 67–270, indexed)
NN IAA

Fellows, Robert E.
Research in New Brunswick.
(IN: *Families*, Toronto, 1972. v. 11, p. 104–9)
NN APW 73-2794

French Canadian and Acadian Genealogical Review.
Haute-Ville, Québec, 1968–. (Roland J. Auger, ed)
(Case Postale 845, Haute-Ville, Québec G1R 4S7)
NN APW 72-1700

Genealogical Society of Church of L.D.S.
Research Paper. series B, no. 3.
NN APA 72-752

Gingras, Raymond.
Précis du Généalogiste Amateur.
(Available from Archives Nationales de Québec, Édifice du Musée, Parc des Champs de Bataille, Québec, P.Q. G1A 1A 3, for $1.00)

Godbout, Archange.
Les Passagers du Saint-André; Le Recue de 1659.
Montréal, 1964. 163 p.
(Société Généalogique Canadiennne Française, pub. no. 5)
NN APW 75-1075

Gregoire, Jeanne.
Le Guide du Généalogist.
Montréal, 1974.
(Available from Société Cana-

dienne Française, C.P. 335, Place d'Armes, Montréal H2Y 3H1 for $3.75)

Gregorovich, Andrew.
Canadian Ethnic Groups Bibliography: A Selected Bibliography of Ethno-Cultural Groups in Canada and the Province of Ontario.
Toronto, 1972. 208 p.
NN HWH 74-1022

Guide to Archives in Toronto Area.
Toronto, 1975. 46 p.
(Available from R. Scott James, City of Toronto Archives, Toronto M5H 2N2)

Heraldry in Canada.
Ottawa, 1966–.
(Hon. Editor, 1922 Alta Vista Dr., Ottawa K1H 7K6)
NN AWA 74-123

Honigmann, John J., and Irma Honigmann.
Eskimo Townsmen.
Ottawa, Research Centre for Anthropology, U. of Ottawa, 1965. 278 p.
NN HBC

Hunter, A.T.
Probated Wills of Persons Prominent in the Public Affairs of Early Upper Canada.
(IN: *Ontario Historical Society Papers and Records.* Toronto, 1926–27. v. 23, p. 328–59; v. 24, p. 381–409.)
NN HWA

Hutton, Samuel King.
An Eskimo Village.
New York, Macmillan, 1929. 156 p.

(Okak, Isle of Kivalek, off the coast of Labrador)
NN HBC

Index to Crownlands, 1763–1890.
Québec, c. 1975.
(Finding Aid no. 876 of the Archives Nationales du Québec)

Jehn, Janet.
Acadian Descendants.
Covington, KY, Acadian Genealogy Exchange, 1972–75. 2 v.
NN APW 75–2766

Jonasson, Eric.
Canadian Genealogical Handbook.
Winnipeg, Wheatfield Press, 1976. 110 p.
(Box 205, St. James Postal Station, Winnipeg, Manitoba R3J 3R 4)

Kirk, Robert F. and Audrey L.
Some References and Sources for Searching for Your Ancestors in the Province of Ontario.
Detroit, DSGR, 1973.

Laliberte, J.M.
Index des Greffes des Notaires Décédés (1645–1948).
Québec, B. Pontbriand, 1967. 219 p.
NN APW

Lapp, Eula A.
To Their Heirs Forever.
Picton, Ontario, 1970. 314 p.
NN APW 74-798

Le Blanc, Robert G.
Acadian Migrations.
(IN: *Acadian Genealogy Exchange*, Covington, KY, 1976. v. 5, p. 83–87, maps)
NN current

Leeson, Francis.
Records of Irish Emigrants to Canada in Sussex Archives, 1839–1847.
(IN: *Irish Ancestor* Dundalk, Ireland, 1974. v. 5, p. 31–42)
NN ARCA 72-1448

Lost in Canada? Canadian American Query Exchange.
Sparta, WI 54656, 1975–.
(% Joy Reisinger, 1020 Central Ave.)
NN current and APW.

Matthews, William.
Canadian Diaries and Autobiographies.
Berkeley, CA, U. of CA, 1950. 130 p. plus index.
NN *RS-AGY- 76-2732

Neville, George A.
Passenger List Resources at Public Archives of Canada (Colonial Office Records Groups 384 and 385)
(IN: *OGS Ottawa Branch News*, Ottawa, 1976. v. 8, p. 13–14)
NN APW

New France. Conseil Supérieur de Québec.
... Lettres de Noblesse, Généalogies, Erections de Comtes et Baronnies Insinuées par le Conseil Souvrain de la Nouvelle France.
Beauceville, L'Éclaireur for Pierre-Georges Roy, 1920.
2 v.
NN APW

New France Courts. Cour de la Prévôté de Québec.
... Inventoire des Insinuation de la Prévôté de Québec.

Beauceville, L'Éclaireur for
Pierre-George Roy.
1936. 2 v.
NN APW

Olivier, Reginald L.
Your Ancient Canadian Family
Ties.
Logan, UT, Everton, 1972. 364 p.

Ontario Genealogical Society Bul-
letin.
Waterloo, 1962–71. v. 1–10.
(Name changed to *Families*)
NN APW- 73-2794

Ontario Genealogical Society, Ot-
tawa Branch. Branch News.
Ottawa, 1970–.
NN APW 76-877

Ontario Register.
Lambertville, NJ, 1968–.
NN APW 72-931

Public Archives of Canada.
Tracing Your Ancestry in Canada.
(IN: *GM*, London, 1966. v. 15, p.
293–94)
(Original 20-page pamphlet avail-
able by mail from Information
Canada, Ottawa)
NN ARCA

Reid, William (d. 1969).
The Loyalists in Ontario: The Sons
and Daughters of the American
Loyalists of Upper Canada.
Lambertville, NJ, Hunterdon
House, 1973. 418 p., index.
NN APW 75-1455

Roy, Antoine.
Bibliographies de Généalogies et
Histories de Familles.
Québec, Archives de Québec, 1941.
95-332 p.
NN APW

Société Généalogique Canadienne
Française.
Memoires.
Montréal, 1944–1976 plus. 27 v.
plus.
NN APW

Tanguay, Cyprien, 1819–1902.
Dictionnaire Généalogique des
Familles Canadiennes Depuis
La Formation de la Colonie
Jusqu'à Nos Jours.
New York, AMS Press, 1967–69
(orig. 1871–90). 7 v.
NN APW

Trudel, Marcel.
Atlas de la Nouvelle-France.
Québec, U. Laval, 1968. 219 p.
NN HWI 72-1370

Trudel, Marcel.
Le Terrier du Saint-Laurent en
1663. (Landowners New France
in 1663)
Ottawa, Ottawa U., 1973. 617 p.

General Sources

Biographie Canadiennes-Fran-
çaises.
Ottawa, 1920–71 plus. 20 v. plus.
NN AGY

Canadian Who's Who.
London, Toronto, 1910–69 plus. 11
v. plus.
NN AGY

Dictionary Catalogue of the Library of the Provincial Archives
of British Columbia (Victoria).
Boston, MA, G.K. Hall, 1971. 8 v.

Dictionary of Canadian Biography.
Toronto, U. of Toronto Press, 1966–
(in progress). 3 v. to 1973.

(v. 1; 1000–1700; v. 2, 1701–1740; v. 3, 1741–1771)
NN *R-AGY 74–739

Eastern Townships Gazetteer and Business Directory ... comp. by Roberts and Reinhold of Montréal.
St. Johns, L.C., Smith & Co., 1867. 133 p.
(1967 reprint available from Mika Pub. Co.)

Fleming, Patricia Lockhart.
A Bibliography of Ontario Directories to 1867.
(IN: *Ontario Library Review*, Toronto, 1975. p. 98–107)

Gazetteer of Canada, British Columbia.
Ottawa, Canadian Board on Geographical Names, 1953.

Gilchrist, J. Brian.
The Ontario Archives: Records and Research Methods.
(IN: *Families*, Toronto, 1976. v. 15, p. 168–76)
NN APW 73-2794

Mackay, R.W.S.
The Canadian Directory for 1857–58: Containing Names of Professional and Business Men and of the Principal Inhabitants in the Cities, Towns and Villages Throughout the Province, etc. ... Corrected to Nov. 1857.
Montréal, John Lowell, 1857. 1,544 p.
(An earlier edition to Nov. 1851 had 692 p.)

Mika, Nick and Helena.
United Empire Loyalists: Pioneers of Upper Canada.

Belleville, Ontario, Mika Pub. Co., 1976. 250 p.

Post-1815 Settlements in Canada.
(IN: *Lost in Canada?* Sparta, WI, 1976. v. 2, p. 74–79, 142–47)
NN APW

Public Archives of Canada. Publications Division.
List of Publications.
Ottawa, 1974–
NN HWA 76-83

Rose, George Maclean.
Cyclopaedia of Canadian Biography: Being Chiefly Men of the Time ...
Toronto, Rose Pub. Co., 1886–88. 2 v., index each v.
NN AGY

Union List of Manuscripts in Canadian Repositories.
Ottawa, 1975. 2 v.
NN *R-*GBI 75-9201

Who's Who in Canada.
Toronto, 1910–66 plus. 53 v. plus.
NN AGY

Parish Registers
Bergeron, Daniel et al.
Mariages de la Parisse Notre-Dame de Montréal, 1642–1850.
Montréal R. et J. Bergeron, 1974–75. 2 v.
(Editions Bergeron et Fils, 9247-24e Ave., Montréal, PQ HIZ 4A2)

Britnell, William.
Irregular Marriages of the Yonge Street Friends, 1806–1828.
(IN: *Families*, Toronto, 1976. v. 15, p. 38–57)
(See also *The Ontario Register*, v. 4, p. 119–26 for marriages 1806–1840)
NN APW 73-2794

Campagna, F. Dominique.
Repertoire des Mariages du Comte
Arthabaska 1840–1925.
Cap Rouge, Québec, F.D. Campagna, 1974. 2 v.
(Pavillon André-Coindre, Cap-Rouge, Québec GOA IKO)
NN APW 75-2579

Coderre, John E., and Paul A. Lavoie.
Parish Registers Held at the Public Archives of Canada.
Ottawa, Ottawa Branch, OGS, 1975.
pub. 75–6.
(Available for $2.00 from Ottawa
Branch OGS, P.O. Box 8346, Ottawa, KIG 3H8)

DeMarce, Virginia.
Checklist of Published Parish Marriage Registers.
(IN: *Lost in Canada?* Sparta, WI,
1975. v. 1, p. 94–101, 139–140)
NN APW

Gareau, G. Robert, and Jean Bergeron.
Marriages of Lachine Saints-Anges-de-Lachine, 1676–1970.
Montréal, R. and J. Bergeron,
1975. 418 p., index.
NN APW 76-1379

Gingras, Frère Robert-Edmond
Mariages de Paroisses, Comte de
Montmorency, St. Gregoire
(1891–1970), Giffard (1914–1970),
St. Louis-de-Courville (1910-1970), St. Thomas-de-Villeneuve
(1948–1970).
Québec (Frère Robert-E. Gingras,
etc., Archiviste, 2567 Chemin
des Quatre-Bourgeois, Sainte-Foy, Québec-10, P.Q.)

Jette, Réné, and Benoit Pontbriand.

Mariages de St. Damase (1823), Ste.
Madeleine (1876), St. Pierre-de-Bagot (1830), Diocese de St. Hyacinthe.
Québec, B. Pontbriand, 1970. 357
p. + index
NN APW 76-562

Mariages et Necrologe de St. Gervais (Co. Bellechasse) 1780–1973.
Montrèal, Roger et Jean Bergeron,
1974. 236, 86 p., alpha cross-index of brides.
(Publication no. 8)
NN APW 75-2755

Nadon, Léon A.
Repertoire des Mariages de Notre-Dame-de-Lourdes, etc., 1887–1971.
Québec, Société de Généalogie de
Québec, 1975.
(Société de Gén. de Québec, Case
Postale 2234, Québec 2, G1K7N8)

Notre-Dame, Montréal.
Premier Registre de l'Église
Notre-Dame de Montréal.
Montréal, Editions des Dix, 1961.
491 p.
(p. 42–491 facsimiles)
NN APW

Parish Registers of Canada on
Microfilm: New Brunswick,
Newfoundland, Nova Scotia,
Prince Edward Island, Ontario.
(IN: *Lost in Canada?* Sparta, WI,
1976. v. 2, p. 80–83)
NN APW

Pontbriand, Benoit.
Repertoire des Mariages de Notre-Dame-de-Québec (1618–1908).
Sillery, Québec, B. Pontbriand,
1962–63. 6 v.
(NYPL has v. 1–3, 6. Benoit Pontbriand, 2390 Marie-Victorin, Sillery, Québec, G1T 1K1, has pub-

lished more than 100 volumes of French-Canadian marriages.)
NN APW

Proulx, Abbé Armand.
Repertoire des Mariages de Sainte-Hélène 1850–1969, de St. Joseph 1922–1969, de Saint-Germain, 1893–1969.
La Procatière, A. Proulx, 1971. 125, 27, 33 p., alpha by bride and groom.
(M. L'Abbé Armand Proulx, C.P. 636, Villa St. Jean La Pocatière, Kamouraska, Québec GOR 1Z0
NN APW 75-150

Provencher, Gérard E.
Mariages de l'Outaouais.
Sillery, Québec, B. Pontbriand, 1971–75. 6 v.
NN APW 74-359

Punch, Terrance M.
Some Irish Immigrant Weddings in Nova Scotia.
(IN: *Irish Ancestor*, Dundalk, Ireland, 1974–1976. v.5, p. 101–112: 1801–17; v.6, p. 39–54, 104–30: 1818–30; v.7, p. 53–69, 124–39: 1831–40)
NN ARCA 72-1448

St. Patrick's Parish, Québec.
An Index of Irish and Other Anglophone Marriages in St. Patrick's Parish, Québec, 1856–1973.

Québec, Helena Haberlin, 1974.
(Miss Helena Haberlin, % St. Patrick's High School, 75 Maissoneuve St., Québec, P.Q.)

Smith, Leonard H., Jr.
St. Mary's Bay 1818–1829, Catalog of Families, St. Mary's Bay Roman Catholic Parish, Clare, Digby, Nova Scotia.
Clearwater, FL, the author, 1975. 152 p., index.
(List of Indians, p. 123–25)
NN APW 76-701

La Société Généalogique des Cantons de l'Est.
Repertoire des mariages (Catholique) Comte Sherbrooke de Debut—1970.
Cap Rouge, F.D. Campagna, c. 1974. 3 v.
(F. Dominique Campagna, La Société Généalogique des Cantons de l'Est, Pavillon André-Coindre, Cap Rouge, Québec GOA 1KO)
NN APW 75-668

Table of Parishes in the Province of Québec Arranged by Location and Year of Origin.
(IN: *Lost in Canada?* Sparta, WI, 1975. v. 1, p. 65–70)
NN APW

MEXICO (MEXICO CITY)

Mexico is the ancient land of the Mayas, the Toltecs and the Aztecs, the last of whom founded the city of Tenochtitlan (now Mexico City) in 1325. The Aztec empire was destroyed when Hernando Cortez undertook the conquest in 1519, but descendants of the family of Montezuma, the last Aztec emperor, can be traced to the present day, as indicated in the bibliography of Mexican references. The viceroyalty of New Spain was set up in 1535 under Antonio de Mendoza. Most of this area and its former holdings in the United States were occupied in the sixteenth century, but it was not until the middle of the eighteenth century that these later areas were settled to any large degree. General Augustin Iturbe led the country to independence, which became effective on September 27, 1821, after a decade of struggle. Iturbe set up an empire and declared himself Augustin I, but in 1823 a republic was chosen, when Santa Anna and Guadalupe Victoria drove Iturbe out of power. The political road of the country has not been smooth. Santa Anna was in power much of the time from 1829 until 1855, when he was finally overthrown by revolution. Benito Juarez was in control after that, until the conservative forces of the country sought the help of Napoleon III and set up an empire under Maximilian of Austria from 1864 to 1867. Juarez ruled again after the fall of this empire, until he was overthrown in 1876 by Porfirio Diaz, who held sway until 1911. The leaders of the revolt that led to his downfall were ineffectual, and in their stead Venustiano Carranza, Francisco Villa and Emiliana Zapata gained control of the country. Under Carranza, the revolutionary constitution of 1917, which restored communal lands to the Indians and separated church and state, was framed. Carranza was deposed in 1920 by General Alvaro Obregon, who ruled until he was assassinated in 1928. Since that time the government has been more stable.

The first survey of the population of Mexico was made between 1579 and 1582, and the original manuscript of the count is in the Mirabeau B. Lamar Library at the University of Texas in Austin. Two more population censuses were made in the late sixteenth century. In the seventeenth, population counts were conducted in 1607–10, 1614, 1625, 1652, 1662 and 1664. Another general inventory of the population was made in 1742, and in 1791 the first attempt at a full census was undertaken, but many Indians did not cooperate. Similar problems were encountered in the post-colonial censuses of 1895 and 1900. The census of 1921 required the heads of households to fill out the census questionnaires themselves, in the European manner. More care was taken with later censuses, recorded every ten years since 1930.

The names noted most frequently in the Guadalajara telephone books in the early 1970's were Garcia, Gonzalez, Hernandez, Lopez and Martinez. In Mexico City, they were Garcia, Gonzalez, Hernandez, Lopez, Sanchez and Martinez; and in Monterrey, Garcia, Garza, Gonzalez, Martinez, Trevino and Villarreal.

Many of the early Spanish families in California had Mexican connections; the same has been true in ensuing centuries. Many Mexican entrepreneurs did business farther afield in New Orleans and New York. Among them was Joaquin A. Medina, a native of Mérida, Yucatán, a merchant who settled in New York in the 1880's. He married Elizabeth Fash (d. 1954), who was of Dutch descent, in Brooklyn, and their son, the noted Judge Harold R. Medina, was born there on February 16, 1888.

Archives

Archivo General De La Nación
Palacio Nacional
México 1, D.F.

Public and Church Records

Certificates are issued by the appropriate Oficial del Registro Civil (Office of Civil Registry). Write the Archivo General de Gobierno, Palacio de Gobierno, at the capital of the state where the birth, marriage or death occurred. Certificates are also issued in the Federal District of Mexico City, where records of subordinate registries of the Federal District are consolidated.

Jefe de la Oficina del Registro Civil del Distrito Federal Mexico City, México

Libraries

Church of Jesus Christ of Latter-day Saints

Mexico City, Mexico, Branch Genealogical Library
Mexico City, México

Biblioteca Nacional de Mexico
República del Salvador 70
Mexico City, México

Biblioteca Central del Universidad Nacional Autónoma de México
Ciudad Universitaria
Mexico City, México

Books and Articles

El Archivo de Hidalgo del Parral, 1631–1821.
Wooster, OH, Bell & Howell, c. 1973. 323 reels of microfilm.
(Covers Mexico—North and West; United States—Southwest)

Barrett, Ellen C.
Baja California.
Los Angeles, CA, Westernlore Press, 1957–67. 2 v.
(v. 1, 1535–1956; v. 2, 1535–1964)
NN HTT

Camara Peon, Oswalda, and Joaquin de A. Peron.
Indice-Resumen, Alfabético y Cronológico de los Matrimonios de Sargario de Merida, Yucatán.
Merida, 1971–73. 3 v.
(v. 1, 1883–1900; v. 2, 1821–50; v. 3, 1850–65. NYPL has v. 1)
NN APY + 73-2137

Carralbo, Marques de.
Una Crónica de los Mocteczuma.
(IN: *Hidalgua*, Madrid, 1954. año 2, p. 341–76)
NN ASM

Dahl, Torsten.
Linajes en México.
Mexico City, Cegiasa, 1967. 1 v.
NN APY

Diccionario Biográfico de México.
Monterey, Editorial N.L. Revesa, 1968. 1st ed., v. 1 (643 p.), alpha.
NN AGX

Fernandez de Recas, Guillermos.
Mayorazgos de la Nueva España.
México, Instituto Bibliográfico Mexicano, 1965.
(Biblioteca Nacional de México. Instituto Bibliográfico Mexicano, no. 10)
NN APY

Flores Olea, Aurora.
Les Regidores de la Ciudad de México en la Primera Mitad del Siglo XVII.
(IN: *Mexico City Universidad Nacional, Instituto de Historia, Etudios de Historia Novohispaña*, Mexico City, 1970. v. 3, p. 149–72)
NN HTA

Garcia, Richard A.
The Chicanos in America, 1540–1974.
Dobbs Ferry, NY, Oceana, 1977. 231 p., index. (Ethnic Chronology Series no. 26)
NN IEE (Mexicans) 77-603

Gomez, David F.
Somos Chicanos: Strangers in Our Own Land.
Boston, MA, Beacon, 1973. 204 p.
NN IEE (Mexicans) 74-1899

Grebler, Leo et al.
The Mexican American People: the Nation's Second Largest Minority.
New York, Collier-Macmillan, 1970. 777 p., index.
NN IEE (Mexicans)

Greenleaf, Richard E.
Research in Mexican History.
Lincoln, NE, U. of Nebraska Press, 1973. 226 p.
NN HTB 73-2754

Houston, Texas, University Libraries. Office of the Assistant Director for Development of Collections.
Mexicano-Americas.
Houston, TX, 1972. 732 p.
NN IEE (Mexicans) 74-985

Ibarrola Arriaga, Gabriel.
Familias y Casas de la Vieja Valladolid.
Morelia, Michocan, México, Fimax Publicistas, 1969. 599 p., index.
APY 73-262

Latorre, Felipe A.
The Mexican Kickapoo Indians.

Austin, TX, U. of Texas Press, 1976. 410 p., index.
(The Texas Pan American Series)
NN HBC 76-1180

Liss, Peggy K.
Mexico under Spain, 1521–1556: Society and Origins.
Chicago, IL, U. of Chicago Press, 1975. 229 p., index.

Lopez de Meneses, Amada.
Gradezas y Titulo de Nobleza a los Descendientes de Moteczuma.
(IN: *Revista de Indias*, Madrid, 1962. año 22, no. 89–90, p. 341–52)
NN HCA

Mexican Archives of New Mexico and Territorial Archives of New Mexico. 189 reels, 43 reels.
NN microfilm

México. Archivo General de la Nación.
Publicaciones.
Segunda Series.
NN HTA 73-2891

Mexico (City) Santa Paula (Cemetery).
Cementerio de Santa Paula.
México, Auila, c. 1841. 16 p.
NN APY

Motezuma, Diego Luís de.
Corona Mexicana; ó Historia de los Nueve Motezumas.
Madrid, Biblioteca Hispania, 1914. 505 p.
(Colección Hispana-Americana)
NN HTH

Ortega y Perez Gallardo, Ricardo.
Historia Genealógica de la Familias mas Antiguas de México. 3rd ed. corr.

Mexico, A. Carranza, 1908–10. 3 v.
NN APY

Rangel, Marc.
Emperor Moctezuma II (and His Descendants).
(IN: *The Amorial*, London, 1963. v. 4, p. 83–85)
NN AWA

Sosa, Francisco.
Biografías de Mexicanos Distinguidos.
México, Liberia Abadiano, 1884. 1,115 p., index.
NN AGX

Swadesh, Frances Leon.
Los Primeros Pobladores: Hispanic Americans of the Ute Frontier.
Notre Dame, IN, U. of Notre Dame Press, 1974. 262 p., index.
NN IEE (Spanish) 74-1758

Talbot, Jane M., and Gilbert R. Cruz.
A Comprehensive Chicano Bibliography 1960–1972.
Austin, TX, Jenkins Pub., 1973. 275 p., index.
NN IEE (Mexicans) 75-1798

Teja Zabre, Alfonso.
Guide to the History of Mexico.
Austin, TX, 1969. 370 p.
NN HTB 70-195

Vaillant, George Clapp.
Aztecs of Mexico; Origin; Rise of the Aztec Nation.
Revised by S.B. Vaillant.
Garden City, Doubleday, 1962. 363 p., index.
NN *R-HBC

SAINT PIERRE AND MIQUELON (SAINT PIERRE)

A French overseas territory, these island groups fifteen miles off the Newfoundland coast were settled by the French in 1660. The area was captured by the British in 1702, but in 1814 the islands were returned to the French on the condition that they not be fortified. Administration of the territory consists of a Paris-appointed governor and an elected general council; a deputy and a senator are elected to the French Chamber of Deputies. The population is made up almost entirely of fishermen and their families.

A census of St. Pierre and Miquelon was conducted in 1967.

Public and Church Records

Certificates can be obtained from the office of the mayor (*La Mairie*) of the town in which a birth or marriage took place.

Paris, Horizona de France, 1963. 158 p.
NN HXC

Rannie, William F.
Saint-Pierre and Miquelon.
Beamsville, Ontario, Rannie Pub., 1963. 132 p.
NN HXC

Books and Articles

Aubert de la Rue, Edgar
Saint-Pierre et Miquelon: un Coin de France au Seuil de l'Amerique.

Saint-Pierre and Miquelon.
... Les Iles Saint-Pierre et Miquelon.
Saint-Pierre, 1922. 111 p.
NN HWE p.v. 24 no. 5

ARGENTINA (BUENOS AIRES)

Amerigo Vespucci was probably one of the first Europeans to see this land, during his voyage of 1502. Juan Diaz de Solis, Magellan and Cabot all visited in their search for the Southwest Passage to the Orient in the early sixteenth century. Pedro de Mendoza founded the first settlement at Buenos Aires in 1536, but attacks by Indians forced the Spanish to abandon the site, and Asunción, now the capital of Paraguay, became the leading settlement of the Río de la Plata area. Buenos Aires was re-founded by Juan de Garay in 1580. Under the administration of Hernando Arias de Saaverda, son-in-law of de Garay, the Río de la Plata territories were separated, and Buenos Aires attained semi-independence under the viceroyalty of Peru. In 1776 Buenos Aires became the capital of a viceroyalty that included the present countries of Argentina, Uruguay, Paraguay and, for a short time, Bolivia. Independence was declared by the United Provinces of La Plata on July 9, 1816, and was supported by the famed liberator, José de San Martín, among others. Uruguay and Paraguay became separate countries. Argentina remained unstable internally until the constitution of 1853 was adopted. Conquest of the Indians in the south and southwest led to the opening up of that territory. The pampas attracted Italians, French, Germans, Swiss, British and other Europeans, who immigrated and mixed with the earlier settlers of Spanish and Basque origin.

A count of the population was planned for 1810 but was carried out only in the city of Buenos Aires. Other local censuses were taken in Buenos Aires in 1887, 1904, 1909 and 1936, in Mendoza in 1942 and in Santa Fe in 1912, 1918, 1925 and 1937. National censuses were recorded in 1869, 1895, 1914, 1920, 1947, 1960 and 1970.

Some of the most common surnames in Buenos Aires in the 1970's are Fernández, García, González, López and Rodríguez.

Archives

Archivo General de la Nación
Av. Leandro N. Alem 246
Buenos Aires, Argentina

Archivo Histórico y Biblioteca de
la Ciudad de Buenos Aires
Av. Córdoba 1556
Buenos Aires, Argentina

Archivo Histórico de la Universi-
dad de Buenos Aires
Viamonte 430
Buenos Aires, Argentina

Centro de Documentación Inter-
nacional
Avenida Figueroa Alcorta 2263
Buenos Aires, Argentina

Public and Church Records

Birth and marriage certificates
can be obtained from the Civil
Registry (Registro Civil) of the
municipality or rural district in
which the event occurred.

Libraries

Biblioteca Nacional
México 564
Buenos Aires, Argentina

Biblioteca de la Universidad de
Buenos Aires
Calle Viamonte 444
Buenos Aires, Argentina

Biblioteca de la Universidad Ca-
tólica de Córdoba
Trejo 323
Córdoba, Argentina

Books and Articles

Azarola Gil, Luis Enrique.
. . . Apellidos de la Patria Vieja.
Buenos Aires, La Facultad, 1942.
233 p.
NN APY

Azarola Gil, Luis Enrique.
. . . Croicas y Linajes de la Gober-
nación de Plata; Documentos in
Editos de nos Siglos XVII y
XVIII.
Buenos Aires, J. Lajouane, 1927.
142 p.
NN APY

Calvo, Carlos.
. . . Nobiliario del Antiguo Virreyn-
ato del Río de la Plata.
Buenos Aires, La Facultad,
1936–43. v. 1–6, 3 v.
NN APY

Diccionario Biográfico Contempor-
aneo Personalidades de la Argentina.
Buenos Aires, Veritas, 1945–1948.
3 v., alpha.
NN AGU

Fitzgibbon, Russell Humke.
Argentina: A Chronology and Fact
Book, 1516–1973.
Dobbs Ferry, NY, Oceana, 1974.
148 p.
NN HKB 75-2040

Foppa, Tito Livio.
Diccionario Teatral de Río de la
Plata.
Buenos Aires, 1961. 1,046 p.
(Biographical dictionary of theat-
rical personalities in Argentina
and Uruguay)
NN MWEL (Argentina)

Instituto Argentino de Ciencias.
Revista.
Buenos Aires, 1942–1951. v. 1–7.
Genealogía: Revista del IAC.
Buenos Aires, 1955–.
Boletín Interno.
Buenos Aires, 1969–.
(Instituto Argentino de Ciencias
Genealógica, Circulo Militar,
Av. Santa Fe 750, Buenos Aires,
Argentina)
NN APA

Lazcano Colodrero, Arturo Gus-
tavo do.
Linajares de la Gobernación de
Tucuman los de Córdoba ...
Córdoba, A. Biffigandi, 1936–69. 3
v.
NN APY

Maedar, Ernesto J.A.
Nomina de Gobernantes Civiles y
Eclesiasticos de la Argentina
Durante la Época Española
1500–1800.
Resistencia, c. 1972. 173 p.
NN HKB 73-2252

Otarola, Alfredo J.
Antecedentes Históricos y Geneal-
ógicos ...
Buenos Aires, Casa Pardo, 1967.
185 p.
NN D-18 7045

Otarola, Alfredo J.
Cunas de Ilustres Linajes; Descendencia de Domingo Martinez
de Irala y Ortas de la Época de
la Conquista.
Buenos Aires, Casa Pardo, 1970.
213 p., index.
NN APY 72-2547

Otarola, Alfredo J.
Estudios Genealógicos Sobre An-
tiguos Appedidos del Río de la
Plata y Remotos Origenes del
Patriarcado Argentino.
Buenos Aires, Casa Pardo, 1969.
211 p.
NN APY

Otarola, Alfredo J.
Mar del Plata y Genealogía de sus
Fundadores ...
Buenos Aires, Casa Pardo, 1972.
212 p.
NN APY 74-1417

Quién es Quién en la Argentina.
Buenos Aires, 1939–1968. v. 1–9.
NN AGU

Rosa, José Maria.
Histórica Argentina.
Buenos Aires, 1974. 8 v.
NN HKB 76-319

Solari, Juan A.
Perfiles Parlamentarios Argenti-
nos.
Buenos Aires, 1965. 194 p.
NN JFC 73-24

Udaondo, Enrique.
Diccionario Biográfico Colonial
Argentino.
Buenos Aires, Haurpes, 1945. 981
p., alpha.
NN AGU

Williams, Glyn.
The Structure and Process of
Welsh Emigration to Patagonia.
(IN: *Welsh History Review*, Cardiff,
1976. v. 8, p. 42–74)
NN CVA

BOLIVIA (LA PAZ AND SUCRE)

The Incas conquered the region of Bolivia during the thirteenth century. In the 1530's, Spaniards, attracted by rich silver deposits, gained control of Bolivia—then called Upper Peru—and enslaved its Indians to work in the mines. In 1809, while Napoleon occupied Spain, Bolivia revolted against Spanish rule, the first of the colonies to do so. In 1824 a revolutionary army led by Antonio José de Sucre, chief lieutenant of Simón Bolívar, defeated the Spanish at Ayacucho; in 1825 independence was proclaimed, and in 1826 a republican form of government was adopted. From 1879 to 1884 Bolivia and Peru fought against Chile in the War of the Pacific, and after Chile's victory Bolivia was forced to cede the province of Atacama, its only coastal territory. Sucre, where the Supreme Court meets, is the legal capital of the country, while other government activities are centered in La Paz.

Archives

Archivo Nacional de Bolivia
Calle España 23 (Postal add.: Casilla 338)
Sucre, Bolivia

Public and Church Records

Birth certificates can be obtained from the Registro Civil of the district of birth or from the Dirección General de Registro Civil in La Paz. Marriage certificates can be obtained from the Civil Registry office in the place of marriage.

Libraries

Biblioteca Central de la Universidad Mayor de San Andres
Av. Villazón 465
La Paz, Bolivia

Biblioteca del Congresso Nacional
(Contains newspaper library)
Palacio Legislativo
La Paz, Bolivia

Biblioteca Nacional de Bolivia
Calle Bolívar
Sucre, Bolivia

Historical and Genealogical Societies

Sociedad de Estudios Geográficos e Históricos
Plaza 24 de Septiembre
Santa Cruz de la Sierra, Bolivia

Books and Articles

Costa de la Torre, Arturo.
El Archivo Histórico y la Biblioteca de Nicolas
Acosta en Estados Unidos.
La Paz, 1970. 203 p.
NN HLB 76-659

Heath Dwight B.
Historical Dictionary of Bolivia.
Metuchen, NJ, Scarecrow, 1972. 324
p.
NN HLB 73-677

Hombres Celebres de Bolivia.
La Paz, Gonzolez y Medina, 1920.
544 p., index.
NN AGU

Montenegro, R. Edmundo.
Diccionario Biográfico de Personalidades en Bolivia.

La Paz, 1968. 152 p.
NN JFD 73-2987

Otero, Gustavo Adolfo.
Figuras de la Cultura Boliviana.
Quito, Ecuador, Ruminahui, 1952.
353 p., t of c called index.
NN AGU

Parker, William B.
Bolivians of Today.
London, Hispanic Society, 1920–22.
2 v.
NN AGU

BRAZIL (BRASÍLIA)

Brazil, the largest country in Latin America, occupies nearly
half of the continent of South America. The basic culture and
language is Portuguese rather than Spanish. Pedro Alvares
Cabral claimed the land for Portugal in 1500, but the first
permanent settlement was not made until 1532 at São Vincente
in São Paulo Province. This was followed by the founding of
Salvador in 1539. French Huguenots established a colony on an
island in Río de Janeiro Harbor, but they were ousted in 1567.
From 1580 to 1640, when Portugal was united with Spain, the
country was vulnerable. The Dutch attacked Salvador unsuccess-
fully in 1632, but in 1633 the Dutch West Indies Company
captured the city and controlled the whole northeast of the
area of rich sugar plantations until they were driven out in
1654. Some of the Dutch colonists then fled to New Amsterdam,
where the Jews among them were the first to settle in North
America.

Beginning in the seventeenth century, the Portuguese settlers gradually extended their control westward into Spanish
territory. In the northeast, many black slaves were imported to
work on the sugar plantations, and their descendants have
contributed much to the culture of modern Brazil. In 1763, Río
de Janeiro became the capital, supplanting the port of Bahia.
After the invasion of Portugal by Napoleon in 1807, John VI,
the King of Portugal of the House of Braganza, fled to Río and

transferred the seat of his government there in 1808. When King John returned to Portugal in 1821, he left his son, Pedro, as regent. On September 7, 1822, independence was declared, and he became Pedro I, Emperor of Brazil.

The empire under the house of Braganza lasted for more than sixty years. Pedro I abdicated in favor of his son Pedro II in 1831. Gradual emancipation of slaves was begun in 1871, and in 1888, while Pedro II was visiting Europe and the country was under the regency of his daughter Isabel, slavery was completely abolished. The plantation owners withdrew their support for the empire in protest, and after a bloodless revolution in 1889 a republic was proclaimed under Manuel Deodoro da Fonseca, the first President. It was under the late Joscelino Kubitschek, who was elected President in 1955, that the construction of Brasília began. The new capital, deep in the jungle, was dedicated in 1960. São Paulo is the largest city in South America and is still growing rapidly.

There are twenty-one states, a federal district and four territories in the structure of the modern Federative Republic of Brazil. The ethnic makeup of the country is a mixture of Portuguese, German, Italian, Spanish, British, Japanese, Chinese, Indian and Black. The most common surnames in Río de Janeiro in the 1970's are Oliveira, Pereira, Santos, Silva and Souza; in São Paulo, they are Carvalho, Oliveira, Ferreira, Pereira, Santos and Silva.

There were national censuses in 1890 and 1920 and every ten years since 1940.

Archives

Arquivo Nacional
Praça da República 26-ZC 14
20000 Río de Janeiro, Brazil

Arquivo Do Instituto Histórico e
  Geográfico Brasileiro
Av. Augusto Severo 8
20000 Río de Janeiro, Brazil

Public and Church Records

Civil registration of births, marriages and deaths was introduced on January 1, 1889; records are maintained by the Registro Civil (Civil Registry Office) of the individual district or city. Before this date, registers were kept by Catholic churches. Although civil registration is fully established, church registers are still accepted wherever civil offices are difficult to reach, because of the vastness of the country.

Libraries

Biblioteca Nacional
Secão de Manuscritos, Av. Río
Branco 219/239
3° andar, 20000 Río de Janeiro,
Brazil

Biblioteca Central da Universidade de São Paulo
Cidade Universitária Butantan,
C.P. 8191
São Paulo, Brazil

Historical and Genealogical Societies

Instituto Genealógico Brasileiro
Rua Dr. Zuquim 1525
São Paulo, Brazil

Instituto Histórico e Geográfico
Brasileiro
Avenida Augusto Severo 8
Río de Janeiro, Brazil

Books and Articles

Anuario Genealógico Latino.
São Paulo, 1949–.
NN APA

Behar, Eli.
Vultos de Brasil.
São Paulo, 1967. 222 p.
NN JFD 71-1245

Biblioteca Genealógica Brasileira.
São Paulo, 1942–56. 8 v.
NN APY

Borges da Fonesca, Antonio J.V.
(1718–1786).
Nobilarchia Permanbucana Río de
Janeiro, 1935. 2 v.
(IN: *Brazil*, Biblioteca Nacional.

Río de Janeiro Annaes, 1925–26.
v. 47–48)
NN *GY

Botelho de Souza Aranha, Maria
Amelia.
Sombras Que Renascem. Memorias
de Familia ...
Costumes Deumaépoca 1862–1881.
Solar de Botelha, Fazendu Santa
Francisca do Lobo, c. 1966. 310
p., no index, t of c, illus. in color.
(Ports. of Empresses of Brazil)
NN APY 76-398

Carbalho, José.
Candidode de Ninguem Mata o
Arco-Iris.
Río de Janeiro, 1972. 233 p.

Gardel, Luis Delgado.
Les Armoiries Ecclésiastiques au
Brésil (1551–1962).
Río de Janeiro, 1963. 557 p., plus
index.
NN AWT

Gonzaga Da Silva Leme, Luis de.
Genealogia Paulistana.
São Paulo, Duprat & Co., 1903–1905.
9 v.

Haus Brasilien (Maison de Bresil)
Bourbon-Orléans, Formerly
Braganza.
(IN: *GHF*, Limburg/Lahn, C.A.
Starke, 1956, 1968. v. 4, p. 101–5
[Portugal-Braganza] v. 8, p.
40–44 [Brazil-Bourbon-Orleans].)
NN ATC

... Indiced Organizado por Salvador de Moya.
São Paulo, c. 1952. 2 v.
(*Indices Genealogical Brasileiros.*
ser. 1, nos. 6–7)
NN APY

670 • *Tracing Your Family's History Abroad*

Instituto Genealógico de Bahia.
Revista ...
1945–60. v. 1–12.
NN APY

Instituto Genealógico Brasileiro.
São Paulo.
Subsidios Genealógicos Familias
Brasileiras de Origem Germa-
nica.
São Paulo, 1962–67. 5 v.
NN APY

Lacombe, Lourenco Luis.
O Tronco da Familia Nabuco de
Araujo.
Río de Janeiro, 1957. 25 p., ports.,
no index.
NN AVHH (Nabuco) 72-1295

Macedo Soares, Antonio J. de.
Nobiliarquia   Flumianense   ...
Familias da Côrte e Provincia
do Río de Janeiro, 1878.
Río de Janeiro, N.R. Macedo
Soares, 1947. 2 v.
NN APY

Marcondes de Moura, Carlos E.
Os Galvaode Franca no Povoa-
mento de Santo Antonio de
Guarantinquetá (1733–1972).
São Paula, Grafica da Escola de
Comunaccoes e Artes Universi-
dade de São Paulo, 1973. 2 v.
(Gives Portuguese origins of set-
tlers of the city of Franca and
genealogy of their descendants)
NN AVHH (Franca) 75-1719

Moya, Salvador de.
Bibliografía de Apelidos no Brasil.
São Paulo, 1958. 540 p.
(*Anuario Genealógico Latino* v. 10)
NN APA

Moya, Salvador de.

Bibliografía   Heráldico-Genealó-
gica.
São Paulo, 1955. 1 v.
NN AP 75-2468

Moya, Salvador de.
Catalogo de Autores Genealógicos.
(IN: *Revista do Arquivo Municipal.*
ano 4, v. 38 [1937], p. 81–160)
NN HFA

Moya, Salvador de.
Catalogo Genealógico de Antonio
de Santa Maria Jaboatao.
São Paulo, 1943–48. 2 v. in 1.
(*Indice Genealógicos Brasileiros.*
ser. 1, no. 1; ser. 2, no. 1)
NN APY

Moya, Salvador de.
Nobiliarquia Paulistana do Pedro
de Almeida Leme.
São Paulo, c. 1944.
(*Indices Genealógicos Brasileiros.*
ser. 1, no. 3/4)
NN APY

Moya, Salvador de.
Origem de Algumas Familias Por-
tuguesas que tem Brasao de Ar-
mas.
(IN: *Anuario Genealógica Latino*,
São Paulo, 1949–53. v. 1, p. 3–99;
v. 4, p. 15–31; v. 5, p. 45–67)
NN APA

Moya, Salvador de.
Simbologia Heráldica.
São Paulo, 1961. 405 p.
(*Biblioteca Genealógica Latina* no.
5)
NN AWD

Quem é Quem no Brasil. 3rd ed.
São Paulo, 1953.
NN AGU

Resende, Oswaldo.

Genealogía Dos Resendes. São
Paulo, the author, 1974. 390 p.,
index.
NN APY 77-593

Sass, Roselis, Baroness von.
Revelacoes Ineditas da História do
Brasil.
São Paulo, 1973. 222 p.
NN JFD 75-6993

Vaconcellos, Barao.
Archio Nobilarchico Brasileiro.
Lausanne, Switzerland, La Con-
corde, 1918. 622 p., index.
NN APY+

Who's Who in Brazil.
São Paulo, W.W. in B. Ltda.,
1973–74. 3 v., A-Z.
NN AGU 73-2691

CHILE (SANTIAGO)

Diego de Almagro marched into Chile from Peru under orders
from Pizarro in 1536 but met fierce opposition from the Arau-
canian Indians. Pedro de Valdivia had more success when he
brought an army into Chile in 1540 and founded the city of
Santiago the next year. The cities of La Serena, Concepción and
Valdivia were established within a few years. The Araucanians
continued to resist Spanish authority and remained hostile until
the late nineteenth century. Chile was a captaincy-general under
the rule of the viceroyalty of Peru until it became a separate
entity in 1778. The struggle for independence from Spain began
in 1810 under the leadership of Bernardo O'Higgins and Juan
Martinez de Rozas. The aid of the Argentine Liberator, José de
San Martin, which began in 1817 and culminated in the battle
of Maipu on April 5, 1818, led to O'Higgins' proclamation of
Chilean independence on February 12, 1818. It was not until
1826 that the last royalists were driven from the country. Outside of the cities, the Spanish had developed large ranches worked
by Indian labor, and a hardy mestizo class became tenant
farmers. Today, nearly 70 percent of the population is mestizo;
some 2 percent is pure Indian, and the balance is of pure
European descent—a mixture of Spanish, Italians, Germans,
Irish and English. The language and culture is Spanish, with
Indian influences.

A census was attempted in 1813 and 1814, but little of it has
survived. In 1831 a census of Maule, Concepción, Valdivia, Chile
and Santiago was taken, and in 1835 the remaining provinces
were counted. Censuses of the entire country were made in

1843, 1854, 1865, 1875, 1888, 1895, 1907, 1920, 1930, 1940, 1952, 1960 and 1970.

Archives

Archivo Nacional
Edificio Biblioteca Nacional
Av. Bernardo O'Higgins 651
Santiago, Chile

Archivo General del Registro Civil
  (Civil Registration Archives)
C. Huerfanos 1579, 1° piso
Santiago, Chile

Public and Church Records

Civil registration dates from 1885. Birth certificates can be obtained from: Dirección General del Registro Civil e Identificacion
Santiago, Chile

Marriage certificates are available from the Civil Registry of the place where the marriage took place.

Libraries

Biblioteca Nacional de Chile
Avenida B. O'Higgins 651
Santiago, Chile

Biblioteca Central del la Universidad de Chile
Avenida Bernardo O'Higgins 1058,
  Casilla 10D
Santiago, Chile

Historical and Genealogical Societies

Sociedad de Genealogía
Santiago, Chile

Sociedad Chilena de Historia y Geografía
Casilla 1386
Santiago, Chile

Books and Articles

Aranguiz Donoso, Horacia.
Bibliografía Histórica, 1959–1967.
Santiago, 1970. 84 p.
NN HIB 74-2146

Bizzarro, Salvatore.
Historical Dictionary of Chile.
Metuchen, NJ, Scarecrow Press, 1972. 309 p., alpha, no index.
HIB 76-1705

Crisostomo, Juan Pablo.
Descendencia de Don Juan Nicolas Merino de Heredia en Chile 1650–1971.
Santiago, the author, 1971. 167 leaves.
NN APY+ 72-3026

Cuadra Gormaz, Guillermo de la.
Familias Chilenas.
Santiago, Editoria Zamorano y Caperan, 1948. v. 1 (Bad paper).
A8L1 only
NN APY

Cuadra Gormaz, Guillermo de la.
Familias Coloniales de Santiago.
Santiago, Imprenta Universitaria, 1918–32. 3 v. (v. 2–4).
NN *ZI-87 film
(v. 1 IN: *Revista Chilena de Historia y Geografía.* v. 11, p.

173–217; v. 12, p. 81–128; v. 13, 35–72; v. 14, 46–84)
NN HIA

Derrick-Jehu, L.C.
The Anglo Chilean Community.
(IN: *Family History*, Canterbury, 1965. v. 3, no. 17–18, p. 157–84)
NN ARCA

Diccionario Biográfico de Chile. 1936–.
Santiago, Empresa Periodistica, v. 1–14, 1968.
NN AGU

Espejo, Juan Luis.
Nobiliario de la Capitania General de Chile.
Santiago, Andres Bello, 1967. 946 p.
NN APY

Fernández-Pradel, Pedro Xavier.
Linajes Vascos y Montañeses en Chile.
Santiago de Chile, Talleres Gráficos San Rafael, 1930.
NN APY

Germans in Chile
A. *Genealogishches Jahrbuch*, Neustadt an der Aisch, 1965. band 5, p. 23–75.
   NN ATA
B. *Sudwestdeutsche Blatter für Familien und Wappenkunde*.
Stuttgart, 1957. Jahrb. 9, heft 3, p. 479–82
   NN ATF (Württemberg)
C. *Zeitschrift für Niedersachsische Familienkunde*.
Hamburg, 1959. Jahrb. 34, heft 1, p. 1–17
   NN ATF (Saxony)

Instituto Chileno de Investigaciones Genealógicas.

Revista de Estudios Históricos.
Santiago, 1949–1954/55. nos. 1–4/5, 5 no. in 2 v.
(Genealogical periodical)
NN APY 75-292

Mansilla Vidal, Luis.
Relacion Genealogía de Varias Familias Chileonsis.
Angol, El Colono, 1927. 307 p.
NN APY 74-217

Mattar, Ahmad Hassan.
Guía Social de la Colonia Arabe en Chile (Siria-Palestina-Libanesa).
Santiago, Ahues Hnos, 1941. 379 p., alpha by city and then by surname under city.
NN AGU

Mujica de la Fuente, J.
Linajes Españoles Nobleza Colonial de Chile.
Santiago, Zamorano y Caperan, 1927. 385 p. (Bad paper).
NN APY

Orrego Barros, Carlos.
Bosquejos y Perfiles.
Santiago, Andres Bello, 1961. 209 p.
NN HIB

Roa y Ursua, Luis de.
Reyno de Chile, 1535–1810. Estudo Histórico Genealógico.
Valladolid, Talleres Tipográficos, 1945. 1,029 p.
NN AGU

Thayer Ojeda, Tomas.
Formacíon de la Sociedad Chilena y Censo de la Población de Chile en los Años de 1540 en 1565.
Santiago, Universidad de Chile, 1939–43. 3 v., alpha.
NN AGU

COLOMBIA (BOGOTÁ)

Colombia was part of the Spanish colony of New Granada, which also included Ecuador, Panama and Venezuela. Columbus, Vespucci and others explored the Caribbean coast of this area between 1499 and 1510, and Pedro Arias de Avila established the cities of Santa Marta in 1525 and Cartagena in 1533. In 1536 Gonzalo Jimenez de Quesada ascended into the Andes, where he subdued the powerful Chibcha Indians. In 1538 he founded the city of Santa Fé, now Bogotá, and it was he who gave the name Granada to the colony, after his homeland. It was under the jurisdiction of Peru for many years, until a separate viceroyalty was created in 1717. Antonio Nariño, one of the first revolutionary leaders, participated in an uprising in Bogotá in 1810, and Simón Bolívar secured the independence of Greater Colombia at the battle of Boyaca in 1819. This new nation had its capital at Cucuta, with Bolívar as President. Venezuela and Ecuador became separate countries in 1830, and the remaining territory became the republic of New Granada. The name was changed to the United States of Colombia in 1863, and in 1886 it became the Republic of Colombia. Panama declared its independence from Colombia in 1903, and in 1914 Colombia recognized Panama in return for rights in the Canal Zone.

A census of Greater Colombia was taken in 1825, and after the area became New Granada censuses were taken in 1835, 1843 and 1851. Censuses of the United States of Colombia were recorded in 1864 and 1870. In 1912 the first census of Colombia as it is today—without Panama—was taken. An incomplete count was made in 1928, and more recent censuses were taken in 1964 and 1970.

Archives

Archivo Nacional de Colombia
Calle 24 No. 5-60, 4° piso
Bogotá, D.E. 1, Colombia

Academia Colombiana de Historia
Sección de Archivos y Microfilmes
Calle 10 No. 8-95 (Postal add.:
  Apdo. nacional 1959)
Bogotá, Colombia

Departamento Administrativo Nacional de Estadistica (DANE)
Centro Administrativo Nacional (CAN)
Bogotá, Colombia

Public and Church Records

Births and marriages are registered with notaries or municipal authorities.

Libraries

Biblioteca Nacional de Colombia
Calle 24, No. 5-60, Apdo. 2525
Bogotá, Colombia

Biblioteca de la Universidad Nacional de Colombia
Bogotá, Colombia

Biblioteca del Centro de Historia
Popayán, Colombia

Books and Articles

Arango Mejia, Gabriel.
... Genealogías de las Familias de Antioquia.
Medellin, Imprenta Editorial, 1911. 774 p.
NN APY

Diaz, Carlos A.
Paginas de Historia Colombiana.
Bucaramange, 1967. 423 p.
NN HDB 71-293

Florez de Ocariz, Juan.
Genealogías del Nuevo Reino de Granada.
Bogotá, Biblioteca Nacional, 1943-55. 3 v.
(Colombia Archivo Nacional, pub. no. 14)
NN APY

Quién es Quién en Colombia.
Bogotá, Kelly, 1944-48. 2 v.
NN AGU

Restrepo Saenz, José M.
Genealogías de Santa Fé de Bogota.
Bogotá, Colombiana, 1928. v. 1.
NN APY

ECUADOR (QUITO)

Once the kingdom of Quito, which was conquered by the Incas in the latter part of the fifteenth century, this land was explored by Benalcázar, a soldier under Pizarro, in 1533. The conquistadors who followed him did not find the wealth attributed to the area in myth and let it become a colonial backwash. As the presidency of Quito, the territory was under the rule of Peru and later of New Granada. It was liberated by Sucre in the battle of Pichincha in 1822 and became part of Greater Colombia; in 1830 it became a separate republic. The majority of the population is of Indian and mestizo descent, but in the coastal regions there are many blacks and mulattos. The white population is small, but as landowners, whites play an important role in the unstable government.

Ecuador was included in the census of Greater Colombia in 1825. In 1864 a partial census was taken, and in 1906 a census of the city of Quito was made. After many abortive attempts, national censuses were recorded in 1950 and 1962.

Archives

Archivo Nacional de Historia
Av. 6 de Diciembre N° 332
Quito, Ecuador

Archivo Nacional de Guayaquil
Apartado 1333
Guayaquil, Ecuador

Public and Church Records

Certificates for births and marriages since 1901 are issued by the Civil Registry of each "canton" and "parroquia" and also by the Direccion General del Registro Civil in Quito. Earlier records may be available at the parish churches.

Libraries

Biblioteca Nacional
Adpo. 163
Quito, Ecuador

Biblioteca de la Universidad Central del Ecuador
García Moreno 887 y Espejo 945
Casilla 166
Quito, Ecuador

Biblioteca Histórica y Archivo Colonial
Palacion de la Municipalidad, P.O. Box 75
Quito, Ecuador

Historical and Genealogical Societies

Centre de Investigaciones Históricas
P.O. Box 75
Guayaquil, Ecuador
(*Revista*)

Books and Articles

Andrade, Manuel de Jesús.
Ecuador. Próceres de la Independences ... Biografías.
Quito, 1909. 418 p.
NN AGU

Arboleda, Gustavo.
Diccionario Biográfico de la República del Ecuador.
Quito, 1910. 194 p.
NN Ref. Cat. 755

Bork, Albert W., and Georg Maier.
Historical Dictionary of Ecuador.
Metuchen, NJ, Scarecrow Press, 1973. 192 p.
NN HGN 76-1418

Destruge, Camilo.
Album Biográfico Ecuadoriano.
Guayaquil, 1903–05. 5 v., indexed.
NN AGU

Empressa Editorial Ecuador.
Diccionario Biografía del Ecuador.
Quito, 1928. 515 p.
NN AGU+

Guzman Rodriguez, José Alejandro.

Titulos Nobiliarios en el Ecuador.
Madrid, 1957. 334 p.
NN APY

Martinez Delgado, Luis.
... Apuntes Histórico-Biográficos.
Bogotá, Editorial ABC, 1940. 410
p.
NN AGU

Quién es Quién en Quito.

Guayaquil, Senefelder, 1966–67–. v.
1–.
NN *RR-AGU

Robles y Chambers, Pedro.
... Contribucio Para el Estudio de
la Sociedad Colonial de Guayaquil
Guayaquil, La Reforma, 1938. 657
p.
NN APY

FRENCH GUIANA (CAYENNE)

A French Overseas Department, French Guiana stretches 200
miles along the northeast coast of South America and 250 miles
into the interior. Devil's Island, a former French penal colony
eight miles offshore, was closed by France in 1944, and it's 2,800
inmates were repatriated. Ninety percent of the people, a mixture of blacks and whites, live in coastal areas, while the interior
is inhabited by Carib, Arawak and Tupi-Guarani Indians and
descendants of escaped African slaves. The territory is administered by a Paris-appointed prefect and an elected general
council; a deputy and senator are elected to the French Chamber
of Deputies.

Public and Church Records

Birth and marriage certificates
can be obtained from the office
of the mayor (*La Mairie*) where
the event took place.

Libraries

Bibliothèque Franconie
Cayenne, French Guiana

Musée Local (Contains historical
documents)
Cayenne, French Guiana

Books and Articles

Almanach de la Guyane Français
pour l'An de Grâce 1821.
Cayenne, 1820. 1 v.
NN *KSA

Jean-Louis, Paul.
La Guyane Française Historique.
Besançon, 1962. 81 p.
NN HAE p.v.874

Mourie, J.F.H.
La Guyane Française
Paris, P. Dupont, 1874. 360 p.
NN HET

GUYANA (GEORGETOWN)

When this area was visited by Spanish sailors in 1499, it was inhabited by Carib, Arawak and Warrau Indians. In the late seventeenth century it was settled by the Dutch, but by 1814 it was a British possession. African slaves and indentured Indian servants were brought in to work the plantations; the Indians soon outnumbered the blacks, as they do to this day. In 1831 the colonies of Berbice, Essequibo and Demerara were united as the colony of British Guiana. The slaves were emancipated in 1837. In 1928 limited representative government was granted, and a new constitution providing for a bicameral legislature and ministerial responsibility was adopted in 1953. In 1961 the colony received full internal self-government. British Guiana became the independent nation of Guyana on May 26, 1966, and a republic in 1970.

Censuses of British Guiana were taken in 1861, 1871, 1881, 1891, 1911, 1921 and 1931.

Archives

National Archives of Guyana
River Police Compound
Water Street
Georgetown, Guyana

Public and Church Records

For vital statistics:
General Register Office
GPO Building
Georgetown, Guyana

For census information:
The Statistical Bureau
Ministry of Economic Development
Georgetown, Guyana

For wills and deeds:
Registrar of Deeds
Victoria Law Courts
Georgetown, Guyana

For religious records:
Guyana Council of Churches
71 Murray Street
Georgetown, Guyana

Libraries

Public Free Library
P.O. Box 110
Georgetown, Guyana

Library, University of Guyana
P.O. Box 841
Georgetown, Guyana

Books and Articles

Bacon, Margaret.
Journey to Guyana.
London, Dobson, 1970. 208 p.
NN HEC

Cabrera Sifontes, Horacio.
Guyana Esequiba.

Caracas, 1970. 139 p.
NN Sc S988.1-C

Daly, Vere T.
The Making of Guyana.
Georgetown, 1967. 158 p.
NN Sc 988.1-D

Georgetown, Guyana, Public Library Reference Department.
A Select Bibliography of the Works of Guyanese and on Guyana.

Georgetown, 1967. 51 p.
NN Sc 016.988-G

MacInnes, Hamish.
Climb to the Lost World.
London, 1974. 224 p.
NN HEC 75-1084

Who's Who in British Guiana, 1945–1948. 4th ed.
Georgetown, 1948. 845 p., ports.
NN AGH

PARAGUAY (ASUNCIÓN)

Paraguay was first explored by Juan Diaz de Solis, and Sebastian Cabot visited the area shortly thereafter, in 1527. The first settlement began in 1535 at Asunción. In 1776 the area became part of the viceroyalty of Río de la Plata, and in 1811 the country gained its independence from Spain. A land-locked country, Paraguay managed to maintain its sovereignty in the War of the Triple Alliance fought with Brazil, Argentina and Uruguay from 1865 to 1870. The population is of mixed Spanish and Guarani Indian origin, with some German, Italian, French, Irish and Scottish immigrants adding new strains.

Estimates of the population of Paraguay were made in 1536, 1775, 1828, 1852, 1857, 1861 and 1872. The first national census was attempted March 1, 1886, but it is doubtful whether it was completed. Another was taken in 1899–1900, and an electoral census was made in 1917. The census planned for 1936–37 was impeded by revolution.

Archives

Archivo Nacional/Museo Nacional
Mariscal Estigarriba e Iturbe
Asunción, Paraguay

Libraries

Biblioteca
Mariscal Estigarriba 93
Asunción, Paraguay

Biblioteca de la Universidad Nacional de Asunción
Colon 63
Asunción, Paraguay

Historical and Genealogical Societies

Instituto Paraguayo de Investigaciones Históricas

Calle 25 de Noviembre, 436
Asunción, Paraguay

Books and Articles

Bray, Arturo.
Hombres y Épocas del Paraguay
. . .
Buenos Aires, Nizza, 1957. 2 v.
NN K-10 1559

Chaves, Julio Cesar.
Historia General del Paraguay.
Asunción, Nizza, 1968. 1 v.
NN HLN

Kolinski, Charles J.
Historical Dictionary of Paraguay.
Metuchen, NJ, Scarecrow Press,
1973. 282 p., alpha, no index.
NN HLN 76-1420

Paraguay. Archivo Nacional
. . . Catálogo de Testamentos y Cod-
icilos del Archivo Nacional.
Asunción, Imprenta Nacional,
1936. 70 p.
NN APB p.v. 20

Parker, William B.
Paraguayans of Today.
London, Hispanic Society, 1920. 315
p., index.
NN AGU

Quién es Quién en el Paraguay.
Buenos Aires, F. Monte Domecq,
1941–55. 6 v.
NN L-10 4074 (NN has v. 2, 4, 6)

Warren, Harris G.
Paraguay: An Informal History.
Norman, OK, U. of Oklahoma
Press, 1949. 392 p.
NN HLN

PERU (LIMA)

Peru was the seat of the ancient Empire of the Incas, with its
capital at Cuzco, high in the Andes. The Spanish conquistadors
under Francisco Pizarro (1478–1541) arrived in 1532 and within
a few years subdued the Inca nation. José de San Martin, the
Argentine liberator, captured Lima in 1821, and a revolutionary
war, fought from 1821 to 1824, established the independence of
Peru, declared July 28, 1821. Today some 47 percent of the
population is Indian. The rest is mainly of Spanish and mestizo
descent, with a small percentage of blacks, Chinese and Japanese. The National Library at Lima was established in 1821,
but in the Pacific War of 1879–1882, the Chileans looted the
collection. Most of the books and manuscripts were recovered,
but in 1943 the historical section of the library suffered heavy
damage by fire.

Partial census enumerations were undertaken in the Spanish period, particularly in 1741 and 1795. The first national census was attempted in 1862, but it was not until 1876 that the first comprehensive Peruvian census was accomplished. Another was not taken until 1940, and since then it has been taken on a fairly regular basis—in 1950, 1961 and 1972.

In the early 1970's the most common surnames in Lima were Fernandez, Garcia, Perez, Rodriguez and Vargas.

Archives

Archivo General de la Nación
Palacio de Justica
Jirón Manuel Cuadros (Casilla N°
   3124)
Lima, Peru

Public and Church Records

A system of local civil registration was set up in 1828, and a central Vital Statistics Division was established in 1876. Birth and marriage certificates are issued by the Provincial Council (Consejo Provincial) or District Council (Consejo Distrital) of the province or district in which the event occurred.

Libraries

Biblioteca Nacional
Avenida Abancay, Apdo. 2335
Lima, Peru

Biblioteca Central de la Universidad Nacional Mayor de San Marcos
Apdo. 454
Lima, Peru

Historical and Genealogical Societies

Instituto Histórico del Peru
Lima, Peru
(*Revista*)

Instituto Peruano de Investigaciones Genealógicas
Santa Luisa 205, San Isidro
Lima, Peru
(*Revista*)

Books and Articles

Gardiner, C. Harvey.
The Japanese and Peru, 1873–1973.
Albuquerque, NM, U. of New Mexico Press, 1975. 202 p., index.
NN HHF 76-2306

Hemming, John.
The Conquest of the Incas.
New York, Harcourt Brace Jovanovich, 1970. 641 p., index.
NN HHK

Inquisition Peru.
Informaciones Genealógicas de Peruanos Seguidas Ante et Santo Officio.
Madrid, 1957. 260 p.
NN APY

Instituto Peruano de Investigaciones Genealógicas.

Revista.
Lima, 1946–
(Genealogical periodical)
NN APY

Izucue, Luis de.
... La Nobleza Titulada en el Perú
Colonia. 2nd ed.
Lima, Emp. edit. Cervantes, 1929.
66 p.
NN APY

Lockhart, James.
Spanish Peru, 1532–1560: A Colonial Society.
Madison, WI, U. of Wisconsin
Press, 1974 (orig. 1968). 285, 8 p.
NN

Martin, Luis.
The Kingdom of the Sun: A Short
History of Peru.

New York, Charles Scribner's Sons,
1974. 288 p., index.
NN HHB 75-613

Millones, Luis.
Etnicas en el Peru.
Lima, 1973. 97 p.
NN Sc S301.45-M

Morales, Adolfo de.
Catálogo de Pasajèros al Reino del
Perú desde 1560.
(IN: *Instituto Peruano de Investigaciones Genealógicas. Revista.*
Lima, 1952–55. Año 6–8, p. 79–95,
152–65, 239–57)
NN APY

Vargas Ugarte, Ruben.
Tutulos Nobiliarios en el Peru. 2nd
ed.
Lima, 1948. 48 p.
NN APB p.v. 45

URUGUAY (MONTEVIDEO)

Uruguay was explored by the Spanish in 1515, but the first permanent settlement was not made until 1624 at Soriano. Uruguay was part of the viceroyalty of Rio de la Plata from 1726 to 1814, when it became a province of Brazil. The country declared its independence August 25, 1825, and the republic was inaugurated in 1830. The University of Montevideo was founded in 1849. The population, concentrated in the south, is mainly of Spanish and Italian descent, with a few blacks and Indians.

Population enumerations for Montevideo were recorded in 1813 and 1816. The first national census was carried out in 1852–53, and others were taken in 1860 and 1900. An industrial census was made in 1937.

Archives

Archivo General de la Nación
Calle Convencion N° 1474
Montevideo, Uruguay

Public and Church Records

Civil registration began in 1879.
The justice of the peace (*juez
de paz*) keeps the civil register

(*registro del estado civil*) for four categories—birth, marriage, death and recognition of natural children—in duplicate books. Divorce and recognition of children are noted in the margin of the original record of marriage or birth. At the close of each year, one copy of each book is deposited with the respective departmental council, and the other is deposited at the office of the Director General of the Civil Register.

Dirección General del Registro del Estado Civil
Canelones 968
Montevideo, Uruguay

For census information:

Dirección General de Estadística y Censos
Cuareim 2052
Montevideo, Uruguay

For wills and deeds:

Suprema Corte de Justicia—Sección Informes
Ibicuy 1310
Montevideo, Uruguay

For religious records:

Instituto de Profesores Artigas
Sección Historia
Eduardo Acevedo 1419
Montevideo, Uruguay

Facultad de Humanidades y Ciencias
Cerrito 75
Montevideo, Uruguay

Libraries

Biblioteca Nacional del Uruguay
Guayabo 1793
Montevideo, Uruguay

Biblioteca del Museo Histórico Nacional
Casa Lavalleja, Zabala 1469, and Casa Rivera, Rincon 437
Montevideo, Uruguay

Biblioteca de la Universidad de la República
Av. 18 de Julio 1824
Montevideo, Uruguay

Books and Articles

Azarola Gil, Luis Enrique.
... Appelidos de la Patria Vieja.
Buenos Aires, La Facultad, 1942. 233 p.
NN APY

Azarola Gil, Luis Enrique.
... Cronicas y Linajes de la Gobernación del Plata ...
Buenos Aires, J. Lajouane, 1927. 142 p.
NN APY

Campos, Ricardo D.
Los Garcia de Zuniga y los Warnes.
Montevideo, Prometeo, 1948. 99 p.
(Las Grandes Familias Patricias Rioplatenses)
NN APB p.v. 52

Fernandez de Burzaco y Barrios, Hugo.
Fundadores de Linajes en El Plata.
(IN: *Genealogía*, Buenos Aires, 1955. no. 11, p. 154–64)
NN APA

Goldaracena, Ricardo.
El Libro de los Linajes: Familias Históricas Uruguayas del Siglo XIX.

Montevideo, Arca, 1976. 300 p.
NN

Lamb, Wilfrid J.
River Plate Personalities: A Bio-
graphical Dictionary.
Buenos Aires, Lamb, 1937. 246 p.
NN AGU

Llambias de Olivar, R.
Ensayo Sobre el Linaje de los Ar-
tigas en el Uruguay.
(IN: *Uruguay, Archivo y Museo
Histórico Nacional Revista His-
tórica*. Montevideo, 1923–24. v.
11, pp. 1055–1159; v. 12, p. 99–352)
NN HGA

Parker, William B.
Uruguayans of Today.
London, Hispanic Society, 1921. 575
p., alpha.
NN AGU

Rodriquez Vigoy, J.
... España en el Uruguay ...
Buenos Aires, Iberia, 1924. 207 p.
NN AGU+

Salterain, Herrera, Eduardo.
Hombres y Faenas: Estudios Uru-
guayos.
Montevideo, 1960. 493 p.
NN HGB

Scarone, Arturo.
... Uruguayos Contemporaneos
...
Montevideo, 1937. 610 p.
NN *RR-AGU

Willis, Jean L.
Historical Dictionary of Uruguay
Metuchen, NJ, Scarecrow Press,
1974. 275 p., alpha, no index.
NN HGB 75-1988

VENEZUELA (CARACAS)

Christopher Columbus discovered the mouth of the Orinoco
River in what is now Venezuela in 1498, and Amerigo Vespucci
visited the following year. Spanish settlement began in 1520 at
Cumana, and German merchant adventurers and British buccaneers were in and out of the area from the sixteenth to the
eighteenth centuries. From 1795 to 1821, as a member of the
Federal Republic of Greater Colombia, the country fought for
and won its independence from Spain, aided by Simón Bolívar, a
Venezuelan native. In 1830 Venezuela declared its independence
from the Colombia Federation. The population is mainly mestizo,
with some mulattos, zambos (people of Indian and black blood)
and pure Indians.

Only about half of the country was covered in the colonial
census of Venezuela taken between 1772 and 1784. National
population censuses have been recorded in 1874, 1881, 1891,
1920, 1926, 1936, 1941, 1950 and 1961.

The most popular surnames in Caracas in the early 1970's
were Garcia, Gonzalez, Hernandez, Perez and Rodriguez.

Archives

Archivo General de la Nación
Santa Capilla a Carmelitas 15
Avenida Urdenata (Apdo. 5935)
Caracas 101, Venezuela

Public and Church Records

Birth certificates are issued by the civil or religious authority having charge of such birth records. Marriage certificates can be procured from the Municipal Council (Consejo Municipal) of a city or the chief civil authority (Jefe Civil) of a district. A General Bureau of Statistics was set up in 1937.

Libraries

Biblioteca Nacional
San Francisco a Bolsa
Caracas, Venezuela

Biblioteca de la Academia Nacional de la Historia
Palacio de las Academias
Caracas, Venezuela

Biblioteca de la Universidad Católica "Andrés Bellow"
Esq. de Jesuítas 37, Apdo. 422
Caracas, Venezuela

Books and Articles

Campos, Antonio J.
... Venezuela Heráldica.
San Carlos, Estado Cojedes, 1939.
70 p.
NN APB p.v. 17

Capriles, Alejandro.
Coronas de Castilla en Venezuela.

Madrid, 1967. 590 p.
NN APY

Cova, Jesus Antonio.
Bocetos de Hoy Para Retratos de Mana.
Madrid, T. Villegas, 1953. 255 p.
NN AGU

Dávila, Vincente.
... Diccionario Biográfico de Ilustres Próceres de la Independencia Suramericana.
Caracas, Bolivar, 1924–26. 2 v.
NN AGU

Davila, Vincente.
... Investigaciones Históricas.
Caracas, Bolivar, 1923–27. 2 v.
NN HDN

Diccionario Biográfico de Venezuela. 1st ed.
Madrid, Garrido Mezquita, 1953.
1,558 p.
NN F-11 1844

Garcia Chuecos, Hector.
... Estudios de Historia Colonial Venezuela.
Caracas, Tip. Americana, 1937–38.
2 v.
NN HDN

Grases, Pedro.
Nuevos Temas de Bibliografía y Cultura Venezuelanas.
Mérida, 1967. 404 p.
NN HDM 72-2970

Nagel von Jess, Kurt.
Algunas Familias Maracaiberas.
Maracaibo, Venezuela, U. del Zulia, 1969. 504 p. Index
NN AVH (Venezuela) 76-1136
NN AVH (Venezuela) 76-754

Quién es Quién en Venezuela, Panama, Ecuador, Colombia.

Bogotá, Oliveira, 1952. 1,074 p.
NN *RR-AGU

Rodriguez Llamosa, Manuel V.
Genealogía del Liberator.
Caracas, Bolivar, 1928. 21 p.
(The Bolivar family)
NN APY

Sangroniz, José Antonio de.
Familias Coloniales de Venezuela.
Caracas, Editorial Bolivar, 1943–.
 v. 1, 1 v.
NN APY

Suárez, Ramón Darío.
Genealogía del Liberator.
Mérida, Venezuela, 1970. 449, 14 p.
(Bolivar family)
NN JFD 72-3889

GENERAL LATIN AMERICAN SOURCES

Brownrigg, Edwin.
Guide to the Rich Collection of Colonial Latin American Manuscripts.
New York, NYPL, 1977.

Garcia, Carraffa, Alberto and Arturo.
Enciclopedia Heráldica y Genealógica.
Madrid, 1920–63. 88 v. A–Urriza.
NN APY

Gerhard, Peter.
A Guide to the Historical Geography of New Spain.
Cambridge, England; Cambridge U. Press, 1972. 476 p.
NN HTK 74-7

Gorden, Raymond.
Spanish Personal Names as Barriers to Communications Between Latin Americans and North Americans.
Yellow Springs, OH, Antioch College, 1968. 142 p.
NN APD 75-356

Gropp, Arthur.
A Bibliography of Latin American Bibliographies.
Metuchen, NJ, Scarecrow Press, 1968. 515 p.
NN *R-HC 73-121

Guía de Bibliotecas de la America Latina.
Washington, DC, Pan-American Union, 1963. 166 p.
(Bibliographic Series no. 51)

Index of Latin American Periodical Literature 1929–1960, Columbus Memorial Library, Pan-American Union (Washington, DC).
Boston, G.K. Hall, 1976. 8 v.

Latin American Newspapers in the United States Libraries: A Union List, comp. by Steven Charno.
Austin, TX, U. of Texas Press, 1968. 619 p.
NN *RS-*A 76-7817

Letters and People of the Spanish Indies: Sixteenth Century.
Cambridge, MA, Harvard U. Press, 1976. 267 p.
(Cambridge Latin American Series, v. 22)

Montalvão Machado, J.T.
Dos Pizarros de Espanha aos de Portugal e Brasil, Historia e Genealogica.
Lisbon, 1970. 535 p., index.

(Conquistadors)
NN ASP (Pizarro) 73-239

Nieto y Cortadellas, Rafael.
Los Descendientes de Cristóbal Colón (Obra Genealógica).
La Habana, Sociedad Colombista Pan Americana, 1952. 485 p., t of c called index.
(The descendants of Christopher Columbus)
NN ASP (Colon)

Spain. Archivo General de Indias.
Catálogo de Pasajeros a Indias.

Seville, Editorial de la Gavida, 1940–46. 3 v., indexed.
(Passenger lists of Spanish to the New World; covers 1509–59)
NN APY

Walne, Peter.
A Guide to Manuscript Sources for the History of Latin America and the Caribbean in the British Isles.
London, 1973. 580 p.
NN HBC 73-2904

ADEN

See Yemen, People's Democratic Republic

AFGHANISTAN (KABUL)

The mountainous central Asian country of Afghanistan, occupying a key position on the land route to India, was a continual temptation to foreign conquerors. Greece, Mongolia, Persia and Turkey all played a part in her history. After the second century B.C. Buddhism spread from the East, but Muslim conquests established Islam as the stable religion. In the eleventh century Mahmud of Ghazni, the strongest of the Muslim rulers, consolidated the diverse petty kingdoms into one which stretched from the Caspian Sea to the Ganges River. In 1152 hordes from Ghor overran the country, to be followed by Genghis Khan in the thirteenth century. In the sixteenth century Babar used the capital city of Kabul for his conquest of India and subsequent establishment of the Mogul Empire. Nadir Shah led Persia in the conquest of Afghanistan in the eighteenth century, and upon his death in 1747 his lieutenant, Ahmed Shah, established the Durani dynasty and Afghanistan as a state.

The Durani line came to an end in 1826, and Dost Muhammed assumed power. His rule saw the emergence of Anglo-Russian rivalry in the area. The First Afghan War (1838–1842) erupted when Dost Muhammed tried to exploit these rivalries and seize British possessions in India. The Second Afghan War occurred when Dost Muhammed's son, Shere Ali, turned to Russia for aid. In 1907 an Anglo-Russian agreement guaranteed the independence of Afghanistan under British influence. In 1933 Muhammed Zahir Shah presented the people with their first democratic constitution. In 1965 a more liberal constitution was adopted, only to be suspended in 1973 by a military coup. Muhammed Daud, spearhead of the coup, proclaimed Afghanistan a republic, designating himself as President and Premier.

Public and Church Records

Statistical Bureau of the Ministry
of Interior
Kabul, Afghanistan

Libraries

Library of the Royal Palace
Kabul, Afghanistan

Public Library
Kabul, Afghanistan

University Library
Kabul, Afghanistan

Historical and Genealogical Societies

Da Tarikh Tolana (Historical Society)
Kabul, Afghanistan

Books and Articles

Ali, Mohammed.
The Afghans.
Kabul, 1969. 183 p.
NN JFC 72-551

Ali, Mohammed.
A Cultural History of Afghanistan.
Kabul, 1964. 255 p.
NN JFD 72-133

Caroe, Olaf.
The Pathans, 550 B.C.–A.D. 1957.
London, St. Martin's Press, 1958.
521 , index.
NN *R-BCW

Sykes, Sir Percy.
A History of Afghanistan.
London, Macmillan, 1940. 2 v., index v. 2.
NN *RR-BCW

Tate, George P.
The Kingdom of Afghanistan.
Dusseldorf, c. 1971. 270 p.
NN JFE 75-1776

BAHREIN (MANAMA)

Bahrein consists of several islands situated in the Persian Gulf, twenty miles off the Arabian Peninsula's northeast coast. The Khalifa family ruled Bahrein until 1861, when Bahrein signed a treaty giving Great Britain responsibility for defense and foreign relations. When Britain announced that its troops would be removed by 1971, Bahrein attempted to federate with seven Trucial Sheikdoms and Qatar, but the effort failed, and Bahrein declared its independence. It is ruled by an Emir, a Prime

Minister and a Council of Ministers. The great majority of Bahreinians are of northern Arabian descent, half of them Sunni Muslims, half of them Sh'ites. Persian and English are both spoken, but the official language is Arabic.

Censuses were taken in 1950 and 1959.

Books and Articles

Esmaili, Malek.
... Le Golfe Persique et les Iles de Bahrein.
Paris, 1936. 288 p.
NN BCP

Faroughy, Abbas.
The Bahrein Islands, 750–1951 ...
New York, Verry, Fisher and Co., 1951. 128 p.
NN BCP

BANGLADESH (DACCA)

In 1947, when India and Pakistan became independent from the British, the government of Pakistan was located in West Pakistan. The East Pakistanis, who made up 56 percent of the population, rioted in 1968–69 when their demands for greater autonomy went unheeded. In 1971 a general strike in East Pakistan prompted West Pakistani troops to attack the Bengalis. The Awami League, spokesmen for an autonomous East Pakistan, declared the independence of East Pakistan on May 26, 1971, and the ensuing war in East Pakistan between West Pakistan troops and guerrilla forces was atrociously violent. Ten million Bengalis fled to India, which supported their cause. Hostilities then commenced between Pakistan and India. East Pakistan won independence in 1971 as Bangladesh. Nearly all its people are Muslim Bengalis.

Archives

Directorate of Archives and Libraries
103 Elephant Road
Dacca 5, Bangladesh

Books and Articles

Farque, Md. Omar.
Emergence of Bangladesh.
Dacca, 1972. 106 p.
NN JFD 74-5013

Hasan, Sayed Mahmudul.
A Guide to Ancient Monuments of
   East Pakistan.
Dacca, 1970. 180 p.
NN JFD 74-7636

Kamruddin, Ahmad.
A Social History of Bengal.
Dacca, 1970. 205 p.
NN JFD 75-860

BHUTAN (THIMPU)

Bhutan, a small kingdom in the eastern Himalayas bordered
by Tibet and India, was conquered by Tibet in the sixteenth
century. In 1865 the British occupied the southern section of
the territory and annexed it to India. In 1949 a treaty signed
by India and Bhutan recognized the British as director of their
foreign relations, and India returned the annexed territory. In
1964, after Prime Minister Jigme Dorji was assassinated, his
brother, Lendup Dorji, assumed his office but was expelled
because he was suspected of plotting a coup. King Jigme Singye
Wangchuck assumed full power, and in 1969 a constitutional
monarchy was declared.

Most of the people of Bhutan are Bhotias of Tibetan ancestry
and are Buddhists; the minority are Hindus of Nepalese descent.

Books and Articles

Das, Nirmala.
The Dragon Country: The General
   History of Bhutan.
Bombay, Orient Longman, 1974. 99
   p.
NN JFF 76-465

Rennie, David Field.
Bhutan and the Story of the Doar
   War.
New Delhi, 1970. 408 p.
NN JFD 72-6979

Shakya'i dge-slong.
A History of Bhutan from the 7th
   Century A.D. to the 18th Cen-
   tury A.D.
Bothell, WA, 1969. 222 leaves.
NN *OZ 75-744

Singh, Nagendra.
Bhutan: A Kingdom in the Hima-
   layas.
New Delhi, 1972. 202 p.
NN JFE 74-523

BURMA (RANGOON)

The valley of the Irrawaddy River in the Southeast Asian country of Burma was settled in the ninth century A.D. by a Mongoloid race from Tibet. In 1044, King Anawratha established control over the delta and introduced Hinayana Buddhism. Anawratha's capital city was Pagan, known as the "city of a thousand temples." The Mongol invasion under Kublai Khan ripped Anawratha's kingdom to pieces in 1287. When the Mongols departed, Burma split into a patchwork of petty states ruled by Shan chieftains who were tributaries of China until 1546. New Burmese dynasties arose with the major ones seated at Ava, Pegu and Toungoo. The country was united in the sixteenth century under the Toungoo dynasty, which initiated a series of wars against Siam that did not end until the nineteenth century.

Burma was first visited by Europeans in the sixteenth century, when Portuguese traders passed through. English and Dutch visited later, and by the eighteenth century the French and English were competing for Burmese trade. Both countries suspended activities in the area after 1760. In a drive to expand Burma's frontiers, the Alaungpaya dynasty conflicted with the British. The Anglo-Burmese wars (1824–85) resulted in the annexation of Burma by the British, who ruled it as part of India. In 1937 Burma achieved Dominion status. Burma obtained independence from Britain in 1948 and became the Union of Burma, an independent republic.

Censuses were recorded in 1872, 1881, 1891, 1901, and 1953.

Public and Church Records

Registrar of Births, Deaths and
   Marriages
Office of the Excise Commissioner
Rangoon, Burma

Libraries

National Library, Museum and
   Art Gallery
Jubilee Hall (temporary address)
Pagoda Road
Rangoon, Burma

State Library and Museum
Kyaukpyu, Burma

University of Rangoon Library
University Estate
Rangoon, Burma

Books and Articles

Cady, John F.
A History of Modern Burma.
Ithaca, New York, Cornell U.
   Press, 1960. (orig. 1958). 682 p.
NN *RR-BGD

Chatterjie, S.
Meeting the Personalities. Burma Series.
Rangoon, 1956. 70 p.
NN JFD 73-1787

Foucar, Emilie C
... They Reigned in Mandalay.
London, D. Dobson, 1946. 165 p.
(Kings and rulers)
NN BGD

Harvey, Godfrey Eric.
History of Burma from the Earliest Times to 10 March 1824, the Beginning of the English Conquest.
London, Longmans, 1925. 415 p.
NN *R-BGD

Jesse, Fryniwyd Tennyson.
The Story of Burma.
London, Macmillan, 1946. 206 p.
NN *RR-BGD

Maha Yaza Win Taw Kyi.
The Glass Palace: Chronicle of the Kings of Burma.
London, Oxford U. Press, 1923. 179 p.
NN *OY

Maring, Joel M.
Historical and Cultural Dictionary of Burma.
Metuchen, NJ, Scarecrow Press, 1973. 290 p.
NN JFD 74-2411

Mi Mi Khaing, Daw.
Burmese Family.
Bloomington, IL, c. 1962. 200 p.
NN JFE 74-1992

Traeger, Frank N.
Burma: A Selected and Annotated Bibliography.
New Haven, CT, 1973. 356 p.
NN JFD 75-4443

CAMBODIA (PHNOM-PENH)

Cambodia was dominant in Indochina during the years of the great Khmer Empire. By the thirteenth century the Cambodian empire was at its height, stretching from the South China Sea westward into Burma. In time, Cambodia fell prey to foreign invasions and was drastically reduced in size. Three provinces were lost to the Siamese, and the Annamese took the provinces of what is now known as Cochin China. The Cambodian king asked for French protection in 1854, and a French protectorate was set up in 1863. In 1887 Cambodia was included in the Union of Indochina. A French-Siamese treaty restored Cambodia's western provinces in 1907. The Japanese invaded the country during the Second World War and drove out the French. In 1946 the French returned, and steps were taken to grant Cambodia autonomy within the French Union. Cambodia became fully independent in 1955. Late that year King Norodom Sihanouk abdicated in favor of his father.

Archives

Archives Nationales
Rukhavithei Daun Penh (B.P. No. 4)
Phnom-Penh, Cambodia

Annales du Musée d'Art et d'Histoire Ex-Palais Royal
Phnom-Penh, Cambodia

Libraries

Bibliothèque du Centre Royal de Documentation et D'Edition
Phnom-Penh, Cambodia

Bibliothèque Nationale
Phnom-Penh, Cambodia

Bibliothèque Royale
Phnom-Penh, Cambodia

Books and Articles

Cheminais, Louis.
Le Cambodge.
Paris, A. Maisonneuve, 1960. 534 p.
NN B-10 1861

Edmonds, I.G.
The Khmers of Cambodia.
Indianapolis, IN, Bobbs-Merrill, 1970. 160 p., index.
NN JFE 71-229

Ghosh, Manomohan.
A History of Cambodia from the Earliest Time to the End of the French Protectorate.
Saigon, J.K. Gupta, 1960. 290 p.
NN C-12 1464

Mignon, Georges.
Une Royauté Millénaire.
(IN: *Asie Nouvelle Illustré*, Saigon, Sept. 30, 1936 p. 5–12)
NN BBA+

Russier, Henri.
Histoire Sommaire du Royaume de Cambodge des Origines à Nos Jours.
Saigon, C. Ardin, 1914. 159 p.

CHINA (PEKING)

Earliest recorded history in China begins with the Shang dynasty (1523–1027 B.C.). The turbulent but culturally active Chou dynasty (1027–256 B.C.) produced the philosopher and teacher Confucius. A centralized imperial system was first established under the Ch'in dynasty (256–221 B.C.). During the Three Kingdoms period (220 B.C.–A.D. 265), when a four-centuries-long era of warfare set in among petty states and against the Huns from the north, Buddhism and Taoism emerged as serious threats to Confucianism. During the years of the Sung dynasty (960–1279) the barbarians created a northern empire that was ultimately overrun by Genghis Khan, chieftain of the Mongols. His grandson, Kublai Khan, founded the Yuan dynasty (1260–1368).

The Manchu people, who had been steadily advancing south during the sixteenth and seventeenth centuries, completely conquered China in 1644 and established the Ch'ing dynasty, which lasted until 1912. Though initially opposed to trade with foreign nations, the Ch'ing opened Canton to limited overseas trade in 1834. Great Britain provoked the Opium War (1839–42) and won some concessions, notably the ceding of Hong Kong to them. After the first Sino-Japanese War (1894–95)—fought for control of the co-protectorate of Korea—the Chinese lost Formosa, the Liaotung Peninsula and the Pescadores to Japan, and Korea became independent under Japanese influence. In 1898 the United States promoted the Open Door Policy, which sought to create equal access to Chinese trade for all nations. Chinese resentment of foreign intrusion erupted in the Boxer Rebellion, which was quelled by Japanese, American and European forces. In 1911–12 the Manchu dynasty was overthrown by the forces of Sun Yat-sen, who became President of the Republic but resigned early in 1912 in favor of Yuan Shih-kai, who established a repressive military rule. From 1917 to 1930 civil war raged between Sun's party—the Kuomintang—and the national government. The Kuomintang, led by Chiang Kai-shek, defeated the government and established a dictatorship at Nanking in 1928, but civil war broke out again when Chiang broke an alliance formed by Sun with the Chinese Communists. After Japan invaded Manchuria in 1931 and set up a puppet government, the second Sino-Japanese War was waged. In 1937 Chiang and the Communists agreed to cooperate against the Japanese threat. During World War II, although the Chinese received aid from the United States and Britain to fight the Japanese, Chinese losses were severe. In 1945 civil war erupted again. With United States aid, Chiang was successful against the Communists until 1947, but at last the superior military force of the Communists, led by Mao Tse-tung, became decisive, and in 1949 Chiang was driven from mainland China to Taiwan. The People's Republic of China was proclaimed October 1, 1949.

It would be difficult to speak of Chinese genealogy without mentioning the Soongs, one of the Chinese families best known to Americans. Charles Jones Soong (1863–1918) was born in Shansi, the son of a family of poor shopkeepers. In 1872, at the age of nine, he was sent to Boston to train with his mother's brother, one of the first Chinese merchants in that city. Young Soong ran away from his uncle and stowed away on a ship headed south. He made friends, was converted to Christianity as a Methodist and was sent to Vanderbilt University in Nashville, Tennessee, where he graduated in 1885. After returning to China as a missionary, he married the daughter of a Christian family, Miss Ni (Ni Kwei-tseng, d. 1931) in about 1887. They had six children—three daughters and three sons. Ei-ling Soong (Soong Ai-ling, 1888–1971) was educated at Wesleyan College in Macon, Georgia, and was married in 1913 to H.H. Kung (K'ung Hsiang-hsi, 1880–1967) of Taiku, Shansi. Kung, seventy-fifth in descent from Confucius (c. 551–479? B.C.), graduated from Oberlin College in Ohio in 1906 and went on to get a Master's degree from Yale. He held many offices in the Nationalist Chinese Government, including Minister of Finance, from 1933–44. The Kungs, who had four children—Rosamunde (Ling-yi), David (Ling-kai), Jeanette (Ling-wei) and Louis (Ling-chieh)—spent their last years in a mansion on Feeks Lane in Locust Valley, New York. Ching-ling Soong (Soong Ch'ing-ling, 1890–) was also educated at Wesleyan College and in 1915 married her father's friend, Sun Yat-sen (1866–1925), the founder of modern China. She has held many offices in the Communist Chinese Government. They had no children. T.V. Soong (Soong Tse-vung, 1894–1971), educated at Harvard, Columbia and at St. John's University in Shanghai, founded the Bank of China in 1936. He came to New York in 1949 and lived in a Park Avenue apartment with his wife, Laura, who survived him. They had three daughters: Laurette Soong, the wife of Ivan Feng of New York; Mary Jane Soong, who married Charles Eu of Singapore; and Catherine Soong, the wife of Arthur Young of Manila. By 1971 they had produced nine grandchildren. May-ling Soong (Soong Mei-ling, 1896–) is perhaps the most famous of the family and most often in the public eye. She was graduated from Wellesley College in 1917 and returned to China, where she met Chiang Kai-shek (1887–1975), a native of Feng-hua and an aide of her brother-in-law, Sun Yat-sen. For nearly fifty years they were one of the most famous couples in the world as they attempted to gain world support for their cause. They had no children, but Generalissimo Chiang had a son, Ching-Kuo, by his former wife, Miss Mao, and a son, Chiang Wei-kuo, by an unknown woman. T.L.

Soong (Soong Tse-liang) graduated from Vanderbilt, while his younger brother T.A. Soong (Soong Tse-an, d. 1960's) was a graduate of Harvard (Illustration 44).

As the Soong genealogy indicates, many Chinese in America have more than one name, often one for use with family members and other Chinese and one for Western use. Westerners are often unable to determine which name is the surname, as you will learn if you begin searching city directories, newspaper indexes, census and vital records and similar documents. Many lines, such as that of H.H. Kung, go far back into antiquity, but to trace Kung's seventy-five generations back to Confucius would truly take the patience of Buddha.

In contemporary Canton, the most common surnames are Li, He, Chen, Zhang, Liang and Huang; in Peking, Wang, Li, Zhang, Chen and Liu.

Libraries

Central Library of the Chinese Academy of Sciences
Peking, China

Nanking Library
Nanking, China

National Library of Peking
Peking, China

Peking University Library
Peking, China

Historical and Genealogical Societies

Chinese Historical Society
Peking, China

United States Sources

Chinese Historical Society of America
17 Adler Place
San Francisco, CA 94133

Books and Articles

BeDunnah, Gary P.
A History of the Chinese in Nevada, 1855–1904.
San Francisco, CA 1973. 90 p.
NN IEA 74-1660

Biographical Dictionary of Republican China, ed. by Howard L. Boorman.
New York, Columbia U. Press, 1967–71. 4 v. (A–Y).
NN *R-AGA

Chang, Kwang-Chih.
Early Chinese Civilization: Anthropological Perspectives.
Cambridge, MA, Harvard U. Press, 1976. 229 p., gen. tables.
(Harvard-Yenching Institute, Monograph Series v. 23)

Char, Tin-Yuke.
The Sandalwood Mountain ... Early Chinese in Hawaii.

Honolulu, HI, U. Press of Hawaii, 1974.
NN

Ch'en, Ch'eng-chih.
A Standard Romanized Dictionary of Chinese and Japanese Popular Surnames.
Hanover, NJ, 1971. 681 p.
NN *R-Oriental 74-761

Ch'en, Ta, 1896–.
Emigrant Communities in South China ...
New York, Secretariat, Institute of Pacific Relations, 1940. 287 p.
NN SEV

China Who's Who (Foreign): A Biographical Dictionary.
Shanghai, 1924–.
NN AGA

Chinese Genealogical Records.
(IN: Studies in Asian Genealogy, Provo, UT, Brigham Young U., 1972. p. 11–56)
NN ARB 73-1060

Chinese Genealogy.
(IN: *Utah Genealogical Magazine*, Salt Lake City, UT, 1915. v. 6, p. 189–202)
NN APR (Utah)

Chinese Written History.
(IN: Studies in Asian Genealogy, Provo, UT, Brigham Young U., 1972. p. 57–80)
NN APB 73-1060

Cohen, Barry, and David Black.
Asian Quartet: A Modern History of China, Japan, India (and Pakistan) and Indonesia.
Sydney, McGraw-Hill, 1975 (orig. 1971). 209 p., index.
NN

Conwell, Russell H.
Why and How. Why the Chinese Emigrate ...
Boston, MA, Lee & Shepard, 1871. 283 p.
NN IEA

Corbitt, Duvon Clough.
A Study of the Chinese in Cuba, 1847–1947.
Wilmore, KY, 142 p.
NN HOB 73-1715

Dictionary of Ming Biography, 1368–1644, ed. by Carrington Goodrich and Chaoying Fang.
New York, Columbia U. Press, 1976. 2 v. v. 1, A–L; v. 2, M–Z.
NN * OVP 76-938

Dobie, Charles L.
San Francisco's Chinatown.
New York, D. Appleton-Century, 1936. 336 p., index.
NN IXH (San Francisco)

Edson, Christopher H.
The Chinese in Eastern Oregon, 1860–1890.
San Francisco, CA, 1974. 84 p.
NN IEA 75-1282

Endacott, George B.
A History of Hong Kong.
London, Oxford U. Press, 1958. 322 p.
NN D-12 91

Engelborghs-Bertels, Marthe.
La Chine Rurale.
Brussels, 1974. 190 p.
NN JLE 76-1627

Fairbank, John King, et. al.
Japanese Studies of Modern China: A Bibliographical Guide to Historical and Social Science Re-

search on the 19th and 20th Centuries.
Cambridge, MA, East Asian Research Center, 1975. 603 p.
(*Harvard East Asian Monographs no. 60*)
NN M-11 435

Fan, Tin-Chiu.
Chinese Residents in Chicago.
Saratoga, CA, 1974. 90 p.
NN IEA 75-1553

Fitzgerald, Stephen.
China and the Overseas Chinese.
Cambridge, England, 1972. 268 p.
NN JLE 73-457

Freedman, Maurice.
Chinese Lineage and Society: Fükien and Kwangtung.
London, Athlone Press, 1966. 207 p.
(Monographs on Social Anthropology no. 33)
NN *QOA

Genealogical Sources of Chinese Immigrants to the United States.
(IN: Studies in Asian Genealogy, Provo, UT, Brigham Young U., 1972. p. 221–28)
NN APB 73-1060

Giles, Herbert.
... A Chinese Biographical Dictionary.
Shanghai, Kelly & Walsh, 1898 ... sup. and index, 1936, 1,022 p.
NN *OVP

Han, Suyin.
The Crippled Tree.
NY, Putnam, 1965. 416 p.
(Story of the Chou family)
NN D-16 3591

Hong Kong Album.
Hong Kong, P.C. Lee, 1965–67. 4th and 5th ed., 2 v., alpha, index (1965/66, 1967/68).
NN M-11 986

... The Hong Kong Directory and Hong List for the Far East.
Hong Kong, R. Frazer-Smith, 1858–84. 2 v.
(Text in English with Chinese trans.)
NN BAZ

Hong Kong Who's Who.
Hong Kong, R. Luzzatto, 1958–60–.
NN K-10 1622

Hopkinson, H.S.P.
Macao Burials.
(IN: *GM*, London. v. 8, p. 325–30)
(184 British and American burials, 18th and 19th cent.)
NN ARCA

Hsieh, Chiao-min.
Atlas of China, ed. by Christopher L. Salter.
New York, McGraw-Hill, 1973. 282 p., index.
NN Map Div. 74-71

Hsu, Immanuel Chung-yuch.
The Rise of Modern China. 2nd ed.
New York, Oxford U. Press, 1975. 1,002 p., index.
NN * R-BEC 76-3637

Hucker, Charles O.
China's Imperial Past: An Introduction to Chinese History and Culture.
London, Duckworth, 1975. 474 p., index.
NN JFE 76-2439

Jan, Antonio S.
The Chinese in the Philippines, 1898–1935.
Quezon City, Philippines, 1972. 417 p.
NN JFD 72-8611

Leslie, Donald D., Colin Mackerras, and Wang Gungwu.
Essays and Sources for Chinese History.
Columbia, SC, U. of South Carolina Press, 1975. 378 p., index.
NN *OVO 75-2029

Liang, Yu-kao.
Village and Town Life in China.
London, Allen & Unwin, 1915. 155 p.
(*Studies in Economics and Political Science Monographs in Sociology, v. 4*)
NN BEB

Liu, Hui-chen Wang.
The Traditional Chinese Clan Rules.
Locust Valley, NY, Assoc. for Asian Studies, 1959.
264 p., biblio., p. 194–208 (many v. on families in Chinese and trans.), no index.
NN E-11 237

Millones, Luis.
Minorias Etnicas en el Peru.
Lima, 1973. 97 p.
NN Sc 301.45-M

Nee, Victor G., and Brett de B. Nee.
Longtime California: A Documentary History of an American Chinatown.
New York, Pantheon Books, 1973. 411 p., t of c, map of district from which they came, no index.
NN IEA 73-2900

Noms Chinois, Thai et Vietnamiens.
(IN: Vroonen, Eugene, Encyclopédie des Noms des Personnes, Paris, 1972. p. 531–81)
NN APD 76-439

Oxnam, Robert Bromley.
Ruling from Horseback: Manchu Politics in the Oboi Regency, 1661–1669.
Chicago, IL, U. of Chicago Press, 1974. 250 p., index.
NN JEF 75-3186

Perleberg, Max.
Who's Who in Modern China.
Hong Kong, 1954. 428 p. (In English and Chinese.)
NN AGA

Pong, David.
A Critical Guide to the Kwangtung Provincial Archives Deposited at the Public Record Office of London.
Cambridge, MA, East Asian Research Center, 1975. 203 p.
(*Harvard East Asian Monographs v. 63*)
NN M-11 435

Rishi, W.R.
Marriages of the Orient.
Singapore, 1970. 140 p.
NN JLC 72-434

Rubicam, Milton.
Americans in China Since 1794.
(IN: *TAG*, New Haven, CT, 1962. v. 38, p. 212–14)
NN APGA

Sih, Paul K.T., and Leonard B. Allen
The Chinese in America.
New York, St. John's U. Press, c. 1976. 177 p.

(Asia in the Modern World Series)
NN K-10 6118

Tung, William.
The Chinese in America, 1820–1973.
Dobbs Ferry, NY, Oceana, 1974.
150 p.
NN IEA 75-194

U.S. Library of Congress. Division
of Bibliographies.
... Select List of References on
Chinese Immigration.
Washington, DC, U.S. Government
Printing Office, 1904. 31 p.
NN *SAB and IEA

Van Norden, Warner M.
Who's Who of the Chinese in New
York.
New York, W.M. Van Norden, 1918.
148 p., illus., ports.
NN *ZH-260

Wang Pun She Ke.
Wang's Editions of Sze-Ma Tseen's
Historical Records ... in 130
Books (In Chinese).
China, 1870. 6 v. (v. 1, histories; v.
2, chronological tables; v. 3,
family histories; v. 4–6, biogra-
phies)
NN *OVO+

Watson, James L.
Emigration and the Chinese Lineage: The Mans in Hong Kong
and London.
Berkeley, CA, U. of California,
1975. 242 p., index.

Who's Who in China.
Shanghai, *Millard's Review*, 1920–.
NN *OVP

Who's Who in Communist China.
Kowloon, Hong Kong, Union Research Inst., 1966–69.

(1966, 1 v. with 754 p.; 1969/70, 2 v.
with 897 p.)
NN *RR-AGA and E-14 2356

Who's Who in the Far East 1906–07.
Hong Kong, 1906. 352 p. plus alpha
both Orientals and foreigners.
NN AGA

Young, Nancy Foon.
The Chinese in Hawaii.
Honolulu, HI, 1973. 149 p.
NN IAA (Hawaii) 72-302 no. 4

Tibet

Aoki, Bunkyo.
Study on Early Tibetan Chronicles,
Regarding Discrepancies of
Dates and Their Adjustments.
Tokyo, 1958. 161 p.
NN *OZ 75-428

Bell, Charles A.
Tibet Past and Present.
Oxford, 1968. 326 p.
NN *R-BDS 73-2060

Bulletin of Tibetology.
Gantok, Sikkim, 1974–.
NN *OZ 72-378

Haah, Erick.
The Yar-Lun Dynasty: A Study
with Particular Regard to the
Contribution by Myths and
Legends to the History of An-
cient Tibet and the Origin and
Nature of Its Kings.
Copenhagen, G.E.C. Gad, 1969. 481
p.
NN G-10 2694

Lo Ch'an-P'ei
The Genealogical Patronymic
Linkage System of the Tibeto-
Burman Speaking Tribes.
(IN: *Harvard Journal of Asiatic*

Studies, Baltimore, MD, 1945. v. 8, p. 349–63)
NN *OAA

Sandberg, Graham.
The Exploration of Tibet: History and Particulars.

Delhi, 1973. 324 p.
NN JFD 74-1301

Warren, Virginia Lee.
Tibetans Adapt to the U.S., but Miss Their Lofty Homeland.
(IN: *New York Times*, New York, April 7, 1976, p. 55)

REPUBLIC OF CHINA: TAIWAN (TAIPEI) (formerly Formosa)

Chinese immigration to this island began in the seventh century. The Portuguese, who arrived in the sixteenth century, called the island Formosa, meaning "beautiful." The Dutch controlled the island by 1641, but they were expelled in the same century by Ming dynasty forces who were fleeing the Manchu take-over in China. In 1683 the Manchus took over Taiwan. After the Sino-Japanese war (1894–95) Taiwan was ceded to Japan, who held it until after World War II, when it was returned to China. In 1949 the nationalist government of Chiang Kai-shek fled to Taiwan, while the forces of Mao Tse-tung won control of the mainland.

A census of Formosa was made in 1905.

Archives

Archives Section of the National Palace Museum
Waishuang-hsi, Shih-lin
Taipei, Republic of China

Academia Historica (National Academy of History and Historical Archives)
The Milky Way, New-Village
Chingtan Hsintien
Taipei 231, Republic of China

Academia Sinica
Taipei, Republic of China

Historical Archives Commission of the Kuomintang (KMT)
Taipei, Republic of China

Libraries

National Central Library
43 Nan-hai Road
Taipei, Republic of China

Institute of History and Philology Library
Academia Sinica
Taipei, Republic of China

Taipei Municipal Library
10-3 Chin-men Street
Taipei, Republic of China

Taiwan Provincial Library in Taipei
1430-1 Chung Cheng Road
Taipei, Republic of China

Historical and Genealogical Societies

Chinese Statistical Association
2 Kwang Chow Street
Taipei, Republic of China
(*Chinese Statistical Journal*)

Books and Articles

Campbell, William.
Formosa under the Dutch.
London, Kegan Paul, 1903. 629 p.
NN BET

A Record of Taiwan's Progress,
1936/37.

Tokyo, 1936–. (Includes Who's Who
in Taiwan)
NN M-10 4646

Taiwan: Studies in Chinese Local
History.
New York, Columbia U. Press,
1970. 124 p.
NN D-20 892

Takeekoshi, Yosaburo.
Japanese Rule in Formosa.
New York, Longmans Green, 1907.
342 p.
NN BEY

CYPRUS (NICOSIA)

The island of Cyprus was successively settled by Greeks, Phoenicians, Macedonians, Egyptians and Romans before the time of Christ and eventually became part of the Byzantine empire. In 1191 Richard I of England took the island from Byzantium and made it a base of operations during the Crusades. Cyprus was annexed by Venice in 1489 and conquered by the Turks in 1571. At the Congress of Berlin in 1878, the island was placed under British administration and in 1914 was annexed by Britain. In 1947 the people of Cyprus voted for union with Greece. Cyprus became independent in 1959, and Archbishop Makarios, political and spiritual leader of Greek Cypriotes, became the first President. In 1963 tension between ethnic Greeks and Turks erupted in violence in Nicosia and led to Turkish refusal to participate in the government. In 1975, after years of violence, a separate Turkish Cypriot federated state was voted by Turkish Cypriotes.

Censuses were taken in Cyprus in 1901, 1911, 1921, 1931, 1946 and 1960.

Public and Church Records

Birth and marriage certificates are issued by the commissioner of the district where the event took place. Records in the district of Nicosia date from 1900, with earlier, incomplete records for 1890, 1893 and 1895; in Famagusta, from 1914, with incomplete records back to 1830; in Larnaca, from 1914, incomplete back to 1895; in Limassol, from 1899, with records of British births since 1896; in Paphos, from 1850, incomplete for several earlier years; and in Kyrenia from April 1, 1915, to March 31, 1920, and from January 1, 1926. Completed marriage registers deposited with the Registration Officer in Nicosia date from 1923.

Libraries

Cyprus Public Library
Nicosia, Cyprus

Library of the Archbishopric
P.O. Box 1130
Nicosia, Cyprus

Municipal Library
Limassol, Cyprus

Sultan's Library
Evcaf
Nicosia, Cyprus

Turkish Public Library
49 Mecediye Street
Nicosia, Cyprus

Historical and Genealogical Societies

Etaireia Kypriakon Spoudon (Society of Cyprus Studies)
P.O. Box 1436
Nicosia, Cyprus

Books and Articles

Cyprus Research Centre.
Texts and Studies of the History of Cyprus.
Nicosia, 1965–.
NN M-11 3138

Genealogy of Some Families of Cyprus from the 18th Century to the Present, Written in Greek.
Nicosia, 1972. 125 p., many illus.
NN AVH (Cyprus) 75-919

Hill, Sir George F.
A History of Cyprus.
Cambridge, Cambridge U. Press, 1940–52. 4 v.
NN *RR-BVX

Koumoulides, John T. A.
Cyprus and the War of Greek Independence, 1821–1829.
London, 1974. 117 p.
NN JFD 75-6164

Lee, Michael.
Cyprus.
Newton Abbot, England, D & C, 1973. 208 p.
NN *R-KFD 75-8466

Luke, Harry C.
Cyprus under the Turks, 1571–1878 . . .
London, Oxford U. Press, 1921. 281 p.
NN BVX

Philippe of Novara.
The Wars of Frederick II against the Ibelins in Syria and Cyprus . . .
New York, Columbia U. Press, 1936. 230 p., gen. table.
NN BVX

Who's Who in Cyprus.
Nicosia, 1968–.
NN L-11 2801

FORMOSA:

See Republic of China, Taiwan

INDIA (NEW DELHI)

In the fourth and fifth centuries A.D. the Gupta dynasty ruled northern India. In 1192 the legions of Ghor invaded India and established the Delhi Sultanate, the first Muslim kingdom in the country, which ended when Tamerlane conquered Delhi in 1398. In 1526 Babur, a Muslim invader, founded the Mogul Empire. Vasco da Gama visited India in 1498, and by 1691 the British East India Company became the dominant power. The Treaty of Paris of 1763 recognized the British Empire in India. There was an Indian mutiny in 1857, and a Viceroy replaced the East India Company in power. After the First World War, Mohandas K. Gandhi organized passive-resistance campaigns, and in 1935 entirely Indian provincial governments were elected and a federal legislature in Delhi was largely elected. In 1947 British India divided into India and Pakistan, and Muslims and Hindus fled to safety across the established borders. In a border dispute in 1962 China gained much territory in northeast India. In 1971, after unrest and hardship, India brought peace to East Pakistan by renaming it Bangladesh, a home for the Hindus, distinct from the Muslims, who reside in West Pakistan.

The first all-India census was recorded in 1872, and censuses have been taken regularly, every ten years, since 1881.

The most common surnames in Bombay are Desai, Mehta, Mody (Modi), Patel and Shah; in Calcutta, Banerjee (several spellings), Das, Ghosh, Mukherjee (several spellings) and Roy; and in Delhi and New Delhi, Gupta, Jain, Kapoor (Kapur), Ram and Sharma.

Archives

National Archives of India
Janpath
New Delhi 1, India

West Bengal Archives
Writers' Building (Current section, 1901–)

Binoy-Badal, Dinesh Bag
Calcutta-1, West Bengal, India
    and 6 Bhowani Dutta Land (Historical section, pre-1901)
Calcutta-7, West Bengal, India

General Register Office
St. Catherine's House 10 Kingsway
London WC2B 6JP, England

India Office Library (records of
the East India Company)
Commonwealth Library
197 Blackfriars Road
London SE11, England

Public and Church Records

Birth and marriage certificates
can be obtained from the State
Registrars General of Births,
Deaths and Marriages and from
the municipal authorities.

Libraries

National Library
Belvedere
Calcutta 27, India

State Central Library
Hyderabad 12, A.P., India

Delhi Public Library
S.P. Mukerji Marg
Delhi 6, India

Historical and Genealogical
Societies

Andhra Historical Research Society
Godavari Bund Road, Rajahmun-
dry
Andhra Pradesh, South India

Bombay Historical Society
Prince of Wales Museum
Bombay 1, India

Books and Articles

Athar Ali, M.
The Moghal Nobility under Au-
rangzeb.
London, Aligarh Muslim U., 1966.
294 p.
NN E-13 803

Banerjee, Hiranmay.
The House of the Tagores. 2nd rev.
ed.
Calcutta, Rabindra Bharati, 1965.
68 p., 4 gen. tables, no index.
NN AVHH (Tagore) 75-181

Basu, Jogiraji.
India in the Age of the Brāh-
manas.
Calcutta, 1969. 295 p.
NN *OHO 73-991

Burgess, James, 1832–1916.
The Chronology of Indian History
. . .
Delhi, 1972. 483 p.
NN *R-Oriental 75-2822

Central India.
Ruling Princes and Chiefs and
Leading Families in Central In-
dia.
Calcutta, 1923. 67 p.
NN BAC+ p.v. 112 no. 7

Dictionary of National Biography
(India).
Calcutta, Institute of Historical
Studies, 1972–74.
v. 1–3, alpha, A–R in progress.
NN *R-AGA 74-2325

Furrell, James W.
The Tagore Family: A Memoir.
2nd ed.
Calcutta, Thacker, Spink & Co.,
1892. 187 p.
NN AVHH (Tagore)

Gaudert, Michael.
Généalogie des Familles de l'Inde
Française XVI–XX Siècle.

Eaubonne, 95600, France, M. Hubert Lamant, 51 rue des Robinettes, c. 1975.

Holmes and Company, Calcutta.
The Bengal Obituary ... A Compilation of Tablets and Monumental Inscriptions from ... Bengal and Agra Presidencies.
London, Holmes and Co. 1851. 426 p.
NN AGA

Indian Tribal Genealogies.
(IN: *Studies in Asian Genealogy*, Provo, UT, Brigham Young U., 1972. p. 179–88)
NN APB 73–1060

Kaul, H.K.
Early Writings on India: A Union Catalogue of Books on India in the English Language, published up to 1900, available in Delhi libraries.
London, Curzon Press, 1975. 324 p., index.

Kennedy, Pringle.
History of the Great Moghuls.
Calcutta, 1968. 556 p.
NN JFD 74-1722

Khosla, Ram Prasid.
Mughal Kingship and Nobility.
Allahabad, Indian Press, 1934. 311 p.
NN *OLO

Lakshminarasimhaiya, N.
Kashi Sesha Sastri and His Descendants.
Madras, *Madras Law Journal*, 1970. 146 p., 10 gen. tables, plus charts and illus. in English and Indian.
NN AVHH (Sastri) 73-1131

Lal, Kishori Saran.
History of the Khaljis.
Bombay, 1967. 288 p.
NN JFD 74-7206

Lethbridge, Sir Roper.
The Golden Book of India: A Genealogical and Biographical Dictionary of Ruling Princes, Chiefs, Nobles and Other Personages, Titled and Decorated, of the Indian Empire.
London, Macmillan, 1893. 584 p.
NN *OHO

Nigram, Shiva B.P.
Nobility under the Sultans of Delhi, A.D. 1206–1398.
Delhi, c. 1968. 223 p.
NN D-20 219

Pargiter, Frederick E.
Ancient Indian Genealogy and Chronology.
(IN: *Royal Asiatic Journal*, London, 1910. p. 1–56)
NN *OAA

Pargiter, Frederick E.
Ancient Indian Historical Tradition.
London, Oxford U. Press, 1972. 368 p.
NN *ZO-35 film

Scholberg, Henry.
The District Gazetteers of British India.
Zug, Switerland, 1970. 131 p.
NN JFD 71-2519

Stokes, Samuel E., Jr.
The Construction of the Hindu Family and the Facilities It Would Afford for Genealogical Research.
(IN: Genealogical Society of Penn-

sylvania Pub., Philadelphia, 1916. v. 6 p. 107–29)
NN APR (Pennsylvania)

Sutherland, Dennis
His Highness Prince Frederick Duleep Singh.
(IN: *East Anglian Magazine*, Ipswich, 1976. v. 35, p. 434–37, illus.)
NN CO (East Anglia)

Triveda, Devasahya.
Indian Chronology.
Bombay, 1963. 112 p.
NN *R-Oriental 75-2821

Who's Who in India.
Poona, Sun Pub. House, 1936. 893 p.
NN AGH

Who's Who in India. Kothari Hemraj, ed.
Calcutta, 1973. 464 p.
NN *R-Oriental 75-2063

Who's Who in India, 1967.
New Delhi, Guide Pub., 1967.
NN *R-Oriental 75-2604

Sikkim

Basnet, Lal Bahadur.
Sikkim.
New Delhi, 1974. 216 p.
NN JFD 76-6493

Coelho, V.H.
Sikkim and Bhutan.
New Delhi, 1970 138 p.
NN JFE 71-821

Kandell, Alice S.
Mountaintop Kingdom: Sikkim
New York, c. 1971. 205 p.
NN JFF 72-161

Kennedy, Shawn G.
Hope Cooke: From Queen of Sikkim to "Regular" New Yorker.
(IN: *New York Times*, June 18, 1976, p. B4)

INDONESIA (JAKARTA)

The people of Indonesia are chiefly Malayan and Papuan. In the seventh and eighth centuries Indian kingdoms were introduced. In Sumatra, a Buddhist kingdom, Sri Vijaya ruled through the thirteenth century, while the Hindu kingdom of Majapahit held sway in Java. In the fourteenth and fifteenth centuries Arab traders established Islam as the dominant religion, supplanting Buddhism and Hinduism. In 1511 the Portuguese occupied Malacca, but they were ousted by the Dutch in 1596. Between 1610 and 1623 the English and Dutch fought for control, and in 1799 the Dutch government established the Dutch East Indies. The Indonesians waged guerrilla war against the Dutch colonists throughout the nineteenth century. In 1927 Sukarno organized the Indonesian Nationalist party; in 1942 the Japanese drove the Dutch out of the islands; and in 1945 Sukarno proclaimed Indonesia a republic. General Suharto was elected

President in 1968. In 1969 Netherlands New Guinea was annexed by Indonesia and its name was changed to Irian Barat.

A census is conducted every five years.

The most common surnames in Jakarta are Lie, Li(e)m, Oey, Tan and The.

Archives

Arsip Nasional Republik Indonesia
111 Djalan Gadjah Mada
Jakarta, Indonesia

Public and Church Records

Birth and marriage certificates can be obtained from the Civil Registrar's Office (Kantor Tjatan Sipil) of the place where the event took place.

Central address for vital records and census information:
Departemen Kehakiman R.I. (Dept. of Justice)
Biro Research, Pejambon 2
Jakarta, Indonesia

For religious records, write:
The Dept. of Religious Affairs (Dep. Agama R.I.)
Jl. Thamring
Jakarta, Indonesia

Libraries

Central Library of the Department of Information
Medan Merdeka Barat 9
Jakarta, Indonesia

Perpustakaan Biro Pusat Statistik (Library of Central Bureau of Statistics)
Djalan Dr. Sutomo 7
Jakarta, Indonesia

Tman Batjaan dan Perpustakaan Umum (Public Library Jakarta)
Dj. Budi Kemuliaan 3
Jakarta, Indonesia

Perpustakaan Islam (Islamic Library)
Jalan P. Mangkubumi
Jogjakarta, Indonesia

Books and Magazines

Andelman, David A.
To Many a South Moluccan Price of Spice is the Key to Life.
(IN: *New York Times*, N.Y., July 9, 1977. p. D5)

Bloys van Treslong Prins, Paul
Genealogische en Heraldische Gedenwaardigheden
Betreffende Europeanen op Java.
Den Haag (Batavia), 1934–39. 4 v.
(Epitaphs and genealogy of the Dutch in Java)
NN AVDH (Java)

Chatterjee, Bijan Raj.
History of Indonesia, Early and Medieval.
Meerut, 1967. 205 p.
NN JFD 75-6279

Emmerson, Donald K.
Indonesia's Elite.
Ithaca, NY, Cornell U. Press, 1976. 303 p.
NN JLD 76-3414

Hague-Koloniale Bibliotheek.
Catalogues der Koloniale Bibliotheek.
's-Gravenhage, 1908. 1,053 p.
(Koloniale Bibliotheek, The Hague, Catalogues)
NN GAY

Klerck, Eduard S. de.
History of the Netherlands East
Indies.
Rotterdam, W.L. & J. Brusse, 1938.
2 v.
NN- BFK

Neill, Wilfred L.
Twentieth Century Indonesia.
New York, 1973. 413 p.
NN JFD 74-1642

Roeder, O.G.
Who's Who in Indonesia.
Jakarta, 1971. 544 p.
NN JFD 73–324

Simandjuntak, I.J.
Tarombo-Partuturan ni Radja
Marsundung Marga Simandjun-
tak.
(Medan, Indonesia), 1965. 426 p.,
index.
NN AVHH (Simandjuntak) 76-182

Van Niel, Robert.
A Survey of Historical Source Ma-
terial in Java and Manila.
Honolulu, HI, 1970. 255 p.
NN *OAA 72-643 no.5

Vlekke, Bernard H.M.
Nusantara: A History of the East
Indian Archipelago. revised ed.
The Hague, W. van Hoeve, 1959.
479 p., gen. table.
NN D-12 3822 (1943 ed. in BFK)

Zainu' Doin, Ailsa G.
A Short History of Indonesia.
New York, Praeger, 1970. 299 p.
NN *R-BFK

IRAN (TEHERAN)

There were ancient settlements in the Caspian coastal region
in 4000 B.C. The Aryans came in 2000 B.C., and the population
split into Medes and Persians. In 550 B.C. Cyrus the Great
founded the Persian Empire. There were Greek and Parthian
occupations, and in the third century A.D. Sassanid ruled. In 636
Arab invaders brought Islam to Persia, and in the tenth century
the Turks founded states there. In the thirteenth century the
Mongols invaded, led by Genghis Khan, and in the fourteenth
century Tamerlane led an invasion. Between 1502 and 1736 the
Safavid dynasty was in power. During the sixteenth century
Shah Abbas drove Portuguese colonists from the Persian Gulf
and established trade with Britain. The Afshar and Zand dynas-
ties (1736–94) were succeeded by the Kajar dynasty under Aga
Muhammad Khan. In 1813 and 1828 treaties with Russia forced
Persia to give up Caucasian lands, and in 1857 Persia recognized

Afghan independence. A Parliament was established in Persia in 1906. In 1925 Reza Shah Pahlevi founded a new dynasty. By royal decree Persia's name was changed to Iran in 1935. In 1941 Muhammad Reza Shah Pahlevi succeeded his father.

A census was conducted in 1966.

The most common surnames in Teheran are Amir-, Haj, Haji, Mir-, Pur-, Cali, Mohammed, -pur, Seyyed and -zadeh.

Archives

Iran National Archives Organization
Behjatabad, 66 Zahed Avenue
Teheran, Iran

Imperial Archives
Golestan Place
Teheran, Iran

Foreign Office Archives
Teheran, Iran

Libraries

Central Library, University of Teheran
Shahreza Avenue
Teheran, Iran

Malek Library
Bazzar
Teheran, Iran

National Library
Ghavamo Saltané Street
Teheran, Iran

Imperial Library
Teheran, Iran

Books and Articles

Avery, Peter.
Modern Persia.
London, E. Benn, 1965. 527 p., index.
NN *R-BCP

Bausani, Alessandro.
The Persians from the Earliest Days to the Twentieth Century.
New York, 1971. 204 p.
NN JFD 73-3185

The Cambridge History of Iran.
London, Cambridge U. Press, 1968–75 in progress v. 1, 4–5 published; 8 v. projected.
Gen. tables of Chingiz-Khan (Jhenghiz Kahn), v. 5, p. 418–21
NN *R-BCP (Cambridge History of Iran)

Frye, Richard N.
The Heritage of Persia.
Cleveland, OH, World, 1963. 301 p., index.
NN *R-BCP 76-1729

The Iran Review, pub. of the Irano-American Society.
New York, 1948–50. v. 1–2.
NN BCP

Iran Review.
Washington, DC, 1956–61.
NN M-10 607

Ismail, Sir Mirza.
My Public Life: Recollections and Reflections.

London, George Allen and Unwin for Ruskin House, Museum St., 1954. 180 p., index.

(His grandfather, Ali Asker Shirazi, 1808–91, was born in Shiraz, Persia, and settled in Bangalore in 1824.)

NN AN (Ismail, M.)

Katrak, Jamshed Cawasji.
Marriage in Ancient Iran.
Bombay, 1965. 120 p., index.
NN JLE 74-3141

Oberling, Pierre.
The Qashqa'i, Nomads of Fars.

The Hague, 1974. 277 p.
NN JFE 76-1869

Pearson, James Douglas.
A Bibliography of Pre-Islamic Persia.
London, Mansell, 1975. 288 p., index. (Persian Studies Series no. 2)
NN JFE 76-2303

Sanghvi, Ramesh.
Aryamehr: The Shah of Iran.
London, Macmillan, 1968. 390 p., index.
NN *RR-BCP

IRAQ (BAGHDAD)

Iraq is located in the region of ancient Mesopotamia, where 7,000 years ago, there was a Sumerian civilization in which Babylon was established by Nebuchadnezzar and Hammurabi wrote the first code of justice. Arabs conquered the land in the seventh century, Ottoman Turks in the sixteenth century. In the nineteenth century the territory was occupied by the Turkish provinces of Basra, Baghdad and Mosul. In 1920 Iraq was established as a mandate of the League of Nations under British administration. In 1921 a kingdom was formed under Faisal I, and in 1932 the British mandate was terminated. A republic was proclaimed in 1958 after a military coup.

Archives

National Centre on Archives
Wazeeriya, Amr bin Kalthoom
Street 15/10/9
Baghdad, Iraq

Public and Church Records

Birth certificates for persons born prior to 1921 can be obtained from heads of religious communities, priests, rabbis or other ecclesiastics, or from local dignitaries (Mukhtars). Official birth certificates for people born after 1921 are issued by municipal offices or by the census department. Marriage certificates are issued only by religious authorities.

Libraries

Central Library, University of Baghdad
Baghdad, Iraq

National Library
Zahawi Street
Baghdad, Iraq

Mohamad Ahmad Library
Basra, Iraq

Books and Articles

Fensham, Frank C.
Heersers van did ou Nabye ooste.
Kaapstad (Cape Town), 1970. 143
p. (Iraq kings and rulers)
NN JFD 72-8068

Foster, Henry A.
The Making of Modern Iraq ...
Norman, OK, U. of Oklahoma
Press, 1935. 319 p.
NN E-13 4581

The Iraq Directory: A General and
Commercial Directory of Iraq.
Baghdad, *The Times*, 1936–.
(Includes Who's Who in Iraq)
NN *SAM

Longrigg, Stephen H., and Frank
Stoakes.
Iraq.
New York, Praeger, 1958. 264 p.,
index.
NN *R-BCB 73-1806

Roux, Georges.
Ancient Iraq.
Harmondsworth, England, Pen-
quin, 1976. 480 p., index.
NN

ISRAEL (JERUSALEM)
(formerly Palestine and the Kingdom of Jerusalem)

Canaan, later Palestine, was the ancient home of Hebrew tribes.
In 1000 B.C. a Jewish kingdom was established in Jerusalem
under King David. It was conquered successively by Assyrians,
Babylonians, Greeks and Romans and, in the seventh century,
by Muslims. During World War I it was under British control.
In 1947 the United Nations adopted the Palestine partition plan,
creating the Israeli and Arab state of Palestine. Israel was
proclaimed a nation in 1948. In 1971 Israeli citizenship was
extended to all Jews wishing to emigrate to Israel while still in
their country of residence. Persons born in Israel are called
Sabras.

Censuses of Palestine were conducted in 1922 and 1931. Israeli
censuses were recorded in 1948, 1961, 1967 and 1972.

The most common surnames in Tel Aviv are Cohen, Friedman,
Katz, Levi, Mizrahi and Schwartz.

Archives

Gansakhha-Medinah (State Archives)

Prime Minister's Office
Hakirivah
Jerusalem, Israel

The Jewish Historical General Archives
P.O. Box 1062
Jerusalem, Israel

Ha-Arkhiyon Ha-Tziyoni Ha-Merkasi (Central Zionist Archives)
I Ibn Gabirol Street (P.O. Box 92)
Jerusalem, Israel

Central Archives for the History of the Jewish People
P.O. Box 1149
Jerusalem, Istael

General Archives of the City of Tel-Aviv-Yafo
Municipality Building, P.O. Box 4001
Tel Aviv, Israel

Public and Church Records

Because Israel is a comparatively young state and most inhabitants were born abroad, there is little genealogical data available in official records. Civil registration began in 1948. Records for births and deaths are housed at the Ministry of the Interior, and marriage and divorce records are kept at the Ministry of Religious Affairs.

Libraries

Jewish National and University Library
P.O. Box 503
Jerusalem, Israel

Municipal Library
25 King Saul Boulevard, P.O. Box 32
Tel Aviv, Israel

Tel Aviv University Library
P.O. Box 17038, 155 Herzl Street
Tel Aviv, Israel

Historical and Genealogical Societies

Historical Society of Israel
P.O. Box 1062
Jerusalem, Israel

See also: Jewish bibliography

Books and Articles

Ben-Gurion, David, 1886–1972.
The Jews in Their Land.
Garden City, NY, Doubleday, 1974.
352 p.
NN *PXLB+ 74-6081

Du Cange, Charles D.
Les Families d'Outre-Mer.
Paris, 1869. 998 p., gen. tables.
NN ASB

Faerber, Meir.
... Die Israel Fuhren.
Tel Aviv, 1971. 321 p.
NN *PWR 72-2567

The Generations of Israel.
New York, 1968. 205 p.
NN *PXLB+ 75-2566

Grousset, Réné.
Histoire des Croisades et du Royaume Franc de Jerusalem.
Paris, Plon, 1934–36. 3 v.
NN BTR

Gruber, Ruth.
Destination Palestine: the Story of the Haganah Ship *Exodus*, 1947.
New York, Current Books, 1948.
128 p.
NN *PWC

Jiskor: ein Buch des Gedenkens an Gefallene Wachter und Arbeiter im Lande Israel. 2nd ed.
Berlin, Judischer Verlag, 1920. 223 p.
NN *PWR

Kaganoff, Benzion C.
A Dictionary of Jewish Names and Their History.
New York, Schocken Books, 1977.

Litvinoff, Barret.
Israel 2500 B.C.–1972.
Dobbs Ferry, NY, Oceana, 1974. 136 p., index.
NN *PXLB 74-3829

Lucas, Noah.
The Modern History of Israel.
London, 1975. 500 p.
NN *PXLB 75-8856

Palestine Personalia.
Tel Aviv, 1947. 359 p.
NN *PWR

Prawer, Joshua.
Histoire du Royaume Latin de Jerusalem.

Paris, 1969–70. 2 v.
NN *PWC

Riley-Smith, Jonathan S.C., ed.
Ayyubibs, Mamlukes and Crusaders.
Cambridge, Cambridge U. Press, 1971. 2 v.
NN *OFI 74-149

Riley-Smith, Jonathan S.C.
The Feudal Nobiblity and the Kingdom of Jerusalem, 1174–1277.
London, Macmillan, 1973. 351 p.
NN *PXLL (Jerusalem) 73-5036

Sachar, Howard M.
Aliyah: The Peoples of Israel.
Cleveland, OH, World, 1961. 475 p.
NN *PXLB

Sachar, Howard M.
A History of Israel: From the Rise of Zionism to Our Time.
New York, Knopf, 1977. 950 p., maps, index.

Who's Who in Israel.
Tel Aviv, 1952–.
NN *RR-AGA and *PWR

JAPAN (TOKYO)

Jimmu Tenno—according to legend a lineal descendant of the Sun Goddess—established the Japanese nation in 660 B.C. His descendants, members of the House of Yamato, unified the islands in about A.D. 200. Emperor Hirohito (1901–), on the throne today, is the 124th ruler in this line. The influence of the Chinese T'ang dynasty was felt in Japan from the sixth to the eighth centuries, when Buddhism and Chinese arts were introduced. In the ninth century the Fujiwara family established firm control over the imperial court, and a feudal system developed. In 1192 a *shogun* (military governor) seized power from the Yamato dynasty, establishing a feudal system that lasted for nearly 700 years. In 1542 Portuguese sailors initiated Western trade, and in 1549 St. Francis Xavier brought Christianity. To prevent European domination, the Tokugawa Shogunate barred trade and contact with the outside world in 1634. In 1867–68 Mutsohito, a member of the House of Yamato, regained power as Emperor and assumed the name of "Meji," meaning "enlightened government." He abolished Japan's feudal system in 1871, and in 1889 he and his supporters created a modern constitutional government. Japan gained extensive territories in its victories in the Sino-Japanese War (1894–95) and the Russo-Japanese War (1904–05). In 1910 Japan annexed Korea, and in 1931 it seized Manchuria from China, establishing the puppet state of Manchukuo. Through the 1930's Japan penetrated North China economically and politically. In 1939 Japan allied itself with Germany and Italy. In 1941 it attacked the United States at Pearl Harbor and made wide military gains before its defeat in 1945. In 1952 the Japanese people assumed full sovereignty, with the Emperor remaining as the symbolic head of government.

Because of the Tokugawa edict that severed contacts with foreign lands in 1634, the people of Japan did not even hear of the American Revolution for some fifty years after it took place. In 1851 some shipwrecked Japanese fishermen became the first of their race known to visit the United States. After Commodore Matthew Perry opened relations in 1854, some Japanese students and diplomats visited this country, but it was not until 1886 that Japanese laws allowed workmen to go abroad. In that year, 194 Japanese immigrated to the United States. By 1891 there were only a thousand Japanese in this country. In 1924 Japanese immigration was halted by American authorities and was not resumed until after World War II. California and the western states received most immigrants, while some settled temporarily in Washington and New York for diplomatic and business reasons. The Nippon Club of New York, established in 1905, was going strong at the outbreak of World War II. In 1939 a list of members was recorded in both Japanese and English, and it is interesting to note that in some cases when English surnames were spelled the same, the Japanese characters, or *kanji*, were different, showing different clans and genealogical connections.

Adoption is a major consideration in Japanese genealogy at all class levels, as evidenced by the case of Prince Ito, whose father was adopted by a distant relative so that his line would not die out (see Kengi Hamada's *Prince Ito* in the Japanese bibliography). Matsukichi Yamashita, a laborer from Kagawaken, Japan, who first went to work in Brazil in 1903 and then settled in Orange County, California, in 1909, was also aware of this tradition. He had a daughter who was an only child. In order to carry on his family name, his son-in-law, Tsurukichi Ikegami, took the surname Yamashita so that the lineage could be continued. The family settled in the Moapa Valley of Nevada in 1925, where some of them live today (see "Yamashita Family," Japanese bibliography).

As related in Edwin Seller's *Jaudon Family of Pennsylvania*, Samuel Peyton Jaudon (1831–96), a native of New Orleans, was one of the first Americans to settle and marry in Japan. It was in the late 1870's that he married Isami Matsura (1855–96) of Tokyo, who belonged to the Hatamoto, a rank between the nobility and gentry. They had a daughter, Julia Auame, who was born in Tokyo in 1880. Robert Irwin of Philadelphia, a descendant of Benjamin Franklin, was another American who married in Japan. His descendant, Yukiko Irwin, who lives in New York, is a member of the Descendants of the Signers of the Declaration of Independence. She is the author of the recent book *Shiatzu*, which deals with a Japanese system of acupuncture without needles.

Censuses of Japan were conducted in 1913, 1920, 1926, 1935, 1940, 1950, 1955, 1960 and 1965.

The most common surnames in Osaka are Tanaka, Nakamura, Matsumoto, Yamamoto, Yoshida and Inoue; in Tokyo, Kobayashi, Sato, Suzuki, Takahashi and Tanaka.

Archives

Kokuritsu Kôbunshokan (National Archives)
3-2 Kitanomaru Park
Chiyoda-ku, Tokyo 102, Japan

Public and Church Records

Civil registration began in 1872 for births and deaths and in 1884 for marriages and divorces. Vital records, housed in each municipality, are called *Koseki* (family registers). When all the persons entered in a family register have been removed from it because of death or other reasons, such as transfer to other family registers, that register is kept as *Josekibo* (struck-off family register), separate from ordinary registers. *Josekibo* are destroyed after eighty years.

Bureau of Statistics
Office of the Prime Minister
95 Wakamatsu-cho
Shinjuku-ku
Tokyo, Japan

Buddhist temples keep *Kakocho* (necrologies) that may be helpful. In order to inspect them, you must identify the temple of your ancestors and obtain permission to inspect their records.

Libraries

Mombushô Shiryôkan (Institute of Historical Documents and Folklore)
16 Yutakamachi, I-chome, Shinagauraku, Tokyo

National Diet Library
10–1, 1-chome, Nagata-cho
Chiyoda-ku, Tokyo

Oriental Library (Tokyo Bunko)
Honkomagome 2-chome, 28-21
Bunkyo

University Library, Tokyo
Hongo 7-chome, Bunkyo-ku

Historical and Genealogical Societies

Academy of Japanese History
Kokugakuin University
10-28, Higashi 4-chome Shibuya-ku, Tokyo
(*Kokushigaku*—Journal of Japanese History)

Nippon-shi Kenkyukai (The Japanese Society of Historical Studies)
58 Sakuraya-cho, Shishigadani Sakyo-ku
Kyoto
(*Journal*)

Shigaku-kai (Historical Society of Japan)
University of Tokyo
Hongo, Bunkyo-ku, Tokyo
(*Shigaku-Zasshi*—Historical Journal of Japan)

Books and Articles

Akiyama, Aisaburo.
... A Chronological List of Japan and China.
Tokyo, 1942. 79 p. (Shows the kings and rulers)
NN *OSL

Asakawa, Kanichi, ed.
The Documents of Iriki Illustrative of the Development of the Feudal Institutions of Japan.
New Haven, CT, Yale U. Press, 1929. xvi, 442, 134, 6, 2 p., including gen. tables. (Iriki, Kyushu, Japan, land tenure in the Shibuya and Shimadzu families)
NN *OSD

Bolton, Sheila.
Some Aspects of Japanese Heraldry and Genealogy.

(IN: *Coat of Arms*, London, 1953. v. 7, p. 110–15)
NN AWA

Conroy, Hilda.
East Across the Pacific.
Santa Barbara, CA, American Bibliographic Center, Clio Press, 1972. 322 p., index.
NN IEA 73-2055

Dictionnaire Historique du Japon.
Tokyo, 1963–.
NN *OSL 75-97

Gillis, Irvin van Gorder, and Pai Ping-ch'i.
Japanese Personal Names.
Peking, Hwa Hsing Press, 1940. 70, 70 p.
NN *OSG

Gillis, Irvin van Gorder, and Pai Ping-ch'i.
Japanese Surnames.
Ann Arbor, MI, Edwards Bros., 1943. 171, 5, 18 p., alpha and cross-index to characters, 18 p. of chronological tables of Emperors at end.

Hamada, Kengi.
Prince Ito.
Tokyo, Sanseido Co., 1936. 240 p., index.
(Juzo Hayashi, a descendant of Emperor Korei, was adopted by Buhei Ito, and his son, Hirobumi, 1841–1909, statesman, was made a prince.)
NN AN (Ito)

Herman, Masako.
The Japanese in America, 1843–1973.
Dobbs Ferry, NY, Oceana, 1974. 152 p., index.
NN IEA 75-316

Hurst, G. Cameron.
Insei.
New York, 1976. 337 p. (The Emperors of Japan)
NN JFE 76-1950

Japan Gazette.
Peerage of Japan.
Yokohama, 1912. 951 p. plus index, illus.
NN AVH (Japan)

Japan Year Book.
Tokyo, 1905–1931.
22 v. Who's Who section in each v.
NN BERA

Japanese and Micronesian Descendants in the Family of George Washington Higgins, n.p., 1956.
(John Adams Higgins, thrice descended from William Brewster of the *Mayflower*, settled in Mokil, Caroline Islands, in 1852, and some of his descendants live there and others named Kishu live in Japan.)
NN APTF (Higgins)

Japanese Family Records.
(IN: *Studies in Asian Genealogy*, Provo, UT, Brigham Young U. Press, 1972. p. 81–138)
NN APB 73-1060

Komatsu, Y., and K. Shoda.
Local History in Japan.
(IN: *Amateur Historian*, London, 1964. v. 6, p. 79–85)
NN CA

Lanman, Charles.
Japan: Its Leading Men . . .
Boston, MA, D. Lothrop, 1886. 421 p.
NN AGA

Matsuda, Mitsugu.
The Japanese in Hawaii.
Honolulu, HI, 1975. 304 p.
NN IAA (Hawaii) 72-302 no. 5

Mori, Senzo.
Taisho Jimbutsu Itsuwa Jiten.
Tokyo, 1966. 438 p.
(Japanese biographical dictionary)
NN *R-Oriental 75-708

Morris, J.
Makers of Japan.
London, Methuen, 1906. 330 p.
NN BES

Mosley, Leonard.
Hirohito, Emperor of Japan.
Englewood Cliffs, NJ, Prentice-
Hall, 1966. 371 p.
NN JFE 74-2020

Murdoch, James.
A History of Japan (Foreword by
John L. Mish)
New York, F. Ungar, 1964. 3 v. in
6.
NN *OSL

Oom, Herman.
Charismatic Bureaucrat: A Politi-
cal Biography of Matsudaira
Sadnobu, 1758–1829.
Chicago, IL, U. of Chicago Press,
1975. 225 p., gen. table, index.
NN

Papinot, E.
Historical and Geographical Dic-
tionary of Japan.
Ann Arbor, MI, Overbeck, 1948.
842 p.
NN *OSL

Parish, H. Carroll.
Japan's Imperial Princes: A Historical Study.

(IN: *The Augustan*, Torrance, CA,
1971. v. 14, p. 92–121)
NN APA

Prominent Americans Interested
in Japan and Prominent Japanese in America.
New York, 1903. 97 p.
NN AGS

Reischauer, Edwin.
Japan: Story of a Nation.
New York, Knopf, 1970. 345 p.
NN *R-BES

Sellers, Edwin J.
Jaudon Family of Pennsylvania.
Philadelphia, the author, 1924. p.
31–32.
NN APV (Jaudon)

Shulman, Frank J.
Japan and Korea (A Bibliography).
Chicago, IL, ALA, 1970. 340 p.
NN *OSD 71-103

Stephenson, Edward S.
Famous People of Japan (Ancient
and Modern)
Yokohama, Kelly and Walsh, 1911.
230 p.
NN D-13 9924

Teng, Ssu-yu.
Japanese Studies on Japan and the
Far East ...
Biographical and Bibliographical
Introduction.
Hong Kong, Hong Kong U. Press,
1961. 485 p.
NN *OSB

Webb, Herschel.
The Japanese Imperial Institution
in the Tokugawa Period.
New York, Columbia U. Press,
1968. 296 p.
NN D-18 3016

Weglyn, Michi.
Years of Infamy: The Untold Story of America's Concentration Camps, with an introduction by James A. Michener.
New York, William Morrow, 1976. 341 p.
NN IEA 76-1363

Who's Who Hakushi in Great Japan.
Tokyo, Hattenska, 1921–22. 2 v.
NN *OSA

Who's Who in Japan by Shunjiro Kurita.

Tokyo, 1911–19. 2 v.
NN *OSA

Yamashita Family.
(IN: Hafner, Arabell Lee, *100 Years on the Muddy*. Springville, UT, Art. Pub., 1967. p. 241–45)
(Typical Japanese-American family)
NN APR (Clarke Co., NV) 72-2074

Yoshimura, Akiji.
A Brief History of the Japanese in Colusa County.
(IN: *Wagon Wheels*, Colusa, CA, 1969. v. 19, p. 4–12)
NN IXH (Colusa Co., CA)

JORDAN (AMMAN)

In Biblical times, Samaritans and Israelites inhabited the area that is the modern state of Jordan. The Arabs conquered the area in the seventh century A.D. From the sixteenth century until World War I it was part of the Ottoman Empire. When France and Great Britain divided the Ottoman domain in the Sykes-Picot agreement in 1916, Trans Jordan—now the East Bank—became a British sphere of influence. The Hashemite dynasty was founded when the British recognized Abdullah as the ruler of Trans Jordan in 1921. In 1946 the independent Kingdom of Trans Jordan was proclaimed. The British mandate ended in 1948, and the Hashemite Kingdom of Jordan was declared in 1949. King Abdullah was assassinated in Jerusalem in 1951, and in 1952 King Hussein assumed power. In 1967 Jordan experienced severe losses in the Six-Day War against Israel. The West Bank and Jerusalem were occupied by the Israelis, and Jordan consequently lost half its population, almost all of its agriculture and the spiritual centers of Hebron and Jerusalem.

A Trans Jordan census was taken in 1961.

Archives

Reference and Documentation Section

Press and Publication Dept. (P.O. Box 960)
Amman, Jordan

Public and Church Records

Birth certificates can be obtained from the Ministry of Health in Amman and its district offices in the principal cities and towns. Muslim marriage certificates can be obtained through the "Sharia" Court in Amman and principal cities, and Christian marriage certificates are maintained by church authorities.

Libraries

American Library
Kabarday Street
Amman, Jordan

Gulbenkian Library
Armenian Patriarchate, P.O. Box 4001
Old City, Jerusalem, Israel

Public Library
P.O. Box 132
Amman Jordan

Public Library
Jerusalem, Israel

Supreme Mosque Library
Mosque of Omar
Jerusalem, Israel

University of Jordan Library
P.O. Box 1682
Amman, Jordan

Books and Articles

'Abd Allan ibn Husain. Hashemite King of Jordan.
Memoirs of King Abdullah, ed. by Philip P. Graves.
London, J. Cape, 1950. 278 p.
NN BCB

Dearden, Ann.
Jordan.
London, Hale, 1958. 224 p.
NN D-11 4372

Glubb, Sir John Bagot.
A Soldier with the Arabs.
London, Hodder and Stoughton, 1957. 460 p.
NN D-10 9841

Harris, George L.
Jordan, Its People, Its Society, Its Culture.
New Haven, CT, HRAF Press, 1958. 246 p.
NN D-11 4213

Lapp, Paul W.
The Dhar Mirzbaneh Tombs.
New Haven, CT, 1966. 116, 87 p.
NN *OFG 74-823

Morris, James.
The Hashemite Kings.
New York, Pantheon, 1959. 208 p.
NN D-12 719

Patai, Raphael.
Jordan, Lebanon and Syria: An Annotated Bibliography.
New Haven, CT, HRAF Press, 1957. 289 p.
NN D-10 8941

KOREA

The founding of a colony at Pyongyang by a Chinese scholar (Ki-Tze) in the twelfth century B.C., the first event in Korea's recorded history, foreshadowed China's centuries-long influence in this country. Buddhism and Confucianism were introduced from China in the fourth century A.D. In 1392 a Chinese general, Yi Sung-jeu, seized the Korean throne and established the Yi dynasty. In 1637 the Chinese Manchu rulers assumed loose authority, not renouncing it until defeated by Japan in the Sino-Japanese War (1894–95). Following the Russo-Japanese War (1904–05), Japan made Korea a virtual protectorate, and in 1910 Korea was formally annexed to the Japanese Empire, which ruled it until the end of World War II. After the Japanese defeat, Korea was divided at the 38th Parallel into two zones; the Soviet Union occupied the north, while the United States took over the south. In 1948 the northern sector became the Democratic People's Republic of Korea, with its capital at Pyongyang, and the south became the Republic of Korea, with its capital at Seoul. When supporters of the People's Republic began a guerrilla campaign in the south to unify the country under northern leadership, the United States helped to suppress their movement. Full-scale war between the two Koreas broke out in 1950. The cease-fire in 1953 reestablished the line of division at the 38th Parallel.

The most common surnames in Pusan and Seoul are Kim, Pak, Yi, Chŏng and Ch'oe.

Public and Church Records

Births and marriages are entered on family registers filed by family heads, which constitute the only official records of these events. For Koreans who are Christians, church records of birth, baptism and marriage are available.

North Korea (Pyongyang)

Libraries

State Central Library
Pyongyang Chief Librarian
Huh Jung Sook, Democratic People's Republic of Korea

North Pyongan Provincial Library
Shinuiju, Librarian
Cha Kyung Ryoon, Democratic People's Republic of Korea

South Pyongan Provincial Library
Pyongyang, Librarian
Li Eui Suk, Democratic People's Republic of Korea

South Korea (Seoul)

Libraries

Korea University Library
1 Anam-dong, Sungbuk-ku
Seoul, Republic of Korea

Namdaimoon Library
Seoul, Republic of Korea

National Central Library
Sogong-dong 6, Jung-Gu
Seoul, Republic of Korea

Seoul National University Library
Seoul, Republic of Korea

Historical and Genealogical Societies

Korean Historical Association
2-5, Myong-nyun-dong 3-ga
chong-no-ku
Seoul, Republic of Korea
(*Yoksa Hakbo* [*The Korean Historical Review*])

Books and Articles

Gardner, Arthur L.
Koreans in Hawaii.
Honolulu, 1970. 83 leaves.
NN IAA (Hawaii) 72-302 no. 2

Ha, Tae-Hŭng.
Korea—Forty-Three Centuries.
Seoul, Yonsei U. Press, 1962. 301 p.
(*Korean Cultural Series v.1*)
NN L-10 5243 v. 1

Han, U-gŭn.
The History of Korea.
Seoul, 1972. 551 p.
NN *R-BEO 72-831

Hulbert, Homer B., 1863–1949.
History of Korea, ed. by Clarence N. Weems.
New York, Hillary House Pub., 1962. 2 v.
NN E-11 7593

Kim, Hyung-chan.
The Koreans in America, 1882–1974.
Dobbs Ferry, NY, Oceana, 1974.
index.
NN IEA 75-195

Kim, Wŏn-Yong.
Koreans in America
Seoul, Po Chin Chai Print Co., 1971.
161 p., no index.
(Migration to Hawaii, 1882; to Mexico, 1905; to Cuba, 1921)
NN IEA 74-1032

Koh, Hesung Chung.
Korea: An Analytical Guide to Bibliographies.
New Haven, CT, Yale U. Press, 1971. 344 p.
NN JFD 72-2285

Korean Genealogical Sources.
(IN: *Studies in Asian Genealogy*, Salt Lake City, UT, Brigham Young U. Press, 1972. p. 139–76)
NN APB 73-1060

Kwak, Hyso-sŏk.
The Korean Handbook.
Seoul, Yungmoonsa Pub., c. 1962. 315 p.
NN C-12 8801

Osgood, Cornelius.
The Koreans and Their Culture.
New York, Ronald Press, 1951. 387 p.
NN *R-BEO

Shiratori, Kurakichi.
Über die Altkoreanischen Königs Titel.
(IN: *Revue Orientale*, Budapest, 1903. v. 4, p. 4–17)
(Korean kings and rulers)
NN *OO

Shulman, Frank J.
Japan and Korea.
Chicago, IL, 1970. 340 p.
NN *OSD 71-103

Sohn, Pow-Key
Biographical Tables of the Koryo
  Period.
Berkeley, CA, 1958. 179 p.

(U. of California Institute of International Studies, East Asia Series)
NN *OTU

KUWAIT (KUWAIT)

Kuwait was inhabited by Arab tribes in the eighteenth century. The Al-Sabah dynasty founded in 1756 prevails to this day. The Ottoman Empire had nominal control of the country until 1897, when the Sheik asked for British protection. In 1914 Britain declared Kuwait independent of Turkey. In 1934 a British-American enterprise, the Kuwait Oil Company, began drilling for oil. Kuwait achieved independence in 1961, with the promise of British protection until 1971.

Archives

Pending the establishment of archives, records are kept in the Library Department of Kuwait University.
The Library Department, Kuwait University
P.O. Box 5969
Kuwait City, Kuwait

Libraries

Kuwait Central Library
Kuwait City, Kuwait

Books and Articles

Abu Hakima, Ahmad Mustafa.
History of Eastern Arabia, 1750–1800: The Rise and Development of Bahrain and Kuwait.
Beirut, Khayats, 1965. 213 p., gen. tables.
NN D-17 4740

Hewins, Ralph.
A Golden Dream: The Miracle of Kuwait.
London, W.H. Allen, 1963. 317 p.
NN D-14 6243

Kabeel, Soraya.
Selected Bibliography on Kuwait and the Arabian Gulf.
Kuwait, 1969. 104 p.
NN JFF 75-1686

Lockhart, Laurence.
Outline of the History of Kuwait.
(IN: *Royal Central Asian Society Journal*, London, 1947. v. 34, pt. 3–4, p. 262–74)
NN BBA

Shaw, Ralph.
Kuwait.
London, Macmillan, 1976. 1 v.

Winstone, Harry V.
Kuwait: Prospect and Reality.
New York, 1972. 232 p.
NN JFF 74-691

LAOS (VIENTIANE, LUANG PRABANG)

The ethnic Lao migrated from China in the ninth century, and for many centuries thereafter the Laotians were preyed upon by neighboring feudal states in Khmer, Burma, Siam and Annam (now Vietnam). Most of what is now Laos and northeast Thailand were united by a ruler of the Luang Prabang state in a new state called the Kingdom of Lan Xang ("Land of the Million Elephants"). By the early 1800's, Thailand dominated the two Laotian Kingdoms of Luang Prabang and Vientiane, although Vietnam disputed its authority. In 1893 the French established a protectorate over Laos, incorporating it into the Union of Indochina. In 1949 Laos became an independent state within the French Union, and two years later the Pathet Lao, a Communist nationalist movement, was formed. The Geneva Conference of 1954 proclaimed Laos fully independent and permitted the Pathet Lao to occupy two provinces. Conflicts among neutralist, Communist and conservative factions created a chaotic political situation. By May 1975 the Pathet Lao, through large military gains, had taken over control of the country, though a formal coalition government remained in effect.

The administrative capital of Laos is at Vientiane, while the royal capital is at Luang Prabang.

Archives

Archives Nationales
rue Sam sène Thai (B.P. 59)
Vientiane, Laos

Public and Church Records

Births and marriages are recorded
  at the Bureau of Vital Statistics
  of the *Muong* (District) where
  the event took place.

Books and Articles

Abhay, Nhouy.
Aspects of Pays Lao.
Vientiane, 1958. 128 p.
NN E-119908

Berval, Réné de.
Kingdom of Laos.
Saigon, Vietnam, France-Asie,
  1959. 506 p.
NN E-12 5646

Le Boulanger, Paul.
... Histoire du Laos Français ...
Paris, Plon, 1931. 381 p.
NN BFV

Manich, M.L.
History of Laos, Including the History of Lannathai, Chiengmai.
Bangkok, 1967. 337 p.
NN D-18 5438

Muller, Hendrik P.N.
Do Oost-Indische Compagnie in
  Cambodia en Laos ...

1636 tot 1670.
's' Gravenhage, N. Nijhoff, 1917.
463 p.

(Werken Uitg door Linschoten-Vereening XIII)
NN KBD (Linschoten)

LEBANON (BEIRUT)

Lebanon was occupied by the Hittites and Aramaeans in ancient times. The Phoenicians later set up coastal cites that became part of their great sea-trading empire. The Assyrians and the Persians later conquered the cities, followed by Alexander the Great, who took the whole region. Lebanon, with Syria, came under Roman domination and eventually became a part of the Byzantine Empire. The Maronite Christians established themselves in Lebanon around this time, and the arrival of Islam, via Arab invasion in the seventh century, did not supersede Christianity in Lebanon. In 1516 Lebanon and Syria were made a part of the Ottoman Empire. From 1832 to 1840 the Egyptians occupied the Levant (Lebanon and Syria), and the area was opened to European contact. In 1841, and again in 1860, Islamic Druses massacred Maronite Christians. The Europeans finally intervened, forcing the Ottoman sultans to permit a pro-Christian government and to establish an autonomous province, Mount Lebanon. In 1918, with the collapse of the Ottoman Empire, the French and British occupied Lebanon, which, along with Syria, became a French mandate in 1920. In 1941 Lebanon, then occupied by the Free French, was declared independent. A full-scale civil war between the Christians (the Phalange) and Palestinian and leftist Muslims erupted in 1975 and lasted for nineteen months.

Archives

Archives du Ministère des Affaires
    Étrangères et d'Outre-Mer
rue Miche Boustross
Beirut, Lebanon

Archives de La Direction Générale des Antiquités
Musée national, rue Damas
Beirut, Lebanon

Public and Church Records

Birth and marriage certificates can be obtained from various district (*caza*) or central offices of the Census Bureau (Recensement, État-Civil).

Libraries

Bibliothèque Nationale du Liban
Beirut, Lebanon

Bibliothèque Orientale
Université St. Joseph
Beirut, Lebanon

Library of the American University
Beirut, Lebanon

Jafet Memorial Library, American University of Beirut
rue Pliss
Beirut, Lebanon

Books and Articles

Abu-Izzeddin, Halim Said.
Lebanon and Its Provinces.
Beirut, 1963. 115 p.
NN JFD 75-4771

Bastani, Tanus J.
O Libano e os Libaneses no Brazil.
Río de Janeiro, 1945. 180 p.
(Lebanese in Brazil)
NN BCB

Chevalier, Dominique.
La Société du Mont Liban à l'Epoque de la Révolution Industrielle en Europe.
Paris, 1971. 316 p.
NN JFF 73-415

Ismael, Adel
Histoire du Liban de XVIIe Siècle à Nos Jours.
Paris, G.P. Maissoneuve, 1955–58. 2 v.
NN *OFP

Kalleel, John G.
Mount Lebanon Trembled; A True Story of One Man's Pilgrimage and Proud Return.
New York, Greenwich Book Publishers, 1960. 72 p.
NN IEA

Moanack, Georges.
... Les Libanais de Colombie, de Latouf à Turbas.
Beirut, 1943. 28 p.
NN HCC p.v. 449

Safa, Elie.
L'Émigration Libanaise.
Beirut, 1960. 324 p.
NN D-15 3430

Sáfady, Wadih.
Cenas e Cenariós dos Caminhos de Mina Vida...
São Paulo, 1966. 1 v. (Lebanon Emigration and Immigration)
HFB 71-216

Salib, Kamal S.
The Modern History of Lebanon.
New York, Praeger, 1965. 227 p.
NN *R-BCB

Touma, Toufic.
Paysans et Institutions Feodales Chez les Druses et Les Maronites du Liban du XVIIe Siècle à 1914.
Beirut, 1971–72. 862 p.
NN JFL 75-14

Who's Who in Lebanon.
Beirut, Les Editions Publitec, 1963–73. 5 v. (1963–64—1973–74)
NN K-10 7086

MALAYSIA (KUALA LUMPUR)

In the thirteenth century there were Malay trading ports, with fishing and the production of spices the chief enterprises. The

Portuguese occupied Malacca, on the west coast of Malaya, in 1571. The British East India Company was established at Penang in 1592, and in 1819 Britain founded Singapore. In 1867 Penang, Malacca and Singapore formed a British Crown Colony called the Straits Settlements. Britain declared North Borneo (Sabah and Sarawak) a British protectorate in 1888. The Japanese invaded in 1941. Malaya became independent and a member of the British Commonwealth in 1957. A Communist insurrection was put down in 1960, and in 1962–63 a new Federation of Malaysia including Malaya, Sarawak, Sabah and Singapore joined the Commonwealth. In 1965 Singapore seceded from the federation. A parliamentary government was established under Prime Minister Abdul Razak after Prime Minister Abdul Rahman resigned in 1971 over tension and rioting between Chinese and Malays.

Censuses of Singapore were made in 1947 and 1957. A census of Malaysia was recorded in 1970.

Archives

Arkib Negara Malaysia (National Archives of Malaysia)
Bangunan Persekutuan, Jalan Sultan
Petaling Jaya, Selangor, Malaysia

Public and Church Records

Vital records can be obtained from the Superintendent Registrar of Births and Deaths or the Registrar of Marriages in the area in which the event took place, or from the nation's central registration office:

National Registration Department
Bangunan Persekutuan
Petaling Jaya, Malaysia

Civil registration of marriages began in 1952.

Libraries

British Council Library
P.O. Box 539
Jalan Bluff, Kuala Lumpur, Malaysia

Library of University of Malaya
Pantai Valley, Kuala Lumpur, Malaysia

Penang Library
Farquhar St.
Penang, Malaysia

Historical and Genealogical Societies

Malayan Historical Society
Muzium Negar
Kuala Lumpur, Malaysia
(*Malaya in History*)

Books and Articles

Adul, Rahman bin Yusop.
Collins Malay Gem Dictionary: Ba-

hasa Malaysia-English, English-Bahasa Malaysia. Revised Edition.
London, Collins, 1975. 614 p.
NN *ORE 77-1328

Andaya, Leonard Y.
The Kingdom of Jahore, 1641–1728.
London, Oxford U. Press, 1975. 394 p., index.
(East Asian History Monographs)

Directory of the State of Singapore, Including Trade Index and Biographical Section.
London, Diplomatic Press, 1960–61–.
NN L-10 7309

Kennedy, J.
A History of Malaysia.
London, Macmillan, 1970. 364 p., index.
NN *R-BFS 76-3127

Linehan, W.
The Kings of 14th Century Singapore.
(IN: *Royal Asiatic Society of Great Britain and Ireland—Malaysian Branch.* London, 1947. p. 117–27) illus.
NN *OAA

Miller, Harry.
The Story of Malaysia.
London, Faber & Faber, 1965. 264 p.
NN *R-BFK

Moore, Donald, and Joanna Moore.
The First 150 Years of Singapore.
Singapore, Donald Moore Press, 1969. 731 p.
NN *RR-BFT

Pearson, H.F.
People of Early Singapore.

London, U. of London Press, 1955. 128 p.
NN BFT

Tregonning, K.G.
A History of Modern Malaysia and Singapore.
Singapore, 1972. 298 p.
NN JFD 74-5948

Wales, Horace G.Q.
The Malay Peninsula in Hindu Times.
London, Quaritch, 1976. 199 p., index (Covers 400–1478).

Who's Who in Malaysia and Singapore.
Kuala Lumpur, J. Victor Morais, 1955–. (Formerly *Leaders of Malaya and Who's Who*)
NN M-11 3902 (NN has 1967, 1971–72)

Sarawak

Brooke of Sarawak (IN: *Burke's Landed Gentry.* 18th ed. London 1972. v. 3 pp. 120–121.)
NN ARF 73-1915

Brooke, Sylvia L., Lady, Ranee of Sarawak.
Queen of the Head Hunters. London, Sidgwick & Jackson, 1970. 194 p.
NN D-20 933

Runciman, Steven.
The White Rajahs: A History of Sarawak from 1841 to 1946. Cambridge, Cambridge U. Press, 1960. 320 p.

Tarling, Nicholas.
Britain, the Brookes and Brunei. Kuala Lampur, 1971. 578 p.
NN JFF 72-427

MALDIVES (MALE)

Islam was brought to the Maldive Islands in the twelfth century. In the sixteenth century Portuguese sailors visited. The British established a protectorate and a military base in 1887, but the islands retained self-government. In 1965 the Maldives declared independence as a sultanate and in 1968 the ad-Din dynasty, which had ruled the islands since the fourteenth century, was ended and a republic was declared.

Books and Articles

Hockley, T.W.
Two Thousand Isles: A Short Account of the People, History and Customs of the Maldive Archipelago.
London, Witherby, 1935. 191 p.
NN BGR

MUSCAT AND OMAN: See Oman

NEPAL (KATMANDU)

Little is known about Nepal before the fifteenth century, after which time the country was often divided. In the eighteenth century the ruler of Gurkha, a principality west of Nepal's capital city of Katmandu, conquered Nepal. The Gurkhas established most of Nepal's present borders and introduced Hinduism, which became the official religion. In 1790 the Gurkhas invaded Tibet and were met by a large Chinese army; in 1792 Nepal entered into a treaty relationship with the British as protection against the Chinese. A series of border incidents led to war between Britain and Nepal in 1814–16 and ultimately to British direction of Nepal's affairs, though the full sovereignty of Nepal was affirmed in a treaty with Britain in 1923. In 1951 King Tribjubana assumed full power after more than a century of rule by hereditary Prime Ministers. In 1959, under King Mahendra, the country held its first elections. In 1960, however, King Mahendra dissolved the cabinet, parliament and all political parties and took full control of the government.

Archives

One public archives institute exists in Nepal under the Department of Archaeology, Government of Nepal, Singha Durbar, Katmandu. It is still not yet fully developed, and most documents are still with various government agencies.

Rastriya Abhilekhalaya (National Archives)
Ram Shah Path
Katmandu, Nepal

Libraries

American Library
Katmandu, Nepal

British Library
"Adza Shar," King's Road
Katmandu, Nepal

Central Library
Lal Darbar
Katmandu, Nepal

Indian Library
Katmandu, Nepal

National Library
Katmandu, Nepal

Library, Tribhuvan University
Kirtipur
Katmandu, Nepal

Books and Articles

Aryal, I.R.
A New History of Nepal.
Katmandu, 1970. 274 p.
NN JFD 72-705

Buchanan, Francis H., 1762–1829.
An Account of the Kingdom of Nepal and the Territories Annexed by the House of Gorkha.
New Delhi, Mañjuśrī Pub. House 1971. 364 p.
NN *OKZE+ 76-548

Hedrick, Basil C.
Historical and Cultural Dictionary of Nepal.
Metuchen, NJ, Scarecrow, 1972. 198 p.
NN JFD 74-2561

Jain, M.S.
Emergence of a New Aristocracy in Nepal (1837–58).
Arga, 1972. 220 p.
NN JFD 73-10087

McFarland, Alan.
Resources and Population: A Study of the Gurungs of Nepal.
Cambridge, Cambridge U. Press, 1976. 364 p., index.
(Cambridge Studies in Social Anthropology v. 12)

Nepal: Chitta Ranhan.
The Shah Kings of Nepal. Revised 2nd ed.
Katmandu, 1965. 22 p.
(Introducing Nepal Series, no. 1)
NN D-17 6604

Northey, William B.
The Gurkhas: Their Manners, Customs and Country.
London, J. Lane, 1928. 282 p.
NN BGR

Regmi, D.R.
Ancient Nepal.
Calcutta, 1969. 364 p.
NN JFD 72-8417

Regmi, D.R.
A Century of Family Autocracy in Nepal ... The Last Hundred Years of Rana Aristocracy, 1846–1949.
Nepal, 1958. 267 p.

Regmi, D.R.
Medieval Nepal.
Calcutta, 1965–66. 4 v.
NN D-17 453 (NN lacks v. 3)

Sama, Bala Krishna.
Heroes of Nepal.
Katmandu, 1971. 49 p.
NN *OKZE 74–827

Vaṃśāvali, English.
History of Nepal, trans. by Shew S. Singh.
Katmandu, Antiquated Books, 1972. 320 p.
NN *OKZE 74–183

OMAN (MUSCAT)
(formerly Muscat and Oman)

Muscat, the capital of Oman, was occupied by the Portuguese from 1508 to 1648, when it fell to Persian princes, who were expelled in 1744. Although an independent state ruled by a sultan, the country has been under British protection since the early 1800's. In 1970 Sultan Said bin Taimur was overthrown by his son, who became Sultan Qabus bin Said, and changed the country's name to Oman. With the help of Iran the Sultan did battle with leftist guerillas, who were aided by the U.S.S.R., Iraq and southern Yemen. With the shrinkage of British power, the country has moved into the Iranian military orbit.

Books and Articles

Darlow, Michael, and Richard Fawkes.
The Last Corner of Arabia.
London, Namara Pub., Quartet Books, 1976. 128 p. plus.
NN JFG 76–259

King, R.A.
A Bibliography of Oman, 1900–1970.
Durham, England, 1973. 14 leaves.
NN *XM 7753

Miles, Samuel B.
The Countries and Tribes of the Persian Gulf.

London, Harrison, 1919. 2 v.
NN *OFK

Nicholls, Christine S.
The Swahilli Coast.
New York, 1971. 419 p.
NN JFD 72–5445

Salil ibn Ruzaik.
History of the Imans and Seyyids of 'Oman ... from A.D. 661–1856.
London, Hakluyt Society, 1871. 435 p. (Hakluyt Society Works no. 44)
NN KBD (Hakluyt)

Skeet, Ian.
Muscat and Oman.
London, 1974. 224 p.
NN JFD 75–9095

Thomas, Bertram.
Arab Rule under the Al Bu Sa'id
   Dynasty of Oman, 1741–1937.

London, H. Milford, 1937. 29 p.
(British Academy, London, The
   Raleigh Lecture on History,
   1938)
NN BAA

PAKISTAN (ISLAMABAD)

Under British rule of the Indian subcontinent, the Muslims maintained a separate identity from the Hindus. In 1916 the Muslim league was founded, and its leader, Mohammad Ali Jinnah, demanded that a Muslim state be set up in India. In 1947 Pakistan was created as a separate British dominion, with Jinnah as Governor-General. The establishment of the new state precipitated a civil war between Muslims and Hindus in which millions lost their lives. In 1948 a state of undeclared war existed between India and Pakistan; the following year a cease-fire was arranged and a temporary demarcation line was traced between the two states. Pakistan became a republic in 1956, with East and West Pakistan represented equally in the national assembly. In 1969, after a long period of unrest, East Pakistan began to demand autonomy. In 1971 riots broke out in the east, and government troops invaded from the west. The independent state of Bangladesh was proclaimed by the easterners, and in the ensuing war thousands were killed and ten million easterners fled to India. After a brief war between Pakistan and India in December 1971, Bangladesh was recognized as a separate nation. In 1972 Pakistan and India signed a pact for the peaceful solution of problems, and in 1973 a new constitution made Pakistan a federal Islamic Republic.

A census of Pakistan was taken in 1961.

Archives

National Archives
Block D, Pakistan Secretariat
Islamabad, Pakistan

Public and Church Records

Where a record of birth exists, a certificate can be obtained from the registrar in a municipality or, in rural areas, from the "union board." If a marriage has been made a matter civil record, a certificate witnessed by the magistrate can be obtained from the registrar in the district where the marriage was performed.

Libraries

Anjuman Taraqqi-e-Urdu Pakistan Libraries
(Comprises Kutub Khana-i-'Am Public Library and Kutub Khana-e-Khas Special Library)
Urdu Road
Karachi 1, Pakistan

Liaquat National Library
Karachi, Pakistan

University of Karachi Library
Karachi 32, Pakistan

Historical and Genealogical Societies

Pakistan Historical Society
30 New Karachi Co-operative Housing Society
Karachi 5, Pakistan

Books and Articles

Abdulla, Ahmed.
The Historical Background of Pakistan and Its People.
Karachi, 1973. 212 p.
NN JFD 74-6767

Baillie, Alexander Francis.

Kurrachee, Past, Present and Future.
London, Oxford U. Press, 1975 (orig. 1890). 269 p.
(Oxford in Asia Historical Reprints from Pakistan)
NN JFE 76-3384

Barque's Who's Who in Pakistan, 1971/72.
Lahore Pakistan, Barque and Company, 1971. 280 p.
NN *R-Oriental 75-2606 and JFK 76-269

Bhatti, Allah Ditta.
Review of Some Selected Aspects of Population Censuses Taken in the Area of Pakistan Since 1867.
Karachi, 1968. 18 leaves.
NN JLG 74-128

Biographical Encyclopedia of Pakistan, 1971/72.
Lahore, Pakistan, International Printing Press, 1971. 990 p.
NN *OHM 76-169

Cousens, Henry.
The Antiquities of Sind, with Historical Outline.
Karachi, London, etc , Oxford U. Press, c. 1976 (orig. 1929). 184 p.
(Oxford in Asia Historical Reprints from Pakistan.)
NN *OHN 77-1893

Safdar Mahmood.
Founders of Pakistan.
Lahore, 1968. 249 p.
NN JFD 75-8677

A Short History of Pakistan.
Karachi 1967. 4 v.
NN JFD 75-1429

PHILIPPINES (QUEZON CITY)

These islands had been settled by peoples of Malay stock for centuries before Ferdinand Magellan of Portugal, the first European explorer, arrived in 1521. The Spanish, who gained control by 1571 and held sway until the end of the nineteenth century, called the islands the Philippines, after Philip II. After the Spanish-American War in 1898, the Philippines were ceded to the United States. In 1932 the American Congress passed the Hawes–Cutting Act, which provided for a ten-year period of increasing self-government culminating in full independence. In 1941 the Japanese attacked the Philippines and occupied the islands until they were finally defeated in 1945. On July 4, 1946, the Republic of the Philippines was proclaimed. Widespread violence was provoked by the Communist-led Huk guerillas, who were put down by 1954. Terrorist activities by leftist groups again became a problem after 1970, and President Ferdinand E. Marcos declared martial law in 1972. In 1973 a new constitution was drafted that provided for a parliamentary government.

The most common surnames in Manila are Chua, Cruz, Lim, Reyes, Santos and Tan.

Archives

National Archives (Bureau of Records Management)
T.M. Kalaw Street, Ermita
Manila, Philippines

Public and Church Records

Certificates can be obtained from the local civil registrar at the place of birth or marriage.

National Census and Statistics Office
Solicerel Bldg., R. Magsaysay Blvd.
Manila, Philippines

Libraries

Bureau of Public Libraries (National Library)
San Luis, Ermita
Manila, Philippines

Far Eastern University Library
Quezon Boulevard
Manila, Philippines

Manila City Library
Manila, Philippines

University of Manila Central Library
546 Alejandro VI, Sampaloc
Manila, Philippines

University of the Philippines Library
Diliman, Quezon City, Philippines

Historical and Genealogical Societies

Institute of History
% University of Santo Tomás
España St.
Manila, Philippines

Philippine Historical Association
%University of the East
Manila, Phillipines

Books and Articles

Galang, Zoilo M.
Encyclopedia of the Philippines. 3rd ed.
Manila, 1950–58. 20 v., alpha, v. 20 index. NN *R-BFG

Hanson, Mariano A.
The Province of Pampanga and Its Towns (A.D. 1300–1955). With Genealogy of the Rulers of Central Luzon. 2nd ed.
Angeles, Pampanga, M.A. Hanson, c. 1955. 169 p.
NN F-10 4332

Kim Hyung-chan.
The Filipinos in America 1898–1974.
Dobbs Ferry, Oceana, 1976. 143 p. index.
NN IEA 76-1429

Know Them: A Book of Biographies.
Manila, 1958. v. 1.
NN M-11 1942

Lim, Rodrigo.
Who's Who in the Philippines.
Manila, C. Nera, 1929. 1 v.
NN AGS

Manuel, E. Arsenio.
Dictionary of Philippine Biography.

Quezon City, Filipinana Pub. 1955. 1 v.
NN *RR-AGS

Maring, Ester G.
Historical and Cultural Dictionary of the Philippines.
Metuchen, NJ, Scarecrow Press, 1973. 240 p.
NN JFD 74-2502

Philippines Who's Who.
Quezon City, Capitol Pub., 1957. 1 v., 327 p.
NN *RR-AGA

Resena Biográfica de los Religiosos de la Provincia del Santismo Rosario de Filipinas desde su Fundacíon ...
Manila, Real de Colegio de Santo Tomás, 1891. 1 v.
NN M-10 1106

Retana y Gamboa, Wenceslao E.
Indice de Personas Nobles y Otras de Calidad que han Estado en Filipinas desde 1521 hasta 1898.
Madrid, V. Suarez, 1921. 84 p.
NN APB p.v. 24

Tableau: Encyclopedia of Distinguished Personalities in the Philippines.
Manila, National Souvenir, 1957. 1 v.
NN M-10 7631

U.S. Insular Affairs Bureau.
A Pronouncing Gazetteer and Geographical Dictionary of the Philippine Islands.
Washington, DC, Government Printing Office, 1902. 933 p.
NN Map Division

Van Niel, Robert.

738 • *Tracing Your Family's History Abroad*

A Survey of Historical Source Materials in Java and Manila. Honolulu, HI, 1970. 255 p.
NN *OAA 72-643 no. 5

Who's Who in the Philippines. Manila, McCullough, 1940. v. 2 1940–41.
NN AGS

QATAR (DOHA)

Qatar, occupying a peninsula extending into the Persian Gulf from the Arabian coast, was under Turkish rule from 1872 to 1915. It was a British Protected State from 1916 to 1971, when it declared itself independent. The government is a monarchy, ruled by an emir, who is assisted by a prime minister and advisory council. In 1972 Emir Ahmed bin Ali al-Thani was replaced by his cousin Khalifa bin Hamad al-Thani by a military coup.

Books and Articles

Qatar. Idārat al-I'lām.
Qatar Into The Seventies.

Doha; Information Department, State of Qatar; 1973. 143 p.
NN JFD 75-9178

SÃO TOMÉ AND PRINCIPE (SÃO TOMÉ)

These islands were uninhabited when they were discovered in 1471 by Portuguese explorers. In 1483 the São Tomé settlement was founded, and Portugal proclaimed it a colony in 1522. The Dutch held the islands from 1641 to 1740, when Portugal recovered them. In the eighteenth century a plantation economy was established, and many native inhabitants today are descendants of slaves imported from the mainland. The Democratic Republic of São Tomé and Principe became independent on July 12, 1975.

Archives

Arquivo Histórico de São Tomé e Principe

Caixa Postal 87
São Tomé, São Tomé and Principe

Books and Articles

Soutelinho, José Manoel.
Indice Alfabético e Cronológico de
  Todos os Diplomas de Carácter
  Permanente...

São Tomé, 1941. 101 p.
NN JLD 76-428

SAUDI ARABIA (RIYADH, JIDDA)

This area was originally inhabited by nomadic Semitic tribes. In the sixth century A.D. Mohammed was born in Mecca. His followers later conquered the territory between Persia and Spain, but Arabia remained isolated and poor. In the eighteenth century the Saud family, of the Wahabi movement, gained control of most of the peninsula, but in 1811 the Egyptians crushed the Wahabi. The Rashid dynasty gained control of central Arabia and expelled the Saud family. Between 1902 and 1932 Ibn Saud conquered the area and formed the kingdom of Saudi Arabia. In 1953 Saud succeeded his father to the throne. A pro-Nasser revolution broke out in Yemen in 1962, causing Saudi Arabia to sever relations with Egypt. Crown Prince Faisal, Saud's brother, was appointed Prime Minister. Saud was deposed in 1964 and was succeeded by Faisal, who abolished slavery and restored relations with Egypt.

The administrative capital of Saudi Arabia is at Jidda, while the royal capital is at Riyadh.

Archives

A system of national archives is being considered for the King Abdul Aziz Centre, Khazzan Street, Riyadh.

Library of University of Riyadh
Riyadh, Saudi Arabia

The Saudi Library
Riyadh, Saudi Arabia

Libraries

Abbas Kattan Library
Mecca, Saudi Arabia

Library of Islamic University
Medina, Saudi Arabia

Books and Articles

Arabische Führergestalten.
Heidelberg, Vowinckel, 1944. 159 p.
  (Kings of Arabia)
NN *OFS

Assah, Ahmed.
Miracle of the Desert Kingdom.
London, Johnson, 1969. 330 p.
NN *RR-*OFW

Deakin, Michael.
Ras al-Khaimah: Flame in the
Desert.
London: Namara Pub., Quartet
Books, 1976. 144 p.
NN

Lipsky, George A.
Saudi-Arabia: Its People, Its Society, Its Culture.

New Haven, CT, HRAF Press,
1959. 366 p.
NN D-12 1226

Meulen, Daniel van der.
The Wells of Ibn Sa'ud.
New York, Praeger, 1957. 270 p.
NN D-10 8643

Winder, Richard B.
Saudi Arabia in the Nineteenth
Century.
New York, Macmillan, 1965. 312 p.
NN D-164526

SEYCHELLES (VICTORIA)

These islands were discovered by Vasco da Gama in 1502. In
1756 the French claimed the islands and in 1768 began to
colonize them with French planters and their slaves from Mauritius (then Ile de France). Britain took possession of the islands
in 1794 and was given permanent control in 1814 by the Treaty
of Paris. The Seychelles were administered as part of Mauritius
until 1930, when they were constituted a Crown Colony. Independence was declared June 29, 1976.

The population descends almost entirely from early French
settlers and African slaves.

Censuses were conducted in 1901, 1911 and 1931.

Public and Church Records

The Chief Civil Status Officer has
the records, which begin in 1794
for births and in 1808 for marriages and deaths.

Books and Articles

Hill, Ken.
The Seychelles and Sri Lanka (For-
merly Ceylon).
London, 1973. 178 p.
NN *R-KCV 75-9125

Ozanne, James A. F.
Coconuts and Creoles.
London, P. Allen and Co., 1936. 336
p.
NN BLT

Sauer, Jonathan D.
Plants and Man on the Seychelles
Coast.
Madison, WI, U. of Wisconsin
Press, 1967. 132 p.
NN AD-10 1411

SINGAPORE (CITY OF SINGAPORE)

The island was a trading center in the Srivijaya empire, which was destroyed in the fourteenth century by the Majapahit empire. Later the island became part of Johore in the Malacca Sultanate. It was ceded in 1819 to the British East India Company, and the city of Singapore was founded in that year by Sir T. Stamford Raffles. In 1824 it came under complete British control. Chinese and Malay merchants were attracted to Singapore. With Penang and Malacca, Singapore formed the Straits Settlements in 1826. Japan conquered Singapore in 1942, but Britain reoccupied it in 1945. In 1946 Singapore became a Crown Colony and was no longer part of the Straits Settlements. In 1959 Singapore became a self-governing state. In 1962 it merged with Malaya, Sarawak and Sabah to form the Federation of Malaysia but withdrew in 1965 because of Malay fear of Chinese domination, as Singapore's population is 76 percent Chinese. Singapore is an independent republic.

Archives

National Archives and Records Centre
17–18 Lewin Terrace, Fort Canning
Singapore 6, Singapore

Public and Church Records

Birth certificates can be obtained from the Registrars of Births, Deaths, and Marriages.

Libraries

National Library
Stamford Road
Singapore 6, Singapore

Nanyang University Library
Jurong Road
Singapore 22, Singapore

University of Singapore Library
Bukit Timah Road
Singapore 10, Singapore

See also: Malaysian bibliography.

SRI LANKA (COLOMBO)
(formerly Ceylon)

The island of Ceylon was inhabitated in ancient times by ancestors of the Veddas, a primitive people now living in isolated mountain areas. The Veddas were conquered by the Singhalese from northern India in the sixth century B.C. The capital city of Anuradhapura, founded by the Singhalese in 437 B.C., became a major religious haven after the introduction of Buddhism from India in the third century B.C. Invasions from southern India, primarily by the Tamils, forced the Singhalese into the southwest of the island. Muslim Arab traders controlled most of Ceylon's foreign trade in the twelfth century. The coastal areas were conquered by the Portuguese in the sixteenth century, but the Dutch, prompted by the avaricious Dutch East India Company, took them in the seventeenth century. The British conquered the whole island in 1795, and by 1815 Ceylon was firmly under British rule. Discontent within the country pressured Britain into granting Ceylon independence and Dominion status in 1948. In 1972 Ceylon became the Republic of Sri Lanka.

Censuses have been taken approximately every ten years since 1871.

Archives

Natika Lekhanarakshaka Departamentuwa (Department of the National Archives)
7 Reid Avenue (Post. Add: P.O. Box No. 1414)
Colombo 7, Sri Lanka

Public and Church Records

The central address for vital records is:

Dept. of the Registrar-General
York St.
Colombo 1, Sri Lanka

Libraries

Office of the Registrar of Books and Newspapers
Nangodavila, Nugegoda, Sri Lanka

(Catalogue of Books; Catalogue of Newspapers)
(Preserves copies of all books printed in Sri Lanka after 1885)

Public Library
18 Edinburgh Crescent
Colombo 7, Sri Lanka

Historical and Genealogical Societies

Royal Asiatic Society
University Building
Thurstan Road
Colombo 3, Sri Lanka

Books and Articles

All in the Family.
(Ratwatte-Bandaranaike family with chart)
(IN: *Time*, New York, 15 Dec. 1975., p. 36)

Arasaratnam, Sinnappah.
Dutch Power in Ceylon, 1658–1687.
Amsterdam, Djambatan, c. 1959.
  246 p.
NN E-10 7378

Goonetileke, H.A.I.
A Bibliography of Ceylon; A Sys-
  tematic Guide to the Literature
  on the Land, People and Culture Published in Western Languages ...
Zug, Switzerland; International
  Documentation Co., 1970–76. 3
  v. index.
(Covers 16th century to 1973)
NN JFD 74-6326

History of Ceylon.
Colombo, Ceylon U. Press, 1954–60.
  1 v. in 2.
NN M-10 6980

Ludovici, Leopold.
Lapidarium Zeylanicum. Being a
  Collection of Monumental In-
scriptions of Dutch Churches
  and Churchyards of Ceylon.
Colombo, J. Maitland & Co., 1877.
  17 p., 98 plates.
NN AVH+ (Ceylon)

Pieris, Paulus E.
Ceylon, the Portuguese Era ...
  1505–1658.
Colombo, Colombo Apothecaries,
  1913–14. 2 v.
NN BGV

Pieris, Paulus E.
Notes on some Sinhalese Fam-
  ilies ...
Colombo, *The Times* of Ceylon, c.
  1933. part 4, Ilangakon.
NN AVH (Ceylon)

Toussaint, James R.
Annals of the Ceylon Civil Service.
Colombo, Colombo Apothecaries,
  1935. 204 p.
NN SEN

SYRIA (DAMASCUS)

Ancient Syria was inhabited by Hebrews, Phoenicians, Amorites
and Aramaeans and was subjected to invasions by the Assyrians,
Babylonians, Egyptians, Hittites and Persians. The land was
united under Alexander the Great in 331 B.C. and later came
under Byzantine control. Syria was conquered in the seventh
century by the Arabs. In the eleventh century Seljuk Turks
invaded from Asia Minor, and in the twelfth century they battled
against the Crusaders, who were attempting to gain a foothold
on the coast. Syria was conquered by the Ottoman Empire in
1516 and remained under its rule until 1918. In 1920 Syria was
made a French mandate. Independence was achieved in 1944.

The first census was taken in 1922 but has not been preserved;
the census of 1963 is the first to survive.

Archives

Direction du Département des Archives Historiques
14 rue Roukn-el-Din
Damascus, Syria

Public and Church Records

Ministry of Interior
Department of Civil Status
Demascus, Syria

Libraries

Al Maktabah Al Wataniah (National Library)
Bab El-Faradj
Alleppo, Syria

Damascus University Library
Damascus, Syria

Dar al-Kutub al-Wataniah (National Library)
Homs, Syria

Dar al-Kutub Al Zahiriah (National Library)
Damascus, Syria

National Library of Latakia
Latakia, Syria

Books and Articles

Adallis, D.
Thirteenth Memorial Anniversary. Historical and Business Brochure Greek, Syrian, Armenian Colonies of Williamson, West Virginia.
Williamson, WV, 1937 (unpaged—30 p.)
NN IXZ p. v. 26 no. 4

Glubb, Sir John Bagot.
Syria, Lebanon, Jordan.
New York, Walker, 1967. 236 p.
NN D-18 3467

Hitti, Philip Khuri.
The Syrians in America.
New York, George H. Doran, 1924. 139 p.
NN IEA

Kayal, Philip M., and Joseph M. Kayal.
The Syrian-Lebanese in America: A Study on Religion and Assimilation.
Boston, MA, Twayne, 1975. 260 p. index.
NN IEE (Syrians) 76-258

Longgrigg, Stephen.
Syrian and Lebanon under French Mandate.
London, Oxford U. Press, 1958. 404 p.
NN D-11 4585

Miller, Lucius H.
Our Syrian Population.
San Francisco, CA, 1969. 48 leaves.
NN IEA 73-1329

Rey, Emmanuel Guillaume, baron.
Les Colonies Franques de Syrie aux XIIme et XIIIme Siècles.
New York, AMS Press, 1972. 537 p.
NN JFD 72-8921

Stark, Juegen K.
Personal Names in Palmyrene Inscriptions.
Oxford, Oxford U. Press, 1972. 152 p.
NN APD 72-2003

Syrian Business Directory, ed. by   New York, 1908.
S. A. Mokarzel and H. F. Otash.   NN *OEL

THAILAND (BANGKOK)
(formerly Siam)

In the eleventh century the Thai people lived in a province of what is now China, but the Chinese pressed them southward, where they settled in the Chao Phyray and Mekong River deltas and founded city-states. In the sixteenth century the Portuguese arrived, followed by trade and missionaries, and in the seventeenth century the Dutch and British opened contact in the area. The French tried to get the upper hand, but in an antiforeign *coup d'état* in 1688 Thailand was closed to European contact. In 1767 the Burmese destroyed the capital city of Ayuthia, which had been established around 1350, and the Thai capital was moved to Bangkok. Thailand was subsequently restored as a state. In 1782 the Chakkri dynasty assumed power, and in the nineteenth century the authority of Bangkok was established over northern Thailand. In 1932 a bloodless revolution resulted in the absolute monarchy being replaced by a constitutional government.

Censuses were recorded in 1954 and 1960.

The most common surnames in Bangkok are Kim, Lim, Saeng, Sri, Tang and Yong.

Archives

National Archives
Fine Arts Department
Na Phra That Street
Bangkok, Thailand

Public and Church Records

Birth and marriage certificates are issued by the Nai Amphur of the district of registration.

Libraries

Chulalongkorn University Library
Phya Thai Road
Bangkok, Thailand

Library of the Kasetsart University
Bangkhen
Bangkok, Thailand

Thammasat University Library
Bangkok, Thailand

Books and Articles

Basche, James R.
Thailand: Land of the Free.
New York, 1971. 273 p.
NN JFE 71-763

Chang and Eng (Bunker).
(IN: *DAB*, New York, 1943. v. 4, p. 2–3)
(Chang and Eng Bunker, Siam, 1811—Surrey Co., NC, 1874—the Siamese Twins)
NN *R-AGZ

Chula, Prince.
Lords of Life, the Paternal Monarchy of Bangkok, 1732–1932, with Earlier and More Recent History of Thailand.
London, A. Redman, 1960. 352 p., many ports., 1 long gen. table, index.
NN D-12 7817

The Directory for Bangkok and Siam.
Bangkok, Bangkok *Times*, 1889– (NN has 1915–)
NN *SAM(Siam)

Hunter, Kay.

Duet for a Lifetime: The Story of the Original Siamese Twins.
London, M. Joseph, 1964. 126 p.
NN MWES (Bunker, C.) and D-15 7838

Mason, John Brown.
Thailand Bibliography.
Gainesville, U. of Florida Library, 1958. 247 p.
(University of Florida Library Bibliographic Series, no. 4)
NN *GAA

Siam Directory.
Bangkok, 1892. no. 15.
NN *OWB

Siam Directory.
Bangkok, 1909/10, 1919. 2 v.
NN *BAZ

The Siam Directory.
Bangkok, Thai Co., 1947–.
NN *SAM

Waugh, Alec.
Bangkok: The Story of a City.
London, W. H. Allen, 1970. 222 p. gen. tables.
NN D-20 3250

TURKEY (ANKARA)

Probably the first Turks to settle permanently in America were Jacobus Turk (Turck) and his son Paulus the Turk, or Paulus Jacobson Turck, who were living in New Amsterdam in 1660. When Paulus Turk married Aeltje Barnets Cole, a native of New Amsterdam, on September 12, 1660, he gave his birthplace as the Hague, and it is probable that his father was of Armenian-Turkish descent. Paulus and Aeltje Turk had eleven children born between 1662 and 1682. The first name Ahassuerus (Asuerus), reminiscent of the names of the ancient Assyrian Empire that covered the territory of modern Turkey, is the only remnant of the ethnic culture of this family that survived into the eighteenth century, when there were still many members of the family living in New York. Ahassuerus Turk, Jr., married Jane Anthony in the old New York Dutch Church on February 11, 1790.

Turkey's recorded history stretches back centuries before the birth of Christ. The first real traces of modern Turkey appeared in the thirteenth century with the birth of the Turkish Ottoman Empire, which reached its height in the sixteenth century. Ottoman power began to decline in the seventeenth century, and after World War I Turkey, which had fought on the side of the Central Powers, was reduced to a small state. In 1922 Turkish nationalists overthrew the Sultan and declared Turkey a republic; Kemal Ataturk, leader of the nationalists, became President but ruled as a dictator until he died in 1938. In 1968 a new constitution was drafted that provided for a bicameral legislature and a strong executive.

A census was first recorded in 1927 and has been taken every five years since 1935.

The most common surnames in Istanbul are Behar, Eskenazi, Guven, Kohen, Levi and Yilmaz.

Archives

Topkapi Palace Archives (National Archives)
Istanbul, Turkey

Public and Church Records

Civil registration began with the establishment of the Ottoman Empire in 1312, and early records are in the Topkapi Palace Archives. Since 1923 all vital records are kept at Population Registration Departments in cities, towns and villages. To request a copy, you must provide the full names and at least an approximate address of the people involved. Non-citizens who were born in Turkey may obtain a baptismal certificate or other religious record. Marriages since October 4, 1926, are recorded in the birth certificate of both parties.

For census information:
Devlet Istatistik Enstitusu (State Statistics Institute)
Ankara, Turkey

Libraries

Ankara University Library
Ankara Üníversítesí (University of Ankara)
Ankara, Turkey

Beyazit Library
Istanbul, Turkey

Istanbul University Library
İstanbul Üníversítesí (Istanbul
    University)
Bayezit
Istanbul, Turkey

Millî Kütüphane (National Li-
brary)
Yenişehir
Ankara, Turkey

Public Library
Ankara, Turkey

Historical and Genealogical Societies

Türk Tarih Kurumu (Turkish His-
    torical Society)
Ankara, Turkey
(*Belleten*, 1937–)
NN *OPB

Books and Articles

Acar, Bekir.
Mufassal Osmanli Seceresi. 2.
    Baski.
Istanbul?, 1966. 2 gen. charts.
NN AVH + Turkey

Berkes, Niyazi.
The Development of Secularism in
    Turkey.
Montréal, McGill U. Press, 1964.
    537 p.
NN F-10 9842

Damon, Theron.
Turkey and the Turks.

(IN: *Asia*, New York, 1920. v. 20,
    p. 95–98, port.)
NN *OAA

Findikoglu, Ziyaeddin.
Le Problème des Noms de Famille
    Considérér comme un Courant
    Culturel en Turquie.
(IN: *Revue International d'Ono-
    mastique*, Paris, 1952. anne 4, p.
    277–286)
NN APA

Gordon, Leland J.
Immigration from Turkey.
(IN: *Sociology and Social Research*,
    Los Angeles, 1930. v. 15, pp. 153–66)
NNSA

Hotham, David.
The Turks.
London, J. Murray, 1972. 220 p.
NN JFD 73-5744

Kinross, John Patrick, D. B.
    Baron.
The Ottoman Centuries: The Rise
    and Fall of the Turkish Empire.
New York, William Morrow, 1977.

Nicol, Donald M.
The Byzantine Family of Kanta-
    kouzenos (Cantacuzenus) ca.
    1100–1460.
Washington, Center for Byzantine
    Studies, 1968. 265 p., 3 indexes,
    2 gen. tables.
(Dumbarton Oaks Studies no. 11)
NN AVHH (Kantakouzenos)

Tugay, Emine Foat.
Three Centuries: Chronicles of
    Turkey and Egypt.
London, Oxford U. Press, 1963. 324
    p.
NN D-14 9943

Turkiye Ter Achimiahva Ansiklo-
pedis.
Constantinople, 1928–. v. 1–.
NN *OPB

Who's Who in Turkey 1960.
Ankara, Cyclopedic, 1959. 192 p.,
alpha.
NN M-10 4530

Who's Who in Turkey, comp. by
Osman Nebioglu.
Washington, DC, 1961–62. 1,067 p.,
alpha.
NN M-10 9528

UNITED ARAB EMIRATES (ABU DHABI)

British influence was strong in this area beginning in the early
1800's, and the Trucial States or Trucial Sheikdoms were British
Protected States until they merged as the independent nation
of the United Arab Emirates on December 2, 1971. Nearly three-
quarters of the population is Arab; the rest consists of Iranians,
Pakistanis and Indians.

Books and Articles

Fenelon, Kevin Gerard.
The United Arab Emirates . . . 2nd
ed.
London, Longman, 1976. (orig.
1973). (6), 164 p., index.
NN JLE 75-1353 (1973 ed.)

Gérard, Bernard.

Les Émirats Arabes Unis-The
United Arab Emirates.
Boulogne, 1973. 144 p.
NN JFF 76-558

Tomkinson, Michael.
The United Arab Emirates.
Hammamet, London, Michael
Tomkinson Pub., 1975. 192 p.,
index.

VIETNAM
(formerly French Indo-China)

The Vietnamese migrated to the Red River Valley, now in North
Vietnam, from southern China during the third century B.C.,
and China conquered the area a century later. Independence
was not achieved until the Vietnamese expelled the Chinese in
A.D. 939 and expanded southward to form the general boundaries
of modern Vietnam. Conquest by France began in 1858 and
culminated in protectorate status in 1884. Japan occupied Vietnam during World War II, and after the Japanese surrendered

in August 1945 the Viet Minh fought against the French, finally defeating them at Dienbienphu. The armistice concluded at Geneva in 1954 divided the country along the 17th Parallel, and the Viet Minh established the Democratic Republic of Vietnam in the north, while Ngo Dinh Diem, an anti-Communist Catholic with American backing, established the Saigon-based Republic of Vietnam in the South. The reunification elections called for by the peace agreement were never held. The National Liberation Front took up arms against Diem, aided by the North Vietnamese government. The conflict assumed major proportions after 1963, with the United States entering the struggle on the side of the Republic of Vietnam, first with supplies and advisers and eventually with some 550,000 troops. On January 27, 1973, a ceasefire agreement was reached between the United States, North and South Vietnam and the Vietcong. In 1975 North Vietnamese troops attacked South Vietnamese government outposts, and Saigon surrendered in April 1975 to the NLF's Provisional Revolutionary Government. Some 130,000 South Vietnamese have settled in the United States in recent years.

The most common surnames in Saigon are Huỳnh-, Lê-, Nguyen-, Pham and Trañ.

North Vietnam (*Hanoi*)

Libraries

Central Library
Hanoi, Democratic Republic of Vietnam

Library, University of Hanoi
(Truòng Dai-Hoc Tông-Ho'P)
Hanoi, Democratic Republic of Vietnam

South Vietnam (*Saigon*)

Archives

Só' Lu'U-Tru Cong-Van (Public Archives)

Nha Văn-Kho Quoc-Gia
8 Nguyen-Trung-Tru'c
Saigon, Republic of Vietnam

Chi-Nhánh Van-Kho Dalat (Regional Archives at Dalat)
24 Yersin
Dalat, Republic of Vietnam

Public and Church Records

Birth and marriage certificates can be obtained from the administrative office of the district where the event was registered.

Libraries

Bibliothèque Générale
Pétrus-Ky High School
Tran binh Trong Street
Saigon, Republic of Vietnam

Bibliothèque Nationale
34 Gia-Long Street
Saigon, Republic of Vietnam

Central Library of the Department of Information
Saigon, Republic of Vietnam

Institute of Historical Research Library
66-68 Le-Thanh-Tôn
Saigon, Republic of Vietnam

Municipal Library
Dalat, Republic of Vietnam

Books and Articles

Boudet, Paul, and Rémy Bourgeois.

Bibliographie de l'Indochine Française.
Hanoi, Extrême-Orient, 1929–67. 4 v. in 3.
NN BFV

Caruso, Bruno.
Vietnam.
Rome, 1972. 90 p. (Bibliography of history)
NN JFF 76-440

Taboulet, Georges.
Le Geste Française en Indochine.
Histoire par les Textes de la France en Indochine des Origines à 1914.
Paris, Adrien Maisoneuve, 1955–56. 2 v.
NN F-10 429

Thompson, Virginia M.
French Indo-China.
New York, Macmillan, 1937. 516 p.
NN *R-BFV

YEMEN, ARAB REPUBLIC OF (SANA)

Yemen was the site of the great kingdom of Sheba from 750 to 115 B.C. The Himyanite people came later and introduced Judaism and Christianity. In A.D. 525 Yemen was invaded by Christian Ethiopians, who were driven out by the Persians in 575. Islam was introduced in the seventh century. The Rassite dynasty took control and established a political structure based on the leadership of imams (religious leaders) during the ninth century. The Ottoman Empire assumed nominal control over Yemen from 1517–1918. In 1948 Imam Yahya was assassinated, and his son, Crown Prince Ahmad, succeeded. In 1962 civil war broke out between Royalists and Republicans and a pro-Nasser element in the army overthrew the imam and proclaimed a republic.

Archives

Dar-al-Kitab (Library)
Sana, Arab Republic of Yemen

Books and Articles

Beeston, Alfred F.L.
Qantan: Studies in Old South Arabian Epigraphy.
London, Luzac, 1976. 72 p.

City of San'a: Nomad and City Exhibition, ed. by James Kirkham.

London, World of Islam Festival Pub. Co., Ltd., 1976. 83 p.

Fayein, Claude.
Yemen.
Paris, 1975. 188 p.
NN JFC 76-225

Smith, Gerald R.
The Ayyubids and Early Rasulids in the Yemen 567–694, 1173–1295.
London, Luzac, 1974. v. 1–. 1 v. (589 p.)

YEMEN, PEOPLE'S DEMOCRATIC REPUBLIC OF (ADEN)

This country became independent as the Republic of Southern Yemen in 1967 after 129 years of British administration. The name was changed to the People's Democratic Republic of Yemen in 1970. In 1969 the left wing of the national liberation front seized control, and the new government broke off relations with the United States. The country includes the former colony of Aden.

Archives

Some records date from the pre-Islamic period.
Minister of Culture and Tourism
Tawah, Aden, People's Democratic Republic of Yemen

Books and Articles

Abū Makrama, 1465—1540.
Arabische Texte zur Kenntis der Stadt Aden im Mittelalter ...
Uppsala, 1936–50. 2 v.
(*Arbeten Utgivna med Understöd av Vilhelm Ekmans Universitetsfond*, Uppsala, no. 42, jafte 1–2)
NN *OFK

Jacob, Harold F.
Kings of Arabia: The Rise and Set of the Turkish Sovereignty in the Arabian Peninsula.
London, Mills & Boon, 1923. 294 p.
NN *OFK

Trevaskis, Gerald, and Nicholas Kennedy.
Shades of Amber: A South Arabian Episode.
London, Hutchinson, 1968. 256 p.
NN E-13 2426

GENERAL ASIAN SOURCES

Clyde, Paul H., and Burton F. Beers.

The Far East: A History of Western Impacts and Eastern Responses, 1830–75. 6th ed.
Englewood Cliffs, NJ, Prentice-Hall, 1975. 545 p., index.

Cressey, George B.
Asia's Lands and Peoples: A Geography of One-third of the Earth and Two-thirds of Its Peoples. 3rd ed.
New York, McGraw-Hill, 1963 (orig. 1944). 663 p.
NN *RR-BBF 75-2827

East Asian Genealogist.
Harbor City, CA, The Hartwell Company, 1977–. v. 1–.

The Far East and Australasia: A Survey and Directory of the Pacific. 7th ed.
London, Europa, 1975/76. 1,349 p., maps, index.
NN *R-Economics 72-1052

Hall, D.G.E.
A History of South East Asia. 3rd ed.
New York, St. Martin's Press, 1968. 1,019 p., index.
NN *R-BE 72-849

Palmer, Spencer P., ed.
Studies in Asian Genealogy.
Provo, UT, BYU Press, 1972. 281 p., index.
NN APB 73-1060

Vinacke, Harold Monck.
A History of the Far East in Modern Times.
London, 1971 (orig. 1959). 877 p.
NN *R-BE 76-396

Who's Who in the Far East. 1906/07.

Hong Kong, China Mail, 1906. 351 p. +.
NN AGA

ISLAM

Abdul-Rauf.
Marriage in Islam.
New York, 1972. 87 p.
NN *OGO- 73-175

Arabische Fuhrergestalten.
Heidelberg, K. von Winckel, 1944. 159 p.
NN *OFS

Aswad, Barbara C.
Arabic Speaking Communities in American Cities.
New York, Center for Migration Studies of New York, Inc., 1974. 191 p., t of c, no index.
NN IEE (Arabs) 75-212

Balyuzi, Hasan Muvaqqar.
Muhammad and the Course of Islam.
Oxford, Ronald, 1976. 457 p., index, gen. tables.
NN *OFI 77-1340

Blandford, Linda.
Oil Sheiks.
London, Weidenfeld and Nicolson, 1976. 286 p., index.
NN JLD 77-1827

Bosworth, Clifford E.
The Islamic Dynasties: A Chronological and Genealogical Handbook.
Edinburgh, U. of Edinburgh Press, 1967. 245 p.
(*Islamic Surveys no. 5*) NN *OFI

Bureau des Documentation Arabes.

Recueil des Archives Biogra-
phiques Permanentes du Monde
Arabe. 2nd ed.
Damascus, c. 1965. 2 v., loose-leaf
to receive additions.
NN G-10 977

The Cambridge History of Islam.
Cambridge, Cambridge U. Press,
1970. 2 v., indexed.
(v. 1, The Central and Islamic
Lands; v. 2, The Further Islamic Lands, Islamic Society
and Civilization)
NN *R-*OGC

Dennett, D.C.
Conversion and the Poll-tax in
Early Islam.
Cambridge, MA, Harvard U. Press,
1956.

Dozy, Reinhart P.A.
Spanish Islam: A History of the
Moslems and Spain.
London, Chatto and Windus, 1913.
769 p.
NN *OFN

Evans, Charles F.H.
Princess Zaida.
(IN: *TAG*, New Haven, CT, 1963.
v. 39, p. 157–60. Corrects an article by George Washington
that appeared in *TAG* New Haven, CT, 1962. v. 38, p. 245–48)
NN APGA

Glubb, Sir John.
The Empire of the Arabs (from
Muhammad 570–632 Who Con-
quered Mecca).
London, Hodder & Stoughton, 1963.
384 p., index, gen. tables.
NN *R-OFI

Hazen, William Edward.

Middle Eastern Sub Cultures: a Re-
gional Approach.
Lexington, MA, and London, D.C.
Health, 1975. 219 p., index.
NN JLE 76-1538

Iqbal, Muhammad.
Understanding Your Muslim
Neighbor.
Guilford, Lutterworth Press, 1976.
45 p.

Irving, Thomas B.
Falcon of Spain: A Study of Eighth
Century Spain with Special Em-
phasis on the Life of Umayyad
Ruler Abdurrahman I 756–788.
Lahore, 1962. 203 p.
NN D-14 7626

Kalbi, Hishau Ibn Muhammad al-
Gamharat an-Nasab.
Das Genealogische Werk des
Hisam ibn Muhammad al-Kalbi.
Leiden, Brill, 1966. 2 v.
NN *OFS+

Katibah, Habib I.
Arabic-Speaking Americans.
New York, 1946. 29 p.
(Institute of Arab American Af-
fairs, New York, pamphlet no. 2)
NN *PWC

Lewis, Bernard, ed.
Islam and the Arab World: Faith,
People, Culture.
New York, American Heritage,
1976. 360 p., index.

Mattar, Ahmad.
Guía Social de la Communidades da
Habla Arabe
(Libanesas, Sirias, Palestinas) en
Antigua, Cuba, Costa Rica.
New York, 1947. 167 p.
NN HAE p. v. 318

Mayer, Leo A.
New Material for Mamjuk Her-
aldry.
Jerusalem, Syrian Orphanage
Press, 1937. 11 p.
NN *OAC p. v. 197

Mayer, Leo A.
Saracenic Heraldry: A Survey.
Oxford, Clarendon Press, 1933. 302
p.
NN *OFG+

The Middle East and North Africa.
London, Europe, 1975–76. 22nd ed.
930 p.

New York Public Library. Refer-
ence Department.
Oriental Division Collection Dic-
tionary Catalog.
Boston, MA, G.K. Hall, 1960. 18 v.
NN Ref. Cat. 1960

Schuon, Frithjof.
Islam and the Perennial Philoso-
phy, trans. from French by J.
Peter Hobson.
London, The World of Islam Festival Pub. Co. Ltd., 1976. 217 p.,
index.

Shaban, M.A.
Islamic History: A New Interpre-
tation.
Cambridge, Cambridge U. Press,
1971–76. 2 v., index.
NN *OFL

Sheean, Vincent.
Faisal, the King and His Kingdom.
Tavistock, U. Press of Arabia,
1975. 162 p., index.
NN JFD 76-3133

Stokvis, A.M.H.J.
Manuel d'Histoire, de Généalogie
et de Chronologie de Tous les
États du Globe ...

Amsterdam (?), B.M. Israel, 1966
(orig. 1888–93).
Chapt. III–VII, p. 42–106.
NN ATC

Trimingham, John S.
Islam in East Africa.
Oxford, Clarendon Press, 1964. 198
p.
NN *OGC

Trimingham, John S.
Islam in Ethiopia.
Oxford, Oxford U. Press, 1952. 299
p.
NN *OGC

Trimingham, John S.
Islam in the Sudan.
London, Oxford U. Press, 1949. 280
p.
NN *OGC

Trimingham, John S.
Islam in West Africa.
Oxford, Clarendon Press, 1959. 262
p.
NN *OGC

Turton, William Henry.
The Plantagenet Ancestry.
Baltimore, MD, GPC, 1968 (orig.
1928) p. 271.
(Ibn Nuseir Musa, b. Mecca 660,
d. Mecca 718. Conq. Spain 712,
ancestor of King Edward IV of
England)
NN ARF+

Walker, Rodney C.
Dynasties of Al-Islam.
(IN: *The Augustan*, Torrance, CA,
1967. v. 10, no. 5, p. 204–)
NN APA

Who's Who in the Arab World.
Beirut, Publitec Editions,
1965–1971. 3 v.
NN F-10 7127

AUSTRALIA (CANBERRA)

The island continent of Australia was settled by primitive native tribes before it was visited by white explorers. It was first sighted by the Portuguese in 1601, and a century later the Dutch passed by and dubbed it "Little Holland." In 1770 Captain James Cook explored the east coast and claimed it for Britain. The first British settlement, in 1788, was a penal colony. By 1829 the entire continent was a British dependency. From 1851 to 1859 a gold strike in Victoria attracted thousands of new settlers. Six self-governing colonies were established. When they were federated in 1901 by a constitution approved by the British, the Commonwealth of Australia was born. Under a government immigration program established in 1946, new settlers, predominantly from Britain, Italy, Greece and the Netherlands, poured into the country; they totaled two million by 1965.

A census is conducted every five years. Censuses of Tasmania, an Australian state, were conducted in 1891 and 1901.

The most common surnames in Melbourne and Sydney are Brown, Jones, Smith, Williams and Wilson.

Archives

National Archives
71 Leichhardt Street, Kingston
Australian Capital Territory 2604,
   Australia

State Library, Archives Branch
3 Francis Street
6000 Perth, West Australia

State Library, Archives Department
North Terrace
5001 Adelaide, South Australia

Archives Office
Wynnum Road. Cannon Hill
4000 Brisbane, Queensland

State Library, Archives Department
91 Murray Street
7000 Hobart, Tasmania

State Library, Archives Division
304-324 Swanston Street
3000 Melbourne, Victoria

State Library Archives Department

Macquarie Street
2000 Sydney, New South Wales, Australia

Public and Church Records

New South Wales
Registers in the custody of the District Registrar date back to March 1, 1856, or the subsequent date of opening of the office. Copies are also held in the General Registry, Sydney. Copies of church registers of baptisms, burials and marriages prior to 1856 are also kept.

The Registrar-General
Prince Albert Road
2000 Sydney, New South Wales, Australia

Queensland
Official records of births, deaths and marriages date from 1856. There are also some records of baptisms and burials that date from 1829 and marriages from 1839. The Registrar-General's Office at Brisbane receives copies of the quarterly registers of births, marriages and deaths from the district registrars.

The Registrar-General
Treasury Building
4000 Brisbane, B7, Queensland, Australia

South Australia
Records date back to 1842.

The Principal Registrar
Box 1351 H. GPO
5001 Adelaide, South Australia

Tasmania
Civil records in the Registrar-General's keeping date back to 1838. Church records of baptisms, burials and marriages going back to 1803 are in the same office.

The Registrar-General
Box 875, GPO J
7001 Hobart, Tasmania, Australia

Victoria
Civil records date back to 1853. Extant church records of baptisms, burials and marriages back to 1837 are also with the Government Statist but are incomplete.

Government Statist
295 Queen Street
3000 Melbourne, Victoria, Australia

Western Australia
Civil records date from July 25, 1841; some are earlier.

On arrival at any port in Western Australia, all masters or commanders of British or colonial vessels are required to furnish particulars of every birth or death that has occurred on board to the District Registrar.

The Registrar-General
Oakleigh Bldg.
22 St. George's Terrace
6000 Perth, Western Australia

Northern Territory
Civil registration began in 1874. There are some birth records from 1870 and some death and marriage records from 1872.

For records since 1912:
Registrar-General of Births, Deaths and Marriages
P.O. Box 367
5794 Darwin, Northern Territory, Australia

For records prior to 1912:
Registrar-General of Births, Deaths and Marriages
Adelaide, South Australia

Australian Capital Territory (Canberra)

Records before January 1, 1930, within the boundaries of what is now the Australian Capital Territory, are held by the Registrar-General. Prior to 1930 registration was in Queanbeyan, New South Wales.

The Registrar-General
P.O. Box 1515
Canberra City, Australian Capital Territory 2600, Australia

Norfolk Island (Territory under Commonwealth Administration)

Records kept by the Registrar of Births, Marriages and Deaths are extracts from church registers at Pitcairn Island and Norfolk Island containing particulars of births, marriages and deaths from 1790 to 1881 and official civil registers of births, deaths and marriages from 1882.

Libraries

Mitchell Library and the Public Library of New South Wales
Macquarie St.
Sydney, N.S.W., Australia

Oxley Memorial Library
William Street
Brisbane, Queensland, Australia

Church of Jesus Christ of Latter-day Saints
Sydney, Australia, Branch Genealogical Library
55 Greenwich Road, Greenwich
Sydney, Australia

Australian National University Library
Canberra, Australian Capital Territory, Australia

National Library of Australia
Canberra, Australian Capital Territory

Central Catholic Library
343 Elizabeth Street
Melbourne, Victoria, Australia

State Library of Victoria
Swanston Street
Melbourne, C.1, Victoria

Library of the University of Western Australia
Perth, Western Australia

Public Library of South Australia
North Terrace
Adelaide, South Australia

State Library of Tasmania
Murray Street
Hobart, Tasmania, Australia

Historical and Genealogical Societies

Historical Division, Royal Geographical Society of Australasia
(S. Australia Branch)

Institute Building, North Terrace
Adelaide, Australia
(*Proceedings*)

Royal Australian Historical Society
History House
8 Young Street
Sydney, New South Wales, Australia
(*Journal*)

Royal Historical Society of Victoria
19 Queen Street
Melbourne 3000, Australia
(*Victorian Historical Magazine; Newsletter*)

Royal Western Australian Historical Society
49 Broadway
Nedlands, Western Australia

Society of Australian Genealogists, Inc.
History House, 8 Young Street
Sydney, New South Wales, Australia

Society of Australian Genealogists
413 Riley Street
Surry Hills, New South Wales 2010
(*Australian Genealogists' Newsletter*; and *Descent*)

The Genealogical Society of Victoria
77 Alma Street
Chadstone
3148 Victoria, Australia
(*Ancestor*)

Genealogical Society of Victoria, Inc.
Room 3, 3rd floor
The Block Building, Collins Street
3000 Melbourne, Australia

The Heraldry and Genealogy Society of Canberra
P.O. Box 1194
2601 Canberra, Australia

Port Phillip Pioneers Group (1834–51)
% Mrs. F. Dubbyn
11 Patterson St.
Nunawading, Victoria, Australia 3131
(Membership requirements—an ancestor who arrived prior to July 1, 1851)

The South Australian Genealogy and Heraldry Society, Inc.
G.P.O. Box 1100
5001 Adelaide, South Australia
(*The South Australian Genealogist*, 1973–)
NN APW

Books and Articles

An Alphabetical List of Passengers Arriving at Port Adelaide from South Australia Coastal and Intercolonial Ports between 1837–1845.
(IN: *South Australian Genealogist*, Adelaide, Marden, 1973–76. v. 1, no. 1, p. 5–8; v. 3, p. 58–65, etc.)
(A-Lefroy)
NN APW

Ancestor.
Melbourne, Genealogical Society of Victoria, 1961–.
% Hon. Sec. Miss M.E. Runting, 77 Alma St., Chadstone 3148, Victoria
NN APW

The Australian Genealogist.
Sydney, 1933–59. 9 v. in 7 v.
(Superseded by *Descent*)
NN APW

Australian Genealogists Newsletter.
Surry Hills, 1974–.
(See *Descent*)

Australians in America, 1876–1976, ed. by John Hammond Moore.
St. Lucia, U. of Queensland Press, 1977. 1 v.

Ballarat Historical Society.
Roll Book Ballarat Pioneers.
Ballarat, Victoria, BHS, 1974. 68 leaves.

Billis, R.V., and A.S. Kenyon.
Pastoral Pioneers of Port Phillip. 2nd ed.
Melbourne, Stockland Press, 1974. 318 p., alpha, no index.
NN AVH (Australia) 76-1109

Blainey, Geoffrey.
Triumph of the Nomads: A History of Ancient Australia.
London, Macmillan, 1976. 285 p., index (Australia to 1788)
NN JFD 76-5816

Blaze, B.R., and Muriel E. Runting.
Ancestors for Australians: A Guidebook for Beginners Which Points the Way to Wider Horizons of Genealogy, ed. by B.R. Blaze, comp. by Muriel E. Runting. Melbourne, Genealogical Society of Victoria, 1974. 100 p.

Cole, William A., and Elwin W. Jensen.
Israel in the Pacific: A Genealogical Text for Polynesia.
Salt Lake City, UT, the Genealogical Society, 1961. 458 p., index.

(Central Polynesia, Hawaii, New Zealand, Australia)
NN APB

Dalkin, R. Nixon.
Colonial Era Cemetery of Norfolk Island.
Sydney, Pacific Pub., 1974. 91 p.
NN AVH (Australia) 76-912

Descent.
Surry Hills, New South Wales, Society of Australian Genealogists, 1968–.
NN APW

The Genealogist.
Hampton, Australian Institute of Genealogical Studies, 1974–.
P.O. Box 89, Hampton, Victoria 3188.

Hall, N.J. Vine.
Gore Hill Cemetery (Sydney), N.S.W. (Dedicated 1868)
(IN: *Descent*, Surry Hills, 1976. v. 7, p. 143–49, etc.)
(Sections devoted to different denominations)
NN APW 73-834

Hansen, Neil T.
Guide to Genealogical Sources Australia and New Zealand.
Melbourne, 1961.

Henderson, Alexander.
Early Pioneer Families of Victoria and Riverina: A Genealogical and Biographical Record.
Melbourne, McCarron, Bird, 1936. 583 p., index, ports.
NN APW

Henderson, Alexander.
Henderson's Australian Families: A Genealogical and Biographical Record.

Melbourne, A. Henderson, 1941. 408 p., index, ports.
NN APW

Ireland, Kingsley J.
Registration of Births, Deaths and Marriages in South Australia, July 1842 to date.
(IN: *SAG*, Marden, 1975. v. 2, no. 2, p. 42–48)
NN APW

John's Notable Australians and Who's Who in Australia.
Adelaide, Fred Johns, 1908. 370 p., alpha.
NN AGH

Johnson, Keith A.
Some Irish Inscriptions in Old Burial Grounds of New South Wales, Australia.
(IN: *Irish Ancestor*, Dundalk, Ireland, 1971. v. 3, p. 5–10; v. 5, p. 76–83)
NN ARCA 72-1448

Kiernan, Thomas Joseph.
Transportation from Ireland to Sydney: 1791–1816.
Canberra, 1954. 184 p.
NN BHM

Lea-Scarlett, Errol J.
Ourselves and Britain: A Record of the Society's Activities in England and Scotland to 1939.
(IN: *Descent*, Surry Hills, 1976. v. 7, p. 115–42)
(The story of the Society of Australian Genealogists)
NN APW 73-834

Lea-Scarlett, Errol J.
St. Thomas's Church of England, North Sydney—Monumental Inscriptions in the Cemetery.
Sydney, 1963. 909 entries, indexed.
NN APW plus 72-2464

Le Pelley, Jean.
Guernsey Pioneers in Australia 1841–1862.
(IN: *Société Guernsey, Report*, 1966. St. Peterport, 1967. v. 18, p. 64–86)
NN CO (Guernsey)

Levi, John Simon.
The Forefathers: A Dictionary of Biography of the Jews of Australia 1788–1830.
Sydney, Australian Jewish Hist. Soc., 1976. [6], 139 p.

List of Cemeteries Transcribed in South Australia.
(IN: *SAG*, Marden, 1976. v. 3, no. 3, p. 69–74)
NN APW

Lord, Richard.
Inscriptions in Stone: St. David's Burial Ground, 1804–1872: A Record of Some Early History of Hobart Town from the Head Stones of Van Diemen's Land's First Cemetery.
Battery Point, St. George's Church, 1976. 210 p.

Major Genealogical Sources in Australia.
Salt Lake City, UT, LDS, Nov. 15, 1968. Series E, no. 2.
NN APA 72-755

McLean, Donald.
Hard Times and Rough Justice.
Sydney, Angus & Robertson, 1975. 1 v. (New South Wales 1788–1801)
(The Story of Australia, book 3)

Men of the Time in Australia.
Victorian Series 1878.
Melbourne, 1878. 274 p. (Only v. in this series)

Mowle, Perseval C.
A Genealogical History of Pioneer
Families of Australia. 4th ed.
Sydney, J. Sands, 1942. 190 p.
NN APW

Potts, Eli David, and Annette
Potts.
Young American and Australian
Gold: Americans and the Gold-
rush of the 1850's.
St. Lucia, Queensland, U. of
Queensland Press, 1974. 1 v., in-
dex.
NN JFO 75-9762

Puttock, Arthur Geoffrey.
Trace Your Family Tree.
Adelaide, Rigby, 1974. 64 p.
(Rigby Instant Book)

Quaife, Geoffrey, ed.
Gold and the Colonial Society, 1851–
1870.
Stanhope, New South Wales, Cas-
sell Australia, 1975. 1 v.
(Problems in Australian History)

Rydon, Joan.
A Biographical Register of the
Commonwealth Parliament,
1901–1972.
Canberra, Aus. Nat. U. Press,
1975. 1 v.
(Australian Parl. Bio. Notes no. 5)

The South Australian Genealogist.
Marden, South Australia, 1974–.
(*SAG* is abbreviation)
The South Aust. Gen. and Heraldry
Soc., P.O. Box 13, Marden, S.A.
5070
NN APW

Sydney *Morning Herald.*
Births, Marriages, Deaths, and
Funeral Newspaper Notices.

Sydney, 1972–75. v. 1–4 (1831–53),
index.
NN APW + 75-343

Tindale, Norman B.
Aboriginal Tribes of Australia,
Their Terrain, Environmental
Controls, Distribution Limits
and Proper Names ... with an
Appendix on Tasmanian Tribes
by Rhys Jones.
Berkeley, CA, U. of California,
1974. 404 p., index.

Who's Who in Australia.
Melbourne, *Herald & Weekly
Times*, 1922–74 plus, 21 v. plus.
NN *RR-AGH and AGH

Wills Among Land Records.
(IN: *SAG*, Adelaide, 1974. v. 1, no.
1, p. 9–12, A–W complete; v. 2,
no. 2, p. 4–6, A–W complete)
NN APW

Norfolk Island
Clune, Frank.
The Norfolk Island Story.
Sydney, Angus and Robertson,
1967. 308 p., no index.
NN E-13 798

Dillon, Claude.
Norfolk Island Data 1788 to 1957.
Mosman, New South Wales, the au-
thor, 1957. 33 leaves.
NN F-10 7865

Shapiro, Harry Lionel.
Descendants of the Mutineers of
the Bounty.
Honolulu, 1929. 106 p.
(Memoirs of the Bernice P. Bishop
Museum, v. 11, no. 1)
NN QPH +

Tasmania

Bonwick, James.
The Lost Tasmanian Race.
New York, Johnson Reprint, 1970
   (orig. 1884). 216 p.
NN D-20 5016

Giblin, Ronald W.
The Early History of Tasmania.

London, Methuen, 1928–39. 2 v.
NN BHW

Tasmania, Western Australia,
   Fiji, Samoa, Tonga, Hawaiian
   Islands Directory.
1898.
NN BAZ (Tasmania)

FIJI (SUVA)

Fiji is composed of 840 islands (106 inhabited) located in the South Pacific. The largest island is Viti Levu, where the capital city of Suva is located. Fiji became a British colony in 1874 and a fully independent member of the Commonwealth in 1970. The population is comprised of native Fijians (Polynesians and Melanesians), descendants of Indian contract workers (over half the population) and a minority of people of Chinese and European descent.

Censuses were recorded in 1921, 1936 and 1956.

Archives

National Archives of Fiji
Government House Grounds
Government Buildings (P.O. Box
   2125)
Suva, Fiji

Library Service of Fiji, Western
   Regional Library
Lautoka, Viti Levu, Fiji

Ramkrishna Library
Nandi, Fiji

Public and Church Records

Records kept by the Registrar-General, Suva, go back to January 1, 1875. The Registrar-General also has consular records of marriages 1861–1874, births 1870–74 and deaths 1870–72.

Historical and Genealogical Societies

The Fiji Society
Suva, Fiji
(*Transactions*)

Books and Articles

Brewster, Adolph B.
King of the Cannibal Isles ...
London, R. Hale, 1937. 286 p.
NN BIR

Libraries

Carnegie Library
Suva, Fiji

Burns, Sir Alan C.
Fiji.
London, HMSO, 1963. 355 p.
NN D-14 4720

Cyclopedia of Fiji.
Sydney, 1907. 4 parts in 1 v.
(Samoa, Tonga, Tahiti, Cook Islands included)
NN BIR

De Ricci, James H.
Fiji: Our New Province in the South Seas.
London, E. Stanford, 1875. 334 p.
NN BIR

Derrick, R.A.
The Fiji Islands: A Genealogical Handbook. revised ed.
Suva, 1957. 334 p.
NN F-10 4138

Nayacakalou, R. R.
The Fijian System of Kinship and Marriage.
(IN: *Polynesian Society Journal*, Wellington, 1955. v. 64, p. 44–55, gen. table)
NN BH

Sahlins, Marshall D.
Moala: Culture and Nature of a Fijian Island.
Ann Arbor, MI, U. of Michigan Press, 1962. 453 p., gen. tables.
NN E-11 5046

Snow, Philip.
A Bibliography of Fiji, Tonga and Rotunda.
Canberra, Aust. Nat. Lib. U. Press, 1969. 418 p.
NN E-14 699 & JFF 70-53

Turpin's Fijian Almanac and Directory.
Levuka, Ovalu, Fiji, 1873–. 1 v.
NN *DW

GUAM (AGANA)

The largest and southernmost of the Mariana Islands, Guam is an unincorporated territory of the United States. Chamorros, a mixture of Spanish, Filipino and Micronesian descent, are the chief inhabitants, while United States military personnel and their dependents comprise a quarter of the population.

Ferdinand Magellan discovered the island in 1521. It belonged to Spain until 1898, when it was taken by the United States in the Spanish-American War. The island was captured by Japan in 1941 and retaken by the United States in 1944. The residents are United States citizens but cannot vote in United States elections.

Public and Church Records

Records of births and deaths are on file since October 26, 1901.

Office of Vital Statistics
Department of Public Health and Social Services

Government of Guam
P.O. Box 2816
Agaña, Guam, M.I. 96910

Books and Articles

Blakeslee, George H.
Japan's New Island Possession in
the Pacific: History and Present
Condition.
(IN: *Journal of International Re-
lations*, Baltimore, MD, 1921 v.
12, p. 173–91)
NN BAA

Bryan, E.H., Jr.
Guam and the Chamorros.
(IN: *Americana*, Somerville, NJ,
1939. v. 33, p. 15–22)
NN IAA

Caldwell, John Cope.
Let's Visit Micronesia: Guam
(USA) and Trust Territories of
the Pacific Islands.
New York, John Day, 1969. 95 p.
NN D-19 4613

MARIANA ISLANDS

The Marianas were discovered by Magellan, who named them
the Thieves Islands, in 1521. Spanish Jesuits in 1668 renamed
them Marianas. They were possessed by Spain until 1898, then
sold to Germany, except for Guam, which was ceded to the United
States. In 1914 Japan seized the German-held islands, and they
were mandated to Japan by the League of Nations in 1920.
United States forces occupied the islands in 1944. Since 1947 they
have been part of the Trust Territory of the Pacific Islands
assigned to United States administration by the United Nations.
The U.S. Senate voted in 1976 to grant Commonwealth status to
the Northern Marianas (all the Marianas except Guam), leading
toward the first United States territorial expansion since 1924.
The House of Representatives approved a covenant to establish
a political union with the Marianas, thereby making the Marianas' 14,500 inhabitants American citizens.

Public and Church Records

Births, marriages and deaths since
November 21, 1952: Clerk of
Court of District where the
event occurred, or Director of
Medical Services, Department
of Medical Services, Saipan, Mariana Islands 96950 to have the
inquiry forwarded to the correct
address.

Books and Articles

Ibanez y Garcia, Luis de.
Historia de las Marianas ... y las
Carolinas y Palaos, desde el Des-
cubrimientos.
NN BIH

Munoz, Barreda V.
La Micronesia Española o los Ar-

chipiélagos de Marianas, Palaos
y Carolinas, 2nd ed.

Manila, 1894. 295 p.
NN BIH

NAURU (Yaren)

An American whaling team discovered the island of Nauru in 1798 and called it Pleasant Island. In 1888 it was annexed by Germany and the native name of Nauru was adopted. In the 1890's phosphate, a substance that continues to provide the island's sole economic support, was discovered. During the First World War, the island was occupied by Australian forces and was administered by Australia under a League of Nations mandate following the war. In the Second World War, Nauru was taken by the Japanese and 1,200 islanders were deported as forced labor. In 1947 Nauru was placed under United Nations trusteeship, and the island was administered by Australia. In 1964 Australia proposed that the inhabitants be resettled on Curtis Island, off the Queensland coast, because of the expected exhaustion of the phosphate deposits, but the islanders rejected the proposal. In 1968 Nauru became an independent republic.

Public and Church Records

Records of birth date from January 25, 1915; of death, from January 2, 1915; and of marriage, from July 7, 1921.

Clerk of the District Court
Yaren, Nauru

Books and Articles

Krauss, Noel L.H.

Bibliography of Nauru, Western Pacific.
Honolulu, 1970. 14 p.
NN D-20 5356

Vivani, Nancy.
Nauru: Phosphate and Political Progress.
Honolulu, HI, U. of Hawaii Press, 1970. 215 p.
NN D-20 2224

NEW CALEDONIA (NOUMEA)

The islands grouped under this name are New Caledonia, Isle of Pines, the Loyalty Islands, Walpole Islands and the Huon, Chesterfield and Belep groups. As a French Overseas Territory, they are ruled by a governor appointed by France and an elected territorial body. The inhabitants are Melanesians, with Polynesians in the outlying islands. In 1774 Captain James Cook sighted and named the main island. France annexed the islands in 1853. Censuses were recorded in 1963 and 1969.

Public and Church Records

Birth certificates can be obtained from the City Hall at the person's birthplace or from the Court Clerk in Noumea, New Caledonia. Marriage certificates can be obtained from the City Hall of the city or town in which the persons were married.

Libraries

Bibliothèque Bernheim
B.P. 7, Noumea, New Caledonia

Library, South Pacific Commission H.Q.
B.P. 9, Noumea, New Caledonia

Books and Articles

Saunier, Gabriel
La Réalité sur le Bagne.
Paris, 1971. 125 p.
NN JLC 73-1052

Thompson, Virginia, Mc L.
The French Pacific Islands.
Berkeley, CA, 1971. 539 p.
NN JFE 73-1776

NEW ZEALAND (WELLINGTON)

New Zealand, comprised of North Island and South Island, was discovered for Europeans by a Dutch explorer in 1642, but hostile Maori natives prevented him from landing. In 1769 Captain James Cook of Britain visited the islands, and the first missionary arrived in 1814. The islands were made a dependency of New South Wales in 1840, and New Zealand became a separate British colony the following year. The Treaty of Waitangi guaranteed the Maori natives possession of their lands in exchange for British sovereignty. The British New Zealand Company began to organize settlement in the islands from 1845 to 1848. The Maoris rebelled against British rule during those years but were put down by British military force. After the discovery of gold in 1861, immigrants began to pour into the country. In 1907 New Zealand attained Dominion status.

National census records were destroyed by law until 1975, the date of the first surviving census. Enumerations are made every five years.

Archives

National Archives
Borthwick House
85 The Terrace
Wellington 1, New Zealand

Public and Church Records

Copies of registers of births, deaths
and marriages held by the Registrar-General go back to January 1848, and some incomplete
entries of births and marriages
go back to 1840.

Maori births and deaths are registered under the Maori Births
and Deaths Registration Regu-
lations, 1935. Registration of
Maori marriages is not compulsory.

The Registrar-General
P.O. Box 5023
Lambton Quay
Wellington 1, New Zealand

Records of births, marriages and
deaths before 1848 are kept by
the churches. Some Methodist
records are at the Connexional
Office (Christchurch, New Zealand).

Libraries

Alexander Turnbull Library (National Library)
44-46 The Terrace
Wellington, New Zealand

National Library of New Zealand
Private Bag
Wellington, New Zealand

Hocken Library, University of
Otago
Otago Museum, Great King Street
(P.O. Box 56)
Dunedin, New Zealand

New Plymouth Public Library
Brougham Street (P.O. Box 48)
New Plymouth, New Zealand

Church of Jesus Christ of Latter-
day Saints
Temple View, New Zealand,
Branch Genealogical Library
Temple View, New Zealand

Auckland Public Library
Wellesley Street
Auckland, C.1, New Zealand

Dunedin Public Library
P.O.B. 906
Dunedin, C.1, New Zealand

Victoria University Library
P.O.B. 196
Wellington, New Zealand

Historical and Genealogical Societies

New Zealand Society of Genealo-
gists, Inc.
P.O. Box 8795
Auckland, New Zealand
(*New Zealand Genealogist*)

Marlborough Historical Society,
Inc.
Box 308
Blenheim, New Zealand

Books and Articles

Acland, L. G. D.
The Early Canterbury Runs and
Glossary of Station Words.

Christchurch, New Zealand, Whitcombe & Tombs, 1951. 427 p., index.
NN APW

Encyclopedia of New Zealand.
Wellington, R.E. Owen, 1966. 3 v.
NN *R-BAX 75-8116

Major Genealogical Sources in New Zealand.
Salt Lake City, UT, LDS 1, Nov. 1967. Series E. no. 1.
NN APA 72-755

Metge, Joan.
The Maoris of New Zealand: Rautahi. rev. ed.
London, Routledge and Kegan Paul, 1976 (orig. 1967).
382, 16 p.
NN JFD 77-1241

The New Zealand Army: A Bibliography.
Corwallville, NY, Hope Farm Press, 1961. 116 p.
NN D-13 708

The New Zealand Genealogist.
Auckland, New Zealand, 1970–.
The New Zealand Society of Genealogists, P.O. Box 8795, Auckland.
NN APW

New Zealand Society of Genealogists.
Surname Index to Record of Ancestry Sheets.
Auckland, 1973–.
(Annual)
NN APW

Passenger List of *Westminster, 1842.*
(IN: *New Zealand Genealogist,* Auckland, 1974. v. 5, no. 41, p. 4–7)
NN APW

Patea Historical Society Journal.
Patea, 1974–.
% Secretary, Patea Historical Society, 34 Norfolk St., Patea.

Robertson, J. B. W.
The Tangata Whenua.
(IN: *Tauranga Historical Society Journal,* Tauranga South, New Zealand, 1976. no. 56, p. 16–18)
NN *XL-410

Salmond, Anne.
Hui: A Study of Maori Ceremonial Gatherings.
Wellington, London, A. H. and A. W. Reed, 1975. 226 p., index.
NN JFE 76-451

Steedman, J. W.
The Fleet Question.
(IN: *Tauranga Historical Society Journal,* Tauranga South, 1976. no. 56; p. 18–22, gen. table p.21)
NN *XL-410

Tauranga Historical Society.
Journal.
Tauranga Historical Society, P.O. Box 2080, Tauranga South, N.Z.
NN *XL-410

Who's Who in New Zealand and the Western Pacific.
Masterton, 1908–51 plus.
NN AGH

PAPUA NEW GUINEA (PORT MORESBY)

Papua New Guinea occupies the eastern half of the island of New Guinea. The area formerly known as the Territory of New

Guinea comprises the southeastern quarter of the island plus a variety of small island groups. The former Territory of New Guinea is composed of the northeastern quarter of the island, plus the northern Solomon Islands and the Bismarck Archipelago. The administrative union of the two Australian-administered territories was promulgated in 1949, although they retained separate identities and status. The name of the territory was changed, officially condensed from Papua and New Guinea to Papua New Guinea in 1971 to encourage unity as independence approached. Self-government was granted in 1973 and full independence in 1975.

Public and Church Records

Records for the former territory of Papua date from September 4, 1888. All records for New Guinea before 1945 were lost or destroyed during the Japanese occupation, although re-registration was made when possible.

Books and Articles

Biskup, Peter, et al.
A Short History of New Guinea.
Sydney, Angus & Robertson, 1968. 174 p.
NN D-19 4105

Encyclopedia of Papua and New Guinea.
Melbourne, U. Press, 1972. 2 v., alpha.
NN *R-BFR 73-1562

Ruhen, Olaf.
Mountains in the Clouds.
Adelaide, Rigby, 1963. 239 p.
NN D-16 1891

White, Osmar.
Parliament of a Thousand Tribes: A Study of New Guinea.
London, Heinemann, 1965. 256 p.
NN D-16 9578

Bismarck Archipeligo

Pullem-Burry, Bessie.
In a German Colony.
London, Methuen, 1909. 238 p.
NN BFR

PITCAIRN ISLAND

This island, a British possession since 1839, is officially administered by the British High Commissioner to New Zealand, with local matters handled by a council of islanders. It was discovered in 1767 by Philip Carteret, a British admiral, and named after Robert Pitcairn, the midshipman who first sighted it. In 1790 it was colonized by mutineers from the *Bounty* and Tahitian women.

Their descendants, who speak English, are still there, and all are descended from Fletcher Christian, leader of the mutineers, who, himself, was a descendant of King Edward I. In 1856 overpopulation caused removal to Norfolk Island, at the request of the inhabitants, but some soon returned to Pitcairn. The remains of the *Bounty* were found off the southern end of the island in 1957.

Books and Articles

Barrow, Sir John.
... A Description of Pitcairn Island and Its Inhabitants.
New York, J.J. Harper, 1832. 303 p.
NN BH

Belcher, Diana T.
The Mutineers of the Bounty and Their Descendants in Pitcairn and Norfolk Islands.
New York, Harper, 1871. 377 p.
NN BH

Chauvel, Charles.
In the Wake of "The Bounty" ...
Sydney, Endeavour Press, 1938. 157 p.
NN BH

Christian, formerly of Milntown and Ewanrigg.
(IN: *Burke's Landed Gentry*, 18th ed., London, 1969. v. 2, p. 96–101)
NN ARF 73-1915

Hudleston of Hutton John.
(IN: *Burke's Landed Gentry*, 18th ed., London, 1969. v. 2, p. 326–329)
NN ARF 73-1915

Nicolson, Robert B.
The Pitcairners.
Sydney, Angus and Robertson, 1965. 222 p.
Appendix I, Genealogies; II, Census of Pitcairners at Tahiti, 1831.
(This is the best book for genealogical purposes.)
NN E-12 6050

The Pitcairn Island Register Book, ed. by Sir Charles Lucas.
London, Macmillan, 1929. 181 p.
NN BH

Silverman, David.
Pitcairn Island.
Cleveland, OH, World, 1967. 258 p.
NN E-12 9047

SAMOA

American Samoa, an unincorporated United States territory consisting of six small islands of the Samoan group, became a United States territory by treaty with the United Kingdom and Germany in 1899, confirmed by local chiefs in 1900 and 1904. Previously it had been a United States coaling station under an 1872 commercial treaty. American Samoans of Polynesian origin are U.S. nationals.

Western Samoa, comprising the larger islands of the Samoan group, was a German colony from 1899 to 1914, when New Zealand took over. It became a New Zealand mandate under the League of Nations and, in 1945, a United Nations Trusteeship. The country became independent on January 1, 1962. Censuses of Western Samoa were recorded in 1951, 1956, 1961, and 1966.

American Samoa (*Pago Pago on Tutuila*)

Public and Church Records

Records of births and deaths are on file since before 1900.

Office of the Territorial Registrar
Government of American Samoa
Pago Pago, American Samoa 96799

Western Samoa (*Apia*)

Libraries

Nelson Memorial Public Library
Apia, Western Samoa

Books and Articles

Churchward, William B.
My Consulate in Samoa: A Record of Four Years' Sojourn in the Navigators Islands, with Personal Experiences of King Malietoa Laupepa, His Country and His Men.
London, R. Bentley, 1887. 403 p.
NN BIF

Davidson, James W.
Samoa mo Samoa: The Emergence of the Independent State of Western Samoa.
Melbourne, Oxford U. Press, 1967. 467 p.
NN D-18 2388

McKay, C.G.R.
Samoana: a Personal Story of the Samoan Islands.
Wellington, A.H. and A.W. Reed, 1968. 177 p.
NN E-13 5736

Major Genealogical Sources in Samoa.
Salt Lake City, UT, LDS, series E, no. 3.
NN APA 72-755

Marsack, C.G.
Samoan Medley.
London, R. Hale, 1961. 192 p.
NN D-13 3666

Rose, Ronald.
South Seas Magic.
London, Hale, 1959. 192 p.
NN D-12 1060

Rowe, Newton A.
... Samoa under Sailing Gods.
London, Putnam, 1930. 339 p.
NN BIF

SOLOMON ISLANDS (HONIARA ON GAUDALCANAL)

First visited by a Spanish explorer in 1568, the islands were settled by Europeans in the eighteenth and nineteenth centuries. In 1885 the German New Guinea Company established control over the Northern Solomons. A British protectorate was placed over the southern islands in 1893 and over the eastern islands in 1898. In 1900 Germany withdrew from all the islands except Bougainville and Buka, in return for British withdrawal from Western Samoa. Bougainville and Buka were occupied by Australian forces during World War I and were placed under Australian mandate in 1920. During World War II Japan occupied Choiseul, New Georgia, Ysabel and Guadalcanal. The islands were liberated by the United States (1943–44). Today, Bougainville and Buka belong to Papua New Guinea. In the British Solomon Islands Protectorate are Guadalcanal, Malaita, New Georgia, Santa Cruz Islands, Choiseul, Ysabel (Santa Isabel), San Cristobal and the Shortland Islands. Melanesians are the chief inhabitants, with some Polynesians in the outlying atolls.

Public and Church Records

Civil registration began in 1893; records are kept by the Registrar of Births, Deaths and Marriages at Suva, Fiji.

Books and Articles

Fox, C.E.
Social Organization in San Cristobal, Solomon Islands.
(IN: *Royal Anthropological Institute ... Journal*, London, 1919.
v. 49, p. 94–179)
NN QOA

Graves, Robert.
The Islands of Unwisdom.
Garden City, New York, Doubleday, 1949. 328 p.
NN NCW

Hocart, A.M.
Medicine and Witchcraft in Eddystone of the Solomon Islands.
(IN: *Royal Anthropological Institute ... Journal*, London, 1925.
v. 55, p. 229–70)
NN QOA

TAHITI (PAPEETE)

Tahiti, formerly called Otaheite and King George III Island, is in the Windward group of the Society Islands, French Polynesia. Most of the inhabitants are Polynesian, but there is a large Chinese minority. Settled by Polynesians in the fourteenth century, the island was visited by Captain Cook in 1769 and 1777 and by the *Bounty*, under Captain William Bligh, in 1788. In the latter part of the eighteenth century English and French missionaries came. The Tahitian queen, Pomare IV, agreed in 1843 to the establishment of a French protectorate. Her son, Pomare V, abdicated in 1880, and France made Tahiti a colony. In 1946 all the indigenous inhabitants became French citizens.

Books and Articles

Adams, Henry.
Memoires d'Arii Taimai.
Paris, 1964 (orig. 1901). 165 p.
(Société des Oceanistes Publications, no. 12)
NN F-10 8968

Adams, Henry.
Tahiti ...
New York, Scholars Facsimilies, 1947. 196 p., gen. tables.
NN BH

Deschamps, Hubert Jules.
Tahiti, la Polynésie Français.
Paris, Berger-Levrault, 1957. 311 p.
NN C-10 9506

O'Reilly, Patrick.
Tahitiens: Répertoire Bio-bibliographique de la Polynésie Français.
Paris, 1962. 534 p. . . . sup. Paris, 1966. 10 p.
(Société des Oceanistes Publications, no. 10, 17)
NN F-10 7361

Price, William.
Adventures in Paradise: Tahiti, Samoa, Fiji.
London, Heinemann, 1956. 245 p.
NN E-10 184

TONGA (NUKU'ALOFA)

Tonga, or Friendly Islands, comprises 150 islands (45 inhabited) in the South Pacific. The main island is Tongatapu, where the capital city is located. The Portuguese visited the islands in the seventeenth century. Years of civil war ended in 1845 with the ascension of the Tupou dynasty. Tonga became a British protectorate in 1900 and, in 1970, an independent nation within the Commonwealth. The government is a constitutional monarchy. The late Queen Salote gained world popularity at the coronation of Queen Elizabeth II in 1953.

Censuses were recorded in 1931 and 1956.

Public and Church Records

Registers of births and deaths date from 1867; of marriages, from 1892.

Registrar of the Supreme Court
Naku'alofa, Tonga

Books and Articles

Bain, K.R.
The Friendly Islanders: A Story of Queen Salote and Her People with a Foreword by Taufa'ahau Tupou IV.
London, Hodder & Stoughton, 1967. 207 p., ports.
NN D-17 8303

Luke, Sir Harry Charles, Jr.
Queen Salote and Her Kingdom.
London, 1954. 136 p., ports.
NN BH

MacQuarrie, Hector.
Friendly Queen.
London, Heinemann, 1955. 193 p., illus., ports.
NN BH

Packet, Charles N.
The Kingdom of Tonga ... rev. ed.
Bradford, Yorks, the author, 1976. 24 p.

BAHAMAS (NASSAU ON NEW PROVIDENCE ISLAND)

The Bahamas consist of 700 islands—30 of which are inhabited—that extend 760 miles in the western Atlantic from a point 50 miles off the coast of Florida to about 70 miles from Haiti. It was on the island of San Salvador that Christopher Columbus first set foot in the New World in 1492. The British began to settle the area in 1647, and the islands were a British colony by 1783. Britain granted internal self-government in 1964, and the Commonwealth of the Bahamas became fully independent on July 10, 1973. Eighty-five percent of the population is of African descent, and Anglicanism is the main religion.

Censuses were conducted in 1731, 1911, 1921, 1931 and 1953.

Archives

Bahamas Public Records Office
% Ministry of Education and Culture (P.O. Box N3913/14)
Nassau, Bahamas

Public and Church Records

Records in the custody of the Registrar-General date back to 1851 for births, 1850 for deaths and 1799 for marriages.
Write:

Registrar General's Office
P.O. Box 532
Nassau, Bahamas

Libraries

Public Library
Rawson Square
Nassau, Bahamas

Library, Queen's College
Nassau, Bahamas

Books and Articles

Bahama Islands Blue Book.
Nassau, 1902–1931.
NN *SF+

Bethell, Arnold Talbot.
The Early Settlers of the Bahama Islands . . .
Jacksonville, FL, A.B. Vance, 1914. 116 p.
NN APW

Hunte, George.
The Bahamas.
London, Batsford, 1975. 200 p.
NN SC 917,296H

Moseley, Mary.
The Bahamas Handbook.
Nassau, Nassau *Guardian*, 1926. 237 p.
NN HRG

Peters, Thelma.
The American Loyalists in the Bahama Islands, Who They Were.

(IN: *Florida Historical Society Quarterly*, Jacksonville, FL, 1962. v. 40, p. 226–40)
NN IAA

Peters, Thelma.
The Loyalist Migration from East Florida to the Bahama Islands.
(IN: *Florida Historical Society Quarterly*, Jacksonville, FL, 1961. v. 40, p. 123–41)
NN IAA

Saunders, D. Gail.
Guide to the Records of the Bahamas.
Nassau, The Commonwealth, 1973. 109, 28 p., index.
NN HRG 76-607

Whittledon, Eric H.
Family History in the Bahamas.
(IN: *GM*, London, 1975. v. 18, p 187–91)
NN ARCA

BARBADOS (BRIDGETOWN)

Barbados was apparently inhabited by Carib and Arawak Indians at one time but was uninhabited when the first English settlers arrived during the seventeenth century. Slaves were brought from Africa to work the sugar plantations but were freed in 1834. In 1954 Sir Grantley Adams, a black Barbadian and founder of the Labour Party, became the island's first Prime Minister. In 1958 Barbados joined the West Indian Federation of ten British colonies, which dissolved four years later, and in 1966 the country achieved full independence.The population is mainly black. English is the language and Anglicanism the predominant religion.

Transcripts of censuses of the white population conducted in 1679–80 and 1715 are available at the Department of Archives. There have been regular censuses since 1844, but there are no surviving enumerations before 1960.

Archives

Department of Archives
Black Rock
St. Michael, Barbados

Public and Church Records

Civil registration began in 1890 for births, 1885 for marriages, 1924 for deaths and 1937 for divorces.

In the nineteenth century, when a central registry was established, existing church registers were transcribed and the copies deposited in the Registration Office. All "Parochial Registers" are arranged according to the boundaries of the eleven original parishes that existed in the seventeenth and eighteenth centuries, and there is a fine series of indexes covering all registers to the present day. Moravian (from 1769), Methodist, Roman Catholic, Garrison and Jewish (from 1660) records were copied in a separate series indexed up to 1886. For information on vital statistics:

Registration Office
Coleridge Street
Bridgetown, Barbados

Libraries

Public Library
Coleridge Street
Bridgetown, Barbados

University of the West Indies Library
Bridgetown, Barbados

Historical and Genealogical Societies

Barbados Museum and Historical Society
St. Ann's Garrison, Barbados
(*Journal*, Bridgetown, 1933–. v.1–.)
NN HRG

Books and Articles

Barbados Notes.
(IN: *GM*, London, 1974. v. 17, p. 563–64)
NN ARCA

Barbados Parish Registers 1678–1679.
(IN: Hotten, John C., *Original List of Persons of Quality*. Baltimore, MD, GPC, 1962 (orig. 1880). p. 421–508)
NN APK

A Census of the Island of Barbados, W.I. (1715).
(IN: *Barbados Museum and Historical Society Journal*, Bridgetown, 1937. v. 4, p. 72–82)
NN HRG

Chandler, M.J.
A Guide to Records in Barbados.
Oxford, Basil Blackwell, 1965. 204 p.
NN HR

Dunn, Richard S.
Barbados Census of 1680.
(IN: *WMCQ*, Williamsburg, VA, 1969. series 3, v. 26, p. 3–30)
NN APR (Virginia)

Peck, Brainerd T.
Researching in Barbados.
(IN: *Connecticut Nutmegger*, Hartford, CT, 1973. v. 6, p. 277–82)
NN APR (Connecticut) 74-726

CAYMAN ISLANDS (GEORGETOWN)

The three Cayman Islands are situated about 180 miles northwest of Jamaica. They were dependencies of Jamaica until 1959, when they became a unit territory within the Federation of the

West Indies. In 1962, after the dissolution of the federation, the Cayman Islands became a British dependency.

Public and Church Records

The Registrar-General keeps registers that go back to 1886. Registration is governed by an extension of the statutes of Jamaica.

CUBA (HAVANA)

Cuba, discovered by Christopher Columbus in 1492, is the largest island in the West Indies. It was a Spanish colony until 1898, except for a brief British occupation in 1762–63. Cuba was under United States military rule from 1899 to 1902 and from 1906 to 1909, when a republican government was instituted. The government was unstable for many years, until Fidel Castro took control in 1959. Since his rise to power, thousands of Cubans have fled the island and settled in the United States, particularly in Florida. The main educational institution in Cuba is the University of Havana, founded in 1721.

There were inaccurate censuses of Cuba taken during the colonial period in 1774, 1792, 1817 and 1827. More realistic enumerations were made in 1841, 1846, 1861 (the year after the census in Spain), 1877 and 1887 (these last two in conjunction with the Spanish census). The United States took censuses in 1899 and 1907, and the Cuban Republic did so in 1919 and 1931.

Archives

Archivo Nacional
Copostela y San Isidro
Havana 1, Cuba

Archivo Histórico Municipal de la
    Habana
Plaza de Catedral
Havana, Cuba

Public and Church Records

Birth and marriage certificates can be obtained from the Civil Registry (Registro Civil) or Municipal Court (Juzgado Municipal) of the district or town where the event took place.

Libraries

Biblioteca Central "Rubén Martínez Villena" de la Universidad de Habana
San Lazaro y L, Vedado
Havana, Cuba

Biblioteca Nacional "José Martí"
Apdo. Official No. 3
Plaza de la República
Havana, Cuba

Books and Articles

Anuario de Familias Cubanas.
Puerto Rico, Joaquín de Posada,
  1971–76. 3 v.
NN APY 74-37

García Kohly, Mario.
... Grandes Hombres de Cuba. 2nd
  ed.
Madrid, 1930. 294 p.
NN AGW

Nieto y Cortadellas, Rafael.
Dignidades Nobiliarias en Cuba.
Madrid, Ediciones Cultura His-
  panica, 1954. 669 p., index.
NN APY

Parker, William B.
Cubans of Today.

New York, G.P. Putnam's, 1919.
  684 p.
NN AGW

Peraza Sarusa, Fermin.
Diccionario Biográfico Cubano.
Havana and Coral Gables, FL,
  Bibliográfica Cubano, 1951–68.
  14 v., alpha, index.
NN AGW

Peraza Sarusa, Fermin.
Personalidades Cubanas.
Havana, 1957–1967. 9 v.
NN F-10 2427

Santa Cruz y Mallen, Francisco X.
  de.
Historia de Familias Cubanas.
Havana,   Editorial   Hercules,
  1940–50. 6 v.
NN APY

Vallellano, Fernando Suarez de
  Tangil y de Angul, Conde de.
Nobiliario Cubano ...
Madrid, F. Beltran, 1921. 2 v.
NN APY

DOMINICAN REPUBLIC (SANTO DOMINGO)

The Dominican Republic occupies the eastern two-thirds, and
Haiti the western third, of the island of Hispaniola, which was
discovered by Columbus in 1492. In 1795 Spain ceded the eastern
part, then known as Santo Domingo, to France. Touissaint
L'Ouverture of Haiti seized Santo Domingo in 1801 but was
overthrown by a Spanish-supported French invasion of Haiti
under General Leclerc. The French were driven out in 1809,
and the area reverted to Spain in 1814. In 1821 the Dominicans
expelled their Spanish governor and proclaimed their independence, but the following year they were reconquered by the
Haitians under Jean Pierre Boyer. In 1844 the Dominicans
revolted and defeated the Haitians; a constitution was adopted

and the Dominican Republic was proclaimed under the leadership of Pedro Santana, who made the country a province of Spain because of revolts and continued Haitian attacks. In 1865 Spain withdrew because of strong opposition headed by Buenventura Baez; the continuously unsettled political situation led to the dictatorship of Ulises Heureaux from 1882 to 1899. The country was occupied by United States Marines from 1916 until 1924, when a constitutional government was installed. In 1930 Rafael Leonidas Trujillo Molina came into power and ruled as a dictator until he was assassinated in 1961. The 1960's saw repeated revolution, civil war, U.S. military intervention and a final mediation under the auspices of the Organization of American States. Juan Balaguer, originally appointed President by Trujillo in 1960, was elected to that office in 1966, 1970 and 1974.

Various censuses were recorded in 1920, 1935, 1950, 1955 and 1960.

Archives

Archivo General de la Nación
Calle Modesto Diaz
Santo Domingo, Dominican Republic

Public and Church Records

Contact the Official del Estado Civil in the place where a birth or marriage occurred or the central office for vital records:

Oficina del Estado Civil
% Junta Central Electoral
Centro de los Heroes
Santo Domingo, Dominican Republic

For census information:

Oficina Nacional de Estadística y Censos
Santo Domingo, Dominican Republic

For religious records:

Palacio del Arzobispado
Santo Domingo, Dominican Republic

Libraries

Biblioteca de la Universidad de Santo Domingo
Ciudad Universitaria
Santo Domingo, Dominican Republic

Biblioteca Municipal de Santo Domingo
Padre Billini No. 18
Santo Domingo, Dominician Republic

Historical and Genealogical Societies

Instituto de Investigaciones Históricas

José Reyes 24 (altos)
Santo Domingo, Dominician Republic
(*Revista de Historia*)

Books and Articles

Garrido, Miquel Angel.
... Siluetas.
Santo Domingo, El Progresso, 1914. 252 p.
NN AGW

Gonzalez-Blanco, Pedro.
Genealogía de los Appelidos Trujillo, Molina, Valdes, Monagas y Chevalier.
Madrid, 1956. 226 p., cursory index.
(The family of Hector Trujillo y Molina)
MM ASP (Trujillo)

La Peron, Gregorio.
Notas Autobiografias y Apuntes Históricos. 2nd ed.
Santiago, R.D., El Diario, 1939. 3 v.
NN HPM

Larrazabel Blanco, Carlos.
Los Negros y la Esclavitud en Santo Domingo.
Santo Domingo, 1967. 200 p.
NN HPM 75-1384

Logan, Rayford Whittingham.
Haiti and the Dominican Republic.
New York, Oxford, 1968. 220 p.
NN HPB

Marrero, Aristy R.
La República Dominicana.
Ciudad Trujillo, 1957–58. 2 v.
NN HPM+

Mejia Billini de Espaillat, Gisela.
Figuras y Retablos de Ayer.
Santo Domingo, 1964. 132 p.
NN E-12-5765

Mejia, Gustavo A.
Historia de Santo Domingo.
Ciudad Trujillo, 1948–54. 7 v.
(Includes bios)
NN HPB

FRENCH ANTILLES:
GUADELOUPE (BASSE-TERRE)
AND MARTINIQUE (FORT-DE-FRANCE)

Guadeloupe and Martinique, both French Overseas Departments, make up the French Antilles. Guadeloupe consists of two large islands, Basse-Terre and Grande-Terre, plus Marie Galante and the Saintes group to the south and St. Barthélemy and over half of St. Martin (the Dutch portion is St. Maarten) to the north. The territory has been a French possession since 1635. The population consists mainly of descendants of slaves.

Martinique is an island 130 miles south of Guadeloupe. The population is made up of descendants of black slaves, Europeans and Carib Indians.

Public and Church Records

Birth and marriage certificates can be obtained from the office of the Mayor (*La Mairie*) of the place of birth or marriage.

Historical and Genealogical Societies

Association Historique Internationale del'Ocean Indien
B.P. 349
Saint-Denis, Martinique

See also: Windward Islands; Leeward Islands.

Books and Articles

Bourgeois, Jean T.
Martinique et Guadeloupe Terres Français des Antilles.
Paris, 1958. 154 p.
NN HRN

Chauleau, Liliane.
La Société à la Martinique aux XVIIe Siècle (1635–1713) ...
Caen, Ozanne, 1966. 252 p.
NN HRN

Debien, Gabriel.
... Le Peuplement des Antilles Française au XVIIe Siècle:
Les Engagés Partis de la Rochelle (1683–1715).
Cairo, 1942. 222 p.
(His: Notes d'Histoire Coloniale, 2)
NN APY

Martineau, Alfred H.
Trois Siècles d'Histoire Antillaise: Martinique et Guadeloupe de 1635 à nos Jours.
Paris, 1935. 282 p.
NN HRN

Oriol, T.
... Les Hommes Célèbres de la Guadeloupe ...
Basse-Terre, L'Imprimerie Catholique, 1935. 352 p., t of c at end, no index.
NN AGW

Rennaud, Joseph.
La Martinique Histoire des Paroisses des Origines à la Séparation.
Thonon-les-Bains, 1951. 349 p.
NN HRN

HAITI (PORT-AU-PRINCE)

In 1492 Columbus discovered the island of Hispaniola. Spanish colonists settled the eastern part of the island, while Haiti, on the western third, became a center for French and English pirates. It became a French colony in 1677, and settlers brought in black slaves to work the sugar plantations. In the late eighteenth century the slaves rebelled. Toussaint L'Ouverture, a former slave, led guerrilla groups who defeated an invading French army in 1793 and went on to occupy the entire island of Hispaniola. Although he was captured by an army sent by Napoleon and died in prison, the revolt went on, and independence was declared in 1804. For a time, north and south were ruled separately, but in 1820 Jean Pierre Boyer reunited Haiti and controlled Santo Domingo. He was overthrown, and Santo Domingo regained its independence in 1844. The United States controlled Haiti from 1905 to 1934. In 1937 years of border clashes with the Dominican Republic (formerly Santo Domingo) resulted in a bloody massacre of between 10,000 and 15,000 Haitains. François Duvalier, a black physician, was elected President in 1957 and ruled as a dictator. In 1964 a new constitution made him President for life, an office in which he was succeeded by his son, Jean-Claude Duvalier, after his death in 1971.

Archives

Archives Nationales
Port-au-Prince, Haiti

Public and Church Records

Birth and marriage certificates can be obtained from the Officer de l'État Civil of a person's native town or from the National Archives.

Libraries

Bibliothèque Nationale d'Haiti
rue Hammerton Killick
Port-au-Prince, Haiti

Bibliothèque, Université d'Haiti
Place des Heros de L'Independence
Port-au-Prince, Haiti

Historical and Genealogical Societies

Société d'Histoire et de Géographie
Port-au-Prince, Haiti

Books and Articles

Begouen Demeaux, Maurice.
Memorial d'une Famille du Havre.

Le Havre, 1948. 2 v.
(NYPL's Schomburg Collection has
v. 2 only)
NN Sc FB-Begouen

David, Placide.
L'Heritage Colonial en Haiti.
Madrid, 1959. 292 p.
NN Sc F309.172-D

Garcia, José Gabriel.
Compendio de la Historia de Santo
Domingo. 4th ed.
Santo Domingo, R.D., 1968. 4 v.
NN HPB 73-220

Léon, Rulx.
Propos d'Histoire d'Haïti.
Port-au-Prince, Impr. de l'Etat
1945–74. 2 v.
NN Sc F972.94-L

Nemours, Alfred.
Histoire de la Famille et de a Descendance   de   Toussaint
L'Ouverture.
Port-au-Prince, Imprimerie de
l'État, 1941. 303 p., t of c, no
index.
NN APY

West Indian (Haiti) Manuscript
Collection. 1716–1817, 1857.
New York, 1971. 1 reel, 120 items.
NN Sc Micro R-1527

JAMAICA (KINGSTON)

The island of Jamaica was inhabited by Arawak Indians when it was discovered by Columbus in 1494. The first Spanish colonists arrived in 1509. The island was attacked by the British in 1596 and 1643, and in 1655 it was captured by Admiral William Penn and Robert Venables. In 1670 Jamaica was ceded to Britain by the Treaty of Madrid. The Buccaneers, led by Sir Henry Morgan, brought great wealth to the island. The capital city of Port Royal was destroyed by an earthquake in 1692, and the capital was moved to Spanish Town. During the next century the island suffered hurricanes, earthquakes and slave revolts. In 1833, when the black slaves who had been imported to replace the nearly extinct Indians were freed, the plantation economy was dealt a severe blow and poverty and social unrest developed. In 1865 a black uprising resulted in the imposition of martial law; a Crown Colony government was set up, and economic and social reform was begun. Full internal autonomy was achieved in 1953, and in 1962 the island became independent, with Sir Alexander Bustamente as its first Prime Minister.

Archives

Island Record Office and Archives
Spanish Town, Jamaica

Public and Church Records

Compulsory registration of births and deaths was established in 1878; certificates can be obtained from the Registrar General's Department in the Island Record Office and Archives (above). Divorce records are filed at the office of the Registrar, Supreme Court, King Street, Kingston. Records of baptisms, burials and marriages before the period of civil registration were kept by the Church of England.

For census information:

Director, Department of Statistics
23½ Charles Street
Kingston, Jamaica

For wills and deeds:

Deputy Keeper of the Records
Island Record Office
Spanish Town, Jamaica

Libraries

Jamaica Library Service
P.O. Box 58, 2 Tom Redcam Drive
Kingston, Jamaica

University of the West Indies
Mona, Kingston 7, Jamaica

Books and Articles

Cundall, Frank.
The Governors of Jamaica in the First Half of the Eighteenth Century.
London, 1937. 229 p.
NN Sc 923.272-C

Feurtado, Walter A.
Official and Other Personages of Jamaica from 1655 to 1790 ...
Kingston, W.A. Feurtado's Sons, 1896. 135 p.
NN APW

Giuseppi, Montague S.
Naturalizations of Foreign Protestants in the American and West Indian Colonies.
Baltimore, MD, GPC, 1964. 195 p.
(Orig. Huguenot Society of London pub., London, 1921. v. 24.)
NN ARCA
NN APK

Jamaica. Registrar General's Department.
Civil Status Records, 1664–1800, in the Registrar General's Office, Spanish Town.
Spanish Town, Jamaica Archives, 1974. 54 p.

Kopytoff, Barbara K.
The Maroons of Jamaica: An Ethnohistorical Study of Incomplete Politics 1655–1905.

Ann Arbor, MI, University Microfilms, 1973. 392 leaves.
(A U. of Pennsylvania thesis)

Livingston, Noel B.
Sketch Pedigrees of Some of the Early Settlers in Jamaica ... with a List of the Inhabitants in 1670 ...
Kingston, Educational Supply Co., 1909. 139 p.
NN APW

Port Royal. Jamaica Record Office.
Real Estate Transactions Before 1692 Earthquake, City of Port Royal, Jamaica.
Washington, DC, National Geographical Society, 1960. 946 cards.
NN APW

Who's Who in Jamaica.
Kingston, 1916–1963. 11 v.
NN AGH

Wright, Philip.
Materials for Family History in Jamaica.
(IN: *GM*, London, 1966. p. 239–50)
NN ARCA

Wright, Philip.
Monumental Inscriptions of Jamaica.
London, Society of Genealogists, 1966. 361 p., index.
NN APW

LEEWARD ISLANDS

The northern group of the Lesser Antilles in the West Indies, the Leeward Islands, include the Virgin Islands of the United States, Guadeloupe and its dependencies (French), St. Eustatius and Saba (Dutch), St. Martin (Maartein) (French and Dutch) and the British-owned Antigua, St. Kitts-Nevis, Montserrat, and the British Virgin Islands.

Columbus discovered the islands in 1493. In the seventeenth century the British came and settled. In 1623, when Sir Thomas Warner was governor-general of St. Kitts and the neighboring islands—Nevis, Antigua, Montserrat and Barbuda—Pierre Belain d'Esnambuc (1585–1636) also established a colony on St. Kitts. Ownership of the islands changed every time a treaty was signed ending an Anglo-French war. Final disposition was made at the end of the Napoleonic Wars in 1815.

See also: U.S. Virgin Islands; French Antilles.

Antigua (St. John)

Public and Church Records

Vital records date back to 1856.

Registrar of the Supreme Court
Antigua, West Indies

Libraries

St. John's Public Library
St. John's, Antigua

British Virgin Islands (Tortola)

Public and Church Records

Records, deposited with the Commissioner of the Presidency, date back to 1859. Anglican records date from 1816; Wesleyan, from 1800.

Registrar-General
Tortola, British Virgin Islands

Montserrat (Plymouth)

Public and Church Records

Vital records date back to 1869, and records prior to this date are kept by the clergy of various denominations.

Libraries

Montserrat Public Library
Plymouth, Montserrat, West Indies

St. Kitts-Nevis-Anguilla (Basseterre)

Public and Church Records

Registration in St. Kitts dates to 1859 for births and deaths and 1885 for marriages; in Nevis, to 1860 for births, 1861 for deaths and 1925 for marriages; in Anguilla, to 1901 for births and deaths and to 1925 for marriages. Earlier records are in the possession of ministers of various religious denominations.

Books and Articles

Baker, E.C.
A Guide to Records in the Leeward Islands.

Oxford, Basil Blackwell for the U. of West Indies, 1965. 102 p.
NN HR

Davis, Margo, and Gregson Davis. Antiqua Black: Portrait of an Island People.
San Francisco, CA, Scrimshaw, 1971. 141 p.
NN Sc 917.2974-D

Oliver, Vere Langford.
The History of Antigua, One of the Leeward Caribbees in the West Indies ... 1635 to the Present Day.
London, Hughes & Mitchell, 1894–99. 3 v., index each v., appendix v. 3, p. 285–460.
(Parishes: St. John's—v. 3, p. 355–79; Registers [1689–1819] p. 363–73; MI p. 373–78. St. Peter's—v. 3, p. 379–82; Registers [1773–1823] p. 380–81; MI p. 381–82. St. George's—v. 3, p.

382–84; Registers [1754–1818] p. 382–83; MI p. 383–84. St. Paul's—v. 3, p. 384–89; Registers [1729–1835] p. 385–87; MI p. 387–89. St. Philip's—v. 3, p. 389–92; Registers [1767–1843] p. 391; MI p. 392. St. Mary's—v. 3, p. 392–98; Registers [1734] p. 397; MI p. 397–98. Grants and warrants—v. 3, p. 285–305. Slave compensations and claims—v. 3, p. 305–18. Officers and officials—v. 3, p. 318–25. Abstracts of wills [c. 1636–c. 1820]—v. 3, Appendix, p. 325–54, 401–5)
NN APW + +

St. Thomas Middle Island, St. Christopher.
The Registers of St. Thomas, Middle Island, St. Kitts, by Vere Langford Oliver.
London, Mitchell and Hughes, 1915. 64 p.
NN APW

NETHERLANDS ANTILLES (WILLEMSTAD)
(formerly the Dutch West Indies)

The Netherlands Antilles consists of two island groups: Curaçao, Aruba and Bonaire; and St. Eustatius, Saba and the southern part of St. Maarten. The islands were discovered in 1499 by Ojeda and Vespucci, and in 1527 Spanish colonization began. In 1634 the Dutch took control, but in 1790, and again from 1807 to 1814, the islands were occupied by the British. The population is largely black; the culture, a unique blend of Afro-Spanish-Dutch.

The first census of the island of Aruba was taken in 1931.

Archives

Historisch Archief of the Netherlands Antilles
Willemstad, Curaçao

Public and Church Records

Birth and marriage certificates can be obtained from the Civil Registrar's Office of the island of birth.

There is a central Register of Wills kept by the Directeur der Belastingen (Director of Taxes) in Curaçao. The register of deeds is kept by the Inspecteur der Belastingen (Tax Inspector) in Curaçao.

Libraries

Openbare Leeszaalen Bibliotheek
Curaçao, Netherlands Antilles

Openbare Leeszaal en Boekerij
Eilandgebied, Aruba

Books and Articles

De Architektuur van Suriname 1667–1930.

Zutphen, 1973. 364 p.
NN JFM 73-802

Encyclopedie van de Nederlandse Antillen.
Amsterdam, 1969. 708 p.
NN HRR 72-890

Essai Historique sur la Colonie de Surinam.
Amsterdam, 1968. 192, 197 p.
NN HEL 75-2217

Hartog, Jan.
History of the Netherlands Antilles. English ed.
Aruba, De Witt, 1961–68. 2 v: v. 1 and 3.
(v. 1, Aruba Past and Present; v. 3, Curaçao)
NN HRR 73-1886

Krafft, Arnoldus, J.C.
Historie en oude Families van de Nederlandse Antillen . . .
's-Gravenhage, M. Nijhoff, 1951. 448 p., index.
NN AVH+ (West Indies, Dutch)

Surinaame Historische Kring.
Emancipatie, 1863–1963.
Paramaribo, 1964. 198 p.
NN Sc Du.920.068S

PUERTO RICO (SAN JUAN)

When Columbus discovered the island in 1493 it was inhabited by Arawak Indians. Juan Ponce de Leon began the Spanish conquest of the island in 1508 and was appointed governor the following year. The Indians revolted in 1511 but were put down and soon wiped out. Blacks were then imported from Africa to replace the Indians at forced labor, and plantation existence became established. In 1873 slavery was abolished. Puerto Rico was given autonomy by the Spanish in 1898, but a few months later the Spanish-American War broke out and Americans landed on the island and established a military occupation. Military rule ended in 1900, and administration of the island was placed in the hands of a United States governor, an executive council appointed by the American President and an elected house of delegates. In 1946 President Truman appointed the first Puerto Rican to hold the office of governor, Jesús T. Piñero. In 1947 the Jones Act, which had previously provided for an elected senate and American citizenship, was amended to provide for the governor to be elected by the Puerto Rican people. Since the Second World War there has been heavy immigration to the United States.

Archives

Archivo General de Puerto Rico
Av. Ponce de Leon 500
Puerta de Tierra, San Juan
(Postal address: Apartado 4184, San Juan, Puerto Rico 00905)

Public and Church Records

The central office has records of births and deaths since July 22, 1931. Earlier records dating from about 1892 may be obtained by writing the local Registrar (Registrador Demográfico) in the municipality where the birth or death occurred.

Division of Demographic Registry and Vital Statistics
Department of Health
San Juan, Puerto Rico 00908

Further information can be obtained from Commonwealth of Puerto Rico
304 Park Avenue South, 23rd Floor
New York, NY 10010.

Libraries

Ateneo Puertorriqueño Library
San Juan, Puerto Rico

Inter-American University of Puerto Rico Library
San Juan Campus, P.O.B. 1293
Hato Rey, Puerto Rico 00919

University of Puerto Rico General Library
San German, Puerto Rico 00753

Books and Articles

Brooklyn College.
Institute of Puerto Rican Studies.
Revista.
New York, c. 1974. v. 1–2.
NN IEE (Puerto Ricans) 76-172

Careras, Carlos N.
Hombres y Mujeres de Puerto Rico.
Mexico City, Orion, 1957. 256 p.
NN C-10 9712

Cifre de Loubriel, Estela.
Catálogo de Extranjeros Resi-

dentes en Puerto Rico en el Siglo XIX.
Río Piedras, Puerto Rico, U. of Puerto Rico, 1962. 160 p.
NN E-12 514

Coll y Toste, Cayetano.
Puertorriqueños Ilustres ...
Barcelona, Rumbos, 1963. 357 p.
NN D-15 9668

Coll y Toste, Cayetano.
Puertorriqueños Ilustres ...
New York, Las Americas Pub. Co., 1957 (orig. 1915–17). 191 p.
NN D-12 10

Cordasco, Francesco.
Puerto Ricans on the U.S. Mainland.
Totowa, NJ, 1972. 146 p.
NN *R-IEE 73-3393

Farr, Kenneth.
Historical Dictionary of Puerto Rico and the U.S. Virgin Islands.
Metuchen, NJ, Scarecrow Press, 1973. 143 p.
NN HPR 76-1414

Figueroa, S.
Ensayo Biográfico de los que Mas han Contribuido al Progreso de Puerto Rico.
Ponce, Puerto Rico, El Vapor, 1888. 356 p.
NN AGW

Gaudier, Martin.
Genealogía, Biografías e Historia del Mayaguez de Ayer y Hoy, y Antología.
San Juan, 1959. 493 p.
NN *ZAN-3020 no. 001450

Geigel de Gandia, Luisa.
La Genealogía y el Apellido de Campeche.

San Juan de Puerto Rico, Instituto de Cultura
Puertorriqueña, 1972. 58 p.
NN APY 74-24

Hill, Marnesba.
Puerto Rican Authors: A Bibliographic Handbook.
Metuchen, NJ, Scarecrow Press, 1974. 267 p.
NN*RS-NPV 74-4510

Libro del Año: Enciclopedia de Datos Utiles y Conocientos Practicos Sobre Puerto Rico.
San Juan Bautista, 1956/57–. v. 1–.
(A Who's Who section included)
NN HPR

Mapp, Edward.
Puerto Rican Perspectives.
Metuchen, NJ, Scarecrow Press, 1974. 171 p.
NN IEE (Puerto Ricans) 74-1724

Melon de Diaz.
Puerto Rico: Figuras del Presente y del Pasado y Apuntes Historicos.
Rio Piedras, 1972. 225 p.
NN JFD 74-739

Puerto Rican Research and Resources Center.
The Puerto Ricans: An Annotated Bibliography.
New York, 1973. 299 p.
NN *R-IEE (Puerto Ricans) 75-1828

Quien es Quien en Puerto Rico.
San Juan, Real Hermanos, 1933–.
NN *RR-AGN

Ribes Tovat, Frederico.
Enciclopedia Puertorriqueña Ilustrada.

San Juan, Ultra Educational Pub.,
   1970. 3 v.
NN HPR

Rosa-Nieves, Cesareo.
Biografías Puertorriqueñas.
Sharon, CT, c. 1970. 487 p.
NN JFF 72-105

Wagenheim, K.
A Survey of Puerto Ricans on the
   U.S. Mainland in the 1970's.
New York, 1975. 133 p.
NN IEE (Puerto Ricans) 75-2618

TRINIDAD AND TOBAGO (PORT-OF-SPAIN)

These two islands in the West Indies were discovered by Christopher Columbus in 1498. In the seventeenth century Spanish colonists began to build plantations on Trinidad, importing African slaves to work them. The British captured Trinidad in 1797, and it was formally ceded to them in 1802; Tobago finally passed to the British in 1814. In 1834 slavery was abolished, and in 1845 contract workers were imported from India to replace the slaves. Trinidad and Tobago became independent. The nation is one of the most prosperous in the West Indies, but because unemployment is high, immigration to England and North America is encouraged by the government. The population is about 43 percent black and 36 percent East Indian. Lebanese, Syrians, Europeans and Chinese make up the rest.

Censuses were conducted in 1891, 1911, 1921, 1931, 1946 and 1960.

Among the most valuable printed sources for research in Trinidad and Tobago is the *Register of Baptisms, Marriages, Deaths from 1781 to 1817* of the English Protestant Church of Tobago, a copy of records which include all races, published in Port-of-Spain in 1936.

Archives

National Archives
Prime Minister's Office
Whitehall, Port-of-Spain, Trinidad

Public and Church Records

Birth and marriage certificates can be obtained from the Registrar General's Office, Port-of-Spain, Trinidad.

Libraries

Central Library of Trinidad and Tobago
20 Queens Park East (P.O. Box 547)
Port-of-Spain, Trinidad

Eastern Caribbean Regional Library
P.O. Box 67
Port-of-Spain, Trinidad

Trinidad Public Library
Knox Street
Port-of-Spain, Trinidad

University of the West Indies Library
St. Augustine, Trinidad

Historical and Genealogical Societies

Historical Society of Trinidad and Tobago
20 Henry Street
Port-of-Spain, Trinidad

St. Andrew's Society of Trinidad
P.O. Box 331
Port-of-Spain, Trinidad

Books and Articles

Borde, Pierre G. L.
Histoire de l'Ile de la Trinidad sous le Gouvernement Espagnol.
Paris, 1876–82. 2 v.
NN HRG

Carmichael, Gertrude.
The History of the West Indian Islands of Trinidad and Tobago 1498–1900.
London, Redman, 1961. 463 p.
NN *R-HRG

Fraser, Lionel M.
History of Trinidad.
London, 1971. 2 v.
NN HRG 72-2457

Historical Society of Trinidad and Tobago Publications.
Port of Spain, 1932–52. no. 1–1,042, index no. 1–299, 1 v.; 300–1,000 1 v.
NN HRG

Register of Baptisms, Marriages, and Deaths from 1781 to 1817.
Port-of-Spain, Gov. Printer, 1936, various paging.
(Faithful copy of records that shows all races)
NN APW

Ryan, Selwyn D.
Race and Nationalism in Trinidad and Tobago.
Toronto, Buffalo, 1972. 509 p.

The Trinidad Almanac and Public Register. . . .
Port-of-Spain, H. J. Mills, 1835. 73 p.
NN HRG

Who's Who in Trinidad and Tobago.
Port-of-Spain.
NN *R-AGW 74-289 and JFK 74-224

Williams, Eric.
History of the People of Trinidad and Tobago.
Trinidad, PNM Pub., 1962. 294 p.
NN HRG

Wood, Donald.
Trinidad in Transition: The Years After Slavery.
London, Oxford U. Press, 1968. 318 p.
NN *R-HRG

VIRGIN ISLANDS, UNITED STATES (CHARLOTTE AMALIE)

The Virgin Islands were discovered by Columbus in 1493. They comprise 100 islands in the West Indies, 68 of which belong to the United States and the rest to Great Britain. The three main islands are St. Thomas, St. John and St. Croix. Settlement of St. Thomas was begun by the Danish West Indies Company in 1672, and St. John was claimed by the company in 1683. St. Croix was purchased by the company from France in 1733. The company retained control of the islands until 1754, when they were purchased by Frederick V of Denmark and became a royal colony. In 1801 and again from 1807 to 1815 the islands were in British hands. In 1917 the United States purchased them from Denmark for $25,000,000. Their importance to the United States was primarily strategic, and they were under the supervision of the Department of the Navy until 1931, when they were transferred to the Department of the Interior. The population is predominantly black.

Public and Church Records

St. Thomas
Birth records are on file since July 1, 1906, and death records since January 1, 1906.

Registrar of Vital Statistics
Charlotte Amalie
St. Thomas, Virgin Islands 00802

St. Croix
Birth and death records are on file since 1840.

Registrar of Vital Statistics
Charles Harwood Memorial Hospital
St. Croix, Virgin Islands

Books and Articles

Creque, Darwin D.
The U.S. Virgin Islands and the Eastern Caribbean.
Philadelphia, Whitmore, 1968. 266 p.
NN HRR

Knox, John.
A Historical Account of St. Thomas, W.I. . . . and Incidental Notices of St. Croix and St. John.
New York, Negro U. Press, 1970 (orig. 1852). 271 p.
NN HRR

Larsen, Jens Peter Mouritz.
Virgin Islands Story.
Philadelphia, Fortress Press, c. 1950. 265 p.
NN HRR

Lewisohn, Florence.
St. Croix under Seven Flags ...
Hollywood, FL, Dukane Press,
1970. 432 p.
NN HRR 71-156

Reid, Charles I.
Bibliography of the Virgin Islands
of the U.S.
New York, H.W. Wilson, 1941.
225 p.
NN HRR

Virgin Islands of the U.S., St.
Thomas Public Library, Charlotte Amalie.

Catalog of the Microfilms Available in the Van Scholton Collection.
St. Thomas, 1969/70.
NN HRR

Westergaard, Walden.
The Danish West Indies under
Company Rule (1671–1754) with
a Supplementary Chapter,
1755–1917 ...
New York, Macmillan, 1917. 359 p.
NN HRR

WINDWARD ISLANDS

The southern group of the Lesser Antilles in the West Indies, the Windward Islands include French Martinique, Grenada, the British Windward Islands of Dominica, St. Lucia and St. Vincent and the Grenadines, an archipelago of islands strung out between St. Vincent and Grenada whose administration is divided between Grenada and the Windward Islands.

Aboriginal Caribs were on the islands when Columbus discovered them. When the British and French colonized the islands in the early seventeenth century, settlements and sovereignty overlapped. Struggle for dominance in the islands was part of worldwide Anglo-French conflict. Present ownership was established in 1815. The islands are largely inhabited by persons of black descent, with some admixture of Carib Indians, Portuguese, East Indians and a small percentage of white families, mostly British.

See also: French Antilles.

Dominica (Roseau)

Public and Church Records

The Registrar General's Office
Roseau, Dominica, West Indies

Grenada (St. George's)

Public and Church Records

Civil registration for births and deaths began in 1866; for marriages, in 1903.

Ministry of Health and Housing
Melville Street, St. George's

For wills and deeds:
Chief Registrar of the Supreme
Court
York House, St. George's

St. Lucia (Castries)

Public and Church Records

Birth certificates can be obtained
from the registrar of Civil Status; marriage certificates, from
the Parish Register of Marriages and Burials.

Libraries

Central Library (Branch library
at Soufrière)
St. Lucia

St. Vincent (Kingstown)

Public and Church Records

Registrar General's Office
Kingstown, St. Vincent

Books and Articles

Baker, E.C.
A Guide to the Records in the
Windward Islands.
Oxford, Basil Blackwell for the U.
of West Indies, 1968. 95 p.
NN HRG

Devas, Raymond.
Conception Island . . .
London, Sands, 1932. 436 p.
NN HRG

General Caribbean Sources

Burns, Sir Alan.
History of the British West Indies.
2nd rev. ed.

London, Allen and Unwin, 1965.
849 p., index.
NN *R-HR

Caribbeana, ed. by Vere L. Oliver.
London, 1909–19. 6 v.
NN APW

Caribbeana, 1900–1965: a Topical
Bibliography.
Seattle, WA, U. of Washington
Press, 1968. 909 p.
NN *R-HN

Journal of Caribbean History.
Barbados, Caribbean Press, 1970–.
v. 1–.
NN Sc. Ser-L.J633

Lawrence-Archer, J.H.
Monumental Inscriptions of the
British West Indies from the
Earliest Date.
London, Chatto & Windus, 1975.
442 p., index.
NN APW

Lux, William.
Historical Dictionary of the Brit-
ish Caribbean.
Metuchen, NJ, Scarecrow Press,
1975. 266 p.
NN HR 76-1417

Personalities Caribbean.
1972–73, 5th ed.
Kingston, Jamaica, 1973. 1,061 p.
NN *RR-AGW

Williams, Eric.
From Columbus to Castro: The
History of the Caribbean, 1492–
1969.
London, André Deutsch, 1970. 576
p., index.
NN *R-HNB

ALBANIA (TIRANA)

The People's Republic of Albania is situated in southeastern Europe on the Adriatic coast, bordered by Yugoslavia and Greece. The old race of Albanians were descended from the ancient Illyrians, but two thousand years of invasions by Romans, Ostrogoths, Byzantines, Slavs, Italians, Normans and Turks have changed the racial mix of the country. Turkish dominance was firm from the fifteenth century until the early part of this century, and as a result of this influence the majority of the people today are Muslims. In 1912 Albania declared its independence, but when the borders were retraced by an international commission, large areas inhabited by Albanians were assigned to Montenegro, Serbia and Greece. Ahmed Zog (Ahmed Bey Zogu) seized control of the country in 1925 and declared himself King Zog I in 1928. His regime lasted until 1939, when he was forced into exile. His widow, Queen Geraldine, who was born Countess Apponyi de Nagy-Apponyi of Hungary and lives with her son King Leka I (1939–), is the granddaughter of John H. Stewart of Baltimore and Pittsburgh. Albania has been a republic since 1946.

Archives

Archives D'État D'Albanie
Tirana, Albania

Public and Church Records

Roman Catholic and Orthodox churches kept parish records until 1929, when civil registration began. Vital records are kept by local officers in each municipality. Muslim records are incomplete, and many Christian records were destroyed by Communists, making Albania a difficult country in which to do genealogical research.

Libraries

National Library
Tirana, Albania

University Library
Tirana, Albania

Books and Articles

Albanian Royal Family
(House of Wied and House of Zogu)
(IN: *CDS*, Paris, 1966. p. 9–15)
NN ARB

(IN: *GHF*, Limburg/Lahn, 1968. v. 8, p. 1–3)
NN ATC

Amers, Julian.
Sons of the Eagle.
London, 1948. 354 p.
NN JFD 73-9784

Iogoreci, Anton.
The Albanians: Europe's Forgotten Survivors.
London, Gollanz, 1977. 230 p. index.

Keefe, Eugene K.
Area Handbook for Albania.
Washington, DC, 1971. 223 p.
NN JFE 72-1399

Pan-Albanian Federation of America "Vatra."
Seminari Nderkombetar i Federates Panshqiptare "Vatra."
New York, 28-29-30 Nanduer, 1969.
Rome, Dario Detti, 1971. 286 p.
NN IEE (Albanians)

Reitwiesner, William Adams.
A Hitherto Unnoted Descendant of Henry Adams of Braintree: Leka I, King (Claimant) of Albania.
(IN: *TAG*, Des Moines, IA, 1977. v. 53, p. 18–20)
NN APGA

Swire, J.
Albania: The Rise of a Kingdom.
New York, Arno, 1971 (orig. 1929). 560 p., index.
NN *R-GIK 76-4082

Tomic, Jovan N.
Les Albanais en Vielle-Servie et dans le Sandjak de Novi-Bazar.
Paris, Hachette, 1913. 81 p.
NN GIK

U.S.W.P.A.
The Albanian Struggle in the Old World and New.
Boston, MA, Albanian Historical Society of Massachusetts, 1939. 168 p., index.
NN IEE (Albanians)

ANDORRA (ANDORRA LA VELLA)

Andorra is a tiny nation of 18,000 people, situated in the eastern Pyrenees between France and Spain. Charlemagne is traditionally thought to have given the Andorrans a charter because of their assistance against the Moors. Emperor Charles II made the Spanish Count of Urgel overlord of Andorra in 843, and the Bishop of Urgel was made joint Suzerain in 1278. The right of the Count eventually passed through inheritance to Henry IV of France and then to the Presidents of France. Andorra is actually independent and sends nominal yearly gifts to its two Suzerains.

Archives

Archives Nationales (Servei D'Arxius)
Assessoria Pedagògica del M.I. Consell General
Casa de la Valle
Andorra la Vella, Andorra

Archives can also be found in the depositories of Spain (particularly in the See of Urgel), France and in the Segreto Archives of the Vatican.

Public and Church Records

Marriage and baptismal certificates can be obtained from church authorities in the parish, or *parroco*, of residence or from civil authorities—the Mayor, or *Alcalde*—of the municipality or district.

Books and Articles

Bacquier, Jean.
La Co-Principaute d'Andorre, Dernier État Feodal.
Andorre-La-Vielle, V. Claverol, 195–?. 73 p.
NN C-10 1727

Guilera, Josep Maria.
Una Historia d'Andorra.
Barcelona, Editions Dedos, 1960. 339 p.
NN D-12 8737

Johnson, Virginia W.
Two Quaint Republics, Andorra and San Marino.
Boston, MA, D. Estes, 1913. 228 p.
NN BWO

Nagel Pub.
Six Little States of Europe.
Geneva, 1961. 166 p.
(Andorra, Liechtenstein, Luxembourg, San Marino, Vatican City, Monaco)
NN D-10 1906

AUSTRIA (VIENNA)

Charlemagne created the first Austrian (eastern) March, a province of his empire, in 788. It fell to the Magyars but was recovered for the Holy Roman Empire in 955. The long reign of the House of Hapsburg began when Rudolf of Hapsburg, who was elected German king in 1278, brought the four duchies of Austria, Styria, Carinthia and Carniola under his control to form the nucelus of the future empire. In 1453 Frederick III raised Austria to an Archduchy, and in 1526 a lasting union was established under the same crown among Austria, Bohemia and Hungary. The Thirty Years War (1618–1648) wreaked havoc on the country, and some of the seventeenth-century migration of Austrians to the New World was undoubtedly one result of this conflict. Another was the loss of the Hapsburg power in Germany. In the late eighteenth century Francis II, son of the famed Empress Maria Theresa, having realized that the Holy Roman Empire (of which the Hapsburgs had become hereditary rulers) was crumbling, declared himself Francis I, Emperor of Austria. A coalition spearheaded by Austria in 1813 was successful against Napoleon, and the new empire, controlling much of central Europe, emerged as a leading power at the Congress of Vienna in 1814–15.

In 1848 the Austrian monarchy was shaken by a revolution, part of general European unrest, which sent many Austrians to America. Although the revolt was initially successful, the rebels were put down. In 1866 Austria battled the emerging German state of Prussia in the Austro-Prussian War, was defeated and lost her influence in the German confederation established at the Congress of Vienna. In 1867 a dual state was established with Hungary. The Austro-Hungarian monarchy endured until after the First World War in 1918, in which Austria, along with Germany and the other Central Powers, was defeated. Under terms of the treaty, Austria was separated from Hungary, and its borders were fixed approximately as they are today.

The first census was taken in 1754, and others were recorded in 1855, 1869, 1880, 1900, 1910, 1920, 1923, 1934 and every ten years since 1951. The 1971 enumeration is the first known to have survived.

The most common surnames in Vienna in the 1970's are Bauer, Fischer, Mayer, Muller, Schneider and Wagner.

Archives

Österreichisches Staatsarchiv (Central Archives)
Generaldirektion
1010 Vienna I.
Minoritenplatz I Austria

Archiv der Stadt Wien (Municipal Archives)
A-1082 Vienna, Felderstrasse I
Rathaus, Austria

Archiv der Universität Wien (Archives of the University of Vienna)
Vienna I, Austria
(Dr. Karl Lueger-Ring I)

Niederösterreichisches Landesarchiv (Lower Austrian Provincial Archives)
Vienna I
Herrengasse 11–13, Austria

Wiener Diözesanarchiv (Vienna Diocesan Archives)
Vienna I
Wollzeile 2, erzbisch. Palais 2, Austria

Public and Church Records

Civil registration began in 1784 for births, deaths and marriages and in 1886 for divorces. Non-Jews who were born before January 1, 1939, whose parents at the time of their birth professed a religion legally recognized in Austria, can apply for birth certificates at the rectory (Pfarramt) of the parish in which they were born. Persons born into the Jewish faith before the same date can apply to the Jewish Community Headquarters (Kultus-Gemeinde) of the community where they were born. All others must apply to the civil district authorities (Politische Bezirksbehoerde) of the district in which they were born. For census information:

Österreichisches Statistisches Zentralamt
Neue Hofburg, Heldenplatz
A-1010 Vienna, Austria

Libraries

Bibliothek des Österreichischen Statistischen Zentralamtes
(Library of the Austrian Central Office of Statistics)
Postfach 41
A-1014 Vienna, Austria

Österreichische Nationalbibliothek (Austrian National Library)
Vienna I
Josefplatz, Austria

Historical and Genealogical Societies

Genealogische-Heraldische Gesellschaft "Adler," Haarhof 4 a
Vienna, Austria

Books and Articles

Adler: Monatsblatt . . .
Vienna, 1939–44. 6 v. (v. 3–6 on film)
NN ATIA and *ZAN-G24 film

Adler: Zeitschrift . . .
Vienna, 1947–.
NN ATIA

Austrian Royal Family.
(House of Hapsburg)
(IN: *CDS*, Paris, 1966. p. 16–88)
NN ARB
(IN: *GHF*, Limburg/Lahn, 1971. v. 9, p. 67–91)
NN ATC

Clark, Francis.
Old Homes for New Americans: The Country and the People of the Austro-Hungarian Monarchy and Their Contribution to the New World.
Boston, MA, Houghton Mifflin, 1913. 265 p.
NN FAY

Davis, David B., and Lilith S. Davis.
The Descendants of Wenzel Blumrich of Friedland, Austria.

Ada, MN, the authors, 1969. 116 p., index.
NN APV (Blumrich) 73-1757

Deutsch-Österreichisches Kunstlerund
Schriftstellerlexikon.
Vienna, 1902–5. 2 v.
NN AGK

Dugast Rouille, Michel.
Les Grandes Mariages des Habsbourgs.
Paris, 1955. 374 p.
NN ATH (Hapsburg)

Genealogisches der Adeligen Hauser Österreichs.
Vienna, Otta Marss'sohne, 1905–13. 5 v.
NN ATIA

Gessner, Gerhard.
Öesterreichisches Familienarchiv.
Neustadt an der Aisch, Degener and Co., 1959–69. 3 v.
NN ATK

Goldinger, Walter.
Österreich in Hübners Bibliotheca Genealogica von 1729.
(IN: *Upper Austria*, Landsarchiv, Mitteilungen, Graz, 1964. v. 8, p. 287–97)
NN FHI

Grass-Cornet, Marie.
Aus der Geschichte der Nortiroler Bürgerkultur Familie Fuchs.
Munich, Wagner, 197–. 360 p., index, handsome illus.
NN ATM (Fuchs) 72-30

Guertler, Alfred.
Die Volkszahlungen Maria Theresias und Josef II, 1753–1790.
Innsbruck, Wagner, 1909. 152 p.

(Austrian census records 1753–90)
NN FAG

Hantich, Teja.
... Familienforscher in Österreich und ihre Arbeitsgebiete.
Vienna, 1972. 24 p.
NN *XMG-232P

Heraldisch-Genealogische Gesellschraft "Adler."
Jahrbuch.
Vienna, 1874–.
NN ATIA+

Hermann, Herman.
Genealogie und Heraldik Burgerlicher Familien Österreich-Ungarns.
Vienna, H. Hermann, 1894–1902. 2 v.
NN ATK

Kann, Robert A.
A History of the Hapsburg Empire, 1526–1918.
Berkeley, CA, 1974. 646 p.
NN *R-FAD 75-6733

Kronsteiner, Otto.
Worterbuch der Gewassernamen von Österreich.
Vienna, 1971. 215 p.
(Austrian gazetteer)
NN JFB-72-300

Maar, Grete.
Problems of Historical Research in Burgenland, the Easternmost Province of Austria.
(IN: *The Local Historian*, London, 1974. v. 14, p. 207–17)
NN CA 72-1598

Megerle von Mühlfeld, Johann G.
Österreichisches Adels-Lexikon ...

Vienna, Morschner und Jasper,
1822. 503 p.
NN ATK

Neu Österreichische Biographie
1815–1918.
Vienna, 1923–72. 18 v.
NN *RR-AGL

Österreicheches Biographisches
Lexikon 1815–1950.
Graz, H. Bohlaus, 1957–75, plus
(A–Musger) in progress.
NN *RR-AGL

Pollak, Walter, ed.
Tausend Jahre Österreich.
Vienna, 1973–74. 3 v.
NN JFL 73-414

Der Schussel.
Gottingern, Heinz Reise, 1970.
Band 6.
(Indexes genealogical and heraldic
periodicals in Austria and
Czechoslovakia 1871–1944)
NN ATA

Spaulding, Ernest W.
The Quiet Invaders: The Story of
the Austrian Impact on America.
Vienna, Östereicher Bundesver-
lag, 1968. 364 p.
NN IEE (Austrians)

Wer ist Wer?
Vienna, 1937–.
NN *RR-AGL

Wer ist Wer in Österreich.
Vienna, 1951. 224 p.
NN *RR-AGL+

Wer ist Wer in Österreich.
Vienna, 1953. 255 p.
NN *RR-AGL

Who's Who in Austria.
Zurich, *Central European Times*,
1954–71. 8 v.
NN *RR-AGL

Wurzbach, Constantin.
Biographisches Lexikon des Kais-
erthums Österreich ...
Vienna, K.K. Hof, 1856–91. 60 v. in
41.
NN D-10 7430

Bohemia
Procházka, Roman, Freiherr von.
Böhmischer Adels-Familien.
Neustadt (Aisch), Degener, 1969.

Procházka, Roman, Freiherr von.
Genealogische Handbuch Erloschener Böhmischer Herrenstandsfamilien.
Neustadt (Aisch), Degener, 1973.
395 p., index.
NN ATL (Bohemia) 74-870

Carinthia
Beckh-Widmanstetter, Leopold
von.
Studien an den Grabstätten alter
Geschlechter der Steiermark
und Kärntens.
Berlin, 1877–78. 218 p.
NN ATL (Styria) 74-1416

Salzburg
Dorn, Conrad.
Der Friedhof zum Herligen Sebas-
tian in Salzburg.
Salzburg, Kulturamt der Stadt,
1969. 224 p., index.
NN ATL (Salzburg) 73-1800

Tyrol
Granichstaedten-Czeova, Rudolf.
Beiträge zur Familiengeschichte
Tirols.

Innsbruck, Universitätsverlag Wagner, 1954. 271 p., index.
NN ATL (Tyrol)

Vienna
Mansfield, Herbert A.
Index Nominum Ex Libris Copulatorum Vindobonensibus
Tomus IV (1780–1850).
Vienna, Bergmann, 1964. 514 p., alpha.
NN ATL (Vienna)

Maurer, Casper.
Wiennerische Chronica.
Vienna, 1973. 205 p.
NN JFB 76-250

Tschechische Familiennamen in Wien.
Vienna, Verlag Adolph Holzhausens, 1972. 269 p., alpha.
NN APD 73-1334

Wiener Genealogische Taschenbuch.
Vienna, Hans Stratowa, 1926–37. 8 v.
NN ATIA

Waldviertl
Pongratz, Walter.
Die Altesten Waldviertler Familiennamen.
Krems, J. Faber, 1960. 183 p.
NN APD

BELGIUM (BRUSSELS)

Belgium, known as Belgae and Belgica in ancient times, was the birthplace of the Frankish Carolingian dynasty that had its roots at Herstal. After the division of Charlemagne's empire in the ninth century, Belgium occupied all the western Low Countries as the duchy of Lower Lorraine. Lower Lorraine disintegrated in the twelfth century, and the duchies of Luxembourg and Brabant and the Bishopric of Liege took its place. The current Belgian cities of Ghent, Bruges and Ypres rose and flourished. By the sixteenth century the Hapsburgs of Austria and Spain had gained control of the region, and the Low Countries revolted against Spanish rule. While the Netherlands won independence, Belgium was successively under Spanish, Austrian, French and Dutch rule until 1830, when Roman Catholic Belgium revolted against affiliation with the Protestant Netherlands. In 1831 Leopold of Saxe-Coburg (died 1865), maternal uncle of Queen Victoria of Great Britain, was elected King of Belgium, and his descendant, King Baudouin I (1930–), is the current ruler. In the nineteenth century Belgium extensively colonized the Congo region of Africa and in 1960 granted the area independence.

The most common surnames in Brussels are De Smet (Desmet, De Smedt, Desmedt), Dubois (Du Bois), Jacobs, Janssens, Mertens and Peeters.

Archives

Archives Générales du Royaume (National Archives)
rue de Ruysbroeck 2-6
1000-Brussels, Belgium

Archives de L'Archevêché de Malines-Bruxelles
(Archief Van Het Aartsbisdom Mechelen-Brussel)
Wollemarkt 15
2800 Mechelen, Belgium

Archives de L'Université Libre de Bruxelles
50 avenue F.D. Roosevelt
1050 Brussels, Belgium

Public and Church Records

Births, marriages, deaths and divorces have been registered since 1796/97. Copies of local records up to 1870 can usually be found at the State Archives; more recent documents are at the "Greffes des Tribunaux de Premiere Instance." Many religious documents for the period before 1796–97 are preserved at the State Archives, but large cities have in some cases preserved their old parochial registers themselves. More recent registers are preserved by the presbytery.

Libraries

Bibliothèque Royale de Belgique (The Belgian National Library)

4 boulevard de l'Empereur
Brussels I, Belgium

Historical and Genealogical Societies

Flemish Society for Familiekunde
E.A. Van Haverbeke, Secr.
Hyacintenloon, 33 Oostende, Belgium

Service de Centralisation des Études Généalogiques et Démographique de Belgique
26 rue au Laines
Brussels, Belgium

Books and Articles

Anthroponymica-Onomastica Neerlandica Institut voor Naamkuned.
Brussels, 1950–. 17 v. to 1967.
NN AVE

L'Association de la Noblesse de Belgique.
Bulletin.
Brussels, 1938–.
NN AVE

Bayer, Henry G.
Belgians, First Settlers in New York.
New York, Devin-Adair, 1925. 373 p., index.
NN IEE (Belgians)

... Les Belges Illustres.
Brussels, A. Jaman, 1844–45. 3 v.
NN AGM

Belgian Royal Family.
(House of Saxe-Coburg and Gotha)
(IN: *CDS*, Paris, 1966. p. 112–24)
NN ARB
(IN: *GHF*, Limburg/Lahn, 1968. v.
8, p. 18–21)
NN ATC

Belgium. Institut Royal Colonial.
Biographie Coloniale Belge.
Brussels, G. van Campenhout,
1948–58. 5 v.
NN F-10 9314

BE-NE-LUX Genealogist.
Harbor City, CA, Hartwell, 1977–.
v. 1–.

Bibliographie Courante.
(IN: *L'Intermediaire des Généalo-
gistes*, Brussels, 1973.
no. 166, p. 259–62; 1976, no. 182, p.
116–21)
NN AVE

Douchamps, Herve.
Inventaire des Fonds d'Archives
de l'Office
Généalogique et Héraldique de
Belgique.
(IN: *Le Parchemin*, Brussels, 1976.
no. 182, p. 82–93)
NN APA

Ghellinck Vaernewyck, Xavier de.
Armorial au Historique de Alliances Contemporaines de la Noblesse du Royaume Belgique.
Brussels, Tradition et Vie, 1962. 2
v.
NN AWT

Ghellinck Vaernewyck, Xavier de.
Bibliothèque Héraldique de Bel-
gique.
(IN: *Archivum Heraldicum Inter-*

nationales Bulletin, Lausanne,
1954. A 68, no. 3–4, p. 53–56)
NN AWT

Ghellinck Vaernewyck, Xavier de.
Petit Traite de la Noblesse en Bel-
gique.
Brussels, Editions "Tradition et
Vie," 1948. 1 v.
NN AWT

Griffis, William E.
The Story of the Walloons ...
Boston, MA, Houghton Mifflin,
1923. 299 p.
NN IEE (Belgians)

Hille, Phillipe van.
Genealogy in Belgium.
(IN: *GM*, London, 1968. v. 15, p.
647–51)
NN ARCA

Hille, Willy von.
Historie de la Famille van Hille.
Bruges, Tablettes des Flandres,
1954–56. 1 v. plus 2 sup.
NN AVEI (Hille)

L'Intermediaire des Généalo-
gistes.
Brussels, 1946–. (Subject index
1946–55 bound with 1955,
1956–60 bound with 1960)
(NYPL has 1952–)
NN AVE

Koller, F.
Armorial Général de Belgique.
Brussels, L'Imprimerie H. Des-
medt, 1958. 265 p., alpha.
NN AWT

Leenaerts, Remy T.
Algemeen Genealogisch-Heraldisch Repertorium voor de Zui-

delijke Nederlanden Genealogisch.
(Genealogical and Heraldic Index
of Southern Netherlands)
Handzame, Familia et Patria,
1969–72. 4 v.
NN AVE 74-2124

Le Livre Bleu: Recueil Biogra-
phie.
Brussels, Larcier, 1950.
NN *R-AGM and K-10 2338

National Biographisch Woorden-
boek.
Brussels, Paleis der Academien,
1964–.
NN *RR-AGM

Noblesse Belge (Annuaire de la).
Brussels, 1847–1945.
NN AVE

Nord Généalogie.
(See France; covers Flanders—Hainaut and Artois)

Office Généalogique et Héraldique
de Belgique.
Recueils Généalogiques et Héraldiques.
Brussels, 1952–.
1st series v. 1–10, 2nd series v. 1–,
indexes for 1st and 2nd series.
NN AVE 75-359

Le Parchemin.
Brussels, 1954–
(NYPL has no. 38, 1958 to date)
NN APA

Poplimont, Charles
Le Belgique Héraldique.
Brussels, G. Adriaens, 1863–67. 11
v., alpha.
NN AVE

Le Registres Paroissiaux et Leur
Conservation en Belgique.
(IN: *Archivum*, Paris, 1961. v. 9
[for 1959], p. 3–13)
NN BAA

Ruzette, J.P.
Liste Alphabétique de Généalogies
Imprimés.
(IN: *L'Intermediaire des Généalo-
gistes*, Brussels, 1958. no. 74, p.
73–129)
NN AVE

Ryckman de Betz, Fernand de
Baron.
Armorial Général de la Noblesse
Belge.
Liege, H. Dessain, 1957. 1,814 p.
NN AWT

Sabbe, Philemon D., and Léon
Buyse.
Belgians in America.
Tielt, Belgium, Lannoo, 1960. 317
p., no index, no t of c.
NN IEE (Belgians)

Vlaamse Stam.
Antwerp, Handzame, 1965–.
NN AVE

Warlop, E.
The Flemish Nobility Before 1300.
Kortrijk, Belgium, Desmet-Huys-
man, 1975. 1 v. in 2.
(Translation of work below)
NN JFM 76-12

Warlop, E.
Vlaamse Adel voor 1300.
Handzame, Familia et Patria,
1968. 2 v. in 3.
NN AVE 72-1784

Who's Who in Belgium, Including
Belgian Congo.

Brussels, 1957–.
NN *RR-AGM and K-10 1626

Brabant
Brabantica.
Brussels, 1956–.
NN AVEH (Brabant)

Bruges
Verbruggen, J.F.
Het Gemeenteleger van Brugges
   van 1338 tot 1340 . . .
Brussels, Palais des Academies,
   1962. 243 p., alpha.
NN AVEH (Bruges)

Brussels
Les Lignages de Bruxelles.
Brussels, 1962–67. v. 1–6.
NN AVE

Parys, H.C. van, and Fr. de Camp.
Généalogie des Familles Incrites
   aux Lignages de Bruxelles en
   1376.
Brussels, Généalogicum Belgicum,
   1971. 3 v., index v. 3.
NN AVEH (Brussels) 73-2101

Flanders
Roggeman, G.
Archif voor Familienkunke voor
   het Vlaams Nederscheldege-
   bied. Handzame, Familia et Patria, 1969–. (5 v. by 1972)
NN AVEH (Flanders) 72-2330

Tablettes des Flandres.
Bruges, 1948–.
NN AVE

Vlaam Kwartierstatenboek, ed. by
   W. Van Hille.
Bruges, 1969. Deel 1 (100 p.), index.
NN AVEH (Flanders) 72-2715

Hainaut
Paternostre de la Mairieu, C.L.R.
Tablettes du Hainaut.
Hombeck, 1955–66. 10 v., index
   each v.
NN AVEH (Hainaut)

Liege
Berg, J.J. van den.
Armorial Liegeois . . .
Liege, 1882. 2 v.
NN AWT 76-239

Pitgam
Hille, W. van.
Inventoire des États de Biens de
   Pitgam.
Ghent, the author, 1973–74. 2 v.
NN ASD (Pitgam Co.) 75-1156

Ursel
Smessaert, Marcel.
De Staten van Goed van Ursel.
Zomergen, Bauwerwaan, 1973–74.
   2 v.
NN AVEH (Ursel) 75-476

BULGARIA (SOFIA)

The southeastern European country of Bulgaria occupies what
was ancient Thrace and Moesia. It was settled by Slavic tribes
in the sixth century A.D. and in 660 was conquered by the
nomadic tribe of Bulgars, who were assimilated into the Slavic

population and adopted their language. The Bulgarian territories were greatly increased until the tenth century, when the Byzantines attacked and ultimately annexed them under Emperor Basil II in 1018. Byzantine rule ended in the twelfth century when, in 1186, a new Bulgarian empire rose under Ivan Asen (Ivan I), who made himself czar. His son, Kaloyan, was crowned in 1204 with the Pope's blessing, went on to defeat Emperor Baldwin I of Constantinople and extended his control over the entire Balkan peninsula, except for Greece. A Turkish invasion in the fourteenth century overwhelmed the country, and it was absorbed into the Ottoman Empire, where it was to remain until 1875, when the Bulgarians, under Stefan Stambulov, revolted against their Turkish masters. The reprisals were so barbaric that they were dubbed the "Bulgarian atrocities" and prompted the Russians to war against the Turks. The Treaty of San Stefano, which terminated the Russo-Turkish Wars of 1877–78, created a larger Bulgaria, but a subsequent revision at the Congress of Berlin made northern Bulgaria a suzerainty of Turkey. Southern Bulgaria—then known as East Rumelia—and Macedonia remained under Turkish rule.

In 1885 Alexander of Battenberg, first prince of Bulgaria, annexed East Rumelia and drove out attacking Serbian forces. His successor, Prince Ferdinand of Saxe-Coburg-Gotha, took advantage of the revolution of the Young Turks in 1908 and proclaimed Bulgaria's independence, with himself as Czar. In the First Balkan War of 1912 the Turks were driven out of Europe, with the exception of Constantinople, by the combined forces of Bulgaria, Serbia, Greece and Montenegro. Bulgaria found itself on the other side when it attempted to win Macedonia, which sparked the Second Balkan War of 1913. Bulgaria was ultimately unsuccessful and lost territory to all its enemies. By 1946 the monarchy was abolished and the Communists took over the Bulgarian government.

Censuses of Bulgaria were conducted in 1881, 1893, 1905, 1920, 1926 and 1934. The most common surnames in the capital city of Sofia are Georgiev, Dimitrov, Ivanov, Petrov and Popov.

Archives

Centralen Dăržaven Arhiv Na Narodna Republika Bălgarija
(Central Archives of the State) Sofia, ul. Slavjanska, Bulgaria

Centralen Dǎržaven Istoričeski Arhiv
(Central Historical Archives of the State)
Sofia, ul. Ždanov 5, Bulgaria

Public and Church Records

Birth and marriage certificates can be obtained from the district People's Council with jurisdiction over the place where the event occurred. Certificates of baptism and records of church weddings can be obtained from the church where the ceremony was performed.

Libraries

Central Library of the Bulgarian Academy of Sciences (Deposit library for all Bulgarian books, newspapers and periodicals)
Sofia, ul. Noemvri I, Bulgaria

"Kiril i Metodi" National Library
Sofia, Boul. Tolbuhin II, Bulgaria

Sofia University Library
Sofia, Boul. Ruski 15, Bulgaria

Books and Articles

American Bulgarian Review.
Mt. Vernon, NY, 1955–62. v. 5–12, incomplete.
NN IEE (Bulgarians)

Bulgaria: Territorial Administrative Organization.
Washington, DC, c. 1956. 310 p.
NN Map Div.

Bulgarian Royal Family.
(House of Saxe-Coburg and Gotha).
(IN: *CDS*, Paris, 1966. p. 138–42)
NN ARB
(IN: *GHF*, Limburg/Lahn, 1968. v. 8, p. 44–46)
NN ATC

Izvori Za Bulgarskata istoriia.
Sofiia, 1954.
(Bulgarian Historical Sources)
NN *QKA-74-632

Lang, David Marshall.
The Bulgarians from Pagan Times to the Ottoman Conquest.
London, Thames & Hudson, 1976. 208 p.
(Ancient Peoples and Places, no. 184; covers Bulgaria to 1396)
NN JFD 76-7775

Macdermott, Mercia.
A History of Bulgaria 1393–1885.
London, Allen and Unwin, 1962. 354 p.
NN R-GIVE 76-1526

Nurigiani, Giorgio.
... Glorie Bulgare.
Sofia, 1942. 205 p.
NN AGO

Orientator: Periodical for Americans of Bulgarian Descent.
Oak Park, IL, 1943–47. no. 1–8.
NN IEE (Bulgarians)

Revue Bulgare d'Histoire.
Sofia, 1973–.
NN Current Slavonic Div.

Roucek, Joseph S.
Les Bulgares d'Amérique.
(IN: *Les Balkans*, Athens, 1937. v. 9, p. 55–70)
NN GIV

Weftner, Mortiz.
Glossen zur Bulgarischen Zaren-
Genealogie: Beitrag zur Kennt-
niss der Ungarische-Bulgari-
schen Beziehungen.

(IN: *Ungarische Rev.*, Budapest,
1890–91. Jahrg. 10, p. 809–14;
Jahrg. 11, p. 17–34, 145–68)
NN *DF

CZECHOSLOVAKIA (PRAGUE)

In the ninth century A.D. the Great Moravian Empire was
comprised of the Czechs in Bohemia and Moravia and the Slavs
in Slovakia. The empire fell apart in the tenth century, and the
Slovaks became part of the Kingdom of Hungary, while the
Czechs set up the Kingdom of Bohemia. Religious wars beginning in the fourteenth century led to the decline of the Kingdom
of Bohemia, which eventually became a part of the Austro-
Hungarian Empire. The Czechs resisted Austrian rule. In World
War I Czech units fought on the Allied side and were rewarded
at the war's conclusion by the unification of Slovakian and Czech
lands and the declaration of an independent republic. Thomas
Masaryk became the first President. In 1938, when Britain,
France and Italy signed the Munich Pact in an effort to concili-
ate the Germans, the Sudetenland—a border region of Bohemia
with a large German population—was given to Germany.

The most common surnames in Prague are Černý, Dvořák,
Novák, Novotný, Svoboda and Procházka.

Censuses were taken in 1920–21 and in 1930.

Archives

Státní Ústřední Archiv (Central
State Archives)
Karmelitská 2
Prague I, Czechoslavakia

Public and Church Records

Civil registration began in a limited way after 1918. All people
who were not members of a
church were required to register with a district office. All others registered with the clergy
of their parish. The parish registers were taken over by the
state archives in 1950. Vital records certificates are issued by
the Local National Committee
in the place where the event
took place.

Libraries

Mětská knihovna (Public Library)
Prague I, Staré Město
nám. primátora dr. V. Vacka I
Prague, Czechoslavakia

Books and Articles

Aberle, George P.
From the Steppes to the Prairies: The Story of the Germans Settling in Russia and the Bohemians in the Crimea, Their Resettlement in the Americas ...
Bismarck, ND, c. 1964. 213 p.
NN IEK

Cada, Joseph.
Czech-American Catholics, 1850–1920.
Chicago, IL, Benedictine Abbey Press, 1964. 124 p.
NN IEE (Czechs)

Capek, Thomas.
The Czech (Bohemian) Community of New York.
New York, Czechoslovak Section of America's Making Inc., 1921. 93 p.
NN IAG p.v. 119

Capek, Thomas.
The Czechs (Bohemians) in America.
Boston, MA, Houghton Mifflin, 1920. 293 p.
NN IEE (Czechs)

Česká Akademie věd a Uměni, Prague.
Památnik na Oslavu Padesátiletého Panovického ...1848–1898.
Prague, 1898. 6 v. in 1.
NN *QW

Czechoslovakian Bibliography.
(IN: Service Bureau for Intercultural Education, pub. SL, New York, 1936. no. 9, p. 1–6)
NN IEE (Slavs)

Dinzenhofer, Wenzel.
XXVIII Genealogische Tafeln der Böhmischen Fürsten, Herzoge und Könige ...
Prague, Karl Barth, 1805. 200,50 p., 25 tables.
NN AVH (Czechoslovakia)

Droba, Daniel D.
Czech and Slovak Leaders in Metropolitan Chicago: A Biographical Study of 300 Prominent Men and Women.
Chicago, IL, Slavonic Club, U. of Chicago, 1934. 307 p.
NN *R-Slavonic Div.

Duben, Vojtech N.
Czech and Slovak Periodicals Outside Czechoslovakia as of Sept. 1964.
New York, Columbia U. Press, 1964. 26 leaves.
NN Desk Slavonic Div.

Fongon, Mihály.
Gömor-Kishont Vármegye Nemes Családai.
Kolozsvárt, Nyomatott Gámán J. Orokose Konyvsajtojan, 1909. 2 v. in 1, alpha.
NN AVH (Czechoslovakia)

Fries, Adelaide L.
Records of the Moravians in North Carolina.
Raleigh, NC, 1922–69. 11 v.
Covers 1752–1879

Fuhn, Heinrich.
Biographisches Handbuch de Tschechoslowakei.
Munich, R. Lerche, 1961. 640 p.
NN *RR-AGG and K-10 8603

Herman, Adolf Hanus.
A History of the Czechs.
London, Allen Lane, 1975. 342 p.

Hudson, Estelle.
Czech Pioneers of the Southwest.

Dallas, TX, Southwest Press, c. 1934. 418 p.
NN IEE (Czechs)

Král von Dobra Vody, Adalbert, Ritter.
Der Adel von Böhmen, Mähren und Schesien.
Prague, I. Taussig, 1904. 312 p., alpha.
NN ATK

Kucera, Vladimir.
Czechs and Nebraska.
Ord, NE, Quiz Graphics, c. 1967. 424 p.
NN IEE (Czechs)

Kulturní, Adresář ČSR: Biografický Slovník ...
Prague, J. Zeibrdlich, 1934–.
NN Desk Slavonic Div.

Gellner, John
The Czechs and Slovaks in Canada.
Toronto, U. of Toronto Press, c. 1968. 172 p.
NN HWH

Genealogische Tafeln zur Mitteleuropaischen Geschichte, ed. by Wilhelm Wegener.
Gottingen, Heinz Reise Verlag, 1964–. Lieferung 1–.
(no. 1, Die Premysliden (Kings óf Bohemia), c. 850–1306, etc.)
NN ARB 74-459

Miller, Olga K.
Ways to a Successful Genealogical Research in Czechoslovakia.
(IN: *GH*, Logan, UT, 1977. v. 31, p. 155–57)
NN APA

Nalevka, Vladimir.
La Colonia Checoslovaca en Cuba Durante la Segunda Guerra Mundial.

(IN: *Ibero-Americana Pragensia*, Prague, 1970. v. 4, p. 231–35)
NN HCA

Prochazka, Roman von.
Genealogisches Handbuch Erloschener Bohmischer Herrenstandsfamilien.
Neustadt/Aisch, Degener, 1973. 395 p.
NN ATL (Bohemia) 74-870

Renoff, Richard, and Stephen Reynolds.
Proceedings of the Conference on Carpatho-Ruthenian Immigration, 8 June 1974.
Cambridge, MA, Harvard Ukrainian Research Institute, 1975. 111 p.
NN IEE (Ruthenians) 76-1228

Rybak, Josef.
S Orlimi Kridly.
Prague, Mlada Fronta, 1954. 185 p.
NN *QW

Schacherl, Lilian.
Wege ins Exil: Emigrantenschicksale aus Böhmen und Mähren in Fünf Jahrhunderten.
Munich, E. Gans, 1964. 215 p.
(*Adabene Stifter Verenin Munich Veroffentlichunger. Abeteilung 8*)
NN L-10 2671 v. 8

Sousek, Charles J.
Czechs in South Africa. Johannesburg, 1942. 17 p.
NN BNS

Tabery, Erhard G.
Briesen im Schönhengst, Seine Geschichte und Seine Familien.
Frankfurt am Main, Zentralstelle fur Personen-und Familiengeschichte, 1965.
2 v., alpha.
NN AVH (Czechoslovakia)

Wallace, William V.
Czechoslovakia.
Boulder, CO, Westview Press,
    1976. index.
(Nations of the World Series)

Zeman, Zbynek A.B.
The Masaryks.
London, Weidenfeld and Nicolson,
    1976. 230 p. index
NN JFD 77-544

Zmizele Praha.
Prague, V. Polacek, 1946–48. 5 v.
    in 4.
(*Umelecke Parmatks II Rada sv.*
    6, 7, 11, 13, 16)
NN *QW

DENMARK (COPENHAGEN)

During the Viking Age in Denmark, which lasted from the ninth through the eleventh century, Danes participated in the Norse raids on Western Europe. Christianity was introduced during this period and Harold Bluetooth (c. 985) was Denmark's first Christian king. Denmark, England and Norway were united under King Canute from 1018 to 1035, but civil war broke out after his death. Waldemar I (1157–82) and Waldemar II (1202–41) were powerful rulers who stabilized Denmark and established its hegemony over the North. Waldemar IV brought Denmark to the acme of its power but was humbled by the Hanseatic League by the Treaty of Straisund in 1370. Denmark, Norway and Sweden were united under one crown by Waldemar's daughter, Queen Margaret, in 1397; Denmark's union with Norway endured until 1814. In 1448 Christian I became king, united Schleswig and Holstein with the Danish crown and established the House of Oldenburg. The present ruler, Queen Margrethe II (1940–), wife of Count Henri de Laborde de Monpezat, is his descendant.

Wars with Sweden from 1643 to 1660 ended with Denmark's defeat and the reduction of her eastern borders to their present position. Fighting on the French side in the Napoleonic wars, Denmark lost Norway, which was ceded to Sweden in 1815. After the Prusso-Danish War (1848–49) Denmark lost Schleswig-Holstein—a third of her territory—to Prussia. Denmark remained neutral during the First World War. In 1920 Denmark's southern border was established when northern Schleswig was recovered in a plebiscite.

The most common surnames in Copenhagen in the 1970's are Anderson, Hansen, Jensen, Larsen and Nielsen.

The oldest censuses date from 1787, 1801, 1834, and 1840, and censuses have contained information on birthplaces since 1845.

Genealogical Guidebook and Atlas of Denmark by Frank Smith and Finn A. Thomsen is a helpful reference. A fact sheet about genealogically valuable Danish records can be obtained from the country's Press and Cultural Relations Department (Dept. of the Ministry of Foreign Affairs, 2 Stormgade, DK-1470, Copenhagen K, Denmark).

Archives

Rigsarkivet (National Archives)
9 Rigsdagsgarden, DK 1218
Copenhagen K, Denmark

Danes Worldwide Archives (Udvandrerarkivet)
2 Konvalvej
DK 9000 Alborg, Denmark

Public and Church Records

Some parish registers of births, deaths and marriages date before 1660, although many early documents have been lost. Since 1814 all parish registers have been kept in duplicate, with one copy deposited in the provincial archives thirty years after completion and the other retained by the church. Draft registers in the National Archives go back to 1788.

Libraries

Det Kongelige Bibliotek (The Royal Library)
Christians Brygge 8
Copenhagen, Denmark

Greenland (Godthaab)

Greenland, part of the kingdom of Denmark, lies mostly within the Arctic Circle. A Danish colony until 1953, it is now represented in the government of Denmark. The land was known in ancient times by the Greeks and later by the Irish. In 982 it was discovered and colonized by Eric the Red, a Norseman, who named it Greenland to make it sound attractive to settlers. It became a bishopric in 1110, and in 1261 it came under Norweigian rule but was neglected so that no trace of Norsemen was left in the sixteenth century. In 1721 colonization was begun by a Norwegian missionary. The Danes came and established trading posts. Greenland was given to Denmark by treaty in 1815.

Books and Articles

Achen, Sven Tito.
Dansk Adelsvabener en Heraldisk Nogle.
Copenhagen, Politikens Forlag, 1973. 623 p., index.
NN AWT 74-1571

Aronson, Theo.
A Family of Kings: The Descendants of Christian IX of Denmark.
London, Cassell, 1976. 253 p., index, gen. tables.

Baekhoj, Lars.
Danske i Argentina.
Copenhagen, Danske Forlage, 1948. 256 p.
NN HKB

Barford, Poul F.
Die Borerlige Rigsdagsmaend, 1660 ...
Copenhagen, G.E.C. Cad, 1925. 272 p.
NN AGQ

Bricka, C.F.
Dansk Biografisk Lexikon, Tillige Amfattende Norge for ... 1537–1814.
Copenhagen, F. Hegel and Son, 1887–1905. 19 v.
NN D-15 4415

Christensen, Thomas P.
A History of the Danes in Iowa.
Solvang, CA, Dansk Folkesamfund, 1952. 281 p.
NN IEP

Christensen, Thomas P.
Danish Settlers in Minnesota.
(IN: *Minnesota History*, St. Paul, 1927. v. 8, p. 363–85)
NN IAA

Dahl, Svend, and P. Englestort.
Dansk Biografisk Haandleksikon.
Copenhagen, Gyldendalske Boghandel, 1918–26. 3 v.
NN *R-AGQ

Danish Royal Family
(IN: *GHF*, Limburg/Lahn, 1968. v. 8, p. 46–53)

(House of Schleswig-Holstein-Sonderburg-Glucksburg)
NN ATC

Danmark 1940 ...
Copenhagen, A. Jensen, 1940. 719 p.
NN AGO

Danmarks Adels Aarbog.
Copenhagen, J.H. Schultz, 1884–1974. 86 v., alpha, index, index to v. 1–86 in v. 86.
NN AVC

Dansk Biografisk Leksikon Grundlagt af C.F. Bricka.
Copenhagen, J.H. Schultz, 1933–44. 27 v.
NN *RR-AGQ

Denmark: An Official Handbook.
Copenhagen, Royal Danish Ministry of Foreign Affairs, 1974. 902 p., index.
NN *R-GHC 75–1152

Erichser, Balder V.A.
Dansk Historisk Bibliografi.
Copenhagen, G.E.C. Gad, 1917–27. 3 v.
NN GE

Favrholdt, E.M.
Emigranter: Fortaellinge og Genfortaellinger.
Copenhagen, Kirkeligt Samsfunds, 1930. 145 p.
NN HWH

Haandbog for Dansk i Osten i USA.
New York, H. Ryberg, 1930–.
NN IEP

Hald, Kristian.
Personnavne i Danmark.
Copenhagen, Dansk Historisk Faellesforenings Handboger, 1971–74. 2 v., index each v.

(v. 1, Oldtiden—Ancient period; v. 2, Middelalderen—Middle Ages)
NN APD 73-1592

Hansen, Jakob M.
AF Nordby Sogns Histoire.
Tranebjerg, Samso Boghandel, 1969. 423 p., index.
(History of Nordby, Denmark)
NN AVC

Hofman, Tycho de.
Portraits Historiques des Hommes Illustres de Dannemark.
Copenhagen, 1946. 6 v. in 1.
NN AVC

Hofman, Hans Dreyer de.
Samlinger af Publique og Private Stiftelser ... Danmark og Norge ...
Copenhagen, N. Libme, 1755–65. 10 v.
NN AVC

Hundrup, Ferdinand E.
Biographiske Efterretninger om de Candidator, som ved Kjobenhavns Universitet ...
Roeskilde, J.D.C. Hansons Bogtrykkeri, 1849–51. 2 v.
(Biographies of alumni of the University of Copenhagen)
NN STT Copenhagen

Jensen, Arne Hall.
... Den Dansk-Amerikanske Historie ...
Copenhagen, A. Jensen, 1937. 284 leaves.
NN IEP

Krak's Blaa Bog.
Copenhagen, 1910–1976+, 63 v. to 1976 in progress.
NN AGQ and *RR-AGQ

Lauring, Palle.
Her Skete det.

Copenhagen, 1969–74. 3 v.
(Danish local history)
NN JFK 75-286

LDS Series D
no. 5 (1968), Denmark General; no. 6 (1968), Denmark Church Records; no. 7 (1968),Denmark Census Records; no. 8 (1968), Denmark Military Records; no. 9 (1969), Denmark Probate Records; no. 10 (1969), Denmark Social Background.
NN APA 72-754

Lolland-Falsterske Kirkeboger.
Copenhagen, 1969. 163 p., index.
(This is an important sourcebook for this diocese, as it gives the dates covered by the various parish registers for births, marriages and deaths.)
NN AVC 73-1876

Paulden-Muller, Casper Peter (1805–1882).
De Forste Konger af den Oldenborgske Skaegt.
Copenhagen, 1971. 635 p.
(House of Holstein-Gottrop)
NN JFE 72-242

Petersen, G.C.
Forest Homes: the Story of Scandinavian Settlements in the Forty Mile Bush, New Zealand.
Wellington, A.H. and A.W. Reed, 1956. 137 p.
NN D-10 1782

Pieris, P.E.
The Danes in Ceylon
(IN: *Royal Asiatic Society of Great Britain and Ireland, Ceylon Branch Journals*, Colombo, 1927. v. 30, p. 169–80)
NN *OAA

Sanfundet for Dansk-Norsk Genealogi og Personalhistorie.
Personalhistorisk Tidsskrift.
Copenhagen, 1880–1972+. 34 v. in progress.
NN AVC

Smith, Frank, and Finn A. Thomsen.
Genealogical Guidebook and Atlas of Denmark.
Salt Lake City, UT, Bookcraft, 1969. 164 p., index.
NN AVC 72-382

Tonnesen, Allan.
Helsingors Bomaerker udg af Samfundet for Dansk Genealogi og Personalhistorie.
Copenhagen, 1968. 156 p.
(Property marks of Elsinor, Denmark)
NN AVC

Troelsen, Svend B.
Rejsby Sogns Historie ...
Copenhagen, 1966. 324 p.
(Rejsby, Denmark, genealogy)
NN AVC

Valynseele, Joseph.
Les Laborde de Montpezat et Leurs Alliances.
Paris, the author, 1975. 368 p.
NN ASF (Laborde) 77-677

Vig, P. Sorensen.
Danske i Kamp i og for Amerika, fra ca. 1640 til 1865.
Omaha, NE, N.H. Andersen, 1917. 393 p.
NN IEP

Yearbook for Danish-born Americans in USA.
Copenhagen, H. Ryberg, 1931–33.

(NYPL has 1932–33)
NN IEP

Greenland

Dalgård, Sune.
Grønland: Gengivelser af Akstykker og Breve fra det 16 til det 20 Århundrede.
Copenhagen, Munksgaards Forlag, 1960. 41 facsimiles, 18 p.
(*Denmark, Rigsarkivet, Fra Rigsarkivets Samlinger 4*)
NN GEA+

Lidegaard, Mads.
Grønlands Historie.
Copenhagen, J.H. Schultz, 1961. 166 p., illus., ports., maps, biblio.
NN E-11 3043

Meldgaard, Jorgen.
Nordboenne i Grønland: en Vikingebygds Historie.
Copenhagen, Munksgaard, 1965. 106, 3 p.
NN C-13 8088

Ostermann, Hother B.S.
... Nordmaend paa Grønland 1721–1814.
Oslo, Gyldendal, 1940. 2 v.
NN KBV

Rosing, Jens.
Tin og Undere i Grønland.
Copenhagen, 1968. 177 p.
NN JFG 75-153

Simpson, Colin.
The Viking Circle: Denmark, Greenland, Norway, Sweden, Finland, Iceland.
New York, Fielding Pub., 1968. 366 p.
NN *RKGO 75-7594

FINLAND (HELSINKI)

The Lapps, the earliest inhabitants of Finland, were pushed northward by the Finns, who came from regions south of the Baltic, but by the twelfth century Finland was conquered by the Swedes, who Christianized the land. In the sixteenth century Finland was made a grand duchy under the Swedish crown. In 1696 a great famine wiped out one-third of the population, and Finland suffered because of wars between Sweden and Russia. In 1721, after a Russian victory, Peter I obtained the Finnish province of Vibord by the Treaty of Nystad; the remainder of the duchy was ceded to Russia in 1809. While Finland under Russian rule was semi-independent and possessed democratic institutions, nationalism began to emerge in the mid-1880's. In 1917—the same year that the Bolsheviks seized power in Russia—the Finns declared their independence. The proclamation led to civil war between Whites (Finnish nationalists) and Reds (Russian sympathizers). The Whites, led by General Mannerheim and aided by German troops, were victorious. After a brief military regency, a republic was proclaimed and elections were held in 1919.

The most common surnames in Helsinki are Aalto, Aaltonen, Andersson, Nieminen and Virtanen.

Annual census records dating back to 1635 are preserved at the National Archives.

Alf Brenner's *Släktforskning: Praktisk Handbok för Finland* is an important guide for Finnish genealogical research.

Archives

Valtionarkisto/Riksarkivet (National Archives)
PL 274, SF-00171
Helsinki 17, Finland

Lakkautettujen Seurakuntien Keskusarkisto/Centralarkivet För De Inragna
Forsamlingarna (Central Archives of the Dissolved Parishes)
Pirttiniemenkatu 8
50101 Mikkeli 10, Finland

Suomen Ortodoksinen Kirkollishallitus/Ortodoxa Kyrkostyrelsen I Finland
(Ecclesiastical Board of the Finnish Orthodox Church)
Puistokatu 35
70300 Kuopio 30, Finland

Helsingin Yliopisto/Helsingfors Universitet (University of Helsinki)
Fabianinkatu 33
00170 Helsinki 17, Finland

Suomen Ritarihuone/Finlands Riddarhus (House of Nobility in Finland)
Regeringsgatan 2 A
00170 Helsinki 17, Finland

Public and Church Records

Civil registration is administered by ecclesiastical authorities, predominantly Evangelic Lutheran. Records of births, marriages and deaths generally date from the end of the seventeenth century, but certain wars—especially the Great Northern War (1700–21) and the World Wars—and several fires have greatly reduced this material, and only a limited number of church records prior to 1721 survive.

Parish registers before 1850 are kept at the National Archives, which can supply microfilm or typewritten copies. For local parish records, write to the Kirkhoherranverasto (Church Minister's Office) of the town.

Greek Orthodox records from 1779 to the present are in the custody of local parish offices, with some in the Provincial Archives of Mikkeli and some with the Administration Board of the Finnish Orthodox Church in Kuopio (address above).

Libraries

Helsingin Yliopiston Kirjasto (Helsinki University Library)
Helsinki 17, Unioninkatu 36, Finland

Turun Yliopiston Kirjasto (Turku University Library)
Turku, Finland

Historical and Genealogical Societies

Suomen Sukututkimusseura (Genealogical Society of Finland)
Sukututkimusosasto
Snellmaninkatu 9–11
00170 Helsinki 17, Finland
(*Genos*)

United States Sources

Finnish American Historical Society of Michigan, Inc.
19885 Melrose
Southfield, MI 48075

Finnish American Historical Society of the West
Box 3515
130 N.W. 19th Avenue
Portland, OR 97208

Minnesota Finnish American Historical Society
814 N. 9th Avenue, E.
Duluth, MN 55805

Books and Articles

Brenner, Alf.
Släktforskning: Praktisk Handbok för Finland. Helsinki, Söderström, 1947. 180 p., t or c at end, no index.
(Genealogical guide for Finnish research)
NN APB

Carpelan, Tor Harald, Friherre, 1867–.
Attartavlor för de pa Findlands Riddarhus Inskrivna Atterna.

Helsinki, Frenckellska Tyckeri, 1954–65. 3 v., alpha, gen. tables, coats of arms.
NN AVH (Finland)

Carpelan, Tor Harald, Friherre.
Helsingfors Universitets Student-matrikel, 1828–1852.
Helsinki, 1928–30. 245 p.
NN STT (Helsinki)

Finlands Riddercaps och Adels-Kalendar.
Helsinki, 1906–74 plus.
NN AVH (Finland)

Finnish American Magazine.
New York, Aika Pub. Co., 1939–.
NN *DT

The Finns in North America, ed by Ralph J. Jalkaneni.
Hancock, MI, Michigan State U. Press, 1969. 224 p.
NN IEP

Genos.
Helsinki, 1929–.
(Pub. by Suomen Sukututkimus-seura Genealogiskasamfundet i Finland. P.O. Box 248, SF-00171, Helsinki 17, Finland; NYPL has v.11 (1940) to date)
NN AVH (Finland)

Gentes Finlandiae.
Helsinki, 1966. 153 p.
(Ritarihuone Skrifter v.2)
NN AVB

Irwin, John L.
The Finns and Lapps.
Newton Abbot, DC, 1973. 171p.
NN JFD 74-6082

Kolehmainen, John I.
The Finnish Pioneers of Minnesota.

(IN: *Minnesota History*, St. Paul, 1944. v. 25, p. 317–28)
NN IAA

Kolehmainen, John I.
The Finns in America: A Bibliographical Guide to Their History.
Hancock, MI, Finnish American History Library, Suomi College, 1947. 141 p.
NN IEP

Kuku Kukin Oli (Who Was Who in Finland 1900–1961).
Helsinki, Otava, 1961. 593 p., alpha.
NN *RR-AGN

Kuka Kukin On.
Helsinki, Otava, 1974. 1,135 p., alpha.
NN *R-AGN

Olin, Saul Chalmer.
Finlandia: The Racial Composition ... and a Brief History of the Finnish People.
Hancock, MI, The Book Concern, 1957. 198 p.
NN E-10 5771

Putting It All on Record.
(IN: *Cheshire Family Historian*, Chester, England, 1975. no 5, p. 5–6)
(Reprint from Finnish Tourist Board)
NN ARX(Cheshire) 76-1670

Rosen, Ragnar.
Liber Scholac Helsingforsensis 1691–1865.
(IN: *Suomen Sukututkimusseura Julkaisuja*, Helsinki, 1936. no. 12, the whole number, 316 p.)
NN AVH (Finland)

Sormunen, Eine.
The Churches of Finland in Pictures.
Helsinki, Otava, 1949. 150 p.
NN GMB+

Suomen Sukututkimusseura. Julkaisuja.
Helsinki, 1924–.
NN AVH (Finland)

Suomen Sukututkimusseura.
Vusikirja.
Helsinki, 1917–.
NN AVH(Finland)

Vem och Vad Biografisk Handbok.
Helsinki, 1926–67 plus.
NN AGN

FRANCE (PARIS)

The Romans held the territory known as France until the fifth century A.D, when Teutonic tribes, including the Visigoths and Franks, swept through the area. Clovis, leader of the Franks, captured southern Gaul and western Germany and made himself ruler of all Frankish tribes. He accepted Christianity and founded the Merovingian dynasty. The Saracens invaded Gaul in the eighth century, taking advantage of the weak Merovingian dynasty, but were routed in 732, when Charles Martel led the Franks against them. His son, Pepin the Short, overthrew the Merovingians and established the Carolingian dynasty, whose power was expanded by his son Charlemagne in the ninth century. Charlemagne was crowned emperor at Rome in 800. After his death in 814 his empire was divided, and Charles I (the Bald) became king of what is now France. The Norsemen constantly raided France, obtained Normandy in 911 and crossed the Channel from there to conquer England in 1066.

In 1337 a long series of wars and truces, known as the Hundred Years War, broke out because of claims on French soil made by the English kings who claimed the country as heirs of Isabelle of France, wife of Edward II. (The title King of France was used by the kings of England from 1340 to 1801.) The English were gaining control when Joan of Arc led the French armies from 1429 to 1431 and lifted the siege of Orléans. In 1435 Burgundy returned to a French alliance, and the English were routed from all but Calais. Brittany was united with France, and most of the Bourbon fiefs were confiscated. Under Kings Charles VIII, Louis XII, Francis XI, Henry II and Francis II (1483–1560) France healed itself, despite disruptions such as the

Italian Wars, caused by a dispute with the Hapsburgs. Louis XIV (1643–1715) centralized the country and raised it to a world power, but attempts to expand in Europe were stopped by the War of the Spanish Succession (1701–14). Louis XV's reign saw the bankruptcy of the state, caused by more foreign wars and support of the American Revolution. Irritated by their tax burden, the peasants precipitated the French Revolution, which lasted from 1789 to 1815. Royalists of all classes—including, for example, the parents of Benjamin Nones of Philadelphia (chapter 14)—were marched to the guillotine in huge numbers during the Reign of Terror under Robespierre, which set in after the king's execution.

Napoleon Bonaparte became first consul under the Consulate, and after he defeated an Austrian-British coalition and proclaimed himself emperor, he led France in great victories until he was finally defeated by Russia. A European Coalition conquered Paris, forced the abdication of Napoleon and restored the Bourbons to the throne. In the July revolution of 1830, Charles X was ousted, and his distant kinsman, Louis Phillipe of the House of Bourbon-Orléans, came to power, only to be overthrown in 1848. In June of that year Napoleon's nephew, Louis Napoleon Bonaparte, became President of the Second Republic; he proclaimed himself Emperor Napoleon III after a *coup d' état* in 1852. Crushing defeat in the Franco-Prussian war of 1870–71 led to Napoleon III's downfall. The Third Republic, in 1914–18, shared victory with Russia and England over Germany in World War I, but the economy was devastated. France joined Britain in 1939 at the start of World War II but was defeated by Germany. General Charles De Gaulle formed the Free French Army in London. After the liberation of Paris, he was elected Provisional President of the Fourth Republic. De Gaulle resigned under leftist pressure but was recalled to power in 1958, during the conflict with the French colony of Algeria. Despite opposition, he negotiated Algeria's independence.

The most common surnames in Marseilles are Arnaud, Blanc, Fabre, Martin, Michel and Roux. In Paris the most common names are Bernard, Lévy, Martin, Petit and Richard.

The valuable *Bibliographie Généalogique Héraldique et Nobiliaire de la France* by Gaston Saffroy, published in three volumes between 1970 and 1974, is the single most important reference for French genealogical research. Yann Grandeau's *A La Re-cherche de Vos Ancêtres* and Pierre Durye's *Genealogy: An Intro-duction to Continental Concepts*, translated by Wilson O. Clough, are also excellent guides.

Archives

Archives Nationale de France
60 rue des Franc–Bourgeois
75141 Paris Cedex 03, France

Archives de la Sorbonne (Univer-sité de Paris)
47 rue des Écoles
75230 Paris Cedex 05, France

Public and Church Records

Civil registration began in 1789 for births, deaths, marriages and divorces. For vital records of people born in France, write Greffe de Tribunaux d'Instance. For French nationals born abroad, write Service Central de l'Etat Civil du Ministère des Af-faires Etrangères. For French nationals born in French over-seas territories, write Ministère des DOM* and TOM*; and for naturalized French citizens who did not bear birth certificates, write Ministère de la Population (Etat Civil). Birth and marriage certificates can also be obtained from the office of the Mayor (*la Mairie*) at the place of birth or marriage.
*(Département d'Outre-Mer and Territoire d'Outre-Mer.)

Catholic Church records predate civil registration.

Libraries

Bibliothèque Nationale

58 rue de Richelieu, Paris 2e, France
Bibliothèque de l'Université de Paris
Paris, France

Historical and Genealogical Societies

Les Vieux Noms de France
12 rue Caumartin
Paris Cedex 09, France

Société Française de Généalogie, d'Heraldique et de Sigillographie
Patrice de Viguerie, Treas.
67 Avenue de Paris
78000 Versailles,France
(Héraldique et Généalogie, 1969–)

Le Société du Grand Armorial de France
179 Boulevard Haussmann
Paris, France

Books and Articles

Allen, Cameron.
Antoine Gevaudan of Manakin Town and His Immediate De-scendants.
(IN: *VM*, Richmond, VA, 1965. v. 73, p. 22–28)
NN *R-APR (Virginia)

Allen, Cameron.
Preliminary Notes on the Per-rault-Perrow Family of Roi Guillaume.
(IN: *VG*, Washington, DC 1964. v. 8, p. 67–74, 126–31, 149–55)
NN APR (Virginia)

Annuaire de la Noblesse de France.
Paris, 1843–1960. 89 v., index, 1843–1930, in v. 80, 1931/33, index each v.
NN ASA

Anselme, Père.
Histoire Généalogique et Chronologique de la Maison Royale de France, des Pairs, Grands Officiers ... et des Anciens Barons du Royaume. 3rd ed.
Paris, Edition Royal, 1967–68 (orig. 1726–1890). 11 v., index.
NN ASC & ASC 74-2340

Les Archives Biographiques Contemporaines ...
Paris, 1906–10. 4 v.
NN AGI

Aubert de La Chesnaye-Desbois, François A.
Dictionnaire de la Noblesse de France.
Paris, le Veuve Duchesne, etc., 1770–78. 12 v., alpha.
NN ASB

Baines, James A.
French Surnames in Australia.
(IN: *Ancestor*, Melbourne, 1975. v. 10, p. 182–83)
NN APW

Bartholoni, Fernand.
Guide du Blason. Paris, Editions Stock, 1975. 312 p., t of c.
NN AWP 77-533

Beaurepaire-Froment, Paul de.
... Dictionnaire Biographiques des Hommes du Midi.
Pairs, L'Armorial Français, 1903. 151 p.
NN F-10 9506

Betencourt, Dom Pierre.
Noms Féodaux.
Paris, 1867. 2 v.
NN ASB

Bird, Jack.
Some Sources for French Genealogy and Heraldry.
(IN: *GM*, London, 1960. p. 237–41)
NN ARCA

Blanche, Pierre.
Dictionnaire Armorial des Noms de Famille de France.
Paris, A. Fayard, 1974. 249 p., alpha.
NN AWP 75-1312

Bran, Louis.
Le Livre d'Or de Quelques 6000 Familles de Velay, Auvergne, Gevaudan, Forez, Vivarais, Languedoc, etc.
Lyon, M. Brun, 1910. 2 v. in 1 (843 p.).
NN ASD

Cahiers d'Héraldique.
Paris, Centre National de la Recherche, c. 1975. 2 v.
NN AWA 76-1567

Les Cahiers Nobles.
Paris, 1954–67. no. 1–32.
NN ASA

Carnoy, Henri.
Dictionnaire Biographique des Grands Négociants et Industriels ...
Paris, L'Armorial Français, 1901. 220 p.
NN F-10 9503

Carnoy, Henri.
Dictionnaire Biographique des Hommes de l'Est.

Paris, L'Armorial Français, 1903. 246 p.
NN F-10 9504

Carnoy, Henri.
Dictionnaire Biographique des Hommes du Nord.
Paris, 189–. 272 p.
NN F-10 9505

Carnoy, Henri.
... Dictionnaire Biographique International des Médecins et Chirurgiens.
Paris, L'Armorial Français, 1903. 136 p.
NN F-10 9511

Chaffanjon, Arnaud.
La Fayette et sa Descendance.
Paris, Berger-Levrault, 1976. 362 p.
(Available from Diffusion Frankelve, 8 rue Clapeyron, 75008 Paris)

Chaffanjon, Arnaud.
Le Petit Gotha Illustré.
Paris, Editions Serg, 1968. 606 p.
NN ARB 74-2286

Coutot, Maurice.
Ces Héritiers que Je Cherche.
75006 Paris, Editions Robert Laffont, 6, Place Saint-Sulpice, 1974. 260 p., t. of c., no index.
NN ASB 76-2294

Dauzat, Albert.
Dictionnaire Etymologique des Noms de France.
Paris, Larousse, 1951. 626 p.
NN APD

Denissen, Fr. Christian.
French Families of the Detroit Region, 1701–1911, ed. by Harold F. Powell.

Detroit, MI, DSGR, 1976. 2 v.
NN APR (Detroit) 76-2735

Desvernes, Louis.
La Famille de Tascher Branche de Périgord (1756–1930).
La Famille Bonaparte ...
Paris, G. Saffroy, 1953. 12 p., 3 gen. tables (the family of the Empress Josephine).
NN ASF (Tascher)

Dictionnaire Biographie Française.
Paris, Letouzey, 1933–1975 plus. 13 v. (A—Flers) in progress.
NN *R-AGI

Dictionnaire des Communes (France et Algérie)
Paris, Berger-Levrault, 1913. 819 p.
NN KGB

Dictionnaire National des Canadiens Français, 1608–1760.
Institut Généalogique Drouin, 1958. 3 v.
NN APW

Dioudonnat, Pierre-Marie.
Encyclopédie de la Fausse Noblesse de la Noblesse d'Apparence.
Paris, Sedopols, 1976. 395 p.
NN ASB 77-721

Durye, Pierre.
Genealogy: An Introduction to Continental Concepts.
(Translated by Wilson O. Clough)
New Orleans, LA, Polyanthos, 1976. c. 150 p.

Etat de la Noblesse Française Subsistante.
Nîmes, Le Castellum, 1976. 1 v. v. 4
NN ASB 76-2245

Fawtier, Robert.
The Capetian Kings of France:
Monarchy and Nation, 987–1328.
London, Macmillan, 1974 (orig.
1960). 242 p.
NN *R-DDD 75-5036

Fox, Frank B.
Two Huguenot Families: De Blois-
Lucas.
Cambridge, MA, Harvard U. Press,
1949. 120 p., index.
(18th-century French in Massa-
chusetts and Rhode Island)
NN APV (De Blois)

Forbes, Allan.
The Boston French.
New Orleans, LA, Polyanthos,
1971 (orig. 1938). 98 p.
NN IEE (French) 73-686

France. Archives Nationales.
Guide des Recherches Généalo-
giques aux Archives Nationales.
Paris, Imprimerie Nationale, 1953.
107 p., index.
NN ASB

The French Genealogist.
Harbor City, CA, Hartwell Co.,
1977– .

French Genealogy
LDS Research Paper. Series G no.
1, Salt Lake City, c. 1975.
NN APA 76-1892

French Royal Families
Bourbon (IN: *GHF*, Limberg/
Lahn, 1968. v. 8, p. 21–39)
Bonaparte
(IN: *GHF*, Limberg/Lahn, 1971. v.
9, p. 16–18)
NN ATC

Bourbon and Bonaparte
(IN: *CDS*, Paris, 1966. p. 242–62)
NN ARB

House of Bonaparte
(IN: *CDS*, Paris, 1966. p. 242–47)
NN ARB
(IN: *GHF*, Limberg/Lahn, 1971. v.
9, p. 16–18)
NN ATC

House of Bourbon-Orléans
(IN: *CDS*, Paris, 1966. p. 248–62)
NN ARB
(IN: *GHF*, Limberg/Lahn, 1968. v.
8, p. 21–39)
NN ATC

House of Bourbon-Parma
(IN: *CDS*, Paris, 1966. p. 387–411)
NN ARB

Grandau, Yann.
A la Recherche de Vos Ancêtres:
Guide du Généalogiste.
Paris, Stock, 1974. 348 p., t of c at
end, illus. of documents excel-
lent.
NN ASB 77-395

Guide Officiel des Franco-Améri-
cains.
Auburn, RI, Albert A. Belanger,
1931. 638 p., arranged by state
and town, alpha under this arrangement.
NN IEE (French)

Haag, Eugene.
La France Protestante.
Paris, Joel Cherbuliez, 1846–58. 10
v., alpha.
NN AGI

Héraldique et Généalogie
Paris, 1969–. (Each issue lists addresses of regional French genealogical societies—Gérard de
Villeneuve, ed. 11, Blvd. Persh-
ing. 78000 Versailles)
NN ASA 73-2514

Hill, Glenna See.
Huguenot Ancestors Documented.
Bloomfield, NJ, Huguenot Society
of New Jersey, 1975. 101 p., in-
dex.
NN APK 77-555

Huguenot Society of London.
Proceedings.
London, 1885–1970+. 21 vols.
NN ARCA

Huguenot Society of London.
Publications
London, 1887–1961. v. 1–47.
(Reprinted by Kraus Reprint,
1969, as 47 v. in 36 v.)
NN ARCA

Irish Residents in Bordeaux, 1756.
(IN: *Irish Genealogist*. London,
1973. v. 4 pp. 598–601)
NN ARCA

Jougla de Morenas, Henri.
Grand Armorial de France.
Paris, Éditions Héraldiques,
1934–52. 6 v. and sup.
(v.1, p. 42–100, has a full account
of the royal family of France
since Robert the Strong, with
the arms of the various kings.)
NN AWP+

Labarre de Raillicourt, Domi-
nique.
La Noblesse de Française Titrée.
Paris, the author, 1970. 283 p.
NN ASB 73-2596

Labarre de Raillicourt, Domi-
nique.
Nouveau Dictionnaire de Biogra-
phie Française et Etrangères.
Paris, the author, 1961– .
NN *RR-AA

Labarre de Raillicourt, Dominique.

Origine des Faux Titres Portés à
la A.N.F.
Paris, the author, 1971. 168 p. index
NN ASB 73-1796

Labarre de Raillicourt, Domi-
nique.
Les Titres de Cour au XVIIIe Siè-
cle. Les Comtes.
Paris, the author, 1968–69. 2 v.
NN ASC 76-1011

Levy, Jean Michel.
Y a-t-il eu un Dénombrement Général de la Population en l'Année
1793?
(IN: Société de Antiquité de Normandie Bulletin, Caen, 1959/60.
v. 55, p. 155–90) (Census of 1793)
NN DPM

Morel, Henri.
La Noblesse de la Famille de
Jeanne d'Arc au XVIe Siècle.
Paris, 1972. 48 p.
NN ASF (Du Lys) 75-2391

Morlet, Marie-Thérèse.
Les Noms de Personne sur le Ter-
ritoire de l'Ancienne Gaule du
Vie au XIIe Siècle.
Paris, Centre National de la Re-
cherche Scientifique, 1968–72. 2
v., alpha.
(v. 1, Gallo-German names; v.2,
Latin names)
NN APD 72-2783

La Nobiliare du XXe ... Le Sang
Glorieux de Jeanne d'Arc.
Paris, 1912. 334 p. (v.4)
NN ASB+

Pequinot, Jean and Linda.
We Follow the Trail Across the
Channel.
(IN: *Cheshire Family Historian*,

Chester, England; 1976. no.3, p. 25–27)
NN ARX (Cheshire) 76-1670

Pula, James S.
The French in America, 1488–1974: a Chronology and Fact Book.
Dobbs Ferry, NY, Oceana Pub., 1975. 154 p., index.
(Ethnic Chronicle Series no. 20)
NN IEE (French) 75-1874

Qui est-ce?
Paris, 1934. 611 p.
NN D-19 6378

Qui Etes-vous?
Paris, G. Ruffy, 1908–24. 3 v.
NN AGI

Reamon, G. Elmore.
The Trail of the Huguenots in Europe, the United States, South Africa and Canada.
Baltimore, MD, GPC, 1972 (orig. 1963). 318 p., index.
NN APK 75-710

Les Registres Paroissiaux et d'Etat Civil en France.
(IN: *Archivum*, Paris, 1961. v. 9, p. 55–99)
(This also includes an account of the Jewish registers, p. 77–78.)
NN BAA

Registers of the Births, Marriages and Deaths of the Eglise Française à la Nouvelle York from 1688 to 1804, ed by Alfred V. Wittmeyer.
Baltimore, MD, GPC, 1968 (orig. 1886). 324, xlii p., index.
NN APRN

Revert, Eugène.
La France d'Amérique: Martinique, Guadeloupe, Guyane, Saint-Pierre et Miquelon.

Paris, 1949. 287 p.
NN HRN

Rieder, Milton P., and Norma G. Rieder
The Acadians in France, 1762–1776.
Metairie, LA, 1967–72. 3 v.
NN ASB 72-2340

Saffroy, Gaston.
Bibliographie Généalogique Héraldique et Nobiliaire de le France.
Paris, Librarie Gaston Saffroy, 1968–72. 3 v., index.
(v. 1, general works; v. 2, works by locality and subject; v. 3, genealogical works. The most important French genealogical reference)
NN AS

Saint-Allais, Nicolas V. de
Nobiliaire Universel de France.
Paris, 1872–77. 21 v.
NN ASB

Le Sang de Louis XIV.
Braga, Cruz, 1961–62. 2 v.
(A vast work dealing with the legitimate and illegitimate descendants of the "Sun King," including both M. and Mme Giscard d'Estaing, who are among the latter.)
NN ASC+

Santerre, Richard.
The Franco-Americans of Lowell, Massachusetts.
Lowell, MA, France American Day Committe, 1972.

Schermack, Joseph.
La Maison de France en Bretagne.
Paris, Robert Laffont, 1972. 377 p., plus 5 gen. tables, t. of c., no index. (El Cid, p. 20)
NN ASF (France) 73-2396

Sereville, E. de, and F. de Saint Simon.
Dictionnaire de la Noblesse Française.
Paris, La Société Française au XXe Siècle, 1975.
1,214 p. plus, alpha.
NN ASB 75-282

Les Sources de l'Histoire de France des Origines à la Fin du XVe Siècle.
Paris, 1971. 1 v. in 2.
NN *RS-D 76-3109

Table Généalogique de l'Ancienne Maison de Ravenel.
n.p., n.d., 14 leaves.
NN ASF+ (Ravenel)

Toulouse-Lautrec Family.
(IN: *Annales du Midi*, Toulouse, 1965. v.77, p. 99–107)
NN DA

Valynseele, Joseph.
Le Sang des Bonaparte.
Paris, 1954. 162 p., gen. table, index.
NN ASF (Bonaparte)

Villeneuve, Gérard de
Les Giscard d'Estaing
Versailles, 1975. 113 p.

Who's Who in France.
Paris, Lafitte, 1953–.
NN *RR-AGI and L-11 2882

Willems, J.H., and H. Lamant
Armorial Français.
1973– , alpha.
NN AWP 73-2310

Woelmont de Brumagne, Baron de.

La Noblesse Française Subsistante.
Paris, 1928–31. 3 v. in 4, plus separate cross-index.
NN ASB+

Alsace
Cercle Généalogique d'Alsace.
Strasbourg, 1968– .
NN ASD (Alsace)

Lehr, Ernest.
L'Alsace Noble.
Paris, Berger-Levrault, 1870. 3 v.; index in v. 3.
NN ASD+ (Alsace)

Schweitzer, Jean.
L'Emigration Alsacienne vers la Russie au Debut du XIXe Siècle.
(IN: *Cercle Généalogique d'Alsace Bulletin*, Strasbourg, 1976. no. 33, p. 9–15)
NN ASD (Alsace)

Wolff, Christian.
Les Principales Causes de l'Immigration et de l'Emigration en Alsace du XVe au XIXe Siècle.
(IN: *Cercle Généalogique d'Alsace Bulletin*, Strasbourg, 1976. no. 34, p. 43–47)
NN ASD (Alsace)

Wolf, Christian.
Répertoire Bibliographique des Biographies Collectives d'Alsace.
Strasbourg, 1962. (Fédération des Sociétés d'Histoire et Archéologie d'Alsace, v. 3)

Anjou
Lebrun, François.
Les Hommes et la Mort en Anjou aux 17e et 18e Siècles.

Paris, 1971. 562 p.
NN JLE 73-1826

Brittany
Gourvil, Francis.
Noms de Famille Breton d'Origine
Toponymique.
Brest, Telegrammy, 1970. 330 p.,
alpha, cross-index.
NN APD 73-1631

Burgundy
Speaight, Robert.
The Companion Guide to Bur-
gundy.
London, Collins, 1975. 351 p., biblio.
p. 340–41, index.
NN *R-KGB 76-5103

Colmar
Les Listes d' Admission à la
Bourgeoisie de Colmar 1361–
1494, ed. by Lucien Sittler.
Colmar, Archives de Ville, 1958.
317 p., index.
(Archives de la Ville de Colmar
Pub. v. 1)
NN ASD+ (Colmar)

Corsica
Antionetti, Pierre.
Histoire de la Corse.
Paris, 1973. 486 p.
NN JFE 74-2879

Biancamaria, J.
La Corse dans sa Gloire. . . .
Paris, J. Peyronnet, 1963. 493 p.
NN D-14 4359

Bonaparte-Wyse, Olga.
The Spurious Brood: Princess Letitia Bonaparte and Her Children.
London, Gollancz, 1969. 205 p., index.
NN D-19 5461

Fortescue, B.
Napoleon's Heritage: An Ethnic
Reconstruction.
London, J. Murray, 1934. 317 p.
NN DG

Galletti, Ange.
Histoire Illustrée de la Corse.
Paris, 1972. 577 p.
NN JFG 74-1114

LeVaivre, Jean de.
Les Premiers Comtes Souverains
de Corse. Les Seigneurs d'Orano
et Leurs Descendants.
New York, Mss, 1956. 134 p., gen.
tables.
NN AZ

Palix, Madeleine.
Les Seigneurs Cortinchi. . . .
Vanves (Seine), 1964. 157 p., gen.
tables.
NN F-11 4808

Tupigny, Jacques P.M., Baron de.
. . . Les Barons Mariani et Leurs
Alliances.
Noget-le Rotrou, Daupley-Gouver-
neur, 1933. 118 p., gen. tables.
NN ASF (Mariani)

Dole
Pideux de la Maduere, S.
Les Officiers au Souverain Parle-
ment de Dole et Leur Famille.
Paris, the author, 1961. 4 v., index
in v. 1(P) poor paper.
NN ASD (Dole)

Dunkirk
Bouley de Lesdain, L.A., and
Pierre Daudruy.
Notice Généalogique sur Quelques
Familles Patriciennes de Dun-
kerque.

Fécamp, L. Durand et fils, 1959.
301 p., alpha, index, poor paper.
NN ASD (Dunkirk)

Flanders
Nord Généalogie.
Roubaix, 1971– .
NN ASD (Nord) 75-16

Franche-Comte
Lurion, Roger de.
Nobiliaire de Franche-Comte.
Marseilles, Lafitte Reprints, 1976
(orig. 1890). 848 p., index.
NN ASB 76-1669

Jura
Rais, André.
Livre d'Or des Familles du Jura.
Porrentruy, La Bonne Press, 1968–.
383 p., index, v. 1–. (A—Br)
NN ASD (Jura)

Languedoc
Lands, Neil
History, People and Places in Languedoc Roussillion.
Bourne End, Spurbooks, 1976. 159
p., index.

Limousin
Nadaud, Abbé Joseph.
Nobiliaire du Diocese et de la Généralité de Limoges.
Paris, Editions du Palais Royal,
1974 (orig. 1880–82). 4 v., index
in each v.
NN ASD (Limousin) 74-2033

Lorraine
Cercle Généalogique de Lorraine.
Nancy, 1971– .
NN ASD (Lorraine)

Pelletier, Ambrose.
Nobiliaire de Lorraine.

Paris, Editions Royal, 1974 (orig.
1758). 2 v. in 3.
AWR 75-1228

Pully, Enguerrand.
Les Particularités du Droit Noble
en Lorraine.
Paris, A. Rousseau, 1909. 196 p.
NN ASD (Lorraine)

Loudun
L'Eglise Réformée de Loudun.
The Registers of the Protestant
Church at Loudun, ed. by C. E.
Lart.
Lymington, C. King, 1905. v.1
(1566–1582)
NN ASD (Loudun)

Lunéville
Lunéville, France. Inventaire des
Registres de l'Etat Civil de
Lunéville (1562–1792).
Nancy, Berger-Levrault, 1899. 367
p.
NN ASD+ (Lunéville)

Montelimar
Coston, Baron de.
Histoire de Montelimar et des
Familles Principales Qui Ont
Habité Cette Ville.
Paris, Editions du Palais Royal,
1973 (orig. 1878). 4 v., index.
NN ASD (Montelimar) 74-1109

Montpellier
La Roque, Louis de (1830–1903).
Armorial de la Noblesse de Languedoc Montpellier.
Marseilles, Lafitte Reprints, 1972
(orig. 1860). 2 v.
NN ASD (Montpellier) 75-875

Nantes
Perthuis, Alexandre.
Le Livre Doré de l'Hôtel-de-Ville
de Nantes.
Nantes, Jules Grinsard, 1873. 2 v.,
index in v. 2.
NN ASD (Nantes)

Nevers
Marolles, L'Abbé de.
Inventaire des Titre de Nevers.
Nevers, Paulin Fay, 1873.
NN ASD (Nevers)

Normandy
Mangy, Edouard, Comte de.
Nobiliaire de Normandie.
Paris, 1863–64. 3 v. in 2 v.
NN ASD (Normandy)

Merval, Stephen de.
Catalogue et Armorial ... de
Parlement de Rouen.
Evereux, Auguste Herissey, 1867.
202 p., index.
NN ASD+ (Normandy)

Paris
Bottin Mondain 1976, Tout Paris,
Toute la France.
Paris, Société Didot-Bottin, 1976.
1,798 p., alpha.
NN *RD-TLE and BAZ for earlier
issues

Christian, Arthur.
Etudes sur le Paris d'Autrefois.
Paris, G. Roustan, 1904–7. 6 v.
NN DOH

Lefeuvre, C.
Les Anciennes Maisons de Paris,
Histoire de Paris Rue par Rue,
Maison par Maison.
Paris, C. Reinwald, 1875. 6 v.
NN DOC

Le François, Philippe.
Paris à Travers les Siècles.
Paris, Calmann-Levy, 1948–56. 10
v.
NN DOV

Tardieu, Ambroise.
Dictionnaire Iconographique des
Parisiens.
Herment, Puy de Dome, the au-
thor, 1885. 308 col.
NN AOF

Who's Who in France.
Paris, 1953 / 54, v.1.
(v.1 covers Paris only—running title: Who's Who in Paris)
NN L-11 28882

Pas-de-Calais
Pas-de-Calais, France. Départe-
ment.
Epigraphie du Département du
Pas Calais.
Arras, Sede, 1883–1937. 198 v. in 25
v.
(Arras 5 v., Bethune 4 v., Boulogne
3 v., Montreuil 7 v., Saint Ormer
3 v., Saint Paul 3 v.)
NN ASD (Pas-de-Calais)

Poitou
Beauchet-Filleau, Joseph.
Dictionnaire Historique et Généa-
logique ... des Familles du Poi-
tou. 2nd ed.
Fontenay-le-Comte,   Lussaud,
1974. 6 v. (A—Mar)
NN ASD (Poitou)

Ponthieu
La Gorgue-Rosny,
Recherches Généalogiques sur les
Comtes des Ponthieu ...
Boulogne-sur-Mer, 1874–75. 4 v.
NN ASD (Ponthieu)

Puy

Bourdon (Boudon)-Lashermes, Albert.
Le Vieux Puy Logis et Vieilles Familles.
Grenoble, Ed. des 4 Seigneurs, 1973. 420 p., index.
ASD (Puy) 76-2546

Rhin, Bas

Rhin, Bas. France (Dept.) Archives.
Tables des Noms Roturiers des Inventaires des Archives Anciennes.
Strasbourg, 1962. 355 p. alpha
NN APD+ 74-56

Rouergue

Barrau, H. de.
Documents Historiques et Généalogiques du Rouergue.
Paris, Editions du Palais Royal, 1972 (orig. 1853–60). 4 v., index each v.
NN ASD (Rouergue) 74-1107

Sarthe

Linière, Raoul de.
Armorial de Sarthe.
Le Mans, M. Vilaire, 1948. 2 v., alpha, index.
NN ASD (Sarthe)

Savoy

Bernard, Abbé Felix.
Les Origines Féodales en Savoie et en Dauphine.
Grenoble, Guirimand, 1949. 333 p., index (Poor paper.)
NN ASD (Savoy)

Somme

Boyenval, Réné.
Répertoire des Noms de Familles de la Somme en 1849.
Amiens, Archives de la Somme, 1972. 228 p., index, map.
NN APD 76-2105

Toulon

Teissier, Octave.
. . . Armorial de la Ville de Toulon.
Toulon, Agence du Petit Marseillais, 1900. 88 p.
NN ASD (Toulon)

Toulouse

Roque, L. de la.
Armorial de la Noblesse de Languedoc.
Marseilles, Lafitte Reprints, 1972 (orig. 1863). 335 p., index.
NN ASD (Toulouse) 75-871

Toulouse. Archives Municipales.
Répertoire Numérique des Archives 1800–1840.
Toulouse, 1967. 80 leaves.
NN JFF 73-1013

GERMANY

In the fourth and fifth centuries A.D., the migrating Germanic tribes of the Rhine and Danube regions completely routed the Romans, who had conquered them beginning in the first century B.C., and Slavic tribes occupied Germany east of the Elbe. The Franks swept through in the late fifth century and subdued all of present France, western and southern Germany and Thuringia. Pepin the Short, the Father of Charlemagne, deposed the Frankish Merovingian dynasty in 751. Charlemagne, crowned king at Rome in 800, continued his father's work and conquered the Saxons, and his kingdom dominated Germany to the Elbe. At Charlemagne's death in 814, the empire was divided, and the Kingdom of the Eastern Franks, under his son Louis the German, constituted the nucleus of the German state. A truly unified Germany was to remain elusive until the nineteenth century. The final years of the Carolingian dynasty were disrupted by Norse, Slav and Magyar raids, and their royal power was diminished by the growth of feudalism. The Carolingians' successors were not equal to the task of centralizing the German state, which gradually became a loose network of principalities and free cities joined by the authority of the Holy Roman Emperor. By the thirteenth century, campaigns against the Slavs achieved great eastward expansion of the empire. The fifteenth and sixteenth centuries were characterized by great prosperity in German commerce, but the Reformation led by Martin Luther was the final blow to German unity, as it precipitated the Thirty Years War (1618–1648). Germany lost a large part of its population to starvation and emigration. Prussia emerged as the strong German state during the eighteenth and nineteenth centuries and benefitted from the Congress of Vienna (1814–15), where the German confederation was established. German nationalism surfaced in the revolution of 1848, which sent thousands of Germans and German Jews fleeing from military conscription to the United States. Prussia, led by Bismarck, defeated Austria in 1866 and France in the Franco-Prussian War of 1870–71 and achieved the goal of a Germany unified with Alsace-Lorraine. Wilhelm I, King of Prussia (1797–1888) of the House of Hohenzollern, was proclaimed Emperor of Germany in 1871. His family's rule ended with the ouster of his grandson, Kaiser Wilhelm II, at the end of World War I in 1918. The humiliating Treaty of Versailles in 1918 laid the groundwork for the rise of Hitler and the Second World War. After decisive defeat by the United States, the Soviet Union and England, Germany was occupied and divided. The Soviet sector became the Communist satellite state of East Germany. West Germany adopted a federal constitution in 1948. In 1961 the East Germans erected a wall partitioning the city of Berlin into two sectors.

Some of the earliest German immigrants to the New World, among them Peter Tallman, a native of Hamburg, fled from Germany in the 1640's. Tallman eventually settled in Rhode Island and became Attorney General of the colony and the ancestor of many Americans. He was followed by many different religious and regional groups of Germans, of whom the Pennsylvania Dutch (*Deutsche*) of Lancaster County, Pennsylvania, have retained some of their ethnic customs. The Palatines and Moravians who settled in New York, Pennsylvania and North Carolina were other immigrants of this period.

In the 1970's the most common surnames in Berlin (East and West) are Hoffman, Kruger, Muller, Schmidt and Schul(t)z.

Clifford Neal and Anna P-C. Smith's *Encyclopedia of German-American Research* and *American Genealogical Research in German Archives*, published in 1976 and 1977 respectively, are two excellent guides for German family history.

Federal Republic of Germany (Bonn)

Archives

Bundesarchiv (National Archives)
54 Koblenz
Am Wollershof 12 (Postfach 320), West Germany

Zentrale Archivverwaltung (Central Archives, West Berlin)
Senatsverw. für Wissenschaft u. Kunst, I
Berlin 19, Bredtschneiderstr. 5-8, West Germany

Public and Church Records

Civil registration began in 1908. Vital records certificates are available from the local Standesamt—in the Western Sector of Berlin from Standesamt I (Berlin-Dahlem, Lentzalle 107).

For census information (the census is not conducted regularly) write the Statistisches Bundesamt, Wiesbaden.

Libraries

Amerika-Gedenkbibliothek: Berliner Zentralbibliothek 1-y1, Blücherplatz
Berlin, Federal Republic of Germany

Universitätsbibliothek der Freien Universität Berlin
Berlin 33, Garystrasse 39, Federal Republic of Germany

Historical and Genealogical Societies

Gesamtverein der Deutschen Geschichts und Altertumsvereine (Union of German Historical and Archaeological Societies)
Wiesbaden, Mainzerstrasse 80, Federal Republic of Germany

Der Herold, Verein für Heraldik, Genealogie und Verwandte Wissenschaften

Westfalische Strasse 38
Berlin-Halensee, Federal Republic
of Germany

Berlin:
Arbeitsgemeinschaft für Familiengeschichte im Kulturkreis Siemens
1 Berlin 13 (Siemensstadt) Goebelstrasse 139-145, Germany

Bielefeld:
Salzburger Verein 48
Bielefeld, Postfach 7206, Germany

Bonn:
Westdeutsche Gesellschaft für Familienkunde
Bonn–Bad Godesberg
Loewenburgstrasse 18, Germany

Bretten:
Landesverein Badische Heimat
Ausschuss für Familienforschung
6518 Bretten
Heilbronnerstrasse 3, Germany

Detmold:
Salzburger Verein
493 Detmold
Berliner Allee 24, Germany

Dortmund:
Roland zu Dortmund
46 Dortmund-Wickede
Duettelstrasse 1, Germany

Elmshorn:
Vereinigung für Familienkunde
Sitz Elmshorn
22 Elmshorn, Sandburg 88, Germany

United States Sources
American Historical Society of Germans from Russia

615 D. Street
Lincoln, NE 68502
(*AHSGR Work Paper; AHSGR Clues; AHSGR Newsletter*)

Society for History of the Germans in Maryland
231 St. Paul Place
Baltimore, MD 21202

Democratic Republic of Germany (*East Berlin*)

Archives

Zentrales Staatsarchiv (Central State Archives)
Abteilung Sozialismus U. Historische Abteilung I
15 Potsdam, Berliner Str. 98-101, Democratic Republic of Germany

Zentrales Staatsarchiv (Central State Archives)
Historische Abteilung II
42 Merseburg
Weibe Mauer 48, Democratic Republic of Germany

Staatsarchiv Leipzig (State Archives of Leipzig)
701 Leipzig, Georgi-Dimitroff-Platz I
Democratic Republic of Germany

Stadtarchiv Berlin (Archives of the City of Berlin)
102 Berlin, Marx-Engels-Platz 7
Democratic Republic of Germany

Archiv der Martin-Luther-Universität Halle-Wittenberg
402 Halle/Saale, Weidenplan 12
Democratic Republic of Germany

Zentralstelle für Genealogie in der DDR

(Center for Genealogy in the Democratic Republic of Germany)
701 Leipzig, Georgi-Dimitroff-Platz I
Democratic Republic of Germany

Libraries

Berliner Stadtbibliothek
C.2 Breitestrasse 37
Berlin, Democratic Republic of Germany

Deutsche Staatsbibliothek
(Originally Preussische Staatsbibliothek)
108 Berlin, Unter den Linden 8
Democratic Republic of Germany

Comenius-Bücherei
(Pädagogische Zentralbibliothek)
Schenkendorfstr. 34,
Leipzig, Democratic Republic of Germany

Books and Articles

Allgemeine Deutsche Biographie.
Berlin, Duncker & Humblot, 1967–71 (orig. 1875–1912). 56 v., alpha indexed.
NN *RR-AGK 71–74

Almanach de Gotha.
Gotha, J. Perthes, etc., 1764–1944. 181 v.
NN APC

Archiv für Sipperforschung und alle Verwandten Gebiete.
Limberg/Lahn, C.A. Starke, 1923– .
(Archives for genealogical research)
NN APA (v. 5 [1928] to date in NN)

Arndt, Karl J.R., and May E. Olson.

German-American Newspapers and Periodicals 1732–1955, History and Bibliography.
Heidelberg, Quelle and Meyer, 1961. 794 p.
NN *AK and *RB-*D

Bahlow, Hans.
Deutsches Namenlexikon ...
Munich, Keysersche, 1967. 588 p.
NN APD

Bahlow, Hans.
Niederdeutsches Namenbuch.
Walluf bei Wiesbaden, Martin Sändig, 1972. 572 p., alpha.
NN APD 73-2485

Biggers, Don H.
German Pioneers in Texas.
Fredericksburg, TX, Fredericksburg Pub. Co., 1925. 230 p., t of c called index.
NN IEK

Bird, Jack.
Some Sources for German Genealogy and Heraldry.
(IN: *GM*, London, 1960. v.13, p. 143–44)
NN ARCA

Blätter für Familienkunde und Familienpflage.
Frankfurt, 1965– . bd. 1.
NN *ZAN-674 & Current Room 315G

Braunfels, Wolfgang.
Karl der Grosse: Lebenswerk und Nachleben.
Düsseldorf, L. Schwann, 1965–68. 5 v.
NN N-10 2034

Brandenburg, Erich.
Die Nachkommen Karls des Grossen.

Frankfurt am Main, Zentralstelle für Deutsche Personen-und Familiengeschichte, 1964. (orig. 1935). 122 p. index (*Caroli Magni Progenies v.*)
NN ATC +

Bubolz, George.
Father Julius and Mother Emilie: A Personal Biography of Midwestern Pioneers.
Hicksville, NY, Exposition Press, c. 1975. 172 p., no index.
(From Pomerania to Winchester, Winnebago County, Wisconsin, by 1870)
NN APV (Bubolz) 76-1487

Cunz, Dieter.
The Maryland Germans: A History.
Princeton, NJ, Princeton U. Press, 1948. 476 p.
Biblio. p. 439-449
NN IEK

Deutsches Adelsblatt. (Formerly *Deutsches Adelsarchiv*)
Melle, 1962-. v.1
NN ATA+

Deutsches Adelsarchiv.
Westerbrak, 1948-61. v. 4-17.
NN ATA+

Deutsches Geschlechtebuch.
Limburg/Lahn, Starke, et al., 1889-1975. 175 v. to 1976.
NN ATC

Elkins, Edna Hornberg, et al.
The Hornberg Story.
Austin, TX, Joe G. Garcia, 1974. 468 p., index.
(The Hornberg family of Platendorf, Kingdom of Hanover, who settled in Texas in the 19th century)
NN APV (Hornberg) 76-2308

Eschenbach, Virginia.
A Primer, Searching for Your German Ancestors.
Munster, IN, the author, 1977. 55 p.

Eschenbach, Virginia.
Searching for German Ancestors: East Germany, West Germany.
(IN: *Genealogical Helper*, Logan, UT, 1976. v. 30, p. 83-84, 301-3, 395-98)
NN APA

Familie und Volk.
Neustadt (Aisch), Degener, 1952-61. 10 v. in 5.
NN ATA

Familiengeschichtliche Bibliographie.
Neustadt (Aisch), Degener, 1936-61. Bd. 5-11 incomplete.
(Bd. 1-4 [1900-34] pub. by Zentralle für Deutsch Person-und Familiengeschichte)
NN AT

Frank, Karl F. von.
Standeserhebungen und Gnadenakte für das Deutsche Reich und die Österreichischen Erblande bis 1806 ... Alt-Österreichischen Adels-Lexikon 1823-1918 ...
Schloss Senftenegg ... Selbstverlag, 1967-74. 5 v., A-Z.
NN ATC 73-694

Freidericks, Dr. Heinz F.
How to Find German Ancestors and Relatives.
Neustadt (Aisch), Degener, 1969. 16 p.
NN *XMG-262

Fristch, Thomas Freiherr von.
Die Gothaiscen Taschenbücher, Hofkalender und Almanach.

(Title page—see Der Gotha, spine title)
Limburg/Lahn, C.A. Starke, 1968. 424 p.
NN APC 73-1809

Genealogical Research in German Speaking Lands: A Symposium. Washington, DC, 1958. 23 p. (NSG Special Publication no. 19)
NN APGA

Genealogie Deutsche Zeitschrift für Familienkunde. (Formerly Familie und Volk)
Neustadt (Aisch), Degener, 1962–
v. 11-
NN ATA

Genealogisches Handbuch der Adeligen Häuser.
Limburg/Lahn, C.A. Starke, 1953–75. 24 v., in progress.
NN ATC

Genealogisches Handbuch der Freiherrlichen Häuser.
Limburg/Lahn, C.A. Starke, 1952–75. 14 v., in progress.
NN ATC

Genealogisches Handbuch der Fürstlichen Häuser.
Limburg/Lahn, C.A. Starke, 1951–76. 11 v., in progress.
NN ATC

Genealogisches Handbuch der Grafliche Häuser.
Limburg/Lahn, C.A. Starke, 1952–75. 11 v., in progress.
NN ATC

The German Language Press of the Americas 1732–1968. History and Bibliography v. 2 (Argentina–Venezuela).

Munich, Verlag Dokumentation, 1973. 709 p.
NN *RB-*D

German-American Genealogical Research Monographs.
Thomson, IL, Heritage House, 1973–75. no.1–4, in 6 parts.
(no.1, Smith, Clifford Neal, *Brunswick Deserter Immigrants of the American Revolution.* alpha and unpaged)
NN IEK 76-1607

The German-American Genealogist.
Cleveland, OH, 1975–76. (Merged with Journal of German-American Studies)
NN IEK 77-696

Germanic Genealogist.
Harbor City, CA, the Hartwell Co., 1976–.

Geschichte der Deutscher in Buffalo und Erie County, New York.
Buffalo, NY, Reinecke und Zesch, 1895.
NN IRM (Buffalo)

Gessner, Gerhard.
Deutsches Familienarchiv.
Neustadt an der Aisch, Verlag Degener & Co., 1952–77. 66 v. in progress.
NN ATC

Glenzdorf, Johann, and Fritz Freichel.
Henker Schinder und Arme Sünder.
Bad Munder am Deister, W. Rost, 1970. 2 v.
(The German knacker's trade—executioners' families)
NN ATC

Der Gotha. (Title on spine). See Fristch, and Almanach de Gotha.
Limberg/Lahn, C.A. Starke, 1968. 424 p., alpha.
(Indexes the volumes of the Gotha series from the beginning up to 194– when they ceased publication. The majority of the volumes of these series dealing with the different levels of nobility are in NN)
NN APC 73–1809

Gottschald, Max.
Deutsche Namenkunde.
Berlin, Walter de Gruyter and Co., 1971. 646 p.
NN APD 72–2704

Hall, Charles M.
The Atlantic Bridge to Germany.
Logan, Everton and Midvale, UT, the author, 1974. 4 v.+.
NN AT 74–2180

The Hamburg Passenger Lists 1850–1934.
Salt Lake City, UT, LDS Gen. Soc., 361 reels of which 105 reels are indexes of regular emigrant lists, 1855–1934.
LDS

Handbuch der Genealogie für den Herold, Verein für Heraldik, Genealogie und Verwandte Wissenschaften zu Berlin . . . compiled by Eckart Henning and Wolfgang Ribbe.
Neustadt (Aisch), Degener & Co., 1972. 304 p.
NN APB 74–1096

Holtzclaw, Benjamin Clark.
Ancestry and Descendants of the Nassau-Siegen Immigrants to Virginia 1714–1750.
Harrisburg, PA, 1964. 583 p., index (*Germana Record. no. 5*)
NN APR (Germana)

Houston, J.R.
The Almanach de Gotha.
(IN: *Families*, Toronto, 1973. v.12, p. 109–19)
NN APW 73–2794

Huberty, Michel, Alain Giraud, et al.
L'Allemagne Dynastique.
(15 Families That Made the Empire)
Leperreux, France, 1976. (v.1, Hessen, Reuss, Saxony)
Alain Giraud, 96 Quai d'Artois, 74170 Leperreux, France
NN ATC 77–749

Hussmann, Heinrich.
Über Deutsche Wappenkunst.
Wiesbaden, Guido Pressler, 1973. 133 p., t of c at end, no index.
NN AWR 75–1631

Journal of German American Studies.
Cleveland, OH 44126, Robert E. Ward, ed., 21010 Mastick Road, 1969–.
NN IEK 76–557

Joyner, Mrs. Douglas M., and Fred S. Palmer.
German Genealogical Research.
(IN: *Virginia Tidewater Genealogy*, Hampton, VA, 1975. v. 6, p. 11–18)
NN Current

Kahlenberg, Friedrich P.
Deutsche Archive in West und Ost.
Düsseldorf, 1972. 153 p.
NN JLD 74–577

Konrad, J.
German Family Research Made Simple. 2nd ed.
Munroe Falls, OH, Summit, 1977. 107 p.

Kosch, Wilhelm.
Biographisches Staatahanbuch.
Bern, Switzerland, 1959–63. A–Z.
NN *RR-AB

Kuhn, Oscar.
Studies in Pennsylvania German
  Family Names.
n.p., 1903 (orig. *Germanica*, 1902).
  43 p.
NN APD

Minerva-Handbücher Archiv.
Archiv im Deutschsprachigen ...
Berlin, Walter de Gruyer, 1974. 2
  v. (A–Z)

Neue Deutsche Biographie.
Berlin, Duncker & Humbolt,
  1952–74. 10 v.
(A–Kaffsack) in progress
NN *RR-AGK

Norddeutsche Familienkunde.
Neustadt (Aisch), Degener, 1952–.
  index for v. 17–19 bound with v.
  19–21.
NN ATA

Ostdeutsche Familienkunde.
Neustadt (Aisch), Degener & Co.,
  1953-
NN ATA

Parsons, William T.
The Pennsylvania Dutch: A Per-
  sistent Minority.
Boston, MA, Twayne, 1976. 316 p.,
  index.
NN IEK 76-2482

Passenger List of the Bark "Wie-
  land" from Bremen to New Orleans, January 1853.
(IN: *Louisiana Genealogical Register*, Baton Rouge, LA, 1976. v.
  23, p. 124–29)
NN APR (Louisiana)

Pochmann, Henry A., comp., and
  Arthur R. Schultz, ed.
Bibliography of German Culture
  in America to 1940.
Madison, WI, U. of Wisconsin
  Press, 1953. 483 p., index.
NN IEK

Ross, Donald A.
Genealogical Research Guidelines
  for South Australians of German Descent.
(IN: *SAG*, Marden, South Australia, 1975. v. 2, no. 2, p. 37–39)
NN APW

Ross, Donald A.
Research in Germany.
(IN: *South Australian Genealogist*,
  Marden, S.A., 1975 v. 2, no. 3, p.
  64–66)
NN APW

Roth, Fritz.
Restlose Auswertung von Lei-
  chenpredigten und Personal-
  schriften für Genealogische und
  Kulture-historische.
Zuecke Boppard, Rhein, E. Roth,
  1959–67. 6 v.
(German obituaries)
NN ATC 73–2337

Rubincam, Milton.
New Light on the Hessians in the
  Revolutionary War.
(IN: *Genealogical Journal*, Salt
  Lake City, UT, 1976. v. 5, p. 92–
  95)
NN Current Room 315G

Sartorius, Otto.
Die Nachkommenschaft D. Martin
  Luthers in Vier Jahrhunder-
  ten ...
Göttingen, Verlag der Lutheriden
  Vereinigung, 1926. vii, 195, 86
  p., index.

(500 years of Martin Luther's descendants)
NN ATH (Luther)

Sartorius, Otto.
Verzeichnis der Lebenden Nachkommen D.M. Luthers ... 1 July 1936.
Ostheim v.d. Rhon, R. Werner, 1936. 24 p., index.
(This brings the descendants down to 1936.)
NN ATH (Luther)

Schnee, Heinrich.
Die Hoffinanz und der Moderne Staat.
Berlin, Duncker & Humblot, 1956–67. 5 v. (band 1–3, 5, 6), gen. tables.
(About the Court Jews)
NN *PXS

Der Schlüssel; Gesamtinhaltsverzeichnisse mit Ortsquellennachweisen für Genealogisch Heraldische und Historische Zeitschriftenreihen.
Göttingen, 1949–70. 6 v. (v. 5 [1965], 1,675 p., covers the period 1945–60 and indexes 27 different German periodicals)
NN ATA

Seiter, Floyd Benjamin, and Bessie W. Seiter.
The Johann David Seiter Family: A Family History.
Ann Arbor, MI, Cushing-Malloy, 1972. 235 p.
(A German family who came to America c. 1869; excellent illustrations of a passport, marriage certificate, Bible record, family groups, the family at work, barn raising, etc.)
NN APV (Seiter) 74-1933

Smith, Clifford Neal, and Anna P-C. Smith.
American Genealogical Research in German Archives.
New York, R.R. Bowker, 1977. c. 360 p., index.

Smith, Clifford Neal, and Anna P-C Smith.
Encyclopedia of German-American Research.
New York, R.R. Bowker, 1976. 273 p., index.
NN APG 76–579

Stammfolgen-Verzeichnis.
Limburg/Lahn, C.A. Starke, 1969. 215+ p.
(Indexes *Gen. Handbuch des Adels Series.* Bands 1-42 and *Deutsch-Geschlechtebuch.* v.1–119, 120–50)
NN AT 75–2774

Strassburger, Ralph B.
Pennsylvania German Pioneers, 1727–1775.
Norristown, PA, Pennsylvania German Society, 1934. 3 v., index.
NN APK

Studien zur Fugger Geschichte.
Leipzig, Duncker & Humbolt, etc., 1907–72. 24 v.
(The money of this famous banking family has been put to good use in creating this very detailed account of the family.)
NN ATH (Fugger)

Stump, Karl.
The Emigration from Germany to Russia in the Years 1763 to 1862.
Lincoln, NE 68502, American Historical Society of Germans from Russia, 615 D Street, 1973. 1,018

p., no index, alpha arrangement in various parts; 8 maps in pocket text in English and German.
(There should be more of this type of work for German-Americans.)
NN ATC 75-281

Tolzmann, Don Heinrich.
German-Americana: A Bibliography.
Metuchen, NJ, Scarecrow Press, 1975. 384 p.
(Genealogy p. 326–35; biography p. 316–25; state histories, including local histories, p. 26–66)
NN IEK 75-2424

Verzeichnis de Familienforscher Familienverbande, Familienstiftungen und Familienkundlichen.
Vereintgungen Archive und Biblioteken.
Limburg/Lahn, C.A. Starke, 1956. 719 p.
NN AT

Wer Ist Wer?
Frankfurt am Main. v.1–18 by 1974–75.
NN *RR-AGK

Ward, Robert E.
German and German-American Genealogical Sources and Guides Since 1850.
(IN: *Genealogical Journal*, Salt Lake City, UT, 1977. v.6, p. 3–14)
NN Current Room 315G

Wer Ist's?
Leipzig, 1900–. v.1–17 plus.
NN AGK

Who's Who in Germany. 5th ed.
Ottobrann nr Munich, 1974. 2 v., A–L, M–Z.
NN *RR-AGK

Wust, Klaus.
The Virginia Germans.
Charlottesville, VA, U of Virginia Press, 1969. 301 p., index.
NN IEK

Augsburg
Haemmerle, Albert.
Stamtaflen Augsburger Familien.
Munich, Privatdruck, 1948–50. 2 v.
NN ATF (Augsburg)

Baden
Badische Familienkunde.
Baden, Grafenhausen, 1958–. index, v.1–10, bound with v.10.
NN ATF (Baden)

Baden Royal Family.
(House of Zahringen)
(IN: *GHF*, Limburg/Lahn, 1968. v. 8, p. 4–6)
NN ATC

Bavaria
Bavarian Royal Family.
(House of Wittelsbach)
(IN: *GHF*, Limburg/Lahn, 1971. v. 9, p. 4–16)
NN ATC

Genealogisches Handbuch des in Bayern Immatrikulierten Adels.
Neustadt (Aisch), Degener,1950–75. v.1–11, in progress, alpha index each v.
NN ATF (Bavaria)

Gewin, J.P.J.
Herkunft und Geschichte Fuhrrender Bayerisch-Österreichischer Geschlechter im Hochmittelalter.'s Gravenhage, H.L. Smits, 1957. 192 p., index.
NN ATF (Bavaria)

Tyroller, Franz.
Genealogie des Altbayerischen
Adels im Hochmittelalter.
Göttingen, H. Reise, 1969. 567 p.,
index.
NN ATF (Bavaria) 72-1580

Berlin

Das Aelteste Berliner Buerger-
buch 1453–1700 . . .
Berlin, Gsellius, 1927. 394 p. (*Quellen und Forschungen zur Geschichte Berlins. Bd. 1*)
(Bd. 4 of this work continues the
list of Bürgers from 1700–50)
NN EIF

Berliner Hauserbuch.
Berlin, Gsellius, 1933. teil 2, bd. 1.
(*Historiche Kommission für die
Provinz Brandenburg und die
Reichaupstadt Berlin Veroffen-
tlichungen nr. 7*)
NN TET

Brunswick

Reidemeister, Sophie L.
Genealogien Braunschweiger Pa-
tritier und Ratsgeschlechter aus
der zeit der Selbständigkeit der
Stadt (vor 1671).
Braunschweig, J.H. Meyer, 1948.
194 p., index.
(*Wertstuecke aus Museum Archiv
und Bibliothek der Stadt Braunschweig Bd. 12*)
NN ATF (Brunswick)

Cologne

Gatzen, Wilhelm.
Beitrage zur Geschichte von Hal-
fen-und Adelsfamilien in Kur-
koln und in Herzogtum Julich.
Cologne, Ostern, 1974. 216 p., t of
c, no index.
NN ATF (Cologne) 75–695

Neiderlandisch-Reformierte Ge-
meinle in Köln.
Protokolle der Niederlandisch-Re-
formierten Gemeinde in Köln
von 1651–1803.
Düsseldorf, Rheinland-Verlag,
1971. 2 v. (*Inventare Nichtsta-
atlicher Archive. 12/13*)
NN ATF (Cologne) 75–2614

Elberfeld

Strutz, Edmund.
Die Ahnentafeln der Elberfelder
von 1708–1808.
Neustadt (Aisch), Degener, 1963.
231 gen. tables.
(*Bergische Forschungen Bd. 3*)
NN ATF (Elberfeld) 74-543

Franconia

Blätter für Frankische Familien-
kunde.
Nürnberg, 1934–. v.1–6 on film, in-
dex v.5–7 in v.7.
NN *ZAN-G23 film and ATF
(Franconia)

Frankenthal

Eglise Réformée Neerlandaise,
Frankenthal.
Registres de l'Eglise Réformée
Neerlandaise de Frankenthal
au Palatinat, 1565–1689.
Brussels, Librairie Evangelique,
1911–13. 2 v.
(*Société d'Histoire de Protestant-
isme Belge Doc. Hist. no.2–3*)
NN ATF (Frankenthal)

Frankfurt am Main

Korner, Hans.
Frankfurter; Histor.-Genealog.
Handbuch . . .
Munich, Vogel, 1971. 456 p., t of c,
no index.
NN ATF (*Frankfurt am Main*) 73-
2342

Hamburg

Marchtaler, Hildegard von.
Aus Alt-Hamburger Senatoren-hausen: Familienschicksale im 18 und 19 Jahrhundert.
Hamburg, H. Christians, 1959. 233 p.
(*Verein für Hamburgische Ge-schichte Veroffentichangen Bd. 16*)
NN ATF (Hamburg)

Hanover

Hanover Royal Family.
(House of Welf)
(IN *GHF*, Limburg/Lahn, 1968. v.8, p. 53–58)
NN ATC
(IN: *CDS*, Paris, 1966. p. 310–318)
NN ARB

Hesse

Arndt, Karl J. R.
How to Find Your Hessian Ances-tor.
(IN: *Genealogical Journal*, Salt Lake City, UT, 1977. v.6, p.15–18)
NN Current Room 315G

Hessische Chronik: Montsschrift für Familien-und Ortsge-schichte in Hessen und Hessen-Nassau
Darmstadt, 1912–. (Suspended 1922–23, ceased pub. 1942)
NN ATF (Hesse)

Hilden

Krant, Elsabeth.
Die Register des Personenstandes von Hilden und Eller 1810–1813.
Hilden, F. Peters, 1966. 529 p.
(*Niederbergische Beitrage Bd. 9*)
NN ATF (Hilden)

Kreuznach

Velten, Carl.
Bürgerbuch der Stadt Kreuznach, 1509–1620 . . .
Neustadt (Aisch), Degener, 1965. 184 p.
NN ATF (Kreuznach) 72–3049

Kulmbach

Bürgerbuch der Stadt Kulmbach, 1250–1769 . . .
Kulmbach, Freunde der Plassen-berg, 1967. 369 p.
(*Die Plassenburg: Schriten fur Hei-matkunde und Kulturpflege in ost Franken Bd. 26*)
NN ATF (Kulmbach)

Lunenburg

Witzendorff, Hans J. von.
Stammtaflen Luneburger Patri-ziergeschlecter . . .
Göttingen, H. Reise, 1952. 168 p.
NN ATF (Lunenburg)

Mannheim

Waldeck, Florian.
Alte Mannheimer Familien.
Mannheim, Selbstverlag, 1920–25. 5 v. in 4.
NN ATF (Mannheim)

Mecklenburg

Mecklenburg Genealogical Hand-book.
Bountiful, UT, AIS, 1977. 40 p.
Mecklenburg Royal Family.
(House of Mecklenburg).
(IN: *GHF*, Limburg/Lahn, 1971. v.9, p. 48–53)
NN ATC

Pritzbuer, Joachim von.
Mecklenburger Adelsgeschleter.
Neustrelitz, A.M. Gundlach, 1894. 216 p.
NN ATF (Mecklenburg)

Nassau
Bonnet, Rudolf.
Nassauisches.
Neustadt (Aisch), Degener, 1964–
65. 2 v.
(Genealogie und Landesgeschichte
Bd. 8-9)
NN ATF (Nassau)

Oldenburg
Herold: Verein für Wappen Siege-
lund Familienkunde.
Berlin, Hoffalzgrafen-Register ...
Neustadt (Aisch), Degener, 1964–
68. 2 v. in 3.
NN ATF (Palatinate)

Last, Martin.
Adel und Graf in Oldenburg ...
Oldenburg, H. Holzberg, 1969. 192
p.
(*Oldenburger Studien Bd. 1*)
NN ATF (Oldenburg)

Oldenburger Balkenschild.
Oldenburg, 1943–.
(1943–55 on film)
NN *ZAN-G21 and ATF (Oldenburg)

Pflaizische Familien-und Wappenkunde.
Ludwigschafer, 1952–. v.1–.
(1952–57 on film)
NN *ZAN G16 and ATF (Palatinate)

Pomerania
Spruth, Herbert.
Landes-und Familiengeschicht-
liche: Bibliographie für Pom-
mern.
Neustadt   (Aisch),   Degener,
1962–65. 866 p.
(Genealogie und Landesgeschichte
Bd. 2)
NN ATF (Pomerania)

Prussia
Altpreussische Geschlechterkunde
Familienarchiv.
Hamburg, 1953–70. v.1–4.
NN ATF (Prussia)

Prussian Royal Family.
(House of Hohenzollern)
(IN: *CDS*, Paris, 1966. p. 431–71)
NN ARB
(IN: *GHF*, Limburg/Lahn, 1968.
v.8, p. 70–71)
NN ATC

Reinbeck
Fink, Walter.
Das Amt Reinbeck 1577–1800 ...
Frankfurt (Main), Zentrastelle für
Personen-und   Familienge-
schichte, 1969. 341 p.
(Genealogie   und   Landesge-
schichte Bd. 23)
NN ATF (Reinbeck)

Rheda
Rheda Kirchengemeinde.
Das Taufbuch I (1622/1680) der
Westfalischen   Kirchenge-
meinde Rheda ...
Rheda, F. Scharpenberg, 1967, v. 1.
(Quellen und Forschungen zur
Westfalischen Geschichte 98
Heft)
NN ATF (Rheda) 73–1174

Rhine Province
Gerhard, Oswald.
Zur Geschichte der Rheinischen
Adelsfamilien ...
Düsseldorf, L. Schwann, 1925. 175
p.
NN ATF (Rhine Province)

Saxony, Lower (Ostfalen)
Quellen zur Genealogie
Göttingen, Heinz Reise, 1965–73. 3
  v.
NN ATF (Saxony, Lower)

Saxony Royal Family.
(House of Wettin)
(IN: *GHF*, Limburg/Lahn, 1968.
  v.8, p. 167–83)
NN ATC

Zoder, Rudolf.
Familiennamen in Ostfalen.
Hildesheim, Georg Olms, 1968. 2 v.,
  alpha.
(v.1, A–K, v.2, L–Z)
NN APD

Stade
Bargen, Werner von.
Erzbischof Giselberts Stadler
  Turnier von 1300.
Stade, Schaumberg, 1970. 212 p.
NN ATF (Stade) 73-1069

Strasbourg
Strasbourg.
Le Livre de Bourgeoise de la Ville
  de Strasbourg 1440–1530, ed. by
  Charles Wittmer and J. Charles
  Meyer.
Strasbourg, P.H. Heinz, 1948–61. 3
  v.
NN ATF (Strasbourg)

Stuttgart
Stuttgart.
Bürgerbuch der Stadt Stuttgart
  1660 bis 1706.
Stuttgart, Kohlhammer, 1956. Bd.
  1–.
NN ATF (Stuttgart)

Westphalia
Fahne, Anton.
Geschichte der Westphälischen
  Geschlechter ...Preussen, Cur-
  land und Liefland.
Cologne, J.M. Heberle, 1858. 431 p.
NN ATF+ (Westphalia)

Hömberg, Albert K.
Geschichtliche Nachrichten Über
  Adelssitze und Rittergüter in
  Herzogtum Westfalen ... Muns-
  ter, Historiche Kommission
  Province.
Westfalen, 1969–70. 2 v.
NN ATF (Westphalia) 72-3063

Wittgenstein
Mundel, Hedwig.
A 1725 List of Wittgenstein Emi-
  grants.
(IN: *PGM*, Philadelphia, PA, 1970.
  v.26, p. 133–43)
NN APR (Pennsylvania)

Württemberg
Sudwestdeutsche Blätter für Fam-
  ilien und Wappenkunde.
Stuttgart, 1947–.
NN ATF (Württemberg)

GREECE (ATHENS)

Ancient Greece was a great civilization, the forerunner of modern democracies. Its Golden Age commenced in the fifth century, at the conclusion of the Persian Wars (449 B.C.). In the fourth century Philip II of Macedon had conquered Greece, and his son, Alexander the Great, went on to conquer a vast domain and spread Hellenistic civilization. Greece became a Roman territory in the second century, and after the division of the Roman Empire in 395 it was part of the Byzantine Empire. The victory of the Visigoths over Emperor Valens at Adrianople (378) marked the beginning of barbarian invasions. Greek prestige was finally restored by a Macedonian dynasty of the Byzantine emperors (867–1025). In the eleventh century the Turks began to make inroads into Greece, and the Crusades passed through. In the Fourth Crusade (1204) the Byzantine Empire was temporarily superseded by French, Flemish and Italian nobles who established a feudal state. The revived Byzantine Empire (1261–1453) contained only parts of Greece, while the rest remained under French and Italian princes, until Turkish conquest was complete in 1456. Greece was oppressed and poverty-stricken under Ottoman rule; Greek nationalism emerged in the nineteenth century and led to a war of independence that was partly inspired by the French Revolution and by Turkish reverses in a war with Russia. The rebellion was initially unsuccessful, but Britain, France and Russia sent financial aid and volunteers. Turkey was defeated in 1829, and Greek independence was recognized in 1832. Prince Otto I of Bavaria, chosen as King of Greece by the European powers in 1832, was deposed in 1862. The following year, Prince Christian of Denmark (1845–1913) of the House of Schleswig-Holstein-Sonderburg-Glücksburg was elected ruler as King George I, King of the Hellenes. His great-grandson, King Constantine II (1940–), has been in exile since a military junta seized power in 1967. A grandson of King George I is Prince Philip (formerly Prince Philip of Greece), Duke of Edinburgh (1912–), consort of Queen Elizabeth II of Great Britain.

One of the most important facets of Greek life is the dowry of every woman. Dower rights to a certain degree still exist even in the United States, but in Greece a girl must have a dowry before marriage, and these dowries are registered in the Bureau of the Pica (Pika) in each district. These records could prove valuable in genealogical research.

One of the first Greeks to settle in America was Peter Kemble, who was born in Smyrna, December 12, 1704, the son of Richard

Kemble, the British Consul there, and his wife, a member of the Mavrocadato family, who were prominent on the Island of Chios, as noted in the work of Philip Argenti, the well-known Greek genealogist (see bibliography). Kemble settled in New York City in about 1730 and prospered. In 1760 he moved to Morristown, New Jersey, where he died at his mansion, Mount Kemble, in 1789, leaving many descendants.

The first Greek census was taken in 1825. In recent years the census has been conducted every ten years.

In modern Athens the most common surnames are Konstantinides, Oikonomou, Papageorgiou, Papadopoulos, Papaioannou and Papademetriou.

Archives

Academy of Athens (National Archives)
Panepistimiou Street
Athens, Greece

Genika Archeia Toù Kratous (General State Archives)
Megaron Akadimias
odos Eleftheriou Venizelou 28
Athens, Greece

Historikon Archeion Kritis (Historical Archives of Crete)
odos I. Sfakianaki 20
La Canee, Crete

Public and Church Records

Civil registration began in 1925. Birth certificates in the cities of Athens, Piraeus and Salonika are kept by special registration bureaus, while in other cities, towns and communities the mayors and presidents of communities are charged by law to act as registrars. Marriage certificates are issued by the metropolitan in whose district the marriage was performed.

Recording Office, Ministry of the Interior
(Civil Registration)
57 Panepistimiou Avenue
Athens, Greece

Census records are confidential, but in special cases permission may be given to search them. Only the latest census records exist, as the prior records are destroyed every ten years.

National Statistical Service
14–16 Lykourgou Street
Athens, Greece

Records prior to 1925 can be found in local parish records.

Greek Orthodox Archdiocese
21 Aghias Filotheis Street
Athens, Greece

Libraries

Athens Academy Library
Odos Venizelou, Athens, Greece

National Library
Odos Venizelou, Athens, Greece

Historical and Genealogical Societies

Historical and Ethnological Society
Old Palace
Constitution Square
Athens, Greece

Books and Articles

Argenti, Philip Pandely.
Libro d'Oro de la Noblesse de Chio.
London, Oxford U. Press, 1955. 2
v., coats of arms and gen. tables,
index.
NN AVH+ (Chios)

Argenti, Philip Pandely.
The Religious Minorities of Chios,
Jews and Roman Catholics.
Cambridge, Cambridge U. Press,
1970. 581 p., index.
NN *PXR

Carratelli, Giovanni P.
Le Genti della Luciana Antica e
Lora Relazioni con i Greci
dell'Italia.
(IN: *Archivo Storico per la Calabria
e la Lucania*, 1972. v.40, p. 5–26)
NN BWA

Greek-American Guide and Business Directory
New York, S.G. Canoutas, 1907,
1909–10, 1912, 1915.
NN IEE (Greeks)

Greek Royal Family.
(House of Schleswig-Holstein-Son-
derburg-Glücksburg)
(IN: *CDS*, Paris, 1966. p. 295–309)
NN ARB
(IN: *GHF*, Limburg/Lahn, 1971.
v.9, p. 19–24)
NN ATC

Hellenic Americans of Arizona and
Los Angeles and Vicinity Direc-
tory.
Hollywood, CA, 1947. 24, vii, 84 p.
NN IEE+ (Greeks)

Hellikon Who's Who.
Athens, 1962. 571 p., alpha (in
Greek).
NN *RR-AGO

Ithaca, Greece, Monumental Inscriptions ...
(IN: *GMH*, London, 1914. 5th ser.,
v.5, p. 177–79)
NN ARCA

Koudounares, Aristeides L.
Merikai Palaiai Oikogeneiai tes
Kyprou.
Nicosia, Cyprus, 1972. 125 p. alpha
biblio., p. 123–25.
(Prominent families of Cyprus)
NN AVH (Cyprus) 75-919

Kourvetaris, George A.
First and Second Generation
Greeks in Chicago.
Athens, 1971. 111 p.
NN IEE (Greeks) 72-1394

Ladas, Stephen P.
The Exchange of Minorities: Bul-
garia, Greece and Turkey.
New York, Macmillan, 1932. 849 p.
NN GIV

Livre d'Oro de la Noblesse Ion-
ienne.
Athens, Maison d'Editions "Elef-
theroudakis," 1925–26. 3 v. in 4,
gen. tables. v.1, Corfu; v.2,
Cephalonie; v.3, Zante.
NN AVH+ (Ionian Islands)

Mead, Robin.
Greece.

London, Batsford, 1976. 168 p., index.
NN JFD 76-6501

Melas, Leon I.
(History of the Melas Family)
Athens, 1967. 1,052 p. (The Melas family 1635–1967)
NN AVHH (Melas)

Narain, A.K.
The Indo-Greeks.
Oxford, Oxford U. Press, 1962. 201 p.
NN JFD 74-1217

Panagopoulous, Epaminondas P.
The Background of the Greek Settlers in the New Smyrna Colony.
(IN: *Florida Historical Quarterly*, Jacksonville, FL, 1956. v.35, p. 95–115)
NN IAA

Panagopoulous, Epaminondas P.
New Smyrna in the Eighteenth Century, Greek Odyssey.
Gainesville, FL, U. of Florida Press, 1966. 207 p.
NN ITM (New Smyrna)

Politis, Athaenase G.
... L'Hellenisme et l'Egypte Moderne.
Paris, F. Alcan, 1929–30. 2 v. (1798–1927)
NN BLA

Rackages, Ulysses.
The Rackages Family 1861–1974.
Floral Park, NY, U. Rackages, 1976. 105 p., no index.
NN APV (Rackages) 76-540

Roberts, Steven V.
Beleaguered Greeks in Istanbul Fearful of Future.

(IN: *NYT*, 1 Mar. 1976, p.3)
Greeks Abroad Hearing Call of Home.
(IN: *NYT*, 28 Aug. 1976, p.5.)
Ionian Island Is Domain of a Rich Greek Family (Vergotis)
(IN: *NYT*, 29 Aug. 1976. p.10, col. 1–2)
NN Room 315M

Sakellarios, Michael R.
Le Migration Grecque en Ionie.
Athens, 1958. 568 p.
(Centre d'Etudes d'Asie Mineure. Collection 10, Ionie 1)
NNF-11 1553

Saloutos, Theodore.
The Greeks in the United States.
Cambridge, MA, Harvard U. Press, 1964. 445 p., index.
NN IEE (Greeks)

Saloutos, Theodore.
The Greeks in America: A Student's Guide to Localized History.
New York, Teachers College Press, 1967. 36 p.
NN D-17 71663

Solev'ev, A.V.
Les Archones Grecs dans l'Empire Serbe.
(IN: *Byzantinslavica*, Prague, 1930. rocnik (*volume*) 2, p. 275–87)
(Text in Bulgarian, summary in French)
NN *QVA

Soteriades, Georges.
An Ethnological Map Illustrating Hellenism in the Balkan Peninsula and Asia Minor.
London, E. Stanford, 1918. 16 p.
NN QPW

Strathopoulos, Peter.
The Greek Community of Montréal.
Athens, 1971. 68 p.
NN HWH 72-2491

Tarn, William W.
The Greeks in Bactria and India.
Cambridge, Cambridge U. Press, 1938. 539 p., gen. tables.
NN E-12 2731

Tavuchis, Nicholas.
Family and Mobility Among Greek-Americans.
Athens, 1972. 191 p.
NN IEE (Greeks) 74-913

Thumb, Albert.
The Modern Greek and His Ancestry.
(IN: *John Rylands Library Bulletin*, Manchester, England, 1915. v. 2, p. 22–47)
NN *GX

U.S. and Canada Greek Business Directory. 1921–22.
New York, Greek Commercial and Information Bureau, 1921. 573 p., + index (S.G. Canoutas, ed.)
NN IEE (Greek)

Vlassis, George Demetrios.
The Greeks in Canada.
Ottawa, 1942. 147 p.
NN HWH

Who's Who in Greece. 1958–59.
Athens, Athens News, 1958. 368 p., alpha (in English).
NN *RR-AGO

Zante, Greece, Monumental Inscriptions in the English Cemetery (Protestant and Catholic).
(IN: *GMH*, London, 1914. 4th ser., v.5, p. 19–27)
NN ARCA

HUNGARY (BUDAPEST)

In the ninth century the Magyars, a Finno-Ugric people, conquered land that had been a Roman province hundreds of years before. Arpad founded the first dynasty, which lasted for more than four centuries. Christianity was introduced in the tenth century. Hungarian nobles made Ferdinand I of Austria King of Western Hungary in 1526 and liberated Budapest from the Turks in 1686, when Turkey ceded Hungary and Transylvania to Austria. In 1867 the Austro-Hungarian monarchy was established under Emperor Francis Joseph, King of Hungary. In 1918–19 a Communist regime was suppressed, and Hungary became a monarchy under a regent, Admiral Horthy de Nagybanya. The Treaty of Trianon in 1920 took away three-quarters of Hungary's territory and one third of its population, and the country became a kingdom. In 1944 Hungary was occupied by Russian troops, and in 1948–49 Hungarian Communists seized power with Soviet support. Soviet troops supported János Kádár in putting down an anti-Communist uprising in 1956, and 200,000 Hungarians fled the country.

The most common surnames in Budapest are Horváth, Kovács, Nagy, Szabó and Tóth.

Archives

Magyar Országos Levéltár (National Archives)
1250 Budapest, I
Bécsikapu-ter 2-4 (Pf. 3)
Hungary

Uj Magyar Központi Levéltár (New Central Archives)
1250 Budapest, I
Hess András tér 4 (Pf. 16)
Hungary

Evangélikus Országos Levéltár (Lutheran Archives)
1085 Budapest, VIII
Üllöi ut 24
Hungary

Magyarországi Református Egyház Zsinati Levéltára (Reformed Church Archives)
1091 Budapest, IX
Kálvin tér 8
Hungary

Primási Levéltár (Roman Catholic Archives of the Primate)
2500 Esztergom
Berényi Zsigmond utca 2 (Pf. 25)
Hungary

Public and Church Records

Certificates can be obtained from the registry office of the district where the event took place.

Libraries

Egyetemi Könyvtár (University Library)
1372 Budapest, P.O.B. 483
Károlyi Mihályu, 10
Hungary

Központi Statisztikai Hivatal Könyvtár és Dokumentációs Szolgálat (Library and Documentation Service of the Central Statistical Office)
H-1525 Budapest, Pf. 10, II
Keleti Károly u. 5
Hungary

Magyar Országos Levéltár Könyvtára (Library of the National Archives)
1250 Budapest I
Bécsikapu-tér 4
Hungary

Books and Articles

Andrássy, Gyula, Gróf.
Magyarország Címeres Könyve (Liber Armorum Hungariae).
Budapest, Grill Karoly Konyvkiadovallalata, 1913. 144 p., 176 + plates, text alpha.
NN AWT+

Bognar, Desi K., ed.
Hungarians in America: A Biographical Dictionary ...
Mt. Vernon, NY, Alpha Pub., 1971. 239 p., alpha
NN IEE (Hungarians) 77-690

Ferenc, Ördóg.
Személynévvizsgálatok Gócses és Hetés Teruleten.
Budapest, Akadémiai Kiadó, 1973. 620 p., index.
NN APD 76-1748

Gulyás, Pál.
Magyar Életrajzi Lexikon ...
Budapest, Lantos, 1925–29. 768 columns.
NN AGL

History of the Hungarian Nation.
Astor Park, FL, Danubian Press, 1969. 421 p., gen. tables.
(Hungarian Heritage Books v.2)
NN JFF 72-894

Jensen, Larry.
Hungarian Genealogical Dictionary
(IN:*SGSB*, Regina, Saskatchewan, 1975. v.6, p. 61–64)
(SGSB = *Saskatchewan Genealogical Society Bulletin*)
NN APW

Kempelen, Béla.
Magyar Nemes Családok.
Budapest, Károly, 1911–32. 11 v., alpha.
NN ATO

Köszeghi, Sándor.
Nemes Családok Pestvármegyében.
Budapest, Hungaria Konyvnyomda, 1899. 449 p., alpha.
NN ATP (Pest)

Kosztolányi, Dezsó.
Irók, Festök, Tudósok, Tanulmanyok Magyar Kortársakról.
Budapest, Szepirodalmi, 1958. 2 v.
NN C-11 3712

Magyar Életrajzi Lexikon ...
Budapest, Akadémiai Kiadó, 1967. 2 v.
NN L-11 2944

Magyar Történeti Électrajok.
Budapest, 1885–1916. 32 v.
NN AGL

Nagy, Ivan.
Magyarország Családai Caimerekkel ...
Pest, Kiadja Ráth Mór, 1857–68. 12 v., alpha.
NN ATO 72-2580

Research Institute for Minority Studies on Hungarians Attached to Czechoslovakia and Carpatho-Ruthenia.
New York, 1959. 166 p.
NN D-12 4334

Segner (Szégner), Felix Ladislaus (László) Der Urgarische Adel (A Magyar Nemesség).
Grafenau, Bavaria, Morsak, 1969. 267 p.
NN ATO 72-2580

Steier, Lajos.
... Ungarns Vergewaltigung: Oberungarn unter Tschechischer Herrschaft.
Aurich, A. Malthea, 1929. 1,007 p.
NN FIH

Szeplaki, Joseph.
The Hungarians in America 1583–1974: A Chronology and Fact Book. ·
Dobbs Ferry, NY, Oceana, 1975. 152 p., index.
NN IEE (Hungarians) 75-1998

Szinnyei, Joseph.
Magyar Írók: Elete és Munkái a

Magyar Tudomanyos Akademia Megbizasabel.
Budapest, Kiadja Hornyanszy, 1891–1914. 14 v.
NN D-16 869

Szy, Tibor.
Hungarians in America: A Biographical Directory of Professionals of Hungarian Origin in the Americas.
New York, Kossuth Foundation, 1963–66. 2 v. (606, 488 p.)
NN IEE (Hungarians)

Turul, A.
Magyar Heraldikai es Genealogiai Társaság Közlönye.

Budapest, 1883–1936. v.1–50, index v.11–50. (1893–1936)
NN ATNA

Valentiny, Antal.
Romania Magyar Irodalmanak Bibliografiája.
[IN: Erdélyi Tudományos Füzetck, Cluj, 1938. szam (volume) 102, p. 1–22]
NN FOA

Zarándy, Alfred Gaspar.
Árpád Vére: Hohenlohe.
Budapest, Hornyánszky Viktor, 1904. 136 p.
NN ATR (Árpád)

ICELAND (REYKJAVÍK)

Irish monks came to this island in the 800's but left when the Norseman arrived in the middle of the century with Scottish and Irish slaves. In 930 a General Assembly, the Althing, was established. Christianity was introduced in 1000 by Olaf I. Snorri Sturluson (1179–1241) incorporated Iceland into the Archdiocese of Trondheim. In 1380 Norway and Iceland passed under the Danish crown. Lutheranism was imposed during the sixteenth century, over the resistance of Bishop Jon Aresson. In 1843 Jon Sigurdsson, a great leader for independence, restored the Althing, which had been abolished in 1800. In 1918 Iceland became a sovereign state in union with Denmark. Iceland voted to terminate its union with Denmark in 1944 and was proclaimed the Kingdom of Iceland, a republic.

A census in 1703 noted the name, occupation, residence and age of every person in Iceland. Subsequent censuses were recorded approximately every ten years until 1960. Since then the National Registry has furnished the requisite population information.

Archives

Safnahusid (National Archives)
Hverfisgotu 8-10
Reykjavík, Iceland

Thjodskjalasafn Islands (National Archives)
Hverfisgate 17
Reykjavík, Iceland

Borgarskjalasafn Reykjavikur
(Town Archives of Reykjavík)
Skulatuni 2
Reykjavík, Iceland

Landsbókasafn Islands (National Library)
Reykjavík, Iceland

Public Library
Reykjavík, Iceland

Historical and Genealogical Societies

Íslenzka sögufélag, Hid (Iceland Historical Society)
Reykjavík, Iceland

Public and Church Records

Civil registration for births, deaths and marriages began in 1916 and for divorces in 1952.

Beginning in 1746, the parochial clergy were instructed to keep registers of births, marriages, confirmations and deaths. Some records exist from even earlier dates, but from 1746 the records are generally unbroken. The church statistics are submitted to the Icelandic Bureau of Statistics and to the National Archives (Thjodskjalasafn Islands). Marriage certificates may be issued by either the Icelandic Bureau of Statistics in Reykjavík (Hagstofa Islands) or by the official who performed the ceremony.

Libraries

Háskólabókasafn (University Library)
Reykjavík, Iceland

Books and Articles

Benediktsson, Bogi.
Syslumannaaefir.
Reykjavík, 1881–1915. 4 v.
NN AGQ

Dahlmann, Friedrich C.
Geschichte van Dannemark.
Hamburg, 1840–1902. 5 v.
NN JFD 72–7892

Gislason, Benedikt.
Folk of Saga.
Reykjavík, Nordri, 1958. 240 p.
NN D-12 5362

Haraldur, Petursson.
Kjosarmenn, Aeviskrar: Asamt Sveitarlysingu.
Reykjavík, Kjosverija, 1961. 528 p.; ports.
NN D-15 5837

Iceland. Capitaneus.
The Old Icelandic Land Registers.
Lund, Sweden, Gleerup, 1967. 375 p.
(*Ekonomisk-Historiska Foreningen*, Lund, Sweden v.6)
NN E-13 5393

Jonasson, Eric.
Tracing Your Icelandic Ancestors.
Winnipeg, Manitoba, Canada R3J
1K3, the author, 160 Riverbend
Crescent, c.1974.

Landnamabok.
The Book of the Settlement of Ice-
land. 2nd ed.
Kendal, T. Wilson, 1908. 243 p.
NN GHY

Lindal, Walter Jacobson
The Icelanders in Canada.
Winnipeg, National Pub., 1967. 502
p.

(*Canada Ethnica* v.2)
NN HWH

Olason, Pall Eggert.
Islenzkar Aeviskrar fra Landnam-
stimun til Arskoka 1940.
Reykjavík, 1948–52. 5 v.
NN *RR-AGQ

Porkelsson, Ton.
Islenzkar Artioaskrar, eoa Obitu-
aria Islandica meo Athugasem-
dum.
Kaupmannahofn, 1893–96. 344 p.
(25 gen. tables)
NN AVC

IRELAND (DUBLIN)

In pre-Christian times Ireland was inhabited by Picts in the
north and a people called the Erainn in the south. About the
fourth century B.C. tall, red-haired Celts arrived from Gaul or
Galicia, subdued and assimilated the inhabitants and established
a Gaelic civilization. St. Patrick introduced Christianity in A.D.
432, and the country became a center of Gaelic and Latin learning.
Irish monasteries sent missionaries to many parts of Europe
and, some say, to North America. Norse invasions along the
coasts, starting in 795, ended in 1014 with Norse defeat at the
Battle of Clontarf by forces under Brian, now a popular Irish
ancestor. In the middle of the twelfth century the Pope gave
Ireland to the English Crown as a papal fief. In 1171 Henry II
of England was acknowledged "Lord of Ireland," but local sec-
tional rule continued for centuries, and English control over the
entire island was not really established until the seventeenth
century. By the Act of Union (1800) England and Ireland became
the "United Kingdom of Great Britain and Ireland." A steady
decline in the Irish economy followed. The great potato famine
of 1846–48 took many lives and drove millions to immigrate to
America. At the same time, anti-British agitation and demands
for Irish home rule continued. The Irish Free State was established as a dominion on December 6, 1921, with the six northern

counties as part of the United Kingdom. The Republic of Ireland was proclaimed on April 18, 1949.

The first census was taken in 1841. Censuses were recorded every ten years until 1941 and since then have been taken every five years.

The most common surnames in Dublin are Byrne, Kelly, Murphy, O'Brien and Ryan.

Archives

National Gallery (National Archives)
Kildare Street
Dublin 2, Ireland

Public Record Office of Ireland/Oifig Taifead Poibli
Four Courts
Dublin 7, Ireland

Public and Church Records

Civil registration began in 1864 for births, deaths and marriages; divorce is not granted in Ireland. Certificates are issued by the General Registrar and may also be obtained from District Register Offices.

General Registrar of Births, Deaths and Marriages
Custom House
Dublin 1, Ireland

For census information:
Central Statistics Office
St. Stephen's Green House
Dublin 2, Ireland

For wills and deeds:
Registry of Deeds
Henrietta Street
Dublin 1, Ireland

Libraries

Central Catholic Library
74-75 Merrion Square
Dublin 2, Ireland

National Library of Ireland
Kildare Street
Dublin 2, Ireland

Representative Church Body Library
Braemor Park, Rathgar
Dublin 14, Ireland

Historical and Genealogical Societies

Irish Genealogical Research Society
7a Duke of York St.
St. James Sq.
London, S.W. 1, England
(*The Irish Genealogist*, 1937–)
NN ARCA

Genealogical Office (formerly Office of Arms)
Dublin Castle
Dublin 2, Ireland

Irish Manuscripts Commission
73 Merrion Square
Dublin 2, Ireland

The Irish Ancestor
(Miss Rosemary ffolliott, editor)
Pirton House

Sydenham Villas
Dundrum, Dublin 14, Ireland

United States Sources

Irish Genealogical Society
% Joseph M. Glynn, Jr.
173 Tremont Street
Newton, MA 02158

Scotch-Irish Society of the U.S.A.
2301 Packard Building
Philadelphia, PA 19102

Books and Articles

American Irish Historical Society.
Journal.
Boston, NY, 1898–1941. 32 v.
NN IEH

Analecta Hibernica.
See Ireland (Eire) Manuscript Commission.

Archivum Hibernicum.
Maynooth, Catholic Record Society
of Ireland, St. Patrick's College,
1912–74, plus 32 v. plus, in progress, indexed.
NN CSB

Bannan, Theresa.
Pioneer Irish of Onondaga (about 1776–1847).
New York, G. P. Putnam's Sons, 1911. 333 p., index.
NN IRM (Onondaga)

Bennett, T.J.G.
North Antrim Families.
Longside, Aberdeen, Volturna Press, 1974. 194 p., index.

Black, J. Anderson.
Your Irish Ancestors.

London, Paddington Press, 1974.
253 p., no index.
NN ARF 75-1217

Burke's Irish Family Records.
American Edition.
London, Burke's Peerage Ltd., 1976. 64, 1,237 p., alpha.
(The American Edition contains a Revised Introductory Section of 64 pages with articles by Owen D. Edwards, Sir Iain Moncreiffe, Edward MacLysaght, Gerard Slevin, Lord Dunboyne and Henry McDowell.)
NN ARF 77-357

Burke's Landed Gentry of Ireland.
London, Burke's Peerage, 1899–1958. 4 v.
NN ARF

Campbell, John H.
History of the Friendly Sons of St. Patrick and of the Hibernian Society, 1771–1892.
Philadelphia, Hibernian Society, 1892. 570 p., index.
NN IEH

Campbell, R.G.
Scotch-Irish Family Research Made Simple.
Munroe Falls, OH, Summit Pub., 1974. 28 p., no index.
NN APB 75-563

Casey, Albert E., and Nell Frances Lowrey.
O'Kief, Coshe Mang, Slieve Lougher and Upper Blackwater Ireland (North Cork, East Kerry).
Birmingham, AL, 1952–68. 14 v., index each v.
(Facsimiles of many important Irish manuscripts and books)
NN ARX (Munster)

Chicago Irish Ancestry
7541 N. Oakley Ave.
Chicago, IL 60645

Clare, Wallace.
A Guide to Copies and Abstracts
of Irish Wills.
Baltimore, MD, GPC, 1972 (orig.
1930). 111 p., index.
NN ARF 73-1938

Clare, Wallace.
Simple Guide to Irish Genealogy.
3rd ed. revised by Rosemary ffolliott.
London, Irish Genealogical Society,
1966. 45 p.
NN ARD

Clark, Dennis.
The Irish of Philadelphia.
Philadelphia, PA, 1973. 246 p.
NN IEH 74-1981

Clarke, Richard S.J.
Gravestone Inscriptions.
Belfast, Ulster Scot Historical
Foundation, 1966-76. 16 v. in
progress
(These volumes so far all deal with
County Down.)
NN ARF

Coombes, Rev. James.
Catholic Churches of Nineteenth
Century, Some Newspaper
Sources.
(IN: *Cork Historical and Archaeo-
logical Society Journal*, Cork,
1975. v.81, p. 1–12)
NN CT (Cork)

Cork Historical and Archaeological
Society.
Journal.
Cork, 1892–. 81 v. to 1975.
NN CT (Cork)

County Louth Archaeological
Journal.
Dundalk, 1904–. index v. 1–13
bound with v. 13–14.
NN CT (Louth)

Cullen, John H.
Young Ireland in Exile: The Story
of the Men of '48 in Tasmania.
Dublin, Talbot Press, 1928. 186 p.
NN AGH

DeBreffny, Brian.
Bibliography of Irish Family His-
tory and Genealogy.
Dublin, Golden Eagle Books, 1974.
167 p., alpha.
NN ARD 76-862

Dickason, Graham Brian.
Irish Settlers to the Cape.
Capetown, 1973. 113 p.
NN AVH (Africa, South) 75-1501

Dickson, R.J.
Ulster Immigration to Colonial
America, 1718–1775.
London, Routledge and Kegan
Paul, 1966. 320 p.
(*Ulster-Scot Historical Series v.1*)
NN L-11 961 v.1

Dublin Historical Record.
(Quarterly publication of the Old
Dublin Society)
Dublin, 28 v. to 1975.
NN CT (Dublin)

Ellis, Eilish.
Emigrants from Ireland,
1847–1852, State-Aided Emigration Schemes from Crown Estates in Ireland.
Baltimore, MD, GPC, 1977 (orig.
1960). 68 p.

Eustace, P. Beryl.
Index of Will Abstracts in the Gen-
ealogical Office, Dublin.
(IN: *Analecta Hibernica*, Dublin,
1949. no. 17, p. 147–348, alpha)
NN CSB

Eustace, P. Beryl.
Registry of Deeds, Abstracts of
Wills.
Dublin, Irish Manuscript Commis-
sion, 1954–56. 2 v. (v.1, 1708–54;
v.2, 1746–85)
NN ARX (Dublin)

Falley, Margaret Dickson.
Irish and Scotch-Irish Family Re-
search.
Evanston, IL, M.D. Falley,
1961–62. 2 v.
NN ARD

Farrar, Henry.
Irish Marriages, Being an Index
to the Marriages in Walker's
Hibernian Magazine, 1771–1812,
with an Appendix ... Births,
Marriages, Deaths in the An-
thologia Hibernica 1793 and
1794.
London, Phillimore, 1897. 2 v.
NN ARS

ffolliott, Rosemary.
Biographical Entries Primarily
Relating to Counties Cork and
Kerry Collected from Newspa-
pers 1756–1827 with a Few Ref-
erences 1749–1755.
Dublin, R. ffolliott, 1969. 1 v., alpha.
NN ARX (Cork)

ffolliott, Rosemary.
Genealogy in Ireland.
(IN: *TAG*, Des Moines, IA, 1976. v.
52, p. 210–15)
NN APGA

ffolliott, Rosemary.
Ireland's Records Regained.
(IN: *GM*, London, 1973. v.17, p. 257–
59)
NN ARCA

ffolliott, Rosemary, and Brian
DeBreffny.
The Houses of Ireland.
New York, Viking, 1975. 240 p. in-
dex
NN MQWK 75-993

Fleming-Haigh, Georgia V.
Ireland, the Albert E. Casey Collection and Other Irish Materials in the Samford University
Library.
(Samford University Library Research Series Paper no. 3)
Birmingham, AL, 1976. 113 p.,
plus index.

Gardiner, David E., Derek Howland and Frank Smith.
Genealogical Atlas of Ireland ...
Salt Lake City, UT, Deseret, 1969.
maps alpha by county, unpaged,
41 p. of index.
NN (Map Division)

Gaughan, J. Anthony.
Listowel and Its Vicinity.
Cork, Mercier, 1973. 611 p., index.
NN CT (Listowel)

Griffith, Margaret.
A Short Guide to the Public Record
Office of Ireland.
Dublin, 1964. 16 p.
NN *XM-7039 (microfiche)

Guide to Irish Surnames. 2nd ed.,
revised.
Dublin, Helicon, 1965. 256 p. (Bibliography of Irish families), p.
207–47.

(An index to MacLysaght's *IF*, *MIF* and *SIF*, noted below)
NN APD

Handbook on Irish Genealogy: How to Trace Your Ancestors and Relatives in Ireland. 2nd enlarged ed.
Dublin, Heraldic Artists, 1973. 131 p., small t of c, no index. (Passenger lists with names, p. 105–31)
NN ARF 75-105

Howard, Joseph J., and Frederick A. Crisp.
Visitation of Ireland.
London, 1897–18. 6 v., index each v.
NN ARF

Hughes, James L. J.
Patentee Officers in Ireland 1173–1826, Including High Sheriffs 1661–1684 and 1761–1816.
Dublin, Irish Manuscript Commission, 1960. 142 p., index.
NN ARF

Humphrey-Smith, Cecil R.
Some Aspects of Irish Genealogy and Heraldry.
(IN: *Family History*, Canterbury, Kent, 1967. v.5, no. 27, also called, n.s., no.3 p. 66–74)
NN ARCA+

Hunt, John.
Irish Medieval Figure Sculpture, 1200–1600.
Dublin and London, Irish U. Press and Sotheby Parke Bernet, 1974. 2 v.
NN MGI+ 75-648

Indexes to Irish Wills.
London, Phillimore, 1909–20. 5 v. in 2 v.
NN ART

Ireland (Eire) Manuscript Commission.
Analecta Hibernica.
Dublin, 1930– .
NN CSB

The Irish Ancestor, ed. by Rosemary ffolliott.
Dublin, Dundrum, 1969– .
(Excellent genealogical periodical content and format, superb illustrations)
NN ARCA 72-1448

Irish Archives Bulletin (Journal of the Irish Society for Archives)
Dublin, University College, 1971–.
NN Current

Irish Genealogical Helper.
Harbor City, CA, The Augustan Society, 1974– . no.1–, 2 v. (v.1, A–J; v.2, K–Z and Appendix)
NN ARS

The Irish Genealogist.
London, Irish Genealogical Society, 1937– .
NN ARCA

Irish Genealogy.
(IN: *Family History*, Canterbury, Kent, 1967. v.5, no.27, also called, n.s. no.3, whole issue devoted to Ireland.)
NN ARCA+

Irish Memorial Association Journal
Dublin, 1883–1932. index v.1–7 and indexes in other v.
NN ARCA

Irish Microfilms Limited.
Catalogue.
Dublin, 1976. 40 p.
(35 Kildare St., Dublin 2)

Irish Passengers Aboard the *New World*, Liverpool to New York, Oct.–Dec. 1853.
(IN: *Irish Ancestor*, Dundrum, 1975. v.1, p. 6–10)
NN ARCA 72-1448

Irish Wills and Administrations at Somerset House for the Years 1859–1876 in Calendar.
(IN: *GM*, London, 1967. p.v. 15, p. 275, 384)
NN ARCA

Kelly, Kathleen.
Extracts from the Census of the City of Waterford, 1821.
(IN: *Irish Genealogist*, London, 1968–69. v.4, p. 17–24, 122–30)
NN ARCA

Leader, M.
Irish Records.
(IN: *GM*, London, 1958. v.12, p. 512–15)
NN ARCA

Lodge, J.
The Peerage of Ireland, enlarged by Mervyn Archdall.
Dublin, 1789. 7 v., index.
NN ARM

Lucas, Richard.
Irish Provincial Directories 1788
. . .
(IN: *IG*, London, 1965–68. v.3, p. 392–416—Leinster; v.3, p. 468–76—Tipperary; v.3, p. 529–37, v.4, p. 37–46—Cork; 1788—Ennis Co., Clare, 1788)
NN ARCA

MacLysaght, Edward.
Irish Families. 3rd ed., revised.
New York, Crown, 1972. 365 p., index, map.
NN ARF 72-2357

MacLysaght, Edward.
Irish Surnames.
Dublin, Irish U. Press, 1973. 377 p. (Indexes IF, MIF, SIF of families p. 365)
NN APD 75-1259

MacLysaght, Edward.
More Irish Families.
Galway, O'Gorman, 1960. 320 p., index.
NN APD

MacLysaght, Edward.
Seventeenth Century Hearth Money Rolls with Full Transcripts Relating to Sligo.
(IN: *AH*, Dublin, 1967. no.24, p. 1–85)
NN CSB

MacLysaght, Edward.
Supplement to Irish Families.
Baltimore, MD, GPC, 1964. 163 p., index.
NN APD

Manuscript Collections in Private Keeping.
(IN: *AH*, Dublin, 1966. no.23, p. 371–87)
NN CSB

McGee, Thomas D'Arcy.
A History of the Irish Settlers in North America from the Earliest Period to the Census of 1850.
San Francisco, CA, R. and E. Research, 1970 (orig. 1852). 240 p., index of names following t of c.
NN IEH 74-458

Moorhouse, B. Ann.
A Moorhouse Family of Dublin, Carlow and Kildare.
(IN: *The Irish Ancestor*, Dundrum, 1977. v.9, p. 15–18)
(The work of one of the best Irish-American genealogists)
NN ARCA 72-1448

Murphy, William M.
The Yeats Family and the Polle-
fens of Sligo.
Dublin, Dolmen Press, 1971. 88 p.
(New Yeats Papers 1)
NN ARZ (Yeats) 75-1154

O'Connell, Basil Morgan.
Tracing Your Irish Ancestors.
(IN: *Family History*, Canterbury,
Kent, 1967. v. 5, no. 27, n.s. no.
3, p. 75–80; see also 81–86)
NN ARCA+

Payton, Frank B.
Locating Your Family in Ireland:
Civil Registration and 19th Cen-
tury Census Returns.
(IN: *Cheshire Family Historian*,
Chester, 1974. no. 1, p. 19–20)
NN ARX (Cheshire) 76-1670

Percival-Maxwell, M.
Scottish Migration to Ulster in the
Reign of James I.
Belfast, Ulster Scot. Hist. Founda-
tion, 1973.
NN CT (Ulster) 76-1250

Petty, Sir William.
Census of Ireland 1659,
ed. by Seamus Pender
Dublin, Stationery Office, 1939. 946
p., 2 indexes—names, places.
NN ARF

Phair, P.B.
Guide to the Registry of Deeds.
(IN: *AH*, Dublin, 1966. no. 23, p.
257–76)
NN CSB

The Recorder.
Boston, NY, American Irish Hist.
Soc., 1901–73. 34 v.
NN IEH

Royal Society of Antiquaries of Ireland Journal.

Dublin, 1849–1976. in progress, indexed.
NN CSB

Services of the Genealogical Office,
Dublin.
(IN: *Irish Genealogical Helper*,
Harbor, CA, 1976. no. 6, p. 78–80)

Smythe-Wood, Patrick.
Index to Killala and Achonry Wills.
(IN: *Irish Genealogist*, London,
1967. v. 3, p. 506–19)
NN ARCA

Survey of Documents in Private
Keeping, compiled by John Ainsworth and Edward MacLysaght.
(3 parts)
(IN: *AH* Dublin, 1944–67. no. 15 [458
p., index], no. 20 [393 p., index],
no. 25 [273 p., index])
NN CSB

Thom's Irish Almanac and Official
Directory.
Dublin, 1844–. v. 1–.
(NN has v. 12–, 1855– incomplete)
NN CA

Walsh, Micheline.
Spanish Knights of Irish Origin.
Documented from Continental Ar-
chives.
Dublin, Irish Manuscript Commis-
sion, 1960–70. 3 v., index each v.
NN ASM

Walsh, Paul.
Irish Chiefs and Leaders.
Dublin, at the Sign of the Three
Candles, 1960. 334 p.
NN D-13 1717

Ward, William R.
A Primer for Irish Genealogical
Research.
Logan, UT, Everton, 1977. 35 p.

Waterford and South East of Ireland Archaeological Society.
Journal.
Waterford, 1894–1910. 13 v.
NN CSB

Who's Who and What's What and Where in Ireland.

London, G. Chapman, 1973. 236 p., index.
NN *R-AGH 75-690

Wittke, Carl.
The Irish in America.
Baton Rouge, LA, Louisiana State University Press, 1956. 319 p.
NN IEH

ITALY (ROME)

This is the land of the ancient Etruscans and Romans (from whom no one has a proven line of descent). Until A.D. 467 when the German Odoacer became head of the Roman Empire in the west, the history of Italy was largely the history of Rome. In 493 Theodoric the Great established Ostrogoth rule, which was replaced in 569 by the Lombards. The Papacy then emerged as the bulwark of Latin civilization, and Pope Gregory (590–604) laid the foundation for the Papal States. In 800 Charlemagne defeated the Lombard king and was crowned Emperor of the West at Rome. From then on the Holy Roman Emperors, Popes, Normans and Saracens all vied for control of the Italian peninsula. Numerous city states, such as Venice and Genoa, and many principalities flourished in the late Middle Ages, and the Italian peninsula remained politically fragmented until modern times. In 1713, after the War of the Spanish Succession, Milan, Naples and Sardinia were handed over to Austria, which lost some of its Italian territories in 1735. After 1800 Italy was unified by Napoleon, who crowned himself King of Italy on May 26, 1805, but after the Congress of Vienna in 1814 Austria once again became the dominant power. In the 1830's Joseph Mazzini, a liberal nationalist, organized the Risorgimento (Resurrection), which laid the foundation for Italian unity. Count Camillo di Cavour (1810–61), Prime Minister of Sardinia in 1852 and the architect of United Italy, joined England and France in the Crimean War (1853–56) and in 1859 helped France in a war against Austria, thereby obtaining Lombardy. By plebiscite in 1860, Modena, Parma, Tuscany and the Romagna voted to join Sardinia. In 1860 Giuseppe Garibaldi conquered Sicily and Naples and turned them over to Sardinia. Victor Emmanuel II, King of Sardinia, was proclaimed King of Italy on March 17, 1861. With the seizure of the papal possessions, Italian unification was completed in 1870. In 1922 Benito Mussolini came to power in the wake of severe depression and established a fascist dictatorship that lasted until 1943. Italy became a republic in 1946.

Censuses were recorded in Sardinia in 1848 and 1857. The first census of Italy was taken in 1861, and enumerations are now made every ten years.

The most common surnames in Milan are Bianchi, Brambilla, Colombo, Ferrari and Rossi; in Naples, Coppola, Deluca, DeRosa, Esposito, Romano and Russo; in Rome, De Angelis, De Santis, Mancini, Ricci and Rossi; and in Turin, Bianco, Ferraro, Gallo, Rossi and Rosso.

Archives

Archivio di Stato (National Archives)
Corso Rinascimento 40
00186 Rome, Italy

Archivio Centrale Dello Stato (Central Archives of the State)
Piazzale degli Archivi, E.U.R.
00144 Rome, Italy

Archivio di Stato di Roma (State Archives of Rome)
Corso Rinascimento 40
00136 Rome, Italy

Public and Church Records

Civil registration began in 1851. Certificates may be obtained from the Vital Statistics Office (Ufficio di Stato Civile) of the town (commune) where a birth, marriage or death took place.

For census information:
Istituto Centrale di Statistica

Via Balbo 16
00100 Rome, Italy

For copies of wills and deeds, write the Ufficio del Registro of the town.

For religious records, contact the individual parish.

Libraries

Centro Nazionale per il Catalogo Unico delle Biblioteche Italiane e per le Informazioni Bibliografiche
(National Center of the Union Catalogue of Italian Libraries and Bibliographical Information)
Via Osoppo
Rome, Italy

Biblioteca Universitaria
Via Zamboni 35
Bologna, Italy

Biblioteca Nazionale Centrale
Piazza de'Cavalleggeri IA
Florence, Italy

Biblioteca della Società Italiana per l'Organizzazione Internazionale (S.I.O.I.)
Via di S. Marco 3, Palazzetto di Venezia, Rome, Italy

Historical and Genealogical Societies

Istituto di Genealogia e Araldica
Via Antonio Cerasi 5A
Rome, Italy

Genealogico Italiano
Castelli 19
Florence, Italy

United States Sources

The Istituto Italiana di Cultura
686 Park Avenue
New York, NY 10021

Italian Government Travel Office
St. Francis Hotel
San Francisco, CA 94119

Italian Embassy
1601 Fuller Avenue NW
Washington, DC 20009

Books and Articles

Bellusci, Michael Consalvo.
Origin of the Bellusci Family.
Winchester, MA, c. 1960. 37 p.
NN APV (Bellusci)

Bertelli, Sergio.
Local History in Italy.
(IN: *The Local Historian*, London, 1975. v. 11, p. 251–62)
NN CA 72-1598

Camajani see Guelfi Camajani.

Carlevale, Joseph W.
Leading Americans of Italian Descent in Massachusetts.
Plymouth, MA, Memorial Press, 1946. 816 p., alpha.
NN IEE (Italians)

Carlevale, Joseph W.
Leading Americans of Italian Descent in New Jersey.
Clifton, NJ, New Jersey Press, 1950. 736 p., alpha.
NN IEE (Italians)

Carlevale, Joseph W.
Leading Americans of Italian Descent in Philadelphia and Vicinity.
Philadelphia, PA, G.S. Ferguson, 1954. 492 p., alpha.
NN IEE (Italians)

Carpi, Leone.
Il Risorgimento Italiano.
Milan, F. Vallardi, 1884–88. 4 v.
NN AGF

Chi E?
Rome, Scarano, 1928–61.
NN AGF

Cordasco, Francesco.
Italians in America: A Bibliography.
New York, Oriole, 1972. 137 p., index.
NN IEE (Italians) 73-135

Cordasco, Francesco.
Studies in Italian American Social ... History.
Totowa, NJ, Rowman and Littlefield, 1975. 264 p., index.
NN IEE (Italians) 76-1352

Cordasco, Francesco, and Eugene Bucchiani.

The Italians; Social Backgrounds of an American Group.
Clifton, NJ, Augustus M. Kelley, 1974. 598 p.
NN IEE (Italians) 74-2038

Cox, Eugene L.
The Eagles of Savoy: The House of Savoy in the Thirteenth Century Europe.
Princeton, NJ, Princeton U. Press, 1974. 492 p.
NN JFD 74-6320

Crollanza, Giovanni Battista Di. (d. 1819)
Dizionario Storico-Blasonico.
Bologna, Arnaldo Forni, 1965. (orig. 1886–90) 3 v., alpha.
NN ASX

DiGirolamo, Louis J.
The Stanzione Family History.
Holmdel, NJ, L.J. DiGirolamo, Jr., 1972. 46, 14 p., t of c, no index.
NN APV (Stanzione) 72-3058

Dizionario Biografico.
Rome, Istituto Della Enciclopedia Italiana, 1960–1976. plus v. 1–19 plus (Aaron-Cardona) in progress.
NN *RR-AGF

Dorian, Donald Clayton.
The English Diodatis.
New Brunswick, NJ, Rutgers U. Press, 1950. 365 p. (p. 318, Wm Diodati, son of John of England, settled in Hartford, CT by 1717)
NN ARZ (Diodati)

Frassoni, Raoul Bertini.
Provvedimenti Nobiliari dei Re D'Italia.
Rome, 1968. 106 p.
(Italian titles granted 1860–1968)
NN ASX 71-98

Fumagalli, Giuseppe.
Piccolo Dizionario dei Nomi Propri Italiani di Persone.
Genoa, A. Donath, 1901. 277 p.
NN APD

Fusero, Clemente.
I Doria.
Milan, Dall'Oglio, 1973. 520 p. plus 8 p., 4 gen charts and t of c following p. 520, no index.
NN ASZ (Doria) 75-1527

Fusilla, Joseph G.S
Our Italian Surnames.
Evanston, IL, Chandler's 1949. 299 p., index.
NN APD

Fruttero, Carlo.
Il Libro dei Nomi di Battesimo.
Milan, A. Mondadori, 1969. 207 p.
NN APD 73-2849

Gambino, Richard.
Blood of My Blood: The Dilemma of Italian Americans.
Garden City, NY, Doubleday, 1974. 350 p.
NN IEE (Italians) 74-2026

Gardner, Charles C.
A Genealogical Dictionary of New Jersey.
Alburtis, Burtis.
(IN: *Genealogical Magazine of New Jersey*, Newark, 1938. v. 13, p. 73–78)
(Pietro Caesare Alberti, a native of the island of Malamocco, Venice, settled in New Amsterdam c. 1635.)
NN APR (New Jersey)

Gheno, Antonio.
Contributo Alla Bibliografia Genealogica Italiana.

Bologna, Forni, 1971 (orig. 1924). 297 p., alpha.
NN ASX 73-54

Guelfi Camajani, Luigi, Conte.
Albo d'Oro Delle Famiglie Nobili e Notabili Italiane.
Florence, Archivio Storico Araldico Nobiliare, 1973. 746 p.; alpha; many gen. tables alpha at end.
NN ASX 76-289

Guelfi Camajani, Luigi, Conte.
Alcuni Appunti Sulle Ricerche Genealogiche in Italia.
Stockholm, Sweden, 1960. 13 p.
NN APB p.v. 162 no. 6

Italian American Who's Who.
New York, The Vigo Press, 1937-65. v. 3-20.
NN AGZ

The Italian Genealogist.
Harbor City, CA, The Hartwell Co., 1977-.

Italian Royal Family
(House of Savoy)
(IN: *CDS*, Paris, 1966. p. 319-36)
NN ARB
(IN: *GHF*, Limburg/Lahn, 1968. v. 8, p. 85-92)
NN ATC

Italiani di America ...
New York, S.F. Vanni, 1936-49. 3 v.
NN AGZ

Italy, comp. by Damaris Ring.
(IN: *Genealogy Digest*, Salt Lake City, UT, 1975. v. 6., p. 35-40, 45, 76-77, 94-98 [includes maps])
NN Current Room 315G

Italy. Emigrazione. Commissario Dell'.

... Emigrazione e Colonie.
Rome, G. Bertero, 1903-9. 3 v.
NN SEV

José, Marie.
La Maison de Savoie. Les Origines—Le Comte Vert—Le Comte Rouge.
Paris, Editions Albia Michel, 1956-62. 2 v., index in v. 1.
NN ASZ (Savoy)

Kingdom of the Two Sicilies. Royal Family.
(House of Bourbon)
(IN: *CDS*, Paris, 1966. p. 168-88)
NN ARB

Kirby, J.W.
Alfonso Ferrabosco of Greenwich (1575?-1627), Court Musician.
(IN: *Greenwich and Lewisham Antiquarian Soc. Trans.* Greenwich, England v. 3, p. 207-17)
NN CO (Greenwich)

Lancellotti, Arturo.
... Pionieri Italiani in Africa.
Brescia, La Scuola, 1951. 200 p.
NN AGF

Libro d'Oro Nobilità Italiana.
Rome, Collegio Araldico, 1910-. (v. 16 is for 1969-72) alpha.
NN ASTA

Litta, Pompeo, Conte.
Famiglie Celebri Italiane.
Milan, 1819-1902. 14 v. in 20 (index at desk in Room 315G, NYPL).
NN ASX+

Lord, Eliot.
The Italians in America.
New York, B.F. Buck, 1905. 268 p.
NN IEE (Italians) 71-78 (reprint)

Lui, Chi E? 2nd ed.
Torino, Editrice Torinese, c. 1970.
2 v.
NN *R-AGF 73-4411

Mannucci, Silvio, Conte.
Nobiliario E Blasonario Del Regno
D'Italia.
Rome, Collegio Araldico, 1929–33.
5 v.
NN AWT

Martellone, Anna Maria.
Una Little Italy Nell' Atene
d'America. La Communità Italiana
di Boston dal 1800 al 1920.
Naples, Guida, 1973. 597 p.

Musmanno, Michael.
The Story of the Italians in Amer-
ica.
Garden City, NY, Doubleday, 1965.
300 p.
(Your Ancestor Series)
NN IEE (Italians)

Perria, Antonio.
Storie d'Amore e di Sangue della
Storia d'Italia.
Milan, 1969. 1 v.
NN ASX 73-608

Pitman, Minot H.
American and British Descendants of a Famous Italian Musician, Muzio Clementi.
(IN: *NYGBR*, New York, 1965. v.
96, p. 129–43)
NN APGA

Rolle, Andrew F.
The American Italians, Their His-
tory and Culture.
Belmont, CA, 1972. 130 p.
NN IEE (Italians) 73-1712

Santini, Florio.
Figli d'Italia in America. Lucca
Villagio del Fanciullo.
Pisa, Lischi, 1958. 192 p.
NN IEE (Italians)

Schiavo, Giovanni E.
Four Centuries of Italian-Ameri-
can History.
New York, Vigo Press, 1952. 468 p.
NN IEE+ (Italians)

Schiavo, Giovanni E.
Italian-American History.
New York, The Vigo Press, 1947–
49. 2 v., alpha.
NN IEE (Italians)

Schiavo, Giovanni E.
The Italians in America Before the
Civil War.
New York, The Vigo Press, 1934.
399 p.
NN IEE (Italians)

Schiavo, Giovanni E.
The Italians in Missouri.
New York, Arno Press, 1975 (orig.
1929). 216 p., some alpha sec-
tions, no index.
NN IEE (Italians) 75-686

Scorza, Angelo.
Enciclopedia Araldica Italiana.
Genoa, Studio Ricerche Storiche,
1955–. in progress, v. 1–16 plus.
NN AWT

Spreti, Vittorio, Marchese
Enciclopedia Storico—Nobiliare
Italiana.
Bologna, Forni, 1968–69 (orig.
1928–36). 9 v., alpha.
NN ASX

Spreti, Vittorio, Marchese.
Saggio Bibliografia Araldica Italiana.

Bologna, Forni, 1969 (orig. 1936)
230 p., alpha.
(*Enciclopedia Storico-Nobiliare Italiana. v. 9*)
NN ASX

Storia e Nobilità.
Rome, 1967–. (v. 4, no. 11–12,
Nov.–Dec. 1970)
NN ASTA 76-1550

Wagner, Anthony, and F.S. Andrus.
Bartholomew Taliaferro of Venice
and London.
(IN: *VM*, Richmond, VA, 1969. v. 77,
p. 22–35)
NN *R-APR (Virginia)

Who's Who in Italian Economic
Life.
Milan, 1964–.
NN K-10 8635

Apulia
Fosarini, Amilcare.
Armerista e Notiziario delle Famiglie Nobili, Notabili e Feudatarie di Terra d'Otranto ...
Bologna, Arnaldo Forni, 1971 (orig.
1927). 303 p., alpha.
NN ASY (Apulia) 73-2031

Bari
Noya di Bitetto, Edgardo.
Blasonario Generale di Terra di
Bari.
Bologna, Forni, 1969 (orig. 1912).
216 p.
NN AWT 74-715

Calabria
Ferrari, Umberto.
Armerista Calabrese.
Bassano del Grappa, La Remondiniana, 1971. 87 p. plus index, t
of c, alpha.
NN AWT + 73-632

Capua
Bonazzi, Francesco.
Elenchi delle Famiglie Ricevute
Nell'Ordine Gerosolinitano Formati per Sovrana Disposizione
dai Priorati di Capua e di Barletta Nell'Anno 1801.
Naples, De Angelis, 1879. 80 p.
NN ASY (Capua)

Como
Carpani, Giovanni A.
Stemmario Quattrocentesco delle
Famiglie della Città e Antica
Diocesi di Como, ed. by Carlo
Maspoli.
Lugano, ARS Heraldica, 1973. index.
NN ASY (Como) 75-2404

Cremona
Lancetti, Vincenzo.
Biografia Cremonese.
Bologna, Forni, 1970 (orig.
1819–20). 2 v., alpha.
NN ASY (Cremona)

Ferrara
Maresti, Alfonso.
Teatro Genealogico et Istorico
dell'Antiche e Illustri Famiglie
di Ferrara.
Bologna, Forni, 1973 (orig. 1678). 2
v. in 1.
NN ASY + (Ferrara)

Florence
Mecatt, Giuseppe M.
Storia Genealogica della Nobilità e
Cittadinanza di Firenze.
Bologna, Forni, 1971 (orig.
1753–54). 410 p., index.
NN ASY (Florence) 74-588

Fiesole

Raspini, Giuseppe.
Gli Archivi Parrocchial della Diocesi di Fiesole Inventario.
Rome, 1974. 415 p., index.
NN ASY (Fiesole) 76-2322

Genoa

Battilana, Natale.
Famiglie Nobili di Genova.
Bologna, Forni, 1971 (orig. 1825–33). various pagination.
NN ASY + (Genoa) 73-2111

Scorza, Angelo.
Libro d'Oro della Nobilità di Genova.
Genoa, Waser, 1920. 38 leaves.
NN AWT

Lombardy

Famiglie Nobili in Lombardia.
Milan, E. Milli, 1964–69. 3 v.
NN ASY + (Lombardy)

Matera

Gattini, Giuseppe.
Note Istoriche della Città di Matera ...
Bologna, Forni, 1969 (orig. 1871).
482 p., no index.
NN ASY (Matera) 76-626

Messina

Galluppi, Giuseppe.
Nobiliario della Città di Messina.
Bologna, Forni, 1970 (orig. 1877).
422 p., index.
NN ASY (Messina) 73-987

Milan

Calvi, Felice.
Famiglie Notabili Milanesi.
Bologna, Forni, 1969 (orig. 1875–85). 4 v.
NN ASY + (Milan)

Calvi, Felice.
Il Patriziato Milanese.
Bologna, Forni, 1970 (orig. 1875).
520, LXVIII p., cursory index, part alpha.
NN ASY (Milan) 75-1345

Naples

Bonazzi, Francesco.
Famiglie Nobili e Titolati del Napolitano.
Bologna, Forni, 1969 (orig. 1901).
444 p., index.
NN ASY (Naples) 72-1755

Caldas de Montbuy, Carlos S.
Les Descendientes Legitimados de Alfonson el Magnánimo en el Trono de Nápoles ...
Barcelona, La Hormiga de Oro, 1951. 247 p.
NN ASY (Naples) 73-1523

Lellis, Carlo de.
Famiglie Nobili del Regno di Napoli.
Bologna, Forni, 1968 (orig. 1654–71). 3 v.
NN ASY + (Naples)

Piedmont

Manno, Antonio.
Il Patriziato Subalpino ...
Bologna, Forni, 1972 (orig. 1895–1906). 2 v.
NN ASY (Piedmont) 75-2459

Zucchi, Mario.
Famiglie Nobili e Notabili del Piemonte.
Turin, Postuma, 1950. alpha, index.
NN ASY + (Piedmont)

Romagna

Tabanelli, Mario.
Romagna Medievale.
Faenza, 1972. 207 p.
NN JFD 73-10006

Rome

Amayden, Teodoro.
La Storia Famiglie Romane.
Bologna, Forni, 1967 (orig. 2 v. in
  1 [463 p., 255 p.]), index
NN ASY (Rome)

Checchi, Eugenio.
Giardini Storici Romani ...
Milan, P. Carrara, 1897. 631 p.
NN D-10 9148

Gelzer, Mattias.
The Roman Nobility.
Oxford, Blackwell, 1969. 164 p.
NN D-19 9296

Il Libro d'Oro del Campidoglio.
Bolgona, Forni, 1973 (orig.
  1893–97). 2 v. in 1.
NN ASY (Rome) 74-1471

Istituto di Studi Romani.
Le Grand Famiglie Romane. 1st
  series.
Rome, 1942–60. 12 v.
NN *Zan-632
2nd series.
Rome, 1972–. v. 1–
NN ASY (Rome) 73-1051

Josi, Mario.
La Società Romana della Feudalita
  al Patrizato 1816–1853.
Rome, 1968.
NN D-20 3763

Sardinia

Bianchi, Nicomede.
Storia della Monarchia Piemontese
  dal 1773 sino al 1861.
Rome, Bocca, 1877–85. 4 v.
NN D-11 7052

Le Lannou, Maurice.
Patres et Paysans de la Sardaigne.

Tours, Arrault, 1941. 364 p.
NN F-10 1085

Martini, Pietro.
Biografia Sarda.
Bologna, Forni, 1971. 3 v.
NN JFD 74-4827

Pais, Ettore.
Storia della Sardegna e della
  Corsica ...
Rome, 1923. 2 v.
NN BWW

Tola, Pasquale.
Dizionario Biografico degli Nomini
  Illustri di Sardegna.
Turin, Chiro e Mina, 1837–38. 3 v.
NN AGF

Sepino

Ruotolo, Nicolina.
Uomini Illustri di Sepino.
Matera, 1971. 190 p.
NN JFE 74-815

Sicily

Lowe, Alfonso.
The Barrier and the Bridge: His-
  toric Sicily.
London, Bles, 1972. (pbk 1976) 200
  p., index.
NN JFD 73-2836

Mango di Casalgerardo, A.
Nobiliario di Sicilia.
Bologna, Forni, 1970 (orig.
  1912–15). 2 v., alpha.
v. 1, A–M; v. 2, N–Z.
NN ASY + (Sicily) 76-679

Palazzolo Drago, Francesco.
Famiglie Nobili Siciliane.
Bologna, Forni, 1970 (orig. 1927).
  208 p.
NN ASY (Sicily) 73-357

Tropea
Toraldo, Felice.
Il Sedile e la Nobilità di Tropea.
Bologna, Forni, 1968. 204 p.
NN ASY (Tropea) 71-34

Tuscany
Gamurrini, Eugenio
Istoria Genealogica delle Famiglie
  Nobili Toscanne et Umbre.
Bologna, Forni, 1972 (orig.
  1668–85). 5 v.
NN ASY (Tuscany) 72-2702

Umbria
Vatican. Archivo Vatican.
Rationes Decimarium.
Vatican City, 1952. 2 v., 339 p.
NN ASY (Umbria)

Venice
Beatiano, Giulio Cesare de.
L'Araldo Veneto.
Bologna, Forni, 1970 (orig. 1680).
  360 p., index.
NN AWT 74-1200

Dolcetti, Giovanni.
Il Libro d'Argento delle Famiglie
  Veneto . . .
Bologna, Forni, 1968 (orig.
  1922–28). 5 v. in 2, index in each
  v.
NN ASY (Venice)

Ventimiglia
Bono, Francesco A.
La Nobiltà Ventimigliese.
Bologna, Forni, 1972 (orig. 1924).
  68 p.
NN ASX 74-700

LIECHTENSTEIN (VADUZ)

The little prinicipality of Liechtenstein, located in the Rhine
River Valley and bordered by Austria and Switzerland, was
created in 1719 as a fief of the Holy Roman Empire. The fief
united the barony of Schellenberg with the county of Vaduz,
both of which had been purchased by the Austrian family of
Liechtenstein. The principality was invaded by the French
during the Napoleonic wars; after Napoleon's defeat in 1815,
Liechtenstein joined the brand-new Germanic Confederation.
After Prussia's victory over Austria in 1866 (Liechtenstein had
sent 80 soldiers to the Austrians) the Germanic Confederation
was dissolved. Liechtenstein disbanded its army and declared
itself neutral for all time. In 1919 Switzerland took control of
Liechtenstein's external affairs. In 1938 Prince Francis I abdicated in favor of his great-nephew, who became Franz Josef II
(1906–) and Liechtenstein's first resident ruler.

Archives

Kanzlei der Regierung des Furstentums Liechtenstein
(Chancellery of the Liechtenstein Government)
Vaduz, Liechtenstein

Liechtensteinisches Landesarchiv
FL—9490 Vaduz, Liechtenstein

Public and Church Records

Church records have been kept in various parishes since 1640. Civil registration began in 1878, but the keeping of the civil registers was left to the Catholic clergy. Certificates are obtained from the "pfarramt" (parsonage) of the local community.

Books and Articles

Falke, Jakob.
Geschichte des Fürstlichen Hauses Liechtenstein.
Vienna, W. Braunmuller, 1868–82. 3 v., gen. tables.
NN D-12 1563

Koller, Fortune.
Histoire de la Principauté de Liechtenstein.
Brussels, Editions de Fericks, 196–. 23 p.
NN E-13 1832

Liechtenstein Royal Family
(IN: *CDS*, Paris, 1966. p. 337–52)
NN ARB
(IN: *GHF*, Limburg/Lahn, 1968. v. 8, p. 97–110)
NN ATC

Moore, Russell F.
Principality of Liechtenstein: A Brief History.
New York, Simmons-Boardman, 1960. 44 p.
NN C-11 6535

Raton, Pierre.
Le Liechtenstein: Ses Institutions.
Paris, Recueil Sirey, 1949. 254 p.
NN FKL

LUXEMBOURG (LUXEMBOURG)

The county of Luxembourg (which included the present Belgian province of Luxembourg) came into being in the tenth century and attained prominence in 1308, when its ruler was elected Holy Roman Emperor. In 1354 the county was raised to a duchy; in 1482 the Hapsburgs gained control. The duchy, connected with the Spanish Netherlands for the next three centuries, passed from Spanish to Austrian rule in 1714. During the French revolutionary wars, France occupied the duchy, formally annexing it in 1747. In 1815 the Congress of Vienna proclaimed Luxembourg a Grand Duchy in union with the Netherlands. A major part of the Grand Duchy was annexed by Belgium when Belgium won independence from the Netherlands in 1839. In 1867 the

Treaty of London declared Luxembourg a neutral, independent state. In 1890 Duke Adolf of Nassau became Grand Duke of Luxembourg, and his descendants are still the ruling family.

Luxembourgers are ethnically a mixture of French and German. Throughout the twentieth century numerous immigrants from Italy and other Mediterranean countries have settled there. The first census was taken in 1821.

Archives

Archives de L'État (National Archives)
Plateau du Saint-Esprit (B.P.6)
Luxembourg 2, Luxembourg

Archives de La Ville de Luxembourg
Hôtel de Ville, place Guillaume
Luxembourg, Luxembourg

Public and Church Records

Parish records in some cases go back to 1601. Civil registration began in 1796. Write the Sreffes des Tribunaux of Luxembourg and Kiekirch.

Libraries

Bibliothèque de la Ville
rue Emile Mayrisch 26
Esch-sur-Alzette
Luxembourg, Luxembourg

Bibliothèque Nationale
37 blvd. F.D.-Roosevelt
Luxembourg, Luxembourg

Books and Articles

Bernard, Henri.
Terre Commune: Histoire des Pays de Benelux ... 2nd ed.
Brussels, Brepols, c. 1961. 699 p.
NN C-12 4823

Biographie Nationale du Pays de Luxembourg Depuis ses Origines Jusqu'à Nos Jours ...
Luxembourg, Victor Buck, 1947–73. 2 v.
NN *RR-GCC

Gade, John Allyne.
Luxembourg in the Middle Ages.
Leiden, E. J. Brill, 1951. 238 p.
NN GCC

Krieps, Roger.
Luxembourger in America.
Druck, Bourg-Bourger, 1962. 320 p., index.
NN IEE (Luxembourgers)

Loutsch, Jean-Claude.
Armorial du Pays de Luxembourg.
Luxembourg, Ministre des Arts et des Sciences, 1974. 869 p.
NN AWT 75-2223

Luxembourg Royal Family
(House of Nassau)
(IN: *CDS*, Paris, 1966. p. 353–65)
NN ARB
(IN: *GHF*, Limburg/Lahn, 1968. v.8, p. 111–14)
NN ATC

Oster, Edouard.
Ce que Furent, il y a Cinq Cents Ans, Nos Noms de Famille.
(IN: *Les Cahiers Luxembourgois*, Luxembourg, 1950. v.22, p. 6–18, 86–95, 184–90)
NN GCC

Oster, Edouard.
Nos Noms de Famille au XVIe Siè-cle.
(IN: *Les Cahiers Luxembourgois*, Luxembourg, 1951. v.23, p. 294–318)
NN GCC

Recherches Généalogiques Fami-lienkunde.
(IN: *Ons Hémecht*, Luxembourg, 1935. Jahrg. 41. p. 40–74, etc.)
NN GCA (Annex)

Schleich de Bosse, Jean Robert.
La Noblesse au Grand-duche de Luxembourg.

Luxembourg, Editions du Centre, 1954–57. 2 v.
NN AVF

Van Volxen, Josef.
Ahnen der Luxemburger Ritter-schaft von 1698 bis etwa 1789.
(IN: *Institut Grand-ducal de Lux-embourg. Section Historique Pub.*, Luxembourg, 1938. v.67, p. 537–93)
NN GCA

MALTA (VALLETTA)

In ancient times the island of Malta was invaded successively by Greeks, Carthaginians, Romans, Byzantines and Arabs. In 1091 the Normans conquered the island, and in 1530 it was given to the Knights Hospitallers by Charles V. Napoleon conquered it in 1798, but two years later the French were ousted by Britain, aided by the Maltese. The opening of the Suez Canal in 1869 increased Malta's strategic value. In 1964 the island achieved independence under its own Prime Minister but chose to remain in the British Commonwealth. The country became a republic in 1974.

Censuses were taken in 1911, 1921, 1931, 1957 and 1967.

Archives

Notarial Archives
Scots Street, Valletta and St. Christopher Street
Valletta, Malta

Law Courts
The Palace, Kingsway
Valletta, Malta

Public and Church Records

Vital records certificates for persons born in Malta can be obtained from the Director of the Public Registry Office (L'Insinua, Merchants Street, Valletta, Malta). Certificates for persons born in Gozo can be obtained from the Director of the Public Registry (Victoria, Gozo, Malta).

Libraries

National Library of Malta
Valletta, Malta

Gozo Public Library
Vajrinaa Street
Victoria, Malta

Books and Articles

Bradford, Ernie D.S.
The Shield and the Sword; The Knights of St. John, Jerusalem, Rhodes and Malta.
London, Hodder & Stoughton, 1972. 245 p.

Casasempere Tabone, Ines.
Linajes Malteses en Alcoy
(IN: *International Congress of Heraldry and Genealogy.* 3rd. Congress. Madrid, 1955. p. 147–56)
NN APB

Denaro, V.F.
The Houses of Valletta.
Valletta, Progress Press, 1967.

Dench, Geoffrey.
Maltese in London.
Boston, MA, 1975. 302 p.
NN JLD 75-2546

Engel, Claire E.
L'Ordre de Malte en Mediterranée (1530–1798).
Monaco, Rocher, 1957. 351 p.
NN C-10 5271

Gando, Herbert.
Rajt Malta Tinbidel.

Malta, the author, 1974-c. 1977. 4 v.

Luttrell, Anthony T., ed.
Medieval Malta: Studies on Malta Before the Knights.
London, the British School at Rome, 1975. 232 p., 24 p. of plates, gen. table, index.

Malta Who's Who.
Valletta, Progress Press, 1964–.
NN K-10 5463

Maltese Titles.
(IN: *Burke's Peerage*, London, 1949. 99th ed., p. 2,206–2,215; 1953. 100th ed., p. 2,308–18; 1956. 101th ed., p. 2,390–2,400)
NN ARM

Mangion, Giovanni.
Melitensia 1900–1975; A Classified List of Books and Articles on Maltese History Printed between 1900–1975.
Malta, Malta Historical Society, 1975.

Xuereb, Paul.
Melitensia; A Catalogue of Printed Books and Articles in the Royal University of Malta Library Referring to Malta.
Malta, Malta Univ. Pres., 1974. 76p.
NN JFD 75-3942

Peyrefitte, R.
The Knights of Malta.
London, Panther, 1971.

Riley-Smith, Jonathan.
History of the Order of the Hospitallers of St. John of Jerusalem.
London, Macmillan, 1967. v. 1 (c. 1050–1310).
NN L-11 2394

Sammut Tagliaferro, Brig. A.
History of the Royal Malta Artillery.
Malta, Lux Press, 1976. v. 1 (1800–1929).
NN JFL 77-138

Sciculuna, Sir Hannibal P.
The Church of St. John in Valletta: Its History, Architecture and Monuments.
Malta, San Martin, 1955. 428 p.
NN 3-MRBN+

Vertot, Réné Auberde.

The History of the Knights Hospitallers of St. John of Jerusalem; Styled Afterwards the Knights of Rhodes and at Present Knights of Malta.
Edinburgh, A. Donaldson, 1770. 5 v.
NN BTN

Wettinger, Godfrey.
The Distribution of Surnames in Malta in 1419 and the 1480's.
(IN: *Journal of Maltese Studies*, Valletta, 1968. no. 5, p. 25–48)
NN L-10 6237 no. 5

MONACO (MONACO-VILLE)

Settled by Phoenicians in ancient times, this land was annexed by Marseilles in the first century A.D. In the seventh century it was part of the kingdom of the Lombards and, in the eighth, part of the kingdom of Arles, until it passed under Muslim domination after the Saracens invaded France. During the thirteenth century it was ruled by the Genovese Grimaldi family. In 1731 the French Goyon-Matignon family succeeded by marriage and assumed the name Grimaldi. From 1542 to 1641 Monaco was a Spanish protectorate, from 1641 to 1793 under a French protectorate, and in 1793 it was annexed by France. From 1815–61 it was under the protection of the kingdom of Sardinia. In 1860 it was ceded to France and was again a French protectorate until 1911, when a constitution created an elected council, with the Prince as absolute ruler. Princess Grace, wife of the present ruler, Prince Rainier III, is the former Grace Kelly of Hollywood and Philadelphia (Illustration 46). A census is conducted in Monaco every five years.

Archives

Archives du Palais Princier de Monaco
Palais Princier, Monaco

Public and Church Records

Bureau de l'Etat-Civil
Mairie de Monaco
Principauté de Monaco

Records of divorce are kept by the Clerk of the Court (Greffier).

Libraries

Bibliothèque du Palais de Monaco
8 rue de la Poste
Monaco
Bibliothèque de Monaco
Monaco

Historical and Genealogical Societies

Office National du Tourisme et de l'Information
2a Boulevarde des Moulins
Monte Carlo, Monaco

Books and Articles

Bernardy, Françoise de.
Princes of Monaco: the Remarkable History of the Grimaldi Family.
London, A. Barker, 1961. 272 p., gen. tables.
NN D-13 2326

Damien, Raymond.
Albert Ier, Prince Souverain de Monaco. Précédé de l'Histoire des Origines de Monaco et de la Dynastie des Grimaldi.
Paris, Institut de Valois, 1964. 518 p.
NN E-12 7585

Jackson, Stanley.
Inside Monte Carlo.
London, 1975. 278 p.
NN JFD 76-1266

Labande, Léon H.
... Histoire de la Principauté ...
Monaco, Archives du Palais, A. Picard, 1934. 513 p.
NN DRR

Mayne, Ethel Colburn.
The Romance of Monaco and Its Rulers.
New York, J. Lane, 1910. 370 p.
NN DRR

Monaco Royal Family
(House of Grimaldi)
(IN: *CDS*, Paris, 1966. p. 366–71)
NN ARB
(IN: *GHF*, Limburg/Lahn, 1971. v.9, p. 54–56)
NN ATC

Robyn, Gwen.
Princess Grace.
London, W.H. Allen, 1976. 280 p., index.

Société du Grand Armorial de France. Paris.
Monaco: Ses Princes, ses Princesses.
Paris, 1956. 42 p.
NN APB p.v. 135

THE NETHERLANDS (AMSTERDAM)

The Franks invaded the Low Countries in the third century A.D., conquering the native Saxons and Frisians, and held firm control of the region by the eighth century. After the breakup of the Carolingian empire in the ninth century the Low Countries went to the East Frankish (German) Kingdom and thus to the

Holy Roman Empire. The Lowlands subsequently became a patchwork of duchies and counties. In the fifteenth century the Low Countries passed to the House of Hapsburg when Mary of Burgundy married the Archduke Maximilian (later Maximilian I). By 1555, when Charles V passed the region to his son Philip II of Spain, the northern provinces (the present Netherlands) had attained considerable prosperity. From 1568 to 1581 the Dutch fought a war of independence against Spain. The northern provinces, under William the Silent, Prince of Orange (ancestor of the present ruling house), defeated the Spanish, and in 1579 the Union of Utrecht proclaimed the seven northern provinces as the United Provinces. Independence was declared in 1581. In 1648 the Treaty of Westphalia, ending the Thirty Years War, recognized the the independence of the United Provinces, but the southern provinces remained a Spanish possession. During the seventeenth century the Dutch built a great overseas empire and admitted religious refugees, notably Portuguese and Spanish Jews and French Huguenots. In the early 1700's, after a series of wars with England and France, Dutch power began to decline. In 1794 forces of revolutionary France invaded the Netherlands, and the following year the French established the Republic of Batavia. The Congress of Vienna in 1815 established the Kingdom of the Netherlands, which united Belgium and Holland (the southern provinces) with the United Provinces. Belgium revolted against union with Holland in 1830 and won independence in 1839. The Germans invaded the Netherlands in 1940 and during the Second World War imposed a harsh occupation; Rotterdam was destroyed. In 1948 Queen Wilhelmina abdicated in favor of her daughter, Juliana. In 1949, after four years of warfare, the colony of Indonesia was granted independence. The government of the Netherlands continues to this day as a hereditary, constitutional monarchy. There has always been a close connection between the United States and the Netherlands since the early colonial period, and it is interesting to note that the 12th grandchild of Queen Juliana, Bernardo Federico Tomás Guillermo, born June 12, 1977, is an American citizen, and has American ancestors through his grandfather, Prince Bernhard of the House of Lippe-Biesterfeld, the husband of Queen Juliana.

The most common surnames in Amsterdam are Bakker, Jans(s)en, de Jong, Meijer/Meyer and de Vries. In Rotterdam, they are Vanden, Berg, van Dijk and Jans(s)en.

Archives

Algemeen Rijksarchief (Central Archives of the State)
Bleijenburg 7
's Gravenhage, Netherlands

Rijksarchief in Noord-Holland (Archives of the State, North Holland)
Ceciliasteeg 12
Haarlem, Netherlands

Rijksarchief In Zuid-Holland (Archives of the State, South Holland)
(Deposited in the Central Archives of the State)

Archiefdienst Nederlandse Hervormde Kerk (Archives of the Reformed Church)
Javastraat 100
's Gravenhage, Netherlands

Centraal Historisch Archief (Dutch Antilles)
71 Roodeweg
Willemstad, Curaçao

Church and Public Records

Birth and marriage certificates are available from the Civil Registrar's Office of the Burgomaster of the community where the event occurred.

Libraries

Universiteitsbibliotheek (University Library)
Singel 421-425
Amsterdam, Netherlands

Reoms-Katholieke Openbare Bibliotheek
(Roman Catholic Public Library)
Nieuwe Gracht 30, Utrecht, Netherlands

Bibliotheek der Rijksuniversiteit te Groningen
(Library of the State University)
Oude Kijk in't Jatstraat 5
Groningen, Netherlands

Bibliotheek van het Centraal Bureau voor de Statistiek
(Library of the Netherlands Central Bureau of Statistics)
Prinses Beatrixlaan 428 Voorburg, The Hague, Netherlands

Historical and Genealogical Societies

Centraal Bureau voor Genealogie
(Central Bureau for Genealogy)
Nassaulaan 18
The Hague, Netherlands
(Private and state-owned book and record collections; *Searching for Your Ancestors in the Netherlands*: $3.00, including airmail postage)

Royal Society for Genealogy and Heraldry
5 Bleijensburg
The Hague, Netherlands
(*De Nederlandsche Leeuw*)

Maandblad der Nederlandse Genealogische Vereniging
Postubus 976
Amsterdam, Netherlands
(*Gens Nostra*)

Historische Genootschap (Historical Association)
Utrecht, Wittevrouwenstraat 11
Netherlands

Vereniging "Geire" (Historical Society, Province of Gelderland)
Arnhem, Markt 1, Netherlands
(*Bijdragen en Medeldelingen, Werken*)

Iconographic Bureau
Sophialaan 9
The Hague, Netherlands
(Aims to register all portraits of Dutch subjects and of personalities closely connected with the Netherlands and the House of Orange, from earliest times, wherever located. Maintains card index and reference library as well as collection of portraits and family albums)

Books and Articles

Bailey, Rosalie Fellows.
Dutch Systems in Family Naming.
New York, New Jersey, Washington, 1954.
(*NGSSP no. 12*)
NN APGA 1

Bailey, Rosalie Fellows.
Pre-Revolutionary Dutch House and Families in Northern New Jersey and Southern New York.
New York, Dover, 1968 (orig. 1936).
612 p., index.
NN ISBB 72-2228

Beresteyn, Eltjo A.
Genealogisch Repertorium.
The Hague, Central Bureau voor Genealogie, 1972.
2 v. (A–L, M–Z)
NN AVD 73-1243

Bogaard, P. H.
The Flowering Orchard: Genealogy of an American Branch of the Bogaard Family That Lived in the Medieval Dutch Town of Utrecht.
De Meern, the Netherlands, 1974.
112 p., index.
NN APV (Bogaard) 76-2272

Brouwer, Hans.
Geschreven Verleden: Genealogie en oud Schrift.
's Gravenzande, Europese Bibliotheek, 1963. 91 p.
NN AVD 72-1126

Central Bureau voor Genealogie.
Jaarboek.
The Hague, 1947–.
NN AVD

De Jong, Gerald F.
The Dutch in America, 1609–1974.
Boston, MA, Twayne Pub., 1975.
326 p., index.
NN IEE (Dutch) 75-1654

Delvenne, Mathieu G.
Biographie du Royaume des Pays Bas ...des Belges et des Hollandais ...
Liége, Ve. J. Desoer, 1828–29. 2 v.
NN AGM

Dillen, Johannes Gerard van.
Het Oudste Aandeelhoudersregister van de Kamer Amsterdam der Oost-Indische Compagnie.
's Gravenhage, M. Nijhoff, 1958.
294 p.
(*Nederlandsch Economisch-Historich Archief. Werken. 14*)
(Biographies of members of the Dutch East India Co.)
NN TLH

Dutch Settlers Society of Albany.
Albany, NY, 1924/25–.
NN IRM (Albany)

Eppstein, Georg Freiherr von, and Max Staercke.
Prins Bernhard, het Vorstelijke Huis zur Lippe-Biesterfeld.
Utrecht, A. W. Bruna, 1936. 192 p.
NN ERW

Fahy, T. G.
Genealogical Research in the Netherlands.
(IN: *GM*, London, 1962. v. 14, p. 24–27)
NN ARCA

Fahy, T. G.
Some Sources for Dutch Genealogy.
(IN: *GM*, London, 1962. v. 14, p.24–27)
NN ARCA

Genealogish Repertorium.
The Hague, Central Bureau voor Genealogie, 1972. 2 v. (A–L, M–Z)
NN AVD 73-1243

Genealogy in the Netherlands.
(IN: *Familia*, Capetown, 1974. v. 11, p. 61–65)
NN AVH (Africa, South)

Gens Nostra, "Ons Geslacht."
Amsterdam, 1946– (NN has 1951–)
(Nederlandse Genealogische Vereniging, Postbus 976)
NN AVD

Goslinga, Cornelis C.
The Dutch in the Caribbean and on the Wild Coast 1580–1680.
Assen, 1971. 647 p.
NN HNB 72-1173

De Haalve Maen.
New York, The Holland Society, 1922–.
NN APGA (Holland)

Het Arnemache Geslacht Nijhoff.
's Gravenhage, M. Nijhoff, 1931. 189 p.
NN AVDI (Nijhoff)

Holland Society of New York.
Year Book.
New York, 1886–. index.
NN APGA

Kenney, Alice.
Stubborn for Liberty: The Dutch in New York.
Syracuse, NY, 1975. 301 p., index.
NN IEE (Dutch) 76-567

Kobins, J.C.
Biographisch Handwoordenboek van Nederland ...
Zutphen, van Someren, 1870. 3 v.
NN AGM

Leenaerts, Remy J.
Algemeen Genealogisch-Heraldisch Repertorium voor de Zuidelijke Nederlanden. General Genealogical and Heraldic Index of the Southern Netherlands.
Handzame, Belgium, Uitgaven, "Familia et Patria," 1969–72.
NN AVE 74-2124

Leiby, Adrian Coulter.
The Early Dutch and Swedish Settlers of New Jersey.
Princeton, NJ, Van Nostrand, 1964. 139 p.
(*New Jersey Historical Society Series.* v. 10)
NN IAA

Moller, Walther.
Der Ursprung des Hauses Nassau.
(IN: *Familie und Volk*, Berchtesgaden, 1954. Jahrg. 3, heft 3, p. 129–36, gen. tables)
NN ATA

Nederland's Adelsboek.
's Gravenhage, 1903–.
(67th year 1975)
NN AVD

Nederlands Patriciaat.
's Gravenhage, 1910–.
NN AVD

De Nederlandsche Leeuw.
's Gravenhage, 1883–1976+. 93 v.
to 1976.
NN AVD

De Nederlandse Ridderorden.
Amsterdam, 1900–36. 2 v.
NN AWT 73-2636

Netherlands.
Genealogical Society, LDS, series
C, no. 3-13.
Salt Lake City, UT, 1968–71.
NN APA 72-753

Nienaber, Gabriel S.
Afrikaanse Familiename: 'n geselsie vir Belangstellende Leke oor
die Betekensis van ouer Afrikaanse Vanne.
Capetown, A. A. Balkema, 1955.
108 p.
NN APD

Pieters, Aleida J.
A Dutch Settlement in Michigan.
Grand Rapids, MI, Reformed
Press, 1923. 207 p.
NN IEE (Dutch)

Purple, Edwin R.
Contributions to the History of the
Ancient Families of New Am-
sterdam and New York ... with
Additions by Samuel S. Purple.
New York, 1881. 138 p.
(Rare, only 25 copies)
NN AZ

R. K. "Wie is Dat?"
Leiden, H.J. Dieben, 1925–26. 2 v.
NN ZLO

Romein, Jan M.
... Erflaters van Onze Beschaving.
Amsterdam, Querido's, 1938–40. 4
v.
NN AGM

Saint Nicholas Society of the City
of New York.
Genealogical Record.
New York, 1905–68. 8 v.
NN APGA

Schaat, J. van den.
Uit de Wordingsgeschiedenis der
Hollandse Doop-en Familiena-
men.
Assen, Van Gorcum, 1953. 208 p.
NN APD

Singleton, Esther.
Dutch New York.
New York, Dodd, Mead, 1909. 360
p., index.
NN IRGC

Smit, Pamela, and J.W. Smit.
The Dutch in America, 1609–1970.
Dobbs Ferry, NY, Oceana, 1972.
116 p., index.
NN IEE (Dutch) 75-731

Stellingwerff, Dr. J.
Amsterdamse Emigration ... de
Praire van Iowa 1846–1873.
Amsterdam, Buijten and Schipper-
heijn, 1975. 395 p., index.
NN IEE (Dutch) 77-461

Verzijl, Jan J.M.H.
Huldeblijk, Bundel Opstellen Aan-
geboden aan de Genealoog.

Roermond, Stichting Instituut voor Genealogie en Streekgus-chiedenis, 1967. 224 p., index.
NN AVD 74-1736

Wakefield, Robert S.
The Search for Descendants of Moses Fletcher.
(IN: *NEHGR*, Boston, 1974. v. 128, p. 161–69)
(A *Mayflower* passenger whose descendants stayed in Holland)
NN *R-APGA

Who's Who in the Netherlands.
Amsterdam, 1962–.
NN K-10 6967

Wie is Dat?
s'Gravenhage, M. Mijhoff, 1931–.
NN AGM

Wijnaendts van Resandt, Willem.
Genealogy in the Netherlands.
(IN: *GM*, London, 1974. v. 17, p. 547–50)
NN ARCA

Wijnaendts van Resandt, Willem.
Repertorium DTB (Concise Repertory of Dutch Parish Registers, etc.)
Witgave, Central Bureau voor Genealogie, 1969. 207 p. alpha
(Gives dates of both Christian and Jewish registers and includes the following symbols; C=Besni-jdenisregisters-Records of Circumcision; D=Doopboeken-Baptism Records; O=Registers van Overlijden/en of Begraven-Records of Deaths and Burials; T=Trouwboeken-Marriage Records)
This is a most important reference for original Dutch research.
NN AVB 75-2752

Amsterdam
Elias, Johan E.
De Vroedschap van Amsterdam.
Haarlem, Vicnet Loosjes, 1903–5. 2 v., index in v.2.
NN AVDH (Amsterdam)

Brabant
De Brabant Leeuw.
Rotterdam, 1952–.
NN AVDH (Brabant)

Drenthe
Prakke, H.J.
Drenthe in Michigan.
Assen, 1948. 86 p.
NN IEE (Dutch)

Friesland
Haan Hettema, M. de, et A. van Halmael.
Stamboek van den Friesche Uroe-geren en Lateren Adel.
Leeuwarden, D. Meinderama, 1846. 2 v.
NN AVDH+ (Friesland)

Roarda, R.S.
Nammen ut de Bylagen fan de Sentinsjes fan it Hof fan Frysland.
Ljouwert, Fryske Academy, c. 1958–62. 3v., v.2–4 1710–1811 in NN
NN AVDH (Friesland)

Sminia, H. Baerdt van.
Nieuwe Naamlijst van Grietmannen ...
Leeuwarden, H.C. Schetsberg, 1837. 430 p.
NN AVDH (Friesland)

Tharp, Dorothy R.
Finding Frisian Forebears ...
(In: *Chicago Genealogist* Chicago,

1976–1977. v. 9. pp. 23–27, 51–55,
140–145)
NN APR (Chicago) 73-254

The Hague

English Church in The Hague.
The Eldest Church Book of the
English Congregation . . . trans.
by M.G. Wildeman.
The Hague, De Wappenheraut,
1906. 84 p.
NN AVDH (The Hague)

The Hague.
Naamlijst der Geborenen, Onder-
trouwden en Overledenen.
's Gravenhage, A. van Hoogstra-
ten, 1817–1838 10 v.
NN AVDH (The Hague)

Kloosterkerk, The Hague.
De Registers de Graven in der
Kloosterkerk te 's Gravenhage.
's Gravenhage, Genealogisch-Her-
aldisch Archief, 1887. 151 p.
NN AVDH (The Hague)

Limburg

Belonje, J.
Genealogische en Heraldische Ged-
enkwaardigheden in en uit de
Kerken der Provincie Limburg.
Maastricht, 1961. 523 p., index.
NN AVDH (Limburg)

Venne, J.M., and J. Graafland.
Limburgsche Wapens.
Maastrichtn van Aelst Drukkers-
Uitgevers, 1925 (reprinted c.
1972). 269 p., index.
NN AWT+ 72-2128

North Holland

Bloys van Treslong Prins, P.C. and
J. Belonje.
Genealogische en Heraldische in

en uit de Kerken der Provincie
Noord-Holland.
Utrecht, Oosthoek, 1928–31. 5 v.
NN AVDH (North Holland)

Orange

Leemans, W.F.
La Noblesse de la Principauté
d'Orange.
The Hague, Société Royale Genéal-
ogie et Héraldique des Pays Bas,
1974. 469 p., index
NN AVDH (Orange) 76-427

Renswoude

Laansma, S.
Boerderijen en Boerengeslachten
te Renswoude.
Renswoude, 1972. 156 p., 2 parts, t
of c.
NN AVDH (Renswoude) 76-1071

Rotterdam

Engelbrecht, E.A.
De Vroedschap van Rotterdam
1572–1795.
Rotterdam, Gemeentelijke Archiefdienst 1973. 471 p. index
gen. tables
(*Rotterdam: Bronnen voor de Ges-
chiedenis van Rotterdam. v.5*)
NN GAXZ

Utrecht

Bloys van Treslong Prins, P.C.
Genealogische en Heraldische . . .
in en uit de Kerken de Provincie
Utrecht.
Utrecht, A. Oosthoek, 1919. 342 p.
NN AVDH (Utrecht)

Zuid-Holland (South Holland)

Bloys van Treslong Prins, P.C.
Genealogische en Heraldische . . .

in en uit de Kerken der Provincie Zuid-Holland.
Utrecht, A. Oosthoek, 1922. 2 v. in 3.
NN AVDH (South Holland)

Ons Voorgeslacht Maanblad van de Zuidhollandse Vereniging voor Genealogie.
Rotterdam, 1946–. 30 v. by 1975.
NN AVH (South Holland)

NORWAY (OSLO)

Norway of the eighth century was comprised of petty kingdoms and earldoms. In the ninth century Harold I (who claimed to be descended from the Norse gods) conquered most of the country and achieved a temporary union. After his death the country was divided among his sons, one of whom, Haakon I, reunited the country about 935. Under Olaf II (1015–28), Christianity was established. After a period of decline caused by conflicting claims to the throne, Haakon IV (1217) became king. During his reign and that of Magnus VI (1263–80), Norway reached the acme of its power, and Greenland and Iceland became possessions of the Norwegian crown. In 1319 Norway was united with Sweden, when Magnus VII, who was King of Sweden, became King of Norway. In 1397 Norway was united with Denmark and Sweden by the Kalmar Union, engineered by Margaret of Denmark, and for the next four centuries Norway's history became that of Denmark. In 1814 Denmark, which had sided with France in the Napoleonic wars, was forced to cede Norway to Sweden. The Norwegians resisted by drafting their own constitution and selecting the Danish Prince Christian as Christian VIII King of Norway, but the Swedes invaded and forced Norway to capitulate to Swedish rule. It was not until 1905 that Norway was able to completely dissolve the union with Sweden. At that time they chose another Danish prince, the second son of Frederick VIII of Denmark, who came to the throne as King Haakon VII and who, as nephew and son-in-law of King Edward VII, maintained close ties with Great Britain. In 1957, after the death of King Haakon, his son Olaf V ascended the throne.

The most common surnames in Oslo are Andersen, Hansen, Johansen, Larsen and Olsen.

The first census was taken in 1769, and another was recorded in 1801. Enumerations were made every ten years from 1815 through 1875 and every ten years since 1890. Returns for 1900 and before are available for inspection. They are found in the National Archives, except for the 1875 and 1900 returns, which are in Regional Archives.

Anyone undertaking Norwegian research should obtain *How to Trace Your Ancestors in Norway*, a free pamphlet issued by the Royal Norwegian Ministry of Foreign Affairs in Oslo.

Archives

Riksarkivet (National Archives)
Bankplassen 3
Oslo 1, Norway

Regional Archives (for vital and parish records older than 100 years):

Ostfold, Akerhus, Oslo, Buskerud, Vestfold and Telemark counties:
Statsarkivet I Oslo
Kirkgata 14–18, Prinsensgate 7, Oslo 1, Norway

Hedmark and Oppland counties:
Statsarkivet I Hamar
Strandgata 71, 2300 Hamar

Aust-Agder and Vest-Agder counties:
Statsarkivet I Kristiansand
Vesterveien 4, 4600 Kristiansand S.

Rogaland County:
Statsarkivet I Stavanger
Domkirkeplassen 3, 4000 Stavanger
Møre og Romsdal, Sør-Trondelag, Nord-Trøndelag, Nordland, Troms and Finmark:
Statsarkivet I Trondheim
Høgskoleveien 12 (P.O. Box 2825) 7001 Trondheim

Statsarkivkontoret I Tromsø
Petersborggata 21–29, 9000 Tromsø

Bergen County:
Statsarkivet in Bergen
Arstadveien 22, 5000 Bergen

Public and Church Records

Birth certificates are issued by the Norwegian State Church (Den Norske Kirke) through the priest or minister of the parish where the parents resided. Marriage certificates may be obtained from the priest of the parish where the marriage was solemnized. Civil marriage certificates are issued by the City Judge (Byfogd) in cities and towns and the District Judge (Sorenskriver) in the rural communities.

Some parish registers date from the 1600's but most are from after 1700 (Illustration 45). Registers are transferred to the Regional Archives eighty years after the last entry, and more recent registers remain in the care of the parish ministers. Abstracts of the parish registers of 1873–77 and since 1921 are

held by the Central Bureau of Statistics (Statistisk Sentralbyra) in Oslo. For the periods 1866–72 and 1889–1920, abstracts are deposited in the National Archives.
The Central Bureau of Statistics (Statistisk Sentralbyra)
Dronningen gate 16, Oslo-Dep.
Oslo 1, Norway

Libraries

Deichmanske Bibliotek (City Library of Oslo)
Henrik Ibsens gt. 1
Oslo 1, Norway

Universitetsbiblioteket i Oslo (The Royal University Library)
Drammensveien 42
Oslo, Norway

Historical and Genealogical Societies

Norsk Slektshistorisk Forening (Norwegian Genealogical Society)
Bygdøy alle 123B
Oslo 2, Norway
(*Norsk Slektshistorisk Tidsskrift*)

Nordmanns-Forbundet (League of Norsemen)
Radhusgata 23b
Oslo 1, Norway

Norges Geografiske Oppmaling
St. Olav gt. 32
Oslo, Norway
(Detailed plat maps available)

Kirkehistorisk Samfunn (Church History Society)
Box 116, Voksenlia

Oslo 3, Norway
(*Norvegia Sacra*)

Landsiaget for Bygde-og Byhistorie
Gyldenlovesgt. 22b
Oslo 2, Norway
(Coordinates the work of about 70 local history organizations)
(*Heimen*)

Norsk Historisk Forening (Norwegian Historical Society)
Historisk institutt,
Postboks 23,
5014 Bergen-Universitetet,
Oslo, Norway

Norsk Lokalhistorisk Institutt
Sommerrogt. 17
Oslo 2, Norway

United States Sources

Supreme Lodge of the Sons of Norway
1312 West Lake Street
Minneapolis, MN

Norwegian-American Historical Association
Northfield, MN 55057

Norwegian-American Historical Museum
Decorah, IA 52101

Library of the Lutheran Theological Seminary
St. Paul, MN
(Records of the Norwegian Evangelical Lutheran Church in America)

Several college libraries have rather extensive holdings of material pertaining to Norwegian genealogy and local history:

Luther College
Preus Library
Decorah, IA 52101

St. Olaf College
Northfield, MN 55057

University of Minnesota
Minneapolis, MN 55812

Memorial Library
University of Wisconsin
Madison, WI 53706

Books and Articles

Aett Og By, Festskrift Til S.H.
Finne-Gronn Om Nordisk Slekts-
forskning Og Oslo Byhistorie.
Oslo, 1944. 236 p.
(Contents in Danish, Norwegian
and Swedish)
NN AVB

Anderson, Arlow William.
The Norwegian-Americans.
Boston, MA, Twayne Press, 1974.
274 p.
(The Immigrant Heritage of Amer-
ica series)
NN IEP 75-2142

Bull, Edvard.
Norsk Biografisk Leksikon ...
Kirstiania (Oslo), Aschehoug,
1923–55. 12 v.
NN *RR-AGO

Derry, T.K.
A History of Norway 1814–1972.
Oxford, Clarendon Press, 1973. 503
p. index, maps.
NN *R-GGC 73-4820

Brouse, Gwendolyn I.
Sven Njellson Aarsvoll and Grete
Marie Handsdatter Aarsvoll,

Their Descendants in North America.
Riverside, CA, the author, 1974.
144 p.
(A family from Norway who settled
in Minnesota and Saskatchewan)
NN APV (Aarsvoll) 75-1642

Fried, Ruby Sather.
Our Norwegian Forefathers and
Their American Descendants.
Inglewood, CA, R.S. Fried, 1971. 73
p., t of c, no index.
NN APV (Christenson-Simonson)
73-411

Genealogical Guidebook and Atlas
of Norway, by Smith and Thomsen.
Logan, UT, Everton, c. 1976. 56 p.
NN AVB 77-1067

Hansen, Morten.
Norske Slektsbøker: en Bibliografi.
Oslo, Aschehoug, 1965. 197 p., in-
dex.
NN AVB 72-2134 (Desk Room 315G)

Hvem er Hvem?
Kristiania (Oslo), 1912–64 plus.
NN AGQ

I Manns Minne: Daglegliv ved
Hundreårsskiftet Frå
Nasjonalforeningens Landskonk-
urranse for eldre.
Oslo, Det Norske Samlaget, 1967–
68. 2 v. index v. 2
NN L-11 2010

Jaeren Gards-Og Aettesoga.
Stavanger, Dreyer Aksjeselskap,
1939–63. 3 v.
(Band 1, Gjestal; Band 2, Hoyland
... 1500–1900; Band 3, Klepp
... 1519–1900)
(Local history of Jaeren)
NN AVB+ (Jaeren)

Koht, Halvdan.
Menn i Historia.
Oslo, Aschehoug, 1963. 187 p.
NN E-11 8342

Krag, Hans.
Norsk Heraldisk Mønstring Fra
Frederik IV's
Regjeringstid, 1699–1730.
Drøbak, O.B. Hansens, 1942–55. 2
v.
NN AWT

LDS Series D. no.1 (1967), Norway
general
no.11 (1969), Norway church records
no.12 (1969), Norway census records
no.13 (1960), Norway probate records
no.14 (1969), Norway social background
NN APA 72-754

Lekwa, Verl L.
The Ledwa Family: Familien
Ledwa.
Conesville, IA, Enterprise Print,
1973. 129 p., t of c, no index.
(Lekwa, Lekia name of family farm
in Norway)
NN APV (Ledwa) 76-385

Lind, Erik H.
Norsk-Isländska   Personbinamn
från Medeltiden.
Uppsala, A.B. Lundequistska,
1921. 416 columns.
NN APD

Lindstøl, Tallak Olsen.
Stortinget og Statsraadet 1814–
1914 ...
Kristiania, Steenske Bogtrykkeri,
1914–15. 2 v. in 4, alpha.
NN AGO

Norlie, Olaf M.
History of the Norwegian People
in America.
New York, Haskell House, 1973
(orig. 1924). 512 p., no index.
NN IEP 76-1329

Norsk Slektshistorisk Tidsskrift.
Oslo, 1927–76, plus. 25 v. plus.
NN AVB

Norsk Slektskalender.
Oslo, Cammermeyer, 1949–51. 2 v.
NN AVB

Norwegian Names (Nrske Navn)
Kinship Terms
(IN: *SGSB*, Regina, Saskatchewan
1975. v. 5, p. 49–51)
NN APW

Norwegian Royal Family
(House of Schleswig-Holstein-Son-
derburg-Glücksburg)
(IN: *CDS*, Paris, 1966. p. 379–83)
NN ARB
(IN: *GHF*, Limburg/Lahn, 1971.
v.9, p. 65–66)
NN ATC

Norwegian-American Historical
Association.
Norwegian-American Studies and
Records.
Northfield, MN, 1926–74. (v.1–17,
1926–52, indexed in Jacobus, v.3)
NN IEP

Palmstrom, Henrik.
The Census of Population in Nor-
way, August 15, 1769.
(IN: *Nordic Statistical Journal*,
Stockholm, 1929. v.1, p. 371–80)
NN SDA

Rolf, Fladby.
The Norwegian Institute for Local

History and Local History Research.
(IN: *The Local Historian*, London, 1974. v.11, p. 217–24)
NN CA

Vanberg, Bert.
So Deep Are My Roots.
Minneapolis, MN, Sons of Norway, c. 1973.

Wierenga, Evelyn Ostraat.
Espelands in America.
Sioux Falls, SD, The Modern Press, Inc., 1973. 173 p., t of c, no index.
(Traces mid-19th-century immigrant family back to 1615; good illustrative material.)
NN APV (Espeland) 74-1918

POLAND (WARSAW)

Slavic tribes within Poland achieved unity by the tenth century, and the main dynasty, the Piast, accepted Christianity in 966. The medieval period was a time of constant warfare against Hungary, Moscow, Moldavia and the Tartars and Turks, which ended at last when a united Poland and Lithuania defeated the Teutonic Knights at Tannenberg in 1410. Under the Jagiello dynasty (1386–1572) Poland was a great power. In the sixteenth and seventeenth centuries tension between Poland's Roman Catholic ruling classes and the Greek Orthodox Church led to frequent wars with Russia. The Polish-Swedish wars were precipitated by conflicting claims to the throne. In the eighteenth century, power squabbles between Austria, Prussia and Russia led to the end of Poland's sovereignty until World War I. Three successive partitions—in 1772, 1793 and 1795—divided Poland into spheres of influence for Maria Theresa of Austria, Catherine II of Russia and Frederick II of Prussia, but a nationalist spirit began to appear, manifested by the revolt led by Thaddeus Kosciusko in the still-independent part of Poland in 1794. At the Congress of Vienna in 1814–15, parts of Poland went to Russia, Prussia and Austria, while Cracow was made a separate republic. In 1830 insurrections erupted in Russian Poland but were put down. The following year thousands of Poles immigrated to Paris, which became a center for revolutionary activities. In 1848 rebellions occurred in Austrian and Prussian Poland but were quelled. After World War I Poland became an independent republic. The Treaty of Versailles in 1919 gave Poland access to the Baltic Sea via the Polish Corridor and restored Prussian Poland. Germany and the Soviet Union invaded Poland in 1939, and the country was partitioned once again. After Germany's attack on the Soviet Union in 1941, all of Poland was occupied by the Germans, who devastated the Polish population. Some three million non-Jews were massacred or died of starvation or in extermination camps, while the Jews, who had numbered in excess of three million before the war, were reduced to a mere 100,000 by outright murder. Two and a half million Poles were deported to Germany as slave labor. The Germans were expelled in 1945. The Polish government-in-exile in London was recognized by the United States, but the Soviets pressed their own group. Elections held in 1947 were controlled by the Communists, and a Soviet-dominated government took power. A constitution drafted in 1952 created a "People's Democracy" modeled after the Soviet Union's.

The most common surnames in Warsaw are Dabrowski, Kamiński, Kowalski, Nowak, Szymański, Wiśniewski and Zieliński.

Archives

Naczeina Dyrekcja Archiwów Pań- stoowych (Main Directorate of the Polish State Archives)
Midowa Street 10
Warsaw, Poland

Archiwum Główne Akt Dawnych (Central Archives of Old Records)
Dluga 7
Warsaw, Poland

Archiwum Akt Nowych (Central Archives of Recent Records)
A1. Niepodległości 162
Warsaw, Poland

´Zydowski Instytut Historyczny, Archiwum (Archives of the Institute of Jewish History)
Al. Gen. Swierczewskiego 79
Warsaw, Poland

For information on Pomerania, once part of Germany and since annexed to Poland:

Pommerische Landsmannschaft
Hamburg 13
Johnsalle 18, Germany

Public and Church Records

Civil registration began about 1870. For births or marriages that occured within or near the corporate limits of Warsaw, a copy of the record may be obtained from either the Vital Statistics Office for Central Warsaw (Urzad Stanu Cywilnego, Warszawa-Strodmiescie) or from the Vital Statistics Office for Praga (Urzad Stanu Cywilnego, Warszawa-Praga), depending on the precise area in which the event took place. If the birth or marriage occurred in a city or larger town outside the district of Warsaw, a copy of the record may be obtained from the local Vital Statistics Office. If it occurred in a village or other place for which no Vital Statistics Office is maintained, the record can be obtained from the Communal Vital Statistics Office (Urzad Stanu Cywilnego Gminnej Rady Narodowej) established for the community. Copies of vital records may also be held in the archives of the district court with jurisdiction over the area.

Centralne Archiwum Głównego Urzedu Statystycznego (GUS) (Central Archives of Statistics) Al. Niepodleglości 208 Warsaw, Poland

Libraries

Biblioteka Narodowa (National Library) Ulica Hankiewicza Warsaw 00-973, Poland

Biblioteka Uniwersytecka Jagiellońska (Library of the University of Jagellone), ul. Mickiewicza 22 Kraków 30-059, Poland

Biblioteka Uniwersytecka w Warszawie Oddział Rekopisów (Library of the University of Warsaw, Manuscript Section) Krakowskie Przedmieście 26-28 Warsaw, Poland

Biblioteka Katolickiego Uniwersytetu Lubelskiego w Lublinie (Library of the Catholic University of Lublin), ul. Chopina 27 Lublin, Poland

Biblioteka Uniwersytecka w Toruniu (Library of Toruń University)

Gagarina 13, Bielany Toruń, Poland

Centralna Biblioteka Statystyczna (Central Statistical Library) Al. Niepodległości 208 Warsaw 00-925, Poland

Historical and Genealogical Societies

Polskie Towarzystwo Historyczne (Polish Historical Society) Rynek Starego Miasta 29/31 Warsaw, Poland

The General Sikorski Historical Institute, 20 Princes' Gate London, S.W. 7, England

United States Sources

Polish Historical Commission of Central Council of Polish Organizations of Pittsburgh, Pa. 4291 Stanton Avenue Pittsburgh, PA 15201 (*Polish Day*)

Polish Museum of America 984 N. Milwaukee Avenue Chicago, IL 60622

Books and Articles

Ames, Mary A. Boczón. How to Research Your Personal Polish Family History. Newcarrollton, N.D. 70784, the Author, 6642 Adrian St., 1977. 30 p.

Archiwum Główne Akt Dawnych w Warszawie (AGAD), 7, rue Dluga, Varsovie.

(See: *Archivum*, Paris, 1965. v. 15, p. 275 ff.)
NN BAA

Baker, T. Lindsay.
The Moczygemba Family of Texas and Poland: Initiators of Polish Colonization in America.
(IN: *Stripes*, Fort Worth, TX, 1975. v. 15, p. 124–38, illus.)
NN APR (Texas)

Berent, Wackaw.
Nurt: Opowiesci Biograficzne.
Warsaw, Czytelnik, 1958. 320 p.
NN *QR

Bolesta-Kozlowski, R.A.
An Intro. to Polish Surnames.
(IN: *Families*, Toronto, 1972. v. 11, p. 55–57, 83–86)
NN APW 73-2794

Boniecki-Fredo, Adam J.F.
Herbarz Polski.
Warsaw, Wolff, 1899–1915. 16 v.
NN *QR+

Czerny, Max Karl.
Polnische Umbenennungen der Ortschaften Jenseits Oder-Neisse.
Frankfurt am Main, 1949–52. 2 v. in 3.
Teil A. Deutsch-Polnisch, Teil B. Polnisch-Deutsch, Band 1, A–P; Band 2, R–Z.
(Polish gazetteer)
NN *QR+

Dunn-Borkowski, Jerzy S.T.
Almanach Blekitny.
Lwów, H. Altenberga, 1908. 1,118 p.
NN *QR

Dworaczyk, Edward J.
... Church Records of Panna Maria, Texas.
Chicago, IL, 1945. 64 p.
NN IXZ p.v. 453

Dworaczek, Vlodimierz.
Genealogia.
Warsaw, Państwowe, 1959. 181 p., 10 gen. tables.
NN *QR

Les Familles Princières et Comtales de Pologne avant le Partage en 1771.
Cracow, 1927. 1 v. (Ostaszewski)
NN *QR

Forst, Otto.
Die Polnische Genealogie.
(IN: *Familiengeschichtliche Blätter*, Leipzig, 1911. Jahr. 9, p. 92–93, 127–28, 144–45.)
NN ATA+

Haiman, Mieczyslaw.
Polish Pioneers in California.
Chicago, IL, R.C. Union Archives and Museum Annals and Museum., 1940. v. 5, 83 p.
NN IEE (Poles)

Haiman, Mieczyslaw.
... Polish Pioneers of Virginia and Kentucky ... with notes on the Sadowski Family by A. Clay Sandusky.
Chicago, IL, 1937. 84 p.
NN IEE (Poles)

Heine, Marc E.
The Poles.
Newton Abbot, Devon, David and Charles, 1976. 168 p., index
NN JFD 76-6867

Iwanoski, Eustachy A.
Wspomnienia Polskich Czasów ...
Lwowie, Schmidta, 1894. 2 v.
NN *QR

Jensen, Larry O.
Genealogical Research in Eastern
    Europe. Poland.
(IN: *SGSB*, v. 7, p. 15–37)
(Includes maps and gazetteer in-
    formation)
NN APW

Jocher, Adam B.
Abraz Bibliograficzno-historyczny
    Literatury i Nauk W Polsce . . .
Wilno, Zawadzkiego, 1840–57. 3 v.
NN *QP

Klec-Pileswski, B.
Some Sources for Polish Genealogy.
(IN: *GM*, London, 1969. v. 16, p.
    150–59)
NN ARCA

Kowallis, Otto K. and Vera N.
A Genealogical Guide and Atlas of
    Silesia.
Logan, UT, Everton, 1976. 442 p.

Krzepela, Józef.
Rody Ziem Pruskich.
Kraków, Wolff, 1927. 262 p.
NN *QO

Krzepela, Józef.
Rody Ziemianskie XV i XVI Wieku
    . . .
Kraków, Wolff, 1930. 102 p.
NN *QR

Lewanski, Richard Casimir.
Guide to Polish Libraries and Ar-
    chives.
Boulder, CO, 1974. 209 p.
NN JFD 76-2156

Materiały do Biografii Genealogii
    i Heraldyki Polskiej.
Buenos Aires, 1963–.
NN *QPA

Mizwa, Stephen P.
Great Men and Women of Poland.
New York, Macmillan, 1942. 397 p.
NN AGN

Obal, Thaddeus.
Polish Family Tree Surnames.
Hillsdale, NJ, T.J. Obal, 1975.
NN APK 76-416

Pamietniki o Koniec Polskich
    Przyczynek do Drzie jow Pol-
    skich XVII Wieku.
Lwow, Nakl. L. Rzewuskiego, 1842.
    452 p.
NN *QR

Polish Day Association, Chicago.
Poles in America: Their Contribu-
    tion to a Century of Progress
    . . .
Chicago, Polish Day Association,
    1933. 263 p.
(Filled with portraits, biographies,
    accounts of Polish parish
    churches and other Polish insti-
    tutions in Chicago)
NN IEE (Poles)

Polish American Studies.
New York, Polish Institute,
    1944–70. 27 v.
NN IEE (Poles)

Polskie Towarzystwo Heraldyczne.
Rocznik.
Kraków, 1908–32. (Not published
    1914–18)
NN *QPA

Przygoda, Jacek.
Texas Pioneer from Poland: A
    Study of Ethnic History.
Waco, TX, Texan Press, 1971. 171
    p., index.
NN IEE (Poles) 73-1258

Przyborowski, Walery, 1845–1913.
Z Przeszlosci Warszawy, Skice Historiczne.
Warsaw, A. G. Dubowski, 1899–1902.
NN *QR

Starykón-Kasprzycki, Stefan.
Almanach Szlachecki.
Warsaw, 1939. 2 parts, Tom. (Volume) 1, parts 1–2.
NN *QR

Szczesniak, Boleslaw.
The Knights Hospitallers in Poland and Lithuania.
The Hague, Mouton, 1969. 108 p.
(Studies in European History no. 19)
NN E-13 9675

Taszycki, Witold.
Bibliografia Onomastyki Polskiej.
Kraków, 1972. 392 p.
NN *QOB 73-3491

Verfilmte Kirchenbücher aus den Ehem, Deutschen Ostprovinzen-auch aus Mitteldeutschland, Polen und Bessarabien-im Archive der Genealogical Society, Salt Lake City.
(IN: *Die Fungrube*, Regensburg, 1970. heft 36, p. 1–60)
(This article lists some of the Polish parish registers filmed by the LDS Church and the dates covered by the registers.)
NN ATA

Wytrwal, Joseph A.
Poles in American History and Tradition.
Detroit, MI, Endurance Press, 1969. 485 p., index.
NN IEE (Poles)

Zabriskie, George Olin.
The Zabriskie Family: a Three Hundred Year History of the Descendants of Albrecht Zaborowskij, (ca. 1638–1711) of Bergen County, New Jersey.
Salt Lake City, UT, Publishers Press, 1963. 2 v., index.
NN APV (Zabriskie)

Żernicki-Szeliga, Emilian von.
Geschichte des Polnischen Adels.
Hamburg, H. Grand, 1905. 84, 56 p.
NN AVA

Żernicki-Szeliga, Emilian von.
Der Polnische Adel ...
Hamburg, H. Grand, 1900. 2 v. (A–Z)
NN AVA

Żychliński, Teodor.
Zlota Księga Szlachty Polskiej.
Poznań, Leitgebera, 1879–1907. 30 v. in 10.
NN *QR+

PORTUGAL (LISBON)

Portugal was born as a country in 1095, when a daughter of Alfonso VI of Castile married Henry of Burgundy, whose title became Count of Portucalense. Henry's younger son, Alfonso Henriques, took power in 1128 and fought against both the Moors and the Castilians; in 1139 he became Alfonso I. When he died in 1185 Portugal was an independent state, and by 1249 the

Moors had been completely expelled. The Castilians were a threat to Portuguese independence until 1385, when they were defeated in the battle of Aljubarrota. John I, of the House of Aviz, then ascended the throne, and a brief, glorious chapter in Portuguese history unfolded. Henry the Navigator, son of John I, took Ceuta on the African coast in 1415, and under Henry's aegis Portuguese navigators undertook a series of voyages that led to the exploration of Africa and the colonization of the Madeira Islands and the Azores. Vasco da Gama was the first European to sail to India (1497–99), and in 1520 Magellan became the first person to circumnavigate the world. In 1580 Philip II of Spain seized the Portuguese throne and a sixty-year period of "Spanish captivity" ensued. The Spanish were ousted when John of Braganza led a successful revolt and took over the throne as John IV. In 1801 Napoleon conquered Portugal and King John VI fled to Brazil. After Napoleon's downfall Portugal was restored as an independent kingdom. In 1822 Brazil declared independence, and Pedro I, King John's eldest son, became emperor of Brazil. In 1910 internal strife forced the abdication of King Manuel II and a republic was proclaimed. In 1928 Antonio de Oliveira Salazar, a former finance minister, became premier and ruled as a virtual dictator until 1968, when he retired because of illness. In 1974 the government was seized by a military junta led by General Antonio de Spinola, who became President and espoused the establishment of democracy in Portugal and Portuguese possessions in Africa. Independence was granted to Guinea-Bissau, Mozambique, Cape Verde Islands, Angola and São Tomé and Principe in 1974.

Censuses were recorded in Portugal in 1864, 1870, 1878, 1900, 1911, 1930, 1950 and 1960.

The most common surnames in Lisbon are Costa, Ferriera, Pereira, Santos and Silva.

Archives

Arquivo Nacional da Torre do Tombo (National Archives)
Palacio de S. Bento,
Lisbon, Portugal
Annexes:

Arquivo do Feitos Findos Largo da Estrela
Lisbon 2, Portugal

Arquivo dos Registos Paroquiais
Rua dos Prazeres 41-r/c
Lisbon 2, Portugal

Arquivo da Universidade de Coimbra
Coimbra, Portugal

Arquivo Histórico Ultramarino (Historical Archives, Overseas Provinces)
Calcada da Boa-Hora 30
Junqueira, Lisbon

Praca Luis de Camoes, 46, 2
Lisbon, Portugal

Instituto Português de Heráldica
Largo do Carmo
Lisbon 2, Portugal
(*Armas e Troféus*, 1932-)
NN AWA

Church and Vital Records

Civil registration began officially in 1878. Certificates are issued by the Office of the Civil Registrar (Conservatoria do Registo Civil) located in the district in which the event took place.

Instituto Nacional de Estatistica (National Statistical Institute)
Ministério das Finanças
Av. Dr. A.J. de Almeida
Lisbon, Portugal

Libraries

Biblioteca Nacional (National Library)
Campo Grande 83
Lisbon 5, Portugal

Biblioteca Pública e Arquivo Distrital de Angra do Heroisme
(Public Library and District Archives)
Palácio Bettencourt
Rua Conselheiro Jacinto Cândido
The Azores

Historical and Genealogical Societies

Conselho de Nobleza (Council of Nobility)

Books and Articles

Academia Portugesa da Histórica. Guia da Bibliografia Histórica Portuguesa.
Lisbon, 1959. v. 1–.
NN M-10 5284

(Administrative Divisions of Portugal outlined, 22 districts, 302 Concelhos, 3,977 Frequesias)
(IN: *Anuario Genealogico Latino*, São Paulo, 1951. v. 3, p. 57–150)
NN APA

Armas e Troféus, Revista de História, Heráldica, Genealogia e de Arte.
Lisbon, Instituto Português de Heráldica, (3 series)
NN AWA

Azevedo Soares, Eduardo de Campos de Castro de.
Bibliographia Nobiliarchica Portuguesa.
Braga, 1916-47. 5 v. in 2, indexed.
NN ASM 76-705

Cardozo, Manoelda S. S.
The Portuguese in America 590 B.C.-1976. Dobbs Ferry, NY, Oceana, 1976. 154 p.
NN IEE (Portuguese) 76-1411

Dicionário das Familias (Subsidios).
(IN: *Anuario Genealogico Latino*,
São Paulo, 1950. v. 22, p. 186–216,
etc.)
NN APA

Esteves Pereira, João Manuel.
Portugal: Dicionário Historico,
Chorographhico, Heraldico ...
Lisbon, J. Romano Torres, 1904–15.
7 v.
NN AF 10-637

Ferreira, Carlos Alberto.
Indice Abreviado das Genealogias
Manuscritas da Biblioteca da
Ajuda.
(IN: *Anuario Genealogico Latino*,
São Paulo, 1949. v. 1, p. 119–63)
NN APA

Ferreira, Carlos Alberto.
Indice Abreviado das Genealogias
Manuscritas do Arquivo Na-
cional da Torre do Tombo.
(IN: *Anuario Genealogico Latino*,
São Paulo, 1950. v. 2, p. 17–136)
NN APA

Ferreira Martins, José Frederico.
... Os Vice-Reis da India,
1505–1917 ...
Lisbon, Imprensa Nacional, 1935.
326 p.
(The Portuguese in India)
NN AGG

Greenlee, William B.
A Descriptive Bibliography of the
History of Portugal.
(IN: *Hispanic American Review*,
Durham, NC, 1940. v. 20, p.
491–516)
(See Newberry Library below)
NN HCA

Guérios, Rosário Farâni Mansur.
Dicionário Etimológico de Nomes
e Sobrenomes. 2nd rev. ed.

São Paulo, 1973. 231 p.
NN APD 75-975

Hall, Joseph.
Genealogy in Portugal.
(IN: *The Genealogical Helper*, Salt
Lake City, UT, 1976. v. 30, p.
255–59)
NN APA

Lagoa, Joao A. de Mascarenhas
Judice, Visconde de.
Grandes e Humildes na epopeia
Portuguese do Oriente
(Seculos XV, XVI e XVII).
Lisbon, Grafica Lisbonense,
1942–46. 2 v.
NN AGG (Portuguese in India)

Leite de Vasconcellos, José.
Antroponimia Portugesa.
Lisbon, Imprensa Nacional, 1928.
659 p., index.
NN APD

Livros de Batismos, Casamentos e
Óbitos de Portugal.
(IN: *Anuario Genealogico Latino*,
São Paulo, 1951. v. 3, p. 84–150)
NN APA

Mattos, Armando de.
Manuel de Genealogia Portuguesa.
Pôrto, F. Machado, 1943. 139 p.
NN APB

Moya, Salvador de.
Origen de Algumas Familias Por-
tuguêsas que Tem Brasao de
Armas.
(IN: *Anuario Genealogico Latino*,
São Paulo, 1949–53. v. 1, p. 3–99;
v. 4, p. 15–31; v. 5, p. 45–67.)
NN APA

Newberry Library Chicago. William B. Greenlee Collection.

Catalogue of the Greenlee Collection.
The Newberry Library Chicago.
Boston, MA, G.K. Hall, 1970. 2 v.
NN *RR-BY

Nobreza de Portugal.
Lisbon, Editorial Enciclopedia, 1960–61. 3 v.
NN ASM

Os Grandes Portuguese.
Lisbon, Arcadia, 195–.
NN N-10 902

Portuguese Royal Family.
(House of Braganza)
(IN: *CDS*, Paris, 1966. p. 124–35)
(Brazilian branch, 420–30)
NN ARB

Quem e Alguem (Who's Who in Portugal).
Lisbon, Portugalia, 1947–.
NN *RR-AGG and M-10 9628

Rada y Delgado, Juan de Dias de la.
... Mujeres Celebras de España y Portugal ...
Buenos Aires, 1942. 2 v. in 1.
NN SNE

Silva, Antonio Lambert Pereira da
Nobres Casas de Portugal.
Porto, Livraria Tavares Martins, 1958–. v. 1–46 in 4 v.
NN ASM

Sousa, Antonio Caetano de.
História Genealógica de Casa Real Portuguesa. Nova ed.
Coimbra, Atlantida, 1946–53. 11 v. in 12.
NN ASM

Sousa, Antonio Caetano de.
Provas da História Genealógica ... Nova ed.
Coimbra, Atlantida, 1946–53. 6 v. in 12.
NN ASM

Sousa, Antonio Caetano de.
Indice General da História Genealógica ... Nova ed.
Coimbra, Atlantida, 1955. 501 p.
NN ASM

Sousa, Antonio Caetano de.
História Genealógica da Casa Real Portuguesa.
Lisbon, 1735–1749. 12 v. and index.
NN ASM

Tavares, Belmira E.
Portuguese Pioneers in the United States.
Fall River, MA, R.E. Smith Print. Co., 1973. 178 p.

Vaz, August M.
The Portuguese in California.
Oakland, CA, I.D.E.S., 1965. 235 p., no index, t of c.
(Irmandade do Divino Espirito)
Supreme Council
NN IEE (Portuguese)

Aveiro
Coutinho, Francisco de Moura.
... Genealogia do Distrito de Aveiro ...
Aveiro, 1944–46. 11 v. in 1.
NN ASO (Aveiro)

Braga
Vas-Osorio da Nobrega, Artur.
Pedras de Armas e Armas Tumulares do Distrito de Braga.
Braga, Junat Distrital de Braga, 1970–74+. 4 v., v. 5 in progress, index each v.

(On buildings: large handsome works with excellent photos of arms carved in stone, colored plates of arms, maps, genealogies, etc.)
NN AWT+ 73-2479

Lisbon
Lisbon.
Registo da Freguesia da se Desde 1563 ate 1610.
Coimbra, 1924–27. 2 v. (v. 1, 1563–96; v.2, 1597–1610)
NN ASO+ (Lisbon)

Madeira
Clode, Luiz Peter.
Registo Genealógico de Famílias que Passaram à Madeira.
Funchal, Tipografia Comercial, 1952. 486 p., index.
NN ASO (Madeira)

Menezes Vaz, Cónego Fernando de.
Famílias da Madeira e do Porto Santo.
Funchal, 1964– c. 1970–.
NN ASO (Madeira) [v.1-8] and ASO (Madeira) 76-883 [v.9-13]

Menezes Vaz, Cónego Fernando de.
Famílias da Madeira e Porto Santo.
(IN: *Arquivo Historico da Madeira*, Funchal, Câmara Municipal, 1951. v. 9, p. 117–44)
NN BYR

Pink, Annette.
See Madeira and the Canaries: A Complete Guide with Maps.
London, Format Books, 1976. 144 p.

RUMANIA (BUCHAREST)

Most of Rumania was part of the ancient kingdom of Dacia that became a Roman province in the second and third centuries A.D. and was subsequently overrun by Goths, Huns, Avars, Slavs and Mongols. The principalities of Moldavia and Walachia, after the Mongols withdrew in the thirteenth century, fell to the Turks and remained under Ottoman rule until the nineteenth century. After the Russo-Turkish war of 1828–29 Moldavia and Walachia became Russian protectorates, though technically they remained within the Ottoman Empire. Moldavia and Walachia, declared a principality under Turkish suzerainty in 1856, were united by the election of Alexander John Cuza as Prince in 1859, and the country was officially named Rumania in 1861.

In 1866 Cuza was deposed, Carol I of the House of Hohenzollern-Sigmaringen became king and a liberal constitution was adopted. At the Congress of Berlin in 1878 Rumania was granted full independence but was required to return southern Bessarabia to Russia and take northern Dobruja instead. In 1881 Rumania proclaimed itself a kingdom. The next seventy years were characterized by turmoil expressed most dramatically in anti-Semitic violence by the peasants. In 1913 Rumania entered the Second Balkan War against Bulgaria and won southern Dobruja. After the Allied victory in World War I Rumania took Bessarabia back from Russia, Bukovina from Austria and Transylvania from Hungary. Carol II took the throne from his son, Michael, in 1930 and in 1938 dissolved the parliament and ruled as a virtual dictator. During the Second World War he was overthrown by a fascist group led by Ion Antonescu, who became dictator. In 1941 Rumania entered the war on the Axis side, but after the Russian invasion King Michael returned, overthrew Antonescu and ordered Rumania to fight on the Allied side. The Russian-supported cabinet forced the abdication of King Michael in 1947, and the following year a constitution proclaimed Rumania a People's Republic. Since 1965, when a new constitution proclaimed Rumania a socialist republic, the country has become increasingly independent of Soviet direction. Censuses were recorded in 1848, 1912, 1930, 1941, 1956 and 1966.

The most common surnames in Bucharest are Constantinescu, Dumitrescu, Georgescu, Ionescu and Popescu.

Archives

Directia Generala A Arhivelor Statului (Director General of State Archives)
Bulevardul Gh. Gheorghiu-Dej. 29
Bucharest, Rumania

Public and Church Records

Civil registration was established on May 1, 1831, in Walachia and in January 1832 in Moldavia, with registers held by the Orthodox churches. In December 1865 registration was taken over by civil offices. Registration was introduced in Transylvania on October 1, 1895. Certificates are obtained by contacting the Office of Vital Statistics (Oficiul Starii̇ Civile) of the People's Council (Sfatul Popular).

Libraries

Biblioteca Academiei Republicii Socialiste Romania
Calea Victoriei 125
Bucharest, Rumania

Biblioteca Centrala de Stat (Central State Library)
Str. Ion Ghica 4
Bucharest, Rumania
Biblioteca Centrala Universitara
Str. Onesti 1
Bucharest, Rumania

Colegiul Reformat (Calvinist College Library)
Targu-Mures, Rumania

United States Sources

St. Mary's Rumanian Orthodox Church Ethnic Museum
3256 Warren Road
Cleveland, OH 44111

Books and Articles

Bibliografia Istorică u României.
Bucharest, 1970–72. 2 v.
NN JFM 73-294

Calendarul ... Ziarului ... Romanul American.
Detroit, MI, 1949–.
NN IEE (Rumanians)

Dictionarul Enciclopedic Illustrat Cartea Romanesca.
Bucharest, Editura Cartea Romanesca, 1931. 1 v. in 2. (1,948 p.)
NN AE-10 1215

Draganu, Nicolae.
... Romani in Veacurile IX-XIV pe Baza Toponimiei si u Onomasticei ...
Bucharest, 1933. 682 p.
NN GIVB

Florescu, Radu R. N., and Raymond T. McNally.
Dracula: A Biography of Vlad the Impaler 1431–1476.
New York, Hawthorne, 1973. 239 p., index.
NN JFE 74-1398

Galitzi, Christine A.
A Study of Assimilation among the Roumanians in the United States.
New York, Columbia U. Press, 1929. 282 p.
(*Studies in History, Economics and Public Law* ... Columbia U., no. 315)
NN TB (Columbia)

Girurescu, Constantine C.
Istoria Romaniei in date.
Bucharest, 1971. 527 p.
NN JFD 73-10398

Ionescu, Christian.
Mică Enciclopedie Onomastică
Bucharest, Enciclopedică Română, 1975.
332 p., alpha, index.

Iorga, Nicolae.
America şi Romanii din America ... Vălenii-de-Munte, 1930. 334 p.
NN ILH

Iorga, Nicolae.
Histoire des Roumains de Transylvania et de Hongrie.
Bucharest, Gutenberg, 1916. 2 v.
NN GIVB (Hongrie)

Metes, Stefan.
Emigrari Romanesti din Transylvania in Secolele XIIIXX.
Bucharest, 1971. 440 p.
NN JLD 73-4279

New Pioneer.
Cleveland, OH, 1942–48. 6 v., index v. 1–3 (1942–45).
NN IEE (Rumanians)

Noe, Constantin.
The Rumanians in Bulgaria.
Craiova, Ramuri, 1940. 87 p.
NN D-10 7489

Ravage, Marcus E.
An American in the Making.
New York, 1971. 324 p.
NN IEE (Rumanians) 72-1742

Rumania. Archiva Istorică Centtrală.
Catalogul Documentelor Moldovenşti din Archiva

Istorică Centrală a Statului.
Bucharest, 1957–59. 2 v. (v. 1, 1387–1620; v. 2, 1621–57)
NN M-10 9025

Rumanian Royal Family
(House of Hohenzollern-Sigmaringen)
(IN: *CDS*, Paris, 1966. p. 472–84)
NN ARB
(IN: *GHF*, Limburg/Lahn, 1968. v. 8, p. 153–56)
NN ATC

Soutzos, Dēmētres S.
Hellēnes Hēgemones Valachias Kai Moldavias.
Athens, 1972. 312 p.
NN JLE 76-3643

Stoicescu, Nicolai.
Dictionar al Marilor Dregători din Tara Româneasca şi Moldova, Sec. XIV-XVII.

Bucharest, Editura Enciclopedia Romana, 1971. 456 p., alpha (A8Z)
(Rumanian nobility of the 14th to 17th centuries)
NN AVH (Rumania) 74-557 and AVH (Rumania) 73-2471

Trifa, Valerian D.
Romania; the Land, the History and the People.
Jackson, MI, Romanian Orthodox Episcopate of America, 1961. 1 v.
(*Orthodox Christian Library no. 15*)
NN G-10 1567

Wertsman, Vladimir.
The Romanians in America 1748–1974: A Chronology and Fact Book.
Dobbs Ferry, NY, Oceana Pub., 1975. 118 p., index.
NN IEE (Rumanians) 75-1875

SAN MARINO (SAN MARINO)

According to legend, Marinus, a Christian stonecutter from Dalmatia, took refuge on Mount Titano during the fourth century A.D. By the fifth century a community had formed there. The republic, named San Marino after the canonized St. Marinus, is the world's smallest and oldest, having been independent some 1,600 years.

Archives

Archivio di Stato (State Archives)
Palazzo Valloni
Via Carducci 141 (C.P. 47031), San Marino

Books and Articles

Bent, James Theodore.
A Freak of Freedom, or the Republic of San Marino.

London, Longmans, 1879. 271 p.
NN BWO

Fattori, Marino.
Ricordi Storici della Republica di San Marino.
Florence, F. Le Monnier, 1956. 121 p.
NN C-10 4388

Gozi, Manilo.
San Marino, Leggende e Storia . . .

San Marino, 1926. 444 p.
NN C-10 1511

Koller, Fortune.
Livre d'Or de la Noblesse du Pa-
triat de Saint-Marin.
Brussels, Editions de Feniks, 1964.
384 p., index.
NN AVH (San Marino)

Koller, Fortune.
The Nobility of San Marino.
(IN: *GM*, London, 1959. v. 13, p.
109–10)
NN ARCA

SPAIN (MADRID)

In 409 A.D. the first wave of the Germanic tribes, the Vandals, swept through Spain but were driven into Africa by the Visigoths, who by 419 had consolidated a kingdom in Spain and southern Gaul with Toulouse as its capital. In 507 the Franks, led by Clovis, conquered Gaul, and the Visigoths made Toledo their capital. A Muslim army under Tarik defeated the last of the Visigothic kings, Roderick, in 711, ushering in a long period of Muslim influence. The province of Asturias, never taken by the Muslims, became the focus of the Christian reconquest of Spain. The Asturians conquered large areas of northwestern Spain and consolidated themselves as the province of Leon. In 778 Charlemagne created the Spanish March, which grew into the county of Barcelona. The Basque country, in the western Pyrenees, had resisted both the Franks and the Moors and united in the kingdom of Navarre. Navarre, under a branch of the Asturian line, reached prominence under Sancho III (1000–1035), who also controlled Aragon and Castile. After the death of Sancho III the territory was divided into three kingdoms: Navarre; Aragon, which eventually united with Barcelona in 1139; and Castile, which joined Leon in 1230. The gradual unification of Spain was completed under Isabella I and Ferdinand II with the conquest of the last Moorish stronghold in Granada in 1492. In the same year the Jews were expelled from Spain, and Columbus discovered America, where a vast Spanish empire was to be established. The first of the Hapsburg kings (1516–1700), Charles I, tried to centralize Spain, but a rebellion by the cities was one of the factors that forced his abdication in 1556. The Inquisition reached its height under his successor, Philip II, who completed the process of creating an absolute monarchy. A series of dynastic and religious wars and the depletion of the Spanish population by extensive colonization weakened the crown. The defeat of the Spanish Armada by the English in 1588 was a major blow. Spain entered the Thirty Years War (1618–48), and ensuing peace treaties established France as the chief continental power. France became influential in Spain when the grandson of Louis XIV was appointed King of Spain in the absence of a direct heir to Charles II. Bourbon kings followed. From 1808 to 1814 Napoleon's armies invaded Spain and placed Napoleon's brother, Joseph Bonaparte, on the throne. British troops, together with Spanish resistance fighters, finally drove out the French and returned the Bourbons to power. By 1825 almost all of Latin America had declared independence from Spanish rule, and in the Spanish-American War of 1898 all that remained of the empire—Cuba, Puerto Rico and the Philippines—were lost. In 1931 Alfonso III was deposed and a republic established. In 1936 a great civil war was precipitated by a military revolt against the republic led by General Francisco Franco with the active support of fascist Germany and Italy. The Loyalists were defeated in 1939, and Franco became head of state. At Franco's death in 1975 Juan Carlos I (1938–) of the House of Bourbon (Borbon y Borbon) became king.

Censuses have been taken in Spain since 1857, but they do not contain a great deal of personal information.

The most common surnames in Barcelona are Fernández, García, López, Martínez, Pérez and Sánchez. In Madrid they are Fernández, García, González, López and Rodríguez.

Archives

Instituto Nacional de Estadistica
(National Archives)
Avda. Generalisimo 91
Madrid 16, Spain

Archivo Histórico Nacional (National Historical Archives)
Calle Serrano 115
Madrid, Spain

Archivo General de Indias (Archives of the Indies)
Seville, Spain

Regional Archives

Barcelona
Archivo de la Corona de Aragón
(Royal Archives of Aragon)

Condes de Barcelona 2
Barcelona, Spain

Archivo Diocesano (Diocesan Archives)
Palacio Episcopal
Barcelona, Spain

Granada
Archivo de la Real Chancilleria de Granada (Archives of the Royal Chancery of Granada)
Casa del Padre Suárez
Calle de Pavaneras 17
Granada, Spain

La Coruna
Archivo Regional de Galicia
La Coruna, Spain

Sabadell
Archivo Histórico de la Ciudad
Sabadell, Spain

Seville
Archivo de la Casa de Medinaceli y Camarasa
Plaza de Pilatos 1
Seville, Spain

Simancas, Valladolid
Archivo General de Simancas
Simancas, Valladolid, Spain

Toledo
Archivo y Biblioteca Capitulares (Archives and Library of the Cathedral Chapter)
Catedral de Toledo
Toledo, Spain

Valencia
Archivo del Reino de Valencia
Plaza de Galicia
Valencia, Spain

Palma de Mallorca, Balearic Islands
Archivo Histórico de Mallorca
Palma, Lulio 5
Palma de Mallorca, Balearic Islands

Public and Church Records

Certificates can be obtained from the Juzgado Municipal (Municipal Court) of the local district.

There are 19,000 parishes in Spain, and of these 1,636 have registers that date before 1570, the year in which most parochial registers begin. When seeking access to parish registers of other information from the local priest, address the Revdo Sr. Cura Parocco.

Registro Civil Central
Calle Maria de Molina n° 42
Madrid, Spain

Libraries

Biblioteca Nacional (National Library)
Av. de Calvo Sotelo 20
Madrid, Spain

Biblioteca de la Dirección General de Plazas y Provincias Africanas (Library of the Department for African Provinces)
Paseo de la Castellana 5
Madrid, Spain

Biblioteca de la Universidad de Madrid
Madrid, Spain

Historical and Genealogical Societies

Instituto Municipal de Historia de la Ciudad
Calle de Santa Lucia 1
Casa del Arcediano
Barcelona, Spain.

Instituto Internacional de Genealogía y Heraldica, y Federación de Corporaciones Afines
(International Institute of Genealogy and Heraldry and Federation of Similar Corporations)
Apartado de Correos 12,079
Madrid, Spain
(*Hoja Informativa*, 1954-)
NN ASM

Books and Articles

Amador de los Rios, José.
Historia de la Villa y Corte de Madrid.
Madrid, 1860–64. 4 v.
NN BXVN++

Alvaréz, Grace de Jesús.
Toponimos en Apellidos Hispanos Estios de Hispano Fila.
Garden City, NY, Adelphi U., 1968. 587 p., alpha.
NN APD 75-2249

Alvaréz y Baena, José Antonia.
Hijos de Madrid ...
Madrid, B. Cano, 1789–91. 4 v.
NN AGG

Asociación de Hidalgos a Fuero de España.
Madrid, 1965–70. 4 v., index each v.
NN ASM 74-818

Ballesteros Robles, Luis.
Diccionario Biográfico Matritense.
Madrid, 1912. 702 p.
NN *RR-AGG

Benito, José de.
Estampas de España e Indias.
Mexico City, Leyenda, 1945. 374 p.
NN BXD

Bergamini, John D.
The Spanish Bourbons: The History of a Tenacious Dynasty.
New York, Putnam, 1974. 442 p.
NN JFE 75-2559

Berwick y de Alba, El Duque.
Noticias Historias y Genealógicas de los Estados de Montijo y Teba.
Madrid, 1915. 370 p.
Long "indice," really a t of c, at end. Good reproductions of seals and documents. (The family of the Empress Eugénie of France, 1826–1920)
NN ASM+

Cadenas y Vicent, Vicente de.
Repertorio do Blasones de la Comunidad Hispánica.
Madrid, Hidalguía, for Instituto Salazar y Castro, 1964–1969 (c. 1964). 3 v.
NN AWT 75-693

Canacho, Francisca.
Peninsulares y Cubanos ...
Havana, Mercantil, 1891. 134 p.
NN AGG

Carderera y Solano, Valentan.
Iconografía Española.
Madrid, R. Campuzano, 1855–64. 2 v.
NN AOM+++

Childs, James Rives.
Spanish, Mexican and Venezuelan Branches of the Rives (Ryves) Family.
(IN: *VM*, Richmond, VA, 1963. v. 71, p. 374–86)
NN *R-APR (Virginia)

Cortes, Narciso A.
Indice de Documentos Utile a la Biografía.
(IN: *Biblioteca Menendez y Pelayo*, Santandar, 1922–23. año (volume) 4, p. 171–84, 328–45; ano 5, p. 7–38)
NN *HA

Delgado y Orellana, José Antonio.
La Casa de Domecq d'Usquain.
Madrid, Hidalguía, 1966. 167 p., plus 16 p. index.
NN ASP (Domecq) 76-644

Delgado y Orellana, José Antonio.
Los Ruiz-Matheos de Luna.
Madrid, Hidalguía, 1975. 196 p., index. gen. table
NN JFE 76-2028

Diaz, Nicomedes P.
Galeria de Españoles Celebres Contemporaneos.
Madrid, Sanchiz, 1841–46. 9 v.
NN AGG

Diccionario Biográfico Español e Hispaño americano.
Palma de Mallorca, 1950.
NN JFF 73-799

Diccionario de Histórica de España Desde sus Origenes
Hasta el Fin del Reinado de Alfonso XIII.
Madrid, 1952. 2 v. (1493–1519)
NN D-10 7455

Douglas, William A., and Jon Bilbao.
Amerikanuaki: Basques in the New World.
Reno, NV, U. of Nevada Press, 1975. 519 p.
NN IEE (Basques) 77-273

Edge, P. Granville.
Early Population Records in Spain.
(IN: *Metron*, Rome, 1932. v. 9, p. 229–49)
NN SDA

Emparan, Madie.
The Vallejos of California.
San Francisco, CA, Gleeson Library Associates, 1968. 464 p., index.
NN APV (Vallejo)

Esperbe Arteaga, Enrique.
Diccionario Enciclopédico Ilustrado . . .
Madrid, Ibarra, 1956. 530 p.
NN *RR-AGG

Gordon, Raymond L.
Spanish Personal Names as Barriers to Communications Between Latin Americans and North Americans.
Yellow Springs, OH, Antioch College, 1965. 142 p.
NN APD 75-356

Guía Nobiliaria de España.
Madrid, 1931–.
NN ASM

Heraldica Guía de Sociedad.
Madrid, 1950–.
NN ASM

Hidalguía: La Revista de Genealogía Nobleza y Armas.
Madrid, 1953–.
NN ASM

Hillgarth, Jocelyn N.
The Spanish Kingdoms 1250–1516.
Oxford, Clarendon Press, 1976–77. 2 v. (v. 1, 1250–1410; v. 2, 1411–1516), index.

Los Libros Parraquiales y del Registro Civil en España.
(IN: *Archivum*, Paris, 1961. v. 9 [for 1959], p. 15–53)
NN BAA

Lowery, Woodbury.
The Spanish Settlements Within the Present Limits of the United States ...
New York, Russell & Russell, 1959. 2 v., index each v. (v. 1, 1513–61; v. 2, Florida, 1562–74)
NN IEE (Spanish)

MacArthur, Mildred Yorba.
Anaheim "The Mother Colony."
Los Angeles, Ward Ritchie Press, 1959. 260 p., index.
(Interesting captions of pictures of Spanish settlers including the Yorba Family, and their descendants, not indexed)
NN IXH (Anaheim)

Maudell, Charles R., Jr.
Don Bernando de Galvez y Gallardo, First Count of Galvez. (9 generations of his ancestry, etc.)
(IN: *New Orleans Genesis*, New Orleans, LA, 1976. v. 15, p. 221–27)
NN APR (New Orleans)

Maudell, Charles R., Jr.
Index of Spanish Citizens Entering New Orleans, Jan. 1820 through Dec. 1839.
New Orleans, LA, the author, 1966. 75, xiii p., alpha.
NN IEE (Spanish)

Maudell, Charles R., Jr.
Index of Spanish Citizens Entering the Port of New Orleans, Mid-Nineteenth Century.
New Orleans, LA, the author, 1966.

alpha. (Covers Jan. 1840– Dec. 1865)
NN IEE (Spanish)

Navarrete, Martin Fernandez de.
Biblioteca Maritima Española.
Madrid, Calero, 1851. 2 v.
(Biographies of explorers and soldiers)
NN AGG

Northrop, Marie E.
Spanish-Mexican Families of Early California, 1769–1850.
New Orleans, LA, Polythanos, 1976. 350 p., index.
NN (California) 77-323

Payne, Stanley G.
History of Spain and Portugal.
Madison, WI, U. of Wisconsin Press, 1973. 2 v.
NN *R-BXB 73-5897

Querexeta, Jaime de.
Diccionario Onomástico y Heráldico Vasco.
Bilbao, La Gran Enciclopedia Vasca, 1970–71.
2 v., v. 1 A–Bas, v. 2 Bas–Hypar, in progress.
NN AWT 72-2429

Quinn, Jane.
Minorcans in Florida and Their History.
St. Augustine, Mission Press, 1975. 282 p., index.

Segovia, Angel M.
Figuras y Figurones.
Madrid, Taramillo, 1881–82. 43 v. in 10.
NN AGG

Shinn, Charles H.
Pioneer Spanish Families of California.

(IN: *Journal of San Diego History*, San Diego, 1965. v. 11, p. 1–14)
NN IXH (San Diego)

Spain. Biblioteca Nacional. Madrid.
Bibliográfia Heráldico-Genealógico-Nobiliaria de la Biblioteca Nacional de Madrid (por) Benito M.C y Luis Garcia Cubero.
Madrid, Instituto Luis de Salazar y Castro, 1958. 2 v.
NN AW

Spanish American Genealogical Helper.
Harbor City, CA, The Hartwell Co., 1971–72., 2 v. in 1.
NN APR (California) 76-1713

Spanish Royal Family
(House of Bourbon)
(IN: *CDS*, Paris, 1966. p. 189–241)
NN ARB
(IN: GHF, Limburg/Lahn, 1968. v.8, p. 190–225)
NN ATC
(IN: *The Monarchist*, London, 1975–76. no. 46 and 47, p. 9–55)
NN current 315 G

Vasquez, Nadine Maria.
Sinaloa Roots: Ancestral Records of Some of the Earliest Settlers of California, 1723–1791.
Carmichael, CA, the author, 1972.
(Sinaloa, New Mexico)

Vidal y de Barnola, Luis Alfonso.
Genealogía de la Familia Franco.
Madrid, Editora Nacional, 1975. 198 p.
(Francisco Franco, p. 47, 49, 51)
NN ASP (Franco) 75-2672

Vilar y Pascual, Luis.
Diccionario Historica Genealógico y Heráldico.

Madrid, Sanchez, 1854–66. 8 v.
NN ASM

Wagner, Henry R.
The Spanish Southwest 1542–1794.
New York, 1967. 2 v. (*Quivira Soc. Pub.* v. 7)
NN IAA (Quivira)

Who's Who in Spain.
Montréal, Intercontinental Book and Pub. Co., 1963–.
NN *RR-AGG and K-10 5342

Alicante
Arques Jover, Augustin de.
Nobiliario Alicantino.
Alicante, 1966. 182 p.
NN ASO (Alicante)

Asturias
Alvarez de la Rivera, Senén.
Biblioteca Histórica-Genealógica Asturiana.
Santiago de Chile, Cervantes, 1924–28. 3 v.
NN ASO (Asturias)

Basque Provinces
Biscay. Archivo General. Guernica.
Catálogo de Genealogías, ed. by Florencio Amador Carrandi.
Bilbao, 1958. 1,042 p., alpha, cross-index.
NN ASO (Basque Provinces)

García Carraffa, Alberto y Arturo.
El Solar Vasco Navarro.
Madrid, 1933–35. 6 v., A–Z
NN ASO (Basque Provinces)

Canary Islands
Fernandez de Bethancourt, Francisco.
Nobiliario y Blasón de Canarias.

Santa Cruz de Tenerife, Islena, 1878–82. 5 v. in 3 (poor paper).
NN ASO (Canary Islands)

Mason, John.
The Canary Islands.
London, Batsford, 1976. 180 p., index.
NN JFD 76-9960

Villere, Sidney Louis.
The Canary Islands Migration to Louisiana 1778–1783: The History and Passenger Lists of the Islenos Volunteer Recruits and Their Families.
Baltimore, MD, GPC, 1972. 94 p., index for each ship.
NN APR (Louisiana) 74-1014

Castile

Salazar de Mendoza, Pedro de.
Origen de las Dignidades Seglares de Castilla y León.
Madrid, 1618. 189 p., no index.
NN ASO (Castile)

Catalonia

Serra y Vilaró, Juan.
Los Señores de Portell, Patria de San Ramón.
Barcelona, Editorial Balmes, 1958. 130 p., index.
NN ASO (Catalonia)

Cordoba

Martínez Bara, José Antonio.
Catálogo de Informaciones Genealógicas de la Inquisición de Córdoba Conservadas en el Archivo Histórico Nacional.
Madrid, Clavileno. 1970. 2 v., index.
NN ASO (Córdoba) 73-1902

Galicia

Crespo Pozo, José Santiago.
Blasones y Linajes de Galicia.
Santiago de Compostela, Bibliófilos Gallegos, 1962. 1 v. (A–F), 441 p.
(Enciclopedia Gallego, v. 2)
NN ASO (Galicia)

Infantado

Arteaga y Falguera, Cristina de la Casa del Infantado.
Madrid, Duque del Infantado, 1940–44. 2 v.
NN ASO (Infantado)

Legasa

Trazegníes, Ferdinand de.
Casa Solariegas en Legasa.
Madrid, Hidalguía, 1968. 48 p.
NN ASO (Legasa) 74-853

León

Cadenas y Vincent, Francisco de.
Antigua Nobleza Leonesa.
Madrid, Hidalguía, 1958. 407 p., index.
NN ASO (León)

Navarre

García Carraffa, Alberto y A.
El Solar Vasco Navarro.
Salamanca, 1933–36. 6 v.
NN APB + p.v. 107

Libro de Armeria del Reino de Navarra.
Bilboa, La Gran Enciclopedia Vasca, 1974. 160 p., index.
NN AWT 76-1907

Ubieto Arteta, Antonio.
Obituario de la Catedral de Pamplona.
Viana, 1954. 53 p.
NN APB + p.v. 107

Segovia
Larios Martín, Jesús.
Nobiliario de Segovia.
Segovia, Instituto Diego de Colmenares, 1956–67. 5 v., index.
NN ASO (Segovia)

Túy
Fernández-Valdés Costas, Manuel.
Familias Antiquas de Túy.
Pronteveda, 1958. 163 p., index.
NN ASO (Túy)

Valencia
Esquerdo, Onofre.
Nobiliario Valenciano de Onofre Esquerdo.
Valencia, Ateneo Mercantil, 1963.
NN ASO (Valencia)

Vallodolid
Spain. Archivo de la Real Chanellería de Valladolid.
Catálogo de Todas sus Pleitos ...
Valladolid, Diario Regional, 1920–22. 4 v.
NN ASO (Valladolid)

Valles
Plantada y Aznar, Jorge.
Nobleza Rural Catalana Masias del Valles.
Madrid, Hidalguía, 1968. 123 p., poor index.
NN ASO (Valles)

SWEDEN (STOCKHOLM)

During the Viking age, which lasted from the ninth through the twelfth centuries, the Swedes extended their influence to the Black Sea. From 1150 to 1160, Erik IX crusaded to wipe out paganism in Sweden and Finland; Finland was conquered and joined to the Swedish crown. In 1319 Sweden and Norway were united under Magnus VII. In 1397 they were joined with Denmark under Queen Margaret of Denmark, in the Kalmar Union. Rule from Copenhagen was not tolerated by the Swedes, however, and in 1523, when Gustav Eriksson was elected king of Sweden as Gustavus I, the union with Norway and Denmark was dissolved. Gustavus also broke the grip of the Hanseatic League—a German mercantile organization—over Sweden and established a Lutheran state church. From 1611 to 1632, under Gustavus II Adolphus, Sweden became a great European power, gaining territory and influence in wars with Russia and Poland and in the Thirty Years War against the Hapsburgs. At the Peace of Westphalia in 1648, Sweden obtained German territory, and thus the Swedish kings became princes of the Holy Roman Empire. In 1660 Sweden's southern provinces were recovered from Denmark. In the Northern War (1700–21) Sweden lost many possessions and became a secondary power. Sweden lost the remainder of her German territories to France in a disastrous war against Napoleon in 1803 and in 1808 was forced to cede Finland to Russia. In 1813 Sweden, led by French Marshal Jean Bernadotte, chosen successor to the Swedish throne, again joined the allies against Napoleon. At the Congress of Vienna in 1815 Sweden gained Norway, which remained a separate kingdom in union with Sweden. Bernadotte, who became King Charles XIV in 1818, espoused a policy of neutrality for Sweden. In 1905 the union with Norway was terminated. Between 1870 and 1914 some 1,500,000 Swedes emigrated to the United States. Under Gustavus V, who became king in 1907, Sweden remained neutral in both world wars. A constitutional change in 1975 left King Carl XVI Gustaf (1946–) with only symbolic powers.

Censuses of Sweden have been taken every ten years from 1850 through 1970.

The most common surnames in Stockholm are Andersson, Eriksson, Johansson, Karlsson and Nilsson.

Tracing Your Swedish Ancestry, a 27-page pamphlet by Nils William Olsson, published in 1974, can be obtained from government offices.

Archives

Riksarkivet (National Archives)
Stockholm, Arkivagate 3
Stockholm 2, Sweden

Kammararkivet (Cameral Archives)
Fack, Fyrverkarbacken 13-17
S-1000 26 Stockholm, Sweden

Riddarhuset (House of Nobility)
P.O. Box 2022
S-103 11 Stockholm, Sweden

Emigrantinstitutet (Emigrant Institute)
P.O. Box 201
S-351 04 Växjö, Sweden

Emigrantregistret (Emigrant Register)

P.O. Box 331
Sta Kyrkogatan 4
S-651 05 Karlstad, Sweden

Public and Church Records

The church has had the responsibility for keeping vital statistics records since the latter part of the seventeenth century. Records are issued by the local Parish Office (Pastorsambetet) or, in the case of a civil marriage, by the person who performed the ceremony. After 1947 a reform provided for the transfer of parish records to a central bureau.

Statistiska Centralbyrån (National Central Bureau of Statistics)

Fack, Karlavägen 100
S-102 50 Stockholm, Sweden

Riksarkivet (National Swedish Record Office)
Fack, Fyrverkarbacken 13-17
S-100 26 Stockholm, Sweden

Libraries

Stockholms Stadsbibliotek
(City Library of Stockholm)
Sveavägen 73
Stockholm, Sweden

Kunge, Biblioteket (Royal Library)
Stockholm 5, Sweden

University of Stockholm Libraries
Box 5039, S-102 41
Stockholm, Sweden

Historical and Genealogical Societies

Genealogiska Föreningen
Röksförening för Släktforskning
Box 780
Skarblacka, Sweden
(*Släkt och Hävd*)

Föreningen för Släktforskning
Olof Hermelins Väg 7
Stocksund, Sweden
(*Genealogisk Tidskrift*,-1961.)

Personhistoriska Samfundet
Riksarkivet, Fack
S-100 26 Stockholm, Sweden
(*Personhistorisk Tidskrift*)

United States Sources

American Swedish Historical
Foundation
1900 Pattison Avenue
Philadelphia, PA 19145

American Swedish Institute
2600 Park Avenue
Minneapolis, MN 55407
(*Happenings*)

Swedish Colonial Society
1300 Locust Street
Philadelphia, PA 19107

Swedish Pioneer Historical Society
5125 N. Spaulding Avenue
Chicago, IL 60625
(Swedish Pioneer Quarterly, 1950–)
NN IEP

Books and Articles

Almquist, Johannes A.
Svensk Genealogisk Litteratur.
Stockholm, P.A. Norstedt und
Söner, 1905, 78 p.
(Svenska Autograf Sällskape
Skrifter och Handlingar v. 7)
NN AVB

American Swedish Historical
Foundation.
Yearbook.
Philadelphia, PA, 1944–71. 21 v.
NN IEP

American Swedish Historical
Foundation.
Philadelphia, PA, 1972–.
NN IEP 73-2534

Beijbom, Ulf.
Swedes in Chicago.
Stockholm, 1971. 381 p.
NN IEP 73-1301

Bergsten, Lenn A.
Bergsten Genealogy.
Topsfield, MA, L.A. Bergsten, 1975.
3 v.
(An excellent example of an individual of Swedish descent tracing his ancestry; 3 large vol-

umes filled with letters; birth, marriage, death records; illustrations, etc.), indexed.
APV (Bergsten) 75-254

Biografiskt Lexikon Öfver Namnkunnige Svenske Män ...
Stockholm, F. & G. Beijers förlag, 1874–76. 8 v. in 4.
NN AGR

Fahlbeck, Pontus Erland.
Der Adel Schwedens und Finlands.
Jena, G. Fischer, 1903. 362 p.
NN AVB

Fjellström, Phebe.
Swedish American Colonization in the San Joaquin Valley.
Uppsala, Almquist, 1970. 157 p.
NN IEP + 74-1456

Furtenbach, Börje.
Släktforskning för Alla. Västerås, Börje Furtenbach, 1971. 133+ p.
(A guide to Swedish gen. research)
NN APB 73-1057

Genealogisk Tidskrift.
Stockholm, 1946–61. Bds. 1–6.
NN AVB

Hildebrand, Bengt.
Handbok I Släkt-och Personforskning. Del 1
Metodlära, Medeltidsförhållanden, Historiografi och Bibliografi.
Stockholm, Wahlström & Widstrand, 1961. 399 p.
NN APB

Hofberg, Johan Herman.
Svenskt Biografiskt Handlexikon; Alfabetiskt Ordnade ...
Stockholm, A. Bonnier, 1906. 2 v.
NN E-12 1342

Johansson, Carl-Erik.
Cradled in Sweden: A Practical Help to Genealogical Research in Swedish Records.
Logan, UT, Everton, 1972. 205 p.

Johnson, Amadeus, 1877–1974.
Swedish Contributions to American Freedom, 1776–1783.
Philadelphia, PA, Swedish Colonial Foundation, 1953–57. 2 v., index each v.
(HIS: The Swedes in America Part 7.)
NN IEP

Keen, Gregory B.
The Descendants of Jöran Kyn of New Sweden.
Philadelphia, PA, Swedish Colonial Society, 1913. 318 p., indexed.
(Includes a list of members of the Swedish Colonial Society in 1913 and a map of New Sweden)
NN APV (Kyn)

LDS Series D
no. 3 (1967), Sweden, general;
no. 15 (1971), Sweden, church records
NN APA 72-754

Louise Mountbatten, Queen of Sweden. 2nd ed., enlarged.
London, Allen and Unwin, 1968 (orig. 1965). 232 p., 3 gen tables.
NN JFD 70-548

Matrikel Öfwer Swea Rikes Ridderskap och Adel...
Stockholm, Tryckt uti Kongl., 1754–1823. 8 v.
NN AGR

Nelson, O.N.
History of the Scandinavians and Successful Scandinavians in the United States. 2nd rev. ed.

New York, Haskell House, 1969 (orig. 1904). 2 v.
(Index of biographies in v. 1)
NN IEP 71-65

Olsen, Ernst W.
History of the Swedes in Illinois.
Chicago, IL, Engberg-Holmberg, 1908. 3 v., indexed.
NN IEP

Ostman, Emil L.
Pioneer Finns and Swedes of the Delaware Valley Before William Penn.
Lyndhurst, NJ, 1972. 48 p.
NN IEP 72-3044

Pehrson, Gerda.
Svenska Pionjärer i Sydamerika.
Stockholm (Solna), 1970. 125 p.
(Swedes in South America)
NN HCO 71-365

Personhistorisk Tidskrift.
Stockholm, 1898–1973+. 69 v.+.
NN AVB

Roberts, Michael.
The Early Vasas: A History of Sweden, 1523–1614.
Cambridge, Cambridge U. Press, 1968.
NN *R-GFN 76-2554

Royal Bachelor's Club. Gothenburg.
The Royal Bachelor's Club, 1769–1944: Minnesskrift.
Goteburg, 1947. 474 p.
NN E-10 5250

Runholm, Harald, ed.
From Sweden to America: A History of Migration.
Minneapolis, MN, U. of Minnesota Press, 1976. 300 p.

Släkt och Hävd, Tidskrift utgiven av Genealogiska föreningen, Riksförening för Släktforskning.
Stockholm, 1949–1974+.
Genealogiska Föreningen
NN AVB

Strom, Albert P., ed.
Swedish Pioneers in Saunders County, Nebraska: A Collection of Family History of Early Settlers in Nebraska.
Pittsburgh, PA, A.P. Strom, 1972
90 p., t of c, no index.
NN APR (Saunders Co., Nebraska) 74-278

Svensk Slagt Kalender.
Stockholm, Bonnier, 1885–1963. 16 v.
NN AVB

Svenska Man och Kvinnor: Biografisk Uppsalagsbok.
Stockholm, Bonnier, 1942–55. 8 v.
NN *R-AGR

Svergiges Ridderskap och Adels Kalendar . . .
Stockholm, 1854–1875+. 93 v.+.
NN AVB

Swedish Royal Family
(House of Bernadotte)
(IN: *CDS*, Paris, 1966. p. 528–44)
NN ARB
(IN: *GHF*, Limburg/Lahn, 1968. v. 8, p. 185–89)
NN ATC

U.S.W.P.A.N.J.
The Swedes and Finns in New Jersey.
Bayonne, NJ, State Board of Ed., 1938?. 165 p., index.
NN IEP

Vem ar Det.
Stockholm, 1912–75+.
NN AGR and *RR-AGR 73-2651

Vem ar Det, Svensk Biografisk
Hanbok (1975)
Stockholm, 1912–.
NN *RR-AGR 73-2651

Vem ar Vem.
Stockholm, Bokforlaget Vem ar
Vem, 1962–68. 5 v.
NN *RR-AGR

Vilken var Det?
Stockholm, Svenska Slaktar, 1949–.
NN AGR

Warnstedt, Christopher von.
Adel-vad ar Det?
Solna, Seeling, 1970. 229 p.
(Covers the peerage and nobility
of other countries also)
NN AVB 72-3038

SWITZERLAND (BERN)

Called Helvetia in ancient times, this land was conquered by
Rome in 58 B.C. and was a Roman province for 300 years. Between
the fifth and ninth centuries it was successively overrun by
Alemanni and Burgundii, Franks, Swabia and Transjurane Burgundy. Switzerland was united under the Holy Roman Empire
in 1033. In 1291 the forest cantons (states) of Schwyz, Uri and
Unterwalden created a defensive league against the House of
Hapsburg; the hero of this league was William Tell. In 1386 the
cantons of Lucerne, Zurich, Zug, Glarus and Bern joined the
league and in battles at Sempach (1386) and Nafels (1388) the
Austrians were decisively defeated. In 1499 the Swiss achieved
virtual independence from Maximilian I. Swiss military strength
was broken in 1515 by a defeat at the hands of the French at
Marignano. Protestantism was preached by Zwingli at Zurich
and John Calvin at Geneva, but a battle between Catholics and
Protestants in 1531 arrested the spread of Protestantism in the
seven Catholic cantons. Despite religious fervor and conflict, the
Swiss stayed out of the Thirty Years War. At the Peace of
Westphalia in 1648, Switzerland's independence was formally
recognized. French revolutionary troops occupied Switzerland in
1798 and named it the Helvetic Republic, but in 1803 Napoleon
restored its federal government. At the Congress of Vienna in
1815, the Swiss were guaranteed perpetual neutrality. Economic
depression during the early nineteenth century led to large-
scale emigration to North and South America.

Swiss censuses were conducted in 1841, 1860, 1870, 1873, 1880, 1888, 1895, 1900, 1906, 1910, 1920, 1930, 1941, 1950, and 1960. The census is now taken every ten years.

Archives

Schweizerisches Bundesarchiv/Archives Fédérales Suisses/ Archivio Federale Svizzero (National Archives)
Ch-3003 Bern, Archivstr. 24
Switzerland

Bischöfliches Archiv Chur (Archives of the Roman Catholic Bishop)
700 Chur (Coire)
Bischöfliches Schloss, Hof 19
Switzerland

Public and Church Records

There are a number of archives, genealogical societies and civil registries in Switzerland, and each retains a certain degree of independence. For research prior to 1800, the most valuable sources of genealogical information are generally Haushaltungsregisters, Familienschein and parish registers.

Sometimes several generations can be traced through the "Haushaltungsregisters," censuses of families residing in particular parish areas. The information, which varies from area to area, includes names and dates and places of birth of several family members—brothers and sisters, children, parents and grandparents. In later years on some areas these records were called "burgher rolls."

Because of the nature of Swiss citizenship it is also possible to uncover several generations in the Familienschein, family certificates generally found in the Zivilstandesamt. Family data is recorded at the place of citizenship, and family certificates can be kept up to date for many generations. A Swiss marrying in any country can register his marriage and the birth of his children in the Heimatort, of place of registration, in Switzerland, and this information is then added to the Familienschein. The death certificate of a Swiss citizen may also be sent back to the Heimatort. By law, these records are accessible only to a person of the family blood line.

Prior to 1848, civil registration was the responsibility of each canton, and the dates when registration began vary from canton to canton. Registration was made in the parish records of churches until 1876, when it became the responsibility of civil authorities. The state archives keep duplicates or abstracts of all parish registers before 1870. It is helpful to know that one religion usually predominated in a canton. The predominantly Protestant cantons were Fribourg, Genève and Neuchâtel. The Catholic Cantons were Glarus, Graubünden, Lucerne, Nidwalden, Obwalden, St. Gallen,

Schwyz, Ticino, Uri and Valais. The mixed cantons (Protestant and Catholic) were Aargau, Bern, Basel, Schaffhausen, Solothurn, Thurgau, Vaud, Zug and Zurich. (Civil registration in Vaud began in 1800.)

In German-speaking Switzerland, vital record certificates are issued by the Zivilstandsbeamter; in French-speaking Switzerland, by the Officer de l'Etat Civil, and in Italian-speaking Switzerland, by the Ufficiale della Stato Civale.

Libraries

Bibliothèque Nationale Suisse—
Schweizerische Landesbibliothek 15 Hallwylstrasse
3003 Bern, Switzerland
(Contains all publications issued in Switzerland)

Bibliothèque Publique et Universitaire de Geneve
1211 Geneva 4, Les Bastions
Switzerland

Historical and Genealogical Societies

Schweizerische Heraldische Gesellschaft (Swiss Heraldic Society)
Lützelmattstrasse 4
Lucerne
(*Archives Héraldiques Suisses; Archivum Heraldicum*)

Société Générale Suisse d'Histoire
Bibliothèque de la Ville
Bern, Switzerland
(*Revue Suisse d'Histoire*)

Archives Héraldique Suisses
Chemin du Parc de Valency
11 Lausanne, Switzerland

Genealogisch-Heraldisch Gesellschaft
Leimgrubelstrasse 12
Zurich, Switzerland CH 8052

Société Suisse d'Héraldique
16 Rue St. Michel
Fribourg, Switzerland

Vorstand der Schweizerschen Gesellschaft für Familienforschung
Neuchâtel, Switzerland

United States Sources

Swiss-American Historical Society
216 East 39th Street
Norfolk, VA 23504
(*Swiss-American Historical Society Newsletter*)

Swiss-American Historical Society
Genealogical Committee
2526 Jackson Avenue
Evanston, IL 60201

Books and Articles

Armoriaux et Recueils d'Armoires Familiales
Suisses XIXe et XXe Siècles. Essai Bibliographique . . .
Bern, Bibliothèque Nationale, 1967. 25 p., index.

Archiv für Schweizerische Familienkunde.
Zurich, 1942–53.
NN AVG

Bibliographie der Schweizerischen Familien Geschichte, Bibliographie Généalogique Suisse.
Basel, 1964–.
NN AVG 76-1639

Biographische Lexikon Verstorbener Schweizer in Memoriam.
Zurich, 1947–75 plus. Bands 1–7 plus in progress, index each v.
NN *RR-AGIB+

Choisy, Albert.
Recueil Généalogique Suisse. Première Serie Genève.
Geneva, A. Jullien, 1902–18. 3 v.
NN AVGH (Geneva)

Dessemontet, Olivier, and Louis F. Nicollier.
Armorial des Communes Vaudoises.
Lausanne, Spes S.A. David Perret, 1972. 269 p., index.
NN AWT+ 74-1209

Familiennamenbuch der Schweiz, Repertoire des Noms de Famille Suisse, Repertorio dei Nomi di Famiglia Svizzeri.
Zurich, Editions Polygraphiques, 1968–71. 6 v. A–Z.
NN AVG 72-2663

Faust, Albert B.
List of Swiss Emigrants in the Eighteenth Century to the American Colonies.
Baltimore, MD, GPC, 1976 (orig. 1920, 1925, 1972). 2 v. in 1 (122, 255 p.).
(Reprinted with additions and corrections from *NGSQ*, Washington, March 1972)
NN earlier ed. IEK

Galbreath, Donald L.
... Armorial Vaudois ...

Baugy sur Clarens, the author, 1934–36. 2 v., alpha A–Z.
NN AWT+

Galiffe, Jacques A.
Notices Généalogiques sur les Familles Genevoises.
Geneva, J. Barrezat, 1829–1908. 7 v.
NN AVGH (Geneva)

Genealogical Society of the Church of Jesus Christ of Latter-day Saints.
Research Paper. Series C., no. 2.
Salt Lake City, UT, 1967.
NN APA 72-753

Genealogisches Handbuch zur Schweizer Geschichte.
Zurich, Schulthess, 1900–45. 3 v.
NN AVG

Historisch-Biographisches Lexikon der Schweiz.
Neuenburg, 1921–34. 7 v.
NN *RR-GDB

Hürlimann, Martin.
Grosse Schweizer ...
Zurich, Atlantis, 1938. 762 p.
NN AGIB

Keller, Willy.
Schweizer Biographische Archiv.
Zurich, EPI, 1952–58. 6 v.
NN E-10 1892

Lienhard-Riva, Alfredo.
Armorial Ticinese.
Lausanne, 1945. 517 p., alpha, many colored plates.
NN AWT+

Lutz, Markus.
Baselerisches Burger-Buch.
Basel, 1819. 408 p.
NN AVGH (Basel)

Osman, Rechat.
. . . Le Nom des Personnes dans les
  Codes Civils Suisse et Turc.
Liège, G. Thone, 1934, 202 p.
NN AVG

Perret, Maurice E.
Les Colonies Tessionoises en Cali-
  fornie.
Lausanne, F. Rouge, 1950. 304 p.,
  index.
NN IEE (Swiss)

Schweizer Archiv für Heraldik.
Archives Heráldiques Suisses Annuaire.
Zurich, 1887–. indexes v. 1–25
  (1887–1911), v. 26–35 (1912–31),
  v. 36–67 (1932–53).
NN AWT

Der Schweizer Familienforscher.
Le Généalogiste Suisse.
Bern, 1934–. (v. 1–8 under Der
  Familienforscher), index v.
  1–17 (1934–50)
NN AVG

Schweizer Frauen der Tat . . .
Zurich, Rascher, 1929. 3 v. (bd. 1,
  1659–1827; bd. 2, 1831–54; bd. 3,
  1855–85)
(Biographies of Swiss women)
NN SNE

Der Schweizer Sammler und Fami-
  lienforscher.
Le Collectionneur et Généalogiste/
  Suisse.
Bern, 1927–42. 16 v.
NN AVG

Schweizersche Gesellschaft für
  Familienforschung.
Veröffentlichunger.
Bern, 1935–.
NN AVG

Schweizerasches Geschlecterbuch.
Almanach Généalogique Suisse.
Basel, 1905–55. 10 v., index each v.
(Index v. 1–10 in v. 10)
NN AVG

Secretan, Eugène, 1839–1919.
Galerie Suisse. Biographie Nation-
  ales.
Lausanne, G. Bridel, 1873–80. 3 v.
NN AGIB

Société Vaudoise de Généalogie.
  Lausanne.
Recueil de Généalogies Vaudoises.
Lausanne, G. Bridel, 1912–1940.
NN AVGH (Vaud)

Stewart-Wallace, Mary.
The Zermatt Bourgeoisie.
(IN: *GM*, London, 1968. v. 15, p. 658–
  60)
NN ARCA

Swiss Passenger Lists to U.S. 1845.
(IN: *Historischen Vereins des Kan-
  ton Glarus*, 1970. heft 63, p. 11 ff.)
(p. 89–93 names of persons settling
  in New Glarus, Wisconsin, in
  1845; p. 105–10 account of New
  Glarus in English)
NN GDA

Verzeichnis de Burger der Stadt
  Bern, Jan. 1, 1906.
Bern, 1906. 399 p.
NN AVGH (Bern)

Von Grueninger, John Paul.
The Swiss in the United States.
Madison, WI, Swiss-American His-
  torical Society, 1940.
153 p., index.
NN IEE (Swiss)

Who's Who in Switzerland, Including the Principality of Liechtenstein.

Zurich, etc., 1952. (1950/51—1974/
  75), 1974+.
NN *RR-AGIB and AGIB

Zurich (City) Zivilstandsamt.
Bürgerbuch der Stadt Zurich, 1926.
Zurich, Muller, Werder, 1927. 2,079
  p.
NN AVGH (Zurich)

UNION OF SOVIET SOCIALIST REPUBLICS (MOSCOW)

Tradition says the Viking Rurik came to Russia in 862 A.D. and founded the first Russian dynasty in Novgorod. His successor, Oleg (879–912), transferred his residence to Kiev in 882. The various tribes were united by the spread of Christianity in the tenth and eleventh centuries; Vladimir I adopted the Greek Orthodox rite in 989. From 1237 to 1240 the Mongols invaded and destroyed all Russian cities except Novgorod and Pskov. The Russian territory was split into numerous smaller dukedoms out of which three large centers—Galicia, Moscow and Novgorod—emerged. In 1380 Dmitri Douskoi conquered the Mongols, and rulers of the grand duchy of Vladimir began to be called grand dukes of Moscow, or Muscovy. In 1497 Ivan adopted the first code of laws, and in 1547 Ivan IV (Ivan the Terrible) was crowned czar of all Russia. He established rule over the middle and lower Volga, forming the basis for the colonization and annexation of Siberia. Michael Romanov, chosen by national council, was czar from 1613 to 1645, and the Romanov dynasty ruled until Czar Nicholas was murdered in 1917.

In 1649 serfdom became a legal institution in Russia—a means of establishing nobles on estates, thus isolating them from central power and political influence. Peter I (Peter the Great) conscripted an army and navy and created the Holy Synod, directly subordinate to the emperor, in 1721. He introduced modern industries and elements of Western education. In 1703 he founded St. Petersburg, now Leningrad, on the Gulf of Finland and transferred the capital there in 1712. Under Catherine II (Catherine the Great), who reigned from 1762–96, Russia became the chief power of continental Europe. There were partitions of Poland (1772, 1793, 1795), annexation of the Crimea (1783) and annexation of Courland (1795). Treaties with Turkey in 1774 and 1792 gave Russia vast new territories in the west and south, including Belorussia, the Ukraine west of the Dneiper River and the Black Sea shores. Finland was annexed from Sweden in 1809, Bessarabia was added to Russia by the Treaty of Bucharest of 1812 and Caucasian territories were added by the Treaty of Gulistan of 1813. In 1861 Alexander II liberated the serfs. In 1864–65 territories of present-day Soviet Central Asia, including Turkistan, were taken, and the southern section of the Far Eastern Territory was acquired from China, so that Russia reached the borders of Afghanistan and China and the Pacific Ocean. In 1860 Vladivostok was founded.

In 1917 the Bolsheviks, led by Vladimir I. Lenin, seized the government and proclaimed it as the Russian Soviet Federated Socialist Republic. In the treaty that ended World War I in 1918, Russia lost much territory to the central powers. Civil war ended in 1920 when the Soviet regime was victorious. Poland, Finland and the Baltic countries emerged as independent states. In 1922 the country united with the Ukrainian, Belorussian and Transcaucasian republics to form the Union of Soviet Socialist Republics.

Censuses were conducted in 1897, 1909, 1920, 1926, 1937, 1939 and 1949. Censuses of Latvia, a constituent republic, were taken in 1925 and 1935.

The most common surnames in Kiev (transliterated from Russian orthography) are Bondarenko, Ivanov, Kovalenko and Kravchenko. In Leningrad and Moscow they are Vasil'ev, Ivanov, Kuznetsov, Petrov, Smirnov and Sokolov.

Archives

Archives Centrales des Actes Anciens (CGADA)
Bolšaja Pirogovskaja 17
119435 Moscow, U.S.S.R.

Archives Historiques Centrales de L'URSS (CGIA SSSR)
190000 Leningrad-Centre
Naberež-naja Krasnogo Flota 4
U.S.S.R.

Direction Générale des Archives de la République Socialiste
Federative Sovietique de Russie (RSFSR), Moscou
Berežkovskaja Nab 26
U.S.S.R.

Central State Historical Archives
Leningrad
Naberezhnaya Krasnogo Flota 4
U.S.S.R.

Central State Archives of Early Russian Historical Records
Moscow
Bolshaya Pirogovskaya ul. 17
U.S.S.R.

Libraries

State V.I. Lenin Library of the
U.S.S.R.
Moscow
Pr. Kalinina 3
U.S.S.R.

State M.E. Saltykov-Shchedrin
Public Library
Leningrad D-69
Sadovaya ul. 18
U.S.S.R.

State Public Historical Library of
the RSFSR
Moscow Starosadsky per. 9
U.S.S.R.

United States Sources

The Russian Historical and Gen-
ealogical Society
971 First Avenue
New York, NY
(Maintains no contact with the
U.S.S.R.)

German Sources

Dr. Karl Stumpp
% Landsmannschaft der Deut-
schen aus Russland
Stofflenbergerstrasse 66
Stuttgart Sud-Wuerttemburg, Ger-
many
(Information about Germans from
Russia)

French Sources

President of the Bureau of Généalogique
Union de la Noblesse Russe
8 rue Gabrielle d'Estrées
Vannes, France

(Some records of Russian immigrants have been placed in a
private collection in France.)

Armenia

Provincial Archives
Direction des Archives de la Ré-
publique Socialiste Soviétique
d'Arménie
Erevan, ul. Kočara 5
U.S.S.R.

Libraries
A.F. Myashnikyan State Public Li-
brary of the Armenian S.S.R.
Erevan, Ul. Teroyana 72
U.S.S.R.

Estonia

Provincial Archives
Direction des Archives de la Ré-
publique Socialiste Soviétique
d'Estonie
Tallinn, ul. Manezi 4
U.S.S.R.

Libraries
State Public Library of the Eston-
ian S.S.R.
Tallinn, Raamatukogu pl. 1
U.S.S.R.

Georgia

Provincial Archives
Direction Générale des Archives
de la République Socialiste Sovié-
tique de Géorgie
Tbilisi, Prospekt Važa Pšhaleva 1
U.S.S.R.

Libraries

K. Marx State Public Library of the
Georgian S.S.R.
Tbilisi, Ul. Ketskhoveli 5
U.S.S.R.

Latvia

Provincial Archives

Direction des Archives de la Ré-
publique Socialiste Soviétique de
Lettonie
Riga, ul. Skjunju 11
U.S.S.R.

Libraries

Vilis Lacis State Library of the
Latvian S.S.R.
Riga, Ul. Kr. Baron iela 14
U.S.S.R.

Lithuania

Provincial Archives

Direction des Archives de la Ré-
publique Socialiste Soviétique de
Lituanie
Vilnius, ul. Vrublevskogo 6

Libraries

National Library of the Lith-
uanian S.S.R.
Vilnius, Lenin pr. 51
U.S.S.R.

Mongolia

Archives

State Archives
Ulan Bator, Mongolia

Libraries

State Public Library (Committee of
Sciences of the M.P.R.)
Ulan Bator, Mongolia

Library, Mongol Ulsiin Ikh Surgu-
uli (Mongolian State University)
Ulan Bator, Mongolia

Ukraine

Provincial Archives

Direction Générale des Archives
de la République Socialiste Soviétique d'Ukraine
Kiev, Solomenskaja ul. 24
U.S.S.R.

Libraries

C.P. S.U. State Public Library of the
Ukrainian S.S.R.
Kiev, Ul. Kirova 1
U.S.S.R.

Books and Articles

Auly, Robert, and Dimitri Obolen-
sky.
An Introduction to Russian History.
Cambridge, Cambridge U. Press,
1976. 403 p., gen. tables, index.
(Companion to Russian Studies v.
10)

Benson, Morton.
Dictionary of Russian Personal
Names.
Philadelphia, PA, 1969. 175 p.
NN *QCF 72-108

Berg, Ernst von.
Der Malteserorden und seine Be-
ziehungen zu Russland.
Riga, N. Kymmel, 1879. 282 p.
NN BTN

Bergamini, John D.
The Tragic Dynasty.
New York, Putnam, 1969. 512 p.,
 index, gen. tables.
(The Romanovs)
NN *RR-GLD 70-2

Bespuda, Anastasia.
Guide to Orthodox America.
Tuckahoe, NY, 1965. 150 p.
NN JXE 75-71

Bobrinskoi, Alexander, Count.
Dvoryanskie Rody.
(Noble Families Included in the
 Heraldic Records of the Russian
 Empire up to 1885)
St. Petersburg, 1890. 2 v.

Cowles, Virginia S.
The Romanovs.
London, Collins, 1971. 288 p., index.
NN JFF 72-196

Davis, Jerome D.
The Russian Immigrant.
New York, Macmillan, 1922. 219 p.
(White Russians)
NN IEE (Russians)

Doering, Heinrich.
Russlands Helden.
Leipzig, J.F. Hartknoch, 1935. 348
 p.
NN GLP

Dukes, Paul.
A History of Russia Medieval, Mod-
 ern and Contemporary.
London, 1974. 361 p.
NN JFD 75-4123

Eckhardt, Julius W.A. von.
La Société Russe.
Paris, M. Dreyfous, 1977. 2 v.
NN GLD

Eisenstadt, Mikhail K.
Moscow on the Hudson.
New York, Harper & Bros., 1951.
 182 p.
NN IEE (Russians)

Feodorova, Svetlana.
The Russian Population in Alaska
 and California, late 18th Century–1867. (Trans. from the Russian)
Kingston, Ontario K7L 5C8, Lime-
 stone Press, P.O. Box 1604, 1973.
 376 p., index.
NN IEE (Russians) 75-288

Galitzine, Princess Nicholas.
Spirit to Survive: The Memoirs of
 Princess Nicholas Galitzine.
London, Kimber, 1976. 199 p., 16 p.
 of plates, gen. tables, ports.

Great Soviet Encyclopedia, trans.
 of 3rd ed.
New York, Macmillan, 1970. 10 v.
 plus index v. 1–5.
NN *QAC 75-605

Hatch, Flora F.
The Russian Advance into Califor-
 nia.
San Francisco, CA, 1971. 72 p.
NN IEE (Russians) 73-1635

Hofmann, Rostislav.
Les Grandes Figures Slaves de
 Russe.
Paris, Editions du Sud, 1965, 429 p.
NN D-16 4113

Institut Po Izucheniyu SSSR.
 Munich.
Biographic Dictionary of the
 USSR.
New York City, Scarecrow Press,
 1958. 782 p. alpha
NN *R-Slavonic

Kleimola, Ann M.
Justice in Medieval Russia: Muscovite Charters
(Pravye Gramoty) of the Fifteenth and Sixteenth Century.
Philadelphia, PA, American Philosophical Society, 1975. 93 p.
(*APS, Trans.* N.S. v. 65, pt. 6)
NN *EA A571

Louis, Victor Eugene, and Jennifer Louis.
The Complete Guide to the Soviet Union.
London, Joseph, 1976. 369 p., 24 p. of plates, index.

Maclean, Sir Fitzroy.
To the Back of Beyond: An Illustrated Companion to Central Asia and Mongolia.
London, Cape, 1974. 144 p.
NN JFF 75-598

Maclean, Sir Fitzroy.
To Caucasus, the End of All the Earth ...
London, Cape, 1976. 203 p. 49 L. of plates, index
NN JFF 77-209

Mehnert, Klaus.
The Russians in Hawaii 1804–1819.
(IN: *Hawaii (Territory) University Occasional Papers*, Honolulu, HI, 1939. no. 38, p. i–iii, 1–86)
NN STG

Metzer, Rev. Father H.
Historical Sketch of St. Peters Parish and the Founding of the Colonies of Rastedt, Katharinenthal and Speyer.
(IN: *SGSB*, Regina, Saskatchewan, 1974. v. 5, p. 7–29)
NN APW

New York Public Library.
Dictionary Catalog of the Slavonic Collection. 2nd rev. ed.
Boston, MA, G.K. Hall, 1974. 44 v.
(Material recorded before Jan. 1, 1972; over 727,000 cards)
NN Pub Cat 75-107

Noblesse de Russie, 2nd ed., compiled by Nicholas Ikonnikov.
Paris, 1957–1966. 26 v., alpha, plus cross-index.
NN ATW

Russian Royal Family.
(House of Romanov-Holstein-Gottorp)
(IN: *CDS*, Paris, 1966. p. 485–517)
NN ARB
(IN: *GHF*, Limburg/Lahn, 1968. v. 8, p. 158–67)
NN ATC

Russian Student Fund.
Russians with American College Training ...
Directory of Former Students, 1921–43.
New York, RSF Alumni Assoc., 1944. 96 p.
NN SSD p.v. 684

Sallet, Richard.
Russian German Settlements in the United States.
Fargo, ND, Institute for Regional Studies, 1974. 207 p., index, maps.
NN IED 75-2135

Struve, Catherine Tolstoy Arapoff.
The Genealogy of Alexis Paul Arapoff.
New York, 1971. 46 leaves.
(Tolstoys and other well-known Russian families in English)
NN ATZ (Arapoff) 72-1877

Summers, Anthony, and Tom Mangold.
The File on the Tsar.
London, Gollanz, 1976. 416 p., 24 p. of plates, index.

Unbegaun, B.O.
Russian Surnames.
Oxford, Clarendon Press, 1972. 529 p., index.
NN APD 74-2179

Veselovskii, Stephan B.
Onomastikon.
Moscow, 1974. 381 p.
NN *QCF 74-5260

Volkmann, Hans E.
Die Russische Emigration in Deutschland 1919–1929.
Wurzburg, Holzner, 1966. 154 p., gen. tables.
NN E-12 8417

Wertsman, Vladimir.
The Russians in America, 1727–1970.
Dobbs Ferry, NY, Oceana, 1977. 140 p. index
NN IEE (Russians) 77-611

Who's Who in the USSR.
New York, Scarecrow Press, 1961–1965. 2 v.
(v.1, 1961–62; v. 2, 1965–66)
NN K-10 3729

Who Was Who in the USSR (1917–1967).
Metuchen, New Jersey, Scarecrow Press, 1972. 677 p., alpha.
NN *R-AGN 72-1168

Armenia
Adontz, Nikolai G.
Etudes Armeno-Byzantines.

Lisbon, Bertrand, 1965. 438 p.
(Bibliothèque Armenienne de la Foundation Calouste Gulbenkian)
NN E-13 5319

Adontz, Nikolai G.
Histoire d'Arménie, les Origines du Xe Siècle au XVIe (AV J.C.).
Paris, 1946. 4,441 p.
NN BBX

Agajanian, Esau T.
The Agajanian Genealogy, ed. by Terry Sherf.
North Hollywood, CA, Publications West, 1971. 400 p., t of c, no index, excellent map as end papers. (This is actually the narrative of a people, many other families mentioned, and it is too bad that there is no index. It goes back to the author's great-great-great-grandfather, Bedros, born c. 1775 in the village of Bazirgan, State of Makoo, Persia.)
NN APV (Agajanian) 73-2569

Arlen, Michael.
Passage to Ararat.
New York, Farrar Straus, 1975. 293 p.

Armenian Church in America.
Martyrdom and Rebirth ...
New York, 1965. 105 p.
(Published on the occasion of the 50th anniversary of the massacres of 1915)
NN E-12 6629

Armenian Directory of the State of California.
Los Angeles, 1942–43–.
NN IEZ

Atamian, Sarkis.
The Armenian Community.
New York, Philosophical Society,
1955. 479 p.
NN BBX

Creap, James.
Armenians, Koords and Turks.
London, S. Tinsley, 1880. 2 v.
NN BBP

Directory of Armenians.
New York, 1952. 1 v.
(New York, New Jersey, Connect-
icut)
NN IEE (Armenians)

Directory of the Armenian Colony
of the Metropolitan District.
New York, Yeprad Pub., 1930. 88
p., ports.
NN IEA

Kerr, Stanley Elphinstone.
The Lions of Marash ...
Albany, N.Y., State Univ. of N.Y.
Press, 1973. 318 p.
NN JFE 73-3085

Kulhanjian, Gary A.
The Historical and Sociological As-
pects of Armenian Immigration
to the United States 1890–1930.
San Francisco, CA, 1975. 83 p.
NN IEE (Armenians) 76-391

Malcom, M. Vortan.
Armenians in America.
Boston, MA, Pilgrim Press, 1919.
142 p., t of c, no index, illus.
NN IEE (Armenians)

Medzadourian, Georges.
Les Exiles de la Paix.
Paris, Editions Entente, 1975. 208
p.
NN JLC 76-244

Megerditian, Ervandt Der.
The Life of an Armenian Emi-
grant.
North Quincy, MA, Christopher,
1970. 186 p., t of c, no index, illus.
NN IEE (Armenians)

Sanjian, Avedis K.
The Armenian Communities in
Syria under Ottoman Domina-
tion.
Cambridge, MA, Harvard U. Press,
1955. 390 p.
(Harvard Middle Eastern Studies
v.10)
NN E-12 5121

Sarafian, Kevork A.
Armenian History of Aintas ...
Los Angeles, CA, 1953. 1 v. in 2.
(Armenians in Turkey)
NN *ONR 74-17

Seth, Mesrovb J.
Armenians in India from the Ear-
liest Times to the Present Day.
Revised and enlarged.
Calcutta, the author, 1937. 629 p.
NN *ONR

Surmeyan, Ardavazt.
La Vie et la Culture Arméniennes
à Alep au XVIIe Siècle ...
Paris, Araze, 1934. 47 p.
(Armenians in Aleppo, Syria)
NN D-16 1354

Toumanoff, Cyril.
Studies in Christian Caucasian
History.
Washington, DC, Georgetown U.
Press, 1963. 599 p., index.
NN JFF 72-364

Zorian, K.
Arménien, une Vie, Souvenirs.
Paris, Scorpion, 1964. 252 p.
NN C-13 7061

Estonia

Baltic Review . . .
New York, 1944–.
NN GMC

Beiträge zur Baltischen Ge-
schichte.
Hannover-Dohren, Berlag Harro v.
Hirschheyer, 1973. Band 1, in-
dex.
NN AVH (Estonia) 75-1515

Hehn, Jürgen von.
Von den Baltischen Provinzen zu
den Baltischen Staaten.
Marburg (Lahn), 1971. 343 p.
NN JFE 73-1649

Kleis, Richard.
Eesti Avalikud Tegelased . . .
Tartus, Eesti Kirjanduse Selts,
1932. 412 p.
(Estonian Bio. Dict.)
NN Ref. Cat.+ 169

Napiersky, Karl E.
Beiträge zur Geschichte der
Kirchen und Prediger in Liv-
land.
Mitau, W.F. Häcker, 1843–52. 4 v.
in 2.
NN E-12 4844

Noored Astuvad Ellu.
Tallinn, 1963. 73 p., ports.
NN D-14 8942

Penmar, Jaan, Tonn Parming, and
P. Peter Rebane.
The Estonians in America 1627–
1975.
Dobbs Ferry, NY, Oceana, 1975.
150 p., index.
NN IEE 75-1991

Roucek, Joseph S.
The American Estonians.

(IN: *Baltic Countries*, Toruń, 1936.
v.2, p. 191–94)
NN GLA+

Välis-Eesti Ühing.
Välis-Eesti Tegelased . . .
Tallinn, 1939. 139 p.
NN E-11 2940

Wrangell, Wilhelm, Baron.
Die Estländische Ritterschaft, ihre
Ritterschafts-hauptmänner
und Landräte.
Limburg/Lahn, C.A. Starke, 1967.
361 p.
NN E-13 3436

U.S. Library of Congress. Slavic
and Central European Division.
Estonia: A Selected Bibliography,
comp. by Salme Kuri.
Washington, DC, 1958. 74 p.
NN F-10 4436

Uutalu, Evald.
The History of the Estonian Peo-
ple.
London, Boreas, 1952. 261 p.
NN *QGK

Georgia

Burney, Charles A.
The Peoples of the Hills: Ancient
Ararat and Caucasus.
London, 1971. 323 p.
NN JFE 73-2165

Canard, Marius.
Les Reines de Géorgie dans
l'Histoire et la Légende Musul-
manes.
(IN: *Revue des Etudes Islamiques*,
Paris, 1969. v.37, p. 3–20)
NN *OAA

Georgia. Transcaucasia. Central
Archives.

Bulletin Historique. année 1–2; 1924–25.
(Text in French and Georgian)
NN *OOE

Gugushvili, A.
The Chronological-Genealogical Tables of the Kings of Georgia.
(IN: *Georgica*, London, 1936. p. 103–53)
NN BBV

Lang, David M.
Georgian Studies in Oxford.
(IN: *Oxford Slavonic Papers*, Oxford, 1955. v.6, p. 115–43)
NN *GAA

Lang, David M.
The Georgians
London, Thames and Hudson, 1966. 244 p.
NN D-17 6600

Menabde, Levan V.
Centres of Ancient Georgian Culture.
Tbilisi, Ganatleba, 1968. 63 p.
NN JFC 72-1392

Toumanoff, Cyril.
The Fifteenth-Century Begratids and the Institution of Collegial Sovereignty in Georgia.
(IN: *Traditio*, New York, 1949–51. v.7, p. 169–221), gen. table.
NN BAA

Latvia

Akmentinš, Osvalds.
Latvijas Ideja Amerika.
Boston, c. 1969. 167 p.
NN *QYN 72-1832

Album Lettonornun 1870–1882–1930.
Rija, 1930. 168 p.
NN *QYN+

Dunsdorfs, Edgars.
Deviņvīru Spēks; Deviņu Latviešu Vīru Dzīves Stāsti Deviņos Latvijas Vēstures Gadsimtos.
Stockholm, Daugava, 1956. 289 p.
NN *QYN

Ērmanis, Pēteris.
Trimdas Rakstnieki, Autobiografiju Krājums.
Kempten, Vila Štāla Apgāds, 1947. 3 v.
NN *QYN

Kronlins, Janis.
379 Baigā Gada Dienas; Latviešu Jaunatnes un Tās Audzinātāju Liktensis Baigajā 1940 un 41 Gadā.
Waverly, IA, Latvju Grāmata, 1967. 362 p.
NN *QYN

Latvijas Darbinieku Galerija 1918–1928.
Rīgā, Grāmatu Draugs, 1929. 466 p.
NN *QYN+

Stepermanis, Marġers.
Lielās Liesmas Atblāzma.
Rīgā, 1971. 220 p.
NN *QYN 74-2066

Lithuania

Akstinas, Bronius
Glimpses of Lithuania.
Vilnius, 1972. 237 p.
NN JFD 74-3637

Amžiais su Gimtine.
Vilnius, 1970. 209 p.
NN *QY 73-5945

Jasas, R.
Lietuvos Didžiosios Kunigaikštystės Gyventojų Surašymas 1790m.

Vilnius, 1972. 95 p.
(Lithuanian census of 1790)
NN *QY 74-2112

Kaupas, A.
Les Colonies Lithuaniennes aux
États-Unis.
(IN: *Annales des Nationalités*,
Paris, 1913. année, p. 231–34)
NN *BA

Lietuvos Albumas ...
Berlin, Elsner, c. 1921. 435 p.
NN *QY

Lithuanians in Canada by Prince
Gaida, etc.
Ottawa, Lights Print., 1967. 370 p.
(*Canada Ethnica, no. 5*)
NN HWH

Lukoševičius, Jonas.
Reemigrantai.
Vilnius, 1971. 142 p.
NN *QY 73-2292

Michelsonas, Stasya.
Lietuviu Išeivija Amerikoje, 1868–
1961.
South Boston, Keleivis, 1961. 499 p.
(Lithuanians in U.S., Canada,
South America)
NN *QY

Miluko, Antano.
Lietuviškas Albumas ...
Shenandoah, PA, V.J. Stagaro & Co.,
1900. 3 v. in 1.
NN *QY (Žilinskis)

Norem, Owen J.C.
Timeless Lithuania.
Chicago, IL, Amerlith Press, 1943.
299 p.
NN GMC

Simutis, Anicetas.
Pasaulio Lietuvių Žinynas (Lith-
uanian World Directory).
New York, Lietuvių Prekybos Rū-
mai, 1958. 464 p.
(In Lithuanian and English)
NN Desk Slavonic Division

Sužiedėlis, Simas.
The Story of St. Francis Lithuanian
Parish, trans. by Rev. A. Bružas.
Lawrence, MA, 1953. 416 p.
NN IQH (Lawrence)

Volkaité-Kulikauskiené, Regina.
Lietuviai IX-XII Amžiais.
Vilnius, Mintis, 1970. 294 p.
(Lithuania in the Middle Ages)
NN *QY

Zokas, Antanas.
Nuo Dubysos iki La Platos.
Vilnius, 1972. 264 p.
NN *QY 73-6527

Mongolia
Akademia Nauk SSSR.
History of the Mongolian People's
Republic.
Moscow, 1973. 523 p.

Brent, Peter.
The Mongol Empire: Genghis
Khan, His Triumph and His Leg-
acy.
London, Weidenfeld and Nicolson,
1976. 264 p., index; gen. tables.

Mongolian Studies.
Amsterdam, 1970. 590 p.
NN *OQ 73-753

Saunders, John J.
History of the Mongol Conquests.
London, 1971. 275 p.
NN *R-BD 76-1727

Pskov

Nechaev V., and N. Chulkov.
Pskovi ego Prigorody (Pskov and
Its Surroundings)
Moscow, 1913–14. 2v.
(v.1, Domesday Book of Pskov
1585–87; v.2, documents relating
to Pskov 1580–1733)
(Moscow Archives of the Ministry
of Justice. Collections. v. 5–6)

Siberia

Lessner, Erwin C.
Cradle of the Conquerors: Siberia.
Garden City, NY, Doubleday, 1955.
774 p.
NN *R-GLD

Siberia.
Pamyatniki Sibirskoi Istorii XVIII
Vyeka.
(Documents of Siberian History in
the 18th Century)
St. Petersburg, 1882–85. 2 v. (1700–
24)
NN *QGO

Ukraine

Bodgan, F.
Dictionary of Ukrainian Surnames
in Canada.
Winnipeg/Vancouver, U. of Van-
couver, 1974. 354 p.
NN APD 75-306

Lypyns'kyĭ, Vyacheslav, 1882–
1931, ed.

Echa Przeszlosci: z Kronik i Aktow.
(IN HIS: *Z Dziejow Ukrainy*, Kiev,
1912. p. 68–139)
NN *QGA

Wenzlaff, Theodore C.
Pioneers on two Continents, the
Ochsner-Griess History and
Genealogy.
Sutton, NE, T.C. Wenzlaff, 1974.
139 p., long t of c, no index, maps,
charts, photos of ship S.S. *Thuringia*, July 30, 1873, and S.S.
Cimbria, Aug. 6, 1873, that arrived in New York bringing
55 German-Ukrainian families
from the Bessarabian section
of the Ukraine.
NN APV (Ochsner) 75-2166

Wertsman, Vladimir.
The Ukrainians in America
1608–1975: A Chronology and
Fact Book.
Dobbs Ferry, NY, Oceana, 1976.
140 p. index
NN IEE (Ukrainians) 76-1422

Ukrainians in North America, a
Biographical Directory of Note-
worthy Men and Women of
Ukrainian Origin in the United
States and Canada, edited by
Dmytro Shtohryn.
Champaign, IL, Association for the
Advancement of Ukrainian
Studies, 1975. 424 p. alpha.
NN IEE (Ukrainians) 77-896

VATICAN CITY

For nearly 1000 years the papal states possessed large parts of
Italy and, until the French Revolution, parts of southern France.
In the nineteenth century, during the unification of Italy, the
House of Savoy absorbed most of the papal territories. The city

of Rome remained a papal possession until the Kingdom of Italy annexed it in 1870. Pope Pius IX refused to recognize the loss of temporal power, and for the next fifty years the popes isolated themselves. In 1929 the independent state of the Vatican City came into being with the signing of the Lateran Treaty by Mussolini and the Pontificate.

Archives

Archivio Segreto Vaticano
00120 Vatican City

Libraries

Biblioteca Apostolica Vaticana (Vatican Apostolic Library)
Vatican City

There is a library attached to each of the papal colleges and seminaries.

Books and Articles

Bertini Frassoni, Carlo A.
... La Nobilità nello Stato Pontifico.
Rome, Collegio Araldico, 193–. 540 p.
NN ASY (Papal States)

Counts of Rome.
(IN: *Genealogical Magazine*, London, 1899. v.3, p. 245–48)
NN ARCA

Labarre de Railicourt, Dominique.
Les Comtes du Pape en France, XVIe–XXe Siècles.
Paris, 1965–67. 4 v.
NN AWP

Partner, Peter.
The Lands of St. Peter.
London, 1972. 527 p.
NN JFD 72–3045

Pericoli, Francesco.
Titoli Nobiliari Pontifici Riconsciuti in Italia.
Rome, 1963. 72 p., tables.
(*Rassengna degli Archivi di Stato. Quaderni 25*)
NN L-10 6158 v.25

YUGOSLAVIA (BELGRADE)

The assassination of Archduke Francis Ferdinand by a Serbian nationalist at Sarajevo in Bosnia (one of the Slavic states in the Austro-Hungarian Empire) set the stage for World War I. In 1914 Serbia and Montenegro—at that time the only independent Slavic states—were overrun by the Central Powers, and by the end of the war the Austro-Hungarian Empire had collapsed. In 1918 the Kingdom of Serbs, Croats and Slovenes was created from the provinces of Croatia, Dalmatia, Bosnia, Herzegovina, Slovenia, Voyvodia and Montenegro and was ruled by King Peter I of Serbia of the House of Karageorgevich. When Croatia moved toward separation, Peter's successor, Alexander I, ruled as a dictator. In 1921 the country's name was changed to Yugoslavia. In 1934 A Croat terrorist assassinated Alexander in Marseilles, and Alexander's son became Peter II under the regency of Alexander's cousin, Prince Paul. In 1941 Yugoslavia signed a Berlin-Rome-Tokyo pact that led to the overthrow of Prince Paul's government by a coup, and Crown Prince Peter became king. The new government signed a non-aggression pact with the Soviet Union, and soon after Yugoslavia was invaded by Germany and Italy, joined by Hungary and Bulgaria. The country collapsed in a week, and King Peter II fled to London. In 1943 civil war broke out between Communist partisans, led by Josip Broz (known as Marshal Tito) and the Chetniks, a Serbian resistance group led by Draja Mikhailovich. In 1944, when the Germans were finally expelled, Tito's forces were in control. In 1945 the monarchy was abolished and the Yugoslav People's Republic was proclaimed, headed by Tito, who was elected President for life in 1974.

The most common surnames in Belgrade are Jovanović, Marković, Nicolić, Petrović and Popović.

Archives

Arhiv Jogoslavije (National Archives)
Vase Pelagića 33
11001 Beograd, Yugoslavia

Arhiv Srbije (Archives of Serbia)
Karnedžijeva 2
11000 Belgrade, Yugoslavia

Arhiv Sr Crne Gore (Archives of Montenegro)
Novice Cerovića 2
81250 Cetinje, Yugoslavia

Arhiv Slovenije (Archives of Slovenia)
Levstikov trg 3
61000 Ljubljana, Yugoslavia

Arhiv Hrvatske (Archives of Croatia)
Marulićev trg 21
41000 Zagreb, Yugoslavia

Arhiv Vojvodine (Archives of Vojvodina)
Trg Branka Radičevića 8
21205 Sremski Karlovci, Yugoslavia

Arhiv Na Makedonija (Archives of Macedonia)
Kej Dimitar Vlahov bb
91000 Skopje, Yugoslavia

Arhiv Kosova (Archives of Kosovo)
Nikola Tesla 43
38000 Priština, Yugoslavia

Public and Church Records

Birth certificates are issued by the Registrar (Maticar) attached to the Village People's Committee (Mesni Narodni Odbor), Municipal People's Committee (Cradski Narodni Odbor) or, in the larger cities, by the People's Committee of the pertinent ward (Rejon). Civil registration began in the territory of Voivodina in 1895; since 1946 it has been required throughout Yugoslavia.

Libraries

Serbia
Narodna Biblioteka Socijatističke Republike Srbije
(National Library—the Central Library for the Socialist Republic of Serbia)
Skerlićeva
Belgrade, Yugoslavia

Univerzitetska Biblioteka "Svetozar Markovič"
(University Library)
Bulevar Revolucije 71
Belgrade, Yugoslavia

Croatia
Nacionalna i Sveučilišna Biblioteka
(National University Library)
Marulićev trg 21
Zagreb, Yugoslavia

Naučna Biblioteka (Research Library)
Docla 1
Rijeka, Yugoslavia

Slovenia
Narodna in Univerzitetna Knjižnica (National and University Library)
Turjaska 1
Ljubljana, Yugoslavia

Študijska Knjižnica (Research Library)
Prešernova 1
6200 Maribor, Yugoslavia

Bosnia and Herzegovina
Narodna i univerzitetska biblioteka Bosna i Hercegovine
Obala Vojvode Stepe 42
Sarajevo, Yugoslavia

Macedonia
Narodna i Univerzitetska Biblioteka
(National and University Library)
Bul. Goce Delčer b.b.
Skopje, Yugoslavia

Biblioteka "Braka Milandinovci" (District of Skopje Public Library)
Partizanski odredi b.b.
Skopje, Yugoslavia

Montenegro
Centralna Narodna Biblioteka SR Crne Gore (Central National Library of the S.R. of Montenegro)
Njegoševa 100
Cetinje, Yugoslavia

Biblioteka Istorijskog Instituta NR Crna Gore
(Library of the Historical Institute of the P.R. of Montenegro)
Naselje Kruševac
Titograd, Yugoslavia

Books and Articles

American Slav.
Pittsburgh, PA, 1944–.
NN IEE (Slavs)

Balch, Emily Greene.
Our Slavic Fellow Citizens.
New York, Arno Press, 1969 (orig. 1910). 536 p., index.
NN IEE (Slavs) 73-1467

British Croatian Review.
Henlease, Bristol, 1974–.
(% British Croatian Society, 40 Henley Grove, Henlease, Bristol BS9 4EG)

Colakovic, Branko Mita
Yugoslav Migrations to America.
San Francisco, CA, R. and E. Research Associates, 1973. 190 p.
NN IEE (Yugoslavs) 74-1213

Culinovic, Ferdo.
Dokumenti o Yugoslaviji.
Zagreb, 1968. 591 p.
NN *QKK 71-57

Davolvic, Kosta St.
Vojislav Marinkovic i Njeovo Doba 1876–1935.
London, 1955–60. 5 v.
NN *QKK

Dedijer, Vladimir.
History of Yugoslavia.
New York, McGraw-Hill, 1974. 752 p., index.
NN*OKK 75-4182

Djilas, Milovan.
Land Without Justice.
New York, Harcourt Brace, 1958. 365 p.
NN D-11 1807

Duisin, Viktor Anton, Comte.
Zbornik Plemstva u Hrvatskoj, Slavonaji, Dalmaciji, Bosni-Hercegovini, Dubrovniku, Kotoru i Vojvodini.
Zagreb, 1938–. sv. 1–.
NN *QKK

Eterovich, Adams.
Croatians from Dalmatia and Montenegrin Serbs in the West and South 1800–1900.
San Francisco, CA, R. and E. Research Associates, 1971. 127 p.
NN IEE (Slavs)

Gopcevic, Spiridon.
Geschichte von Montenegro und Albanien . . .
Gotha, F.A. Perthes, 1914. 462 p., 2 tables.
NN *QKK

Govorchin, Gerald G.
Americans from Yugoslavia.
Gainesville, FL, U. of Florida Press, 1961. 352 p., index.
NN IEE (Slavs)

Hefner, Stanislaus.
Studien zur Altservischen Dynastischen Historiography.
2nd ed., revised and enlarged.
Munich, R. Oldenburg, 1964. 141 p.
(Studosteuropaische Arbeitin 62)
NN E-12 4484

Karadzic, Vuf Stefanovic, 1787–1864.
Zivoti Srpskih Vojvoda i Ostalih Znamenitih Srba.
Belgrade, Barnko Donovic, 1963. 303 p.
NN *QKK

Miklosic, Franz.
Die Serbischen Dynasten Crnojevic.

Vienna, C. Gerold's Sohn, 1886. 66
p.
NN GIVI

Miller, William.
The Medieval Serbian Empire.
(IN: *Quarterly Review*, New York,
1916. v. 226, p. 488–507)
NN *DA

Mistruzzi di Frisginga, Carlo.
La Nobilità dei Principato de Gradisca
(IN: *International Congress of Heraldry and Genealogy*, 3rd congress Madrid, 1955. p. 429–34)
NN APB

Montenegrin Royal Family.
(House of Petrovitch Niegosh)
(IN: *CDS*, Paris, 1966. p. 372–78)
NN ARB
(IN: *GHF*, Limburg/Lahn, 1971. v.
9, p. 57–61)
NN ATC

Prpic, George.
The Croatian Immigrants in Amer-
ica.
New York, Philosophical Society,
1971. 519 p., index.
NN IEE (Croats) 72-584

Serbisches Mittelalter: Alterbische
Herrscher-Biographien.
Graz, Verlag Styria, 1963. 1 v., gen.
tables.
(Slavische Geschichtschreiber)
NN K-10 6356

Stevenson, Francis S.
A History of Montenegro.
London, Jarrold, 1912. 214 p.
NN *R-GIVP

Supuk, Ante.
Sibenski Glagoljski Spomenci.

Zagreb, Jugoslavenski Adaemija
Znanosti i Umjetnosti, 1957. 239
p.
(History of the city of Sibenik,
sources)
NN *QKK

Temperley, Harold W.V.
History of Serbs.
London, G. Bell, 1917. 359 p.
NN *QKK

Vuinovic, Ilija-Lee.
Kad Navru Sjecanja …
Sarajevo, 1970. 197 p.
NN *QKK 73-1118

Vujnovich, Milos.
Yugoslavs in Louisiana.
Gretna, Pelican Pub., 1974. 246 p.,
index.
Appendix I, p. 213–20, Yugoslav
businesses in Louisiana
Appendix II, members of the
United Slavonian Benevolent
Association 1874–1974.
Extracts from passenger lists
1821–65, p. 29–30.
1850 census extracts of South
Slavs, p. 31–32.
NN IEE (Yugoslavs) 75-1212

Yugoslav Royal Family.
(House of Karageorgevitch)
(IN: *CDS*, Paris, 1966. p. 565–74)
NN ARB
(IN: *GHF*, Limburg/Lahn, 1971. v.
9, p. 43–47)
NN ATC

The Yugoslav Village.
Zagreb, 1972. 261 p.
NN JLD 2072

The Yugoslavs in America.
Minneapolis, MN, Lerner Pub. Co.,
1977.

Zagreb. Jugoslavenski.
Leksikografski Zavod Bibliografiji Rasprava ...
Zagreb, 1956–.
(Yugoslav history bibliography)
NN Desk Slavonic Div. 73-672

General European Sources

Cambridge Medieval History.
Cambridge, Cambridge U. Press, 1934–1967. 8 v. in 9.
NN *R-BTH

Chaffanjon, Arnaud.
Le Petit Gotha Illustre.
Paris, 1968. 606 p.
NN ARB 74-2286

Coutant de Saisseval, Guy.
Les Maisons Imperiales et Royales d'Europe.
Paris, Editions du Palais-Royal, 1966. 597 p., cursory index.
NN ARB

Davis, John.
People of the Mediterranean ...
London, RKP, 1976. 296 p.

Diesbach, Ghislain de.
Les Secrets du Goths.
Paris, Réné Julliard, 1964. 429 p. plus t of c.
NN ARB

East European Genealogist.
Harbor City, CA, 1977–. v. 1–.

Evans, Ellis.
Gaulish Personal Names: a Study of Some Continental Celtic Formations.
Oxford, Clarendon Press, 1967. 492 p., alpha, index.
NN APD

Foreign Titles of Nobility.
(IN: *Burke's Peerage*, London, 1938. 96th ed., p. 2,678–703)
NN ARM

Gantenbein, James W.
Documentary Background of World War II 1931 to 1941.
New York, Octagon Books, 1975. 1,122 p. Appendix II, Chronology 1938–41.
NN *R-BZAH

Holmes, George.
Europe, Hierarchy and Revolt, 1320–1450.
Hassocks, England, Harvester Press, 1975. 352 p., index.
(Fontana Library of Europe)

Horecky, Paul L.
Southeastern Europe: A Guide to Basic Publications.
Chicago, IL, U. of Chicago Press, 1969. 755 p., index.
NN *RB-GIV

International List of the Nobility ... [Title in Five Languages]
Geneva, International List of Nobility, Rue Cornavin 11, 1973. 433 p. (World-wide Coverage)

Isenburg, Wilhelm Karl, Prinz von.
Europaische Stammtafelin ...
Marburg, J.A. Stargardt, 1956–75. 4 v. (v. 1–2 orig. 1936)
NN ARB + 76-669 & ARB +

Jensen, Larry O.
Genealogical Research in Eastern Europe.
(IN: *Saskatchewan Genealogical Society Bulletin*, Regina, 1975. v. 6, p. 108–21, 171–83)
NN APW

Liddell-Hart, Basil Henry.
History of the Second World War.
London, Cassell, 1970. 768 p., index.
*R-BZAC

Liddell-Hart, Basil Henry.
A History of the World War, 1914–1918.
London, Cassell, 1934. 635 p., index.
NN *R-BTZE

McNaughton, Arnold T.
The Book of Kings.
New York, Quadrangle Press, NYT Books, 1973. 3 v., index.
NN ARB + 75-1925

Methuen's History of Medieval and Modern Europe. (475–1923)
London, Methuen, 1931–74. (2nd ed. of v. 1: 476–911, 1974)
NN *B-BTC

Mitchell, Henri.
The Second World War.
New York, Praeger, 1975. 947 p., index.
NN *R-BZAC 76-905

Newspapers in Microform: Foreign Countries, 1948–1972.
Washington, DC, Library of Congress, 1973. 269 p.
(Covers newspapers from earliest dates that were put on film between 1948 and 1972)
NN Pub. Cat.

Ogg, David.
Europe in the Seventeenth Century.
London, A. and C. Black, 1971. 9th ed. 576 p.
NN *R-BTW 72-1723

Paget, Gerald.
The Lineage and Ancestry of H. R. H. Prince Charles, Prince of Wales.
Baltimore, GPC, 1977. 2 v. (European Royal Houses)

Pounds, Norman J.G.
An Historical Geography of Europe 450 B.C. to A.D. 1330.
Cambridge, Cambridge U. Press, 1973. 475 p.
NN *R-BTH 72-2882

Powell, James H.
Medieval Studies.
Syracuse, NY, Syracuse U. Press, 1976. 389 p. index.
NN *R-BTH 76-7564

The Rise of Modern Europe (1250–1945).
New York, Harper & Row, 1936–71. 20 v.
NN *R-BTE

The Royalty, Peerage and Aristocracy of the World (formerly, Annuaire de la Noblesse de France.)
London, 1966–. v.90–.
NN APC

Rude, George F.E.
Europe in the Eighteenth Century.
London, 1972. 290 p.
NN *R-BTX 73-876

Ruvigny and Raineval, Melville A.H.D., Marquis de.
Titled Nobility of Europe.
London, Harrison, 1914. 1,598 p., alpha.
NN ARB

Sirjean, Gaston.
Encyclopédie Généalogique des Souveraines du Monde.
Paris, 1959–.
NN ARB

Sulzberger, Cyrus L.
The Fall of Eagles.
New York, Crown, 1977. 448 p., 400
 illus.

Tullberg, Hasse W.
Les Maisons Souveraines de
 L'Europe.
Stockholm, 1899–1907. 2 v., illus.
NN ARB

Valko, William G.
The Illustrated Who's Who in
 Reigning Royalty.
Philadelphia, PA, Vasilikon Pub.,
 1969. 263 p. (World-wide Cover-
 age)

Valynseele, Joseph.
Les Prétendants aux Trônes
 d'Europe.
Paris, 1967. 457 p.
NN ARB

Wagener, Wilhelm.
Genealogische Tafeln zur Mitt-
 eleuropaishen Geschichte.
Göttingen, Heinz Reise, 1962–.
NN ARB 74-459

Wagner, Sir Anthony R.
Pedigrees and Progress: Essays in
 the Genealogical Interpretation
 of History.
Chichester, Phillimore, 1975. 333
 p., index.
NN APB 76-2339

Wallace-Hardrill, John Michael.
Early Medieval History.
Oxford, Blackwell, 1975. 247 p., in-
 dex.
(Covers 400–1000)
NN JFK 76-7500

Wellauer, Maralyn.
A Guide to Foreign Genealogical
 Research.
Milwaukee, WI, the author, 1973.
 78 p.
NN AP 74-797

Who's Who in Central and East
 Europe, 1933–34.
Zurich, Central European Times,
 1933. 1,163 p.
(Includes Estonia, Latvia, Yugo-
 slavia, Turkey, etc. Good for
 finding information about peo-
 ple who fled Europe because of
 World War II.)
NN AA

ENGLAND (LONDON)

When Julius Caesar invaded Britain in 55 B.C. it was inhabited by Celts. When the Romans withdrew in the early fifth century the land was open for the invasion of the German Angles, Saxons and Jutes, who pushed the Celts back to the western part of Britain and Wales and formed a group of kingdoms that only began to draw together in the ninth century under King Alfred the Great (c. 848–900) as the threat of Danish marauders grew more pressing. His successors united England and ruled until they were totally subdued by King Canute in 1016. In 1066 William, Duke of Normandy, conquered England in the last invasion to date and established the line from which the present queen, Elizabeth II (Illustration 47), is descended, although the succession has zigzagged down through innumerable female heiresses of the Houses of Plantagenet (Anjou, Lancaster and York), Tudor, Stuart, Hanover (Guelph) and Windsor to the Mountbatten-Windsors. In spite of various periods of war among the royal heirs, a general feeling of continuity has enabled the democracy that we have now in Great Britain and the United States to grow and flourish.

Highlights and milestones in English history are numerous. The Magna Carta of 1215, signed by King John after his defeat by the English barons, is the basis of British and American constitutional government and enabled Parliament to develop into the ruling body as we know it today. The Hundred Years War, begun in 1337, and the War of the Roses between the Houses of Lancaster and York in the fifteenth century devastated the country and paved the way for the rise of the Tudor dynasty founded by Henry VII (1457–1509). It was under his tight reign, begun in 1485, and the reign of his son, Henry VIII (1491–1547), and granddaughter, Elizabeth I (1533–1603), that England prospered. With the establishment of the Church of England and the confiscation of many religious lands, there arose a new class of nobility and gentry who were eager to expand beyond their island and explore the world. King James I (1566–1625), who succeeded his cousin Elizabeth in 1603, encouraged exploration, and the first permanent English colony in the New World was established at Jamestown, Virginia, in 1607. The break with Rome led to the development of Puritanism, which culminated in the settlement of New England, begun by the Pilgrims of Plymouth Colony, who arrived in 1620. Numerous groups followed, led by such men as John Winthrop (Boston, 1629), Roger Williams (Providence, 1636) and Theophilus Eaton and John Davenport (New Haven, 1638). In the period when the Puritan forces under Oliver Cromwell controlled the government after the overthrow and beheading of Charles I in 1649, many royalist supporters fled to the colonies of Virginia and Maryland. Even after the restoration of Charles II eleven years later, the flow of immigrants to the American colonies continued at an increasing rate. In 1707, with the Act of Union, Scotland joined England, Ireland, and Wales to form Great Britain. Colonial expansion in Asia, Africa and the Pacific flourished from the late seventeenth century and culminated when Queen Victoria was proclaimed Empress of India in 1877 and Great Britain officially became an empire. The first setback to colonial power had been in the eighteenth century, when the American colonies revolted against "taxation without representation" and the tyranny of George III. The next great loss leading to the eventual dissolution of the empire came after World War I, when southern Ireland gained independence in 1922. In 1947, when India became a republic, Great Britain could no longer be called an empire, and the term "United Kingdom" became a more realistic description of the country.

The English records that one uses to trace a family are much the same as those used in the United States or any other country, but there are some important differences in where the records are kept. Central registration of births, marriages and deaths began on July 1, 1837 in England and Wales, so if your ancestors emigrated after that date, a vital record in the General Register Office at St. Catherine's House (formerly housed at Somerset House) would indicate the parish and county in which they lived. If they came to the United States or the colonies before 1837, you should check various central indexes of vital records, such as *Boyd's Marriage Index*, which have been gradually made up from printed copies and typescripts of English parish registers, which in a few cases date all the way back to 1538, when the law requiring the clergy to keep registers went into effect. Some clergy neglected to comply with the law, and some early parish registers have not survived. *The National Index of Parish Registers,* edited by Donald J. Steel and others, still being compiled, will ultimately be the best source to check for the availability of parish registers and Bishops' Transcripts—paper copies of the register entries sent to the bishops' offices by parish priests. In many instances these copies predate the surviving parish registers. The English started indexing marriage records early in the last century for various purposes. *Pallot's Marriage Index 1780–1837,* which covers 100 ancient parishes of London, 119 of Middlesex and 400 in the vicinity of London, was compiled by a firm of London solicitors to aid them in searching for heirs. This index is now owned by Achievements Ltd. of Northgate, Canterbury, Kent. *Boyd's Marriage Index,* begun by the late Percival Boyd (d. 1955), covers the period from 1538 to 1837. It is available in bound volumes at the Society of Genealogists in London, on film in the New York Public Library, in the Genealogical Society in Salt Lake City and through its some 190 branch libraries throughout this country. Mr. Boyd left his manuscripts to the Genealogical Society in Salt Lake City with the proviso that they would continue to index marriages from the film copies of parish registers in their vast collection, and they have continued to make additions.

The numerous local genealogical societies that have sprung up in the past few years in England have increased interest in indexing marriage and other vital records, and this is one of their valuable contributions to the literature of genealogy. Among the notable compilations are the Sussex Marriage Index of the Sussex Family History Group c/o Francis Leeson (108 Sea Lane, Ferring, Sussex), which included entries from some 167 parishes by 1973; the Cheshire Marriage Index, also called Merrell's Marriage Index, being compiled by Bertram Merrell (now living near Salt Lake City, Utah); and the Northamptonshire Marriage Index, made up of entries from the Bishops' Transcripts and kept at the Northamptonshire Record Office (Delapré Abbey, Northampton NN4 9AW). If you locate the parish in which your family lived, you should contact the present clergyman in whose custody the records are today. By looking in *Crockford's Clerical Directory,* you will be able to find his name and address, and he will be able to tell you if he has the records for the period in which you are interested, if they have been deposited in the county record office, or if they simply do not exist.

There are some English wills that were centrally probated from the fourteenth century up to 1857 in the prerogative courts of Canterbury (in the south of England) and York (in the north). Published indexes to these records—mainly wills of important people with land in more than one probate district or of people who died overseas—are noted in the bibliography. The Prerogative Court of Canterbury (commonly called PCC) wills prior to 1858 are deposited in the Public Record Office in London, while the wills of the Prerogative Court of York for this same period are housed in the Borthwick Institute in York. Since 1858 wills have been filed centrally at the Principal Probate Registry, Somerset House. The guides to British wills by Anthony Camp and Jeremy Gibson should help you find other wills that were probated in local courts all over the country. Other records connected with probates of wills that should be helpful are *Inquisitiones post mortem* (inquiries after death), which date from the thirteenth century to 1660 and are similar to petitions for probate in this country, and chancery proceedings, which pertain to problems with probates, such as contests to overturn a will. Depositions with information on age, relationship and residence are often noted in these records, some of which have been abstracted and/or indexed in various publications listed in the bibliography.

English deeds and leases were usually held privately, but in recent years many solicitors and old land-owning families have deposited collections of these documents in the various county record offices. The published guides to the record offices often list these collections, and supplements concerning the holdings of these depositories can be obtained by writing to them at the addresses below.

The Domesday Book of 1086 might be called the first census of England, but this document, even in translation from the original Latin, will be of little use to the average genealogist, as the people mentioned in it lived before surnames were in general use. Beware of the genealogist who states that his family name is listed in the Domesday Book. There are manor rolls, fines, poll taxes and other documents that date from the twelfth century, but the first tax assessment of general import is the lay subsidy tax for 1524–25, which exists for most of England. These records for several counties have been published. One of the next fairly comprehensive lists is the muster roll of 1569, taken during the reign of Elizabeth I, and there are musters for other years that will be helpful, depending on the county. In the seventeenth century the Protestation returns of 1642 list all the males over eighteen in every parish who subscribed to the Oath of Protestation, and it was through these lists for Devonshire that I was able to verify and substantiate the parishes where my own family were living (Illustration 44). The Heath Tax Assessments were taken on all the fireplaces in England from 1662–98, and of these taxes the assessment of Lady Day 1664 is the most comprehensive. The first national census of England was taken in 1801 and continued on a decennial basis until the present day, but for the most part these records do not survive until 1841, and the 1851 census was the first to record the parish of birth of each individual, thus giving the genealogist the best clue leading back into the appropriate parish register. The census records of England and Wales for the years from 1841 to 1871 are fully available on microfilm to the public at the Public Record Office in London, and through the LDS libraries in the United States. The census records after that date will not be available until one hundred years has elapsed, since the date that they were taken. Therefore, the 1881 census should be available to researchers in 1981. Limited and restricted searches for genealogical purposes can be made in the census records after 1871, upon application to the Public Record Office and the payment of a fee. Some 1831 copies may survive at a local level, as noted in the account of my Bailey relatives (page 91).

The guides to printed genealogical sources by George Marshall and James Whittmore are of special use to those tracing prosperous middle-class, gentle and noble families. They index the published visitations taken by the heralds of the College of Arms from 1532 to 1689 (page 966), county histories, genealogies and accounts of families in county historical society publications and other periodicals. In pursuing research in Great Britain it is especially important to note the realignment of counties which took place in 1974, since many records have been relocated, as a result of this change. Some of these new borders make great sense, such as separating the Isle of Wight from Hampshire, since in the winter choppy water often prevented boats from going back and forth between the two places and thus delayed the performance of county business. Other results of this new order, such as the elimination of the ancient county of Rutland, only cause consternation and sorrow.

Through the use of the various records and guides mentioned here and in the bibliography below, it is sometimes possible to trace an average English yeoman or middle-class town family back into the 1400's, if they lived in a county where the wills and manorial records survive, or in such cities as London, Lincoln, Exeter and York, where I have had some luck in following several lines backward through wills, parish registers, inquisitions post-mortem, chancery proceedings and similar documents.

In two articles in the *Sussex Family Historian* (1974–76, v. 1, no. 4, p. 85–88; v.2, no. 7, p. 228–33), Michael J. Burchall expertly weaves the information from the Lay Subsidy of 1524 with wills (local wills from Lewes, Sussex, as well as Prerogative Court of Canterbury-PCC-wills), parish register entries, Bishops' Transcripts, marriage licenses, university records and manorial records to piece together the genealogies of the yeoman Pardon and Tillinghast families of Sussex back to the fifteenth century. These are the ancestors of Rev. Pardon Tillinghast (d. Providence, Rhode Island; January 29, 1718), who was pastor of the First Baptist Church in Providence and an ancestor of numerous Americans living today. Among his descendants is Charles Carpenter Tillinghast, Jr. (1911–), former president of Trans-World Airlines, a 1932 graduate of Brown University in Providence who holds the strong Baptist traditions of his forebear.

In contemporary London the most common surnames are Brown(e), Clark(e), Davies(Davis), Jones, Taylor and Williams.

Archives

Public Record Office
Chancery Lane
London WC2A 1LR, England
(Includes PCC wills prior to 1858)
 (Some records moved to PRO,
Ruskin Ave., Kew, London, England)

The College of Arms is the official registry of coats of arms, including crests and badges for England, Wales, Northern Ireland and the Commonwealth.

The College of Arms
Queen Victoria Street
London, EC4V 4BT, England

Public and Church Records

The General Register Office holds certificates of births, deaths and marriages in England and Wales since July 1, 1837. Since Nov. 1976, the original birth certificates of adoptees have been available to them when they reach their majority.
General Register Office
St. Catherine's House
10 Kingsway
London WC2B 6JP, England

For divorce records:
The Chief Clerk
Room G45, Divorce Registry
Somerset House, The Strand,
London WC2R 1LB, England

For wills since 1858:
The Principal Probate Registry
Somerset House, The Strand
London WC2R, ILP England

Libraries

British Museum Library and Reading Rooms
Great Russell Street
London WC1B 3DG, England

British Newspaper Library
Colindale Avenue
London NW9 5HE, England

British Transport Historical Records Office
66 Porchester Road
London W2, England

Congregational Library
Memorial Hall, 2 Fleet Lane
London EC 4, England

Guildhall Library (Library of the Corporation of London)
Aldermanbury
London EC2P 2EJ, England

H.M. Customs and Excise Library
King's Beam House
London EC3, England

Indian Office Library (Foreign and Commonwealth Office)
197 Blackfriars Road,
London SE1 8NG, England
(Relates principally to India and the East)

Lambeth Palace Library
Lambeth
London SE1 7JU, England

Methodist Archives and Research Centre
Epworth House
25-35 City Road
London EC1, England

Historical and Genealogical Societies

Association of Genealogists and Record Agents
% Miss Isobel Mordy, Hon. Secretary
123 West End Road
Ruislip, Middlesex HA4 6JS, England

Canterbury and York Society
The Secretary
79 Whitwell Way, Coton
Combridge CB3 7PW, England
(*Bishops' Registers*)

Catholic Record Society
% 114 Mount Street
London W1Y 6AH, England
(Recusant History)

Council of Social Service
26 Bedford Square
London WC1B 3HU, England
(*The Local Historian*)

Federation of Family History Societies
Mrs. Elizabeth Simpson, Hon. Secretary
Peapkin's End, 2 Stella Grove,
Tollerton
Nottinghamshire NG12 4EY, England

Friends Historical Society
Friends House, Euston Road
London NW1 2BJ, England
(*Journal of the Friends Historical Society*)

Harleian Society
Ardon House, Mill Lane
Godalming, Surrey, England

Heraldry Society
28 Museum St.
London WC1A 1LH, England
(*The Coat of Arms*)

Historical Association
59A Kennington Park Road
London, SE11 4JH, England
(*History: Annual Bulletin of Historical Literature*)

Historical Manuscripts Commission
Quality House, Quality Court
Chancery Lane
London WC2 1HP, England

Huguenot Society of London
% Barclays Bank
1 Pall Mall East
London SW1Y 5AX, England
(*Proceedings*, 20 v.; *Quarto Series*, 47 v.)
NN ARCA

Jewish Historical Society of England
33 Seymour Place
London W1H 5AP England
(*Transactions; Miscellanies*, etc.)
NN *PXQ

Methodist Archives and Research Centre
Epworth House, 25-35 City Road
London EC1Y 1AA, England

Presbyterian Historical Society of England
86 Tavistock Place
London WC1, England
(*Journal*)

Royal Historical Society
University College, Gower St.
London WCIE 6BT
(Publications, 1838–)
NN CA

Society of Genealogists
37 Harrington Gardens
London SW7 4JX, England
(*The Genealogists' Magazine, 1925–*)
NN ARCA

Avon

County Archives

Avon and Bristol Archives
The Council House, College Green
Bristol BS1 5TR, England

Historical and Genealogical Societies

Bristol and Avon Family Society
% S. Emylyn-Jones
108 Newbridge Road
St. Anne's
Bristol BS4 4DR, England
(*BAFS Journal*, Bristol, 1975–)

Bedfordshire

County Archives

Bedfordshire County Record Office
County Hall
Bedford MK42 9AP, England

Historical and Genealogical Societies

Bedfordshire Family History Society
% Royston F. Gambier
45 Falcon Crescent
Flitwick
Bedfordshire, England

Berkshire

County Archives

Berkshire County Record Office
Shire Hall
Reading RG1 3EE, England

Historical and Genealogical Societies

Berkshire Family History Society
Major A.S. Ogden
Bearwood College
Winnersh, Wokingham RG11 5BG,
England
(*Berkshire Family History Group*,
1975–)

Buckinghamshire

County Archives

Buckinghamshire County Record
Office
County Offices
Aylesbury HP20 1UA, England

Historical and Genealogical Societies

Buckinghamshire Family History
Society
Miss B.E. Thorpe
35 Castle Street
Aylesbury, England

Channel Islands

County Archives

Guernsey (Alderney, Sark, Herm,
Jethou and Brechou):
The Greffe
St. Peterport
Guernsey

Jersey:
Judicial Greffe
States Building
St. Helier, Jersey

Public and Church Records

Guernsey vital records (since 1840):
Registrar-General's Office
The Greffe (above)

Guernsey wills:
The Ecclesiastical Court of the
Dean of Guernsey
12 New St.
St. Peterport, Guernsey

Jersey vital records (since 1842):
Superintendent Registrar
States Building
St. Helier, Jersey

Jersey wills:
The Royal Court
Judicial Greffe (above)

Cheshire

County Archives

Cheshire County Record Office
The Castle
Chester CH1 2DN, England

Societies

Family History Society of Cheshire, Western Region
Mr. B. Pollard
4 Eaton Road
Chester, England
(*Family History Society of Cheshire*, 1971–)

Family History Society of North Cheshire
Mrs. Pauline Litton
34 Bramley Lane
Bramhall
Stockport, Cheshire SK7 2DP, England
North Cheshire Family Historian (Nov. 1975–, v.3–.)
(A continuation of the *Cheshire Family Historian*, 1974–1975.)
NN ARX (Cheshire) 76-1670

Cornwall

County Archives

Cornwall County Record Office
County Hall
Truro TR1 3AY, England

Cumbria

County Archives

Cumbria, Cumberland, Westmoreland and Carlisle Record Office
The Castle, Carlisle, and
County Hall, Kendal
England

Historical and Genealogical Societies

Cumbria Family History Society
Ulpha, 32, Granada Road
Denton, Manchester, England

Derbyshire

County Archives

Derbyshire County Record Office
County Offices
Matlock DE4 3AG, England

Devon

County Archives

Devon County Record Office
Castle Street
Exeter EX4 3PQ, England

Historical and Genealogical Societies

Devon Family History Society
% Mrs. A. V. Chiswell, Hon. Sec.
96 Beaumont Road
Plymouth, Devon PL2 4AN
(*The Devon Family Historian*, 1977–)

Dorset

County Archives

Dorset County Record Office
County Hall
Dorchester DT1 1XJ, England

Historical and Genealogical Societies

Somerset and Dorset Family History Society
% Mervyn T. Medlycott, Esq.
5 Hillside Cottages
Sandford Orcas, Sherborne
Dorset, England
(*The Greenwood Tree: Newsletter of the S&DFHS*, 1975–)

Durham

County Archives

Durham County Record Office
County Hall
Durham DH1 5UL, England

Historical and Genealogical Societies

Northumberland and Durham Family History Society
J.A. Readie
38 Archery Rise
Neville's Cross, Durham DH1 4LA, England
(*Northumberland and Durham Family History Society*, 1975–)

Essex

County Archives

Essex County Record Office
County Hall, Chelmsford,
Essex CM1 1LX, England
(*Essex Record Office Publications*, 1947–74+, no.1–66+)
NN CO (Essex)

Historical and Genealogical Societies

Essex Society for Family History
J. W. Peters
6 Windsor Way
Rayleigh, Essex, England
(*Essex Family Historian*, Nov. 1974–; *Essex Society for Family History Handbook*, 1975, 24 p.)

Gloucestershire

County Archives

Gloucestershire County Record Office
Shire Hall,
Gloucester GL1 2TG, England

Greater Manchester

County Archives

Archives Department
Greater Manchester Central Library
St. Peter's Square
Manchester M2 5PD, England

Hampshire

County Archives

Hampshire County Record Office
20 Southgate Street
Winchester SO23 9EF, England

Historical and Genealogical Societies

Hampshire Family History (1974–; continuation of the *Family History Journal of South East Hampshire Genealogical Society*)
% W.G. Wakelin
53 Durley Avenue, Cowplain
Hampshire PO8 8UZ, England

Hereford and Worcester

County Archives

Hereford and Worcester County Record Office
The Old Barracks, Harold Street
Hereford, England

Hertfordshire

County Archives

Hertfordshire County Records Office
County Hall, Room 204,
Hertford SG13 8DE, England

Historical and Genealogical Societies

Hertfordshire Family History Society
% Mrs. Crowley
189 Handside Lane

Welwyn, Garden City AL8 6TE, England

Humberside

County Archives

Humberside County Record Office
County Hall
Beverley, North Humberside England

South Humberside Area Record Office
Central Library
Town Hall Square
Grimsby
South Humberside DN31 1HG, England

Registry of Deeds
Beverly, England

Huntingdon

County Archives

Huntingdonshire Record Office
County Buildings, Grammar School Walk,
Huntingdon PE18 6LF, England

Isle of Wight

County Archives

Isle of Wight County Record Office
26 Hillside
Newport, Isle of Wight PO30 2EB, England

Historical and Genealogical Societies

The Isle of Wight Society
Mr. and Mrs. K. Seiles

"Eaglesfield"
Heathfield   Close,   Bembridge,
    I.O.W.
(Offshoot of the Hampshire Society)

Kent

County Archives

Kent Archives Office
County Hall, Maidstone
Kent ME14 1XH, England

Cathedral Archives and Library
The Precincts
Canterbury, Kent CT1 2EG, England

Historical and Genealogical Societies

Kent Family History Society
% Colin J. Parry, Hon. Sec.
53 St. Lawrence Frostal
Canterbury, Kent, England; or,
Alan Neame, ed. of *Journal*
Fisher Street, Sheldwich near Faversham
Kent ME13 OLB, England
(*Kent Family History Society Journal*, 1975–)

Lancashire

County Archives

Lancashire County Record Office
Bow Lane
Preston PR1 8ND, England

Historical and Genealogical Societies

Manchester and Lancashire Family History Society

Mrs. P. Seddon
54 School Hill, Cheadle
Cheshire, England
(*The Manchester Genealogist*, c. 1964–)

Leicestershire

County Archives

Leicestershire County Record Office
57 New Walk
Leicester LE1 6TD, England

Historical and Genealogical Societies

Leicester Family History Circle
Mrs. H. Glendening
5 Avondale Road
Wigston, Leicester, England
(*LFHC Newsletter*, 1975–)

Lincolnshire

County Archives

Lincolnshire County Archives Office
The Castle
Lincoln LN1 3AB, England

London

County Archives

Greater London Record Office
(London Records)
County Hall, Room B21,
Westminster Bridge,
London SE1 7PB, England

Greater London Record Office
(Middlesex Records)

1 Queen Anne's Gate Buildings,
Dartmouth Street,
London SW1H 9BS, England

Principal Registry, Family Division
Somerset House
The Strand WC2R 1LP, England

British Transport Historical Records Office
66 Porchester Road
London W2, England

Corporation of London Records Office
Guildhall
London EC2P 2EJ, England

University of London Library
Senate House, Malet Street
London WC1E 7HU, England

Man, Isle of

Public and Church Records

Vital records (marriages from 1849; births and deaths from 1878):
Registrar-General
Government Office
Douglas, Isle of Man

For wills and deeds:
Probate Registry
Finch Road
Douglas, Isle of Man

Historical and Genealogical Societies

Manx Society
Manx Records (Douglas, 1859–82)
   NN CW (Manx)

Merseyside

County Archives

Merseyside City Record Office
Central Library
Liverpool L3 8EW, England

Historical and Genealogical Societies

Liverpool Family History Society
% Mr. Arnold Cully
11 Lisburn Lane, Trebrook
Liverpool L13 9AE, England

Middlesex

County Archives

See London

Norfolk

County Archives

Norfolk and Norwich Record Office
Central Library, Bethel Street
Norwich NR2 1NJ, England

Historical and Genealogical Societies

Norfolk & Norwich Genealogical Society
% Hon. Secretary, Patrick Palgrave-Moore, FSG
Grove House, Hethersett
Norfolk, England
(*NNGS Publications*, 1969–) NN
   ARX (Norfolk) 75–1239

Northamptonshire

County Archives

Northamptonshire County Record Office
Delapré Abbey
Northampton NN4 9AW, England
(*Northamptonshire Past and Present*, 1948–date)
NN CO (Northamptonshire)

Historical and Genealogical Societies

Northamptonshire Family History Society
c/o Christopher Glazebrook
294 Birchfield Road East
Northampton NN3 2SY, England.

Northumberland

County Archives

Northumberland County Record Office
Melton Park, North Gosforth
Newcastle-upon-Tyne
NE3 5QX, England

Historical and Genealogical Societies

See Durham & Tyne and Wear

Nottinghamshire

County Archives

Nottinghamshire County Record Office

County House, High Pavement
Nottingham NG1 1HR, England

Southwell Diocesan Registry
Church House, Park Row
Nottingham, England

Historical and Genealogical Societies

Nottingham Family History Society
(Formerly the Genealogical Society of East Midlands)
Mrs. F. B. Payton, Sec.
Glenholme, High Oakham Road,
Mansfield, Nottingham
(*Nottingham Family History Society Journal*)

Oxfordshire

County Archives

Oxfordshire County Record Office
County Hall, New Road,
Oxford, OX1 1ND, England

Archdeaconries of Oxford and Berkshire and Oxford Diocesan Registry
Bodleian Library
Oxford OX1 3BG, England

Historical and Genealogical Societies

Oxford Family History Society
% Hon. Sec., K. Mary Beck

90 Hockmore Tower, Cowley Centre,
Oxford, England
(*Journal of Oxford Family History Society*, 1977–)

Rutland
See Leicestershire and Northamptonshire Record Offices

Salop (Shropshire)

County Archives

Salop County Record Office,
New Shirehall, Abbey Foregate
Shrewsbury SY2 6ND, England

Borough Archives
Guildhall
Shrewsbury, England

Shropshire
See Salop

Somerset

County Archives

Somerset County Record Office
Obridge Road
Taunton TA2 7PU, England

Historical and Genealogical Societies

Somerset & Dorset Family History Society
M. T. Medlycott
5 Hillside Cottages
Sandford Orcas, Sherborne
Dorset, England
(*The Greenwood Tree: Newsletter of the S&DFHS*, 1975–)

Staffordshire

County Archives

Staffordshire County Record Office
County Buildings, Eastgate Street
Stafford ST16 2LZ, England

In association with:
Joint Record Office and Lichfield
    Diocesan Registry
Bird Street
Lichfield WS13 6PN, England

Also in association with:
Stafford Record Society
William Salt Library
19 Eastgate Street
Stafford, England

Suffolk

County Archives

Suffolk County Record Office (Ipswich)
County Hall
Ipswich IP4 2JS, England

Suffolk County Record Office
(Bury St. Edmunds)
Schoolhall St.
Bury St. Edmunds, IP33 1RX, England

Historical and Genealogical Societies

Suffolk Genealogy Society
Mrs. Katherine Bardwell
25 Rushmere Road
Carlton Colville
Lowestoft NR33 8DA, England
(*Suffolk Roots*, formerly *Family History Society of Suffolk*, 1975–)

Surrey

County Archives

Surrey County Record Office
County Hall
Kingston upon Thames KT1 2DN,
England

Museum and Muniment Room
Castle Arch
Guildford GU1 3SX, England

Historical and Genealogical Societies

West Surrey Borders Family History Society
Mrs. Shirley J. Brook
7 Oakfield Road, Hawley
Camberley
Surrey GU17 9EA, England
(*WSBFH Magazine,* "*Root and Branch,*" Autumn 1974–)

Sussex, East

County Archives

East Sussex Record Office
Pelham House, St. Andrews Lane
Lewes, East Sussex BN7 1UN,
England

Historical and Genealogical Societies

Sussex Family History Group
M. T. Burchall
4/33 Sussex Square
Brighton BN2 5AB
Sussex, England
(*Sussex Family History,* 1974–)

Sussex, West

County Archives

West Sussex Record Office
John Edes House, West Street
Chichester, West Sussex POI9 1RN,
England

Tyne and Wear

County Archives

Tyne and Wear County Record Office
109 Pilgrim St.,
Newcastle-upon-Tyne NE1 6QF,
England

Historical and Genealogical Societies

Northumberland & Durham Family History Society
Mr. G. Nicholson, ed.
57 Manor Park,
Concord 11, Washington,
Tyne and Wear NE37 2BU, England
(*Northumberland & Durham Family History Society,* 1975–)

Warwickshire

County Archives

Warwickshire County Record Office,
Priory Park, Cape Road,
Warwick CV34 4JS England

Historical and Genealogical Societies

Warwickshire Local History Society
47 Newbold Terrace, Leamington Spa,
Warwick, England

West Midlands

County Archives

West Midland City Library
Ratcliff Place
Birmingham 1, England

City Record Office
9 Hay Lane
Coventry, CV1, 5RF England

Historical and Genealogical Societies
Birmingham and Midland Society
for Genealogy and Heraldry
c/o F. C. Markwell
48 Howard Road
King's Hearth
Birmingham B14 7PQ
(*Midland Ancestor*, 1971–)

Westmoreland
See Cumbria Record Office

Wight, Isle of
See Isle of Wight

Wiltshire

County Archives

Wiltshire County Record Office
County Hall
Trowbridge BA14 8JG, England

Diocesan Record Office
The Wren Hall, 56C The Close
Salisbury, England

Worcester

County Archives

Worcestershire Record Office
Shirehall
Worcester WR1 1TR, England

Yorkshire, North

County Archives

North Yorkshire County Record
Office,
County Hall,
Northallerton DL7 8SG, England

Registry of Deeds
Northallerton, England

York Diocesan Records, Borthwick
Institute of Historical Research
St. Anthony's Hall, Peasholme
Green
York Y01 2PW, England

Historical and Genealogical Societies

The York Society
Mrs. B. M. Whitehead
10 Hopgrove Lane North
Yorkshire YO3 9TF, England
(Offshoot of Yorkshire Archaeolog-
ical Society—Family Studies
Section)
(*Yorkshire Family History Society
Newsletter*)

Yorkshire, South

County Archives

South Yorkshire
County Archives Service
Cultural Activities Centre, Ellin St.,
Sheffield S1 4PL, England

Yorkshire, West

West Yorkshire

West Riding Archives and Diocesan Records

Archives Department, Sheepscar
  Branch Library
Leeds LS7 3AP, England

Yorkshire Archaeological Society
Claremont, Clarendon Road
Leeds LS2 9N2, England
(*Yorkshire Archaeological Journal*,
  1869–)

County Record Office and Registry
  of Deeds
County Hall
Wakefield WF1 2QW West Yorkshire, England

Historical and Genealogical Societies

Yorkshire Archaeological Society
Family Studies Section
Mrs. M. Morton
21 Bedford Garth,
Leeds LS16 6DU, England
(*York Archaeological Society News-
  letter*)

Books and Articles

Genealogical Guides
Bartrum, Peter C.
Early Welsh Genealogical Tracts.
Cardiff, U. of Wales, 1966. 228 p.
NN ARF

Bateman, John.
The Great Landowners of Great
  Britain and Ireland: A List of
  All Owners of 3,000 Acres and
  Upwards, Worth £3,000 ... New
  Revised Edition with the Addi-
  tion of 1,300 Owners of 2,000
  Acres and Upwards. 4th ed.
London, 1883. 533 p.
NN ARF

Burke's Family Index.
London, Burke's Peerage, 1976. 200
  p., alpha A–Z.
(An index to 20,000 different family
  histories appearing in various
  Burke publications since 1826)

Burke's Landed Gentry ...
London, Burke's Peerage, 1837–
  1972. 18 editions.
(18th ed., 1965–72, 3 v., alpha, index
  v. 3)
NN ARF and ARF 73–1915 (for
  18th ed.)

Camp, Anthony J.
Collections and Indexes of the So-
  ciety of Genealogists.
(IN: *GM*, London 1961. v. 13, p. 311–
  19)
NN ARCA

Camp, Anthony J.
Tracing Your Ancestors. New cor-
  rected ed.
Baltimore, MD, GPC, 1971. 78 p.
NN APB 72-2438

Catalogue of British Family His-
  tories. 3rd ed.
London, Research Pub. Co. and the
  Society of Genealogists, 1976.
  184 p., alpha.
NN ARC 76-2718

Coldham, Peter Wilson.
English Convicts in Colonial Amer-
  ica.
New Orleans, LA, Polyanthos,
  1974–.
(v.1, Middlesex: 1617–1775; v. 2 the
  City of London: 1656–1755)
NN APK 75-16

Colwell, Stella.
Companions of the Conqueror and

Others: An Analysis of Fact and Fancy.
(IN *GM*, London, 1974. p. 611–18)
(Only 15 proven companions of William the Conqueror at Hastings in 1066)
NN ARCA

Dewey, Kathleen Menhinick.
A Monster at the Top of the Tree.
London, 1976. 126 p. (Deals with some early English royal lines)
NN APB 76-1725

Elwell, Charles.
The London Gazette as a Source of Family History.
(IN: *GM*, London, 1969. p. 45–47)
NN ARCA

The English Genealogist (formerly the *English Genealogical Helper*).
Harbor City, CA, 1975–. (Hartwell Co., 1617 W. 261st Street, Harbor City, CA 90710)

Family History.
Northgate, Canterbury, Kent, 1962–.
Institute of Heraldic and Genealogical Studies.
NN ARCA+

Fry, Edward A.
An Index of Marriages in the Gentleman's Magazine 1731–68.
Exeter, William Ollard, 1922. 396 p., alpha.
NN ARF

The Genealogical Quarterly, 1932–1975.
London (Research Pub. Co., 52 Lincoln's Inn Fields, London WC2A 3NW)
NN ARCA

The Genealogist's Magazine.
London, 1925–.
(The Society of Genealogists)
NN ARCA

Hall, Joseph.
The Genealogical Handbook for England and Wales.
Salt Lake City, UT 84103; Genealogy Inn, 157 North State Street, 1977.

Hamilton-Edwards, Gerald.
In Search of Ancestry. New ed.
London, Phillimore, 1974 (orig. 1969). 293, 4 p. index.
NN APB (1st ed.)

Harleian Society.
Publications.
London, 1869–. v. 1–. (116 v. by 1970)
NN ARCA

Harleian Society.
Registers.
London, 1877–. v.1. (88 v. by 1958)
NN ARCA

Howard, Joseph T.
Visitations of England and Wales.
London, 1893–1921. 35 v., index each v.
NN ARF

Huguenot Society of London Proceedings.
London, 1885–. (21 v. to 1970)
NN ARCA

Huguenot Society of London.
Publications.
London, 1887–1961. 47 v. (Reprinted by Kraus)
(Later volumes in Quarto Series)
Huguenot Society of London, Quarto Series, 1962–.
NN ARCA

Humphrey-Smith, Cecil R.
Ancestry Tracing and Genealogists.
(IN: *Family History*, Northgate, Canterbury, 1971. n.s., no. 10–12, p. 1–2)
NN ARCA+

Humphrey-Smith, Cecil R.
An Introduction to Medieval Genealogy. Part 2: Bibliography and Glossary.
Northgate, Canterbury, Institute of Heraldic and Genealogical Studies, 1976. 93 p.

✓ Iredale, David.
Discovering Your Family Tree: A Pocket Guide to Tracing Your English Ancestors. revised ed.
Aylesbury, Shire Pub., 1976 (orig. 1973). 72 p., index.

Jones, Jeremy, and Philip Rahtz.
How to Record Graveyards.
London, Council for British Archaeology, 7 Marylebone Rd., London NW1 5HA, 1976. 40 p.

Kaminkow, Marion.
Genealogical Manuscripts in British Libraries: A Descriptive Guide.
Baltimore, MD, Magna Charta, 1967. 140 p.
NN ARC

Major Genealogical Resources in England and Wales.
Research Papers.
Salt Lake City, UT, Genealogical Society, CJC LDS, Series A, no. 1–37.
NN APA 72-440

Mander, Meda.
Tracing Your Ancestors.

Newton Abbot, DC, 1976. 148 p., index.
NN APB 77-229

Marshall, George W.
The Genealogists' Guide, with a new introduction by Anthony J. Camp. 4th ed.
Baltimore, MD, GPC, 1967 (orig. 1903). 880 p., alpha.
(The majority of the sources noted are in NN)
NN ARC

Matthews, Constance Mary.
Your Family History and How to Discover It.
Guildford & London, Lutterworth Press, 1976. 144 p. index
NN APB 77-977

Miscellanea Genealogica et Heraldica.
London, 1868–1938.
v.1–2 (1868–76), n.s.; v.1–3 (1874, 1877, 1880); ser. 2, v.1–5 (1886–94); ser. 3, v.1–5 (1894–1904); ser. 4, v.1–5 (1904–14); ser. 5, v.1–10 (1916-38). Joseph Howard ed. ser. 1–3, W. Bruce Bannerman ed. ser. 4, A. W. Hughes Clark ed. ser. 5, index each v.
(A wealth of genealogical material)
NN ARCA

Musgrave's Obituaries Prior to 1800.
London, 1899–1901. 6 v., alpha.
(*Harleian Society Publications. v. 44–49*)
NN ARCA

Pine, Leslie G.
Sons of the Conqueror: Descendants of Norman Ancestry.

Rutland, C.E. Tuttle, 1973. 289 p.,
 index.
NN ARF 73-1751

Pine, Leslie G.
Your Family Tree: A Guide to
 Genealogical Sources.
London, Herbert Jenkins, 1961. 191
 p.
NN APB

Poole, Keith B.
Historical Heraldic Families.
Newton Abbot, DC, 1975. 167 p.,
 alpha, t of c, no index.
NN ARF 76-543

Steel, Donald J. and L. Taylor.
Family History in Schools.
London, Phillimore, 1973. (14), 183,
 (2) p. index
NN ARD 75-1003

Thomson, Theodore Radford.
A Catalogue of British Family His-
 tories. 3rd revised edition.
London, Research Pub. Co. for the
 Society of Genealogists, 1976
 (previous ed. 1928, 1935) 184p.
NN ARC 76-2718

Wagner, Sir Anthony R.
English Genealogy.
Oxford, Clarendon Press, 1960. 397
 p., index. (Chap. 6, "Strangers,"
 p. 210-37, deals with foreign
 blood in England and Chap. 7,
 "Settlers," p. 238-76, with immigrants to America.)
NN ARF

Walford, Edward.
County Families of the United
 Kingdom.
London, 1860-1920. 60 v., alpha.
NN ARF

Whitmore, John Beach.
Genealogical Guide: An Index to
 British Pedigrees in Continua-
 tion of Marshall's Genealogist's
 Guide (1903).
London, Walford Brothers, 1953.
 658 p., alpha (Also Harleian So-
 ciety Publications).
NN ARC

Willis, Arthur James.
Genealogy for Beginners.
London, E. Benn, 1955. 144 p.
NN APB

Willis, Arthur James.
Introducing Genealogy.
London, E. Benn, 1961. 95 p.
NN APB p.v. 138

Biography
Annual Register.
General Index, 1758-1819.
London, 1826. 936 p.
Births, p. 681-706; marriages, p.
 706-46; deaths, p. 851-918.
NN BAA

Bence-Jones, Mark.
The Cavaliers.
London, Constable, 1976. 206 p.,
 index.

Burchall, Michael J.
The Jordans of Gatwick in Charl-
 wood: An Outline History 1287-
 1750.
(IN: *Sussex Family Historian*,
 Brighton, 1976. v.2, no.4, p.
 112-21, chart op. p. 120)
(This illustrates long tenure of
 land, and it is indicated that
 there are Jordans still in this
 area of Sussex with 800 years of
 traceable genealogy.)

Cambridge University.
Alumni Cantabrigiensis.
Cambridge, 1922, 1954. 2 parts, 10 v.
(Part 1 to 1751, 4 v., alpha; Part 2 1752–1900, 6 v., alpha)
NN F-111541

Dictionary of National Biography ... from Earliest Times to 1900.
Oxford, Oxford U. Press, 1968 (orig. 1901). 22 v., alpha.
Supplements covering 1901–60, Oxford, 1912–71. 5 v.
NN *R-AGH 75-1514

✓ Gentleman's Magazine.
London, 1731–1868.
Annual indexes of births, marriages, deaths, preferments and bankruptcies 1731–1868.
General indexes 1731–86 v.2, 1787–1818 v.4
NN *DA

Jack, R. Ian.
Entail and Descent: The Hastings Inheritance 1370–1436.
(IN: London University, *Institute of Historical Research Bulletin*, London, 1965. v. 38, p. 1–19)
NN BAA

Keeler, Mary F.
The Long Parliament 1640–1641: A Biographical Study of Its Members.
Philadelphia, PA, 1954. 410 p.
(*American Philosophical Society Memoirs no. 36*)
NN AGH+

Kelly's Handbook.
London, Kelly's Directories, 1875–1976. 100 v. plus, alpha.
NN ARF

Obituaries from *The Times*, 1961–1970,
Including an Index to All Obituaries and Tributes Appearing in *The Times* During the Years 1961–1970.
Reading, Newspaper Archive Developments Ltd., 1975. 952 p.

Oxford University.
Alumni Oxoniensis 1500–1714.
Oxford, 1891. 4 v., alpha.
NN F-11 1539

Oxford University.
Alumni Oxoniensis 1715–1886.
Oxford, 1888. 4 v., alpha.
NN F-11 1540

Reed, Jerome V., Jr.
Index of Biographies of Englishmen 1000–1584 Found in Dissertation Theses.
Westport, CT, Greenwood Press, 1975. 688 p., index, alpha.
NN *RS-AGH 76-1301

Wedgwood, Josiah C.
History of Parliament.
London, HMSO, 1936–38. 2 v. (v.1, biographies, 1439–1509; v.2, registers, 1439–1509)
NN *RR-CM and CM

Who's Who.
London, A. & C. Black, 1849–1976, 128 v.
NN *RR-AA and AA

Who Was Who. (1897–1970)
London, Black, 1920–72. 6 v.
NN AGH

English Surnames
Bardsley, Charles W.
Dictionary of English and Welsh Surnames.

Baltimore, MD, GPC, 1967 (orig. 1901). 837 p., alpha.
NN APD

Bardsley, Charles W.
English Surnames: Their Sources and Significations.
Newton Abbot, DC, 1969 (orig. 1873). 612 p.
NN APD

✓ Dolan, J.R.
English Ancestral Names: The Evolution of the Surname from Medieval Occupations.
New York, Clarkson N. Potter, 1972. 381 p., index.
NN APD 73-722

Dunkling, Leslie.
The Guinness Book of Names.
Enfield, Middlesex, Guinness Superlatives Ltd., 1974. 256 p., index, games p. 226 ff.
(Names in all phases, first, last-name games, etc.)
NN APD 76-1434

Ewen, C. L'Estrange.
A History of Surnames of the British Isles: A Concise Account of their Origin, Evolution, Etymology and Legal Status.
London, Kegan Paul, 1931. 508 p.
(Additions and corrections)
NN APD 74-174 and APB p.v. 34

Hitchin, F. K., and S. Hitchin.
References to English Surnames 1601.
Walton-on-Thames, C.A. Bernau, 1910. lxx p., alpha.
NN ARF

Leeson, Francis.
Aliases.

(IN: *GM*, London, 1968. v.15, p. 594–99)
NN ARCA

Palgrave, D.A.
One-Name Societies.
(IN: *GM*, London, 1976. v.18, p. 296–98)
NN ARCA

Reaney, Percy Hide.
A Dictionary of British Surnames.
2nd ed. revised by R.M. Wilson.
London, Routledge and Kegan Paul, 1976. 398 p.
(1st ed. of 1958 NN APD)

Reaney, Percy Hide.
The Origin of English Surnames.
London, Routledge and Kegan Paul, 1967. 415 p., index.
NN APD

History

The Amateur Historian.
London, National Council of Social Service, 1952–67. 7 v.
(Now *The Local Historian*)
NN CA

Anglo-Saxon England, ed. by Peter Clemoes.
Cambridge, Cambridge U. Press, 1974. 4 v.

Cambridge History of the British Empire.
Cambridge, Cambridge U. Press, 1929–63. 8 v. in 9. v.1, Old Empire to 1783; v.2, Growth, 1783–1870; v.3, Empire Commonwealth, 1870–1919; v.4, British India, 1497–1858; v.5, Indian Empire, 1858–1918; v.6, Canada, Newfoundland; v.7 (1),Australia; v.7 (2), New Zealand; v.8 (2nd ed.),

South Africa, Rhodesia, High Commission Territories.
NN *R-CB

Douglas, David C.
The Domesday Monachorum of Christ Church Canterbury.
London, Royal Historical Society, 1944. 127 p., 8 folios.
NN CO+ (Canterbury)

The English Historical Review.
London, Longman, 1886–.
NN BAA

Green, Howard.
Guide to the Battlefields of Great Britain and Ireland.
London, Constable, 1973. 309 p., index.
NN JFC 75–104

Humble, Richard.
The Fall of Saxon England.
London, Barker, 1975. 242 p., index.
NN JFD 77–2440

Harrison, Kenneth.
The Framework of Anglo-Saxon History to A.D. 900.
Cambridge, Cambridge U. Press, 1976. 107 p., index.
NN JFD 76-1887

Harvey, John.
The Plantagenets. 3rd ed.
London, Severn House, 1976. 248 p., index.
(Previous eds. 1948 NN CF, 1959 NN D-12 347)

Jolliffe, T. E. A.
Angevin Kingship.
London, Adam & Charles, 1955. 358 p., index.
NN CF

Kightly, Charles.
Flodden: The Anglo-Scottish War of 1513.
London, Almark Pub., 1975. 48 p. (Great Battles)
NN JFE 76–1897

Lindsay, Jack.
The Normans and Their World.
London, Hart-Davis, MacGibbon, 1973. 530 p.
NN JFE 75–218

The Local Historian.
London, National Council of Social Service, 1968–.
NN CA 72-1598

London University.
Institute of Historical Research Bulletin.
London, 1923–.
NN BAA

McFarland, Kenneth Bruce.
The Nobility of Later Medieval England.
Oxford, Oxford U. Press, 1973. 315 p.
NN JFD 75-2493

Midland History.
Chichester, Phillimore, for the U. of Birmingham, 1971–.

Northern History.
Leeds, School of History, U. of Leeds, 1966–.
NN CA

Oxford History of England. 2nd ed.
Oxford, Clarendon Press, 1968 (orig. 1937). 15 v. (v.2, 3rd ed., 1971, Anglo-Saxon England)
NN *R-CB

Tuck, Anthony.
Richard II and the English Nobil-
ity.
London, Arnold, 1973. 255 p.
NN *R-CF 74-2084

History Bibliographies

Bibliography of British and Irish
Municipal History, ed. by G.H.
Martin and Sylvia McIntyre.
Leicester, Leicester U. Press, 1972.
v.1 (General Works, 806 p.), in-
dex.
NN JLL 75-580 and C 76-7116

British History: Classification
Schedule, Author and Title List-
ings, Chronological Listings.
Cambridge, MA, Harvard U. Press,
1975. 2 v.
(Widener Library Shelf Lists
Series no. 53–54)
NN*RG-*GR

The British National Bibliography. Annual Volume.
(A subject catalogue of new British
books, British Library, Store
Street, London WC1E 7DC)

Gransden, Antonia.
Historical Writing in England, c.
550 to c. 1307.
Ithaca, NY, Cornell U. Press, 1974.
610 p.
NN *RR-C 75-5846

Graves, Edgar B.
A Bibliography of English History
to 1485 based on "The Sources
and Literature of English History from the Earliest Times to
About 1485" by Charles Gross.
2nd ed.
Oxford, Oxford U. Press, 1975 (orig.
1915) 1,103 p.
NN *RS-CB 76-996

Gross, Charles.
Bibliography of British Municipal
History. 2nd ed.
Revised by Geoffrey H. Martin and
Sylvia McIntyre.
NN JLL 75-580 and C 75-2079

Hanham, Harold John
Bibliography of British History,
1851–1914.
Oxford, Oxford U. Press, 1976. 1636
p.

Keeler, Mary F., ed.
Bibliography of British History:
Stuart Period, 1603–1714. 2nd ed.
Oxford, Clarendon Press, 1970. 734
p.
NN *RB-C

Mullins, E.L.C.
Texts and Calendars.
London, Royal Historical Society,
1958. 674 p., index.
NN C

Norton, Jane E.
Guide to Directories.
London, Royal Historical Society,
1950. 241 p.
NN C

London

Burke, Arthur M.
Indexes to the Ancient Testamen-
tary Records of Westminster.
London, 1913. 104 p.
NN ARX (London: Westminster)

Inquisitions Post-Mortem Relating to the City of London (1485–
1577).
London, 1896–1901. 2 v.
v.1, 1485–1561; v.2, 1561–77.
(British Record Society, *Index Library*. v.15, 26)
NN ARCA

London Record Society.
Publications
London, 1965–.
(Examples: Glass, D.V. London Inhabitants Within the Walls, 1695. London, 1966. 337 p. index [*London Record Society Pub. no. 2*]; Darlington, Ida. London Consistory Wills 1492–1547. London, 1967. 206 p., index [*London Record Society Pub. no.3*]
NN CO (London)

Parish Register Sources
Bernau, Charles A.
Sixteenth Century Marriages 1538-1600.
London, C.A. Bernau, 1911. 335 p., alpha.
NN ARS

✓ Boyd, Percival. (1866–1955)
Boyd's Marriage Index.
Salt Lake City, UT, LDS microfilm, 1967. 3 series, 176 reels.
NN *ZI-126 film

✓ Boyd, Percival. (1866–1955)
Key to Boyd's Marriage Index. 2nd ed, revised.
London, Society of Genealogists, 1963. 37 p.
NN ARS

✓ Boyd, Percival. (1866–1955)
Key to the Parishes Included in Boyd's Marriage Indexes.
Salt Lake City, UT, Claire T. Wells, 1969. unpaged, alpha.
NN ARS

✓ Boyd, Percival (1866–1955)
A List of Parishes in Boyd's Marriage Index.

London, The Society of Genealogists, 1974. 44 p.
NN ARF 76-1106

Burn, John Southerden.
Registrum Ecclesiae Parochialis: The History of Parish Registers in England ... Scotland, Ireland, the East and West Indies, the Dissenters ... with Observations on Bishops' Transcripts ...
London, J.R. Smith, 1862. 296 p.
NN ARC

Canterbury, England (Province).
Faculty Office Calendars of Allegations for Marriage Licenses (1632–1865)*
London, University Microfilms Ltd., 1965. 3 reels.
Reel 1, 1632–1764; reel 2, 1765–1841; reel 3, 1841–64;* filmed at Lambeth Palace, London.
NN *ZI-223

Canterbury, England (Province).
Registry of the Vicar General Calendars of Allegations for Marriage Licences (1660–1864).
London, University Microfilms Ltd., 1965. 4 reels.
Reel 1, 1660–94; reel 2, 1694–1753; reel 3, 1754–1839; reel 4, 1839–64; from records in the Lambeth Palace Library.
NN *ZI-224

Catalogue of Parish Register Copies. Part One.
Society of Genealogists Collection. 3rd ed.
London, Phillimore, 1970. 44 p.
NN ARS 74-160

Catalogue of Parish Register Copies in the Possession of the Society of Genealogists.

Revised and enlarged.
London, the Society, 1968 (orig.
1963). 78 p., alpha.
NN ARC 76-836

Challen, William Harold.
Parish Register Typescripts.
London, Guildhall Library, 1969.
87 v. on 21 reels of microfilm.
(Table of Contents of Parish Reg-
ister Transcripts, William H.
Challen, by Mrs. Mary M. Mid-
dleton. Orange, NJ, 17 p. Desk
Room 315G)
NN *ZI-128

Cox, John Charles.
The Parish Registers of England.
London, Methuen, 1910. 290 p., in-
dex.
NN ARS

✓ Encyclopedia of Inventory of British Church Records.
Bountiful, UT, AIS, 1976. 109 p.
(Church records of England, Scotland, Wales and Ireland)

Guildhall London.
Parish Registers: A Handlist.
London, the Guildhall, 1963–64. 3
parts.
(Part 1, Parishes Within the City
of London; Part 2, Parishes Out-
side the City; Part 3, Provisional
Guide to Foreign Registers)
(Part 3 ed. rev. and enlarged, 1972)
76 p. in ARX 73-2686
NN ARX (London) 72-2613

Inventory of Church Records of
the British Isles.
Bountiful, UT, Accelerated Indexing Systems, Inc., 1976.
109 p., alpha.
(*Encyclopedia of Local History and
Genealogy Series 2, v.1*)

Litton, Pauline.
Pitfalls in Parish Registers.
(IN: *North Cheshire Family His-
torian*, Stockport, 1976. v.2, no.1,
p. 25–26; v.3, no.2, p. 44–46)
NN ARX (Cheshire) 76-1670

Marriages Licenses Bonds and Al-
legations.
(IN: *Family History*, Northgate,
Canterbury, 1967. n.s., v.1 (v.5,
no.25) p. 7–32)
NN ARCA+

National Index of Parish Registers. Donald J. Steel, et al., ed.
London, Society of Genealogists,
1966–.
v.1, General Sources of Births,
Marriages and Deaths before
1837 . . .
v.2, Sources for Nonconformist
Genealogy and Family History
v.3, Sources for Roman Catholic
and Jewish Genealogy and Family History
v.4, Southeast England
v.5, South Midlands and Welsh
Border
v.6, Southwest England
v.7, London and Home Counties
North of the Thames
v.8, Eastern England
v.9, North and East Midlands
v.10, Northwest England
v.11, Northeast England
v.12, Sources for Scottish Genealogy and Family History
v.13, Wales
NN ARS 72-1119

Original Parish Registers in Rec-
ord Offices and Libraries.
Matlock, Local Population Studies,
Derbyshire, 1975. 128 p.
. . . the First Sup. 1976. 60 p.
(Available from Tawney Hall, Mat-

lock, Derbyshire, England DE4 3BT; covers England and Wales. More registers are continually deposited, so write the appropriate office if the one you're looking for isn't listed in this pamphlet.)

Parish Maps of the Counties of England and Wales, compiled by the Institute of Heraldic and Genealogical Studies, Northgate, Canterbury, Cecil Humphrey-Smith, Director.
Logan, UT, Everton, 1977.

Parish Register Searching in England and Wales.
(IN: *Family History*, Northgate, Canterbury, 1971. n.s., v.10–12, p. 13–16)
NN ARCA+

Parish Register Society.
Registers.
London, 1896–1922. v.1–84, extra v.1 (1922).
NN ARS

Parish and Vital Records Listings of the Genealogical Department of the Church of Jesus Christ of Latter-day Saints.
Salt Lake City, UT, LDS, 1976. 246 p.
England, p. 13–184; Ireland, p. 195–98; Scotland, p. 229; Wales, p. 243–46

Society of Genealogists.
Parish Register Copies.
London, Phillimore, 1974–75. 2 parts.
Part 1, Society of Genealogists Collection, 3rd ed. updated;

Part 2, Other Than the Society of Genealogists Collection, 1st ed. updated.

Society of Genealogists.
A List of Parishes in Boyd's Marriage Index.
London, Phillimore, 1974. 44 p.
NN ARF 76-1106

Survey of Parish Registers Diocese of London, Inner London Area.
London, Greater London Record Office, 1972. (1st ed. 1968)
80 p., index.
NN ARX (London) 72-2856

Willis, Arthur J.
Diocesan Records as Sources for Genealogists.
(IN: *GM*, London, 1966. v.15 p. 165–74)
NN ARCA

Willis, Arthur J.
Register of Persons Who Have Provided Certificates of Settlement.
(IN: *Hampshire Family Historian*, 1975. v.2, no.1, p. 10–13)
NN (Geneal. Div.)

The Peerage

Burke, John, and John B. Burke.
Extinct and Dormant Baronetcies. 2nd ed.
London, J.R. Smith, 1844. 645, 5 p.
NN ARL (Reprinted by GPC in 1977)

Burke, Sir John Bernard.
A Genealogical History of the Dormant, Abeyant, Forfeited and Extinct Peerages of the British Empire. New ed.
London, Wm. Clowes for Burke's Peerage, 1962

(orig. 1883). 642 p., alpha, cross-index.
NN ARL

Burke's Guide to the Royal Family.
London, Burke's Peerage, 1973. 358 p., no index.
(Accounts of Anglo-Saxon, English, Scottish and Welsh kings and an attempt to conjugate all the descendants of George II, which is a little confusing in the Burke format.)
NN ARF 75-1005

Burke's Peerage, Baronetage, and Knightage.
London, Burke's Peerage, 1826–1970. 105 v.
(Next edition scheduled for 1980)
NN ARM

Camp, Anthony J.
The Matrilineal Descent of Queen Victoria.
(IN: *GM*, London, 1960. v.13, p. 241–44)
NN ARCA

Clay, John W.
Extinct Peerages of the Northern Counties of England.
London, James Nisbet, 1913. 255 p.
NN ARL

Cokayne, George E.
Complete Baronetage.
Exeter, Wm. Pollard, 1900–06. 5 v., index each v.
NN APK

Cokayne, George E.
Complete Peerage.
London, St. Catherine Press, 1910–59. 13 v. in 15.
(Lists all peers but only the direct line)
NN ARK

(Collins, Arthur.)
Collins' Peerage of England, ed. by Sir Egerton Brydges.
London, 1812. 9 v., index v.9.
(Lists peers of the period with all issue of the peers and their ancestors. Caution should be used with the early ancestry, but many documents are cited as sources.)
NN ARN

Debrett's Peerage of England, Scotland and Ireland . . .
compiled by John Debrett.
London, John Debrett, 1802–.
NN has 1817 (11th ed. with some gaps)
NN ARM

Felberman, Louis.
The House of Teck: A Romance of a Thousand Years.
London, J. Long, 1911. 316 p., 63 plates, 2 charts.
(The ancestry of Queen Mary, wife of King George V)
NN ATR (Teck)

Hamilton, Gerald.
Blood Royal.
London, A. Gibbs and Phillips, 1964. 178 p., ports.,
gen. tables.
NN D-15 1568

Hankinson, Cyril.
My Forty Years with Debrett.
London, Robert Hale, 1963. 223 p., index.
NN ARM

Milner, Walter M.H.
The Royal House of Britain: An Enduring Dynasty.
London, 1933. 44 p., gen. tables.
(Tabular pedigree with a thousand

names showing descents from the royal house of Judah and King David)
NN ARF

Montagu of Beaulieu, Edward J.B. Douglas-Scott-Montagu, Baron.
More Equal than Others: The Changing Fortunes of British and European Aristocracies . . . Foreword by Sir Iain Moncreiffe of That Ilk.
New York, St. Martin's Press, 1972. 222 p.
NN JFD 72-2893

Montague-Smith, Patrick.
The Ancestry of Captain Mark Phillips.
(IN: *GM*, London, 1973. v.17, p. 407–19)
NN ARCA

Montague-Smith, Patrick.
The Royal Line of Succession.
London, Pitkin Pictorials, 1970. 24 p.
NN ARF 72-1298

Pinches, J.H., and R.V. Pinches.
The Royal Heraldry of England.
London, Heraldry Today, 1974. 334 p., index, gen. tables.
NN AWN 75-2008

Pine, Leslie G.
The New Extinct Peerage, 1884–1971
London, Heraldry Today, 1973. 313 p., index.
NN ARL 73-1939

Pryce, Frederick R.
The Princes of Wales Since 1377.
(IN: *GM*, London, 1969. v.16, p. 6–8)
(Genealogical chart showing descendants from five daughters of Llewelyn the Great for the Prince of Wales)
NN ARCA

Pryce, Frederick R.
Royal Descents.
(IN: *GM*, London, 1974. v.17, p. 527–31)
NN ARCA

Roberts, Gary Boyd.
The Mowbray Connection: An Analysis of the Genealogical Evaluation of Continental, British and American Nobilities, Gentries and Upper Classes Since the End of the Middle Ages.
Boston, MA, 1966–75. 16 v. Section I, v.1-4; Section II, v. 1–12, index.
NN ARB 75-858

Roberts, Gary Boyd.
The Mowbray Connection. (IN: *The Connecticut Nutmegger*. Hartford, CT, 1977. v.10 pp. 3–12ff) A description of his vast work on the connections of Thomas Mowbray, Duke of Norfolk.
NN APR (Connecticut) 74-726

Round, John Horace (1854–1928)
Peerage and Pedigree.
London, 1910. 2 v., index.
NN ARN 74-2310

Rowse, Alfred L.
The Churchills: The Story of a Family.
New York, Harper & Row, 1966. (orig. 1956). 577 p., index.
NN ARZ (Churchhill)

Ruvigny and Ravenel, Melville, Marquis de.
Plantagenet Roll of the Blood Royal.

1903–11.
London, 5 v.
NN ARF

Squibb, George Drewry.
Founder's Kin, Privilege and Pedigree.
Oxford, Clarendon Press, 1972. 245 p., index.
NN ARF 77-158

Tauerschmidt, Edward.
Prince Albert's Ancestry: A Brief Historical Account of the Dukedom and Ducal House of Saxe-Coburg and Gotha.
London, Black and Armstrong, 1840. 107 p.
NN EPK

Thomas, Phillip M.
The Paternal Ancestry of the Duke of Edinburgh, Scion of the House of Oldenburg.
(IN: *GM*, London, 1966. v.15, p. 175–81, 305–06)
NN ARCA

Turner, Clare Forbes.
The Name Mountbatten-Windsor.
(IN: *GM*, London, 1972. v.17, p. 123–24)
NN ARCA

Wagner, Sir Anthony R.
The Ancestry of Mr. Anthony Armstrong-Jones.
(IN: *GM*, London, 1959–61. v.13, p. 97–103, 129–33, 280–81)
NN ARCA

Warner, Phillip.
A Guide to Castles in Britain: Where to Find Them and What to Look For.
London, New English Library, 1976. 166 p., 16 p. of plates.

Watney, Vernon J.
The Wallop Family.
Oxford, John Johnson, 1928. 4 v., alpha, index.
(Good guide to many gentle and noble families of Great Britain and royal continental lines of the Middle Ages)
NN ARZ+ (Wallop)

Wotton, Thomas.
English Baronetage.
London, 1741. 4 v. in 5.
NN ARN

Records
Archives: The Journal of the British Records Association.
London, 1949–.
NN C

Batts, John S.
British Manuscript Diaries of the Nineteenth Century ...
Totowa, NJ, Rowan & Littlefield, 1976. 345 p.
NN *RS-AGH 76-5454

Bell, A.S.
The Historical Manuscripts Commission and the Genealogist.
(IN: *GM*, London, 1966. v.15, p. 207–12)
NN ARCA

Beresford, Maurice.
The Lost Villages of England.
London, Lutterworth, 1954. 445 p.
NN CAB

Bond, Maurice.
The Records of Parliament.
Canterbury, Phillimore, 1964. 54 p.
NN APB p.v. 158

British Record Society.
Index Library.

London, 1888–.
(Indexes of wills, administrations, marriages, chancery proceedings, Inquisitiones Post Mortem.)
NN ARCA

Catholic Record Society.
Publications.
London, 1905–73 plus. 64 v. to 1973.
NN ARCA

✓ Chambers, D.S.
Faculty Office Registers 1534–1549.
Oxford, Clarendon Press, 1966. 394 p., surname index.
(Contains dispensations for marriages, wills, etc.)
NN E-13 1912

✓ Crockford's Clerical Directory.
London, 1858–1975 plus.
(1973–74 85th issue by Oxford U. Press, 1975. 1,451 p. plus worldwide map section)
Alphabetical biographies of clergymen with addresses and indexes of parishes in Great Britain, Ireland and Overseas Dominions that give the names of the clergymen associated with them.
NN *RR-A

Devon and Cornwall Record Society.
% Devon and Exeter Institution, 7 the Close, Exeter.
(*DCRS Publications*, Exeter, 1904–, old and new series)
NN ARX (Devon) and CO (Devon) 74-760

Documents in the Public Record Office: 1-3.
(IN: *Amateur Historian*, London, 1965. v.6, p. 192–97, 235–42, 254–59)

1: Michael Godfrey, "Personal Records of Officers in the British Army"
2: Mary McGuiness, "Inquisitions Post-Mortem"
3: J. Fins, "The Early Chancery Proceedings"
NN CA

Emmison, Frederick George.
Archives and Local History. 2nd ed., revised.
Chichester, Phillimore, 1974. 112 p., index.
NN ARF 75-1005

England and Wales . . .
(IN: *Genealogical Helper*, Logan, UT, 1977. v.31, no.1, p. 3–17) Articles by Frank Smith, David Gardner and Lord Teviot.
NN APA

Farrant, Sue.
Some Records of the Old Poor Law as Sources of Local History.
(IN: *The Local Historian*, London, 1976. v.12, p. 136–38)
(Settlement papers, etc.)
NN CA 72-1598

Gardner, David E., and Frank Smith.
Old English Handwriting: Latin Research Standards and Proceedings.
Salt Lake City, UT, Bookcraft, 1964. 158 p., index.
(v.3, Genealogical Research in England and Wales)
NN ARC

Godfrey, M.
British Military Records as Sources of Biography and Genealogy.
(IN: *GM*, London, 1969. v.16, p. 1–5)
NN ARCA

Great Britain Historical Manuscripts Commission.
Guide to Reports. Index of Persons. 1870–1911.
London, HMSO, 1935–38. 2 v., A–Z.
NN C

Great Britain Public Record Office.
Guide to the Contents of the Public Record Office.
(Revised to 1960 from the Guide of the late M.S. Giuseppi)
London, HMSO, 1963. 2 v.
(v.1, Legal Records; v.2, State Papers and Departmental Records)
NN C

Great Britain Public Record Office.
Handbook, by F. S. Thomas.
London, HMSO, 1853. 482 p., index.
NN C

✓ Hamilton-Edwards, Gerald.
Family History Material in Registers of Deeds.
(IN: *GM*, London, 1970–71. v. 16, p. 389–99, 457–99, 517–35)
NN ARCA

Historical Association. London. Local History Committee.
English Local History Handlist ...
London, 1969. 84 p. (Helps for Students of History no. 69)
NN CAB 75-2795

✓ Hogg, Nigel.
Registration of Title to Land.
(IN: *GM*, London, 1966. v.15, p. 212–21)
NN ARCA

Holloway, Derrick R. Le B.
A Probate Handbook. 4th ed.
London, Oyez Pub., 1976. 311 p., index.

Hoskins, W.G.
Local History in England. 2nd ed.
London, Longman, 1972 (orig. 1959).
NN CAB 74-1677

Iredale, David.
Local History Research and Writing ...
Morley, Leeds, Elmfield Press, 1974. 225 p., index.
NN CAB 75-2519

Leeson, Francis.
Government Life Annuity of 1745.
(IN: *Blackmansbury*, Bridge Place, 1968. v. 5, sup. p. 1–40)
NN ARCA

List and Index Society.
Registers.
London, HMSO, 1965–. 132 v. by 1976.
(v.97, 98, 109, Chancery Patent Rolls 1–6, James I in N-10 2403)
NN N-10 2408 and N-10 2403

List and Index Society.
Special Series.
London, 1968–. 10 v. by 1976.
NN N-10 2661

Litton, Pauline M.
Comments on the Census Returns.
(IN: *North Cheshire Family Historian*, Stockport, Cheshire, Aug. 1976. v.3, no.3, 71–74)
NN ARX (Cheshire) 76-1670

Litton, Pauline M.
Fact, Fiction and a Foundling.
(IN: *North Cheshire Family Historian*, Stockport, Cheshire, Feb. 1976. v.3, no.1, p. 7–9)
NN ARX (Cheshire) 76-1670

Marriage Licenses, Bonds and Allegations.
(IN: *Family History*, Canterbury,

Jan. 1967. v.5, no.25, n.s., v.1, p. 7–32)
(Shows where original and printed records can be found)
NN ARCA+

Monger, R.F.
Emigrants in Public Records.
(IN: *GM*, London, 1969–70. v.16, p. 135–43, 197–201)
NN ARCA

Newton, K.C.
Reading Medieval Local Records.
(IN: *Amateur Historian*, London, 1966. v.7, p. 88–91)
NN CA

Peskett, Hugh.
Leases for Lives.
(IN: *GM*, London, 1973. v.17, p. 327–29)
NN ARCA

Preston, Jean.
Collections of English Historical Manuscripts.
(IN: *Archives*, 1963. v.6, p. 95–107)
NN CA

Rendel, Rosemary.
Catholic Record Society Sources and Their Uses in Family History.
(IN: *Cheshire Family Historian*, Chester, Oct. 1974. no.4, p. 15–17)
NN ARX (Cheshire) 76-1670

Richardson, John.
The Local Historian's Encyclopedia.
New Barnet, Historical Publications, 1974. 312 p., index.
(A paperback called "minor masterpiece of compression")
NN JFL 75-3222

Sheppard, Walter Lee, Jr.
Feudal Genealogy.
Washington, DC, 1976. 32 p. (*NSGSP*, no. 39)
NN APGA

Smith, Frank.
Immigrants to America Appearing in English Records.
Logan, UT, Everton, 1976. 117 p., index.

Spufford, Peter.
Population Mobility in Pre-Industrial England.
(IN: *GM*, London, 1973–74. p. 17, 420–29, 475–81, 537–43)
Part 1: The Pattern of Migration
Part 2: The Magnet of the Metropolis
Part 3: Conclusion
NN ARCA

Squibb, George Drewry.
Visitation Pedigrees and the Genealogist.
Canterbury, Phillimore, 1968. 48 p. (Phillimore Handbooks no. 4)
NN ARD 72-19

Stephens, W.B.
Sources for English Local History.
Manchester, Manchester U. Press, 1973. 260 p., index.
NN CAB 74-653

West, John.
Village Records.
London, Macmillan, 1962. 208 p., index.
NN CAB

Wrigley, Edward Anthony.
Identifying People in the Past.
London, Edward Arnold, 1973. 159 p.
NN JFE 74-2184

Wills, Chancery Proceedings, etc.

British Record Society.
Index Library.
London, 1888–. 84 v. by 1969.
Indexes of wills, administrations,
marriages, bonds, IPMS, chancery proceedings, etc.
(PCC wills 1383–1700: v.10–11, 18,
25, 43, 44, 54, 61 (2 pts.), 67, 71,
77, 80; Admin. 1581–1660 v.68,
72, 74, 75, 76, 81, 83)
NN ARCA

Camp, Anthony J.
Wills and Their Whereabouts:
Being a Thorough Revision and
Extension of the Previous Work
of the Same Name by B.G. Bouwens.
Canterbury, Phillimore, 1963 (orig.
1939). 137 p., index.
NN ART

Camp, Anthony J.
Wills and Their Whereabouts. 4th
ed. revised and extended.
London, the author, 84 Cornwall
Gardens, London SW7 4AY,
1974.
263 p., index.

Canterbury, England (Province).
Prerogative Court.
Administrations in the PCC
1559–1580, compiled by Reginald
M. Glencross.
Exeter, William Pollard, 1912–17.
2 v. (v.1, 1559–71; v.2, 1572–80)
NN ART

Canterbury, England (Province).
Prerogative Court.
Letters of Administrations. PCC
Administrations 1620–1630.

London, J.H. Morrison, 1935. 162
p., alpha, index.
NN ART

Canterbury, England (Province).
Prerogative Court.
PCC Wills 1661–1670.
London, J.H. Morrison, 1935. 334 p.
NN ART

Canterbury, England (Province).
Prerogative Court.
... Register "Scroope" (1630); Abstracts and Index.
London, J.H. Morrison, 1934. 280
p., index.
NN ART

Canterbury, England (Province).
Prerogative Court.
Probates and Sentences, 1620–1629.
London, John and George F. Matthews, 1911. v.1, 1620–24.
NN ART

Canterbury Year Book of Probates,
1630–1655.
London, John and George F. Matthews, 1902–28.
v.1–8 plus extra v. (Sentences in
PCC 1630–1639)
NN ART

Coldham, Peter Wilson.
American Administration and Probate Acts in the P.C.C. ...
(IN: *NGSQ*, Washington, DC,
1973–77. v.61, p.183–88, 278–84
(1700–1710); v.62, p.54–59
(1711–15), 91–95 (1716–20),
282–86 (1721–25); v.64, p.128–32
(1726–30), 189–96 (1731–40); v.65,
p. 195–203 (1741–50) ff.)
NN APGA

Coldham, Peter Wilson.

Genealogical Gleanings in England.
(IN: *NGSQ*, Washington, DC, 1971–77. v.59, p.175–81, 283–95; v.60, p.13–21, 88–93, 180–87, 256–66; v.61, p.34–39, 115–17; v.62, p.34–46, 119–212, 270–75; v.63, p.39–48, 130–38, 193–203, 291–95; v.64, p.45–53, 137–46, 213–26, 285–93; v.65 pp.135–45, ff.)
NN APGA

Currier-Briggs, Noel.
English Wills of Colonial Families.
Cottonport, LA, Polyanthos, 1972. 209, [5], 24, [xlvi]p., index.
NN APR (Virginia) 73-688

A Digest of Essex Wills with Particular References to Names of Importance in the American Colonies.
(IN: *NYGBR*, New York, 1909–11. v.40, p.4–9, 108–14, 155–59, 276–80; v.41, p.56–60, 142–45, 175–81, 367–72; v.42, p.50–57, 193–201, 319–21)
NN *R-APGA

Emmison, F.G., and Olwen Hall.
Life and Death in Foulness, 1503–1632.
(IN: *Essex Journal, Incorporating Essex Review*, Chichester, Sussex, Phillimore, 1975. v.10, p. 2–31)
(Abstracts of 48 wills of the inhabitants in this Essex parish)
NH CO (Essex)

Garrett, R.E.F.
Chancery and other Proceedings.
(IN: *GM*, London, 1965. v.15, p. 97–103, 139–44)
NN ARCA

Genealogical Abstracts of Wills Proved in P.C.C. Register.
Wooton, 1658.
Leeds, William Brigg, 1894–1914. 7 v.
NN ART

Gibson, Jeremy S.W.
Wills and Where to Find Them.
Chichester, Sussex, Phillimore, 1974. 210 p., index, maps.
NN ART 74-2638

Great Britain. Courts. Court of Chancery.
Calendar of Inquisitions Miscellaneous (Chancery) Preserved in the Public Record Office.
London, HMSO, 1916–68. 7 v.
(v.1, 1219–1307; v.2, 1307–49; v.3, 1348–77; v.4, 1377–88; v.5, 1387–93; v.6, 1392–99; v.7, 1399–1422)
NN C

Great Britain. Courts. Court of Chancery.
Calendar of the Inquisitions Post-Mortem and Other Analogous Documents Preserved in the Public Record Office.
London, HMSO, 1898–1970. 18 v.
(Series 1, v.1 [Henry III]; v.2–4 [Edward I]; v.5–6 [Edward II]; v.7–14 [Edward III]; v.15 [Richard II]; Series 2, v.1–3 [Henry VII])
NN C (Series 1) and C-75-968 (Series 2)

Great Britain. Courts. Court of Chancery.
Calendar of the Patent Rolls Preserved in the Public Record Office.
London, HMSO, 1891–1966. 69 v.
NN C

Hastings, Mrs. Russell.
Calvert and Darnell Gleanings from England.
(IN: *MHM*, Baltimore, MD, 1926–27. v.21, p. 303–24; v.22, p. 1–22, 115–38, 211–45, 307–49)
NN IAA

Index of Wills in the York Registry. Workshop, 1888–1934. 14 v.
(Wills in the Exchequer and Prerogative Courts of York 1389–1688)
(Yorkshire Archaeological Society. Record Series. v.6, 11, 14, 19, 22, 24, 26, 28, 32, 35, 49, 60, 68, 89)
NN CO (Yorkshire)

Lea, J. Henry, and J.R. Hutchinson.
Clues from English Archives Contributory to American Genealogy.
(IN: *NYGBR*, New York, 1909–13. v.40, p. 80–86, 177–85, 229–40; v.41, p.4–9, 72–82, 183–91, 278–86; v.42, p.92–100, 168–76, 294–301, 430–34; v.43, p.67–73; v.44, p.116–24)
NN *R-APGA

Moore, John S.
The Goods and Chattels of our Forefathers, Frampton Cotterell and District Probate Inventories, 1539–1804.
Chichester, Phillimore, 1976. 320 p.

P.C.C. Wills and Administrations "B" 1801–1804.
(IN: *Blackmansbury*, 1964–69. v.1, no.5 and 6 sup. p.9–12; v.5, no.5 and 6 sup. p.13–16; v.6, Oct./Dec. sup. p.17–40)
NN ARCA

Salley, A.S.
Abstracts from the Records of the Court of Ordinary of the Province of South Carolina, 1692–1700.
(IN: *SCGM*, Charleston, 1907–12. v. 8, p. 164–72, 195–210; v. 9, p. 73–77, 187–88; v. 10, p. 10–19, 83–91, 136–44, 236–44; v. 11, p. 50–56; v. 12, p. 70–77, 146–52, 207–14; v. 13, p. 56–63, 84–88)
NN *R-APR (South Carolina)

Sheehan, Michael M.
A List of Thirteenth Century English Wills.
(IN: *GM* London, 1961. p. 259–65)
NN ARCA

Smith, D.M.
A Guide to the Archive Collections in the Borthwick Institute of Historical Research.
York, University of York, 1973. 218 p. (Borthwick Texts and Calendars 1)
(Sup. 1973–1975. In: *Borthwick Institute Bulletin*, , York, 1975. v.1, no.1)
NN CO (York: Diocese) 74-632

Waters, Henry F.
Genealogical Gleanings in England.
Boston, 1914 (orig. 1901). 2 v. (Also available from GPC in a later reprint)
NN ARF

Withington, Lothrop.
South Carolina Genealogical Gleanings in England.
(IN: *SCGM*, Charleston, 1903–10. v. 4, p. 231–38, 286–95; v.5, 100–7, 218–28; v.6, p. 20–28, 117–25, 169–73; v.7, p. 27–30, 143–152; v.8, p. 211–19; v.9, p. 78–84; v. 11, p. 129–32)
NN *R-APR (South Carolina)

Withington, Lothrop, and Leo Culleton.

✓ Virginia Gleanings in England.
(IN: *VM*, Richmond, VA, 1914–24.
  v.22 [1914], p. 396–400
  v.23[1915] p. 53–61, 161–66, 239–49,
    280–93 [index of abstracts of
    English wills]
  v.24 [1916], p. 22–28, 66–69, 261–70
  v.25 [1917], p. 53–61, 161–66, 239–49,
    389–99
  v.26 [1918], p. 32–40, 145–50, 267–82,
    380–87
  v.27 [1919], p. 50–58, 150–56, 289–
    308 [will of Daniel Horsemanden
    of Maidstone, Kent], 289–90
  v.28 [1920], p. 26–40, 128–41, 235–40,
    340–45
  v.29 [1921], p. 36–44, 344–55, 431–38
  v.30 [1922], p. 38–44, 274–79, 362–67
  v.31 [1923], p. 164–67, 237–44, 319–25
  v.32[1924], p. 175–82, 260–64, 351–59)
NN *R-APR (Virginia)

NORTHERN IRELAND (BELFAST)

Northern Ireland comprises the six predominantly Protestant countries of Antrim, Armagh, Down, Fermanagh, Londonderry and Tyrone, collectively known as Ulster, which form the northern part of the island of Ireland. Ulster was part of Catholic Ireland until the reign of Elizabeth I (1558–1603) when, after crushing three Irish rebellions, the Crown confiscated lands in Ireland and settled in Ulster Scot Presbyterians. Another rebellion in 1641–61, brutally crushed by Oliver Cromwell, resulted in the settlement of Anglican Englishmen in the area and subsequent political policy favored continuing Protestant settlement. The North separated from the South when William Gladstone presented his proposal for home rule in Ireland in 1886. Although, like the Catholics in the south, the Protestants in the north had grievances, they feared domination by the Catholic majority. An act of the British Parliament in 1920 divided northern from southern Ireland, each with a parliament and government. While Ireland became a dominion in 1921 and later a republic, Northern Ireland remained part of the United Kingdom. Relations improved between North and South, but the Irish Republican Army, outlawed in recent years, continued the struggle to end the partition of Ireland. Since 1960 the dispute has been marked by rioting, street fighting and terrorism involving branches of the I.R.A., Protestant groups, police and British troops. More than 1,300 persons were killed between 1969 and 1975. In 1972 Britain imposed direct rule from London after dissolving the Ulster parliament.

Archives

The Public Record Office
66 Balmoral Avenue
Belfast BT9 6NY, Northern Ireland

Chief Herald of Ireland
Dublin Castle
Dublin 2, Ireland

The College of Arms
Queen Victoria Street
London, EC4V 4BT, England

Public and Church Records

The General Register Office holds certificates of births, deaths and marriages in Northern Ireland since 1922. Certified copies of earlier records can be obtained from the Superintendent Registrars and District Registrars of the areas where the events occurred. The main records prior to 1922 are kept at the General Register Office, Custom House, Dublin.

General Register Office
Oxford House
49-55 Chichester Street
Belfast BT1 4HL, Northern Ireland

For divorce records: Chief Registrar
High Court of Justice in Northern Ireland
Principal Registry, Royal Courts of Justice
Belfast 1, Northern Ireland

Libraries

Belfast Public Libraries
Central Library
Royal Avenue,
Belfast BT1 1EA, Northern Ireland

Each of six counties has its own county library.

Historical and Genealogical Societies

The Ulster-Scot Historical Foundation
66 Balmoral Avenue
Belfast BT9 6NY, Northern Ireland

Ulster-Scot Historical Society
Law Courts Bldg., Chichester St.
Belfast, Northern Ireland

Presbyterian Historical Society
Church House, Fisherwick Place
Belfast 1, Northern Ireland

Books and Articles

Deutsch, Richard.
Northern Ireland 1921–1974, A Select Bibliography.
New York, Garland Pub., 1975. 142 p.
NN JFD 76-5624

Falley, Margaret Dickson. ✓
Irish and Scotch-Irish Ancestral Research...
Evanston, IL, the author, 1962. 2 v. index each v.
NN APD

Northern Ireland. Ordnance Survey.
Gazetteer of Northern Ireland. . .
Belfast, HMSO, 1969. 80p.
NN Map Division 74-293

Potterton, Homan.
Irish Church Monuments, 1570–1880.

Belfast, Ulster Architectural Heritage Society, 1975. 98p.
NN 3-MGI 76-1308

See also: Ireland, in European section, for an additional bibliography

SCOTLAND (EDINBURGH)

The Romans were unable to conquer the Picts and Celts of Scotland (which took its name from the Scots, who originally inhabited Ireland and eventually became the dominant race of this country in northern Britain). Christianity was brought to the country by St. Ninian (living 397) and by St. Columba of Ireland, who settled on Iona about 563. In the ninth century Kenneth I MacAlphin (d. 858–59) became the first united King of Scots and Picts. Malcolm III Canmore (c. 1031–93) married the English Princess (St.) Margaret, and her influence brought many English and Norman families to Scotland—among them the Bruces and Walter, son of Alan, ancestor of the Stewarts. In the disputed succession to the throne among the descendants of David, Earl of Huntington, which followed the death of Alexander III in 1286, one of the claimants was Robert De Bruce (1210–95). His grandson, the national hero Robert the Bruce (1274–1329), was crowned at Scone in 1306. His daughter, Marjorie, married Walter, 6th High Steward of Scotland, and their son Robert II (1315–16—1390) was the first of the Stewart (Stuart) family to reign. Queen Elizabeth is Queen of Scotland today as the descendant of this line. The battles of Bannockburn (1314), won by the English, and Flodden (1513), in which the English killed James IV and most of the Scottish nobility, stand out as important events in the continuing dispute between England and Scotland, which persisted until James VI, son of Mary, Queen of Scots, became James I of England at the death of his cousin, Queen Elizabeth I, in 1603. When the Roman Catholic King James II of England was deposed in 1688, he had numerous supporters (called Jacobites) in Scotland and Northern Ireland. Many of them were in the Jacobite forces who were defeated at the Battle of Boyne in 1690 when he attempted to regain the throne. His son, Charles Edward Stuart ("Bonnie Prince Charlie,"

1720–88), is one of the great romantic figures in eighteenth-century Scottish history, along with Flora Macdonald, who helped him escape after the disastrous battle at Culloden Moor in 1746. Great turmoil in Scotland and Northern Ireland in the seventeenth and eighteenth centuries sent many Scots—including shiploads of prisoners who went against their will—to the American colonies. Even Flora Macdonald and and her husband, Angus Macdonald, immigrated to North Carolina in 1774. Today there is a strong Scottish strain in the United States and Canada, reflected in numerous flourishing Scottish organizations, and the chiefs of some clans are Americans. The American Scottish Foundation of New York, under the leadership of Lady Malcolm Douglas-Hamilton, has been active as a liaison with Scottish societies and has recently opened Scotland House (124 East 39th Street, New York, NY) as a center for Americans of Scottish descent. There are some unique features which will be found in undertaking genealogical research in Scottish records. The Scottish parish registers prior to January 1, 1855, when central registration of vital records commenced, are gathered together at the New Register House in Edinburgh. Some of these registers date from the 16th century, but for the most part they begin in the 17th and 18th centuries. The original records are now being replaced by film copies, as they are deteriorating from the constant use that they are receiving. As a rule married Scottish women are listed under their maiden names in the parish registers and other records, which is useful for genealogists.

The registers of sasines (1617-to date) dealing with the descent of land and the centrally registered deeds (1661 to date) are deposited in the Scottish Record Office, and many of the indexes of these records have been and are continuing to be published. The commissariot records dealing with the probate of estates are in this same depository, or in the local Sheriff Courts. The indexes to the service of heirs for Scotland have been published in English for the period from 1700 to 1860 on a decennial basis and annually after that date to the present day. Records of earlier inheritances prior to 1700 have been published in Latin, as noted in the bibliography.

Census records in Scotland are available after 70 years, rather than 100 years. In Scotland since 1930, the original birth certificates of adoptees have been available to them when they reach their majority.

The guides for Scottish genealogy by Margaret Stuart, Joan Ferguson, Gerald Hamilton-Edwards and Donald J. Steel should be consulted by all who are interested in Scottish research. A new guide to the Scottish Record Office will be published in the near future and it should be of great use.

The most common surnames in Glasgow are Brown, Campbell, McDonald (MacDonald), Smith, Thomson (Thompson) and Wilson.

Archives

Scottish Record Office
P.O. Box 36
H.M. General Register House
Edinburgh EH1 3YT, Scotland

The Court of the Lord Lyon is the official registry of coats of arms, including crests and badges for Scotland. It is the equivalent of the College of Arms in England.

Court of the Lord Lyon
H.M. New Register House
Edinburgh EH1 3YT, Scotland

Public and Church Records

The Registrar General's Office holds certificates of births, deaths and marriages in Scotland since January 1, 1855.

Registrar General
New Register House
Edinburgh EH1 3YT, Scotland

For divorce records:
Principal Clerk of Sessions
Parliament House
Parliament Square
Edinburgh EH1 1RQ, Scotland

Libraries

Mitchell Library
North Street
Glasgow G3 7DN, Scotland

National Library of Scotland
George IV Bridge
Edinburgh EH1 1EW Scotland

Royal Society of Edinburgh Library
22-24 George Street
Edinburgh, Scotland

Scottish Central Library
Lawnmarket
Edinburgh EH1 2PJ, Scotland

Historical and Genealogical Societies

Scots Ancestry Research Society
20 York Place
Edinburgh EH1 3EP, Scotland

Scottish Catholic Archives
Columbia House, 16 Drummond Place
Edinburgh EH3 6PL, Scotland

Scottish History Society
% Scottish Record Office
H.M. General Register House
Edinburgh EH1 3YY, Scotland

Scottish History Society
Dept. of History
Kings College
Aberdeen AB9 2UB, Scotland

Scottish Genealogy Society
% Hon. Secretary
21 Howard Place
Edinburgh EH3 5JY, Scotland

Scottish Tartans Society
Old Tollbooth
Stirling, Scotland

United States Sources

There are numerous clan groups
and Scottish societies in the
United States, (see *The Highlander* for addresses)

American Scottish Foundation
P.O. Box 537, Lenox Hill Station
New York, NY 10021

St. Andrew's Society of the State of
New York
281 Park Avenue South
New York, NY 10010

Books and Articles

Adam, Frank.
The Clans, Septs and Regiments of
the Scottish Highlands, revised
by Sir Thomas Innes of Learney.
Edinburgh, W. & F.A.K. Johnston,
1952. 624 p.
112 plates (8th revised ed. 1975.
Available from GPC)
NN CPE and CPE 77-769

Addington, Arthur C.
The Royal House of Stewart: The
Descendants of King James VI
of Scotland; James I of England.
London, C. Skliton, 1969–76. 3 v.
NN ARF+

Aldis, H.G.
A List of Books Published in Scot-
land before 1700. Edinburgh,
National Library of Scotland,
1970. 184 p.
NN *R-GDD 71-73

Anderson, A.
The Scottish Record Office.
(IN: *GM*, London, 1965. v. 15, p. 64–
67)
NN ARCA

Bain, Robert.
The Clans and Tartans of Scotland,
enlarged and re-edited by Mar-
garet O. MacDougall.
London, Collins, 1954. 320 p.
NN CPE

Black, George F.
The Surnames of Scotland: Their
Origin, Meaning and History.
New York, New York Public Li-
brary, 1962. 838 p.
NN APD

Brander, Michael.
Scottish and Border Battles and
Ballads.
London, Seeley, 1975. 300 p.
NN JFE 76-1558

Cargill, David C.
Irishmen in Scottish Census Rec-
ords (1851).
(IN: *Irish Ancestor*, Dundalk, 1972.
v. 4, p. 8–14)
NN ARCA 72-1448

Cargill, David C.
Pre-1855 Tombstone Inscriptions
of Berwickshire.
Edinburgh, D.C. Cargill, 1968–69.
2 v.
Surname index for each parish.
NN ARX+ (Berwick) 75-825

Donaldson, Gordon.
The Scots Overseas. London, Robert Hale, 1966. 232 p., index.
NN D-17 791

Douglas, Hugh.
Portrait of the Burns Country and Galloway.
London, Robert Hale, 1968. 190 p., index.
NN CRB (Ayrshire)

Dumfrieshire and Galloway Natural History and Antiquarian Society. Transactions.
Dumfries, 1862–.
NN *EC D888 and CR (Dumfries) 75-116 for ser. 3, v. 42, 1965–date

Dunbar, Sir Archibald H.
Scottish Kings: A Revised Chronology of Scottish History 1005–1625 ...
Edinburgh, D. Douglas, 1899. 420 p. (Pedigrees, calendars, etc.)
NN *RR-CP

Fenwick, Hubert.
Scotland's Historic Buildings.
London, Hale, 1975. 254 p.
NN JFD 76-735

Ferguson, Joan P.S.
Scottish Family Histories Held in Scottish Libraries
Edinburgh, Scottish Central Library, 1960. 194 p., alpha.
NN ARC

Fischer, Thomas A.
The Scots in Eastern and Western Prussia ...
Edinburgh, 1903. 244 p.
NN CP

Fischer, Thomas A.
The Scots in Germany ...
Edinburgh, O. Schultze, 1902. 324 p.
NN CP

Fischer, Thomas A.
The Scots in Sweden ...
Edinburgh, O. Schultze, 1907. 278 p.
NN CP

Great Britain. Public Record Commission.
Acts of Parliament in Scotland, 1124–1707.
Edinburgh, HMSO, 1844–75. 12 v. in 13.
(v. 12 index in 2 parts: A–F, G–Z)
NN CP+

Grimble, Ian.
Scottish Clans and Tartans.
London, Hamlyn, 1973. 272 p.
NN CPE 74–70

Gilchrist, George.
Memorials of Moffat Parish.
Annan, 1971. 80 p.
NN ARZ (Dumfrieshire: Moffat) 75-2102

Hamilton-Edwards, Gerald.
In Search of Scottish Ancestry.
London, Phillimore, 1972. 252 p.
NN ARF 73-1854.

Hawick Archaeological Society. Transactions.
Hawick, 1856–. index 1856–.
NN CPA (NN has 1864–)

Henderson, John A.
Aberdeenshire Epitaphs and Inscriptions with Historical, Biographical, Genealogical and Antiquarian Notes.
Aberdeen, 1907. 556 p.
NN ARX (Aberdeen)

The Highlander.
Barrington, IL 60010, 1963. (P.O. Box 397)
(A great deal of information concerning clan gatherings, etc.)
NN APGA

An Historical Atlas of Scotland, c. 400–c. 1600, ed. by Peter McNeil and Ranald Nicholson.
St. Andrews, Fife; U. of St. Andrews, 1975. 213 p.
NN Map Div. 76-812

Innes, Sir Thomas of Learney (d. Oct. 16, 1971)
Scots Heraldry. 2nd ed. revised and enlarged.
Edinburgh, Oliver & Boyd, 1956 (orig. 1934). 256 p.
NN AWN

Mackenzie, Agnes, Mure.
Foundations of Scotland, Earliest Times to 1286; Robert the Bruce, King of the Scots; Rise of the Stewarts; Passing of the Stewarts; Scotland in Modern Times.
Edinburgh, Chambers, 1934–41. 5 v.
NN *RR-CP, CP & *R-CP74-4717 (revision)

MacLean, J.
The Entries of Marriages of Scottish Soldiers in the Netherlands 1574–1665.
The Hague, Royal Netherlands Society for Genealogy and Heraldry, 1976. 420 p.
(The author has already published 11 articles in *Gens Nostra* and other Dutch genealogical periodicals covering the period from 1674–1783 since 1965.)

Maitland Club.
Publications.
Edinburgh, 1839–59. 75 v.
NN CP some scattered

Maxwell, Archibald Straith.
Scottish Society of Friends "Quakers" Register of Births, Proposal Marriage, Marriages and Deaths, 1647–1878.
Aberdeen, A.S. Maxwell, c. 1973.
NN ARS 74-1742

Maxwell, Archibald Straith.
Aberdeen, Scotland, Burials.
Aberdeen, A.S. Maxwell, c. 1969. 2 v., index each v. (v.1, 1571–1647; v.2, 1647–70)
NN ARX (Aberdeen) 73-1083

Mitchell, John Fowler and Sheila.
Monumental Inscriptions (Pre-1855) in West Lothian.
Edinburgh, 1969. 178 p.
NN APX+ (Linlithgow) 70-11

Mitchell, John F.
Monumental Inscriptions (Pre-1855) in Dumbartonshire.
Edinburgh, SGS, 1969. 206 p.
NN ARX+ (Dumbartonshire) 73-461

Mitchell, John Fowler and Sheila.
Monumental Inscriptions (Pre-1855) in East Fife.
Edinburgh, 1971. 398 p.
NN ARX+ (Fife) 72-2965

Mitchell, John Fowler and Sheila.
Monumental Inscriptions (Pre-1855) in West Fife.
Edinburgh, 1972. 172 p.
NN ARX+ (Fife) 75-57

A New History of Scotland.
London, Thomas Nelson, 1961–62.

2 v. (v.1 by William Croft, earliest times to 1603; v.2 by George S. Pryde, 1603 to present)
NN *R-CP 74-4722

New Spalding Club.
Publications.
Aberdeen, 1887. 1887–1924. 43 v.
NN CP

New York Public Library.
Works Relating to Scotland, ed. by George F. Black.
New York, NYPL, 1916. 1,233 p., index.
NN CP

Paul, Sir James B.
The Scots Peerage.
Edinburgh, David Douglas, 1904–14. 9 v., alpha by title, index v.9.
NN ARO

Perth Parish Registers.
(IN: *Scottish Antiquary* ... Edinburgh, 1886–88. v.1, p. 69–73, 99–107, 132–36, 165–70)
NN CPA

Pine, Leslie G.
The Highland Clans.
Newton Abbot, DC, 1972. 198 p., index.
NN CPE 77-57

Prebble, John.
Glencoe: The Story of a Massacre.
London, Secker & Warburg, 1966. 336 p., index.
NN CP

Rattray, W.J.
The Scot in British North America.
Toronto, 1880–83. 4 v.
NN HWH

Royal Commission on the Ancient and Historical Monuments of Scotland.
Argyll: An Inventory of the Ancient Monuments.
Edinburgh, HMSO, 1971–75. 2 v. (v.1, Kintyre; v.2, Lorn)
NN JFM 75-369

Sandison, Alexander.
Surnames Found in Shetland in 1804 and 1954.
(IN: *GM*, London, 1968. v.15, p. 500–04)
NN ARCA

Scarlett, James.
Scotland's Clans and Tartans.
Guilford, Lutterworth Press, 1975. 128 p.
NN CPE 76-1459

Scottish History Society. Publications.
Edinburgh, 1887–.
(4 series by 1974)
NN CPA

Scottish Notes and Queries.
Aberdeen, 1887–1935. (3 series)
NN CPA

Scotland.
Inquisitionum ad Capellam Domini Regis Retornatarum Quae in Publicis Archivis Scotiae Adhue Servantur Abbreviatio.
Edinburgh, 1811–16. 3v. indexed.
NN ARF plus

Scotland. Chancery Office.
Decennial Indexes to the Services of Heirs in Scotland, Commencing Jan. 1, 1700-Ending Dec. 31, 1859.
Edinburgh, HMSO, 1863–89. 4v.
2nd Series. 1860–1962 plus.
NN ARF plus

Scotland. General Register House. Indexes.
Edinburgh, HMSO, 1915–1975 plus. 70v. of Deeds (1661–1696) and Sasines of various counties, v.3 contains Gen. Register of Sasines for all counties, 1701–1720.
NN ARF plus

Scotland. General Register House. Registrum Secreti Sigilli Regum Scotorum, 1488–1580.
Edinburgh, HMSO, 1908–1966. 7v. in 8.
NN ARF

Scots Magazine. ✓
Edinburgh, 1739–1826.
Births, marriages, deaths, promotions indexed annually by surname, many American references (for example "Aug. 1802, at Charleston, S.C., James Graham Esq., formerly of His Majesty's 64th Regiment," p. 708).
NN *DA

Scottish American Heritage. Newsletter.
New York
(30 E. 60th St., N.Y. 10022)

Scottish Genealogist.
Harbor City, CA, The Augustan Society, 1974–
Queries, Ancestral lines, passenger lists, etc.
NN Current

The Scottish Genealogist.
Edinburgh, 1953, Quarterly pub. of the Scottish Genealogy Society.
% Hon. Sec. Miss Joan P.S. Ferguson
21 Howard Place
Edinburgh EH4 3PG, England

Queries, articles indexed.
NN ARCA

The Scottish Record Society. Publications.
Edinburgh, 1898–.
The old series had 160 parts by 1952. The new series began in 1969 and by 1972 issued three volumes: v.1 (1969), Fasti Ecclesia Scoticanae Medii Aevis ad Annum 1638, 2nd ed., D.E.R. Watt, ed.; v.2 (1971), Directory of Former Scottish Commonities, ed. by Ian H. Adams; v.3 (1972), Scottish Parish Clergy at the Reformation 1540–1574, ed. by Charles H. Haws. All indexed.
NN ARCA

The 1745 Association and National Military History Society.
Quarterly Notes.
Glencoe, Argyll. (no. 30, Feb. 1976) (Invercoe House, Glencoe, Argyll)
NN (Geneal. Div.)

Simpson, Grant G.
Scottish Handwriting 1150–1650.
Edinburgh, Bratton Pub., 1973. 140 p.
JFF 75-68

Sinclair, James P.
The Highlanders.
Milton, Quebec, 1971. 124 p.
NN JFF 75-1404

Smith, Colin and Robert S. Walker.
Library Resources in Scotland.
Glasgow, Scottish Library Association, 1968. 107 p.
NN JFD 71-2420

A Source Book of Scottish History.
2nd ed., revised, ed. by William C. Dickinson, Gordon Donalson and Isabel A. Milne.

London, T. Nelson, 1958–61. 3 v.
v.1, earliest times–1424; v.2,
1424–1567; v.3, 1567–1707.
NN D-13 7731

Sources for Scottish Local History.
(5 parts: 1. The Scottish Record Office—Margaret Sanderson; 2.
Kirk Session records—Rosalind
Mitchison; 3. The Scottish National Portrait Gallery—Rosalind K. Marshall; 4. Manuscript
Resources in the National Library of Scotland; 5. Estate
Plans—I.H. Adams)
(IN: *The Local Historian*, London,
National Council of Social Service, 1974–76. v.11, p. 123–29,
229–33, 382–84, 445–48, v.12, p.
26–30)
NN CA 72-1598

Spalding Club. Aberdeen.
Publications.
Aberdeen, 1841–71. 39 v.
NN CP

Steel, Donald J.
Sources for Scottish Genealogy and
Family History.
London, Phillimore for the Society
of Genealogists, 1970.
(*National Index of Parish Registers*, v.12) 320 p., index.
NN ARS 72-1119

Stewart, Donald Calder.
The Setts of the Scottish Tartans.
2nd ed., revised.
London, Shepheard-Walwyn, 1974.
xiii, 154 p.
NN CPE 76-1475

The Stewarts
Edinburgh, The Stewart Society,
1902–
(% Hon. Sec. Treas. and Ed. Doug-

las F. Stewart, 48 Castle Street,
Edinburgh EH2 3LX; has a library open to members)
NN AR2 (Stewart)

Stirling Register of Marriages,
Baptisms 1585–1589.
(IN: *Scottish Antiquary*, Edinburgh, 1891–93. v.6, p. 159–68;
v.7, p. 37–42, 70–78, 166–69)
NN CPA

Stuart, Margaret.
Scottish Family History: A Guide
to Works of Reference on the
History and Genealogy of Scottish Families.
Edinburgh, Oliver & Boyd, 1930.
386 p.
NN ARC

The Tartans of Scottish Clans with
an Introduction by Sir Iain Moncrieffe of That Ilk.
Glasgow, Collins, 1975. 176 p.

Tranter, Nigel.
Portrait of the Border Country.
London, Robert Hale, 1972. 208 p.,
index.
NN CR (Borders) 73-806

Whyte, Donald.
A Dictionary of Scottish Emigrants
to the U.S.A.
Baltimore, MD, Magna Carta, 1972.
504 p., alpha, index.
NN APK 73-1027

Whyte, Donald.
Old Parochial Registers of Scotland.
References to Parties from Ireland.
(IN: *Irish Ancestor*, Dundalk,
1971–73. v.3, p. 79–82; v.5, p. 88–
96)
NN ARCA 72-1448

WALES (CARDIFF)

The native Celtic tribes of Wales were conquered by Romans and a structured government was set up that lasted until the Romans withdrew about A.D. 400. This long occupation had a lasting effect on the language, arts, genealogy and general culture of the country. Following the Roman evacuation, from the mid-fifth to the seventh century the tribal kingdoms, including Gwynedd, Powys, Seisyllwg and Deheubarth, formed a loose federation often bound by marriage. Rhodri Mawr (the Great, died c. 878), King of Gwynedd (844), Powys (855) and Seisyllwg (872), was the first of a long line of kings to have some firm historical significance. He fought off the incursions of the Danes and was killed in battle with the English. His descendant, Llewelyn the Great, Prince of Gwynedd (d. 1240), dispossessed his uncle in 1194 and was acknowledged by the other Welsh princes as their overlord. He attempted to strengthen his ties with England in 1205 by marrying Joan (d. 1237), the natural daughter of King John. There are numerous descendants from their daughters. Following the death of his nephew Llewelyn in battle with the English in 1282, the forces of King Edward I conquered the country, and the title Prince of Wales was joined to the Crown of England. The Welsh did not give in quietly to English authority, and in the late fourteenth century Owen Glendower (c. 1359–c. 1416), a descendant of the Welsh princes, attempted without success to regain Welsh independence. The Act of Union of 1535 officially united England and Wales. In spite of obstacles the Welsh language and culture have continued to flourish to this day.

In the drastic rearrangement of local boundaries which took place in Great Britain in 1974, the counties of Wales were greatly affected. The old counties of Anglesey, Caernarvonshire (Caernarfonshire) and Merionethshire are now the new county of Gwynedd. Cardinganshire, Carmarthonshire and Pembrokeshire form the new county of Dyfed, while Denbighshire and Flintshire make up the new county of Clwyd. The name of Monmouthshire was changed to Gwent, and Brecknockshire, Radnorshire and Montgomeryshire became the new county of Powys.

Archives

National Library of Wales
Aberystwyth, Dyfed, SY23 3BU
  Wales

The College of Arms
Queen Victoria Street
London, EC4V 4BT, England

County and Local Record Offices

Clywd

Clywd County Record Office
The Old Rectory, Hawarden
Deeside, Clwyd CH5 3NR, Wales

Denbighshire Record Office
46 Clwyd Street
Ruthin, Clwyd, Wales

Dyfed

Carmarthenshire County Record
  Office
County Hall
Carmarthen SA31 1JP, Wales

Pembrokeshire Record Office
The Castle
Haverfordwest, Dyfed, Wales

Cardiganshire Record Office
Marine Terrace
Aberystwyth, Dyfed, Wales

Glamorgan

Glamorgan Record Office
County Record Office
County Hall, Cathays Park,
Cardiff, CF1 3NE, Wales

Gwent

Gwent County Record Office
County Hall
Cwmbran, Gwent NP4 2XH, Wales

Gwynedd

Gwynedd Archives Service, Area
  Record Office,
Shire Hall
Llangefni, Gwynedd LL77 7TW,
  Wales

Merionethshire Area Record Office
Y Lawnt
Dolgellau, Gwynedd, Wales

Denbighshire:
See Clwyd

Caernarfonshire Area Record Office
Gwynedd Archives Service.
County Offices.
Shirehall St., Caernarfon LL55
  1SH, Wales

Powys

National Library of Wales
Aberystwyth, Dyfed SY23 3BU,
  Wales

Public and Church Records

See England.

Libraries

Library of the National Museum
  of Wales
Cathays Park
Cardiff CF1 3NP, Glamorgan,
  Wales

National Library of Wales
Aberystwyth, Dyfed, Wales

University of Wales Libraries
Cathays Park
Cardiff CF1 1XQ Glamorgan, Wales

Books and Articles

Anglesey Antiquarian Society and Field Club. Transactions. (Trafodion)
Denbigh, Gee & Son for the Society, 1914–.
NN CVG (Anglesey)

Archeologia Cambrensis.
Journal of the Cambrian Archaeological Association.
London, 1846–.
(Index series 1–4, 1846–86; series 5, 1884–1900)
NN CVA

Bartrum, Peter C.
Welsh Genealogies A.D. 300–1400.
Cardiff, U. of Wales Press for Board of Celtic Studies, 1974. 8 v., each v. alpha., gen. tables.
NN ARF 77–355

Blackwell, Henry (1851–1928).
A Bibliography of Welsh Americana.
Aberystwyth, National Library of Wales, 1942. 92 p.
NN *HPD

Brycheiniog.
Brecknock, 1955–.
NN GVG (Brecknock)

Caernarvonshire Historical Society. Transactions.
Carnarvon, 1939–.
NN CVG (Carnarvon)

Cardiganshire Antiquarian Society. Transactions.
Aberswyth, 1910–39. v.1–14, index v.1–14, 1 v.
NN CVG (Cardiganshire)

Ceredigion. Journal of the Cardiganshire Antiquarian Society.
Llandyssul, 1950–.
NN CVG (Cardiganshire)

Clark, Arthur.
The Story of Monmouthshire.
Llandybie, Davies, 1962. 1 v., index. (Earliest times to the Civil War)
NN CO (Monmouthshire)

Cyfrol.
Aberswyth, the Cardiganshire Antiquarian Society, 1950–.
NN CVG (Cardiganshire)

Cymmrodorian Society Transactions.
London, 1893–.
(Cymmrodorian Society, 118 Newgate St., St. Paul's, London, E.C.1A 7AE)
NN CV

Davies, Sir Leonard T.
Men of Monmouthshire.
Cardiff, Western Mail, 1933. 2 v., t of c, no index.
NN CO (Monmouthshire)

Dwynn, Lewys.
Heraldic Visitations of Wales and Part of the Marches ... ed. by Sir Samuel R. Meyrick ...
Llandovty, Wm. Rees, etc., 1946. 2 v.
NN Desk Room 315G

Eames, Aled.
Ships and Seamen of Anglesey 1558–1918: Studies in Maritime and Coast History.
Denbigh, Anglesey Antiquarian Society, 1973. 674 p.
NN CVG (Anglesey) 75–2582

England. Kings Remembrancer.
The Merioneth Lay Subsidy Roll, 1292–3, ed. Keith Williams-Jones.
Cardiff, U. of Wales Press, 1976. 136 p., index.
(University of Wales, Board of Celtic Studies. History and Law Series, no.26)

Evans, Evan.
The National Library of Wales and Its Genealogical Holdings.
(IN: *Genealogical Journal*, Salt Lake City, UT, 1977. v.6, p.43–45)

Fishlock, Trevor.
Wales and the Welsh.
London, Cassell, 1972. 196 p., index.
NN CVB 77–218

Fraser, David.
Wales in History: Book I to 1066— The Invaders.
Cardiff, U. of Wales Press, 1962. 209 p.
(For children, but good overview for adults)

Gascoigne, Christina.
Castles of Britain.
London, Thames & Hudson, 1975. 224 p., index.
NN JFF 76-344

Glamorgan County History.
Cardiff, U. of Wales, 1936–74. 4 v.
(In progress)
NN CVG (Glamorgan) 73-1608

Great Britain. Ancient and Historical Monuments in Wales . . .
An Inventory of the Ancient Monuments in Caenarvonshire.
London, HMSO, 1956–60. 3 v., index each v.
NN CVG (Carnarvon)

Great Britain Courts of Quarter Sessions of the Peace (Merionethshire)
A Calendar of the Merioneth Quarter Sessions Rolls, ed. by Keith W. Jones.
Merioneth, County Council, 1965. 1 v.
(v. 1, 1733–65)
NN CVG (Merionethshire) 74-645

Gresham, Colin A.
Eifionydd: A Study in Landownership from the Medieval Period to the Present Day.
Cardiff, U. of Wales Press, 1973. 417 p.
NN JLF 73-1263

Guide to the Flintshire Record Office, ed. by A.G. Veysey, County Archivist.
Denbigh, Gee for the Flintshire County Council, 1974. 188 p., index.
(This is now the Clwyd Record Office)
NN CVG (Flintshire) 75-2280

Hilling, John B.
Wales, South and West.
London, Batsford, 1976. 208 p., index.
NN CVB 76-1645

Houses of the Welsh Countryside: A Study in Historical Geography.
Cardiff, HMSO, 1976.

Interpreting the Census Returns for Rural Anglesey and Llyn.
(IN: Anglesey Antiquarian Society and Field Club, Transactions. Denbigh, 1973. p. 111–36)
NN CVG (Anglesey)

Jones, E.D.
Material for the Genealogist in the
National Library of Wales.
(IN: *GM*, London, 1964. v. 14, p. 313–
21)
NN ARCA

Jones, Francis.
An Approach to Welsh Genealogy.
(IN: Cymmrodiorion Society,
Transactions, 1948. London,
1949. p. 303–466)
NN CV

Jones, Francis.
The Princes and Principality of
Wales.
Cardiff, U. of Wales Press, 1969.
204 p., t of c, no index, 8 gen.
charts.
NN CV 71-8

Jones, Howard C.
Place Names in Glamorgan.
Risca, Starling Press, 1976. 56, 32 p.

Kissack, Keith E.
Monmouth: The Making of a
County Town.
London, Phillimore, 1975. 345 p.,
index.
NN CO (Monmouth) 76-2711

Lewis, E.R.
North of the Hills: A History of
the Parishes of Eglwyswen,
Eglwysurn, Llanfair, Nant-
gwyn, Meline, Nevern.
Haverfordwest, C.I., Thomas, 1972.
309 p.
NN CVG (Pembroke) 75-1080

Mason, Edmund J.
Portrait of the Brecon Beacons
. . .
London, Robert Hale, 1975. 224 p.,
index.
NN CVG (Brecknock) 76-1454

Monmouthshire Pages from the
Past.
Newport, Gwent, Monmouthshire
Local History Council, 1973–.
(Monmouthshire is now Gwent.)

Morgannwg.
Transactions of the Glamorgan Lo-
cal History Society.
Cardiff, 1957–.
NN CVG (Glamorgan)

Owen, Geraint Dyfnalt.
Elizabethan Wales (The Social
Scene).
Cardiff, U. of Wales Press, 1962.
258 p.
NN CVB

The Pembrokeshire Historian.
Haverfordwest, Pembrokeshire
Community Council, 1959–.
(Pembrokeshire is now in Dyfed)
NN GVG (Pembrokeshire)

Powys-Land Club.
Collections Historical and Archae-
ological Relating to Montgom-
eryshire.
London, Newton, etc., 1868–1976
plus. 65 v. to 1976.
(Now called Montgomeryshire Col-
lections of the Powys-Land
Club)
NN CO (Montgomeryshire)

Pride, Emrys.
Rhondda My Valley Brave.
Risca, Newport, Gwent, Starling
Press, 1975. 191 p., gen. table (c.
1800–1974).
NN CVG (Rhodda Valley) 76-1990

Pryce, Frederic R.
The Princes of Wales Since 1377.
(IN: *GM*, London, 1969. v. 16, p.
6–8) (Long chart showing the

descendants from the 5 daughters of Llewelyn the Great)
NN ARCA

Pugh, T.B.
The Marcher Lordships of South Wales 1415–1536: Select Documents.
Cardiff, U. of Wales Press, 1963. 326 p.
NN CV

Senior, Michael.
Portrait of South Wales.
London, Robert Hale, 1974. 221 p.
NN CVB 76-2685

Thomas, Gwyn.
Old Rhondda.
Glamorgan, Stuart Willimas, 1974. 189 illus., unpaged.
(Coal-mining area)
NN CVG (Rhondda Valley) 76-1368

Tucker, Norman.
Denbighshire Officers in the Civil War.
Denbigh, Gee, 1968. 197 p.
NN CV

Tucker, Norman.
North Wales in the Civil War.
Denbigh, Gee, 1968. 197 p.
NN CV

Tucker, Norman.
Royalist Officers of North Wales, 1642–1660: A Provisional List.

Denbigh, N. Tucker, 1961. 72 leaves.
NN F-10 6362

Vaughan, Thomas G.
Portrait of Gower.
London, Hale, 1976. 204 p., index.

Wales. University of Wales. Board of Celtic Studies.
Bulletin of the Board of Celtic Studies.
London, 1921–. v. 1–.
NN CVA

The Welsh History Review (Cylch-grawn Hanes Cymru)
Cardiff, Board of Celtic Studies, U. of Wales, 1960–.
NN CVA

Welsh Society Journal.
1974–. (Family history society)

Welsh Wills Abstracts.
(IN: *Archaeologia Cambrensis*, 1876–84. ser. 4, v. 7, p. 220–27; v. 9, p. 149–56; v. 11, p. 217–21; v. 12, p. 80–83; v. 14, p. 14–18; 5th ser., v. 1, p. 63–64)
NN CVA

Williams, Stuart.
Glamorgan Historian.
Barry, South Glamorgan, 1966–. 11 v. in 1976.
NN CVG (Glamorgan)

[Many items in the bibliographies in this book are noted as having been published or reprinted by the Genealogical Publishing Co., Inc., (GPC), 521–523 St. Paul Place, Baltimore, MD 21202. Catalogs can be obtained from them upon request.]

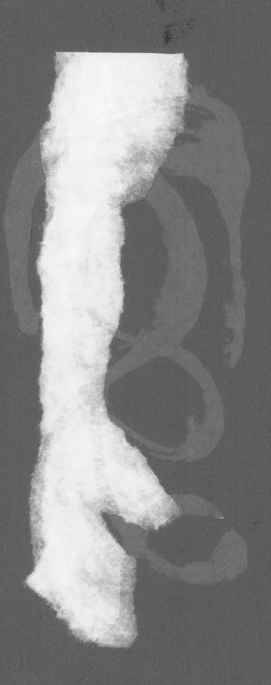